Concepts, Techniques, and Models of Computer Programming

Concepts, Techniques, and Models of Computer Programming

by
Peter Van Roy
Seif Haridi

The MIT Press
Cambridge, Massachusetts
London, England

This book was set in $\LaTeX\,2_\varepsilon$ by the authors and was printed and bound in the United States of America.

Library of Congress Cataloging-in-Publication Data

Van Roy, Peter.
Concepts, techniques, and models of computer programming / Peter Van Roy, Seif Haridi
p. cm.
Includes bibliographical references and index.
ISBN 0-262-22069-5
1. Computer programming. I. Haridi, Seif. II. Title.

QA76.6.V36 2004
005.1—dc22 2003065140

10 9 8 7 6 5 4 3 2

Short Contents

Table of Contents

Preface

Six blind sages were shown an elephant and met to discuss their experience. "It's wonderful," said the first, "an elephant is like a rope: slender and flexible." "No, no, not at all," said the second, "an elephant is like a tree: sturdily planted on the ground." "Marvelous," said the third, "an elephant is like a wall." "Incredible," said the fourth, "an elephant is a tube filled with water." "What a strange piecemeal beast this is," said the fifth. "Strange indeed," said the sixth, "but there must be some underlying harmony. Let us investigate the matter further."
— Freely adapted from a traditional Indian fable.

A programming language is like a natural, human language in that it favors certain metaphors, images, and ways of thinking.
— *Mindstorms: Children, Computers, and Powerful Ideas*, Seymour Papert (1980)

One approach to the study of computer programming is to study programming languages. But there are a tremendously large number of languages, so large that it is impractical to study them all. How can we tackle this immensity? We could pick a small number of languages that are representative of different programming paradigms. But this gives little insight into programming as a unified discipline. This book uses another approach.

We focus on programming concepts and the techniques in using them, not on programming languages. The concepts are organized in terms of computation models. A computation model is a formal system that defines how computations are done. There are many ways to define computation models. Since this book is intended to be practical, it is important that the computation model be directly useful to the programmer. We therefore define it in terms of concepts that are important to programmers: data types, operations, and a programming language. The term *computation model* makes precise the imprecise notion of "programming paradigm." The rest of the book talks about computation models and not programming paradigms. Sometimes we use the phrase "programming model." This refers to what the programmer needs: the programming techniques and design principles made possible by the computation model.

Each computation model has its own set of techniques for programming and reasoning about programs. The number of different computation models that are known to be useful is much smaller than the number of programming languages. This book covers many well-known models as well as some less-known models. The main criterion for presenting a model is whether it is useful in practice.

Each computation model is based on a simple core language called its kernel language. The kernel languages are introduced in a progressive way, by adding concepts one by one. This lets us show the deep relationships between the different models. Often, adding just one new concept makes a world of difference in programming. For example, adding destructive assignment (explicit state) to functional programming allows us to do object-oriented programming.

When should we add a concept to a model and which concept should we add? We touch on these questions many times. The main criterion is the *creative extension principle*. Roughly, a new concept is added when programs become complicated for technical reasons unrelated to the problem being solved. Adding a concept to the kernel language can keep programs simple, if the concept is chosen carefully. This is explained further in appendix D. This principle underlies the progression of kernel languages presented in the book.

A nice property of the kernel language approach is that it lets us use different models together in the same program. This is usually called multiparadigm programming. It is quite natural, since it means simply to use the right concepts for the problem, independent of what computation model they originate from. Multiparadigm programming is an old idea. For example, the designers of Lisp and Scheme have long advocated a similar view. However, this book applies it in a much broader and deeper way than has been previously done.

From the vantage point of computation models, the book also sheds new light on important problems in informatics. We present three such areas, namely graphical user interface design, robust distributed programming, and constraint programming. We show how the judicious combined use of several computation models can help solve some of the problems of these areas.

Languages mentioned

We mention many programming languages in the book and relate them to particular computation models. For example, Java and Smalltalk are based on an object-oriented model. Haskell and Standard ML are based on a functional model. Prolog and Mercury are based on a logic model. Not all interesting languages can be so classified. We mention some other languages for their own merits. For example, Lisp and Scheme pioneered many of the concepts presented here. Erlang is functional, inherently concurrent, and supports fault-tolerant distributed programming.

We single out four languages as representatives of important computation models: Erlang, Haskell, Java, and Prolog. We identify the computation model of each language in terms of the book's uniform framework. For more information about them we refer readers to other books. Because of space limitations, we are not able to mention all interesting languages. Omission of a language does not imply any kind of value judgment.

Goals of the book

Teaching programming

The main goal of the book is to teach programming as a unified discipline with a scientific foundation that is useful to the practicing programmer. Let us look closer at what this means.

What is programming?

We define *programming*, as a general human activity, to mean the act of extending or changing a system's functionality. Programming is a widespread activity that is done both by nonspecialists (e.g., consumers who change the settings of their alarm clock or cellular phone) and specialists (computer programmers, the audience for this book).

This book focuses on the construction of software systems. In that setting, programming is the step between the system's specification and a running program that implements it. The step consists in designing the program's architecture and abstractions and coding them into a programming language. This is a broad view, perhaps broader than the usual connotation attached to the word "programming." It covers both programming "in the small" and "in the large." It covers both (language-independent) architectural issues and (language-dependent) coding issues. It is based more on concepts and their use rather than on any one programming language. We find that this general view is natural for teaching programming. It is unbiased by limitations of any particular language or design methodology. When used in a specific situation, the general view is adapted to the tools used, taking into account their abilities and limitations.

Both science and technology

Programming as defined above has two essential parts: a technology and its scientific foundation. The technology consists of tools, practical techniques, and standards, allowing us to do programming. The science consists of a broad and deep theory with predictive power, allowing us to understand programming. Ideally, the science should explain the technology in a way that is as direct and useful as possible.

If either part is left out, we are no longer doing programming. Without the technology, we are doing pure mathematics. Without the science, we are doing a craft, i.e., we lack deep understanding. Teaching programming correctly therefore means teaching both the technology (current tools) and the science (fundamental concepts). Knowing the tools prepares the student for the present. Knowing the concepts prepares the student for future developments.

More than a craft

Despite many efforts to introduce a scientific foundation, programming is almost always taught as a craft. It is usually taught in the context of one (or a few) programming language(s) (e.g., Java, complemented with Haskell, Scheme, or Prolog). The historical accidents of the particular languages chosen are interwoven together so closely with the fundamental concepts that the two cannot be separated. There is a confusion between tools and concepts. What's more, different schools of thought have developed, based on different ways of viewing programming, called "paradigms": object-oriented, logic, functional, etc. Each school of thought has its own science. The unity of programming as a single discipline has been lost.

Teaching programming in this fashion is like having separate schools of bridge building: one school teaches how to build wooden bridges and another school teaches how to build iron bridges. Graduates of either school would implicitly consider the restriction to wood or iron as fundamental and would not think of using wood and iron together.

The result is that programs suffer from poor design. We give an example based on Java, but the problem exists in all languages to some degree. Concurrency in Java is complex to use and expensive in computational resources. Because of these difficulties, Java-taught programmers conclude that concurrency is a fundamentally complex and expensive concept. Program specifications are designed around the difficulties, often in a contorted way. But these difficulties are not fundamental at all. There are forms of concurrency that are quite useful and yet as easy to program with as sequential programs (e.g., stream programming as exemplified by Unix pipes). Furthermore, it is possible to implement threads, the basic unit of concurrency, almost as cheaply as procedure calls. If the programmer were taught about concurrency in the correct way, then he or she would be able to specify for and program in systems without concurrency restrictions (including improved versions of Java).

The kernel language approach

Practical programming languages scale up to programs of millions of lines of code. They provide a rich set of abstractions and syntax. How can we separate the languages' fundamental concepts, which underlie their success, from their historical accidents? The kernel language approach shows one way. In this approach, a practical language is translated into a kernel language that consists of a small number of programmer-significant elements. The rich set of abstractions and syntax is encoded in the kernel language. This gives both programmer and student a clear insight into what the language does. The kernel language has a simple formal semantics that allows reasoning about program correctness and complexity. This gives a solid foundation to the programmer's intuition and the programming techniques built on top of it.

A wide variety of languages and programming paradigms can be modeled by a small set of closely related kernel languages. It follows that the kernel language approach is a truly language-independent way to study programming. Since any given language translates into a kernel language that is a subset of a larger, more complete kernel language, the underlying unity of programming is regained.

Reducing a complex phenomenon to its primitive elements is characteristic of the scientific method. It is a successful approach that is used in all the exact sciences. It gives a deep understanding that has predictive power. For example, structural science lets one design all bridges (whether made of wood, iron, both, or anything else) and predict their behavior in terms of simple concepts such as force, energy, stress, and strain, and the laws they obey [70].

Comparison with other approaches

Let us compare the kernel language approach with three other ways to give programming a broad scientific basis:

- A foundational calculus, like the λ calculus or π calculus, reduces programming to a minimal number of elements. The elements are chosen to simplify mathematical analysis, not to aid programmer intuition. This helps theoreticians, but is not particularly useful to practicing programmers. Foundational calculi are useful for studying the fundamental properties and limits of programming a computer, not for writing or reasoning about general applications.
- A virtual machine defines a language in terms of an implementation on an idealized machine. A virtual machine gives a kind of operational semantics, with concepts that are close to hardware. This is useful for designing computers, implementing languages, or doing simulations. It is not useful for reasoning about programs and their abstractions.
- A multiparadigm language is a language that encompasses several programming paradigms. For example, Scheme is both functional and imperative [43], and Leda has elements that are functional, object-oriented, and logical [31]. The usefulness of a multiparadigm language depends on how well the different paradigms are integrated.

The kernel language approach combines features of all these approaches. A well-designed kernel language covers a wide range of concepts, like a well-designed multiparadigm language. If the concepts are independent, then the kernel language can be given a simple formal semantics, like a foundational calculus. Finally, the formal semantics can be a virtual machine at a high level of abstraction. This makes it easy for programmers to reason about programs.

Designing abstractions

The second goal of the book is to teach how to design programming abstractions. The most difficult work of programmers, and also the most rewarding, is not writing programs but rather designing abstractions. Programming a computer is primarily designing and using abstractions to achieve new goals. We define an *abstraction* loosely as a tool or device that solves a particular problem. Usually the same abstraction can be used to solve many different problems. This versatility is one of the key properties of abstractions.

Abstractions are so deeply part of our daily life that we often forget about them. Some typical abstractions are books, chairs, screwdrivers, and automobiles.[1] Abstractions can be classified into a hierarchy depending on how specialized they are (e.g., "pencil" is more specialized than "writing instrument," but both are abstractions).

Abstractions are particularly numerous inside computer systems. Modern computers are highly complex systems consisting of hardware, operating system, middleware, and application layers, each of which is based on the work of thousands of people over several decades. They contain an enormous number of abstractions, working together in a highly organized manner.

Designing abstractions is not always easy. It can be a long and painful process, as different approaches are tried, discarded, and improved. But the rewards are very great. It is not too much of an exaggeration to say that civilization is built on successful abstractions [153]. New ones are being designed every day. Some ancient ones, like the wheel and the arch, are still with us. Some modern ones, like the cellular phone, quickly become part of our daily life.

We use the following approach to achieve the second goal. We start with programming concepts, which are the raw materials for building abstractions. We introduce most of the relevant concepts known today, in particular lexical scoping, higher-order programming, compositionality, encapsulation, concurrency, exceptions, lazy execution, security, explicit state, inheritance, and nondeterministic choice. For each concept, we give techniques for building abstractions with it. We give many examples of sequential, concurrent, and distributed abstractions. We give some general laws for building abstractions. Many of these general laws have counterparts in other applied sciences, so that books like [63], [70], and [80] can be an inspiration to programmers.

Main features

Pedagogical approach

There are two complementary approaches to teaching programming as a rigorous discipline:

- The computation-based approach presents programming as a way to define

1. Also, pencils, nuts and bolts, wires, transistors, corporations, songs, and differential equations. They do not have to be material entities!

executions on machines. It grounds the student's intuition in the real world by means of actual executions on real systems. This is especially effective with an interactive system: the student can create program fragments and immediately see what they do. Reducing the time between thinking "what if" and seeing the result is an enormous aid to understanding. Precision is not sacrificed, since the formal semantics of a program can be given in terms of an abstract machine.

- The logic-based approach presents programming as a branch of mathematical logic. Logic does not speak of execution but of program properties, which is a higher level of abstraction. Programs are mathematical constructions that obey logical laws. The formal semantics of a program is given in terms of a mathematical logic. Reasoning is done with logical assertions. The logic-based approach is harder for students to grasp yet it is essential for defining precise specifications of what programs do.

Like Structure and Interpretation of Computer Programs [1, 2], our book mostly uses the computation-based approach. Concepts are illustrated with program fragments that can be run interactively on an accompanying software package, the Mozart Programming System [148]. Programs are constructed with a building-block approach, using lower-level abstractions to build higher-level ones. A small amount of logical reasoning is introduced in later chapters, e.g., for defining specifications and for using invariants to reason about programs with state.

Formalism used

This book uses a single formalism for presenting all computation models and programs, namely the Oz language and its computation model. To be precise, the computation models of the book are all carefully chosen subsets of Oz. Why did we choose Oz? The main reason is that it supports the kernel language approach well. Another reason is the existence of the Mozart Programming System.

Panorama of computation models

This book presents a broad overview of many of the most useful computation models. The models are designed not just with formal simplicity in mind (although it is important), but on the basis of how a programmer can express himself or herself and reason within the model. There are many different practical computation models, with different levels of expressiveness, different programming techniques, and different ways of reasoning about them. We find that each model has its domain of application. This book explains many of these models, how they are related, how to program in them, and how to combine them to greatest advantage.

More is not better (or worse), just different

All computation models have their place. It is not true that models with more concepts are better or worse. This is because a new concept is like a two-edged sword. Adding a concept to a computation model introduces new forms of expression, making some programs simpler, but it also makes reasoning about programs harder. For example, by adding explicit state (mutable variables) to a functional programming model we can express the full range of object-oriented programming techniques. However, reasoning about object-oriented programs is harder than reasoning about functional programs. Functional programming is about calculating values with mathematical functions. Neither the values nor the functions change over time. Explicit state is one way to model things that change over time: it provides a container whose content can be updated. The very power of this concept makes it harder to reason about.

The importance of using models together

Each computation model was originally designed to be used in isolation. It might therefore seem like an aberration to use several of them together in the same program. We find that this is not at all the case. This is because models are not just monolithic blocks with nothing in common. On the contrary, they have much in common. For example, the differences between declarative and imperative models (and between concurrent and sequential models) are very small compared to what they have in common. Because of this, it is easy to use several models together.

But even though it is technically possible, why would one want to use several models in the same program? The deep answer to this question is simple: because one does not program with models, but with programming concepts and ways to combine them. Depending on which concepts one uses, it is possible to consider that one is programming in a particular model. The model appears as a kind of epiphenomenon. Certain things become easy, other things become harder, and reasoning about the program is done in a particular way. It is quite natural for a well-written program to use different models. At this early point this answer may seem cryptic. It will become clear later in the book.

An important principle we will see in the book is that concepts traditionally associated with one model can be used to great effect in more general models. For example, the concepts of lexical scoping and higher-order programming, which are usually associated with functional programming, are useful in all models. This is well-known in the functional programming community. Functional languages have long been extended with explicit state (e.g., Scheme [43] and Standard ML [145, 213]) and more recently with concurrency (e.g., Concurrent ML [176] and Concurrent Haskell [167, 165]).

The limits of single models

We find that a good programming style requires using programming concepts that are usually associated with different computation models. Languages that implement just one computation model make this difficult:

- Object-oriented languages encourage the overuse of state and inheritance. Objects are stateful by default. While this seems simple and intuitive, it actually complicates programming, e.g., it makes concurrency difficult (see section 8.2). Design patterns, which define a common terminology for describing good programming techniques, are usually explained in terms of inheritance [66]. In many cases, simpler higher-order programming techniques would suffice (see section 7.4.7). In addition, inheritance is often misused. For example, object-oriented graphical user interfaces often recommend using inheritance to extend generic widget classes with application-specific functionality (e.g., in the Swing components for Java). This is counter to separation of concerns.

- Functional languages encourage the overuse of higher-order programming. Typical examples are monads and currying. Monads are used to encode state by threading it throughout the program. This makes programs more intricate but does not achieve the modularity properties of true explicit state (see section 4.8). Currying lets you apply a function partially by giving only some of its arguments. This returns a new function that expects the remaining arguments. The function body will not execute until all arguments are there. The flip side is that it is not clear by inspection whether a function has all its arguments or is still curried ("waiting" for the rest).

- Logic languages in the Prolog tradition encourage the overuse of Horn clause syntax and search. These languages define all programs as collections of Horn clauses, which resemble simple logical axioms in an "if-then" style. Many algorithms are obfuscated when written in this style. Backtracking-based search must always be used even though it is almost never needed (see [217]).

These examples are to some extent subjective; it is difficult to be completely objective regarding good programming style and language expressiveness. Therefore they should not be read as passing any judgment on these models. Rather, they are hints that none of these models is a panacea when used alone. Each model is well-adapted to some problems but less to others. This book tries to present a balanced approach, sometimes using a single model in isolation but not shying away from using several models together when it is appropriate.

Teaching from the book

We explain how the book fits in an informatics curriculum and what courses can be taught with it. By *informatics* we mean the whole field of information technology, including computer science, computer engineering, and information systems. Informatics is sometimes called *computing*.

Role in informatics curriculum

Let us consider the discipline of programming independent of any other domain in informatics. In our experience, it divides naturally into three core topics:

1. Concepts and techniques
2. Algorithms and data structures
3. Program design and software engineering

The book gives a thorough treatment of topic (1) and an introduction to (2) and (3). In which order should the topics be given? There is a strong interdependency between (1) and (3). Experience shows that program design should be taught early on, so that students avoid bad habits. However, this is only part of the story since students need to know about concepts to express their designs. Parnas has used an approach that starts with topic (3) and uses an imperative computation model [161]. Because this book uses many computation models, we recommend using it to teach (1) and (3) concurrently, introducing new concepts and design principles together. In the informatics program at the Université catholique de Louvain at Louvain-la-Neuve, Belgium (UCL), we attribute eight semester-hours to each topic. This includes lectures and lab sessions. Together the three topics make up one sixth of the full informatics curriculum for licentiate and engineering degrees.

There is another point we would like to make, which concerns how to teach concurrent programming. In a traditional informatics curriculum, concurrency is taught by extending a stateful model, just as chapter 8 extends chapter 6. This is rightly considered to be complex and difficult to program with. There are other, simpler forms of concurrent programming. The declarative concurrency of chapter 4 is much simpler to program with and can often be used in place of stateful concurrency (see the epigraph that starts chapter 4). Stream concurrency, a simple form of declarative concurrency, has been taught in first-year courses at MIT and other institutions. Another simple form of concurrency, message passing between threads, is explained in chapter 5. We suggest that both declarative concurrency and message-passing concurrency be part of the standard curriculum and be taught before stateful concurrency.

Courses

We have used the book as a textbook for several courses ranging from second-year undergraduate to graduate courses [175, 220, 221]. In its present form, the book is not intended as a first programming course, but the approach could likely be adapted for such a course.[2] Students should have some basic programming

2. We will gladly help anyone willing to tackle this adaptation.

experience (e.g., a practical introduction to programming and knowledge of simple data structures such as sequences, sets, and stacks) and some basic mathematical knowledge (e.g., a first course on analysis, discrete mathematics, or algebra). The book has enough material for at least four semester-hours worth of lectures and as many lab sessions. Some of the possible courses are:

- An undergraduate course on programming concepts and techniques. Chapter 1 gives a light introduction. The course continues with chapters 2 through 8. Depending on the desired depth of coverage, more or less emphasis can be put on algorithms (to teach algorithms along with programming), concurrency (which can be left out completely, if so desired), or formal semantics (to make intuitions precise).
- An undergraduate course on applied programming models. This includes relational programming (chapter 9), specific programming languages (especially Erlang, Haskell, Java, and Prolog), graphical user interface programming (chapter 10), distributed programming (chapter 11), and constraint programming (chapter 12). This course is a natural sequel to the previous one.
- An undergraduate course on concurrent and distributed programming (chapters 4, 5, 8, and 11). Students should have some programming experience. The course can start with small parts of chapters 2, 3, 6, and 7 to introduce declarative and stateful programming.
- A graduate course on computation models (the whole book, including the semantics in chapter 13). The course can concentrate on the relationships between the models and on their semantics.

The book's Web site has more information on courses, including transparencies and lab assignments for some of them. The Web site has an animated interpreter that shows how the kernel languages execute according to the abstract machine semantics. The book can be used as a complement to other courses:

- Part of an undergraduate course on constraint programming (chapters 4, 9, and 12).
- Part of a graduate course on intelligent collaborative applications (parts of the whole book, with emphasis on part II). If desired, the book can be complemented by texts on artificial intelligence (e.g., [179]) or multi-agent systems (e.g., [226]).
- Part of an undergraduate course on semantics. All the models are formally defined in the chapters that introduce them, and this semantics is sharpened in chapter 13. This gives a real-sized case study of how to define the semantics of a complete modern programming language.

The book, while it has a solid theoretical underpinning, is intended to give a practical education in these subjects. Each chapter has many program fragments, all of which can be executed on the Mozart system (see below). With these fragments, course lectures can have live interactive demonstrations of the concepts. We find that students very much appreciate this style of lecture.

Each chapter ends with a set of exercises that usually involve some programming. They can be solved on the Mozart system. To best learn the material in the chapter, we encourage students to do as many exercises as possible. Exercises marked (advanced exercise) can take from several days up to several weeks. Exercises marked (research project) are open-ended and can result in significant research contributions.

Software

A useful feature of the book is that all program fragments can be run on a software platform, the Mozart Programming System. Mozart is a full-featured production-quality programming system that comes with an interactive incremental development environment and a full set of tools. It compiles to an efficient platform-independent bytecode that runs on many varieties of Unix and Windows, and on Mac OS X. Distributed programs can be spread out over all these systems. The Mozart Web site, `http://www.mozart-oz.org`, has complete information, including downloadable binaries, documentation, scientific publications, source code, and mailing lists.

The Mozart system implements efficiently all the computation models covered in the book. This makes it ideal for using models together in the same program and for comparing models by writing programs to solve a problem in different models. Because each model is implemented efficiently, whole programs can be written in just one model. Other models can be brought in later, if needed, in a pedagogically justified way. For example, programs can be completely written in an object-oriented style, complemented by small declarative components where they are most useful.

The Mozart system is the result of a long-term development effort by the Mozart Consortium, an informal research and development collaboration of three laboratories. It has been under continuing development since 1991. The system is released with full source code under an Open Source license agreement. The first public release was in 1995. The first public release with distribution support was in 1999. The book is based on an ideal implementation that is close to Mozart version 1.3.0, released in April 2004. The differences between the ideal implementation and Mozart are listed on the book's Web site.

History and acknowledgments

The ideas in this book did not come easily. They came after more than a decade of discussion, programming, evaluation, throwing out the bad, and bringing in the good and convincing others that it is good. Many people contributed ideas, implementations, tools, and applications. We are lucky to have had a coherent vision among our colleagues for such a long period. Thanks to this, we have been able to make progress.

Our main research vehicle and "test bed" of new ideas is the Mozart system, which implements the Oz language. The system's main designers and developers are (in alphabetical order) Per Brand, Thorsten Brunklaus, Denys Duchier, Kevin Glynn, Donatien Grolaux, Seif Haridi, Dragan Havelka, Martin Henz, Erik Klintskog, Leif Kornstaedt, Michael Mehl, Martin Müller, Tobias Müller, Anna Neiderud, Konstantin Popov, Ralf Scheidhauer, Christian Schulte, Gert Smolka, Peter Van Roy, and Jörg Würtz. Other important contributors are (in alphabetical order) Iliès Alouini, Raphaël Collet, Frej Drejhammar, Sameh El-Ansary, Nils Franzén, Martin Homik, Simon Lindblom, Benjamin Lorenz, Valentin Mesaros, and Andreas Simon. We thank Konstantin Popov and Kevin Glynn for managing the release of Mozart version 1.3.0, which is designed to accompany the book.

We would also like to thank the following researchers and indirect contributors: Hassan Aït-Kaci, Joe Armstrong, Joachim Durchholz, Andreas Franke, Claire Gardent, Fredrik Holmgren, Sverker Janson, Torbjörn Lager, Elie Milgrom, Johan Montelius, Al-Metwally Mostafa, Joachim Niehren, Luc Onana, Marc-Antoine Parent, Dave Parnas, Mathias Picker, Andreas Podelski, Christophe Ponsard, Mahmoud Rafea, Juris Reinfelds, Thomas Sjöland, Fred Spiessens, Joe Turner, and Jean Vanderdonckt.

We give special thanks to the following people for their help with material related to the book. Raphaël Collet for co-authoring chapters 12 and 13, for his work on the practical part of LINF1251, a course taught at UCL, and for his help with the $\LaTeX\,2_\varepsilon$ formatting. Donatien Grolaux for three graphical user interface case studies (used in sections 10.4.2–10.4.4). Kevin Glynn for writing the Haskell introduction (section 4.7). William Cook for his comments on data abstraction. Frej Drejhammar, Sameh El-Ansary, and Dragan Havelka for their help with the practical part of Datalogi II, a course taught at KTH (the Royal Institute of Technology, Stockholm). Christian Schulte for completely rethinking and redeveloping a subsequent edition of Datalogi II and for his comments on a draft of the book. Ali Ghodsi, Johan Montelius, and the other three assistants for their help with the practical part of this edition. Luis Quesada and Kevin Glynn for their work on the practical part of INGI2131, a course taught at UCL. Bruno Carton, Raphaël Collet, Kevin Glynn, Donatien Grolaux, Stefano Gualandi, Valentin Mesaros, Al-Metwally Mostafa, Luis Quesada, and Fred Spiessens for their efforts in proofreading and testing the example programs. We thank other people too numerous to mention for their comments on the book. Finally, we thank the members of the Department of Computing Science and Engineering at UCL, SICS (the Swedish Institute of Computer Science, Stockholm), and the Department of Microelectronics and Information Technology at KTH. We apologize to anyone we may have inadvertently omitted.

How did we manage to keep the result so simple with such a large crowd of developers working together? No miracle, but the consequence of a strong vision and a carefully crafted design methodology that took more than a decade to create and polish.[3] Around 1990, some of us came together with already strong system-building and theoretical backgrounds. These people initiated the ACCLAIM project, funded by the European Union (1991–1994). For some reason, this project became a focal point. Three important milestones among many were the papers by Sverker Janson and Seif Haridi in 1991 [105] (multiple paradigms in the Andorra Kernel Language AKL), by Gert Smolka in 1995 [199] (building abstractions in Oz), and by Seif Haridi et al. in 1998 [83] (dependable open distribution in Oz). The first paper on Oz was published in 1993 and already had many important ideas [89]. After ACCLAIM, two laboratories continued working together on the Oz ideas: the Programming Systems Lab (DFKI, Saarland University, and Collaborative Research Center SFB 378) at Saarbrücken, Germany, and the Intelligent Systems Laboratory at SICS.

The Oz language was originally designed by Gert Smolka and his students in the Programming Systems Lab [85, 89, 90, 190, 192, 198, 199]. The well-factorized design of the language and the high quality of its implementation are due in large part to Smolka's inspired leadership and his lab's system-building expertise. Among the developers, we mention Christian Schulte for his role in coordinating general development, Denys Duchier for his active support of users, and Per Brand for his role in coordinating development of the distributed implementation. In 1996, the German and Swedish labs were joined by the Department of Computing Science and Engineering at UCL when the first author moved there. Together the three laboratories formed the Mozart Consortium with its neutral Web site `http://www.mozart-oz.org` so that the work would not be tied down to a single institution.

This book was written using $\LaTeX\,2_\varepsilon$, flex, xfig, xv, vi/vim, emacs, and Mozart, first on a Dell Latitude with Red Hat Linux and KDE, and then on an Apple Macintosh PowerBook G4 with Mac OS X and X11. The screenshots were taken on a Sun workstation running Solaris. The first author thanks the Walloon Region of Belgium for their generous support of the Oz/Mozart work at UCL in the PIRATES and MILOS projects.

Final comments

We have tried to make this book useful both as a textbook and as a reference. It is up to you to judge how well it succeeds in this. Because of its size, it is likely that some errors remain. If you find any, we would appreciate hearing from you. Please send them and all other constructive comments you may have to the following address:

3. We can summarize the methodology in two rules (see [217] for more information). First, a new abstraction must either simplify the system or greatly increase its expressive power. Second, a new abstraction must have both an efficient implementation and a simple formalization.

Concepts, Techniques, and Models of Computer Programming
Department of Computing Science and Engineering
Université catholique de Louvain
B-1348 Louvain-la-Neuve, Belgium

As a final word, we would like to thank our families and friends for their support and encouragement during the four years it took us to write this book. Seif Haridi would like to give a special thanks to his parents Ali and Amina and to his family Eeva, Rebecca, and Alexander. Peter Van Roy would like to give a special thanks to his parents Frans and Hendrika and to his family Marie-Thérèse, Johan, and Lucile.

Louvain-la-Neuve, Belgium
Kista, Sweden
September 2003

PETER VAN ROY
SEIF HARIDI

Running the Example Programs

This book gives many example programs and program fragments. All of these can be run on the Mozart Programming System. To make this as easy as possible, please keep the following points in mind:

- The Mozart system can be downloaded without charge from the Mozart Consortium Web site `http://www.mozart-oz.org`. Releases exist for various flavors of Windows and Unix and for Mac OS X.
- All examples, except those intended for standalone applications, can be run in Mozart's interactive development environment. Appendix A gives an introduction to this environment.
- New variables in the interactive examples must be declared with the **`declare`** statement. The examples of chapter 1 show how to do this. Forgetting these declarations can result in strange errors if older versions of the variables exist. Starting with chapter 2 and for all following chapters, the **`declare`** statement is omitted in the text when it is obvious what the new variables are. It should be added to run the examples.
- Some chapters use operations that are not part of the standard Mozart release. The source code for these additional operations (along with much other useful material) is given on the book's Web site. We recommend putting these definitions in your `.ozrc` file, so they will be loaded automatically when the system starts up.
- The book occasionally gives screenshots and timing measurements of programs. The screenshots were taken on a Sun workstation running Solaris and the timing measurements were done on Mozart 1.1.0 under Red Hat Linux release 6.1 on a Dell Latitude CPx notebook computer with Pentium III processor at 500 MHz, unless otherwise indicated. Screenshot appearance and timing numbers may vary on your system.
- The book assumes an ideal implementation whose semantics is given in chapter 13 (general computation model) and chapter 12 (computation spaces). There are a few differences between this ideal implementation and the Mozart system. They are explained on the book's Web site.

1 Introduction to Programming Concepts

There is no royal road to geometry.
— Euclid's reply to Ptolemy, Euclid (*fl.* *c.* 300 B.C.)

Just follow the yellow brick road.
— *The Wonderful Wizard of Oz*, L. Frank Baum (1856–1919)

Programming is telling a computer how it should do its job. This chapter gives a gentle, hands-on introduction to many of the most important concepts in programming. We assume you have had some previous exposure to computers. We use the interactive interface of Mozart to introduce programming concepts in a progressive way. We encourage you to try the examples in this chapter on a running Mozart system.

This introduction only scratches the surface of the programming concepts we will see in this book. Later chapters give a deep understanding of these concepts and add many other concepts and techniques.

1.1 A calculator

Let us start by using the system to do calculations. Start the Mozart system by typing:

```
oz
```

or by double-clicking a Mozart icon. This opens an editor window with two frames. In the top frame, type the following line:

```
{Browse 9999*9999}
```

Use the mouse to select this line. Now go to the `Oz` menu and select `Feed Region`. This feeds the selected text to the system. The system then does the calculation `9999*9999` and displays the result, `99980001`, in a special window called the browser. The curly braces { ... } are used for a procedure or function call. `Browse` is a procedure with one argument, which is called as `{Browse X}`. This opens the browser window, if it is not already open, and displays `X` in it.

1.2 Variables

While working with the calculator, we would like to remember an old result, so that we can use it later without retyping it. We can do this by declaring a variable:

```
declare
V=9999*9999
```

This declares V and binds it to 99980001. We can use this variable later on:

```
{Browse V*V}
```

This displays the answer 9996000599960001. Variables are just shortcuts for values. They cannot be assigned more than once. But you can declare another variable with the same name as a previous one. The previous variable then becomes inaccessible. Previous calculations that used it are not changed. This is because there are two concepts hiding behind the word "variable":

- The identifier. This is what you type in. Variables start with a capital letter and can be followed by any number of letters or digits. For example, the character sequence Var1 can be a variable identifier.
- The store variable. This is what the system uses to calculate with. It is part of the system's memory, which we call its store.

The **declare** statement creates a new store variable and makes the variable identifier refer to it. Previous calculations using the same identifier are not changed because the identifier refers to another store variable.

1.3 Functions

Let us do a more involved calculation. Assume we want to calculate the factorial function $n!$, which is defined as $1 \times 2 \times \cdots \times (n-1) \times n$. This gives the number of permutations of n items, i.e., the number of different ways these items can be put in a row. Factorial of 10 is:

```
{Browse 1*2*3*4*5*6*7*8*9*10}
```

This displays 3628800. What if we want to calculate the factorial of 100? We would like the system to do the tedious work of typing in all the integers from 1 to 100. We will do more: we will tell the system how to calculate the factorial of any n. We do this by defining a function:

```
declare
fun {Fact N}
   if N==0 then 1 else N*{Fact N-1} end
end
```

The **declare** statement creates the new variable Fact. The **fun** statement defines a function. The variable Fact is bound to the function. The function has one argument `N`, which is a local variable, i.e., it is known only inside the function body. Each time we call the function a new local variable is created.

Recursion

The function body is an instruction called an **`if`** expression. When the function is called, then the **`if`** expression does the following steps:

- It first checks whether `N` is equal to 0 by doing the test `N==0`.
- If the test succeeds, then the expression after the **`then`** is calculated. This just returns the number 1. This is because the factorial of 0 is 1.
- If the test fails, then the expression after the **`else`** is calculated. That is, if `N` is not 0, then the expression `N*{Fact N-1}` is calculated. This expression uses `Fact`, the very function we are defining! This is called recursion. It is perfectly normal and no cause for alarm.

`Fact` uses the following mathematical definition of factorial:

$0! = 1$

$n! = n \times (n-1)! \text{ if } n > 0$

This definition is recursive because the factorial of `N` is `N` times the factorial of `N-1`. Let us try out the function `Fact`:

```
{Browse {Fact 10}}
```

This should display `3628800` as before. This gives us confidence that `Fact` is doing the right calculation. Let us try a bigger input:

```
{Browse {Fact 100}}
```

This will display a huge number (which we show in groups of five digits to improve readability):

```
                                                      933 26215
44394 41526 81699 23885 62667 00490 71596 82643 81621 46859
29638 95217 59999 32299 15608 94146 39761 56518 28625 36979
20827 22375 82511 85210 91686 40000 00000 00000 00000 00000
```

This is an example of arbitrary precision arithmetic, sometimes called "infinite precision," although it is not infinite. The precision is limited by how much memory your system has. A typical low-cost personal computer with 256 MB of memory can handle hundreds of thousands of digits. The skeptical reader will ask: is this huge number really the factorial of 100? How can we tell? Doing the calculation by hand would take a long time and probably be incorrect. We will see later on how to gain confidence that the system is doing the right thing.

Combinations

Let us write a function to calculate the number of combinations of k items taken from n. This is equal to the number of subsets of size k that can be made from a set of size n. This is written $\binom{n}{k}$ in mathematical notation and pronounced "n choose k." It can be defined as follows using the factorial:

$$\binom{n}{k} = \frac{n!}{k!\,(n-k)!}$$

which leads naturally to the following function:

```
declare
fun {Comb N K}
   {Fact N} div ({Fact K}*{Fact N-K})
end
```

For example, `{Comb 10 3}` is 120, which is the number of ways that 3 items can be taken from 10. This is not the most efficient way to write `Comb`, but it is probably the simplest.

Functional abstraction

The definition of `Comb` uses the existing function `Fact` in its definition. It is always possible to use existing functions when defining new functions. Using functions to build abstractions is called functional abstraction. In this way, programs are like onions, with layers upon layers of functions calling functions. This style of programming is covered in chapter 3.

1.4 Lists

Now we can calculate functions of integers. But an integer is really not very much to look at. Say we want to calculate with lots of integers. For example, we would like to calculate Pascal's triangle[1]:

$$\begin{array}{ccccccccc} & & & & 1 & & & & \\ & & & 1 & & 1 & & & \\ & & 1 & & 2 & & 1 & & \\ & 1 & & 3 & & 3 & & 1 & \\ 1 & & 4 & & 6 & & 4 & & 1 \\ . & . & . & . & . & . & . & . & . \end{array}$$

1. Pascal's triangle is a key concept in combinatorics. The elements of the nth row are the combinations $\binom{n}{k}$, where k ranges from 0 to n. This is closely related to the binomial theorem, which states $(x+y)^n = \sum_{k=0}^{n} \binom{n}{k} x^k y^{(n-k)}$ for integer $n \geq 0$.

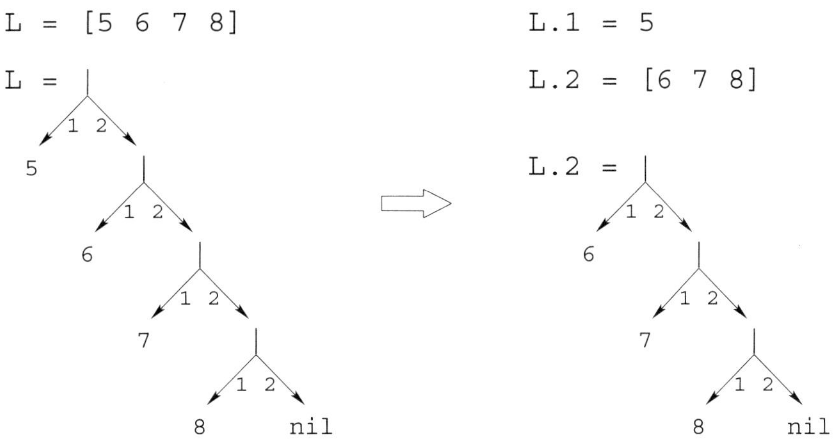

Figure 1.1: Taking apart the list `[5 6 7 8]`.

This triangle is named after scientist and philosopher Blaise Pascal. It starts with 1 in the first row. Each element is the sum of the two elements just above it to the left and right. (If there is no element, as on the edges, then zero is taken.) We would like to define one function that calculates the whole nth row in one swoop. The nth row has n integers in it. We can do it by using lists of integers.

A list is just a sequence of elements, bracketed at the left and right, like `[5 6 7 8]`. For historical reasons, the empty list is written `nil` (and not `[]`). Lists can be displayed just like numbers:

```
{Browse [5 6 7 8]}
```

The notation `[5 6 7 8]` is a shortcut. A list is actually a chain of links, where each link contains two things: one list element and a reference to the rest of the chain. Lists are always created one element at a time, starting with `nil` and adding links one by one. A new link is written `H|T`, where `H` is the new element and `T` is the old part of the chain. Let us build a list. We start with `Z=nil`. We add a first link `Y=7|Z` and then a second link `X=6|Y`. Now `X` references a list with two links, a list that can also be written as `[6 7]`.

The link `H|T` is often called a cons, a term that comes from Lisp.[2] We also call it a list pair. Creating a new link is called consing. If `T` is a list, then consing `H` and `T` together makes a new list `H|T`:

2. Much list terminology was introduced with the Lisp language in the late 1950s and has stuck ever since [137]. Our use of the vertical bar comes from Prolog, a logic programming language that was invented in the early 1970s [45, 201]. Lisp itself writes the cons as `(H . T)`, which it calls a dotted pair.

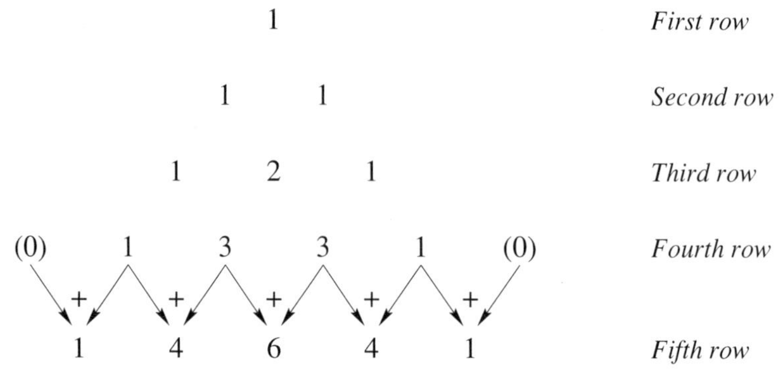

Figure 1.2: Calculating the fifth row of Pascal's triangle.

```
declare
H=5
T=[6 7 8]
{Browse H|T}
```

The list `H|T` can be written `[5 6 7 8]`. It has head `5` and tail `[6 7 8]`. The cons `H|T` can be taken apart, to get back the head and tail:

```
declare
L=[5 6 7 8]
{Browse L.1}
{Browse L.2}
```

This uses the dot operator "`.`", which is used to select the first or second argument of a list pair. Doing `L.1` gives the head of `L`, the integer `5`. Doing `L.2` gives the tail of `L`, the list `[6 7 8]`. Figure 1.1 gives a picture: `L` is a chain in which each link has one list element and `nil` marks the end. Doing `L.1` gets the first element and doing `L.2` gets the rest of the chain.

Pattern matching

A more compact way to take apart a list is by using the **case** instruction, which gets both head and tail in one step:

```
declare
L=[5 6 7 8]
case L of H|T then {Browse H} {Browse T} end
```

This displays `5` and `[6 7 8]`, just like before. The **case** instruction declares two local variables, `H` and `T`, and binds them to the head and tail of the list `L`. We say the **case** instruction does pattern matching, because it decomposes `L` according to the "pattern" `H|T`. Local variables declared with a **case** are just like variables declared with **declare**, except that the variable exists only in the body of the **case** statement, i.e., between the **then** and the **end**.

1.5 Functions over lists

Now that we can calculate with lists, let us define a function, `{Pascal N}`, to calculate the nth row of Pascal's triangle. Let us first understand how to do the calculation by hand. Figure 1.2 shows how to calculate the fifth row from the fourth. Let us see how this works if each row is a list of integers. To calculate a row, we start from the previous row. We shift it left by one position and shift it right by one position. We then add the two shifted rows together. For example, take the fourth row:

```
[1  3  3  1]
```

We shift this row left and right and then add them together element by element:

```
  [1  3  3  1  0]
+ [0  1  3  3  1]
```

Note that shifting left adds a zero to the right and shifting right adds a zero to the left. Doing the addition gives

```
[1  4  6  4  1]
```

which is the fifth row.

The main function

Now that we understand how to solve the problem, we can write a function to do the same operations. Here it is:

```
declare Pascal AddList ShiftLeft ShiftRight
fun {Pascal N}
   if N==1 then [1]
   else
      {AddList {ShiftLeft {Pascal N-1}} {ShiftRight {Pascal N-1}}}
   end
end
```

In addition to defining `Pascal`, we declare the variables for the three auxiliary functions that remain to be defined.

The auxiliary functions

To solve the problem completely, we still have to define three functions: `ShiftLeft`, which shifts left by one position, `ShiftRight`, which shifts right by one position, and `AddList`, which adds two lists. Here are `ShiftLeft` and `ShiftRight`:

```
fun {ShiftLeft L}
   case L of H|T then
      H|{ShiftLeft T}
   else [0] end
end

fun {ShiftRight L} 0|L end
```

`ShiftRight` just adds a zero to the left. `ShiftLeft` traverses `L` one element at a time and builds the output one element at a time. We have added an **else** to the **case** instruction. This is similar to an **else** in an **if**: it is executed if the pattern of the **case** does not match. That is, when `L` is empty, then the output is `[0]`, i.e., a list with just zero inside.

Here is `AddList`:

```
fun {AddList L1 L2}
   case L1 of H1|T1 then
      case L2 of H2|T2 then
         H1+H2|{AddList T1 T2}
      end
   else nil end
end
```

This is the most complicated function we have seen so far. It uses two **case** instructions, one inside another, because we have to take apart two lists, `L1` and `L2`. Now we have the complete definition of `Pascal`. We can calculate any row of Pascal's triangle. For example, calling `{Pascal 20}` returns the 20th row:

```
[1 19 171 969 3876 11628 27132 50388 75582 92378
 92378 75582 50388 27132 11628 3876 969 171 19 1]
```

Is this answer correct? How can we tell? It looks right: it is symmetric (reversing the list gives the same list) and the first and second arguments are 1 and 19, which are right. Looking at figure 1.2, it is easy to see that the second element of the nth row is always $n-1$ (it is always one more than the previous row and it starts out zero for the first row). In the next section, we will see how to reason about correctness.

Top-down software development

Let us summarize the methodology we used to write `Pascal`:

- The first step is to understand how to do the calculation by hand.
- The second step is to write a main function to solve the problem, assuming that some auxiliary functions are known (here, `ShiftLeft`, `ShiftRight`, and `AddList`).
- The third step is to complete the solution by writing the auxiliary functions.

The methodology of first writing the main function and filling in the blanks afterward is known as *top-down* software development. It is one of the best known approaches to program design, but it gives only part of the story as we shall see.

1.6 Correctness

A program is correct if it does what we would like it to do. How can we tell whether a program is correct? Usually it is impossible to duplicate the program's calculation by hand. We need other ways. One simple way, which we used before, is to verify that the program is correct for outputs that we know. This increases confidence in the program. But it does not go very far. To prove correctness in general, we have to reason about the program. This means three things:

- We need a mathematical model of the operations of the programming language, defining what they should do. This model is called the language's semantics.
- We need to define what we would like the program to do. Usually, this is a mathematical definition of the inputs that the program needs and the output that it calculates. This is called the program's specification.
- We use mathematical techniques to reason about the program, using the semantics. We would like to demonstrate that the program satisfies the specification.

A program that is proved correct can still give incorrect results, if the system on which it runs is incorrectly implemented. How can we be confident that the system satisfies the semantics? Verifying this is a major undertaking: it means verifying the compiler, the run-time system, the operating system, the hardware, and the physics upon which the hardware is based! These are all important tasks, but they are beyond the scope of the book. We place our trust in the Mozart developers, software companies, hardware manufacturers, and physicists.[3]

Mathematical induction

One very useful technique is mathematical induction. This proceeds in two steps. We first show that the program is correct for the simplest case. Then we show that, if the program is correct for a given case, then it is correct for the next case. If we can be sure that all cases are eventually covered, then mathematical induction lets us conclude that the program is always correct. This technique can be applied for integers and lists:

- For integers, the simplest case is 0 and for a given integer n the next case is $n+1$.
- For lists, the simplest case is `nil` (the empty list) and for a given list `T` the next case is `H|T` (with no conditions on `H`).

Let us see how induction works for the factorial function:

- `{Fact 0}` returns the correct answer, namely 1.

3. Some would say that this is foolish. Paraphrasing Thomas Jefferson, they would say that the price of correctness is eternal vigilance.

■ Assume that {Fact N-1} is correct. Then look at the call {Fact N}. We see that the **if** instruction takes the **else** case (since N is not zero), and calculates N*{Fact N-1}. By hypothesis, {Fact N-1} returns the right answer. Therefore, assuming that the multiplication is correct, {Fact N} also returns the right answer.

This reasoning uses the mathematical definition of factorial, namely $n! = n\times(n-1)!$ if $n > 0$, and $0! = 1$. Later in the book we will see more sophisticated reasoning techniques. But the basic approach is always the same: start with the language semantics and problem specification, and use mathematical reasoning to show that the program correctly implements the specification.

1.7 Complexity

The Pascal function we defined above gets very slow if we try to calculate higher-numbered rows. Row 20 takes a second or two. Row 30 takes many minutes.[4] If you try it, wait patiently for the result. How come it takes this much time? Let us look again at the function Pascal:

```
fun {Pascal N}
   if N==1 then [1]
   else
     {AddList {ShiftLeft {Pascal N-1}} {ShiftRight {Pascal N-1}}}
   end
end
```

Calling {Pascal N} will call {Pascal N-1} two times. Therefore, calling {Pascal 30} will call {Pascal 29} twice, giving four calls to {Pascal 28}, eight to {Pascal 27}, and so forth, doubling with each lower row. This gives 2^{29} calls to {Pascal 1}, which is about half a billion. No wonder that {Pascal 30} is slow. Can we speed it up? Yes, there is an easy way: just call {Pascal N-1} once instead of twice. The second call gives the same result as the first. If we could just remember it, then one call would be enough. We can remember it by using a local variable. Here is a new function, FastPascal, that uses a local variable:

```
fun {FastPascal N}
   if N==1 then [1]
   else L in
      L={FastPascal N-1}
      {AddList {ShiftLeft L} {ShiftRight L}}
   end
end
```

We declare the local variable L by adding "L **in**" to the **else** part. This is just like using **declare**, except that the identifier can only be used between the **else** and the **end**. We bind L to the result of {FastPascal N-1}. Now we can use L wherever we need it. How fast is FastPascal? Try calculating row 30. This takes minutes

4. These times may vary depending on the speed of your machine.

with `Pascal`, but is done practically instantaneously with `FastPascal`. A lesson we can learn from this example is that using a good algorithm is more important than having the best possible compiler or fastest machine.

Run-time guarantees of execution time

As this example shows, it is important to know something about a program's execution time. Knowing the exact time is less important than knowing that the time will not blow up with input size. The execution time of a program as a function of input size, up to a constant factor, is called the program's *time complexity*. What this function is depends on how the input size is measured. We assume that it is measured in a way that makes sense for how the program is used. For example, we take the input size of `{Pascal N}` to be simply the integer `N` (and not, e.g., the amount of memory needed to store `N`).

The time complexity of `{Pascal N}` is proportional to 2^n. This is an exponential function in n, which grows very quickly as n increases. What is the time complexity of `{FastPascal N}`? There are n recursive calls and each call takes time proportional to n. The time complexity is therefore proportional to n^2. This is a polynomial function in n, which grows at a much slower rate than an exponential function. Programs whose time complexity is exponential are impractical except for very small inputs. Programs whose time complexity is a low-order polynomial are practical.

1.8 Lazy evaluation

The functions we have written so far will do their calculation as soon as they are called. This is called eager evaluation. There is another way to evaluate functions called lazy evaluation.[5] In lazy evaluation, a calculation is done only when the result is needed. This is covered in chapter 4 (see section 4.5). Here is a simple lazy function that calculates a list of integers:

```
fun lazy {Ints N}
   N|{Ints N+1}
end
```

Calling `{Ints 0}` calculates the infinite list `0|1|2|3|4|5|...`. This looks like an infinite loop, but it is not. The `lazy` annotation ensures that the function will only be evaluated when it is needed. This is one of the advantages of lazy evaluation: we can calculate with potentially infinite data structures without any loop boundary conditions. For example:

5. Eager and lazy evaluation are sometimes called data-driven and demand-driven evaluation, respectively.

```
L={Ints 0}
{Browse L}
```

This displays the following, i.e., nothing at all about the elements of `L`:

```
L<Future>
```

(The browser does not cause lazy functions to be evaluated.) The "`<Future>`" annotation means that `L` has a lazy function attached to it. If some elements of `L` are needed, then this function will be called automatically. Here is a calculation that needs an element of `L`:

```
{Browse L.1}
```

This displays the first element, namely 0. We can calculate with the list as if it were completely there:

```
case L of A|B|C|_ then {Browse A+B+C} end
```

This causes the first three elements of `L` to be calculated, and no more. What does it display?

Lazy calculation of Pascal's triangle

Let us do something useful with lazy evaluation. We would like to write a function that calculates as many rows of Pascal's triangle as are needed, but we do not know beforehand how many. That is, we have to look at the rows to decide when there are enough. Here is a lazy function that generates an infinite list of rows:

```
fun lazy {PascalList Row}
   Row|{PascalList
          {AddList {ShiftLeft Row} {ShiftRight Row}}}
end
```

Calling this function and browsing it will display nothing:

```
declare
L={PascalList [1]}
{Browse L}
```

(The argument `[1]` is the first row of the triangle.) To display more results, they have to be needed:

```
{Browse L.1}
{Browse L.2.1}
```

This displays the first and second rows.

Instead of writing a lazy function, we could write a function that takes `N`, the number of rows we need, and directly calculates those rows starting from an initial row:

```
fun {PascalList2 N Row}
   if N==1 then [Row]
   else
      Row|{PascalList2 N-1
               {AddList {ShiftLeft Row} {ShiftRight Row}}}
   end
end
```

We can display 10 rows by calling `{Browse {PascalList2 10 [1]}}`. But what if later on we decide that we need 11 rows? We would have to call `PascalList2` again, with argument 11. This would redo all the work of defining the first 10 rows. The lazy version avoids redoing all this work. It is always ready to continue where it left off.

1.9 Higher-order programming

We have written an efficient function, `FastPascal`, that calculates rows of Pascal's triangle. Now we would like to experiment with variations on Pascal's triangle. For example, instead of adding numbers to get each row, we would like to subtract them, exclusive-or them (to calculate just whether they are odd or even), or many other possibilities. One way to do this is to write a new version of `FastPascal` for each variation. But this quickly becomes tiresome. Is it possible to have just a single version that can be used for all variations? This is indeed possible. Let us call it `GenericPascal`. Whenever we call it, we pass it the customizing function (adding, exclusive-oring, etc.) as an argument. The ability to pass functions as arguments is known as higher-order programming.

Here is the definition of `GenericPascal`. It has one extra argument `Op` to hold the function that calculates each number:

```
fun {GenericPascal Op N}
   if N==1 then [1]
   else L in
      L={GenericPascal Op N-1}
      {OpList Op {ShiftLeft L} {ShiftRight L}}
   end
end
```

`AddList` is replaced by `OpList`. The extra argument `Op` is passed to `OpList`. `ShiftLeft` and `ShiftRight` do not need to know `Op`, so we can use the old versions. Here is the definition of `OpList`:

```
fun {OpList Op L1 L2}
   case L1 of H1|T1 then
      case L2 of H2|T2 then
         {Op H1 H2}|{OpList Op T1 T2}
      end
   else nil end
end
```

Instead of doing the addition `H1+H2`, this version does `{Op H1 H2}`.

Variations on Pascal's triangle

Let us define some functions to try out `GenericPascal`. To get the original Pascal's triangle, we can define the addition function:

```
fun {Add X Y} X+Y end
```

Now we can run `{GenericPascal Add 5}`.[6] This gives the fifth row exactly as before. We can define `FastPascal` using `GenericPascal`:

```
fun {FastPascal N} {GenericPascal Add N} end
```

Let us define another function:

```
fun {Xor X Y} if X==Y then 0 else 1 end end
```

This does an *exclusive-or* operation, which is defined as follows:

X	Y	{Xor X Y}
0	0	0
0	1	1
1	0	1
1	1	0

Exclusive-or lets us calculate the parity of each number in Pascal's triangle, i.e., whether the number is odd or even. The numbers themselves are not calculated. Calling `{GenericPascal Xor N}` gives the result:

```
                    1
                 1     1
              1     0     1
           1     1     1     1
        1     0     0     0     1
     1     1     0     0     1     1
  .  .  .  .  .  .  .  .  .  .  .  .  .
```

Some other functions are given in the exercises.

1.10 Concurrency

We would like our program to have several independent activities, each of which executes at its own pace. This is called *concurrency*. There should be no interference

6. We can also call `{GenericPascal Number.´+´ 5}`, since the addition operation `´+´` is part of the module `Number`. But modules are not introduced in this chapter.

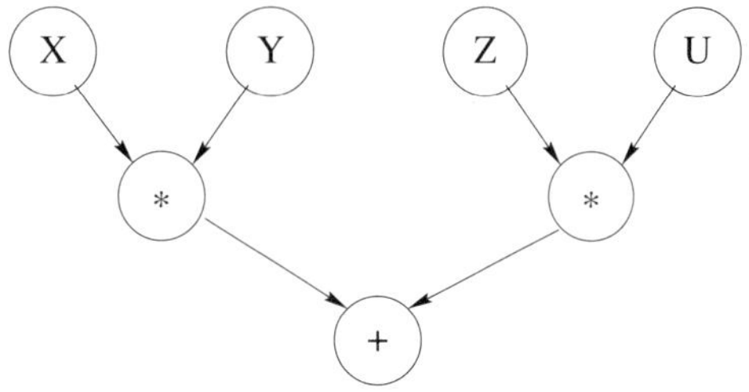

Figure 1.3: A simple example of dataflow execution.

among the activities, unless the programmer decides that they need to communicate. This is how the real world works outside of the system. We would like to be able to do this inside the system as well.

We introduce concurrency by creating threads. A thread is simply an executing program like the functions we saw before. The difference is that a program can have more than one thread. Threads are created with the **thread** instruction. Do you remember how slow the original `Pascal` function was? We can call `Pascal` inside its own thread. This means that it will not keep other calculations from continuing. They may slow down, if `Pascal` really has a lot of work to do. This is because the threads share the same underlying computer. But none of the threads will stop. Here is an example:

```
thread P in
   P={Pascal 30}
   {Browse P}
end
{Browse 99*99}
```

This creates a new thread. Inside this new thread, we call `{Pascal 30}` and then call `Browse` to display the result. The new thread has a lot of work to do. But this does not keep the system from displaying `99*99` immediately.

1.11 Dataflow

What happens if an operation tries to use a variable that is not yet bound? From a purely aesthetic point of view, it would be nice if the operation would simply wait. Perhaps some other thread will bind the variable, and then the operation can continue. This civilized behavior is known as dataflow. Figure 1.3 gives a simple example: the two multiplications wait until their arguments are bound and the addition waits until the multiplications complete. As we will see later in the book, there are many good reasons to have dataflow behavior. For now, let us see how dataflow and concurrency work together. Take, e.g.:

```
declare X in
thread {Delay 10000} X=99 end
{Browse start} {Browse X*X}
```

The multiplication `X*X` waits until `X` is bound. The first `Browse` immediately displays `start`. The second `Browse` waits for the multiplication, so it displays nothing yet. The `{Delay 10000}` call pauses for 10000 ms (i.e., 10 seconds). `X` is bound only after the delay continues. When `X` is bound, then the multiplication continues and the second browse displays 9801. The two operations `X=99` and `X*X` can be done in any order with any kind of delay; dataflow execution will always give the same result. The only effect a delay can have is to slow things down. For example:

```
declare X in
thread {Browse start} {Browse X*X} end
{Delay 10000} X=99
```

This behaves exactly as before: the browser displays 9801 after 10 seconds. This illustrates two nice properties of dataflow. First, calculations work correctly independent of how they are partitioned between threads. Second, calculations are patient: they do not signal errors, but simply wait.

Adding threads and delays to a program can radically change a program's appearance. But as long as the same operations are invoked with the same arguments, it does not change the program's results at all. This is the key property of dataflow concurrency. This is why dataflow concurrency gives most of the advantages of concurrency without the complexities that are usually associated with it. Dataflow concurrency is covered in chapter 4.

1.12 Explicit state

How can we let a function learn from its past? That is, we would like the function to have some kind of internal memory, which helps it do its job. Memory is needed for functions that can change their behavior and learn from their past. This kind of memory is called explicit state. Just like for concurrency, explicit state models an essential aspect of how the real world works. We would like to be able to do this in the system as well. Later in the book we will see deeper reasons for having explicit state (see chapter 6). For now, let us just see how it works.

For example, we would like to see how often the `FastPascal` function is used. Is there some way `FastPascal` can remember how many times it was called? We can do this by adding explicit state.

A memory cell

There are lots of ways to define explicit state. The simplest way is to define a single memory cell. This is a kind of box in which you can put any content. Many programming languages call this a "variable." We call it a "cell" to avoid confusion with the variables we used before, which are more like mathematical variables, i.e., just shortcuts for values. There are three functions on cells: `NewCell` creates a new cell, `:=` (assignment) puts a new value in a cell, and `@` (access) gets the current value stored in the cell. Access and assignment are also called read and write. For example:

```
declare
C={NewCell 0}
C:=@C+1
{Browse @C}
```

This creates a cell `C` with initial content 0, adds one to the content, and displays it.

Adding memory to `FastPascal`

With a memory cell, we can let `FastPascal` count how many times it is called. First we create a cell outside of `FastPascal`. Then, inside of `FastPascal`, we add 1 to the cell's content. This gives the following:

```
declare
C={NewCell 0}
fun {FastPascal N}
   C:=@C+1
   {GenericPascal Add N}
end
```

(To keep it short, this definition uses `GenericPascal`.)

1.13 Objects

A function with internal memory is usually called an *object*. The extended version of `FastPascal` we defined in the previous section is an object. It turns out that objects are very useful beasts. Let us give another example. We will define a counter object. The counter has a cell that keeps track of the current count. The counter has two operations, `Bump` and `Read`, which we call its interface. `Bump` adds 1 and then returns the resulting count. `Read` just returns the count. Here is the definition:

```
declare
local C in
   C={NewCell 0}
   fun {Bump}
      C:=@C+1
      @C
   end
   fun {Read}
      @C
   end
end
```

The **local** statement declares a new variable `C` that is visible only up to the matching **end**. There is something special going on here: the cell is referenced by a local variable, so it is completely invisible from the outside. This is called encapsulation. Encapsulation implies that users cannot mess with the counter's internals. We can guarantee that the counter will always work correctly no matter how it is used. This was not true for the extended `FastPascal` because anyone could look at and modify the cell.

It follows that as long as the interface to the counter object is the same, the user program does not need to know the implementation. The separation of interface and implementation is the essence of data abstraction. It can greatly simplify the user program. A program that uses a counter will work correctly for any implementation as long as the interface is the same. This property is called polymorphism. Data abstraction with encapsulation and polymorphism is covered in chapter 6 (see section 6.4).

We can bump the counter up:

```
{Browse {Bump}}
{Browse {Bump}}
```

What does this display? `Bump` can be used anywhere in a program to count how many times something happens. For example, `FastPascal` could use `Bump`:

```
declare
fun {FastPascal N}
   {Browse {Bump}}
   {GenericPascal Add N}
end
```

1.14 Classes

The last section defined one counter object. What if we need more than one counter? It would be nice to have a "factory" that can make as many counters as we need. Such a factory is called a *class*. Here is one way to define it:

```
declare
fun {NewCounter}
C Bump Read in
   C={NewCell 0}
   fun {Bump}
      C:=@C+1
      @C
   end
   fun {Read}
      @C
   end
   counter(bump:Bump read:Read)
end
```

`NewCounter` is a function that creates a new cell and returns new `Bump` and `Read` functions that use the cell. Returning functions as results of functions is another form of higher-order programming.

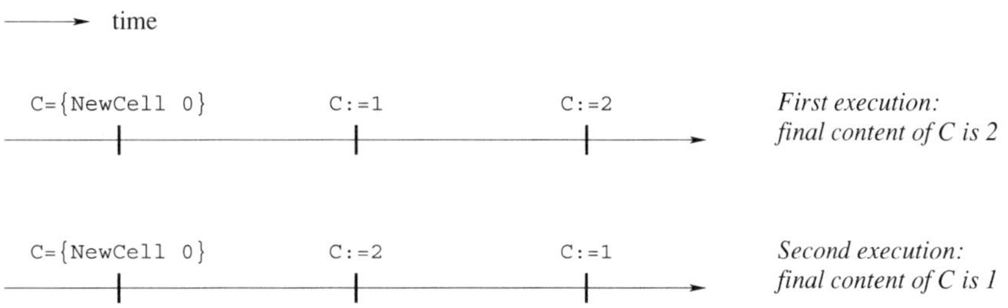

Figure 1.4: All possible executions of the first nondeterministic example.

We group the `Bump` and `Read` functions together into a record, which is a compound data structure that allows easy access to its parts. The record `counter(bump:Bump read:Read)` is characterized by its label `counter` and by its two fields, called `bump` and `read`. Let us create two counters:

```
declare
Ctr1={NewCounter}
Ctr2={NewCounter}
```

Each counter has its own internal memory and its own `Bump` and `Read` functions. We can access these functions by using the "`.`" (dot) operator. `Ctr1.bump` accesses the `Bump` function of the first counter. Let us bump the first counter and display its result:

```
{Browse {Ctr1.bump}}
```

Toward object-oriented programming

We have given an example of a simple class, `NewCounter`, that defines two operations, `Bump` and `Read`. Operations defined inside classes are usually called methods. The class can be used to make as many counter objects as we need. All these objects share the same methods, but each has its own separate internal memory. Programming with classes and objects is called object-based programming.

Adding one new idea, inheritance, to object-based programming gives object-oriented programming. Inheritance means that a new class can be defined in terms of existing classes by specifying just how the new class is different. For example, say we have a counter class with just a `Bump` method. We can define a new class that is the same as the first class except that it adds a `Read` method. We say the new class inherits from the first class. Inheritance is a powerful concept for structuring programs. It lets a class be defined incrementally, in different parts of the program. Inheritance is quite a tricky concept to use correctly. To make inheritance easy to use, object-oriented languages add special syntax for it. Chapter 7 covers object-oriented programming and shows how to program with inheritance.

1.15 Nondeterminism and time

We have seen how to add concurrency and state to a program separately. What happens when a program has both? It turns out that having both at the same time is a tricky business, because the same program can give different results from one execution to the next. This is because the order in which threads access the state can change from one execution to the next. This variability is called nondeterminism. Nondeterminism exists because we lack knowledge of the exact time when each basic operation executes. If we would know the exact time, then there would be no nondeterminism. But we cannot know this time, simply because threads are independent. Since they know nothing of each other, they also do not know which instructions each has executed.

Nondeterminism by itself is not a problem; we already have it with concurrency. The difficulties occur if the nondeterminism shows up in the program, i.e., if it is observable. An observable nondeterminism is sometimes called a race condition. Here is an example:

```
declare
C={NewCell 0}
thread
   C:=1
end
thread
   C:=2
end
```

What is the content of C after this program executes? Figure 1.4 shows the two possible executions of this program. Depending on which one is done, the final cell content can be either 1 or 2. The problem is that we cannot say which. This is a simple case of observable nondeterminism. Things can get much trickier. For example, let us use a cell to hold a counter that can be incremented by several threads:

```
declare
C={NewCell 0}
thread I in
   I=@C
   C:=I+1
end
thread J in
   J=@C
   C:=J+1
end
```

What is the content of C after this program executes? It looks like each thread just adds 1 to the content, making it 2. But there is a surprise lurking: the final content can also be 1! How is this possible? Try to figure out why before continuing.

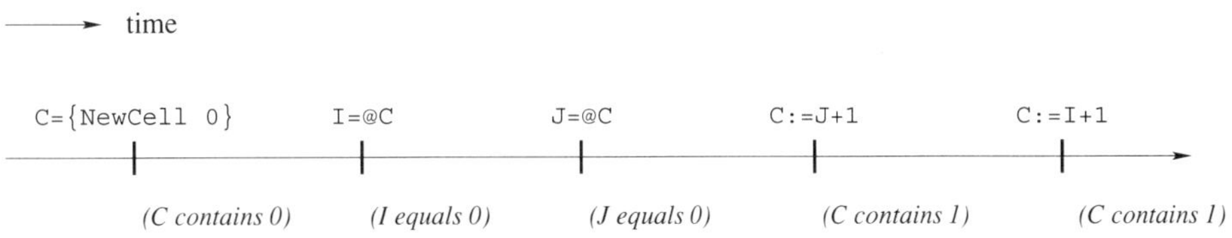

Figure 1.5: One possible execution of the second nondeterministic example.

Interleaving

The content can be 1 because thread execution is interleaved. That is, threads take turns each executing a little. We have to assume that any possible interleaving can occur. For example, consider the execution of figure 1.5. Both `I` and `J` are bound to 0. Then, since `I+1` and `J+1` are both 1, the cell gets assigned 1 twice. The final result is that the cell content is 1.

This is a simple example. More complicated programs have many more possible interleavings. Programming with concurrency and state together is largely a question of mastering the interleavings. In the history of computer technology, many famous and dangerous bugs were due to designers not realizing how difficult this really is. The Therac-25 radiation therapy machine is an infamous example. Because of concurrent programming errors, it sometimes gave its patients radiation doses that were thousands of times greater than normal, resulting in death or serious injury [128].

This leads us to a first lesson for programming with state and concurrency: if at all possible, do not use them together! It turns out that we often do not need both together. When a program does need to have both, it can almost always be designed so that their interaction is limited to a very small part of the program.

1.16 Atomicity

Let us think some more about how to program with concurrency and state. One way to make it easier is to use atomic operations. An operation is *atomic* if no intermediate states can be observed. It seems to jump directly from the initial state to the result state. Programming with atomic actions is covered in chapter 8.

With atomic operations we can solve the interleaving problem of the cell counter. The idea is to make sure that each thread body is atomic. To do this, we need a way to build atomic operations. We introduce a new language entity, called a lock, for this. A lock has an inside and an outside. The programmer defines the instructions that are inside. A lock has the property that only one thread at a time can be executing inside. If a second thread tries to get in, then it will wait until the first gets out. Therefore what happens inside the lock is atomic.

We need two operations on locks. First, we create a new lock by calling the function `NewLock`. Second, we define the lock's inside with the instruction **lock** `L` **then** ... **end**, where `L` is a lock. Now we can fix the cell counter:

```
declare
C={NewCell 0}
L={NewLock}
thread
   lock L then I in
      I=@C
      C:=I+1
   end
end
thread
   lock L then J in
      J=@C
      C:=J+1
   end
end
```

In this version, the final result is always 2. Both thread bodies have to be guarded by the same lock, otherwise the undesirable interleaving can still occur. Do you see why?

1.17 Where do we go from here?

This chapter has given a quick overview of many of the most important concepts in programming. The intuitions given here will serve you well in the chapters to come, when we define in a precise way the concepts and the computation models they are part of. This chapter has introduced the following computation models:

- Declarative model (chapters 2 and 3). Declarative programs define mathematical functions. They are the easiest to reason about and to test. The declarative model is important also because it contains many of the ideas that will be used in later, more expressive models.
- Concurrent declarative model (chapter 4). Adding dataflow concurrency gives a model that is still declarative but that allows a more flexible, incremental execution.
- Lazy declarative model (section 4.5). Adding laziness allows calculating with potentially infinite data structures. This is good for resource management and program structure.
- Stateful model (chapter 6). Adding explicit state allows writing programs whose behavior changes over time. This is good for program modularity. If written well, i.e., using encapsulation and invariants, these programs are almost as easy to reason about as declarative programs.
- Object-oriented model (chapter 7). Object-oriented programming is a programming style for stateful programming with data abstractions. It makes it easy to use

powerful techniques such as polymorphism and inheritance.

- Shared-state concurrent model (chapter 8). This model adds both concurrency and explicit state. If programmed carefully, using techniques for mastering interleaving such as monitors and transactions, this gives the advantages of both the stateful and concurrent models.

In addition to these models, the book covers many other useful models such as the declarative model with exceptions (section 2.7), the message-passing concurrent model (chapter 5), the relational model (chapter 9), and the specialized models of part II.

1.18 Exercises

1. *A calculator.* Section 1.1 uses the system as a calculator. Let us explore the possibilities:

   (a) Calculate the exact value of 2^{100} without using any new functions. Try to think of shortcuts to do it without having to type `2*2*2*...*2` with one hundred 2s. *Hint*: use variables to store intermediate results.

   (b) Calculate the exact value of 100! without using any new functions. Are there any possible shortcuts in this case?

2. *Calculating combinations.* Section 1.3 defines the function `Comb` to calculate combinations. This function is not very efficient because it might require calculating very large factorials. The purpose of this exercise is to write a more efficient version of `Comb`.

   (a) As a first step, use the following alternative definition to write a more efficient function:

   $$\binom{n}{k} = \frac{n \times (n-1) \times \cdots \times (n-k+1)}{k \times (k-1) \times \cdots \times 1}$$

   Calculate the numerator and denominator separately and then divide them. Make sure that the result is 1 when $k = 0$.

   (b) As a second step, use the following identity:

   $$\binom{n}{k} = \binom{n}{n-k}$$

   to increase efficiency even more. That is, if $k > n/2$, then do the calculation with $n - k$ instead of with k.

3. *Program correctness.* Section 1.6 explains the basic ideas of program correctness and applies them to show that the factorial function defined in section 1.3 is correct. In this exercise, apply the same ideas to the function `Pascal` of section 1.5 to show that it is correct.

4. *Program complexity.* What does section 1.7 say about programs whose time complexity is a high-order polynomial? Are they practical or not? What do you

think?

5. *Lazy evaluation.* Section 1.8 defines the lazy function `Ints` that lazily calculates an infinite list of integers. Let us define a function that calculates the sum of a list of integers:

```
fun {SumList L}
   case L of X|L1 then X+{SumList L1}
   else 0 end
end
```

What happens if we call `{SumList {Ints 0}}`? Is this a good idea?

6. *Higher-order programming.* Section 1.9 explains how to use higher-order programming to calculate variations on Pascal's triangle. The purpose of this exercise is to explore these variations.

   (a) Calculate individual rows using subtraction, multiplication, and other operations. Why does using multiplication give a triangle with all zeros? Try the following kind of multiplication instead:

   ```
   fun {Mul1 X Y} (X+1)*(Y+1) end
   ```

   What does the 10th row look like when calculated with `Mul1`?

   (b) The following loop instruction will calculate and display 10 rows at a time:

   ```
   for I in 1..10 do {Browse {GenericPascal Op I}} end
   ```

   Use this loop instruction to make it easier to explore the variations.

7. *Explicit state.* This exercise compares variables and cells. We give two code fragments. The first uses variables:

```
local X in
   X=23
   local X in
      X=44
   end
   {Browse X}
end
```

The second uses a cell:

```
local X in
   X={NewCell 23}
   X:=44
   {Browse @X}
end
```

In the first, the identifier `X` refers to two different variables. In the second, `X` refers to a cell. What does `Browse` display in each fragment? Explain.

8. *Explicit state and functions.* This exercise investigates how to use cells together with functions. Let us define a function `{Accumulate N}` that accumulates all its inputs, i.e., it adds together all the arguments of all calls. Here is an example:

```
{Browse {Accumulate 5}}
{Browse {Accumulate 100}}
{Browse {Accumulate 45}}
```

This should display 5, 105, and 150, assuming that the accumulator contains zero at the start. Here is a wrong way to write `Accumulate`:

```
declare
fun {Accumulate N}
Acc in
   Acc={NewCell 0}
   Acc:=@Acc+N
   @Acc
end
```

What is wrong with this definition? How would you correct it?

9. *Memory store.* This exercise investigates another way of introducing state: a memory store. The memory store can be used to make an improved version of `FastPascal` that remembers previously calculated rows.

(a) A memory store is similar to the memory of a computer. It has a series of memory cells, numbered from 1 up to the maximum used so far. There are four functions on memory stores: `NewStore` creates a new store, `Put` puts a new value in a memory cell, `Get` gets the current value stored in a memory cell, and `Size` gives the number of cells used so far. For example:

```
declare
S={NewStore}
{Put S 2 [22 33]}
{Browse {Get S 2}}
{Browse {Size S}}
```

This stores `[22 33]` in memory cell 2, displays `[22 33]`, and then displays 1. Load into the Mozart system the memory store as defined in the supplements file on the book's Web site. Then use the interactive interface to understand how the store works.

(b) Now use the memory store to write an improved version of `FastPascal`, called `FasterPascal`, that remembers previously calculated rows. If a call asks for one of these rows, then the function can return it directly without having to recalculate it. This technique is sometimes called memoization since the function makes a "memo" of its previous work. This improves its performance. Here's how it works:

- First make a store S available to `FasterPascal`.
- For the call `{FasterPascal N}`, let m be the number of rows stored in S, i.e., rows 1 up to m are in S.
- If $n > m$, then compute rows $m+1$ up to n and store them in S.
- Return the nth row by looking it up in S.

Viewed from the outside, `FasterPascal` behaves identically to `FastPascal` except that it is faster.

(c) We have given the memory store as a library. It turns out that the memory store can be defined by using a memory cell. We outline how it can be done and you can write the definitions. The cell holds the store contents as a list of the form `[N1|X1 ... Nn|Xn]`, where the cons `Ni|Xi` means that cell number `Ni` has content `Xi`. This means that memory stores, while they are convenient, do not introduce any additional expressive power over memory cells.

(d) Section 1.13 defines a counter object. Change your implementation of the memory store so that it uses this counter to keep track of the store's size.

10. *Explicit state and concurrency.* Section 1.15 gives an example using a cell to store a counter that is incremented by two threads.

(a) Try executing this example several times. What results do you get? Do you ever get the result 1? Why could this be?

(b) Modify the example by adding calls to `Delay` in each thread. This changes the thread interleaving without changing what calculations the thread does. Can you devise a scheme that always results in 1?

(c) Section 1.16 gives a version of the counter that never gives the result 1. What happens if you use the delay technique to try to get a 1 anyway?

I GENERAL COMPUTATION MODELS

2 Declarative Computation Model

Non sunt multiplicanda entia praeter necessitatem.
Do not multiply entities beyond necessity.
– Ockham's razor, after William of Ockham (1285?–1347/49)

Programming encompasses three things:

- First, a computation model, which is a formal system that defines a language and how sentences of the language (e.g., expressions and statements) are executed by an abstract machine. For this book, we are interested in computation models that are useful and intuitive for programmers. This will become clearer when we define the first one later in this chapter.
- Second, a set of programming techniques and design principles used to write programs in the language of the computation model. We will sometimes call this a programming model. A programming model is always built on top of a computation model.
- Third, a set of reasoning techniques to let you reason about programs, to increase confidence that they behave correctly, and to calculate their efficiency.

The above definition of computation model is very general. Not all computation models defined in this way will be useful for programmers. What is a reasonable computation model? Intuitively, we will say that a reasonable model is one that can be used to solve many problems, that has straightforward and practical reasoning techniques, and that can be implemented efficiently. We will have more to say about this question later on. The first and simplest computation model we will study is declarative programming. For now, we define this as evaluating functions over partial data structures. This is sometimes called stateless programming, as opposed to stateful programming (also called imperative programming) which is explained in chapter 6.

The declarative model of this chapter is one of the most fundamental computation models. It encompasses the core ideas of the two main declarative paradigms, namely functional and logic programming. It encompasses programming with functions over complete values, as in Scheme and Standard ML. It also encompasses deterministic logic programming, as in Prolog when search is not used. And finally, it can be made concurrent without losing its good properties (see chapter 4).

Declarative programming is a rich area—it has most of the ideas of the more expressive computation models, at least in embryonic form. We therefore present it in two chapters. This chapter defines the computation model and a practical language based on it. The next chapter, chapter 3, gives the programming techniques of this language. Later chapters enrich the basic model with many concepts. Some of the most important are exception handling, concurrency, components (for programming in the large), capabilities (for encapsulation and security), and state (leading to objects and classes). In the context of concurrency, we will talk about dataflow, lazy execution, message passing, active objects, monitors, and transactions. We will also talk about user interface design, distribution (including fault tolerance), and constraints (including search).

Structure of the chapter

The chapter consists of eight sections:

- Section 2.1 explains how to define the syntax and semantics of practical programming languages. Syntax is defined by a context-free grammar extended with language constraints. Semantics is defined in two steps: by translating a practical language into a simple kernel language and then giving the semantics of the kernel language. These techniques will be used throughout the book. This chapter uses them to define the declarative computation model.
- The next three sections define the syntax and semantics of the declarative model:
    - Section 2.2 gives the data structures: the single-assignment store and its contents, partial values and dataflow variables.
    - Section 2.3 defines the kernel language syntax.
    - Section 2.4 defines the kernel language semantics in terms of a simple abstract machine. The semantics is designed to be intuitive and to permit straightforward reasoning about correctness and complexity.
- Section 2.5 uses the abstract machine to explore the memory behavior of computations. We look at last call optimization and the concept of memory life cycle.
- Section 2.6 defines a practical programming language on top of the kernel language.
- Section 2.7 extends the declarative model with exception handling, which allows programs to handle unpredictable and exceptional situations.
- Section 2.8 gives a few advanced topics to let interested readers deepen their understanding of the model.

2.1 Defining practical programming languages

Programming languages are much simpler than natural languages, but they can still have a surprisingly rich syntax, set of abstractions, and libraries. This is especially

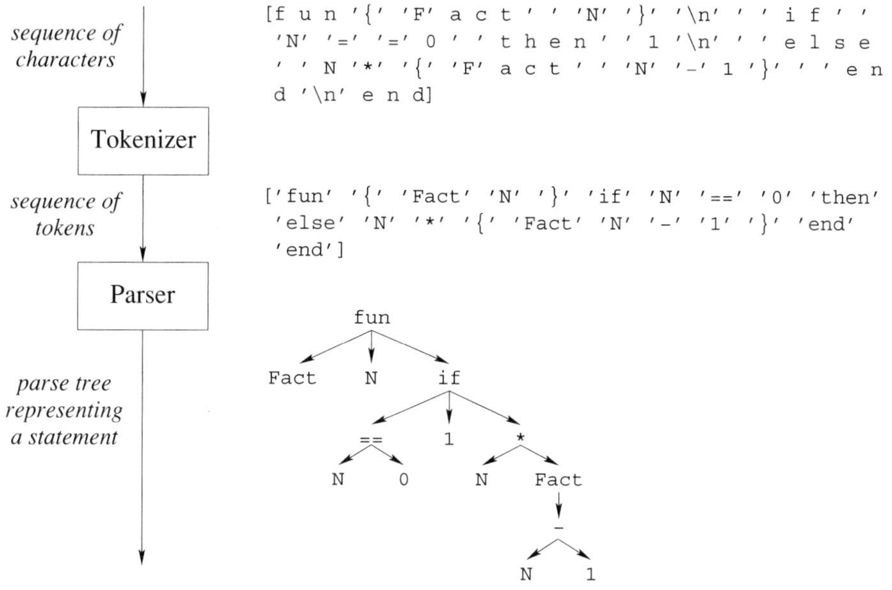

Figure 2.1: From characters to statements.

true for languages that are used to solve real-world problems, which we call practical languages. A practical language is like the toolbox of an experienced mechanic: there are many different tools for many different purposes and all tools are there for a reason.

This section sets the stage for the rest of the book by explaining how we will present the syntax ("grammar") and semantics ("meaning") of practical programming languages. With this foundation we will be ready to present the first computation model of the book, namely the declarative computation model. We will continue to use these techniques throughout the book to define computation models.

2.1.1 Language syntax

The syntax of a language defines what are the legal programs, i.e., programs that can be successfully executed. At this stage we do not care what the programs are actually doing. That is semantics and will be handled in section 2.1.2.

Grammars

A grammar is a set of rules that defines how to make 'sentences' out of 'words'. Grammars can be used for natural languages, like English or Swedish, as well as for artificial languages, like programming languages. For programming languages, 'sentences' are usually called 'statements' and 'words' are usually called 'tokens'. Just as words are made of letters, tokens are made of characters. This gives us two levels of structure:

statement ('sentence')	=	sequence of tokens ('words')
token ('word')	=	sequence of characters ('letters')

Grammars are useful both for defining statements and tokens. Figure 2.1 gives an example to show how character input is transformed into a statement. The example in the figure is the definition of `Fact`:

```
fun {Fact N}
   if N==0 then 1
   else N*{Fact N-1} end
end
```

The input is a sequence of characters, where `' '` represents the space and `'\n'` represents the newline. This is first transformed into a sequence of tokens and subsequently into a parse tree. The syntax of both sequences in the figure is compatible with the list syntax we use throughout the book. Whereas the sequences are "flat," the parse tree shows the structure of the statement. A program that accepts a sequence of characters and returns a sequence of tokens is called a tokenizer or lexical analyzer. A program that accepts a sequence of tokens and returns a parse tree is called a parser.

Extended Backus-Naur Form

One of the most common notations for defining grammars is called Extended Backus-Naur Form (EBNF), after its inventors John Backus and Peter Naur. The EBNF notation distinguishes terminal symbols and nonterminal symbols. A terminal symbol is simply a token. A nonterminal symbol represents a sequence of tokens. The nonterminal is defined by means of a grammar rule, which shows how to expand it into tokens. For example, the following rule defines the nonterminal $\langle\text{digit}\rangle$:

$$\langle\text{digit}\rangle \quad ::= \quad 0 \mid 1 \mid 2 \mid 3 \mid 4 \mid 5 \mid 6 \mid 7 \mid 8 \mid 9$$

It says that $\langle\text{digit}\rangle$ represents one of the ten tokens 0, 1, ..., 9. The symbol "|" is read as "or"; it means to pick one of the alternatives. Grammar rules can themselves refer to other nonterminals. For example, we can define a nonterminal $\langle\text{int}\rangle$ that defines how to write positive integers:

$$\langle\text{int}\rangle \quad ::= \quad \langle\text{digit}\rangle \; \{ \; \langle\text{digit}\rangle \; \}$$

This rule says that an integer is a digit followed by any number of digits, including none. The braces "{ ... }" mean to repeat whatever is inside any number of times, including none.

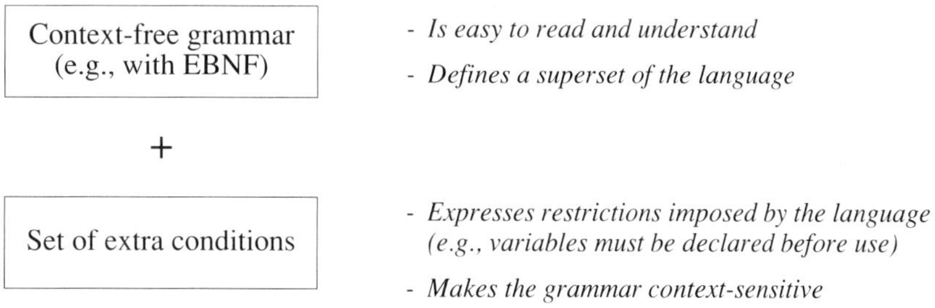

Figure 2.2: The context-free approach to language syntax.

How to read grammars

To read a grammar, start with any nonterminal symbol, say ⟨int⟩. Reading the corresponding grammar rule from left to right gives a sequence of tokens according to the following scheme:

- Each terminal symbol encountered is added to the sequence.
- For each nonterminal symbol encountered, read its grammar rule and replace the nonterminal by the sequence of tokens that it expands into.
- Each time there is a choice (with |), pick any of the alternatives.

The grammar can be used both to verify that a statement is legal and to generate statements.

Context-free and context-sensitive grammars

Any well-defined set of statements is called a formal language, or language for short. For example, the set of all possible statements generated by a grammar and one nonterminal symbol is a language. Techniques to define grammars can be classified according to how expressive they are, i.e., what kinds of languages they can generate. For example, the EBNF notation given above defines a class of grammars called context-free grammars. They are so-called because the expansion of a nonterminal, e.g., ⟨digit⟩, is always the same no matter where it is used.

For most practical programming languages, there is usually no context-free grammar that generates all legal programs and no others. For example, in many languages a variable has to be declared before it is used. This condition cannot be expressed in a context-free grammar because the nonterminal that uses the variable must only allow using already-declared variables. This is a context dependency. A grammar that contains a nonterminal whose use depends on the context where it is used is called a context-sensitive grammar.

The syntax of most practical programming languages is therefore defined in two parts (see figure 2.2): as a context-free grammar supplemented with a set of extra

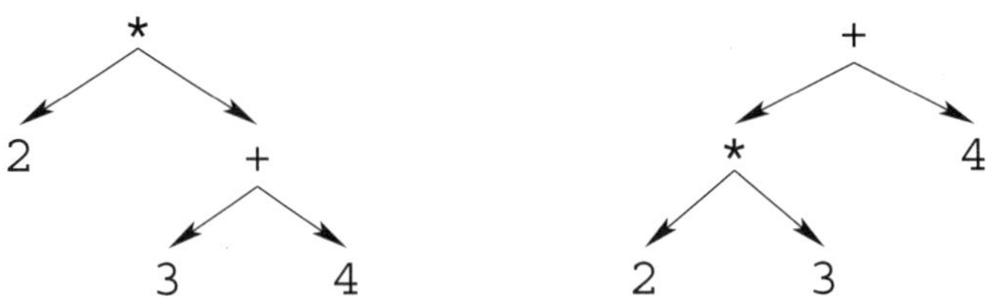

Figure 2.3: Ambiguity in a context-free grammar.

conditions imposed by the language. The context-free grammar is kept instead of some more expressive notation because it is easy to read and understand. It has an important locality property: a nonterminal symbol can be understood by examining only the rules needed to define it; the (possibly much more numerous) rules that use it can be ignored. The context-free grammar is corrected by imposing a set of extra conditions, like the declare-before-use restriction on variables. Taking these conditions into account gives a context-sensitive grammar.

Ambiguity

Context-free grammars can be ambiguous, i.e., there can be several parse trees that correspond to a given token sequence. For example, here is a simple grammar for arithmetic expressions with addition and multiplication:

$\langle\mathsf{exp}\rangle$ ::= $\langle\mathsf{int}\rangle \mid \langle\mathsf{exp}\rangle\ \langle\mathsf{op}\rangle\ \langle\mathsf{exp}\rangle$
$\langle\mathsf{op}\rangle$ ::= + | *

The expression `2*3+4` has two parse trees, depending on how the two occurrences of ⟨exp⟩ are read. Figure 2.3 shows the two trees. In one tree, the first ⟨exp⟩ is `2` and the second ⟨exp⟩ is `3+4`. In the other tree, they are `2*3` and `4`, respectively.

Ambiguity is usually an undesirable property of a grammar since it is unclear exactly what program is being written. In the expression `2*3+4`, the two parse trees give different results when evaluating the expression: one gives 14 (the result of computing 2*(3+4)) and the other gives 10 (the result of computing (2*3)+4). Sometimes the grammar rules can be rewritten to remove the ambiguity, but this can make the rules more complicated. A more convenient approach is to add extra conditions. These conditions restrict the parser so that only one parse tree is possible. We say that they disambiguate the grammar.

For expressions with binary operators such as the arithmetic expressions given above, the usual approach is to add two conditions, precedence and associativity:

- Precedence is a condition on an expression with different operators, like `2*3+4`. Each operator is given a precedence level. Operators with high precedences are put as deep in the parse tree as possible, i.e., as far away from the root as possible. If `*` has higher precedence than `+`, then the parse tree `(2*3)+4` is chosen over the alternative `2*(3+4)`. If `*` is deeper in the tree than `+`, then we say that `*` binds tighter than `+`.

- Associativity is a condition on an expression with the same operator, like `2-3-4`. In this case, precedence is not enough to disambiguate because all operators have the same precedence. We have to choose between the trees `(2-3)-4` and `2-(3-4)`. Associativity determines whether the leftmost or the rightmost operator binds tighter. If the associativity of `-` is `left`, then the tree `(2-3)-4` is chosen. If the associativity of `-` is `right`, then the other tree `2-(3-4)` is chosen.

Precedence and associativity are enough to disambiguate all expressions defined with operators. Appendix C gives the precedence and associativity of all the operators used in the book.

Syntax notation used in the book

In this chapter and the rest of the book, each new data type and language construct is introduced together with a small syntax diagram that shows how it fits in the whole language. The syntax diagram gives grammar rules for a simple context-free grammar of tokens. The notation is carefully designed to satisfy two basic principles:

- All grammar rules stand on their own. No later information will ever invalidate a grammar rule. That is, we never give an incorrect grammar rule just to "simplify" the presentation.
- It is always clear by inspection when a grammar rule completely defines a nonterminal symbol or when it gives only a partial definition. A partial definition always ends in three dots "...".

All syntax diagrams used in the book are collected in appendix C. This appendix also gives the lexical syntax of tokens, i.e., the syntax of tokens in terms of characters. Here is an example of a syntax diagram with two grammar rules that illustrates our notation:

$$\langle \text{statement} \rangle \quad ::= \quad \textbf{skip} \mid \langle \text{expression} \rangle \text{ ´=´ } \langle \text{expression} \rangle \mid \ldots$$
$$\langle \text{expression} \rangle \quad ::= \quad \langle \text{variable} \rangle \mid \langle \text{int} \rangle \mid \ldots$$

These rules give partial definitions of two nonterminals, ⟨statement⟩ and ⟨expression⟩. The first rule says that a statement can be the keyword **`skip`**, or two expressions separated by the equals symbol `=`, or something else. The second rule says that an expression can be a variable, an integer, or something else. A choice between different possibilities in the grammar rule is given by a vertical bar |. To avoid confusion with the grammar rule's own syntax, we will sometimes quote a symbol that occurs literally in the text with single quotes. For example, the equals symbol is shown as ´=´. Keywords are not quoted, since for them no confusion is possible.

Here is a second example to give the remaining notation:

⟨statement⟩	::=	**if** ⟨expression⟩ **then** ⟨statement⟩
		{ **elseif** ⟨expression⟩ **then** ⟨statement⟩ }
		[**else** ⟨statement⟩] **end** | ...
⟨expression⟩	::=	´[´ { ⟨expression⟩ }+ ´]´ | ...
⟨label⟩	::=	**unit** | **true** | **false** | ⟨variable⟩ | ⟨atom⟩

The first rule defines the **if** statement. There is an optional sequence of **elseif** clauses, i.e., there can be any number of occurrences including zero. This is denoted by the braces { ... }. This is followed by an optional **else** clause, i.e., it can occur zero or one times. This is denoted by the brackets [...]. The second rule defines the syntax of explicit lists. They must have at least one element, e.g., `[5 6 7]` is valid but `[ ]` is not (note the space that separates the `[` and the `]`). This is denoted by { ... }+. The third rule defines the syntax of record labels. The third rule is a complete definition since there are no three dots "...". There are five possibilities and no more will ever be given.

2.1.2 Language semantics

The semantics of a language defines what a program does when it executes. Ideally, the semantics should be defined in a simple mathematical structure that lets us reason about the program (including its correctness, execution time, and memory use) without introducing any irrelevant details. Can we achieve this for a practical language without making the semantics too complicated? The technique we use, which we call the kernel language approach, gives an affirmative answer to this question.

Modern programming languages have evolved through more than five decades of experience in constructing programmed solutions to complex, real-world problems.[1] Modern programs can be quite complex, reaching sizes measured in millions of lines of code, written by large teams of human programmers over many years. In our view, languages that scale to this level of complexity are successful in part because they model some essential aspects of how to construct complex programs. In this sense, these languages are not just arbitrary constructions of the human mind. We would therefore like to understand them in a scientific way, i.e., by explaining their behavior in terms of a simple underlying model. This is the deep motivation behind the kernel language approach.

1. The figure of five decades is somewhat arbitrary. We measure it from the first working stored-program computer, the Manchester Mark I. According to lab documents, it ran its first program on June 21, 1948 [197].

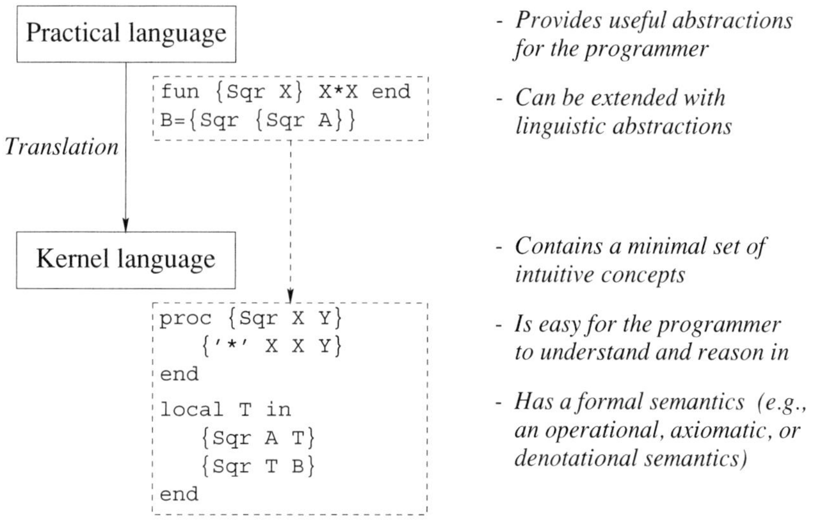

Figure 2.4: The kernel language approach to semantics.

The kernel language approach

This book uses the kernel language approach to define the semantics of programming languages. In this approach, all language constructs are defined in terms of translations into a core language known as the kernel language. The kernel language approach consists of two parts (see figure 2.4):

- First, define a very simple language, called the kernel language. This language should be easy to reason in and be faithful to the space and time efficiency of the implementation. The kernel language and the data structures it manipulates together form the kernel computation model.
- Second, define a translation scheme from the full programming language to the kernel language. Each grammatical construct in the full language is translated into the kernel language. The translation should be as simple as possible. There are two kinds of translation, namely linguistic abstraction and syntactic sugar. Both are explained below.

The kernel language approach is used throughout the book. Each computation model has its kernel language, which builds on its predecessor by adding one new concept. The first kernel language, which is presented in this chapter, is called the declarative kernel language. Many other kernel languages are presented later on in the book.

Formal semantics

The kernel language approach lets us define the semantics of the kernel language in any way we want. There are four widely used approaches to language semantics:

- An operational semantics shows how a statement executes in terms of an abstract machine. This approach always works well, since at the end of the day all languages execute on a computer.
- An axiomatic semantics defines a statement's semantics as the relation between the input state (the situation before executing the statement) and the output state (the situation after executing the statement). This relation is given as a logical assertion. This is a good way to reason about statement sequences, since the output assertion of each statement is the input assertion of the next. It therefore works well with stateful models, since a state is a sequence of values. Section 6.6 gives an axiomatic semantics of chapter 6's stateful model.
- A denotational semantics defines a statement as a function over an abstract domain. This works well for declarative models, but can be applied to other models as well. It gets complicated when applied to concurrent languages. Sections 2.8.1 and 4.9.2 explain functional programming, which is particularly close to denotational semantics.
- A logical semantics defines a statement as a model of a logical theory. This works well for declarative and relational computation models, but is hard to apply to other models. Section 9.3 gives a logical semantics of the declarative and relational computation models.

Much of the theory underlying these different semantics is of interest primarily to mathematicians, not to programmers. It is outside the scope of the book to give this theory. The principal formal semantics we give in the book is an operational semantics. We define it for each computation model. It is detailed enough to be useful for reasoning about correctness and complexity yet abstract enough to avoid irrelevant clutter. Chapter 13 collects all these operational semantics into a single formalism with a compact and readable notation.

Throughout the book, we give an informal semantics for every new language construct and we often reason informally about programs. These informal presentations are always based on the operational semantics.

Linguistic abstraction

Both programming languages and natural languages can evolve to meet their needs. When using a programming language, at some point we may feel the need to extend the language, i.e., to add a new linguistic construct. For example, the declarative model of this chapter has no looping constructs. Section 3.6.3 defines a **`for`** construct to express certain kinds of loops that are useful for writing declarative programs. The new construct is both an abstraction and an addition to the language syntax.

We therefore call it a linguistic abstraction. A practical programming language contains many linguistic abstractions.

There are two phases to defining a linguistic abstraction. First, define a new grammatical construct. Second, define its translation into the kernel language. The kernel language is not changed. This book gives many examples of useful linguistic abstractions, e.g., functions (**fun**), loops (**for**), lazy functions (**fun** `lazy`), classes (**class**), reentrant locks (**lock**), and others.[2] Some of these are part of the Mozart system. The others can be added to Mozart with the `gump` parser-generator tool [117]. Using this tool is beyond the scope of the book.

Some languages have facilities for programming linguistic abstractions directly in the language. A simple yet powerful example is the Lisp macro. A Lisp macro resembles a function that generates Lisp code when executed. Partly because of Lisp's simple syntax, macros have been extraordinarily successful in Lisp and its successors. Lisp has built-in support for macros, such as quote (turning a program expression into a data structure) and backquote (doing the inverse, inside a quoted structure). For a detailed discussion of Lisp macros and related ideas we refer the reader to any good book on Lisp [72, 200].

A simple example of a linguistic abstraction is the function, which uses the keyword **fun**. This is explained in section 2.6.2. We have already programmed with functions in chapter 1. But the kernel language of this chapter only has procedures. Procedures are used since all arguments are explicit and there can be multiple outputs. There are other, deeper reasons for choosing procedures which are explained later in this chapter. Because functions are so useful, though, we add them as a linguistic abstraction.

We define a syntax for both function definitions and function calls, and a translation into procedure definitions and procedure calls. The translation lets us answer all questions about function calls. For example, what does `{F1 {F2 X} {F3 Y}}` mean exactly (nested function calls)? Is the order of these function calls defined? If so, what is the order? There are many possibilities. Some languages leave the order of argument evaluation unspecified, but assume that a function's arguments are evaluated before the function. Other languages assume that an argument is evaluated when and if its result is needed, not before. So even as simple a thing as nested function calls does not necessarily have an obvious semantics. The translation makes it clear what the semantics is.

Linguistic abstractions are useful for more than just increasing the expressiveness of a program. They can also improve other properties such as correctness, security, and efficiency. By hiding the abstraction's implementation from the programmer, the linguistic support makes it impossible to use the abstraction in the wrong way. The compiler can use this information to give more efficient code.

---

2. Logic gates (**gate**) for circuit descriptions, mailboxes (**receive**) for message-passing concurrency, and currying and list comprehensions as in modern functional languages, cf. Haskell.

Syntactic sugar

It is often convenient to provide a shortcut notation for frequently occurring idioms. This notation is part of the language syntax and is defined by grammar rules. This notation is called syntactic sugar. Syntactic sugar is analogous to linguistic abstraction in that its meaning is defined precisely by translating it into the full language. But it should not be confused with linguistic abstraction: it does not provide a new abstraction, but just reduces program size and improves program readability.

We give an example of syntactic sugar that is based on the **local** statement. Local variables can always be defined by using the statement **local** X **in** ... **end**. When this statement is used inside another, it is convenient to have syntactic sugar that lets us leave out the keywords **local** and **end**. Instead of

```
if N==1 then [1]
else
   local L in
      ...
   end
end
```

we can write

```
if N==1 then [1]
else L in
   ...
end
```

which is both shorter and more readable than the full notation. Other examples of syntactic sugar are given in section 2.6.1.

Language design

Linguistic abstractions are a basic tool for language design. They have a natural place in the life cycle of an abstraction. An abstraction has three phases in its life cycle. When first we define it, it has no linguistic support, i.e., there is no syntax in the language designed to make it easy to use. If at some point, we suspect that it is especially basic and useful, we can decide to give it linguistic support. It then becomes a linguistic abstraction. This is an exploratory phase, i.e., there is no commitment that the linguistic abstraction will become part of the language. If the linguistic abstraction is successful, i.e., it simplifies programs and is useful to programmers, then it becomes part of the language.

Other translation approaches

The kernel language approach is an example of a translation approach to semantics, i.e., it is based on a translation from one language to another. Figure 2.5 shows the three ways that the translation approach has been used for defining programming languages:

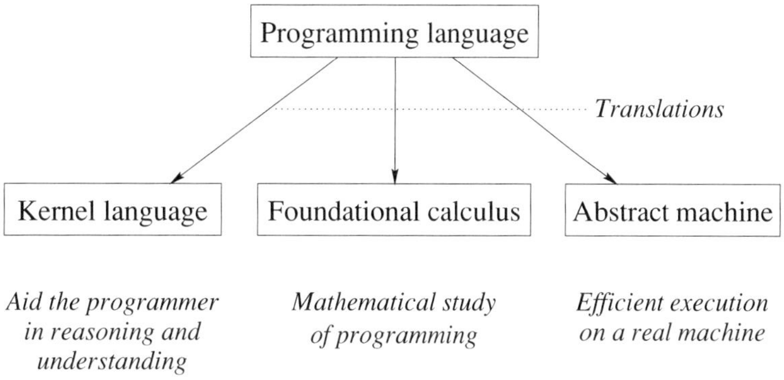

Figure 2.5: Translation approaches to language semantics.

- The kernel language approach, used throughout the book, is intended for the programmer. Its concepts correspond directly to programming concepts.
- The foundational approach is intended for the mathematician. Examples are the Turing machine, the λ calculus (underlying functional programming), first-order logic (underlying logic programming), and the π calculus (to model concurrency). Because these calculi are intended for formal mathematical study, they have as few elements as possible.
- The abstract machine approach is intended for the implementor. Programs are translated into an idealized machine, which is traditionally called an *abstract machine* or a *virtual machine*.[3] It is relatively easy to translate idealized machine code into real machine code.

Because we focus on practical programming techniques, the book uses only the kernel language approach. The other two approaches have the problem that any realistic program written in them is cluttered with technical details about language mechanisms. The kernel language approach avoids this clutter by a careful choice of concepts.

The interpreter approach

An alternative to the translation approach is the interpreter approach. The language semantics is defined by giving an interpreter for the language. New language features

---

3. Strictly speaking, a virtual machine is a software emulation of a real machine, running on the real machine, that is almost as efficient as the real machine. It achieves this efficiency by executing most virtual instructions directly as real instructions. The concept was pioneered by IBM in the early 1960s in the VM operating system. Because of the success of Java, which uses the term "virtual machine," modern usage also uses the term virtual machine in the sense of abstract machine.

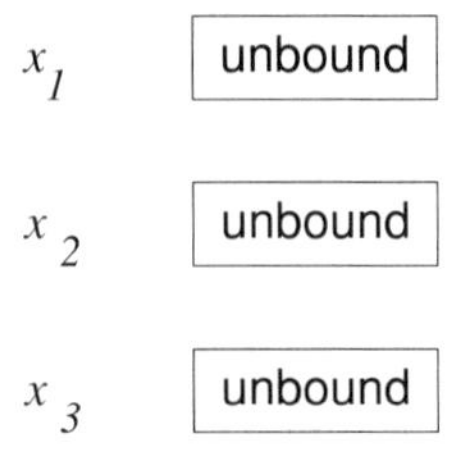

Figure 2.6: A single-assignment store with three unbound variables.

are defined by extending the interpreter. An interpreter is a program written in language L_1 that accepts programs written in another language L_2 and executes them. This approach is used by Abelson, Sussman, and Sussman [2]. In their case, the interpreter is metacircular, i.e., L_1 and L_2 are the same language L. Adding new language features, e.g., for concurrency and lazy evaluation, gives a new language L' which is implemented by extending the interpreter for L.

The interpreter approach has the advantage that it shows a self-contained implementation of the linguistic abstractions. We do not use the interpreter approach in this book because it does not in general preserve the execution-time complexity of programs (the number of operations needed as a function of input size). A second difficulty is that the basic concepts interact with each other in the interpreter, which makes them harder to understand. The translation approach makes it easier to keep the concepts separate.

2.2 The single-assignment store

We introduce the declarative model by first explaining its data structures. The model uses a single-assignment store, which is a set of variables that are initially unbound and that can be bound to one value. Figure 2.6 shows a store with three unbound variables x_1, x_2, and x_3. We can write this store as $\{x_1, x_2, x_3\}$. For now, let us assume we can use integers, lists, and records as values. Figure 2.7 shows the store where x_1 is bound to the integer 314 and x_2 is bound to the list `[1 2 3]`. We write this as $\{x_1 = 314, x_2 =$ `[1 2 3]`$, x_3\}$.

2.2.1 Declarative variables

Variables in the single-assignment store are called declarative variables. We use this term whenever there is a possible confusion with other kinds of variables. Later on in the book, we will also call these variables dataflow variables because of their role in dataflow execution.

Once bound, a declarative variable stays bound throughout the computation and is indistinguishable from its value. What this means is that it can be used in

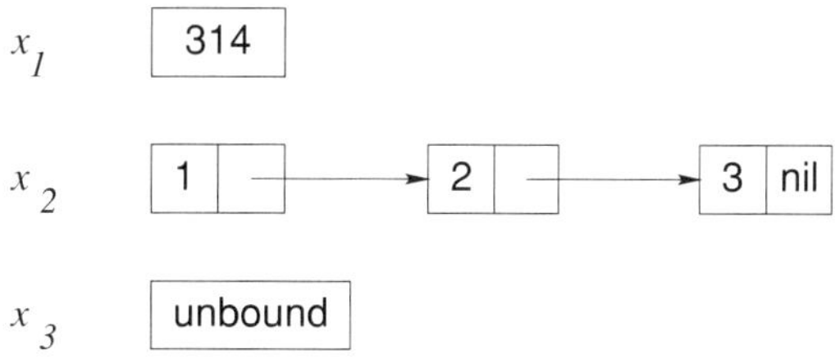

Figure 2.7: Two of the variables are bound to values.

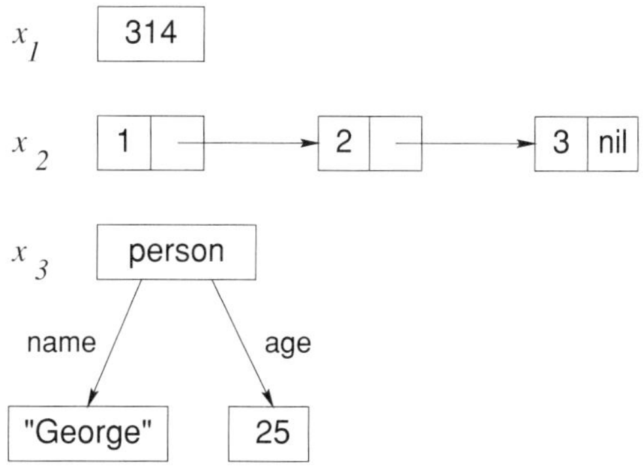

Figure 2.8: A value store: all variables are bound to values.

calculations as if it were the value. Doing the operation $x + y$ is the same as doing $11 + 22$, if the store is $\{x = 11, y = 22\}$.

2.2.2 Value store

A store where all variables are bound to values is called a value store. Another way to say this is that a value store is a persistent mapping from variables to values. A value is a mathematical constant. For example, the integer 314 is a value. Values can also be compound entities, i.e., entities that contain one or more other values. For example, the list `[1 2 3]` and the record `person(name:"George" age:25)` are values. Figure 2.8 shows a value store where x_1 is bound to the integer 314, x_2 is bound to the list `[1 2 3]`, and x_3 is bound to the record `person(name:"George" age:25)`. Functional languages such as Standard ML, Haskell, and Scheme get by with a value store since they compute functions on values. (Object-oriented languages such as Smalltalk, C++, and Java need a cell store, which consists of cells whose content can be modified.)

At this point, a reader with some programming experience may wonder why we are introducing a single-assignment store, when other languages get by with

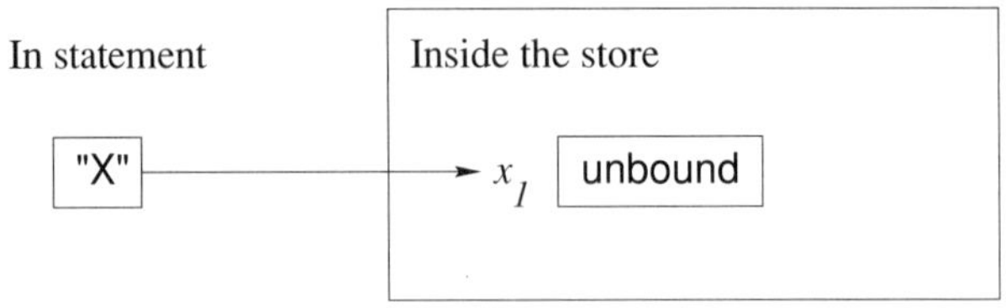

Figure 2.9: A variable identifier referring to an unbound variable.

a value store or a cell store. There are many reasons. A first reason is that we want to compute with partial values. For example, a procedure can return an output by binding an unbound variable argument. A second reason is declarative concurrency, which is the subject of chapter 4. It is possible because of the single-assignment store. A third reason is that a single-assignment store is needed for relational (logic) programming and constraint programming. Other reasons having to do with efficiency (e.g., tail recursion and difference lists) will become clear in the next chapter.

2.2.3 Value creation

The basic operation on a store is binding a variable to a newly created value. We will write this as x_i=*value*. Here x_i refers directly to a variable in the store (it is not the variable's textual name in a program!) and *value* refers to a value, e.g., 314 or `[1 2 3]`. For example, figure 2.7 shows the store of figure 2.6 after the two bindings:

$x_1 = 314$
$x_2 =$ `[1 2 3]`

The single-assignment operation x_i=*value* constructs *value* in the store and then binds the variable x_i to this value. If the variable is already bound, the operation will test whether the two values are compatible. If they are not compatible, an error is signaled (using the exception-handling mechanism; see section 2.7).

2.2.4 Variable identifiers

So far, we have looked at a store that contains variables and values, i.e., store entities, with which calculations can be done. It would be nice if we could refer to a store entity from outside the store. This is the role of variable identifiers. A variable identifier is a textual name that refers to a store entity from outside the store. The mapping from variable identifiers to store entities is called an environment.

The variable names in program source code are in fact variable identifiers. For example, figure 2.9 has an identifier "`X`" (the capital letter X) that refers to the store variable x_1. This corresponds to the environment {`X` $\rightarrow x_1$}. To talk about

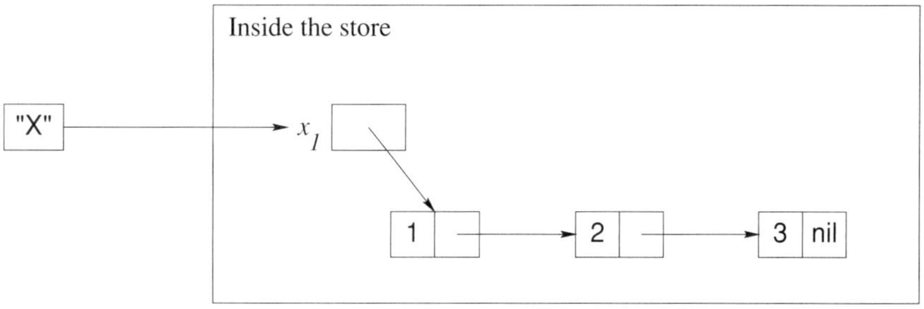

Figure 2.10: A variable identifier referring to a bound variable.

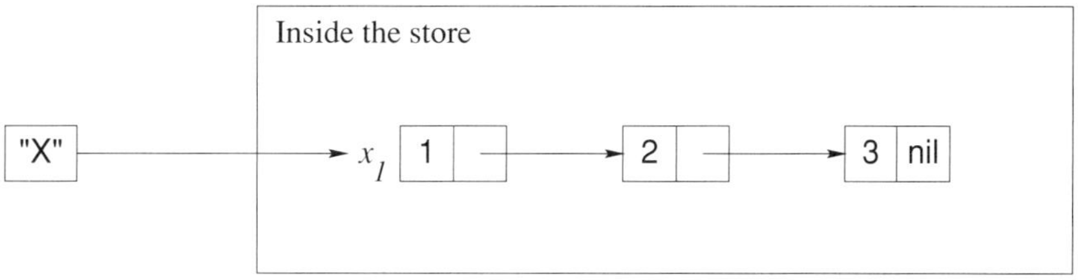

Figure 2.11: A variable identifier referring to a value.

any identifier, we will use the notation ⟨x⟩. The environment $\{\langle x\rangle \rightarrow x_1\}$ is the same as before, if ⟨x⟩ represents `X`. As we will see later, variable identifiers and their corresponding store entities are added to the environment by the **`local`** and **`declare`** statements.

2.2.5 Value creation with identifiers

Once bound, a variable is indistinguishable from its value. Figure 2.10 shows what happens when x_1 is bound to `[1 2 3]` in figure 2.9. With the variable identifier `X`, we can write the binding as `X=[1 2 3]`. This is the text a programmer would write to express the binding. We can also use the notation ⟨x⟩`=[1 2 3]` if we want to be able to talk about any identifier. To make this notation legal in a program, ⟨x⟩ has to be replaced by an identifier.

The equality sign "`=`" refers to the bind operation. After the bind completes, the identifier "`X`" still refers to x_1, which is now bound to `[1 2 3]`. This is indistinguishable from figure 2.11, where `X` refers directly to `[1 2 3]`. Following the links of bound variables to get the value is called dereferencing. It is invisible to the programmer.

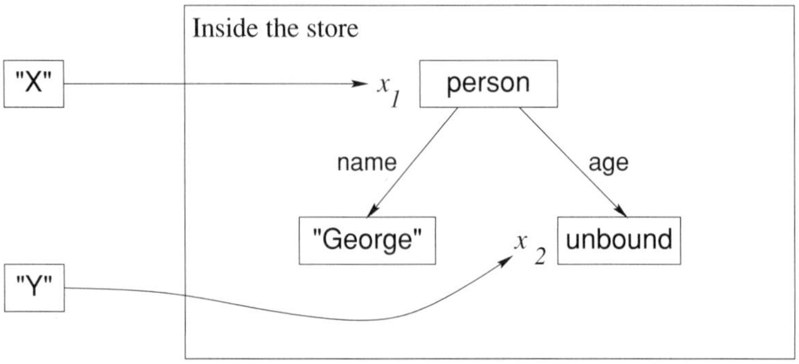

Figure 2.12: A partial value.

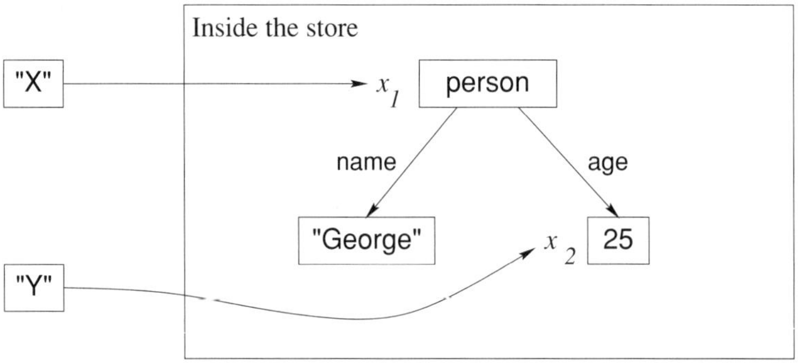

Figure 2.13: A partial value with no unbound variables, i.e., a complete value.

2.2.6 Partial values

A partial value is a data structure that may contain unbound variables. Figure 2.12 shows the record `person(name:"George" age:`x_2`)`, referred to by the identifier `X`. This is a partial value because it contains the unbound variable x_2. The identifier `Y` refers to x_2. Figure 2.13 shows the situation after x_2 is bound to 25 (through the bind operation `Y=25`). Now x_1 is a partial value with no unbound variables, which we call a complete value. A declarative variable can be bound to several partial values, as long as they are compatible with each other. We say a set of partial values is compatible if the unbound variables in them can be bound in such a way as to make them all equal. For example, `person(age:25)` and `person(age:`x`)` are compatible (because x can be bound to 25), but `person(age:25)` and `person(age:26)` are not.

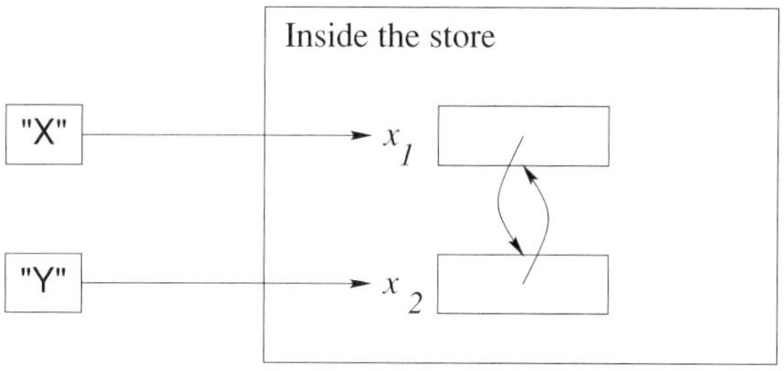

Figure 2.14: Two variables bound together.

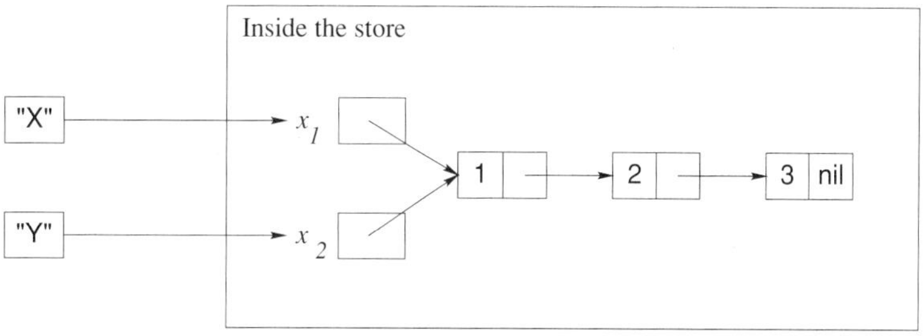

Figure 2.15: The store after binding one of the variables.

2.2.7 Variable-variable binding

Variables can be bound to variables. For example, consider two unbound variables x_1 and x_2 referred to by the identifiers `X` and `Y`. After doing the bind `X=Y`, we get the situation in figure 2.14. The two variables x_1 and x_2 are equal to each other. The figure shows this by letting each variable refer to the other. We say that $\{x_1, x_2\}$ form an equivalence set.[4] We also write this as $x_1 = x_2$. Three variables that are bound together are written as $x_1 = x_2 = x_3$ or $\{x_1, x_2, x_3\}$. Drawn in a figure, these variables would form a circular chain. Whenever one variable in an equivalence set is bound, then all variables see the binding. Figure 2.15 shows the result of doing `X=[1 2 3]`.

2.2.8 Dataflow variables

In the declarative model, creating a variable and binding it are done separately. What happens if we try to use the variable before it is bound? We call this a

4. From a formal viewpoint, the two variables form an equivalence class with respect to equality.

variable use error. Some languages create and bind variables in one step, so that use errors cannot occur. This is the case for functional programming languages. Other languages allow creating and binding to be separate. Then we have the following possibilities when there is a use error:

1. Execution continues and no error message is given. The variable's content is undefined, i.e. it is "garbage": whatever is found in memory. This is what C++ does.

2. Execution continues and no error message is given. The variable is initialized to a default value when it is declared, e.g., to 0 for an integer. This is what Java does for fields in objects and data structures, such as arrays. The default value depends on the type.

3. Execution stops with an error message (or an exception is raised). This is what Prolog does for arithmetic operations.

4. Execution is not possible because the compiler detects that there is an execution path to the variable's use that does not initialize it. This is what Java does for local variables.

5. Execution waits until the variable is bound and then continues. This is what Oz does, to support dataflow programming.

These cases are listed in increasing order of niceness. The first case is very bad, since different executions of the same program can give different results. What's more, since the existence of the error is not signaled, the programmer is not even aware when this happens. The second case is somewhat better. If the program has a use error, then at least it will always give the same result, even if it is a wrong one. Again the programmer is not made aware of the error's existence.

The third and fourth cases can be reasonable in certain situations. In both cases, a program with a use error will signal this fact, either during execution or at compile time. This is reasonable in a sequential system, since there really is an error. The third case is unreasonable in a concurrent system, since the result becomes nondeterministic: depending on the execution timing, sometimes an error is signaled and sometimes not.

In the fifth case, the program will wait until the variable is bound and then continue. The computation models of the book use the fifth case. This is unreasonable in a sequential system, since the program will wait forever. It is reasonable in a concurrent system, where it could be part of normal operation that some other thread binds the variable. The fifth case introduces a new kind of program error, namely a suspension that waits forever. For example, if a variable name is misspelled then it will never be bound. A good debugger should detect when this occurs.

Declarative variables that cause the program to wait until they are bound are called *dataflow variables*. The declarative model uses dataflow variables because they are tremendously useful in concurrent programming, i.e., for programs with activities that run independently. If we do two concurrent operations, say `A=23` and `B=A+1`, then with the fifth case this will always run correctly and give the answer

⟨s⟩ ::=	
skip	Empty statement
| ⟨s⟩$_1$ ⟨s⟩$_2$	Statement sequence
| **local** ⟨x⟩ **in** ⟨s⟩ **end**	Variable creation
| ⟨x⟩$_1$=⟨x⟩$_2$	Variable-variable binding
| ⟨x⟩=⟨v⟩	Value creation
| **if** ⟨x⟩ **then** ⟨s⟩$_1$ **else** ⟨s⟩$_2$ **end**	Conditional
| **case** ⟨x⟩ **of** ⟨pattern⟩ **then** ⟨s⟩$_1$ **else** ⟨s⟩$_2$ **end**	Pattern matching
| { ⟨x⟩ ⟨y⟩$_1$ ... ⟨y⟩$_n$ }	Procedure application

Table 2.1: The declarative kernel language.

`B=24`. It doesn't matter whether `A=23` is run first or whether `B=A+1` is run first. With the other cases, there is no guarantee of this. This property of order-independence makes possible the declarative concurrency of chapter 4. It is at the heart of why dataflow variables are a good idea.

2.3 Kernel language

The declarative model defines a simple kernel language. All programs in the model can be expressed in this language. We first define the kernel language syntax and semantics. Then we explain how to build a full language on top of the kernel language.

2.3.1 Syntax

The kernel syntax is given in tables 2.1 and 2.2. It is carefully designed to be a subset of the full language syntax, i.e., all statements in the kernel language are valid statements in the full language.

Statement syntax

Table 2.1 defines the syntax of ⟨s⟩, which denotes a statement. There are eight statements in all, which we will explain later.

Value syntax

Table 2.2 defines the syntax of ⟨v⟩, which denotes a value. There are three kinds of value expressions, denoting numbers, records, and procedures. For records and patterns, the arguments ⟨x⟩$_1$, ..., ⟨x⟩$_n$ must all be distinct identifiers. This ensures

⟨v⟩	::=	⟨number⟩ | ⟨record⟩ | ⟨procedure⟩
⟨number⟩	::=	⟨int⟩ | ⟨float⟩
⟨record⟩, ⟨pattern⟩	::=	⟨literal⟩
	|	⟨literal⟩(⟨feature⟩$_1$: ⟨x⟩$_1$ ··· ⟨feature⟩$_n$: ⟨x⟩$_n$)
⟨procedure⟩	::=	**proc** { $ ⟨x⟩$_1$ ··· ⟨x⟩$_n$} ⟨s⟩ **end**
⟨literal⟩	::=	⟨atom⟩ | ⟨bool⟩
⟨feature⟩	::=	⟨atom⟩ | ⟨bool⟩ | ⟨int⟩
⟨bool⟩	::=	**true** | **false**

Table 2.2: Value expressions in the declarative kernel language.

that all variable-variable bindings are written as explicit kernel operations.

Variable identifier syntax

Table 2.1 uses the nonterminals ⟨x⟩ and ⟨y⟩ to denote a variable identifier. We will also use ⟨z⟩ to denote identifiers. There are two ways to write a variable identifier:

- An uppercase letter followed by zero or more alphanumeric characters (letters or digits or underscores), e.g., `X`, `X1`, or `ThisIsALongVariable_IsntIt`.
- Any sequence of printable characters enclosed within ` (backquote) characters, e.g., `` `this is a 25$\variable!` ``.

A precise definition of identifier syntax is given in appendix C. All newly declared variables are unbound before any statement is executed. All variable identifiers must be declared explicitly.

2.3.2 Values and types

A type or data type is a set of values together with a set of operations on those values. A value is "of a type" if it is in the type's set. The declarative model is typed in the sense that it has a well-defined set of types, called basic types. For example, programs can calculate with integers or with records, which are all of integer type or record type, respectively. Any attempt to use an operation with values of the wrong type is detected by the system and will raise an error condition (see section 2.7). The model imposes no other restrictions on the use of types.

Because all uses of types are checked, it is not possible for a program to behave outside of the model, e.g., to crash because of undefined operations on its internal data structures. It is still possible for a program to raise an error condition, e.g., by dividing by zero. In the declarative model, a program that raises an error condition will terminate immediately. There is nothing in the model to handle errors. In section 2.7 we extend the declarative model with a new concept, exceptions, to

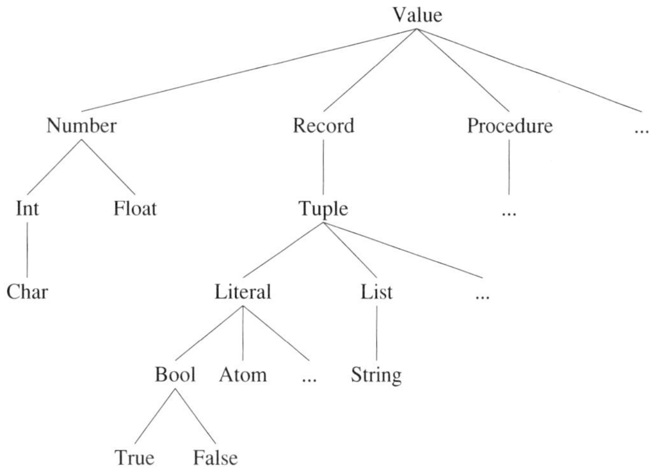

Figure 2.16: The type hierarchy of the declarative model.

handle errors. In the extended model, type errors can be handled within the model.

In addition to basic types, programs can define their own types. These are called abstract data types, or ADTs. Chapter 3 and later chapters show how to define ADTs. There are other kinds of data abstraction in addition to ADTs. Section 6.4 gives an overview of the different possibilities.

Basic types

The basic types of the declarative model are numbers (integers and floats), records (including atoms, booleans, tuples, lists, and strings), and procedures. Table 2.2 gives their syntax. The nonterminal ⟨v⟩ denotes a partially constructed value. Later in the book we will see other basic types, including chunks, functors, cells, dictionaries, arrays, ports, classes, and objects. Some of these are explained in appendix B.

Dynamic typing

There are two basic approaches to typing, namely dynamic and static typing. In static typing, all variable types are known at compile time. In dynamic typing, the variable type is known only when the variable is bound. The declarative model is dynamically typed. The compiler tries to verify that all operations use values of the correct type. But because of dynamic typing, some type checks are necessarily left for run time.

The type hierarchy

The basic types of the declarative model can be classified into a hierarchy. Figure 2.16 shows this hierarchy, where each node denotes a type. The hierarchy is ordered by set inclusion, i.e., all values of a node's type are also values of the parent node's type. For example, all tuples are records and all lists are tuples. This implies that all operations of a type are also legal for a subtype, e.g., all list operations work also for strings. Later on in the book we extend this hierarchy. For example, literals can be either atoms (explained below) or another kind of constant called names (see section 3.7.5). The parts where the hierarchy is incomplete are given as "...".

2.3.3 Basic types

We give some examples of the basic types and how to write them. See appendix B for more complete information.

- *Numbers.* Numbers are either integers or floating point numbers. Examples of integers are `314`, `0`, and `~10` (minus 10). Note that the minus sign is written with a tilde "~". Examples of floating point numbers are `1.0`, `3.4`, `2.0e2`, and `~2.0E~2`.
- *Atoms.* An atom is a kind of symbolic constant that can be used as a single element in calculations. There are several different ways to write atoms. An atom can be written as a sequence of characters starting with a lowercase letter followed by any number of alphanumeric characters. An atom can also be written as any sequence of printable characters enclosed in single quotes. Examples of atoms are `a_person`, `donkeyKong3`, and `'#### hello ####'`.
- *Booleans.* A boolean is either the symbol **`true`** or the symbol **`false`**.
- *Records.* A record is a compound data structure. It consists of a label followed by a set of pairs of features and variable identifiers. Features can be atoms, integers, or booleans. Examples of records are `person(age:X1 name:X2)` (with features `age` and `name`), `person(1:X1 2:X2)`, `'|'(1:H 2:T)`, `'#'(1:H 2:T)`, `nil`, and `person`. An atom is a record with no features.
- *Tuples.* A tuple is a record whose features are consecutive integers starting from 1. The features do not have to be written in this case. Examples of tuples are `person(1:X1 2:X2)` and `person(X1 X2)`, both of which mean the same.
- *Lists.* A list is either the atom `nil` or the tuple `'|'(H T)` (label is vertical bar), where `T` is either unbound or bound to a list. This tuple is called a list pair or a cons. There is syntactic sugar for lists:
  - The `'|'` label can be written as an infix operator, so that `H|T` means the same as `'|'(H T)`.
  - The `'|'` operator associates to the right, so that `1|2|3|nil` means the same as `1|(2|(3|nil))`.

- Lists that end in `nil` can be written with brackets `[ ... ]`, so that `[1 2 3]` means the same as `1|2|3|nil`. These lists are called complete lists.

- *Strings.* A string is a list of character codes. Strings can be written with double quotes, so that `"E=mc^2"` means the same as `[69 61 109 99 94 50]`.
- *Procedures.* A procedure is a value of the procedure type. The statement

$\langle x \rangle$ = **proc** {\$ $\langle y \rangle_1 \cdots \langle y \rangle_n$} $\langle s \rangle$ **end**

binds $\langle x \rangle$ to a new procedure value. That is, it simply declares a new procedure. The `$` indicates that the procedure value is anonymous, i.e., created without being bound to an identifier. There is a syntactic shortcut that is more familiar:

proc {$\langle x \rangle$ $\langle y \rangle_1 \cdots \langle y \rangle_n$} $\langle s \rangle$ **end**

The `$` is replaced by the identifier $\langle x \rangle$. This creates the procedure value and immediately tries to bind it to $\langle x \rangle$. This shortcut is perhaps easier to read, but it blurs the distinction between creating the value and binding it to an identifier.

2.3.4 Records and procedures

We explain why we chose records and procedures as basic concepts in the kernel language. This section is intended for readers with some programming experience who wonder why we designed the kernel language the way we did.

The power of records

Records are the basic way to structure data. They are the building blocks of most data structures including lists, trees, queues, graphs, etc., as we will see in chapter 3. Records play this role to some degree in most programming languages. But we shall see that their power can go much beyond this role. The extra power appears in greater or lesser degree depending on how well or how poorly the language supports them. For maximum power, the language should make it easy to create them, take them apart, and manipulate them. In the declarative model, a record is created by simply writing it down, with a compact syntax. A record is taken apart by simply writing down a pattern, also with a compact syntax. Finally, there are many operations to manipulate records: to add, remove, or select fields; to convert to a list and back, etc. In general, languages that provide this level of support for records are called symbolic languages.

When records are strongly supported, they can be used to increase the effectiveness of many other techniques. This book focuses on three in particular: object-oriented programming, graphical user interface (GUI) design, and component-based programming. In object-oriented programming, chapter 7 shows how records can represent messages and method heads, which are what objects use to communicate. In GUI design, chapter 10 shows how records can represent "widgets," the basic building blocks of a user interface. In component-based programming, section 3.9

shows how records can represent first-class modules, which group together related operations.

Why procedures?

A reader with some programming experience may wonder why our kernel language has procedures as a basic construct. Fans of object-oriented programming may wonder why we do not use objects instead. Fans of functional programming may wonder why we do not use functions. We could have chosen either possibility, but we did not. The reasons are quite straightforward.

Procedures are more appropriate than objects because they are simpler. Objects are actually quite complicated, as chapter 7 explains. Procedures are more appropriate than functions because they do not necessarily define entities that behave like mathematical functions.[5] For example, we define both components and objects as abstractions based on procedures. In addition, procedures are flexible because they do not make any assumptions about the number of inputs and outputs. A function always has exactly one output. A procedure can have any number of inputs and outputs, including zero. We will see that procedures are extremely powerful building blocks, when we talk about higher-order programming in section 3.6.

2.3.5 Basic operations

Table 2.3 gives the basic operations that we will use in this chapter and the next. There is syntactic sugar for many of these operations so that they can be written concisely as expressions. For example, `X=A*B` is syntactic sugar for `{Number.´*´ A B X}`, where `Number.´*´` is a procedure associated with the type `Number`.[6] All operations can be denoted in some long way, e.g., `Value.´==´`, `Value.´<´`, `Int.´div´`, `Float.´/´`. The table uses the syntactic sugar when it exists.

- *Arithmetic.* Floating point numbers have the four basic operations, `+`, `-`, `*`, and `/`, with the usual meanings. Integers have the basic operations `+`, `-`, `*`, **`div`**, and **`mod`**, where **`div`** is integer division (truncate the fractional part) and **`mod`** is the integer modulo, i.e., the remainder after a division. For example, `10 mod 3`=1.
- *Record operations.* Three basic operations on records are `Arity`, `Label`, and "." (dot, which means field selection). For example, given

```
X=person(name:"George" age:25)
```

5. From a theoretical point of view, procedures are "processes" as used in concurrent calculi such as the π calculus. The arguments are channels. In this chapter we use processes that are composed sequentially with single-shot channels. Chapters 4 and 5 show other types of channels (with sequences of messages) and do concurrent composition of processes.
6. To be precise, `Number` is a module that groups the operations of the `Number` type and `Number.´*´` selects the multiplication operation.

Operation	Description	Argument type
`A==B`	Equality comparison	Value
`A\=B`	Inequality comparison	Value
`{IsProcedure P}`	Test if procedure	Value
`A=<B`	Less than or equal comparison	Number or Atom
`A<B`	Less than comparison	Number or Atom
`A>=B`	Greater than or equal comparison	Number or Atom
`A>B`	Greater than comparison	Number or Atom
`A+B`	Addition	Number
`A-B`	Subtraction	Number
`A*B`	Multiplication	Number
`A div B`	Division	Int
`A mod B`	Modulo	Int
`A/B`	Division	Float
`{Arity R}`	Arity	Record
`{Label R}`	Label	Record
`R.F`	Field selection	Record

Table 2.3: Examples of basic operations.

then `{Arity X}=[age name]`, `{Label X}=person`, and `X.age=25`. The call to `Arity` returns a list that contains first the integer features in ascending order and then the atom features in ascending lexicographic order.

- *Comparisons.* The boolean comparison functions include `==` and `\=`, which can compare any two values for equality, as well as the numeric comparisons `=<`, `<`, `>=`, and `>`, which can compare two integers, two floats, or two atoms. Atoms are compared according to the lexicographic order of their print representations. In the following example, `Z` is bound to the maximum of `X` and `Y`:

```
declare X Y Z T in
X=5 Y=10
T=(X>=Y)
if T then Z=X else Z=Y end
```

There is syntactic sugar so that an **if** statement accepts an expression as its condition. The above example can be rewritten as:

```
declare X Y Z in
X=5 Y=10
if X>=Y then Z=X else Z=Y end
```

- *Procedure operations.* There are three basic operations on procedures: defining them (with the **proc** statement), calling them (with the curly brace notation), and testing whether a value is a procedure with the `IsProcedure` function. The call `{IsProcedure P}` returns **true** if `P` is a procedure and **false** otherwise.

Appendix B gives a more complete set of basic operations.

2.4 Kernel language semantics

The kernel language execution consists in evaluating functions over partial values. To see this, we give the semantics of the kernel language in terms of a simple operational model. The model is designed to let the programmer reason about both correctness and complexity in a simple way. It is a kind of abstract machine, but at a high level of abstraction that leaves out details such as registers and explicit memory addresses.

2.4.1 Basic concepts

Before giving the formal semantics, let us give some examples to give intuition on how the kernel language executes. This will motivate the semantics and make it easier to understand.

A simple execution

During normal execution, statements are executed one by one in textual order. Let us look at a simple execution:

```
local A B C D in
   A=11
   B=2
   C=A+B
   D=C*C
end
```

This seems simple enough; it will bind `D` to 169. Let us see exactly what it does. The **`local`** statement creates four new variables in the store, and makes the four identifiers `A`, `B`, `C`, `D` refer to them. (For convenience, this extends slightly the **`local`** statement of table 2.1.) This is followed by two bindings, `A=11` and `B=2`. The addition `C=A+B` adds the values of `A` and `B` and binds `C` to the result 13. The multiplication `D` multiples the value of `C` by itself and binds `D` to the result 169. This is quite simple.

Variable identifiers and static scoping

We saw that the **`local`** statement does two things: it creates a new variable and it sets up an identifier to refer to the variable. The identifier only refers to the variable inside the **`local`** statement, i.e., between the **`local`** and the **`end`**. The program region in which an identifier refers to a particular variable is called the *scope* of the identifier. Outside of the scope, the identifier does not mean the same thing. Let us look closer at what this implies. Consider the following fragment:

```
local X in
   X=1
   local X in
      X=2
      {Browse X}
   end
   {Browse X}
end
```

What does it display? It displays first 2 and then 1. There is just one identifier, `X`, but at different points during the execution, it refers to different variables.

Let us summarize this idea. The meaning of an identifier like `X` is determined by the innermost **`local`** statement that declares `X`. The area of the program where `X` keeps this meaning is called the scope of `X`. We can find out the scope of an identifier by simply inspecting the text of the program; we do not have to do anything complicated like execute or analyze the program. This scoping rule is called lexical scoping or static scoping. Later we will see another kind of scoping rule, dynamic scoping, that is sometimes useful. But lexical scoping is by far the most important kind of scoping rule. One reason is because it is localized, i.e., the meaning of an identifier can be determined by looking at a small part of the program. We will see another reason shortly.

Procedures

Procedures are one of the most important basic building blocks of any language. We give a simple example that shows how to define and call a procedure. Here is a procedure that binds `Z` to the maximum of `X` and `Y`:

```
proc {Max X Y ?Z}
   if X>=Y then Z=X else Z=Y end
end
```

To make the definition easier to read, we mark the output argument with a question mark "`?`". This has absolutely no effect on execution; it is just a comment. Calling `{Max 3 5 C}` binds `C` to 5. How does the procedure work, exactly? When `Max` is called, the identifiers `X`, `Y`, and `Z` are bound to 3, 5, and the unbound variable referenced by `C`. When `Max` binds `Z`, then it binds this variable. Since `C` also references this variable, this also binds `C`. This way of passing parameters is called call by reference. Procedures output results by being passed references to unbound variables, which are bound inside the procedure. This book mostly uses call by reference, both for dataflow variables and for mutable variables. Section 6.4.4 explains some other parameter-passing mechanisms.

Procedures with external references

Let us examine the body of `Max`. It is just an **`if`** statement:

```
if X>=Y then Z=X else Z=Y end
```

This statement has one particularity, though: it cannot be executed! This is because it does not define the identifiers X, Y, and Z. These undefined identifiers are called free identifiers. (Sometimes they are called free variables, although strictly speaking they are not variables.) When put inside the procedure Max, the statement can be executed, because all the free identifiers are declared as procedure arguments.

What happens if we define a procedure that only declares some of the free identifiers as arguments? For example, let's define the procedure LB with the same procedure body as Max, but only two arguments:

```
proc {LB X ?Z}
   if X>=Y then Z=X else Z=Y end
end
```

What does this procedure do when executed? Apparently, it takes any number X and binds Z to X if X>=Y, but to Y otherwise. That is, Z is always at least Y. What is the value of Y? It is not one of the procedure arguments. It has to be the value of Y when the procedure is defined. This is a consequence of static scoping. If Y=9 when the procedure is defined, then calling {LB 3 Z} binds Z to 9. Consider the following program fragment:

```
local Y LB in
   Y=10
   proc {LB X ?Z}
      if X>=Y then Z=X else Z=Y end
   end
   local Y=15 Z in
      {LB 5 Z}
   end
end
```

What does the call {LB 5 Z} bind Z to? It will be bound to 10. The binding Y=15 when LB is called is ignored; it is the binding Y=10 at the procedure definition that is important.

Dynamic scoping versus static scoping

Consider the following simple example:

```
local P Q in
   proc {Q X} {Browse stat(X)} end
   proc {P X} {Q X} end
   local Q in
      proc {Q X} {Browse dyn(X)} end
      {P hello}
   end
end
```

What should this display, stat(hello) or dyn(hello)? Static scoping says that it will display stat(hello). In other words, P uses the version of Q that exists at P's definition. But there is another solution: P could use the version of Q that exists at P's call. This is called dynamic scoping.

Both static and dynamic scoping have been used as the default in programming languages. Let us compare the two by first giving their definitions side by side:

- *Static scope.* The variable corresponding to an identifier occurrence is the one defined in the textually innermost declaration surrounding the occurrence in the source program.
- *Dynamic scope.* The variable corresponding to an identifier occurrence is the one in the most-recent declaration seen during the execution leading up to the current statement.

The original Lisp language was dynamically scoped. Common Lisp and Scheme, which are descended from Lisp, are statically scoped by default. Common Lisp allows declaring dynamically scoped variables, which it calls special variables [200]. Which default is the right one? The correct default is procedure values with static scoping. This is because a procedure that works when it is defined will continue to work, independent of the environment where it is called. This is an important software engineering property.

Dynamic scoping remains useful in some well-defined areas. For example, consider the case of a procedure whose code is transferred across a network from one computer to another. Some of this procedure's external references, e.g., calls to common library operations, can use dynamic scoping. This way, the procedure will use local code for these operations instead of remote code. This is much more efficient.[7]

Procedural abstraction

Let us summarize what we learned from `Max` and `LB`. Three concepts play an important role:

1. Procedural abstraction. Any statement can be made into a procedure by putting it inside a procedure declaration. This is called procedural abstraction. We also say that the statement is abstracted into a procedure.
2. Free identifiers. A free identifier in a statement is an identifier that is not defined in that statement. It might be defined in an enclosing statement.
3. Static scoping. A procedure can have external references, which are free identifiers in the procedure body that are not declared as arguments. `LB` has one external reference. `Max` has none. The value of an external reference is its value when the procedure is defined. This is a consequence of static scoping.

Procedural abstraction and static scoping together form one of the most powerful tools presented in the book. In the semantics, we will see that they can be

7. However, there is no guarantee that the operation will behave in the same way on the target machine. So even for distributed programs the default should be static scoping.

implemented in a simple way.

Dataflow behavior

In the single-assignment store, variables can be unbound. On the other hand, some statements need bound variables, otherwise they cannot execute. For example, what happens when we execute:

```
local X Y Z in
   X=10
   if X>=Y then Z=X else Z=Y end
end
```

The comparison `X>=Y` returns **`true`** or **`false`**, if it can decide which is the case. If `Y` is unbound, it cannot decide, strictly speaking. What does it do? Continuing with either **`true`** or **`false`** would be incorrect. Raising an error would be a drastic measure, since the program has done nothing wrong (it has done nothing right either). We decide that the program will simply stop its execution, without signaling any kind of error. If some other activity (to be determined later) binds `Y`, then the stopped execution can continue as if nothing had perturbed the normal flow of execution. This is called dataflow behavior. Dataflow behavior underlies a second powerful tool presented in the book, namely concurrency. In the semantics, we will see that dataflow behavior can be implemented in a simple way.

2.4.2 The abstract machine

We define the semantics of the kernel language as an operational semantics, i.e., it defines the meaning of the kernel language through its execution on an abstract machine. We first define the basic concepts of the abstract machine: environments, semantic statement, statement stack, execution state, and computation. We then show how to execute a program. Finally, we explain how to calculate with environments, which is a common semantic operation.

Definitions

A running program is defined in terms of a computation, which is a sequence of execution states. Let us define exactly what this means. We need the following concepts:

- A *single-assignment store* σ is a set of store variables. These variables are partitioned into (1) sets of variables that are equal but unbound and (2) variables that are bound to a number, record, or procedure. For example, in the store $\{x_1, x_2 = x_3, x_4 = \mathsf{a}|x_2\}$, x_1 is unbound, x_2 and x_3 are equal and unbound, and x_4 is bound to the partial value $\mathsf{a}|x_2$. A store variable bound to a value is indistinguishable from that value. This is why a store variable is sometimes called a store entity.

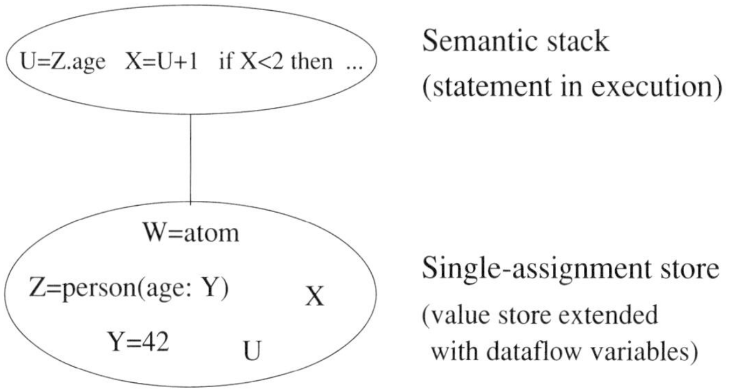

Figure 2.17: The declarative computation model.

- An *environment* E is a mapping from variable identifiers to entities in σ. This is explained in section 2.2. We will write E as a set of pairs, e.g., $\{\texttt{X} \rightarrow x, \texttt{Y} \rightarrow y\}$, where X, Y are identifiers and x, y refer to store entities.
- A *semantic statement* is a pair $(\langle \mathsf{s} \rangle, E)$ where $\langle \mathsf{s} \rangle$ is a statement and E is an environment. The semantic statement relates a statement to what it references in the store. The set of possible statements is given in section 2.3.
- An *execution state* is a pair (ST, σ) where ST is a stack of semantic statements and σ is a single-assignment store. Figure 2.17 gives a picture of the execution state.
- A *computation* is a sequence of execution states starting from an initial state: $(ST_0, \sigma_0) \rightarrow (ST_1, \sigma_1) \rightarrow (ST_2, \sigma_2) \rightarrow \cdots$.

A single transition in a computation is called a computation step. A computation step is atomic, i.e., there are no visible intermediate states. It is as if the step is done "all at once." In this chapter, all computations are sequential, i.e., the execution state contains exactly one statement stack, which is transformed by a linear sequence of computation steps.

Program execution

Let us execute a program in this semantics. A program is simply a statement $\langle \mathsf{s} \rangle$. Here is how to execute the program:

- The initial execution state is:

$([(\langle \mathsf{s} \rangle, \phi)], \phi)$

That is, the initial store is empty (no variables, empty set ϕ) and the initial execution state has just one semantic statement $(\langle \mathsf{s} \rangle, \phi)$ in the stack ST. The semantic statement contains $\langle \mathsf{s} \rangle$ and an empty environment (ϕ). We use brackets $[\ldots]$ to denote the stack.

- At each step, the first element of ST is popped and execution proceeds according to the form of the element.
- The final execution state (if there is one) is a state in which the semantic stack is empty.

A semantic stack ST can be in one of three run-time states:

- Runnable: ST can do a computation step.
- Terminated: ST is empty.
- Suspended: ST is not empty, but it cannot do any computation step.

Calculating with environments

A program execution often does calculations with environments. An environment E is a function that maps variable identifiers $\langle \mathsf{x} \rangle$ to store entities (both unbound variables and values). The notation $E(\langle \mathsf{x} \rangle)$ retrieves the entity associated with the identifier $\langle \mathsf{x} \rangle$ from the store. To define the semantics of the abstract machine instructions, we need two common operations on environments, namely adjunction and restriction.

Adjunction defines a new environment by adding a mapping to an existing one. The notation

$$E + \{\langle \mathsf{x} \rangle \rightarrow x\}$$

denotes a new environment E' constructed from E by adding the mapping $\{\langle \mathsf{x} \rangle \rightarrow x\}$. This mapping overrides any other mapping from the identifier $\langle \mathsf{x} \rangle$. That is, $E'(\langle \mathsf{x} \rangle)$ is equal to x, and $E'(\langle \mathsf{y} \rangle)$ is equal to $E(\langle \mathsf{y} \rangle)$ for all identifiers $\langle \mathsf{y} \rangle$ different from $\langle \mathsf{x} \rangle$. When we need to add more than one mapping at once, we write $E + \{\langle \mathsf{x} \rangle_1 \rightarrow x_1, \ldots, \langle \mathsf{x} \rangle_n \rightarrow x_n\}$.

Restriction defines a new environment whose domain is a subset of an existing one. The notation

$$E|_{\{\langle \mathsf{x} \rangle_1, \ldots, \langle \mathsf{x} \rangle_n\}}$$

denotes a new environment E' such that $\mathrm{dom}(E') = \mathrm{dom}(E) \cap \{\langle \mathsf{x} \rangle_1, \ldots, \langle \mathsf{x} \rangle_n\}$ and $E'(\langle \mathsf{x} \rangle) = E(\langle \mathsf{x} \rangle)$ for all $\langle \mathsf{x} \rangle \in \mathrm{dom}(E')$. That is, the new environment does not contain any identifiers other than those mentioned in the set.

2.4.3 Nonsuspendable statements

We first give the semantics of the statements that can never suspend.

The `skip` statement

The semantic statement is:

(**skip**, E)

Execution is complete after this pair is popped from the semantic stack.

Sequential composition

The semantic statement is:

$(\langle \mathsf{s} \rangle_1\ \langle \mathsf{s} \rangle_2, E)$

Execution consists of the following actions:

- Push $(\langle \mathsf{s} \rangle_2, E)$ on the stack.
- Push $(\langle \mathsf{s} \rangle_1, E)$ on the stack.

Variable declaration (the `local` statement)

The semantic statement is:

(**local** $\langle \mathsf{x} \rangle$ **in** $\langle \mathsf{s} \rangle$ **end**, E)

Execution consists of the following actions:

- Create a new variable x in the store.
- Let E' be $E + \{\langle \mathsf{x} \rangle \rightarrow x\}$, i.e., E' is the same as E except that it adds a mapping from $\langle \mathsf{x} \rangle$ to x.
- Push $(\langle \mathsf{s} \rangle, E')$ on the stack.

Variable-variable binding

The semantic statement is:

$(\langle \mathsf{x} \rangle_1 = \langle \mathsf{x} \rangle_2, E)$

Execution consists of the following action:

- Bind $E(\langle \mathsf{x} \rangle_1)$ and $E(\langle \mathsf{x} \rangle_2)$ in the store.

Value creation

The semantic statement is:

$(\langle \mathsf{x} \rangle = \langle \mathsf{v} \rangle, E)$

where $\langle \mathsf{v} \rangle$ is a partially constructed value that is either a record, number, or procedure. Execution consists of the following actions:

- Create a new variable x in the store.
- Construct the value represented by $\langle \mathsf{v} \rangle$ in the store and let x refer to it. All

identifiers in ⟨v⟩ are replaced by their store contents as given by E.

- Bind $E(\langle x \rangle)$ and x in the store.

We have seen how to construct record and number values, but what about procedure values? In order to explain them, we have first to explain the concept of lexical scoping.

Free and bound identifier occurrences

A statement ⟨s⟩ can contain many occurrences of variable identifiers. For each identifier occurrence, we can ask the question: where was this identifier declared? If the declaration is in some statement (part of ⟨s⟩ or not) that textually surrounds (i.e., encloses) the occurrence, then we say that the declaration obeys lexical scoping. Because the scope is determined by the source code text, this is also called static scoping.

Identifier occurrences in a statement can be bound or free with respect to that statement. An identifier occurrence `X` is bound with respect to a statement ⟨s⟩ if it is declared inside ⟨s⟩, i.e., in a **`local`** statement, in the pattern of a **`case`** statement, or as argument of a procedure declaration. An identifier occurrence that is not bound is free. Free occurrences can only exist in incomplete program fragments, i.e., statements that cannot run. In a running program, it is always true that every identifier occurrence is bound.

> Bound identifier occurrences and bound variables
>
> Do not confuse a bound identifier occurrence with a bound variable! A bound identifier occurrence does not exist at run time; it is a textual variable name that textually occurs inside a construct that declares it (e.g., a procedure or variable declaration). A bound variable exists at run time; it is a dataflow variable that is bound to a partial value.

Here is an example with both free and bound occurrences:

```
local Arg1 Arg2 in
   Arg1=111*111
   Arg2=999*999
   Res=Arg1+Arg2
end
```

In this statement, all variable identifiers are declared with lexical scoping. All occurrences of the identifiers `Arg1` and `Arg2` are bound and the single occurrence of `Res` is free. This statement cannot be run. To make it runnable, it has to be part of a bigger statement that declares `Res`. Here is an extension that can run:

```
local Res in
   local Arg1 Arg2 in
      Arg1=111*111
      Arg2=999*999
      Res=Arg1+Arg2
   end
   {Browse Res}
end
```

This can run since it has no free identifier occurrences.

Procedure values (closures)

Let us see how to construct a procedure value in the store. It is not as simple as one might imagine because procedures can have external references. For example:

```
proc {LowerBound X ?Z}
   if X>=Y then Z=X else Z=Y end
end
```

In this example, the `if` statement has three free variables, `X`, `Y`, and `Z`. Two of them, `X` and `Z`, are also formal parameters. The third, `Y`, is not a formal parameter. It has to be defined by the environment where the procedure is declared. The procedure value itself must have a mapping from `Y` to the store. Otherwise, we could not call the procedure since `Y` would be a kind of dangling reference.

Let us see what happens in the general case. A procedure expression is written as:

proc { \$ $\langle y\rangle_1 \cdots \langle y\rangle_n$ } $\langle s\rangle$ **end**

The statement $\langle s\rangle$ can have free variable identifiers. Each free identifier is either a formal parameter or not. The first kind are defined anew each time the procedure is called. They form a subset of the formal parameters $\{\langle y\rangle_1, \ldots, \langle y\rangle_n\}$. The second kind are defined once and for all when the procedure is declared. We call them the external references of the procedure. Let us write them as $\{\langle z\rangle_1, \ldots, \langle z\rangle_k\}$. Then the procedure value is a pair:

(**proc** { \$ $\langle y\rangle_1 \cdots \langle y\rangle_n$ } $\langle s\rangle$ **end**, CE)

Here CE (the contextual environment) is $E|_{\{\langle z\rangle_1,\ldots,\langle z\rangle_n\}}$, where E is the environment when the procedure is declared. This pair is put in the store just like any other value.

Because it contains an environment as well as a procedure definition, a procedure value is often called a closure or a lexically scoped closure. This is because it "closes" (i.e., packages up) the environment at procedure definition time. This is also called environment capture. When the procedure is called, the contextual environment is used to construct the environment of the executing procedure body.

2.4.4 Suspendable statements

There are three statements remaining in the kernel language:

$\langle s \rangle$ ::= ...
| **if** $\langle x \rangle$ **then** $\langle s \rangle_1$ **else** $\langle s \rangle_2$ **end**
| **case** $\langle x \rangle$ **of** $\langle \text{pattern} \rangle$ **then** $\langle s \rangle_1$ **else** $\langle s \rangle_2$ **end**
| ´{´ $\langle x \rangle$ $\langle y \rangle_1 \cdots \langle y \rangle_n$ ´}´

What should happen with these statements if $\langle x \rangle$ is unbound? From the discussion in section 2.2.8, we know what should happen. The statements should simply wait until $\langle x \rangle$ is bound. We say that they are suspendable statements. They have an *activation condition*, which we define as a condition that must be true for execution to continue. The condition is that $E(\langle x \rangle)$ must be determined, i.e., bound to a number, record, or procedure.

In the declarative model of this chapter, once a statement suspends it will never continue. The program simply stops executing. This is because there is no other execution that could make the activation condition true. In chapter 4, when we introduce concurrent programming, we will have executions with more than one semantic stack. A suspended stack ST can become runnable again if another stack does an operation that makes ST's activation condition true. This is the basis of dataflow execution. For now, let us investigate sequential programming and stick with just a single semantic stack.

Conditional (the `if` *statement)*

The semantic statement is:

$(\texttt{if}\ \langle x \rangle\ \texttt{then}\ \langle s \rangle_1\ \texttt{else}\ \langle s \rangle_2\ \texttt{end}, E)$

Execution consists of the following actions:

- If the activation condition is true ($E(\langle x \rangle)$ is determined), then do the following actions:
  - If $E(\langle x \rangle)$ is not a boolean (**true** or **false**) then raise an error condition.
  - If $E(\langle x \rangle)$ is **true**, then push $(\langle s \rangle_1, E)$ on the stack.
  - If $E(\langle x \rangle)$ is **false**, then push $(\langle s \rangle_2, E)$ on the stack.
- If the activation condition is false, then execution does not continue. The execution state is kept as is. We say that execution suspends. The stop can be temporary. If some other activity in the system makes the activation condition true, then execution can resume.

Procedure application

The semantic statement is:

$(\{\langle x \rangle\ \langle y \rangle_1 \cdots \langle y \rangle_n\}, E)$

Execution consists of the following actions:

- If the activation condition is true ($E(\langle \mathsf{x}\rangle)$ is determined), then do the following actions:
  - If $E(\langle \mathsf{x}\rangle)$ is not a procedure value or is a procedure with a number of arguments different from n, then raise an error condition.
  - If $E(\langle \mathsf{x}\rangle)$ has the form $(\textbf{proc}\ \{\ \$\ \langle \mathsf{z}\rangle_1 \cdots \langle \mathsf{z}\rangle_n\}\ \langle \mathsf{s}\rangle\ \textbf{end}, CE)$ then push $(\langle \mathsf{s}\rangle, CE + \{\langle \mathsf{z}\rangle_1 \rightarrow E(\langle \mathsf{y}\rangle_1), \ldots, \langle \mathsf{z}\rangle_n \rightarrow E(\langle \mathsf{y}\rangle_n)\})$ on the stack.
- If the activation condition is false, then suspend execution.

Pattern matching (the `case` *statement)*

The semantic statement is:

$(\textbf{case}\ \langle \mathsf{x}\rangle\ \textbf{of}\ \langle \mathsf{lit}\rangle(\langle \mathsf{feat}\rangle_1\texttt{:}\ \langle \mathsf{x}\rangle_1 \cdots \langle \mathsf{feat}\rangle_n\texttt{:}\ \langle \mathsf{x}\rangle_n)\ \textbf{then}\ \langle \mathsf{s}\rangle_1\ \textbf{else}\ \langle \mathsf{s}\rangle_2\ \textbf{end}, E)$

(Here $\langle \mathsf{lit}\rangle$ and $\langle \mathsf{feat}\rangle$ are synonyms for $\langle \mathsf{literal}\rangle$ and $\langle \mathsf{feature}\rangle$.) Execution consists of the following actions:

- If the activation condition is true ($E(\langle \mathsf{x}\rangle)$ is determined), then do the following actions:
  - If the label of $E(\langle \mathsf{x}\rangle)$ is $\langle \mathsf{lit}\rangle$ and its arity is $[\langle \mathsf{feat}\rangle_1 \cdots \langle \mathsf{feat}\rangle_n]$, then push $(\langle \mathsf{s}\rangle_1, E + \{\langle \mathsf{x}\rangle_1 \rightarrow E(\langle \mathsf{x}\rangle).\langle \mathsf{feat}\rangle_1, \ldots, \langle \mathsf{x}\rangle_n \rightarrow E(\langle \mathsf{x}\rangle).\langle \mathsf{feat}\rangle_n\})$ on the stack.
  - Otherwise push $(\langle \mathsf{s}\rangle_2, E)$ on the stack.
- If the activation condition is false, then suspend execution.

2.4.5 Basic concepts revisited

Now that we have seen the kernel semantics, let us look again at the examples of section 2.4.1 to see exactly what they are doing. We look at three examples; we suggest you do the others as exercises.

Variable identifiers and static scoping

We saw before that the following statement $\langle \mathsf{s}\rangle$ displays first 2 and then 1:

```
⟨s⟩ ≡ local X in
         X=1
         ⟨s⟩1 ≡ local X in
                   X=2
                   {Browse X}
                end
         ⟨s⟩2 ≡ {Browse X}
      end
```

The same identifier X first refers to 2 and then refers to 1. We can understand better what happens by executing $\langle \mathsf{s} \rangle$ in our abstract machine.

1. The initial execution state is:

$$([(\langle \mathsf{s} \rangle, \phi)],\ \phi)$$

Both the environment and the store are empty ($E = \phi$ and $\sigma = \phi$).

2. After executing the outermost **local** statement and the binding `X=1`, we get:

$$([(\langle \mathsf{s} \rangle_1 \langle \mathsf{s} \rangle_2, \{\mathtt{X} \rightarrow x\})],$$
$$\{y = 1, x = y\})$$

We simplify $\{y = 1, x = y\}$ to $\{x = 1\}$. The identifier X refers to the store variable x, which is bound to 1. The next statement is the sequential composition $\langle \mathsf{s} \rangle_1 \langle \mathsf{s} \rangle_2$.

3. After executing the sequential composition, we get:

$$([(\langle \mathsf{s} \rangle_1, \{\mathtt{X} \rightarrow x\}),\ (\langle \mathsf{s} \rangle_2, \{\mathtt{X} \rightarrow x\})],$$
$$\{x = 1\})$$

Each of the statements $\langle \mathsf{s} \rangle_1$ and $\langle \mathsf{s} \rangle_2$ has its own environment. At this point, the two environments have identical values.

4. Let us start executing $\langle \mathsf{s} \rangle_1$. The first statement in $\langle \mathsf{s} \rangle_1$ is a **local** statement. Executing it gives

$$([(\mathtt{X=2}\ \{\mathtt{Browse\ X}\}, \{\mathtt{X} \rightarrow x'\}),\ (\langle \mathsf{s} \rangle_2, \{\mathtt{X} \rightarrow x\})],$$
$$\{x', x = 1\})$$

This creates the new variable x' and calculates the new environment $\{\mathtt{X} \rightarrow x\} + \{\mathtt{X} \rightarrow x'\}$, which is $\{\mathtt{X} \rightarrow x'\}$. The second mapping of X overrides the first.

5. After the binding `X=2` we get:

$$([(\{\mathtt{Browse\ X}\}, \{\mathtt{X} \rightarrow x'\}),\ (\{\mathtt{Browse\ X}\}, \{\mathtt{X} \rightarrow x\})],$$
$$\{x' = 2, x = 1\})$$

(Remember that $\langle \mathsf{s} \rangle_2$ is a `Browse`.) Now we see why the two `Browse` calls display different values. It is because they have different environments. The inner **local** statement is given its own environment, in which X refers to another variable. This does not affect the outer **local** statement, which keeps its environment no matter what happens in any other instruction.

Procedure definition and call

Our next example defines and calls the procedure `Max`, which calculates the maximum of two numbers. With the semantics we can see precisely what happens during the definition and execution of `Max`. Here is source code for the example, written with some syntactic shortcuts:

```
local Max C in
   proc {Max X Y ?Z}
      if X>=Y then Z=X else Z=Y end
   end
   {Max 3 5 C}
end
```

Translating into kernel syntax and rearranging slightly gives

```
      local Max in
         local A in
            local B in
               local C in
                     Max=proc {$ X Y Z}
                              local T in
                                 T=(X>=Y)
⟨s⟩ ≡ ⟨s⟩1 ≡  ⟨s⟩3 ≡  ⟨s⟩4 ≡ if T then Z=X else Z=Y end
                              end
                          end
                     A=3
                     B=5
                  ⟨s⟩2 ≡ {Max A B C}
               end
            end
         end
      end
```

You can see that the kernel syntax is rather verbose. This is because of the simplicity of the kernel language. This simplicity is important because it lets us keep the semantics simple too. The original source code uses the following three syntactic shortcuts for readability:

- Declaring more than one variable in a `local` declaration. This is translated into nested `local` declarations.
- Using "in-line" values instead of variables, e.g., `{P 3}` is a shortcut for `local X in X=3 {P X} end`.
- Using nested operations, e.g., putting the operation `X>=Y` in place of the boolean in the `if` statement.

We will use these shortcuts in all examples from now on.

Let us now execute statement ⟨s⟩. For clarity, we omit some of the intermediate steps.

1. The initial execution state is:

$(\; [(\langle \texttt{s} \rangle, \phi)], \; \phi \;)$

Both the environment and the store are empty ($E = \phi$ and $\sigma = \phi$).

2. After executing the four **local** declarations, we get:

$(\; [(\langle \texttt{s} \rangle_1, \{\texttt{Max} \rightarrow m, \texttt{A} \rightarrow a, \texttt{B} \rightarrow b, \texttt{C} \rightarrow c\})],$
$\quad \{m, a, b, c\} \;)$

The store contains the four variables m, a, b, and c. The environment of $\langle \texttt{s} \rangle_1$ has mappings to these variables.

3. After executing the bindings of `Max`, `A`, and `B`, we get:

$(\; [(\{\texttt{Max A B C}\}, \{\texttt{Max} \rightarrow m, \texttt{A} \rightarrow a, \texttt{B} \rightarrow b, \texttt{C} \rightarrow c\})],$
$\quad \{m = (\textbf{proc} \; \{\$ \; \texttt{X Y Z}\} \; \langle \texttt{s} \rangle_3 \; \textbf{end}, \; \phi), a = 3, b = 5, c\} \;)$

The variables m, a, and b are now bound to values. The procedure is ready to be called. Notice that the contextual environment of `Max` is empty because it has no free identifiers.

4. After executing the procedure application, we get:

$(\; [(\langle \texttt{s} \rangle_3, \{\texttt{X} \rightarrow a, \texttt{Y} \rightarrow b, \texttt{Z} \rightarrow c\})],$
$\quad \{m = (\textbf{proc} \; \{\$ \; \texttt{X Y Z}\} \; \langle \texttt{s} \rangle_3 \; \textbf{end}, \; \phi), a = 3, b = 5, c\} \;)$

The environment of $\langle \texttt{s} \rangle_3$ now has mappings from the new identifiers `X`, `Y`, and `Z`.

5. After executing the comparison `X>=Y`, we get:

$(\; [(\langle \texttt{s} \rangle_4, \{\texttt{X} \rightarrow a, \texttt{Y} \rightarrow b, \texttt{Z} \rightarrow c, \texttt{T} \rightarrow t\})],$
$\quad \{m = (\textbf{proc} \; \{\$ \; \texttt{X Y Z}\} \; \langle \texttt{s} \rangle_3 \; \textbf{end}, \; \phi), a = 3, b = 5, c, t = \textbf{false}\} \;)$

This adds the new identifier `T` and its variable t bound to **false**.

6. Execution is complete after statement $\langle \texttt{s} \rangle_4$ (the conditional):

$(\; [], \{m = (\textbf{proc} \; \{\$ \; \texttt{X Y Z}\} \; \langle \texttt{s} \rangle_3 \; \textbf{end}, \; \phi), a = 3, b = 5, c = 5, t = \textbf{false}\} \;)$

The statement stack is empty and c is bound to 5.

Procedure with external references (part 1)

Our third example defines and calls the procedure `LowerBound`, which ensures that a number will never go below a given lower bound. The example is interesting because `LowerBound` has an external reference. Let us see how the following code executes:

```
local LowerBound Y C in
   Y=5
   proc {LowerBound X ?Z}
      if X>=Y then Z=X else Z=Y end
   end
   {LowerBound 3 C}
end
```

This is very close to the `Max` example. The body of `LowerBound` is identical to the body of `Max`. The only difference is that `LowerBound` has an external reference. The procedure value is

(**proc** {$ X Z} **if** X>=Y **then** Z=X **else** Z=Y **end** **end**, $\{$Y $\rightarrow y\}$)

where the store contains:

$y = 5$

When the procedure is defined, i.e., when the procedure value is created, the environment has to contain a mapping of `Y`. Now let us apply this procedure. We assume that the procedure is called as `{LowerBound A C}`, where `A` is bound to 3. Before the application we have:

([({LowerBound A C}, {Y $\rightarrow y$, LowerBound $\rightarrow lb$, A $\rightarrow a$, C $\rightarrow c$})],
{ lb = (**proc** {$ X Z} **if** X>=Y **then** Z=X **else** Z=Y **end** **end**, {Y $\rightarrow y$}),
$y = 5, a = 3, c$})

After the application we get:

([(**if** X>=Y **then** Z=X **else** Z=Y **end**, {Y $\rightarrow y$, X $\rightarrow a$, Z $\rightarrow c$})],
{ lb = (**proc** {$ X Z} **if** X>=Y **then** Z=X **else** Z=Y **end** **end**, {Y $\rightarrow y$}),
$y = 5, a = 3, c$})

The new environment is calculated by starting with the contextual environment ({Y $\rightarrow y$} in the procedure value) and adding mappings from the formal arguments `X` and `Z` to the actual arguments a and c.

Procedure with external references (part 2)

In the above execution, the identifier `Y` refers to y in both the calling environment as well as the contextual environment of `LowerBound`. How would the execution change if the following statement were executed instead of `{LowerBound 3 C}`?:

```
local Y in
   Y=10
   {LowerBound 3 C}
end
```

Here `Y` no longer refers to y in the calling environment. Before looking at the answer, please put down the book, take a piece of paper, and work it out. Just before the application we have almost the same situation as before:

([({LowerBound A C}, {Y → y', LowerBound → lb, A → a, C → c})],
{ lb = (**proc** {$ X Z} **if** X>=Y **then** Z=X **else** Z=Y **end** **end**, {Y → y}),
$y' = 10, y = 5, a = 3, c$})

The calling environment has changed slightly: Y refers to a new variable y', which is bound to 10. When doing the application, the new environment is calculated in exactly the same way as before, starting from the contextual environment and adding the formal arguments. This means that the y' is ignored! We get exactly the same situation as before in the semantic stack:

([(**if** X>=Y **then** Z=X **else** Z=Y **end**, {Y → y, X → a, Z → c})],
{ lb = (**proc** {$ X Z} **if** X>=Y **then** Z=X **else** Z=Y **end** **end**, {Y → y}),
$y' = 10, y = 5, a = 3, c$})

The store still has the binding $y' = 10$. But y' is not referenced by the semantic stack, so this binding makes no difference to the execution.

2.5 Memory management

The abstract machine we defined in the previous section is a powerful tool with which we can investigate properties of computations. As a first exploration, let us look at memory behavior, i.e., how the sizes of the semantic stack and store evolve as a computation progresses. We will look at the principle of last call optimization and explain it by means of the abstract machine. This will lead us to the concepts of memory life cycle and garbage collection.

2.5.1 Last call optimization

Consider a recursive procedure with just one recursive call which happens to be the last call in the procedure body. We call such a procedure tail-recursive. We will show that the abstract machine executes a tail-recursive procedure with a constant stack size. This property is called last call optimization or tail call optimization. The term tail recursion optimization is sometimes used, but is less precise since the optimization works for any last call, not just tail-recursive calls (see Exercises, section 2.9). Consider the following procedure:

```
proc {Loop10 I}
   if I==10 then skip
   else
      {Browse I}
      {Loop10 I+1}
   end
end
```

Calling {Loop10 0} displays successive integers from 0 up to 9. Let us see how this procedure executes.

- The initial execution state is:

$$(\ [(\{\texttt{Loop10 0}\}, E_0)], \\ \sigma \ )$$

where E_0 is the environment at the call and σ the initial store.

- After executing the **if** statement, this becomes:

$$(\ [(\{\texttt{Browse I}\}, \{\texttt{I} \rightarrow i_0\}) \ (\{\texttt{Loop10 I+1}\}, \{\texttt{I} \rightarrow i_0\})], \\ \{i_0 = 0\} \cup \sigma \ )$$

- After executing the `Browse`, we get to the first recursive call:

$$(\ [(\{\texttt{Loop10 I+1}\}, \{\texttt{I} \rightarrow i_0\})], \\ \{i_0 = 0\} \cup \sigma \ )$$

- After executing the **if** statement in the recursive call, this becomes:

$$(\ [(\{\texttt{Browse I}\}, \{\texttt{I} \rightarrow i_1\}) \ (\{\texttt{Loop10 I+1}\}, \{\texttt{I} \rightarrow i_1\})], \\ \{i_0 = 0, i_1 = 1\} \cup \sigma \ )$$

- After executing the `Browse` again, we get to the second recursive call:

$$(\ [(\{\texttt{Loop10 I+1}\}, \{\texttt{I} \rightarrow i_1\})], \\ \{i_0 = 0, i_1 = 1\} \cup \sigma \ )$$

It is clear that the stack at the kth recursive call is always of the form:

$$[(\{\texttt{Loop10 I+1}\}, \{\texttt{I} \rightarrow i_{k-1}\})]$$

There is just one semantic statement and its environment is of constant size. This is the last call optimization. This shows that the efficient way to program loops in the declarative model is to program the loop as a tail-recursive procedure.

We can further see that the sizes of the semantic stack and the store evolve quite differently. The semantic stack is bounded by a constant size. On the other hand, the store grows bigger at each call. At the kth recursive call, the store has the form:

$$\{i_0 = 0, i_1 = 1, \ldots, i_{k-1} = k-1\} \cup \sigma$$

The store size is proportional to the number of recursive calls. Let us see why this growth is not a problem in practice. Look carefully at the semantic stack of the kth recursive call. It does not need the variables $\{i_0, i_1, \ldots, i_{k-2}\}$. The only variable needed is i_{k-1}. This means that we can remove the not-needed variables from the store without changing the results of the computation. This gives a smaller store:

$$\{i_{k-1} = k-1\} \cup \sigma$$

This smaller store is of constant size. If we could somehow ensure that the not-needed variables are always removed, then the program could execute indefinitely with a constant memory size.

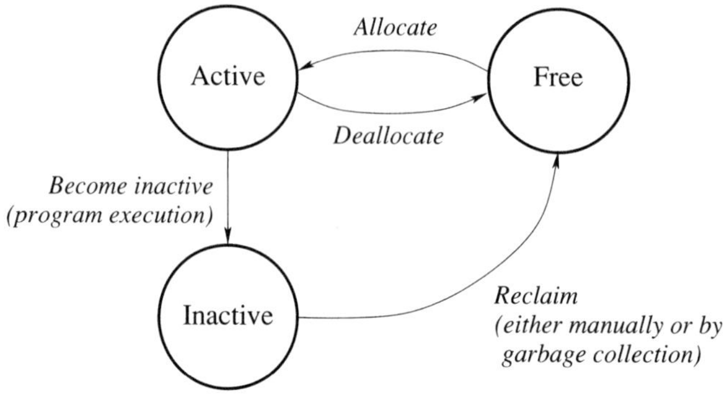

Figure 2.18: Life cycle of a memory block.

For this example we can solve the problem by storing the variables on the stack instead of in the store. This is possible because the variables are bound to small integers that fit in a machine word (e.g., 32 bits). So the stack can store the integers directly instead of storing variable references into the store.[8] This example is atypical; almost all realistic programs have large amounts of long-lived or shared data that cannot easily be stored on the stack. So we still have to solve the general problem of removing the not-needed variables. In the next sections we will see how to do this.

2.5.2 Memory life cycle

From the abstract machine semantics it follows that a running program needs only the information in the semantic stack and in that part of the store reachable from the semantic stack. A partial value is reachable if it is referenced by a statement on the semantic stack or by another reachable partial value. The semantic stack and the reachable part of the store are together called the active memory. All the memory that is not active can safely be reclaimed, i.e., it can be reused in the computation. We saw that the active memory size of the `Loop10` example is bounded by a constant, which means that it can loop indefinitely without exhausting system memory.

Now we can introduce the concept of memory life cycle. Programs execute in main memory, which consists of a sequence of memory words. At the time of writing, low-cost personal computers have 32-bit words and high-end computers have 64-bit or longer words. The sequence of words is divided up into blocks, where a block consists of a sequence of one or more words used to store part of an execution state.

8. A further optimization that is often done is to store part of the stack in machine registers. This is important since machine registers are much faster to read and write than main memory.

Blocks are the basic unit of memory allocation. Figure 2.18 shows the life cycle of a memory block. Each memory block continuously cycles through three states: active, inactive, and free. Memory management is the task of making sure that blocks circulate correctly along this cycle. A running program that needs a block will allocate it from a pool of free memory blocks. The block then becomes active. During its execution, the running program may no longer need some of its allocated memory blocks:

- If it can determine this directly, then it deallocates the blocks. This makes them become free again immediately. This is what happens with the semantic stack in the `Loop10` example.
- If it cannot determine this directly, then the blocks become inactive. They are no longer reachable by the running program, but the program does not know this, so it cannot make the blocks free. This is what happens with the store in the `Loop10` example.

Usually, memory blocks used for managing control flow (the semantic stack) can be deallocated and memory blocks used for data structures (the store) become inactive.

Inactive memory must eventually be reclaimed, i.e., the system must recognize that it is inactive and put it back in the pool of free memory. Otherwise, the system has a memory leak and will soon run out of memory. Reclaiming inactive memory is the hardest part of memory management, because recognizing that memory is unreachable is a global condition. It depends on the whole execution state of the running program. Low-level languages like C or C++ often leave reclaiming to the programmer, which is a major source of program errors. There are two kinds of program error that can occur:

- *Dangling reference.* This happens when a block is reclaimed even though it is still reachable. The system will eventually reuse this block. This means that data structures will be corrupted in unpredictable ways, causing the program to crash. This error is especially pernicious since the effect (the crash) is usually very far away from the cause (the incorrect reclaiming). This makes dangling references hard to debug.
- *Memory leak.* This happens when a block is not reclaimed even though it is unreachable. The effect is that active memory size keeps growing indefinitely until eventually the system's memory resources are exhausted. Memory leaks are less dangerous than dangling references because programs can continue running for some time before the error forces them to stop. Long-lived programs, such as operating systems and servers, must not have any memory leaks.

2.5.3 Garbage collection

Many high-level languages, such as Erlang, Haskell, Java, Lisp, Prolog, Smalltalk, and so forth, do automatic reclaiming. That is, reclaiming is done by the system independently of the running program. This completely eliminates dangling references and greatly reduces memory leaks. This relieves the programmer of most of the difficulties of manual memory management. Automatic reclaiming is called garbage collection. Garbage collection is a well-known technique that has been used for a long time. It was used in the 1960s for early Lisp systems. Until the 1990s, mainstream languages did not use it because it was judged (erroneously) as being too inefficient. It has finally become acceptable in mainstream programming because of the popularity of the Java language.

A typical garbage collector has two phases. In the first phase, it determines what the active memory is. It does this by finding all data structures reachable from an initial set of pointers called the root set. The original meaning of "pointer" is an address in the address space of a process. In the context of our abstract machine, a pointer is a variable reference in the store. The root set is the set of pointers that are always needed by the program. In the abstract machine of the previous section, the root set is simply the semantic stack. In general, the root set includes all pointers in ready threads and all pointers in operating system data structures. We will see this when we extend the abstract machine in later chapters to implement new concepts. The root set also includes some pointers related to distributed programming (namely references from remote sites; see chapter 11).

In the second phase, the garbage collector compacts the memory. That is, it collects all the active memory blocks into one contiguous block (a block without holes) and the free memory blocks into one contiguous block.

Modern garbage collection algorithms are efficient enough that most applications can use them with only small memory and time penalties [107]. The most widely used garbage collectors run in a "batch" mode, i.e., they are dormant most of the time and run only when the total amount of active and inactive memory reaches a predefined threshold. While the garbage collector runs, there is a pause in program execution. Usually the pause is small enough not to be disruptive.

There exist garbage collection algorithms, called real-time garbage collectors, that can run continuously, interleaved with the program execution. They can be used in cases, such as hard real-time programming, in which there must not be any pauses.

2.5.4 Garbage collection is not magic

Having garbage collection lightens the burden of memory management for the developer, but it does not eliminate it completely. There are two cases that remain the developer's responsibility: avoiding memory leaks and managing external resources.

Avoiding memory leaks

The programmer still has some responsibility regarding memory leaks. If the program continues to reference a data structure that it no longer needs, then that data structure's memory will never be recovered. The program should be careful to lose all references to data structures no longer needed.

For example, take a recursive function that traverses a list. If the list's head is passed to the recursive call, then list memory will not be recovered during the function's execution. Here is an example:

```
L=[1 2 3 ... 1000000]

fun {Sum X L1 L}
   case L1 of Y|L2 then {Sum X+Y L2 L}
   else X end
end

{Browse {Sum 0 L L}}
```

`Sum` sums the elements of a list. But it also keeps a reference to `L`, the original list, even though it does not need `L`. This means `L` will stay in memory during the whole execution of `Sum`. A better definition is as follows:

```
fun {Sum X L1}
   case L1 of Y|L2 then {Sum X+Y L2}
   else X end
end

{Browse {Sum 0 L}}
```

Here the reference to `L` is lost immediately. This example is trivial. But things can be more subtle. For example, consider an active data structure `S` that contains a list of other data structures `D1`, `D2`, ..., `Dn`. If one of these, say `Di`, is no longer needed by the program, then it should be removed from the list. Otherwise its memory will never be recovered.

A well-written program therefore has to do some "cleanup" after itself, making sure that it no longer references data structures that it no longer needs. The cleanup can be done in the declarative model, but it is cumbersome.[9]

Managing external resources

A Mozart program often needs data structures that are external to its operating system process. We call such a data structure an external resource. External resources affect memory management in two ways. An internal Mozart data structure can refer to an external resource, and vice versa. Both possibilities need some programmer intervention. Let us consider each case separately.

The first case is when a Mozart data structure refers to an external resource. For example, a record can correspond to a graphic entity in a graphics display or to an open file in a file system. If the record is no longer needed, then the graphic entity has to be removed or the file has to be closed. Otherwise, the graphics display or the file system will have a memory leak. This is done with a technique

9. It is more efficiently done with explicit state (see chapter 6).

called finalization, which defines actions to be taken when data structures become unreachable. Finalization is explained in section 6.9.2.

The second case is when an external resource needs a Mozart data structure. This is often straightforward to handle. For example, consider a scenario where the Mozart program implements a database server that is accessed by external clients. This scenario has a simple solution: never do automatic reclaiming of the database storage. Other scenarios may not be so simple. A general solution is to set aside a part of the Mozart program to represent the external resource. This part should be active (i.e., have its own thread) so that it is not reclaimed haphazardly. It can be seen as a "proxy" for the resource. The proxy keeps a reference to the Mozart data structure as long as the resource needs it. The resource informs the proxy when it no longer needs the data structure. Section 6.9.2 gives another technique.

2.5.5 The Mozart garbage collector

The Mozart system does automatic memory management. It has both a local garbage collector and a distributed garbage collector. The latter is used for distributed programming and is explained in chapter 11. The local garbage collector uses a copying dual-space algorithm.

The garbage collector divides memory into two spaces, of which each takes up half of available memory space. At any instant, the running program sits completely in one half. Garbage collection is done when there is no more free memory in that half. The garbage collector finds all data structures that are reachable from the root set and copies them to the other half of memory. Since they are copied to one contiguous memory block this also does compaction.

The advantage of a copying garbage collector is that its execution time is proportional to the active memory size, not to the total memory size. Small programs will garbage-collect quickly, even if they are running in a large memory space. The two disadvantages of a copying garbage collector are that half the memory is unusable at any given time and that long-lived data structures (like system tables) have to be copied at each garbage collection. Let us see how to remove these two disadvantages. Copying long-lived data can be avoided by using a modified algorithm called a generational garbage collector. This partitions active memory into generations. Long-lived data structures are put in older generations, which are collected less often.

The memory disadvantage is only important if the active memory size approaches the maximum addressable memory size of the underlying architecture. Mainstream computer technology is currently in a transition period from 32-bit to 64-bit addressing. In a computer with 32-bit addresses, the limit is reached when active memory size is 1000 MB or more. (The limit is usually not 2^{32} bytes, i.e., 4096 MB, due to limitations in the operating system.) At the time of writing, this limit is reached by large programs in high-end personal computers. For such programs, we recommend using a computer with 64-bit addresses, which has no such problem.

2.6 From kernel language to practical language

The kernel language has all the concepts needed for declarative programming. But trying to use it for practical declarative programming shows that it is too minimal. Kernel programs are just too verbose. Most of this verbosity can be eliminated by judiciously adding syntactic sugar and linguistic abstractions. This section does just that:

- It defines a set of syntactic conveniences that give a more concise and readable full syntax.
- It defines an important linguistic abstraction, namely functions, that is useful for concise and readable programming.
- It explains the interactive interface of the Mozart system and shows how it relates to the declarative model. This brings in the **declare** statement, which is a variant of the **local** statement designed for interactive use.

The resulting language is used in chapter 3 to explain the programming techniques of the declarative model.

2.6.1 Syntactic conveniences

The kernel language defines a simple syntax for all its constructs and types. The full language has the following conveniences to make this syntax more usable:

- Nested partial values can be written in a concise way.
- Variables can be both declared and initialized in one step.
- Expressions can be written in a concise way.
- The **if** and **case** statements can be nested in a concise way.
- The operators **andthen** and **orelse** are defined for nested **if** statements.
- Statements can be converted into expressions by using a nesting marker.

The nonterminal symbols used in the kernel syntax and semantics correspond as follows to those in the full syntax:

Kernel syntax	Full syntax
⟨x⟩, ⟨y⟩, ⟨z⟩	⟨variable⟩
⟨s⟩	⟨statement⟩, ⟨stmt⟩

Nested partial values

In table 2.2, the syntax of records and patterns implies that their arguments are variables. In practice, many partial values are nested deeper than this. Because nested values are so often used, we give syntactic sugar for them. For example, we extend the syntax to let us write `person(name:"George" age:25)` instead of the more cumbersome version:

```
local A B in A="George" B=25 X=person(name:A age:B) end
```

where `X` is bound to the nested record.

Implicit variable initialization

To make programs shorter and easier to read, there is syntactic sugar to bind a variable immediately when it is declared. The idea is to put a bind operation between **local** and **in**. Instead of **local** `X` **in** `X=10 {Browse X}` **end**, in which `X` is mentioned three times, the shortcut lets one write **local** `X=10` **in** `{Browse X}` **end**, which mentions `X` only twice. A simple case is the following:

```
local X=⟨expression⟩ in ⟨statement⟩ end
```

This declares `X` and binds it to the result of ⟨expression⟩. The general case is:

```
local ⟨pattern⟩=⟨expression⟩ in ⟨statement⟩ end
```

where ⟨pattern⟩ is any partial value. This first declares all the variables in ⟨pattern⟩ and then binds ⟨pattern⟩ to the result of ⟨expression⟩. The general rule in both examples is that variable identifiers occurring on the left-hand side of the equality, i.e., `X` or the identifiers in ⟨pattern⟩, are the ones declared. Variable identifiers on the right-hand side are not declared.

Implicit variable initialization is convenient for building a complex data structure when we need variable references inside the structure. For example, if `T` is unbound, then the following:

```
local tree(key:A left:B right:C value:D)=T in ⟨statement⟩ end
```

builds the `tree` record, binds it to `T`, and declares `A`, `B`, `C`, and `D` as referring to parts of `T`. This is strictly equivalent to:

```
local A B C D in
   T=tree(key:A left:B right:C value:D) ⟨statement⟩
end
```

It is interesting to compare implicit variable initialization with the **case** statement. Both use patterns and implicitly declare variables. The first uses them to build data structures and the second uses them to take data structures apart.[10]

10. Implicit variable initialization can also be used to take data structures apart. If `T` is already bound to a `tree` record, then its four fields will be bound to `A`, `B`, `C`, and `D`. This works because the binding operation is actually doing unification, which is a symmetric operation (see section 2.8.2). We do not recommend this use.

```
⟨expression⟩ ::= ⟨variable⟩ | ⟨int⟩ | ⟨float⟩
               | ⟨unaryOp⟩ ⟨expression⟩
               | ⟨expression⟩ ⟨evalBinOp⟩ ⟨expression⟩
               | '(' ⟨expression⟩ ')'
               | '{' ⟨expression⟩ { ⟨expression⟩ } '}'
               | ...
⟨unaryOp⟩    ::= '~' | ...
⟨evalBinOp⟩  ::= '+' | '-' | '*' | '/' | div | mod
               | '==' | '\=' | '<' | '=<' | '>' | '>=' | ...
```

Table 2.4: Expressions for calculating with numbers.

```
⟨statement⟩   ::= if ⟨expression⟩ then ⟨inStatement⟩
                  { elseif ⟨expression⟩ then ⟨inStatement⟩ }
                  [ else ⟨inStatement⟩ ] end
                | ...
⟨inStatement⟩ ::= [ { ⟨declarationPart⟩ }+ in ] ⟨statement⟩
```

Table 2.5: The **if** statement.

Expressions

An expression is syntactic sugar for a sequence of operations that returns a value. It is different from a statement, which is also a sequence of operations but does not return a value. An expression can be used inside a statement whenever a value is needed. For example, `11*11` is an expression and `X=11*11` is a statement. Semantically, an expression is defined by a straightforward translation into kernel syntax. So `X=11*11` is translated into `{Mul 11 11 X}`, where `Mul` is a three-argument procedure that does multiplication.[11]

Table 2.4 shows the syntax of expressions that calculate with numbers. Later on we will see expressions for calculating with other data types. Expressions are built hierarchically, starting from basic expressions (e.g., variables and numbers) and combining them together. There are two ways to combine them: using operators (e.g., the addition `1+2+3+4`) or using function calls (e.g., the square root `{Sqrt 5.0}`).

11. Its real name is `Number.'*'`, since it is part of the `Number` module.

```
⟨statement⟩  ::= case ⟨expression⟩
                 of ⟨pattern⟩ [ andthen ⟨expression⟩ ] then ⟨inStatement⟩
                 { ´[]´ ⟨pattern⟩ [ andthen ⟨expression⟩ ] then ⟨inStatement⟩ }
                 [ else ⟨inStatement⟩ ] end
               | ...
⟨pattern⟩    ::= ⟨variable⟩ | ⟨atom⟩ | ⟨int⟩ | ⟨float⟩
               | ⟨string⟩ | unit | true | false
               | ⟨label⟩ ´(´ { [ ⟨feature⟩ ´:´ ] ⟨pattern⟩ } [ ´...´ ] ´)´
               | ⟨pattern⟩ ⟨consBinOp⟩ ⟨pattern⟩
               | ´[´ { ⟨pattern⟩ }+ ´]´
⟨consBinOp⟩ ::= ´#´ | ´|´
```

Table 2.6: The **case** statement.

Nested `if` *and* `case` *statements*

We add syntactic sugar to make it easy to write **if** and **case** statements with multiple alternatives and complicated conditions. Table 2.5 gives the syntax of the full **if** statement. Table 2.6 gives the syntax of the full **case** statement and its patterns. (Some of the nonterminals in these tables are defined in appendix C.) These statements are translated into the primitive **if** and **case** statements of the kernel language. Here is an example of a full **case** statement:

```
case Xs#Ys
of nil#Ys then ⟨s⟩1
[] Xs#nil then ⟨s⟩2
[] (X|Xr)#(Y|Yr) andthen X=<Y then ⟨s⟩3
else ⟨s⟩4 end
```

It consists of a sequence of alternative cases delimited with the "`[]`" symbol. The alternatives are often called clauses. This statement translates into the following kernel syntax:

```
case Xs of nil then ⟨s⟩1
else
   case Ys of nil then ⟨s⟩2
   else
      case Xs of X|Xr then
         case Ys of Y|Yr then
            if X=<Y then ⟨s⟩3 else ⟨s⟩4 end
         else ⟨s⟩4 end
      else ⟨s⟩4 end
   end
end
```

The translation illustrates an important property of the full **case** statement: clauses are tested sequentially starting with the first clause. Execution continues past a clause only if the clause's pattern is inconsistent with the input argument.

Nested patterns are handled by looking first at the outermost pattern and then working inward. The nested pattern `(X|Xr)#(Y|Yr)` has one outer pattern of the form `A#B` and two inner patterns of the form `A|B`. All three patterns are tuples that are written with infix syntax, using the infix operators `'#'` and `'|'`. They could have been written with the usual syntax as `'#'(A B)` and `'|'(A B)`. Each inner pattern `(X|Xr)` and `(Y|Yr)` is put in its own primitive **case** statement. The outer pattern using `'#'` disappears from the translation because it occurs also in the **case**'s input argument. The matching with `'#'` can therefore be done at translation time.

The operators andthen *and* orelse

The operators **andthen** and **orelse** are used in calculations with boolean values. The expression

```
⟨expression⟩1 andthen ⟨expression⟩2
```

translates into

```
if ⟨expression⟩1 then ⟨expression⟩2 else false end
```

The advantage of using **andthen** is that ⟨expression⟩$_2$ is not evaluated if ⟨expression⟩$_1$ is **false**. There is an analogous operator **orelse**. The expression

```
⟨expression⟩1 orelse ⟨expression⟩2
```

translates into

```
if ⟨expression⟩1 then true else ⟨expression⟩2 end
```

That is, ⟨expression⟩$_2$ is not evaluated if ⟨expression⟩$_1$ is **true**.

Nesting markers

The nesting marker "`$`" turns any statement into an expression. The expression's value is what is at the position indicated by the nesting marker. For example, the statement `{P X1 X2 X3}` can be written as `{P X1 $ X3}`, which is an expression whose value is `X2`. This makes the source code more concise, since it avoids having to declare and use the identifier `X2`. The variable corresponding to `X2` is hidden from the source code.

Nesting markers can make source code more readable to a proficient programmer, while making it harder for a beginner to see how the code translates to the kernel language. We use them only when they greatly increase readability. For example, instead of writing

```
local X in {Obj get(X)} {Browse X} end
```

<table>
<tr><td>⟨statement⟩</td><td>::=</td><td>fun '{' ⟨variable⟩ { ⟨pattern⟩ } '}' ⟨inExpression⟩ end</td></tr>
<tr><td></td><td>|</td><td>...</td></tr>
<tr><td>⟨expression⟩</td><td>::=</td><td>fun '{' '$' { ⟨pattern⟩ } '}' ⟨inExpression⟩ end</td></tr>
<tr><td></td><td>|</td><td>proc '{' '$' { ⟨pattern⟩ } '}' ⟨inStatement⟩ end</td></tr>
<tr><td></td><td>|</td><td>'{' ⟨expression⟩ { ⟨expression⟩ } '}'</td></tr>
<tr><td></td><td>|</td><td>local { ⟨declarationPart⟩ }+ in ⟨expression⟩ end</td></tr>
<tr><td></td><td>|</td><td>if ⟨expression⟩ then ⟨inExpression⟩
{ elseif ⟨expression⟩ then ⟨inExpression⟩ }
[else ⟨inExpression⟩] end</td></tr>
<tr><td></td><td>|</td><td>case ⟨expression⟩
of ⟨pattern⟩ [andthen ⟨expression⟩] then ⟨inExpression⟩
{ '[]' ⟨pattern⟩ [andthen ⟨expression⟩] then ⟨inExpression⟩ }
[else ⟨inExpression⟩] end</td></tr>
<tr><td></td><td>|</td><td>...</td></tr>
<tr><td>⟨inStatement⟩</td><td>::=</td><td>[{ ⟨declarationPart⟩ }+ in] ⟨statement⟩</td></tr>
<tr><td>⟨inExpression⟩</td><td>::=</td><td>[{ ⟨declarationPart⟩ }+ in] [⟨statement⟩] ⟨expression⟩</td></tr>
</table>

Table 2.7: Function syntax.

we will instead write `{Browse {Obj get($)}}`. Once you get used to nesting markers, they are both concise and clear. Note that the syntax of procedure values as explained in section 2.3.3 is consistent with the nesting marker syntax.

2.6.2 Functions (the `fun` statement)

The declarative model provides a linguistic abstraction for programming with functions. This is our first example of a linguistic abstraction, as defined in section 2.1.2. We define the new syntax for function definitions and function calls and show how they are translated into the kernel language.

Function definitions

A function definition differs from a procedure definition in two ways: it is introduced with the keyword **fun** and the body must end with an expression. For example, a simple definition is:

fun `{F X1 ... XN}` ⟨statement⟩ ⟨expression⟩ **end**

This translates to the following procedure definition:

proc `{F X1 ... XN ?R}` ⟨statement⟩ `R=`⟨expression⟩ **end**

The extra argument `R` is bound to the expression in the procedure body. If the function body is an **if** statement, then each alternative of the **if** can end in an expression:

```
fun {Max X Y}
   if X>=Y then X else Y end
end
```

This translates to:

```
proc {Max X Y ?R}
   R = if X>=Y then X else Y end
end
```

We can further translate this by transforming the **if** from an expression to a statement. This gives the final result:

```
proc {Max X Y ?R}
   if X>=Y then R=X else R=Y end
end
```

Similar rules apply for the **local** and **case** statements, and for other statements we will see later. Each statement can be used as an expression. Roughly speaking, whenever an execution sequence in a procedure ends in a statement, the corresponding sequence in a function ends in an expression. Table 2.7 gives the complete syntax of expressions after applying this rule. This table takes all the statements we have seen so far and shows how to use them as expressions. In particular, there are also function values, which are simply procedure values written in functional syntax.

Function calls

A function call `{F X1 ... XN}` translates to the procedure call `{F X1 ... XN R}`, where `R` replaces the function call where it is used. For example, the following nested call of `F`:

```
{Q {F X1 ... XN} ...}
```

is translated to:

```
local R in
   {F X1 ... XN R}
   {Q R ...}
end
```

In general, nested function calls are evaluated before the function call in which they are nested. If there are several, then they are evaluated in the order they appear in the program.

Function calls in data structures

There is one more rule to remember for function calls. It has to do with a call inside a data structure (record, tuple, or list). Here is an example:

⟨interStatement⟩	::=	⟨statement⟩
		| **declare** { ⟨declarationPart⟩ }+ [⟨interStatement⟩]
		| **declare** { ⟨declarationPart⟩ }+ **in** ⟨interStatement⟩
⟨declarationPart⟩	::=	⟨variable⟩ | ⟨pattern⟩ ´=´ ⟨expression⟩ | ⟨statement⟩

Table 2.8: Interactive statement syntax.

```
Ys={F X}|{Map Xr F}
```

In this case, the translation puts the nested calls after the bind operation:

```
local Y Yr in
   Ys=Y|Yr
   {F X Y}
   {Map Xr F Yr}
end
```

This ensures that the recursive call is last. Section 2.5.1 explains why this is important for execution efficiency. The full `Map` function is defined as follows:

```
fun {Map Xs F}
   case Xs
   of nil then nil
   [] X|Xr then {F X}|{Map Xr F}
   end
end
```

`Map` applies the function `F` to all elements of a list and returns the result. Here is an example call:

```
{Browse {Map [1 2 3 4] fun {$ X} X*X end}}
```

This displays `[1 4 9 16]`. The definition of `Map` translates as follows to the kernel language:

```
proc {Map Xs F ?Ys}
   case Xs of nil then Ys=nil
   else case Xs of X|Xr then
      local Y Yr in
         Ys=Y|Yr {F X Y} {Map Xr F Yr}
      end
   end end
end
```

The dataflow variable `Yr` is used as a "placeholder" for the result in the recursive call `{Map Xr F Yr}`. This lets the recursive call be the last call. In our model, this means that the recursion executes with the same space and time efficiency as an iterative construct like a **while** loop.

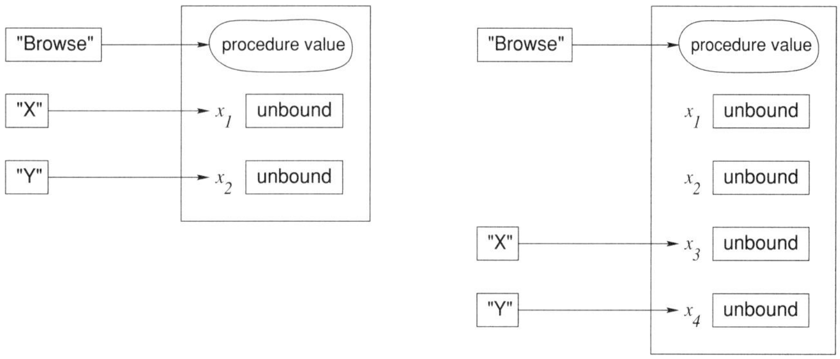

Result of first `declare X Y`   Result of second `declare X Y`

Figure 2.19: Declaring global variables.

2.6.3 Interactive interface (the **`declare`** statement)

The Mozart system has an interactive interface that allows introducing program fragments incrementally and execute them as they are introduced. The fragments have to respect the syntax of interactive statements, which is given in table 2.8. An interactive statement is either any legal statement or a new form, the **`declare`** statement. We assume that the user feeds interactive statements to the system one by one. (In the examples given throughout the book, the **`declare`** statement is often left out. It should be added if the example declares new variables.)

The interactive interface allows much more than just feeding statements. It has all the functionality needed for software development. Appendix A gives a summary of some of this functionality. For now, we assume that the user just knows how to feed statements.

The interactive interface has a single, global environment. The **`declare`** statement adds new mappings to this environment. It follows that **`declare`** can *only* be used interactively, not in standalone programs. Feeding the following declaration:

```
declare X Y
```

creates two new variables in the store, x_1 and x_2, and adds mappings from `X` and `Y` to them. Because the mappings are in the global environment we say that `X` and `Y` are global variables or interactive variables. Feeding the same declaration a second time will cause `X` and `Y` to map to two other new variables, x_3 and x_4. Figure 2.19 shows what happens. The original variables, x_1 and x_2, are still in the store, but they are no longer referred to by `X` and `Y`. In the figure, `Browse` maps to a procedure value that implements the browser. The **`declare`** statement adds new variables and mappings, but leaves existing variables in the store unchanged.

Adding a new mapping to an identifier that already maps to a variable may

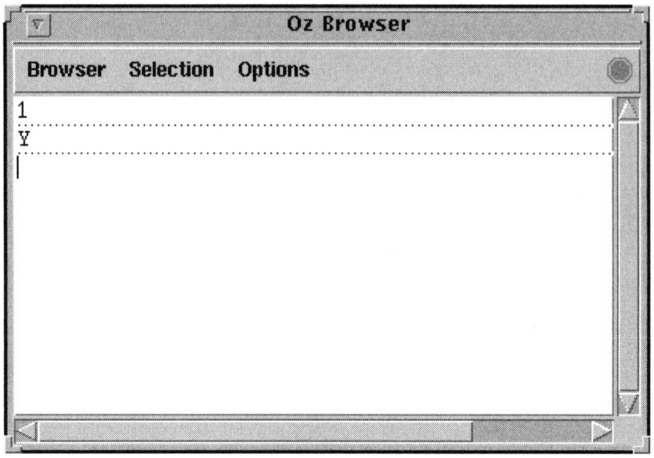

Figure 2.20: The Browser.

cause the variable to become inaccessible if there are no other references to it. If the variable is part of a calculation, then it is still accessible from within the calculation. For example:

```
declare X Y
X=25
declare A
A=person(age:X)
declare X Y
```

Just after the binding `X=25`, `X` maps to 25, but after the second **`declare`** `X Y` it maps to a new unbound variable. The 25 is still accessible through the global variable `A`, which is bound to the record `person(age:25)`. The record contains 25 because `X` mapped to 25 when the binding `A=person(age:X)` was executed. The second **`declare`** `X Y` changes the mapping of `X`, but not the record `person(age:25)` since the record already exists in the store. This behavior of **`declare`** is designed to support a modular programming style. Executing a program fragment will not cause the results of any previously executed fragment to change.

There is a second form of **`declare`**:

```
declare X Y in ⟨stmt⟩
```

which declares two global variables, as before, and then executes ⟨stmt⟩. The difference with the first form is that ⟨stmt⟩ declares no global variables (unless it contains a **`declare`**).

The Browser

The interactive interface has a tool, called the *Browser*, which allows looking into the store. This tool is available to the programmer as a procedure called `Browse`.

The procedure Browse has one argument. It is called as {Browse ⟨expr⟩}, where ⟨expr⟩ is any expression. It can display partial values and it will update the display whenever the partial values are bound more. Feeding the following:

```
{Browse 1}
```

displays the integer 1. Feeding:

```
declare Y in
{Browse Y}
```

displays just the name of the variable, namely Y. No value is displayed. This means that Y is currently unbound. Figure 2.20 shows the browser window after these two operations. If Y is bound, e.g., by doing Y=2, then the browser will update its display to show this binding.

Dataflow execution

We saw earlier that declarative variables support dataflow execution, i.e., an operation waits until all arguments are bound before executing. For sequential programs this is not very useful, since the program will wait forever. On the other hand, it is useful for concurrent programs, in which more than one instruction sequence can be executing at the same time. An independently executing instruction sequence is called a thread. Programming with more than one thread is called concurrent programming; it is introduced in chapter 4.

Each program fragment fed into the interactive interface executes in its own thread. This lets us give simple examples of dataflow execution in this chapter. For example, feed the following statement:

```
declare A B C in
C=A+B
{Browse C}
```

This will display nothing, since the instruction C=A+B blocks (both of its arguments are unbound). Now, feed the following statement:

```
A=10
```

This will bind A, but the instruction C=A+B still blocks since B is still unbound. Finally, feed the following:

```
B=200
```

This displays 210 in the browser. Any operation, not just addition, will block if it does not get enough input information to calculate its result. For example, comparisons can block. The equality comparison X==Y will block if it cannot decide whether or not X is equal to or different from Y. This happens, e.g., if one or both of the variables are unbound.

Programming errors often result in dataflow suspensions. If you feed a statement that should display a result and nothing is displayed, then the probable cause of the problem is a blocked operation. Carefully check all operations to make sure that their arguments are bound. Ideally, the system's debugger should detect when a program has blocked operations that cannot continue.

2.7 Exceptions

First let us find the rule, then we will try to explain the exceptions.
– *The Name of the Rose*, Umberto Eco (1932–)

How do we handle exceptional situations within a program? For example, dividing by zero, opening a nonexistent file, or selecting a nonexistent field of a record? These operations do not occur in a correct program, so they should not encumber normal programming style. On the other hand, they do occur sometimes. It should be possible for programs to manage them in a simple way. The declarative model cannot do this without adding cumbersome checks throughout the program. A more elegant way is to extend the model with an exception-handling mechanism. This section does exactly that. We give the syntax and semantics of the extended model and explain what exceptions look like in the full language.

2.7.1 Motivation and basic concepts

In the semantics of section 2.4, we speak of "raising an error" when a statement cannot continue correctly. For example, a conditional raises an error when its argument is a non-boolean value. Up to now, we have been deliberately vague about exactly what happens next. Let us now be more precise. We define an error as a difference between the actual behavior of a program and its desired behavior. There are many sources of errors, both internal and external to the program. An internal error could result from invoking an operation with an argument of illegal type or illegal value. An external error could result from opening a nonexistent file.

We would like to be able to detect errors and handle them from within a running program. The program should not stop when they occur. Rather, it should in a controlled way transfer execution to another part, called the exception handler, and pass the exception handler a value that describes the error.

What should the exception-handling mechanism look like? We can make two observations. First, it should be able to confine the error, i.e., quarantine it so that it does not contaminate the whole program. We call this the error confinement principle. Assume that the program is made up of interacting "components" organized in hierarchical fashion. Each component is built of smaller components. We put "component" in quotes because the language does not need to have a component concept. It just needs to be compositional, i.e., programs are built in layered fashion. Then the error confinement principle states that an error in a component should be catchable at the component boundary. Outside the component, the error is either invisible or reported in a nice way.

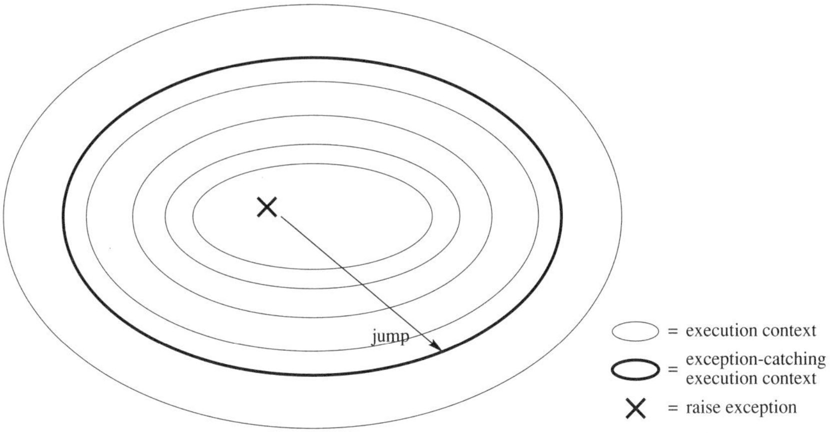

Figure 2.21: Exception handling.

Therefore, the mechanism causes a "jump" from inside the component to its boundary. The second observation is that this jump should be a single operation. The mechanism should be able, in a single operation, to exit from arbitrarily many levels of nested context. Figure 2.21 illustrates this. In our semantics, we define a context as an entry on the semantic stack, i.e., an instruction that has to be executed later. Nested contexts are created by procedure calls and sequential compositions.

The declarative model cannot jump out in a single operation. The jump has to be coded explicitly as little hops, one per context, using boolean variables and conditionals. This makes programs more cumbersome, especially since the extra coding has to be added everywhere that an error can possibly occur. It can be shown theoretically that the only way to keep programs simple is to extend the model [116, 118].

We propose a simple extension to the model that satisfies these conditions. We add two statements: the **try** statement and the **raise** statement. The **try** statement creates an exception-catching context together with an exception handler. The **raise** statement jumps to the boundary of the innermost exception-catching context and invokes the exception handler there. Nested **try** statements create nested contexts. Executing **try** ⟨s⟩ **catch** ⟨x⟩ **then** $\langle s \rangle_1$ **end** is equivalent to executing ⟨s⟩, if ⟨s⟩ does not raise an exception. On the other hand, if ⟨s⟩ raises an exception, i.e., by executing a **raise** statement, then the (still ongoing) execution of ⟨s⟩ is aborted. All information related to ⟨s⟩ is popped from the semantic stack. Control is transferred to $\langle s \rangle_1$, passing it a reference to the exception in ⟨x⟩.

Any partial value can be an exception. This means that the exception-handling mechanism is extensible by the programmer, i.e., new exceptions can be defined as they are needed by the program. This lets the programmer foresee new exceptional situations. Because an exception can be an unbound variable, raising an exception and determining what the exception is can be done concurrently. In other words, an exception can be raised (and caught) before it is known which exception it is! This is quite reasonable in a language with dataflow variables: we may at some point know that there exists a problem but not know yet which problem.

An example

Let us give a simple example of exception handling. Consider the following function, which evaluates simple arithmetic expressions and returns the result:

```
fun {Eval E}
   if {IsNumber E} then E
   else
      case E
      of   plus(X Y) then {Eval X}+{Eval Y}
      []   times(X Y) then {Eval X}*{Eval Y}
      else raise illFormedExpr(E) end
      end
   end
end
```

For this example, we say an expression is ill-formed if it is not recognized by `Eval`, i.e., if it contains other values than numbers, `plus`, and `times`. Trying to evaluate an ill-formed expression `E` will raise an exception. The exception is a tuple, `illFormedExpr(E)`, that contains the ill-formed expression. Here is an example of using `Eval`:

```
try
   {Browse {Eval plus(plus(5 5) 10)}}
   {Browse {Eval times(6 11)}}
   {Browse {Eval minus(7 10)}}
catch illFormedExpr(E) then
   {Browse ´*** Illegal expression ´#E#´ ***´}
end
```

If any call to `Eval` raises an exception, then control transfers to the **catch** clause, which displays an error message.

2.7.2 The declarative model with exceptions

We extend the declarative computation model with exceptions. Table 2.9 gives the syntax of the extended kernel language. Programs can use two new statements, **try** and **raise**. In addition, there is a third statement, **catch** ⟨x⟩ **then** ⟨s⟩ **end**, that is needed internally for the semantics and is not allowed in programs. The **catch** statement is a "marker" on the semantic stack that defines the boundary of the exception-catching context. We now give the semantics of these statements.

The try statement

The semantic statement is:

⟨s⟩ ::=	
skip	Empty statement
| ⟨s⟩$_1$ ⟨s⟩$_2$	Statement sequence
| **local** ⟨x⟩ **in** ⟨s⟩ **end**	Variable creation
| ⟨x⟩$_1$=⟨x⟩$_2$	Variable-variable binding
| ⟨x⟩=⟨v⟩	Value creation
| **if** ⟨x⟩ **then** ⟨s⟩$_1$ **else** ⟨s⟩$_2$ **end**	Conditional
| **case** ⟨x⟩ **of** ⟨pattern⟩ **then** ⟨s⟩$_1$ **else** ⟨s⟩$_2$ **end**	Pattern matching
| { ⟨x⟩ ⟨y⟩$_1$ ⋯ ⟨y⟩$_n$ }	Procedure application
| **try** ⟨s⟩$_1$ **catch** ⟨x⟩ **then** ⟨s⟩$_2$ **end**	**Exception context**
| **raise** ⟨x⟩ **end**	**Raise exception**

Table 2.9: The declarative kernel language with exceptions.

(**try** ⟨s⟩$_1$ **catch** ⟨x⟩ **then** ⟨s⟩$_2$ **end**, E)

Execution consists of the following actions:

- Push the semantic statement (**catch** ⟨x⟩ **then** ⟨s⟩$_2$ **end**, E) on the stack.
- Push (⟨s⟩$_1$, E) on the stack.

The `raise` *statement*

The semantic statement is:

(**raise** ⟨x⟩ **end**, E)

Execution consists of the following actions:

- Pop elements off the stack looking for a **catch** statement.
  - If a **catch** statement is found, pop it from the stack.
  - If the stack is emptied and no **catch** is found, then stop execution with the error message "`Uncaught exception`".
- Let (**catch** ⟨y⟩ **then** ⟨s⟩ **end**, E_c) be the **catch** statement that is found.
- Push (⟨s⟩, $E_c + \{$⟨y⟩ $\rightarrow E($⟨x⟩$)\}$) on the stack.

Let us see how an uncaught exception is handled by the Mozart system. For interactive execution, an error message is printed in the Oz emulator window. For standalone applications, the application terminates and an error message is sent on the standard error output of the process. It is possible to change this behavior to something else that is more desirable for particular applications, by using the System module `Property`.

⟨statement⟩	::=	**try** ⟨inStatement⟩
		[**catch** ⟨pattern⟩ **then** ⟨inStatement⟩
		{ ´[]´ ⟨pattern⟩ **then** ⟨inStatement⟩ }]
		[**finally** ⟨inStatement⟩] **end**
	|	**raise** ⟨inExpression⟩ **end**
	|	...
⟨inStatement⟩	::=	[{ ⟨declarationPart⟩ }+ **in**] ⟨statement⟩
⟨inExpression⟩	::=	[{ ⟨declarationPart⟩ }+ **in**] [⟨statement⟩] ⟨expression⟩

Table 2.10: Exception syntax.

The `catch` *statement*

The semantic statement is:

(**catch** ⟨x⟩ **then** ⟨s⟩ **end**, E)

Execution is complete after this pair is popped from the semantic stack. That is, the **catch** statement does nothing, just like **skip**.

2.7.3 Full syntax

Table 2.10 gives the syntax of the **try** statement in the full language. It has an optional **finally** clause. The **catch** clause has an optional series of patterns. Let us see how these extensions are defined.

The `finally` *clause*

A **try** statement can specify a **finally** clause which is always executed, whether or not the statement raises an exception. The new syntax

```
try ⟨s⟩1 finally ⟨s⟩2 end
```

is translated to the kernel language as:

```
try ⟨s⟩1
catch X then
   ⟨s⟩2
   raise X end
end
⟨s⟩2
```

(where an identifier X is chosen that is not free in $\langle s \rangle_2$). It is possible to define a translation in which $\langle s \rangle_2$ only occurs once; we leave this to the exercises.

The **finally** clause is useful when dealing with entities that are external to the computation model. With **finally**, we can guarantee that some "cleanup" action gets performed on the entity, whether or not an exception occurs. A typical example is reading a file. Assume `F` is an open file,[12] the procedure `ProcessFile` manipulates the file in some way, and the procedure `CloseFile` closes the file. Then the following program ensures that `F` is always closed after `ProcessFile` completes, whether or not an exception was raised:

```
try
   {ProcessFile F}
finally {CloseFile F} end
```

Note that this **try** statement does not catch the exception; it just executes `CloseFile` whenever `ProcessFile` completes. We can combine both catching the exception and executing a final statement:

```
try
   {ProcessFile F}
catch X then
   {Browse '*** Exception '#X#' when processing file ***'}
finally {CloseFile F} end
```

This behaves like two nested **try** statements: the innermost with just a **catch** clause and the outermost with just a **finally** clause.

Pattern matching

A **try** statement can use pattern matching to catch only exceptions that match a given pattern. Other exceptions are passed to the next enclosing **try** statement. The new syntax:

```
try ⟨s⟩
catch ⟨p⟩1 then ⟨s⟩1
   [] ⟨p⟩2 then ⟨s⟩2
   ...
   [] ⟨p⟩n then ⟨s⟩n
end
```

is translated to the kernel language as:

```
try ⟨s⟩
catch X then
   case X
   of ⟨p⟩1 then ⟨s⟩1
   [] ⟨p⟩2 then ⟨s⟩2
   ...
   [] ⟨p⟩n then ⟨s⟩n
   else raise X end
   end
end
```

If the exception does not match any of the patterns, then it is simply raised again.

12. We will see later how file input/output is handled.

2.7.4 System exceptions

The Mozart system itself raises a few exceptions. They are called system exceptions. They are all records with one of the three labels `failure`, `error`, or `system`:

- `failure`: indicates an attempt to perform an inconsistent bind operation (e.g., `1=2`) in the store (see section 2.8.2.1). This is also called a unification failure.
- `error`: indicates a run-time error inside the program, i.e., a situation that should not occur during normal operation. These errors are either type or domain errors. A type error occurs when invoking an operation with an argument of incorrect type, e.g., applying a nonprocedure to some argument (`{foo 1}`, where `foo` is an atom), or adding an integer to an atom (e.g., `X=1+a`). A domain error occurs when invoking an operation with an argument that is outside of its domain (even if it has the right type), e.g., taking the square root of a negative number, dividing by zero, or selecting a nonexistent field of a record.
- `system`: indicates a run-time condition occurring in the environment of the Mozart operating system process, e.g., an unforeseeable situation like a closed file or window or a failure to open a connection between two Mozart processes in distributed programming (see chapter 11).

What is stored inside the exception record depends on the Mozart system version. Therefore programmers should rely only on the label. For example:

```
fun {One} 1 end
fun {Two} 2 end
try {One}={Two}
catch
   failure(...) then {Browse caughtFailure}
end
```

The pattern `failure(...)` catches any record whose label is `failure`.

2.8 Advanced topics

This section gives additional information for deeper understanding of the declarative model, its trade-offs, and possible variations.

2.8.1 Functional programming languages

Functional programming consists in defining functions on complete values, where the functions are true functions in the mathematical sense. A language in which this is the only possible way to calculate is called a pure functional language. Let us examine how the declarative model relates to pure functional programming. For further reading on the history, formal foundations, and motivations for functional programming, we recommend the survey article by Hudak [96].

The λ calculus

Pure functional languages are based on a formalism called the λ calculus. There are many variants of the λ calculus. All of these variants have in common two basic operations, namely defining and evaluating functions. For example, the function value **fun** {$ X} X*X **end** is identical to the λ expression $\lambda x.\ x{*}x$. This expression consists of two parts: the x before the dot, which is the function's argument, and the expression $x * x$, which is the function's result. The `Append` function, which appends two lists together, can be defined as a function value:

```
Append=fun {$ Xs Ys}
          if {IsNil Xs} then Ys
          else {Cons {Car Xs} {Append {Cdr Xs} Ys}}
          end
       end
```

This is equivalent to the following λ expression:

$$\begin{aligned} \mathit{append} = \lambda xs, ys\ .\ &\text{if } \mathit{isNil}(xs) \text{ then } ys \\ &\text{else } \mathit{cons}(\mathit{car}(xs), \mathit{append}(\mathit{cdr}(xs), ys)) \end{aligned}$$

This definition of `Append` uses the following helper functions:

```
fun {IsNil X} X==nil end
fun {IsCons X} case X of _|_ then true else false end end
fun {Car H|T} H end
fun {Cdr H|T} T end
fun {Cons H T} H|T end
```

Restricting the declarative model

The declarative model is more general than the λ calculus in two ways. First, it defines functions on partial values, i.e., with unbound variables. Second, it uses a procedural syntax. We can define a pure functional language by putting two syntactic restrictions on the declarative model so that it always calculates functions on complete values:

- Always bind a variable to a value immediately when it is declared. That is, the **local** statement always has one of the following two forms:

```
local ⟨x⟩=⟨v⟩ in ⟨s⟩ end
local ⟨x⟩={⟨y⟩ ⟨y⟩1 ... ⟨y⟩n} in ⟨s⟩ end
```

- Use only the function syntax, not the procedure syntax. For function calls inside data structures, do the nested call before creating the data structure (instead of after, as in section 2.6.2). This avoids putting unbound variables in data structures.

With these restrictions, the model no longer needs unbound variables. The declarative model with these restrictions is called the (strict) functional model. This model is close to well-known functional programming languages such as Scheme and Standard ML. The full range of higher-order programming techniques is possible. Pattern matching is possible using the **case** statement.

Varieties of functional programming

Let us explore some variations on the theme of functional programming:

- The functional model of this chapter is dynamically typed like Scheme. Many functional languages are statically typed. Section 2.8.3 explains the differences between the two approaches. Furthermore, many statically typed languages, e.g., Haskell and Standard ML, do type inferencing, which allows the compiler to infer the types of all functions.
- Thanks to dataflow variables and the single-assignment store, the declarative model allows programming techniques that are not found in most functional languages, including Scheme, Standard ML, Haskell, and Erlang. This includes certain forms of last call optimization and techniques to compute with partial values as shown in chapter 3.
- The declarative concurrent model of chapter 4 adds concurrency while still keeping all the good properties of functional programming. This is possible because of dataflow variables and the single-assignment store.
- In the declarative model, functions are eager by default, i.e., function arguments are evaluated before the function body is executed. This is also called strict evaluation. The functional languages Scheme and Standard ML are strict. There is another useful execution order, lazy evaluation, in which function arguments are evaluated only if their result is needed. Haskell is a lazy functional language.[13] Lazy evaluation is a powerful flow control technique in functional programming [98]. It allows programming with potentially infinite data structures without giving explicit bounds. Section 4.5 explains this in detail. An eager declarative program can evaluate functions and then never use them, thus doing superfluous work. A lazy declarative program, on the other hand, does the absolute minimum amount of work to get its result.
- Many functional languages support a higher-order programming technique called currying, which is explained in section 3.6.6.

2.8.2 Unification and entailment

In section 2.2 we have seen how to bind dataflow variables to partial values and to each other, using the equality (´=´) operation as shown in table 2.11. In section 2.3.5 we have seen how to compare values, using the equality test (´==´ and ´\=´) operations. So far, we have seen only the simple cases of these operations. Let us

13. To be precise, Haskell is a nonstrict language. This is identical to laziness for most practical purposes. The difference is explained in section 4.9.2.

⟨statement⟩	::=	⟨expression⟩ ´=´ ⟨expression⟩ | ...
⟨expression⟩	::=	⟨expression⟩ ´==´ ⟨expression⟩
	|	⟨expression⟩ ´\=´ ⟨expression⟩ | ...
⟨binaryOp⟩	::=	´=´ | ´==´ | ´\=´ | ...

Table 2.11: Equality (unification) and equality test (entailment check).

now examine the general cases.

Binding a variable to a value is a special case of an operation called unification. The unification ⟨Term1⟩=⟨Term2⟩ makes the partial values ⟨Term1⟩ and ⟨Term2⟩ equal, if possible, by adding zero or more bindings to the store. For example, `f(X Y)=f(1 2)` does two bindings: `X=1` and `Y=2`. If the two terms cannot be made equal, then an exception is raised. Unification exists because of partial values; if there would be only complete values, then it would have no meaning.

Testing whether a variable is equal to a value is a special case of the entailment check and disentailment check operations. The entailment check ⟨Term1⟩==⟨Term2⟩ (and its opposite, the disentailment check ⟨Term1⟩\=⟨Term2⟩) is a two-argument boolean function that blocks until it is known whether ⟨Term1⟩ and ⟨Term2⟩ are equal or not equal.[14] Entailment and disentailment checks never do any binding.

2.8.2.1 Unification (the = operation)

A good way to conceptualize unification is as an operation that adds information to the single-assignment store. The store is a set of dataflow variables, where each variable is either unbound or bound to some other store entity. The store's information is just the set of all its bindings. Doing a new binding, e.g., `X=Y`, will add the information that `X` and `Y` are equal. If `X` and `Y` are already bound when doing `X=Y`, then some other bindings may be added to the store. For example, if the store already has `X=foo(A)` and `Y=foo(25)`, then doing `X=Y` will bind `A` to 25. Unification is a kind of "compiler" that is given new information and "compiles it into the store," taking into account the bindings that are already there. To understand how this works, let us look at some possibilities.

- The simplest cases are bindings to values, e.g., `X=person(name:X1 age:X2)`, and variable-variable bindings, e.g., `X=Y`. If `X` and `Y` are unbound, then these operations each add one binding to the store.
- Unification is symmetric. For example, `person(name:X1 age:X2)=X` means the

14. The word "entailment" comes from logic. It is a form of logical implication. This is because the equality ⟨Term1⟩==⟨Term2⟩ is true if the store, considered as a conjunction of equalities, "logically implies" ⟨Term1⟩==⟨Term2⟩.

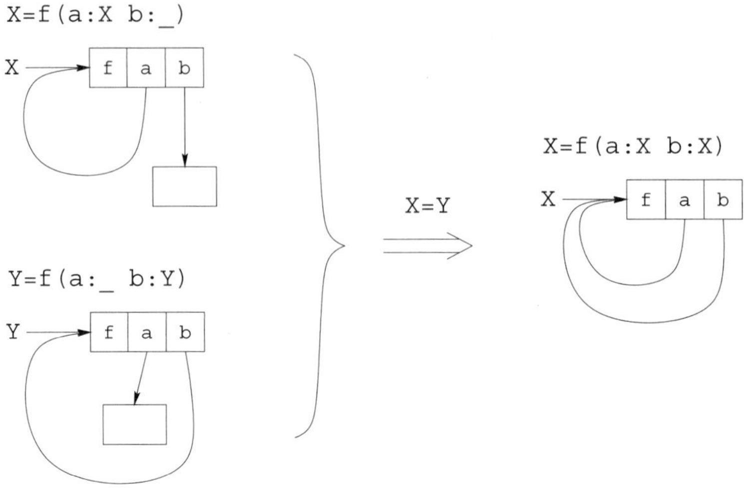

Figure 2.22: Unification of cyclic structures.

same as `X=person(name:X1 age:X2)`.

- Any two partial values can be unified. For example, unifying the two records:

```
person(name:X1 age:X2)
person(name:"George" age:25)
```

This binds `X1` to `"George"` and `X2` to 25.

- If the partial values are already equal, then unification does nothing. For example, unifying `X` and `Y` where the store contains the two records:

```
X=person(name:"George" age:25)
Y=person(name:"George" age:25)
```

This does nothing.

- If the partial values are incompatible, then they cannot be unified. For example, unifying the two records:

```
person(name:X1 age:26)
person(name:"George" age:25)
```

The records have different values for their `age` fields, namely 25 and 26, so they cannot be unified. This unification will raise a `failure` exception, which can be caught by a **`try`** statement. The unification might or might not bind `X1` to `"George"`; it depends on exactly when it finds out that there is an incompatibility. Another way to get a unification failure is by executing the statement **`fail`**.

- Unification is symmetric in the arguments. For example, unifying the two records:

```
person(name:"George" age:X2)
person(name:X1 age:25)
```

This binds `X1` to `"George"` and `X2` to 25, just like before.

- Unification can create cyclic structures, i.e., structures that refer to themselves. For example, the unification `X=person(grandfather:X)`. This creates a record whose `grandfather` field refers to itself. This situation happens in some crazy time-travel stories.
- Unification can bind cyclic structures. For example, let's create two cyclic structures, in `X` and `Y`, by doing `X=f(a:X b:_)` and `Y=f(a:_ b:Y)`. Now, doing the unification `X=Y` creates a structure with two cycles, which we can write as `X=f(a:X b:X)`. This example is illustrated in figure 2.22.

2.8.2.2 *The unification algorithm*

Let us give a precise definition of unification. We will define the operation unify(x, y) that unifies two partial values x and y in the store σ. Unification is a basic operation of logic programming. When used in the context of unification, store variables are called logic variables. Logic programming, which is also called relational programming, is discussed in chapter 9.

The store The store consists of a set of k variables, x_1, ..., x_k, that are partitioned as follows:

- Sets of unbound variables that are equal (also called equivalence sets of variables). The variables in each set are equal to each other but not to any other variables.
- Variables bound to a number, record, or procedure (also called determined variables).

An example is the store $\{x_1 = \texttt{foo(a:}x_2\texttt{)}, x_2 = 25, x_3 = x_4 = x_5, x_6, x_7 = x_8\}$ that has eight variables. It has three equivalence sets, namely $\{x_3, x_4, x_5\}$, $\{x_6\}$, and $\{x_7, x_8\}$. It has two determined variables, namely x_1 and x_2.

The primitive bind operation We define unification in terms of a primitive bind operation on the store σ. The operation binds all variables in an equivalence set:

- bind$(ES, \langle\mathsf{v}\rangle)$ binds all variables in the equivalence set ES to the number or record $\langle\mathsf{v}\rangle$. For example, the operation bind$(\{x_7, x_8\}, \texttt{foo(a:}x_2\texttt{)})$ modifies the example store so that x_7 and x_8 are no longer in an equivalence set but both become bound to $\texttt{foo(a:}x_2\texttt{)}$.
- bind(ES_1, ES_2) merges the equivalence set ES_1 with the equivalence set ES_2. For example, the operation bind$(\{x_3, x_4, x_5\}, \{x_6\})$ modifies the example store so that x_3, x_4, x_5, and x_6 are in a single equivalence set, namely $\{x_3, x_4, x_5, x_6\}$.

The algorithm We now define the operation unify(x, y) as follows:

1. If x is in the equivalence set ES_x and y is in the equivalence set ES_y, then do bind(ES_x, ES_y). If x and y are in the same equivalence set, this is the same as

doing nothing.

2. If x is in the equivalence set ES_x and y is determined, then do bind(ES_x, y).

3. If y is in the equivalence set ES_y and x is determined, then do bind(ES_y, x).

4. If x is bound to $l(l_1 : x_1, \ldots, l_n : x_n)$ and y is bound to $l'(l'_1 : y_1, \ldots, l'_m : y_m)$ with $l \neq l'$ or $\{l_1, \ldots, l_n\} \neq \{l'_1, \ldots, l'_m\}$, then raise a failure exception.

5. If x is bound to $l(l_1 : x_1, \ldots, l_n : x_n)$ and y is bound to $l(l_1 : y_1, \ldots, l_n : y_n)$, then for i from 1 to n do unify(x_i, y_i).

Handling cycles The above algorithm does not handle unification of partial values with cycles. For example, assume the store contains x = `f(a:`x`)` and y = `f(a:`y`)`. Calling unify(x, y) results in the recursive call unify(x, y), which is identical to the original call. The algorithm loops forever! Yet it is clear that x and y have exactly the same structure: what the unification *should* do is add exactly zero bindings to the store and then terminate. How can we fix this problem?

A simple fix is to make sure that unify(x, y) is called at most once for each possible pair of two variables (x, y). Since any attempt to call it again will not do anything new, it can return immediately. With k variables in the store, this means at most k^2 unify calls, so the algorithm is guaranteed to terminate. In practice, the number of unify calls is much less than this. We can implement the fix with a table that stores all called pairs. This gives the new algorithm unify$'(x, y)$:

- Let M be a new, empty table.
- Call unify$''(x, y)$.

This needs the definition of unify$''(x, y)$:

- If $(x, y) \in M$, then we are done.
- Otherwise, insert (x, y) in M and then do the original algorithm for unify(x, y), in which the recursive calls to unify are replaced by calls to unify$''$.

This algorithm can be written in the declarative model by passing M as two extra arguments to unify$''$. A table that remembers previous calls so that they can be avoided in the future is called a memoization table.

2.8.2.3 Displaying cyclic structures

We have seen that unification can create cyclic structures. To display these in the browser, it has to be configured right. In the browser's `Options` menu, pick the `Representation` entry and choose the `Graph` mode. There are three display modes, namely `Tree` (the default), `Graph`, and `Minimal Graph`. `Tree` does not take sharing or cycles into account. `Graph` correctly handles sharing and cycles by displaying a graph. `Minimal Graph` shows the smallest graph that is consistent with the data. We give some examples. Consider the following two unifications:

```
local X Y Z in
   f(X b)=f(a Y)
   f(Z a)=Z
   {Browse [X Y Z]}
end
```

This shows the list `[a b R14=f(R14 a)]` in the browser, if the browser is set up to show the `Graph` representation. The term `R14=f(R14 a)` is the textual representation of a cyclic graph. The variable name `R14` is introduced by the browser; different versions of Mozart might introduce different variable names. As a second example, feed the following unification when the browser is set up for `Graph`, as before:

```
declare X Y Z in
a(X c(Z) Z)=a(b(Y) Y d(X))
{Browse X#Y#Z}
```

Now set up the browser for the `Minimal Graph` mode and display the term again. How do you explain the difference?

2.8.2.4 Entailment and disentailment checks (the `==` and `\=` operations)

The entailment check `X==Y` is a boolean function that tests whether `X` and `Y` are equal or not. The opposite check, `X\=Y`, is called a disentailment check. Both checks use essentially the same algorithm.[15] The entailment check returns **`true`** if the store implies the information `X=Y` in a way that is verifiable (the store "entails" `X=Y`) and **`false`** if the store will never imply `X=Y`, again in a way that is verifiable (the store "disentails" `X=Y`). The check blocks if it cannot determine whether `X` and `Y` are equal or will never be equal. It is defined as follows:

- It returns the value **`true`** if the graphs starting from the nodes of `X` and `Y` have the same structure, i.e., all pairwise corresponding nodes have identical values or are the same node. We call this structure equality.
- It returns the value **`false`** if the graphs have different structure, or some pairwise corresponding nodes have different values.
- It blocks when it arrives at pairwise corresponding nodes that are different, but at least one of them is unbound.

Here is an example:

15. Strictly speaking, there is a single algorithm that does both the entailment and disentailment checks simultaneously. It returns **`true`** or **`false`** depending on which check calls it.

```
declare L1 L2 L3 Head Tail in
L1=Head|Tail
Head=1
Tail=2|nil

L2=[1 2]
{Browse L1==L2}

L3='|'(1:1 2:'|'(2 nil))
{Browse L1==L3}
```

All three lists, `L1`, `L2`, and `L3`, are identical. Here is an example where the entailment check cannot decide:

```
declare L1 L2 X in
L1=[1]
L2=[X]
{Browse L1==L2}
```

Feeding this example will not display anything, since the entailment check cannot decide whether `L1` and `L2` are equal or not. In fact, both are possible: if `X` is bound to `1`, then they are equal, and if `X` is bound to `2`, then they are not. Try feeding `X=1` or `X=2` to see what happens. What about the following example?:

```
declare L1 L2 X in
L1=[X]
L2=[X]
{Browse L1==L2}
```

Both lists contain the same unbound variable `X`. What will happen? Think about it before reading the answer in the footnote.[16] Here is a final example:

```
declare L1 L2 X in
L1=[1 a]
L2=[X b]
{Browse L1==L2}
```

This will display **`false`**. While the comparison `1==X` blocks, further inspection of the two graphs shows that there is a definite difference, so the full check returns **`false`**.

2.8.3 Dynamic and static typing

The only way of discovering the limits of the possible is to venture a little way past them into the impossible.
– Clarke's second law, Arthur C. Clarke (1917–)

It is important for a language to be strongly typed, i.e., to have a type system that is enforced by the language. (This is in contrast to a weakly typed language, in which the internal representation of a type can be manipulated by a program. We

16. The browser will display **`true`**, since `L1` and `L2` are equal no matter what `X` might be bound to.

will not speak further of weakly typed languages.) There are two major families of strong typing: dynamic typing and static typing. We have introduced the declarative model as being dynamically typed, but we have not yet explained the motivation for this design decision, nor the differences between static and dynamic typing that underlie it.

- In a dynamically typed language, variables can be bound to entities of any type, so in general their type is known only at run time.
- In a statically typed language, on the other hand, all variable types are known at compile time. The type can be declared by the programmer or inferred by the compiler.

When designing a language, one of the major decisions to make is whether the language is to be dynamically typed, statically typed, or some mixture of both. What are the advantages and disadvantages of dynamic and static typing? The basic principle is that static typing puts restrictions on what programs one can write, reducing expressiveness of the language in return for giving advantages such as improved error-catching ability, efficiency, security, and partial program verification. Let us examine this closer:

- Dynamic typing puts no restrictions on what programs one can write. To be precise, all syntactically legal programs can be run. Some of these programs will raise exceptions, possibly due to type errors, which can be caught by an exception handler. Dynamic typing gives the widest possible variety of programming techniques. The increased flexibility is noticeable in practice. The programmer spends less time adjusting the program to fit the type system.
- Dynamic typing makes it a trivial matter to do separate compilation, i.e., modules can be compiled without knowing anything about each other. This allows truly open programming, in which independently written modules can come together at run time and interact with each other. It also makes program development scalable, i.e., extremely large programs can be divided into modules that can be compiled individually without recompiling other modules. This is harder to do with static typing because the type discipline must be enforced across module boundaries.
- Dynamic typing shortens the turnaround time between an idea and its implementation. It enables an incremental development environment that is part of the run-time system. It allows testing programs or program fragments even when they are in an incomplete or inconsistent state.
- Static typing allows catching more program errors at compile time. The static type declarations are a partial specification of the program, i.e., they specify part of the program's behavior. The compiler's type checker verifies that the program satisfies this partial specification. This can be quite powerful. Modern static type systems can catch a surprising number of semantic errors.
- Static typing allows a more efficient implementation. Since the compiler has more information about what values a variable can contain, it can choose a more

efficient representation. For example, if a variable is of boolean type, the compile can implement it with a single bit. In a dynamically typed language, the compiler cannot always deduce the type of a variable. When it cannot, then it usually has to allocate a full memory word, so that any possible value (or a pointer to a value) can be accommodated.

- Static typing can improve the security of a program. Secure data abstractions can be constructed based solely on the protection offered by the type system.

Unfortunately, the choice between dynamic and static typing is most often based on emotional ("gut") reactions, not on rational argument. Adherents of dynamic typing relish the expressive freedom and rapid turnaround it gives them and criticize the reduced expressiveness of static typing. On the other hand, adherents of static typing emphasize the aid it gives them in writing correct and efficient programs and point out that it finds many program errors at compile time. Little hard data exist to quantify these differences. In our experience, the differences are not great. Programming with static typing is like word processing with a spelling checker: a good writer can get along without it, but it can improve the quality of a text.

Each approach has a role in practical application development. Static typing is recommended when the programming techniques are well understood and when efficiency and correctness are paramount. Dynamic typing is recommended for rapid development and when programs must be as flexible as possible, such as application prototypes, operating systems, and some artificial intelligence applications.

The choice between static and dynamic typing does not have to be all-or-nothing. In each approach, a bit of the other can be added, gaining some of its advantages. For example, different kinds of polymorphism (where a variable might have values of several different types) add flexibility to statically typed functional and object-oriented languages. It is an active research area to design static type systems that capture as much as possible of the flexibility of dynamic type systems, while encouraging good programming style and still permitting compile time verification.

The computation models given in the book are all subsets of the Oz language, which is dynamically typed. One research goal of the Oz project is to explore what programming techniques are possible in a computation model that integrates several programming paradigms. The only way to achieve this goal is with dynamic typing.

When the programming techniques are known, then a possible next step is to design a static type system. While research into increasing the functionality and expressiveness of Oz is still ongoing in the Mozart Consortium, the Alice project at Saarland University in Saarbrücken, Germany, has chosen to add a static type system. Alice is a statically typed language that has much of the expressiveness of Oz. At the time of writing, Alice is interoperable with Oz (programs can be written partly in Alice and partly in Oz) since it is based on the Mozart implementation.

2.9 Exercises

1. *Free and bound identifiers.* Consider the following statement:

```
proc {P X}
   if X>0 then {P X-1} end
end
```

Is the second occurrence of the identifier P free or bound? Justify your answer. *Hint*: this is easy to answer if you first translate to kernel syntax.

2. *Contextual environment.* Section 2.4 explains how a procedure call is executed. Consider the following procedure MulByN:

```
declare MulByN N in
N=3
proc {MulByN X ?Y}
   Y=N*X
end
```

together with the call {MulByN A B}. Assume that the environment at the call contains {A $\rightarrow$ 10, B $\rightarrow$ x_1}. When the procedure body is executed, the mapping N $\rightarrow$ 3 is added to the environment. Why is this a necessary step? In particular, would not N $\rightarrow$ 3 already exist somewhere in the environment at the call? Would not this be enough to ensure that the identifier N already maps to 3? Give an example where N does not exist in the environment at the call. Then give a second example where N does exist there, but is bound to a different value than 3.

3. *Functions and procedures.* If a function body has an **if** statement with a missing **else** case, then an exception is raised if the **if** condition is false. Explain why this behavior is correct. This situation does not occur for procedures. Explain why not.

4. *The* **if** *and* **case** *statements.* This exercise explores the relationship between the **if** statement and the **case** statement.

   (a) Define the **if** statement in terms of the **case** statement. This shows that the conditional does not add any expressiveness over pattern matching. It could have been added as a linguistic abstraction.

   (b) Define the **case** statement in terms of the **if** statement, using the operations Label, Arity, and ´.´ (feature selection).

This shows that the **if** statement is essentially a more primitive version of the **case** statement.

5. *The* **case** *statement.* This exercise tests your understanding of the full **case** statement. Given the following procedure:

```
proc {Test X}
   case X
   of a|Z then {Browse ´case´(1)}
   [] f(a) then {Browse ´case´(2)}
   [] Y|Z andthen Y==Z then {Browse ´case´(3)}
   [] Y|Z then {Browse ´case´(4)}
   [] f(Y) then {Browse ´case´(5)}
   else {Browse ´case´(6)} end
end
```

Without executing any code, predict what will happen when you feed `{Test [b c a]}`, `{Test f(b(3))}`, `{Test f(a)}`, `{Test f(a(3))}`, `{Test f(d)}`, `{Test [a b c]}`, `{Test [c a b]}`, `{Test a|a}`, and `{Test ´|´(a b c)}`. Use the kernel translation and the semantics if necessary to make the predictions. After making the predictions, check your understanding by running the examples in Mozart.

6. *The* **case** *statement again.* Given the following procedure:

```
proc {Test X}
   case X of f(a Y c) then {Browse ´case´(1)}
   else {Browse ´case´(2)} end
end
```

Without executing any code, predict what will happen when you feed:

```
declare X Y {Test f(X b Y)}
```

Same for:

```
declare X Y {Test f(a Y d)}
```

Same for:

```
declare X Y {Test f(X Y d)}
```

Use the kernel translation and the semantics if necessary to make the predictions. After making the predictions, check your understanding by running the examples in Mozart. Now run the following example:

```
declare X Y
if f(X Y d)==f(a Y c) then {Browse ´case´(1)}
else {Browse ´case´(2)} end
```

Does this give the same result or a different result than the previous example? Explain the result.

7. *Lexically scoped closures.* Given the following code:

```
declare Max3 Max5
proc {SpecialMax Value ?SMax}
   fun {SMax X}
      if X>Value then X else Value end
   end
end
{SpecialMax 3 Max3}
{SpecialMax 5 Max5}
```

Without executing any code, predict what will happen when you feed:

```
{Browse [{Max3 4} {Max5 4}]}
```

Check your understanding by running this example in Mozart.

8. *Control abstraction.* This exercise explores the relationship between linguistic abstractions and higher-order programming.

   (a) Define the function `AndThen` as follows:

   ```
   fun {AndThen BP1 BP2}
      if {BP1} then {BP2} else false end
   end
   ```

   Does the call

   ```
   {AndThen fun {$} ⟨expression⟩1 end fun {$} ⟨expression⟩2 end}
   ```

   give the same result as $\langle\text{expression}\rangle_1$ **andthen** $\langle\text{expression}\rangle_2$? Does it avoid the evaluation of $\langle\text{expression}\rangle_2$ in the same situations?

   (b) Write a function `OrElse` that is to **orelse** as `AndThen` is to **andthen**. Explain its behavior.

9. *Tail recursion.* This exercise examines the importance of tail recursion, in the light of the semantics given in the chapter. Consider the following two functions:

```
fun {Sum1 N}
   if N==0 then 0 else N+{Sum1 N-1} end
end
fun {Sum2 N S}
   if N==0 then S else {Sum2 N-1 N+S} end
end
```

Now do the following:

   (a) Expand the two definitions into kernel syntax. It should be clear that `Sum2` is tail recursive and `Sum1` is not.

   (b) Execute the two calls `{Sum1 10}` and `{Sum2 10 0}` by hand, using the semantics of this chapter to follow what happens to the stack and the store. How large does the stack become in either case?

   (c) What would happen in the Mozart system if you would call `{Sum1 100000000}` or `{Sum2 100000000 0}`? Which one is likely to work? Which one is not? Try both on Mozart to verify your reasoning.

10. *Expansion into kernel syntax.* Consider the following function `SMerge` that merges two sorted lists:

```
fun {SMerge Xs Ys}
   case Xs#Ys
   of nil#Ys then Ys
   [] Xs#nil then Xs
   [] (X|Xr)#(Y|Yr) then
      if X=<Y then X|{SMerge Xr Ys}
      else Y|{SMerge Xs Yr} end
   end
end
```

Expand `SMerge` into the kernel syntax. Note that `X#Y` is a tuple of two arguments that can also be written `'#'(X Y)`. The resulting procedure should be tail recursive, if the rules of section 2.6.2 are followed correctly.

11. *Mutual recursion.* Last call optimization is important for much more than just recursive calls. Consider the following mutually recursive definition of the functions `IsOdd` and `IsEven`:

```
fun {IsEven X}
   if X==0 then true else {IsOdd X-1} end
end

fun {IsOdd X}
   if X==0 then false else {IsEven X-1} end
end
```

We say that these functions are mutually recursive since each function calls the other. Mutual recursion can be generalized to any number of functions. A set of functions is mutually recursive if they can be put in a sequence such that each function calls the next and the last calls the first. For this exercise, show that the calls `{IsOdd N}` and `{IsEven N}` execute with constant stack size for all non-negative `N`. In general, if each function in a mutually recursive set has just one function call in its body, and this function call is a last call, then all functions in the set will execute with their stack size bounded by a constant.

12. *Exceptions with a* **finally** *clause.* Section 2.7 shows how to define the **try/finally** statement by translating it into a **try/catch** statement. For this exercise, define another translation of

```
try ⟨s⟩1 finally ⟨s⟩2 end
```

in which $\langle s\rangle_1$ and $\langle s\rangle_2$ only occur once. *Hint*: it needs a boolean variable.

13. *Unification.* Section 2.8.2 explains that the bind operation is actually much more general than just binding variables: it makes two partial values equal (if they are compatible). This operation is called unification. The purpose of this exercise is to explore why unification is interesting. Consider the three unifications `X=[a Z]`, `Y=[W b]`, and `X=Y`. Show that the variables `X`, `Y`, `Z`, and `W` are bound to the same values, no matter in which order the three unifications are done. In chapter 4 we will see that this order-independence is important for declarative concurrency.

3 Declarative Programming Techniques

S'il vous plaît... dessine-moi un arbre!
If you please—draw me a tree!
– Freely adapted from *Le Petit Prince*, Antoine de Saint-Exupéry (1900–1944)

The nice thing about declarative programming is that you can write a specification and run it as a program. The nasty thing about declarative programming is that some clear specifications make incredibly bad programs. The hope of declarative programming is that you can move from a specification to a reasonable program without leaving the language.
– *The Craft of Prolog*, Richard O'Keefe (1990)

Consider any computational operation, i.e., a program fragment with inputs and outputs. We say the operation is declarative if, whenever called with the same arguments, it returns the same results independent of any other computation state. Figure 3.1 illustrates the concept. A declarative operation is independent (does not depend on any execution state outside of itself), stateless (has no internal execution state that is remembered between calls), and deterministic (always gives the same results when given the same arguments). We will show that all programs written using the computation model of the last chapter are declarative.

Why declarative programming is important

Declarative programming is important because of two properties:

- *Declarative programs are compositional.* A declarative program consists of components that can each be written, tested, and proved correct independently of other components and of its own past history (previous calls).
- *Reasoning about declarative programs is simple.* Programs written in the declarative model are easier to reason about than programs written in more expressive models. Since declarative programs compute only values, simple algebraic and logical reasoning techniques can be used.

These two properties are important both for programming in the large and in the small. It would be nice if all programs could easily be written in the declarative model. Unfortunately, this is not the case. The declarative model is a good fit for certain kinds of programs and a bad fit for others. This chapter and the next

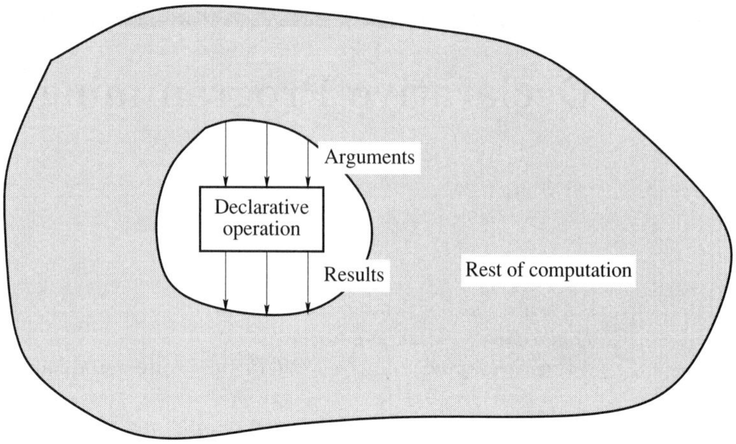

Figure 3.1: A declarative operation inside a general computation.

examine the programming techniques of the declarative model and explain what kinds of programs can and cannot be easily written in it.

We start by looking more closely at the first property. Let us define a *component* as a precisely delimited program fragment with well-defined inputs and outputs. A component can be defined in terms of a set of simpler components. For example, in the declarative model a procedure is one kind of component. The application program is the topmost component in a hierarchy of components. The hierarchy bottoms out in primitive components which are provided by the system.

In a declarative program, the interaction between components is determined solely by each component's inputs and outputs. Consider a program with a declarative component. This component can be understood on its own, without having to understand the rest of the program. The effort needed to understand the whole program is the sum of the efforts needed for the declarative component and for the rest.

If there would be a more intimate interaction between the component and the rest of the program, then they could not be understood independently. They would have to be understood together, and the effort needed would be much bigger. For example, it might be (roughly) proportional to the product of the efforts needed for each part. For a program with many components that interact intimately, this very quickly explodes, making understanding difficult or impossible. An example of such an intimate interaction is a concurrent program with shared state, as explained in chapter 8.

Intimate interactions are often necessary. They cannot be "legislated away" by programming in a model that does not directly support them (as section 4.8 clearly explains). But an important principle is that they should only be used when necessary and not otherwise. To support this principle, as many components as possible should be declarative.

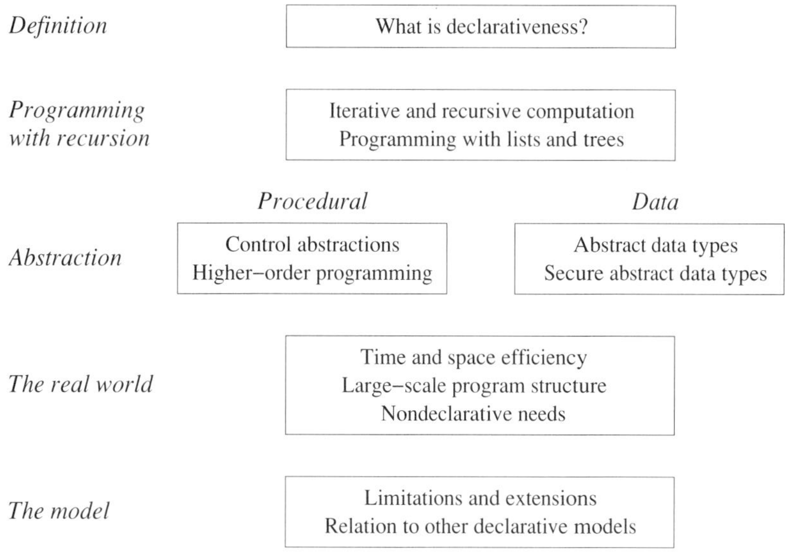

Figure 3.2: Structure of the chapter.

Writing declarative programs

The simplest way to write a declarative program is to use the declarative model of chapter 2. The basic operations on data types are declarative, e.g., the arithmetic, list, and record operations. It is possible to combine declarative operations to make new declarative operations, if certain rules are followed. Combining declarative operations according to the operations of the declarative model will result in a declarative operation. This is explained in section 3.1.3.

The standard rule in algebra that "equals can be replaced by equals" is another example of a declarative combination. In programming languages, this property is called referential transparency. It greatly simplifies reasoning about programs. For example, if we know that $f(a) = a^2$, then we can replace $f(a)$ by a^2 in any other place where it occurs. The equation $b = 7f(a)^2$ then becomes $b = 7a^4$. This is possible because $f(a)$ is declarative: it depends only on its arguments and not on any other computation state.

The basic technique for writing declarative programs is to consider the program as a set of recursive function definitions, using higher-order programming to simplify the program structure. A recursive function is one whose definition body refers to the function itself, either directly or indirectly. Direct recursion means that the function itself is used in the body. Indirect recursion means that the function refers to another function that directly or indirectly refers to the original function. Higher-order programming means that functions can have other functions as arguments and results. This ability underlies all the techniques for building abstractions that we

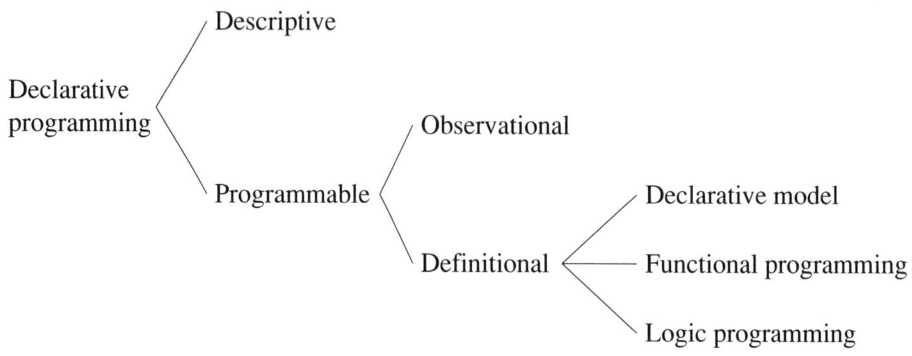

Figure 3.3: A classification of declarative programming.

will show in the book. Higher-orderness can compensate somewhat for the lack of expressiveness of the declarative model, i.e., it makes it easy to code limited forms of concurrency and state in the declarative model.

Structure of the chapter

This chapter explains how to write practical declarative programs. The chapter is roughly organized into the six parts shown in figure 3.2. The first part defines "declarativeness." The second part gives an overview of programming techniques. The third and fourth parts explain procedural and data abstraction. The fifth part shows how declarative programming interacts with the rest of the computing environment. The sixth part steps back to reflect on the usefulness of the declarative model and situate it with respect to other models.

3.1 What is declarativeness?

The declarative model of chapter 2 is an especially powerful way of writing declarative programs, since all programs written in it will be declarative by this fact alone. But it is still only one way out of many for doing declarative programming. Before explaining how to program in the declarative model, let us situate it with respect to the other ways of being declarative. Let us also explain why programs written in it are always declarative.

3.1.1 A classification of declarative programming

We have defined declarativeness in one particular way, so that reasoning about programs is simplified. But this is not the only way to make precise what declarative programming is. Intuitively, it is programming by defining the what (the results

⟨s⟩ ::=		
	skip	Empty statement
|	⟨s⟩$_1$ ⟨s⟩$_2$	Statement sequence
|	**local** ⟨x⟩ **in** ⟨s⟩ **end**	Variable creation
|	⟨x⟩$_1$=⟨x⟩$_2$	Variable-variable binding
|	⟨x⟩=⟨v⟩	Value creation

Table 3.1: The descriptive declarative kernel language.

we want to achieve) without explaining the how (the algorithms, etc., needed to achieve the results). This vague intuition covers many different ideas. Figure 3.3 gives a classification. The first level of classification is based on the expressiveness. There are two possibilities:

- A descriptive declarativeness. This is the least expressive. The declarative "program" just defines a data structure. Table 3.1 defines a language at this level. This language can only define records! It contains just the first five statements of the kernel language in table 2.1. Section 3.8.2 shows how to use this language to define graphical user interfaces. Other examples are a formatting language like HTML (Hypertext Markup Language), which gives the structure of a document without telling how to do the formatting, or an information exchange language like XML (Extensible Markup Language), which is used to exchange information in an open format that is easily readable by all. The descriptive level is too weak to write general programs. So why is it interesting? Because it consists of data structures that are easy to calculate with. The records of table 3.1, HTML and XML documents, and the declarative user interfaces of section 3.8.2 can all be created and transformed easily by a program.
- A programmable declarativeness. This is as expressive as a Turing machine.[1] For example, table 2.1 defines a language at this level. See the introduction to chapter 6 for more on the relationship between the descriptive and programmable levels.

There are two fundamentally different ways to view programmable declarativeness:

- A definitional view, where declarativeness is a property of the component implementation. For example, programs written in the declarative model are guaranteed to be declarative, because of properties of the model.
- An observational view, where declarativeness is a property of the component in-

1. A Turing machine is a simple formal model of computation, first defined by Alan Turing, that is as powerful as any computer that can be built, as far as is known in the current state of computer science. That is, any computation that can be programmed on any computer can also be programmed on a Turing machine.

terface. The observational view follows the principle of abstraction: that to use a component it is enough to know its specification without knowing its implementation. The component just has to behave declaratively, i.e., as if it were independent, stateless, and deterministic, without necessarily being written in a declarative computation model.

This book uses both the definitional and observational views. When we are interested in looking inside a component, we will use the definitional view. When we are interested in how a component behaves, we will use the observational view.

Two styles of definitional declarative programming have become particularly popular: the functional and the logical. In the functional style, we say that a component defined as a mathematical function is declarative. Functional languages such as Haskell and Standard ML follow this approach. In the logical style, we say that a component defined as a logical relation is declarative. Logic languages such as Prolog and Mercury follow this approach. It is harder to formally manipulate functional or logical programs than descriptive programs, but they still follow simple algebraic laws.[2] The declarative model used in this chapter encompasses both functional and logic styles.

The observational view lets us use declarative components in a declarative program even if they are written in a nondeclarative model. For example, a database interface can be a valuable addition to a declarative language. Yet, the implementation of this interface is almost certainly not going to be logical or functional. It suffices that it could have been defined declaratively. Sometimes a declarative component will be written in a functional or logical style, and sometimes it will not be. In later chapters we build declarative components in nondeclarative models. We will not be dogmatic about the matter; we will consider the component to be declarative if it behaves declaratively.

3.1.2 Specification languages

Proponents of declarative programming sometimes claim that it allows dispensing with the implementation, since the specification is all there is. That is, the specification is the program. This is true in a formal sense, but not in a practical sense. Practically, declarative programs are very much like other programs: they require algorithms, data structures, structuring, and reasoning about the order of operations. This is because declarative languages can only use mathematics that can be implemented efficiently. There is a trade-off between expressiveness and efficiency. Declarative programs are usually a lot longer than what a specification could be. So the distinction between specification and implementation still makes sense, even for declarative programs.

It is possible to define a declarative language that is much more expressive than what we use in the book. Such a language is called a specification language. It is

2. For programs that do not use the nondeclarative abilities of these languages.

usually impossible to implement specification languages efficiently. This does not mean that they are impractical. On the contrary, they are an important tool for thinking about programs. They can be used together with a theorem prover, i.e., a program that can do certain kinds of mathematical reasoning. Practical theorem provers are not completely automatic; they need human help. But they can take over much of the drudgery of reasoning about programs, i.e., the tedious manipulation of mathematical formulas. With the aid of the theorem prover, a developer can often prove very strong properties about his or her program. Using a theorem prover in this way is called proof engineering. Up to now, proof engineering is only practical for small programs. But this is enough for it to be used successfully when safety is of critical importance, e.g., when lives are at stake, such as in medical apparatus or public transportation.

Specification languages are outside the scope of the book.

3.1.3 Implementing components in the declarative model

Combining declarative operations according to the operations of the declarative model always results in a declarative operation. This section explains why this is so. We first define more precisely what it means for a statement to be declarative. Given any statement in the declarative model, partition the free variable identifiers in the statement into inputs and outputs. Then, given any binding of the input identifiers to partial values and the output identifiers to unbound variables, executing the statement will give one of three results: (1) some binding of the output variables, (2) suspension, or (3) an exception. If the statement is declarative, then for the same bindings of the inputs, the result is always the same.

For example, consider the statement `Z=X`. Assume that `X` is the input and `Z` is the output. For any binding of `X` to a partial value, executing this statement will bind `Z` to the same partial value. Therefore the statement is declarative.

We can use this result to prove that the statement

```
if X>Y then Z=X else Z=Y end
```

is declarative. Partition the statement's three free identifiers, `X`, `Y`, `Z`, into two input identifiers `X` and `Y` and one output identifier `Z`. Then, if `X` and `Y` are bound to any partial values, the statement's execution will either block or bind `Z` to the same partial value. Therefore the statement is declarative.

We can do this reasoning for all operations in the declarative model:

- First, all basic operations in the declarative model are declarative. This includes all operations on basic types, which are explained in chapter 2.

- Second, combining declarative operations with the constructs of the declarative model gives a declarative operation. The following five compound statements exist in the declarative model:

  - The statement sequence.
  - The **`local`** statement.

- The **if** statement.
- The **case** statement.
- Procedure declaration, i.e., the statement ⟨x⟩=⟨v⟩ where ⟨v⟩ is a procedure value.

They allow building statements out of other statements. All these ways of combining statements are deterministic (if their component statements are deterministic, then so are they) and they do not depend on any context.

3.2 Iterative computation

We will now look at how to program in the declarative model. We start by looking at a very simple kind of program, the iterative computation. An iterative computation is a loop whose stack size is bounded by a constant, independent of the number of iterations. This kind of computation is a basic programming tool. There are many ways to write iterative programs. It is not always obvious when a program is iterative. Therefore, we start by giving a general schema that shows how to construct many interesting iterative computations in the declarative model.

3.2.1 A general schema

An important class of iterative computations starts with an initial state S_0 and transforms the state in successive steps until reaching a final state S_{final}:

$$S_0 \rightarrow S_1 \rightarrow \cdots \rightarrow S_{\text{final}}$$

An iterative computation of this class can be written as a general schema:

```
fun {Iterate Si}
   if {IsDone Si} then Si
   else Si+1 in
      Si+1={Transform Si}
      {Iterate Si+1}
   end
end
```

In this schema, the functions `IsDone` and `Transform` are problem-dependent. Let us prove that any program that follows this schema is iterative. We will show that the stack size does not grow when executing `Iterate`. For clarity, we give just the statements on the semantic stack, leaving out the environments and the store:

- Assume the initial semantic stack is [`R={Iterate` S_0`}`].
- Assume that {`IsDone` S_0} returns **false**. Just after executing the **if**, the semantic stack is [S_1`={Transform` S_0`}`, `R={Iterate` S_1`}`].
- After executing {`Transform` S_0}, the semantic stack is [`R={Iterate` S_1`}`].

```
fun {Sqrt X}
   Guess=1.0
in
   {SqrtIter Guess X}
end
fun {SqrtIter Guess X}
   if {GoodEnough Guess X} then Guess
   else
      {SqrtIter {Improve Guess X} X}
   end
end
fun {Improve Guess X}
  (Guess + X/Guess) / 2.0
end
fun {GoodEnough Guess X}
  {Abs X-Guess*Guess}/X < 0.00001
end
fun {Abs X} if X<0.0 then ~X else X end end
```

Figure 3.4: Finding roots using Newton's method (first version).

We see that the semantic stack has just one element at every recursive call, namely the statement `R={Iterate` S_{i+1}`}`. This is the same argument we used to show last call optimization in section 2.5.1, but presented more concisely.

3.2.2 Iteration with numbers

A good example of iterative computation is Newton's method for calculating the square root of a positive real number x. The idea is to start with a guess g of the square root, and to improve this guess iteratively until it is accurate enough. The improved guess g' is the average of g and x/g:

$$g' = (g + x/g)/2.$$

To see that the improved guess is better, let us study the difference between the guess and $\sqrt{x}$:

$$\varepsilon = g - \sqrt{x}$$

Then the difference between g' and $\sqrt{x}$ is

$$\varepsilon' = g' - \sqrt{x} = (g + x/g)/2 - \sqrt{x} = \varepsilon^2/2g$$

For convergence, ε' should be smaller than ε. Let us see what conditions that this imposes on x and g. The condition $\varepsilon' < \varepsilon$ is the same as $\varepsilon^2/2g < \varepsilon$, which is the same as $\varepsilon < 2g$. (Assuming that $\varepsilon > 0$, since if it is not, we start with ε', which is always greater than 0.) Substituting the definition of ε, we get the condition $\sqrt{x} + g > 0$. If $x > 0$ and the initial guess $g > 0$, then this is always true. The algorithm therefore always converges.

Figure 3.4 shows one way of defining Newton's method as an iterative computation. The function `{SqrtIter Guess X}` calls `{SqrtIter {Improve Guess X} X}` until `Guess` satisfies the condition `{GoodEnough Guess X}`. It is clear that this is an instance of the general schema, so it is an iterative computation. The improved guess is calculated according to the formula given above. The "good enough" check is $|x - g^2|/x < 0.00001$, i.e., the square root has to be accurate to five decimal places. This check is relative, i.e., the error is divided by x. We could also use an absolute check, e.g., something like $|x - g^2| < 0.00001$, where the magnitude of the error has to be less than some constant. Why is using a relative check better when calculating square roots?

3.2.3 Using local procedures

In the Newton's method program of figure 3.4, several "helper" routines are defined: `SqrtIter`, `Improve`, `GoodEnough`, and `Abs`. These routines are used as building blocks for the main function `Sqrt`. In this section, we discuss where to define helper routines. The basic principle is that a helper routine defined only as an aid to define another routine should not be visible elsewhere. (We use the word "routine" for both functions and procedures.)

In the Newton example, `SqrtIter` is only needed inside `Sqrt`, `Improve` and `GoodEnough` are only needed inside `SqrtIter`, and `Abs` is a utility function that could be used elsewhere. There are two basic ways to express this visibility, with somewhat different semantics. The first way is shown in figure 3.5: the helper routines are defined outside of `Sqrt` in a **`local`** statement. The second way is shown in figure 3.6: each helper routine is defined inside of the routine that needs it.[3]

In figure 3.5, there is a trade-off between readability and visibility: `Improve` and `GoodEnough` could be defined local to `SqrtIter` only. This would result in two levels of local declarations, which is harder to read. We have decided to put all three helper routines in the same local declaration.

In figure 3.6, each helper routine sees the arguments of its enclosing routine as external references. These arguments are precisely those with which the helper routines are called. This means we could simplify the definition by removing these arguments from the helper routines. This gives figure 3.7.

There is a trade-off between putting the helper definitions outside the routine that needs them or putting them inside:

- Putting them inside (figures 3.6 and 3.7) lets them see the arguments of the main routines as external references, according to the lexical scoping rule (see section 2.4.3). Therefore, they need fewer arguments. But each time the main routine is invoked, new helper routines are created. This means that new procedure

3. We leave out the definition of `Abs` to avoid needless repetition.

```
local
   fun {Improve Guess X}
     (Guess + X/Guess) / 2.0
   end
   fun {GoodEnough Guess X}
     {Abs X-Guess*Guess}/X < 0.00001
   end
   fun {SqrtIter Guess X}
      if {GoodEnough Guess X} then Guess
      else
         {SqrtIter {Improve Guess X} X}
      end
   end
in
   fun {Sqrt X}
      Guess=1.0
   in
      {SqrtIter Guess X}
   end
end
```

Figure 3.5: Finding roots using Newton's method (second version).

```
fun {Sqrt X}
   fun {SqrtIter Guess X}
      fun {Improve Guess X}
        (Guess + X/Guess) / 2.0
      end
      fun {GoodEnough Guess X}
        {Abs X-Guess*Guess}/X < 0.00001
      end
   in
      if {GoodEnough Guess X} then Guess
      else
         {SqrtIter {Improve Guess X} X}
      end
   end
   Guess=1.0
in
   {SqrtIter Guess X}
end
```

Figure 3.6: Finding roots using Newton's method (third version).

```
fun {Sqrt X}
   fun {SqrtIter Guess}
      fun {Improve}
         (Guess + X/Guess) / 2.0
      end
      fun {GoodEnough}
         {Abs X-Guess*Guess}/X < 0.00001
      end
   in
      if {GoodEnough} then Guess
      else
         {SqrtIter {Improve}}
      end
   end
   Guess=1.0
in
   {SqrtIter Guess}
end
```

Figure 3.7: Finding roots using Newton's method (fourth version).

values are created.

- Putting them outside (figures 3.4 and 3.5) means that the procedure values are created once and for all, for all calls to the main routine. But then the helper routines need more arguments so that the main routine can pass information to them.

In figure 3.7, new definitions of `Improve` and `GoodEnough` are created on each iteration of `SqrtIter`, whereas `SqrtIter` itself is only created once. This suggests a good trade-off, where `SqrtIter` is local to `Sqrt` and both `Improve` and `GoodEnough` are outside `SqrtIter`. This gives the final definition of figure 3.8, which we consider the best in terms of both efficiency and visibility.

3.2.4 From general schema to control abstraction

The general schema of section 3.2.1 is a programmer aid. It helps the programmer design efficient programs but it is not seen by the computation model. Let us go one step further and provide the general schema as a program component that can be used by other components. We say that the schema becomes a control abstraction, i.e., an abstraction that can be used to provide a desired control flow. Here is the general schema:

```
fun {Sqrt X}
   fun {Improve Guess}
      (Guess + X/Guess) / 2.0
   end
   fun {GoodEnough Guess}
      {Abs X-Guess*Guess}/X < 0.00001
   end
   fun {SqrtIter Guess}
      if {GoodEnough Guess} then Guess
      else
         {SqrtIter {Improve Guess}}
      end
   end
   Guess=1.0
in
   {SqrtIter Guess}
end
```

Figure 3.8: Finding roots using Newton's method (fifth version).

```
fun {Iterate S_i}
   if {IsDone S_i} then S_i
   else S_{i+1} in
      S_{i+1}={Transform S_i}
      {Iterate S_{i+1}}
   end
end
```

This schema implements a general **while** loop with a calculated result. To make the schema into a control abstraction, we have to parameterize it by extracting the parts that vary from one use to another. There are two such parts: the functions *IsDone* and *Transform*. We make these two parts into parameters of `Iterate`:

```
fun {Iterate S IsDone Transform}
   if {IsDone S} then S
   else S1 in
      S1={Transform S}
      {Iterate S1 IsDone Transform}
   end
end
```

To use this control abstraction, the arguments `IsDone` and `Transform` are given one-argument functions. Passing functions as arguments to functions is part of a range of programming techniques called higher-order programming. These techniques are further explained in section 3.6. We can make `Iterate` behave exactly like `SqrtIter` by passing it the functions `GoodEnough` and `Improve`. This can be written as follows:

```
fun {Sqrt X}
   {Iterate
      1.0
      fun {$ G} {Abs X-G*G}/X<0.00001 end
      fun {$ G} (G+X/G)/2.0 end}
end
```

This uses two function values as arguments to the control abstraction. This is a powerful way to structure a program because it separates the general control flow from this particular use. Higher-order programming is especially helpful for structuring programs in this way. If this control abstraction is used often, the next step could be to provide it as a linguistic abstraction.

3.3 Recursive computation

Iterative computations are a special case of a more general kind of computation, called recursive computation. Let us see the difference between the two. Recall that an iterative computation can be considered as simply a loop in which a certain action is repeated some number of times. Section 3.2 implements this in the declarative model by introducing a control abstraction, the function `Iterate`. The function first tests a condition. If the condition is false, it does an action and then calls itself.

Recursion is more general than this. A recursive function can call itself anywhere in the body and can call itself more than once. In programming, recursion occurs in two major ways: in functions and in data types. A function is recursive if its definition has at least one call to itself. The iteration abstraction of Section 3.2 is a simple case. A data type is recursive if it is defined in terms of itself. For example, a list is defined in terms of a smaller list. The two forms of recursion are strongly related since recursive functions can be used to calculate with recursive data types.

We saw that an iterative computation has a constant stack size, as a consequence of the last call optimization. This is not always the case for a recursive computation. Its stack size may grow as the input grows. Sometimes this is unavoidable, e.g., when doing calculations with trees, as we will see later. In other cases, it can be avoided. An important part of declarative programming is to avoid a growing stack size whenever possible. This section gives an example of how this is done. We start with a typical case of a recursive computation that is not iterative, namely the naive definition of the factorial function. The mathematical definition is:

$0! = 1$
$n! = n \cdot (n-1)! \text{ if } n > 0$

This is a recurrence equation, i.e., the factorial $n!$ is defined in terms of a factorial with a smaller argument, namely $(n-1)!$. The naive program follows this mathematical definition. To calculate `{Fact N}` there are two possibilities, namely `N=0` or `N>0`. In the first case, return `1`. In the second case, calculate `{Fact N-1}`, multiply by N, and return the result. This gives the following program:

```
fun {Fact N}
   if N==0 then 1
   elseif N>0 then N*{Fact N-1}
   else raise domainError end
   end
end
```

This defines the factorial of a big number in terms of the factorial of a smaller number. Since all numbers are non-negative, they will bottom out at zero and the execution will finish.

Note that factorial is a partial function. It is not defined for negative N. The program reflects this by raising an exception for negative N. The definition in chapter 1 has an error since for negative N it goes into an infinite loop.

We have done two things when writing Fact. First, we followed the mathematical definition to get a correct implementation. Second, we reasoned about termination, i.e., we showed that the program terminates for all legal arguments, i.e., arguments inside the function's domain.

3.3.1 Growing stack size

This definition of factorial gives a computation whose maximum stack size is proportional to the function argument N. We can see this by using the semantics. First translate Fact into the kernel language:

```
proc {Fact N ?R}
   if N==0 then R=1
   elseif N>0 then N1 R1 in
      N1=N-1
      {Fact N1 R1}
      R=N*R1
   else raise domainError end
   end
end
```

Already we can guess that the stack size might grow, since the multiplication comes after the recursive call. That is, during the recursive call the stack has to keep information about the multiplication for when the recursive call returns. Let us follow the semantics and calculate by hand what happens when executing the call {Fact 5 R}. For clarity, we simplify slightly the presentation of the abstract machine by substituting the value of a store variable into the environment. That is, the environment $\{\ldots,\mathtt{N} \rightarrow n,\ldots\}$ is written as $\{\ldots,\mathtt{N} \rightarrow 5,\ldots\}$ if the store is $\{\ldots,n=5,\ldots\}$.

- The initial semantic stack is $[(\{\mathtt{Fact\ N\ R}\},\{\mathtt{N} \rightarrow 5, \mathtt{R} \rightarrow r_0\})]$.
- At the first call:

$[(\{\mathtt{Fact\ N1\ R1}\},\{\mathtt{N1} \rightarrow 4, \mathtt{R1} \rightarrow r_1,\ldots\}),$
$(\mathtt{R{=}N{*}R1},\{\mathtt{R} \rightarrow r_0, \mathtt{R1} \rightarrow r_1, \mathtt{N} \rightarrow 5,\ldots\})]$

- At the second call:

$[(\{$`Fact N1 R1`$\}, \{$`N1`$\rightarrow 3,$ `R1` $\rightarrow r_2, \ldots\}),$
$($`R=N*R1`$, \{$`R`$\rightarrow r_1,$ `R1` $\rightarrow r_2,$ `N` $\rightarrow 4, \ldots\}),$
$($`R=N*R1`$, \{$`R`$\rightarrow r_0,$ `R1` $\rightarrow r_1,$ `N` $\rightarrow 5, \ldots\})]$

- At the third call:

$[(\{$`Fact N1 R1`$\}, \{$`N1`$\rightarrow 2,$ `R1` $\rightarrow r_3, \ldots\}),$
$($`R=N*R1`$, \{$`R`$\rightarrow r_2,$ `R1` $\rightarrow r_3,$ `N` $\rightarrow 3, \ldots\}),$
$($`R=N*R1`$, \{$`R`$\rightarrow r_1,$ `R1` $\rightarrow r_2,$ `N` $\rightarrow 4, \ldots\}),$
$($`R=N*R1`$, \{$`R`$\rightarrow r_0,$ `R1` $\rightarrow r_1,$ `N` $\rightarrow 5, \ldots\})]$

It is clear that the stack grows bigger by one statement per call. The last recursive call is the fifth, which returns immediately with $r_5 = 1$. Then five multiplications are done to get the final result $r_0 = 120$.

3.3.2 Substitution-based abstract machine

This example shows that the abstract machine of chapter 2 can be rather cumbersome for hand calculation. This is because it keeps both variable identifiers and store variables, using environments to map from one to the other. This is realistic; it is how the abstract machine is implemented on a real computer. But it is not so nice for hand calculation.

We can make a simple change to the abstract machine that makes it much easier to use for hand calculation. The idea is to replace the identifiers in the statements by the store entities that they refer to. This operation is called a substitution. For example, the statement `R=N*R1` becomes $r_2 = 3 * r_3$ when substituted according to $\{$`R`$\rightarrow r_2,$ `N` $\rightarrow 3,$ `R1` $\rightarrow r_3\}$.

The substitution-based abstract machine has no environments. It directly substitutes identifiers by store entities in statements. For the recursive factorial example, this gives the following:

- The initial semantic stack is $[\{$`Fact 5` $r_0\}]$.
- At the first call: $[\{$`Fact 4` $r_1\}, r_0$=5*$r_1]$.
- At the second call: $[\{$`Fact 3` $r_2\}, r_1$=4*r_2, r_0=5*$r_1]$.
- At the third call: $[\{$`Fact 2` $r_3\}, r_2$=3*r_3, r_1=4*r_2, r_0=5*$r_1]$.

As before, we see that the stack grows by one statement per call. We summarize the differences between the two versions of the abstract machine:

- The environment-based abstract machine, defined in chapter 2, is faithful to the implementation on a real computer, which uses environments. However, environments introduce an extra level of indirection, so they are hard to use for hand calculation.
- The substitution-based abstract machine is easier to use for hand calculation,

because there are many fewer symbols to manipulate. However, substitutions are costly to implement, so they are generally not used in a real implementation.

Both versions do the same store bindings and the same manipulations of the semantic stack.

3.3.3 Converting a recursive to an iterative computation

Factorial is simple enough that it can be rearranged to become iterative. Let us see how this is done. Later on, we will give a systematic way of making iterative computations. For now, we just give a hint. In the previous calculation:

```
R=(5*(4*(3*(2*(1*1)))))
```

it is enough to rearrange the numbers:

```
R=(((((1*5)*4)*3)*2)*1)
```

Then the calculation can be done incrementally, starting with `1*5`. This gives `5`, then `20`, then `60`, then `120`, and finally `120`. The iterative definition of factorial that does things this way is

```
fun {Fact N}
   fun {FactIter N A}
      if N==0 then A
      elseif N>0 then {FactIter N-1 A*N}
      else raise domainError end
      end
   end
in
   {FactIter N 1}
end
```

The function that does the iteration, `FactIter`, has a second argument `A`. This argument is crucial; without it an iterative factorial is impossible. The second argument is not apparent in the simple mathematical definition of factorial we used first. We had to do some reasoning to bring it in.

3.4 Programming with recursion

Recursive computations are at the heart of declarative programming. This section shows how to write in this style. We show the basic techniques for programming with lists, trees, and other recursive data types. We show how to make the computation iterative when possible. The section is organized as follows:

- The first step is *defining* recursive data types. Section 3.4.1 gives a simple notation that lets us define the most important recursive data types.
- The most important recursive data type is the *list*. Section 3.4.2 presents the

basic programming techniques for lists.

- Efficient declarative programs have to define iterative computations. Section 3.4.3 presents *accumulators*, a systematic technique to achieve this.
- Computations often build data structures incrementally. Section 3.4.4 presents *difference lists*, an efficient technique to achieve this while keeping the computation iterative.
- An important data type related to the list is the *queue*. Section 3.4.5 shows how to implement queues efficiently. It also introduces the basic idea of amortized efficiency.
- The second most important recursive data type, next to linear structures such as lists and queues, is the *tree*. Section 3.4.6 gives the basic programming techniques for trees.
- Sections 3.4.7 and 3.4.8 give two realistic *case studies*, a tree-drawing algorithm and a parser, that between them use many of the techniques of this section.

3.4.1 Type notation

The list type is a subset of the record type. There are other useful subsets of the record type, e.g., binary trees. Before going into writing programs, let us introduce a simple notation to define lists, trees, and other subtypes of records. This will help us to write functions on these types.

A list `Xs` is defined to be either `nil` or `X|Xr` where `Xr` is a list. Other subsets of the record type are also useful. For example, a binary tree can be defined as a leaf node `leaf` or a non-leaf node `tree(key:K value:V left:LT right:RT)` where `LT` and `RT` are both binary trees. How can we write these types in a concise way? Let us create a notation based on the context-free grammar notation for defining the syntax of the kernel language. The nonterminals represent either types or values. Let us use the type hierarchy of figure 2.16 as a basis: all the types in this hierarchy will be available as predefined nonterminals. So ⟨Value⟩ and ⟨Record⟩ both exist, and since they are sets of values, we can say ⟨Record⟩ ⊂ ⟨Value⟩. Now we can define lists:

```
⟨List⟩  ::=  nil
          |  ⟨Value⟩ ´|´ ⟨List⟩
```

This means that a value is in ⟨List⟩ if it has one of two forms. Either it is `X|Xr` where `X` is in ⟨Value⟩ and `Xr` is in ⟨List⟩. Or it is the atom `nil`. This is a recursive definition of ⟨List⟩. It can be proved that there is just one set ⟨List⟩ that is the smallest set that satisfies this definition. The proof is beyond the scope of the book, but can be found in any introductory book on semantics, e.g., [229]. We take this smallest set as the value of ⟨List⟩. Intuitively, ⟨List⟩ can be constructed by starting with `nil` and repeatedly applying the grammar rule to build bigger and bigger lists.

We can also define lists whose elements are of a given type:

```
⟨List T⟩  ::=  nil
            |  T '|' ⟨List T⟩
```

Here T is a type variable and ⟨List T⟩ is a type function. Applying the type function to any type returns the type of a list of that type. For example, ⟨List ⟨Int⟩⟩ is the list of integer type. Observe that ⟨List ⟨Value⟩⟩ is equal to ⟨List⟩ (since they have identical definitions).

Let us define a binary tree with literals as keys and elements of type T:

```
⟨BTree T⟩  ::=  leaf
             |  tree(key: ⟨Literal⟩ value: T
                      left: ⟨BTree T⟩ right: ⟨BTree T⟩)
```

The type of a procedure is ⟨**proc** {$ $T_1 \cdots T_n$}⟩, where $T_1, \ldots, T_n$ are the types of its arguments. The procedure's type is sometimes called the signature of the procedure, because it gives some key information about the procedure in a concise form. The type of a function is ⟨**fun** {$ $T_1 \cdots T_n$}: T⟩, which is equivalent to ⟨**proc** {$ $T_1 \cdots T_n$, T}⟩. For example, the type ⟨**fun** {$ ⟨List⟩ ⟨List⟩}: ⟨List⟩ ⟩ is a function with two list arguments that returns a list.

Limits of the notation

This type notation can define many useful sets of values, but its expressiveness is definitely limited. Here are some cases where the notation is not good enough:

- The notation cannot define the positive integers, i.e., the subset of ⟨Int⟩ whose elements are all greater than zero.
- The notation cannot define sets of partial values. For example, difference lists cannot be defined.

We can extend the notation to handle the first case, e.g., by adding boolean conditions.[4] In the examples that follow, we will add these conditions in the text when they are needed. This means that the type notation is descriptive: it gives logical assertions about the set of values that a variable may take. There is no claim that the types could be checkable by a compiler. On the contrary, they often cannot be checked. Even types that are simple to specify, such as the positive integers, cannot in general be checked by a compiler.

3.4.2 Programming with lists

List values are very concise to create and to take apart, yet they are powerful enough to encode any kind of complex data structure. The original Lisp language

---

4. This is similar to the way we define language syntax in section 2.1.1: a context-free notation with extra conditions when they are needed.

got much of its power from this idea [137]. Because of lists' simple structure, declarative programming with them is easy and powerful. This section gives the basic techniques of programming with lists:

- *Thinking recursively.* The basic approach is to solve a problem in terms of smaller versions of the problem.
- *Converting recursive to iterative computations.* Naive list programs are often wasteful because their stack size grows with the input size. We show how to use state transformations to make them practical.
- *Correctness of iterative computations.* A simple and powerful way to reason about iterative computations is by using state invariants.
- *Constructing programs by following the type.* A function that calculates with a given type almost always has a recursive structure that closely mirrors the type definition.

We end this section with a bigger example, the mergesort algorithm. Later sections show how to make the writing of iterative functions more systematic by introducing accumulators and difference lists. This lets us write iterative functions from the start. We find that these techniques "scale up," i.e., they work well even for large declarative programs.

3.4.2.1 Thinking recursively

A list is a recursive data structure, i.e., it is defined in terms of a smaller version of itself. To write a function that calculates on lists we have to follow this recursive structure. The function consists of two parts:

- A base case. For small lists (say, of zero, one, or two elements), the function computes the answer directly.
- A recursive case. For bigger lists, the function computes the result in terms of the results of one or more smaller lists.

As our first example, we take a simple recursive function that calculates the length of a list according to this technique:

```
fun {Length Ls}
   case Ls
   of nil then 0
   [] _|Lr then 1+{Length Lr}
   end
end
{Browse {Length [a b c]}}
```

Its type signature is ⟨**fun** {$ ⟨List⟩}: ⟨Int⟩⟩, a function of one list that returns an integer. The base case is the empty list `nil`, for which the function returns `0`. The recursive case is any other list. If the list has length n, then its tail has length $n-1$. The tail is smaller than the original list, so the program will terminate.

Our second example is a function that appends two lists `Ls` and `Ms` together to make a third list. The question is, on which list do we use induction? Is it the first or the second? We claim that the induction has to be done on the first list. Here is the function:

```
fun {Append Ls Ms}
   case Ls
   of nil then Ms
   [] X|Lr then X|{Append Lr Ms}
   end
end
```

Its type signature is ⟨**fun** {$ ⟨List⟩ ⟨List⟩}: ⟨List⟩⟩. This function follows exactly the following two properties of append:

$$\text{append}(\texttt{nil},\ m) \quad = \quad m$$
$$\text{append}(x\,|\,l,\ m) \quad = \quad x \mid \text{append}(l, m)$$

The recursive case always calls `Append` with a smaller first argument, so the program terminates.

3.4.2.2 Recursive functions and their domains

Let us define the function `Nth` to get the nth element of a list.

```
fun {Nth Xs N}
   if N==1 then Xs.1
   elseif N>1 then {Nth Xs.2 N-1}
   end
end
```

Its type is ⟨**fun** {$ ⟨List⟩ ⟨Int⟩}: ⟨Value⟩⟩. Remember that a list `Xs` is either `nil` or a tuple `X|Y` with two arguments. `Xs.1` gives `X` and `Xs.2` gives `Y`. What happens when we feed the following?:

```
{Browse {Nth [a b c d] 5}}
```

The list has only four elements. Trying to ask for the fifth element means trying to do `Xs.1` or `Xs.2` when `Xs=nil`. This will raise an exception. An exception is also raised if `N` is not a positive integer, e.g., when `N=0`. This is because there is no **else** clause in the **if** statement.

This is an example of a general technique to define functions: always use statements that raise exceptions when values are given outside their domains. This will maximize the chances that the function as a whole will raise an exception when called with an input outside its domain. We cannot guarantee that an exception will always be raised in this case, e.g., `{Nth 1|2|3 2}` returns 2 while `1|2|3` is not a list. Such guarantees are hard to come by. They can sometimes be obtained in statically typed languages.

The **case** statement also behaves correctly in this regard. Using a **case** statement to recurse over a list will raise an exception when its argument is not a list. For example, let us define a function that sums all the elements of a list of integers:

```
fun {SumList Xs}
   case Xs
   of nil then 0
   [] X|Xr then X+{SumList Xr}
   end
end
```

Its type is ⟨**fun** {$ ⟨List ⟨Int⟩⟩}: ⟨Int⟩⟩. The input must be a list of integers because `SumList` internally uses the integer 0. The following call

```
{Browse {SumList [1 2 3]}}
```

displays 6. Since `Xs` can be one of two values, namely `nil` or `X|Xr`, it is natural to use a **case** statement. As in the `Nth` example, not using an **else** in the case will raise an exception if the argument is outside the domain of the function. For example:

```
{Browse {SumList 1|foo}}
```

raises an exception because `1|foo` is not a list, and the definition of `SumList` assumes that its input is a list.

3.4.2.3 Naive definitions are often slow

Let us define a function to reverse the elements of a list. Start with a recursive definition of list reversal:

- Reverse of `nil` is `nil`.
- Reverse of `X|Xs` is `Z`, where
  reverse of `Xs` is `Ys`, and
  append `Ys` and `[X]` to get `Z`.

This works because `X` is moved from the front to the back. Following this recursive definition, we can immediately write a function:

```
fun {Reverse Xs}
   case Xs
   of nil then nil
   [] X|Xr then
      {Append {Reverse Xr} [X]}
   end
end
```

Its type is ⟨**fun** {$ ⟨List⟩}: ⟨List⟩⟩. Is this function efficient? To find out, we have to calculate its execution time given an input list of length n. We can do this rigorously with the techniques of section 3.5. But even without these techniques, we can see intuitively what happens. There will be n recursive calls followed by n calls to `Append`. Each `Append` call will have a list of length $n/2$ on average. The total execution time is therefore proportional to $n \cdot n/2$, namely n^2. This is rather slow. We would expect that reversing a list, which is not exactly a complex calculation, would take time proportional to the input length and not to its square.

This program has a second defect: the stack size grows with the input list length, i.e., it defines a recursive computation that is not iterative. Naively following the recursive definition of reverse has given us a rather inefficient result! Luckily, there are simple techniques for getting around both these inefficiencies. They will let us define linear-time iterative computations whenever possible. We will see two useful techniques: state transformations and difference lists.

3.4.2.4 Converting recursive to iterative computations

Let us see how to convert recursive computations into iterative ones. Instead of using `Reverse`, we take a simpler function that calculates the length of a list:

```
fun {Length Xs}
   case Xs of nil then 0
   [] _|Xr then 1+{Length Xr}
   end
end
```

Note that the `SumList` function has the same structure. This function is linear-time but the stack size is proportional to the recursion depth, which is equal to the length of `Xs`. Why does this problem occur? It is because the addition `1+{Length Xr}` happens after the recursive call. The recursive call is not last, so the function's environment cannot be recovered before it.

How can we calculate the list length with an iterative computation, which has bounded stack size? To do this, we have to formulate the problem as a sequence of state transformations. That is, we start with a state S_0 and we transform it successively, giving S_1, S_2, ..., until we reach the final state S_{final}, which contains the answer. To calculate the list length, we can take the length i of the part of the list already seen as the state. Actually, this is only part of the state. The rest of the state is the part `Ys` of the list not yet seen. The complete state S_i is then the pair $(i, \texttt{Ys})$. The general intermediate case is as follows for state S_i (where the full list `Xs` is $[e_1\ e_2\ \cdots\ e_n]$):

$$\overbrace{e_1\ e_2\ \cdots\ e_i\ \underbrace{e_{i+1}\ \cdots\ e_n}_{\texttt{Ys}}}^{\texttt{Xs}}$$

At each recursive call, i will be incremented by 1 and `Ys` reduced by one element. This gives us the function:

```
fun {IterLength I Ys}
   case Ys
   of nil then I
   [] _|Yr then {IterLength I+1 Yr}
   end
end
```

Its type is ⟨**fun** {$ ⟨Int⟩ ⟨List⟩}: ⟨Int⟩⟩. Note the difference from the previous definition. Here the addition `I+1` is done before the recursive call to `IterLength`, which is the last call. We have defined an iterative computation.

In the call {IterLength I Ys}, the initial value of I is 0. We can hide this initialization by defining IterLength as a local procedure. The final definition of Length is therefore

```
local
   fun {IterLength I Ys}
      case Ys
      of nil then I
      [] _|Yr then {IterLength I+1 Yr}
      end
   end
in
   fun {Length Xs}
      {IterLength 0 Xs}
   end
end
```

This defines an iterative computation to calculate the list length. Note that we define IterLength outside of Length. This avoids creating a new procedure value each time Length is called. There is no advantage to defining IterLength inside Length, since it does not use Length's argument Xs.

We can use the same technique on Reverse as we used for Length. The state is different. In the case of Reverse, the state contains the reverse of the part of the list already seen instead of its length. Updating the state is easy: we just put a new list element in front. The initial state is nil. This gives the following version of Reverse:

```
local
   fun {IterReverse Rs Ys}
      case Ys
      of nil then Rs
      [] Y|Yr then {IterReverse Y|Rs Yr}
      end
   end
in
   fun {Reverse Xs}
      {IterReverse nil Xs}
   end
end
```

This version of Reverse is both a linear-time and an iterative computation.

3.4.2.5 Correctness with state invariants

Let us prove that IterLength is correct. We will use a general technique that works well for IterReverse and other iterative computations. The idea is to define a property $P(S_i)$ of the state that we can prove is always true, i.e., it is a state invariant. If P is chosen well, then the correctness of the computation follows from $P(S_{\text{final}})$. For IterLength we define P as follows:

$$P((i, \texttt{Ys})) \equiv (\text{length}(\texttt{Xs}) = i + \text{length}(\texttt{Ys}))$$

where length(L) gives the length of the list L. This combines i and Ys in such a way that we suspect it is a state invariant. We use induction to prove this:

- First prove $P(S_0)$. This follows directly from $S_0 = (0, \texttt{Xs})$.
- Assuming $P(S_i)$ and S_i is not the final state, prove $P(S_{i+1})$. This follows from the semantics of the **case** statement and the function call. Write $S_i = (i, \texttt{Ys})$. We are not in the final state, so Ys is of nonzero length. From the semantics, I+1 adds 1 to i and the **case** statement removes one element from Ys. Therefore $P(S_{i+1})$ holds.

Since Ys is reduced by one element at each call, we eventually arrive at the final state $S_{\text{final}} = (i, \texttt{nil})$, and the function returns i. Since length(nil) $= 0$, from $P(S_{\text{final}})$ it follows that $i =$ length(Xs).

The difficult step in this proof is to choose the property P. It has to satisfy two constraints. First, it has to combine the arguments of the iterative computation such that the result does not change as the computation progresses. Second, it has to be strong enough that the correctness follows from $P(S_{\text{final}})$. A rule of thumb for finding a good P is to execute the program by hand in a few small cases, and from them to picture what the general intermediate case is.

3.4.2.6 Constructing programs by following the type

The above examples of list functions all have a curious property. They all have a list argument, ⟨List T⟩, which is defined as:

```
⟨List T⟩  ::=  nil
            |  T '|' ⟨List T⟩
```

and they all use a **case** statement which has the form:

```
case Xs
of nil then ⟨expr⟩   % Base case
[] X|Xr then ⟨expr⟩  % Recursive call
end
```

What is going on here? The recursive structure of the list functions exactly follows the recursive structure of the type definition. We find that this is almost always true of list functions.

We can use this property to help us write list functions. This can be a tremendous help when type definitions become complicated. For example, let us write a function that counts the elements of a nested list. A nested list is a list in which each element can itself be a list, e.g., [[1 2] 4 nil [[5] 10]]. We define the type ⟨NestedList T⟩ as follows:

```
⟨NestedList T⟩  ::=  nil
                  |  ⟨NestedList T⟩ '|' ⟨NestedList T⟩
                  |  T '|' ⟨NestedList T⟩
```

To avoid ambiguity, we have to add a condition on T, namely that T is neither `nil` nor a cons. Now let us write the function `{LengthL ⟨NestedList T⟩}: ⟨Int⟩` which counts the number of elements in a nested list. Following the type definition gives this skeleton:

```
fun {LengthL Xs}
   case Xs
   of nil then ⟨expr⟩
   [] X|Xr andthen {IsList X} then
      ⟨expr⟩ % Recursive calls for X and Xr
   [] X|Xr then
      ⟨expr⟩ % Recursive call for Xr
   end
end
```

(The third case does not have to mention `{Not {IsList X}}` since it follows from the negation of the second case.) Here `{IsList X}` is a function that checks whether `X` is `nil` or a cons:

```
fun {IsCons X} case X of _|_ then true else false end end
fun {IsList X} X==nil orelse {IsCons X} end
```

Fleshing out the skeleton gives the following function:

```
fun {LengthL Xs}
   case Xs
   of nil then 0
   [] X|Xr andthen {IsList X} then
      {LengthL X}+{LengthL Xr}
   [] X|Xr then
      1+{LengthL Xr}
   end
end
```

Here are two example calls:

```
X=[[1 2] 4 nil [[5] 10]]
{Browse {LengthL X}}
{Browse {LengthL [X X]}}
```

What do these calls display?

Using a different type definition for nested lists gives a different length function. For example, let us define the type ⟨NestedList2 T⟩ as follows:

⟨NestedList2 T⟩	::=	`nil`
	|	⟨NestedList2 T⟩ ´|´ ⟨NestedList2 T⟩
	|	T

Again, we have to add the condition that T is neither `nil` nor a cons. Note the subtle difference between ⟨NestedList T⟩ and ⟨NestedList2 T⟩! Following the definition of ⟨NestedList2 T⟩ gives a different and simpler function `LengthL2`:

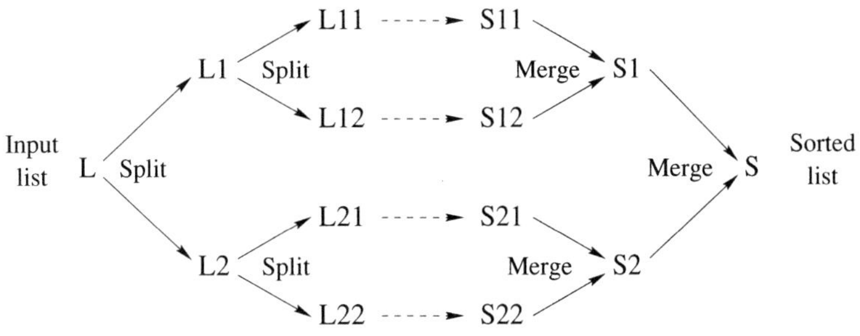

Figure 3.9: Sorting with mergesort.

```
fun {LengthL2 Xs}
   case Xs
   of nil then 0
   [] X|Xr then
      {LengthL2 X}+{LengthL2 Xr}
   else 1 end
end
```

What is the difference between `LengthL` and `LengthL2`? We can deduce it by comparing the types ⟨NestedList T⟩ and ⟨NestedList2 T⟩. A ⟨NestedList T⟩ always has to be a list, whereas a ⟨NestedList2 T⟩ can also be of type T. Therefore the call `{LengthL2 foo}` is legal (it returns 1), whereas `{LengthL foo}` is illegal (it raises an exception). From the standpoint of desired behavior (the input should be a list), we think it is reasonable to consider `LengthL2` as being in error and `LengthL` as being correct.

There is an important lesson to be learned here. Defining a recursive type should be done before writing the recursive function that uses it. Otherwise it is easy to be misled by an apparently simple function that is incorrect. This is true even in functional languages that do type inference, such as Standard ML and Haskell. Type inference can verify that a recursive type is used correctly, but the design of a recursive type remains the programmer's responsibility.

3.4.2.7 Sorting with mergesort

We define a function that takes a list of numbers or atoms and returns a new list sorted in ascending order. It uses the comparison operator `<`, so all elements have to be of the same type (all integers, all floats, or all atoms). We use the mergesort algorithm, which is efficient and can be programmed easily in a declarative model. The mergesort algorithm is based on a simple strategy called divide-and-conquer:

- Split the list into two smaller lists of approximately equal length.
- Use mergesort recursively to sort the two smaller lists.
- Merge the two sorted lists together to get the final result.

Figure 3.9 shows the recursive structure. Mergesort is efficient because the split and merge operations are both linear-time iterative computations. We first define the merge and split operations and then mergesort itself:

```
fun {Merge Xs Ys}
   case Xs # Ys
   of nil # Ys then Ys
   [] Xs # nil then Xs
   [] (X|Xr) # (Y|Yr) then
      if X<Y then X|{Merge Xr Ys}
      else Y|{Merge Xs Yr}
      end
   end
end
```

The type is ⟨**fun** {$ ⟨List T⟩ ⟨List T⟩}: ⟨List T⟩⟩, where T is either ⟨Int⟩, ⟨Float⟩, or ⟨Atom⟩. We define split as a procedure because it has two outputs. It could also be defined as a function returning a pair as a single output.

```
proc {Split Xs ?Ys ?Zs}
   case Xs
   of nil then Ys=nil Zs=nil
   [] [X] then Ys=[X] Zs=nil
   [] X1|X2|Xr then Yr Zr in
      Ys=X1|Yr
      Zs=X2|Zr
      {Split Xr Yr Zr}
   end
end
```

The type is ⟨**proc** {$ ⟨List T⟩ ⟨List T⟩ ⟨List T⟩}⟩. Here is the definition of mergesort itself:

```
fun {MergeSort Xs}
   case Xs
   of nil then nil
   [] [X] then [X]
   else Ys Zs in
      {Split Xs Ys Zs}
      {Merge {MergeSort Ys} {MergeSort Zs}}
   end
end
```

Its type is ⟨**fun** {$ ⟨List T⟩}: ⟨List T⟩⟩ with the same restriction on T as in `Merge`. The splitting up of the input list bottoms out at lists of length zero and one, which can be sorted immediately.

3.4.3 Accumulators

We have seen how to program simple list functions and how to make them iterative. Realistic declarative programming is usually done in a different way, namely by writing functions that are iterative from the start. The idea is to carry state forward at all times and never do a return calculation. A state `S` is represented by adding a

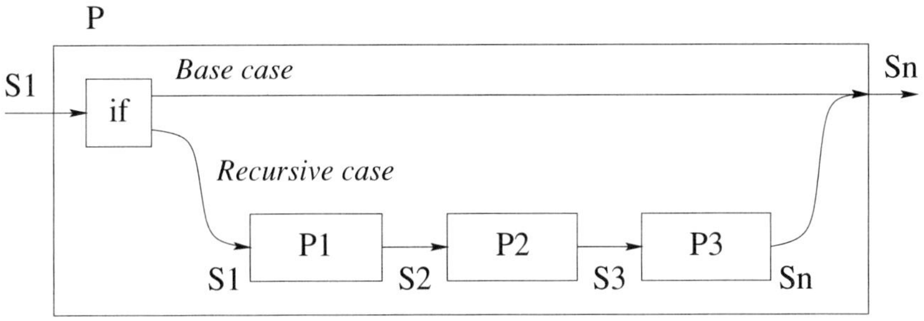

Figure 3.10: Control flow with threaded state.

pair of arguments, `S1` and `Sn`, to each procedure. This pair is called an *accumulator*. `S1` represents the input state and `Sn` represents the output state. Each procedure definition is then written in a style that looks like this:

```
proc {P X S1 ?Sn}
   if {BaseCase X} then Sn=S1
   else
      {P1 S1 S2}
      {P2 S2 S3}
      {P3 S3 Sn}
   end
end
```

The base case does no calculation, so the output state is the same as the input state (`Sn=S1`). The recursive case threads the state through each recursive call (`P1`, `P2`, and `P3`) and eventually returns it to `P`. Figure 3.10 gives an illustration. Each arrow represents one state variable. The state value is given at the arrow's tail and passed to the arrow's head. By state threading we mean that each procedure's output is the next procedure's input. The technique of threading a state through nested procedure calls is called accumulator programming.

Accumulator programming is used in the `IterLength` and `IterReverse` functions we saw before. In these functions the accumulator structure is not so clear, because they are functions. What is happening is that the input state is passed to the function and the output state is what the function returns.

Multiple accumulators

Consider the following procedure, which takes an expression containing identifiers, integers, and addition operations (using label `plus`). It calculates two results: it translates the expression into machine code for a simple stack machine and it calculates the number of instructions in the resulting code.

```
proc {ExprCode E C1 ?Cn S1 ?Sn}
   case E
   of plus(A B) then C2 C3 S2 S3 in
      C2=plus|C1
      S2=S1+1
      {ExprCode B C2 C3 S2 S3}
      {ExprCode A C3 Cn S3 Sn}
   [] I then
      Cn=push(I)|C1
      Sn=S1+1
   end
end
```

This procedure has two accumulators: one to build the list of machine instructions and another to hold the number of instructions. Here is a sample execution:

```
declare Code Size in
{ExprCode plus(plus(a 3) b) nil Code 0 Size}
{Browse Size#Code}
```

This displays

```
5#[push(a) push(3) plus push(b) plus]
```

More complicated programs usually need more accumulators. When writing large declarative programs, we have typically used around a half-dozen accumulators simultaneously. The Aquarius Prolog compiler was written in this style [219, 215]. Some of its procedures have as many as twelve accumulators. This means twenty-four additional arguments! This is difficult to do without mechanical aid. We used an extended DCG preprocessor[5] that takes declarations of accumulators and adds the arguments automatically [108].

We no longer program in this style; we find that programming with explicit state is simpler and more efficient (see chapter 6). It is reasonable to use a few accumulators in a declarative program; it is actually quite rare that a declarative program does not need a few. On the other hand, using many is a sign that some of them would probably be better written with explicit state.

Mergesort with an accumulator

In the previous definition of mergesort, we first called the function `Split` to divide the input list into two halves. There is a simpler way to do the mergesort, by using an accumulator. The parameter represents the part of the list still to be sorted. The specification of `MergeSortAcc` is:

- `S#L2={MergeSortAcc L1 N}` takes an input list `L1` and an integer `N`. It returns two results: `S`, the sorted list of the first `N` elements of `L1`, and `L2`, the remaining elements of `L1`. The two results are paired together with the `#` tupling constructor.

5. DCG (Definite Clause Grammar) is a grammar notation that is used to hide the explicit threading of accumulators.

The accumulator is defined by L1 and L2. This gives the following definition:

```
fun {MergeSort Xs}
   fun {MergeSortAcc L1 N}
      if N==0 then
         nil # L1
      elseif N==1 then
         [L1.1] # L1.2
      elseif N>1 then
         NL=N div 2
         NR=N-NL
         Ys # L2 = {MergeSortAcc L1 NL}
         Zs # L3 = {MergeSortAcc L2 NR}
      in
         {Merge Ys Zs} # L3
      end
   end
in
   {MergeSortAcc Xs {Length Xs}}.1
end
```

The Merge function is unchanged. Remark that this mergesort does a different split than the previous one. In this version, the split separates the first half of the input list from the second half. In the previous version, split separates the odd-numbered list elements from the even-numbered elements.

This version has the same time complexity as the previous version. It uses less memory because it does not create the two split lists. They are defined implicitly by the combination of the accumulating parameter and the number of elements.

3.4.4 Difference lists

A difference list is a pair of two lists, each of which might have an unbound tail. The two lists have a special relationship: it must be possible to get the second list from the first by removing zero or more elements from the front. Here are some examples:

```
X#X                  % Represents the empty list
nil#nil              % idem
[a]#[a]              % idem
(a|b|c|X)#X          % Represents [a b c]
(a|b|c|d|X)#(d|X)    % idem
[a b c d]#[d]        % idem
```

A difference list is a representation of a standard list. We will talk of the difference list sometimes as a data structure by itself, and sometimes as representing a standard list. Be careful not to confuse these two viewpoints. The difference list [a b c d]#[d] might contain the lists [a b c d] and [d], but it represents neither of these. It represents the list [a b c].

Difference lists are a special case of difference structures. A difference structure is a pair of two partial values where the second value is embedded in the first. The difference structure represents a value that is the first structure minus the second structure. Using difference structures makes it easy to construct iterative computations on many recursive data types, e.g., lists or trees. Difference lists and difference structures are special cases of accumulators in which one of the accumulator arguments can be an unbound variable.

The advantage of using difference lists is that when the second list is an unbound variable, another difference list can be appended to it in constant time. To append `(a|b|c|X)#X` and `(d|e|f|Y)#Y`, just bind `X` to `(d|e|f|Y)`. This creates the difference list `(a|b|c|d|e|f|Y)#Y`. We have just appended the lists `[a b c]` and `[d e f]` with a single binding. Here is a function that appends any two difference lists:

```
fun {AppendD D1 D2}
   S1#E1=D1
   S2#E2=D2
in
   E1=S2
   S1#E2
end
```

It can be used like a list append:

```
local X Y in {Browse {AppendD (1|2|3|X)#X (4|5|Y)#Y}} end
```

This displays `(1|2|3|4|5|Y)#Y`. The standard list append function, defined as follows:

```
fun {Append L1 L2}
   case L1
   of X|T then X|{Append T L2}
   [] nil then L2
   end
end
```

iterates on its first argument, and therefore takes time proportional to the length of the first argument. The difference list append is much more efficient: it takes constant time.

The limitation of using difference lists is that they can be appended only once. This property means that difference lists can only be used in special circumstances. For example, they are a natural way to write programs that construct big lists in terms of lots of little lists that must be appended together.

Difference lists as defined here originated from Prolog and logic programming [201]. They are the basis of many advanced Prolog programming techniques. As a concept, a difference list lives somewhere between the concept of value and the concept of state. It has the good properties of a value (programs using them are declarative), but it also has some of the power of state because it can be appended once in constant time.

Flattening a nested list

Consider the problem of flattening a nested list, i.e., calculating a list that has all the elements of the nested list but is no longer nested. We first give a solution using lists and then we show that a much better solution is possible with difference lists. For the list solution, let us reason with mathematical induction based on the type ⟨NestedList⟩ we defined earlier, in the same way we did with the `LengthL` function:

- Flatten of `nil` is `nil`.
- Flatten of `X|Xr` where `X` is a nested list, is `Z` where
  flatten of `X` is `Y`,
  flatten of `Xr` is `Yr`, and
  append `Y` and `Yr` to get `Z`.
- Flatten of `X|Xr` where `X` is not a list, is `Z` where
  flatten of `Xr` is `Yr`, and
  `Z` is `X|Yr`.

Following this reasoning, we get the following definition:

```
fun {Flatten Xs}
   case Xs
   of nil then nil
   [] X|Xr andthen {IsList X} then
      {Append {Flatten X} {Flatten Xr}}
   [] X|Xr then
      X|{Flatten Xr}
   end
end
```

Calling:

```
{Browse {Flatten [[a b] [[c] [d]] nil [e [f]]]}}
```

displays `[a b c d e f]`. This program is very inefficient because it needs to do many append operations (see Exercises, section 3.10). Now let us reason again in the same way, but with difference lists instead of standard lists:

- Flatten of `nil` is `X#X` (empty difference list).
- Flatten of `X|Xr` where `X` is a nested list, is `Y1#Y4` where
  flatten of `X` is `Y1#Y2`,
  flatten of `Xr` is `Y3#Y4`, and
  equate `Y2` and `Y3` to append the difference lists.
- Flatten of `X|Xr` where `X` is not a list, is `(X|Y1)#Y2` where
  flatten of `Xr` is `Y1#Y2`.

We can write the second case as follows:

- Flatten of `X|Xr` where `X` is a nested list, is `Y1#Y4` where
  flatten of `X` is `Y1#Y2` and

flatten of Xr is Y2#Y4.

This gives the following program:

```
fun {Flatten Xs}
   proc {FlattenD Xs ?Ds}
      case Xs
      of nil then Y in Ds=Y#Y
      [] X|Xr andthen {IsList X} then Y1 Y2 Y4 in
         Ds=Y1#Y4
         {FlattenD X Y1#Y2}
         {FlattenD Xr Y2#Y4}
      [] X|Xr then Y1 Y2 in
         Ds=(X|Y1)#Y2
         {FlattenD Xr Y1#Y2}
      end
   end Ys
in {FlattenD Xs Ys#nil} Ys end
```

This program is efficient: it does a single cons operation for each non-list in the input. We convert the difference list returned by `FlattenD` into a regular list by binding its second argument to `nil`. We write `FlattenD` as a procedure because its output is part of its last argument, not the whole argument (see section 2.6.2). It is common style to write a difference list in two arguments:

```
fun {Flatten Xs}
   proc {FlattenD Xs ?S E}
      case Xs
      of nil then S=E
      [] X|Xr andthen {IsList X} then Y2 in
         {FlattenD X S Y2}
         {FlattenD Xr Y2 E}
      [] X|Xr then Y1 in
         S=X|Y1
         {FlattenD Xr Y1 E}
      end
   end Ys
in {FlattenD Xs Ys nil} Ys end
```

As a further simplification, we can write `FlattenD` as a function. To do this, we use the fact that `S` is the output:

```
fun {Flatten Xs}
   fun {FlattenD Xs E}
      case Xs
      of nil then E
      [] X|Xr andthen {IsList X} then
         {FlattenD X {FlattenD Xr E}}
      [] X|Xr then
         X|{FlattenD Xr E}
      end
   end
in {FlattenD Xs nil} end
```

What is the role of `E`? It gives the "rest" of the output, i.e., when the `FlattenD` call exhausts its own contribution to the output.

Reversing a list

Let us look again at the naive list reverse of the last section. The problem with naive reverse is that it uses a costly append function. Will it be more efficient with the constant-time append of difference lists? Let us do the naive reverse with difference lists:

- Reverse of `nil` is `X#X` (empty difference list).
- Reverse of `X|Xs` is `Z`, where
  reverse of `Xs` is `Y1#Y2` and
  append `Y1#Y2` and `(X|Y)#Y` together to get `Z`.

Rewrite the last case as follows, by doing the append:

- Reverse of `X|Xs` is `Y1#Y`, where
  reverse of `Xs` is `Y1#Y2` and
  equate `Y2` and `X|Y`.

It is perfectly allowable to move the equate before the reverse (why?). This gives

- Reverse of `X|Xs` is `Y1#Y`, where
  reverse of `Xs` is `Y1#(X|Y)`.

Here is the final definition:

```
fun {Reverse Xs}
   proc {ReverseD Xs ?Y1 Y}
      case Xs
      of nil then Y1=Y
      [] X|Xr then {ReverseD Xr Y1 X|Y}
      end
   end Y1
in {ReverseD Xs Y1 nil} Y1 end
```

Look carefully and you will see that this is almost exactly the same iterative solution as in the last section. The only difference between `IterReverse` and `ReverseD` is the argument order: the output of `IterReverse` is the second argument of `ReverseD`. So what's the advantage of using difference lists? With them, we derived `ReverseD` without thinking, whereas to derive `IterReverse` we had to guess an intermediate state that could be updated.

3.4.5 Queues

A queue is a sequence of elements with an insert and a delete operation. The insert operation adds an element to one end of the queue and the delete operation removes an element from the other end. We say the queue has FIFO (first-in, first-out) behavior. Let us investigate how to program queues in the declarative model.

A naive queue

An obvious way to implement queues is by using lists. If `L` represents the queue content, then inserting `X` gives the new queue `X|L` and deleting `X` is done by calling `{ButLast L X L1}`, which binds `X` to the deleted element and returns the new queue in `L1`. `ButLast` returns the last element of `L` in `X` and all elements but the last in `L1`. It can be defined as:

```
proc {ButLast L ?X ?L1}
   case L
   of [Y] then X=Y L1=nil
   [] Y|L2 then L3 in
      L1=Y|L3
      {ButLast L2 X L3}
   end
end
```

The problem with this implementation is that `ButLast` is slow: it takes time proportional to the number of elements in the queue. On the contrary, we would like both the insert and delete operations to be constant-time. That is, doing an operation on a given implementation and machine always takes time less than some constant number of seconds. The value of the constant depends on the implementation and machine. Whether or not we can achieve the constant-time goal depends on the expressiveness of the computation model:

- In a strict functional programming language, i.e., the declarative model without dataflow variables (see section 2.8.1), we cannot achieve it. The best we can do is to get amortized constant-time operations [157]. That is, any sequence of n insert and delete operations takes a total time that is proportional to some constant times n. Any individual operation might not be constant-time, however.
- In the declarative model, which extends the strict functional model with dataflow variables, we can achieve the constant-time goal.

We will show how to define both solutions. In both definitions, each operation takes a queue as input and returns a new queue as output. As soon as a queue is used by the program as input to an operation, then it can no longer be used as input to another operation. In other words, there can be only one version of the queue in use at any time. We say that the queue is ephemeral.[6] Each version exists from the moment it is created to the moment it can no longer be used.

---

6. Queues implemented with explicit state (see chapters 6 and 7) are also usually ephemeral.

Amortized constant-time ephemeral queue

Here is the definition of a queue whose insert and delete operations have constant amortized time bounds. The definition is taken from [157]:

```
fun {NewQueue} q(nil nil) end

fun {Check Q}
   case Q of q(nil R) then q({Reverse R} nil) else Q end
end

fun {Insert Q X}
   case Q of q(F R) then {Check q(F X|R)} end
end

fun {Delete Q X}
   case Q of q(F R) then F1 in F=X|F1 {Check q(F1 R)} end
end

fun {IsEmpty Q}
   case Q of q(F R) then F==nil end
end
```

This uses the pair `q(F R)` to represent the queue. `F` and `R` are lists. `F` represents the front of the queue and `R` represents the back of the queue in reversed form. At any instant, the queue content is given by `{Append F {Reverse R}}`. An element can be inserted by adding it to the front of `R` and deleted by removing it from the front of `F`. For example, say that `F=[a b]` and `R=[d c]`. Deleting the first element returns `a` and makes `F=[b]`. Inserting the element `e` makes `R=[e d c]`. Both operations are constant-time.

To make this representation work, each element in `R` has to be moved to `F` sooner or later. When should the move be done? Doing it element by element is inefficient, since it means replacing `F` by `{Append F {Reverse R}}` each time, which takes time at least proportional to the length of `F`. The trick is to do it only occasionally. We do it when `F` becomes empty, so that `F` is non-nil if and only if the queue is nonempty. This invariant is maintained by the `Check` function, which moves the content of `R` to `F` whenever `F` is nil.

The `Check` function does a list reverse operation on `R`. The reverse takes time proportional to the length of `R`, i.e., to the number of elements it reverses. Each element that goes through the queue is passed exactly once from `R` to `F`. Allocating the reverse's execution time to each element therefore gives a constant time per element. This is why the queue is amortized.

Worst-case constant-time ephemeral queue

We can use difference lists to implement queues whose insert and delete operations have constant worst-case execution times. We use a difference list that ends in an unbound dataflow variable. This lets us insert elements in constant time by binding the dataflow variable. Here is the definition:

```
fun {NewQueue} X in q(0 X X) end

fun {Insert Q X}
   case Q of q(N S E) then E1 in E=X|E1 q(N+1 S E1) end
end

fun {Delete Q X}
   case Q of q(N S E) then S1 in S=X|S1 q(N-1 S1 E) end
end

fun {IsEmpty Q}
   case Q of q(N S E) then N==0 end
end
```

This uses the triple `q(N S E)` to represent the queue. At any instant, the queue content is given by the difference list `S#E`. `N` is the number of elements in the queue. Why is `N` needed? Without it, we would not know how many elements were in the queue.

Example use

The following example works with both the amortized and worst-case definitions:

```
declare Q1 Q2 Q3 Q4 Q5 Q6 Q7 in
Q1={NewQueue}
Q2={Insert Q1 peter}
Q3={Insert Q2 paul}
local X in Q4={Delete Q3 X} {Browse X} end
Q5={Insert Q4 mary}
local X in Q6={Delete Q5 X} {Browse X} end
local X in Q7={Delete Q6 X} {Browse X} end
```

This inserts three elements and deletes them. Each element is inserted before it is deleted. Now let us see what each definition can do that the other cannot.

With the worst-case definition, we can delete an element before it is inserted. This may seem surprising, but it is perfectly natural. Doing such a delete returns an unbound variable that will be bound to the next inserted element. So the last four calls in the above example can be changed as follows:

```
local X in Q4={Delete Q3 X} {Browse X} end
local X in Q5={Delete Q4 X} {Browse X} end
local X in Q6={Delete Q5 X} {Browse X} end
Q7={Insert Q6 mary}
```

This works because the bind operation of dataflow variables, which is used both to insert and delete elements, is symmetric.

With the amortized definition, maintaining multiple versions of the queue simultaneously gives correct results, although the amortized time bounds no longer hold.[7] Here is an example with two versions:

```
declare Q1 Q2 Q3 Q4 Q5 Q6 in
Q1={NewQueue}
Q2={Insert Q1 peter}
Q3={Insert Q2 paul}
Q4={Insert Q2 mary}
local X in Q5={Delete Q3 X} {Browse X} end
local X in Q6={Delete Q4 X} {Browse X} end
```

Both `Q3` and `Q4` are calculated from their common ancestor `Q2`. `Q3` contains `peter` and `paul`. `Q4` contains `peter` and `mary`. What do the two `Browse` calls display?

Persistent queues

Both definitions given above are ephemeral. What can we do if we need to use multiple versions and still require constant-time execution? A queue that supports multiple simultaneous versions is called persistent.[8] Some applications need persistent queues. For example, if during a calculation we pass a queue value to another routine:

```
...
{SomeProc Qa}
Qb={Insert Qa x}
Qc={Insert Qb y}
...
```

We assume that `SomeProc` can do queue operations but that the caller does not want to see their effects. It follows that we may have two versions of the queue. Can we write queues that keep the time bounds for this case? It can be done if we extend the declarative model with lazy execution. Then both the amortized and worst-case queues can be made persistent. We defer this solution until we present lazy execution in section 4.5.

For now, let us propose a simple workaround that is often sufficient to make the worst-case queue persistent. It depends on there not being too many simultaneous versions. We define an operation `ForkQ` that takes a queue `Q` and creates two identical versions `Q1` and `Q2`. As a preliminary, we first define a procedure `ForkD` that creates two versions of a difference list:

---

7. To see why not, consider any sequence of n queue operations. For the amortized constant-time bound to hold, the total time for all operations in the sequence must be proportional to n. But what happens if the sequence repeats an "expensive" operation in many versions? This is possible, since we are talking of any sequence. Since both the time for an expensive operation and the number of versions can be proportional to n, the total time bound grows as n^2.

8. This meaning of persistence should not be confused with persistence as used in transactions and databases (see sections 8.5 and 9.6), which is a completely different concept.

```
proc {ForkD D ?E ?F}
   D1#nil=D
   E1#E0=E {Append D1 E0 E1}
   F1#F0=F {Append D1 F0 F1}
in skip end
```

The call `{ForkD D E F}` takes a difference list `D` and returns two fresh copies of it, `E` and `F`. `Append` is used to convert a list into a fresh difference list. Note that `ForkD` consumes `D`, i.e., `D` can no longer be used afterward since its tail is bound. Now we can define `ForkQ`, which uses `ForkD` to make two versions of a queue:

```
proc {ForkQ Q ?Q1 ?Q2}
   q(N S E)=Q
   q(N S1 E1)=Q1
   q(N S2 E2)=Q2
in
   {ForkD S#E S1#E1 S2#E2}
end
```

`ForkQ` consumes `Q` and takes time proportional to the size of the queue. We can rewrite the example as follows using `ForkQ`:

```
...
{ForkQ Qa Qa1 Qa2}
{SomeProc Qa1}
Qb={Insert Qa2 x}
Qc={Insert Qb y}
...
```

This works well if it is acceptable for `ForkQ` to be an expensive operation.

3.4.6 Trees

Next to linear data structures such as lists and queues, trees are the most important recursive data structure in a programmer's repertory. A tree is either a leaf node or a node that contains one or more trees. Usually we are interested in finite trees, e.g., trees with a finite number of nodes. Nodes can carry additional information. Here is one possible definition:

$$\langle \mathsf{Tree} \rangle \ ::= \ \texttt{leaf} \ \mid \ \texttt{tree(} \langle \mathsf{Value} \rangle \ \langle \mathsf{Tree} \rangle_1 \ \cdots \ \langle \mathsf{Tree} \rangle_n \texttt{)}$$

The basic difference between a list and a tree is that a list always has a linear structure whereas a tree can have a branching structure. A list always has an element followed by exactly one smaller list. A tree has an element followed by some number of smaller trees. This number can be any natural number, i.e., zero for leaf nodes and any positive number for non-leaf nodes.

There exist many different kinds of trees, with different branching structures and node contents. For example, a list is a tree in which non-leaf nodes always have exactly one subtree (it could be called a unary tree). In a binary tree the non-leaf nodes always have exactly two subtrees. In a ternary tree they have exactly three subtrees. In a balanced tree, all subtrees of the same node have the same size (i.e.,

3.4.6.4 Tree traversal

Traversing a tree means to perform an operation on its nodes in some well-defined order. There are many ways to traverse a tree. Many of these are derived from one of two basic traversals, called depth-first and breadth-first traversal. Let us look at these traversals.

Depth-first traversal Depth-first is the simplest traversal. For each node, it visits first the node itself, then the leftmost subtree, and then the rightmost subtree. This makes it easy to program since it closely follows how nested procedure calls execute. Here is a traversal that displays each node's key and information:

```
proc {DFS T}
   case T
   of leaf then skip
   [] tree(Key Val L R) then
      {Browse Key#Val}
      {DFS L}
      {DFS R}
   end
end
```

The astute reader will realize that this depth-first traversal does not make much sense in the declarative model, because it does not calculate any result.[9] We can fix this by adding an accumulator. Here is a traversal that calculates a list of all key/value pairs:

```
proc {DFSAccLoop T S1 ?Sn}
   case T
   of leaf then Sn=S1
   [] tree(Key Val L R) then S2 S3 in
      S2=Key#Val|S1
      {DFSAccLoop L S2 S3}
      {DFSAccLoop R S3 Sn}
   end
end
fun {DFSAcc T} {Reverse {DFSAccLoop T nil $}} end
```

This uses the accumulator in the same way as we saw before, with input state `S1` and output state `Sn`. The result is that `DFSAccLoop` calculates the list in reverse, so `DFSAcc` has to call `Reverse` to put it in the right order. Here is another version that calculates the list in the right order directly:

9. `Browse` cannot be defined in the declarative model.

```
proc {BFS T}
   fun {TreeInsert Q T}
      if T\=leaf then {Insert Q T} else Q end
   end

   proc {BFSQueue Q1}
      if {IsEmpty Q1} then skip
      else X Q2 Key Val L R in
         Q2={Delete Q1 X}
         tree(Key Val L R)=X
         {Browse Key#Val}
         {BFSQueue {TreeInsert {TreeInsert Q2 L} R}}
      end
   end
in
   {BFSQueue {TreeInsert {NewQueue} T}}
end
```

Figure 3.13: Breadth-first traversal.

```
proc {DFSAccLoop2 T ?S1 Sn}
   case T
   of leaf then S1=Sn
   [] tree(Key Val L R) then S2 S3 in
      S1=Key#Val|S2
      {DFSAccLoop2 L S2 S3}
      {DFSAccLoop2 R S3 Sn}
   end
end
fun {DFSAcc2 T} {DFSAccLoop2 T $ nil} end
```

Do you see how the two versions differ? The second version uses unbound dataflow variables. It considers `S1#Sn` as a difference list. This gives a more natural program that does not need to call `Reverse`.

Breadth-first traversal Breadth-first is a second basic traversal. It first traverses all nodes at depth 0, then all nodes at depth 1, and so forth, going one level deeper at a time. At each level, it traverses the nodes from left to right. The depth of a node is the length of the path from the root to the current node, not including the current node. To implement breadth-first traversal, we need a queue to keep track of all the nodes at a given depth. Figure 3.13 shows how it is done. It uses the queue data type we defined in the previous section. The next node to visit comes from the head of the queue. The node's two subtrees are added to the tail of the queue. The traversal will get around to visiting them when all the other nodes of the queue have been visited, i.e., all the nodes at the current depth.

Just like for the depth-first traversal, breadth-first traversal is only useful in the declarative model if supplemented by an accumulator. Figure 3.14 gives an example that calculates a list of all key/value pairs in a tree.

```
fun {BFSAcc T}
   fun {TreeInsert Q T}
      if T\=leaf then {Insert Q T} else Q end
   end

   proc {BFSQueue Q1 ?S1 Sn}
      if {IsEmpty Q1} then S1=Sn
      else X Q2 Key Val L R S2 in
         Q2={Delete Q1 X}
         tree(Key Val L R)=X
         S1=Key#Val|S2
         {BFSQueue {TreeInsert {TreeInsert Q2 L} R} S2 Sn}
      end
   end
in
   {BFSQueue {TreeInsert {NewQueue} T} $ nil}
end
```

Figure 3.14: Breadth-first traversal with accumulator.

```
proc {DFS T}
   fun {TreeInsert S T}
      if T\=leaf then T|S else S end
   end

   proc {DFSStack S1}
      case S1
      of nil then skip
      [] X|S2 then
         tree(Key Val L R)=X
      in
         {Browse Key#Val}
         {DFSStack {TreeInsert {TreeInsert S2 R} L}}
      end
   end
in
   {DFSStack {TreeInsert nil T}}
end
```

Figure 3.15: Depth-first traversal with explicit stack.

Depth-first traversal can be implemented in a similar way to breadth-first traversal by using an explicit data structure to keep track of the nodes to visit. To make the traversal depth-first, we simply use a stack instead of a queue. Figure 3.15 defines the traversal, using a list to implement the stack.

How does the new version of `DFS` compare with the original? Both versions use a stack to remember the subtrees to be visited. In the original version, the stack is hidden: it is the semantic stack. There are two recursive calls. During the execution of the first call, the second call is kept on the semantic stack. In the new version, the stack is an explicit data structure. Since the new version is tail recursive, like `BFS`, the semantic stack does not grow. The new version simply trades space on the semantic stack for space in the store.

Let us see how much memory the `DFS` and `BFS` algorithms use. Assume we have a tree of depth n with 2^n leaf nodes and $2^n - 1$ non-leaf nodes. How big do the stack and queue arguments get? We can prove that the stack has at most $n+1$ elements and the queue has at most 2^n elements. Therefore, `DFS` is much more economical: it uses memory proportional to the tree depth. `BFS` uses memory proportional to the size of the tree.

3.4.7 Drawing trees

Now that we have introduced trees and programming with them, let us write a more significant program. We will write a program to draw a binary tree in an aesthetically pleasing way. The program calculates the coordinates of each node. This program is interesting because it traverses the tree for two reasons: to calculate the coordinates and to add the coordinates to the tree itself.

The tree-drawing constraints

We first define the tree's type:

```
⟨Tree⟩  ::=  tree(key:⟨Literal⟩ val:⟨Value⟩ left: ⟨Tree⟩ right: ⟨Tree⟩)
          |  leaf
```

Each node is either a leaf or has two children. In contrast to section 3.4.6, this uses a record to define the tree instead of a tuple. There is a very good reason for this which will become clear when we talk about the principle of independence. Assume that we have the following constraints on how the tree is drawn:

1. There is a minimum horizontal spacing between both subtrees of every node. To be precise, the rightmost node of the left subtree is at a minimal horizontal distance from the leftmost node of the right subtree.

2. If a node has two child nodes, then its horizontal position is the arithmetic average of their horizontal positions.

3. If a node has only one child node, then the child is directly underneath it.

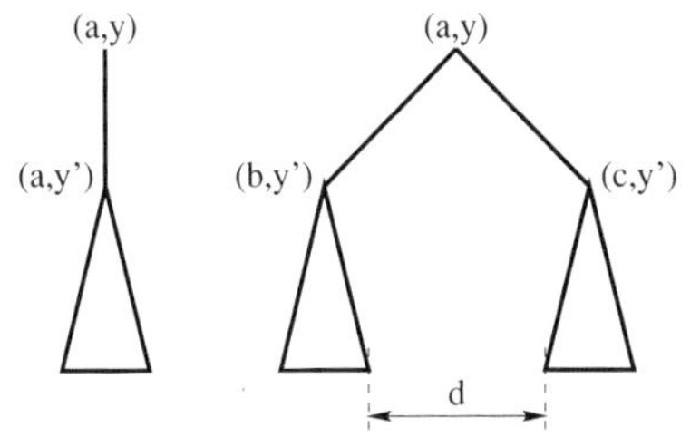
(a,y)
(a,y')
(a,y)
(b,y')
(c,y')
d
1. Distance d between subtrees has minimum value
2. If two children exist, a is average of b and c
3. If only one child exists, it is directly below parent
4. Vertical position y is proportional to level in the tree

Figure 3.16: The tree-drawing constraints.

```
tree(key:a val:111
 left:tree(key:b val:55
       left:tree(key:x val:100
             left:tree(key:z val:56 left:leaf right:leaf)
             right:tree(key:w val:23 left:leaf right:leaf))
       right:tree(key:y val:105 left:leaf
             right:tree(key:r val:77 left:leaf right:leaf)))
 right:tree(key:c val:123
       left:tree(key:d val:119
             left:tree(key:g val:44 left:leaf right:leaf)
             right:tree(key:h val:50
                   left:tree(key:i val:5 left:leaf right:leaf)
                   right:tree(key:j val:6 left:leaf right:leaf)))
       right:tree(key:e val:133 left:leaf right:leaf)))
```

Figure 3.17: An example tree.

4. The vertical position of a node is proportional to its level in the tree.

In addition, to avoid clutter the drawing shows only the nodes of type `tree`. Figure 3.16 shows these constraints graphically in terms of the coordinates of each node. The example tree of figure 3.17 is drawn as shown in figure 3.19.

Calculating the node positions

The tree-drawing algorithm calculates node positions by traversing the tree, passing information between nodes, and calculating values at each node. The traversal has to be done carefully so that all the information is available at the right time. Exactly what traversal is the right one depends on what the constraints are. For the above four constraints, it is sufficient to traverse the tree in a depth-first order. In this order, each left subtree of a node is visited before the right subtree. A basic depth-first traversal looks like this:

```
Scale=30
proc {DepthFirst Tree Level LeftLim ?RootX ?RightLim}
   case Tree
   of tree(x:X y:Y left:leaf right:leaf ...) then
      X=RootX=RightLim=LeftLim
      Y=Scale*Level
   [] tree(x:X y:Y left:L right:leaf ...) then
      X=RootX
      Y=Scale*Level
      {DepthFirst L Level+1 LeftLim RootX RightLim}
   [] tree(x:X y:Y left:leaf right:R ...) then
      X=RootX
      Y=Scale*Level
      {DepthFirst R Level+1 LeftLim RootX RightLim}
   [] tree(x:X y:Y left:L right:R ...) then
         LRootX LRightLim RRootX RLeftLim
      in
         Y=Scale*Level
         {DepthFirst L Level+1 LeftLim LRootX LRightLim}
         RLeftLim=LRightLim+Scale
         {DepthFirst R Level+1 RLeftLim RRootX RightLim}
         X=RootX=(LRootX+RRootX) div 2
   end
end
```

Figure 3.18: Tree-drawing algorithm.

```
proc {DepthFirst Tree}
   case Tree
   of tree(left:L right:R ...) then
      {DepthFirst L}
      {DepthFirst R}
   [] leaf then
      skip
   end
end
```

The tree-drawing algorithm does a depth-first traversal and calculates the (x,y) coordinates of each node during the traversal. As a preliminary to running the algorithm, we extend the `tree` nodes with the fields `x` and `y` at each node:

```
fun {AddXY Tree}
   case Tree
   of tree(left:L right:R ...) then
      {Adjoin Tree
         tree(x:_ y:_ left:{AddXY L} right:{AddXY R})}
   [] leaf then
      leaf
   end
end
```

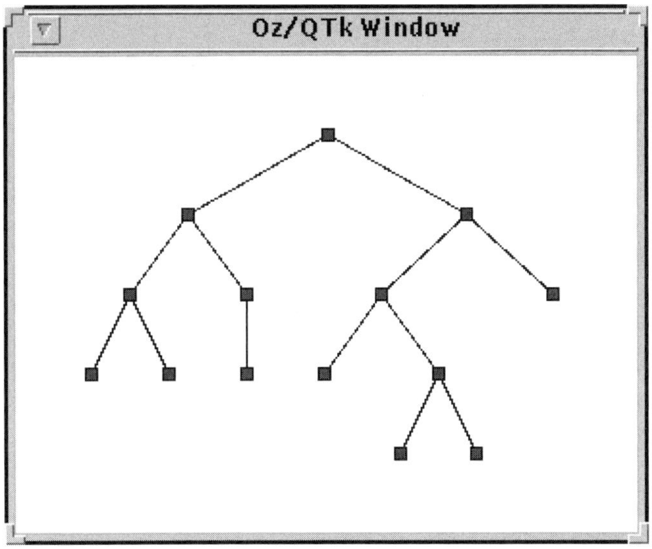

Figure 3.19: The example tree displayed with the tree-drawing algorithm.

The function `AddXY` returns a new tree with the two fields `x` and `y` added to all nodes. It uses the `Adjoin` function which can add new fields to records and override old ones. This is explained in appendix B.3.2. The tree-drawing algorithm will fill in these two fields with the coordinates of each node. If the two fields exist nowhere else in the record, then there is no conflict with any other information in the record.

To implement the tree-drawing algorithm, we extend the depth-first traversal by passing two arguments down (namely, level in the tree and limit on leftmost position of subtree) and two arguments up (namely, horizontal position of the subtree's root and rightmost position of subtree). Downward-passed arguments are sometimes called inherited arguments. Upward-passed arguments are sometimes called synthesized arguments. With these extra arguments, we have enough information to calculate the positions of all nodes. Figure 3.18 gives the complete tree-drawing algorithm. The `Scale` parameter gives the basic size unit of the drawn tree, i.e., the minimum distance between nodes. The initial arguments are `Level`=1 and `LeftLim`=`Scale`. There are four cases, depending on whether a node has two subtrees, one subtree (left or right), or zero subtrees. Pattern matching in the **`case`** statement always picks the correct case. This works because the tests are done in sequential order.

3.4.8 Parsing

As a second case study of declarative programming, let us write a parser for a small imperative language with syntax similar to Pascal. This uses many of the techniques we have seen; in particular, it uses an accumulator and builds a tree.

⟨Prog⟩	::=	`program` ⟨Id⟩ `;` ⟨Stat⟩ `end`
⟨Stat⟩	::=	`begin` ⟨Stat⟩ { `;` ⟨Stat⟩ } `end`
	|	⟨Id⟩ `:=` ⟨Expr⟩
	|	`if` ⟨Comp⟩ `then` ⟨Stat⟩ `else` ⟨Stat⟩
	|	`while` ⟨Comp⟩ `do` ⟨Stat⟩
	|	`read` ⟨Id⟩
	|	`write` ⟨Expr⟩
⟨Comp⟩	::=	⟨Expr⟩ { ⟨COP⟩ ⟨Expr⟩ }
⟨Expr⟩	::=	⟨Term⟩ { ⟨EOP⟩ ⟨Term⟩ }
⟨Term⟩	::=	⟨Fact⟩ { ⟨TOP⟩ ⟨Fact⟩ }
⟨Fact⟩	::=	⟨Integer⟩ | ⟨Id⟩ | `(` ⟨Expr⟩ `)`
⟨COP⟩	::=	`´==´` | `´!=´` | `´>´` | `´<´` | `´=<´` | `´>=´`
⟨EOP⟩	::=	`´+´` | `´-´`
⟨TOP⟩	::=	`´*´` | `´/´`
⟨Integer⟩	::=	(integer)
⟨Id⟩	::=	(atom)

Table 3.2: The parser's input language (which is a token sequence).

What is a parser?

A parser is part of a compiler. A compiler is a program that translates a sequence of characters, which represents a program, into a sequence of low-level instructions that can be executed on a machine. In its most basic form, a compiler consists of three parts:

1. *Tokenizer.* The tokenizer reads a sequence of characters and outputs a sequence of tokens.

2. *Parser.* The parser reads a sequence of tokens and outputs an abstract syntax tree. This is sometimes called a parse tree.

3. *Code generator.* The code generator traverses the syntax tree and generates low-level instructions for a real machine or an abstract machine.

Usually this structure is extended by optimizers to improve the generated code. In this section, we will just write the parser. We first define the input and output formats of the parser.

The parser's input and output languages

The parser accepts a sequence of tokens according to the grammar given in table 3.2 and outputs an abstract syntax tree. The grammar is carefully designed to be right recursive and deterministic. This means that the choice of grammar rule is

<table>
<tr><td>⟨Prog⟩</td><td>::=</td><td>prog(⟨Id⟩ ⟨Stat⟩)</td></tr>
<tr><td>⟨Stat⟩</td><td>::=</td><td>';'(⟨Stat⟩ ⟨Stat⟩)</td></tr>
<tr><td></td><td>|</td><td>assign(⟨Id⟩ ⟨Expr⟩)</td></tr>
<tr><td></td><td>|</td><td>'if'(⟨Comp⟩ ⟨Stat⟩ ⟨Stat⟩)</td></tr>
<tr><td></td><td>|</td><td>while(⟨Comp⟩ ⟨Stat⟩)</td></tr>
<tr><td></td><td>|</td><td>read(⟨Id⟩)</td></tr>
<tr><td></td><td>|</td><td>write(⟨Expr⟩)</td></tr>
<tr><td>⟨Comp⟩</td><td>::=</td><td>⟨COP⟩(⟨Expr⟩ ⟨Expr⟩)</td></tr>
<tr><td>⟨Expr⟩</td><td>::=</td><td>⟨Id⟩ | ⟨Integer⟩ | ⟨OP⟩(⟨Expr⟩ ⟨Expr⟩)</td></tr>
<tr><td>⟨COP⟩</td><td>::=</td><td>'==' | '!=' | '>' | '<' | '=<' | '>='</td></tr>
<tr><td>⟨OP⟩</td><td>::=</td><td>'+' | '-' | '*' | '/'</td></tr>
<tr><td>⟨Integer⟩</td><td>::=</td><td>(integer)</td></tr>
<tr><td>⟨Id⟩</td><td>::=</td><td>(atom)</td></tr>
</table>

Table 3.3: The parser's output language (which is a tree).

completely determined by the next token. This makes it possible to write a top-down, left-to-right parser with only one token lookahead.

For example, say we want to parse a ⟨Term⟩. It consists of a nonempty series of ⟨Fact⟩ separated by ⟨TOP⟩ tokens. To parse it, we first parse a ⟨Fact⟩. Then we examine the next token. If it is a ⟨TOP⟩, then we know the series continues. If it is not a ⟨TOP⟩, then we know the series has ended, i.e., the ⟨Term⟩ has ended. For this parsing strategy to work, there must be no overlap between ⟨TOP⟩ tokens and the other possible tokens that come after a ⟨Fact⟩. By inspecting the grammar rules, we see that the other tokens must be taken from {⟨EOP⟩, ⟨COP⟩, `;`, `end`, `then`, `do`, `else`, `)`}. We confirm that all the tokens defined by this set are different from the tokens defined by ⟨TOP⟩.

There are two kinds of symbols in table 3.2: nonterminals and terminals. A nonterminal symbol is one that is further expanded according to a grammar rule. A terminal symbol corresponds directly to a token in the input. It is not expanded. The nonterminal symbols are ⟨Prog⟩ (complete program), ⟨Stat⟩ (statement), ⟨Comp⟩ (comparison), ⟨Expr⟩ (expression), ⟨Term⟩ (term), ⟨Fact⟩ (factor), ⟨COP⟩ (comparison operator), ⟨EOP⟩ (expression operator), and ⟨TOP⟩ (term operator). To parse a program, start with ⟨Prog⟩ and expand until finding a sequence of tokens that matches the input.

The parser output is a tree (i.e., a nested record) with syntax given in table 3.3. Superficially, tables 3.2 and 3.3 have very similar content, but they are actually quite different: the first defines a sequence of tokens and the second defines a tree. The first does not show the structure of the input program—we say it is flat. The second exposes this structure—we say it is nested. Because it exposes the program's structure, we call the nested record an abstract syntax tree. It is abstract because it

```
fun {Stat S1 Sn}
T|S2=S1 in
   case T
   of begin then
      {Sequence Stat fun {$ X} X==´;´ end S2 ´end´|Sn}
   [] ´if´ then C X1 X2 S3 S4 S5 S6 in
      C={Comp S2 S3}
      S3=´then´|S4
      X1={Stat S4 S5}
      S5=´else´|S6
      X2={Stat S6 Sn}
      ´if´(C X1 X2)
   [] while then C X S3 S4 in
      C={Comp S2 S3}
      S3=´do´|S4
      X={Stat S4 Sn}
      while(C X)
   [] read then I in
      I={Id S2 Sn}
      read(I)
   [] write then E in
      E={Expr S2 Sn}
      write(E)
   elseif {IsIdent T} then E S3 in
      S2=´:=´|S3
      E={Expr S3 Sn}
      assign(T E)
   else
      S1=Sn
      raise error(S1) end
   end
end
```

Figure 3.20: Left-to-right top-down parser with one token lookahead.

is encoded as a data structure in the language, and no longer in terms of tokens. The parser's role is to extract the structure from the flat input. Without this structure, it is extremely difficult to write the code generator and code optimizers.

The parser program

The main parser call is the function `{Prog S1 Sn}`, where `S1` is an input list of tokens and `Sn` is the rest of the list after parsing. This call returns the parsed output. For example:

```
declare A Sn in
A={Prog
   [program foo ´;´
    while a ´+´ 3 ´<´ b ´do´ b ´:=´ b ´+´ 1 ´end´]
   Sn}
{Browse A}
```

displays the following parser output:

```
prog(foo while(´<´(´+´(a 3) b) assign(b ´+´(b 1))))
```

We now give annotated program code for the parser. `Prog` is written as follows:

```
fun {Prog S1 Sn}
   Y Z S2 S3 S4 S5
in
   S1=program|S2    Y={Id S2 S3}   S3=´;´|S4
   Z={Stat S4 S5}   S5=´end´|Sn
   prog(Y Z)
end
```

The accumulator is threaded through all terminal and nonterminal symbols. Each nonterminal symbol has a procedure to parse it. Statements are parsed with the function `Stat`, which is shown in Figure 3.20. The one-token lookahead is put in `T` and used in a **case** statement to find the correct branch of the `Stat` grammar rule.

Statement sequences are parsed by the procedure `Sequence`, a generic procedure that also handles comparison sequences, expression sequences, and term sequences. `Sequence` is written as follows:

```
fun {Sequence NonTerm Sep S1 Sn}
   fun {SequenceLoop Prefix S2 Sn}
      case S2 of T|S3 andthen {Sep T} then Next S4 in
         Next={NonTerm S3 S4}
         {SequenceLoop T(Prefix Next) S4 Sn}
      else
         Sn=S2 Prefix
      end
   end
   First S2
in
   First={NonTerm S1 S2}
   {SequenceLoop First S2 Sn}
end
```

It takes two input functions: `NonTerm` (which is passed any nonterminal) and `Sep` (which detects the separator symbol in a sequence). The syntax `T(X1 X2)` does dynamic record creation according to a label that is known only at run time; it is syntactic sugar for

```
local R={MakeRecord T [1 2]} in X1=R.1 X2=R.2 R end
```

Comparisons, expressions, and terms are parsed as follows with `Sequence`:

```
fun {Comp S1 Sn} {Sequence Expr COP S1 Sn} end
fun {Expr S1 Sn} {Sequence Term EOP S1 Sn} end
fun {Term S1 Sn} {Sequence Fact TOP S1 Sn} end
```

Each of these three functions has its corresponding function for detecting separators:

```
fun {COP Y}
   Y=='<' orelse Y=='>' orelse Y=='=<' orelse
   Y=='>=' orelse Y=='==' orelse Y=='!='
end
fun {EOP Y} Y=='+' orelse Y=='-' end
fun {TOP Y} Y=='*' orelse Y=='/' end
```

Finally, factors and identifiers are parsed as follows:

```
fun {Fact S1 Sn}
T|S2=S1 in
   if {IsInt T} orelse {IsIdent T} then
      S2=Sn
      T
   else E S2 S3 in
      S1='('|S2
      E={Expr S2 S3}
      S3=')'|Sn
      E
   end
end

fun {Id S1 Sn} X in S1=X|Sn true={IsIdent X} X end
fun {IsIdent X} {IsAtom X} end
```

Integers are represented as built-in integer values and detected using the built-in `IsInt` function.

This parsing technique works for grammars where one-token lookahead is enough. Some grammars, called ambiguous grammars, require looking at more than one token to decide which grammar rule is needed. A simple way to parse them is with nondeterministic choice, as explained in chapter 9.

3.5 Time and space efficiency

Declarative programming is still programming; even though it has strong mathematical properties it still results in real programs that run on real computers. Therefore, it is important to think about computational efficiency. There are two parts to efficiency: execution time (e.g., in seconds) and memory usage (e.g., in bytes). We will show how to calculate both of these.

3.5.1 Execution time

Using the kernel language and its semantics, we can calculate the execution time up to a constant factor. For example, for a mergesort algorithm we will be able to say that the execution time is proportional to $n \log n$, given an input list of length n. The asymptotic time complexity of an algorithm is the tightest upper bound on its execution time as a function of the input size, up to a constant factor. This is sometimes called the worst-case time complexity.

To find the constant factor, it is necessary to measure actual runs of the program on its implementation. Calculating the constant factor a priori is extremely difficult. This is because modern computer systems have a complex hardware and software structure that introduces much unpredictability in the execution time: they do memory management (see section 2.5), they have complex memory systems (with virtual memory and several levels of caches), they have complex pipelined and superscalar architectures (many instructions are simultaneously in various stages of execution; an instruction's execution time often depends on the other instructions present), and the operating system does context switches at unpredictable times. This unpredictability improves the average performance at the price of increasing performance fluctuations. For more information on measuring performance and its pitfalls, we recommend [103].

Big-oh notation

We will give the execution time of the program in terms of the "big-oh" notation $O(f(n))$. This notation lets us talk about the execution time without having to specify the constant factor. Let $T(n)$ be a function that gives the execution time of some program, measured in the size of the input n. Let $f(n)$ be some other function defined on non-negative integers. Then we say $T(n)$ is of order $f(n)$ if $T(n) \le c.f(n)$ for some positive constant c, for all n except for some small values $n \le n_0$. That is, as n grows there is a point after which $T(n)$ never gets bigger than $c.f(n)$.

Sometimes this is written $T(n) = O(f(n))$. Be careful! This use of equals is an abuse of notation, since there is no equality involved. If $g(n) = O(f(n))$ and $h(n) = O(f(n))$, then it is not true that $g(n) = h(n)$. A better way to understand the big-oh notation is in terms of sets and membership: $O(f(n))$ is a set of functions, and saying $T(n)$ is of $O(f(n))$ means simply that $T(n)$ is a member of the set.

Calculating the execution time

We use the kernel language as a guide. Each kernel instruction has a well-defined execution time, which may be a function of the size of its arguments. Assume we have a program that consists of the p functions `F1`, ..., `Fp`. We would like to calculate the p functions $T_{\texttt{F1}}, \ldots, T_{\texttt{Fp}}$. This is done in three steps:

1. Translate the program into the kernel language.

2. Use the kernel execution times to set up a collection of equations that contain $T_{\texttt{F1}}, \ldots, T_{\texttt{Fp}}$. We call these equations recurrence equations since they define the result for n in terms of results for values smaller than n.

3. Solve the recurrence equations for $T_{\texttt{F1}}, \ldots, T_{\texttt{Fp}}$.

⟨s⟩ ::=	
skip	k
| ⟨x⟩$_1$=⟨x⟩$_2$	k
| ⟨x⟩=⟨v⟩	k
| ⟨s⟩$_1$ ⟨s⟩$_2$	$T(s_1) + T(s_2)$
| **local** ⟨x⟩ **in** ⟨s⟩ **end**	$k + T(s)$
| **proc** {⟨x⟩ ⟨y⟩$_1$ ··· ⟨y⟩$_n$} ⟨s⟩ **end**	k
| **if** ⟨x⟩ **then** ⟨s⟩$_1$ **else** ⟨s⟩$_2$ **end**	$k + \max(T(s_1), T(s_2))$
| **case** ⟨x⟩ **of** ⟨pattern⟩ **then** ⟨s⟩$_1$ **else** ⟨s⟩$_2$ **end**	$k + \max(T(s_1), T(s_2))$
| {⟨x⟩ ⟨y⟩$_1$ ··· ⟨y⟩$_n$}	$T_x(\text{size}_x(I_x(\{y_1, \ldots, y_n\})))$

Table 3.4: Execution times of kernel instructions.

Table 3.4 gives the execution time $T(s)$ for each kernel statement ⟨s⟩. In this table, s is an integer and the arguments $y_i = E(\langle\text{y}\rangle_i)$ for $1 \le i \le n$, for the appropriate environment E. Each instance of k is a different positive real constant. The function $I_x(\{y_1, \ldots, y_n\})$ returns the subset of a procedure's arguments that are used as inputs.[10] The function $\text{size}_x(\{y_1, \ldots, y_k\})$ is the "size" of the input arguments for the procedure x. We are free to define size in any way we like; if it is defined badly, then the recurrence equations will have no solution. For the instructions ⟨x⟩=⟨y⟩ and ⟨x⟩=⟨v⟩ there is a rare case when they can take more than constant time, namely, when both arguments are bound to large partial values. In that case, the time is proportional to the size of the common part of the two partial values.

Example: `Append` *function*

Let us give a simple example to show how this works. Consider the `Append` function:

```
fun {Append Xs Ys}
   case Xs
   of nil then Ys
   [] X|Xr then X|{Append Xr Ys}
   end
end
```

This has the following translation into the kernel language:

10. This can sometimes differ from call to call, e.g., when a procedure is used to perform different tasks at different calls.

Equation	Solution
$T(n) = k + T(n-1)$	$O(n)$
$T(n) = k_1 + k_2.n + T(n-1)$	$O(n^2)$
$T(n) = k + T(n/2)$	$O(\log n)$
$T(n) = k_1 + k_2.n + T(n/2)$	$O(n)$
$T(n) = k + 2.T(n/2)$	$O(n)$
$T(n) = k_1 + k_2.n + 2.T(n/2)$	$O(n \log n)$
$T(n) = k_1.n^{k_2} + k_3.T(n-1)$	$O({k_3}^n)$ (if $k_3 > 1$)

Table 3.5: Some common recurrence equations and their solutions.

```
proc {Append Xs Ys ?Zs}
   case Xs
   of nil then Zs=Ys
   [] X|Xr then Zr in
      Zs=X|Zr
      {Append Xr Ys Zr}
   end
end
```

Using table 3.4, we get the following recurrence equation for the recursive call:

$$T_{\texttt{Append}}(\text{size}(I(\{\texttt{Xs}, \texttt{Ys}, \texttt{Zs}\}))) = k_1 + \max(k_2, k_3 + T_{\texttt{Append}}(\text{size}(I(\{\texttt{Xr}, \texttt{Ys}, \texttt{Zr}\}))))$$

(The subscripts for size and I are not needed here.) Let us simplify this. We know that $I(\{\texttt{Xs}, \texttt{Ys}, \texttt{Zs}\}) = \{\texttt{Xs}\}$ and we assume that $\text{size}(\{\texttt{Xs}\}) = n$, where n is the length of `Xs`. This gives

$$T_{\texttt{Append}}(n) = k_1 + \max(k_2, k_3 + T_{\texttt{Append}}(n-1))$$

Further simplifying gives

$$T_{\texttt{Append}}(n) = k_4 + T_{\texttt{Append}}(n-1)$$

We handle the base case by picking a particular value of `Xs` for which we can directly calculate the result. Let us pick `Xs=nil`. This gives

$$T_{\texttt{Append}}(0) = k_5$$

Solving the two equations gives

$$T_{\texttt{Append}}(n) = k_4.n + k_5$$

Therefore $T_{\texttt{Append}}(n)$ is of $O(n)$.

Recurrence equations

Before looking at more examples, let us take a step back and look at recurrence equations in general. A recurrence equation has one of two forms:

> Solving recurrence equations
>
> The following techniques are often useful:
>
> - A simple three-step technique that almost always works in practice. First, get exact numbers for some small inputs (e.g.: $T(0) = k$, $T(1) = k+3$, $T(2) = k+6$). Second, guess the form of the result (e.g.: $T(n) = an+b$, for some as yet unknown a and b). Third, plug the guessed form into the equations. In our example this gives $b = k$ and $(an + b) = 3 + (a.(n-1) + b)$. This gives $a = 3$, for a final result of $T(n) = 3n + k$. The three-step technique works if the guessed form is correct.
> - A much more powerful technique, called generating functions, that gives closed-form or asymptotic results in a wide variety of cases without having to guess the form. It requires some technical knowledge of infinite series and calculus, but not more than is seen in a first university-level course on these subjects. See Knuth [115] and Wilf [228] for good introductions to generating functions.

- An equation that defines a function $T(n)$ in terms of $T(m_1), \ldots, T(m_k)$, where $m_1, \ldots, m_k < n$.
- An equation that gives $T(n)$ directly for certain values of n, e.g., $T(0)$ or $T(1)$.

When calculating execution times, recurrence equations of many different kinds pop up. Table 3.5 gives some frequently occurring equations and their solutions. The table assumes that the k's are nonzero constants. There are many techniques to derive these solutions. We will see a few in the examples that follow. The box explains two of the most generally useful ones.

Example: `FastPascal`

In chapter 1, we introduced the function `FastPascal` and claimed with a bit of hand waving that `{FastPascal N}` is of $O(n^2)$. Let us see if we can derive this more rigorously. Here is the definition again:

```
fun {FastPascal N}
   if N==1 then [1]
   else L in
      L={FastPascal N-1}
      {AddList {ShiftLeft L} {ShiftRight L}}
   end
end
```

We can derive the equations directly from looking at this definition, without translating functions into procedures. Looking at the definition, it is easy to see that `ShiftRight` is of $O(1)$, i.e., it is constant-time. Using similar reasoning as for `Append`, we can derive that `AddList` and `ShiftLeft` are of $O(n)$ where n is the length of `L`. This gives us the following recurrence equation for the recursive call:

$$T_{\texttt{FastPascal}}(n) = k_1 + \max(k_2, k_3 + T_{\texttt{FastPascal}}(n-1) + k_4.n)$$

where n is the value of the argument `N`. Simplifying gives

$$T_{\texttt{FastPascal}}(n) = k_5 + k_4.n + T_{\texttt{FastPascal}}(n-1)$$

For the base case, we pick `N`=1. This gives

$$T_{\texttt{FastPascal}}(1) = k_6$$

To solve these two equations, we first "guess" that the solution is of the form:

$$T_{\texttt{FastPascal}}(n) = a.n^2 + b.n + c$$

This guess comes from an intuitive argument like the one given in chapter 1. We then insert this form into the two equations. If we can successfully solve for a, b, and c, then this means that our guess was correct. Inserting the form into the two equations gives the following three equations in a, b, and c:

$$\begin{aligned} k_4 - 2a &= 0 \\ k_5 + a - b &= 0 \\ a + b + c - k_6 &= 0 \end{aligned}$$

We do not have to solve this system completely; it suffices to verify that $a \neq 0$.[11] Therefore $T_{\texttt{FastPascal}}(n)$ is of $O(n^2)$.

Example: `MergeSort`

In the previous section we saw three mergesort algorithms. They all have the same execution time, with different constant factors. Let us calculate the execution time of the first algorithm. Here is the main function again:

```
fun {MergeSort Xs}
   case Xs
   of nil then nil
   [] [X] then [X]
   else Ys Zs in
      {Split Xs Ys Zs}
      {Merge {MergeSort Ys} {MergeSort Zs}}
   end
end
```

Let $T(n)$ be the execution time of `{MergeSort Xs}`, where n is the length of `Xs`. Assume that `Split` and `Merge` are of $O(n)$ in the length of their inputs. We know that `Split` outputs two lists of lengths $\lceil n/2 \rceil$ and $\lfloor n/2 \rfloor$, From the definition of

11. If we guess $a.n^2 + b.n + c$ and the actual solution is of the form $b.n + c$, then we will get $a = 0$.

`MergeSort`, this lets us define the following recurrence equations:

$$T(0) = k_1$$
$$T(1) = k_2$$
$$T(n) = k_3 + k_4 n + T(\lceil n/2 \rceil) + T(\lfloor n/2 \rfloor) \text{ if } n \geq 2$$

This uses the ceiling and floor functions, which are a bit tricky. To get rid of them, assume that n is a power of 2, i.e., $n = 2^k$ for some k. Then the equations become:

$$T(0) = k_1$$
$$T(1) = k_2$$
$$T(n) = k_3 + k_4 n + 2T(n/2) \text{ if } n \geq 2$$

Expanding the last equation gives (where $L(n) = k_3 + k_4 n$):

$$T(n) = \overbrace{L(n) + 2L(n/2) + 4L(n/4) + \cdots + (n/2)L(2)}^{k} \; + \; 2T(1)$$

Replacing $L(n)$ and $T(1)$ by their values gives

$$T(n) = \overbrace{(k_4 n + k_3) + (k_4 n + 2k_3) + (k_4 n + 4k_3) + \cdots + (k_4 n + (n/2)k_3)}^{k} \; + \; k_2$$

Doing the sum gives

$$T(n) = k_4 k n + (n-1)k_3 + k_2$$

We conclude that $T(n) = O(n \log n)$. For values of n that are not powers of 2, we use the easily proved fact that $n \leq m \Rightarrow T(n) \leq T(m)$ to show that the big-oh bound still holds. The bound is independent of the content of the input list. This means that the $O(n \log n)$ bound is also a worst-case bound.

3.5.2 Memory usage

Memory usage is not a single figure like execution time. It consists of two quite different concepts:

- The instantaneous active memory size $m_a(t)$, in memory words. This number gives how much memory the program needs to continue to execute successfully. A related number is the maximum active memory size, $M_a(t) = \max_{0 \leq u \leq t} m_a(u)$. This number is useful for calculating how much physical memory your computer needs to execute the program successfully.
- The instantaneous memory consumption $m_c(t)$, in memory words/second. This number gives how much memory the program allocates during its execution. A large value for this number means that memory management has more work to do, e.g., the garbage collector will be invoked more often. This will increase execution time. A related number is the total memory consumption, $M_c(t) = \int_0^t m_c(u)du$, which is a measure of how much total work memory management has to do to run the

⟨s⟩ ::=	
`skip`	0
| ⟨x⟩$_1$=⟨x⟩$_2$	0
| ⟨x⟩=⟨v⟩	memsize(v)
| ⟨s⟩$_1$ ⟨s⟩$_2$	$M(s_1) + M(s_2)$
| **local** ⟨x⟩ **in** ⟨s⟩ **end**	$1 + T(s)$
| **if** ⟨x⟩ **then** ⟨s⟩$_1$ **else** ⟨s⟩$_2$ **end**	$\max(M(s_1), M(s_2))$
| **case** ⟨x⟩ **of** ⟨pattern⟩ **then** ⟨s⟩$_1$ **else** ⟨s⟩$_2$ **end**	$\max(M(s_1), M(s_2))$
| { ⟨x⟩ ⟨y⟩$_1$ ⋯ ⟨y⟩$_n$ }	$M_x(\text{size}_x(I_x(\{y_1, \ldots, y_n\})))$

Table 3.6: Memory consumption of kernel instructions.

program.

These two numbers should not be confused. The first is much more important. A program can allocate memory very slowly (e.g., 1 KB/s) and yet have a large active memory (e.g., 100 MB); e.g., a large in-memory database that handles only simple queries. The opposite is also possible. A program can consume memory at a high rate (e.g., 100 MB/s) and yet have a quite small active memory (e.g., 10 KB); e.g., a simulation algorithm running in the declarative model.[12]

Instantaneous active memory size

The active memory size can be calculated at any point during execution by following all the references from the semantic stack into the store and totaling the size of all the reachable variables and partial values. It is roughly equal to the size of all the data structures needed by the program during its execution.

Total memory consumption

The total memory consumption can be calculated with a technique similar to that used for execution time. Each kernel language operation has a well-defined memory consumption. Table 3.6 gives the memory consumption $M(s)$ for each kernel statement ⟨s⟩. Using this table, recurrence equations can be set up for the program, from which the total memory consumption of the program can be calculated as a function of the input size. To this number should be added the memory consumption of the semantic stack. For the instruction ⟨x⟩=⟨v⟩ there is a rare case in which memory consumption is less than memsize(v), namely when ⟨x⟩ is partly instantiated. In that case, only the memory of the new entities should be

12. Because of this behavior, the declarative model is not good for running simulations unless it has an excellent garbage collector!

counted. The function memsize(v) is defined as follows, according to the type and value of v:

- For an integer: 0 for small integers, otherwise proportional to integer size. Calculate the number of bits needed to represent the integer in 2's complement form. If this number is less than 28, then 0. Else divide by 32 and round up to the nearest integer.
- For a float: 2.
- For a list pair: 2.
- For a tuple or record: $1 + n$, where $n = \text{length}(\text{arity}(v))$.
- For a procedure value: $k + n$, where n is the number of external references of the procedure body and k is a constant that depends on the implementation.

All figures are in number of 32-bit memory words and are correct for Mozart 1.3.0. For nested values, take the sum of all the values. For records and procedure values there is an additional one-time cost. For each distinct record arity the additional cost is roughly proportional to n (because the arity is stored once in a symbol table). For each distinct procedure in the source code, the additional cost depends on the size of the compiled code, which is roughly proportional to the total number of statements and identifiers in the procedure body. In most cases, these one-time costs add a constant to the total memory consumption; for the calculation they can usually be ignored.

3.5.3 Amortized complexity

Sometimes we are not interested in the complexity of single operations, but rather in the total complexity of a sequence of operations. As long as the total complexity is reasonable, we might not care whether individual operations are sometimes more expensive. Section 3.4.5 gives an example with queues: as long as a sequence of n insert and delete operations has a total execution time that is $O(n)$, we might not care whether individual operations are always $O(1)$. They are allowed occasionally to be more expensive, as long as this does not happen too frequently. In general, if a sequence of n operations has a total execution time $O(f(n))$, then we say that it has an amortized complexity of $O(f(n)/n)$.

Amortized versus worst-case complexity

For many application domains, having a good amortized complexity is good enough. However, there are three application domains that need guarantees on the execution time of individual operations. They are hard real-time systems, parallel systems, and high-performance interactive systems.

A hard real-time system has to satisfy strict deadlines on the completion of calculations. Missing such a deadline can have dire consequences, including loss of life. Such systems exist, e.g., in pacemakers and train collision avoidance (see also section 4.6.1).

A parallel system executes several calculations simultaneously to achieve speedup of the whole computation. Often, the whole computation can only advance after all the simultaneous calculations complete. If one of these calculations occasionally takes much more time, then the whole computation slows down.

An interactive system, such as a computer game, should have a uniform reaction time. For example, if a multiuser action game sometimes delays its reaction to a player's input, then the player's satisfaction is much reduced.

The banker's method and the physicist's method

Calculating the amortized complexity is a little harder than calculating the worst-case complexity. (And it will get harder still when we introduce lazy execution in section 4.5.) There are basically two methods, called the banker's method and the physicist's method.

The banker's method counts credits, where a "credit" represents a unit of execution time or memory space. Each operation puts aside some credits. An expensive operation is allowed when enough credits have been put aside to cover its execution.

The physicist's method is based on finding a potential function. This is a kind of "height above sea level." Each operation changes the potential, i.e., it climbs or descends a bit. The cost of each operation is the change in potential, namely, how much it climbs or descends. The total complexity is a function of the difference between the initial and final potentials. As long as this difference remains small, large variations are allowed in between.

For more information on these methods and many examples of their use with declarative algorithms, we recommend the book by Okasaki [157].

3.5.4 Reflections on performance

Ever since the beginning of the computer era in the 1940s, both space and time have been becoming cheaper at an exponential rate (a constant factor improvement each year). They are currently very cheap, both in absolute terms and in perceived terms: a low-cost personal computer of the year 2003 typically has 512 MB of random-access memory and 80 GB of persistent storage on disk with a clock frequency of 2 GHz. This gives a sustained maximum performance of around one billion instructions per second, where each instruction can perform a full 64-bit operation, including floating point. It is significantly faster than a Cray-1 supercomputer, the world's fastest computer in 1975. A supercomputer is defined to be one of the fastest computers existing at a particular time. The first Cray-1 had a clock frequency of 80 MHz and could perform several 64-bit floating point operations per cycle [197]. At constant cost, personal computer performance is still improving at an exponential rate (doubling about every two years), and this is predicted to continue at least throughout the first decade of the 21st century. This follows from Moore's law.

Moore's law

Moore's law states that the circuit density of integrated circuits doubles approximately every 18 months. This was first observed by Gordon Moore around 1965 and has continued to hold until the present day. Experts believe this law may slow down but will continue to hold substantially for at least another two decades. A common misinterpretation of the original Moore's law is that performance doubles approximately every two years. This also seems to be substantially correct.

Moore's law looks only at a small time period compared to the time in which machine-based computation has been done. Since the 19th century, there have been at least five technologies used for computing, including mechanical, electromechanical, vacuum tubes, discrete transistors, and integrated circuits. Throughout this longer period, it can be seen that the growth in computational power has always been exponential. According to Raymond Kurzweil, who has studied this growth pattern, the next technology will be three-dimensional molecular computing [122].[13]

Because of this situation, performance is usually not a critical issue. If your problem is tractable, i.e., if there exists an efficient algorithm for it, then if you use good techniques for algorithm design, the actual time and space that the algorithm takes will almost always be acceptable. In other words, given a reasonable asymptotic complexity of a program, the constant factor is almost never critical. This is even true for most multimedia applications (which use video and audio) because of the excellent graphics libraries that exist.

Intractable problems

Not all problems are tractable, though. There are many problems that are computationally expensive, e.g., in the areas of combinatorial optimization, operational research, scientific computation and simulation, machine learning, speech and vision recognition, and computer graphics. Some of these problems are expensive simply because they have to do a lot of work. For example, games with realistic graphics, which by definition are always at the edge of what is possible. Other problems are expensive for more fundamental reasons. For example, NP-complete problems. These problems are in the class NP, i.e., it is easy to check a solution, if you are given a candidate.[14] But finding a solution may be much harder. A simple example is the circuit satisfiability problem. Given a combinational digital circuit that consists of `And`, `Or`, and `Not` gates, does there exist a set of input values that makes the output 1? This problem is NP-complete [47]. An NP-complete problem is a special kind of NP problem with the property that if you can solve one in polynomial time, then you can solve all in polynomial time. Many computer scientists have tried over several decades to find polynomial-time solutions to NP-complete problems,

13. Kurzweil claims that the growth rate is increasing and will lead to a "singularity" somewhere near the middle of the 21st century.
14. NP stands for "nondeterministic polynomial time."

and none have succeeded. Therefore, most computer scientists suspect that NP-complete problems cannot be solved in polynomial time. In this book, we will not talk any more about computationally expensive problems. Since our purpose is to show how to program, we limit ourselves to tractable problems.

Optimization

In some cases, the performance of a program can be insufficient, even if the problem is theoretically tractable. Then the program has to be rewritten to improve performance. Rewriting a program to improve some characteristic is called optimizing it, although it is never "optimal" in any mathematical sense. Usually, the program can easily be improved up to a point, after which diminishing returns set in and the program rapidly becomes more complex for ever smaller improvements. Optimization should therefore not be done unless necessary. Premature optimization is the bane of computing.

Optimization has a good side and a bad side. The good side is that the overall execution time of most applications is largely determined by a very small part of the program text. Therefore performance optimization, if necessary, can almost always be done by rewriting just this small part (sometimes a few lines suffice). The bad side is that it is usually not obvious, even to experienced programmers, where this part is a priori. Therefore, this part should be identified after the application is running and only if a performance problem is noticed. If no such problem exists, then no performance optimization should be done. The best technique to identify the "hot spots" is profiling, which instruments the application to measure its run-time characteristics.

Reducing a program's space use is easier than reducing its execution time. The overall space use of a program depends on the data representation chosen. If space is a critical issue, then a good technique is to use a compression algorithm on the data when it is not part of an immediate computation. This trades space for time.

3.6 Higher-order programming

Higher-order programming is the collection of programming techniques that become available when using procedure values in programs. Procedure values are also known as lexically scoped closures. The term higher order comes from the concept of *order* of a procedure. A procedure all of whose arguments are not procedures is of first order. A language that allows only this kind of procedure is called a first-order language. A procedure that has at least one first-order procedure in an argument is of second order. And so forth: a procedure is of order $n + 1$ if it has at least one argument of order n and none of higher order. Higher-order programming then means simply that procedures can be of any order. A language that allows this is called a higher-order language.

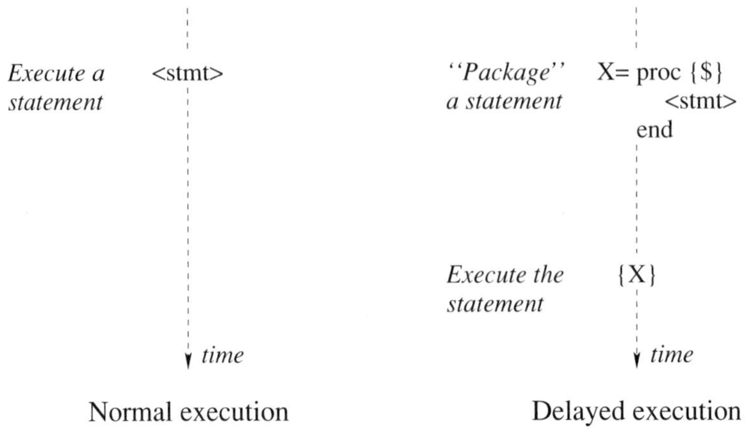

Figure 3.21: Delayed execution of a procedure value.

3.6.1 Basic operations

There are four basic operations that underlie all the techniques of higher-order programming:

1. *Procedural abstraction*: the ability to convert any statement into a procedure value.
2. *Genericity*: the ability to pass procedure values as arguments to a procedure call.
3. *Instantiation*: the ability to return procedure values as results from a procedure call.
4. *Embedding*: the ability to put procedure values in data structures.

Let us first examine each of these operations in turn. Subsequently, we will see more sophisticated techniques, such as loop abstractions, that use these basic operations.

Procedural abstraction

We have already introduced procedural abstraction. Let us briefly recall the basic idea. Any statement ⟨stmt⟩ can be "packaged" into a procedure by writing it as **proc** {$} ⟨stmt⟩ **end**. This does not execute the statement, but instead creates a procedure value (a closure). Because the procedure value contains a contextual environment, executing it gives exactly the same result as executing ⟨stmt⟩. The decision whether or not to execute the statement is not made where the statement is defined, but somewhere else in the program. Figure 3.21 shows the two possibilities: either executing ⟨stmt⟩ immediately or with a delay.

Procedure values allow more than just delaying execution of a statement. They can have arguments, which allows some of their behavior to be influenced by the call.

As we will see throughout the book, procedural abstraction is enormously powerful. It underlies higher-order programming and object-oriented programming, and is the principle tool for building abstractions. Let us give another example of procedural abstraction. Consider the statement:

```
local A=1.0 B=3.0 C=2.0 D RealSol X1 X2 in
   D=B*B-4.0*A*C
   if D>=0.0 then
       RealSol=true
       X1=(~B+{Sqrt D})/(2.0*A)
       X2=(~B-{Sqrt D})/(2.0*A)
   else
       RealSol=false
       X1=~B/(2.0*A)
       X2={Sqrt ~D}/(2.0*A)
   end
   {Browse RealSol#X1#X2}
end
```

This calculates the solutions of the quadratic equation $x^2 + 3x + 2 = 0$. It uses the quadratic formula $(-b \pm \sqrt{b^2 - 4ac})/2a$, which gives the two solutions of the equation $ax^2 + bx + c = 0$. The value $d = b^2 - 4ac$ is called the discriminant. If it is positive, then there are two different real solutions. If it is zero, then there are two identical real solutions. Otherwise, the two solutions are conjugate complex numbers. The above statement can be converted into a procedure by using it as the body of a procedure definition and passing the free variables as arguments:

```
proc {QuadraticEquation A B C ?RealSol ?X1 ?X2}
   D=B*B-4.0*A*C
in
   if D>=0.0 then
       RealSol=true
       X1=(~B+{Sqrt D})/(2.0*A)
       X2=(~B-{Sqrt D})/(2.0*A)
   else
       RealSol=false
       X1=~B/(2.0*A)
       X2={Sqrt ~D}/(2.0*A)
   end
end
```

This procedure will solve any quadratic equation. Just call it with the equation's coefficients as arguments:

```
declare RS X1 X2 in
{QuadraticEquation 1.0 3.0 2.0 RS X1 X2}
{Browse RS#X1#X2}
```

Restricted forms of procedural abstraction

Many older imperative languages have a restricted form of procedural abstraction. To understand this, let us look at Pascal and C [106, 112]. In C, all procedure definitions are global (they cannot be nested). This means that only one procedure value can exist corresponding to each procedure definition. In Pascal, procedure definitions can be nested, but procedure values can only be used in the same scope as the procedure definition, and then only while the program is executing in that scope. These restrictions make it impossible in general to "package up" a statement and execute it somewhere else.

This means that many higher-order programming techniques are impossible. For example, it is impossible to program new control abstractions. Instead, Pascal and C each provide a predefined set of control abstractions (such as loops, conditionals, and exceptions). A few higher-order techniques are still possible. For example, the quadratic equation example works because it has no external references: it can be defined as a global procedure in Pascal and C. Generic operations also often work for the same reason (see below).

The restrictions of Pascal and C are a consequence of the way these languages do memory management. In both languages, the implementation puts part of the store on the semantic stack. This part of the store is usually called local variables. Allocation is done using a stack discipline. For example, some local variables are allocated at each procedure entry and deallocated at the corresponding exit. This is a form of automatic memory management that is much simpler to implement than garbage collection. Unfortunately, it is easy to create dangling references. It is extremely difficult to debug a large program that occasionally behaves incorrectly because of a dangling reference.

Now we can explain the restrictions. In both Pascal and C, creating a procedure value is restricted so that the contextual environment never has any dangling references. There are some language-specific techniques that can be used to lighten this restriction. For example, in object-oriented languages such as C++ or Java it is possible for objects to play the role of procedure values. This technique is explained in chapter 7.

Genericity

We have already seen an example of higher-order programming in an earlier section. It was introduced so gently that perhaps you have not noticed that it is doing higher-order programming. It is the control abstraction `Iterate` of section 3.2.4, which uses two procedure arguments, `Transform` and `IsDone`.

To make a function generic is to let any specific entity (i.e., any operation or value) in the function body become an argument of the function. We say the entity is abstracted out of the function body. The specific entity is given when the function is called. Each time the function is called another entity can be given.

Let us look at a second example of a generic function. Consider the function `SumList`:

```
fun {SumList L}
   case L
   of nil then 0
   [] X|L1 then X+{SumList L1}
   end
end
```

This function has two specific entities: the number zero (`0`) and the operation plus (+). The zero is a neutral element for the plus operation. These two entities can be abstracted out. Any neutral element and any operation are possible. We give them as parameters. This gives the following generic function:

```
fun {FoldR L F U}
   case L
   of nil then U
   [] X|L1 then {F X {FoldR L1 F U}}
   end
end
```

This function is usually called `FoldR` because it associates to the right. We can define `SumList` as a special case of `FoldR`:

```
fun {SumList L}
   {FoldR L fun {$ X Y} X+Y end 0}
end
```

We can use `FoldR` to define other functions on lists. Here is function that calculates the product:

```
fun {ProductList L}
   {FoldR L fun {$ X Y} X*Y end 1}
end
```

Here is another that returns **`true`** if there is at least one **`true`** in the list:

```
fun {Some L}
   {FoldR L fun {$ X Y} X orelse Y end false}
end
```

`FoldR` is an example of a loop abstraction. Section 3.6.2 looks at other kinds of loop abstraction.

An example: mergesort made generic

The mergesort algorithm we saw in section 3.4.2 is hardwired to use the `'<'` comparison function. Let us make mergesort generic by passing the comparison function as an argument. We change the `Merge` function to reference the function argument `F` and the `MergeSort` function to reference the new `Merge`:

```
fun {GenericMergeSort F Xs}
   fun {Merge Xs Ys}
      case Xs # Ys
      of nil # Ys then Ys
      [] Xs # nil then Xs
      [] (X|Xr) # (Y|Yr) then
         if {F X Y} then X|{Merge Xr Ys}
         else Y|{Merge Xs Yr} end
      end
   end
   fun {MergeSort Xs}
      case Xs
      of nil then nil
      [] [X] then [X]
      else Ys Zs in
         {Split Xs Ys Zs}
         {Merge {MergeSort Ys} {MergeSort Zs}}
      end
   end
in
   {MergeSort Xs}
end
```

This uses the old definition of `Split`. We put the definitions of `Merge` and `MergeSort` inside the new function `GenericMergeSort`. This avoids passing the function `F` as an argument to `Merge` and `MergeSort`. Instead, the two procedures are defined once per call of `GenericMergeSort`. We can define the original mergesort in terms of `GenericMergeSort`:

```
fun {MergeSort Xs}
   {GenericMergeSort fun {$ A B} A<B end Xs}
end
```

Instead of `fun {$ A B} A<B end`, we could have written `Number.´<´` because the comparison `´<´` is part of the module `Number`.

Instantiation

An example of instantiation is a function `MakeSort` that returns a sorting function. Functions like `MakeSort` are sometimes called "factories" or "generators." `MakeSort` takes a boolean comparison function `F` and returns a sorting routine that uses `F` as comparison function. Let us see how to build `MakeSort` using a generic sorting routine `Sort`. Assume that `Sort` takes two inputs, a list `L` and a boolean function `F`, and returns a sorted list. Now we can define `MakeSort`:

```
fun {MakeSort F}
   fun {$ L}
      {Sort L F}
   end
end
```

We can see `MakeSort` as specifying a set of possible sorting routines. Calling `MakeSort` instantiates the specification. It returns an element of the set, which

```
proc {For A B S P}
   proc {LoopUp C}
      if C=<B then {P C} {LoopUp C+S} end
   end
   proc {LoopDown C}
      if C>=B then {P C} {LoopDown C+S} end
   end
in
   if S>0 then {LoopUp A} end
   if S<0 then {LoopDown A} end
end
```

Figure 3.22: Defining an integer loop.

```
proc {ForAll L P}
   case L
   of nil then skip
   [] X|L2 then
      {P X}
      {ForAll L2 P}
   end
end
```

Figure 3.23: Defining a list loop.

we call an instance of the specification.

Embedding

Procedure values can be put in data structures. This has many uses:

- *Explicit lazy evaluation*, also called *delayed evaluation*. The idea is not to build a complete data structure in one go, but to build it on demand. Build only a small part of the data structure with procedures at the extremities that can be called to build more. For example, the consumer of a data structure is given a pair: part of the data structure and a new function to calculate another pair. This means the consumer can control explicitly how much of the data structure is evaluated.
- *Modules*. A module is a record that groups together a set of related operations.
- *Software components*. A software component is a generic procedure that takes a set of modules as input arguments and returns a new module. It can be seen as specifying a module in terms of the modules it needs (see section 6.7).

```
Integer loop                      List loop
{For A B S P}                     {ForAll L P}
   {P A      }                       {P X1}
   {P A+S    }                       {P X2}
   {P A+2*S}                         {P X3}
      .                                 .
      .                                 .
      .                                 .
   {P A+n*S}                         {P Xn}
(if S>0: as long as A+n*S=<B)     (where L=[X1 X2 ... Xn])
(if S<0: as long as A+n*S>=B)
```

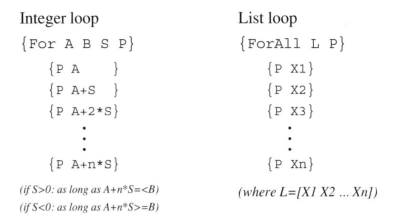

Figure 3.24: Simple loops over integers and lists.

3.6.2 Loop abstractions

As the examples in the previous sections show, loops in the declarative model tend to be verbose because they need explicit recursive calls. Loops can be made more concise by defining them as control abstractions. There are many different kinds of loops that we can define. In this section, we first define simple for-loops over integers and lists and then we add accumulators to them to make them more useful.

Integer loop

Let us define an integer loop, i.e., a loop that repeats an operation with a sequence of integers. The procedure `{For A B S P}` calls `{P I}` for integers `I` that start with `A` and continue to `B`, in steps of `S`. For example, executing `{For 1 10 1 Browse}` displays the integers 1, 2, ..., 10. Executing `{For 10 1 ~2 Browse}` displays 10, 8, 6, 4, 2. The `For` loop is defined in figure 3.22. This definition works for both positive and negative steps. It uses `LoopUp` for positive `S` and `LoopDown` for negative `S`. Because of lexical scoping, `LoopUp` and `LoopDown` each needs only one argument. They see `B`, `S`, and `P` as external references.

List loop

Let us define a list loop, i.e., a loop that repeats an operation for all elements of a list. The procedure `{ForAll L P}` calls `{P X}` for all elements `X` of the list `L`. For example, `{ForAll [a b c] Browse}` displays `a`, `b`, `c`. The `ForAll` loop is defined in figure 3.23. Figure 3.24 compares `For` and `ForAll` in a graphic way.

```
proc {ForAcc A B S P In ?Out}
   proc {LoopUp C In ?Out}
   Mid in
      if C=<B then {P In C Mid} {LoopUp C+S Mid Out}
      else In=Out end
   end
   proc {LoopDown C In ?Out}
   Mid in
      if C>=B then {P In C Mid} {LoopDown C+S Mid Out}
      else In=Out end
   end
in
   if S>0 then {LoopUp A In Out} end
   if S<0 then {LoopDown A In Out} end
end

proc {ForAllAcc L P In ?Out}
   case L
   of nil then In=Out
   [] X|L2 then Mid in
      {P In X Mid}
      {ForAllAcc L2 P Mid Out}
   end
end
```

Figure 3.25: Defining accumulator loops.

Accumulator loops

The `For` and `ForAll` loops just repeat an action on different arguments, but they do not calculate any result. This makes them quite useless in the declarative model. They will show their worth only in the stateful model of chapter 6. To be useful in the declarative model, the loops can be extended with an accumulator. In this way, they can calculate a result. Figure 3.25 defines `ForAcc` and `ForAllAcc`, which extend `For` and `ForAll` with an accumulator.[15] `ForAcc` and `ForAllAcc` are the workhorses of the declarative model. They are both defined with a variable `Mid` that is used to pass the current state of the accumulator to the rest of the loop. Figure 3.26 compares `ForAcc` and `ForAllAcc` in a graphic way.

Folding a list

There is another way to look at accumulator loops over lists. They can be seen as a "folding" operation on a list, where folding means to insert an infix operator

15. In the Mozart system, `ForAcc` and `ForAllAcc` are called `ForThread` and `FoldL`, respectively.

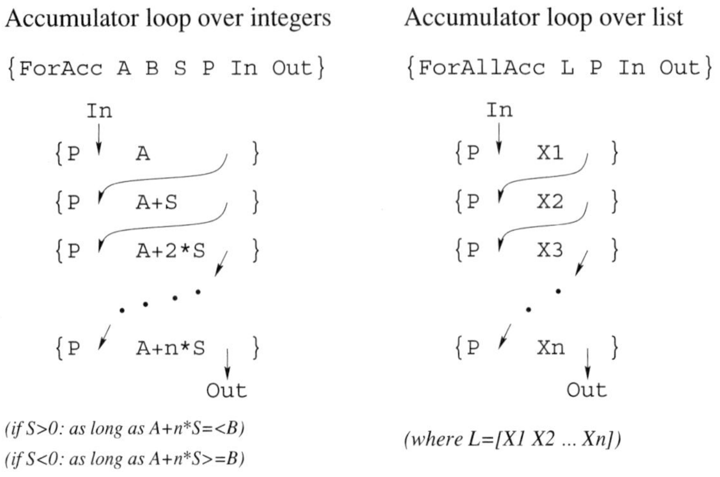

Figure 3.26: Accumulator loops over integers and lists.

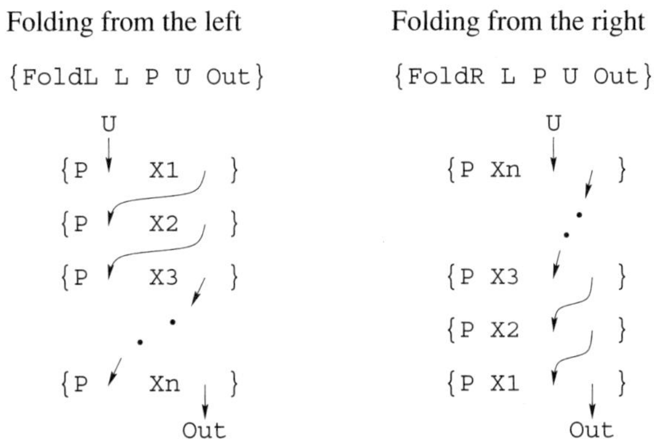

Figure 3.27: Folding a list.

between elements of the list. Consider the list $l = [x_1\ x_2\ x_3\ \cdots\ x_n]$. Then folding l with the infix operator f gives

$$x_1\ f\ x_2\ f\ x_3\ f\ \cdots\ f\ x_n$$

To calculate this expression unambiguously we have to add parentheses. There are two possibilities. We can do the leftmost operations first (associate to the left):

$$((\cdots((x_1\ f\ x_2)\ f\ x_3)\ f\ \cdots\ x_{n-1})\ f\ x_n)$$

or do the rightmost operations first (associate to the right):

$(x_1\ f\ (x_2\ f\ (x_3\ f\ \cdots\ (x_{n-1}\ f\ x_n)\cdots)))$

As a finishing touch, we slightly modify these expressions so that each application of f involves just one new element of l. This makes them easier to calculate and reason with. To do this, we add a neutral element u. This gives the following two expressions:

$((\cdots(((u\ f\ x_1)\ f\ x_2)\ f\ x_3)\ f\ \cdots\ x_{n-1})\ f\ x_n)$

$(x_1\ f\ (x_2\ f\ (x_3\ f\ \cdots\ (x_{n-1}\ f\ (x_n\ f\ u))\cdots)))$

To calculate these expressions we define the two functions `{FoldL L F U}` and `{FoldR L F U}`. The function `{FoldL L F U}` does the following:

```
{F ... {F {F {F U X1} X2} X3} ... Xn}
```

The function `{FoldR L F U}` does the following:

```
{F X1 {F X2 {F X3 ... {F Xn U} ...}}}
```

Figure 3.27 shows `FoldL` and `FoldR` in a graphic way. We can relate `FoldL` and `FoldR` to the accumulator loops we saw before. Comparing figure 3.26 and figure 3.27, we can see that `FoldL` is just another name for `ForAllAcc`.

Iterative definitions of folding

Figure 3.25 defines `ForAllAcc` iteratively, and therefore also `FoldL`. Here is the same definition in functional notation:

```
fun {FoldL L F U}
   case L
   of nil then U
   [] X|L2 then
      {FoldL L2 F {F U X}}
   end
end
```

This is more concise than the procedural definition but it hides the accumulator, which obscures its relationship with the other kinds of loops. Conciseness is not always a good thing.

What about `FoldR`? The discussion on genericity in section 3.6.1 gives a recursive definition, not an iterative one. At first glance, it does not seem so easy to define `FoldR` iteratively. Can you give an iterative definition of `FoldR`? The way to do it is to define an intermediate state and a state transformation function. Look at the expression given above: what is the intermediate state? How do you get to the next state? Before peeking at the answer, we suggest you put down the book and try to define an iterative `FoldR`. Here is one possible definition:

```
fun {FoldR L F U}
   fun {Loop L U}
      case L
      of nil then U
      [] X|L2 then
         {Loop L2 {F X U}}
      end
   end
in
   {Loop {Reverse L} U}
end
```

Since `FoldR` starts by calculating with `Xn`, the last element of `L`, the idea is to iterate over the reverse of `L`. We have seen before how to define an iterative reverse.

3.6.3 Linguistic support for loops

Because loops are so useful, they are a perfect candidate for a linguistic abstraction. This section defines the declarative **for** loop, which is one way to do this. The **for** loop is defined as part of the Mozart system [55]. The **for** loop is closely related to the loop abstractions of the previous section. Using **for** loops is often easier than using loop abstractions. When writing loops we recommend trying **for** loops first.

Iterating over integers

A common operation is iterating for successive integers from a lower bound `I` to a higher bound `J`. Without loop syntax, the standard declarative way to do this uses the `{For A B S P}` abstraction:

```
{For A B S proc {$ I} ⟨stmt⟩ end}
```

This is equivalent to the following **for** loop:

```
for I in A..B do ⟨stmt⟩ end
```

when the step `S` is 1, or:

```
for I in A..B;S do ⟨stmt⟩ end
```

when `S` is different from 1. The **for** loop declares the loop counter `I`, which is a variable whose scope extends over the loop body ⟨stmt⟩.

Declarative versus imperative loops

There is a fundamental difference between a declarative loop and an imperative loop, i.e., a loop in an imperative language such as C or Java. In the latter, the loop counter is an assignable variable which is assigned a different value on each iteration. The declarative loop is quite different: on each iteration it declares a new variable. All these variables are referred to by the same identifier. There is no destructive assignment at all. This difference can have major consequences. For example, the iterations of a declarative loop are completely independent of each other. Therefore, it is possible to run them concurrently without changing the loop's final result. For example:

```
for I in A..B do thread ⟨stmt⟩ end end
```

runs all iterations concurrently but each of them still accesses the right value of `I`. Putting ⟨stmt⟩ inside the statement **thread ... end** runs it as an independent activity. This is an example of declarative concurrency, which is the subject of chapter 4. Doing this in an imperative loop would raise havoc since each iteration would no longer be sure it accesses the right value of `I`. The increments of the loop counter would no longer be synchronized with the iterations.

Iterating over lists

The **for** loop can be extended to iterate over lists as well as over integer intervals. For example, the call

```
{ForAll L proc {$ X} ⟨stmt⟩ end end}
```

is equivalent to

```
for X in L do ⟨stmt⟩ end
```

Just as with `ForAll`, the list can be a stream of elements.

Patterns

The **for** loop can be extended to contain patterns that implicitly declare variables. For example, if the elements of `L` are triplets of the form `obj(name:N price:P coordinates:C)`, then we can loop over them as follows:

```
for obj(name:N price:P coordinates:C) in L do
   if P<1000 then {Browse N} end
end
```

This declares and binds the new variables `N`, `P`, and `C` for each iteration. Their scope ranges over the loop body.

Collecting results

A useful extension of the **for** loop is to collect results. For example, let us make a list of all integers from 1 to 1000 that are not multiples of either 2 or 3:

```
L=for I in 1..1000 collect:C do
     if I mod 2 \= 0 andthen I mod 3 \= 0 then {C I} end
  end
```

The **for** loop is an expression that returns a list. The "`collect:C`" declaration defines a collection procedure `C` that can be used anywhere in the loop body. The collection procedure uses an accumulator to collect the elements. The above example is equivalent to

```
{ForAcc 1 1000 1
   proc {$ ?L1 I L2}
      if I mod 2 \= 0 andthen I mod 3 \= 0 then L1=I|L2
      else L1=L2 end
   end
   L nil}
```

In general, the **for** loop is more expressive than this, since the collection procedure can be called deep inside nested loops and other procedures without having to thread the accumulator explicitly. Here is an example with two nested loops:

```
L=for I in 1..1000 collect:C do
     if I mod 2 \= 0 andthen I mod 3 \= 0 then
        for J in 2..10 do
           if I mod J == 0 then {C I#J} end
        end
     end
  end
```

How does the **for** loop achieve this without threading the accumulator? It uses explicit state, as we will see in chapter 6.

Other useful extensions

The above examples give some of the most-used looping idioms in a declarative loop syntax. Many more looping idioms are possible. For example: immediately exiting the loop (`break`), immediately exiting and returning an explicit result (`return`), immediately continuing with the next iteration (`continue`), multiple iterators that advance in lockstep, and other collection procedures (e.g., `append` and `prepend` for lists and `sum` and `maximize` for integers) [55]. For other example designs of declarative loops we recommend studying the loop macro of Common Lisp [200] and the state threads package of SICStus Prolog [108].

3.6.4 Data-driven techniques

A common task is to do some operation over a big data structure, traversing the data structure and calculating some other data structure based on this traversal. This idea is used most often with lists and trees.

3.6.4.1 List-based techniques

Higher-order programming is often used together with lists. Some of the loop abstractions can be seen in this way, e.g., `FoldL` and `FoldR`. Let us look at some other list-based techniques.

A common list operation is `Map`, which calculates a new list from an old list by applying a function to each element. For example, `{Map [1 2 3] fun {$ I} I*I`

end} returns [1 4 9]. It is defined as follows:

```
fun {Map Xs F}
   case Xs
   of nil then nil
   [] X|Xr then {F X}|{Map Xr F}
   end
end
```

Its type is ⟨**fun** {$ ⟨List T⟩ ⟨**fun** {$ T}: U⟩}: ⟨List U⟩⟩. Map can be defined with FoldR. The output list is constructed using FoldR's accumulator:

```
fun {Map Xs F}
   {FoldR Xs fun {$ I A} {F I}|A end nil}
end
```

What would happen if we would use FoldL instead of FoldR? Another common list operation is Filter, which applies a boolean function to each list element and outputs the list of all elements that give **true**. For example, {Filter [1 2 3 4] **fun** {$ A B} A<3 **end**} returns [1 2]. It is defined as follows:

```
fun {Filter Xs F}
   case Xs
   of nil then nil
   [] X|Xr andthen {F X} then X|{Filter Xr F}
   [] X|Xr then {Filter Xr F}
   end
end
```

Its type is ⟨**fun** {$ ⟨List T⟩ ⟨**fun** {$ T T}: ⟨bool⟩⟩}: ⟨List T⟩⟩. Filter can also be defined with FoldR:

```
fun {Filter Xs F}
   {FoldR Xs fun {$ I A} if {F I} then I|A else A end end nil}
end
```

It seems that FoldR is a surprisingly versatile function. This should not be a surprise, since FoldR is simply a for-loop with an accumulator! FoldR itself can be implemented in terms of the generic iterator Iterate of section 3.2:

```
fun {FoldR Xs F U}
   {Iterate
     {Reverse Xs}#U
     fun {$ S} Xr#A=S in Xr==nil end
     fun {$ S} Xr#A=S in Xr.2#{F Xr.1 A} end}.2
end
```

Since Iterate is a while-loop with accumulator, it is the most versatile loop abstraction of them all. All other loop abstractions can be programmed in terms of Iterate. For example, to program FoldR we only have to encode the state in the right way with the right termination function. Here we encode the state as a pair Xr#A, where Xr is the not-yet-used part of the input list and A is the accumulated result of the FoldR. Watch out for the details: the initial Reverse call and the .2 at the end to get the final accumulated result.

3.6.4.2 Tree-based techniques

As we saw in section 3.4.6 and elsewhere, a common operation on a tree is to visit all its nodes in some particular order and do certain operations while visiting the nodes. For example, the code generator mentioned in section 3.4.8 has to traverse the nodes of the abstract syntax tree to generate machine code. The tree-drawing program of section 3.4.7, after it calculates the node's positions, has to traverse the nodes in order to draw them. Higher-order techniques can be used to help in these traversals.

Let us consider n-ary trees, which are more general than the binary trees we looked at so far. An n-ary tree can be defined as follows:

⟨Tree T⟩ ::= `tree(node:`T `sons:`⟨List ⟨Tree T⟩⟩`)`

In this tree, each node can have any number of sons. Depth-first traversal of this tree is just as simple as for binary trees:

```
proc {DFS Tree}
   case Tree of tree(node:N sons:Sons ...) then
      {Browse N}
      for T in Sons do {DFS T} end
   end
end
```

We can "decorate" this routine to do something at each node it visits. For example, let us call `{P T}` at each node `T`. This gives the following generic procedure:

```
proc {VisitNodes Tree P}
   case Tree of tree(sons:Sons ...) then
      {P Tree}
      for T in Sons do {VisitNodes T P} end
   end
end
```

A slightly more involved traversal is to call `{P Tree T}` for each father-son link between a father node `Tree` and one of its sons `T`:

```
proc {VisitLinks Tree P}
   case Tree of tree(sons:Sons ...) then
      for T in Sons do {P Tree T} {VisitLinks T P} end
   end
end
```

These two generic procedures were used to draw the trees of section 3.4.7 after the node positions were calculated. `VisitLinks` drew the lines between nodes and `VisitNodes` drew the nodes themselves.

Following the development of section 3.4.6, we extend these traversals with an accumulator. There are as many ways to accumulate as there are possible traversals. Accumulation techniques can be top-down (the result is calculated by propagating from a father to its sons), bottom-up (from the sons to the father), or use some other order (e.g., across the breadth of the tree, for a breadth-first traversal). Comparing with lists, top-down is like `FoldL` and bottom-up is like `FoldR`. Let us do a bottom-up accumulation. We first calculate a folded value for each node. Then the folded value for a father is a function of the father's node and the values for the sons. There are two functions: LF to fold together all sons of a given father, and TF to fold their result together with the father. This gives the following generic function with accumulator:

```
local
   fun {FoldTreeR Sons TF LF U}
      case Sons
      of nil then U
      [] S|Sons2 then
         {LF {FoldTree S TF LF U} {FoldTreeR Sons2 TF LF U}}
      end
   end
in
   fun {FoldTree Tree TF LF U}
      case Tree of tree(node:N sons:Sons ...) then
         {TF N {FoldTreeR Sons TF LF U}}
      end
   end
end
```

Here is an example call:

```
fun {Add A B} A+B end
T=tree(node:1
       sons:[tree(node:2 sons:nil)
             tree(node:3 sons:[tree(node:4 sons:nil)])])
{Browse {FoldTree T Add Add 0}}
```

This displays 10, the sum of all the node values.

3.6.5 Explicit lazy evaluation

Modern functional languages have a built-in execution strategy called lazy evaluation. Here we show how to program lazy evaluation explicitly with higher-order programming. Section 4.5 shows how to make lazy evaluation implicit, i.e., where the mechanics of triggering the execution are handled by the system. As we shall see in chapter 4, implicit lazy evaluation is closely connected to concurrency.

In lazy evaluation, a data structure (such as a list) is constructed incrementally. The consumer of the list structure asks for new list elements when they are needed. This is an example of demand-driven execution. It is very different from the usual, supply-driven evaluation, where the list is completely calculated independent of whether the elements are needed or not.

To implement lazy evaluation, the consumer needs to ask for new elements. One technique for doing this is called a programmed trigger. There are two natural ways to express programmed triggers in the declarative model: as a dataflow variable or with higher-order programming. Section 4.3.3 explains how with a dataflow variable. Here we explain how with higher-order programming. The consumer has a function that it calls when it needs a new list element. The function call returns a pair: the list element and a new function. The new function is the new trigger: calling it returns the next data item and another new function. And so forth.

3.6.6 Currying

Currying is a technique that can simplify programs that heavily use higher-order programming. The idea is to write functions of n arguments as n nested functions of one argument. For example, the maximum function:

```
fun {Max X Y}
   if X>=Y then X else Y end
end
```

is rewritten as follows:

```
fun {Max X}
   fun {$ Y}
      if X>=Y then X else Y end
   end
end
```

This keeps the same function body. It is called as `{{Max 10} 20}`, giving `20`. The advantage of using currying is that the intermediate functions can be useful in themselves. For example, the function `{Max 10}` returns a result that is never less than `10`. It is called a partially applied function. We can give it the name `LowerBound10`:

```
LowerBound10={Max 10}
```

In many functional programming languages, in particular, Standard ML and Haskell, all functions are implicitly curried. To use currying to maximum advantage, these languages give it a simple syntax and an efficient implementation. They define the syntax so that curried functions can be defined without nesting any keywords and called without parentheses. If the function call `max 10 20` is possible, then `max 10` is also possible. The implementation makes currying as cheap as possible. It costs nothing when not used and the construction of partially applied functions is avoided whenever possible.

The declarative computation model of this chapter does not have any special support for currying. Neither does the Mozart system have any syntactic or implementation support for it. Most uses of currying in Mozart are simple ones. However, intensive use of higher-order programming as is done in functional languages may justify currying support for them. In Mozart, the partially applied functions have to be defined explicitly. For example, the `max 10` function can be defined as

```
fun {LowerBound10 Y}
   {Max 10 Y}
end
```

The original function definition does not change, which is efficient in the declarative model. Only the partially applied functions themselves become more expensive.

3.7 Abstract data types

A data type, or simply type, is a set of values together with a set of operations on these values. The declarative model comes with a predefined set of types, called the basic types (see section 2.3). In addition to these, the user is free to define new types. We say a type is abstract if it is completely defined by its set of operations, regardless of the implementation. The term "abstract data type" is abbreviated as ADT. Using an ADT means that it is possible to change the implementation of the type without changing its use. Let us investigate how the user can define new ADTs.

3.7.1 A declarative stack

To start this section, let us give a simple example of an abstract data type, a stack ⟨Stack T⟩ whose elements are of type T. Assume the stack has four operations, with the following types:

⟨**fun** {NewStack}: ⟨Stack T⟩⟩
⟨**fun** {Push ⟨Stack T⟩ T}: ⟨Stack T⟩⟩
⟨**fun** {Pop ⟨Stack T⟩ T}: ⟨Stack T⟩⟩
⟨**fun** {IsEmpty ⟨Stack T⟩}: ⟨Bool⟩⟩

This set of operations and their types defines the interface of the ADT. These operations satisfy certain laws:

- {IsEmpty {NewStack}}=**true**. A new stack is always empty.
- For any E and S0, S1={Push S0 E} and S0={Pop S1 E} hold. Pushing an element and then popping gives the same element back.
- {Pop {EmptyStack}} raises an error. No elements can be popped off an empty stack.

These laws are independent of any particular implementation, i.e., all implementations have to satisfy these laws. Here is an implementation of the stack that satisfies the laws:

```
fun {NewStack} nil end
fun {Push S E} E|S end
fun {Pop S E} case S of X|S1 then E=X S1 end end
fun {IsEmpty S} S==nil end
```

Here is another implementation that satisfies the laws:

```
fun {NewStack} stackEmpty end
fun {Push S E} stack(E S) end
fun {Pop S E} case S of stack(X S1) then E=X S1 end end
fun {IsEmpty S} S==stackEmpty end
```

A program that uses the stack will work with either implementation. This is what we mean by saying that the stack is abstract.

A functional programming look

Attentive readers will notice an unusual aspect of these two definitions: `Pop` is written using a functional syntax, but one of its arguments is an output! We could have written `Pop` as follows:

```
fun {Pop S} case S of X|S1 then X#S1 end end
```

which returns the two outputs as a pair, but we chose not to. Writing `{Pop S E}` is an example of programming with a functional look, which uses functional syntax for operations that are not necessarily mathematical functions. We consider that this is justified for programs that have a clear directionality in the flow of data. It can be interesting to highlight this directionality even if the program is not functional. In some cases this can make the program more concise and more readable. The functional look should be used sparingly, though, and only in cases where it is clear that the operation is not a mathematical function. We will use the functional look occasionally throughout the book, when we judge it appropriate.

For the stack, the functional look lets us highlight the symmetry between `Push` and `Pop`. It makes it clear syntactically that both operations take a stack and return a stack. Then, e.g., the output of `Pop` can be immediately passed as input to a `Push`, without needing an intermediate **`case`** statement.

3.7.2 A declarative dictionary

Let us give another example, an extremely useful ADT called a dictionary. A dictionary is a finite mapping from a set of simple constants to a set of language entities. Each constant maps to one language entity. The constants are called keys because they unlock the path to the entity, in some intuitive sense. We will use atoms or integers as constants. We would like to be able to create the mapping dynamically, i.e., by adding new keys during the execution. This gives the following set of basic functions on the new type ⟨Dict⟩:

- ⟨**fun** `{NewDictionary}`: ⟨Dict⟩⟩ returns a new empty dictionary.
- ⟨**fun** `{Put` ⟨Dict⟩ ⟨Feature⟩ ⟨Value⟩`}`: ⟨Dict⟩⟩ takes a dictionary and returns a new dictionary that adds the mapping ⟨Feature⟩→⟨Value⟩. If ⟨Feature⟩ already exists, then the new dictionary replaces it with ⟨Value⟩.
- ⟨**fun** `{Get` ⟨Dict⟩ ⟨Feature⟩`}`: ⟨Value⟩⟩ returns the value corresponding to ⟨Feature⟩. If there is none, an exception is raised.
- ⟨**fun** `{Domain` ⟨Dict⟩`}`: ⟨List ⟨Feature⟩⟩⟩ returns a list of the keys in ⟨Dict⟩.

For this example we define the ⟨Feature⟩ type as ⟨Atom⟩ | ⟨Int⟩.

```
fun {NewDictionary} nil end
fun {Put Ds Key Value}
   case Ds
   of nil then [Key#Value]
   [] (K#V)|Dr andthen K==Key then
      (Key#Value) | Dr
   [] (K#V)|Dr andthen K>Key then
      (Key#Value)|(K#V)|Dr
   [] (K#V)|Dr andthen K<Key then
      (K#V)|{Put Dr Key Value}
   end
end
fun {CondGet Ds Key Default}
   case Ds
   of nil then Default
   [] (K#V)|Dr andthen K==Key then
      V
   [] (K#V)|Dr andthen K>Key then
      Default
   [] (K#V)|Dr andthen K<Key then
      {CondGet Dr Key Default}
   end
end
fun {Domain Ds}
   {Map Ds fun {$ K#_} K end}
end
```

Figure 3.28: Declarative dictionary (with linear list).

List-based implementation

Figure 3.28 shows an implementation in which the dictionary is represented as a list of pairs `Key#Value` that are sorted on the key. Instead of `Get`, we define a slightly more general access operation, `CondGet`:

- ⟨**fun** {`CondGet` ⟨Dict⟩ ⟨Feature⟩ ⟨Value⟩$_1$}: ⟨Value⟩$_2$⟩ returns the value corresponding to ⟨Feature⟩. If ⟨Feature⟩ is not present, then it returns ⟨Value⟩$_1$.

`CondGet` is almost as easy to implement as `Get` and is very useful, as we will see in the next example.

This implementation is extremely slow for large dictionaries. Given a uniform distribution of keys, `Put` needs on average to look at half the list. `CondGet` needs on average to look at half the list, whether the element is present or not. We see that the number of operations is $O(n)$ for dictionaries with n keys. We say that the implementation does a linear search.

```
fun {NewDictionary} leaf end
fun {Put Ds Key Value}
   % ... similar to Insert
end
fun {CondGet Ds Key Default}
   % ... similar to Lookup
end
fun {Domain Ds}
   proc {DomainD Ds ?S1 Sn}
      case Ds
      of leaf then
         S1=Sn
      [] tree(K _ L R) then S2 S3 in
         {DomainD L S1 S2}
         S2=K|S3
         {DomainD R S3 Sn}
      end
   end D
in
   {DomainD Ds D nil} D
end
```

Figure 3.29: Declarative dictionary (with ordered binary tree).

Tree-based implementation

A more efficient implementation of dictionaries is possible by using an ordered binary tree, as defined in section 3.4.6. `Put` is simply `Insert` and `CondGet` is very similar to `Lookup`. This gives the definitions of figure 3.29. In this implementation, the `Put` and `CondGet` operations take $O(\log n)$ time and space for a tree with n nodes, given that the tree is "reasonably balanced." That is, for each node, the sizes of the left and right subtrees should not be "too different."

State-based implementation

We can do even better than the tree-based implementation by leaving the declarative model behind and using explicit state (see section 6.5.1). This gives a stateful dictionary, which is a slightly different type than the declarative dictionary. But it gives the same functionality. Using state is an advantage because it reduces the execution time of `Put` and `CondGet` operations to amortized constant time.

3.7.3 A word frequency application

To compare our four dictionary implementations, let us use them in a simple application. Let us write a program to count word frequencies in a string. Later on, we will see how to use this to count words in a file. Figure 3.30 defines the function

```
fun {WordChar C}
   (&a=<C andthen C=<&z) orelse
   (&A=<C andthen C=<&Z) orelse (&0=<C andthen C=<&9)
end

fun {WordToAtom PW}
   {StringToAtom {Reverse PW}}
end

fun {IncWord D W}
   {Put D W {CondGet D W 0}+1}
end

fun {CharsToWords PW Cs}
   case Cs
   of nil andthen PW==nil then
      nil
   [] nil then
      [{WordToAtom PW}]
   [] C|Cr andthen {WordChar C} then
      {CharsToWords {Char.toLower C}|PW Cr}
   [] C|Cr andthen PW==nil then
      {CharsToWords nil Cr}
   [] C|Cr then
      {WordToAtom PW}|{CharsToWords nil Cr}
   end
end

fun {CountWords D Ws}
   case Ws
   of W|Wr then {CountWords {IncWord D W} Wr}
   [] nil then D
   end
end

fun {WordFreq Cs}
   {CountWords {NewDictionary} {CharsToWords nil Cs}}
end
```

Figure 3.30: Word frequencies (with declarative dictionary).

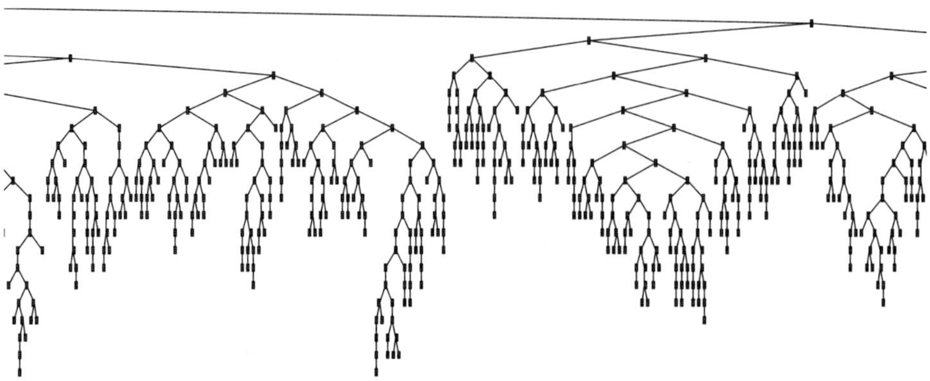

Figure 3.31: Internal structure of binary tree dictionary in WordFreq (in part).

WordFreq, which is given a list of characters Cs and returns a list of pairs W#N, where W is a word (a maximal sequence of letters and digits) and N is the number of times the word occurs in Cs. The function WordFreq is defined in terms of the following functions:

- {WordChar C} returns true if and only if C is a letter or digit.
- {WordToAtom PW} converts a reversed list of word characters into an atom containing those characters. The function StringToAtom is used to create the atom.
- {IncWord D W} takes a dictionary D and an atom W. Returns a new dictionary in which the W field is incremented by 1. Remark how easy this is to write with CondGet, which takes care of the case when W is not yet in the dictionary.
- {CharsToWords nil Cs} takes a list of characters Cs and returns a list of atoms, where the characters in each atom's print name form a word in Cs. The function Char.toLower is used to convert uppercase letters to lowercase, so that "The" and "the" are considered the same word.
- {CountWords D Ws} takes an empty dictionary and the output of CharsToWords. It returns a dictionary in which each key maps to the number of times the word occurs.

Here is a sample execution. The following input:

```
declare
T="Oh my darling, oh my darling, oh my darling Clementine.
   She is lost and gone forever, oh my darling Clementine."
{Browse {WordFreq T}}
```

displays this word frequency count:

```
[she#1 is#1 clementine#2 lost#1 my#4 darling#4 gone#1 and#1
 oh#4 forever#1]
```

We have run `WordFreq` on a more substantial text, namely an early draft of the book. The text contains 712626 characters, giving a total of 110457 words of which 5561 are different. We have run `WordFreq` with three implementations of dictionaries: using lists (see previous example), using binary trees (see section 3.7.2), and using state (the built-in implementation of dictionaries; see section 6.8.2). Figure 3.31 shows part of the internal structure of the binary tree dictionary, drawn with the algorithm of section 3.4.7. The code we measured is in section 3.8.1. Running it gives the following times (accurate to 10%)[16]:

Dictionary implementation	Execution time	Time complexity
Using lists	620 seconds	$O(n)$
Using ordered binary trees	8 seconds	$O(\log n)$
Using state	2 seconds	$O(1)$

The time is the wall-clock time to do everything, i.e., read the text file, run `WordFreq`, and write a file containing the word counts. The difference between the three times is due completely to the different dictionary implementations. Comparing the times gives a good example of the practical effect of using different implementations of an important data type. The complexity shows how the time to insert or look up one item depends on the size of the dictionary.

3.7.4 Secure abstract data types

In both the stack and dictionary data types, the internal representation of values is visible to users of the type. If the users are disciplined programmers, then this might not be a problem. But this is not always the case. A user can be tempted to look at a representation or even to construct new values of the representation.

For example, a user of the stack type can use `Length` to see how many elements are on the stack, if the stack is implemented as a list. The temptation to do this can be very strong if there is no other way to find out what the size of the stack is. Another temptation is to fiddle with the stack contents. Since any list is also a legal stack value, the user can build new stack values, e.g., by removing or adding elements.

In short, any user can add new stack operations anywhere in the program. This means that the stack's implementation is potentially spread out over the whole program instead of being limited to a small part. This is a disastrous state of affairs, for two reasons:

- The program is much harder to maintain. For example, say we want to improve the efficiency of a dictionary by replacing the list-based implementation by a tree-based implementation. We would have to scour the whole program to find out which parts depend on the list-based implementation. There is also a problem of

16. Using Mozart 1.1.0 on a Pentium III processor at 500 MHz.

fault confinement: if the program has bugs in one part, then this can spill over into the ADTs, making them buggy as well, which then contaminates other parts of the program.

- The program is susceptible to malicious interference. This is a more subtle problem that has to do with security. It does not occur with programs written by people who trust each other. It occurs rather with open programs. An open program is one that can interact with other programs that are only known at run time. What if the other program is malicious and wants to disrupt the execution of the open program? Because of the evolution of the Internet, the proportion of open programs is increasing.[17]

How do we solve these problems? The basic idea is to protect the internal representation of the ADT's values, e.g., the stack values, from unauthorized interference. The value to be protected is put inside a protection boundary. There are two ways to use this boundary:

- Stationary value. The value never leaves the boundary. A well-defined set of operations can enter the boundary to calculate with the value. The result of the calculation stays inside the boundary.
- Mobile value. The value can leave and reenter the boundary. When it is outside, operations can be done on it. Operations with proper authorization can take the value out of the boundary and calculate with it. The result is put back inside the boundary.

With either of these solutions, reasoning about the type's implementation is much simplified. Instead of looking at the whole program, we need only look at how the type's operations are implemented.

The first solution is like computerized banking. Each client has an account with some amount of money. A client can do a transaction that transfers money from his or her account to another account. But since clients never actually go to the bank, the money never actually leaves the bank. The second solution is like a safe. It stores money and can be opened by clients who have the key. Each client can take money out of the safe or put money in. Once out, the client can give the money to another client. But when the money is in the safe, it is safe.

In the next section we build a secure ADT using the second solution. This way is the easiest to understand for the declarative model. The authorization we need to enter the protection boundary is a kind of "key." We add it as a new concept to the declarative model, and call it a name. Section 3.7.7 then explains that a key is an example of a very general security idea, called a capability. In chapter 6, section 6.4 completes the story on secure ADTs by showing how to implement the first solution and by explaining the effect of explicit state on security.

17. Chapter 11 shows how to write open programs in Mozart.

⟨s⟩ ::=	
skip	Empty statement
| ⟨s⟩$_1$ ⟨s⟩$_2$	Statement sequence
| **local** ⟨x⟩ **in** ⟨s⟩ **end**	Variable creation
| ⟨x⟩$_1$=⟨x⟩$_2$	Variable-variable binding
| ⟨x⟩=⟨v⟩	Value creation
| **if** ⟨x⟩ **then** ⟨s⟩$_1$ **else** ⟨s⟩$_2$ **end**	Conditional
| **case** ⟨x⟩ **of** ⟨pattern⟩ **then** ⟨s⟩$_1$ **else** ⟨s⟩$_2$ **end**	Pattern matching
| { ⟨x⟩ ⟨y⟩$_1$ ··· ⟨y⟩$_n$ }	Procedure application
| **try** ⟨s⟩$_1$ **catch** ⟨x⟩ **then** ⟨s⟩$_2$ **end**	Exception context
| **raise** ⟨x⟩ **end**	Raise exception
| {NewName ⟨x⟩}	**Name creation**
| ⟨y⟩=!!⟨x⟩	**Read-only view**

Table 3.7: The declarative kernel language with secure types.

3.7.5 The declarative model with secure types

The declarative model defined so far does not let us construct a protection boundary. To do it, we need to extend the model. We need two extensions, one to protect values and one to protect unbound variables. Table 3.7 shows the resulting kernel language with its two new operations. We now explain these two operations.

Protecting values

One way to make values secure is by adding a "wrapping" operation with a "key." That is, the internal representation is put inside a data structure that is inaccessible except to those that know a special value, the key. Knowing the key allows the creation of new wrappings and a look inside existing wrappings made with the same key.

We implement this with a new basic type called a name. A name is a constant like an atom except that it has a much more restricted set of operations. In particular, names do not have a textual representation: they cannot be printed or typed in at the keyboard. Unlike for atoms, it is not possible to convert between names and strings. The only way to know a name is by being passed a reference to it within a program. The name type comes with just two operations:

Operation	Description
`{NewName}`	Return a fresh name
`N1==N2`	Compare names `N1` and `N2`

A fresh name is one that is guaranteed to be different from all other names in the system. Alert readers will notice that `NewName` is not declarative because calling it twice returns different results. In fact, the creation of fresh names is a stateful operation. The guarantee of uniqueness means that `NewName` has some internal memory. However, if we use `NewName` just for making declarative ADTs secure, then this is not a problem. The resulting secure ADT is still declarative.

To make a data type secure, it suffices to put it inside a data structure that can only be accessed through a name. For example, take the value `S`:

```
S=[a b c]
```

`S` is an internal state of the stack we defined before. We make it secure as follows:

```
Key={NewName}
SS={Chunk.new w(Key:S)}
```

This first creates a new name in `Key`. Then it makes a chunk `SS` that contains `S`, so that `S` can only be extracted if `Key` is known. A chunk is a limited record with only one operation, the selection operator "`.`" (see appendix B.4). We say that this "wraps" the value `S` inside `SS`. If one knows `Key`, then accessing `S` from `SS` is easy:

```
S=try SS.Key catch _ then raise error(unwrap(SS)) end end
```

We say this "unwraps" the value `S` from `SS`. If one does not know `Key`, unwrapping is impossible. There is no way to know `Key` except by being passed it explicitly in the program. Calling `SS` with a wrong argument will simply raise an exception. The **try** ensures that the key is not leaked through the exception.

A wrapper

We can define a data abstraction to do the wrapping and unwrapping. The abstraction defines two operations, `Wrap` and `Unwrap`. `Wrap` takes any value and returns a protected value. `Unwrap` takes any protected value and returns the original value. The `Wrap` and `Unwrap` operations come in pairs. The only way to unwrap a wrapped value is by using the corresponding unwrap operation. With names we can define a procedure `NewWrapper` that returns new `Wrap`/`Unwrap` pairs:

```
proc {NewWrapper ?Wrap ?Unwrap}
Key={NewName} in
   fun {Wrap X}
      {Chunk.new w(Key:X)}
   end
   fun {Unwrap W}
      try W.Key catch _ then raise error(unwrap(W)) end end
   end
end
```

For maximum protection, each secure ADT we define can use its own `Wrap`/`Unwrap` pair. Then they are protected from each other as well as from the main program. Given the value `S` as before:

```
S=[a b c]
```

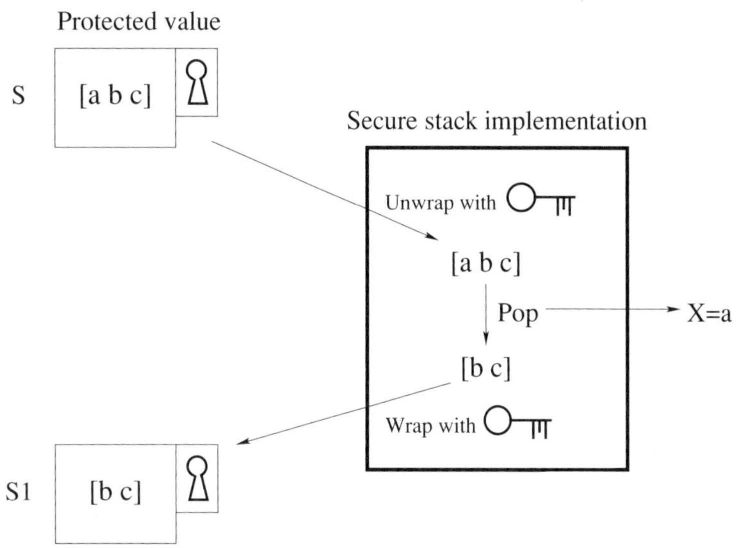

Figure 3.32: Doing `S1={Pop S X}` with a secure stack.

we protect it as follows:

```
SS={Wrap S}
```

We can get the original value back as follows:

```
S={Unwrap SS}
```

A secure stack

Now we can make the stack secure. The idea is to unwrap incoming values and wrap outgoing values. To perform a legal operation on a secure type value, the routine unwraps the secure value, performs the intended operation to get a new value, and then wraps the new value to guarantee security. This gives the following implementation:

```
local Wrap Unwrap in
   {NewWrapper Wrap Unwrap}
   fun {NewStack} {Wrap nil} end
   fun {Push S E} {Wrap E|{Unwrap S}} end
   fun {Pop S E}
      case {Unwrap S} of X|S1 then E=X {Wrap S1} end
   end
   fun {IsEmpty S} {Unwrap S}==nil end
end
```

Figure 3.32 illustrates the `Pop` operation. The box with keyhole represents a protected value. The key represents the name, which is used internally by `Wrap` and `Unwrap` to lock and unlock a box. Lexical scoping guarantees that wrapping and unwrapping are only possible inside the stack implementation. Namely, the identifiers `Wrap` and `Unwrap` are only visible inside the **`local`** statement. Outside this scope, they are hidden. Because `Unwrap` is hidden, there is absolutely no way to see inside a stack value. Because `Wrap` is hidden, there is absolutely no way to "forge" stack values.

Protecting unbound variables

Sometimes it is useful for a data type to output an unbound variable. For example, a stream is a list with an unbound tail. We would like anyone to be able to read the stream but only the data type implementation to be able to extend it. Using standard unbound variables, this does not work. For example:

```
S=a|b|c|X
```

The variable `X` is not secure since anyone who knows `S` can bind `X`.

The problem is that anyone who has a reference to an unbound variable can bind the variable. One solution is to have a restricted version of the variable that can only be read, not bound. We call this a read-only view of a variable. We extend the declarative model with one function:

Operation	Description
`!!X`	Return a read-only view of `X`

Any attempt to bind a read-only view will block. Any binding of `X` will be transferred to the read-only view. To protect a stream, its tail should be a read-only view.

In the abstract machine, read-only views sit in a new store called the read-only store. We modify the bind operation so that before binding a variable to a determined value, it checks whether the variable is in the read-only store. If so, the bind suspends. When the variable becomes determined, then the bind operation can continue.

Creating fresh names

To conclude this section, let us see how to create fresh names in the implementation of the declarative model. How can we guarantee that a name is globally unique? This is easy for programs running in one process: names can be implemented as successive integers. But this approach fails miserably for open programs. For them, globally potentially means among all running programs in all the world's computers. There are basically two approaches to creating names that are globally unique:

1. The centralized approach. There is a name factory somewhere in the world. To get a fresh name, you need to send a message to this factory and the reply contains a fresh name. The name factory does not have to be physically in one place; it can be spread out over many computers. For example, the Internet Protocol (IP)

supposes a unique IP address for every computer in the world that is connected to the Internet. IP addresses can change over time, though, e.g., if network address translation is done or dynamic allocation of IP addresses is done using the DHCP protocol. We therefore complement the IP address with a high-resolution timestamp giving the creation time of `NewName`. This gives a unique constant that can be used to implement a local name factory on each computer.

2. The decentralized approach. A fresh name is just a vector of random bits. The random bits are generated by an algorithm that depends on enough external information so that different computers will not generate the same vector. If the vector is long enough, then the probability that names are not unique will be arbitrarily small. Theoretically, the probability is always nonzero, but in practice this technique works well.

Now that we have a unique name, how do we make sure that it is unforgeable? This requires cryptographic techniques that are beyond the scope of the book [185].

3.7.6 A secure declarative dictionary

Now let us see how to make the declarative dictionary secure. It is quite easy. We can use the same technique as for the stack, namely by using a wrapper and an unwrapper. Here is the new definition:

```
local
   Wrap Unwrap
   {NewWrapper Wrap Unwrap}
   % Previous definitions:
   fun {NewDictionary2} ... end
   fun {Put2 Ds K Value} ... end
   fun {CondGet2 Ds K Default} ... end
   fun {Domain2 Ds} ... end
in
   fun {NewDictionary}
      {Wrap {NewDictionary2}}
   end
   fun {Put Ds K Value}
      {Wrap {Put2 {Unwrap Ds} K Value}}
   end
   fun {CondGet Ds K Default}
      {CondGet2 {Unwrap Ds} K Default}
   end
   fun {Domain Ds}
      {Domain2 {Unwrap Ds}}
   end
end
```

Because `Wrap` and `Unwrap` are only known inside the scope of the **`local`**, the wrapped dictionary cannot be unwrapped by anyone outside of this scope. This technique works for both the list and tree implementations of dictionaries.

3.7.7 Capabilities and security

We say a computation is secure if it has well-defined and controllable properties, independent of the existence of other (possibly malicious) entities (either computations or humans) in the system [4]. We call these entities "adversaries." Security allows protection from both malicious computations and innocent (but buggy) computations. The property of being secure is global; "cracks" in a system can occur at any level, from the hardware to the software to the human organization housing the system. Making a computer system secure involves not only computer science but also many aspects of human society [5].

A short, precise, and concrete description of how the system will ensure its security is called its security policy. Designing, implementing, and verifying security policies is crucial for building secure systems, but is outside the scope of the book.

In this section, we consider only a small part of the vast discipline of security, namely the programming language viewpoint. To implement a security policy, a system uses security mechanisms. Throughout the book, we will discuss security mechanisms that are part of a programming language, such as lexical scoping and names. We will ask ourselves what properties a language must possess in order to build secure programs, i.e., programs that can resist attacks by adversaries that stay within the language.[18] We call such a language a secure language. Having a secure language is an important requirement for building secure computer programs. Designing and implementing a secure language is an important topic in programming language research. It involves both semantic properties and properties of the implementation.

Capabilities

The protection techniques we have introduced to make secure ADTs are special cases of a security concept called a capability. Capabilities are at the heart of modern research on secure languages. For example, the secure language E hardens references to language entities so that they behave as capabilities [142, 202]. The `Wrap`/`Unwrap` pairs we introduced previously are called sealer/unsealer pairs in E. Instead of using external references to protect values, sealer/unsealer pairs encrypt and decrypt the values. In this view, the name is used as an encryption and decryption key.

The capability concept was invented in the 1960s in the context of operating system design [52, 129]. Operating systems have always had to protect users from each other while still allowing them do their work. Since this early work, it has become clear that the concept belongs in the programming language and is generally useful for building secure programs [143]. Capabilities can be defined in many ways, but the following definition is reasonable for a programming language. A

18. Staying within the language can be guaranteed by always running programs on a virtual machine that accepts only binaries of legal programs.

capability is defined as an unforgeable language entity that gives its owner the right to perform a given set of actions. The set of actions is defined inside the capability and may change over time. By unforgeable we mean that it is not possible for any implementation, even one that is intimately connected to the hardware architecture such as one written in assembly language, to create a capability. In the E literature this property is summarized by the phrase "connectivity begets connectivity": the only way to get a new capability is by being passed it explicitly through an existing capability [144].

All values of data types are capabilities in this sense, since they give their owners the ability to do all operations of that type, but no more. An owner of a language entity is any program fragment that references that entity. For example, a record `R` gives its owner the ability to do many operations, including field selection `R.F` and arity `{Arity R}`. A procedure `P` gives its owner the ability to call `P`. A name gives its owner the ability to compare its value with other values. An unbound variable gives its owner the ability to bind it and to read its value. A read-only variable gives its owner the ability to read its value, but not to bind it.

New capabilities can be defined during a program's execution as instances of data abstractions such as ADTs. For the models of the book, the simplest way is to use procedure values. A reference to a procedure value gives its owner the right to call the procedure, i.e., to do whatever action the procedure was designed to do. Furthermore, a procedure reference cannot be forged. In a program, the only way to know the reference is if it is passed explicitly. The procedure can hide all its sensitive information in its external references. For this to work, the language must guarantee that knowing a procedure does not automatically give one the right to examine the procedure's external references!

Principle of least privilege

An important design principle for secure systems is the principle of least privilege: each entity should be given the least authority (or "privilege") that is necessary for it to get its job done. This is also called the principle of least authority (POLA) or the "need to know" principle. Determining exactly what the least authority is in all cases is an undecidable problem: there cannot exist an algorithm to solve it in all cases. This is because the authority depends on what the entity does during its execution. If we would have an algorithm, it would be powerful enough to solve the halting problem, which has been proved not to have a solution.

In practice, we do not need to know the exact least authority. Adequate security can be achieved with approximations. The programming language should make it easy to do these approximations. Capabilities, as we defined them above, have this ability. With them, it is easy to make the approximation as precise as is needed. For example, an entity can be given the authority to create a file with a given name and maximum size in a given directory. For files, coarser granularities are usually enough, such as the authority to create a file in a given directory. Capabilities can handle both the fine and coarse-grained cases easily.

Capabilities and explicit state

Declarative capabilities, i.e., capabilities written in a declarative computation model, lack one crucial property to make them useful in practice. The set of actions they authorize cannot be changed over time. In particular, none of their actions can be revoked. To make a capability revocable, the computation model needs an additional concept, namely explicit state. This is explained in section 6.4.5.

3.8 Nondeclarative needs

Declarative programming, because of its "pure functional" view of programming, is somewhat detached from the real world, in which entities have memories (state) and can evolve independently and proactively (concurrency). To connect a declarative program to the real world, some nondeclarative operations are needed. This section talks about two classes of such operations: file I/O (input/output) and graphical user interfaces. A third class of operations, standalone compilation, is given in section 3.9.

Later on we will see that the nondeclarative operations of this section fit into more general computation models than the declarative one, in particular stateful and concurrent models. In a general sense, this section ties in with the discussion on the limits of declarative programming in section 4.8. Some of the operations manipulate state that is external to the program; this is just a special case of the system decomposition principle explained in section 6.7.2.

The new operations introduced by this section are collected in modules. A module is simply a record that groups together related operations. For example, the module `List` groups many list operations, such as `List.append` and `List.member` (which can also be referenced as `Append` and `Member`). This section introduces the three modules `File` (for file I/O of text), `QTk` (for graphical user interfaces), and `Pickle` (for file I/O of any values). Some of these modules (like `Pickle`) are immediately known by Mozart when it starts up. The other modules can be loaded by calling `Module.link`. In what follows, we show how to do this for `File` and `QTk`. More information about modules and how to use them is given later, in section 3.9.

3.8.1 Text input/output with a file

A simple way to interface declarative programming with the real world is by using files. A file is a sequence of values that is stored external to the program on a permanent storage medium such as a hard disk. A text file is a file containing a sequence of characters. In this section, we show how to read and write text files. This is enough for using declarative programs in a practical way. The basic pattern of access is simple:

Input file $\stackrel{read}{\longrightarrow}$ compute function $\stackrel{write}{\longrightarrow}$ output file

We use the module `File`, which can be found on the book's Web site. Later on we will do more sophisticated file operations, but this is enough for now.

Loading the module `File`

The first step is to load the module `File` into the system, as explained in appendix A.1.2. We assume that you have a compiled version of the module `File`, in the file **`File.ozf`**. Then execute the following:

```
declare [File]={Module.link ['File.ozf']}
```

This calls `Module.link` with a list of paths to compiled modules. Here there is just one. The module is loaded, linked it into the system, initialized, and bound to `File`.[19] Now we are ready to do file operations.

Reading a file

The operation `File.readList` reads the whole content of the file into a string:

```
L={File.readList "foo.txt"}
```

This example reads the file **`foo.txt`** into `L`. We can also write this as:

```
L={File.readList 'foo.txt'}
```

Remember that `"foo.txt"` is a string (a list of character codes) and `'foo.txt'` is an atom (a constant with a print representation). The file name can be represented in both ways. There is a third way to represent file names: as virtual strings. A virtual string is a tuple with label `'#'` that represents a string. We could therefore just as well have entered the following:

```
L={File.readList foo#'.'#txt}
```

The tuple `foo#'.'#txt`, which we can also write as `'#'(foo '.' txt)`, represents the string `"foo.txt"`. Using virtual strings avoids the need to do explicit string concatenations. All Mozart built-in operations that expect strings will work also with virtual strings. All three ways of loading **`foo.txt`** have the same effect. They bind `L` to a list of the character codes in the file **`foo.txt`**.

Files can also be referred to by URL. An URL (Uniform Resource Locator) gives a convenient global address for files since it is widely supported through the World Wide Web infrastructure. It is just as easy to read a file through its URL as through its file name:

```
L={File.readList 'http://www.mozart-oz.org/features.html'}
```

---

19. To be precise, the module is loaded lazily: it will only actually be loaded the first time that we use it.

That's all there is to it. URLs can only be used to read files, but not to write files. This is because URLs are handled by Web servers, which are usually set up to allow only reading.

Mozart has other operations that allow reading a file either incrementally or lazily, instead of all at once. This is important for very large files that do not fit into the memory space of the Mozart process. To keep things simple for now, we recommend that you read files all at once. Later on we will see how to read a file incrementally.

Writing a file

Writing a file is usually done incrementally, by appending one string at a time to the file. The module `File` provides three operations: `File.writeOpen` to open the file, which must be done first; `File.write` to append a string to the file; and `File.writeClose` to close the file, which must be done last. Here is an example:

```
{File.writeOpen ´foo.txt´}
{File.write ´This comes in the file.\n´}
{File.write ´The result of 43*43 is ´#43*43#´.\n´}
{File.write "Strings are ok too.\n"}
{File.writeClose}
```

After these operations, the file `'foo.txt'` has three lines of text, as follows:

```
This comes in the file.
The result of 43*43 is 1849.
Strings are ok too.
```

Example execution

In section 3.7.3 we defined the function `WordFreq` that calculates the word frequencies in a string. We can use this function to calculate word frequencies and store them in a file:

```
% 1. Read input file
L={File.readList ´book.raw´}
% 2. Compute function
D={WordFreq L}
% 3. Write output file
{File.writeOpen ´word.freq´}
for X in {Domain D} do
   {File.write {Get D X}#´ occurrences of word ´#X#´\n´}
end
{File.writeClose}
```

Section 3.7.3 gives some timing figures of this code using different dictionary implementations.

3.8.2 Text input/output with a graphical user interface

The most direct way to interface programs with a human user is through a graphical user interface. This section shows a simple yet powerful way to define graphical user interfaces, namely by means of concise, mostly declarative specifications. This is an excellent example of a descriptive declarative language, as defined in section 3.1. The descriptive language is recognized by the `QTk` module of the Mozart system. The user interface is specified as a nested record, supplemented with objects and procedures. (Objects are introduced in chapter 7. For now, you can consider them as procedures with internal state, like the examples of chapter 1.)

This section shows how to build user interfaces to input and output textual data to a window. This is enough for many declarative programs. We give a brief overview of the `QTk` module, just enough to build these user interfaces. Later on we will build more sophisticated graphical user interfaces. Chapter 10 gives a fuller discussion of declarative user interface programming in general and of its realization in `QTk`.

Declarative specification of widgets

A window on the screen consists of a set of widgets. A widget is a rectangular area in the window that has a particular interactive behavior. For example, some widgets can display text or graphic information, and other widgets can accept user interaction such as keyboard input and mouse clicks. We specify each widget declaratively with a record whose label and features define the widget type and initial state. We specify the window declaratively as a nested record (i.e., a tree) that defines the logical structure of the widgets in the window. Here are the five widgets we will use for now:

- The `label` widget can display a text. The widget is specified by the record:

```
label(text:VS)
```

where `VS` is a virtual string.

- The `text` widget is used to display and enter large quantities of text. It can use scrollbars to display more text than can fit on screen. With a vertical (i.e., top-down) scrollbar, the widget is specified by the record:

```
text(handle:H tdscrollbar:true)
```

When the window is created, the variable `H` will be bound to an object used to control the widget. We call such an object a handler. You can consider the object as a one-argument procedure: {`H set(VS)`} displays a text and {`H get(VS)`} reads the text.

- The `button` widget specifies a button and an action to execute when the button is pressed. The widget is specified by the record:

```
button(text:VS action:P)
```

where VS is a virtual string and P is a zero-argument procedure. {P} is called whenever the button is pressed.[20] For each window, all its actions are executed sequentially.

- The td (top-down) and lr (left-to-right) widgets specify an arrangement of other widgets in top-down or left-to-right order:

```
lr(W1 W2 ... Wn)
td(W1 W2 ... Wn)
```

where W1, W2, ..., Wn are other widget specifications.

Declarative specification of resize behavior

When a window is resized, the widgets inside should behave properly, i.e., either changing size or staying the same size, depending on what the interface should do. We specify each widget's resize behavior declaratively, by means of an optional glue feature in the widget's record. The glue feature indicates whether the widget's borders should or should not be "glued" to its enclosing widget. The glue feature's argument is an atom consisting of any combination of the four characters n (north), s (south), w (west), e (east), indicating for each direction whether the border should be glued or not. Here are some examples:

- No glue. The widget keeps its natural size and is centered in the space allotted to it, both horizontally and vertically.
- glue:nswe glues to all four borders, stretching to fit both horizontally and vertically.
- glue:we glues horizontally left and right, stretching to fit. Vertically, the widget is not stretched but centered in the space allotted to it.
- glue:w glues to the left edge and does not stretch.
- glue:wns glues vertically top and bottom, stretching to fit vertically, and glues to the left edge, not stretching horizontally.

Installing the QTk *module*

The first step is to install the QTk module into the system. Since QTk is part of the Mozart Standard Library, it suffices to know the right path name. We load it into the interactive interface as follows:

```
declare [QTk]={Module.link ['x-oz://system/wp/QTk.ozf']}
```

Now that QTk is installed, we can use it to build interfaces according to the specifications of the previous section.

20. To be precise, whenever the left mouse button is both clicked and released while the mouse is over the button. This allows the user to correct any mistaken click on the button.

```
declare In Out
A1=proc {$} X in {In get(X)} {Out set(X)} end
A2=proc {$} {W close} end
D=td(title:"Simple text I/O interface"
     lr(label(text:"Input:")
        text(handle:In  tdscrollbar:true glue:nswe)
        glue:nswe)
     lr(label(text:"Output:")
        text(handle:Out tdscrollbar:true glue:nswe)
        glue:nswe)
     lr(button(text:"Do It" action:A1 glue:nswe)
        button(text:"Quit"  action:A2 glue:nswe)
        glue:we))
W={QTk.build D}
{W show}
```

Figure 3.33: A simple graphical I/O interface for text.

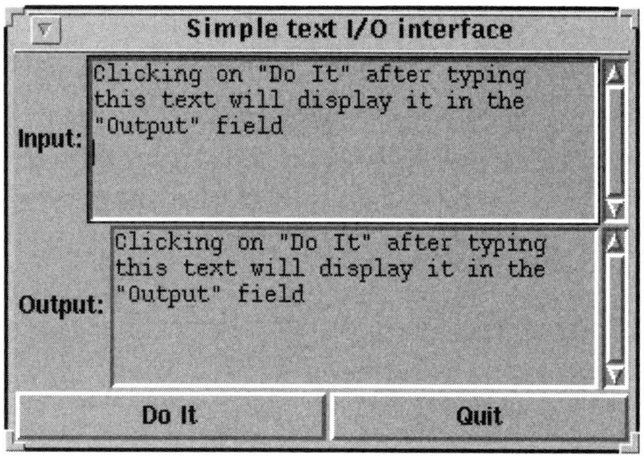

Figure 3.34: Screenshot of the interface.

Building the interface

The `QTk` module has a function `QTk.build` that takes an interface specification, which is just a nested record of widgets, and builds a window containing these widgets. Let us build a simple interface with one button that displays `ouch` in the browser whenever the button is clicked:

```
D=td(button(text:"Press me"
            action:proc {$} {Browse ouch} end))
W={QTk.build D}
{W show}
```

The record `D` always has to start with `td` or `lr`, even if the window has just one widget. `QTk.build` returns an object `W` that represents the window. The window starts out being hidden. It can be displayed or hidden again by calling `{W show}` or `{W hide}`. Figure 3.33 gives a bigger example that implements a complete text I/O interface. Figure 3.34 shows the resulting window. At first glance, this program may seem complicated, but look again: there are six widgets (two `label`, two `text`, two `button`) arranged with `td` and `lr` widgets. The `QTk.build` function takes the description `D`, builds the window, and creates the handler objects `In` and `Out`. Compare the record `D` in figure 3.33 with the screenshot in figure 3.34.

There are two action procedures, `A1` and `A2`, one for each button. The action `A1` is attached to the "`Do It`" button. Clicking on the button calls `A1`, which transfers text from the first text widget to the second text widget. This works as follows. The call `{In get(X)}` gets the text of the first text widget and binds it to `X`. Then `{Out set(X)}` sets the text in the second text widget to `X`. The action `A2` is attached to the "`Quit`" button. It calls `{W close}`, which closes the window permanently.

Putting `nswe` glue almost everywhere allows the window to behave properly when resized. The `lr` widget with the two buttons has `we` glue only, so that the buttons do not expand vertically. The `label` widgets have no glue, so they have fixed sizes. The `td` widget at the top level needs no glue since we assume it is always glued to its window.

3.8.3 Stateless data I/O with files

Input/output of a string is simple, since a string consists of characters that can be stored directly in a file. What about other values? It would be a great help to the programmer if it would be possible to save any value to a file and to load it back later. The System module `Pickle` provides exactly this ability. It can save and load any complete value:

```
{Pickle.save X FN}      % Save X in file FN
{Pickle.load FNURL ?X} % Load X from file (or URL) FNURL
```

All data structures used in declarative programming can be saved and loaded except for those containing unbound variables. For example, consider this program fragment:

```
declare
fun {Fact N}
   if N==0 then 1 else N*{Fact N-1} end
end
F100={Fact 100}
F100Gen1=fun {$} F100 end
F100Gen2=fun {$} {Fact 100} end
FNGen1=fun {$ N} F={Fact N} in fun {$} F end end
FNGen2=fun {$ N} fun {$} {Fact N} end end
```

`F100` is a (rather big) integer; the four other entities are functions. The following operation saves the four functions to a file:

```
{Pickle.save [F100Gen1 F100Gen2 FNGen1 FNGen2] ´factfile´}
```

To be precise, this saves a value consisting of a list of four elements in the file `factfile`. In this example, all elements are functions. The functions have been chosen to illustrate various degrees of delayed calculation. The first two return the result of calculating 100!. The first, `F100Gen1`, knows the integer and returns it directly, and the second, `F100Gen2`, calculates the value each time it is called. The third and fourth, when called with an integer argument n, return a function that when itself called, returns $n!$. The third, `FNGen1`, calculates $n!$ when called, so the returned function just returns a known integer. The fourth, `FNGen2`, does no calculation but lets the returned function calculate $n!$ when called.

To use the contents of `factfile`, it must first be loaded:

```
declare [F1 F2 F3 F4]={Pickle.load ´factfile´} in
{Browse {F1}}
{Browse {F2}}
{Browse {{F3 100}}}
{Browse {{F4 100}}}
```

This displays 100! four times. Of course, the following is also possible:

```
declare F1 F2 F3 F4 in
{Browse {F1}}
{Browse {F2}}
{Browse {{F3 100}}}
{Browse {{F4 100}}}
[F1 F2 F3 F4]={Pickle.load ´factfile´}
```

After the file is loaded, this displays exactly the same as before. This illustrates yet again how dataflow makes it possible to use a variable before binding it.

We emphasize that the loaded value is exactly the same as the one that was saved. There is no difference at all between them. This is true for all possible values: numbers, records, procedures, names, atoms, lists, and so on, including other values that we will see later on in the book. Executing this on one process:

```
... % First statement (defines X)
{Pickle.save X ´myfile´}
```

and then this on a second process:

```
X={Pickle.load ´myfile´}
... % Second statement (uses X)
```

is rigorously identical to executing the following on a single process:

```
... % First statement (defines X)
{Pickle.save X ´myfile´}
_={Pickle.load ´myfile´}
... % Second statement (uses X)
```

If the calls to `Pickle` are removed, like this:

```
... % First statement (defines X)
... % Second statement (uses X)
```

then there are two minor differences:

- The first case creates and reads the file `'myfile'`. The second case does not.
- The first case raises an exception if there was a problem in creating or reading the file.

3.9 Program design in the small

Now that we have seen many programming techniques, the next logical step is to use them to solve problems. This step is called program design. It starts from a problem we want to solve (usually explained in words, sometimes not very precisely); gives the high-level structure of the program, i.e., what programming techniques we need to use and how they are connected together; and ends up with a complete program that solves the problem.

In program design, there is an important distinction between "programming in the small" and "programming in the large." We will call the resulting programs "small programs" and "large programs." The distinction has nothing to do with the program's size in number of lines of source code, but rather with how many people were involved in its development. Small programs are written by one person over a short period of time. Large programs are written by more than one person or over a long period of time. The same person now and one year from now should be considered as two people, since the person will forget many details over a year. This section gives an introduction to programming in the small; we leave programming in the large to section 6.7.

3.9.1 Design methodology

Assume we have a problem that can be solved by writing a small program. Let us see how to design the program. We recommend the following design methodology, which is a mixture of creativity and rigorous thinking:

- *Informal specification.* We start by writing down as precisely as we can what the program should do: what its inputs and outputs are and how the outputs relate to the inputs. This description is called an informal specification. Even though it is precise, we call it "informal" because it is written in English. "Formal" specifications are written in a mathematical notation.
- *Examples.* To make the specification perfectly clear, it is always a good idea to imagine examples of what the program does in particular cases. The examples should "stress" the program: use it in boundary conditions and in the most unexpected ways we can imagine.
- *Exploration.* To find out what programming techniques we will need, a good way is to use the interactive interface to experiment with program fragments. The idea is to write small operations that we think might be needed for the program. We use the operations that the system already provides as a basis. This step gives us a clearer view of what the program's structure should be.

- *Structure and coding.* At this point we can lay out the program's structure. We make a rough outline of the operations needed to calculate the outputs from the inputs and how they fit together. We then fill in the blanks by writing the actual program code. The operations should be simple: each operation should do just one thing. To improve the structure we can group related operations in modules.
- *Testing and reasoning.* Now that we have a program, we must verify that it does the right thing. We try it on a series of test cases, including the examples we came up with before. We correct errors until the program works well. We can also reason about the program and its complexity, using the formal semantics for parts that are not clear. Testing and reasoning are complementary: it is important to do both to get a high-quality program.
- *Judging the quality.* The final point is to step back and judge the design's quality. There are many factors involved in quality: does the design solve the right problem, is it correct, is it efficient, is it maintainable, is it extensible, is it simple? Simplicity is especially important, since it makes many of the other factors easier to achieve. If a design is complex, the best we can say is that it is not yet in its definitive form. Next to simplicity is completeness, that is, the design (potentially) has all the functionality it needs, so that it can be used as a building block.

These steps are not meant to be obligatory, but rather to serve as inspiration. Feel free to adapt them to your own circumstances. For example, when imagining examples it can be clear that the specification has to be changed. However, take care not to forget the most important step, which is testing. It is important since it closes the loop: it gives feedback from the coding step back to the specification step.

3.9.2 Example of program design

To illustrate these steps, let us retrace the development of the word frequency application of section 3.7.3. Here is a first attempt at an informal specification:

> Given a file name, the application opens a window and displays a list of pairs, where each pair consists of a word and an integer giving the number of times the word occurs in the file.

Is this specification precise enough? What about a file containing a word that is not valid English or a file containing non-ASCII (American Standard Code for Information Interchange) characters? Our specification is not precise enough: it does not define what a "word" is. To make it more precise we have to know the purpose of the application. Say that we just want to get a general idea of word frequencies, independent of any particular language. Then we can define a word simply as:

> A "word" is a maximal contiguous sequence of letters and digits.

This means that words are separated by at least one character that is not a letter or a digit. This accepts a word that is not valid English but does not accept words containing non-ASCII characters. Is this good enough? What about words with a hyphen (such as "true-blue") or idiomatic expressions that act as units (such as "trial and error")? In the interest of simplicity, let us reject these for now. But we may have to change the specification later to accept them, depending on how we use the word frequency application.

Now we have arrived at our specification. Note the essential role played by examples. They are important signposts on the way to a precise specification. The examples were expressly designed to test the limits of the specification.

The next step is to design the program's structure. The appropriate structure seems to be a pipeline: first read the file into a list of characters and then convert the list of characters into a list of words, where a word is represented as a character string. To count the words we need a data structure that is indexed by words. The declarative dictionary of section 3.7.2 would be ideal, but it is indexed by atoms. Luckily, there is an operation to convert character strings to atoms: `StringToAtom` (see appendix B). With this we can write our program. Figure 3.30 gives the heart: a function `WordFreq` that takes a list of characters and returns a dictionary. We can test this code on various examples, and especially on the examples we used to write the specification. To this we will add the code to read the file and display the output in a window; for this we use the file operations and graphical user interface operations of section 3.8. It is important to package the application cleanly, as a software component. This is explained in the next two sections.

3.9.3 Software components

What is a good way to organize a program? One could write the program as one big monolithic whole, but this can be confusing. A better way is to partition the program into logical units, each of which implements a set of operations that are related in some way. Each logical unit has two parts, an interface and an implementation. Only the interface is visible from outside the logical unit. A logical unit may use others as part of its implementation.

A program is then simply a directed graph of logical units, where an edge between two logical units means that the first needs the second for its implementation. Popular usage calls these logical units "modules" or "components," without defining precisely what these words mean. This section introduces the basic concepts, defines them precisely, and shows how they can be used to help design small declarative programs. Section 6.7 explains how these ideas can be used to help design large programs.

Modules and functors

A module groups together related operations into an entity that has an interface and an implementation. We represent modules in a simple way:

```
⟨statement⟩ ::= functor ⟨variable⟩
                [ import{ ⟨variable⟩ [ at ⟨atom⟩ ]
                        | ⟨variable⟩ ´(´ { (⟨atom⟩ | ⟨int⟩) [ ´:´ ⟨variable⟩ ] }+ ´)´
                        }+ ]
                [ export { [ (⟨atom⟩ | ⟨int⟩) ´:´ ] ⟨variable⟩ }+ ]
                define { ⟨declarationPart⟩ }+ [ in ⟨statement⟩ ] end
              | ...
```

Table 3.8: Functor syntax.

- The module's interface is a record that groups together related language entities (usually procedures, but anything is allowed, including classes, objects, etc.).
- The module's implementation is a set of language entities that are accessible by the interface operations but hidden from the outside. The implementation is hidden using lexical scoping.

We will consider module specifications as entities separate from modules. A module specification is a kind of template that creates a module each time it is instantiated. A module specification is sometimes called a software component. Unfortunately, the term "software component" is widely used with many different meanings [208]. To avoid confusion, we will call the book's module specifications functors. A functor is a function whose arguments are the modules it needs and whose result is a new module. (To be precise, the functor takes module interfaces as arguments, creates a new module, and returns that module's interface!) Because of the functor's role in structuring programs, we provide it as a linguistic abstraction. A functor has three parts: an **import** part, which specifies what other modules it needs, an **export** part, which specifies the module interface, and a **define** part, which gives the module implementation including initialization code. The syntax for functor declarations allows using them as either statements or expressions, like the syntax for procedures. Table 3.8 gives the syntax of functor declarations as statements. Functor declarations can also be used as expressions if the first ⟨variable⟩ is replaced by a nesting marker "`$`".

In the terminology of software engineering, a software component is a unit of independent deployment, a unit of third-party development, and has no persistent state (following the definition given in [208]). Functors satisfy this definition and are therefore a kind of software component. With this terminology, a module is a component instance; it is the result of installing a functor in a particular module environment. The module environment consists of a set of modules, each of which may have an execution state.

Functors in the Mozart system are compilation units. That is, the system has support for handling functors in files, both as source code (i.e., human-readable text) and object code (i.e., compiled form). Source code can be compiled, i.e., translated, into object code. This makes it easy to use functors to exchange software between developers. For example, the Mozart system has a library, called MOGUL (Mozart Global User Library), in which third-party developers can put any kind of information. Usually, they put in functors and applications.

An application is standalone if it can be run without the interactive interface. It consists of a main functor, which is evaluated when the program starts. It imports the modules it needs, which causes other functors to be evaluated. The main functor is used for its effect of starting the application and not for its resulting module, which is silently ignored. Evaluating, or "installing," a functor creates a new module in three steps. First, the modules it needs are identified. Second, the initialization code is executed. Third, the module is loaded the first time it is needed during execution. This technique is called dynamic linking, as opposed to static linking, in which the modules are already loaded when execution starts. At any time, the set of currently installed modules is called the module environment.

Implementing modules and functors

Let us see how to construct software components in steps. First we give an example module. Then we show how to convert this module into a software component. Finally, we turn it into a linguistic abstraction.

Example module In general, a module is a record, and its interface is accessed through the record's fields. We construct a module called `MyList` that provides interface procedures for appending, sorting, and testing membership of lists. This can be written as follows:

```
declare MyList in
local
   proc {Append ... }  ... end
   proc {MergeSort ...} ... end
   proc {Sort ... } ... {MergeSort ...} ... end
   proc {Member ...} ... end
in
   MyList='export'(append: Append
                   sort: Sort
                   member: Member
                   ...)
end
```

The procedure `MergeSort` is inaccessible outside of the **`local`** statement. The other procedures cannot be accessed directly, but only through the fields of the `MyList` module, which is a record. For example, `Append` is accessible as `MyList.append`. Most of the library modules of Mozart, i.e., the Base and System modules, follow this structure.

A software component Using procedural abstraction, we can turn this module into a software component. The software component is a function that returns a module:

```
fun {MyListFunctor}
   proc {Append ... }  ... end
   proc {MergeSort ...} ... end
   proc {Sort ... } ... {MergeSort ...} ... end
   proc {Member ...} ... end
in
   ´export´(append: Append
            sort: Sort
            member: Member
            ...)
end
```

Each time `MyListFunctor` is called, it creates and returns another `MyList` module. In general, `MyListFunctor` could have arguments, which are the other modules needed for `MyList`.

From this definition, it is clear that functors are just values in the language. They share the following properties with procedure values:

- A functor definition can be evaluated at run time, giving a functor.
- A functor can have external references to other language entities. For example, it is easy to make a functor that contains data calculated at run time. This is useful, e.g., to include large tables or image data in source form.
- A functor can be stored in a file by using the `Pickle` module. This file can be read by any Mozart process. This makes it easy to create libraries of third-party functors, such as MOGUL.
- A functor is lightweight; it can be used to encapsulate a single entity such as one object or class, in order to make explicit the modules needed by the entity.

Because functors are values, it is possible to manipulate them in sophisticated ways within the language. For example, a software component can be built that implements component-based programming, in which components determine at run time which components they need and when to link them. Even more flexibility is possible when dynamic typing is used. A component can link an arbitrary component at run time, by installing any functors and calling them according to their needs.

Linguistic support This software component abstraction is a reasonable one to organize large programs. To make it easier to use, to ensure that it is not used incorrectly, and to make clear the intention of the programmer (avoiding confusion with other higher-order programming techniques), we turn it into a linguistic abstraction. The function `MyListFunctor` corresponds to the following functor syntax:

```
functor
export
   append:Append
   sort:Sort
   member:Member
   ...
define
   proc {Append ... }  ... end
   proc {MergeSort ...} ... end
   proc {Sort ... } ... {MergeSort ...} ... end
   proc {Member ...} ... end
end
```

Note that the statement between **define** and **end** does implicit variable declaration, exactly like the statement between **local** and **in**.

Assume that this functor has been compiled and stored in the file `MyList.ozf` (we will see below how to compile a functor). Then the module can be created as follows in the interactive interface:

```
declare [MyList]={Module.link ['MyList.ozf']}
```

The function `Module.link` is defined in the System module `Module`. It takes a list of functors, loads them from the file system, links them together (i.e., evaluates them together, so that each module sees its imported modules), and returns a corresponding list of modules. The `Module` module allows doing many other operations on functors and modules.

Importing modules Software components can depend on other software components. To be precise, instantiating a software component creates a module. The instantiation might need other modules. In the new syntax, we declare this with **import** declarations. To import a library module it is enough to give the name of its functor. On the other hand, to import a user-defined module requires stating the file name or URL of the file where the functor is stored.[21] This is reasonable, since the system knows where the library modules are stored, but does not know where you have stored your own functors. Consider the following functor:

```
functor
import
   Browser
   FO at 'file:///home/mydir/FileOps.ozf'
define
   {Browser.browse {FO.countLines '/etc/passwd'}}
end
```

The **import** declaration imports the System module `Browser` and the user-defined module `FO` specified by the functor stored in the file `/home/mydir/FileOps.ozf`. When this functor is linked, the statement between **define** ... **end** is executed.

21. Other naming schemes are possible, in which functors have some logical name in a component management system.

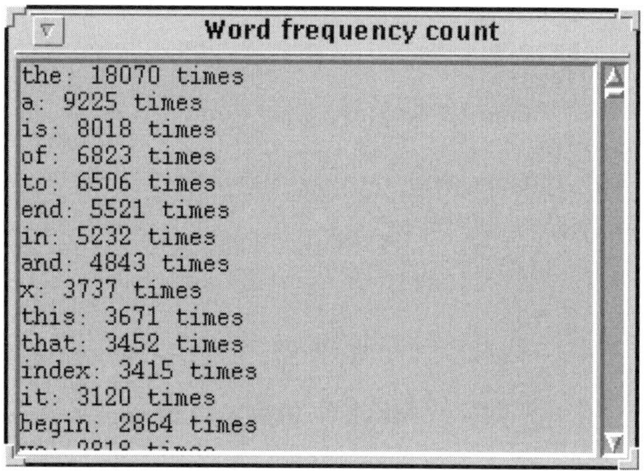

Figure 3.35: Screenshot of the word frequency application.

This calls the function `FO.countLines`, which counts the number of lines in a given file, and then calls the procedure `Browser.browse` to display the result. This particular functor is defined for its effect, not for the module that it creates. It therefore does not export any interface.

3.9.4 Example of a standalone program

Now let us package the word frequency application using components and make it into a standalone program. Figure 3.35 gives a screenshot of the program's execution. The program consists of two components, `Dict` and `WordApp`, which are functors whose source code is in the files `Dict.oz` and `WordApp.oz`. The components implement the declarative dictionary and the word frequency application. In addition to importing `Dict`, the `WordApp` component also imports the modules `File` and `QTk`. It uses these modules to read from the file and create an output window.

The complete source code of the `Dict` and `WordApp` components is given in figures 3.36 and 3.37. The principal difference between these components and the code of sections 3.7.3 and 3.7.2 is that the components are enclosed in **`functor ... end`** with the right **`import`** and **`export`** clauses. Figure 3.38 shows the dependencies. The `Open` and `Finalize` modules are Mozart System modules. The `File` component can be found on the book's Web site. The `QTk` component is in the Mozart Standard Library. It can be used from within a functor by adding the following clause:

```
import QTk at 'x-oz://system/wp/QTk.ozf'
```

The `Dict` component differs slightly from the declarative dictionary of section 3.7.2: it replaces `Domain` by `Entries`, which gives a list of pairs `Key#Value` instead of just a list of keys.

This application can easily be extended in many ways. For example, the window

```
functor
export new:NewDict put:Put condGet:CondGet entries:Entries
define
   fun {NewDict} leaf end

   fun {Put Ds Key Value}
      case Ds
      of leaf then tree(Key Value leaf leaf)
      [] tree(K _ L R) andthen K==Key then
                          tree(K Value L R)
      [] tree(K V L R) andthen K>Key then
                          tree(K V {Put L Key Value} R)
      [] tree(K V L R) andthen K<Key then
                          tree(K V L {Put R Key Value})
      end
   end

   fun {CondGet Ds Key Default}
      case Ds
      of leaf then Default
      [] tree(K V _ _) andthen K==Key then V
      [] tree(K _ L _) andthen K>Key then
                          {CondGet L Key Default}
      [] tree(K _ _ R) andthen K<Key then
                          {CondGet R Key Default}
      end
   end

   fun {Entries Ds}
      proc {EntriesD Ds S1 ?Sn}
         case Ds
         of leaf then
            S1=Sn
         [] tree(K V L R) then S2 S3 in
            {EntriesD L S1 S2}
            S2=K#V|S3
            {EntriesD R S3 Sn}
         end
      end
   in {EntriesD Ds $ nil} end
end
```

Figure 3.36: Standalone dictionary library (file `Dict.oz`).

```
functor
import
   Dict File
   QTk at ´x-oz://system/wp/QTk.ozf´
define
   fun {WordChar C}
      (&a=<C andthen C=<&z) orelse
      (&A=<C andthen C=<&Z) orelse (&0=<C andthen C=<&9) end

   fun {WordToAtom PW} {StringToAtom {Reverse PW}} end

   fun {IncWord D W} {Dict.put D W {Dict.condGet D W 0}+1} end

   fun {CharsToWords PW Cs}
      case Cs
      of nil andthen PW==nil then
         nil
      [] nil then
         [{WordToAtom PW}]
      [] C|Cr andthen {WordChar C} then
         {CharsToWords {Char.toLower C}|PW Cr}
      [] _|Cr andthen PW==nil then
         {CharsToWords nil Cr}
      [] _|Cr then
         {WordToAtom PW}|{CharsToWords nil Cr}
      end
   end

   fun {CountWords D Ws}
      case Ws of W|Wr then {CountWords {IncWord D W} Wr}
      [] nil then D end
   end

   fun {WordFreq Cs}
      {CountWords {Dict.new} {CharsToWords nil Cs}} end

   L={File.readList stdin}
   E={Dict.entries {WordFreq L}}
   S={Sort E fun {$ A B} A.2>B.2 end}

   H Des=td(title:´Word frequency count´
            text(handle:H tdscrollbar:true glue:nswe))
   W={QTk.build Des} {W show}
   for X#Y in S do {H insert(´end´ X#´: ´#Y#´ times\n´)} end
end
```

Figure 3.37: Standalone word frequency application (file `WordApp.oz`).

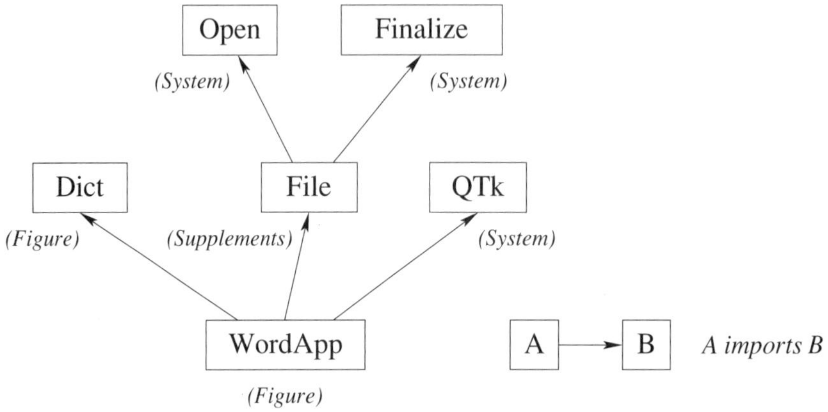

Figure 3.38: Component dependencies for the word frequency application.

display code in `WordApp.oz` could be replaced by the following:

```
H1 H2 Des=td(title:"Word frequency count"
             text(handle:H1 tdscrollbar:true glue:nswe)
             text(handle:H2 tdscrollbar:true glue:nswe))
W={QTk.build Des} {W show}

E={Dict.entries {WordFreq L}}
SE1={Sort E fun {$ A B} A.1<B.1 end}
SE2={Sort E fun {$ A B} A.2>B.2 end}
for X#Y in SE1 do
   {H1 insert('end' X#': '#Y#' times\n')}
end
for X#Y in SE2 do
   {H2 insert('end' X#': '#Y#' times\n')}
end
```

This displays two frames, one in alphabetic order and the other in order of decreasing word frequency.

Standalone compilation and execution

Let us now compile the word frequency application as a standalone program. A functor can be used in two ways: as a compiled functor (which is importable by other functors) or as a standalone program (which can be executed directly from the command line). Any functor can be compiled to make a standalone program. In that case, no export part is necessary and the initialization part defines the program's effect. Given the file `Dict.oz` defining a functor, the compiled functor `Dict.ozf` is created with the command `ozc` from a shell interface:

```
ozc -c Dict.oz
```

Given the file `WordApp.oz` defining a functor to be used as a standalone program, the standalone executable `WordApp` is created with the following command:

```
ozc -x WordApp.oz
```

This can be executed as follows:

```
WordApp < book.raw
```

where `book.raw` is a file containing a text. The text is passed to the program's standard input, which is seen inside the program as a file with the name `stdin`. This will dynamically link `Dict.ozf` when dictionaries are first accessed. It is also possible to statically link `Dict.ozf` in the compiled code of the `WordApp` application, so that no dynamic linking is needed. These possibilities are documented in the Mozart system.

Library modules

The word frequency application uses the `QTk` module, which is part of the Mozart system. Any programming language, to be practically useful, must be accompanied by a large set of useful abstractions. These are organized into libraries. A library is a coherent collection of one or more related abstractions that are useful in a particular problem domain. Depending on the language and the library, the library can be considered as part of the language or as being outside of the language. The dividing line can be quite vague: in almost all cases, many of a language's basic operations are in fact implemented in libraries. For example, higher functions on real numbers (sine, cosine, logarithm, etc.) are usually implemented in libraries. Since the number of libraries can be very great, it is a good idea to organize libraries as modules.

The importance of libraries has become increasingly important. It is fueled on the one side by the increasing speed and memory capacity of computers and on the other side by the increasing demands of users. A new language that does not come with a significant set of libraries, e.g., for network operations, graphic operations, database operations, etc., is either a toy, unsuited for real application development, or only useful in a narrow problem domain. Implementing libraries is a major effort. To alleviate this problem, new languages almost always come with an external language interface. This lets them communicate with programs written in other languages.

Library modules in Mozart The library modules available in the Mozart system consist of Base modules and System modules. The Base modules are available immediately upon startup, both in the interactive interface and in standalone applications. They provide basic operations on the language data types. The number, list, and record operations given in this chapter are in the Base modules. The System modules are available immediately upon startup in the interactive interface, but in standalone applications (i.e., functors) they must be imported. (Modules in the Mozart Standard Library, such as `QTk`, must always be installed explicitly, including in the interactive interface.) System modules provide additional functionality such as file I/O, graphical user interfaces, distributed programming, logic and constraint programming, operating system access, and so forth.

The Mozart interactive interface can give a list of the installed library modules. In the interactive `Oz` menu, open the `Compiler Panel` and click on the Environment tab. This shows all the defined variables in the global environment, including the modules.

3.10 Exercises

1. *Absolute value of real numbers.* We would like to define a function `Abs` that calculates the absolute value of a real number. The following definition does not work:

```
fun {Abs X} if X<0 then ~X else X end end
```

Why not? How would you correct it? *Hint*: the problem is trivial.

2. *Cube roots.* This chapter uses Newton's method to calculate square roots. The method can be extended to calculate roots of any degree. For example, the following method calculates cube roots. Given a guess g for the cube root of x, an improved guess is given by $(x/g^2+2g)/3$. Write a declarative program to calculate cube roots using Newton's method.

3. *The half-interval method.*[22] The half-interval method is a simple but powerful technique for finding roots of the equation $f(x) = 0$, where f is a continuous real function. The idea is that, if we are given real numbers a and b such that $f(a) < 0 < f(b)$, then f must have at least one root between a and b. To locate a root, let $x = (a+b)/2$ and compute $f(x)$. If $f(x) > 0$, then f must have a root between a and x. If $f(x) < 0$ then f must have a root between x and b. Repeating this process will define smaller and smaller intervals that converge on a root. Write a declarative program to solve this problem using the techniques of iterative computation.

4. *Iterative factorial.* This chapter gives a definition of factorial whose maximum stack depth is proportional to the input argument. Give another definition of factorial which results in an iterative computation. Use the technique of state transformations from an initial state, as shown in the `IterLength` example.

5. *An iterative* `SumList`. Rewrite the function `SumList` of section 3.4.2 to be iterative using the techniques developed for `Length`.

6. *State invariants.* Write down a state invariant for the `IterReverse` function.

7. *Another append function.* Section 3.4.2 defines the `Append` function by doing

22. This exercise is taken from [1].

recursion on the first argument. What happens if we try to do recursion on the second argument? Here is a possible solution:

```
fun {Append Ls Ms}
   case Ms
   of nil then Ls
   [] X|Mr then {Append {Append Ls [X]} Mr}
   end
end
```

Is this program correct? Does it terminate? Why or why not?

8. *An iterative append.* This exercise explores the expressive power of dataflow variables. In the declarative model, the following definition of append is iterative:

```
fun {Append Xs Ys}
   case Xs
   of nil then Ys
   [] X|Xr then X|{Append Xr Ys}
   end
end
```

We can see this by looking at the expansion:

```
proc {Append Xs Ys ?Zs}
   case Xs
   of nil then Zs=Ys
   [] X|Xr then Zr in
      Zs=X|Zr
      {Append Xr Ys Zr}
   end
end
```

This can do a last call optimization because the unbound variable `Zr` can be put in the list `Zs` and bound later. Now let us restrict the computation model to calculate with values only. How can we write an iterative append? One approach is to define two functions: (1) an iterative list reversal and (2) an iterative function that appends the reverse of a list to another list. Write an iterative append using this approach.

9. *Iterative computations and dataflow variables.* The previous exercise shows that using dataflow variables sometimes makes it simpler to write iterative list operations. This leads to the following question. For any iterative operation defined with dataflow variables, is it possible to give another iterative definition of the same operation that does not use dataflow variables?

10. *Checking if something is a list.* Section 3.4.3 defines a function `LengthL` that calculates the number of elements in a nested list. To see whether `X` is a list or not, `LengthL` uses the function `Leaf` defined in this way:

```
fun {Leaf X} case X of _|_ then false else true end end
```

What happens if we replace this by the following definition?:

```
fun {Leaf X} X\=(_|_) end
```

What goes wrong if we use this version of `Leaf`?

11. *Limitations of difference lists.* What goes wrong when trying to append the same difference list more than once?

12. *Complexity of list flattening.* Calculate the number of operations needed by the two versions of the `Flatten` function given in section 3.4.4. With n elements and maximal nesting depth k, what is the worst-case complexity of each version?

13. *Matrix operations.* Assume that we represent a matrix as a list of lists of integers, where each internal list gives one row of the matrix. Define functions to do standard matrix operations such as matrix transposition and matrix multiplication.

14. *FIFO queues.* Consider the FIFO queue defined in section 3.4.4. Answer the following two questions:

   (a) What happens if you delete an element from an empty queue?

   (b) Why is it wrong to define `IsEmpty` as follows?

```
fun {IsEmpty q(N S E)} S==E end
```

15. *Quicksort.* The following is a possible algorithm for sorting lists. Its inventor, C.A.R. Hoare, called it quicksort, because it was the fastest known general-purpose sorting algorithm at the time it was invented. It uses a divide and conquer strategy to give an average time complexity of $O(n \log n)$. Here is an informal description of the algorithm for the declarative model. Given an input list `L`, then do the following operations:

   (a) Pick `L`'s first element, `X`, to use as a pivot.

   (b) Partition `L` into two lists, `L1` and `L2`, such that all elements in `L1` are less than `X` and all elements in `L2` are greater than or equal to `X`.

   (c) Use quicksort to sort `L1` giving `S1` and to sort `L2` giving `S2`.

   (d) Append the lists `S1` and `S2` to get the answer.

Write this program with difference lists to avoid the linear cost of append.

16. (advanced exercise) *Tail-recursive convolution.*[23] For this exercise, write a function that takes two lists $[x_1\ x_2\ \cdots\ x_n]$ and $[y_1\ y_2\ \cdots\ y_n]$ and returns their symbolic convolution $[x_1\#y_n\ x_2\#y_{n-1}\ \cdots\ x_n\#y_1]$. The function should be tail recursive and do no more than n recursive calls. *Hint*: the function can calculate the reverse of the second list and pass it as an argument to itself. Because unification is order-independent, this works perfectly well.

17. (advanced exercise) *Currying.* The purpose of this exercise is to define a linguistic abstraction to add currying to Oz. First define a scheme for translating function definitions and calls. Then use the **gump** parser-generator tool to add the linguistic abstraction to Mozart.

---

23. This exercise is inspired by an exercise from Olivier Danvy.

4 Declarative Concurrency

Twenty years ago, parallel skiing was thought to be a skill attainable only after many years of training and practice. Today, it is routinely achieved during the course of a single skiing season. ... All the goals of the parents are achieved by the children: ... But the movements they make in order to produce these results are quite different.
– *Mindstorms: Children, Computers, and Powerful Ideas*, Seymour Papert (1980)

The declarative model of chapter 2 lets us write many programs and use powerful reasoning techniques on them. But, as section 4.8 explains, there exist useful programs that cannot be written easily or efficiently in it. For example, some programs are best written as a set of activities that execute independently. Such programs are called concurrent. Concurrency is essential for programs that interact with their environment, e.g., for agents, graphical user interface (GUI) programming, operating system (OS) interaction, and so forth. Concurrency also lets a program be organized into parts that execute independently and interact only when needed, i.e., client/server and producer/consumer programs. This is an important software engineering property.

Concurrency can be simple

This chapter extends the declarative model of chapter 2 with concurrency while still being declarative. That is, all the programming and reasoning techniques for declarative programming still apply. This is a remarkable property that deserves to be more widely known. We explore it throughout this chapter. The intuition underlying it is quite simple. It is based on the fact that a dataflow variable can be bound to only one value. This gives the following consequences:

- What stays the same: The result of a program is the same whether or not it is concurrent. Putting any part of the program in a thread does not change the result.
- What is new: The result of a program can be calculated incrementally. If the input to a concurrent program is given incrementally, then the program will calculate its output incrementally as well.

Let us give an example to fix this intuition. Consider the following sequential program that calculates a list of successive squares by generating a list of successive integers and then mapping each to its square:

```
fun {Gen L H}
   {Delay 100}
   if L>H then nil else L|{Gen L+1 H} end
end

Xs={Gen 1 10}
Ys={Map Xs fun {$ X} X*X end}
{Browse Ys}
```

(The `{Delay 100}` call waits for 100 ms before continuing.) We can make this concurrent by doing the generation and mapping in their own threads:

```
thread Xs={Gen 1 10} end
thread Ys={Map Xs fun {$ X} X*X end} end
{Browse Ys}
```

This uses the **thread** ⟨s⟩ **end** statement, which executes ⟨s⟩ concurrently. What is the difference between the concurrent and the sequential versions? The result of the calculation is the same in both cases, namely `[1 4 9 16 ... 81 100]`. In the sequential version, `Gen` calculates the whole list before `Map` starts. The final result is displayed all at once when the calculation is complete, after one second. In the concurrent version, `Gen` and `Map` both execute simultaneously. Whenever `Gen` adds an element to its list, `Map` will immediately calculate its square. The result is displayed incrementally, as the elements are generated, one element each tenth of a second.

We will see that the deep reason why this form of concurrency is so simple is that programs have no observable nondeterminism. A program in the declarative concurrent model always has this property, if the program does not try to bind the same variable to incompatible values. This is explained in section 4.1. Another way to say it is that there are no race conditions in a declarative concurrent program. A race condition is just an observable nondeterministic behavior.

Structure of the chapter

The chapter can be divided into six parts:

- *Programming with threads.* This part explains the first form of declarative concurrency, namely data-driven concurrency, also known as supply-driven concurrency. There are four sections. Section 4.1 defines the data-driven concurrent model, which extends the declarative model with threads. This section also explains what declarative concurrency means. Section 4.2 gives the basics of programming with threads. Section 4.3 explains the most popular technique, stream communication. Section 4.4 gives some other techniques, namely order-determining concurrency, coroutines, and concurrent composition.
- *Lazy execution.* This part explains the second form of declarative concurrency, namely demand-driven concurrency, also known as lazy execution. Section 4.5 introduces the lazy concurrent model and gives some of the most important programming techniques, including lazy streams and list comprehensions.

- *Soft real-time programming.* Section 4.6 explains how to program with time in the declarative concurrent model.
- *The Haskell language.* Section 4.7 gives an introduction to Haskell, a purely functional programming language based on lazy evaluation. Lazy evaluation is the sequential form of lazy execution.
- *Limitations and extensions of declarative programming.* How far can declarative programming go? Section 4.8 explores the limitations of declarative programming and how to overcome them. This section gives the primary motivations for explicit state, which is introduced and studied in the next four chapters.
- *Advanced topics and history.* Section 4.9 shows how to extend the declarative concurrent model with exceptions. It also goes deeper into various topics, including the different kinds of nondeterminism, lazy execution, dataflow variables, and synchronization (both explicit and implicit). Section 4.10 concludes by giving some historical notes on the roots of declarative concurrency.

Concurrency is also a key part of three other chapters. Chapter 5 extends the eager model of this chapter with a simple kind of communication channel. Chapter 8 explains how to use concurrency together with state, e.g., for concurrent object-oriented programming. Chapter 11 shows how to do distributed programming, i.e., programming a set of computers that are connected by a network. Including this chapter, all four chapters taken together give a comprehensive introduction to practical concurrent programming.

4.1 The data-driven concurrent model

In chapter 2 we presented the declarative computation model. This model is sequential, i.e., there is just one statement that executes over a single-assignment store. Let us extend the model in two steps, adding just one concept in each step:

- The first step is the most important. We add threads and the single instruction **thread** ⟨s⟩ **end**. A thread is simply an executing statement, i.e., a semantic stack. This is all we need to start programming with declarative concurrency. As we will see, adding threads to the declarative model keeps all the good properties of the model. We call the resulting model the data-driven concurrent model.
- The second step extends the model with another execution order. We add by-need triggers and the single instruction `{ByNeed P X}`. This adds the possibility to do demand-driven computation, or lazy execution. This second extension also keeps the good properties of the declarative model. We call the resulting model the demand-driven concurrent model or the lazy concurrent model. We put off explaining lazy execution until section 4.5.

For most of this chapter, we leave out exceptions from the model. This is because with exceptions the model is no longer declarative. Section 4.9.1 looks closer at the

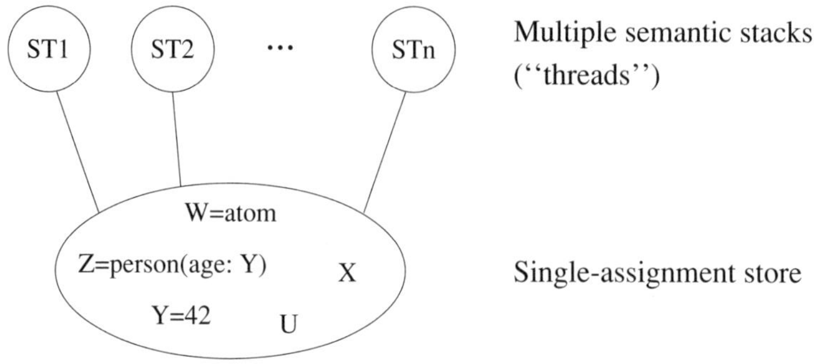

Figure 4.1: The declarative concurrent model.

⟨s⟩ ::=	
skip	Empty statement
| $\langle s\rangle_1$ $\langle s\rangle_2$	Statement sequence
| **local** ⟨x⟩ **in** ⟨s⟩ **end**	Variable creation
| $\langle x\rangle_1$=$\langle x\rangle_2$	Variable-variable binding
| ⟨x⟩=⟨v⟩	Value creation
| **if** ⟨x⟩ **then** $\langle s\rangle_1$ **else** $\langle s\rangle_2$ **end**	Conditional
| **case** ⟨x⟩ **of** ⟨pattern⟩ **then** $\langle s\rangle_1$ **else** $\langle s\rangle_2$ **end**	Pattern matching
| { ⟨x⟩ $\langle y\rangle_1 \cdots \langle y\rangle_n$ }	Procedure application
| **thread** ⟨s⟩ **end**	**Thread creation**

Table 4.1: The data-driven concurrent kernel language.

interaction of concurrency and exceptions.

4.1.1 Basic concepts

Our approach to concurrency is a simple extension to the declarative model that allows more than one executing statement to reference the store. Roughly, all these statements are executing "at the same time." This gives the model illustrated in figure 4.1, whose kernel language is in table 4.1. The kernel language extends figure 2.1 with just one new instruction, the **thread** statement.

Interleaving

Let us pause to consider precisely what "at the same time" means. There are two ways to look at the issue, which we call the language viewpoint and the

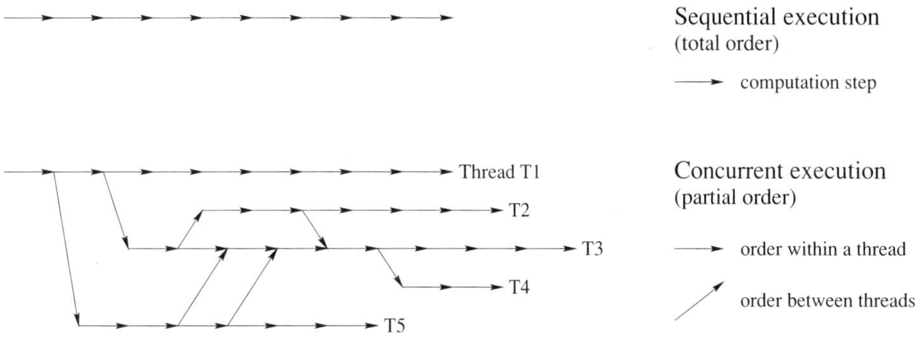

Figure 4.2: Causal orders of sequential and concurrent executions.

implementation viewpoint:

- The language viewpoint is the semantics of the language, as seen by the programmer. From this viewpoint, the simplest assumption is to let the threads do an interleaving execution; there is one global sequence of computation steps and threads take turns doing computation steps. Computation steps do not overlap; in other words, each computation step is atomic. This simplifies reasoning about programs.
- The implementation viewpoint is how the multiple threads are actually implemented on a real machine. If the system is implemented on a single processor, then the implementation could also do interleaving. However, the system might be implemented on multiple processors, so that threads can do several computation steps simultaneously. This takes advantage of parallelism to improve performance.

We use the interleaving semantics throughout the book. Whatever the parallel execution is, there is always at least one interleaving that is observationally equivalent to it. That is, if we observe the store during the execution, we can always find an interleaving execution that makes the store evolve in the same way.

Causal order

Another way to see the difference between sequential and concurrent execution is in terms of an order defined among all execution states of a given program:

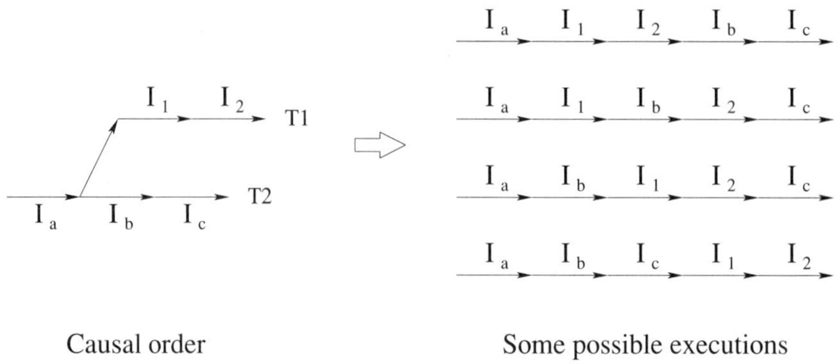

Figure 4.3: Relationship between causal order and interleaving executions.

> Causal order of computation steps
>
> For a given program, all computation steps form a partial order, called the causal order. A computation step occurs before another step if in all possible executions of the program it happens before the other. Similarly for a computation step that occurs after another step. Sometimes a step is neither before nor after another step. In that case, we say that the two steps are concurrent.

In a sequential program, all computation steps are totally ordered. There are no concurrent steps. In a concurrent program, all computation steps of a given thread are totally ordered. The computation steps of the whole program form a partial order. Two steps in this partial order are causally ordered if the first binds a dataflow variable X and the second needs the value of X.

Figure 4.2 shows the difference between sequential and concurrent execution. Figure 4.3 gives an example that shows some of the possible executions corresponding to a particular causal order. Here the causal order has two threads, T1 and T2, where T1 has two operations (I_1 and I_2) and T2 has three operations (I_a, I_b, and I_c). Four possible executions are shown. Each execution respects the causal order, i.e., all instructions that are related in the causal order are related in the same way in the execution. How many executions are possible in all? *Hint*: there are not so many in this example.

Nondeterminism

An execution is called nondeterministic if there is an execution state in which there is a choice of what to do next, i.e., a choice of which thread to reduce. Nondeterminism appears naturally when there are concurrent states. If there are several threads, then in each execution state the system has to choose which thread to execute next. For example, in figure 4.3, after the first step, which always does

I_a, there is a choice of either I_1 or I_b for the next step.

In a declarative concurrent model, the nondeterminism is not visible to the programmer.[1] There are two reasons for this. First, dataflow variables can be bound to only one value. The nondeterminism affects only the exact moment when each binding takes place; it does not affect the plain fact that the binding does take place. Second, any operation that needs the value of a variable has no choice but to wait until the variable is bound. If we allow operations that could choose whether to wait or not, the nondeterminism would become visible.

As a consequence, a declarative concurrent model keeps the good properties of the declarative model of chapter 2. The concurrent model removes some but not all of the limitations of the declarative model, as we will see in this chapter.

Scheduling

The choice of which thread to execute next is done by part of the system called the scheduler. At each computation step, the scheduler picks one among all the ready threads to execute next. We say a thread is ready, also called runnable, if its statement has all the information it needs to execute at least one computation step. Once a thread is ready, it stays ready indefinitely. We say that thread reduction in the declarative concurrent model is monotonic. A ready thread can be executed at any time.

A thread that is not ready is called suspended. Its first statement cannot continue because it does not have all the information it needs. We say the first statement is blocked. Blocking is an important concept that we will come across again.

We say the system is fair if it does not let any ready thread "starve"; i.e., all ready threads will eventually execute. This is an important property to make program behavior predictable and to simplify reasoning about programs. It is related to modularity: fairness implies that a thread's execution does not depend on that of any other thread, unless the dependency is programmed explicitly. In the rest of the book, we will assume that threads are scheduled fairly.

4.1.2 Semantics of threads

We extend the abstract machine of section 2.4 by letting it execute with several semantic stacks instead of just one. Each semantic stack corresponds to the intuitive concept "thread." All semantic stacks access the same store. Threads communicate through this shared store.

---

1. If there are no unification failures, i.e., attempts to bind the same variable to incompatible partial values. Usually we consider a unification failure as a consequence of a programmer error.

Concepts

We keep the concepts of single-assignment store σ, environment E, semantic statement $(\langle \mathsf{s}\rangle, E)$, and semantic stack ST. We extend the concepts of execution state and computation to take into account multiple semantic stacks:

- An execution state is a pair (MST, σ) where MST is a multiset of semantic stacks and σ is a single-assignment store. A multiset is a set in which the same element can occur more than once. MST has to be a multiset because we might have two different semantic stacks with identical contents, e.g., two threads that execute the same statements.
- A computation is a sequence of execution states starting from an initial state: $(MST_0, \sigma_0) \rightarrow (MST_1, \sigma_1) \rightarrow (MST_2, \sigma_2) \rightarrow \cdots$.

Program execution

As before, a program is simply a statement $\langle \mathsf{s}\rangle$. Here is how to execute the program:

- The initial execution state is

$$(\underbrace{\{\underbrace{[\overbrace{(\langle \mathsf{s}\rangle, \phi)}^{\text{statement}}]}_{\text{stack}}\}}_{\text{multiset}}, \phi)$$

That is, the initial store is empty (no variables, empty set ϕ) and the initial execution state has one semantic stack that has just one semantic statement $(\langle \mathsf{s}\rangle, \phi)$ on it. The only difference with chapter 2 is that the semantic stack is in a multiset.

- At each step, one runnable semantic stack ST is selected from MST, leaving MST'. We can say $MST = \{ST\} \uplus MST'$. (The operator $\uplus$ denotes multiset union.) One computation step is then done in ST according to the semantics of chapter 2, giving

$$(ST, \sigma) \rightarrow (ST', \sigma')$$

The computation step of the full computation is then

$$(\{ST\} \uplus MST', \sigma) \rightarrow (\{ST'\} \uplus MST', \sigma')$$

We call this an interleaving semantics because there is one global sequence of computation steps. The threads take turns, each doing a little bit of work.

- The choice of which ST to select is done by the scheduler according to a well-defined set of rules called the scheduling algorithm. This algorithm is careful to make sure that good properties, e.g., fairness, hold for any computation. A real scheduler has to take much more than just fairness into account. Section 4.2.4 discusses many of these issues and explains how the Mozart scheduler works.
- If there are no runnable semantic stacks in MST, then the computation cannot

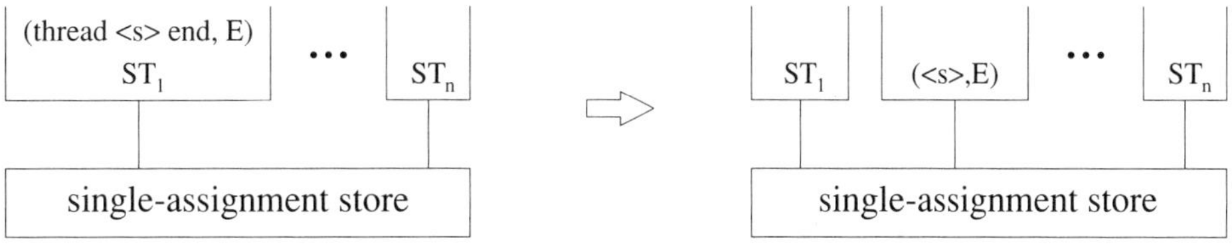

Figure 4.4: Execution of the `thread` statement.

continue:

- If all ST in MST are terminated, then we say the computation terminates.
- If there exists at least one suspended ST in MST that cannot be reclaimed (see below), then we say the computation blocks.

The `thread` *statement*

The semantics of the `thread` statement is defined in terms of how it alters the multiset MST. A `thread` statement never blocks. If the selected ST is of the form $[(\texttt{thread}\ \langle\mathsf{s}\rangle\ \texttt{end}, E)] + ST'$, then the new multiset is $\{[(\langle\mathsf{s}\rangle, E)]\} \uplus \{ST'\} \uplus MST'$. In other words, we add a new semantic stack $[(\langle\mathsf{s}\rangle, E)]$ that corresponds to the new thread. Figure 4.4 illustrates this. We can summarize this in the following computation step:

$$(\{[(\texttt{thread}\ \langle\mathsf{s}\rangle\ \texttt{end}, E)] + ST'\} \uplus MST', \sigma) \rightarrow (\{[(\langle\mathsf{s}\rangle, E)]\} \uplus \{ST'\} \uplus MST', \sigma)$$

Memory management

Memory management is extended to the multiset as follows:

- A terminated semantic stack can be deallocated.
- A blocked semantic stack can be reclaimed if its activation condition depends on an unreachable variable. In that case, the semantic stack would never become runnable again, so removing it changes nothing during the execution.

This means that the simple intuition of chapter 2, that "control structures are deallocated and data structures are reclaimed," is no longer completely true in the concurrent model.

4.1.3 Example execution

The first example shows how threads are created and how they communicate through dataflow synchronization. Consider the following statement:

```
local B in
   thread B=true end
   if B then {Browse yes} end
end
```

For simplicity, we will use the substitution-based abstract machine introduced in section 3.3.

- We skip the initial computation steps and go directly to the situation when the **thread** and **if** statements are each on the semantic stack. This gives

({[**thread** b=**true end**, **if** b **then** {Browse yes} **end**]},
  $\{b\} \cup \sigma$)

where b is a variable in the store. There is just one semantic stack, which contains two statements.

- After executing the **thread** statement, we get

({[b=**true**], [**if** b **then** {Browse yes} **end**]},
  $\{b\} \cup \sigma$)

There are now two semantic stacks ("threads"). The first, containing b=**true**, is ready. The second, containing the **if** statement, is suspended because the activation condition (b determined) is false.

- The scheduler picks the ready thread. After executing one step, we get

({[], [**if** b **then** {Browse yes} **end**]},
  $\{b = \texttt{true}\} \cup \sigma$)

The first thread has terminated (empty semantic stack). The second thread is now ready, since b is determined.

- We remove the empty semantic stack and execute the **if** statement. This gives

({[{Browse yes}]},
  $\{b = \texttt{true}\} \cup \sigma$)

One ready thread remains. Further calculation will display `yes`.

4.1.4 What is declarative concurrency?

Let us see why we can consider the data-driven concurrent model as a form of declarative programming. The basic principle of declarative programming is that the output of a declarative program should be a mathematical function of its input. In functional programming, it is clear what this means: the program executes with some input values and when it terminates, it has returned some output values. The output values are functions of the input values. But what does this mean in the data-driven concurrent model? There are two important differences with functional programming. First, the inputs and outputs are not necessarily values since they can contain unbound variables. And second, execution might not terminate since the inputs can be streams that grow indefinitely! Let us look at these two problems one at a time and then define what we mean by declarative concurrency.[2]

Partial termination

As a first step, let us factor out the indefinite growth. We will present the execution of a concurrent program as a series of stages, where each stage has a natural ending. Here is a simple example:

```
fun {Double Xs}
   case Xs of X|Xr then 2*X|{Double Xr} end
end

Ys={Double Xs}
```

The output stream `Ys` contains the elements of the input stream `Xs` multiplied by 2. As long as `Xs` grows, then `Ys` grows too. The program never terminates. However, if the input stream stops growing, then the program will eventually stop executing too. This is an important insight. We say that the program does a partial termination. It has not terminated completely yet, since further binding the inputs would cause it to execute further (up to the next partial termination!). But if the inputs do not change, then the program will execute no further.

Logical equivalence

If the inputs are bound to some partial values, then the program will eventually end up in partial termination, and the outputs will be bound to other partial values. But in what sense are the outputs "functions" of the inputs? Both inputs and outputs can contain unbound variables! For example, if `Xs=1|2|3|Xr`, then the `Ys={Double Xs}` call returns `Ys=2|4|6|Yr`, where `Xr` and `Yr` are unbound variables. What does it mean that `Ys` is a function of `Xs`?

To answer this question, we have to understand what it means for store contents to be "the same." Let us give a simple definition from first principles. (Chapters 9 and 13 give a more formal definition based on mathematical logic.) Before giving the definition, we look at two examples to get an understanding of what is going on. The first example can bind `X` and `Y` in two different ways:

```
X=1 Y=X    % First case
Y=X X=1    % Second case
```

In the first case, the store ends up with `X=1` and `Y=X`. In the second case, the store ends up with `X=1` and `Y=1`. In both cases, `X` and `Y` end up being bound to 1. This means that the store contents are the same for both cases. (We assume that the identifiers denote the same store variables in both cases.) Let us give a second

2. Chapter 13 gives a formal definition of declarative concurrency that makes precise the ideas of this section.

example, this time with some unbound variables:

```
X=foo(Y W) Y=Z    % First case
X=foo(Z W) Y=Z    % Second case
```

In both cases, X is bound to the same record, except that the first argument can be different, Y or Z. Since Y=Z (Y and Z are in the same equivalence set), we again expect the store contents to be the same for both cases.

Now let us define what logical equivalence means. We will define logical equivalence in terms of store variables. The above examples used identifiers, but that was just so that we could execute them. A set of store bindings, like each of the four cases given above, is called a constraint. For each variable x and constraint c, we define values(x, c) to be the set of all possible values x can have, given that c holds. Then we define:

Two constraints c_1 and c_2 are *logically equivalent* if: (1) they contain the same variables, and (2) for each variable x, values(x, c_1) = values(x, c_2).

For example, the constraint $x = \texttt{foo(}y\ w\texttt{)} \wedge y = z$ (where x, y, z, and w are store variables) is logically equivalent to the constraint $x = \texttt{foo(}z\ w\texttt{)} \wedge y = z$. This is because $y = z$ forces y and z to have the same set of possible values, so that $\texttt{foo(}y\ w\texttt{)}$ defines the same set of values as $\texttt{foo(}z\ w\texttt{)}$. Note that variables in an equivalence set (like $\{y, z\}$) always have the same set of possible values.

Declarative concurrency

Now we can define what it means for a concurrent program to be declarative. In general, a concurrent program can have many possible executions. The thread example given above has at least two, depending on the order in which the bindings X=1 and Y=X are done.[3] The key insight is that all these executions have to end up with the same result. But "the same" does not mean that each variable has to be bound to the same thing. It just means logical equivalence. This leads to the following definition:

> A concurrent program is *declarative* if the following holds for all possible inputs. All executions with a given set of inputs have one of two results: (1) they all do not terminate or (2) they all eventually reach partial termination and give results that are logically equivalent. Different executions may introduce new variables; we assume that the new variables in corresponding positions are equal.

Another way to say this is that there is no observable nondeterminism. This definition is valid for eager as well as lazy execution. What's more, when we introduce nondeclarative models (e.g., with exceptions or explicit state), we will use this definition as a criterion: if part of a nondeclarative program obeys the

3. In fact, there are more than two, because the binding X=1 can be done either before or after the second thread is created.

definition, we can consider it as declarative for the rest of the program.

We can prove that the data-driven concurrent model is declarative according to this definition. But even more general declarative models exist. The demand-driven concurrent model of section 4.5 is also declarative. This model is quite general: it has threads and can do both eager and lazy execution. The fact that it is declarative is astonishing.

Failure

A failure is an abnormal termination of a declarative program that occurs when we attempt to put conflicting information in the store, e.g., if we would bind `X` both to 1 and to 2. The declarative program cannot continue because there is no correct value for `X`.

Failure is an all-or-nothing property: if a declarative concurrent program results in failure for a given set of inputs, then all possible executions with those inputs will result in failure. This must be so, else the output would not be a mathematical function of the input (some executions would lead to failure and others would not). Take the following example:

```
thread X=1 end
thread Y=2 end
thread X=Y end
```

We see that all executions will eventually reach a conflicting binding and subsequently terminate.

Most failures are due to programmer errors. It is rather drastic to terminate the whole program because of a single programmer error. Often we would like to continue execution instead of terminating, perhaps to repair the error or simply to report it. A natural way to do this is by using exceptions. At the point where a failure would occur, we raise an exception instead of terminating. The program can catch the exception and continue executing. The store contents are what they were just before the failure.

However, it is important to realize that execution after raising the exception is no longer declarative! This is because the store contents are not always the same in all executions. In the above example, just before failure occurs, there are three possibilities for the values of `X` & `Y`: 1 & 1, 2 & 2, and 1 & 2. If the program continues execution, then we can observe these values. This is an observable nondeterminism. We say that we have "left the declarative model." From the instant when the exception is raised, the execution is no longer part of a declarative model, but is part of a more general (nondeclarative) model.

Failure confinement

If we want execution to become declarative again after a failure, then we have to hide the nondeterminism. This is the responsibility of the programmer. For the reader who is curious as to how to do this, let us get ahead of ourselves a little and show how to repair the previous example. Assume that X and Y are visible to the rest of the program. If there is an exception, we arrange for X and Y to be bound to default values. If there is no exception, then they are bound as before.

```
declare X Y
local X1 Y1 S1 S2 S3 in
   thread
      try X1=1  S1=ok catch _ then S1=error end
   end
   thread
      try Y1=2  S2=ok catch _ then S2=error end
   end
   thread
      try X1=Y1 S3=ok catch _ then S3=error end
   end
   if S1==error orelse S2==error orelse S3==error then
      X=1  % Default for X
      Y=1  % Default for Y
   else X=X1 Y=Y1 end
end
```

Two things have to be repaired. First, we catch the failure exceptions with the **try** statements, so that execution will not stop with an error. (See section 4.9.1 for more on the declarative concurrent model with exceptions.) A **try** statement is needed for each binding since each binding could fail. Second, we do the bindings in local variables X1 and Y1, which are invisible to the rest of the program. We make the bindings global only when we are sure that there is no failure.[4]

4.2 Basic thread programming techniques

There are many new programming techniques that become possible in the concurrent model with respect to the sequential model. This section examines the simplest ones, which are based on a simple use of the dataflow property of thread execution. We also look at the scheduler and see what operations are possible on threads. Later sections explain more sophisticated techniques, including stream communication, order-determining concurrency, and others.

4.2.1 Creating threads

The **thread** statement creates a new thread:

```
thread
   proc {Count N} if N>0 then {Count N-1} end end
in
   {Count 1000000}
end
```

4. This assumes that X=X1 and Y=Y1 will not fail.

This creates a new thread that runs concurrently with the main thread. The **thread** ... **end** notation can also be used as an expression:

```
declare X in
X = thread 10*10 end + 100*100
{Browse X}
```

This is just syntactic sugar for:

```
declare X in
local Y in
   thread Y=10*10 end
   X=Y+100*100
end
```

A new dataflow variable, `Y`, is created to communicate between the main thread and the new thread. The addition blocks until the calculation `10*10` is finished.

When a thread has no more statements to execute, then it terminates. Each nonterminated thread that is not suspended will eventually be run. We say that threads are scheduled fairly. Thread execution is implemented with preemptive scheduling. That is, if more than one thread is ready to execute, then each thread will get processor time in discrete intervals called time slices. It is not possible for one thread to take over all the processor time.

4.2.2 Threads and the browser

The browser is a good example of a program that works well in a concurrent environment. For example:

```
thread {Browse 111} end
{Browse 222}
```

In what order are the values `111` and `222` displayed? The answer is, either order is possible! Is it possible that something like `112122` will be displayed, or worse, that the browser will behave erroneously? At first glance, it might seem so, since the browser has to execute many statements to display each value `111` and `222`. If no special precautions are taken, then these statements can indeed be executed in almost any order. But the browser is designed for a concurrent environment. It will never display strange interleavings. Each browser call is given its own part of the browser window to display its argument. If the argument contains an unbound variable that is bound later, then the display will be updated when the variable is bound. In this way, the browser will correctly display multiple streams that grow concurrently, for example:

```
declare X1 X2 Y1 Y2 in
thread {Browse X1} end
thread {Browse Y1} end
thread X1=all|roads|X2 end
thread Y1=all|roams|Y2 end
thread X2=lead|to|rome|_ end
thread Y2=lead|to|rhodes|_ end
```

This correctly displays the two streams

```
all|roads|lead|to|rome|_
all|roams|lead|to|rhodes|_
```

in separate parts of the browser window. In this chapter and later chapters we will see how to write concurrent programs that behave correctly, like the browser.

4.2.3 Dataflow computation with threads

Let us see what we can do by adding threads to simple programs. It is important to remember that each thread is a dataflow thread, i.e., it suspends on availability of data.

Simple dataflow behavior

We start by observing dataflow behavior in a simple calculation. Consider the following program:

```
declare X0 X1 X2 X3 in
thread
Y0 Y1 Y2 Y3 in
   {Browse [Y0 Y1 Y2 Y3]}
   Y0=X0+1
   Y1=X1+Y0
   Y2=X2+Y1
   Y3=X3+Y2
   {Browse completed}
end
{Browse [X0 X1 X2 X3]}
```

If you feed this program, then the browser will display all the variables as being unbound. Observe what happens when you input the following statements one at a time:

```
X0=0
X1=1
X2=2
X3=3
```

With each statement, the thread resumes, executes one addition, and then suspends again. That is, when `X0` is bound, the thread can execute `Y0=X0+1`. It suspends again because it needs the value of `X1` while executing `Y1=X1+Y0`, and so on.

Using a declarative program in a concurrent setting

Let us take a program from chapter 3 and see how it behaves when used in a concurrent setting. Consider the `ForAll` loop, which is defined as follows:

```
proc {ForAll L P}
   case L of nil then skip
   [] X|L2 then {P X} {ForAll L2 P} end
end
```

What happens when we execute it in a thread?:

```
declare L in
thread {ForAll L Browse} end
```

If L is unbound, then this will immediately suspend. We can bind L in other threads:

```
declare L1 L2 in
thread L=1|L1 end
thread L1=2|3|L2 end
thread L2=4|nil end
```

What is the output? Is the result any different from the result of the sequential call `{ForAll [1 2 3 4] Browse}`? What is the effect of using `ForAll` in a concurrent setting?

A concurrent map function

Here is a concurrent version of the `Map` function defined in section 3.6.4:

```
fun {Map Xs F}
   case Xs of nil then nil
   [] X|Xr then thread {F X} end|{Map Xr F} end
end
```

The **thread** statement is used here as an expression. Let us explore the behavior of this program. If we enter the following statements:

```
declare F Xs Ys Zs
{Browse thread {Map Xs F} end}
```

then a new thread executing `{Map Xs F}` is created. It will suspend immediately in the **case** statement because `Xs` is unbound. If we enter the following statements (without a **declare**!):

```
Xs=1|2|Ys
fun {F X} X*X end
```

then the main thread will traverse the list, creating two threads for the first two arguments of the list, `thread {F 1} end` and `thread {F 2} end`, and then it will suspend again on the tail of the list `Y`. Finally, doing

```
Ys=3|Zs
Zs=nil
```

will create a third thread with `thread {F 3} end` and terminate the computation of the main thread. The three threads will also terminate, resulting in the final list `[1 4 9]`. Remark that the result is the same as the sequential map function, only it can be obtained incrementally if the input is given incrementally. The sequential map function executes as a "batch": the calculation gives no result until the complete input is given, and then it gives the complete result.

A concurrent Fibonacci function

Here is a concurrent divide-and-conquer program to calculate the Fibonacci function:

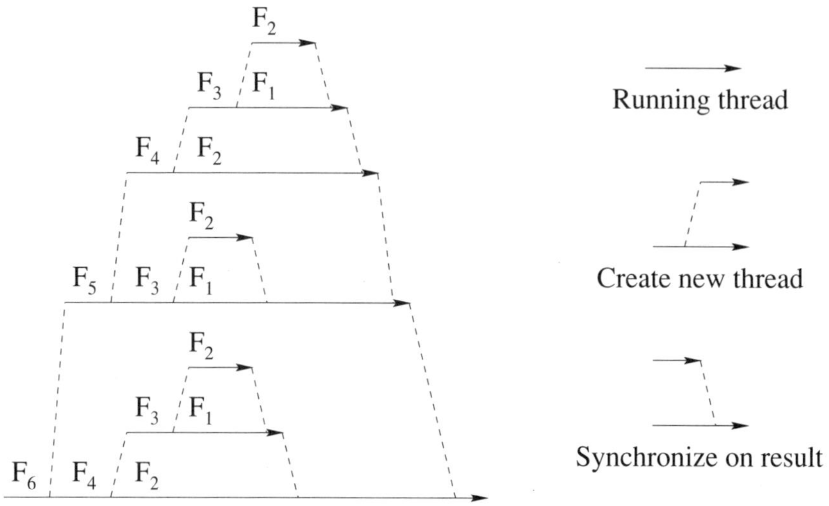

Figure 4.5: Thread creations for the call {Fib 6}.

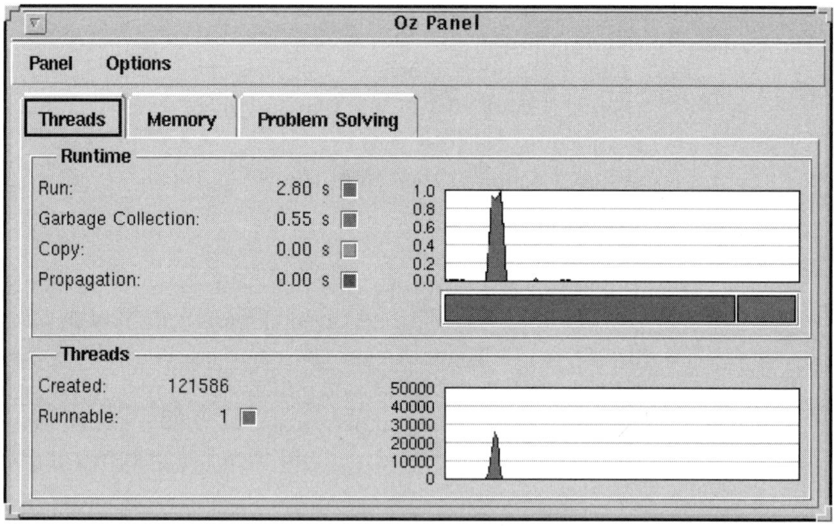

Figure 4.6: The Oz Panel showing thread creation in X={Fib 26}.

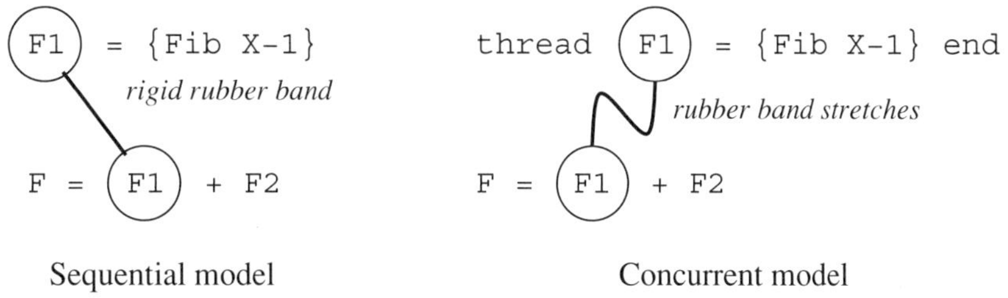

Figure 4.7: Dataflow and rubber bands.

```
fun {Fib X}
   if X=<2 then 1
   else thread {Fib X-1} end + {Fib X-2} end
end
```

This program is based on the sequential recursive Fibonacci function; the only difference is that the first recursive call is done in its own thread. This program creates an exponential number of threads! Figure 4.5 shows all the thread creations and synchronizations for the call `{Fib 6}`. A total of eight threads are involved in this calculation. You can use this program to test how many threads your Mozart installation can create. For example, feed

```
{Browse {Fib 26}}
```

while observing the `Oz Panel` to see how many threads are running. If `{Fib 26}` completes too quickly, try a larger argument. The `Oz Panel`, shown in figure 4.6, is a Mozart tool that gives information on system behavior (run time, memory usage, threads, etc.). To start the `Oz Panel`, select the `Oz Panel` entry of the `Oz` menu in the interactive interface.

Dataflow and rubber bands

By now, it is clear that any declarative program of chapter 3 can be made concurrent by putting **thread** ... **end** around some of its statements and expressions. Because each dataflow variable will be bound to the same value as before, the final result of the concurrent version will be exactly the same as the original sequential version.

One way to see this intuitively is by means of rubber bands. Each dataflow variable has its own rubber band. One end of the rubber band is attached to where the variable is bound and the other end to where the variable is used. Figure 4.7 shows what happens in the sequential and concurrent models. In the sequential model, binding and using are usually close to each other, so the rubber bands do not stretch much. In the concurrent model, binding and using can be done in different threads, so the rubber band is stretched. But it never breaks: the user always sees the right value.

Cheap concurrency and program structure

By using threads, it is often possible to improve the structure of a program, e.g., to make it more modular. Most large programs have many places in which threads could be used for this. Ideally, the programming system should support this with threads that use few computational resources. In this respect the Mozart system is excellent. Threads are so cheap that one can afford to create them in large numbers. For example, entry-level personal computers of the year 2003 typically have at least 256 MB of active memory, with which they can support more than 100000 simultaneous active threads.

If using concurrency lets your program have a simpler structure, then use it without hesitation. But keep in mind that even though threads are cheap, sequential programs are even cheaper. Sequential programs are always faster than concurrent programs having the same structure. The `Fib` program in section 4.2.3 is faster if the **`thread`** statement is removed. You should create threads only when the program needs them. On the other hand, you should not hesitate to create a thread if it improves program structure.

4.2.4 Thread scheduling

We have seen that the scheduler should be fair, i.e., every ready thread will eventually execute. A real scheduler has to do much more than just guarantee fairness. Let us see what other issues arise and how the scheduler takes care of them.

Time slices

The scheduler puts all ready threads in a queue. At each step, it takes the first thread out of the queue, lets it execute some number of steps, and then puts it back in the queue. This is called round-robin scheduling. It guarantees that processor time is spread out equitably over the ready threads.

It would be inefficient to let each thread execute only one computation step before putting it back in the queue. The overhead of queue management (taking threads out and putting them in) relative to the actual computation would be quite high. Therefore, the scheduler lets each thread execute for many computation steps before putting it back in the queue. Each thread has a maximum time that it is allowed to run before the scheduler stops it. This time interval is called its time slice or quantum. After a thread's time slice has run out, the scheduler stops its execution and puts it back in the queue. Stopping a running thread in this way is called preemption.

To make sure that each thread gets roughly the same fraction of the processor time, a thread scheduler has two approaches. The first way is to count computation steps and give the same number to each thread. The second way is to use a hardware timer that gives the same time to each thread. Both approaches are practical. Let us compare the two:

- The counting approach has the advantage that scheduler execution is deterministic, i.e., running the same program twice will preempt threads at exactly the same instants. A deterministic scheduler is often used for hard real-time applications, where guarantees must be given on timings.
- The timer approach is more efficient, because the timer is supported by hardware. However, the scheduler is no longer deterministic. Any event in the operating system, e.g., a disk or network operation, will change the exact instants when preemption occurs.

The Mozart system uses a hardware timer.

Priority levels

For many applications, more control is needed over how processor time is shared between threads. For example, during the course of a computation, an event may happen that requires urgent treatment, bypassing the "normal" computation. On the other hand, it should not be possible for urgent computations to starve normal computations, i.e., to cause them to slow down inordinately.

A compromise that seems to work well in practice is to have priority levels for threads. Each priority level is given a minimum percentage of the processor time. Within each priority level, threads share the processor time fairly as before. The Mozart system uses this technique. It has three priority levels, high, medium, and low. There are three queues, one for each priority level. By default, processor time is divided among the priorities in the ratios 100:10:1 for high-medium-low priorities. This is implemented in a very simple way: for every tenth time slice of a high-priority thread, a medium-priority thread is given one slice. Similarly, for every tenth time slice of a medium-priority thread, a low-priority thread is given one slice. This means that high-priority threads, if there are any, divide at least 100/111 (about 90%) of the processor time among themselves. Similarly, medium-priority threads, if there are any, divide at least 10/111 (about 9%) of the processor time among themselves. And last of all, low-priority threads, if there are any, divide at least 1/111 (about 1%) of the processor time among themselves. These percentages are guaranteed lower bounds. If there are fewer threads, then they might be higher. For example, if there are no high-priority threads, then a medium-priority thread can get up to 10/11 of the processor time. In Mozart, the ratios high-medium and medium-low are both 10 by default. They can be changed with the `Property` module.

Priority inheritance

When a thread creates a child thread, then the child is given the same priority as the parent. This is particularly important for high-priority threads. In an application, these threads are used for "urgency management," i.e., to do work that must be handled in advance of the normal work. The part of the application doing urgency management can be concurrent. If the child of a high-priority thread would have, say, medium priority, then there is a short "window" of time during which the child thread is medium priority, until the parent or child can change the thread's priority. The existence of this window would be enough to keep the child thread from being scheduled for many time slices, because the thread is put in the queue of medium priority. This could result in hard-to-trace timing bugs. Therefore a child thread should never get a lower priority than its parent.

Time slice duration

What is the effect of the time slice's duration? A short slice gives very "fine-grained" concurrency: threads react quickly to external events. But if the slice is too short, then the overhead of switching between threads becomes significant. Another question is how to implement preemption: does the thread itself keep track of how long it has run, or is it done externally? Both solutions are viable, but the second is much easier to implement. Modern multitasking operating systems, such as Unix, Windows 2000/XP, or Mac OS X, have timer interrupts that can be used to trigger preemption. These interrupts arrive at a fairly low frequency, 60 or 100 per second. The Mozart system uses this technique.

A time slice of 10 ms may seem short enough, but for some applications it is too long. For example, assume the application has 100000 active threads. Then each thread gets one time slice every 1000 seconds. This may be too long a wait. In practice, we find that this is not a problem. In applications with many threads, such as large constraint programs (see chapter 12), the threads usually depend strongly on each other and not on the external world. Each thread only uses a small part of its time slice before yielding to another thread.

On the other hand, it is possible to imagine an application with many threads, each of which interacts with the external world independently of the other threads. For such an application, it is clear that Mozart, as well as recent Unix, Windows, or Mac OS X operating systems, is unsatisfactory. The hardware itself of a personal computer is unsatisfactory. What is needed is a hard real-time computing system, which uses a special kind of hardware together with a special kind of operating system. Hard real time is outside the scope of the book.

4.2.5 Cooperative and competitive concurrency

Threads are intended for cooperative concurrency, not for competitive concurrency. Cooperative concurrency is for entities that are working together on some global goal. Threads support this, e.g., any thread can change the time ratios between the three priorities, as we will see. Threads are intended for applications that run in an environment where all parts trust one another.

On the other hand, competitive concurrency is for entities that have a local goal, i.e., they are working just for themselves. They are interested only in their own performance, not in the global performance. Competitive concurrency is usually

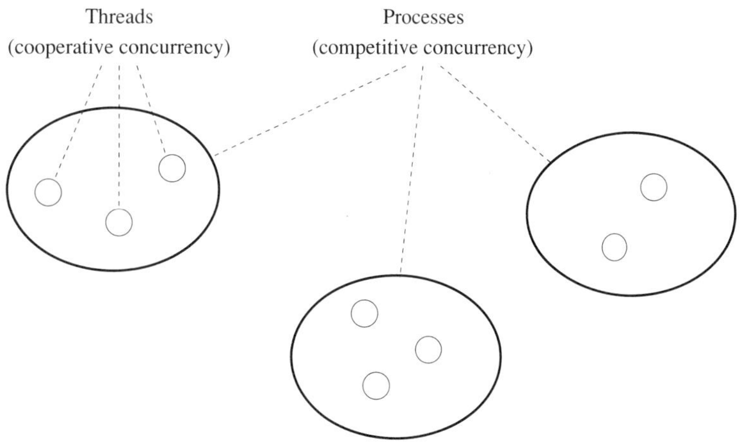

Figure 4.8: Cooperative and competitive concurrency.

managed by the operating system in terms of a concept called a process.

This means that computations often have a two-level structure, as shown in figure 4.8. At the highest level, there is a set of operating system processes interacting with each other, doing competitive concurrency. Processes are usually owned by different applications, with different, perhaps conflicting goals. Within each process, there is a set of threads interacting with each other, doing cooperative concurrency. Threads in one process are usually owned by the same application.

Competitive concurrency is supported in Mozart by its distributed computation model and by the `Remote` module. The `Remote` module creates a separate operating system process with its own computational resources. A competitive computation can then be put in this process. This is relatively easy to program because the distributed model is network-transparent: the same program can run with different distribution structures, i.e., on different sets of processes, and it will always give the same result.[5]

4.2.6 Thread operations

The modules `Thread` and `Property` provide a number of operations pertinent to threads. Some of these operations are summarized in table 4.2. The priority `P` of a thread is one of the three atoms `low`, `medium`, and `high`. The state of a thread is one of the three atoms `runnable`, `blocked`, and `terminated`. Each thread has a unique name, which refers to the thread when doing operations on it. The thread name is a value of `Name` type. The only way to get a thread's name is for the thread

5. This is true as long as no process fails. See chapter 11 for examples and more information.

Operation	Description
{Thread.this}	Return the current thread's name
{Thread.state T}	Return the current state of T
{Thread.suspend T}	Suspend T (stop its execution)
{Thread.resume T}	Resume T (undo suspension)
{Thread.preempt T}	Preempt T
{Thread.terminate T}	Terminate T immediately
{Thread.injectException T E}	Raise exception E in T
{Thread.setPriority T P}	Set T's priority to P
{Thread.setThisPriority P}	Set current thread's priority to P
{Property.get priorities}	Return the system priority ratios
{Property.put priorities p(high:X medium:Y)}	Set the system priority ratios

Table 4.2: Operations on threads.

itself to call `Thread.this`. It is not possible for another thread to get the name without cooperation from the original thread. This makes it possible to rigorously control access to thread names. The system procedure

```
{Property.put priorities p(high:X medium:Y)}
```

sets the processor time ratio to `X:1` between high priority and medium priority and to `Y:1` between medium priority and low priority. `X` and `Y` are integers. If we execute

```
{Property.put priorities p(high:10 medium:10)}
```

then for each ten time slices allocated to runnable high-priority threads, the system will allocate one time slice to medium-priority threads, and similarly between medium-priority and low-priority threads. This is the default. Within the same priority level, scheduling is fair and round robin.

4.3 Streams

The most useful technique for concurrent programming in the declarative concurrent model is using streams to communicate between threads. A stream is a potentially unbounded list of messages, i.e., it is a list whose tail is an unbound dataflow variable. Sending a message is done by extending the stream by one element: bind the tail to a list pair containing the message and a new unbound tail. Receiving a message is reading a stream element. A thread communicating through streams is a kind of "active object" that we will call a stream object. No locking or mutual exclusion is necessary since each variable is bound by only one thread.

Stream programming is a quite general approach that can be applied in many

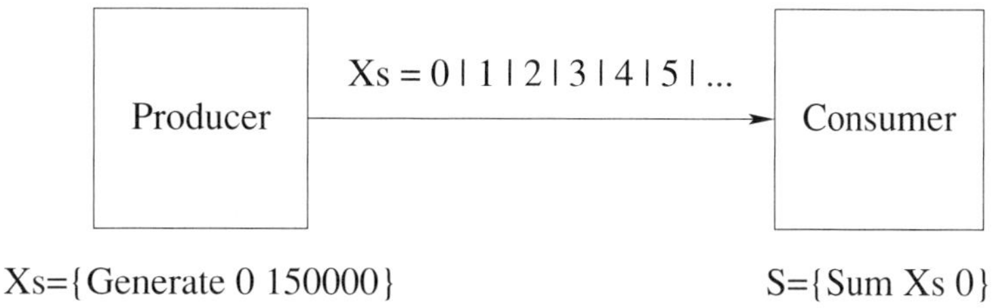

Figure 4.9: Producer/consumer stream communication.

domains. It is the concept underlying Unix pipes. Morrison uses it to good effect in business applications, in an approach he calls "flow-based programming" [146]. This chapter looks at a special case of stream programming, namely deterministic stream programming, in which each stream object always knows for each input where the next message will come from. This case is interesting because it is declarative. Yet it is already quite useful. We put off looking at nondeterministic stream programming until chapter 5.

4.3.1 Basic producer/consumer

This section explains how streams work and shows how to program an asynchronous producer/consumer with streams. In the declarative concurrent model, a stream is represented by a list whose tail is an unbound variable:

```
declare Xs Xs2 in
Xs=0|1|2|3|4|Xs2
```

A stream is created incrementally by binding the tail to a new list pair and a new tail:

```
declare Xs3 in
Xs2=5|6|7|Xs3
```

One thread, called the producer, creates the stream in this way, and other threads, called the consumers, read the stream. Because the stream's tail is a dataflow variable, the consumers will read the stream as it is created. The following program asynchronously generates a stream of integers and sums them:

```
fun {Generate N Limit}
   if N<Limit then
      N|{Generate N+1 Limit}
   else nil end
end
fun {Sum Xs A}
   case Xs
   of X|Xr then {Sum Xr A+X}
   [] nil then A
   end
end
```

```
local Xs S in
   thread Xs={Generate 0 150000} end  % Producer thread
   thread S={Sum Xs 0} end            % Consumer thread
   {Browse S}
end
```

Figure 4.9 gives a particularly nice way to define this pattern, using a precise graphic notation. Each rectangle denotes a recursive function inside a thread, the solid arrow denotes a stream, and the arrow's direction is from producer to consumer. After the calculation is finished, this displays `11249925000`. The producer, `Generate`, and the consumer, `Sum`, run in their own threads. They communicate through the shared variable `Xs`, which is bound to a stream of integers. The **`case`** statement in `Sum` blocks when `Xs` is unbound (no more elements), and resumes when `Xs` is bound (new elements arrive).

In the consumer, dataflow behavior of the **`case`** statement blocks execution until the arrival of the next stream element. This synchronizes the consumer thread with the producer thread. Waiting for a dataflow variable to be bound is the basic mechanism for synchronization and communication in the declarative concurrent model.

Using a higher-order iterator

The recursive call to `Sum` has an argument `A` that is the sum of all elements seen so far. This argument and the function's output together make an accumulator, as we saw in chapter 3. We can get rid of the accumulator by using a loop abstraction:

```
local Xs S in
   thread Xs={Generate 0 150000} end
   thread S={FoldL Xs fun {$ X Y} X+Y end 0} end
   {Browse S}
end
```

Because of dataflow variables, the `FoldL` function has no problems working in a concurrent setting. Getting rid of an accumulator by using a higher-order iterator is a general technique. The accumulator is not really gone, it is just hidden inside the iterator. But writing the program is simpler since the programmer no longer has to reason in terms of state. The `List` module has many loop abstractions and other higher-order operations that can be used to help implement recursive functions.

Multiple readers

We can introduce multiple consumers without changing the program in any way. For example, here are three consumers, reading the same stream:

```
local Xs S1 S2 S3 in
   thread Xs={Generate 0 150000} end
   thread S1={Sum Xs 0} end
   thread S2={Sum Xs 0} end
   thread S3={Sum Xs 0} end
end
```

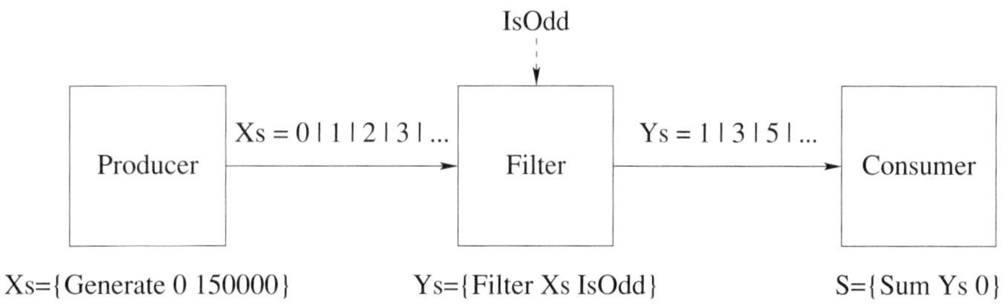

Figure 4.10: Filtering a stream.

Each consumer thread will receive stream elements independently of the others. The consumers do not interfere with each other because they do not actually "consume" the stream; they just read it.

4.3.2 Transducers and pipelines

We can put a third stream object in between the producer and consumer. This stream object reads the producer's stream and creates another stream which is read by the consumer. We call it a transducer. In general, a sequence of stream objects each of which feeds the next is called a pipeline. The producer is sometimes called the source and the consumer is sometimes called the sink. Let us look at some pipelines with different kinds of transducers.

Filtering a stream

One of the simplest transducers is the filter, which outputs only those elements of the input stream that satisfy a given condition. A simple way to make a filter is to put a call to the function `Filter`, which we saw in chapter 3, inside its own thread. For example, we can pass only those elements that are odd integers:

```
local Xs Ys S in
   thread Xs={Generate 0 150000} end
   thread Ys={Filter Xs IsOdd} end
   thread S={Sum Ys 0} end
   {Browse S}
end
```

where `IsOdd` is a one-argument boolean function that is true only for odd integers:

```
fun {IsOdd X} X mod 2 \= 0 end
```

Figure 4.10 shows this pattern. This figure introduces another bit of graphic notation, the dotted arrow, which denotes a single value (a non-stream argument to the function).

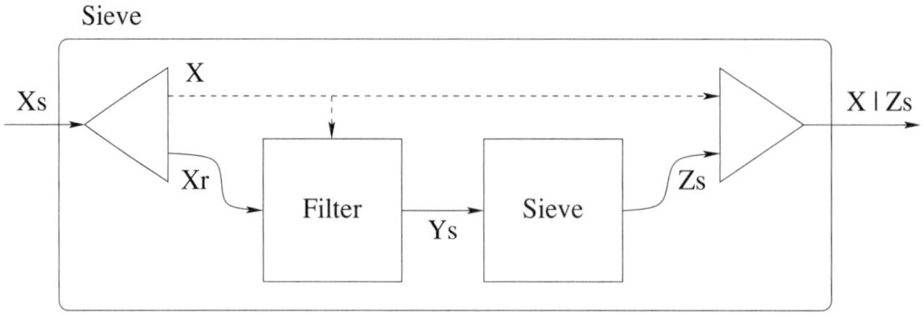

Figure 4.11: A prime-number sieve with streams.

Sieve of Eratosthenes

As a bigger example, let us define a pipeline that implements the prime-number sieve of Eratosthenes. The output of the sieve is a stream containing only prime numbers. This program is called a "sieve" since it works by successively filtering out nonprimes from streams, until only primes remain. The filters are created dynamically when they are first needed. The producer generates a stream of consecutive integers starting from 2. The sieve peels off an element and creates a filter to remove multiples of that element. It then calls itself recursively on the stream of remaining elements. Filter 4.11 gives a picture. This introduces yet another bit of graphic notation, the triangle, which denotes either peeling off the first element of a stream or prefixing a new first element to a stream. Here is the sieve definition:

```
fun {Sieve Xs}
   case Xs
   of nil then nil
   [] X|Xr then Ys in
      thread Ys={Filter Xr fun {$ Y} Y mod X \= 0 end} end
      X|{Sieve Ys}
   end
end
```

This definition is quite simple, considering that it is dynamically setting up a pipeline of concurrent activities. Let us call the sieve:

```
local Xs Ys in
   thread Xs={Generate 2 100000} end
   thread Ys={Sieve Xs} end
   {Browse Ys}
end
```

This displays prime numbers up to 100000. This program is a bit simplistic because it creates too many threads, namely one per prime number. Such a large number of threads is not necessary since it is easy to see that generating prime numbers

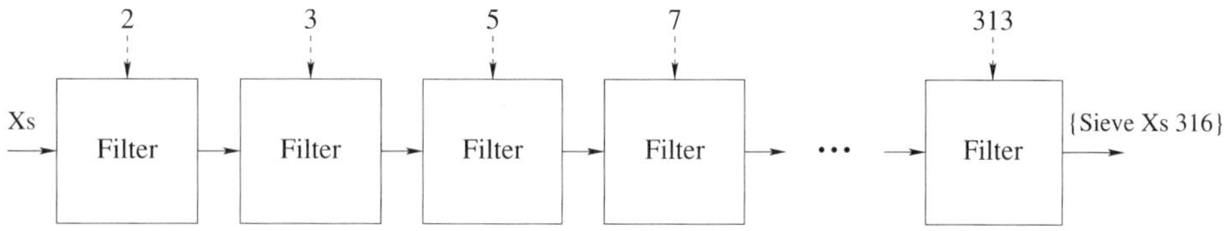

Figure 4.12: Pipeline of filters generated by {Sieve Xs 316}.

up to n requires filtering multiples only up to $\sqrt{n}$.[6] We can modify the program to create filters only up to this limit:

```
fun {Sieve Xs M}
   case Xs
   of nil then nil
   [] X|Xr then Ys in
      if X=<M then
         thread Ys={Filter Xr fun {$ Y} Y mod X \= 0 end} end
      else Ys=Xr end
      X|{Sieve Ys M}
   end
end
```

With a list of 100000 elements, we can call this as {Sieve Xs 316} (since $316 = \lfloor\sqrt{100000}\rfloor$). This dynamically creates the pipeline of filters shown in figure 4.12. Since small factors are more common than large factors, most of the actual filtering is done in the early filters.

4.3.3 Managing resources and improving throughput

What happens if the producer generates elements faster than the consumer can consume them? If this goes on long enough, then unconsumed elements will pile up and monopolize system resources. The examples we saw so far do nothing to prevent this. One way to solve this problem is to limit the rate at which the producer generates new elements, so that some global condition (like a maximum resource usage) is satisfied. This is called flow control. It requires that some information be sent back from the consumer to the producer. Let us see how to implement it.

4.3.3.1 Flow control with demand-driven concurrency

The simplest flow control is called demand-driven concurrency, or lazy execution. In this technique, the producer only generates elements when the consumer explicitly demands them. (The previous technique, where the producer generates an element whenever it likes, is called supply-driven execution, or eager execution.) Lazy

6. If the factor f is greater than $\sqrt{n}$, then there is another factor n/f less than $\sqrt{n}$.

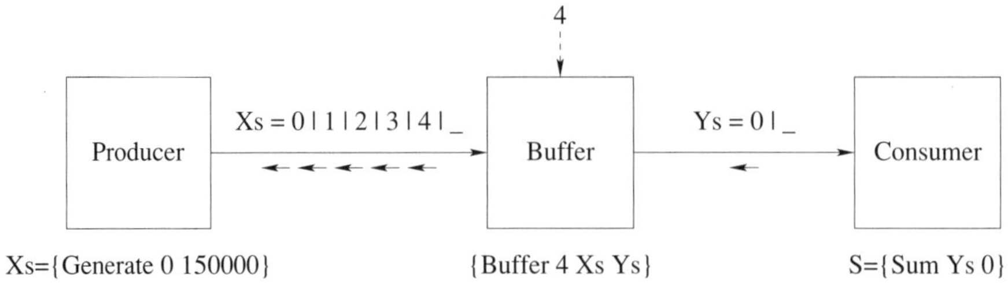

Figure 4.13: Bounded buffer.

execution requires a mechanism for the consumer to signal the producer whenever it needs a new element. The simplest way to do this is to use dataflow. For example, the consumer can extend its input stream whenever it needs a new element. That is, the consumer binds the stream's end to a list pair `X|Xr`, where `X` is unbound. The producer waits for this list pair and then binds `X` to the next element. Here is how to program it:

```
proc {DGenerate N Xs}
   case Xs of X|Xr then
      X=N
      {DGenerate N+1 Xr}
   end
end
fun {DSum ?Xs A Limit}
   if Limit>0 then
      X|Xr=Xs
   in
      {DSum Xr A+X Limit-1}
   else A end
end
local Xs S in
   thread {DGenerate 0 Xs} end       % Producer thread
   thread S={DSum Xs 0 150000} end % Consumer thread
   {Browse S}
end
```

It is now the consumer that controls how many elements are needed (150000 is an argument of `DSum`, not `DGenerate`). This implements lazy execution by programming it explicitly. This is an example of a programmed trigger as defined in section 3.6.5.[7]

7. There is another way to implement lazy execution, namely by extending the computation model with a new concept: an implicit trigger. This is explained in section 4.5. We will see that implicit triggers are easier to program with than programmed triggers.

```
proc {Buffer N ?Xs Ys}
   fun {Startup N ?Xs}
      if N==0 then Xs
      else Xr in Xs=_|Xr {Startup N-1 Xr} end
   end

   proc {AskLoop Ys ?Xs ?End}
      case Ys of Y|Yr then Xr End2 in
         Xs=Y|Xr     % Get element from buffer
         End=_|End2 % Replenish the buffer
         {AskLoop Yr Xr End2}
      end
   end

   End={Startup N Xs}
in
   {AskLoop Ys Xs End}
end
```

Figure 4.14: Bounded buffer (data-driven concurrent version).

4.3.3.2 Flow control with a bounded buffer

Up to now we have seen two techniques for managing stream communication, namely eager and lazy execution. In eager execution, the producer is completely free: there are no restrictions on how far it can get ahead of the consumer. In lazy execution, the producer is completely constrained: it can generate nothing without an explicit request from the consumer. Both techniques have problems. We have seen that eager execution leads to an explosion in resource usage. But lazy execution also has a serious problem. It leads to a strong reduction in throughput. By throughput we mean the number of messages that can be sent per unit of time. (Throughput is usually contrasted with latency, which is defined as the time taken from the send to the arrival of a single message.) If the consumer requests a message, then the producer has to calculate it, and meanwhile the consumer waits. If the producer were allowed to get ahead of the consumer, then the consumer would not have to wait.

Is there a way we can get the best of both worlds, i.e., both avoid the resource problem and not reduce throughput? Yes, this is indeed possible. It can be done with a combination of eager and lazy execution called a bounded buffer. A bounded buffer is a transducer that stores elements up to a maximum number, say n. The producer is allowed to get ahead of the consumer, but only until the buffer is full. This limits the extra resource usage to n elements. The consumer can take elements from the buffer immediately without waiting. This keeps throughput high. When the buffer has less than n elements, the producer is allowed to produce more elements, until the buffer is full.

Figure 4.14 shows how to program the bounded buffer. Figure 4.13 gives a picture. This picture introduces a further bit of graphic notation, small inverse arrows on a stream, which denote requests for new stream elements (i.e., the stream is lazy). To understand how the buffer works, remember that both `Xs` and `Ys` are lazy streams. The buffer executes in two phases:

- The first phase is the initialization. It calls `Startup` to ask for n elements from the producer. In other words, it extends `Xs` with n elements that are unbound. The producer detects this and can generate these n elements.
- The second phase is the buffer management. It calls `AskLoop` to satisfy requests from the consumer and initiate requests to the producer. Whenever the consumer asks for an element, `AskLoop` does two things: it gives the consumer an element from the buffer and it asks the producer for another element to replenish the buffer.

Here is a sample execution:

```
local Xs Ys S in
   thread {DGenerate 0 Xs} end      % Producer thread
   thread {Buffer 4 Xs Ys} end     % Buffer thread
   thread S={DSum Ys 0 150000} end % Consumer thread
   {Browse Xs} {Browse Ys}
   {Browse S}
end
```

One way to see for yourself how this works is to slow down its execution to a human scale. This can be done by adding a `{Delay 1000}` call inside `Sum`. This way, you can see the buffer: `Xs` always has four more elements than `Ys`.

The bounded buffer program is a bit tricky to understand and write. This is because a lot of bookkeeping is needed to implement the lazy execution. This bookkeeping is there for technical reasons only; it has no effect on how the producer and consumer are written. This is a good indication that extending the computation model might be a good alternative way to implement laziness. This is indeed the case, as we will see in section 4.5. The implicit laziness introduced there is much easier to program with than the explicit laziness we use here.

There is one defect of the bounded buffer we give here. It takes up $O(n)$ memory space even if nothing is stored in it (e.g., when the producer is slow). This extra memory space is small: it consists of n unbound list elements, which are the n requests to the producer. Yet, as sticklers for program frugality, we ask if it is possible to avoid this extra memory space. A simple way to avoid it is by using explicit state, as defined in chapter 6. This allows us to define a data abstraction that represents a bounded buffer and that has two operations, `Put` and `Get`. Internally, the data abstraction can save space by using an integer to count producer requests instead of list elements.

We conclude this discussion by remarking that eager and lazy execution are just extreme cases of a bounded buffer. Execution is eager when the buffer has infinite size. Execution is lazy when the buffer has zero size. When the buffer has a finite nonzero size, then its behavior is in between these two extremes.

4.3.3.3 Flow control with thread priorities

Using a bounded buffer is the best way to implement flow control, because it works for all relative producer/consumer speeds without twiddling with any "magic numbers." A different and inferior way to do flow control is to change the relative priorities between producer and consumer threads, so that consumers consume faster than producers can produce. It is inferior because it is fragile: its success depends on the amount of work needed for an element to be produced w_p and consumed w_c. It succeeds only if the speed ratio s_c/s_p between the consumer thread and the producer thread is greater than w_c/w_p. The latter depends not only on thread priorities but also on how many other threads exist.

That said, let us show how to implement it anyway. Let us give the producer low priority and the consumer high priority. We also set both priority ratios high-medium and medium-low to `10:1` and `10:1`. We use the original, data-driven versions of `Generate` and `Sum`:

```
{Property.put priorities p(high:10 medium:10)}
local Xs S in
   thread
      {Thread.setThisPriority low}
      Xs={Generate 0 150000}
   end
   thread
      {Thread.setThisPriority high}
      S={Sum Xs 0}
   end
   {Browse S}
end
```

This works in our case since the time to consume an element is not 100 times greater than the time to produce an element. But it might no longer work for a modified producer or consumer which might take more or less time. The general lesson is that changing thread priorities should never be used to get a program to work correctly. The program should work correctly, no matter what the priorities are. Changing thread priorities is then a performance optimization; it can be used to improve the throughput of a program that is already working.

4.3.4 Stream objects

Let us now step back and reflect on what stream programming is really doing. We have written concurrent programs as networks of threads that communicate through streams. This introduces a new concept which we can call a stream object: a recursive procedure that executes in its own thread and communicates with other stream objects through input and output streams. The stream object can maintain an internal state in the arguments of its procedure, which are accumulators.

We call a stream object an object because it is a single entity that combines the notion of value and operation. This is in contrast to an ADT, in which values and operations are separate entities (see section 6.4). Furthermore, it has an internal state that is accessed in a controlled way (by messages on streams). Throughout the book, we will use the term "object" for several such entities, including port objects, passive objects, and active objects. These entities differ in how the internal state is stored and how the controlled access is defined. The stream object is the first and simplest of these entities.

Here is a general way to create stream objects:

```
proc {StreamObject S1 X1 ?T1}
   case S1
   of M|S2 then N X2 T2 in
      {NextState M X1 N X2}
      T1=N|T2
      {StreamObject S2 X2 T2}
   [] nil then T1=nil end
end
declare S0 X0 T0 in
thread
   {StreamObject S0 X0 T0}
end
```

`StreamObject` is a template for creating a stream object. Its behavior is defined by `NextState`, which takes an input message `M` and a state `X1`, and calculates an output message `N` and a new state `X2`. Executing `StreamObject` in a new thread creates a new stream object with input stream `S0`, output stream `T0`, and initial state `X0`. The stream object reads messages from the input stream, does internal calculations, and sends messages on the output stream. In general, an object can have any fixed number of input and output streams.

Stream objects can be linked together in a graph, where each object receives messages from one or more other objects and sends messages to one or more other objects. For example, here is a pipeline of three stream objects:

```
declare S0 T0 U0 V0 in
thread {StreamObject S0 0 T0} end
thread {StreamObject T0 0 U0} end
thread {StreamObject U0 0 V0} end
```

The first object receives from `S0` and sends on `T0`, which is received by the second object, and so forth.

4.3.5 Digital logic simulation

Programming with a directed graph of stream objects is called synchronous programming. This is because a stream object can only perform a calculation after it reads one element from each input stream. This implies that all the stream objects in the graph are synchronized with each other. It is possible for a stream object to get ahead of its successors in the graph, but it cannot get ahead of its predecessors. (In chapter 8 we will see how to build active objects which can run completely independently of each other.)

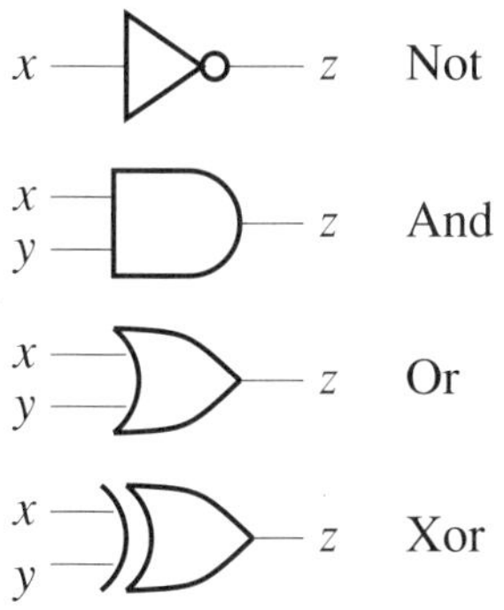

x	y	z Not	And	Or	Xor
0	0	1	0	0	0
0	1	1	0	1	1
1	0	0	0	1	1
1	1	0	1	1	0

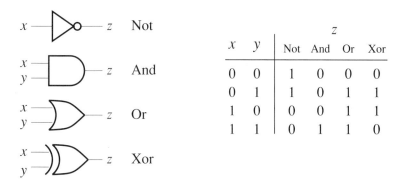

Figure 4.15: Digital logic gates.

All the examples of stream communication we have seen so far are very simple kinds of graphs, namely linear chains. Let us now look at an example where the graph is not a linear chain. We will build a digital logic simulator, i.e., a program that faithfully models the execution of electronic circuits consisting of interconnected logic gates. The gates communicate through time-varying signals that can only take discrete values, such as 0 and 1. In synchronous digital logic the whole circuit executes in lockstep. At each step, each logic gate reads its input wires, calculates the result, and puts it on the output wires. The steps are cadenced by a circuit called a clock. Most current digital electronic technology is synchronous. Our simulator will be synchronous as well.

How do we model signals on a wire and circuits that read these signals? In a synchronous circuit, a signal varies only in discrete time steps. So we can model a signal as a stream of 0s and 1s. A logic gate is then simply a stream object: a recursive procedure, running in its own thread, that reads input streams and calculates output streams. A clock is a recursive procedure that produces an initial stream at a fixed rate.

4.3.5.1 Combinational logic

Let us first see how to build simple logic gates. Figure 4.15 shows some typical gates with their standard pictorial symbols and the boolean functions that define them. The exclusive-or gate is usually called `Xor`. Each gate has one or more inputs and an output. The simplest is the `Not` gate, whose output is simply the negation of the input. With streams we can define it as follows:

```
fun {NotGate Xs}
   case Xs of X|Xr then (1-X)|{NotGate Xr} end
end
```

This gate works instantaneously, i.e., the first element of the output stream is calculated from the first element of the input stream. This is a reasonable way to model a real gate if the clock period is much longer than the gate delay. It allows us to model *combinational* logic, i.e., logic circuits that have no internal memory. Their outputs are boolean functions of their inputs, and they are totally dependent on the inputs.

How do we connect several gates together? Connecting streams is easy: the output stream of one gate can be directly connected to the input stream of another. Because all gates can execute simultaneously, each gate needs to execute inside its own thread. This gives the final definition of NotG:

```
local
   fun {NotLoop Xs}
      case Xs of X|Xr then (1-X)|{NotLoop Xr} end
   end
in
   fun {NotG Xs}
      thread {NotLoop Xs} end
   end
end
```

Calling NotG creates a new Not gate in its own thread. We see that a working logic gate is much more than just a boolean function; it is actually a concurrent entity that communicates with other concurrent entities. Let us build other kinds of gates. Here is a generic function that can build any kind of two-input gate:

```
fun {GateMaker F}
   fun {$ Xs Ys}
      fun {GateLoop Xs Ys}
         case Xs#Ys of (X|Xr)#(Y|Yr) then
            {F X Y}|{GateLoop Xr Yr}
         end
      end
   in
      thread {GateLoop Xs Ys} end
   end
end
```

This function is a good example of higher-order programming: it combines genericity with instantiation. With it we can build many gates:

```
AndG ={GateMaker fun {$ X Y} X*Y end}
OrG  ={GateMaker fun {$ X Y} X+Y-X*Y end}
NandG={GateMaker fun {$ X Y} 1-X*Y end}
NorG ={GateMaker fun {$ X Y} 1-X-Y+X*Y end}
XorG ={GateMaker fun {$ X Y} X+Y-2*X*Y end}
```

Each of these functions creates a gate whenever it is called. The logical operations are implemented as arithmetic operations on the integers 0 and 1.

Now we can build combinational circuits. A typical circuit is a full adder, which adds three one-bit numbers, giving a two-bit result. Full adders can be chained together to make adders of any number of bits. A full adder has three inputs, x, y, z, and two outputs, c and s. It satisfies the equation $x+y+z=(cs)_2$. For example, if $x=1$, $y=1$, and $z=0$, then the result is $c=1$ and $s=0$, which is $(10)_2$ in binary, namely 2. Figure 4.16 defines the circuit. Let us see how it works. c is 1 if

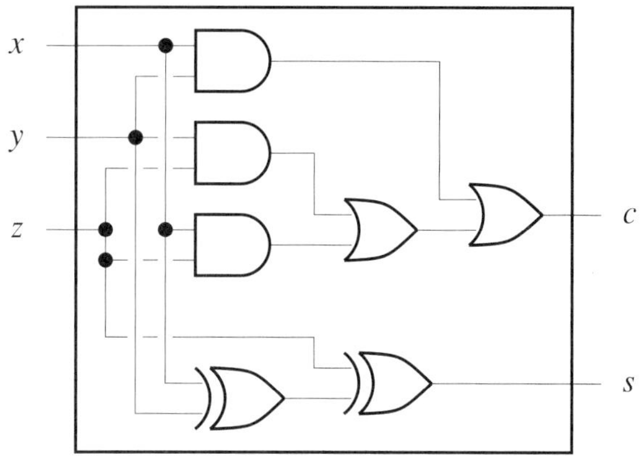

Figure 4.16: A full adder.

at least two inputs are 1. There are three ways that this can happen, each of which is covered by an `AndG` call. s is 1 if the number of 1 inputs is odd, which is exactly the definition of exclusive-or. Here is the same circuit defined in our simulation framework:

```
proc {FullAdder X Y Z ?C ?S}
   K L M
in
   K={AndG X Y}
   L={AndG Y Z}
   M={AndG X Z}
   C={OrG K {OrG L M}}
   S={XorG Z {XorG X Y}}
end
```

We use procedural notation for `FullAdder` because it has two outputs. Here is an example of using the full adder:

```
declare
X=1|1|0|_
Y=0|1|0|_
Z=1|1|1|_ C S in
{FullAdder X Y Z C S}
{Browse inp(X Y Z)#sum(C S)}
```

This adds three sets of input bits.

4.3.5.2 *Sequential logic*

Combinational circuits are limited because they cannot store information. Let us be more ambitious in the kinds of circuits we wish to model. Let us model sequential circuits, i.e., circuits whose behavior depends on their own past output. This means simply that some outputs are fed back as inputs. Using this idea, we can build

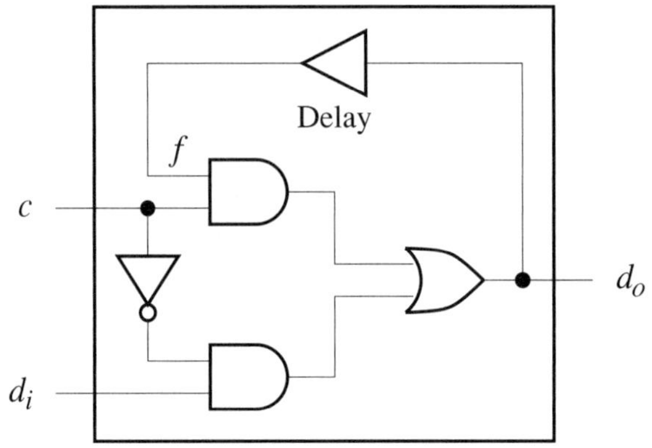

Figure 4.17: A latch.

bistable circuits, i.e., circuits with two stable states. A bistable circuit is a memory cell that can store one bit of information. Bistable circuits are often called flip-flops.

We cannot model sequential circuits with the approach of the previous section. What happens if we try? Let us connect an output to an input. To produce an output, the circuit has to read an input. But there is no input, so no output is produced either. In fact, this is a deadlock situation since there is a cyclic dependency: output waits for input and input waits for output.

To correctly model sequential circuits, we have to introduce some kind of time delay between the inputs and the outputs. Then the circuit will take its input from the previous output. There is no longer a deadlock. We can model the time delay by a delay gate, which simply adds one or more elements to the head of the stream:

```
fun {DelayG Xs}
   0|Xs
end
```

For an input $a|b|c|d|\ldots$, `DelayG` outputs `0`$|a|b|c|d|\ldots$, which is just a delayed version of the input. With `DelayG` we can model sequential circuits. Let us build a latch, which is a simple kind of bistable circuit that can memorize its input. Figure 4.17 defines a simple latch. Here is the program:

```
fun {Latch C DI}
   DO X Y Z F
in
   F={DelayG DO}
   X={AndG F C}
   Z={NotG C}
   Y={AndG Z DI}
   DO={OrG X Y}
   DO
end
```

The latch has two inputs, `C` and `DI`, and one output, `DO`. If `C` is 0, then the output tracks DI, i.e., it always has the same value as DI. If C is 1, then the output is frozen at the last value of DI. The latch is bistable since DO can be either 0 or 1. The latch works because of the delayed feedback from DO to F.

4.3.5.3 Clocking

Assume we have modeled a complex circuit. To simulate its execution, we have to create an initial input stream of values that are discretized over time. One way to do it is by defining a clock, which is a timed source of periodic signals. Here is a simple clock:

```
fun {Clock}
   fun {Loop B}
      B|{Loop B}
   end
in
   thread {Loop 1} end
end
```

Calling {Clock} creates a stream that grows very quickly, which makes the simulation go at the maximum rate of the Mozart implementation. We can slow down the simulation to a human time scale by adding a delay to the clock:

```
fun {Clock}
   fun {Loop B}
      {Delay 1000} B|{Loop B}
   end
in
   thread {Loop 1} end
end
```

The call {Delay N} causes its thread to suspend for N ms and then to become running again.

4.3.5.4 A linguistic abstraction for logic gates

In most of the above examples, logic gates are programmed with a construction that always has the same shape. The construction defines a procedure with stream arguments and at its heart there is a procedure with boolean arguments. Figure 4.18 shows how to make this construction systematic. Given a procedure GateStep, it defines another procedure Gate. The arguments of GateStep are booleans (or integers) and the arguments of Gate are streams. We distinguish the gate's inputs and outputs. The arguments X1, X2, ..., Xn are the gate's inputs. The arguments Y1, Y2, ..., Ym are the gate's outputs. GateStep defines the instantaneous behavior of the gate, i.e., it calculates the boolean outputs of the gate from its boolean inputs at a given instant. Gate defines the behavior in terms of streams. We can say that the construction lifts a calculation with booleans to become a calculation with streams. We could define an abstraction that implements this construction. This gives the function GateMaker we defined before. But we can go further and

```
proc {Gate X1 X2 ... Xn Y1 Y2 ... Ym}
   proc {P S1 S2 ... Sn U1 U2 ... Um}
      case S1#S2#...#Sn
      of (X1|T1)#(X2|T2)#...#(Xn|Tn) then
         Y1 Y2 ... Ym
         V1 V2 ... Vm
      in
         {GateStep X1 X2 ... Xn Y1 Y2 ... Ym}
         U1=Y1|V1
         U2=Y2|V2
         ...
         Um=Ym|Vm
         {P T1 T2 ... Tn V1 V2 ... Vm}
      end
   end
in
   thread {P X1 X2 ... Xn Y1 Y2 ... Ym} end
end
```

Figure 4.18: A linguistic abstraction for logic gates.

define a linguistic abstraction, the **gate** statement:

gate input ⟨x⟩$_1$ $\cdots$ ⟨x⟩$_n$ **output** ⟨y⟩$_1$ $\cdots$ ⟨y⟩$_m$ **then** ⟨s⟩ **end**

This statement translates into the construction of figure 4.18. The body ⟨s⟩ corresponds to the definition of `GateStep`: it does a boolean calculation with inputs ⟨x⟩$_1$ $\cdots$ ⟨x⟩$_n$ and outputs ⟨y⟩$_1$ $\cdots$ ⟨y⟩$_m$. With the **gate** statement, we can define an `And` gate as follows:

```
proc {AndG X1 X2 ?X3}
   gate input X1 X2 output X3 then X3=X1*X2 end
end
```

The identifiers `X1`, `X2`, and `X3` refer to different variables inside and outside the statement. Inside they refer to booleans and outside to streams. We can embed **gate** statements in procedures and use them to build large circuits.

We could implement the **gate** statement using Mozart's parser-generator tool gump. Many symbolic languages, notably Haskell and Prolog, have the ability to extend their syntax, which makes this kind of addition easy. This is often convenient for special-purpose applications.

4.4 Using the declarative concurrent model directly

Stream communication is not the only way to program in the declarative concurrent model. This section explores some other techniques. These techniques use the declarative concurrent model directly, without taking advantage of an abstraction

```
proc {DepthFirst Tree Level LeftLim ?RootX ?RightLim}
   case Tree
   of tree(x:X y:Y left:leaf right:leaf ...) then
      X=LeftLim
      RootX=X
      RightLim=X
      thread Y=Scale*Level end
   [] tree(x:X y:Y left:L right:leaf ...) then
      X=RootX
      thread Y=Scale*Level end
      {DepthFirst L Level+1 LeftLim RootX RightLim}
   [] tree(x:X y:Y left:leaf right:R ...) then
      X=RootX
      thread Y=Scale*Level end
      {DepthFirst R Level+1 LeftLim RootX RightLim}
   [] tree(x:X y:Y left:L right:R ...) then
         LRootX LRightLim RRootX RLeftLim
      in
         RootX=X
         thread X=(LRootX+RRootX) div 2 end
         thread Y=Scale*Level end
         thread RLeftLim=LRightLim+Scale end
         {DepthFirst L Level+1 LeftLim LRootX LRightLim}
         {DepthFirst R Level+1 RLeftLim RRootX RightLim}
   end
end
```

Figure 4.19: Tree-drawing algorithm with order-determining concurrency.

such as stream objects.

4.4.1 Order-determining concurrency

In whichever order these twenty-four cards are laid side by side, the result will be a perfectly harmonious landscape.
– From *"The Endless Landscape": 24-piece Myriorama*, Leipzig (1830s).

A simple use of concurrency in a declarative program is to find the order of calculations. That is, we know which calculations have to be done, but because of data dependencies, we do not know their order. What's more, the order may depend on the values of the data, i.e., there is no one static order that is always right. In this case, we can use dataflow concurrency to find the order automatically.

We give an example of order-determining concurrency using the tree-drawing algorithm of chapter 3. This algorithm is given a tree and calculates the positions of all the tree's nodes so that the tree can be drawn in an aesthetically pleasing way. The algorithm traverses the tree in two directions: first from the root to the leaves and then from the leaves back up to the root. During the traversals, all the node positions are calculated. One of the tricky details in this algorithm is the order in which the node positions are calculated. Consider the algorithm definition given in section 3.4.7. In this definition, `Level` and `LeftLim` are inputs (they propagate down toward the leaves), `RootX` and `RightLim` are outputs (they propagate up toward the root), and the calculations have to be done in the correct order to avoid deadlock. There are two ways to find the correct order:

- The first way is for the programmer to deduce the order and to program accordingly. This is what section 3.4.7 does. This gives the most efficient code, but if the programmer makes an error, then the program blocks without giving a result.
- The second way is for the system to deduce the order dynamically. The simplest way to do this is to put each calculation in a different thread. Dataflow execution then finds the correct order at run time.

Figure 4.19 gives a version of the tree-drawing algorithm that uses order-determining concurrency to find the correct calculation order at run time. Each calculation that might block is done in a thread of its own.[8] The algorithm's result is the same as before. This is true because the concurrency is used only to change the calculation order, not to change which calculations are done. This is an example of how to use concurrency in declarative programming and remain declarative. In the above code, the threads are created before the recursive calls. In fact, the threads can be created at any time and the algorithm will still work.

Constraint programming

Compared to the sequential algorithm of section 3.4.7, the algorithm of this section is simpler to design because it moves part of the design burden from the programmer to the system. There is an even simpler way: by using constraint programming. This approach is explained in chapter 12.

Constraint programming lightens the design burden of the programmer even more, at the cost of needing fairly sophisticated constraint-solving algorithms that might need large execution times. Order-determining concurrency does local propagation, where simple local conditions (e.g., dataflow dependencies) determine when constraints run. Constraint programming is a natural step beyond this: it extends local propagation by also doing search, which looks at candidate solutions until it finds one that is a complete solution.

4.4.2 Coroutines

A coroutine is a nonpreemptive thread. To explain this precisely, let us use the term locus of control, which is defined as an executing sequence of instructions.

8. Binding operations are not put in their own threads because they never block. What would be the difference if each binding were put in its own thread?

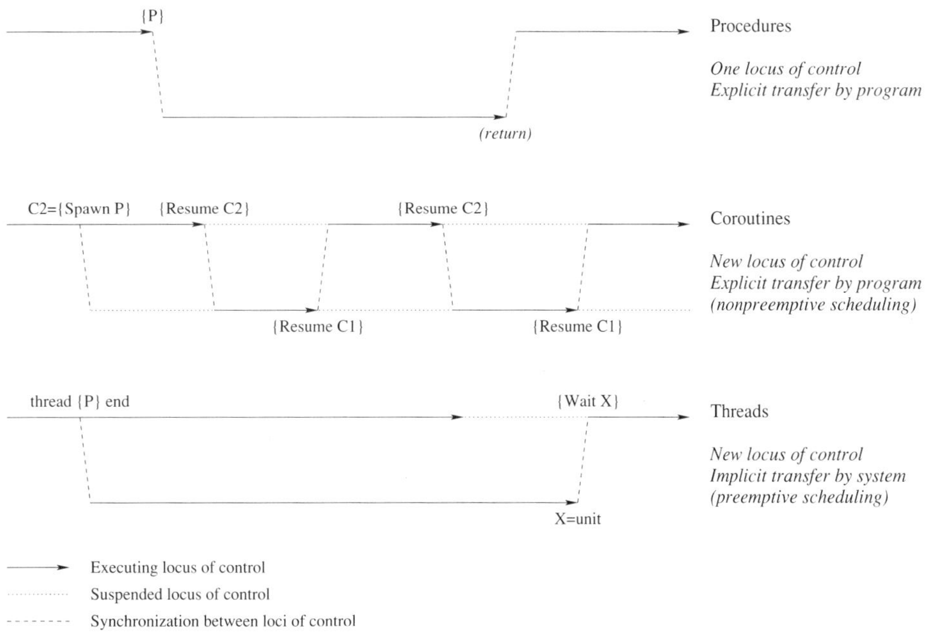

Figure 4.20: Procedures, coroutines, and threads.

Figure 4.20 compares coroutines with procedure calls and threads. A procedure call transfers control once to the procedure body (the call), and then back (the return). There is only one locus of control in the program. A coroutine is called explicitly like a procedure, but each coroutine has its has its own locus of control, like a thread. The difference with a thread is that the latter is controlled implicitly: the system automatically switches execution between threads without any programmer intervention.

Coroutines have two operations, `Spawn` and `Resume`. The `CId={Spawn P}` function creates a new coroutine and returns its identity `CId`. This is a bit like creating a new thread. The new coroutine is initially suspended but will execute the zero-argument procedure `P` when it is resumed. The `{Resume CId}` operation transfers control from the current coroutine to the coroutine with identity `CId`. Each coroutine has the responsibility to transfer control often enough so that the others have a chance to execute. If this is not done correctly, then a coroutine might never have a chance to execute. This is called starvation and is usually due to programmer error. (Starvation is not possible with threads if they are scheduled fairly.)

Since coroutines do not introduce nondeterminism in the model, programs using them are still declarative. However, coroutines themselves cannot be implemented in the declarative concurrent model because their implementation needs explicit state. They can be implemented using the shared-state concurrent model of chapter 8. Section 8.2.2 explains how to implement simple versions of `Spawn` and `Resume` using

```
fun {Spawn P}
PId in
   thread
      PId={Thread.this}
      {Thread.suspend PId}
      {P}
   end
   PId
end

proc {Resume Id}
   {Thread.resume Id}
   {Thread.suspend {Thread.this}}
end
```

Figure 4.21: Implementing coroutines using the `Thread` module.

this model. Another way to implement them is by using the `Thread` module.

Implementation using the* `Thread` *module

Thread scheduling is often made controllable in ways that resemble coroutines. For example, we can introduce an operation similar to `Resume` that immediately preempts a thread, i.e., switches execution to another runnable thread (if one exists). This is called `Thread.preempt` in Mozart. We can also introduce operations to control whether a thread is allowed to execute or not. In Mozart, these operations are called `Thread.suspend` and `Thread.resume`. A thread `T` can be suspended indefinitely by calling `{Thread.suspend T}`. Here `T` is the thread identity, which is obtained by calling `T={Thread.this}`. The thread can be resumed by calling `{Thread.resume T}`. Figure 4.21 shows how to implement `Spawn` and `Resume` in terms of `Thread.this`, `Thread.suspend`, and `Thread.resume`.

4.4.3 Concurrent composition

We have seen how threads are forked using the **`thread`** statement. A natural question that arises is how to join back a forked thread into the original thread of control. That is, how can the original thread wait until the forked thread has terminated? This is a special case of detecting termination of multiple threads, and making another thread wait on that event. The general scheme is quite easy when using dataflow execution. Assume that we have n statements $\langle \mathsf{stmt} \rangle_1$, ..., $\langle \mathsf{stmt} \rangle_n$. Assume that the statements create no threads while executing.[9] Then the following

9. The general case in which threads can create new threads, and so forth recursively, is handled in section 5.6.3.

```
proc {Barrier Ps}
   fun {BarrierLoop Ps L}
      case Ps of P|Pr then M in
         thread {P} M=L end
         {BarrierLoop Pr M}
      [] nil then L
      end
   end
   S={BarrierLoop Ps unit}
in
   {Wait S}
end
```

Figure 4.22: Concurrent composition.

code will execute each statement in a different thread and wait until they have all completed:

```
local X1 X2 X3 ... Xn1 Xn in
   thread ⟨stmt⟩1 X1=unit end
   thread ⟨stmt⟩2 X2=X1 end
   thread ⟨stmt⟩3 X3=X2 end
   ...
   thread ⟨stmt⟩n Xn=Xn1 end
   {Wait Xn}
end
```

This works by using the unification operation of dataflow variables (see section 2.8.2.1). When thread T_i terminates, it binds the variables $\mathtt{X}_{i-1}$ and $\mathtt{X}_i$. This "short-circuits" the variables. When all threads have terminated then the variables X1, X2, ..., Xn will be unified ("merged together") and bound to **unit**. The operation {Wait Xn} blocks until Xn is bound.

There is a different way to detect termination with dataflow variables that does not depend on binding variables to variables, but uses an auxiliary thread:

```
local X1 X2 X3 ... Xn1 Xn Done in
   thread ⟨stmt⟩1 X1=unit end
   thread ⟨stmt⟩2 X2=unit end
   thread ⟨stmt⟩3 X3=unit end
   ...
   thread ⟨stmt⟩n Xn=unit end
   thread
      {Wait X1} {Wait X2} {Wait X3} ... {Wait Xn}
      Done=unit
   end
   {Wait Done}
end
```

Using explicit state gives another set of approaches to detect termination. For example, section 5.6.3 shows an algorithm that works even when threads can themselves create new threads.

Control abstraction

Figure 4.22 defines the combinator `Barrier` that implements concurrent composition. A combinator is just a control abstraction. The term combinator emphasizes that the operation is compositional, i.e., that combinators can be nested. This is also true of control abstractions if they are based on lexically scoped closures, i.e., procedure values.

`Barrier` takes a list of zero-argument procedures, starts each procedure in its own thread, and terminates after all these threads terminate. It does termination detection using the unification scheme of the previous section. `Barrier` can be the basis of a linguistic abstraction, the **conc** statement:

```
conc
   ⟨stmt⟩1 [] ⟨stmt⟩2 [] ... [] ⟨stmt⟩n
end
```

defined as

```
{Barrier
 [proc {$} ⟨stmt⟩1 end
  proc {$} ⟨stmt⟩2 end
  ...
  proc {$} ⟨stmt⟩n end]}
```

`Barrier` is more general than the **conc** statement since the number of statements does not have to be known at compile time.

4.5 Lazy execution

All things spring up without a word spoken,
and grow without a claim for their production.
– Tao-te Ching, *Lao-tzu* (6th century B.C.)

"Necessity is the mother of invention."
"But who is the father?"
"Laziness!"
– Freely adapted from a traditional proverb.

Up to now, we have always executed statements in order, from left to right. In a statement sequence, we start by executing the first statement. When it is finished we continue to the next.[10] This fact may seem too obvious to require mentioning. Why should it be any other way? But it is a healthy reflex to question the obvious! Many significant discoveries have been made by people questioning the obvious: it led Newton to discover that white light consists of a spectrum of colors and Einstein to discover that the speed of light is constant for all observers. Let us

10. Statement order may be determined statically by textual sequence or dynamically by dataflow synchronization.

therefore question the obvious and see where it leads us.

Are there other execution strategies for declarative programs? It turns out that there is a second execution strategy fundamentally different from the usual left-to-right execution. We call this strategy lazy evaluation or demand-driven evaluation. This in contrast to the usual strategy, which is called eager evaluation or data-driven evaluation. In lazy evaluation, a statement is only executed when its result is needed somewhere else in the program. For example, take the following program fragment:

```
fun lazy {F1 X} 1+X*(3+X*(3+X)) end
fun lazy {F2 X} Y=X*X in Y*Y end
fun lazy {F3 X} (X+1)*(X+1) end
A={F1 10}
B={F2 20}
C={F3 30}
D=A+B
```

The three functions `F1`, `F2`, and `F3` are lazy functions. This is indicated with the annotation "`lazy`" in the syntax. Lazy functions are not executed when they are called. They do not block either. What happens is that they create "stopped executions" that will be continued only when their results are needed. In our example, the function calls `A={F1 10}`, `B={F2 20}`, and `C={F3 30}` all create stopped executions. When the addition `D=A+B` is invoked, then the values of `A` and `B` are needed. This triggers the execution of the first two calls. After the calls finish, the addition can continue. Since `C` is not needed, the third call is not executed.

The importance of lazy evaluation

Lazy evaluation is a powerful concept that can simplify many programming tasks. It was first discovered in functional programming, where it has a long and distinguished history [96]. Lazy evaluation was originally studied as an execution strategy that is useful only for declarative programs. However, as we will see later, laziness also has a role to play in more expressive computation models that contain declarative models as subsets.

Lazy evaluation has a role both in programming in the large (for modularization and resource management) and in programming in the small (for algorithm design). In programming in the small, it can help in the design of declarative algorithms that have good amortized or worst-case time bounds [157]. Section 4.5.8 gives the main ideas. In programming in the large, it can help modularize programs [98]. For example, consider an application where a producer sends a stream of data to a consumer. In an eager model, the producer decides when enough data has been sent. With laziness, it is the consumer that decides. Sections 4.5.3 through 4.5.6 give this example and others.

The lazy computation model of the book is slightly different from lazy evaluation as used in functional languages such as Haskell and Miranda. Since these languages are sequential, lazy evaluation does coroutining between the lazy function and the function that needs the result. This book studies laziness in the more general context

⟨s⟩ ::=	
skip	Empty statement
| ⟨s⟩$_1$ ⟨s⟩$_2$	Statement sequence
| **local** ⟨x⟩ **in** ⟨s⟩ **end**	Variable creation
| ⟨x⟩$_1$=⟨x⟩$_2$	Variable-variable binding
| ⟨x⟩=⟨v⟩	Value creation
| **if** ⟨x⟩ **then** ⟨s⟩$_1$ **else** ⟨s⟩$_2$ **end**	Conditional
| **case** ⟨x⟩ **of** ⟨pattern⟩ **then** ⟨s⟩$_1$ **else** ⟨s⟩$_2$ **end**	Pattern matching
| { ⟨x⟩ ⟨y⟩$_1$ ⋯ ⟨y⟩$_n$ }	Procedure application
| **thread** ⟨s⟩ **end**	Thread creation
| {ByNeed ⟨x⟩ ⟨y⟩}	**Trigger creation**

Table 4.3: The demand-driven concurrent kernel language.

of concurrent models. To avoid confusion with lazy evaluation, which is always sequential, we will use the term lazy execution to cover the general case which can be either sequential or concurrent.

Structure of the section

This section defines the concept of lazy execution and surveys the new programming techniques that it makes possible. It has the following structure:

- The first two sections give the fundamentals of lazy execution and show how it interacts with eager execution and concurrency. Section 4.5.1 defines the demand-driven concurrent model and gives its semantics. This model extends the data-driven concurrent model with laziness as a new concept. It is an amazing fact that this model is declarative. Section 4.5.2 shows six different declarative computation models that are possible with different combinations of laziness, dataflow variables, and declarative concurrency. All of these models are practical and some of them have been used as the basis of functional programming languages.
- The next four sections, sections 4.5.3 through 4.5.6, give programming techniques using lazy streams. Streams are the most common use of laziness.
- The final three sections give more advanced uses of laziness. Section 4.5.7 introduces the subject by showing what happens when standard list functions are made lazy. Section 4.5.8 shows how to use laziness to design persistent data structures, with good amortized or worst-case complexities. Section 4.5.9 explains list comprehensions, which are a higher level of abstraction in which to view lazy streams.

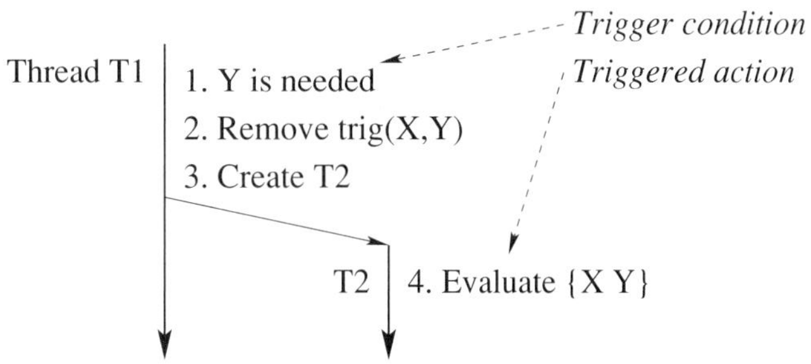

Figure 4.23: The by-need protocol.

4.5.1 The demand-driven concurrent model

The demand-driven concurrent model extends the data-driven concurrent model with just one new concept, the by-need trigger. An important principle in the design of this concept was that the resulting model satisfy the definition of declarative concurrency given in section 4.1.4. This section defines the semantics of by-need triggers and shows how lazy functions can be expressed with it.

How can both data-driven and demand-driven concurrency coexist in the same computation model? The way we have chosen is to make data-driven concurrency the default and to add an extra operation to introduce a demand-driven part. It is reasonable to make data-driven concurrency the default because it is much easier to reason about time and space complexity and to implement efficiently. We find that often the best way to structure an application is to build it in data-driven fashion around a demand-driven core.

By-need triggers

To do demand-driven concurrency, we add one instruction, `ByNeed`, to the kernel language (see table 4.3). Its operation is extremely simple. The statement `{ByNeed P Y}` has the same effect as the statement **`thread`** `{P Y}` **`end`**, except for scheduling. Both statements call the procedure `P` in its own thread with argument `Y`. The difference between the statements is when the procedure call is executed. For **`thread`** `{P Y}` **`end`**, we know that `{P Y}` will always be executed eventually. For `{ByNeed P Y}`, we know that `{P Y}` will be executed only if the value of `Y` is needed. If the value of `Y` is never needed, then `{P Y}` will never be executed. Here is an example:

```
{ByNeed proc {$ A} A=111*111 end Y}
{Browse Y}
```

This displays `Y` without calculating its value, since the browser does not need the value of `Y`. Invoking an operation that needs the value of `Y`, e.g., `Z=Y+1` or `{Wait Y}`, will trigger the calculation of `Y`. This causes `12321` to be displayed.

Semantics of by-need triggers

We implement `ByNeed` in the computation model by adding just one concept, the by-need trigger. In general, a trigger is a pair consisting of an activation condition, which is a boolean expression, and an action, which is a procedure. When the activation condition becomes true, then the action is executed once. When this happens we say the trigger is activated. For a by-need trigger, the activation condition is the need for the value of a variable.

We distinguish between programmed triggers, which are written explicitly by the programmer, and implicit triggers, which are part of the computation model. Programmed triggers are explained in sections 3.6.5 and 4.3.3. A by-need trigger is a kind of implicit trigger.

We define the semantics of by-need triggers in three steps. We first add a trigger store to the execution state. We then define two operations, trigger creation and activation. Finally, we make precise what we mean by "needing" a variable.

Extension of execution state A by-need trigger is a pair $trig(x, y)$ of a dataflow variable y and a one-argument procedure x. Next to the single-assignment store σ, we add a new store τ called the trigger store. The trigger store contains all the by-need triggers and is initially empty. The execution state becomes a triple (MST, σ, τ).

Trigger creation The semantic statement is

$(\{\texttt{ByNeed}\ \langle\mathsf{x}\rangle\ \langle\mathsf{y}\rangle\}, E)$

Execution consists of the following actions:

- If $E(\langle\mathsf{y}\rangle)$ is not determined, then add the trigger $trig(E(\langle\mathsf{x}\rangle), E(\langle\mathsf{y}\rangle))$ to the trigger store.
- Otherwise, if $E(\langle\mathsf{y}\rangle)$ is determined, then create a new thread with initial semantic statement $(\{\langle\mathsf{x}\rangle\ \langle\mathsf{y}\rangle\}, E)$ (see section 4.1 for thread semantics).

Trigger activation If the trigger store contains $trig(x, y)$ and a need for y is detected, i.e., there is either a thread that is suspended waiting for y to be determined, or an attempt to bind y to make it determined, then do the following:

- Remove the trigger from the trigger store.
- Create a new thread with initial semantic statement $(\{\langle\mathsf{x}\rangle\ \langle\mathsf{y}\rangle\}, \{\langle\mathsf{x}\rangle \rightarrow x, \langle\mathsf{y}\rangle \rightarrow y\})$ (see section 4.1). In this semantic statement, $\langle\mathsf{x}\rangle$ and $\langle\mathsf{y}\rangle$ are any two different identifiers.

These actions can be done at any point in time after the need is detected, since the need will not go away. The semantics of trigger activation is called the by-need protocol. It is illustrated in figure 4.23.

Memory management There are two modifications to memory management:

- Extending the definition of reachability: A variable x is reachable if the trigger store contains $trig(x, y)$ and y is reachable.
- Reclaiming triggers: If a variable y becomes unreachable and the trigger store contains $trig(x, y)$, then remove the trigger.

Needing a variable

What does it mean for a variable to be needed? The definition of need is carefully designed so that lazy execution is declarative, i.e., all executions lead to logically equivalent stores. A variable is needed by a suspended operation if the variable must be determined for the operation to continue. Here is an example:

```
thread X={ByNeed fun {$} 3 end} end
thread Y={ByNeed fun {$} 4 end} end
thread Z=X+Y end
```

To keep the example simple, let us consider that each thread executes atomically. This means there are six possible executions. For lazy execution to be declarative, all of these executions must lead to equivalent stores. Is this true? Yes, it is true, because the addition will wait until the other two triggers are created, and these triggers will then be activated.

There is a second way a variable can be needed. A variable is needed if it is determined. If this were not true, then the demand-driven concurrent model would not be declarative. Here is an example:

```
thread X={ByNeed fun {$} 3 end} end
thread X=2 end
thread Z=X+4 end
```

The correct behavior is that all executions should fail. If `X=2` executes last, then the trigger has already been activated, binding `X` to 3, so this is clear. But if `X=2` is executed first, then the trigger should also be activated.

Let us conclude by giving a more subtle example:

```
thread X={ByNeed fun {$} 3 end} end
thread X=Y end
thread if X==Y then Z=10 end end
```

Should the comparison `X==Y` activate the trigger on `X`? According to our definition the answer is no. If `X` is made determined then the comparison will still not execute (since `Y` is unbound). It is only later on, if `Y` is made determined, that the trigger on `X` should be activated.

Being needed is a monotonic property of a variable. Once a variable is needed, it stays needed forever. Figure 4.24 shows the stages in a variable's lifetime. Note that a determined variable is always needed, just by the fact of being determined. Monotonicity of the need property is essential to prove that the demand-driven concurrent model is declarative.

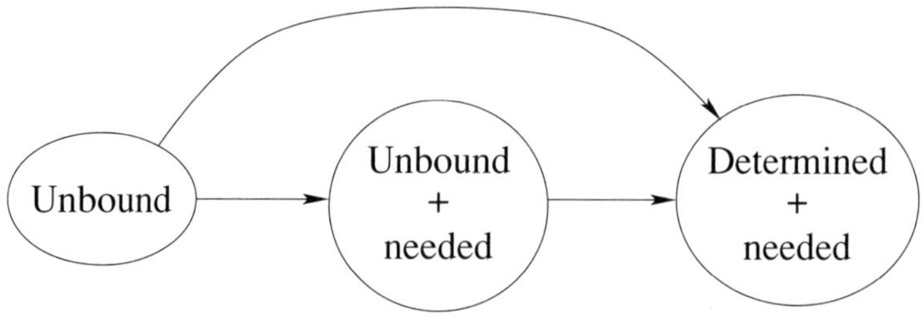

Figure 4.24: Stages in a variable's lifetime.

Using by-need triggers

By-need triggers can be used to implement other concepts that have some "lazy" or "demand-driven" behavior. For example, they underlie lazy functions and dynamic linking. Let us examine each in turn.

Implementing lazy functions with by-need A lazy function is evaluated only when its result is needed. For example, the following function generates a lazy list of integers:

```
fun lazy {Generate N} N|{Generate N+1} end
```

This is a linguistic abstraction that is defined in terms of `ByNeed`. It is called like a regular function:

```
L={Generate 0}
{Browse L}
```

This will display nothing until `L` is needed. Let us ask for the third element of `L`:

```
{Browse L.2.2.1}
```

This will calculate the third element, 2, and then display it. The linguistic abstraction is translated into the following code that uses `ByNeed`:

```
fun {Generate N}
   {ByNeed fun {$} N|{Generate N+1} end}
end
```

This uses procedural abstraction to delay the execution of the function body. The body is packaged into a zero-argument function which is only called when the value of `{Generate N}` is needed. It is easy to see that this works for all lazy functions. Threads are cheap enough in Mozart that this definition of lazy execution is practical.

Implementing dynamic linking with by-need We briefly explain what dynamic linking is all about and the role played by lazy execution. Dynamic linking is used to implement a general approach to structuring applications called component-based programming. This approach was introduced in section 3.9 and is explained fully in chapters 5 and 6. Briefly, an application's source code consists of a set of component specifications, called functors. A running application consists of instantiated components, called modules. A module is represented by a record that groups together the module's operations. Each record field references one operation. Components are linked when they are needed, i.e., their functors are loaded into memory and instantiated. As long as the module is not needed, then the component is not linked. When a program attempts to access a module field, then the component is needed and by-need execution is used to link the component.

4.5.2 Declarative computation models

At this point, we have defined a computation model with both laziness and concurrency. It is important to realize that these are independent concepts. Concurrency can make batch computations incremental. Laziness can reduce the amount of computation needed to get a result. A language can have neither, either, or both of these concepts. For example, a language with laziness but no concurrency does coroutining between a producer and a consumer.

Let us now give an overview of all the declarative computation models we know. All together, we have added three concepts to strict functional programming that preserve declarativeness while increasing expressiveness: dataflow variables, declarative concurrency, and laziness. Adding these concepts in various combinations gives six different practical computation models, as summarized in figure 4.25.[11] Dataflow variables are a prerequisite of declarative concurrency, since they are the mechanism by which threads synchronize and communicate. However, a sequential language, like the model of chapter 2, can also have dataflow variables and use them to good effect.

Since laziness and dataflow variables are independent concepts, this means there are three special moments in a variable's lifetime:

1. Creation of the variable as an entity in the language, such that it can be placed inside data structures and passed to or from a function or procedure. The variable is not yet bound to its value. We call such a variable a "dataflow variable."

2. Specification of the function or procedure call that will evaluate the value of the variable (but the evaluation is not done yet).

3. Evaluation of the function. When the result is available, it is bound to the variable. The evaluation might be done according to a trigger, which may be implicit, such as a "need" for the value. Lazy execution uses implicit need.

These three moments can be done separately or at the same time. Different languages enforce different possibilities. This gives four variant models in all.

11. This diagram leaves out search, which leads to another kind of declarative programming called relational programming. This is explained in chapter 9.

	sequential with values	*sequential with values and dataflow variables*	*concurrent with values and dataflow variables*
eager execution (strictness)	strict functional programming (e.g., Scheme, ML) (1)&(2)&(3)	declarative model (e.g., Chapter 2, Prolog) (1), (2)&(3)	data–driven concurrent model (e.g., Section 4.1) (1), (2)&(3)
lazy execution	lazy functional programming (e.g., Haskell) (1)&(2), (3)	lazy FP with dataflow variables (1), (2), (3)	demand–driven concurrent model (e.g., Section 4.5.1) (1), (2), (3)

(1): Declare a variable in the store
(2): Specify the function to calculate the variable's value
(3): Evaluate the function and bind the variable

(1)&(2)&(3): Declaring, specifying, and evaluating all coincide
(1)&(2), (3): Declaring and specifying coincide; evaluating is done later
(1), (2)&(3): Declaring is done first; specifying and evaluating are done later and coincide
(1), (2), (3): Declaring, specifying, and evaluating are done separately

Figure 4.25: Practical declarative computation models.

Figure 4.25 lists these models, as well as the two additional models that result when concurrency is added as well. (In this figure and in the following discussion, we use the ampersand "&" to group together moments that coincide.) For each of the variants, we show an example with a variable `X` that will eventually be bound to the result of the computation `11*11`. Here are the models:

- In a strict functional language with values, such as Scheme or Standard ML, moments (1) & (2) & (3) must always coincide. This is the model of section 2.8.1. For example:

```
declare X=11*11            % (1)&(2)&(3) together
```

- In a lazy functional language with values, such as Haskell, moments (1) & (2) always coincide, but (3) may be separate. For example (defining first a lazy function):

```
declare fun lazy {LazyMul A B} A*B end
declare X={LazyMul 11 11}  % (1)&(2) together
{Wait X}                   % (3) separate
```

This can also be written as

```
declare X={fun lazy {$} 11*11 end}  % (1)&(2) together
{Wait X}                            % (3) separate
```

- In a strict language with dataflow variables, moment (1) may be separate and (2) & (3) always coincide. This is the declarative model, which is defined in chapter 2.

This is also used in logic programming languages such as Prolog. For example:

```
declare X                        % (1) separate
X=11*11                          % (2)&(3) together
```

If concurrency is added, this gives the data-driven concurrent model defined at the beginning of this chapter. This is used in concurrent logic programming languages. For example:

```
declare X                        % (1) separate
thread X=11*11 end               % (2)&(3) together
thread if X>100 then {Browse big} end end  % Conditional
```

Because dataflow variables are single-assignment, the conditional always gives the same result.

- In the demand-driven concurrent model of this chapter, moments (1), (2), (3) may all be separate. For example:

```
declare X                        % (1) separate
X={fun lazy {$} 11*11 end}       % (2) separate
{Wait X}                         % (3) separate
```

When concurrency is used explicitly, this gives

```
declare X                                  % (1)
thread X={fun lazy {$} 11*11 end} end      % (2)
thread {Wait X} end                        % (3)
```

This is the most general variant model. The only connection between the three moments is that they act on the same variable. The execution of (2) and (3) is concurrent, with an implicit synchronization between (2) and (3): (3) waits until (2) has defined the function.

In all these examples, `X` is eventually bound to `121`. Allowing the three moments to be separate gives maximum expressiveness within a declarative framework.[12] For example, laziness allows doing declarative calculations with potentially infinite lists. Laziness allows implementation of many data structures as efficiently as with explicit state, yet still declaratively (see, e.g., [157]). Dataflow variables allow writing concurrent programs that are still declarative. Using both together allows writing concurrent programs that consist of stream objects communicating through potentially infinite streams.

Why laziness with dataflow must be concurrent

In a functional language without dataflow variables, laziness can be sequential. In other words, demand-driven arguments to a lazy function can be evaluated sequentially (i.e., using coroutining). If dataflow variables are added, this is no longer the case. A deadlock can occur if the arguments are evaluated sequentially.

12. One way to understand the added expressiveness is to realize that dataflow variables and laziness each add a weak form of state to the model. In both cases, restrictions on using the state ensure the model is still declarative.

To solve the problem, the arguments must be evaluated concurrently. Here is an example:

```
local
   Z
   fun lazy {F1 X}      X+Z end
   fun lazy {F2 Y} Z=1 Y+Z end
in
   {Browse {F1 1}+{F2 2}}
end
```

This defines `F1` and `F2` as lazy functions. Executing this fragment displays 5 (do you see why?). If `{F1 1}` and `{F2 2}` were executed sequentially instead of concurrently, then this fragment would deadlock. This is because `X+Z` would block and `Z=1` would never be reached. A question for the astute reader: which of the models in figure 4.25 has this problem? The binding of `Z` done by `F2` is a kind of "declarative side effect," since `F2` changes its surroundings through a means separate from its arguments. Declarative side effects are usually benign.

It is important to remember that a language with dataflow variables and concurrent laziness is still declarative. There is no observable nondeterminism. `{F1 1}+{F2 2}` always gives the same result.

4.5.3 Lazy streams

In the producer/consumer example of section 4.3.1, it is the producer that decides how many list elements to generate, i.e., execution is eager. This is a reasonable technique if the total amount of work is finite and does not use many system resources (e.g., memory or processor time). On the other hand, if the total work potentially uses many resources, then it may be better to use lazy execution. With lazy execution, the consumer decides how many list elements to generate. If an extremely large or a potentially unbounded number of list elements are needed, then lazy execution will use many fewer system resources at any given point in time. Problems that are impractical with eager execution can become practical with lazy execution. On the other hand, lazy execution may use many more total resources, because of the cost of its implementation. The need for laziness must take both of these factors into account.

Lazy execution can be implemented in two ways in the declarative concurrent model: with programmed triggers or with implicit triggers. Section 4.3.3 gives an example with programmed triggers. Programmed triggers require explicit communication from the consumer to the producer. Implicit triggers, where the language supports laziness directly, are simpler. The language semantics ensures that a function is evaluated only if its result is needed. This simplifies the function definition because it does not have to do the "bookkeeping" of the trigger messages. In the demand-driven concurrent model we give syntactic support to this technique: the function can be annotated with the keyword "`lazy`". Here is how to do the previous example with a lazy function that generates a potentially infinite list:

```
fun lazy {Generate N}
   N|{Generate N+1}
end
fun {Sum Xs A Limit}
   if Limit>0 then
      case Xs of X|Xr then
         {Sum Xr A+X Limit-1}
      end
   else A end
end
local Xs S in
   Xs={Generate 0}       % Producer
   S={Sum Xs 0 150000}  % Consumer
   {Browse S}
end
```

As before, this displays `11249925000`. Note that the `Generate` call does not need to be put in its own thread, in contrast to the eager version. This is because `Generate` creates a by-need trigger and then completes.

In this example, it is the consumer that decides how many list elements should be generated. With eager execution it was the producer that decided. In the consumer, it is the **`case`** statement that needs a list pair, so it implicitly triggers the generation of a new list element `X`. To see the difference in resource consumption between this version and the preceding version, try both with 150000 and then with 15000000 elements. With 150000 elements, there are no memory problems (even on a small personal computer with 64 MB memory) and the eager version is faster. This is because of the overhead of the lazy version's implicit triggering mechanism. With 15000000 elements the situation changes. The lazy version needs only a very small memory space during execution, while the eager version needs a huge memory space. Lazy execution is implemented with the `ByNeed` operation (see section 4.5.1).

Declaring lazy functions

In lazy functional languages, *all* functions are lazy by default. In contrast to this, the demand-driven concurrent model requires laziness to be declared explicitly, with the `lazy` annotation. We find that this makes things simpler both for the programmer and the compiler, in several ways. The first way has to do with efficiency and compilation. Eager evaluation is several times more efficient than lazy evaluation because there is no triggering mechanism. To get good performance in a lazy functional language, this implies that the compiler has to determine which functions can safely be implemented with eager evaluation. This is called strictness analysis. The second way has to do with language design. An eager language is much easier to extend with nondeclarative concepts, e.g., exceptions and state, than a lazy language.

```
fun {Buffer1 In N}
   End={List.drop In N}
   fun lazy {Loop In End}
      case In of I|In2 then
         I|{Loop In2 End.2}
      end
   end
in
   {Loop In End}
end
```

Figure 4.26: Bounded buffer (naive lazy version).

Multiple readers

The multiple reader example of section 4.3.1 will also work with lazy execution. For example, here are three lazy consumers using the `Generate` and `Sum` functions defined in the previous section:

```
local Xs S1 S2 S3 in
   Xs={Generate 0}
   thread S1={Sum Xs 0 150000} end
   thread S2={Sum Xs 0 100000} end
   thread S3={Sum Xs 0  50000} end
end
```

Each consumer thread asks for stream elements independently of the others. If one consumer is faster than the others, then the others may not have to ask for the stream elements, if they have already been calculated.

4.5.4 Bounded buffer

In the previous section we built a bounded buffer for eager streams by explicitly programming the laziness. Let us now build a bounded buffer using the laziness of the computation model. Our bounded buffer will take a lazy input stream and return a lazy output stream.

Defining a lazy bounded buffer is a good exercise in lazy programming because it shows how lazy execution and data-driven concurrency interact. Let us do the design in stages. We first specify its behavior. When the buffer is first called, it fills itself with n elements by asking the producer. Afterward, whenever the consumer asks for an element, the buffer in its turn asks the producer for another element. In this way, the buffer always contains up to n elements. Figure 4.26 shows the resulting definition. The call `{List.drop In N}` skips over `N` elements of the stream `In`, giving the stream `End`. This means that `End` always "looks ahead" `N` elements with respect to `In`. The lazy function `Loop` is iterated whenever a stream element is needed. It returns the next element `I` but also asks the producer for one more element, by calling `End.2`. In this way, the buffer always contains up to `N` elements.

```
fun {Buffer2 In N}
   End=thread {List.drop In N} end
   fun lazy {Loop In End}
      case In of I|In2 then
         I|{Loop In2 thread End.2 end}
      end
   end
in
   {Loop In End}
end
```

Figure 4.27: Bounded buffer (correct lazy version).

However, the buffer of figure 4.26 is incorrect. The major problem is due to the way lazy execution works: the calculation that needs the result will block while the result is being calculated. This means that when the buffer is first called, it cannot serve any consumer requests until the producer generates n elements. Furthermore, whenever the buffer serves a consumer request, it cannot give an answer until the producer has generated the next element. This is too much synchronization: it links together the producer and consumer in lockstep! A usable buffer should on the contrary decouple the producer and consumer. Consumer requests should be serviced whenever the buffer is nonempty, independent of the producer.

It is not difficult to fix this problem. In the definition of `Buffer1`, there are two places where producer requests are generated: in the call to `List.drop` and in the operation `End.2`. Putting a **thread** ... **end** in both places solves the problem. Figure 4.27 shows the fixed definition.

Example execution

Let us see how this buffer works. We define a producer that generates an infinite list of successive integers, but only one integer per second:

```
fun lazy {Ints N}
   {Delay 1000}
   N|{Ints N+1}
end
```

Now let us create this list and add a buffer of five elements:

```
declare
In={Ints 1}
Out={Buffer2 In 5}
{Browse Out}
{Browse Out.1}
```

The call `Out.1` requests one element. Calculating this element takes one second. Therefore, the browser first displays `Out<Future>` and one second later adds the first element, which updates the display to `1|_<Future>`. The notation "`_<Future>`" denotes a read-only variable. In the case of lazy execution, this variable has an implicit trigger attached to it. Now wait at least five seconds, to let the buffer fill up. Then enter

```
{Browse Out.2.2.2.2.2.2.2.2.2.2}
```

This requests ten elements. Because the buffer only has five elements, it is immediately emptied, displaying

```
1|2|3|4|5|6|_<Future>
```

One more element is added each second for four seconds. The final result is:

```
1|2|3|4|5|6|7|8|9|10|_<Future>
```

At this point, all consumer requests are satisfied and the buffer will start filling up again at the rate of one element per second.

4.5.5 Reading a file lazily

The simplest way to read a file is as a list of characters. However, if the file is very large, this uses an enormous amount of memory. This is why files are usually read incrementally, a block at a time (where a block is a contiguous piece of the file). The program is careful to keep in memory only the blocks that are needed. This is memory-efficient, but is cumbersome to program.

Can we have the best of both worlds: to read the file as a list of characters (which keeps programs simple), yet to read in only the parts we need (which saves memory)? With lazy execution the answer is yes. Here is the function `ReadListLazy` that solves the problem:

```
fun {ReadListLazy FN}
   {File.readOpen FN}
   fun lazy {ReadNext}
   L T I in
      {File.readBlock I L T}
      if I==0 then T=nil {File.readClose} else T={ReadNext} end
      L
   end
in
   {ReadNext}
end
```

It uses three operations in the `File` module (which is available on the book's Web site): `{File.readOpen FN}`, which opens file `FN` for reading; `{File.readBlock I L T}`, which reads a block in the difference list `L#T` and returns its size in `I`; and `{File.readClose}`, which closes the file.

The `ReadListLazy` function reads a file lazily, a block at a time. Whenever a block is exhausted then another block is read automatically. Reading blocks is much more efficient than reading single characters since only one lazy call is needed for a whole block. This means that `ReadListLazy` is, practically speaking, just as efficient as the solution in which we read blocks explicitly. When the end of file is

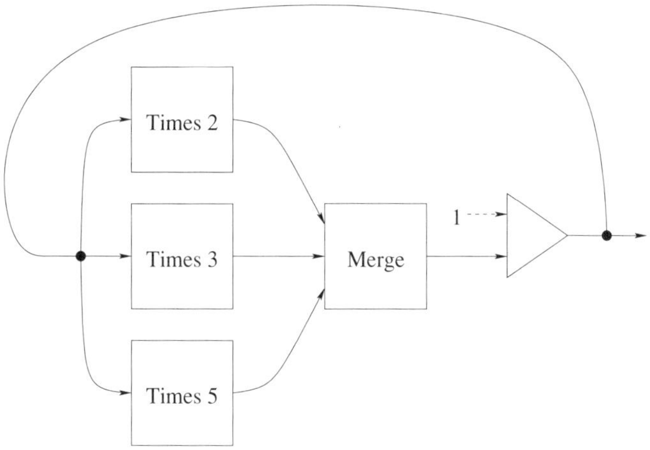

Figure 4.28: Lazy solution to the Hamming problem.

reached, then the tail of the list is bound to `nil` and the file is closed.

The `ReadListLazy` function is acceptable if the program reads all of the file, but if it only reads part of the file, then it is not good enough. Do you see why not? Think carefully before reading the answer in the footnote![13] Section 6.9.2 shows the right way to use laziness together with external resources such as files.

4.5.6 The Hamming problem

The Hamming problem, named after Richard Hamming, is a classic problem of demand-driven concurrency. The problem is to generate the first n integers of the form $2^a 3^b 5^c$ with $a, b, c \geq 0$. Hamming actually solved a more general version, which considers products of the first k primes. We leave this one as an exercise! The idea is to generate the integers in increasing order in a potentially infinite stream. At all times, a finite part h of this stream is known. To generate the next element of h, we take the least element x of h such that $2x$ is bigger than the last element of h. We do the same for 3 and 5, giving y and z. Then the next element of h is $\min(2x, 3y, 5z)$. We start the process by initializing h to have the single element 1. Figure 4.28 gives a picture of the algorithm. The simplest way to program this algorithm is with two lazy functions. The first function multiplies all elements of a list by a constant:

```
fun lazy {Times N H}
   case H of X|H2 then N*X|{Times N H2} end
end
```

13. It is because the file stays open during the whole execution of the program—this consumes valuable system resources, including a file descriptor and a read buffer.

The second function takes two lists of integers in increasing order and merges them into a single list:

```
fun lazy {Merge Xs Ys}
   case Xs#Ys of (X|Xr)#(Y|Yr) then
      if X<Y then X|{Merge Xr Ys}
      elseif X>Y then Y|{Merge Xs Yr}
      else X|{Merge Xr Yr}
      end
   end
end
```

Each value should appear only once in the output. This means that when `X==Y`, it is important to skip the value in both lists `Xs` and `Ys`. With these two functions, it is easy to solve the Hamming problem:

```
H=1|{Merge {Times 2 H}
           {Merge {Times 3 H}
                  {Times 5 H}}}
{Browse H}
```

This builds a three-argument merge function using two two-argument merge functions. If we execute this as is, then it displays very little:

```
1|_<Future>
```

No elements are calculated. To get the first n elements of `H`, we need to ask that they be calculated. For example, we can define the procedure `Touch`:

```
proc {Touch N H}
   if N>0 then {Touch N-1 H.2} else skip end
end
```

This traverses `N` elements of `H`, which causes them to be calculated. Now we can calculate 20 elements by calling `Touch`:

```
{Touch 20 H}
```

This displays

```
1|2|3|4|5|6|8|9|10|12|15|16|18|20|24|25|27|30|32|36|_<Future>
```

4.5.7 Lazy list operations

All the list functions of section 3.4 can be made lazy. It is insightful to see how this changes their behavior.

Lazy append

We start with a simple function, a lazy version of `Append`:

```
fun lazy {LAppend As Bs}
   case As
   of nil then Bs
   [] A|Ar then A|{LAppend Ar Bs}
   end
end
```

The only difference with the eager version is the "`lazy`" annotation. The lazy definition works because it is recursive: it calculates part of the answer and then calls itself. Calling `LAppend` with two lists will append them lazily:

```
L={LAppend "foo" "bar"}
{Browse L}
```

We say this function is incremental: forcing its evaluation only does enough of the calculation to generate one additional output element, and then creates another suspension. If we "touch" successive elements of `L` this will successively show `f`, `o`, `o`, one character at a time. However, after we have exhausted `"foo"`, then `LAppend` is finished, so it will show `"bar"` all at once. How do we make a list append that returns a completely lazy list? One way is to give `LAppend` a lazy list as second argument. First define a function that takes any list and returns a lazy version:

```
fun lazy {MakeLazy Ls}
   case Ls
   of X|Lr then X|{MakeLazy Lr}
   else nil end
end
```

`MakeLazy` works by iterating over its input list, i.e., like `LAppend`, it calculates part of the answer and then calls itself. This only changes the control flow; considered as a function between lists, `MakeLazy` is an identity. Now call `LAppend` as follows:

```
L={LAppend "foo" {MakeLazy "bar"}}
{Browse L}
```

This will lazily enumerate both lists, i.e., it successively returns the characters `f`, `o`, `o`, `b`, `a`, and `r`.

Lazy mapping

We have seen `Map` in section 3.6; it evaluates a function on all elements of a list. It is easy to define a lazy version of this function:

```
fun lazy {LMap Xs F}
   case Xs
   of nil then nil
   [] X|Xr then {F X}|{LMap Xr F}
   end
end
```

This function takes any list or lazy list `Xs` and returns a lazy list. Is it incremental?

Lazy integer lists

We define the function {LFrom I J} that generates a lazy list of integers from I to J:

```
fun {LFrom I J}
   fun lazy {LFromLoop I}
      if I>J then nil else I|{LFromLoop I+1} end
   end
   fun lazy {LFromInf I} I|{LFromInf I+1} end
in
   if J==inf then {LFromInf I} else {LFromLoop I} end
end
```

Why is LFrom itself not annotated as lazy?[14] This definition allows J=inf, in which case an infinite lazy stream of integers is generated.

Lazy flatten

This definition shows that lazy difference lists are as easy to generate as lazy lists. As with the other lazy functions, it suffices to annotate as lazy all recursive functions that calculate part of the solution on each iteration.

```
fun {LFlatten Xs}
   fun lazy {LFlattenD Xs E}
      case Xs
      of nil then E
      [] X|Xr then
         {LFlattenD X {LFlattenD Xr E}}
      [] X then X|E
      end
   end
in
   {LFlattenD Xs nil}
end
```

We remark that this definition has the same asymptotic efficiency as the eager definition, i.e., it takes advantage of the constant-time append property of difference lists.

Lazy reverse

Up to now, all the lazy list functions we introduced are incremental, i.e., they are able to produce one element at a time efficiently. Sometimes this is not possible. For some list functions, the work required to produce one element is enough to produce them all. We call these functions monolithic. A typical example is list reversal. Here is a lazy definition:

---

14. Only recursive functions need to be controlled, since they would otherwise do a potentially unbounded calculation.

```
fun {LReverse S}
   fun lazy {Rev S R}
      case S
      of nil then R
      [] X|S2 then {Rev S2 X|R} end
   end
in {Rev S nil} end
```

Let us call this function:

```
L={LReverse [a b c]}
{Browse L}
```

What happens if we touch the first element of `L`? This will calculate and display the whole reversed list! Why does this happen? Touching `L` activates the suspension `{Rev [a b c] nil}` (remember that `LReverse` itself is not annotated as lazy). This executes `Rev` and creates a new suspension for `{Rev [b c] [a]}` (the recursive call), but no list pair. Therefore the new suspension is immediately activated. This does another iteration and creates a second suspension, `{Rev [c] [b a]}`. Again, no list pair is available, so the second suspension is immediately activated. This continues until `Rev` returns `[c b a]`. At this point, there is a list pair so the evaluation completes. The need for one list pair has caused the whole list reversal to be done. This is what we mean by a monolithic function. For list reversal, another way to understand this behavior is to think of what list reversal means: the first element of a reversed list is the last element of the input list. We therefore have to traverse the whole input list, which lets us construct the whole reversed list.

Lazy filter

To complete this section, we give another example of an incremental function, namely filtering an input list according to a condition `F`:

```
fun lazy {LFilter L F}
   case L
   of nil then nil
   [] X|L2 then
      if {F X} then X|{LFilter L2 F} else {LFilter L2 F} end
   end
end
```

We give this function because we will need it for list comprehensions in section 4.5.9.

4.5.8 Persistent queues and algorithm design

In section 3.4.5 we saw how to build queues with constant-time insert and delete operations. Those queues only work in the ephemeral case, i.e., only one version exists at a time. It turns out we can use laziness to build persistent queues with the same time bounds. A persistent queue is one that supports multiple versions. We first show how to make an amortized persistent queue with constant-time insert and delete operations. We then show how to achieve worst-case constant-time.

4.5.8.1 Amortized persistent queue

We first tackle the amortized case. The reason why the amortized queue of section 3.4.5 is not persistent is that `Delete` sometimes does a list reversal, which is not constant-time. Each time a `Delete` is done on the same version, another list reversal is done. This breaks the amortized complexity if there are multiple versions.

We can regain the amortized complexity by doing the reverse as part of a lazy function call. Invoking the lazy function creates a suspension instead of doing the reverse right away. Sometime later, when the result of the reverse is needed, the lazy function does the reverse. With some cleverness, this can solve our problem:

- Between the creation of the suspension and the actual execution of the reverse, we arrange that there are enough operations to pay back the costs incurred by the reverse.
- But the reverse can be paid for only once. What if several versions want to do the reverse? This is not a problem. Laziness guarantees that the reverse is only done once, even if more than one version triggers it. The first version that needs it will activate the trigger and save the result. Subsequent versions will use the result without doing any calculation.

This sounds nice, but it depends on being able to create the suspension far enough in advance of the actual reverse. Can we do it? In the case of a queue, we can. Let us represent the queue as a 4-tuple:

```
q(LenF F LenR R)
```

`F` and `R` are the front and rear lists, as in the ephemeral case. We add the integers `LenF` and `LenR`, which give the lengths of `F` and `R`. We need these integers to test when it is time to create the suspension. At some magic instant, we move the elements of `R` to `F`. The queue then becomes

```
q(LenF+LenR {LAppend F {fun lazy {$} {Reverse R} end}} 0 nil)
```

In section 3.4.5 we did this (eagerly) when `F` became empty, so the `Append` did not take any time. But this is too late to keep the amortized complexity, since the reverse is not paid for (e.g., maybe `R` is a very big list). We remark that the reverse gets evaluated in any case when the `LAppend` has finished, i.e., after |`F`| elements are removed from the queue. Can we arrange that the elements of `F` pay for the reverse? We can, if we create the suspension when |`R`| $\approx$ |`F`|. Then removing each element of `F` pays for part of the reverse. By the time we have to evaluate the reverse, it is completely paid for. Using the lazy append makes the payment incremental. This gives the following implementation:

```
fun {NewQueue} q(0 nil 0 nil) end

fun {Check Q}
   case Q of q(LenF F LenR R) then
      if LenF>=LenR then Q
      else q(LenF+LenR {LAppend F {fun lazy {$} {Reverse R} end}}
             0 nil) end
   end
end

fun {Insert Q X}
   case Q of q(LenF F LenR R) then
      {Check q(LenF F LenR+1 X|R)}
   end
end

fun {Delete Q X}
   case Q of q(LenF F LenR R) then F1 in
      F=X|F1 {Check q(LenF-1 F1 LenR R)}
   end
end
```

Both `Insert` and `Delete` call the function `Check`, which chooses the moment to do the lazy call. Since `Insert` increases |`R`| and `Delete` decreases |`F`|, eventually |`R`| becomes as large as |`F`|. When |`R`| = |`F`|+1, `Check` does the lazy call `{LAppend F {fun lazy {$} {Reverse R} end}}`. The function `LAppend` is defined in section 4.5.7.

Let us summarize this technique. We replace the original eager function call by a lazy function call. The lazy call is partly incremental and partly monolithic. The trick is that the lazy call starts off being incremental. By the time the monolithic part is reached, there have been enough incremental steps so that the monolithic part is paid for. It follows that the result is amortized constant-time.

For a deeper discussion of this technique, including its application to other data structures and a proof of correctness, we recommend [157].

4.5.8.2 Worst-case persistent queue

The reason the above definition is not worst-case constant-time is because `Reverse` is monolithic. If we could rewrite it to be incremental, then we would have a solution with worst-case constant-time behavior. But list reversal cannot be made incremental, so this does not work. Let us try another approach.

Look at the context of the `Reverse` call. It is called together with a lazy append:

```
{LAppend F {fun lazy {$} {Reverse R} end}}
```

This first executes the append incrementally. When all elements of `F` have been passed to the output, then the reverse is executed monolithically. The cost of the reverse is amortized over the steps of the append.

Instead of amortizing the cost of the reverse, perhaps we can actually do the reverse together with the steps of the append. When the append is finished, the reverse will be finished as well. This is the heart of the solution. To implement it, let us compare the definitions of reverse and append. Reverse uses the recursive function `Rev`:

```
fun {Reverse R}
   fun {Rev R A}
      case R
      of nil then A
      [] X|R2 then {Rev R2 X|A} end
   end
in {Rev R nil} end
```

`Rev` traverses `R`, accumulates a solution in `A`, and then returns the solution. Can we do both `Rev` and `LAppend` in a single loop? Here is `LAppend`:

```
fun lazy {LAppend F B}
   case F
   of nil then B
   [] X|F2 then X|{LAppend F2 B}
   end
end
```

This traverses `F` and returns `B`. The recursive call is passed `B` unchanged. Let us change this to use `B` to accumulate the result of the reverse! This gives the following combined function:

```
fun lazy {LAppRev F R B}
   case F#R
   of nil#[Y] then Y|B
   [] (X|F2)#(Y|R2) then X|{LAppRev F2 R2 Y|B}
   end
end
```

`LAppRev` traverses both `F` and `R`. During each iteration, it calculates one element of the append and accumulates one element of the reverse. This definition only works if `R` has exactly one more element than `F`, which is true for our queue. The original call

```
{LAppend F {fun lazy {$} {Reverse R} end}}
```

is replaced by

```
{LAppRev F R nil}
```

which gives exactly the same result except that `LAppRev` is completely incremental. The definition of `Check` then becomes:

```
fun {Check Q}
   case Q of q(LenF F LenR R) then
      if LenR=<LenF then Q
      else q(LenF+LenR {LAppRev F R nil} 0 nil) end
   end
end
```

Careful analysis shows that the worst-case bound of this queue is $O(\log n)$, and not $O(1)$ as our intuition might expect it to be. The bound is much better than

$O(n)$, but it is not constant. See Exercises (section 4.11) for an explanation and a suggestion on how to achieve a constant bound.

Taking a program with a worst-case bound and adding laziness naively will give an amortized bound. This is because laziness changes where the function calls are executed, but does not do more of them (the eager case is an upper bound). The definition of this section is remarkable because it does just the opposite: it starts with an amortized bound and uses laziness to give a worst-case bound.

4.5.8.3 Lessons for algorithm design

Laziness is able to shuffle calculations around, spreading them out or bunching them together without changing the final result. This is a powerful tool for designing declarative algorithms. It has to be used carefully, however. Used naively, laziness can destroy perfectly good worst-case bounds, turning them into amortized bounds. Used wisely, laziness can improve amortized algorithms: it can sometimes make the algorithm persistent and it can sometimes transform the amortized bound into a worst-case bound.

We can outline a general scheme. Start with an algorithm A that has an amortized bound $O(f(n))$ when used ephemerally. For example, the first queue of section 3.4.5 has an amortized bound of $O(1)$. We can use laziness to move from ephemeral to persistent while keeping this time bound. There are two possibilities:

- Often we can get a modified algorithm A' that keeps the amortized bound $O(f(n))$ when used persistently. This is possible when the expensive operations can be spread out to be mostly incremental but with a few remaining monolithic operations.
- In a few cases, we can go farther and get a modified algorithm A" with worst-case bound $O(f(n))$ when used persistently. This is possible when the expensive operations can be spread out to be completely incremental.

This section realizes both possibilities with the first queue of section 3.4.5. The persistent algorithms so obtained are often quite efficient, especially if used by applications that really need the persistence. They compare favorably with algorithms in stateful models.

4.5.9 List comprehensions

List comprehensions are a notational convenience for defining streams. The streams can be either bounded, i.e., they are lists, or potentially unbounded. In the latter case, it is often useful to calculate them lazily. List comprehensions can be useful for all of these possibilities. We introduce them here, in the context of lazy execution, because they are especially interesting with lazy streams. List comprehensions allow specifying streams in a way that closely resembles the mathematical notation of set comprehensions. For example, the mathematical notation $\{x * y \mid 1 \le x \le 10,\ 1 \le y \le x\}$ specifies the set $\{1*1, 2*1, 2*2, 3*1, 3*2, 3*3, \ldots, 10*10\}$, i.e. $\{1, 2, 3, 4, 5, \ldots, 100\}$. We turn this notation into a practical programming tool by modifying it to specify not sets, but lazy streams. This makes the notation very efficient to implement, while keeping it at a high level of abstraction. For example, the list comprehension $[x * y \mid 1 \le x \le 10,\ 1 \le y \le x]$ (notice the square list brackets!) specifies the list `[1*1 2*1 2*2 3*1 3*2 3*3 ··· 10*10]` (in this order), i.e., the list `[1 2 4 3 6 9 ··· 100]`. The list is calculated lazily. Because of laziness the list comprehension can generate a potentially unbounded stream, not just a finite list.

List comprehensions have the following basic form:

$$[f(x) \mid x \leftarrow \mathit{generator}(a_1, \ldots, a_n),\ \mathit{guard}(x, a_1, \ldots, a_n)]$$

The generator $x \leftarrow \mathit{generator}(a_1, \ldots, a_n)$ calculates a lazy list whose elements are successively assigned to x. The guard $\mathit{guard}(x, a_1, \ldots, a_n)$ is a boolean function. The list comprehension specifies a lazy list containing the elements $f(x)$, where f is any function and x takes on values from the generator for which the guard is true. In the general case, there can be any number of variables, generators, and guards. A typical generator is *from*:

$$x \leftarrow \mathit{from}(a, b)$$

Here x takes on the integer values a, $a+1$, ..., b, in that order. Calculation is done from left to right. The generators, when taken from left to right, are considered as nested loops: the rightmost generator is the innermost loop.

There is a close connection between list comprehensions and the relational programming of chapter 9. Both provide lazy interfaces to infinitely long sequences and make it easy to write "generate-and-test" programs. Both allow specifying the sequences in a declarative way.

While list comprehensions are usually considered to be lazy, they can in fact be programmed in both eager and lazy versions. For example, the list comprehension:

$$z = [x\#x \mid x \leftarrow \mathit{from}(1, 10)]$$

can be programmed in two ways. An eager version is

```
Z={Map {From 1 10} fun {$ X} X#X end}
```

For the eager version, the declarative model of chapter 2 is good enough. It uses the `Map` function of section 3.6.3 and the `From` function which generates a list of integers. A lazy version is

```
Z={LMap {LFrom 1 10} fun {$ X} X#X end}
```

The lazy version uses the `LMap` and `LFrom` functions of the previous section. This example and most examples in this section can be done with either a lazy or eager version. Using the lazy version is always correct. Using the eager version is a performance optimization. It is several times faster if the cost of calculating the list elements is not counted. The optimization is only possible if the whole list fits in memory. In the rest of this section, we always use the lazy version.

Here is a list comprehension with two variables:

$$z = [x\#y \mid x \leftarrow \mathit{from}(1,10),\ y \leftarrow \mathit{from}(1,x)]$$

This can be programmed as

```
Z={LFlatten
      {LMap {LFrom 1 10} fun {$ X}
         {LMap {LFrom 1 X} fun {$ Y}
            X#Y
          end}
       end}}
```

We have seen `LFlatten` in the previous section; it converts a list of lists to a "flat" lazy list, i.e., a lazy list that contains all the elements, but no lists. We need `LFlatten` because otherwise we have a list of lists. We can put `LFlatten` inside `LMap`:

```
fun {FMap L F}
   {LFlatten {LMap L F}}
end
```

This simplifies the program:

```
Z={FMap {LFrom 1 10} fun {$ X}
      {LMap {LFrom 1 X} fun {$ Y}
         X#Y
       end}
    end}
```

Here is an example with two variables and a guard:

$$z = [x\#y \mid x \leftarrow \mathit{from}(1,10),\ y \leftarrow \mathit{from}(1,10),\ x+y \leq 10]$$

This gives the list of all pairs $x\#y$ such that the sum $x+y$ is at most 10. It can be programmed as

```
Z={LFilter
      {FMap {LFrom 1 10} fun {$ X}
         {LMap {LFrom 1 10} fun {$ Y}
            X#Y
          end}
       end}
      fun {$ X#Y} X+Y=<10 end}
```

This uses the function `LFilter` defined in the previous section. We can reformulate this example to be more efficient. The idea is to generate as few elements as possible. In the above example, 100 (=10*10) elements are generated. From $2 \leq x+y \leq 10$ and $1 \leq y \leq 10$, we derive that $1 \leq y \leq 10-x$. This gives the following solution:

$$z = [x\#y \mid x \leftarrow \mathit{from}(1,10),\ y \leftarrow \mathit{from}(1,10-x)]$$

The program then becomes:

```
Z={FMap {LFrom 1 10} fun {$ X}
      {LMap {LFrom 1 10-X} fun {$ Y}
         X#Y
        end}
   end}
```

This gives the same list as before, but only generates about half as many elements.

4.6 Soft real-time programming

4.6.1 Basic operations

The `Time` module contains a number of useful soft real-time operations. A real-time operation has a set of deadlines (particular times) at which certain calculations must be completed. A soft real-time operation requires only that the real-time deadlines be respected most of the time. This is opposed to hard real time, which has hard deadlines, i.e., that must be respected all the time, without any exception. Hard real time is needed when lives are at stake, e.g., in medical equipment and air traffic control. Soft real time is used in other cases, e.g., for telephony and consumer electronics. Hard real time requires special techniques for both hardware and software. Standard personal computers cannot do hard real time because they have unpredictable hardware delays (e.g., virtual memory, caching, process scheduling). Soft real time is much easier to implement and is often sufficient. Three soft real-time operations provided by `Time` are:

1. `{Delay I}`: suspends the executing thread for at least `I` ms and then continues.

2. `{Alarm I U}`: creates a new thread that binds `U` to **`unit`** after at least `I` ms. `Alarm` can be implemented with `Delay`.

3. `{Time.time}`: returns the integer number of seconds that have passed since the current year started.

The semantics of `Delay` is simple: it communicates to the scheduler that the thread is to be considered suspended for a given time period. After this time is up, the scheduler marks the thread as runnable again. The thread is not necessarily run immediately. If there are lots of other runnable threads, it may take some time before the thread actually runs.

We illustrate the use of `Delay` by means of a simple example that shows the interleaving execution of two threads. The program is called `´Ping Pong´` and is defined in figure 4.29. It starts two threads. One displays `ping` periodically each 500 ms and the other displays `pong` each 600 ms. Because pongs come out slower than pings, it is possible for two pings to be displayed without any pongs in between. Can the same thing happen with two pongs? That is, can two pongs ever be displayed with no pings in between? Assume that the `Ping` thread has not yet terminated, otherwise the question would be too easy. Think carefully before reading the answer

```
local
   proc {Ping N}
      if N==0 then {Browse ´ping terminated´}
      else {Delay 500} {Browse ping} {Ping N-1} end
   end
   proc {Pong N}
      {For 1 N 1
         proc {$ I} {Delay 600} {Browse pong} end}
      {Browse ´pong terminated´}
   end
in
   {Browse ´game started´}
   thread {Ping 50} end
   thread {Pong 50} end
end
```

Figure 4.29: A simple 'Ping Pong' program.

in the footnote.[15]

A simple standalone application

Section 3.9 shows how to make standalone applications in Oz. To make the `´Ping Pong´` program standalone, the first step is to make a functor of it, as shown in figure 4.30. If the source code is stored in file `PingPong.oz`, then the program can be compiled with the following command:

```
ozc -x PingPong.oz
```

Type `PingPong` in your shell to start the program. To terminate this program in a Unix shell you have to type CTRL-C.

The program of figure 4.30 does not terminate properly when the `Ping` and the `Pong` threads terminate. It does not detect when the threads terminate. We can fix this problem using the techniques of section 4.4.3. Figure 4.31 adds a termination detection that terminates the main thread only when both the `Ping` and the `Pong` threads terminate. We could also use the `Barrier` abstraction directly. After detecting termination, we use the call `{Application.exit 0}` to cleanly exit the application.

---

15. The language does indeed allow two pongs to be displayed with no intervening pings because the definition of `Delay` only gives the minimum suspension time. The thread suspending for 500 ms can occasionally suspend for a longer time, e.g., for 700 ms. But this is a rare occurrence in practice because it depends on external events in the operating system or in other threads.

```
functor
import
   Browser(browse:Browse)
define
   proc {Ping N}
      if N==0 then {Browse ´ping terminated´}
      else {Delay 500} {Browse ping} {Ping N-1} end
   end
   proc {Pong N}
      {For 1 N 1
         proc {$ I} {Delay 600} {Browse pong} end }
      {Browse ´pong terminated´}
   end
in
   {Browse ´game started´}
   thread {Ping 50} end
   thread {Pong 50} end
end
```

Figure 4.30: A standalone 'Ping Pong' program.

```
functor
import
   Browser(browse:Browse)
   Application
define
   ...
   X1 X2
in
   {Browse ´game started´}
   thread {Ping 50} X1=unit end
   thread {Pong 50} X2=unit end
   {Wait X1} {Wait X2}
   {Application.exit 0}
end
```

Figure 4.31: A standalone 'Ping Pong' program that exits cleanly.

4.6.2 Ticking

We would like to invoke an action (e.g., send a message to a stream object, call a procedure, etc.) exactly once per second, giving it the local time as argument. We have three operations at our disposal: {Delay D}, which delays for at least D ms, {Time.time}, which returns the number of seconds since January 1 of the current year, and {OS.localTime}, which returns a record giving local time accurate to one second. How does the following function measure up?:

```
fun {NewTicker}
   fun {Loop}
      X={OS.localTime}
   in
      {Delay 1000}
      X|{Loop}
   end
in
   thread {Loop} end
end
```

This function creates a stream that grows by one element per second. To execute an action once every second, create a thread that reads the stream and performs the action:

```
thread for X in {NewTicker} do {Browse X} end end
```

Any number of threads can read the same stream. The problem is, this solution is not quite right. The stream is extended almost exactly once per second. The problem is the "almost." Every once in a while, one second is lost, i.e., successive elements on the stream show a difference of two seconds. However, there is one good point: the same second cannot be sent twice, since {Delay 1000} guarantees a delay of at least 1000 ms, to which is added the execution of the instructions in Loop. This gives a total delay of at least $1000 + \varepsilon$ ms, where ε is a fraction of a microsecond.

How can we correct this problem? A simple way is to compare the current result of OS.localTime with the previous result, and to add an element to the stream only when the local time changes. This gives

```
fun {NewTicker}
   fun {Loop T}
      T1={OS.localTime}
   in
      {Delay 900}
      if T1\=T then T1|{Loop T1} else {Loop T1} end
   end
in
   thread {Loop {OS.localTime}} end
end
```

This version guarantees that exactly one tick will be sent per second, if {Delay 900} always delays for less than one second. The latter condition holds if there are not too many active threads and garbage collection does not take too long. One way to guarantee the first condition is to give the `Loop` thread high priority and all other threads medium or low priority. To guarantee the second condition, the program must ensure that there is not too much active data, since garbage collection time is proportional to the amount of active data.

This version has the minor problem that it "hesitates" every nine seconds. That is, it can happen that `{OS.localTime}` gives the same result twice in a row, since the two calls are separated by just slightly more than 900 ms. This means that the stream will not be updated for 1800 ms. Another way to see this problem is that ten intervals of 900 ms are needed to cover nine seconds, which means that nothing happens during one of the intervals. How can we avoid this hesitation? A simple way is to make the delay smaller. With a delay of 100 ms, the hesitation will never be greater than 100 ms plus the garbage collection time.

A better way to avoid the hesitation is to use synchronized clocks. That is, we create a free-running counter that runs at approximately one second per tick, and we adjust its speed so that it remains synchronized with the operating system time. Here is how it is done:

```
fun {NewTicker}
   fun {Loop N}
      T={Time.time}
   in
      if T>N then {Delay 900}
      elseif T<N then {Delay 1100}
      else {Delay 1000} end
      N|{Loop N+1}
   end
in
   thread {Loop {Time.time}} end
end
```

The loop has a counter, `N`, that is always incremented by 1. We compare the counter value to the result of `{Time.time}`.[16] If the counter is slower (`T>N`), we speed it up. Likewise, if the counter is faster (`T<N`), we slow it down. The speedup and slowdown factors are small (10% in the example), which makes the hesitation unnoticeable.

4.7 The Haskell language

We give a brief introduction to Haskell, a popular functional programming language supported by a number of interpreters and compilers [96, 166].[17] It is perhaps the most successful attempt to define a practical, completely declarative language. Haskell is a nonstrict, strongly typed functional language that supports currying

16. How would you fix `NewTicker` to work correctly when `Time.time` turns over, i.e., goes back to 0?
17. The author of this section is Kevin Glynn.

and the monadic programming style. "Strongly typed" means that the types of all expressions are computed at compile time and all function applications must be type-correct. The monadic style is a set of higher-order programming techniques that can be used to replace explicit state in many cases. The monadic style can do much more than just simulate state; we do not explain it in this brief introduction but we refer to any of the many papers and tutorials written about it [97, 230, 154].

Before giving the computation model, let us start with a simple example. We can write a factorial function in Haskell as follows:

```
factorial :: Integer -> Integer
factorial 0         = 1
factorial n | n > 0 = n * factorial (n-1)
```

The first line is the type signature. It specifies that `factorial` is a function that expects an argument of type `Integer` and returns a result of type `Integer`. Haskell does type inferencing, i.e., the compiler is able to automatically infer the type signatures, for almost all functions.[18] This happens even when the type signature is provided: the compiler then checks that the signature is accurate. Type signatures provide useful documentation.

The next two lines are the code for `factorial`. In Haskell a function definition can consist of many equations. To apply a function to an argument we do pattern matching; we examine the equations one by one from top to bottom until we find the first one whose pattern matches the argument. The first line of `factorial` only matches an argument of 0; in this case the answer is immediate, namely 1. If the argument is nonzero we try to match the second equation. This equation has a boolean guard which must be true for the match to succeed. The second equation matches all arguments that are greater than 0; in that case we evaluate `n * factorial (n-1)`. What happens if we apply `factorial` to a negative argument? None of the equations match and the program will give a run-time error.

4.7.1 Computation model

A Haskell program consists of a single expression. This expression may contain many reducible subexpressions. In which order should they be evaluated? Haskell is a nonstrict language, so no expression should be evaluated unless its result is definitely needed. Intuitively then, we should first reduce the leftmost expression until it is a function, substitute arguments in the function body (without evaluating them!) and then reduce the resulting expression. This evaluation order is called normal order. For example, consider the following expression:

```
(if n >= 0 then factorial else error) (factorial (factorial n))
```

18. Except in a very few special cases which are beyond the scope of this section, such as polymorphic recursion.

This uses `n` to choose which function, `factorial` or `error`, to apply to the argument `(factorial (factorial n))`. It is pointless evaluating the argument until we have evaluated the `if then else` statement. Once this is evaluated we can substitute `factorial (factorial n)` in the body of `factorial` or `error` as appropriate and continue evaluation.

Let us explain in a more precise way how expressions reduce in Haskell. Imagine the expression as a tree.[19] Haskell first evaluates the leftmost subexpression until it evaluates to a data constructor or function:

- If it evaluates to a data constructor, then evaluation is finished. Any remaining subexpressions remain unevaluated.
- If it evaluates to a function and it is not applied to any arguments, then evaluation is finished.
- Otherwise, it evaluates to a function and is applied to arguments. Apply the function to the first argument (without evaluating it) by substituting it in the body of the function and re-evaluate.

Built-in functions such as addition and pattern matching cause their arguments to be evaluated before they can evaluate. For declarative programs this evaluation order has the nice property that it always terminates if any evaluation order could.

4.7.2 Lazy evaluation

Since arguments to functions are not automatically evaluated before function calls, we say that function calls in Haskell are nonstrict. Although not mandated by the Haskell language, most Haskell implementations are in fact lazy, i.e., they ensure that expressions are evaluated at most once. The differences between lazy and nonstrict evaluation are explained in section 4.9.2.

Optimizing Haskell compilers perform an analysis called strictness analysis to determine when the laziness is not necessary for termination or resource control. Functions that do not need laziness are compiled as eager ("strict") functions, which is much more efficient.

As an example of laziness we reconsider the calculation of a square root by Newton's method given in section 3.2. The idea is that we first create an "infinite" list containing better and better approximations to the square root. We then traverse the list until we find the first approximation which is accurate enough and return it. Because of laziness we will only create as much of the list of approximations as we need.

19. For efficiency reasons, most Haskell implementations represent expressions as graphs, i.e., shared expressions are only evaluated once.

```
sqrt x = head (dropWhile (not . goodEnough) sqrtGuesses)
   where
      goodEnough guess = (abs (x - guess*guess))/x < 0.00001
      improve guess = (guess + x/guess)/2.0
      sqrtGuesses = 1:(map improve sqrtGuesses)
```

The definitions following the `where` keyword are local definitions, i.e., they are only visible within `sqrt`. `goodEnough` returns true if the current guess is close enough. `improve` takes a guess and returns a better guess. `sqrtGuesses` produces the infinite list of approximations. The colon `:` is the list constructor, equivalent to | in Oz. The first approximation is 1. The following approximations are calculated by applying the `improve` function to the list of approximations. `map` is a function that applies a function to all elements of a list, similar to `Map` in Oz.[20] So the second element of `sqrtGuesses` will be `improve 1`, the third element will be `improve (improve 1)`. To calculate the nth element of the list we evaluate `improve` on the $(n-1)^{th}$ element.

The expression `dropWhile (not . goodEnough) sqrtGuesses` drops the approximations from the front of the list that are not close enough. `(not . goodEnough)` is a function composition. It applies `goodEnough` to the approximation and then applies the boolean function `not` to the result. So `(not . goodEnough)` is a function that returns true if `goodEnough` returns false.

Finally, `head` returns the first element of the resulting list, which is the first approximation that was close enough. Notice how we have separated the calculation of the approximations from the calculation that chooses the appropriate answer.

4.7.3 Currying

From the reduction rules we see that a function that expects multiple arguments is actually applied to its arguments one at a time. In fact, applying an n-argument function to a single argument evaluates to an $(n-1)$ argument function specialized to the value of the first argument. This process is called currying (see also section 3.6.6). We can write a function which doubles all the elements in a list by calling `map` with just one argument:

```
doubleList = map (\x -> 2*x)
```

The notation `\x -> 2*x` is Haskell's way of writing an anonymous function, i.e., a λ expression. The ASCII backslash character \ represents the symbol λ. In Oz the same expression would be written **fun** `{$ X} 2*X` **end**. Let us see how `doubleList` evaluates:

---

20. Note that the function and list arguments appear in a different order in the Haskell and Oz versions.

```
doubleList [1,2,3,4]
 =>  map (\x -> 2*x) [1,2,3,4]
 =>  [2,4,6,8]
```

Note that list elements are separated by commas in Haskell.

4.7.4 Polymorphic types

All Haskell expressions have a statically determined type. However, we are not limited to Haskell's predefined types. A program can introduce new types. For example, we can introduce a new type `BinTree` for binary trees:

```
data BinTree a = Empty | Node a (BinTree a) (BinTree a)
```

A `BinTree` is either `Empty` or a `Node` consisting of an element and two subtrees. `Empty` and `Node` are data constructors: they build data structures of type `BinTree`. In the definition `a` is a type variable and stands for an arbitrary type, the type of elements contained in the tree. `BinTree Integer` is then the type of binary trees of integers. Notice how in a `Node` the element and the elements in subtrees are restricted to have the same type. We can write a `size` function that returns the number of elements in a binary tree as follows:

```
size :: BinTree a -> Integer
size Empty              = 0
size (Node val lt rt) = 1 + (size lt) + (size rt)
```

The first line is the type signature. It can be read as "For all types `a`, `size` takes an argument of type `BinTree a` and returns an `Integer`." Since `size` works on trees containing any type of element it is called a polymorphic function. The code for the function consists of two lines. The first line matches trees that are empty; their size is 0. The second line matches trees that are nonempty; their size is 1 plus the size of the left subtree plus the size of the right subtree.

Let us write a `lookup` function for an ordered binary tree. The tree contains tuples consisting of an integer key and a string value. It has type `BinTree (Integer,String)`. The lookup function returns a value with type `Maybe String`. This value will be `Nothing` if the key does not exist in the tree and `Just val` if `(k,val)` is in the tree:

```
lookup :: Integer -> BinTree (Integer,String) -> Maybe String
lookup k Empty = Nothing
lookup k (Node (nk,nv) lt rt) | k == nk = Just nv
lookup k (Node (nk,nv) lt rt) | k < nk  = lookup k lt
lookup k (Node (nk,nv) lt rt) | k > nk  = lookup k rt
```

At first sight, the type signature of `lookup` may look strange. Why is there a `->` between the `Integer` and tree arguments? This is due to currying. When we apply `lookup` to an integer key we get back a new function which when applied to a binary tree always looks up the same key.

4.7.5 Type classes

A disadvantage of the above definition of `lookup` is that the given type is very restrictive. We would like to make it polymorphic as we did with `size`. Then the same code could be used to search trees containing tuples of almost any type. However, we must restrict the first element of the tuple to be a type that supports the comparison operations `==`, `<`, and `>` (e.g., there is not a computable ordering for functions, so we do not want to allow functions as keys).

To support this Haskell has type classes. A type class gives a name to a group of functions. If a type supports those functions we say the type is a member of that type class. In Haskell there is a built-in type class called `Ord` which supports `==`, `<`, and `>`. The following type signature specifies that the type of the tree's keys must be in type class `Ord`:

```
lookup :: (Ord a) => a -> BinTree (a,b) -> Maybe b
```

and indeed this is the type Haskell will infer for `lookup`. Type classes allow function names to be *overloaded*. The `<` operator for `Integers` is not the same as the `<` operator for `Strings`. Since a Haskell compiler knows the types of all expressions, it can substitute the appropriate type-specific operation at each use. Type classes are supported by functional languages such as Clean and Mercury. (Mercury is a logic language with functional programming support.) Other languages, including Standard ML and Oz, can achieve a similar overloading effect by using functors.

Programmers can add their own types to type classes. For example, we could add the `BinTree` type to `Ord` by providing appropriate definitions for the comparison operators. If we created a type for complex numbers we could make it a member of the numeric type class `Num` by providing appropriate numerical operators. The most general type signature for `factorial` is

```
factorial :: (Num a, Ord a) => a -> a
```

So `factorial` can be applied to an argument of any type supporting numerical and comparison operations, returning a value of the same type.

4.8 Limitations and extensions of declarative programming

Declarative programming has the major advantage that it considerably simplifies system building. Declarative components can be built and debugged independently of each other. The complexity of a system is the sum of the complexities of its components. A natural question to ask is, how far can declarative programming go? Can everything be programmed in a declarative way, such that programs are both natural and efficient? This would be a major boon for system building. We say a program is *efficient* if its performance differs by just a constant factor from the performance of an assembly language program to solve the same problem. We say a program is *natural* if very little code is needed just for technical reasons unrelated to the problem at hand. Let us consider efficiency and naturalness issues separately. There are three naturalness issues: modularity, nondeterminism, and interfacing with the real world.

We recommend using the declarative model of this chapter or the sequential version of chapter 2 except when any of the above issues are critical. This makes it easier to write correct and efficient components.

4.8.1 Efficiency

Is declarative programming efficient? There is a fundamental mismatch between the declarative model and a standard computer, such as presented in [164]. The computer is optimized for modifying data in-place, while the declarative model never modifies data but always creates new data. This is not as severe a problem as it seems at first glance. The declarative model may have a large inherent memory consumption, but its active memory size remains small. The task remains, though, to implement the declarative model with in-place assignment. This depends first on the sophistication of the compiler.

Can a compiler map declarative programs effectively to a standard computer? Paraphrasing science fiction author and futurologist Arthur C. Clarke, we can say that "any sufficiently advanced compiler is indistinguishable from magic" [42].[21] That is, it is unrealistic to expect the compiler to rewrite your program. Even after several decades of research, no such compiler exists for general-purpose programming. The farthest we have come are compilers that can rewrite the program in particular cases. Computer scientist Paul Hudak calls them "smart-aleck" compilers. Because of their unpredictable optimizations, they are hard to use. Therefore, for the rest of the discussion, we assume that the compiler does a straightforward mapping from the source program to the target, in the sense that time and space complexities of compiled code can be derived in a simple way from language semantics.

Now we can answer the question whether declarative programming is efficient. Given a straightforward compiler, the pedantic answer to the question is no. But in fact the practical answer is yes, with one caveat: declarative programming is efficient if one is allowed to rewrite the program to be less natural. Here are three typical examples:

1. A program that does incremental modifications of large data structures, e.g., a simulation that modifies large graphs (see section 6.8.4), cannot in general be compiled efficiently. Even after decades of research, there is no straightforward compiler that can take such a program and implement it efficiently. However, if one is allowed to rewrite the program, then there is a simple trick that is often sufficient

21. Clarke's third law: "Any sufficiently advanced technology is indistinguishable from magic."

in practice. If the state is threaded (e.g., kept in an accumulator) and the program is careful never to access an old state, then the accumulator can be implemented with destructive assignment.

2. A function that does memoization cannot be programmed without changing its interface. Assume we have a function that uses many computational resources. To improve its performance, we would like to add memoization to it, i.e., an internal cache of previously calculated results, indexed by the function arguments. At each function call, we first check the cache to see if the result is already there. This internal cache cannot be added without rewriting the program by threading an accumulator everywhere that the function is called. Section 10.4.2 gives an example.

3. A function that implements a complex algorithm often needs intricate code. That is, even though the program can be written declaratively with the same efficiency as a stateful program, doing so makes it more complex. This follows because the declarative model is less expressive than the stateful model. Section 6.8.1 shows an example: a transitive closure algorithm written in both the declarative and the stateful models. Both versions have time efficiency $O(n^3)$. The stateful algorithm is simpler to write than the declarative one.

We conclude that declarative programming cannot always be efficient and natural simultaneously. Let us now look at the naturalness issues.

4.8.2 Modularity

We say a program is modular with respect to a change in a given part if the change can be done without changing the rest of the program. Modularity cannot be achieved in general with a declarative model, but it can be achieved if the model is extended with explicit state. Here are two examples where declarative programs are not modular:

1. The first example is the memoization cache we saw before. Adding this cache to a function is not modular, since an accumulator must be threaded in many places outside the function.

2. A second example is instrumenting a program. We would like to know how many times some of its subcomponents are invoked. We would like to add counters to these subcomponents, preferably without changing either the subcomponent interfaces or the rest of the program. If the program is declarative, this is impossible, since the only way is to thread an accumulator throughout the program.

Let us look closer at the second example, to understand exactly why the declarative model is inadequate. Assume that we are using the declarative model to implement a large declarative component. The component definition looks something like this:

```
fun {SC ...}
   proc {P1 ...}
      ...
   end
   proc {P2 ...}
      ...
      {P1 ...}
      {P2 ...}
   end
   proc {P3 ...}
      ...
      {P2 ...}
      {P3 ...}
   end
in
   'export'(p1:P1 p2:P2 p3:P3)
end
```

Calling `SC` instantiates the component: it returns a module with three operations, `P1`, `P2`, and `P3`. We would like to instrument the component by counting the number of times procedure `P1` is called. The successive values of the count are a state. We can encode this state as an accumulator, i.e., by adding two arguments to each procedure. With this added instrumentation, the component definition looks something like this:

```
fun {SC ...}
   proc {P1 ... S1 ?Sn}
      Sn=S1+1
      ...
   end
   proc {P2 ... T1 ?Tn}
      ...
      {P1 ... T1 T2}
      {P2 ... T2 Tn}
   end
   proc {P3 ... U1 ?Un}
      ...
      {P2 ... U1 U2}
      {P3 ... U2 Un}
   end
in
   'export'(p1:P1 p2:P2 p3:P3)
end
```

Each procedure defined by `SC` has a changed interface: it has two extra arguments that together form an accumulator. The procedure `P1` is called as `{P1 ... Sin Sout}`, where `Sin` is the input count and `Sout` is the output count. The accumulator has to be threaded between the procedure calls. This technique requires both `SC` and the calling module to do a fair amount of bookkeeping, but it works.

Another solution is to write the component in a stateful model. One such model is defined in chapter 6; for now assume that we have a new language entity, called "cell," that we can assign and access (with the `:=` and `@` operators), similar to an

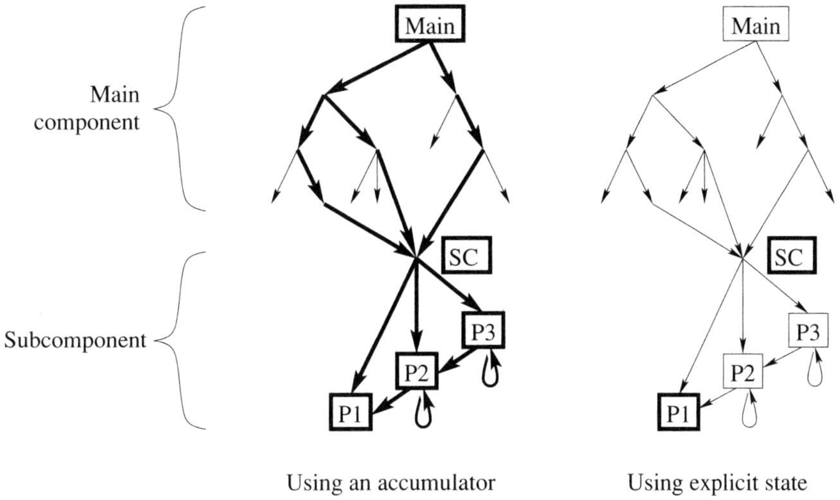

Figure 4.32: Changes needed for instrumenting procedure P1.

assignable variable in imperative programming languages. Cells were introduced in chapter 1. Then the component definition looks something like this:

```
fun {SC ...}
   Ctr={NewCell 0}
   proc {P1 ...}
      Ctr:=@Ctr+1
      ...
   end
   proc {P2 ...}
      ...
      {P1 ...}
      {P2 ...}
   end
   proc {P3 ...}
      ...
      {P2 ...}
      {P3 ...}
   end
   fun {Count} @Ctr end
in
   ´export´(p1:P1 p2:P2 p3:P3 count:Count)
end
```

In this case, the component interface has one extra function, `Count`, and the interfaces to `P1`, `P2`, and `P3` are unchanged. The calling module has no bookkeeping to do whatsoever. The count is automatically initialized to zero when the component is instantiated. The calling module can call `Count` at any time to get the current value of the count. The calling module can also ignore `Count` completely, if it likes, in which case the component has exactly the same behavior as before (except for a very slight difference in performance).

Figure 4.32 compares the two approaches. The figure shows the call graph of a program with a component `Main` that calls subcomponent `SC`. A call graph is a directed graph where each node represents a procedure and there is an edge from each procedure to the procedures it calls. In figure 4.32, `SC` is called from three places in the main component. Now let us instrument `SC`. In the declarative approach (at left), an accumulator has to be added to each procedure on the path from `Main` to `P1`. In the stateful approach (at right), the only changes are the extra operation `Count` and the body of `P1`. In both cases, the changes are shown with thick lines. Let us compare the two approaches:

- The declarative approach is not modular with respect to instrumenting `P1`, because every procedure definition and call on the path from `Main` to `P1` needs two extra arguments. The interfaces to `P1`, `P2`, and `P3` are all changed. This means that other components calling `SC` have to be changed too.
- The stateful approach is modular because the cell is mentioned only where it is needed, in the initialization of `SC` and in `P1`. In particular, the interfaces to `P1`, `P2`, and `P3` remain the same in the stateful approach. Since the extra operation `Count` can be ignored, other components calling `SC` do not have to be changed.
- The declarative approach is slower because it does much extra argument passing. All procedures are slowed down for the sake of one. The stateful approach is efficient; it only spends time when necessary.

Which approach is simpler: the first or the second? The first has a simpler model but a more complex program. The second has a more complex model but a simpler program. In our view, the declarative approach is not natural. Because it is modular, the stateful approach is clearly the simplest overall.

The fallacy of the preprocessor

Maybe there is a way we can have our cake and eat it too. Let us define a preprocessor to add the arguments so we do not have to write them everywhere. A preprocessor is a program that takes another program's source code as input, transforms it according to some simple rules, and returns the result. We define a preprocessor that takes the syntax of the stateful approach as input and translates it into a program that looks like the declarative approach. Voilà! It seems that we can now program with state in the declarative model. We have overcome a limitation of the declarative model. But have we? In fact, we have done nothing of the sort. All we have succeeded in doing is build an inefficient implementation of a stateful model. Let us see why:

- When using the preprocessor, we see only programs that look like the stateful version, i.e., stateful programs. This obliges us to reason in the stateful model. We have therefore de facto extended the declarative model with explicit state.
- The preprocessor transforms these stateful programs into programs with threaded

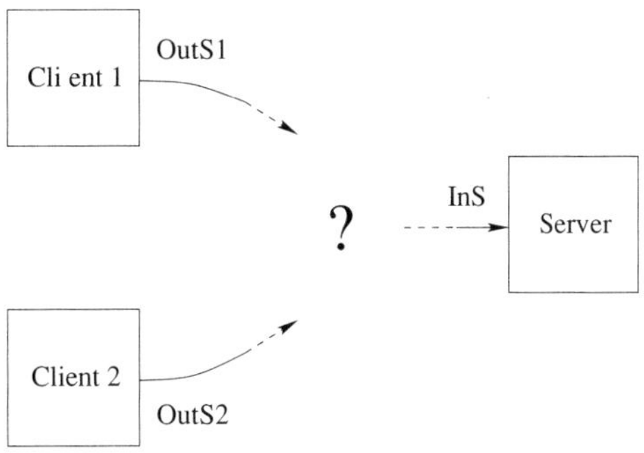

Figure 4.33: How can two clients send to the same server? They cannot!.

state, which are inefficient because of all the argument passing.

4.8.3 Nondeterminism

The declarative concurrent model seems to be quite powerful for building concurrent programs. For example, we can easily build a simulator for digital electronic circuits. However, despite this apparent power, the model has a limitation that cripples it for many concurrent applications: it always behaves deterministically. If a program has observable nondeterminism, then it is not declarative. This limitation is closely related to modularity: components that are truly independent behave nondeterministically with respect to each other. To show that this is not a purely theoretical limitation, we give two realistic examples: a client/server application and a video display application.

The limitation can be removed by adding a nondeterministic operation to the model. The extended model is no longer declarative. There are many possible nondeterministic operations we could add. Chapters 5 and 8 explain the possibilities in detail. Let us briefly go over them here:

- A first solution is to add a nondeterministic wait operation, such as `WaitTwo` which waits for one of two variables to become bound, and indicates one of the bound ones. Its definition is given in the supplements file on the book's Web site. `WaitTwo` is nice for the client/server application.
- A second solution is to add `IsDet`, a boolean function that tests immediately whether a dataflow variable is bound or not. This allows using dataflow variables as a weak form of state. `IsDet` is nice for the video display application.
- A third solution is to add explicit state to the model, e.g., in the form of ports (communication channels) or cells (mutable variables).

How do these three solutions compare in expressiveness? `WaitTwo` can be programmed in the declarative concurrent model with explicit state. Therefore, it seems that the most expressive model needs just explicit state and `IsDet`.

4.8.3.1 A client/server application

Let us investigate a simple client/server application. Assume that there are two independent clients. Being independent implies that they are concurrent. What happens if they communicate with the same server? Because they are independent, the server can receive information in any order from the two clients. This is observable nondeterministic behavior.

Let us examine this closer and see why it cannot be expressed in the declarative concurrent model. The server has an input stream from which it reads commands. Let us start with one client, which sends commands to the server. This works perfectly. How can a second client connect to the server? The second client has to obtain a reference to a stream that it can bind and that is read by the server. The problem is that such a stream does not exist! There is only one stream, between the first client and the server. The second client cannot bind that stream, since this would conflict with the first client's bindings.

How can we solve this problem? Let us approach it naively and see if we can find a solution. One approach might be to let the server have two input streams, like this:

```
fun {Server InS1 InS2}
   ...
end
```

But how does the server read the streams? Does it first read one element from `InS1` and then one element from `InS2`? Does it simultaneously read one element from both streams? Neither of these solutions is correct. In fact, it is not possible to write a solution in the declarative concurrent model. The only thing we can do is have two independent servers, one for each client. But these servers cannot communicate with each other, since otherwise we would have the same problem all over again.

Figure 4.33 illustrates the problem: `InS` is the server's input stream and `OutS1` and `OutS2` are the two client's output streams. How can the messages appearing on both client streams be given to the server? The simple answer is that in the declarative concurrent model they cannot! In the declarative concurrent model, an active object always has to know from which stream it will read next.

How can we solve this problem? If the clients execute in coordinated fashion, so that the server always knows which client will send the next command, then the program is declarative. But this is unrealistic. To write a true solution, we have to add a nondeterministic operation to the model, like the `WaitTwo` operation we mentioned above. With `WaitTwo`, the server can wait for a command from either client. Chapter 5 gives a solution using `WaitTwo`, in the nondeterministic concurrent model (see section 5.8).

4.8.3.2 A video display application

Let us look at a simple video display application. It consists of a displayer that receives a stream of video frames and displays them. The frames arrive at a particular rate, i.e., some number of frames arrive per second. For various reasons, this rate can fluctuate: the frames have different resolutions, some processing might be done on them, or the transmission network has varying bandwidth and latency.

Because of the varying arrival rate, the displayer cannot always display all frames. Sometimes it has to skip over frames. For example, it might want to skip quickly to the latest frame that was sent. This kind of stream management cannot be done in the declarative concurrent model, because there is no way to detect the end of the stream. It can be done by extending the model with one new operation, `IsDet`. The boolean test `{IsDet Xs}` checks immediately whether `Xs` is already bound or not (returning **`true`** or **`false`**), and does not wait if it is not bound. Using `IsDet`, we can define the function `Skip` that takes a stream and returns its unbound tail:

```
fun {Skip Xs}
   if {IsDet Xs} then
      case Xs of _|Xr then {Skip Xr} [] nil then nil end
   else Xs end
end
```

This iterates down the stream until it finds an unbound tail. Here is a slightly different version that always waits until there is at least one element:

```
fun {Skip1 Xs}
   case Xs of X|Xr then
      if {IsDet Xr} then {Skip1 Xr} else Xs end
   [] nil then nil end
end
```

With `Skip1`, we can write a video displayer that, after it has displayed a frame, immediately skips to the latest transmitted frame:

```
proc {Display Xs}
   case {Skip1 Xs}
   of X|Xr then
      {DisplayFrame X}
      {Display Xr}
   [] nil then skip
   end
end
```

This will work well even if there are variations in the frame arrival rate and the time to display a frame.

4.8.4 The real world

The real world is not declarative. It has both state (entities have an internal memory) and concurrency (entities evolve independently).[22] Since declarative programs interact with the real world, either directly or indirectly, they are part of an environment that contains these concepts. This has two consequences:

1. Interfacing problems. Declarative components lack the expressivity to interface with nondeclarative components. The latter are omnipresent, e.g., hardware peripherals and user interfaces are both inherently concurrent and stateful (see section 3.8). Operating systems also use concurrency and state for their own purposes, because of the reasons mentioned previously. One might think that these nondeclarative properties could be either masked or encoded somehow, but somehow this never works. Reality always peeks through.

2. Specification problems. Program specifications, because they are targeted for the real world, often mention state and concurrency. If the program is declarative, then it has to encode this in some way. For example, a specification for a collaborative tool may require that users lock what they are working on to prevent conflicts during concurrent access. In the implementation, the locks have to be encoded in some way. Using locks directly in a stateful model gives an implementation that is closer to the specification.

4.8.5 Picking the right model

There exist many computation models that differ in how expressive they are and how hard it is to reason about programs written in them. The declarative model is one of the simplest of all. However, as we have explained, it has serious limitations for some applications. There are more expressive models that overcome these limitations, at the price of sometimes making reasoning more complicated. For example, concurrency is often needed when interacting with the external world. When such interactions are important, then a concurrent model should be used instead of trying to get by with just the declarative model.

The more expressive models are not "better" than the others, since they do not always give simpler programs and reasoning in them is usually harder.[23] In our experience, all models have their place and can be used together to good effect in the same program. For example, in a program with concurrent state, many components can be declarative. Conversely, in a declarative program, some components (e.g.,

---

22. In fact, the real world is parallel, but this is modeled inside a program with concurrency. Concurrency is a language concept that expresses logically independent computations. Parallelism is an implementation concept that expresses activities that happen simultaneously. In a computer, parallelism is used only to increase performance.

23. Another reason why they are not better has to do with distributed programming and network awareness, which is explained in chapter 11.

graph algorithms) need state to be implemented well. We summarize this experience in the following rule:

> Rule of least expressiveness
>
> When programming a component, the right computation model for the component is the least expressive model that results in a natural program.

The idea is that each component should be programmed in its "natural" model. Using a less expressive model would give a more complex program and using a more expressive model would not give a simpler program but would make reasoning about it harder.

The problem with this rule is that we have not really defined "natural." This is because to some degree, naturalness is a subjective property. Different people may find different models easier to use, because of their differing knowledge and background. The issue is not the precise definition of "natural," but the fact that such a definition exists for each person, even though it might be different for different people. This lets each person apply the rule in a consistent way.

4.8.6 Extended models

Now we have some idea of the limitations of the declarative model and a few intuitions on how extended models with state and concurrency can overcome these limitations. This is a good place to give a brief overview of these models, starting with the declarative model:

- *Declarative sequential model* (see chapters 2 and 3). This model encompasses strict functional programming and deterministic logic programming. It extends the former with partial values (using dataflow variables, which are also called "logic variables") and the latter with higher-order procedures. Reasoning with this model is based on algebraic calculations with values. Equals can be substituted for equals and algebraic identities can be applied. A component's behavior is independent of when it is executed or of what happens in the rest of the computation.
- *Declarative concurrent model* (in this chapter; defined in sections 4.1 and 4.5). This is the declarative model extended with explicit threads and by-need computation. This model keeps most of the nice properties of the declarative model, e.g., reasoning is almost as simple, while being truly concurrent. This model can do both data-driven and demand-driven concurrency. It subsumes lazy functional programming and deterministic concurrent logic programming. Components interact by binding and using sharing dataflow variables.
- *Declarative model with exceptions* (defined in sections 2.7.2 and 4.9.1). The concurrent declarative model with exceptions is no longer declarative, since programs can be written that expose nondeterminism.

- *Message-passing concurrent model* (see chapter 5). This is the declarative model extended with communication channels (ports). This removes the limitation of the declarative concurrent model that it cannot implement programs with some nondeterminism, e.g., a client/server where several clients talk to a server. This is a useful generalization of the declarative concurrent model that is easy to program in and allows restricting the nondeterminism to small parts of the program.
- *Stateful model* (see chapters 6 and 7; defined in section 6.3). This is the declarative model extended with explicit state. This model can express sequential object-oriented programming as it is usually understood. A state is a sequence of values that is extended as the computation proceeds. Having explicit state means that a component does not always give the same result when called with the same arguments. The component can "remember" information from one call to the next. This allows the component to have a "history," which lets it interact more meaningfully with its environment by adapting and learning from its past. Reasoning with this model requires reasoning on the history.
- *Shared-state concurrent model* (see chapter 8; defined in section 8.1). This is the declarative model extended with both explicit state and threads. This model contains concurrent object-oriented programming. The concurrency is more expressive than the declarative concurrent model since it can use explicit state to wait simultaneously on one of several events occurring (this is called nondeterministic choice). Reasoning with this model is the most complex since there can be multiple histories interacting in unpredictable ways.
- *Relational model* (see chapter 9; defined in section 9.1). This is the declarative model extended with search (which is sometimes called "don't know nondeterminism," although the search algorithm is almost always deterministic). In the program, the search is expressed as sequence of choices. The search space is explored by making different choices until the result is satisfactory. This model allows programming with relations. It encompasses nondeterministic logic programming in the Prolog style. This model is a precursor to constraint programming, which is introduced in chapter 12.

Later on, we devote whole chapters to each of these models to explain what they are good for, how to program in them, and how to reason with them.

4.8.7 Using different models together

Typically, any well-written program of reasonable size has different parts written in different models. There are many ways to use different models together. This section gives an example of a particularly useful technique, which we call impedance matching, that naturally leads to using different models together in the same program.

Impedance matching is one of the most powerful and practical ways to implement the general principle of separation of concerns. Consider two computation models `Big` and `Small`, such that model `Big` is more expressive than `Small`, but harder to

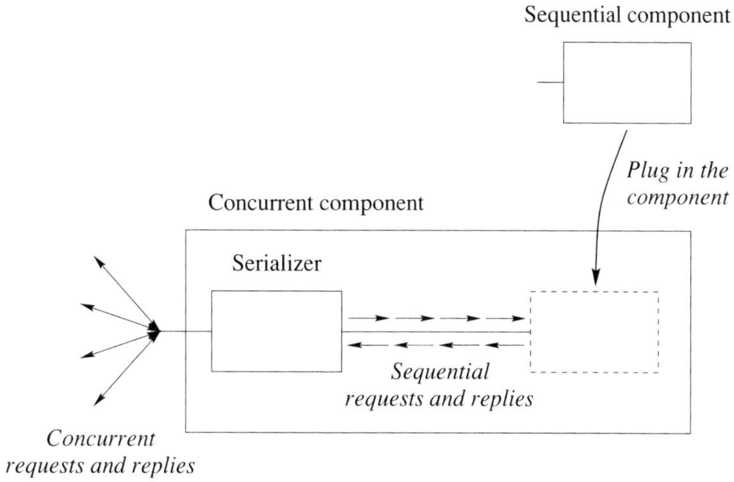

Figure 4.34: Impedance matching: example of a serializer.

reason in. For example, model `Big` could be stateful and model `Small` declarative. With impedance matching, we can write a program in model `Small` that can live in the computational environment of model `Big`.

Impedance matching works by building an abstraction in model `Big` that is parameterized with a program in model `Small`. The heart of impedance matching is finding and implementing the right abstraction. This hard work only needs to be done once; afterward there is only the easy work of using the abstraction. Perhaps surprisingly, it turns out that it is almost always possible to find and implement an appropriate abstraction. Here are some typical cases of impedance matching:

- Using a sequential component in a concurrent model. For example, the abstraction can be a serializer that accepts concurrent requests, passes them sequentially, and returns the replies correctly. Figure 4.34 gives an illustration. Plugging a sequential component into the serializer gives a concurrent component.
- Using a declarative component in a stateful model. For example, the abstraction can be a storage manager that passes its content to the declarative program and stores the result as its new content.
- Using a centralized component in a distributed model. A distributed model executes over more than one operating system process. For example, the abstraction can be a collector that accepts requests from any site and passes them to a single site.
- Using a component that is intended for a secure model in an insecure model. A insecure model is one that assumes the existence of malicious entities that can disturb programs in well-defined ways. A secure model assumes that no such entities exist. The abstraction can be a protector that insulates a computation by verifying

all requests from other computations. The abstraction handles all the details of coping with the presence of malicious adversaries. A firewall is a kind of protector.

- Using a component that is intended for a closed model in an open model. An open model is one that lets independent computations find each other and interact. A closed model assumes that all computations are initially known. The abstraction can be a connector that accepts requests from one computation to connect to another, using an open addressing scheme.
- Using a component that assumes a reliable model in a model with partial failure. Partial failure occurs in a distributed system when part of the system fails. For example, the abstraction can be a replicator that implements fault tolerance by doing active replication between several sites and managing recovery when one fails.

These cases are orthogonal. As the examples show, it is often a good idea to implement several cases in one abstraction. This book has abstractions that illustrate all these cases and more. Usually, the abstraction puts a minor condition on the program written in model `Small`. For example, a replicator often assumes that the function it is replicating is deterministic.

Impedance matching is extensively used in the Erlang project at Ericsson [10]. A typical Erlang abstraction takes a declarative program written in a functional language and makes it stateful, concurrent, and fault tolerant.

4.9 Advanced topics

4.9.1 The declarative concurrent model with exceptions

In section 2.7 we added exceptions to sequential declarative programming. Let us now see what happens when we add exceptions to concurrent declarative programming. We first explain how exceptions interact with concurrency. Then we explain how exceptions interact with by-need computation.

Exceptions and concurrency

So far, we have ignored exceptions in concurrent declarative programming. There is a very simple reason for this: if a component raises an exception in the declarative concurrent model, then the model is no longer declarative! Let us add exceptions to the declarative concurrent model and see what happens. For the data-driven model, the resulting kernel language is given in table 4.4. This table contains the **`thread`** and `ByNeed` instructions, the **`try`** and **`raise`** statements, and also one new operation, `FailedValue`, which handles the interaction between exceptions and by-need computation. We first explain the interaction between concurrency and exceptions; we leave `FailedValue` to the next section.

Let us investigate how exceptions can make the model nondeclarative. There are

⟨s⟩ ::=	
skip	Empty statement
| ⟨s⟩$_1$ ⟨s⟩$_2$	Statement sequence
| **local** ⟨x⟩ **in** ⟨s⟩ **end**	Variable creation
| ⟨x⟩$_1$=⟨x⟩$_2$	Variable-variable binding
| ⟨x⟩=⟨v⟩	Value creation
| **if** ⟨x⟩ **then** ⟨s⟩$_1$ **else** ⟨s⟩$_2$ **end**	Conditional
| **case** ⟨x⟩ **of** ⟨pattern⟩ **then** ⟨s⟩$_1$ **else** ⟨s⟩$_2$ **end**	Pattern matching
| {⟨x⟩ ⟨y⟩$_1$ ··· ⟨y⟩$_n$}	Procedure application
| **thread** ⟨s⟩ **end**	Thread creation
| {ByNeed ⟨x⟩ ⟨y⟩}	Trigger creation
| **try** ⟨s⟩$_1$ **catch** ⟨x⟩ **then** ⟨s⟩$_2$ **end**	Exception context
| **raise** ⟨x⟩ **end**	Raise exception
| {FailedValue ⟨x⟩ ⟨y⟩}	**Failed value**

Table 4.4: The declarative concurrent kernel language with exceptions.

two basic ways. First, to be declarative, a component has to be deterministic. If the statements `X=1` and `X=2` are executed concurrently, then execution is no longer deterministic: one of them will succeed and the other will raise an exception. In the store, `X` will be bound either to 1 or to 2; both cases are possible. This is a clear case of observable nondeterminism. The exception is a witness to this; it is raised on unification failure, which means that there is potentially an observable nondeterminism. The exception is not a guarantee of this; e.g., executing `X=1` and `X=2` in order in the same thread will raise an exception, yet `X` is always bound to 1. But if there are no exceptions, then execution is surely deterministic and hence declarative.

A second way that an exception can be raised is when an operation cannot complete normally. This can be due to internal reasons, e.g., the arguments are outside the operation's domain (such as dividing by zero), or external reasons, e.g., the external environment has a problem (such as trying to open a file that does not exist). In both cases, the exception indicates that an operation was attempted outside of its specification. When this happens, all bets are off, so to speak. From the viewpoint of semantics, there is no guarantee on what the operation has done; it could have done anything. Again, the operation has potentially become nondeterministic.

To summarize, when an exception is raised, this is an indication either of nondeterministic execution or of an execution outside specification. In either case, the component is no longer declarative. We say that the declarative concurrent model is declarative modulo exceptions. It turns out that the declarative concurrent model with exceptions is similar to the shared-state concurrent model of chapter 8. This is explained in section 8.1.

So what do we do when an exception occurs? Are we completely powerless to write a declarative program? Not at all. In some cases, the component can "fix things" so that it is still declarative when viewed from the outside. The basic problem is to make the component deterministic. All sources of nondeterminism have to be hidden from the outside. For example, if a component executes `X=1` and `X=2` concurrently, then the minimum it has to do is (1) catch the exception by putting a **`try`** around each binding, and (2) encapsulate `X` so its value is not observable from the outside. See the failure confinement example in section 4.1.4.

Exceptions and by-need computation

In section 2.7, we added exceptions to the declarative model as a way to handle abnormal conditions without encumbering the code with error checks. If a binding fails, it raises a failure exception, which can be caught and handled by another part of the application.

Let us see how to extend this idea to by-need computation. What happens if the execution of a by-need trigger cannot complete normally? In that case it does not calculate a value. For example:

```
X={ByNeed fun {$} A=foo(1) B=foo(2) in A=B A end}
```

What should happen if a thread needs `X`? Triggering the calculation causes a failure when attempting the binding `A=B`. It is clear that `X` cannot be bound to a value, since the by-need computation is not able to complete. On the other hand, we cannot simply leave `X` unbound since the thread that needs `X` expects a value. The right solution is for that thread to raise an exception. To ensure this, we can bind `X` to a special value called a failed value. Any thread that needs a failed value will raise an exception.

We extend the kernel language with the operation `FailedValue`, which creates a failed value:

```
X={FailedValue cannotCalculate}
```

Its definition is given in the supplements file on the book's Web site. It creates a failed value that encapsulates the exception `cannotCalculate`. Any thread that attempts to use `X` will raise the exception `cannotCalculate`. Any partial value can be encapsulated inside the failed value.

With `FailedValue` we can define a "robust" version of `ByNeed` that automatically creates a failed value when a by-need computation raises an exception:

```
proc {ByNeed2 P X}
   {ByNeed
      proc {$ X}
         try Y in {P Y} X=Y
         catch E then X={FailedValue E} end
      end X}
end
```

`ByNeed2` is called in the same way as `ByNeed`. If there is any chance that the by-need computation will raise an exception, then `ByNeed2` will encapsulate the exception in a failed value.

Table 4.4 gives the kernel language for the complete declarative concurrent model, including both by-need computation and exceptions. The kernel language contains the operations `ByNeed` and `FailedValue` as well as the **try** and **raise** statements. The operation {`FailedValue` ⟨x⟩ ⟨y⟩} encapsulates the exception ⟨x⟩ in the failed value ⟨y⟩. Whenever a thread needs ⟨y⟩, the statement **raise** ⟨x⟩ **end** is executed in the thread.

One important use of failed values is in the implementation of dynamic linking. Recall that by-need computation is used to load and link modules on need. If the module could not be found, then the module reference is bound to a failed value. Then, whenever a thread tries to use the nonexistent module, an exception is raised.

4.9.2 More on lazy execution

There is a rich literature on lazy execution. Section 4.5 just touches the tip of the iceberg. Let us now continue the discussion of lazy execution. We bring up two topics:

- *Language design issues.* When designing a new language, what is the role of laziness? We briefly summarize the issues involved.
- *Reduction order and parallelism.* Modern functional programming languages, as exemplified by Haskell, often use a variant of laziness called nonstrict evaluation. We give a brief overview of this concept and why it is useful.

Language design issues

Should a declarative language be lazy or eager or both? This is part of a larger question: should a declarative language be a subset of an extended, nondeclarative language? Limiting a language to one computation model allows optimizing its syntax and semantics for that model. For programs that "fit" the model, this can give amazingly concise and readable code. Haskell and Prolog are particularly striking examples of this approach to language design [21, 201]. Haskell uses lazy evaluation throughout and Prolog uses Horn clause resolution throughout. See sections 4.7 and 9.7, respectively, for more information on these two languages. FP, an early and influential functional language, carried this to an extreme with a special character set, which paradoxically reduces readability [13]. However, as we saw in section 4.8, many programs require more than one computation model. This is true also for lazy versus eager execution. Let us see why:

- For programming in the small, e.g., designing algorithms, eagerness is important when execution complexity is an issue. Eagerness makes it easy to design and reason about algorithms with desired worst-case complexities. Laziness makes this much harder; even experts get confused. On the other hand, laziness is important when designing algorithms with persistence, i.e., that can have multiple coexisting versions. Section 4.5.8 explains why this is so and gives an example. We find that a good approach is to use eagerness by default and to put in laziness explicitly, exactly where it is needed. Okasaki does this with a version of the eager functional language Standard ML extended with explicit laziness [157].

- For programming in the large, eagerness and laziness both have important roles when interfacing components. For example, consider a pipeline communication between a producer and consumer component. There are two basic ways to control this execution: either the producer decides when to calculate new elements ("push" style) or the consumer asks for elements as it needs them ("pull" style). A push style implies an eager execution and a pull style implies a lazy execution. Both styles can be useful. For example, a bounded buffer enforces a push style when it is not full and a pull style when it is full.

We conclude that a declarative language intended for general-purpose programming should support both eager and lazy execution, with eager being the default and lazy available through a declaration. If one is left out, it can always be encoded, but this makes programs unnecessarily complex.

Reduction order and parallelism

We saw that lazy evaluation will evaluate a function's arguments only when they are needed. Technically speaking, this is called normal order reduction. When executing a declarative program, normal order reduction will always choose to reduce first the leftmost expression. After doing one reduction step, it chooses the leftmost expression again, and so forth. Let us look at an example to see how this works. Consider the function `F1` defined as follows:

```
fun {F1 A B}
   if B then A else 0 end
end
```

Let us evaluate the expression `{F1 {F2 X} {F3 Y}}`. The first reduction step applies `F1` to its arguments. This substitutes the arguments into the body of `F1`. This gives `if {F3 Y} then {F2 X} else 0 end`. The second step starts the evaluation of `F3`. If this returns `false`, then `F2` is not evaluated at all. We can see intuitively that normal order reduction only evaluates expressions when they are needed.

There are many possible reduction orders. This is because every execution step gives a choice of which function to reduce next. With declarative concurrency, many of these orders can appear during execution. This makes no difference in the result of the calculation: we say that there is no observable nondeterminism.

Besides normal order reduction, there is another interesting order called applicative order reduction. It always evaluates a function's arguments before evaluating the function. This is the same as eager evaluation. In the expression `{F1 {F2 X} {F3 Y}}`, this evaluates both `{F2 X}` and `{F3 Y}` before evaluating `F1`. With applicative order reduction, if either `{F2 X}` or `{F3 Y}` goes into an infinite loop, then the whole computation will go into an infinite loop. This is true even though the results of {F2 X} or {F3 Y} might not be needed by the rest of the computation. We say that applicative order reduction is strict.

For all declarative programs, we can prove that all reduction orders that terminate give the same result. This result is a consequence of the Church-Rosser theorem, which shows that reduction in the λ calculus is confluent, i.e., reductions that start from the same expression and follow different paths can always be brought back together again. We can say this another way: changing the reduction order only affects whether or not the program terminates but does not change its result. We can also prove that normal order reduction gives the smallest number of reduction steps when compared to any other reduction order.

Nonstrict evaluation A functional programming language whose computation model terminates when normal order reduction terminates is called a nonstrict language. We mention nonstrict evaluation because it is used in Haskell, a popular functional language. The difference between nonstrict and lazy evaluation is subtle. A lazy language does the absolute minimum number of reduction steps. A nonstrict language might do more steps, but it is still guaranteed to terminate in those cases when the lazy language terminates. To better see the difference between lazy and nonstrict, consider the following example:

```
local X={F 4} in X+X end
```

In a nonstrict language {F 4} may be computed twice. In a lazy language {F 4} will be computed exactly once when X is first needed and the result reused for each subsequent occurrence of X. A lazy language is always nonstrict, but not the other way around.

The difference between nonstrict and lazy evaluation becomes important in a parallel processor. For example, during the execution of {F1 {F2 X} {F3 Y}} we might start executing {F2 X} on an available processor, even before we know whether it is really needed or not. This is called speculative execution. If later on we find out that {F2 X} is needed, then we have a head start in its execution. If {F2 X} is not needed, then we abort it as soon as we know this. This might waste some work, but since it is on another processor it will not cause a slowdown. A nonstrict language can be implemented with speculative execution.

Nonstrictness is problematic when we want to extend a language with explicit state (as we will do in chapter 6). A nonstrict language is hard to extend with explicit state because nonstrictness introduces a fundamental unpredictability in a language's execution. We can never be sure how many times a function is evaluated. In a declarative model this is not serious since it does not change computations' results. It becomes serious when we add explicit state. Functions with explicit state can have unpredictable results. Lazy evaluation has the same problem but to a lesser degree: evaluation order is data-dependent but at least we know that a function is evaluated at most once. The solution used in the declarative concurrent model is to make eager evaluation the default and lazy evaluation require an explicit

	Asynchronous	Synchronous
Send	bind a variable	wait until variable needed
Receive	use variable immediately	wait until variable bound

Table 4.5: Dataflow variable as communication channel.

declaration. The solution used in Haskell is more complicated: to avoid explicit state and instead use a kind of accumulator called a monad. The monadic approach uses higher-order programming to make the state threading implicit. The extra arguments are part of function inputs and outputs. They are threaded by defining a new function composition operator.

4.9.3 Dataflow variables as communication channels

In the declarative concurrent model, threads communicate through shared dataflow variables. There is a close correspondence between operations on dataflow variables and operations on a communication channel. We consider a dataflow variable as a kind of communication channel and a thread as a kind of object. Then binding a variable is a kind of send, and waiting until a variable is bound is a kind of receive. The channel has the property that only one message can be sent but the message can be received many times. Let us investigate this analogy further.

Consider a communication that involves two parties, a sender and a receiver. As part of the act of communication, each party does one operation: a send or a receive. An asynchronous operation completes immediately, without any interaction with the other party. A synchronous operation continues only after a successful interaction with the other party. On a communication channel, send and receive operations can each be asynchronous or synchronous. This gives four possibilities in all. Can we express these possibilities with dataflow variables? Two of the possibilities are straightforward since they correspond to a standard use of dataflow execution:

- Binding a variable corresponds to an asynchronous send. The binding can be done independent of whether any threads have received the message.
- Waiting until a variable is bound corresponds to a synchronous receive. The binding must exist for the thread to continue execution.

What about asynchronous receive and synchronous send? In fact, they are both possible:

- Asynchronous receive means simply to use a variable before it is bound. For example, the variable can be inserted in a data structure before it is bound. Of course, any operation that needs the variable's value will wait until the value arrives.
- Synchronous send means to wait with binding until the variable's value is received.

Let us consider that a value is received if it is needed by some operation. Then the synchronous send can be implemented with by-need triggers:

```
proc {SyncSend X M}
Sync in
   {ByNeed proc {$ _} X=M Sync=unit end X}
   {Wait Sync}
end
```

Doing `{SyncSend X M}` sends `M` on channel `X` and waits until it has been received.

Table 4.5 summarizes these four possibilities.

Communication channels sometimes have nonblocking send and receive operations. These are not the same as asynchronous operations. The defining characteristic of a nonblocking operation is that it returns immediately with a boolean result telling whether the operation was successful or not. With dataflow variables, a nonblocking send is trivial since a send is always successful. A nonblocking receive is more interesting. It consists in checking whether the variable is bound or not, and returning **`true`** or **`false`** accordingly. This can be implemented with the `IsDet` function. `{IsDet X}` returns immediately with **`true`** if `X` is bound and with **`false`** otherwise. To be precise, `IsDet` returns true if `X` is determined, i.e., bound to a number, record, or procedure. Needless to say, `IsDet` is not a declarative operation.

4.9.4 More on synchronization

We have seen that threads can communicate through shared dataflow variables. When a thread needs the result of a calculation done by another thread, then it waits until this result is available. We say that it synchronizes on the availability of the result. Synchronization is one of the fundamental concepts in concurrent programming. Let us now investigate this concept more closely.

We first define precisely the basic concept of synchronization point. Consider threads T1 and T2, each doing a sequence of computation steps. T1 does $\alpha_0 \rightarrow \alpha_1 \rightarrow \alpha_2 \rightarrow \cdots$ and T2 does $\beta_0 \rightarrow \beta_1 \rightarrow \beta_2 \rightarrow \cdots$. The threads actually execute together in one global computation. This means that there is one global sequence of computation steps that contains the steps of each thread, interleaved: $\alpha_0 \rightarrow \beta_0 \rightarrow \beta_1 \rightarrow \alpha_1 \rightarrow \alpha_2 \rightarrow \cdots$. There are many ways that the two computations can be interleaved. But not all interleavings can occur in real computations:

- Because of fairness, it is not possible to have an infinite sequence of α steps without some β steps. Fairness is a global property that is enforced by the system.
- If the threads depend on each other's results in some way, then there are additional constraints called synchronization points. A synchronization point links two computation steps β_i and α_j. We say that β_i synchronizes on α_j if in every interleaving that can occur in a real computation, β_i occurs *after* α_j. Synchronization is a local property that is enforced by operations happening in the threads.

	Supply-driven	Demand-driven
Implicit	dataflow execution	lazy execution
Explicit	locks, monitors, etc.	programmed trigger

Table 4.6: Classifying synchronization.

How does the program specify when to synchronize? There are two broad approaches:

- *Implicit synchronization.* In this approach, the synchronization operations are not visible in the program text; they are part of the operational semantics of the language. For example, using a dataflow variable will synchronize on the variable being bound to a value.
- *Explicit synchronization.* In this approach, the synchronization operations are visible in the program text; they consist of explicit operations put there by the programmer. For example, section 4.3.3 shows a demand-driven producer/consumer that uses a programmed trigger. Later on in the book we will see other ways to do explicit synchronization, e.g., by using locks or monitors (see chapter 8).

There are two directions of synchronization:

- *Supply-driven synchronization (eager execution).* Attempting to execute an operation causes the operation to wait until its arguments are available. In other words, the operation synchronizes on the availability of its arguments. This waiting has no effect on whether or not the arguments will be calculated; if some other thread does not calculate them, then the operation will wait indefinitely.
- *Demand-driven synchronization (lazy execution).* Attempting to execute an operation causes the calculation of its arguments. In other words, the calculation of the arguments synchronizes on the operation needing them.

Table 4.6 shows the four possibilities that result. All four are practical and exist in real systems. Explicit synchronization is the primary mechanism in most languages that are based on a stateful model, e.g., Java, Smalltalk, and C++. This mechanism is explained in chapter 8. Implicit synchronization is the primary mechanism in most languages that are based on a declarative model, e.g., functional languages such as Haskell use lazy evaluation and logic languages such as Prolog and concurrent logic languages use dataflow execution. This mechanism is presented in this chapter.

All four possibilities can be used efficiently in the computation models of the book. This lets us compare their expressiveness and ease of use. We find that concurrent programming is simpler with implicit synchronization than with explicit synchronization. In particular, we find that programming with dataflow execution makes concurrent programs simpler. Even in a stateful model, like the one in chapter 8, dataflow execution is advantageous. After comparing languages with explicit and implicit synchronization, Bal, Steiner, and Tanenbaum come to the same conclusion: that dataflow variables are "spectacularly expressive" in concurrent programming when compared to explicit synchronization, even without explicit state [15]. This expressiveness is one of the reasons why we emphasize implicit synchronization in the book. Let us now examine more closely the usefulness of dataflow execution.

4.9.5 Usefulness of dataflow variables

Section 4.2.3 shows how dataflow execution is used for synchronization in the declarative concurrent model. There are many other uses for dataflow execution. This section summarizes these uses. We give pointers to examples throughout the book to illustrate them. Dataflow execution is useful because:

- It is a powerful primitive for concurrent programming (see this chapter and chapter 8). It can be used for synchronizing and communicating between concurrent computations. Many concurrent programming techniques become simplified and new techniques become possible when using dataflow variables.
- It removes order dependencies between parts of a program (see this chapter and chapter 8). To be precise, it replaces static dependencies (decided by the programmer) with dynamic dependencies (decided by the data). This is the basic reason why dataflow computation is useful for parallel programming. The output of one part can be passed directly as input to the next part, independent of the order in which the two parts are executed. When the parts execute, the second one will block only if necessary, i.e., only if it needs the result of the first and it is not yet available.
- It is a powerful primitive for distributed programming (see chapter 11). It improves latency tolerance and third-party independence. A dataflow variable can be passed among sites arbitrarily. At all times, it "remembers its origins," i.e., when the value becomes known, then the variable will receive it. The communication needed to bind the variable is part of the variable and not part of the program manipulating the variable.
- It makes it possible to do declarative calculations with partial information. This was exploited in chapter 3 with difference lists. One way to look at partial values is as complete values that are only partially known. This is a powerful idea that is further exploited in constraint programming (see chapter 12).
- It allows the declarative model to support logic programming (see section 9.3). That is, it is possible to give a logical semantics to many declarative programs. This allows reasoning about these programs at a very high level of abstraction. From a historical viewpoint, dataflow variables were originally discovered in the context of concurrent logic programming, where they are called logic variables.

An insightful way to understand dataflow variables is to see them as a middle ground between having no state and having state:

- A dataflow variable is stateful, because it can change state (i.e., be bound to a value), but it can be bound to just one value in its lifetime. The stateful aspect can be used to get some of the advantages of programming with state (as explained in chapter 6) while staying within a declarative model. For example, difference lists can be appended in constant time, which is not possible for lists in a pure functional model.
- A dataflow variable is stateless, because binding is monotonic. By monotonic we mean that more information can be added to the binding, but no information can be changed or removed. Assume the variable is bound to a partial value. Later on, more and more of the partial value can be bound, which amounts to binding the unbound variables inside the partial value. But these bindings cannot be changed or undone.
The stateless aspect can be used to get some of the advantages of declarative programming within a nondeclarative model. For example, it is possible to add concurrency to the declarative model, giving the declarative concurrent model of this chapter, precisely because threads communicate through shared dataflow variables.

Futures and I-structures

Dataflow variables are but one technique to implement dataflow execution. Another, quite popular technique is based on a slightly different concept, the single-assignment variable. This is a mutable variable that can be assigned only once. This differs from a dataflow variable in that the latter can be assigned (perhaps multiple times) to many partial values, as long as the partial values are compatible with each other.

Two of the best known instances of the single-assignment variable are futures and I-structures. The purpose of futures and I-structures is to increase the potential parallelism of a program by removing inessential dependencies between calculations. They allow concurrency between a computation that calculates a value and one that uses the value. This concurrency can be exploited on a parallel machine. We define futures and I-structures and compare them with dataflow variables.

Futures were first introduced in Multilisp, a language intended for writing parallel programs [79]. Multilisp introduces the function call `(future E)` (in Lisp syntax), where E is any expression. This does two things: it immediately returns a placeholder for the result of E and it initiates a concurrent evaluation of E. When the value of E is needed, i.e., a computation tries to access the placeholder, then the computation blocks until the value is available. We model this as follows in the declarative concurrent model (where E is a zero-argument function):

```
fun {Future E}
X in
   thread X={E} end
   !!X
end
```

A future can only be bound by the concurrent computation that is created along with it. This is enforced by returning a read-only variable. Multilisp also has a `delay` construct that does not initiate any evaluation but uses by-need execution. It causes evaluation of its argument only when the result is needed.

An I-structure (for "incomplete structure") is an array of single-assignment variables. Individual elements can be accessed before all the elements are computed. I-structures were introduced as a language construct for writing parallel programs on dataflow machines, e.g., in the dataflow language Id [12, 99, 150, 223]. I-structures are also used in pH ("parallel Haskell"), a recent language design that extends Haskell for implicit parallelism [151, 152]. An I-structure permits concurrency between a computation that calculates the array elements and a computation that uses their values. When the value of an element is needed, then the computation blocks until it is available. Like a future and a read-only variable, an element of an I-structure can only be bound by the computation that calculates it.

There is a fundamental difference between dataflow variables on one side and futures and I-structures on the other side. The latter can be bound only once, whereas dataflow variables can be bound more than once, as long as the bindings are consistent with each other. Two partial values are consistent if they are unifiable. A dataflow variable can be bound many times to different partial values, as long as the partial values are unifiable. Section 4.3.1 gives an example when doing stream communication with multiple readers. Multiple readers are each allowed to bind the list's tail, since they bind it in a consistent way.

4.10 Historical notes

Declarative concurrency has a long and respectable history. We give some of the highlights. In 1974, Gilles Kahn defined a simple Algol-like language with threads that communicate by channels that behave like FIFO queues with blocking wait and nonblocking send [109]. He called this model determinate parallel programming.[24] In Kahn's model, a thread can wait on only one channel at a time, i.e., each thread always knows from what channel the next input will come. Furthermore, only one thread can send on each channel. This last restriction is actually a bit too strong. Kahn's model could be extended to be like the declarative concurrent model. More than one thread could send on a channel, as long as the sends are ordered deterministically. For example, two threads could take turns sending on the same channel.

In 1977, Kahn and David MacQueen extended Kahn's original model in significant ways [110]. The extended model is demand-driven, supports dynamic recon-

24. By "parallelism" he means concurrency. In those days the term parallelism was used to cover both concepts.

figuration of the communication structure, and allows multiple readers on the same channel.

In 1990, Saraswat, Rinard, and Panangaden generalized Kahn's original model to concurrent constraints [183]. This adds partial values to the model and reifies communication channels as streams. Saraswat et al. define first a determinate concurrent constraint language, which is essentially the same as the data-driven model of this chapter. It generalizes Kahn's original model to make possible programming techniques such as dynamic reconfiguration, channels with multiple readers, incomplete messages, difference structures, and tail-recursive append.

Saraswat et al. define the concept of resting point, which is closely related to partial termination, as defined in section 13.2. A resting point of a program is a store σ that satisfies the following property. When the program executes with this store, no information is ever added (the store is unchanged). The store existing when a program is partially terminated is a resting point.

The declarative concurrent models of the book have strong relationships to the papers cited above. The basic concept of determinate concurrency was defined by Kahn. The existence of the data-driven model is implicit in the work of Saraswat et al. The demand-driven model is related to the model of Kahn and MacQueen. The contribution of the book is to place these models in a uniform framework that subsumes all of them. Section 4.5 defines a demand-driven model by adding by-need synchronization to the data-driven model. By-need synchronization is based on the concept of needing a variable. Because need is defined as a monotonic property, this gives a quite general declarative model that has both concurrency and laziness.

4.11 Exercises

1. *Thread semantics.* Consider the following variation of the statement used in section 4.1.3 to illustrate thread semantics:

```
local B in
   thread B=true end
   thread B=false end
   if B then {Browse yes} end
end
```

For this exercise, do the following:

(a) Enumerate all possible executions of this statement.

(b) Some of these executions cause the program to terminate abnormally. Make a small change to the program to avoid these abnormal terminations.

2. *Threads and garbage collection.* This exercise examines how garbage collection behaves with threads and dataflow variables. Consider the following program:

```
proc {B _}
   {Wait _}
end

proc {A}
   Collectible={NewDictionary}
in
   {B Collectible}
end
```

After the call `{A}` is done, will `Collectible` become garbage? That is, will the memory occupied by `Collectible` be recovered? Give an answer by thinking about the semantics. Verify that the Mozart system behaves in this way.

3. *Concurrent Fibonacci.* Consider the following sequential definition of the Fibonacci function:

```
fun {Fib X}
   if X=<2 then 1
   else {Fib X-1}+{Fib X-2} end
end
```

and compare it with the concurrent definition given in section 4.2.3. Run both on the Mozart system and compare their performance. How much faster is the sequential definition? How many threads are created by the concurrent call `{Fib N}` as a function of `N`?

4. *Order-determining concurrency.* Explain what happens when executing the following:

```
declare A B C D in
thread D=C+1 end
thread C=B+1 end
thread A=1 end
thread B=A+1 end
{Browse D}
```

In what order are the threads created? In what order are the additions done? What is the final result? Compare with the following:

```
declare A B C D in
A=1
B=A+1
C=B+1
D=C+1
{Browse D}
```

Here there is only one thread. In what order are the additions done? What is the final result? What do you conclude?

5. *The* `Wait` *operation.* Explain why the `{Wait X}` operation could be defined as:

```
proc {Wait X}
   if X==unit then skip else skip end
end
```

Use your understanding of the dataflow behavior of the **`if`** statement and `==` operation.

6. *Thread scheduling.* Section 4.8.3.2 shows how to skip over already-calculated elements of a stream. If we use this technique to sum the elements of the integer stream in section 4.3.1, the result is much smaller than 11249925000, which is the sum of the integers in the stream. Why is it so much smaller? Explain this result in terms of thread scheduling.

7. *Programmed triggers using higher-order programming.* Programmed triggers can be implemented by using higher-order programming instead of concurrency and dataflow variables. The producer passes a zero-argument function `F` to the consumer. Whenever the consumer needs an element, it calls the function. This returns a pair `X#F2` where `X` is the next stream element and `F2` is a function that has the same behavior as `F`. Modify the example of section 4.3.3 to use this technique.

8. *Dataflow behavior in a concurrent setting.* Consider the function `{Filter In F}`, which returns the elements of `In` for which the boolean function `F` returns **`true`**. Here is a possible definition of `Filter`:

```
fun {Filter In F}
   case In
   of X|In2 then
      if {F X} then X|{Filter In2 F}
      else {Filter In2 F} end
   else
      nil
   end
end
```

Executing the following:

```
{Show {Filter [5 1 2 4 0] fun {$ X} X>2 end}}
```

displays

```
[5 4]
```

(We use the procedure `Show`, which displays the instantaneous value of its argument in Mozart's emulator window. Unlike `Browse`, this output is not updated if the argument is subsequently bound.) So `Filter` works as expected in the case of a sequential execution when all the input values are available. Let us now explore the dataflow behavior of `Filter`.

(a) What happens when we execute the following?:

```
declare A
{Show {Filter [5 1 A 4 0] fun {$ X} X>2 end}}
```

One of the list elements is a variable `A` that is not yet bound to a value. Remember that the **`case`** and **`if`** statements will suspend the thread in which they execute, until they can decide which alternative path to take.

(b) What happens when we execute the following?:

```
declare Out A
thread Out={Filter [5 1 A 4 0] fun {$ X} X>2 end} end
{Show Out}
```

Remember that calling `Show` displays its argument as it exists at the instant of the call. Several possible results can be displayed. Which and why? Is the `Filter` function deterministic? Why or why not?

(c) What happens when we execute the following?:

```
declare Out A
thread Out={Filter [5 1 A 4 0] fun {$ X} X>2 end} end
{Delay 1000}
{Show Out}
```

Remember that the call `{Delay N}` suspends its thread for at least `N` ms. During this time, other ready threads can be executed.

(d) What happens when we execute the following?:

```
declare Out A
thread Out={Filter [5 1 A 4 0] fun {$ X} X>2 end} end
thread A=6 end
{Delay 1000}
{Show Out}
```

What is displayed and why?

9. *Digital logic simulation.* In this exercise we will design a circuit to add n-bit numbers and simulate it using the technique of section 4.3.5. Given two n-bit binary numbers, $(x_{n-1} \ldots x_0)_2$ and $(y_{n-1} \ldots y_0)_2$, we will build a circuit to add these numbers by using a chain of full adders, similar to doing long addition by hand. The idea is to add each pair of bits separately, passing the carry to the next pair. We start with the low-order bits x_0 and y_0. Feed them to a full adder with the third input $z = 0$. This gives a sum bit s_0 and a carry c_0. Now feed x_1, y_1, and c_0 to a second full adder. This gives a new sum s_1 and carry c_1. Continue this for all n bits. The final sum is $(s_{n-1} \ldots s_0)_2$. For this exercise, program the addition circuit using full adders. Verify that it works correctly by feeding it several additions.

10. *Basics of laziness.* Consider the following program fragment:

```
fun lazy {Three} {Delay 1000} 3 end
```

Calculating `{Three}+0` returns 3 after a 1000 ms delay. This is as expected, since the addition needs the result of `{Three}`. Now calculate `{Three}+0` three times in succession. Each calculation waits 1000 ms. How can this be, since `Three` is supposed to be lazy? Shouldn't its result be calculated only once?

11. *Laziness and concurrency.* This exercise looks closer at the concurrent behavior of lazy execution. Execute the following:

```
fun lazy {MakeX} {Browse x} {Delay 3000} 1 end
fun lazy {MakeY} {Browse y} {Delay 6000} 2 end
fun lazy {MakeZ} {Browse z} {Delay 9000} 3 end

X={MakeX}
Y={MakeY}
Z={MakeZ}

{Browse (X+Y)+Z}
```

This displays `x` and `y` immediately, `z` after six seconds, and the result 6 after fifteen seconds. Explain this behavior. What happens if `(X+Y)+Z` is replaced by `X+(Y+Z)` or by **thread** `X+Y` **end** `+ Z`? Which form gives the final result the quickest? How would you program the addition of n integers $i_1, \ldots, i_n$, given that integer i_j only appears after t_j ms, so that the final result appears the quickest?

12. *Laziness and incrementality.* Let us compare the kind of incrementality we get from laziness and from concurrency. Section 4.3.1 gives a producer/consumer example using concurrency. Section 4.5.3 gives the same producer/consumer example using laziness. In both cases, it is possible for the output stream to appear incrementally. What is the difference? What happens if you use both concurrency and laziness in the producer/consumer example?

13. *Laziness and monolithic functions.* Consider the following two definitions of lazy list reversal:

```
fun lazy {Reverse1 S}
   fun {Rev S R}
      case S of nil then R
      [] X|S2 then {Rev S2 X|R} end
   end
in {Rev S nil} end

fun lazy {Reverse2 S}
   fun lazy {Rev S R}
      case S of nil then R
      [] X|S2 then {Rev S2 X|R} end
   end
in {Rev S nil} end
```

What is the difference in behavior between `{Reverse1 [a b c]}` and `{Reverse2 [a b c]}`? Do the two definitions calculate the same result? Do they have the same lazy behavior? Explain your answer in each case. Finally, compare the execution efficiency of the two definitions. Which definition would you use in a lazy program?

14. *Laziness and iterative computation.* In the declarative model, one advantage of dataflow variables is that the straightforward definition of `Append` is iterative. For this exercise, consider the straightforward lazy version of `Append` without dataflow variables, as defined in section 4.5.7. Is it iterative? Why or why not?

15. *Performance of laziness.* For this exercise, take some declarative programs you have written and make them lazy by declaring all routines as lazy. Use lazy versions of all built-in operations, e.g., addition becomes `Add`, which is defined as **fun** `lazy {Add X Y} X+Y` **end**. Compare the behavior of the original eager programs with the new lazy ones. What is the difference in efficiency? Some functional languages, such as Haskell and Miranda, implicitly consider all functions as lazy. To achieve reasonable performance, these languages do strictness analysis, which tries to find as many functions as possible that can safely be compiled as eager functions.

16. *By-need execution.* Define an operation that requests the calculation of `X` but that does not wait.

17. *Hamming problem.* The Hamming problem of section 4.5.6 is actually a special case of the original problem, which asks for the first n integers of the form

$p_1^{a_1} p_2^{a_2} \cdots p_k^{a_k}$ with $a_1, a_2, \ldots, a_k \geq 0$ using the first k primes $p_1, \ldots, p_k$. For this exercise, write a program that solves this problem for any n when given k.

18. *Concurrency and exceptions.* Consider the following control abstraction that implements **try–finally**:

```
proc {TryFinally S1 S2}
B Y in
   try {S1} B=false catch X then B=true Y=X end
   {S2}
   if B then raise Y end end
end
```

Using the abstract machine semantics as a guide, determine the different possible results of the following program:

```
local U=1 V=2 in
   {TryFinally
    proc {$}
       thread
          {TryFinally proc {$} U=V end
                      proc {$} {Browse bing} end}
       end
    end
    proc {$} {Browse bong} end}
end
```

How many different results are possible? How many different executions are possible?

19. *Limitations of declarative concurrency.* Section 4.8 states that declarative concurrency cannot model client/server applications, because the server cannot read commands from more than one client. Yet, the declarative `Merge` function of section 4.5.6 reads from three input streams to generate one output stream. How can this be?

20. (advanced exercise) *Worst-case bounds with laziness.* Section 4.5.8 explains how to design a queue with worst-case time bound of $O(\log n)$. The logarithm appears because the variable `F` can have logarithmically many suspensions attached to it. Let us see how this happens. Consider an empty queue to which we repeatedly add new elements. The tuple $(|\texttt{F}|, |\texttt{R}|)$ starts out as $(0, 0)$. It then becomes $(0, 1)$, which immediately initiates a lazy computation that will eventually make it become $(1, 0)$. (Note that `F` remains unbound and has one suspension attached.) When two more elements are added, the tuple becomes $(1, 2)$, and a second lazy computation is initiated that will eventually make it become $(3, 0)$. Each time that `R` is reversed and appended to `F`, one new suspension is created on `F`. The size of `R` that triggers the lazy computation doubles with each iteration. The doubling is what causes the logarithmic bound. For this exercise, investigate how to write a queue with a constant worst-case time bound. One approach that works is to use the idea of a schedule, as defined in [157].

21. (advanced exercise) *List comprehensions.* Define a linguistic abstraction for list comprehensions (both lazy and eager) and add it to the Mozart system. Use the

gump parser-generator tool documented in [117].

22. (research project) *Controlling concurrency.* The declarative concurrent model gives three primitive operations that affect execution order without changing the results of a computation: sequential composition (total order, supply-driven), lazy execution (total order, demand-driven), and concurrency (partial order, determined by data dependencies). These operations can be used to "tune" the order in which a program accepts input and gives results, e.g., to be more or less incremental. This is a good example of separation of concerns. For this exercise, investigate this topic further and answer the following questions. Are these three operations complete? That is, can all possible partial execution orders be specified with them? What is the relationship with reduction strategies in the λ calculus (e.g., applicative order reduction, normal order reduction)? Are dataflow or single-assignment variables essential?

23. (research project) *Parallel implementation of functional languages.* Section 4.9.2 explains that nonstrict evaluation allows taking advantage of speculative execution when implementing a parallel functional language. However, using nonstrict evaluation makes it difficult to use explicit state. For this exercise, study this trade-off. Can a parallel functional language take advantage of both speculative execution and explicit state? Design, implement, and evaluate a language to verify your ideas.

5 Message-Passing Concurrency

Only then did Atreyu notice that the monster was not a single, solid body, but was made up of innumerable small steel-blue insects which buzzed like angry hornets. It was their compact swarm that kept taking different shapes.
– *The Neverending Story*, Michael Ende (1929–1995)

Message passing is a programming style in which a program consists of independent entities that interact by sending each other messages asynchronously, i.e., without waiting for a reply. This programming style was first studied by Carl Hewitt in the actor model [91, 92]. Message passing is important in three areas:

- It is the basic framework for multi-agent systems, a discipline that views complex systems as a set of interacting "agents." Agents are independent entities that work toward their own, local goals. If the interaction is designed properly, then the agents can also achieve global goals. For example, resource allocation can be done efficiently by selfish agents that interact according to mechanisms inspired by a market economy [179, 226].
- It is the natural style for a distributed system, i.e., a set of computers that can communicate with each other through a network. It is natural because it reflects the structure of the system and its costs. Distributed systems are becoming ubiquitous because of the continued expansion of the Internet. Older technologies for programming distributed systems, such as RPC, CORBA, and RMI, are based on synchronous communication. Newer technologies, such as Web services, are asynchronous. The techniques of this chapter apply directly to asynchronous technologies. (The particularities of programming distributed systems are explored further in chapter 11.)
- It lends itself well to building highly reliable systems. Since the message-passing entities are independent, if one fails the others can continue executing. In a properly designed system, the others reorganize themselves to continue providing a service. This idea is used by the Erlang language, which is used in telecommunications and high-speed networking (see section 5.7).

We define a computation model for message passing as an extension of the declarative concurrent model. We then use this model to show how to program with message passing.

Extending the declarative concurrent model

The declarative concurrent model of the last chapter cannot have observable nondeterminism. This limits the kinds of programs we can write in the model. For example, we saw that it is impossible to write a client/server program where the server does not know which client will send it the next message.

The message-passing concurrent model extends the declarative concurrent model by adding just one new concept, an asynchronous communication channel. This means that any client can send messages to the channel at any time and the server can read all the messages from the channel. This removes the limitation on what kinds of programs we can write. A client/server program can give different results on different executions because the order of client sends is not determined. This means that the message-passing model is nondeterministic and therefore no longer declarative.

We use a simple kind of channel called a port that has an associated stream. Sending a message to the port causes the message to appear on the port's stream. A useful programming technique is to associate a port with a stream object. We call the resulting entity a port object. A port object reads all its messages from the port's stream, and sends messages to other port objects through their ports. Each port object is defined by a recursive procedure that is declarative. This keeps some of the advantages of the declarative model.

Structure of the chapter

The chapter consists of the following parts:

- Section 5.1 defines the message-passing concurrent model. It defines the port concept and the kernel language.
- Section 5.2 introduces the concept of port objects, which we get by combining ports with stream objects.
- Section 5.3 shows how to do simple kinds of message protocols with port objects.
- Section 5.4 explains how to design programs with concurrent components. It defines the basic concepts and gives a methodology for managing the concurrency.
- Section 5.5 gives a case study of this methodology. It uses port objects to build a lift control system.
- Section 5.6 shows how to use the message-passing model directly, without using the port object abstraction. This can be harder to reason about than using port objects, but it is sometimes useful.
- Section 5.7 gives an introduction to Erlang, a programming language based on port objects that is used to build highly reliable systems.
- Section 5.8 explains one advanced topic: the nondeterministic concurrent model, which is intermediate in expressiveness between the declarative concurrent model and the message-passing model of this chapter.

⟨s⟩ ::=	
skip	Empty statement
| ⟨s⟩$_1$ ⟨s⟩$_2$	Statement sequence
| **local** ⟨x⟩ **in** ⟨s⟩ **end**	Variable creation
| ⟨x⟩$_1$=⟨x⟩$_2$	Variable-variable binding
| ⟨x⟩=⟨v⟩	Value creation
| **if** ⟨x⟩ **then** ⟨s⟩$_1$ **else** ⟨s⟩$_2$ **end**	Conditional
| **case** ⟨x⟩ **of** ⟨pattern⟩ **then** ⟨s⟩$_1$ **else** ⟨s⟩$_2$ **end**	Pattern matching
| {⟨x⟩ ⟨y⟩$_1$ ··· ⟨y⟩$_n$}	Procedure application
| **thread** ⟨s⟩ **end**	Thread creation
| {NewName ⟨x⟩}	Name creation
| ⟨y⟩=!!⟨x⟩	Read-only view
| **try** ⟨s⟩$_1$ **catch** ⟨x⟩ **then** ⟨s⟩$_2$ **end**	Exception context
| **raise** ⟨x⟩ **end**	Raise exception
| {NewPort ⟨y⟩ ⟨x⟩}	**Port creation**
| {Send ⟨x⟩ ⟨y⟩}	**Port send**

Table 5.1: The kernel language with message-passing concurrency.

5.1 The message-passing concurrent model

The message-passing concurrent model extends the declarative concurrent model by adding ports. Table 5.1 shows the kernel language. Ports are a kind of communication channel. Ports are no longer declarative since they allow observable nondeterminism: many threads can send a message on a port and their order is not determined. However, the part of the computation that does not use ports can still be declarative. This means that with care we can still use many of the reasoning techniques of the declarative concurrent model.

5.1.1 Ports

A port is an ADT with two operations, namely creating a channel and sending to it:

- `{NewPort S P}`: create a new port with entry point `P` and stream `S`.
- `{Send P X}`: append `X` to the stream corresponding to the entry point `P`.

Successive sends from the same thread appear on the stream in the same order in which they were executed. This property implies that a port is an asynchronous FIFO (first-in, first-out) communication channel. For example:

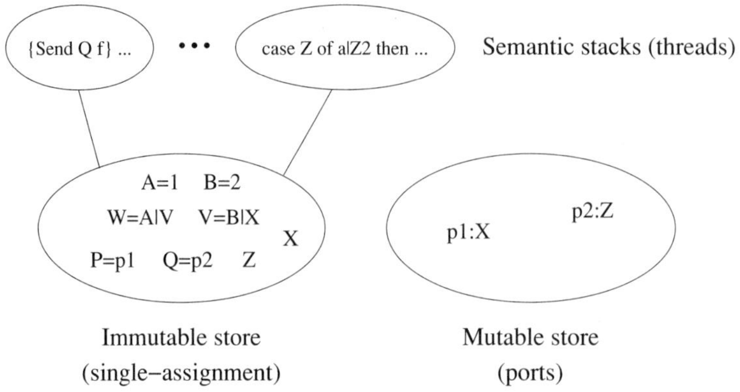

Figure 5.1: The message-passing concurrent model.

```
declare S P in
{NewPort S P}
{Browse S}
{Send P a}
{Send P b}
```

This displays the stream `a|b|_`. Doing more sends will extend the stream. Say the current end of the stream is `S`. Doing the send `{Send P a}` will bind `S` to `a|S1`, and `S1` becomes the new end of the stream. Internally, the port always remembers the current end of the stream. The end of the stream is a read-only variable. This means that a port is a secure ADT.

By asynchronous we mean that a thread that sends a message does not wait for any reply. As soon as the message is in the communication channel, the thread can continue executing. This means that the communication channel can contain many pending messages, which are waiting to be handled.

5.1.2 Semantics of ports

The semantics of ports is quite straightforward. To define it, we first extend the execution state of the declarative model by adding a mutable store. Figure 5.1 shows the mutable store. Then we define the operations `NewPort` and `Send` in terms of the mutable store.

Extension of execution state

Next to the single-assignment store σ (and the trigger store τ, if laziness is important) we add a new store μ called the mutable store. This store contains ports, which are pairs of the form $x : y$, where x and y are variables of the single-assignment store. The mutable store is initially empty. The semantics guarantees that x is always bound to a name value that represents a port and that y is unbound. We use name values to identify ports because name values are unique unforgeable constants. The execution state becomes a triple (MST, σ, μ) (or a quadruple (MST, σ, μ, τ) if the trigger store is considered).

The `NewPort` *operation*

The semantic statement $(\{$`NewPort` $\langle x\rangle\ \langle y\rangle\}, E)$ does the following:

- Create a fresh port name n.
- Bind $E(\langle y\rangle)$ and n in the store.
- If the binding is successful, then add the pair $E(\langle y\rangle) : E(\langle x\rangle)$ to the mutable store μ.
- If the binding fails, then raise an error condition.

The `Send` *operation*

The semantic statement $(\{$`Send` $\langle x\rangle\ \langle y\rangle\}, E)$ does the following:

- If the activation condition is true ($E(\langle x\rangle)$ is determined), then do the following actions:
  - If $E(\langle x\rangle)$ is not bound to the name of a port, then raise an error condition.
  - If the mutable store contains $E(\langle x\rangle) : z$, then do the following actions:
    - Create a new variable z' in the store.
    - Update the mutable store to be $E(\langle x\rangle) : z'$.
    - Create a new list pair $E(\langle y\rangle)\,|\,z'$ and bind z with it in the store.
- If the activation condition is false, then suspend execution.

This semantics is slightly simplified with respect to the complete port semantics. In a correct port, the end of the stream should always be a read-only view. This requires a straightforward extension to the `NewPort` and `Send` semantics. We leave this as an exercise for the reader.

Memory management

Two modifications to memory management are needed because of the mutable store:

- Extending the definition of reachability: A variable y is reachable if the mutable store contains $x : y$ and x is reachable.
- Reclaiming ports: If a variable x becomes unreachable, and the mutable store contains the pair $x : y$, then remove this pair.

5.2 Port objects

A port object is a combination of one or more ports and a stream object. This extends stream objects in two ways. First, many-to-one communication is possible: many threads can reference a given port object and send to it independently. This is not possible with a stream object because it has to know where its next message will come from. Second, port objects can be embedded inside data structures (including messages). This is not possible with a stream object because it is referenced by a stream that can be extended by just one thread.

The concept of port object has many popular variations. Sometimes the word "agent" is used to cover a similar idea: an active entity with which one can exchange messages. The Erlang system has the "process" concept, which is like a port object except that it adds an attached mailbox that allows filtering of incoming messages by pattern matching. Another often-used term is "active object." It is similar to a port object except that it is defined in an object-oriented way, by a class (as we shall see in chapter 7). In this chapter we use only port objects.

In the message-passing model, a program consists of a set of port objects sending and receiving messages. Port objects can create new port objects. Port objects can send messages containing references to other port objects. This means that the set of port objects forms a graph that can evolve during execution.

Port objects can be used to model distributed systems. A port object models a computer or an OS process. A distributed algorithm is simply an algorithm between port objects.

A port object has the following structure:

```
declare P1 P2 ... Pn in
local S1 S2 ... Sn in
   {NewPort S1 P1}
   {NewPort S2 P2}
   ...
   {NewPort Sn Pn}
   thread {RP S1 S2 ... Sn} end
end
```

The thread contains a recursive procedure `RP` that reads the port streams and performs some action for each message received. Sending a message to the port object is just sending a message to one of the ports. Here is an example port object with one port that displays all the messages it receives:

```
declare P in
local S in
   {NewPort S P}
   thread {ForAll S Browse} end
end
```

Remember that `Browse` is a one-argument procedure. With the **`for`** loop syntax, this can also be written as:

```
declare P in
local S in
   {NewPort S P}
   thread for M in S do {Browse M} end end
end
```

Doing `{Send P hi}` will eventually display `hi`. We can compare this with the stream objects of chapter 4. The difference is that port objects allow many-to-one communication, i.e., any thread that references the port can send a message to the port object at any time. The object does not know from which thread the next message will come. This is in contrast to stream objects, where the object always knows from which thread the next message will come.

5.2.1 The `NewPortObject` abstraction

We can define an abstraction to make it easier to program with port objects. Let us define an abstraction in the case that the port object has just one port. To define the port object, we only have to give the initial state `Init` and the state transition function `Fun`. This function is of type ⟨**fun** {\$ T_s T_m}: T_s⟩ where T_s is the state type and T_m is the message type.

```
fun {NewPortObject Init Fun}
Sin Sout in
   thread {FoldL Sin Fun Init Sout} end
   {NewPort Sin}
end
```

This uses `FoldL` to implement the accumulator loop. This is an excellent example of declarative concurrency. When the input stream terminates, the final state appears in `Sout`. Some port objects are purely reactive, i.e., they have no internal state. The abstraction is even simpler for them since no accumulator is needed:

```
fun {NewPortObject2 Proc}
Sin in
   thread for Msg in Sin do {Proc Msg} end end
   {NewPort Sin}
end
```

There is no state transition function, but simply a procedure that is invoked for each message.

5.2.2 An example

There are three players standing in a circle, tossing a ball among themselves. When a player catches the ball, he or she picks one of the other two randomly to throw the ball to. We can model this situation with port objects. Consider three port objects, where each object has a reference to the others. There is a ball that is sent between the objects. When a port object receives the ball, it immediately sends it to another, picked at random. Figure 5.2 shows the three objects and what messages each object can send and where. Such a diagram is called a component diagram.

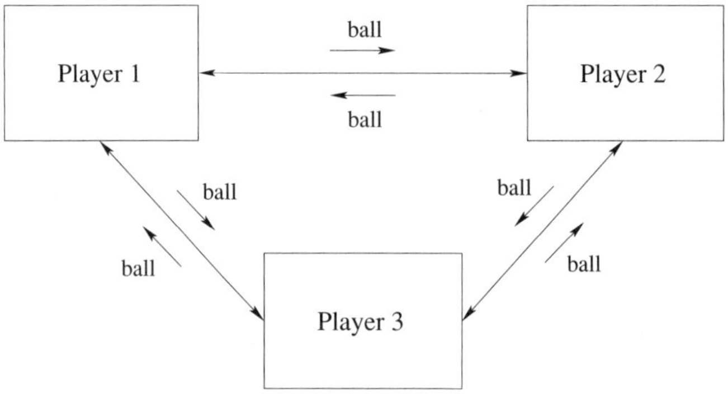

Figure 5.2: Three port objects playing ball.

To program this, we first define a component that creates a new player:

```
fun {Player Others}
   {NewPortObject2
    proc {$ Msg}
       case Msg of ball then
          Ran={OS.rand} mod {Width Others} + 1
       in
          {Send Others.Ran ball}
       end
    end}
end
```

Others is a tuple that contains the other players. Now we can set up the game:

```
P1={Player others(P2 P3)}
P2={Player others(P1 P3)}
P3={Player others(P1 P2)}
```

In this program, Player is a component and P1, P2, P3 are its instances. To start the game, we toss a ball to one of the players:

```
{Send P1 ball}
```

This starts a furiously fast game of tossing the ball. To slow it down, we can add a {Delay 1000} in each player.

5.2.3 Reasoning with port objects

Consider a program that consists of port objects which send each other messages. Proving that the program is correct consists of two parts: proving that each port object is correct (when considered by itself) and proving that the port objects work together correctly. The first step is to show that each port object is correct. Each port object defines a data abstraction. The abstraction should have an invariant assertion, i.e., an assertion that is true whenever an abstract operation has completed and before the next operation has started. To show that the abstraction is correct, it is enough to show that the assertion is an invariant. We showed how to do this for the declarative model in chapter 3. Since the inside of a port object is declarative (it is a recursive function reading a stream), we can use the techniques we showed there.

Because the port object has just one thread, its operations are executed sequentially. This means we can use mathematical induction to show that the assertion is an invariant. We have to prove two things:

- When the port object is first created, the assertion is satisfied.
- If the assertion is satisfied before a message is handled, then the assertion is satisfied after the message is handled.

The existence of the invariant shows that the port object itself is correct. The next step is to show that the program using the port objects is correct. This requires a whole different set of techniques.

A program in the message-passing model is a set of port objects that send each other messages. To show that this is correct, we have to determine what the possible sequences of messages are that each port object can receive. To determine this, we start by classifying all the events in the system. The events are of three kinds: message sends, message receives, and internal state changes of a port object. We can then define causality between events (whether an event happens before another). Considering the system of port objects as a state transition system, we can then reason about the whole program. Explaining this in detail is beyond the scope of this chapter. We refer interested readers to books on distributed algorithms, such as Lynch [133] or Tel [210].

5.3 Simple message protocols

Port objects work together by exchanging messages in coordinated ways. It is interesting to study what kinds of coordination are important. This leads us to define a protocol as a sequence of messages between two or more parties that can be understood at a higher level of abstraction than just its individual messages. Let us take a closer look at message protocols and see how to realize them with port objects.

Most well-known protocols are rather complicated ones such as the Internet protocols (TCP/IP, HTTP, FTP, etc.) or LAN (local area network) protocols such as Ethernet, DHCP (Dynamic Host Connection Protocol), and so forth [121]. In this section we show some simpler protocols and how to implement them using port objects. All the examples use `NewPortObject2` to create port objects.

Figure 5.3 shows the message diagrams of many of the simple protocols (we leave the other diagrams up to the reader!). These diagrams show the messages passed between a client (denoted `C`) and a server (denoted `S`). Time flows downward. The

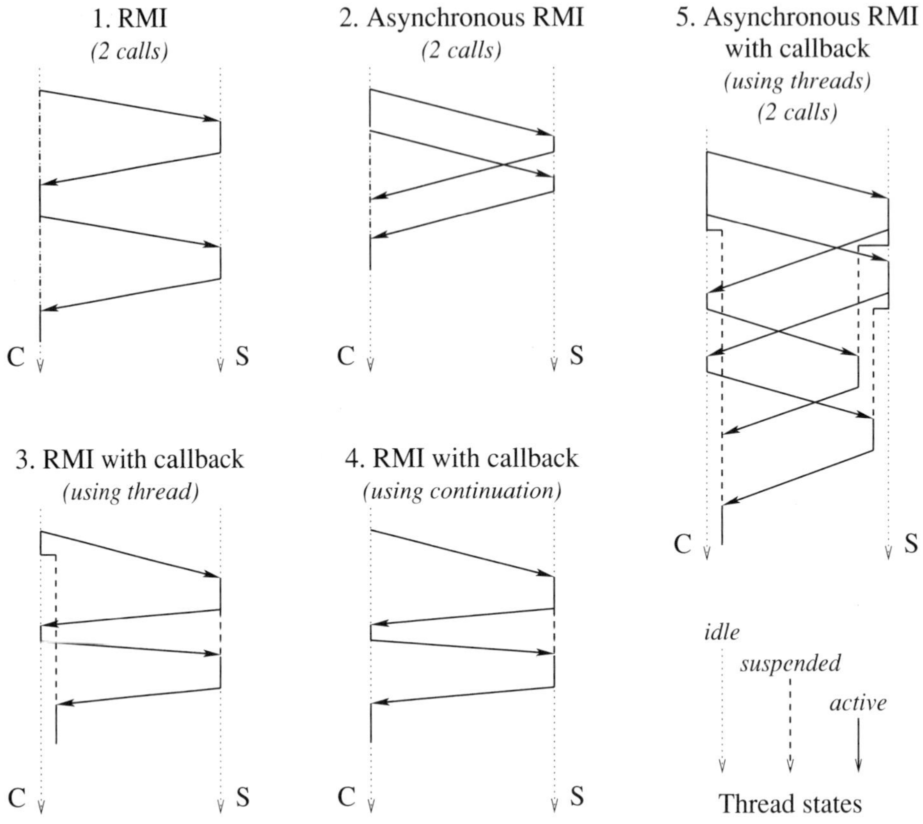

Figure 5.3: Message diagrams of simple protocols.

figure is careful to distinguish idle threads (which are available to service requests) from suspended threads (which are not available).

5.3.1 RMI (Remote Method Invocation)

Perhaps the most popular of the simple protocols is the RMI. It allows an object to call another object in a different operating system process, either on the same machine or on another machine connected by a network [207]. Historically, the RMI is a descendant of the RPC (remote procedure call), which was invented in the early 1980s, before object-oriented programming became popular [22]. The term RMI became popular once objects started replacing procedures as the remote entities to be called. We apply the term RMI somewhat loosely to port objects, even though they do not have methods in the sense of object-oriented programming (see chapter 7 for more on methods). For now, we assume that a "method" is simply what a port object does when it receives a particular message.

From the programmer's viewpoint, the RMI and RPC protocols are quite simple:

a client sends a request to a server and then waits for the server to send back a reply. (This viewpoint abstracts from implementation details such as how data structures are passed from one address space to another.) Let us give an example. We first define the server as a port object:

```
proc {ServerProc Msg}
   case Msg
   of calc(X Y) then
      Y=X*X+2.0*X+2.0
   end
end
Server={NewPortObject2 ServerProc}
```

This particular server has no internal state. The second argument `Y` of `calc` is bound by the server. We assume the server does a complex calculation, which we model by the polynomial `X*X+2.0*X+2.0`. We define the client:

```
proc {ClientProc Msg}
   case Msg
   of work(Y) then Y1 Y2 in
      {Send Server calc(10.0 Y1)}
      {Wait Y1}
      {Send Server calc(20.0 Y2)}
      {Wait Y2}
      Y=Y1+Y2
   end
end
Client={NewPortObject2 ClientProc}
{Browse {Send Client work($)}}
```

Note that we are using a nesting marker "`$`". We recall that the last line is equivalent to

```
local X in {Send Client work(X)} {Browse X} end
```

Nesting markers are a convenient way to turn statements into expressions. There is an interesting difference between the client and server definitions. The client definition references the server directly but the server definition does not know its clients. The server gets a client reference indirectly, through the argument `Y`. This is a dataflow variable that is bound to the answer by the server. The client waits until receiving the reply before continuing.

In this example, all messages are executed sequentially by the server. In our experience, this is the best way to implement RMI. It is simple to program with and reason about. Some RMI implementations do things somewhat differently. They allow multiple calls from different clients to be processed concurrently. This is done by allowing multiple threads at the server side to accept requests for the same object. The server no longer serves requests sequentially. This is much harder to program with: it requires the server to protect its internal state data. We examine this case later, in chapter 8. When programming in a language that provides RMI or RPC, such as C or Java, it is important to know whether or not messages are executed sequentially by the server.

In this example, the client and server are both written in the same language and both execute in the same operating system process. This is true for all programs of this chapter. When programming a distributed system, this is no longer true. For example, two OS processes running Java programs can communicate with Java RMI. Two processes running programs written in different languages can communicate by using CORBA (Common Object Request Broker Architecture) or Web services. The general programming techniques of this chapter still hold for these cases, with some modifications due to the nature of distributed systems. This is explained in chapter 11.

5.3.2 Asynchronous RMI

Another useful protocol is the asynchronous RMI. This is similar to RMI, except that the client continues execution immediately after sending the request. The client is informed when the reply arrives. With this protocol, two requests can be done in rapid succession. If communications between client and server are slow, then this will give a large performance advantage over RMI. In RMI, we can only send the second request after the first is completed, i.e., after one round trip from client to server. Here is the client:

```
proc {ClientProc Msg}
   case Msg
   of work(?Y) then Y1 Y2 in
      {Send Server calc(10.0 Y1)}
      {Send Server calc(20.0 Y2)}
      Y=Y1+Y2
   end
end
Client={NewPortObject2 ClientProc}
{Browse {Send Client work($)}}
```

The message sends overlap. The client waits for both results `Y1` and `Y2` before doing the addition `Y1+Y2`.

Note that the server is the same as with standard RMI. It still receives messages one by one and executes them sequentially. Requests are handled by the server in the same order as they are sent and the replies arrive in that order as well.

5.3.3 RMI with callback (using thread)

The RMI with callback is like an RMI except that the server needs to call the client in order to fulfill the request. Let us see an example. Here is a server that does a callback to find the value of a special parameter called `delta`, which is known only by the client:

```
proc {ServerProc Msg}
   case Msg
   of calc(X ?Y Client) then X1 D in
      {Send Client delta(D)}
      X1=X+D
      Y=X1*X1+2.0*X1+2.0
   end
end
Server={NewPortObject2 ServerProc}
```

The server knows the client reference because it is an argument of the `calc` message. We leave out the `{Wait D}` since it is implicit in the addition `X+D`. Here is a client that calls the server in the same way as for RMI:

```
proc {ClientProc Msg}
   case Msg
   of work(?Z) then Y in
      {Send Server calc(10.0 Y Client)}
      Z=Y+100.0
   [] delta(?D) then
      D=1.0
   end
end
Client={NewPortObject2 ClientProc}
{Browse {Send Client work($)}}
```

(As before, the `Wait` is implicit.) Unfortunately, this solution does not work. It deadlocks during the call `{Send Client work(Z)}`. Do you see why? Draw a message diagram to see why.[1] This shows that a simple RMI is not the right concept for doing callbacks.

The solution to this problem is for the client call not to wait for the reply. The client must continue immediately after making its call, so that it is ready to accept the callback. When the reply comes eventually, the client must handle it correctly. Here is one way to write a correct client:

```
proc {ClientProc Msg}
   case Msg
   of work(?Z) then Y in
      {Send Server calc(10.0 Y Client)}
      thread Z=Y+100.0 end
   [] delta(?D) then
      D=1.0
   end
end
Client={NewPortObject2 ClientProc}
{Browse {Send Client work($)}}
```

Instead of waiting for the server to bind `Y`, the client creates a new thread to do the waiting. The new thread's body is the work to do when `Y` is bound. When the

1. It is because the client suspends when it calls the server, so that the server cannot call the client.

reply comes eventually, the new thread does the work and binds `Z`.

It is interesting to see what happens when we call this client from outside. For example, let us do the call `{Send Client work(Z)}`. When this call returns, `Z` will usually not be bound yet. Usually this is not a problem, since the operation that uses `Z` will block until `Z` is bound. If this is undesirable, then the client call can itself be treated like an RMI:

```
{Send Client work(Z)}
{Wait Z}
```

This lifts the synchronization from the client to the application that uses the client. This is the right way to handle the problem. The problem with the original, buggy solution is that the synchronization is done in the wrong place.

5.3.4 RMI with callback (using record continuation)

The solution of the previous example creates a new thread for each client call. This assumes that threads are inexpensive. How do we solve the problem if we are not allowed to create a new thread? The solution is for the client to pass a continuation to the server. After the server is done, it passes the continuation back to the client so that the client can continue. In that way, the client never waits and deadlock is avoided. Here is the server definition:

```
proc {ServerProc Msg}
   case Msg
   of calc(X Client Cont) then X1 D Y in
      {Send Client delta(D)}
      X1=X+D
      Y=X1*X1+2.0*X1+2.0
      {Send Client Cont#Y}
   end
end
Server={NewPortObject2 ServerProc}
```

After finishing its own work, the server passes `Cont#Y` back to the client. It adds `Y` to the continuation since `Y` is needed by the client!

```
proc {ClientProc Msg}
   case Msg
   of work(?Z) then
      {Send Server calc(10.0 Client cont(Z))}
   [] cont(Z)#Y then
      Z=Y+100.0
   [] delta(?D) then
      D=1.0
   end
end
Client={NewPortObject2 ClientProc}
{Browse {Send Client work($)}}
```

The part of `work` after the server call is put into a new method, `cont`. The client passes the server the continuation `cont(Z)`. The server calculates `Y` and then lets the client continue its work by passing it `cont(Z)#Y`.

When the client is called from outside, the continuation-based solution to callbacks behaves in the same way as the thread-based solution. Namely, `Z` will usually not be bound yet when the client call returns. We handle this in the same way as the thread-based solution, by lifting the synchronization from the client to its caller.

5.3.5 RMI with callback (using procedure continuation)

The previous example can be generalized in a powerful way by passing a procedure instead of a record. We change the client as follows (the server is unchanged):

```
proc {ClientProc Msg}
   case Msg
   of work(?Z) then
      C=proc {$ Y} Z=Y+100.0 end
   in
      {Send Server calc(10.0 Client cont(C))}
   [] cont(C)#Y then
      {C Y}
   [] delta(?D) then
      D=1.0
   end
end
Client={NewPortObject2 ClientProc}
{Browse {Send Client work($)}}
```

The continuation contains the work that the client has to do after the server call returns. Since the continuation is a procedure value, it is self-contained: it can be executed by anyone without knowing what is inside.

5.3.6 Error reporting

All the protocols we covered so far assume that the server will always do its job correctly. What should we do if this is not the case, i.e., if the server can occasionally make an error? For example, it might be due to a network problem between the client and server, or the server process is no longer running. In any case, the client should be notified that an error has occurred. The natural way to notify the client is by raising an exception. Here is how we can modify the server to do this:

```
proc {ServerProc Msg}
   case Msg
   of sqrt(X Y E) then
      try
         Y={Sqrt X}
         E=normal
      catch Exc then
         E=exception(Exc)
      end
   end
end
Server={NewPortObject2 ServerProc}
```

The extra argument `E` signals whether execution was normal or not. The server calculates square roots. If the argument is negative, `Sqrt` raises an exception, which is caught and passed to the client.

This server can be called by both synchronous and asynchronous protocols. In a synchronous protocol, the client can call it as follows:

```
{Send Server sqrt(X Y E)}
case E of exception(Exc) then raise Exc end end
```

The **case** statement blocks the client until `E` is bound. In this way, the client synchronizes on one of two things happening: a normal result or an exception. If an exception was raised at the server, then the exception is raised again at the client. This guarantees that `Y` is not used unless it is bound to a normal result. In an asynchronous protocol there is no guarantee. It is the client's responsibility to check `E` before using `Y`.

This example makes the basic assumption that the server can catch the exception and pass it back to the client. What happens when the server fails or the communication link between the client and server is cut or too slow for the client to wait? These cases are handled in chapter 11.

5.3.7 Asynchronous RMI with callback

Protocols can be combined to make more sophisticated ones. For example, we might want to do two asynchronous RMIs where each RMI does a callback. Here is the server:

```
proc {ServerProc Msg}
   case Msg
   of calc(X ?Y Client) then X1 D in
      {Send Client delta(D)}
      thread
         X1=X+D
         Y=X1*X1+2.0*X1+2.0
      end
   end
end
```

Here is the client:

```
proc {ClientProc Msg}
   case Msg
   of work(?Y) then Y1 Y2 in
      {Send Server calc(10.0 Y1 Client)}
      {Send Server calc(20.0 Y2 Client)}
      thread Y=Y1+Y2 end
   [] delta(?D) then
      D=1.0
   end
end
```

What is the message diagram for the call `{Send Client work(Y)}`? What would happen if the server did not create a thread for doing the work after the callback?

5.3.8 Double callbacks

Sometimes the server does a first callback to the client, which itself does a second callback to the server. To handle this, both the client and the server must continue immediately and not wait until the result comes back. Here is the server:

```
proc {ServerProc Msg}
   case Msg
   of calc(X ?Y Client) then X1 D in
      {Send Client delta(D)}
      thread
         X1=X+D
         Y=X1*X1+2.0*X1+2.0
      end
   [] serverdelta(?S) then
      S=0.01
   end
end
```

Here is the client:

```
proc {ClientProc Msg}
   case Msg
   of work(Z) then Y in
      {Send Server calc(10.0 Y Client)}
      thread Z=Y+100.0 end
   [] delta(?D) then S in
      {Send Server serverdelta(S)}
      thread D=1.0+S end
   end
end
```

Calling `{Send Client work(Z)}` calls the server, which calls the client method `delta(D)`, which itself calls the server method `serverdelta(S)`. A question for an alert reader: why is the last statement `D=1.0+S` also put in a thread?[2]

2. Strictly speaking, it is not needed in this example. But in general, the client does not know whether the server will do another callback!

5.4 Program design for concurrency

This section gives an introduction to component-based programming with concurrent components.

In section 4.3.5 we saw how to do digital logic design using the declarative concurrent model. We defined logic gates as basic circuit components and showed how to compose them to get bigger and bigger circuits. Each circuit had inputs and outputs, which were modeled as streams.

This section continues that discussion in a more general setting. We put it in the larger context of component-based programming. Because of message-passing concurrency we no longer have the limitations of the synchronous "lockstep" execution of chapter 4.

We first introduce the basic concepts of concurrent modeling. Then we give a practical example, a lift control system. We show how to design and implement this system using high-level component diagrams and state diagrams. We start by explaining these concepts.

5.4.1 Programming with concurrent components

To design a concurrent application, the first step is to model it as a set of concurrent activities that interact in well-defined ways. Each concurrent activity is modeled by exactly one concurrent component. A concurrent component is sometimes known as an "agent." Agents can be reactive (have no internal state) or have internal state. The science of programming with agents is sometimes known as multi-agent systems, often abbreviated as MAS. Many different protocols of varying complexities have been devised in MAS. This section only briefly touches on these protocols. In component-based programming, agents are usually considered as quite simple entities with little intelligence built in. In the artificial intelligence community, agents are usually considered as doing some kind of reasoning.

Let us define a simple model for programming with concurrent components. The model has primitive components and ways to combine components. The primitive components are used to create port objects.

A concurrent component

Let us define a simple model for component-based programming that is based on port objects and executes with concurrent message-passing. In this model, a concurrent component is a procedure with inputs and outputs. When invoked, the procedure creates a component instance, which is a port object. An input is a port whose stream is read by the component. An output is a port to which the component can send.

For various reasons, procedures are the right concept to model concurrent components. They are compositional and they can have an arbitrary number of inputs and outputs. When composing subcomponents, they allow the visibility of inputs and outputs to be controlled, e.g., some might have visibility restricted to inside the component.

Interface

A concurrent component interacts with its environment through its interface. The interface consists of the set of its inputs and outputs, which are collectively known as its wires. A wire connects one or more outputs to one or more inputs. The message-passing model of this chapter provides two basic kinds of wires: one-shot and many-shot. One-shot wires are implemented by dataflow variables. They are used for values that do not change or for one-time messages (like acknowledgments). Only one message can be passed and only one output can be connected to a given input. Many-shot wires are implemented by ports. They are used for message streams. Any number of messages can be passed and any number of outputs can write to a given input.

The declarative concurrent model of chapter 4 also has one-shot and many-shot wires, but the many-shot wires are restricted in that only one output can write to a given input.[3]

Basic operations

There are four basic operations in component-based programming:

1. Instantiation: creating an instance of a component. By default, each instance is independent of each other instance. In some cases, instances might all have a dependency on a shared instance.

2. Composition: building a new component out of other components. The latter can be called subcomponents to emphasize their relationship with the new component. We assume that the default is that the components we wish to compose are independent. This means that they are concurrent! Perhaps surprisingly, compound components in a sequential system have dependencies even if they share no arguments. This follows because execution is sequential.

3. Linking: combining component instances by connecting inputs and outputs together. There are different kinds of links: one-shot or many-shot; inputs that can be connected to one output only or to many outputs; outputs that can be connected to one input only or to many inputs. Usually, one-shot links go from one output to many inputs. All inputs see the same value when it is available. Many-shot links go from many outputs to many inputs. All inputs see the same stream of input values.

---

3. To be precise, there can be many writers to an input, but they must all write compatible information.

4. Restriction: restricting visibility of inputs or outputs to within a compound component. Restriction means to limit some of the interface wires of the subcomponents to the interior of the new component, i.e., they do not appear in the new component's interface.

Let us give an example to illustrate these concepts. In section 4.3.5 we showed how to model digital logic circuits as components. We defined procedures AndG, OrG, NotG, and DelayG to implement logic gates. Executing one of these procedures creates a component instance. These instances are stream objects, but they could have been port objects. (A simple exercise is to generalize the logic gates to become port objects.) We defined a latch as a compound component as follows in terms of gates:

```
proc {Latch C DI ?DO}
   X Y Z F
in
   {DelayG DO F}
   {AndG F C X}
   {NotG C Z}
   {AndG Z DI Y}
   {OrG X Y DO}
end
```

The latch component has five subcomponents. These are linked together by connecting outputs and inputs. For example, the output X of the first And gate is given as input to the Or gate. Only the wires DI and DO are visible to the outside of the latch. The wires X, Y, Z, and F are restricted to the inside of the component.

5.4.2 Design methodology

Designing a concurrent program is more difficult than designing a sequential program, because there are usually many more potential interactions between the different parts. To have confidence that the concurrent program is correct, we need to follow a sequence of unambiguous design rules. From our experience, the design rules of this section give good results if they are followed with some rigor.

- *Informal specification.* Write down a possibly informal, but precise specification of what the system should do.
- *Components.* Enumerate all the different forms of concurrent activity in the specification. Each activity will become one component. Draw a block diagram of the system that shows all component instances.
- *Message protocols.* Decide on what messages the components will send and design the message protocols between them. Draw the component diagram with all message protocols.
- *State diagrams.* For each concurrent entity, write down its state diagram. For each state, verify that all the appropriate messages are received and sent with the right conditions and actions.

- *Implement and schedule.* Code the system in your favorite programming language. Decide on the scheduling algorithm to be used for implementing the concurrency between the components.
- *Test and iterate.* Test the system and reiterate until it satisfies the initial specification.

We use these rules for designing the lift control system that is presented later on.

5.4.3 Functional building blocks as concurrency patterns

Programming with concurrent components results in many message protocols. Some simple protocols are illustrated in section 5.3. Much more complicated protocols are possible. Because message-passing concurrency is so close to declarative concurrency, many of these can be programmed as simple list operations.

All the standard list operations (e.g., of the `List` module) can be interpreted as concurrency patterns. We will see that this is a powerful way to write concurrent programs. For example, the standard `Map` function can be used as a pattern that broadcasts queries and collects their replies in a list. Consider a list `PL` of ports, each of which is the input port of a port object. We would like to send the message `query(foo Ans)` to each port object, which will eventually bind `Ans` to the answer. By using `Map` we can send all the messages and collect the answers in a single line:

```
AL={Map PL fun {$ P} Ans in {Send P query(foo Ans)} Ans end}
```

The queries are sent asynchronously and the answers will eventually appear in the list `AL`. We can simplify the notation even more by using the `$` nesting marker with the `Send`. This completely avoids mentioning the variable `Ans`:

```
AL={Map PL fun {$ P} {Send P query(foo $)} end}
```

We can calculate with `AL` as if the answers were already there; the calculation will automatically wait if needed. For example, if the answers are positive integers, then we can calculate their maximum in the same way as a sequential program:

```
M={FoldL AL Max 0}
```

Section 5.2.1 shows another way to use `FoldL` as a concurrency pattern.

5.5 Lift control system

Lifts are a part of our everyday life.[4] Yet, have you ever wondered how they work? How do lifts communicate with floors and how does a lift decide which floor to go

4. Lifts are useful for those who live in flats, in the same way that elevators are useful for those who live in apartments.

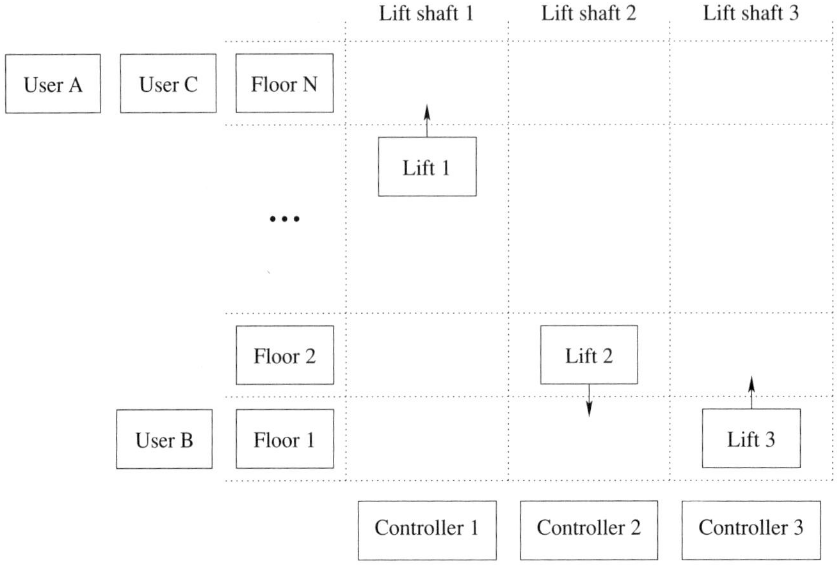

Figure 5.4: Schematic overview of a building with lifts.

to? There are many ways to program a lift control system.

In this section we will design a simple lift control system as a concurrent program, using the methodology of the previous section. Our first design will be quite simple. Nevertheless, as you will see, the concurrent program that results will still be fairly complex. Therefore we take care to follow the design methodology given earlier.

We will model the operation of the hypothetical lift control system of a building, with a fixed number of lifts, a fixed number of floors between which lifts travel, and users. Figure 5.4 gives an abstract view of what our building looks like. There are floors, lifts, controllers for lift movement, and users that come and go. We will model what happens when a user calls a lift to go to another floor. Our model will focus on concurrency and timing, to show correctly how the concurrent activities interact in time. But we will put in enough detail to get a running program.

The first task is the specification. In this case, we will be satisfied with a partial specification of the problem. There are a set of floors and a set of lifts. Each floor has a call button that users can press. The call button does not specify an up or down direction. The floor randomly chooses the lift that will service its request. Each lift has a series of call(I) buttons numbered for all floors I, to tell it to stop at a given floor. Each lift has a schedule, which is the list of floors that it will visit in order.

The scheduling algorithm we will use is called FCFS (first-come, first-served): a new floor is always added at the end of the schedule. This is the same as FIFO scheduling. Both the call and call(I) buttons do FCFS. This is not the best scheduling algorithm for lifts, but it has the advantage of simplicity. Later we will

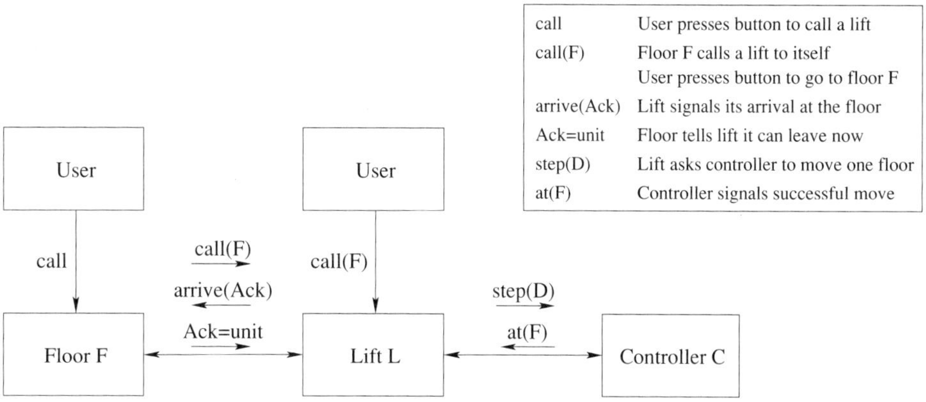

Figure 5.5: Component diagram of the lift control system.

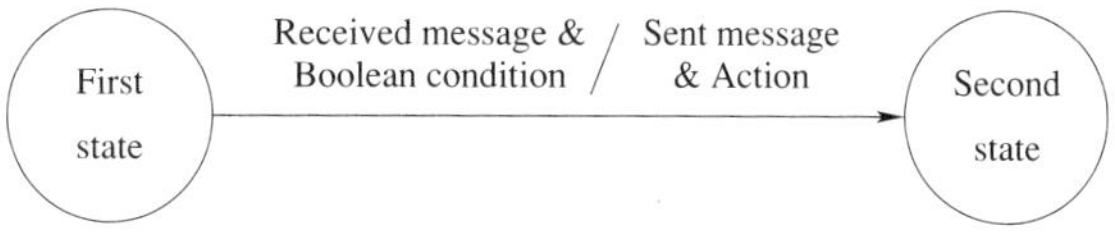

Figure 5.6: Notation for state diagrams.

see how to improve it. When a lift arrives at a scheduled floor, the doors open and stay open for a fixed time before closing. Moving lifts take a fixed time to go from one floor to the next.

The lift control system is designed as a set of interacting concurrent components. Figure 5.5 shows the block diagram of their interactions. Each rectangle represents an instance of a concurrent component. In our design, there are four kinds of components, namely floors, lifts, controllers, and timers. All component instances are port objects. Controllers are used to handle lift motion. Timers handle the real-time aspect of the system.

Because of FCFS scheduling, lifts will often move much farther than necessary. If a lift is already at a floor, then calling that floor again may call another lift. If a lift is on its way from one floor to another, then calling an intermediate floor will not cause the lift to stop there. We can avoid these problems by making the scheduler more intelligent. Once we have determined the structure of the whole application, it will become clear how to do this and other improvements.

5.5.1 State transition diagrams

A good way to design a port object is to start by enumerating the states it can be in and the messages it can send and receive. This makes it easy to check that all messages are properly handled in all states. We will go over the state diagrams of each component. First we introduce the notation for state transition diagrams (sometimes called state diagrams for short).

A state transition diagram is a finite state automaton. It consists of a finite set of states and a set of transitions between states. At each instant, it is in a particular state. It starts in an initial state and evolves by doing transitions. A transition is an atomic operation that does the following. The transition is enabled when the appropriate message is received and a boolean condition on it and the state is true. The transition can then send a message and change the state. Figure 5.6 shows the graphical notation. Each circle represents a state. Arrows between circles represent transitions.

Messages can be sent in two ways: to a port or by binding a dataflow variable. Messages can be received on the port's stream or by waiting for the binding. Dataflow variables are used as a lightweight channel on which only one message can be sent (a "one-shot wire"). To model time delays, we use a timer protocol: the caller `Pid` sends the message `starttimer(N Pid)` to a timer agent to request a delay of `N` ms. The caller then continues immediately. When time is up, the timer agent sends a message `stoptimer` back to the caller. (The timer protocol is similar to the `{Delay N}` operation, reformulated in the style of concurrent components.)

5.5.2 Implementation

We present the implementation of the lift control system by showing each part separately, namely the controller, the floor, and the lift. We will define functions to create them:

- `{Floor Num Init Lifts}` returns a floor `Fid` with number `Num`, initial state `Init`, and lifts `Lifts`.
- `{Lift Num Init Cid Floors}` returns a lift `Lid` with number `Num`, initial state `Init`, controller `Cid`, and floors `Floors`.
- `{Controller Init}` returns a controller `Cid`.

For each function, we explain how it works and give the state diagram and the source code. We then create a building with a lift control system and show how the components interact.

The controller

The controller is the easiest to explain. It has two states, motor stopped and motor running. At the motor stopped state the controller can receive a `step(Dest)` from

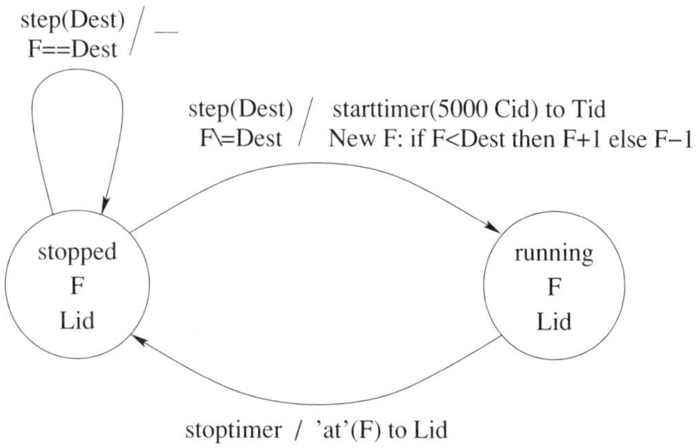

Figure 5.7: State diagram of a lift controller.

the lift, where `Dest` is the destination floor number. The controller then goes to the motor running state. Depending on the direction, the controller moves up or down one floor. Using the timer protocol, the motor running state automatically makes a transition to the motor stopped state after a fixed time. This is the time needed to move from one floor to the next (either up or down). In the example, we assume this time to be 5000 ms. The timer protocol models a real implementation which would have a sensor at each floor. When the lift has arrived at floor `F`, the controller sends the message `'at'(F)` to the lift. Figure 5.7 gives the state diagram of controller Cid.

The source code of the timer and the controller is given in figure 5.8. It is interesting to compare the controller code with the state diagram. The timer defined here is used also in the floor component.

Attentive readers will notice that the controller actually has more than two states, since strictly speaking the floor number is also part of the state. To keep the state diagram simple, we parameterize the motor stopped and motor running states by the floor number. Representing several states as one state with variables inside is a kind of syntactic sugar for state diagrams. It lets us represent very big diagrams in a compact way. We will use this technique also for the floor and lift state diagrams.

The floor

Floors are more complicated because they can be in one of three states: no lift called, lift called but not yet arrived, and lift arrived and doors open. Figure 5.9 gives the state diagram of floor Fid. Each floor can receive a `call` message from a user, an `arrive(Ack)` message from a lift, and an internal timer message. The floor can send a `call(F)` message to a lift.

The source code of the floor is shown in figure 5.10. It uses the random number

```
fun {Timer}
   {NewPortObject2
    proc {$ Msg}
       case Msg of starttimer(T Pid) then
          thread {Delay T} {Send Pid stoptimer} end
       end
    end}
end

fun {Controller Init}
   Tid={Timer}
   Cid={NewPortObject Init
        fun {$ state(Motor F Lid) Msg}
           case Motor
           of running then
              case Msg
              of stoptimer then
                 {Send Lid 'at'(F)}
                 state(stopped F Lid)
              end
           [] stopped then
              case Msg
              of step(Dest) then
                 if F==Dest then
                    state(stopped F Lid)
                 elseif F<Dest then
                    {Send Tid starttimer(5000 Cid)}
                    state(running F+1 Lid)
                 else % F>Dest
                    {Send Tid starttimer(5000 Cid)}
                    state(running F-1 Lid)
                 end
              end
           end
        end}
in Cid end
```

Figure 5.8: Implementation of the timer and controller components.

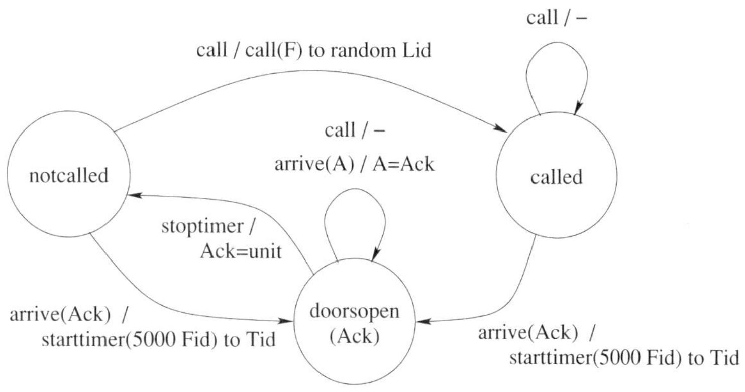

Figure 5.9: State diagram of a floor.

function `OS.rand` to pick a lift at random. It uses `Browse` to display when a lift is called and when the doors open and close. The total time needed for opening and closing the doors is assumed to be 5000 ms.

The lift

Lifts are the most complicated of all. Figure 5.11 gives the state diagram of lift Lid. Each lift can be in one of four states: empty schedule and lift stopped (idle), nonempty schedule and lift moving past a given floor, waiting for doors when moving past a scheduled floor, and waiting for doors when idle at a called floor. The way to understand this figure is to trace through some execution scenarios. For example, here is a simple scenario. A user presses the call button at floor 1. The floor then sends `call(1)` to a lift. The lift receives this and sends `step(1)` to the controller. Say the lift is currently at floor 3. The controller sends `´at´(2)` to the lift, which then sends `step(1)` to the controller again. The controller sends `´at´(1)` to the lift, which then sends `arrive(Ack)` to floor 1 and waits until the floor acknowledges that it can leave.

Each lift can receive a `call(N)` message and an `´at´(N)` message. The lift can send an `arrive(Ack)` message to a floor and a `step(Dest)` message to its controller. After sending the `arrive(Ack)` message, the lift waits until the floor acknowledges that the door actions have finished. The acknowledgment is done by using the dataflow variable `Ack` as a one-shot wire. The floor sends an acknowledgment by binding `Ack=`**`unit`** and the lift waits with `{Wait Ack}`.

The source code of the lift component is shown in figure 5.12. It uses a series of **`if`** statements to implement the conditions for the different transitions. It uses `Browse` to display when a lift will go to a called floor and when the lift arrives at a called floor. The function `{ScheduleLast L N}` implements the scheduler: it adds `N` to the end of the schedule `L` and returns the new schedule.

```
fun {Floor Num Init Lifts}
   Tid={Timer}
   Fid={NewPortObject Init
        fun {$ state(Called) Msg}
           case Called
           of notcalled then Lran in
              case Msg
              of arrive(Ack) then
                 {Browse ´Lift at floor ´#Num#´: open doors´}
                 {Send Tid starttimer(5000 Fid)}
                 state(doorsopen(Ack))
              [] call then
                 {Browse ´Floor ´#Num#´ calls a lift!´}
                 Lran=Lifts.(1+{OS.rand} mod {Width Lifts})
                 {Send Lran call(Num)}
                 state(called)
              end
           [] called then
              case Msg
              of arrive(Ack) then
                 {Browse ´Lift at floor ´#Num#´: open doors´}
                 {Send Tid starttimer(5000 Fid)}
                 state(doorsopen(Ack))
              [] call then
                 state(called)
              end
           [] doorsopen(Ack) then
              case Msg
              of stoptimer then
                 {Browse ´Lift at floor ´#Num#´: close doors´}
                 Ack=unit
                 state(notcalled)
              [] arrive(A) then
                 A=Ack
                 state(doorsopen(Ack))
              [] call then
                 state(doorsopen(Ack))
              end
           end
        end}
in Fid end
```

Figure 5.10: Implementation of the floor component.

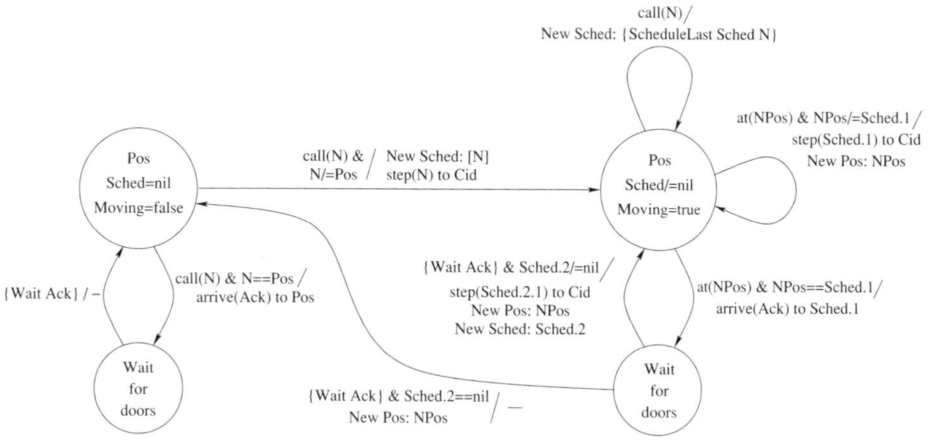

Figure 5.11: State diagram of a lift.

The building

We have now specified the complete system. It is instructive to trace through the execution by hand, following the flow of control in the floors, lifts, controllers, and timers. For example, say that there are ten floors and two lifts. Both lifts are on floor 1, and floors 9 and 10 each call a lift. What are the possible executions of the system? Let us define a compound component that creates a building with `FN` floors and `LN` lifts:

```
proc {Building FN LN ?Floors ?Lifts}
   Lifts={MakeTuple lifts LN}
   for I in 1..LN do Cid in
      Cid={Controller state(stopped 1 Lifts.I)}
      Lifts.I={Lift I state(1 nil false) Cid Floors}
   end
   Floors={MakeTuple floors FN}
   for I in 1..FN do
      Floors.I={Floor I state(notcalled) Lifts}
   end
end
```

This uses `MakeTuple` to create a new tuple containing unbound variables. Each component instance will run in its own thread. Here is a sample execution:

```
declare F L in
{Building 10 2 F L}
{Send F.9 call}
{Send F.10 call}
{Send L.1 call(4)}
{Send L.2 call(5)}
```

The first lift goes to floor 4 and the second to floor 5.

```
fun {ScheduleLast L N}
   if L\=nil andthen {List.last L}==N then L
   else {Append L [N]} end
end

fun {Lift Num Init Cid Floors}
   {NewPortObject Init
    fun {$ state(Pos Sched Moving) Msg}
       case Msg
       of call(N) then
          {Browse ´Lift ´#Num#´ needed at floor ´#N}
          if N==Pos andthen {Not Moving} then
             {Wait {Send Floors.Pos arrive($)}}
             state(Pos Sched false)
          else Sched2 in
             Sched2={ScheduleLast Sched N}
             if {Not Moving} then
                {Send Cid step(N)} end
             state(Pos Sched2 true)
          end
       [] ´at´(NewPos) then
          {Browse ´Lift ´#Num#´ at floor ´#NewPos}
          case Sched
          of S|Sched2 then
             if NewPos==S then
                {Wait {Send Floors.S arrive($)}}
                if Sched2==nil then
                   state(NewPos nil false)
                else
                   {Send Cid step(Sched2.1)}
                   state(NewPos Sched2 true)
                end
             else
                {Send Cid step(S)}
                state(NewPos Sched Moving)
             end
          end
       end
    end}
end
```

Figure 5.12: Implementation of the lift component.

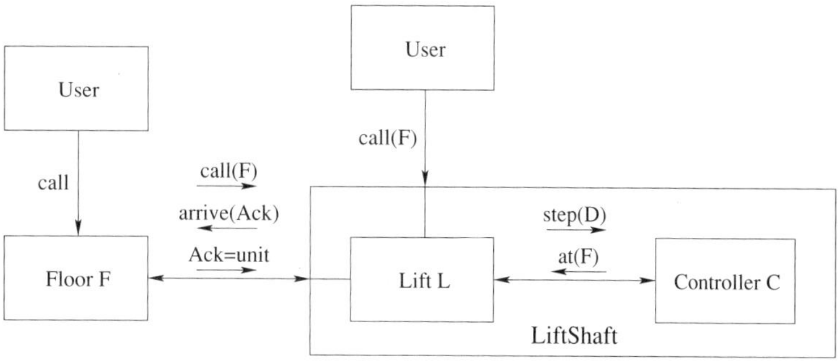

Figure 5.13: Hierarchical component diagram of the lift control system.

Reasoning about the lift control system

To show that the lift works correctly, we can reason about its invariant properties. For example, an `'at'(_)` message can only be received when `Sched\=nil`. This is a simple invariant that can be proved easily from the fact that `'at'` and `step` messages occur in pairs. It is easy to see by inspection that a `step` message is always done when the lift goes into a state where `Sched\=nil`, and that the only transition out of this state (triggered by a `call` message) preserves the invariant. Another invariant is that successive elements of a schedule are always different (can you prove this?).

5.5.3 Improvements to the lift control system

The lift control system of the previous section is somewhat naive. In this section we will indicate five ways in which it can be improved: by using component composition to make it hierarchical, by improving how it opens and closes doors, by using negotiation to find the best lift to call, by improving scheduling to reduce the amount of lift motion, and by handling faults (lifts that stop working). We leave the last three improvements as exercises for the reader.

Hierarchical organization

Looking at the component diagram of figure 5.5, we see that each controller talks only with its corresponding lift. This is visible also in the definition of `Building`. This means that we can improve the organization by combining controller and lift into a compound component, which we call a lift shaft. Figure 5.13 shows the updated component diagram with a lift shaft. We implement this by defining the component `LiftShaft` as follows:

```
fun {LiftShaft I state(F S M) Floors}
   Cid={Controller state(stopped F Lid)}
   Lid={Lift I state(F S M) Cid Floors}
in Lid end
```

Then the Building procedure can be simplified:

```
proc {Building FN LN ?Floors ?Lifts}
   Lifts={MakeTuple lifts LN}
   for I in 1..LN do Cid in
      Lifts.I={LiftShaft I state(1 nil false) Floors}
   end
   Floors={MakeTuple floors FN}
   for I in 1..FN do
      Floors.I={Floor I state(notcalled) Lifts}
   end
end
```

The encapsulation provided by LiftShaft improves the modularity of the program. We can change the internal organization of a lift shaft without changing its interface.

Improved door management

Our system opens all doors at a floor when the first lift arrives and closes them a fixed time later. So what happens if a lift arrives at a floor when the doors are already open? The doors may be just about to close. This behavior is unacceptable for a real lift. We need to improve our lift control system so that each lift has its own set of doors.

Improved negotiation

We can improve our lift control system so that the floor picks the closest lift instead of a random lift. The idea is for the floor to send messages to all lifts asking them to give an estimate of the time it would take to reach the floor. The floor can then pick the lift with the least time. This is an example of a simple negotiation protocol.

Improved scheduling

We can improve the lift scheduling. For example, assume the lift is moving from floor 1 to floor 5 and is currently at floor 2. Calling floor 3 should cause the lift to stop on its way up, instead of the naive solution where it first goes to floor 5 and then down to floor 3. The improved algorithm moves in one direction until there are no more floors to stop at and then changes direction. Variations on this algorithm, which is called the elevator algorithm for obvious reasons, are used to schedule the head movement of a hard disk. With this scheduler we can have two call buttons to call upgoing and downgoing lifts separately.

```
proc {NewPortObjects ?AddPortObject ?Call}
   Sin P={NewPort Sin}

   proc {MsgLoop S1 Procs}
      case S1
      of add(I Proc Sync)|S2 then Procs2 in
         Procs2={AdjoinAt Procs I Proc}
         Sync=unit
         {MsgLoop S2 Procs2}
      [] msg(I M)|S2 then
         try {Procs.I M} catch _ then skip end
         {MsgLoop S2 Procs}
      [] nil then skip end
   end
in
   thread {MsgLoop Sin procs} end

   proc {AddPortObject I Proc}
   Sync in
      {Send P add(I Proc Sync)}
      {Wait Sync}
   end

   proc {Call I M}
      {Send P msg(I M)}
   end
end
```

Figure 5.14: Defining port objects that share one thread.

Fault tolerance

What happens if part of the system stops working? For example, a lift can be out of order, either because of maintenance, because it has broken down, or simply because someone is blocking open the doors at a particular floor. Floors can also be "out of order," e.g., a lift may be forbidden to stop at a floor for some reason. We can extend the lift control system to continue providing at least part of its service in these cases. The basic ideas are explained in the exercises (section 5.9).

5.6 Using the message-passing model directly

The message-passing model can be used in other ways rather than just programming with port objects. One way is to program directly with threads, procedures, ports, and dataflow variables. Another way is to use other abstractions. This section gives some examples.

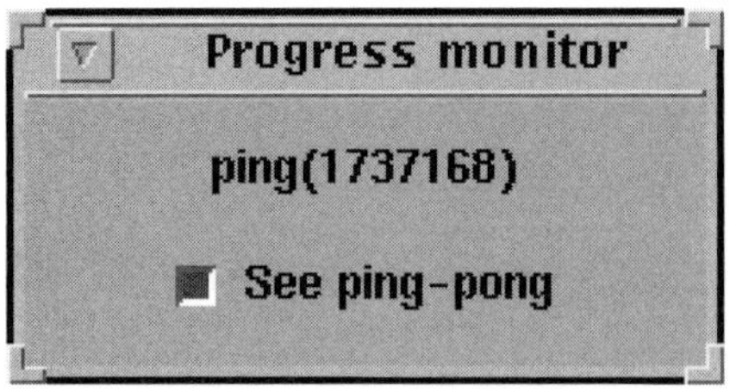

Figure 5.15: Screenshot of the Ping-Pong program.

5.6.1 Port objects that share one thread

It is possible to run many port objects on just one thread, if the thread serializes all their messages. This can be more efficient than using one thread per port object. According to David Wood of Symbian Ltd., this solution was used in the operating system of the Psion Series 3 palmtop computers, where memory is at a premium [231]. Execution is efficient since no thread scheduling has to be done. Objects can access shared data without any particular precautions since all the objects run in the same thread. The main disadvantage is that synchronization is harder. Execution cannot wait inside an object for a calculation done in another object. Attempting this will block the program. This means that programs must be written in a particular style. State must be either global or stored in the message arguments, not in the objects. Messages are a kind of continuation, i.e., there is no return. Each object execution finishes by sending a message.

Figure 5.14 defines the abstraction `NewPortObjects`. It sets up the single thread and returns two procedures, `AddPortObject` and `Call`:

- `{AddPortObject PO Proc}` adds a new port object with name `PO` to the thread. The name should be a literal or a number. Any number of new port objects can be added to the thread.
- `{Call PO Msg}` asynchronously sends the message `Msg` to the port object `PO`. All message executions of all port objects are executed in the single thread. Exceptions raised during message execution are simply ignored.

Note that the abstraction stores the port objects' procedures in a record and uses `AdjoinAt` to extend this record when a new port object is added.

Ping-Pong program

Figure 5.15 gives a screenshot of a small concurrent program, Ping-Pong, which uses port objects that share one thread. Figure 5.16 gives the full source code of Ping-Pong. It uses `NewProgWindow`, the simple progress monitor defined in section 10.4.1. Two objects are created initially, `pingobj` and `pongobj`. Each object understands two messages, `ping(N)` and `pong(N)`. The `pingobj` object asynchronously sends a

```
declare AddPortObject Call
{NewPortObjects AddPortObject Call}

InfoMsg={NewProgWindow "See ping-pong"}

fun {PingPongProc Other}
   proc {$ Msg}
      case Msg
      of ping(N) then
         {InfoMsg "ping("#N#")"}
         {Call Other pong(N+1)}
      [] pong(N) then
         {InfoMsg "pong("#N#")"}
         {Call Other ping(N+1)}
      end
   end
end

{AddPortObject pingobj {PingPongProc pongobj}}
{AddPortObject pongobj {PingPongProc pingobj}}
{Call pingobj ping(0)}
```

Figure 5.16: The Ping-Pong program: using port objects that share one thread.

`pong(N)` message to the `pongobj` object and vice versa. Each message executes by displaying a text and then continuing execution by sending a message to the other object. The integer argument `N` counts messages by being incremented at each call. Execution is started with the initial call `{Call pingobj ping(0)}`.

When the program starts, it creates a window that displays a term of the form `ping(123)` or `pong(123)`, where the integer gives the message count. This monitors execution progress. When the checkbutton is enabled, then each term is displayed for 50 ms. When the checkbutton is disabled, then the messages are passed internally at a much faster rate, limited only by the speed of the Mozart run-time system.[5]

5.6.2 A concurrent queue with ports

The program shown in figure 5.17 defines a thread that acts as a FIFO queue. The function `NewQueue` returns a new queue `Q`, which is a record `queue(put:PutProc get:GetProc)` that contains two procedures, one for inserting an element in the queue and one for fetching an element from the queue. The queue is implemented with two ports. The use of dataflow variables makes the queue insensitive to the relative arrival order of `Q.get` and `Q.put` requests. For example, the `Q.get` requests

5. Using a prerelease of Mozart 1.3.0 on a PowerPC processor at 1 GHz (PowerBook G4 running Mac OS X), the rate is about 300000 asynchronous method calls per second.

```
fun {NewQueue}
   Given GivePort={NewPort Given}
   Taken TakePort={NewPort Taken}
in
   Given=Taken
   queue(put:proc {$ X} {Send GivePort X} end
         get:proc {$ X} {Send TakePort X} end)
end
```

Figure 5.17: Queue (naive version with ports).

can arrive even when the queue is empty. To insert an element `X`, call `{Q.put X}`. To fetch an element in `Y`, call `{Q.get Y}`.

The program in figure 5.17 is almost correct, but it does not work because port streams are read-only variables. To see this, try the following sequence of statements:

```
declare Q in
thread Q={NewQueue} end
{Q.put 1}
{Browse {Q.get $}}
{Browse {Q.get $}}
{Browse {Q.get $}}
{Q.put 2}
{Q.put 3}
```

The problem is that `Given=Taken` tries to impose equality between two read-only variables, i.e., bind them. But a read-only variable can only be read and not bound. So the thread defining the queue will suspend in the statement `Given=Taken`. We can fix the problem by defining a procedure `Match` and running it in its own thread, as shown in figure 5.18. You can verify that the above sequence of statements now works.

Let us look closer to see why the correct version works. Doing a series of put operations:

```
{Q.put I0} {Q.put I1} ... {Q.put In}
```

incrementally adds the elements `I0`, `I1`, ..., `In`, to the stream `Given`, resulting in

```
I0|I1|...|In|F1
```

where `F1` is a read-only variable. In the same way, doing a series of get operations:

```
{Q.get X0} {Q.get X1} ... {Q.get Xn}
```

adds the elements `X0`, `X1`, ..., `Xn` to the stream `Taken`, resulting in

```
X0|X1|...|Xn|F2
```

where `F2` is another read-only variable. The call `{Match Given Taken}` binds the

```
fun {NewQueue}
   Given GivePort={NewPort Given}
   Taken TakePort={NewPort Taken}
   proc {Match Xs Ys}
      case Xs # Ys
      of (X|Xr) # (Y|Yr) then
         X=Y {Match Xr Yr}
      [] nil # nil then skip
      end
   end
in
   thread {Match Given Taken} end
   queue(put:proc {$ X} {Send GivePort X} end
         get:proc {$ X} {Send TakePort X} end)
end
```

Figure 5.18: Queue (correct version with ports).

`Xi`'s to `Ii`'s and blocks again for `F1=F2`.

This concurrent queue is completely symmetric with respect to inserting and retrieving elements. That is, `Q.put` and `Q.get` are defined in exactly the same way. Furthermore, because they use dataflow variables to reference queue elements, these operations never block. This gives the queue the remarkable property that it can be used to insert and retrieve elements before the elements are known. For example, if you do a `{Q.get X}` when there are no elements in the queue, then an unbound variable is returned in `X`. The next element that is inserted will be bound to `X`. To do a blocking retrieval, i.e., one that waits when there are no elements in the queue, the call to `Q.get` should be followed by a `Wait`:

```
{Q.get X}
{Wait X}
```

Similarly, if you do `{Q.put X}` when `X` is unbound, i.e., when there is no element to insert, then the unbound variable `X` will be put in the queue. Binding `X` will make the element known. To do an insert only when the element is known, the call to `Q.put` should be preceded by a `Wait`:

```
{Wait X}
{Q.put X}
```

We have captured the essential asymmetry between put and get: it is in the `Wait` operation. Another way to see this is that put and get reserve places in the queue. The reservation can be done independent of whether the values of the elements are known or not.

Attentive readers will see that there is an even simpler solution to the problem of figure 5.17. The procedure `Match` is not really necessary. It is enough to run `Given=Taken` in its own thread. This is because the unification algorithm does exactly what `Match` does.[6]

5.6.3 A thread abstraction with termination detection

"Ladies and gentlemen, we will be arriving shortly in Brussels Midi station, where this train terminates."
– Announcement, Thalys high-speed train, Paris–Brussels line, January 2002

Thread creation with **thread** ⟨stmt⟩ **end** can itself create new threads during the execution of ⟨stmt⟩. We would like to detect when all these new threads have terminated. This does not seem easy: new threads may themselves create new threads, and so forth. A termination detection algorithm like the one of section 4.4.3 is needed. The algorithm of that section requires explicitly passing variables between threads. We require a solution that is encapsulated, i.e., it does not have this awkwardness. To be precise, we require a procedure `NewThread` with the following properties:

- The call `{NewThread P SubThread}` creates a new thread that executes the zero-argument procedure `P`. It also returns a one-argument procedure `SubThread`.
- During the execution of `P`, new threads can be created by calling `{SubThread P1}`, where the zero-argument procedure `P1` is the thread body. We call these subthreads. `SubThread` can be called recursively, that is, inside `P` and inside the `P1` argument of any `SubThread` call.
- The `NewThread` call returns after the new thread and all subthreads have terminated.

That is, there are three ways to create a new thread:

```
thread ⟨stmt⟩ end
{NewThread proc {$} ⟨stmt⟩ end ?SubThread}
{SubThread proc {$} ⟨stmt⟩ end}
```

They have identical concurrency behavior except for `NewThread`, which has a different termination behavior. `NewThread` can be defined using the message-passing model as shown in figure 5.19. This definition uses a port. When a subthread is created, then +1 is sent to the port. When a subthread terminates, then −1 is sent. The procedure `ZeroExit` accumulates a running total of these numbers. If the total ever reaches zero, then all subthreads have terminated and `ZeroExit` returns.

We can prove that this definition is correct by using invariant assertions. Consider the following assertion: "the sum of the elements on the port's stream is greater than or equal to the number of active threads." When the sum is zero, this implies that the number of active threads is zero as well. We can use induction to show that the assertion is true at every part of every possible execution, starting from the call to `NewThread`. It is clearly true when `NewThread` starts since both numbers are zero. During an execution, there are four relevant actions: sending +1, sending −1,

6. This FIFO queue design was first given by Denys Duchier.

```
local
   proc {ZeroExit N Is}
      case Is of I|Ir then
         if N+I\=0 then {ZeroExit N+I Ir} end
      end
   end
in
   proc {NewThread P ?SubThread}
      Is Pt={NewPort Is}
   in
      proc {SubThread P}
         {Send Pt 1}
         thread
            {P} {Send Pt ~1}
         end
      end
      {SubThread P}
      {ZeroExit 0 Is}
   end
end
```

Figure 5.19: A thread abstraction with termination detection.

starting a thread, and terminating a thread. By inspection of the program, each of these actions keeps the assertion true. (We can assume without loss of generality that thread termination occurs just before sending -1, since the thread then no longer executes any part of the user program.)

This definition of `NewThread` has two restrictions. First, `P` and `P1` should always call `SubThread` to create subthreads, never any other operation (such as **`thread`** ... **`end`** or a `SubThread` created elsewhere). Second, `SubThread` should not be called anywhere else in the program. The definition can be extended to relax these restrictions or to check them. We leave these tasks as exercises for the reader.

Port send semantics and distributed systems

We know that the `Send` operation is asynchronous, i.e., it completes immediately. The termination detection algorithm relies on another property of `Send`: that `{Send Pt 1}` (in the parent thread) arrives before `{Send Pt ~1}` (in the child thread). Can we assume that sends in different threads behave in this way? Yes we can, if we are sure the `Send` operation reserves a slot in the port stream. Look back to the semantics we have defined for ports in the beginning of the chapter: the `Send` operation does indeed put its argument in the port stream. We call this the

```
proc {ConcFilter L F ?L2}
   Send Close
in
   {NewPortClose L2 Send Close}
   {Barrier
      {Map L
         fun {$ X}
            proc {$}
               if {F X} then {Send X} end
            end
         end}}
   {Close}
end
```

Figure 5.20: A concurrent filter without sequential dependencies.

slot-reserving semantics of `Send`.[7]

Unfortunately, this semantics is not the right one in general. We really want an *eventual* slot-reserving semantics, where the `Send` operation might not immediately reserve a slot but we are sure that it will eventually. Why is this semantics "right"? It is because it is the natural behavior of a distributed system, where a program is spread out over more than one process and processes can be on different machines. A `Send` can execute on a different process than where the port stream is constructed. Doing a `Send` does not immediately reserve a slot because the slot might be on a different machine (remember that the `Send` should complete immediately)! All we can say is that doing a `Send` will eventually reserve a slot.

With the "right" semantics for `Send`, our termination detection algorithm is incorrect since `{Send Pt ~1}` might arrive before `{Send Pt 1}`. We can fix the problem by defining a slot-reserving port in terms of an eventual slot-reserving port:

```
proc {NewSPort ?S ?SSend}
S1 P={NewPort S1} in
  proc {SSend M} X in {Send P M#X} {Wait X} end
  thread S={Map S1 fun {$ M#X} X=unit M end} end
end
```

`NewSPort` behaves like `NewPort`. If `NewPort` defines an eventual slot-reserving port, then `NewSPort` will define a slot-reserving port. Using `NewSPort` in the termination detection algorithm will ensure that it is correct in case we use the "right" port semantics.

7. This is sometimes called a synchronous `Send`, because it only completes when the message is delivered to the stream. We will avoid this term because the concept of "delivery" is not clear. For example, we might want to talk about delivering a message to an application process instead of a stream.

5.6.4 Eliminating sequential dependencies

Let us examine how to remove useless sequential dependencies between different parts of a program. We take as example the procedure `{Filter L F L2}`, which takes a list `L` and a one-argument boolean function `F`. It outputs a list `L2` that contains the elements `X` of `L` for which `{F X}` is true. This is a library function (it is part of the `List` module) that can be defined declaratively as follows:

```
fun {Filter L F}
   case L
   of nil then nil
   [] X|L2 then
      if {F X} then X|{Filter L2 F} else {Filter L2 F} end
   end
end
```

or equivalently, using the loop syntax:

```
fun {Filter L F}
   for X in L collect:C do
      if {F X} then {C X} end
   end
end
```

This definition is efficient, but it introduces sequential dependencies: `{F X}` can be calculated only after it has been calculated for all elements of `L` before `X`. These dependencies are introduced because all calculations are done sequentially in the same thread. But these dependencies are not really necessary. For example, in the call

```
{Filter [A 5 1 B 4 0 6] fun {$ X} X>2 end Out}
```

it is possible to deduce immediately that `5`, `4`, and `6` will be in the output, without waiting for `A` and `B` to be bound. Later on, if some other thread does `A=10`, then `10` could be added to the result immediately.

We can write a new version of `Filter` that avoids these dependencies. It constructs its output incrementally, as the input information arrives. We use two building blocks:

- Concurrent composition (see section 4.4.3). The procedure `Barrier` implements concurrent composition: it creates a concurrent task for each list element and waits until all are finished.

- Asynchronous channels (ports; see earlier in this chapter). The procedure `NewPortClose` implements a port with a send and a close operation. Its definition is given in the supplements file on the book's Web site. The close operation terminates the port's stream with `nil`.

Figure 5.20 gives the definition. It first creates a port whose stream is the output list. Then `Barrier` is called with a list of procedures, each of which adds `X` to the output list if `{F X}` is true. Finally, when all list elements are taken care of, the output list is ended by closing the port.

Is `ConcFilter` declarative? As it is written, certainly not, since the output list can appear in any order (an observable nondeterminism). It can be made declarative by hiding this nondeterminism, e.g., by sorting the output list. There is another way, using the properties of data abstraction. If the rest of the program does not depend on the order (e.g., the list is a representation of a set data structure), then `ConcFilter` can be treated as if it were declarative. This is easy to see: if the list were in fact hidden inside a set abstraction, then `ConcFilter` would be deterministic and hence declarative.

5.7 The Erlang language

The Erlang language was developed by Ericsson for telecommunications applications, in particular for telephony [10, 227]. Its implementation, the Ericsson OTP (Open Telecom Platform), features fine-grained concurrency (efficient threads), extreme reliability (high-performance software fault tolerance), and hot code replacement ability (update software while the system is running). It is a high-level language that hides the internal representation of data and does automatic memory management. It has been used successfully in several Ericsson products.

5.7.1 Computation model

The Erlang computation model has an elegant layered structure. We first explain the model and then we show how it is extended for distribution and fault tolerance.

The Erlang computation model consists of concurrent entities called "processes." A process consists of a port object and a mailbox. The language can be divided into two layers:

- *Functional core.* Processes are programmed in a dynamically typed strict functional language. Each process contains a port object that is defined by a recursive function. A process that spawns a new process specifies which function should be initially executed inside it.

- *Message-passing extension.* Processes communicate by sending messages to other processes asynchronously in FIFO order. Messages are put in the mailbox of the destination process. Messages can contain any value, including function values. Each process has a process identifier, its PID, which is a unique constant that identifies the process. The PID can be embedded in data structures and messages. A process can read messages from its mailbox. Message receiving can be either blocking or nonblocking. The receiving process uses pattern matching to wait for and remove messages from its mailbox, without disturbing the other messages. This means that messages are not necessarily treated in the order that they are sent.

An important property of Erlang processes is that they are independent by default.

That is, whatever happens in one process has no effect on any other process, unless it is programmed explicitly. This implies that messages are always copied when sent between processes. There are never any shared references between processes. This is also the deep reason why the communication primitive is an asynchronous send. Synchronous communication creates a dependency, since the sending process waits for a reply from the destination process. Process independence makes it easier to build highly reliable systems [9].

Extensions for distribution and fault tolerance

The centralized model is extended for distribution and fault tolerance:

- *Transparent distribution.* Processes can be on the same machine or on different machines. A single machine environment is called a node in Erlang terminology. In a program, communication between local or remote processes is written in exactly the same way. The PID encapsulates the destination and allows the run-time system to decide whether to do a local or remote operation. Processes are stationary; this means that once a process is created in a node it remains there for its entire lifetime. Sending a message to a remote process requires exactly one network operation, i.e., no intermediate nodes are involved. Processes can be created at remote nodes. Programs are network-transparent, i.e., they give the same result no matter on which nodes the processes are placed. Programs are network-aware since the programmer has complete control of process placement and can optimize it according to the network characteristics.
- *Failure detection.* A process can be set up to perform some action when another process fails. In Erlang terminology this is called *linking* the two processes. One possible action is that when the second process fails, a message is sent to the first. This failure detection ability allows many fault-tolerance mechanisms to be programmed entirely in Erlang. Since processes are independent, this style of programming is straightforward.
- *Persistence.* The Erlang run-time system comes with a database, called Mnesia, that helps to build highly available applications. Mnesia is replicated to achieve high availability.

We can summarize by saying that Erlang's computation model, i.e., independent port objects, is strongly optimized for building fault-tolerant distributed systems. The Mnesia database compensates for the lack of a general mutable store. An example of a successful product built using Erlang is Ericsson's AXD 301 ATM switch, which provides telephony over an ATM network. The AXD 301 handles 30 to 40 million calls per week with an availability of 99.9999999% according to Ericsson (about 30 ms downtime per year) and contains 1.7 million lines of Erlang [8, 9].

5.7.2 Introduction to Erlang programming

To give a taste of Erlang, we give some small Erlang programs and show how to do the same thing in the book's computation models. The programs are mostly taken from the Erlang book [10]. We show how to write functions and concurrent programs with message passing. For more information on Erlang programming, we highly recommend the Erlang book.

A simple function

The core of Erlang is a strict functional language with dynamic typing. Here is a simple definition of the factorial function:

```
factorial(0) -> 1;
factorial(N) when N>0 -> N*factorial(N-1).
```

This example introduces the basic syntactic conventions of Erlang. Function names are in lowercase and variable identifiers are capitalized. Variable identifiers are bound to values when defined, which means that Erlang has a value store. An identifier's binding cannot be changed; it is single assignment, just as in the declarative model. These conventions are inherited from Prolog, in which the first Erlang implementation (an interpreter) was written.

Erlang functions are defined by clauses; each clause has a head (with a pattern and optional guard) and a body. The patterns are checked in order starting with the first clause. If a pattern matches, its variables are bound and the clause body is executed. The optional guard is a boolean function that has to return `true`. All the variable identifiers in the pattern must be different. If a pattern does not match, then the next clause is tried. We can translate the factorial as follows in the declarative model:

```
fun {Factorial N}
   case N
   of 0 then 1
   [] N andthen N>0 then N*{Factorial N-1}
   end
end
```

The **case** statement does pattern matching exactly as in Erlang, with a different syntax.

Pattern matching with tuples

Here is a function that does pattern matching with tuples:

```
area({square, Side}) ->
    Side*Side;
area({rectangle, X, Y}) ->
    X*Y;
area({circle, Radius}) ->
    3.14159*Radius*Radius;
area({triangle, A, B, C}) ->
    S=(A+B+C)/2;
    math:sqrt(S*(S-A)*(S-B)*(S-C)).
```

This uses the square root function `sqrt` defined in the module `math`. This function calculates the area of a plane shape. It represents the shape by means of a tuple that identifies the shape and gives its size. Tuples in Erlang are written with curly braces: `{square, Side}` would be written as `square(Side)` in the declarative model. In the declarative model, the function can be written as follows:

```
fun {Area T}
   case T
   of square(Side) then Side*Side
   [] rectangle(X Y) then X*Y
   [] circle(Radius) then 3.14159*Radius*Radius
   [] triangle(A B C) then S=(A+B+C)/2.0 in
      {Sqrt S*(S-A)*(S-B)*(S-C)}
   end
end
```

Concurrency and message passing

In Erlang, threads are created together with a port object and a mailbox. This combination is called a process. There are three primitives:

1. The `spawn` operation (written as `spawn(M,F,A)`) creates a new process and returns a value (called "process identifier") that can be used to send messages to it. The arguments of `spawn` give the initial function call that starts the process, identified by module `M`, function name `F`, and argument list `A`. Note that modules are first-class entities in Erlang.

2. The `send` operation (written as `Pid!Msg`) asynchronously sends the message `Msg` to the process with process identifier `Pid`. The messages are put in the receiver's mailbox.

3. The `receive` operation is used to remove messages from the mailbox. It uses pattern matching to remove messages that match a given pattern. Section 5.7.3 explains this in detail.

Let us take the `area` function and put it inside a process. This makes it into a server that can be called from any other process.

```
-module(areaserver).
-export([start/0, loop/0]).

start() -> spawn(areaserver, loop, []).

loop() ->
    receive
       {From, Shape} ->
            From!area(Shape),
            loop()
    end.
```

This defines the two operations `start` and `loop` in the new module `areaserver`. These two operations are exported outside the module. We need to define them in a module because the `spawn` operation requires the module name as an argument. The `loop` operation repeatedly reads a message (a two-argument tuple `{From, Shape}`) and responds to it by calling `area` and sending the reply to the process `From`. Now let us start a new server and call it

```
Pid=areaserver:start(),
Pid!{self(), {square, 3.4}},
receive
   Ans -> ...
end,
```

Here `self()` is a language operation that returns the process identifier of the current process. This allows the server to return a reply. Let us write this in the concurrent stateful model:

```
fun {Start}
S AreaServer={NewPort S} in
   thread
      for msg(Ans Shape) in S do
         Ans={Area Shape}
      end
   end
   AreaServer
end
```

Let us again start a new server and call it:

```
Pid={Start}
local Ans in
   {Send Pid msg(Ans square(3.4))}
   {Wait Ans}
   ...
end
```

This example uses the dataflow variable `Ans` to get the reply. This mimics the send to `From` done by Erlang. To do exactly what Erlang does, we need to translate the `receive` operation into a computation model of the book. This is a little more complicated. It is explained in the next section.

5.7.3 The `receive` operation

Much of the unique flavor and expressiveness of concurrent programming in Erlang is due to the mailboxes and how they are managed. Messages are taken out of a mailbox with the `receive` operation. It uses pattern matching to pick out a desired message, leaving the other messages unchanged. Using `receive` gives particularly compact, readable, and efficient code. In this section, we implement `receive` as a linguistic abstraction. We show how to translate it into the book's computation models. There are two reasons for giving the translation. First, it gives a precise semantics for `receive`, which aids the understanding of Erlang. Second, it shows how to do Erlang-style programming in Oz.

Because of Erlang's functional core, `receive` is an expression that returns a value. The `receive` expression has the following general form [10]:

```
receive
   Pattern1 [when Guard1] -> Body1;
   ...
   PatternN [when GuardN] -> BodyN;
[ after Expr -> BodyT; ]
end
```

The guards (`when` clauses) and the time-out (`after` clause) are optional. This expression blocks until a message matching one of the patterns arrives in the current thread's mailbox. It then removes this message, binds the corresponding variables in the pattern, and executes the body. Patterns are very similar to patterns in the **case** statement: they introduce new single-assignment variables whose scope ranges over the corresponding body. For example, the Erlang pattern {`rectangle, [X,Y]`} corresponds to the pattern `rectangle([X Y])`. Identifiers starting with lowercase letters correspond to atoms, and identifiers starting with capital letters correspond to variables, like the notation of the book. Compound terms are enclosed in braces { and } and correspond to tuples.

The optional `after` clause defines a time-out; if no matching message arrives after a number of milliseconds given by evaluating the expression `Expr`, then the time-out body is executed. If zero milliseconds are specified, then the `after` clause is executed immediately if there are no messages in the mailbox.

General remarks

Each Erlang process is translated into one thread with one port. Sending to the process means sending to the port. This adds the message to the port's stream, which represents the mailbox contents. All forms of `receive`, when they complete, either take exactly one message out of the mailbox or leave the mailbox unchanged. We model this by giving each translation of `receive` an input stream and an output stream. All translations have two arguments, `Sin` and `Sout`, that reference the input stream and the output stream. These streams do not appear in the Erlang syntax.

```
T(receive ... end Sin Sout) ≡
   local
      fun {Loop S T#E Sout}
         case S of M|S1 then
            case M
            of T(Pattern1) then E=S1 T(Body1 T Sout)
            ...
            [] T(PatternN) then E=S1 T(BodyN T Sout)
            else E1 in E=M|E1 {Loop S1 T#E1 Sout}
            end
         end
      end T
   in
      {Loop Sin T#T Sout}
   end
```

Figure 5.21: Translation of `receive` without time-out.

After executing a `receive`, there are two possibilities for the value of the output stream. Either it is the same as the input stream or it has one less message than the input stream. The latter occurs if the message matches a pattern.

We distinguish three different forms of `receive` that result in different translations. In each form the translation can be directly inserted in a program and it will behave like the respective `receive`. The first form is translated using the declarative model. The second form has a time-out; it uses the nondeterministic concurrent model (see section 8.2). The third form is a special case of the second where the delay is zero, which makes the translation much simpler.

First form (without time-out)

The first form of the `receive` expression is as follows:

```
receive
   Pattern1 -> Body1;
   ...
   PatternN -> BodyN;
end
```

The `receive` blocks until a message arrives that matches one of the patterns. The patterns are checked in order from `Pattern1` to `PatternN`. We leave out the guards to avoid cluttering up the code. Adding them is straightforward. A pattern can be any partial value; in particular an unbound variable will always cause a match. Messages that do not match are put in the output stream and do not cause the `receive` to complete.

Figure 5.21 gives the translation of the first form, which we will write as T(`receive ... end Sin Sout`). The output stream contains the messages that remain after the `receive` expression has removed the ones it needs. Note that the

```
T(receive ... end Sin Sout) ≡
   local
      Cancel={Alarm T(Expr)}
      fun {Loop S T#E Sout}
         if {WaitTwo S Cancel}==1 then
            case S of M|S1 then
               case M
               of T(Pattern1) then E=S1 T(Body1 T Sout)
               ...
               [] T(PatternN) then E=S1 T(BodyN T Sout)
               else E1 in E=M|E1 {Loop S1 T#E1 Sout} end
            end
         else E=S T(BodyT T Sout)
      end T
   in
      {Loop Sin T#T Sout}
   end
```

Figure 5.22: Translation of `receive` with time-out.

translation T(`Body T Sout`) of a body that does *not* contain a `receive` expression must bind `Sout=T`.

The `Loop` function is used to manage out-of-order reception: if a message `M` is received that does not match any pattern, then it is put in the output stream and `Loop` is called recursively. `Loop` uses a difference list to manage the case when a `receive` expression contains a `receive` expression.

Second form (with time-out)

The second form of the `receive` expression is as follows:

```
receive
   Pattern1 -> Body1;
   ...
   PatternN -> BodyN;
after Expr -> BodyT;
end
```

When the `receive` is entered, `Expr` is evaluated first, giving the integer n. If no match is done after n ms, then the time-out action is executed. If a match is done before n ms, then it is handled as if there were no time-out. Figure 5.22 gives the translation.

The translation uses a timer interrupt implemented by `Alarm` and `WaitTwo`. `{Alarm N}`, explained in section 4.6, is guaranteed to wait for at least n ms and then bind the unbound variable `Cancel` to **`unit`**. `{WaitTwo S Cancel}`, which is defined in the supplements file on the book's Web site, waits simultaneously for one of two events: a message (`S` is bound) and a time-out (`Cancel` is bound). It can

```
T(receive ... end Sin Sout) ≡
   if {IsDet Sin} then
      case Sin of M|S1 then
         case M
         of T(Pattern1) then T(Body1 S1 Sout)
         ...
         [] T(PatternN) then T(BodyN) S1 Sout)
         else T(BodyT Sin Sout) end
      end
   else Sout=Sin end
```

Figure 5.23: Translation of `receive` with zero time-out.

return 1 if its first argument is bound and 2 if its second argument is bound.

The Erlang semantics is slightly more complicated than what is defined in figure 5.22. It guarantees that the mailbox is checked at least once, even if the time-out is zero or has expired by the time the mailbox is checked. We can implement this guarantee by stipulating that `WaitTwo` favors its first argument, i.e., that it always returns 1 if its first argument is determined. The Erlang semantics also guarantees that the `receive` is exited quickly after the time-out expires. While this is easily guaranteed by an actual implementation, it is not guaranteed by figure 5.22 since `Loop` could go on forever if messages arrive quicker than the loop iterates. We leave it to the reader to modify figure 5.22 to add this guarantee.

Third form (with zero time-out)

The third form of the `receive` expression is like the second form except that the time-out delay is zero. With zero delay the `receive` is nonblocking. A simpler translation is possible when compared to the case of nonzero time-out. Figure 5.23 gives the translation. Using `IsDet`, it first checks whether there is a message that matches any of the patterns. `{IsDet S}`, explained in section 4.9.3, checks immediately whether `S` is bound or not and returns **`true`** or **`false`**. If there is no message that matches (e.g., if the mailbox is empty), then the default action `BodyT` is done.

5.8 Advanced topic

5.8.1 The nondeterministic concurrent model

This section explains the nondeterministic concurrent model, which is intermediate in expressiveness between the declarative concurrent model and the message-passing concurrent model. It is less expressive than the message-passing model but in return it has a logical semantics (see chapter 9).

⟨s⟩ ::=	
skip	Empty statement
| ⟨s⟩$_1$ ⟨s⟩$_2$	Statement sequence
| **local** ⟨x⟩ **in** ⟨s⟩ **end**	Variable creation
| ⟨x⟩$_1$=⟨x⟩$_2$	Variable-variable binding
| ⟨x⟩=⟨v⟩	Value creation
| **if** ⟨x⟩ **then** ⟨s⟩$_1$ **else** ⟨s⟩$_2$ **end**	Conditional
| **case** ⟨x⟩ **of** ⟨pattern⟩ **then** ⟨s⟩$_1$ **else** ⟨s⟩$_2$ **end**	Pattern matching
| { ⟨x⟩ ⟨y⟩$_1$ ⋯ ⟨y⟩$_n$ }	Procedure application
| **thread** ⟨s⟩ **end**	Thread creation
| {`WaitTwo` ⟨x⟩ ⟨y⟩ ⟨z⟩}	**Nondeterministic choice**

Table 5.2: The nondeterministic concurrent kernel language.

The nondeterministic concurrent model is the model used by concurrent logic programming [196]. It is sometimes called the process model of logic programming, since it models predicates as concurrent computations. It is interesting both for historical reasons and for the insight it gives into practical concurrent programming. We first introduce the nondeterministic concurrent model and show how it solves the stream communication problem of section 4.8.3. We then show how to implement nondeterministic choice in the declarative concurrent model with exceptions, showing that the latter is at least as expressive as the nondeterministic model.

Table 5.2 gives the kernel language of the nondeterministic concurrent model. It adds just one operation to the declarative concurrent model: a nondeterministic choice that waits for either of two events and nondeterministically returns when one has happened with an indication of which one.

Limitation of the declarative concurrent model

In section 4.8.3 we saw a fundamental limitation of the declarative concurrent model: stream objects must access input streams in a fixed pattern. Two streams cannot independently feed the same stream object. How can we solve this problem? Consider the case of two client objects and a server object. We can try to solve it by putting a new stream object, a stream merger, in between the two clients and the server. The stream merger has two input streams and one output stream. All the messages appearing on each of the input streams will be put on the output stream. Figure 5.24 illustrates the solution. This seems to solve our problem: each client sends messages to the stream merger, and the stream merger forwards them to the server. The stream merger is defined as follows:

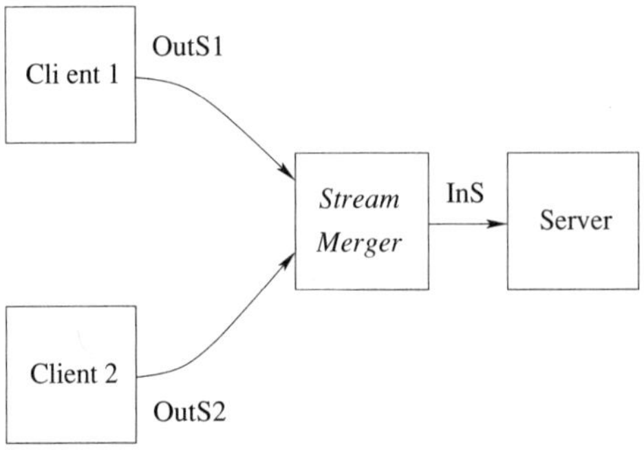

Figure 5.24: Connecting two clients using a stream merger.

```
fun {StreamMerger OutS1 OutS2}
   case OutS1#OutS2
   of (M|NewS1)#OutS2 then
       M|{StreamMerger NewS1 OutS2}
   [] OutS1#(M|NewS2) then
       M|{StreamMerger OutS1 NewS2}
   [] nil#OutS2 then
       OutS2
   [] OutS1#nil then
       OutS1
   end
end
```

The stream merger is executed in its own thread. This definition handles the case of termination, i.e., when either or both clients terminate. Yet this solution has a basic difficulty: it does not work! Why not? Think carefully before reading the answer in the footnote.[8]

Adding nondeterministic choice

But this abortive solution has the germs of a working solution. The problem is that the **case** statement only waits on *one* condition at a time. A possible solution is therefore to extend the declarative concurrent model with an operation that allows waiting concurrently on more than one condition. We call this operation nondeterministic choice. One of the simplest ways is to add an operation that waits concurrently on two dataflow variables being bound. We call this operation `WaitTwo` because it generalizes `Wait`. The function call `{WaitTwo A B}` returns when either `A` or `B` is bound. It returns either 1 or 2. It can return 1 when `A` is bound and 2

8. It is because the **case** statement tests only one pattern at a time, and only goes to the next when the previous ones fail. While it is waiting on stream `OutS1`, it cannot accept an input from stream `OutS2`, and vice versa.

when `B` is bound. A simple Mozart definition is given in the supplements file on the book's Web site. The declarative concurrent model extended with `WaitTwo` is called the nondeterministic concurrent model.

Concurrent logic programming

The nondeterministic concurrent model is the basic model of concurrent logic programming, as pioneered by IC-Prolog, Parlog, Concurrent Prolog, FCP (Flat Concurrent Prolog), GHC (Guarded Horn Clauses), and Flat GHC [39, 40, 41, 194, 195, 212]. It is the principal computation model that was used by the Japanese Fifth Generation Project and many other substantial projects in the 1980s [65, 196, 211]. In the nondeterministic concurrent model, it is possible to write a stream merger. Its definition looks as follows:

```
fun {StreamMerger OutS1 OutS2}
   F={WaitTwo OutS1 OutS2}
in
   case F#OutS1#OutS2
   of 1#(M|NewS1)#OutS2 then
       M|{StreamMerger OutS2 NewS1}
   [] 2#OutS1#(M|NewS2) then
       M|{StreamMerger NewS2 OutS1}
   [] 1#nil#OutS2 then
       OutS2
   [] 2#OutS1#nil then
       OutS1
   end
end
```

This style of programming is exactly what concurrent logic programming does. A typical syntax for this definition in a Prolog-like concurrent logic language would be as follows:

```
streamMerger([M|NewS1], OutS2, InS) :- true |
        InS=[M|NewS],
        streamMerger(OutS2, NewS1, NewS).
streamMerger(OutS1, [M|NewS2], InS) :- true |
        InS=[M|NewS],
        streamMerger(NewS2, OutS1, NewS).
streamMerger([], OutS2, InS) :- true |
        InS=OutS2.
streamMerger(OutS1, [], InS) :- true |
        InS=OutS1.
```

This definition consists of four clauses, each of which defines one nondeterministic choice. Keep in mind that syntactically Prolog uses `[]` for `nil` and `[H|T]` for `H|T`. Each clause consists of a guard and a body. The vertical bar `|` separates the guard from the body. A guard does only tests, blocking if a test cannot be decided. A guard must be true for a clause to be choosable. The body is executed only if the clause is chosen. The body can bind output variables.

The stream merger first calls `WaitTwo` to decide which stream to listen to. Only after `WaitTwo` returns does it enter the **case** statement. Because of the argument `F`, alternatives that do not apply are skipped. Note that each recursive call switches the two stream arguments. This helps guarantee fairness between both streams in systems where the `WaitTwo` statement favors one or the other (which is often the case in an implementation). A message appearing on an input stream will eventually appear on the output stream, independent of what happens in the other input stream.

Is it practical?

What can we say about practical programming in this model? Assume that new clients arrive during execution. Each client wants to communicate with the server. This means that a new stream merger must be created for each client! The final result is a tree of stream mergers feeding the server. Is this a practical solution? It has two problems:

- It is inefficient. Each stream merger executes in its own thread. The tree of stream mergers is extended at run time each time a new object references the server. Furthermore, the tree is not necessarily balanced. It would take extra work to balance it.
- It lacks expressiveness. It is not possible to reference the server directly. For example, it is not possible to put a server reference in a data structure. The only way we have to reference the server is by referencing one of its streams. We can put this in a data structure, but only one client can use this reference. (Remember that declarative data structures cannot be modified.)

How can we solve these two problems? The first problem could hypothetically be solved by a very smart compiler that recognizes the tree of stream mergers and replaces it by a direct many-to-one communication in the implementation. However, after two decades of research in this area, such a compiler does not exist [211]. Some systems solve the problem in another way: by adding an abstraction for multiway merge whose implementation is done outside the model. This amounts to extending the model with ports. The second problem can be partially solved (see Exercises, section 5.9), but the solution is still cumbersome.

We seem to have found an inherent limitation of the nondeterministic concurrent model. Upon closer examination, the problem seems to be that there is no notion of explicit state in the model, where explicit state associates a name with a store reference. Both the name and the store reference are immutable; only their association can be changed. There are many equivalent ways to introduce explicit state. One way is by adding the concept of cell, as will be shown in chapter 6. Another way is by adding the concept of port, as we did in this chapter. Ports and cells are equivalent in a concurrent language: there are simple implementations of each in terms of the other.

```
fun {WaitTwo A B}
X in
   thread {Wait A} try X=1 catch _ then skip end end
   thread {Wait B} try X=2 catch _ then skip end end
   X
end
```

Figure 5.25: Symmetric nondeterministic choice (using exceptions).

```
fun {WaitTwo A B}
U in
   thread {Wait A} U=unit end
   thread {Wait B} U=unit end
   {Wait U}
   if {IsDet A} then 1 else 2 end
end
```

Figure 5.26: Asymmetric nondeterministic choice (using `IsDet`).

Implementing nondeterministic choice

The `WaitTwo` operation can be defined in the declarative concurrent model if exceptions are added.[9] Figure 5.25 gives a simple definition. This returns 1 or 2, depending on whether `A` is bound or `B` is bound. This definition is symmetric; it does not favor either `A` or `B`. We can write an asymmetric version that favors `A` by using `IsDet`, as shown in figure 5.26.[10]

5.9 Exercises

1. *Port objects that share one thread.* Section 5.6.1 gives a small program, called Ping-Pong, that has two port objects. Each object executes a method and then asynchronously calls the other. When one initial message is inserted into the system, this causes an infinite ping-pong of messages to bounce between the objects. What happens if two (or more) initial messages are inserted? For example, what happens if these two initial calls are done?:

9. For practical use, however, we recommend the definition given in the supplements file on the book's Web site.
10. Both definitions have the minor flaw that they can leave threads "hanging around" forever if one variable is never bound. The definitions can be corrected to terminate any hanging threads. We leave these corrections as exercises for the reader.

```
{Call Ping ping(0)}
{Call Pong pong(10000000)}
```

Messages will still ping-pong indefinitely, but how? Which messages will be sent and how will the object executions be interleaved? Will the interleaving be in lockstep (alternating between objects strictly), looser (subject to fluctuations due to thread scheduling), or something in between?

2. *Lift control system.* Section 5.5 gives the design of a simple lift control system. Let us explore it:

(a) The current design has one controller object per lift. To economize on costs, the developer decides to change this to keep just one controller for the whole system. Each lift then communicates with this controller. The controller's internal definition stays the same. Is this a good idea? How does it change the behavior of the lift control system?

(b) In the current design, the controller steps up or down one floor at a time. It stops at all floors that it passes, even if the floor was not requested. Change the lift and controller objects to avoid this jumpy behavior by stopping only at requested floors.

3. *Fault tolerance for the lift control system.* There are two kinds of faults that can happen: components can be blocked temporarily or they can be permanently out of order. Let us see how to handle some common problems that can occur because of these faults:

(a) A lift is blocked. Extend the system to continue working when a lift is temporarily blocked at a floor by a malicious user. First extend the floor to reset the door timer when the floor is called while the doors are open. Then the lift's schedule should be given to other lifts and the floors should no longer call that particular lift. When the lift works again, floors should again be able to call the lift. This can be done with time-outs.

(b) A lift is out of order. The first step is to add generic primitives for failure detection. We might need both synchronous and asynchronous detection. In synchronous detection, when a component goes down, we assume that any message sent to it gets the immediate reply `down(Id)`, where `Id` identifies the component. In asynchronous detection, we "link" a component to another when they are both still working. Then, when the second component crashes, the `down` message is sent to the first one immediately. Now extend the system to continue working when a lift is out of order. The system should reconfigure itself to continue working for a building with one less lift.

(c) A floor is out of order. Extend the system to continue working when a floor is out of order. The system should reconfigure itself to continue working for a building with one less floor.

(d) Lift maintenance. Extend the system so that a lift can be brought down for maintenance and brought back up again later.

(e) Interactions. What happens if several floors and lifts become out of order simultaneously? Does your system handle this properly?

4. *Termination detection.* Replace definition of `SubThread` in section 5.6.3 by:

```
proc {SubThread P}
   thread
      {Send Pt 1} {P} {Send Pt ~1}
   end
end
```

Explain why the result is not correct. Give an execution such that there exists a point where the sum of the elements on the port's stream is zero, yet all threads have not terminated.

5. *Concurrent filter.* Section 5.6.4 defines a concurrent version of `Filter`, called `ConcFilter`, that calculates each output element independently, i.e., without waiting for the previous ones to be calculated.

(a) What happens when the following is executed?:

```
declare Out
{ConcFilter [5 1 2 4 0] fun {$ X} X>2 end Out}
{Show Out}
```

How many elements are displayed by the `Show`? What is the order of the displayed elements? If several displays are possible, give all of them. Is the execution of `ConcFilter` deterministic? Why or why not?

(b) What happens when the following is executed?:

```
declare Out
{ConcFilter [5 1 2 4 0] fun {$ X} X>2 end Out}
{Delay 1000}
{Show Out}
```

What is displayed now by `Show`? If several displays are possible, give all of them.

(c) What happens when the following is executed?:

```
declare Out A
{ConcFilter [5 1 A 4 0] fun {$ X} X>2 end Out}
{Delay 1000}
{Show Out}
```

What is displayed now? What is the order of the displayed elements? If, after the above, `A` is bound to 3, then what happens to the list `Out`?

(d) If the input list has n elements, what is the complexity (in "big-oh" notation) of the number of operations of `ConcFilter`? Discuss the difference in execution time between `Filter` and `ConcFilter`.

6. *Semantics of Erlang's receive.* Section 5.7.3 shows how to translate Erlang's **`receive`** operation. The second form of this operation, with time-out, is the most general one. Let us take a closer look.

(a) Verify that the second form reduces to the third form when the time-out delay is zero.

(b) Verify that the second form reduces to the first form when the time-out delay approaches infinity.

(c) Another way to translate the second form would be to insert a unique message (using a name) after n ms. This requires some care to keep the unique message from appearing in the output stream. Write another translation of the second form that uses this technique. What are the advantages and disadvantages of this translation with respect to the one in the book?

7. *Erlang's receive as a control abstraction.* For this exercise, implement the Erlang `receive` operation, which is defined in section 5.7.3, as the following control abstraction:

- `C={Mailbox.new}` creates a new mailbox `C`.
- `{Mailbox.send C M}` sends message `M` to mailbox `C`.
- `{Mailbox.receive C [P1#E1 P2#E2 ... Pn#En] D}` performs a receive on mailbox `C` and returns the result. Each `Pi` is a one-argument boolean function **fun** `{$ M}` ⟨expr⟩ **end** that represents a pattern and its guard. The function returns **true** if and only if the pattern and guard succeed for message `M`. Each `Ei` is a one-argument function **fun** `{$ M}` ⟨expr⟩ **end** that represents a body. It is called when the message `M` is received successfully and its result is returned as the result of the `Mailbox.receive`. The last argument `D` represents the time-out delay. It is either the atom `infinity`, which says that there is no time-out, or the pair `T#E`, where `T` is an integer in milliseconds giving the delay and `E` is a one-argument function.

8. *Limitations of stream communication.* In this exercise, we explore the limits of stream communication in the nondeterministic concurrent model. Section 5.8.1 claims that we can partially solve the problem of putting server references in a data structure. How far can we go? Consider the following active object:

```
declare NS
thread {NameServer NS nil} end
```

where `NameServer` is defined as follows (together with the helper function `Replace`):

```
fun {Replace InL A OldS NewS}
   case InL
   of B#S|L1 andthen A=B then
      OldS=S
      A#NewS|L1
   [] E|L1 then
      E|{Replace L1 A OldS NewS}
   end
end
```

```
proc {NameServer NS L}
   case NS
   of register(A S)|NS1 then
      {NameServer NS1 A#S|L}
   [] getstream(A S)|NS1 then L1 OldS NewS in
      L1={Replace L A OldS NewS}
      thread {StreamMerger S NewS OldS} end
      {NameServer NS1 L1}
   [] nil then
      skip
   end
end
```

The `NameServer` object understands two commands. Assume that `S` is a server's input stream and `foo` is the name we wish to give the server. Given a reference `NS` to the name server's input stream, doing `NS=register(foo S)|NS1` will add the pair `foo#S` to its internal list `L`. Doing `NS=getstream(foo S1)|NS1` will create a fresh input stream, `S1`, for the server whose name is `foo`, which the name server has stored on its internal list `L`. Since `foo` is a constant, we can put it in a data structure. Therefore, it seems that we can put server references in a data structure, by defining a name server. Is this a practical solution? Why or why not? Think before reading the answer in the footnote.[11]

11. It's not possible to name the name server! It has to be added as an extra argument to all procedures. Eliminating this argument needs explicit state.

6 Explicit State

L'état c'est moi.
I am the state.
– Louis XIV (1638–1715)

If declarative programming is like a crystal, immutable and practically eternal, then stateful programming is organic: it grows and evolves.
– Inspired by *On Growth and Form*, D'Arcy Wentworth Thompson (1860–1948)

At first glance, explicit state is just a minor extension to declarative programming: in addition to depending on its arguments, the component's result also depends on an internal parameter, which is called its "state." This parameter gives the component a long-term memory, a "sense of history" if you will.[1] Without state, a component has only short-term memory, one that exists during a particular invocation of the component. State adds a potentially infinite branch to a finitely running program. By this we mean the following. A component that runs for a finite time can have only gathered a finite amount of information. If the component has state, then to this finite information can be added the information stored by the state. This "history" can be indefinitely long, since the component can have a memory that reaches far into the past.

Oliver Sacks has described the case of people with brain damage who only have a short-term memory [180]. They live in a continuous "present" with no memory beyond a few seconds into the past. The mechanism to "fix" short-term memories into the brain's long-term storage is broken. Strange it must be to live in this way. Perhaps these people use the external world as a kind of long-term memory? This analogy gives some idea of how important state can be for people. We will see that state is just as important for programming.

---

1. Chapter 5 also introduced a form of long-term memory, the port. It was used to define port objects, active entities with an internal memory. The main emphasis there was on concurrency. The emphasis of this chapter is on the expressiveness of state without concurrency.

Degrees of declarativeness

Stateless and stateful programming are often called declarative and imperative programming, respectively. The latter terms are not quite right, but tradition has kept their use. Declarative programming, taken literally, means programming with declarations, i.e., saying what is required and letting the system determine how to achieve it. Imperative programming, taken literally, means to give commands, i.e., to say how to do something. In this sense, the declarative model of chapter 2 is imperative too, because it defines sequences of commands.

The real problem is that "declarative" is not an absolute property, but a matter of degree. The language Fortran, developed in the late 1950s, was the first mainstream language that allowed writing arithmetic expressions in a syntax that resembles mathematical notation [14]. Compared to assembly language, this is definitely declarative! One could tell the computer that `I+J` is required without specifying where in memory to store `I` and `J` and what machine instructions are needed to retrieve and add them. In this relative sense, languages have been getting more declarative over the years. Fortran led to Algol-60 and structured programming [53, 54, 149], which led to Simula-67 and modern object-oriented programming languages [156, 170].[2]

This book sticks to the traditional usage of declarative as stateless and imperative as stateful. We call the computation model of chapter 2 "declarative," even though later models are arguably more declarative, since they are more expressive. We stick to the traditional usage because there is an important sense in which the declarative model really is declarative according to the literal meaning. This sense appears when we look at the declarative model from the viewpoint of logic and functional programming:

- A logic program can be "read" in two ways: either as a set of logical axioms (the what) or as a set of commands (the how). This is summarized by Robert Kowalski's famous equation: Algorithm = Logic + Control [119, 120]. The logical axioms, when supplemented by control flow information (either implicit or explicitly given by the programmer), give a program that can be run on a computer. Section 9.3.3 explains how this works for the declarative model.

- A functional program can also be "read" in two ways: either as a definition of a set of functions in the mathematical sense (the what) or as a set of commands for evaluating those functions (the how). As a set of commands, the definition is executed in a particular order. The two most popular orders are eager and lazy evaluation. When the order is known, the mathematical definition can be run on a computer. Section 4.9.2 explains how this works for the declarative model.

---

2. It is a remarkable fact that all three languages were designed in one ten-year period, from approximately 1957 to 1967. Considering that Lisp and Absys also date from this period and that Prolog is from 1972, we can speak of a veritable golden age of programming language design.

However, in practice, the declarative reading of a logic or functional program can lose much of its "what" aspect because it has to go into a lot of detail on the "how" (see the O'Keefe epigraph at the head of chapter 3). For example, a declarative definition of tree search has to give almost as many orders as an imperative definition. Nevertheless, declarative programming still has three crucial advantages. First, it is easier to build abstractions in a declarative setting, since declarative operations are by nature compositional. Second, declarative programs are easier to test, since it is enough to test single calls (give arguments and check the results). Testing stateful programs is harder because it involves testing sequences of calls (due to the internal history). Third, reasoning with declarative programming is simpler than with imperative programming (e.g., algebraic reasoning is possible).

Structure of the chapter

This chapter gives the basic ideas and techniques of using state in program design. The chapter is structured as follows:

- We first introduce and define the concept of explicit state in the first three sections.
  - Section 6.1 introduces explicit state: it defines the general notion of "state," which is independent of any computation model, and shows the different ways that the declarative and stateful models implement this notion.
  - Section 6.2 explains the basic principles of system design and why state is an essential part of system design. It also gives first definitions of component-based programming and object-oriented programming.
  - Section 6.3 precisely defines the stateful computation model.
- We then introduce data abstraction with state in the next two sections.
  - Section 6.4 explains all the different ways to build data abstractions, both with and without explicit state. It explains the two main styles of building data abstractions, the ADT style and the object style.
  - Section 6.5 gives an overview of some useful stateful ADTs, namely collections of items. It explains the trade-offs of expressiveness and efficiency in these ADTs.
- Section 6.6 shows how to reason with state. We present a technique, the method of invariants, that can make this reasoning almost as simple as reasoning about declarative programs, when it can be applied.
- Section 6.7 explains programming in the large, which is programming by a team of people. This extends the presentation of programming in the small given in section 3.9.
- Section 6.8 gives some case studies of programs that use state, to show more clearly the differences with declarative programs.
- Section 6.9 introduces some more advanced topics: the limitations of stateful

programming and how to extend memory management for external references.

Chapter 7 continues the discussion of state by developing a particularly useful programming style, namely object-oriented programming. Because of the wide applicability of object-oriented programming, we devote a full chapter to it.

6.1 What is state?

We have already programmed with state in the declarative model of chapter 3. For example, the accumulators of section 3.4.3 are state. So why do we need a whole chapter devoted to state? To see why, let us look closely at what state really is. In its simplest form, we can define state as follows:

> A *state* is a sequence of values in time that contains the intermediate results of a desired computation.

Let us examine the different ways that state can be present in a program.

6.1.1 Implicit (declarative) state

The sequence need only exist in the mind of the programmer. It does not need any support at all from the computation model. This kind of state is called implicit state or declarative state. As an example, look at the declarative function `SumList`:

```
fun {SumList Xs S}
   case Xs
   of nil then S
   [] X|Xr then {SumList Xr X+S}
   end
end
```

It is recursive. Each call has two arguments: `Xs`, the unexamined rest of the input list, and `S`, the sum of the examined part of the input list. While calculating the sum of a list, `SumList` calls itself many times. Let us take the pair `(Xs#S)` at each call, since it gives us all the information we need to know to characterize the call. For the call `{SumList [1 2 3 4] 0}` this gives the following sequence:

```
[1 2 3 4] # 0
[2 3 4] # 1
[3 4] # 3
[4] # 6
nil # 10
```

This sequence is a state. When looked at in this way, `SumList` calculates with state. Yet neither the program nor the computation model "knows" this. The state is completely in the mind of the programmer.

6.1.2 Explicit state

It can be useful for a function to have a state that lives across function calls and that is hidden from the callers. For example, we can extend `SumList` to count how many times it is called. There is no reason why the function's callers need to know about this extension. Even stronger: for modularity reasons the callers should not know about the extension. This cannot be programmed in the declarative model. The closest we can come is to add two arguments to `SumList` (an input and output count) and thread them across all the callers. To do it without additional arguments we need an explicit state:

> An *explicit state* in a procedure is a state whose lifetime extends over more than one procedure call without being present in the procedure's arguments.

Explicit state cannot be expressed in the declarative model. To have it, we extend the model with a kind of container that we call a cell. A cell has a name, an indefinite lifetime, and a content that can be changed. If the procedure knows the name, it can change the content. The declarative model extended with cells is called the stateful model. Unlike declarative state, explicit state is not just in the mind of the programmer. It is visible in both the program and the computation model. We can use a cell to add a long-term memory to `SumList`. For example, let us keep track of how many times it is called:

```
local
   C={NewCell 0}
in
   fun {SumList Xs S}
      C:=@C+1
      case Xs
      of nil then S
      [] X|Xr then {SumList Xr X+S}
      end
   end
   fun {SumCount} @C end
end
```

This is the same definition as before, except that we define a cell and update its content in `SumList`. We also add the function `SumCount` to make the state observable. Let us explain the new operations that act on the explicit state. `NewCell` creates a new cell with initial content 0. `@` gets the content and `:=` puts in a new content. If `SumCount` is not used, then this version of `SumList` cannot be distinguished from the previous version: it is called in the same way and gives the same results.[3]

3. The only differences are a minor slowdown and a minor increase in memory use. In almost all cases, these differences are irrelevant in practice.

The ability to have explicit state is very important. It removes the limits of declarative programming (see section 4.8). With explicit state, data abstractions gain tremendously in modularity since it is possible to encapsulate an explicit state inside them. The access to the state is limited according to the operations of the data abstraction. This idea is at the heart of object-oriented programming, a powerful programming style that is elaborated in chapter 7. This chapter and chapter 7 both explore the ramifications of explicit state.

6.2 State and system building

The principle of abstraction

As far as we know, the most successful system-building principle for intelligent beings with finite thinking abilities, such as human beings, is the principle of abstraction. Consider any system. It can be thought of as having two parts: a specification and an implementation. The specification is a contract, in a mathematical sense that is stronger than the legal sense. The contract defines how the system should behave. We say a system is correct if the actual behavior of the system is in accord with the contract. If the system behaves differently, then we say it fails.

The specification defines how the rest of the world interacts with the system, as seen from the outside. The implementation is how the system is constructed, as seen from the inside. The miraculous property of the distinction specification/implementation is that the specification is usually much simpler to understand than the implementation. One does not have to know how to build a watch in order to read time on it. To paraphrase evolutionist Richard Dawkins, it does not matter whether the watchmaker is blind or not, as long as the watch works.

This means that it is possible to build a system as a concentric series of layers. One can proceed step by step, building layer upon layer. At each layer, build an implementation that takes the next lower specification and provides the next higher one. It is not necessary to understand everything at once.

Systems that grow

How is this approach supported by declarative programming? With the declarative model of chapter 2, all that the system "knows" is on the outside, except for the fixed set of knowledge that it was born with. To be precise, because a procedure is stateless, all its knowledge, its "smarts," are in its arguments. The smarter the procedure gets, the "heavier" and more numerous the arguments get. Declarative programming is like an organism that keeps all its knowledge outside of itself, in its environment. Despite his claim to the contrary (see the epigraph at the head of this chapter) this was exactly the situation of Louis XIV: the state was not in his person but all around him, in 17th-century France.[4] We conclude that the principle of abstraction is not well supported by declarative programming, because we cannot put new knowledge inside a component.

Chapter 4 partly alleviated this problem by adding concurrency. Stream objects can accumulate internal knowledge in their internal arguments. Chapter 5 enhanced the expressive power dramatically by adding ports, which makes possible port objects. A port object has an identity and can be viewed from the outside as a stateful entity. But this requires concurrency. In this chapter, we add explicit state without concurrency. We shall see that this promotes a very different programming style than the concurrent component style of chapter 5. There is a total order among all operations in the system. This cements a strong dependency between all parts of the system. Later, in chapter 8, we add concurrency to remove this dependency. The model of that chapter is difficult to program in. Let us first see what we can do with state without concurrency.

6.2.1 System properties

What properties should a system have to best support the principle of abstraction? Here are three:

- *Encapsulation.* It should be possible to hide the internals of a part.
- *Compositionality.* It should be possible to combine parts to make a new part.
- *Instantiation/invocation.* It should be possible to create many instances of a part based on a single definition. These instances "plug" themselves into their environment (the rest of the system in which they will live) when they are created.

These properties need support from the programming language, e.g., lexical scoping supports encapsulation and higher-order programming supports instantiation. The properties do not require state; they can be used in declarative programming as well. For example, encapsulation is orthogonal to state. On the one hand, it is possible to use encapsulation in declarative programs without state. We have already used it many times, e.g., in higher-order programming and stream objects. On the other hand, it is also possible to use state without encapsulation, by defining the state globally so all components have free access to it.

Invariants

Encapsulation and explicit state are most useful when used together. Adding state to declarative programming makes reasoning about the program much harder, because the program's behavior depends on the state. For example, a procedure can do a side effect, i.e., it modifies state that is visible to the rest of the program.

4. To be fair to Louis, what he meant was that the decision-making power of the state was vested in his person.

Side effects make reasoning about the program extremely difficult. Bringing in encapsulation does much to make reasoning tractable again. This is because stateful systems can be designed so that a well-defined property, called an invariant, is always true when viewed from the outside. This makes reasoning about the system independent of reasoning about its environment. This partly gives us back one of the properties that makes declarative programming so attractive.

Invariants are only part of the story. An invariant just says that the component is not behaving incorrectly; it does not guarantee that the component is making progress toward some goal. For that, a second property is needed to mark the progress. This means that even with invariants, programming with state is not quite as simple as declarative programming. We find that a good rule of thumb for complex systems is to keep as many components as possible declarative. State should not be "smeared out" over many components. It should be concentrated in just a few carefully selected components.

6.2.2 Component-based programming

The three properties of encapsulation, compositionality, and instantiation define component-based programming (see section 6.7). A component specifies a program fragment with an inside and an outside, i.e., with a well-defined interface. The inside is hidden from the outside, except for what the interface permits. Components can be combined to make new components. Components can be instantiated, making a new instance that is linked into its environment. Components are a ubiquitous concept. We have already seen them in several guises:

- *Procedural abstraction.* We have seen a first example of components in the declarative computation model. The component is called a procedure definition and its instance is called a procedure invocation. Procedural abstraction underlies the more advanced component models that came later.
- *Functors* (compilation units). A particularly useful kind of component is a compilation unit, i.e., it can be compiled independently of other components. We call such components functors and their instances modules.
- *Concurrent components.* A system with independent, interacting entities can be seen as a graph of concurrent components that send each other messages.

In component-based programming, the natural way to extend a component is by using composition: build a new component that contains the original one. The new component offers a new functionality and uses the old component to implement the functionality.

We give a concrete example from our experience to show the usefulness of components. Component-based programming was an essential part of the Information Cities project, which did extensive multi-agent simulations using the Mozart system [173, 181]. The simulations were intended to model evolution and information flow in parts of the Internet. Different simulation engines (in a single process or distributed, with different forms of synchronization) were defined as reusable components with identical interfaces. Different agent behaviors were defined in the same way. This allowed rapidly setting up many different simulations and extending the simulator without having to recompile the system. The setup was done by a program, using the module manager provided by the System module `Module`. This is possible because components are values in the Oz language (see section 3.9.3).

6.2.3 Object-oriented programming

A popular set of techniques for stateful programming is called object-oriented programming. We devote the whole of chapter 7 to these techniques. Object-oriented programming is based on a particular way to do data abstraction called "objects." Objects and ADTs are fundamentally different. ADTs keep values and operations separate. Objects combine them together into a single entity called an "object" which we can invoke. The distinction between ADTs and objects is explained in section 6.4. Objects are important because they make it easy to use the powerful techniques of polymorphism and inheritance. Because polymorphism can be done in both component-based and object-oriented programming, we do not discuss it further here. Instead, we introduce inheritance, which is a new concept that is not part of component-based programming:

- *Inheritance.* It is possible to build a data abstraction in incremental fashion, as a small extension or modification of another data abstraction.

Incrementally built components are called classes and their instances are called objects. Inheritance is a way of structuring programs so that a new implementation extends an existing one.

The advantage of inheritance is that it factors the implementation to avoid redundancy. But inheritance is not an unmixed blessing. It implies that a component strongly depends on the components it inherits from. This dependency can be difficult to manage. Much of the literature on object-oriented design, e.g., on design patterns [66], focuses on the correct use of inheritance. Although component composition is less flexible than inheritance, it is much simpler to use. We recommend using it whenever possible and to use inheritance only when composition is insufficient (see chapter 7).

6.3 The declarative model with explicit state

One way to introduce state is to have concurrent components that run indefinitely and that can communicate with other components, like the stream objects of chapter 4 or the port objects of chapter 5. In this chapter we directly add explicit state to the declarative model. Unlike in the two previous chapters, the resulting model is still sequential. We will call it the stateful model.

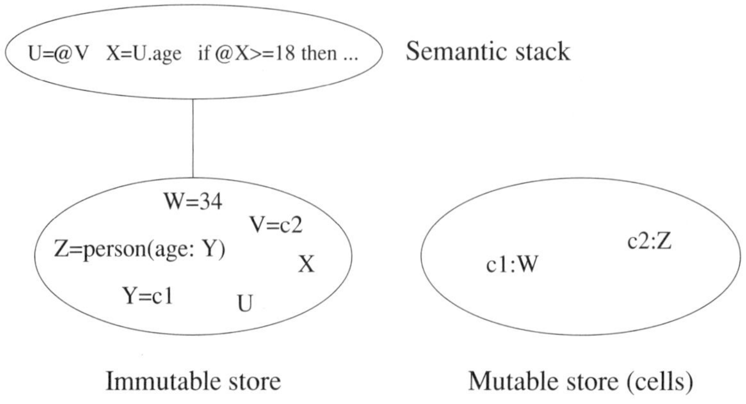

Figure 6.1: The declarative model with explicit state.

Explicit state is a pair of two language entities. The first entity is the state's identity and the second is the state's current content. There exists an operation that when given the state's identity returns the current content. This operation defines a system-wide mapping between state identities and all language entities. What makes it stateful is that the mapping can be modified. Interestingly, neither of the two language entities themselves is modified. It is only the mapping that changes.

6.3.1 Cells

We add explicit state as one new basic type to the computation model. We call the type a cell. A cell is a pair of a constant, which is a name value, and a reference into the single-assignment store. Because names are unforgeable, cells are an example of a secure ADT. The set of all cells lives in the mutable store. Figure 6.1 shows the resulting computation model. There are two stores: the immutable (single-assignment) store, which contains dataflow variables that can be bound to one value, and the mutable store, which contains pairs of names and references. Table 6.1 shows its kernel language. Compared to the declarative model, it adds just two new statements, the cell operations `NewCell` and `Exchange`. These operations are defined informally in table 6.2. For convenience, this table adds two more operations, `@` (access) and `:=` (assignment). These do not provide any new functionality since they can be defined in terms of `Exchange`. Using `C:=Y` as an expression has the effect of an `Exchange`: it gives the old value as the result.

Amazingly, adding cells with their two operations is enough to build all the wonderful concepts that state can provide. All the sophisticated concepts of objects, classes, and other data abstractions can be built with the declarative model extended with cells. Section 7.6.2 explains how to build classes and section 7.6.3 explains how to build objects. In practice, their semantics are defined in this way,

⟨s⟩ ::=	
skip	Empty statement
| ⟨s⟩$_1$ ⟨s⟩$_2$	Statement sequence
| **local** ⟨x⟩ **in** ⟨s⟩ **end**	Variable creation
| ⟨x⟩$_1$=⟨x⟩$_2$	Variable-variable binding
| ⟨x⟩=⟨v⟩	Value creation
| **if** ⟨x⟩ **then** ⟨s⟩$_1$ **else** ⟨s⟩$_2$ **end**	Conditional
| **case** ⟨x⟩ **of** ⟨pattern⟩ **then** ⟨s⟩$_1$ **else** ⟨s⟩$_2$ **end**	Pattern matching
| {⟨x⟩ ⟨y⟩$_1$ ··· ⟨y⟩$_n$}	Procedure application
| {NewName ⟨x⟩}	Name creation
| ⟨y⟩=!!⟨x⟩	Read-only view
| **try** ⟨s⟩$_1$ **catch** ⟨x⟩ **then** ⟨s⟩$_2$ **end**	Exception context
| **raise** ⟨x⟩ **end**	Raise exception
| {NewCell ⟨x⟩ ⟨y⟩}	**Cell creation**
| {Exchange ⟨x⟩ ⟨y⟩ ⟨z⟩}	**Cell exchange**

Table 6.1: The kernel language with explicit state.

Operation	Description
{NewCell X C}	Create a new cell C with initial content X.
{Exchange C X Y}	Atomically bind X with the old content of cell C and set Y to be the new content.
X=@C	Bind X to the current content of cell C.
C:=X	Set X to be the new content of cell C.
X=C:=Y	Another syntax for {Exchange C X Y}.

Table 6.2: Cell operations.

but the language has syntactic support to make them easy to use and the implementation has support to make them more efficient [85].

6.3.2 Semantics of cells

The semantics of cells is quite similar to the semantics of ports given in section 5.1.2. It is instructive to compare them. In similar manner to ports, we first add a mutable store. The same mutable store can hold both ports and cells. Then we define the operations `NewCell` and `Exchange` in terms of the mutable store.

Extension of execution state

Next to the single-assignment store σ and the trigger store τ, we add a new store μ called the mutable store. This store contains cells, which are pairs of the form $x : y$, where x and y are variables of the single-assignment store. The mutable store is initially empty. The semantics guarantees that x is always bound to a name value that represents a cell. On the other hand, y can be any partial value. The execution state becomes a triple (MST, σ, μ) (or a quadruple (MST, σ, μ, τ) if the trigger store is considered).

The `NewCell` *operation*

The semantic statement $(\{$`NewCell` $\langle$x$\rangle$ $\langle$y$\rangle\}, E)$ does the following:

- Create a fresh cell name n.
- Bind $E(\langle$y$\rangle)$ and n in the store.
- If the binding is successful, then add the pair $E(\langle$y$\rangle) : E(\langle$x$\rangle)$ to the mutable store μ.
- If the binding fails, then raise an error condition.

Observant readers will notice that this semantics is almost identical to that of ports. The principal difference is the type. Ports are identified by a port name and cells by a cell name. Because of the type, we can enforce that cells can only be used with `Exchange` and ports can only be used with `Send`.

The `Exchange` *operation*

The semantic statement $(\{$`Exchange` $\langle$x$\rangle$ $\langle$y$\rangle$ $\langle$z$\rangle\}, E)$ does the following:

- If the activation condition is true ($E(\langle$x$\rangle)$ is determined), then do the following actions:
  - If $E(\langle$x$\rangle)$ is not bound to the name of a cell, then raise an error condition.
  - If the mutable store contains $E(\langle$x$\rangle) : w$, then do the following actions:
    - Update the mutable store to be $E(\langle$x$\rangle) : E(\langle$z$\rangle)$.

  * Bind $E(\langle \mathsf{y} \rangle)$ and w in the store.

- If the activation condition is false, then suspend execution.

Memory management

Two modifications to memory management are needed because of the mutable store:

- Extending the definition of reachability: A variable y is reachable if the mutable store contains $x : y$ and x is reachable.
- Reclaiming cells: If a variable x becomes unreachable, and the mutable store contains the pair $x : y$, then remove this pair.

The same modifications are needed independent of whether the mutable store holds cells or ports.

6.3.3 Relation to declarative programming

In general, a stateful program is no longer declarative, since running the program several times with the same inputs can give different outputs depending on the internal state. It is possible, though, to write stateful programs that behave as if they were declarative, i.e., to write them so they satisfy the definition of a declarative operation. It is a good design goal to write stateful components so that they behave declaratively.

A simple example of a stateful program that behaves declaratively is the `SumList` function we gave earlier. Let us show a more interesting example, in which the state is used as an intimate part of the function's calculation. We define a list reversal function by using a cell:

```
fun {Reverse Xs}
   Rs={NewCell nil}
in
   for X in Xs do Rs := X|@Rs end
   @Rs
end
```

Since the cell is encapsulated inside the `Reverse`, there is no way to tell the difference between this implementation and a declarative implementation. It is often possible to take a declarative program and convert it to a stateful program with the same behavior by replacing the declarative state with an explicit state. The reverse direction is often possible as well. We leave it as an exercise for the reader to take any stateful implementation and convert it to a declarative implementation.

Another interesting example is memoization, in which a function remembers the results of previous calls so that future calls can be handled quicker. Chapter 10 gives an example using a simple graphical calendar display. It uses memoization to avoid redrawing the display unless it has changed.

6.3.4 Sharing and equality

By introducing cells we have extended the concept of equality. We have to distinguish the equality of cells from the equality of their contents. This leads to the concepts of sharing and token equality.

Sharing

Sharing, also known as aliasing, happens when two identifiers `X` and `Y` refer to the same cell. We say that the two identifiers are aliases of each other. Changing the content of `X` also changes the content of `Y`. For example, let us create a cell:

```
X={NewCell 0}
```

We can create a second reference `Y` to this cell:

```
declare Y in
Y=X
```

Changing the content of `Y` will change the content of `X`:

```
Y:=10
{Browse @X}
```

This displays 10. In general, when a cell's content is changed, then all the cell's aliases see the changed content. When reasoning about a program, the programmer has to be careful to keep track of aliases. This can be difficult, since they can easily be spread out through the whole program. This problem can be made manageable by encapsulating the state, i.e., using it in just a small part of a program and guaranteeing that it cannot escape from there. This is one of the key reasons why data abstraction is an especially good idea when used together with explicit state.

Token equality and structure equality

Two values are equal if they have the same structure. For example:

```
X=person(age:25 name:"George")
Y=person(age:25 name:"George")
{Browse X==Y}
```

This displays **`true`**. We call this structure equality. It is the equality we have used up to now. With cells, though, we introduce a new notion of equality called token equality. Two cells are not equal if they have the same content, rather they are equal if they are the same cell! For example, let us create two cells:

```
X={NewCell 10}
Y={NewCell 10}
```

These are different cells with different identities. The following comparison:

```
{Browse X==Y}
```

displays **false**. It is logical that the cells are not equal, since changing the content of one cell will not change the content of the other. However, our two cells happen to have the same content:

```
{Browse @X==@Y}
```

This displays **true**. This is a pure coincidence; it does not have to stay true throughout the program. We conclude by remarking that aliases do have the same identities. The following example:

```
X={NewCell 10}
Y=X
{Browse X==Y}
```

displays **true** because `X` and `Y` are aliases, i.e., they refer to the same cell.

6.4 Data abstraction

A data abstraction is a way of using data in abstract fashion, i.e., we can use the data without having to deal with its implementation. A data abstraction consists of a set of instances that can be used according to certain rules, called its interface. We will sometimes use the term "type" loosely to refer to a data abstraction. Using data abstractions has many advantages over using the implementation directly: it can be much simpler (since the implementation can be complicated), reasoning about the data can be much simpler (since it has its own properties), and the system can ensure that the data is used in the right way (since we cannot touch the implementation except through the interface).

Section 3.7 showed one particular kind of data abstraction, namely an abstract data type, or ADT: a set of values together with a set of operations on these values. We defined a stack ADT with stack values and push and pop operations. ADTs are not the only way to deal abstractly with data. Now that we have added explicit state to the model, we can present a more complete set of techniques for doing data abstraction.

6.4.1 Eight ways to organize a data abstraction

A data abstraction with a given functionality can be organized in many different ways. For example, in section 3.7 we saw that a simple data abstraction like a stack can be either open or secure. Here we introduce two more axes, bundling and explicit state. Bundling is a fundamental distinction that was originally observed in 1975 by John Reynolds [46, 77, 177]. Each axis has two choices, which gives eight ways in all to organize a data abstraction. Some are rarely used. Others are common. But each has its advantages and disadvantages. We briefly explain each axis and give some examples. In the examples later on in the book, we choose whichever of the eight ways that is appropriate in each case.

Openness and security

A data abstraction is secure if its encapsulation is enforced by the language. Otherwise it is open. For an open abstraction, the encapsulation should be enforced by programmer discipline. Strictly speaking, if encapsulation is not enforced by the language then a data abstraction is no longer an abstraction. We will still call it an abstraction because it can still be used like an abstraction. The only difference is who is responsible for enforcing the encapsulation, the language or the programmer.

Bundling

A data abstraction is unbundled if it defines two kinds of entities, called value and operation. Values are passed as arguments to operations and returned as results. An unbundled data abstraction is usually called an abstract data type, or ADT. An unbundled data abstraction can be made secure by using a "key." The key is an authorization to access the internal data of an abstract value (and update it, if the value is stateful). All ADT operations know the key. The rest of the program does not know the key. The key can be a name value, which is an unforgeable constant (see appendix B.2).

The best known language based on ADTs is probably CLU, designed and implemented in the 1970s by Barbara Liskov and her students [131]. CLU has the distinction of being the first implemented language with linguistic support for the ADT style.

A data abstraction is bundled if it defines just one kind of entity, called object, that combines the notion of value and operation. A bundled data abstraction is sometimes called a procedural data abstraction, or PDA. An operation is done by invoking the object and informing it which operation it should do. This is sometimes called "sending a message to the object," but this gives the wrong impression since there is no message sending in the sense of chapter 5. An object invocation is synchronous, like a procedure's. It returns only when it is completely finished.

The object style has become immensely popular because it has important advantages with respect to modularity and program structure. These advantages are due to the ease with which the object style supports polymorphism and inheritance. Polymorphism is explained later in this section. Inheritance is explained in chapter 7, which focuses completely on the object style.

Explicit state

A data abstraction is stateful if it uses explicit state. Otherwise it is known as stateless or declarative. Chapter 3 gives some stateless examples: a declarative stack, queue, and dictionary. The present chapter gives some stateful examples: Section 6.5 has a stateful dictionary and array. All these examples are in the ADT style.

The decision to make an abstraction stateful or stateless depends on concerns of

Open, declarative, and unbundled	*The usual open declarative style, as used in Prolog and Scheme*
Secure, declarative, and unbundled	*The ADT style*
Secure, declarative, and bundled	*The PDA style with declarative objects*
Secure, stateful, and bundled	*The PDA style with stateful objects, as used in Smalltalk and Java*
Secure, stateful, and unbundled	*The ADT style with stateful "values"*

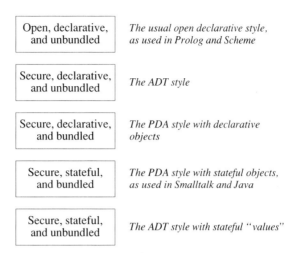

Figure 6.2: Five ways to package a stack.

modularity, conciseness, and ease of reasoning. We remark that "values" in a data abstraction, as defined above, can be stateful with this definition. This is a slight abuse of terminology, since the basic values we define in this book are all stateless.

6.4.2 Variations on a stack

Let us take the ⟨Stack T⟩ type from section 3.7 and see how to adapt it to some of the eight possibilities. We give five useful possibilities. We start from the simplest one, the open declarative version, and then use it to build four different secure versions. Figure 6.2 summarizes them. Figure 6.3 gives a graphic illustration of the four secure versions and their differences. In this figure, the boxes with thick borders labeled "`Pop`" are procedures that can be invoked. Incoming arrows are inputs and outgoing arrows are outputs. The boxes with thin borders and keyholes are wrapped data structures that are the inputs and outputs of the `Pop` procedures. The wrapped data structures can only be unwrapped inside the `Pop` procedures. Two of the `Pop` procedures (the second and third) themselves encapsulate data using lexical scoping.

Open declarative stack

We set the stage for these secure versions by first giving the basic stack functionality in the simplest way:

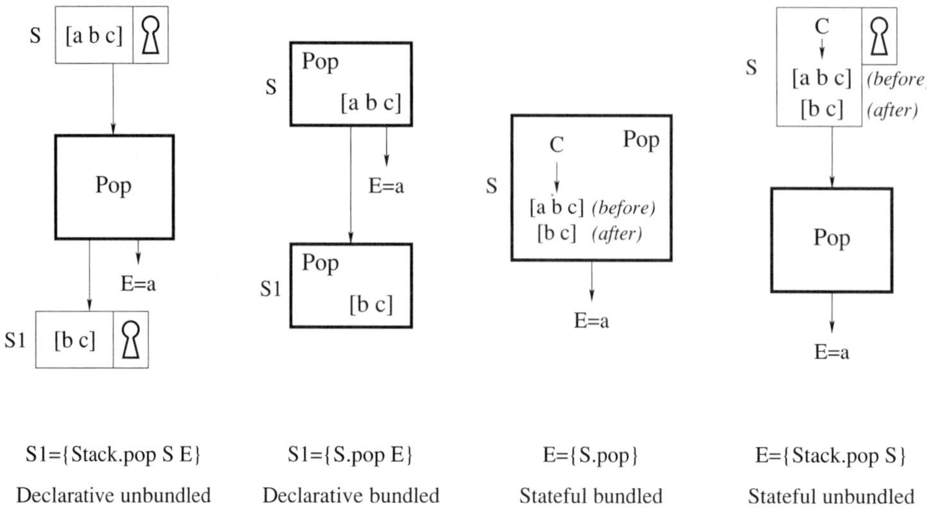

Figure 6.3: Four versions of a secure stack.

```
declare
local
   fun {NewStack} nil end
   fun {Push S E} E|S end
   fun {Pop S ?E} case S of X|S1 then E=X S1 end end
   fun {IsEmpty S} S==nil end
in
   Stack=stack(new:NewStack push:Push pop:Pop isEmpty:IsEmpty)
end
```

`Stack` is a module that groups together the stack operations.[5] This version is open, declarative, and unbundled.

Secure declarative unbundled stack

We make this version secure by using a wrapper/unwrapper pair, as seen in section 3.7:

5. Note that `Stack` is a global variable that needs a **`declare`**, even though it is inside the **`local`** statement.

```
declare
local Wrap Unwrap
   {NewWrapper Wrap Unwrap}
   fun {NewStack} {Wrap nil} end
   fun {Push S E} {Wrap E|{Unwrap S}} end
   fun {Pop S ?E}
      case {Unwrap S} of X|S1 then E=X {Wrap S1} end end
   fun {IsEmpty S} {Unwrap S}==nil end
in
   Stack=stack(new:NewStack push:Push pop:Pop isEmpty:IsEmpty)
end
```

This version is secure, declarative, and unbundled. The stack is unwrapped when entering an ADT operation and wrapped when the operation exits. Outside the ADT, the stack is always wrapped.

Secure declarative bundled stack

Let us now make a bundled version of the declarative stack. The idea is to hide the stack inside the operations, so that it cannot be separated from them. Here is how it is programmed:

```
local
   fun {StackObject S}
      fun {Push E} {StackObject E|S} end
      fun {Pop ?E}
         case S of X|S1 then E=X {StackObject S1} end end
      fun {IsEmpty} S==nil end
   in stack(push:Push pop:Pop isEmpty:IsEmpty) end
in
   fun {NewStack} {StackObject nil} end
end
```

This version is secure, declarative, and bundled. It demonstrates the remarkable fact that making a data abstraction secure needs neither explicit state nor names. It can be done with higher-order programming alone. The function `StackObject` takes a list `S` and returns the record of procedure values `stack(push:Push pop:Pop isEmpty:IsEmpty)`, in which `S` is hidden by lexical scoping. This record represents the object and its fields are the methods. This is very different from the declarative unbundled case, where the record represents a module and its fields are ADT operations. Here is an example use:

```
declare S1 S2 S3 E in
S1={NewStack}
{Browse {S1.isEmpty}}
S2={S1.push 23}
S3={S2.pop E}
{Browse E}
```

Because this version is both bundled and secure, we can consider it as a declarative form of object-oriented programming. The stack `S1` is a declarative object.

Secure stateful bundled stack

Now let us construct a stateful version of the stack. Calling `NewStack` creates a new stack object:

```
fun {NewStack}
   C={NewCell nil}
   proc {Push E} C:=E|@C end
   fun {Pop} case @C of X|S1 then C:=S1 X end end
   fun {IsEmpty} @C==nil end
in
   stack(push:Push pop:Pop isEmpty:IsEmpty)
end
```

This version is secure, stateful, and bundled. In like manner to the declarative bundled version, the object is represented by a record of procedure values. This version provides the basic functionality of object-oriented programming, namely a group of operations ("methods") with a hidden internal state. The result of calling `NewStack` is an object instance with the three methods: `push`, `pop`, and `isEmpty`.

Secure stateful bundled stack (with procedure dispatching)

This is another way to implement a secure stateful bundled stack. It uses a **case** statement inside a procedure instead of a record:

```
fun {NewStack}
   C={NewCell nil}
   proc {Push E} C:=E|@C end
   fun {Pop} case @C of X|S1 then C:=S1 X end end
   fun {IsEmpty} @C==nil end
in
   proc {$ Msg}
      case Msg
      of push(X) then {Push X}
      [] pop(?E) then E={Pop}
      [] isEmpty(?B) then B={IsEmpty}
      end
   end
end
```

This is called procedure dispatching as opposed to the previous version which uses record dispatching. With procedure dispatching, an object `S` is invoked as `{S push(X)}`. With record dispatching, the same invocation is written `{S.push X}`. Procedure dispatching will be used throughout chapter 7.

Secure stateful unbundled stack

It is possible to combine wrapping with cells to make a version that is secure, stateful, and unbundled. This style is little used in object-oriented programming, but deserves to be more widely known. It does not use higher-order programming directly. Each operation has one stack argument instead of two for the declarative version:

```
declare
local Wrap Unwrap
   {NewWrapper Wrap Unwrap}
   fun {NewStack} {Wrap {NewCell nil}} end
   proc {Push S E} C={Unwrap S} in C:=E|@C end
   fun {Pop S}
      C={Unwrap S} in case @C of X|S1 then C:=S1 X end end
   fun {IsEmpty S} @{Unwrap S}==nil end
in
   Stack=stack(new:NewStack push:Push pop:Pop isEmpty:IsEmpty)
end
```

In this version, `NewStack` only needs `Wrap` and the other functions only need `Unwrap`. Like with the declarative unbundled version, we group the four operations together in a module.

6.4.3 Polymorphism

In everyday language, polymorphism is the ability of an entity to take on many forms. In the context of data abstraction, we say an operation is *polymorphic* if it works correctly for arguments of different types.

Polymorphism is important for organizing programs so they are maintainable. In particular, it allows a program to properly apportion responsibility among its component parts [19]. A single responsibility should not be spread out over several components. It should rather be concentrated in one place if possible.

Consider the following analogy: a patient goes to see a medical doctor who is a specialist in the domain of the patient's illness. The patient asks the doctor for a cure. Depending on the doctor's specialty, this may mean doing different things (such as prescribing medicine or performing surgery). In a computer program, the patient object invokes the operation `perform_cure` of the doctor object. Polymorphism means that the doctor object can be of many different types, as long as it understands the `perform_cure` operation. The patient object does not know how to cure itself; it should not *have* to know. The doctor object understands the `perform_cure` operation and will do the right thing.

All the organizations we gave before for data abstractions can provide polymorphism. The basic idea is simple. Assume a program works correctly with one particular data abstraction. Then it can potentially work with any other data abstraction that has the same interface. The real issue here is correctness: is the program still correct with the other data abstraction? It will be, if the other data abstraction satisfies the same mathematical properties that the program assumes the original one satisfies. That is, the reasoning that showed correctness for the original abstraction should also apply for the other one.

The object style has an advantage over the ADT style in that polymorphism is particularly easy to express. Although polymorphism can be expressed in the ADT style, it is more cumbersome since it requires first-class modules. The ADT style has a different advantage: it gives more freedom to make efficient implementations. Let us give an example to make these differences clear. We first define a Collection type and implement it in both ADT and object styles. We add a new operation, `union`, to the Collection type and extend both implementations.

An example: a Collection type

Say we have a Collection type with three operations: a `put` to add an element, a `get` to extract an element, and an `isEmpty` to test whether the collection is empty. We start the example by implementing the Collection type in both the ADT and object styles. We implement the collection as an ADT using the stateful unbundled stack:

```
local Wrap Unwrap
   {NewWrapper Wrap Unwrap}
   fun {NewCollection} {Wrap {Stack.new}} end
   proc {Put C X} S={Unwrap C} in {Stack.push S X} end
   fun {Get C} S={Unwrap C} in {Stack.pop S} end
   fun {IsEmpty C} {Stack.isEmpty {Unwrap C}} end
in
   Collection=collection(new:NewCollection put:Put get:Get
                         isEmpty:IsEmpty)
end
```

Here is an example use:

```
C={Collection.new}
{Collection.put C 1}
{Collection.put C 2}
{Browse {Collection.get C}}
{Browse {Collection.get C}}
```

Now let us implement the collection as an object using the stateful bundled stack:

```
fun {NewCollection}
   S={NewStack}
   proc {Put X} {S.put X} end
   fun {Get X} {S.pop} end
   fun {IsEmpty} {S.isEmpty} end
in
   collection(put:Put get:Pop isEmpty:IsEmpty)
end
```

Here is an example use, doing the same things we did with the ADT:

```
C={NewCollection}
{C.put 1}
{C.put 2}
{Browse {C.get}}
{Browse {C.get}}
```

Adding a `union` *operation in the ADT case*

We would like to extend the Collection type with a `union` operation that takes all elements of one collection and adds them to another collection. In ADT style this is called as `{Collection.union C1 C2}`, where all elements of `C2` are added into `C1`, leaving `C2` empty. To implement `union`, let us first introduce a control abstraction:

```
proc {DoUntil BF S}
   if {BF} then skip else {S} {DoUntil BF S} end
end
```

This executes `{S}` as long as `{BF}` returns **`false`**. With `DoUntil`, we can implement the new Collection type as follows (as an extension of the original implementation):

```
local Wrap Unwrap
   ...
   proc {Union C1 C2}
   S1={Unwrap C1} S2={Unwrap C2} in
      {DoUntil fun {$} {Stack.isEmpty S2} end
       proc {$} {Stack.push S1 {Stack.pop S2}} end}
   end
in
   Collection=collection(... union:Union)
end
```

Note that this implementation uses both internal representations of `C1` and `C2`, i.e., both stacks. Here is an example use:

```
C1={Collection.new} C2={Collection.new}
for I in [1 2 3] do {Collection.put C1 I} end
for I in [4 5 6] do {Collection.put C2 I} end
{Collection.union C1 C2}
{Browse {Collection.isEmpty C2}}
{DoUntil fun {$} {Collection.isEmpty C1} end
 proc {$} {Browse {Collection.get C1}} end}
```

We can do a second implementation that only uses the external interfaces of `C1` and `C2`:

```
local Wrap Unwrap
   ...
   proc {Union C1 C2}
      {DoUntil fun {$} {Collection.isEmpty C2} end
       proc {$} {Collection.put C1 {Collection.get C2}} end}
   end
in
   Collection=collection(... union:Union)
end
```

In summary, we have the choice of whether or not to use the internal representation of each collection argument. This gives us the freedom to make a more efficient implementation, with the caveat that if we use the internal representation we lose polymorphism.

Adding a `union` *operation in the object case*

Let us now add a `union` operation to the Collection object. In object style this is called as `{C1 union(C2)}`. The implementation is as follows:

```
fun {NewCollection}
   S1={NewStack}
   ...
   proc {Union C2}
      {DoUntil C2.isEmpty
       proc {$} {S1.push {C2.get}} end}
   end
in
   collection(... union:Union)
end
```

This implementation uses the internal representation of `C1` but the external interface of `C2`. This is a crucial difference with the ADT style! Can we make an implementation in object style that uses both internal representations, as we did in the ADT case? The simple answer is no, not without breaking the encapsulation of the object `C2`.

To complete the object case, we show how to do an object implementation that only uses external interfaces:

```
fun {NewCollection}
   ...
   proc {Union C2}
      {DoUntil C2.isEmpty
       proc {$} {This.put {C2.get}} end}
   end
   This=collection(... union:Union)
in
   This
end
```

Note that the object `C1` refers to itself through the variable `This`.

Discussion

How do we choose between the ADT and object styles? Let us compare them:

- The ADT style can be more efficient because it allows accessing both internal representations. Using an external interface can be less efficient since the interface might not implement all the operations we need.
- Sometimes the ADT style is the only one that works. Say we are defining an integer type and we want to define the addition of two integers. If no other integer operations are defined, then we really need to access the internal representations. For example, the representation might be in a binary form that we can add by using a machine instruction. This justifies why common object-oriented languages such as Java use the ADT style for the primitive operations of basic types such as

integers.

- The object style provides polymorphism "for free." Say we define a second collection type (with an object `D`) that has the same interface as the first. Then the two collection types can interoperate even though their implementations are independent. In short, `{C union(D)}` works without writing any new code![6]

- The object style is not limited to sequential objects. In particular, stream objects (see chapter 4), port objects (see chapter 5), and active objects (which we will see in section 7.8) are all objects as we define them in this section. All provide polymorphism in the same way as sequential objects.

- The ADT style can provide polymorphism if the language has first-class modules. Say we define a second collection type as a module `Collection2`. The implementation of `union` then has to make sure that `C2` always uses an operation from `Collection2`. We can do this by adding `Collection2` as an argument to the union operation, so that it is called as `{Union C1 Collection2 C2}`. This gives the following definition:

```
proc {Union C1 Collection2 C2}
   {DoUntil fun {$} {Collection2.isEmpty C2} end
    proc {$} {Collection.put C1 {Collection2.get C2}} end}
end
Collection=collection(... union:Union)
```

This technique is used often in languages with first-class modules, such as Erlang.

- If we use the ADT style without first-class modules, then we must write new code to get the types to interoperate. We have to write a `union` operation that knows about *both* internal representations. If we have three or more collection types, it gets even messier: we have to implement all pairwise combinations.

Object-oriented languages use the object style by default, which makes them polymorphic by default. This is one of the key advantages of object-oriented programming, which we will explore further in chapter 7. ADT languages can also be polymorphic, but only if they have first-class modules.

Other kinds of polymorphism

The kind of polymorphism discussed in this section is called *universal* polymorphism. There is a second concept that is also considered as a kind of polymorphism, namely *ad-hoc* polymorphism [33]. In ad-hoc polymorphism, different code is executed for arguments of different types. In universal polymorphism, the same code is executed for all admissible argument types. An example of ad-hoc polymorphism is operator overloading, where the same operator can represent many different functions. For example, the plus operator + is overloaded in many lan-

6. This may seem miraculous. It works because the `C` implementation of `union` only calls the external interface of `D`. Think it over!

guages. The compiler chooses the appropriate plus function depending on the types of the arguments (e.g., integers or floats).

6.4.4 Parameter passing

The operations of a data abstraction can have arguments and results. Many different mechanisms have been devised to pass the arguments and results between a calling program and an abstraction. Let us briefly go over the most prominent ones. For each mechanism, we give an example in a Pascal-like syntax and we code the example in the stateful model of this chapter. This coding can be seen as a semantic definition of the mechanism. We use Pascal because of its simplicity. Java is a more popular language, but explaining its more elaborate syntax is not appropriate for this section. Section 7.7 gives an example of Java syntax.

Call by reference

The identity of a language entity is passed to the procedure. The procedure can then use this language entity freely. This is the primitive mechanism used by the computation models of the book for all language entities including dataflow variables and cells.

Imperative languages often mean something slightly different by call by reference. They assume that the reference is stored in a cell local to the procedure. In our terminology, this is a call by value where the reference is considered as a value (see below). When studying a language that has call by reference, we recommend looking carefully at the language definition to see exactly what is meant.

Call by variable

This is a special case of call by reference. The identity of a cell is passed to the procedure. Here is an example:

```
procedure sqr(var a:integer);
begin
   a:=a*a
end
var c:integer;
c:=25;
sqr(c);
browse(c);
```

We code this example as follows:

```
proc {Sqr A}
   A:=@A*@A
end
local
   C={NewCell 0}
in
   C:=25
   {Sqr C}
   {Browse @C}
end
```

For the call `{Sqr C}`, the `A` inside `Sqr` is a synonym of the `C` outside.

Call by value

A value is passed to the procedure and put into a cell local to the procedure. The implementation is free either to copy the value or to pass a reference, as long as the procedure cannot change the value in the calling environment. Here is an example:

```
procedure sqr(a:integer);
begin
   a:=a+1;
   browse(a*a)
end;
sqr(25);
```

We code this example as follows:

```
proc {Sqr D}
   A={NewCell D}
in
   A:=@A+1
   {Browse @A*@A}
end
{Sqr 25}
```

The cell `A` is initialized with the argument of `Sqr`. The Java language uses call by value for both values and object references. This is explained in section 7.7.

Call by value-result

This is a modification of call by variable. When the procedure is called, the content of a cell (i.e., a mutable variable) is put into another mutable variable local to the procedure. When the procedure returns, the content of the latter is put into the former. Here is an example:

```
procedure sqr(inout a:integer);
begin
   a:=a*a
end
var c:integer;
c:=25;
sqr(c);
browse(c);
```

This uses the keyword "inout" to indicate call by value-result, as is used in the Ada language. We code this example as follows:

```
proc {Sqr A}
   D={NewCell @A}
in
   D:=@D*@D
   A:=@D
end
local
   C={NewCell 0}
in
   C:=25
   {Sqr C}
   {Browse @C}
end
```

There are two mutable variables: one inside `Sqr` (namely `D`) and one outside (namely `C`). Upon entering `Sqr`, `D` is assigned the content of `C`. Upon exiting, `C` is assigned the content of `D`. During the execution of `Sqr`, modifications to `D` are invisible from the outside.

Call by name

This mechanism is the most complex. It creates a function for each argument. Calling the function returns the name of a cell, i.e., the address of a mutable variable. Each time the argument is needed, the function is called. A function used in this way is called a thunk.[7] Thunks were originally invented for the implementation of Algol 60. Here is an example:

7. This is the original meaning of thunk. The term thunk is also used in a more general way to mean any lexically scoped closure.

```
procedure sqr(callbyname a:integer);
begin
   a:=a*a
end;
var c:integer;
c:=25;
sqr(c);
browse(c);
```

This uses the keyword "`callbyname`" to indicate call by name. We code this example as follows:

```
proc {Sqr A}
   {A}:=@{A}*@{A}
end
local C={NewCell 0} in
   C:=25
   {Sqr fun {$} C end}
   {Browse @C}
end
```

The argument `A` is a function that when evaluated returns the name of a mutable variable. The function is evaluated each time the argument is needed. Call by name can give unintuitive results if array indices are used in the argument (see Exercises, section 6.10).

Call by need

This is a modification of call by name in which the function is called at most once. Its result is stored and used for subsequent evaluations. Here is one way to code call by need for the call by name example:

```
proc {Sqr A}
   B={A}
in
   B:=@B*@B
end
local C={NewCell 0} in
   C:=25
   {Sqr fun {$} C end}
   {Browse @C}
end
```

The argument `A` is evaluated when the result is needed. The local variable `B` stores its result. If the argument is needed again, then `B` is used. This avoids reevaluating the function. In the `Sqr` example this is easy to implement since the result is clearly needed three times. If it is not clear from inspection whether the result is needed, then lazy evaluation can be used to implement call by need directly (see Exercises, section 6.10).

Call by need is exactly the same concept as lazy evaluation. The term "call by need" is more often used in a language with state, where the result of the function evaluation can be the name of a cell (a mutable variable). Call by name is lazy evaluation without memoization. The result of the function evaluation is not stored, so it is evaluated again each time it is needed.

Discussion

Which of these mechanisms (if any) is "right" or "best"? This has been the subject of much discussion (see, e.g., [134]). The goal of the kernel language approach is to factorize programming languages into a small set of programmer-significant concepts. For parameter passing, this justifies using call by reference as the primitive mechanism which underlies the other mechanisms. Unlike the others, call by reference does not depend on additional concepts such as cells or procedure values. It has a simple formal semantics and is efficient to implement. On the other hand, this does not mean that call by reference is always the right mechanism for programs. Other parameter-passing mechanisms can be coded by combining call by reference with cells and procedure values. Many languages offer these mechanisms as linguistic abstractions.

6.4.5 Revocable capabilities

It is sometimes necessary to control the security of a data abstraction. Let us show how to use explicit state to build revocable capabilities. This is an example of a data abstraction that controls the security of other data abstractions. Chapter 3 introduced the concept of a capability, which gives its owner an irrevocable right to do something. Sometimes we would like to give a revocable right instead, i.e., a right that can be removed. We can implement this with explicit state. Without loss of generality, we assume the capability is represented as a one-argument procedure.[8] Here is a generic procedure that takes any capability and returns a revocable version of that capability:

```
proc {Revocable Obj ?R ?RObj}
   C={NewCell Obj}
in
   proc {R}
      C:=proc {$ M} raise revokedError end end
   end
   proc {RObj M}
      {@C M}
   end
end
```

Given any one-argument procedure `Obj`, the procedure returns a revoker `R` and a revocable version `RObj`. At first, `RObj` forwards all its messages to `Obj`. After executing `{R}`, calling `RObj` invariably raises a `revokedError` exception. Here is an

8. This is an important case because it covers the object system of chapter 7.

example:

```
fun {NewCollector}
   Lst={NewCell nil}
in
   proc {$ M}
      case M
      of add(X) then T in {Exchange Lst T X|T}
      [] get(L) then L={Reverse @Lst}
      end
   end
end

declare C R in
C={Revocable {NewCollector} R}
```

The function `NewCollector` creates an instance of a data abstraction that we call a collector. It has two operations, `add` and `get`. With `add`, it can collect items into a list in the order that they are collected. With `get`, the current value of the list can be retrieved at any time. We make the collector revocable. When it has finished its job, the collector can be made inoperable by calling `R`.

6.5 Stateful collections

An important kind of ADT is the collection, which groups together a set of partial values into one compound entity. There are different kinds of collection depending on what operations are provided. Along one axis we distinguish indexed collections and unindexed collections, depending on whether or not there is rapid access to individual elements (through an index). Along another axis we distinguish extensible or inextensible collections, depending on whether the number of elements is variable or fixed. We give a brief overview of these different kinds of collections, starting with indexed collections.

6.5.1 Indexed collections

In the context of declarative programming, we have already seen two kinds of indexed collections, namely tuples and records. We can add state to these two data types, allowing them to be updated in certain ways. The stateful versions of tuples and records are called arrays and dictionaries.

In all, this gives four different kinds of indexed collections, each with its particular trade-offs between expressiveness and efficiency (see figure 6.4). With such a proliferation, how does one choose which to use? Section 6.5.2 compares the four and gives advice on how to choose among them.

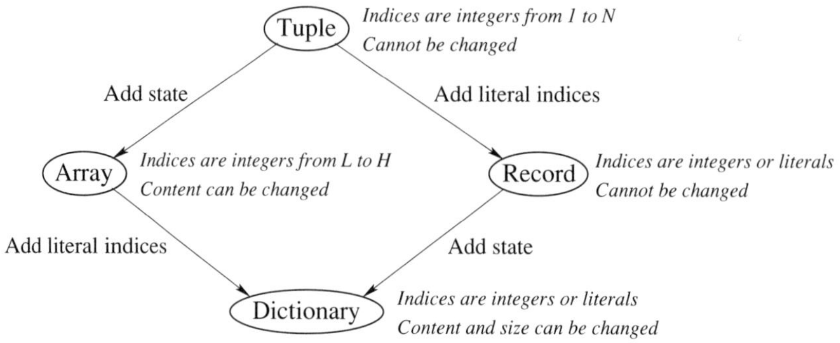

Figure 6.4: Different varieties of indexed collections.

Arrays

An array is a mapping from integers to partial values. The domain is a set of consecutive integers from a lower bound to an upper bound. The domain is given when the array is declared and cannot be changed afterward. The range of the mapping can be changed. Both accessing and changing an array element are done in constant time. If you need to change the domain or if the domain is not known when you declare the array, then you should use a dictionary instead of an array. The Mozart system provides arrays as a predefined ADT in the `Array` module. Here are some of the more common operations:

- `A={NewArray L H I}` returns a new array with indices from `L` to `H`, inclusive, all initialized to `I`.
- `{Array.put A I X}` puts in `A` the mapping of `I` to `X`. This can also be written `A.I:=X`.
- `X={Array.get A I}` returns from `A` the mapping of `I`. This can also be written as `X=A.I`.
- `L={Array.low A}` returns the lower index bound of `A`.
- `H={Array.high A}` returns the higher index bound of `A`.
- `R={Array.toRecord L A}` returns a record with label `L` and the same items as the array `A`. The record is a tuple only if the lower index bound is 1.
- `A={Tuple.toArray T}` returns an array with bounds between 1 and `{Width T}`, where the elements of the array are the elements of `T`.
- `A2={Array.clone A}` returns a new array with exactly the same indices and contents as `A`.

There is a close relationship between arrays and tuples. Each of them maps one of a set of consecutive integers to partial values. The essential difference is that tuples are stateless and arrays are stateful. A tuple has fixed contents for its fields, whereas in an array the contents can be changed. It is possible to create a completely new tuple differing only on one field from an existing tuple, using the `Adjoin` and `AdjoinAt` operations. These take time and memory proportional to the number of features in the tuple. The `put` operation of an array is a constant-time operation, and therefore much more efficient.

Dictionaries

A dictionary is a mapping from simple constants (atoms, names, or integers) to partial values. Both the domain and the range of the mapping can be changed. An item is a pair of one simple constant and a partial value. Items can be accessed, changed, added, or removed during execution. All operations are efficient: accessing and changing are done in constant time and adding/removal are done in amortized constant-time. By amortized constant-time we mean that a sequence of n add or removal operations is done in total time proportional to n, when n becomes large. This means that each individual operation may not be constant-time, since occasionally the dictionary has to be reorganized internally, but reorganizations are relatively rare. The active memory needed by a dictionary is always proportional to the number of items in the mapping. Other than system memory, there are no limits to the number of fields in the mapping. Section 3.7.3 gives some ballpark measurements comparing stateful dictionaries to declarative dictionaries. The Mozart system provides dictionaries as a predefined ADT in the `Dictionary` module. Here are some of the more common operations:

- `D={NewDictionary}` returns a new empty dictionary.
- `{Dictionary.put D LI X}` puts in `D` the mapping of `LI` to `X`. This can also be written `D.LI:=X`.
- `X={Dictionary.get D LI}` returns from `D` the mapping of `LI`. This can also be written `X=D.LI`, i.e., with the same notation as for records.
- `X={Dictionary.condGet D LI Y}` returns from `D` the mapping of `LI`, if it exists. Otherwise, it returns `Y`. This is a minor variation of `get`, but it turns out to be extremely useful in practice.
- `{Dictionary.remove D LI}` removes from `D` the mapping of `LI`.
- `{Dictionary.member D LI B}` tests in `D` whether `LI` exists, and binds `B` to the boolean result.
- `R={Dictionary.toRecord L D}` returns a record with label `L` and the same items as the dictionary `D`. The record is a "snapshot" of the dictionary's state at a given moment in time.
- `D={Record.toDictionary R}` returns a dictionary with the same items as the record `R`. This operation and the previous one are useful for saving and restoring dictionary state in pickles.

■ `D2={Dictionary.clone D}` returns a new dictionary with exactly the same keys and items as `D`.

There is a close relationship between dictionaries and records. Each of them maps simple constants to partial values. The essential difference is that records are stateless and dictionaries are stateful. A record has a fixed set of fields and their contents, whereas in a dictionary the set of fields and their contents can be changed. As for tuples, new records can be created with the `Adjoin` and `AdjoinAt` operations, but these take time proportional to the number of record features. The `put` operation of a dictionary is a constant-time operation, and therefore much more efficient.

6.5.2 Choosing an indexed collection

The different indexed collections have different trade-offs in possible operations, memory use, and execution time. It is not always easy to decide which collection type is the best one in any given situation. We examine the differences between these collections to make this decision easier.

We have seen four types of indexed collections: tuples, records, arrays, and dictionaries. All provide constant-time access to their elements by means of indices, which can be calculated at run time. But apart from this commonality they are quite different. Figure 6.4 gives a hierarchy that shows how the four types are related to each other. Let us compare them:

■ *Tuples.* Tuples are the most restrictive, but they are fastest and require least memory. Their indices are consecutive positive integers from 1 to a maximum `N` which is specified when the tuple is created. They can be used as arrays when the contents do not have to be changed. Accessing a tuple field is extremely efficient because the fields are stored consecutively.

■ *Records.* Records are more flexible than tuples because the indices can be any literals (atoms or names) and integers. The integers do not have to be consecutive. The record type, i.e., the label and arity (set of indices), is specified when the record is created. Accessing record fields is nearly as efficient as accessing tuple fields. To guarantee this, record fields are stored consecutively, as for tuples. This implies that creating a new record type (i.e., one for which no record exists yet) is much more expensive than creating a new tuple type. A hash table is created when the record type is created. The hash table maps each index to its offset in the record. To avoid having to use the hash table on each access, the offset is cached in the access instruction. Creating new records of an already-existing type is as inexpensive as creating a tuple.

■ *Arrays.* Arrays are more flexible than tuples because the content of each field can be changed. Accessing an array field is extremely efficient because the fields are stored consecutively. The indices are consecutive integers from any lower bound to any upper bound. The bounds are specified when the array is created. The bounds

```
fun {NewExtensibleArray L H Init}
   A={NewCell {NewArray L H Init}}#Init
   proc {CheckOverflow I}
      Arr=@(A.1)
      Low={Array.low Arr}
      High={Array.high Arr}
   in
      if I>High then
         High2=Low+{Max I 2*(High-Low)}
         Arr2={NewArray Low High2 A.2}
      in
         for K in Low..High do Arr2.K:=Arr.K end
         (A.1):=Arr2
      end
   end
   proc {Put I X}
      {CheckOverflow I}
      @(A.1).I:=X
   end
   fun {Get I}
      {CheckOverflow I}
      @(A.1).I
   end
in extArray(get:Get put:Put)
end
```

Figure 6.5: Extensible array (stateful implementation).

cannot be changed.

- *Dictionaries.* Dictionaries are the most general. They combine the flexibility of arrays and records. The indices can be any literals and integers and the content of each field can be changed. Dictionaries are created empty. No indices need to be specified. Indices can be added and removed efficiently, in amortized constant time. On the other hand, dictionaries take more memory than the other data types (by a constant factor) and have slower access time (also by a constant factor). Dictionaries are implemented as dynamic hash tables.

Each of these types defines a particular trade-off that is sometimes the right one. Throughout the examples in the book, we select the right indexed collection type whenever we need one.

6.5.3 Other collections

Unindexed collections

Indexed collections are not always the best choice. Sometimes it is better to use an unindexed collection. We have seen two unindexed collections: lists and streams.

Both are declarative data types that collect elements in a linear sequence. The sequence can be traversed from front to back. Any number of traversals can be done simultaneously on the same list or stream. Lists are of finite, fixed length. Streams are also called incomplete lists or partial lists; their tails are unbound variables. This means they can always be extended, i.e., they are potentially unbounded. The stream is one of the most efficient extensible collections, in both memory use and execution time. Extending a stream is more efficient than adding a new index to a dictionary and much more efficient than creating a new record type.

Streams are useful for representing ordered sequences of messages. This is an especially appropriate representation since the message receiver will automatically synchronize on the arrival of new messages. This is the basis of a powerful declarative programming style called stream programming (see chapter 4) and its generalization to message passing (see chapter 5).

Extensible arrays

Up to now we have seen two extensible collections: streams and dictionaries. Streams are efficiently extensible but elements cannot be accessed efficiently (linear search is needed). Dictionaries are more costly to extend (but only by a constant factor) and they can be accessed in constant time. A third extensible collection is the extensible array. This is an array that is resized upon overflow. It has the advantages of constant-time access and significantly less memory usage than dictionaries (by a constant factor). The resize operation is amortized constant-time, since it is only done when an index is encountered that is greater than the current size.

Extensible arrays are not provided as a predefined type by Mozart. We can implement them using standard arrays and cells. Figure 6.5 shows one possible version, which allows an array to increase in size but not decrease. The call `{NewExtensibleArray L H X}` returns a secure extensible array `A` with initial bounds `L` and `H` and initial content `X`. The operation `{A.put I X}` puts `X` at index `I`. The operation `{A.get I}` returns the content at index `I`. Both operations extend the array whenever they encounter an index that is out of bounds. The resize operation always at least doubles the array's size. This guarantees that the amortized cost of the resize operation is constant. For increased efficiency, one could add "unsafe" `put` and `get` operations that do no bounds checking. In that case, the responsibility would be on the programmer to ensure that indices remain in bounds.

6.6 Reasoning with state

Programs that use state in a haphazard way are very difficult to understand. For example, if the state is visible throughout the whole program, then it can be assigned anywhere. The only way to reason is to consider the whole program at once. Practically speaking, this is impossible for big programs. This section introduces a method, called invariant assertions, with which state can be tamed. We show how to use the method for programs that have both stateful and declarative parts. The declarative part appears as logical expressions inside the assertions. We also explain the role of abstraction (deriving new proof rules for linguistic abstractions) and how to take dataflow execution into account.

The technique of invariant assertions is usually called axiomatic semantics, following Floyd, Hoare, and Dijkstra, who initially developed it in the 1960s and 1970s. The correctness rules were called "axioms" and the terminology has stuck ever since. Manna gave an early but still interesting presentation [136].

6.6.1 Invariant assertions

The method of invariant assertions allows independent reasoning about parts of programs. This gets back one of the strongest properties of declarative programming. However, this property is achieved at the price of a rigorous organization of the program. The basic idea is to organize the program as a hierarchy of data abstractions. Each abstraction can use other abstractions in its implementation. This gives a directed graph of data abstractions.

A hierarchical organization of the program is good for more than just reasoning. We will see it many times in the book. We find it again in the component-based programming of Section 6.7 and the object-oriented programming of chapter 7.

Each data abstraction is specified with a series of invariant assertions, also called invariants. An invariant is a logical sentence that defines a relation among the abstraction's arguments and its internal state. Each operation of the abstraction assumes that some invariant is true and, when it completes, assures the truth of another invariant. The operation's implementation guarantees this. In this way, using invariants decouples an abstraction's implementation from its use. We can reason about each separately.

To realize this idea, we use the concept of assertion. An assertion is a logical sentence that is attached to a given point in the program, between two instructions. An assertion can be considered as a kind of boolean expression (we will see later exactly how it differs from boolean expressions in the computation model). Assertions can contain variable and cell identifiers from the program as well as variables and quantifiers that do not occur in the program, but are used just for expressing a particular relation. For now, consider a quantifier as a symbol, such as $\forall$ ("for all") and $\exists$ ("there exists"), that is used to express assertions that hold true over all values of variables in a domain, not just for one value.

Each operation O_i of the data abstraction is specified by giving two assertions A_i and B_i. The specification states that, if A_i is true just before O_i, then when O_i completes B_i will be true. We denote this by:

$$\{ A_i \}\ O_i\ \{ B_i \}$$

This specification is sometimes called a partial correctness assertion. It is partial because it is only valid if O_i terminates normally. A_i is called the precondition and

B_i is called the postcondition. The specification of the complete abstraction then consists of partial correctness assertions for each of its operations.

6.6.2 An example

Now that we have some inkling of how to proceed, let us give an example of how to specify a simple data abstraction and prove it correct. We use the stateful stack abstraction we introduced before. To keep the presentation simple, we will introduce the notation we need gradually during the example. The notation is not complicated; it is just a way of writing boolean expressions that allows us to express what we need to. Section 6.6.3 defines the notation precisely.

Specifying the data abstraction

We begin by specifying the data abstraction independent of its implementation. The first operation creates a stateful bundled instance of a stack:

```
Stack={NewStack}
```

The function `NewStack` creates a new cell c, which is hidden inside the stack by lexical scoping. It returns a record of three operations, `Push`, `Pop`, and `IsEmpty`, which is bound to `Stack`. So we can say that the following is a specification of `NewStack`:

{ **true** }
`Stack={NewStack}`
{ $@c =$ `nil` $\wedge$ `Stack` $=$ `ops(push:Push pop:Pop isEmpty:IsEmpty)` }

The precondition is **`true`**, which means that there are no special conditions. The notation $@c$ denotes the content of the cell c.

This specification is incomplete since it does not define what the references `Push`, `Pop`, and `IsEmpty` mean. Let us define each of them separately. We start with `Push`. Executing `{Stack.push X}` is an operation that pushes `X` on the stack. We specify this as follows:

{ $@c =$ `S` }
`{Stack.push X}`
{ $@c =$ `X|S` }

The specifications of `NewStack` and `Stack.push` both mention the internal cell c. This is reasonable when proving correctness of the stack, but is not reasonable when using the stack, since we want the internal representation to be hidden. We can avoid this by introducing a predicate *stackContent* with following definition:

stackContent(`Stack`, `S`) $\equiv$ $@c =$ `S`

where c is the internal cell corresponding to `Stack`. This hides any mention of the internal cell from programs using the stack. Then the specifications of `NewStack` and `Stack.push` become:

```
{ true }
Stack={NewStack}
{ stackContent(Stack,nil) ∧
  Stack = ops(push:Push pop:Pop isEmpty:IsEmpty) }
```

```
{ stackContent(Stack,S) }
{Stack.push X}
{ stackContent(Stack,X|S) }
```

We continue with the specifications of `Stack.pop` and `Stack.isEmpty`:

```
{ stackContent(Stack,X|S) }
Y={Stack.pop}
{ stackContent(Stack,S) ∧ Y = X }
```

```
{ stackContent(Stack,S) }
X={Stack.isEmpty}
{ stackContent(Stack,S) ∧ X = (S==nil) }
```

The full specification of the stack consists of these four partial correctness assertions. These assertions do not say what happens if a stack operation raises an exception. We discuss this later.

Proving the data abstraction correct

The specification we gave above is how the stack should behave. But does our implementation actually behave in this way? To verify this, we have to check whether each partial correctness assertion is correct for our implementation. Here is the implementation (to make things easier, we have unnested the nested statements):

```
fun {NewStack}
   C={NewCell nil}
   proc {Push X} S in S=@C C:=X|S end
   fun {Pop} S1 in
      S1=@C
      case S1 of X|S then C:=S X end
   end
   fun {IsEmpty} S in S=@C S==nil end
in
   ops(push:Push pop:Pop isEmpty:IsEmpty)
end
```

With respect to this implementation, we have to verify each of the four partial correctness assertions that make up the specification of the stack. Let us focus on the specification of the `Push` operation. We leave the other three verifications up to the reader. The definition of `Push` is:

```
proc {Push X}
S in
   S=@C
   C:=X|S
end
```

The precondition is $\{\ stackContent(\texttt{Stack}, s)\ \}$, which we expand to $\{\ \texttt{@C} = s\ \}$, where `C` refers to the stack's internal cell. This means we have to prove:

$\{\ \texttt{@C} = s\ \}$
`S=@C`
`C:=X|S`
$\{\ \texttt{@C} = \texttt{X|}s\ \}$

The stack abstraction uses the cell abstraction in its implementation. To continue the proof, we therefore need to know the specifications of the cell operations `@` and `:=`. The specification of `@` is

$\{\ P\ \}$
$\langle \mathsf{y} \rangle = \texttt{@}\langle \mathsf{x} \rangle$
$\{\ P \wedge \langle \mathsf{y} \rangle = \texttt{@}\langle \mathsf{x} \rangle\ \}$

where $\langle \mathsf{y} \rangle$ is an identifier, $\langle \mathsf{x} \rangle$ is an identifier bound to a cell, and P is an assertion. The specification of `:=` is

$\{\ P(\langle \mathsf{exp} \rangle)\ \}$
$\langle \mathsf{x} \rangle \texttt{:=} \langle \mathsf{exp} \rangle$
$\{\ P(\texttt{@}\langle \mathsf{x} \rangle)\ \}$

where $\langle \mathsf{x} \rangle$ is an identifier bound to a cell, $P(\texttt{@}\langle \mathsf{x} \rangle)$ is an assertion that contains $\texttt{@}\langle \mathsf{x} \rangle$, and $\langle \mathsf{exp} \rangle$ is an expression that is allowed in an assertion. These specifications are also called proof rules, since they are used as building blocks in a correctness proof. When we apply each rule we are free to choose $\langle \mathsf{x} \rangle$, $\langle \mathsf{y} \rangle$, P, and $\langle \mathsf{exp} \rangle$ to be what we need.

Let us apply the proof rules to the definition of `Push`. We start with the assignment statement and work our way backward: given the postcondition, we determine the precondition. (With assignment, it is often easier to reason in the backward direction.) In our case, the postcondition is $\texttt{@C} = \texttt{X|}s$. Matching this to $P(\texttt{@}\langle \mathsf{x} \rangle)$, we see that $\langle \mathsf{x} \rangle$ is the cell `C` and $P(\texttt{@C}) \equiv \texttt{@C} = \texttt{X|}s$. Using the rule for `:=`, we replace `@C` by `X|S`, giving $\texttt{X|S} = \texttt{X|}s$ as the precondition.

Now let us reason forward from the cell access. The precondition is $\texttt{@C} = s$. From the proof rule, we see that the postcondition is $(\texttt{@C} = s \wedge \texttt{S} = \texttt{@C})$. Bringing the two parts together gives

$\{\ \texttt{@C} = s\ \}$
`S=@C`
$\{\ \texttt{@C} = s \wedge \texttt{S} = \texttt{@C}\ \}$
$\{\ \texttt{X|S} = \texttt{X|}s\ \}$
`C:=X|S`
$\{\ \texttt{@C} = \texttt{X|}s\ \}$

This is a valid proof because of two reasons. First, it strictly respects the proof rules for `@` and `:=`. Second, $(\texttt{@C} = s \wedge \texttt{S} = \texttt{@C})$ implies $(\texttt{X|S} = \texttt{X|}s)$.

6.6.3 Assertions

An assertion $\langle \mathsf{ass} \rangle$ is a boolean expression that is attached to a particular place in a program, which we call a program point. The boolean expression is very similar to boolean expressions in the computation model. There are some differences because assertions are mathematical expressions used for reasoning, not program fragments. An assertion can contain identifiers ⟨x⟩, partial values x, and cell contents @⟨x⟩ (with the operator @). For example, we used the assertion @C $=$ X | s when reasoning about the stack data abstraction. An assertion can also contain quantifiers and their dummy variables. Finally, it can contain mathematical functions. These can correspond directly to functions written in the declarative model.

To evaluate an assertion it has to be attached to a program point. Program points are characterized by the environment that exists there. Evaluating an assertion at a program point means evaluating using this environment. We assume that all dataflow variables are sufficiently bound so that the evaluation gives **true** or **false**.

We use the notations $\wedge$ for logical conjunction (and), $\vee$ for logical disjunction (or), and $\neg$ for logical negation (not). We use the quantifiers *for all* ($\forall$) and *there exists* ($\exists$):

$\forall x$.⟨type⟩: ⟨ass⟩	⟨ass⟩ is true when x has any value of type ⟨type⟩
$\exists x$.⟨type⟩: ⟨ass⟩	⟨ass⟩ is true for at least one value x of type ⟨type⟩

In each of these quantified expressions, ⟨type⟩ is a legal type of the declarative model, as defined in section 2.3.2.

The reasoning techniques we introduce here can be used in all stateful languages. In many of these languages, e.g., C++ and Java, it is clear from the declaration whether an identifier refers to a mutable variable (a cell or attribute) or a value (i.e., a constant). Since there is no ambiguity, the @ symbol can safely be left out for them. In our model, we keep the @ because we can distinguish between the name of a cell (C) and its content (@C).

6.6.4 Proof rules

For each statement S in the kernel language, we have a proof rule that shows all possible correct forms of $\{\ A\ \}\ S\ \{\ B\ \}$. This proof rule is just a specification of S. We can prove the correctness of the rule by using the operational semantics of the kernel language. Let us see what the rules are for the stateful kernel language.

Binding

We have already shown one rule for binding, in the case ⟨y⟩ $=$ @⟨x⟩, where the right-hand side is the content of a cell. The general form of a binding is ⟨x⟩ $=$ ⟨exp⟩, where ⟨exp⟩ is a declarative expression that evaluates to a partial value. The expression may contain cell accesses (calls to @). This gives the following proof rule:

$$\{\ P\ \}\ \langle \mathsf{x} \rangle = \langle \mathsf{exp} \rangle\ \{\ P \wedge \langle \mathsf{x} \rangle = \langle \mathsf{exp} \rangle\ \}$$

where P is an assertion.

Assignment

The following proof rule holds for assignment:

$$\{\ P(\langle\mathsf{exp}\rangle)\ \}\ \langle\mathsf{x}\rangle\,\texttt{:=}\,\langle\mathsf{exp}\rangle\ \{\ P(\texttt{@}\langle\mathsf{x}\rangle)\ \}$$

where $\langle\mathsf{x}\rangle$ refers to a cell, $P(\texttt{@}\langle\mathsf{x}\rangle)$ is an assertion that contains $\texttt{@}\langle\mathsf{x}\rangle$, and $\langle\mathsf{exp}\rangle$ is a declarative expression.

Conditional (`if` statement)

The **`if`** statement has the form:

```
if ⟨x⟩ then ⟨stmt⟩1 else ⟨stmt⟩2 end
```

The behavior depends on whether $\langle\mathsf{x}\rangle$ is bound to **`true`** or **`false`**. If we know:

$\{\ P \wedge \langle\mathsf{x}\rangle = \texttt{true}\ \}\ \langle\mathsf{stmt}\rangle_1\ \{\ Q\ \}$

and also:

$\{\ P \wedge \langle\mathsf{x}\rangle = \texttt{false}\ \}\ \langle\mathsf{stmt}\rangle_2\ \{\ Q\ \}$

then we can conclude:

$\{\ P\ \}\ \texttt{if}\ \langle\mathsf{x}\rangle\ \texttt{then}\ \langle\mathsf{stmt}\rangle_1\ \texttt{else}\ \langle\mathsf{stmt}\rangle_2\ \texttt{end}\ \{\ Q\ \}.$

Here P and Q are assertions and $\langle\mathsf{stmt}\rangle_1$ and $\langle\mathsf{stmt}\rangle_2$ are statements in the kernel language. We summarize this rule with the following notation:

$$\frac{\begin{array}{c}\{\ P \wedge \langle\mathsf{x}\rangle = \texttt{true}\ \}\ \langle\mathsf{stmt}\rangle_1\ \{\ Q\ \}\\ \{\ P \wedge \langle\mathsf{x}\rangle = \texttt{false}\ \}\ \langle\mathsf{stmt}\rangle_2\ \{\ Q\ \}\end{array}}{\{\ P\ \}\ \texttt{if}\ \langle\mathsf{x}\rangle\ \texttt{then}\ \langle\mathsf{stmt}\rangle_1\ \texttt{else}\ \langle\mathsf{stmt}\rangle_2\ \texttt{end}\ \{\ Q\ \}}$$

In this notation, the premises are above the horizontal line and the conclusion is below it. To use the rule, we first have to prove the premises.

Procedure without external references

Assume the procedure has the following form:

```
proc {⟨p⟩ ⟨x⟩1 ... ⟨x⟩n}
   ⟨stmt⟩
end
```

where the only external references of $\langle\mathsf{stmt}\rangle$ are $\{\langle\mathsf{x}\rangle_1, \ldots, \langle\mathsf{x}\rangle_n\}$. Then the following rule holds:

$$\frac{\{\ P(\,\overline{\langle\mathsf{x}\rangle}\,)\ \}\ \langle\mathsf{stmt}\rangle\ \{\ Q(\,\overline{\langle\mathsf{x}\rangle}\,)\ \}}{\{\ P(\,\overline{\langle\mathsf{y}\rangle}\,)\ \}\ \{\langle\mathsf{p}\rangle\ \langle\mathsf{y}\rangle_1 \cdots \langle\mathsf{y}\rangle_n\}\ \{\ Q(\,\overline{\langle\mathsf{y}\rangle}\,)\ \}}$$

where P and Q are assertions and the notation $\overline{\langle \mathsf{x} \rangle}$ means $\langle \mathsf{x} \rangle_1, \ldots, \langle \mathsf{x} \rangle_n$.

Procedure with external references

Assume the procedure has the following form:

```
proc {⟨p⟩ ⟨x⟩1 ... ⟨x⟩n}
   ⟨stmt⟩
end
```

where the external references of ⟨stmt⟩ are $\{\langle \mathsf{x} \rangle_1, \ldots, \langle \mathsf{x} \rangle_n, \langle \mathsf{z} \rangle_1, \ldots, \langle \mathsf{z} \rangle_k\}$. Then the following rule holds:

$$\frac{\{\ P(\ \overline{\langle \mathsf{x} \rangle},\ \overline{\langle \mathsf{z} \rangle}\ )\ \}\ \langle \mathsf{stmt} \rangle\ \{\ Q(\ \overline{\langle \mathsf{x} \rangle},\ \overline{\langle \mathsf{z} \rangle}\ )\ \}}{\{\ P(\ \overline{\langle \mathsf{y} \rangle},\ \overline{\langle \mathsf{z} \rangle}\ )\ \}\ \{\langle \mathsf{p} \rangle\ \langle \mathsf{y} \rangle_1 \cdots \langle \mathsf{y} \rangle_n\}\ \{\ Q(\ \overline{\langle \mathsf{y} \rangle},\ \overline{\langle \mathsf{z} \rangle}\ )\ \}}$$

where P and Q are assertions.

While loops

The previous rules are sufficient to reason about programs that use recursion to do looping. For stateful loops it is convenient to add another basic operation: the **while** loop. Since we can define the **while** loop in terms of the kernel language, it does not add any new expressiveness. Let us therefore define the **while** loop as a linguistic abstraction. We introduce the new syntax:

```
while ⟨expr⟩ do ⟨stmt⟩ end
```

We define the semantics of the **while** loop by translating it into simpler operations:

```
{While fun {$} ⟨expr⟩ end proc {$} ⟨stmt⟩ end}

proc {While Expr Stmt}
   if {Expr} then {Stmt} {While Expr Stmt} end
end
```

Let us add a proof rule specifically for the **while** loop:

$$\frac{\{\ P \wedge \langle \mathsf{expr} \rangle\ \}\ \langle \mathsf{stmt} \rangle\ \{\ P\ \}}{\{\ P\ \}\ \textbf{while}\ \langle \mathsf{expr} \rangle\ \textbf{do}\ \langle \mathsf{stmt} \rangle\ \textbf{end}\ \{\ P \wedge \neg \langle \mathsf{expr} \rangle\ \}}$$

We can prove that the rule is correct by using the definition of the **while** loop and the method of invariant assertions. It is usually easier to use this rule than to reason directly with recursive procedures.

For loops

In section 3.6.3 we saw another loop construct, the **for** loop. In its simplest form, this loops over integers:

```
for ⟨x⟩ in ⟨y⟩..⟨z⟩ do ⟨stmt⟩ end
```

This is also a linguistic abstraction, which we define as follows:

```
{For ⟨y⟩ ⟨z⟩ proc {$ ⟨x⟩} ⟨stmt⟩ end}

proc {For I H Stmt}
   if I=<H then {Stmt I} {For I+1 H Stmt} else skip end
end
```

We add a proof rule specifically for the **for** loop:

$$\frac{\forall i.\langle \mathsf{y}\rangle \le i \le \langle \mathsf{z}\rangle : \{\ P_{i-1} \wedge \langle \mathsf{x}\rangle = i\ \}\ \langle \mathsf{stmt}\rangle\ \{\ P_i\ \}}{\{\ P_{\langle \mathsf{y}\rangle -1}\ \}\ \mathbf{for}\ \langle \mathsf{x}\rangle\ \mathbf{in}\ \langle \mathsf{y}\rangle\,..\,\langle \mathsf{z}\rangle\ \mathbf{do}\ \langle \mathsf{stmt}\rangle\ \mathbf{end}\ \{\ P_{\langle \mathsf{z}\rangle}\ \}}$$

Watch out for the initial index of P! Because a **for** loop starts with $\langle \mathsf{y}\rangle$, the initial index of P has to be $\langle \mathsf{y}\rangle - 1$, which expresses that we have not yet started the loop. Just as for the **while** loop, we can prove that this rule is correct by using the definition of the **for** loop. Let us see how this rule works with a simple example. Consider the following code which sums the elements of an array:

```
local C={NewCell 0} in
   for I in 1..10 do C:=@C+A.I end
end
```

where `A` is an array with indices from 1 to 10. Let us choose an invariant:

$$P_i \equiv \texttt{@C} = \sum_{j=1}^{i} \texttt{A}_j$$

where $\texttt{A}_j$ is the j-th element of `A`. This invariant simply defines an intermediate result of the loop calculation. With this invariant we can prove the premise of the **for** rule:

$\{\ \texttt{@C} = \sum_{j=1}^{i-1} \texttt{A}_j \wedge \texttt{I} = i\ \}$
`C:=@C+A.I`
$\{\ \texttt{@C} = \sum_{j=1}^{i} \texttt{A}_j\ \}$

This follows immediately from the assignment rule. Since P_0 is clearly true just before the loop, it follows from the **for** rule that P_{10} is true. Therefore `C` contains the sum of all array elements.

Reasoning at higher levels of abstraction

The **while** and **for** loops are examples of reasoning at a higher level of abstraction than the kernel language. For each loop, we defined the syntax and its translation into the kernel language, and then gave a proof rule. The idea is to verify the proof rule once and for all and then to use it as often as we like. This approach, defining new concepts and their proof rules, is the way to go for practical reasoning about stateful programs. Always staying at the kernel language level is much too verbose for all but toy programs.

Aliasing

The proof rules given above are correct if there is no aliasing. They need to be modified in obvious ways if aliasing can occur. For example, assume that `C` and `D` both reference the same cell and consider the assignment `C:=@C+1`. Say the postcondition is `@C` $= 5 \wedge$ `@D` $= 5 \wedge$ `C` $=$ `D`. The standard proof rule lets us calculate the precondition by replacing `@C` by `@C` $+ 1$. This gives an incorrect result because it does not take into account that `D` is aliased to `C`. The proof rule can be corrected by doing the replacement for `@D` as well.

6.6.5 Normal termination

Partial correctness reasoning does not say anything about whether or not a program terminates normally. It just says, if a program terminates normally, then such and such is true. This makes reasoning simple, but it is only part of the story. We also have to prove termination. There are three ways that a program can fail to terminate normally:

- Execution goes into an infinite loop. This is a programmer error due to the calculation not making progress toward its goal.
- Execution blocks because a dataflow variable is not sufficiently bound inside an operation. This is a programmer error due to overlooking a calculation or a deadlock situation.
- Execution raises an exception because of an error. The exception is an abnormal exit. In this section we consider only one kind of error, a type error, but similar reasoning can be done for other kinds of errors.

Let us see how to handle each case.

Progress reasoning

Each time there is a loop, there is the danger that it will not terminate. To show that a loop terminates, it suffices to show that there is a function that is non-negative and that always decreases upon successive iterations.

Suspension reasoning

It suffices to show that all variables are sufficiently bound before they are used. For each use of the variable, tracing back all possible execution paths should always come across a binding.

Type checking

To show that there are no type errors, it suffices to show that all variables are of the correct type. This is called type checking. Other kinds of errors need other kinds of checking.

6.7 Program design in the large

Good software is good in the large *and* in the small, in its high-level architecture and in its low-level details.
– *Object-Oriented Software Construction*, 2nd ed., Bertrand Meyer (1997)

An efficient and a successful administration manifests itself equally in small as in great matters.
– Memorandum, August 8, 1943, Winston Churchill (1874–1965)

Programming in the large is programming by a team of people. It involves all aspects of software development that require communication and coordination between people. Managing a team so they work together efficiently is difficult in any area—witness the difficulty of coaching a football team. For programming, it is especially difficult since programs are generally quite unforgiving of small errors. Programs demand an exactness which is hard for human beings to satisfy. Programming in the large is often called software engineering.

This section builds on the introduction to programming in the small (see section 3.9). We explain how to develop software in small teams. We do not explain what to do for larger teams (with hundreds or thousands of members)—that is a topic for another book.

6.7.1 Design methodology

Many things, both true and false, have been published about the correct design methodology for programming in the large. Much of the existing literature consists of extrapolation based on limited experiments, since rigorous validation is so difficult. To validate a new idea, several otherwise identical teams would have to work in identical circumstances. This has rarely been done and we do not attempt it either.

This section summarizes the lessons we have learned from our own systems-building experience. We have designed and built several large software systems [101, 148, 219]. We have thought quite a bit about how to do good program design in a team and looked at how other successful developer teams work. We have tried to isolate the truly useful principles from the others.

Managing the team

The first and most important task is to make sure that the team works together in a coordinated fashion. There are three ideas for achieving this:

1. Compartmentalize the responsibility of each person. For example, each component can be assigned to one person, who is responsible for it. We find that responsibilities should respect component boundaries and not overlap. This avoids interminable discussions about who should have fixed a problem.

2. In contrast to responsibility, knowledge should be freely exchanged, not compartmentalized. Team members should frequently exchange information about different parts of the system. Ideally, there should be no team member who is indispensable. All major changes to the system should be discussed among knowledgeable team members before being implemented. This greatly improves the system's quality. It is important also that a component's owner have the last word on how the component should be changed. Junior team members should be apprenticed to more senior members to learn about the system. Junior members become experienced by being given specific tasks to do, which they do in as independent a fashion as possible. This is important for the system's longevity.

3. Carefully document each component interface, since it is also the interface between the component's owner and other team members. Documentation is especially important, much more so than for programming in the small. Good documentation is a pillar of stability that can be consulted by all team members.

Software development methodology

There are many ways to organize software development. The techniques of top-down, bottom-up, and even "middle-out" development have been much discussed. None of these techniques is really satisfactory for large programs, and combining them does not help much. The main problem is that they all rely on the system's requirements and specification to be fairly complete to start with, i.e., that the designers anticipated most of the functional and nonfunctional requirements. Unless the system is very well understood, this is almost impossible to achieve. In our experience, an approach that works well is incremental development, which is also called iterative development or IID (iterative and incremental development). It is sometimes called evolutionary development, although strictly speaking this metaphor is not applicable since there is no evolution in the Darwinian sense [48].[9] Incremental development has a long history both inside and outside of computing. It has been used successfully for software development at least since the 1950s [17,

9. Darwinian evolution implies a population in which individuals die and new ones are born, a source of variety in newly born individuals, and a filter (natural selection) that weeds out less fit individuals. There is no population in the incremental approach.

124]. Its steps are as follows:

- Start with a small set of requirements, which is a subset of the complete set, and build a complete system that satisfies them. The system specification and architecture are "empty shells": they are just complete enough so that a running program can be built, but they do not solve the user problems.
- Then continuously extend the requirements according to user feedback, extending the system specification and architecture as needed to satisfy the new requirements. Using an organic metaphor, we say the application is "grown." At all times, there is a running system that satisfies its specification and that can be evaluated by its potential users.
- Do not optimize during the development process. That is, do not make the design more complex just to increase performance. Use simple algorithms with acceptable complexity and keep a simple design with the right abstractions. Do not worry about the overhead of these abstractions. Performance optimization can be done near the end of development, but only if there are performance problems. Profiling should then be used to find those parts of the system (usually very small) that should be rewritten.
- Reorganize the design as necessary during development, to keep a good component organization. Components should encapsulate design decisions or implement common abstractions. This reorganization is sometimes called "refactoring." There is a spectrum between the extremes of completely planning a design and completely relying on refactoring. The best approach is somewhere in the middle.

Incremental development has many advantages:

- Bugs of all sizes are detected early and can be fixed quickly.
- Deadline pressure is much relieved, since there is always a working application.
- Developers are more motivated, because they have quick feedback on their efforts.
- Users are more likely to get what they really need, because they have a chance to use the application during the development process.
- The architecture is more likely to be good, since it can be corrected early on.
- The user interface is more likely to be good, since it is continuously improved during the development process.

For most systems, even very small ones, we find that it is almost impossible to determine in advance what the real requirements are, what a good architecture is to implement them, and what the user interface should be. Incremental development works well partly because it makes very few assumptions up front. For a complementary view, we recommend looking at extreme programming, which is another approach that emphasizes the trade-off between planning and refactoring [205]. For a more radical view, we recommend looking at test-driven development, which is incremental in a completely different way. Test-driven development claims that it is possible to write a program without any design phase, by just creating tests and

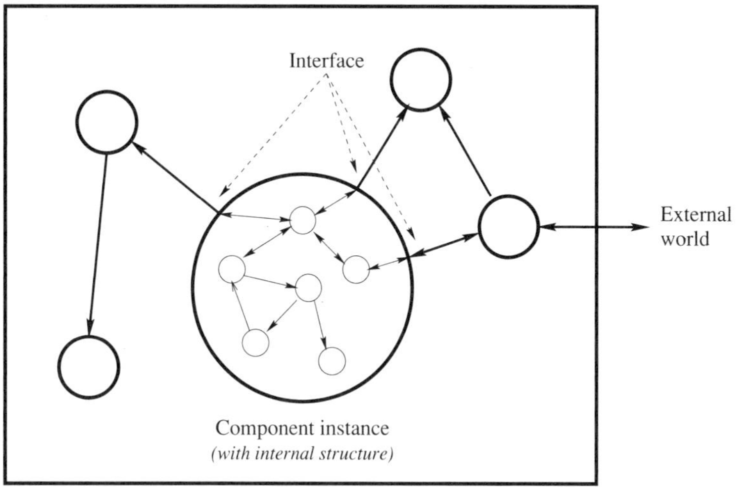

Figure 6.6: A system structured as a hierarchical graph.

refactoring each time the program breaks a new test [18]. We can see that designing good tests is crucial for the success of this approach!

6.7.2 Hierarchical system structure

How should the system be structured to support teamwork and incremental development? One way that works in practice is to structure the application as a hierarchical graph with well-defined interfaces at each level (see figure 6.6). That is, the application consists of a set of nodes where each node interacts with some other nodes. Each node is a component instance. Each node is itself a small application, and can itself be decomposed into a graph. The decomposition bottoms out when we reach primitive components that are provided by the underlying system.

Component connection

The first task when building the system is to connect the components together. This has both a static and a dynamic aspect:

- *Static structure.* This consists of the component graph that is known when the application is designed. These components can be linked as soon as the application starts up. Each component instance corresponds roughly to a bundle of functionality that is sometimes known as a library or a package. For efficiency, we would like each component instance to exist at most once in the system. If a library is needed by different parts of the application, then we want the instances to share this same library. For example, a component may implement a graphics package; the whole application can get by with just one instance.

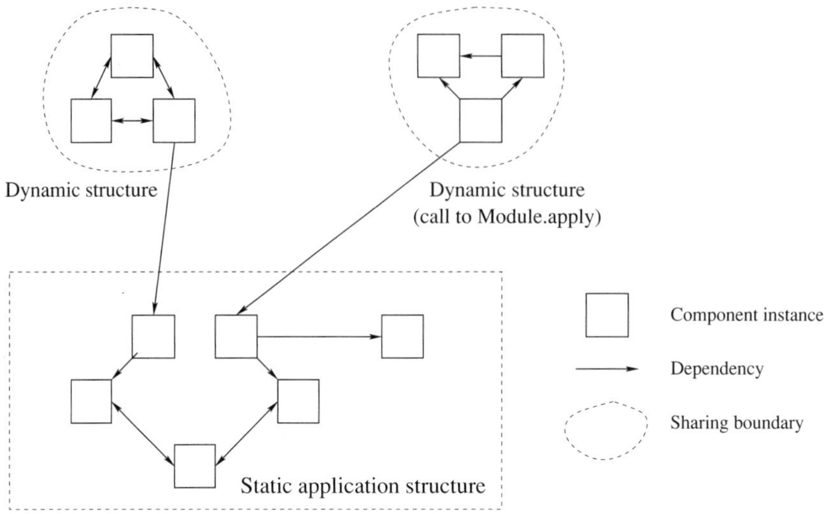

Figure 6.7: Static and dynamic system structure.

- *Dynamic structure.* Often, an application will do calculations with components at run time. It may want to link new components, which are known only at run time. Or it may want to calculate a new component and store it. Component instances need not be shared; perhaps several instances of a component are needed. For example, a component may implement a database interface. Depending on whether there are one or more external databases, one or more instances of the component should be loaded. This is determined at run time, whenever a database is added.

Figure 6.7 shows the resulting structure of the application, with some components linked statically and others linked dynamically.

Static structure To support the static structure, it is useful to make components into compilation units stored in files. We call these components functors and their instances modules. A functor is a component that can be stored in a file. It is a compilation unit because the file can be compiled independently of other functors. The functor's dependencies are given as file names. In order to be accessible by other functors, the functor must be stored in a file. This allows other functors to specify that they need it by giving the file name.

A functor has two representations: a source form, which is just a text, and a compiled form, which is a value in the language. If the source form is in a file `foo.oz`, whose entire content is of the form **`functor ... end`**, then it can be compiled to give another file, `foo.ozf`, that contains the compiled form. The content of file `foo.oz` looks like this:

```
functor
import OtherComp1 at File1
       OtherComp2 at File2
       ...
       OtherCompN at FileN
export op1:X1 op2:X2 ... opK:Xk
define
   % Define X1, ..., Xk
   ...
end
```

This component depends on the other components `OtherComp1`, ..., `OtherCompN`, stored respectively in files `File1`, ..., `FileN`. It defines a module with fields `op1`, ..., `opK`, referenced by `X1`, ..., `Xk` and defined in the functor body.

An application is just one compiled functor. To run the application, all the other compiled functors that it needs, directly or indirectly, must be brought together and instantiated. When the application is run, it loads its components and links them. Linking a component means to evaluate it with its imported modules as arguments and to give the result to the modules that need it. Linking can be done when the application starts up (static linking), or by need, i.e., one by one as they are needed (dynamic linking). We have found that dynamic linking is usually preferable, as long as all the compiled functors are quickly accessible (e.g., exist on the local system). With this default the application starts up quickly and it takes up only as much memory space as it needs.

Dynamic structure A functor is just another language entity. If a program contains a statement of the form `X=`**`functor`** `...` **`end`**, then `X` will be bound to the functor value. Like a procedure, the functor may have external references. Instantiating a functor gives a module, which is the set of language entities created by initializing the functor. An interface is a record giving the externally visible language entities of the module. In a convenient abuse of notation, this record is sometimes called the module. There exists a single operation to instantiate functors:

- `Ms={Module.apply Fs}`. Given a list `Fs` of functors (as language entities), this instantiates all the functors and creates a list `Ms` of modules. Within the scope of a `Module.apply` call, functors are shared. That is, if the same functor is mentioned more than once, then it is only linked once.

Each call to `Module.apply` results in a new, fresh set of modules. This operation is part of the module `Module`. If the functor is stored in a file it must be loaded first before calling `Module.apply`.

Component communication

Once the components are connected together, they have to communicate with each other. Here are six of the most popular protocols for component communication. We give them in order of increasing component independence:

1. *Procedure.* The first organization is where the application is sequential and where one component calls the other like a procedure. The caller is not necessarily the only initiator; there can be nested calls where the locus of control passes back and forth between components. But there is only one global locus of control, which strongly ties together the two components.

2. *Coroutine.* A second organization is where two components each evolve independently, but still in a sequential setting. This introduces the concept of a coroutine (see section 4.4.2). A component calls another, which continues where it left off. There are several loci of control, one for each coroutine. This organization is looser than the previous one, but the components are still dependent because they execute in alternation.

3. *Concurrent synchronous.* A third organization is one in which each component evolves independently of the others and can initiate and terminate communications with another component, according to some protocol that both components agree on. The components execute concurrently. There are several loci of control, called threads, which evolve independently (see chapters 4 and 8). Each component still calls the others synchronously, i.e., each call waits for a response.

4. *Concurrent asynchronous.* A fourth organization is a set of concurrent components that communicate through asynchronous channels. Each component sends messages to others, but does not have to wait for a response. The channels can have FIFO order (messages received in order of sending) or be unordered. The channels are called streams in chapter 4 and ports in chapter 5. In this organization each component still knows the identity of the component with which it communicates.

5. *Concurrent mailbox.* A fifth organization is a variation of the fourth. The asynchronous channels behave like mailboxes. That is, it is possible to do pattern matching to extract messages from the channels, without disturbing the messages that remain. This is very useful for many concurrent programs. It is a basic operation in the Erlang language, which has FIFO mailboxes (see chapter 5). Unordered mailboxes are also possible.

6. *Coordination model.* A sixth organization is where the components can communicate without the senders and receivers knowing each other's identities. An abstraction called tuple space lives at the interface. The components are concurrent and interact solely through the common tuple space. One component can insert a message asynchronously and another can retrieve the message. Section 8.3.2 defines one form of tuple space abstraction and shows how to implement it.

The model independence principle

Each component of the system is written in a particular computation model. Section 4.8.6 has summarized the most popular computation models used to program components. During development, a component's internal structure may change drastically. It is not uncommon for its computation model to change. A stateless component can become stateful (or concurrent, or distributed, etc.), or vice versa. If such a change happens inside a component, then it is not necessary to change its interface. The interface needs to change only if the externally visible functionality of the component changes. This is an important modularity property of the computation models. As long as the interface is the same, this property guarantees that it is not necessary to change anything else in the rest of the system. We consider this property as a basic design principle for the computation models:

> Model independence principle
>
> The interface of a component should be independent of the computation model used to implement the component. The interface should depend only on the externally visible functionality of the component.

A good example of this principle is memoization. Assume the component is a function that calculates its result based on one argument. If the calculation is time-consuming, then keeping a cache of argument-result pairs can greatly reduce the execution time. When the function is called, check whether the argument is in the cache. If so, return the result directly without doing the calculation. If not, do the calculation and add the new argument-result pair to the cache. Section 10.4.2 has an example of memoization. Since the memoization cache is stateful, changing a component to do memoization means that the component may change from using the declarative model to using the stateful model. The model independence principle implies that this can be done without changing anything else in the program.

Efficient compilation versus efficient execution

A component is a compilation unit. We would like to compile a component as quickly and efficiently as possible. This means we would like to compile a component separately, i.e., without knowing about other components. We would also like the final program, in which all components are assembled, to be as efficient and compact as possible. This means we would like to do compile-time analysis, e.g., type checking, Haskell-style type inference, or global optimization.

There is a strong tension between these two desires. If the compilation is truly separate, then analysis cannot cross component boundaries. To do a truly global analysis, the compiler must in general be able to look at the whole program at once. This means that for many statically typed languages, compiling large programs (more than, say, a million lines of source code) requires much time and memory.

There are many clever techniques that try to get the best of both worlds. Ideally, these techniques should not make the compiler too complicated. This is a difficult problem. After five decades of experience in language and compiler design, it is still an active research topic.

Commercial-quality systems span the whole spectrum from completely separate compilation to sophisticated global analysis. Practical application development can be done at any point of the spectrum. The Mozart system is at one extreme of the spectrum. Since it is dynamically typed, components can be compiled without knowing anything about each other. This means that compilation is completely scalable: compiling a component takes the same time, independent of whether it is used in a million-line program or in a thousand-line program. On the other hand, there are disadvantages: less optimization is possible and type mismatches can only be detected at run time. Whether or not these issues are critical depends on the application and the experience of the developer.

6.7.3 Maintainability

Once the system is built and works well, we have to make sure that it keeps working well. The process of keeping a system working well after it is deployed is called maintenance. What is the best way to structure systems so they are maintainable? From our experience, here are some of the most important principles. We look at this from the viewpoint of single components and from the viewpoint of the system.

Component design

There are good ways and bad ways to design components. A bad way is to make a flowchart and carve it up into pieces, where each piece is a component. Much better is to think of a component as an abstraction. For example, assume that we are writing a program that uses lists. Then it is almost always a good idea to gather all list operations into a component, which defines the list abstraction. With this design, lists can be implemented, debugged, changed, and extended without touching the rest of the program. For example, say we want to use the program with lists that are too big for main memory. It is enough to change the list component to store them on files instead of in main memory.

Encapsulate design decisions More generally, we can say that a component should encapsulate a design decision.[10] That way, when the design decision is changed, only that component has to be changed. This a very powerful form of modularity. The usefulness of a component can be evaluated by seeing what changes it accommodates. For example, consider a program that calculates with characters, such as the word frequency example of section 3.9.4. Ideally, the decision as to which character format to use (e.g., ASCII, Latin-1, or Unicode) should be encapsulated in one component. This makes it simple to change from one format to another.

Avoid changing component interfaces A component can be changed by changing its implementation or by changing its interface. Changing the interface is problematic since all components that depend on the changed interface have to be rewritten or recompiled. Therefore, changing the interface should be avoided. But

10. More romantically, it is sometimes said that the component has a "secret."

in practice, interface changes cannot be avoided during the design of a component. All we can do is minimize their frequency. This means that the interfaces of often-needed components should be designed as carefully as possible from the start.

Let us give a simple example to make this clear. Consider a component that sorts lists of character strings. It can change its sorting algorithm without changing its interface. This can often be done without recompiling the rest of the program, simply by linking in the new component. On the other hand, if the character format is changed, then the component might require a different interface. For example, characters can change size from one to two bytes (if ASCII is replaced with Unicode). This requires recompiling all the components that use the changed component (directly or indirectly), since the compiled code may depend on the character format. Recompilation can be onerous; changing a ten-line component might require recompiling most of the program, if the component is used often.

System design

Fewest possible external dependencies A component that depends on another, i.e., it requires the other for its operation, is a source of maintenance problems. If the other is changed, then the first must be changed as well. This is a major source of "software rot," i.e., once-working software that stops working. For example, LaTeX 2_ε is a popular document preparation system in the scientific community that is noted for its high-quality output [123]. A LaTeX 2_ε document can have links to other files, to customize and extend its abilities. Some of these other files, called packages, are fairly standardized and stable. Others are simply local customizations, called style files. In our experience, it is very bad for LaTeX 2_ε documents to have links to style files in other, perhaps global, directories. If these are changed, then the documents can often no longer be pageset. To aid maintenance, it is much preferable to have copies of the style files in each document directory. This satisfies a simple invariant: each document is guaranteed to be typesettable at all times ("working software keeps working"). This invariant is an enormous advantage that far outweighs the two disadvantages: (1) the extra memory needed for the copies and (2) the possibility that a document may use an older style file. If a style file is updated, the programmer is free to use the new version in the document, but only if necessary. Meanwhile, the document stays consistent. A second advantage is that it is easy to send the document from one person to another, since it is self-contained.

Fewest possible levels of indirection This is related to the previous rule. When A points to B, then updating B requires updating A. Any indirection is a kind of "pointer." The idea is to avoid the pointer becoming dangling, i.e., its destination no longer makes sense to the source. An action at B may cause A's pointer to become dangling. B doesn't know about A's pointer and so cannot prevent such a thing. A stopgap is never to change B, but only to make modified copies. This can work well if the system does automatic global memory management.

Two typical examples of problematic pointers are symbolic links in a Unix file system and URLs. Symbolic links are pernicious for system maintenance. They are convenient because they can refer to other mounted directory trees, but in fact they are a big cause of system problems. URLs are known to be extremely flaky. They are often referenced in printed documents, but their lifetime is usually much less than that of the document. This is both because they can quickly become dangling and because the Internet has a low quality of service.

Dependencies should be predictable For example, consider a 'localize' command that is guaranteed to retrieve a file over a network and make a local copy. It has simple and predictable behavior, unlike the "page caching" done by Web browsers. Page caching is a misnomer, because a true cache maintains coherence between the original and the copy. For any such "cache," the replacement policy should be clearly indicated.

Make decisions at the right level For example, time-outs should be made at the right level. It is wrong to implement a time-out as an irrevocable decision made at a low level in the system (a deeply nested component) that propagates all the way to the top level without any way for the intermediate components to intervene. This behavior short-circuits any efforts the application designer may make to mask the problem or solve it.

Documented violations Whenever one of the previous principles is violated, perhaps for a good reason (e.g., physical constraints such as memory limitations or geographic separation force a pointer to exist), then this should be documented! That is, all external dependencies, all levels of indirection, all nonpredictable dependencies, and all irrevocable decisions, should be documented.

Simple bundling hierarchy A system should not be stored in a dispersed way in a file system, but should be together in one place as much as possible. We define a simple hierarchy of how to bundle system components. We have found this hierarchy to be useful for documents as well as applications. The easiest-to-maintain design is first. For example, if the application is stored in a file system, then we can define the following order:

1. If possible, put the whole application in one file. The file may be structured in sections, corresponding to components.
2. If the above is not possible (e.g., there are files of different types or different people are to work on different parts simultaneously), then put the whole application in one directory.
3. If the above is not possible (e.g., the application is to be compiled for multiple platforms), put the application in a directory hierarchy with one root.

6.7.4 Future developments

Components and the future of programming

The increased use of components is changing the programming profession. We see two major ways this change is happening. First, components will make programming accessible to application users, not just professional developers. Given a set of components at a high level of abstraction and an intuitive graphical user interface, a user can do many simple programming tasks by himself or herself. This tendency has existed for a long time in niche applications such as statistics packages, signal processing packages, and packages for control of scientific experiments. The tendency will eventually encompass applications for the general public.

Second, programming will change for professional developers. As more and more useful components are developed, the granularity of programming will increase. That is, the basic elements used by programmers will more often be large components instead of fine-grained language operations. This trend is visible in programming tools such as Visual Basic and in component environments such as Enterprise Java Beans. The main bottleneck limiting this evolution is the specification of component behavior. Current components tend to be overcomplicated and have vague specifications. This limits their possible uses. The solution, in our view, is to make components simpler, better factorize their functionalities, and improve how they can be connected together.

Compositional versus noncompositional design

Hierarchical composition may seem like a very natural way to structure a system. In fact, it is not "natural" at all! Nature uses a very different approach, which can be called noncompositional. Let us compare the two. Let us first compare their component graphs. In a component graph, each node represents a component and there is an edge between nodes if the components know of each other. In a compositional system, the graph is hierarchical. Each component is connected only to its siblings, its children, and its parents. As a result, the system can be decomposed in many ways into independent parts, such that the interface between the parts is small.

In a noncompositional system, the component graph does not have this structure. The graph tends to be bushy and nonlocal. "Bushy" means that each component is connected to many others. "Nonlocal" means that each component is connected to widely different parts of the graph. Decomposing the system into parts is more arbitrary. The interfaces between the parts tend to be larger. This makes it harder to understand the components without taking into account their relation to the rest of the system. One example of a noncompositional graph is a small world graph, which has the property that the graph's diameter is small (each component is within a few hops of any other component).

Let us see why hierarchical composition is suitable for system design by humans.

The main constraint for humans is the limited size of human short-term memory. A human being can only keep a small number of concepts in his or her mind simultaneously [141]. A large design must therefore be chopped up into parts that are each small enough to be kept in a single individual's mind. Without external aid, this leads humans to build compositional systems. On the other hand, design by nature has no such limitation. It works through the principle of natural selection. New systems are built by combining and modifying existing systems. Each system is judged as a whole by how well it performs in the natural environment. The most successful systems are those with the most offspring. Therefore natural systems tend to be noncompositional.

It seems that each approach, in its pure form, is a kind of extreme. Human design is goal-oriented and reductionistic. Natural design is exploratory and holistic. Is it a meaningful quest to try to get the best of both worlds? We can imagine building tools to let human beings use a more "natural" approach to system design. In this book, we do not consider this direction further. We focus on the compositional approach.

6.7.5 Further reading

There are many books on program design and software engineering. We suggest [168, 172] as general texts and [205] for a view on how to balance design and refactoring. The Mythical Man-Month by Frederick Brooks dates from 1975 but is still good reading [29, 30]. Software Fundamentals is a collection of papers by Dave Parnas that spans his career and is good reading [162]. The Cathedral and the Bazaar by Eric Raymond is an interesting account of how to develop open source software [174].

Component Software: Beyond Object-Oriented Programming

For more information specifically about components, we recommend Component Software: Beyond Object-Oriented Programming by Clemens Szyperski [208]. This book gives an overview of the state of the art of component technology at the time of its publication. The book combines a discussion of the fundamentals of components together with an overview of what exists commercially. The fundamentals include the definition of component, the concepts of interface and polymorphism, the difference between inheritance, delegation, and forwarding, the trade-offs in using component composition versus inheritance, and how to connect components together. The three main commercial platforms discussed are the OMG (Object Management Group) with its CORBA standard; Microsoft with COM (Component Object Model) and its derivatives DCOM (Distributed COM), OLE (Object Linking and Embedding), and ActiveX; and Sun Microsystems with Java and JavaBeans. The book gives a reasonably well-balanced technical overview of these platforms.

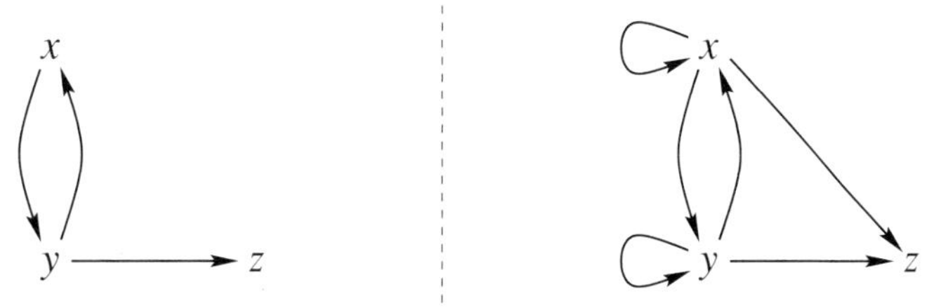

Figure 6.8: A directed graph and its transitive closure.

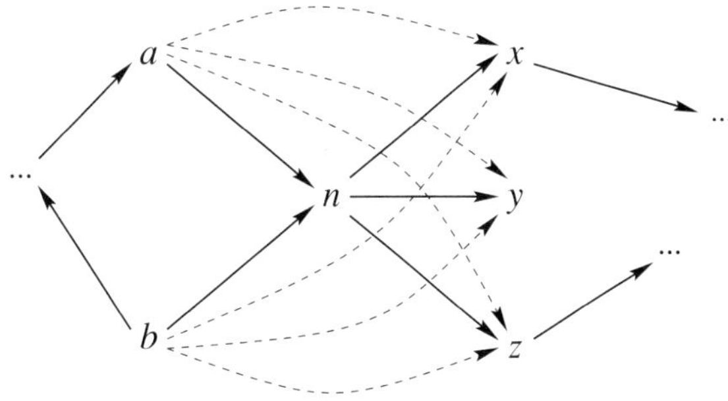

Figure 6.9: One step in the transitive closure algorithm.

6.8 Case studies

6.8.1 Transitive closure

Calculating the transitive closure is an example of a graph problem that can be solved reasonably well both with and without state. We define a directed graph $G = (V, E)$ as a set of nodes (or vertices) V and a set of edges E represented as pairs (x, y) with $x, y \in V$, such that $(x, y) \in E$ if and only if there is an edge from x to y. Then we can state the problem as follows:

> Consider any directed graph. Calculate a new directed graph, called the *transitive closure*, that has an edge between two nodes whenever the original graph has a path (a sequence of one or more edges) between those same two nodes.

Figure 6.8 shows an example graph and its transitive closure. We start with an abstract description of an algorithm that is independent of any particular computation model. Depending on how we represent the graph, this description will lead naturally to a declarative and a stateful implementation of the algorithm.

The algorithm successively adds edges according to the following strategy: for each node in the graph, add edges to connect all the node's predecessors to all its successors. Let us see how this works on an example. Figure 6.9 shows part of a directed graph. Here the node n has predecessors a and b and successors x, y, and z. When the algorithm encounters node n, it adds the six edges $a \to x$, $a \to y$, $a \to z$, $b \to x$, $b \to y$, and $b \to z$. After the algorithm has treated all nodes in this fashion, it is finished. We can state this algorithm as follows:

For each node x in the graph G:
  for each node y in $\text{pred}(x, G)$:
    for each node z in $\text{succ}(x, G)$:
      add the edge (y, z) to G.

We define the function $\text{pred}(x, G)$ as the set of predecessor nodes of x, i.e., the nodes with edges finishing in x, and the function $\text{succ}(x, G)$ as the set of successor nodes of x, i.e., the nodes with edges starting in x.

Why does this algorithm work? Consider any two nodes a and b with a path between them: $a \to n_1 \to n_2 \to \cdots \to n_k \to b$ (where $k \geq 0$). We have to show that the final graph has an edge from a to b. The nodes n_1 through n_k are encountered in some order by the algorithm. When the algorithm encounters a node n_i, it "short-circuits" the node, i.e., it creates a new path from a to b that avoids the node. Therefore, when the algorithm has encountered all nodes, it has created a path that avoids all of them, i.e., it has an edge directly from a to b.

Representing a graph

To write up the algorithm as a program, we first have to choose a representation for directed graphs. Let us consider two possible representations:

- The *adjacency list* representation. The graph is a list with elements of the form `I#Ns` where `I` identifies a node and `Ns` is an ordered list of its immediate successors. As we will see below, ordered lists of successors are more efficient to calculate with than unordered lists.
- The *matrix* representation. The graph is a two-dimensional array. The element with coordinates (`I`,`J`) is true if there is an edge from node `I` to node `J`. Otherwise, the element is false.

We find that the choice of representation strongly influences what is the best computation model. In what follows, we assume that all graphs have at least one node and that the nodes are consecutive integers. We first give a declarative algorithm that uses the adjacency list representation [158]. We then give an in-place stateful algorithm that uses the matrix representation [47]. We then give a second declarative algorithm that also uses the matrix representation. Finally, we compare the three algorithms.

Converting between representations

To make comparing the two algorithms easier, we first define routines to convert from the adjacency list representation to the matrix representation and vice versa. Here is the conversion from adjacency list to matrix:

```
fun {L2M GL}
   M={Map GL fun {$ I#_} I end}
   L={FoldL M Min M.1}
   H={FoldL M Max M.1}
   GM={NewArray L H unit}
in
   for I#Ns in GL do
      GM.I:={NewArray L H false}
      for J in Ns do GM.I.J:=true end
   end
   GM
end
```

In this routine, as in all following routines, we use `GL` for the adjacency list representation and `GM` for the matrix representation. Here is the conversion from matrix to adjacency list:

```
fun {M2L GM}
   L={Array.low GM}
   H={Array.high GM}
in
   for I in L..H collect:C do
      {C I#for J in L..H collect:D do
               if GM.I.J then {D J} end
            end}
   end
end
```

This uses the loop syntax, including the accumulation procedure `collect:C`, to good advantage.

Declarative algorithm

We first give a declarative algorithm for transitive closure. The graph is represented as an adjacency list. The algorithm needs two utility routines, `Succ`, which returns the successor list of a given node, and `Union`, which calculates the union of two ordered lists. We develop the algorithm by successive transformation of the abstract algorithm. This design method is known as stepwise refinement.

The outermost loop in the abstract algorithm transforms the graph in successive steps. Our declarative algorithm does the same by using `FoldL`, which defines a loop with accumulator. This means we can define the main function `DeclTrans` as follows:

```
fun {DeclTrans G}
   Xs={Map G fun {$ X#_} X end}
in
   {FoldL Xs
    fun {$ InG X}
    SX={Succ X InG} in
       {Map InG
        fun {$ Y#SY}
           Y#if {Member X SY} then
              {Union SY SX} else SY end
        end}
    end G}
end
```

Figure 6.10: Transitive closure (first declarative version).

```
fun {DeclTrans G}
Xs={Nodes G} in
   {FoldL Xs
    fun {$ InG X}
    SX={Succ X InG} in
       for each node Y in pred(X, InG):
          for each node Z in SX:
             add edge (Y, Z)
    end G}
end
```

The next step is to implement the two inner loops:

```
for each node Y in pred(X, InG):
   for each node Z in SX:
      add edge (Y, Z)
```

These loops transform one graph into another, by adding edges. Since our graph is represented by a list, a natural choice is to use `Map`, which transforms one list into another. This gives the following code, where `Union` is used to add the successor list of `X` to that of `Y`:

```
{Map InG
 fun {$ Y#SY}
    Y#if "Y in pred(X, InG)" then
       {Union SY SX} else SY end
 end}
```

We finish up by noticing that `Y` is in pred(`X`, `InG`) if and only if `X` is in succ(`Y`, `InG`). This means we can write the **`if`** condition as follows:

```
{Map InG
 fun {$ Y#SY}
    Y#if {Member X SY} then
       {Union SY SX} else SY end
 end}
```

Putting everything together we get the final definition in figure 6.10. This uses `Map`

```
proc {StateTrans GM}
   L={Array.low GM}
   H={Array.high GM}
in
   for K in L..H do
      for I in L..H do
         if GM.I.K then
            for J in L..H do
               if GM.K.J then GM.I.J:=true end
            end
         end
      end
   end
end
```

Figure 6.11: Transitive closure (stateful version).

to calculate {Nodes G}. We conclude by remarking that FoldL, Map, and other routines such as Member, Filter, etc., are basic building blocks that must be mastered when writing declarative algorithms.

To finish up our presentation of the declarative algorithm, we give the definitions of the two utility routines. Succ returns the list of successors of a node:

```
fun {Succ X G}
   case G of Y#SY|G2 then
      if X==Y then SY else {Succ X G2} end
   end
end
```

Succ assumes that X is always in the adjacency list, which is true in our case. Union returns the union of two sets, where all sets are represented as ordered lists:

```
fun {Union A B}
   case A#B
   of nil#B then B
   [] A#nil then A
   [] (X|A2)#(Y|B2) then
      if X==Y then X|{Union A2 B2}
      elseif X<Y then X|{Union A2 B}
      elseif X>Y then Y|{Union A B2}
      end
   end
end
```

Union's execution time is proportional to the length of the smallest input list because its input lists are ordered. If the lists were not ordered, its execution time would be proportional to the product of their lengths (why?), which is usually much larger.

Stateful algorithm

We give a stateful algorithm for transitive closure. The graph is represented as a matrix. This algorithm assumes that the matrix contains the initial graph. It then calculates the transitive closure in-place, i.e., by updating the input matrix itself. Figure 6.11 gives the algorithm. For each node `K`, this looks at each potential edge (`I`, `J`) and adds it if there is both an edge from `I` to `K` and from `K` to `J`. We show now the stepwise transformation that leads to this algorithm. We first restate the abstract algorithm with the proper variable names:

For each node k in the graph G:
  for each node i in pred(k, G):
    for each node j in succ(k, G):
      add the edge (i, j) to G.

This leads to the following refinement:

```
proc {StateTrans GM}
   L={Array.low GM}
   H={Array.high GM}
in
   for K in L..H do
      for I in L..H do
         if GM.I.K then
            for each J in succ(K,GM) do GM.I.J:=true
         end
      end
   end
end
```

We note that `J` is in succ(`K`, `GM`) if `GM.K.J` is true. This means we can replace the inner loop by:

```
for J in L..H do
   if GM.K.J then GM.I.J:=true end
end
```

Second declarative algorithm

Inspired by the stateful algorithm, we develop a second declarative algorithm. The second algorithm uses a series of tuples to store the successive approximations of the transitive closure. We use the variable `GT` instead of `GM` to emphasize this change in representation. A tuple is a record with fields numbered consecutively from 1 to a maximum value. So this algorithm is restricted to nodes whose numbering starts from 1. Note that `MakeTuple` creates a tuple with unbound variables. Figure 6.12 gives the algorithm.

This is somewhat more complicated than the stateful version. Each iteration of the outer loop uses the result of the previous iteration (`InG`) as input to calculate the next iteration (`G`). The recursive function `Loop` passes the result from one iteration

```
fun {DeclTrans2 GT}
   H={Width GT}
   fun {Loop K InG}
      if K=<H then
      G={MakeTuple g H} in
         for I in 1..H do
            G.I={MakeTuple g H}
            for J in 1..H do
               G.I.J = InG.I.J orelse (InG.I.K andthen InG.K.J)
            end
         end
         {Loop K+1 G}
      else InG end
   end
in
   {Loop 1 GT}
end
```

Figure 6.12: Transitive closure (second declarative version).

to the next. While this may seem a bit complicated, it has the advantages of the declarative model. For example, it is straightforward to convert it into a concurrent algorithm for transitive closure using the model of chapter 4. The concurrent algorithm can run efficiently on a parallel processor. We just add **`thread`** ... **`end`** to parallelize the two outer loops, as shown in figure 6.13. This gives a parallel dataflow implementation of the algorithm. Synchronization is done through the tuples which initially contain unbound variables. The tuples behave like I-structures in a dataflow machine (see section 4.9.5). It is an interesting exercise to draw a picture of an executing program, with data structures and threads.

Example executions

Let us calculate the transitive closure of the graph `[1#[2 3] 2#[1] 3#nil]`. This is the same graph we showed in figure 6.8 except that we use integers to represent the nodes. Here is how to use the declarative algorithms:

```
{Browse {DeclTrans [1#[2 3] 2#[1] 3#nil]}}
```

Here is how to use the stateful algorithm:

```
declare GM in
{StateTrans GM={L2M [1#[2 3] 2#[1] 3#nil]}}
{Browse {M2L GM}}
```

This is slightly more complicated because of the calls to `L2M` and `M2L`, which we use to give both the input and output as an adjacency list. All three algorithms give the result `[1#[1 2 3] 2#[1 2 3] 3#nil]`.

```
fun {DeclTrans2 GT}
   H={Width GT}
   fun {Loop K InG}
      if K=<H then
      G={MakeTuple g H} in
         thread
            for I in 1..H do
               thread
                  G.I={MakeTuple g H}
                  for J in 1..H do
                     G.I.J = InG.I.J orelse
                                (InG.I.K andthen InG.K.J)
                  end
               end
            end
         end
         {Loop K+1 G}
      else InG end
   end
in
   {Loop 1 GT}
end
```

Figure 6.13: Transitive closure (concurrent/parallel version).

Discussion

Both the declarative and stateful algorithms are actually variations of the same conceptual algorithm, which is called the Floyd-Warshall algorithm. All three algorithms have an asymptotic running time of $O(n^3)$ for a graph of n nodes. So which algorithm is better? Let us explore different aspects of this question:

- A first aspect is ease of understanding and reasoning. Perhaps surprisingly, the stateful algorithm has the simplest structure. It consists of three simple nested loops that update a matrix in a straightforward way. Both declarative algorithms have a more complex structure:
  - The first one takes an adjacency list and passes it through a sequence of stages in pipelined fashion. Each stage takes an input list and incrementally creates an output list.
  - The second one has a similar structure to the stateful algorithm, but creates a sequence of tuples in pipelined fashion.

Programming in the declarative model forces the algorithm to be structured as a pipeline, written with small, independent components. Programming in the stateful model encourages (but does not force) the algorithm to be structured as a monolithic block, which is harder to decompose. The stateful model gives more freedom in how to write the program. Depending on one's point of view, this can be a good or bad thing.

- A second aspect is performance: running time and memory use. Both algorithms asymptotically have the same running time and active memory sizes. We have measured the running times of both algorithms on several large random graphs. Given a random graph of 200 nodes in which there is an edge between any node pair with probability p. For p greater than about 0.05, the first declarative algorithm takes about 10 seconds, the second about 12 seconds, and the stateful algorithm about 15 seconds. For p tending to 0, the first declarative algorithm tends toward 0 seconds and the other algorithms increase slightly, to 16 and 20 seconds, respectively.[11] We conclude that the first declarative algorithm always has better performance than the two others. The adjacency list representation is better than the matrix representation when the graph is sparse.

Of course, the conclusions of this particular comparison are by no means definitive. We have chosen simple and clean versions of each style, but many variations are possible. For example, the first declarative algorithm can be modified to use a stateful `Union` operation. The stateful algorithm can be modified to stop looping when no more new edges are found. What can we conclude from this comparison?

- Both the declarative and stateful models are reasonable for implementing transitive closure.
- The choice of representation (adjacency list or matrix) can be more important than the choice of computation model.
- Declarative programs tend to be less readable than stateful programs, because they must be written in pipelined fashion.
- Stateful programs tend to be more monolithic than declarative programs, because explicit state can be modified in any order.
- It can be easier to parallelize a declarative program, because there are fewer dependencies between its parts.

6.8.2 Word frequencies (with stateful dictionary)

In section 3.7.3 we showed how to use dictionaries to count the number of different words in a text file. We compared the execution times of three versions of the word frequency counter, each one with a different implementation of dictionaries. The first two versions use declarative dictionaries (implemented lists and binary trees, respectively) and the third uses the built-in definition of dictionaries (implemented with state). The version using stateful dictionaries, shown in figure 6.14, is slightly different from the one using declarative dictionaries, shown in figure 3.30:

- The stateful version needs to pass just one argument as input to each procedure

11. Using Mozart 1.1.0 on a Pentium III processor at 500 MHz.

```
fun {WordChar C} ... end

fun {WordToAtom PW} ... end

fun {CharsToWords PW Cs} ... end

Put=Dictionary.put
CondGet=Dictionary.condGet

proc {IncWord D W}
   {Put D W {CondGet D W 0}+1}
end

proc {CountWords D Ws}
   case Ws
   of W|Wr then
      {IncWord D W}
      {CountWords D Wr}
   [] nil then skip
   end
end

fun {WordFreq Cs}
   D={NewDictionary}
in
   {CountWords D {CharsToWords nil Cs}}
   D
end
```

Figure 6.14: Word frequencies (with stateful dictionary).

that uses a dictionary.

- The declarative version has to use two arguments to these procedures: one for the input dictionary and one for the output dictionary. In figure 3.30, the second output is realized by using functional notation.

The difference shows up in the operations `Put`, `IncWords`, `CountWords`, and `WordFreq`. For example, figure 6.14 uses the stateful `{Put D LI X}`, which updates `D`. Figure 3.30 uses the declarative `{Put D1 LI X D2}`, which reads `D1` and returns a new dictionary `D2`.

6.8.3 Generating random numbers

A very useful primitive operation is a random number generator. It lets the computer "throw dice," so to speak. How do we generate random numbers in a computer? Here we give a few insights; see Knuth [114] for a deep discussion of the theory underlying random number generators and of the concept of randomness.

Different approaches

One could imagine the following ways to generate random numbers:

- A first technique would be to use unpredictable events in the computer, e.g., related to concurrency, as explained in the previous chapter. Alas, their unpredictability does not follow simple laws. For example, using the thread scheduler as a source of randomness will give some fluctuations, but they do not have a useful probability distribution. Furthermore, they are intimately linked with the computation in nonobvious ways, so even if their distribution were known, it would be dependent on the computation. So this is not a good source of random numbers.
- A second technique would be to rely on a source of true randomness. For example, electronic circuits generate noise, which is a completely unpredictable signal whose approximate probability distribution is known. The noise comes from the depths of the quantum world, so for all practical purposes it is truly random. But there are two problems. First, the probability distribution is not exactly known: it might vary slightly from one circuit to the next or with the ambient temperature. The first problem is not serious; there are ways to "normalize" the random numbers so that their distribution is a constant, known one. There is a second, more serious problem: the randomness cannot be reproduced except by storing the random numbers and replaying them. It might seem strange to ask for reproducibility from a source of randomness, but it is perfectly reasonable. For example, the randomness might be input to a simulator. We would like to vary some parameter in the simulator such that any variation in the simulator depends only on the parameter, and not on any variation in the random numbers. For this reason, computers are not usually connected to truly random sources.
- It might seem that we have carefully worked ourselves into a tight corner. We would like true randomness and we would like it to be reproducible. How can we resolve this dilemma? The solution is simple: we calculate the random numbers. How can this generate truly random numbers? The simple answer is, it cannot. But the numbers can appear random, for all practical purposes. They are called pseudorandom numbers. What does this mean? It is not simple to define. Roughly, the generated numbers should give the same behavior as truly random numbers, for the use we make of them.

The third solution, calculating random numbers, is the one that is almost always implemented. The question is, what algorithm do we use? Certainly not an algorithm chosen at random! Knuth [114] shows the pitfalls of this approach. It almost always gives bad results. We need an algorithm that has known good properties. We cannot guarantee that the random numbers will be good enough, but we can try to get what we can. For example, the generated random numbers should satisfy strong statistical properties, have the right distribution, and their period should be sufficiently long. The last point is worth expanding on: since a random number generator does a calculation with finite information, it will eventually repeat itself.

Clearly, the period of repetition should be very long.

Uniformly distributed random numbers

A random number generator stores an internal state, with which it calculates the next random number and the next internal state. The state should be large enough to allow a long period. The random number is initialized with a number called its seed. Initializing it again with the same seed should give the same sequence of random numbers. If we do not want the same sequence, we can initialize it with information that will never be the same, such as the current date and time. Modern computers almost always have an operation to get the time information. Now we can define a random number generator as a data abstraction:

- `{NewRand ?Rand ?Init ?Max}` returns three references: a random number generator `Rand`, its initialization procedure `Init`, and its maximum value `Max`. Each generator has its own internal state. For best results, `Max` should be large. This allows the program to reduce the random numbers to the smaller domains it needs for its own purposes.
- `{Init Seed}` initializes the generator with integer seed `Seed`, that should be in the range 0, 1, ..., `Max-1`. To give many possible sequences, `Max` should be large. Initialization can be done at any time.
- `X={Rand}` generates a new random number `X` and updates the internal state. `X` is an integer in the range 0, 1, ..., `Max-1` and has a uniform distribution, i.e., all integers have the same probability of appearing.

How do we calculate a new random number? It turns out that a good simple method is the linear congruential generator. If x is the internal state and s is the seed, then the internal state is updated as follows:

$$x_0 = s$$
$$x_n = (ax_{n-1} + b) \bmod m$$

The constants a, b, and m have to be carefully chosen so that the sequence x_0, x_1, x_2, ..., has good properties. The internal state x_i is a uniformly distributed integer from 0 to $m - 1$. It is easy to implement this generator:

```
local A=333667 B=213453321 M=1000000000 in
   proc {NewRand ?Rand ?Init ?Max}
   X={NewCell 0} in
      fun {Rand} X:=(A*@X+B) mod M end
      proc {Init Seed} X:=Seed end
      Max=M
   end
end
```

Note that the function body `X:=(A*@X+B) mod M` does an exchange, since it is in an expression position. This is one of the simplest methods that has reasonably good behavior. More sophisticated methods are possible that are even better.

Using laziness instead of state

The linear congruential algorithm can be packaged in a completely different way, namely as a lazy function. To get the next random number, it suffices to read the next element of the stream. Here is the definition:

```
local A=333667 B=213453321 M=1000000000 in
   fun lazy {RandList S0}
      S1=(A*S0+B) mod M in S1|{RandList S1}
   end
end
```

Instead of using a cell, the state is stored in a recursive argument of `RandList`. Instead of calling `Rand` explicitly to get the next number, `RandList` is called implicitly when the next number is needed. Laziness acts as a kind of brake, making sure that the computation advances only as rapidly as its results are needed. We remark that higher-order programming is not needed if we want to create many random number generators. Each call to `RandList` generates a new sequence of random numbers.

Nonuniform distributions

A good technique to generate random numbers of any distribution is to start with a uniformly distributed random number. From this, we calculate a number with another distribution. Using this technique we explain how to generate Gaussian and exponential distributions. We first define a new generator:

```
declare Rand Init Max in {NewRand Rand Init Max}
```

Now we define functions to generate a uniform distribution from 0 to 1 and a uniform integer distribution from `A` to `B` inclusive:

```
FMax={IntToFloat Max}
fun {Uniform}
   {IntToFloat {Rand}}/FMax
end

fun {UniformI A B}
   A+{FloatToInt {Floor {Uniform}*{IntToFloat B-A+1}}}
end
```

We will use `Uniform` to generate random variables with other distributions. First, let us generate random variables with an exponential distribution. For this distribution, the probability that $X \le x$ is $D(x) = 1 - e^{-\lambda x}$, where λ is a parameter called the intensity. Since $X \le x$ if and only if $D(X) \le D(x)$, it follows that the probability that $D(X) \le D(x)$ is $D(x)$. Writing $y = D(x)$, it follows that the probability that $D(X) \le y$ is y. Therefore $D(X)$ is uniformly distributed. Say $D(X) = U$ where U is a uniformly distributed random variable. Then we have $X = -\ln(1-U)/\lambda$. This gives the following function:

```
fun {Exponential Lambda}
   ~{Log 1.0-{Uniform}}/Lambda
end
```

Now let us generate a normal distribution with mean 0 and variance 1. A normal distribution is also called a Gaussian distribution. We use the following technique. Given two variables U_1 and U_2, uniformly distributed from 0 to 1. Let $R = \sqrt{-2 \ln U_1}$ and $\phi = 2\pi U_2$. Then $X_1 = R \cos \phi$ and $X_2 = R \sin \phi$ are independent variables with a Gaussian distribution. The proof of this fact is beyond the scope of the book; it can be found in [114]. This gives the following function:

```
TwoPi=4.0*{Float.acos 0.0}
fun {Gauss}
   {Sqrt ~2.0*{Log {Uniform}}} * {Cos TwoPi*{Uniform}}
end
```

Since each call can give us two Gaussian variables, we can use a cell to remember one result for the next call:

```
local GaussCell={NewCell nil} in
   fun {Gauss}
      Prev={Exchange GaussCell $ nil}
   in
      if Prev\=nil then Prev
      else R Phi in
         R={Sqrt ~2.0*{Log {Uniform}}}
         Phi=TwoPi*{Uniform}
         GaussCell:=R*{Cos Phi}
         R*{Sin Phi}
      end
   end
end
```

Each call of `Gauss` calculates two independent Gaussian variables; we return one and store the other in a cell. The next call returns it without doing any calculation.

6.8.4 "Word-of-mouth" simulation

Let us simulate how Web users "surf" on the Internet. To surf between Web sites means to successively load different Web sites. To keep our simulator simple, we will only look at one aspect of a Web site, namely its performance. This can be reasonable when surfing between Web portals, each of which provides a similar set of services. Assume there are n Web sites with equal content and a total of m users. Each Web site has constant performance. Each user would like to get to the Web site with highest performance. But there is no global measure of performance; the only way a user can find out about performance is by asking others. We say that information passes by "word of mouth." This gives the following simulation rules:

- Each site has a constant performance. We assume the constants are uniformly distributed among the sites.
- Each user knows which site it is on.

- Each site knows how many users are on it.
- Each user tries to step to a site with higher performance. The user asks a few randomly picked users about the performance at their site. The user then goes to the site with highest performance. However, the performance information is not exact: it is perturbed by Gaussian noise.
- One round of the simulation consists of all users doing a single step.

With these rules, we might expect users eventually to swarm among the sites with highest performance. But is it really so? A simulation can give us the answer.

Let us write a small simulation program. First, let us set up the global constants. We use the functions `Init`, `UniformI`, and `Gauss` defined in the previous section. There are n sites, m users, and t simulation rounds. We initialize the random number generator and write information to the file `´wordofmouth.txt´` during the simulation. We use the incremental write operations defined in the `File` module on the book's Web site. With 10000 sites, 500000 users, and 200 rounds, this gives the following:

```
declare
N=10000 M=500000 T=200
{Init 0}
{File.writeOpen ´wordofmouth.txt´}
proc {Out S}
   {File.write {Value.toVirtualString S 10 10}#"\n"}
end
```

Next, we decide how to store the simulation information. We would like to store it in records or tuples, because they are easy to manipulate. But they cannot be modified. Therefore, we store the simulation information in dictionaries. Dictionaries are very similar to records except that they can be changed dynamically (see section 6.5.1). Each site picks its performance randomly. It has a dictionary giving its performance and the number of users on it. The following code creates the initial site information:

```
Sites={MakeTuple sites N}
for I in 1..N do
  Sites.I={Record.toDictionary
           o(hits:0 performance:{IntToFloat {UniformI 1 80000}})}
end
```

Each user picks its site randomly. It has a dictionary giving its current site. It updates the `Sites` information. The following code creates the initial user information:

```
Users={MakeTuple users M}
for I in 1..M do S={UniformI 1 N} in
   Users.I={Record.toDictionary o(currentSite:S)}
   Sites.S.hits := Sites.S.hits + 1
end
```

Now that we have all the data structures, let us do one user step in the simulation. Figure 6.15 defines the function `{UserStep I}`, which does one step for user `I`. In one step, the user asks three other users for the performance of their sites, it

```
proc {UserStep I}
   U=Users.I
   % Ask three users for their performance information
   L={List.map [{UniformI 1 M} {UniformI 1 M} {UniformI 1 M}]
       fun {$ X}
          (Users.X.currentSite) #
          Sites.(Users.X.currentSite).performance
             + {Gauss}*{IntToFloat N}
       end}
   % Calculate the best site
   MS#MP = {List.foldL L
              fun {$ X1 X2} if X2.2>X1.2 then X2 else X1 end end
              U.currentSite #
              Sites.(U.currentSite).performance
                 + {Abs {Gauss}*{IntToFloat N}}}
in
   if MS\=U.currentSite then
      Sites.(U.currentSite).hits :=
         Sites.(U.currentSite).hits - 1
      U.currentSite := MS
      Sites.MS.hits := Sites.MS.hits + 1
   end
end
```

Figure 6.15: One step in the word-of-mouth simulation.

calculates its new site, and it updates the site and user information.

Figure 6.16 does the complete simulation. To make the simulator self-contained, we can put all the simulator code in one procedure with parameters `N` (number of sites), `M` (number of users), `T` (number of rounds), and the output file name. This lets us do many simulations with different parameters.

What is the result of the simulation? Will users cluster around the sites with highest performance, even though they have only a very narrow and inaccurate view of what is going on? Running the above simulation shows that the number of nonzero sites (with at least one user) decreases smoothly in inverse exponential fashion from 10000 initially to less than 100 after eighty-three rounds. Average performance of user sites increases from about 40000 (half of the maximum) to more than 75000 (within 6% of maximum) after just ten rounds. So we can make a preliminary conclusion that the best sites will quickly be found and the worst sites will quickly be abandoned, even by word-of-mouth propagation of very approximate information. Of course, our simulation has some simplifying assumptions. Feel free to change the assumptions and explore. For example, the assumption that a user can pick any three other users is unrealistic—it assumes that each user knows all the others. This makes convergence too fast. See Exercises (section 6.10) for a more realistic assumption of user knowledge.

```
for J in 1..N do
   {Out {Record.adjoinAt
           {Dictionary.toRecord site Sites.J} name J}}
end
{Out endOfRound(time:0 nonZeroSites:N)}
for I in 1..T do X={NewCell 0} in
   for U in 1..M do {UserStep U} end
   for J in 1..N do H=Sites.J.hits in
      if H\=0 then
         {Out {Record.adjoinAt
                 {Dictionary.toRecord site Sites.J} name J}}
         X := @X+1
      end
   end
   {Out endOfRound(time:I nonZeroSites:@X)}
end
{File.writeClose}
```

Figure 6.16: The complete word-of-mouth simulation.

6.9 Advanced topics

6.9.1 Limitations of stateful programming

Stateful programming has some strong limitations due to its use of explicit state. Object-oriented programming is a special case of stateful programming, so it suffers from the same limitations.

The real world is parallel

The main limitation of the stateful model is that programs are sequential. In the real world, entities are both stateful and act in parallel. Sequential stateful programming does not model the parallel execution.

Sometimes this limitation is appropriate, e.g., when writing simulators where all events must be coordinated (stepping from one global state to another in a controlled way). In other cases, e.g., when interacting with the real world, the limitation is an obstacle. To remove the limitation, the model needs to have both state and concurrency. We have seen one simple way to achieve this in chapter 5. Another way is given in chapter 8. As section 4.8.6 explains, concurrency in the model can model parallelism in the real world.

The real world is distributed

Explicit state is hard to use well in a distributed system. Chapter 11 explains this limitation in depth. Here we give just the main points. In a distributed system, the store is partitioned into separate parts. Within one part, the store behaves efficiently, as we have seen. Between parts, communication is many orders of magnitude more expensive. The parts coordinate with one another to maintain the desired level of global consistency. For cells this can be expensive because cell contents can change at any time in any part. The programmer has to decide on both the level of consistency and the coordination algorithm used. This makes it tricky to do distributed programming with state.

The declarative model and its extension to concurrent message passing in chapter 5 are much easier to use. As chapter 5 explains, a system can be decomposed into independent components that communicate with messages. This fits very well with the partitioned store of a distributed system. When programming a distributed system, we recommend using the message-passing model whenever possible for coordinating the parts. Chapter 11 explains how to program a distributed system and when to use the different computation models in a distributed setting.

6.9.2 Memory management and external references

As explained in section 2.5, garbage collection is a technique for automatic memory management that recovers memory for all entities inside the computation model that no longer take part in the computation. This is not good enough for entities outside the computation model. Such entities exist because there is a world outside of the computation model, which interacts with it. How can we do automatic memory management for them? There are two cases:

- From inside the computation model, there is a reference to an entity outside it. We call such a reference a resource pointer. Here are some examples:
    - A file descriptor, which points to a data structure held by the operating system. When the file descriptor is no longer referenced, we would like to close the file.
    - A handle to access an external database. When the handle is no longer referenced, we would like to close the connection to the database.
    - A pointer to a block of memory allocated through the Mozart C++ interface. When the memory is no longer referenced, we would like it to be freed.
- From the external world, there is a reference to inside the computation model. We call such a reference a ticket. Tickets are used in distributed programming as a means to connect processes together (see chapter 11).

In the second case, there is no safe way in general to recover memory. By safe we mean not to release memory as long as external references exist. The external world is so big that the computation model cannot know whether any reference still exists or not. One pragmatic solution is to add the language entity to the root set for a limited period of time. This is known as a time-lease mechanism. The time period can be renewed when the language entity is accessed. If the time period expires without a renewal, we assume that there are no more external references.

The application has to be designed to handle the rare case when this assumption is wrong.

In the first case, there is a simple solution based on parameterizing the garbage collector. This solution, called finalization, gives the ability to perform a user-defined action when a language entity has become unreachable. This is implemented by the System module `Finalize`. We first explain how the module works. We then give some examples of how it is used.

Finalization

Finalization is supported by the `Finalize` module. The design of this module is inspired by the guardian concept of [59]. `Finalize` has the following two operations:

- `{Finalize.register X P}` registers a reference `X` and a procedure `P`. When `X` becomes otherwise unreachable (otherwise than through finalization), `{P X}` is eventually executed in its own thread. During this execution, `X` is reachable again until its reference is no longer accessible.
- `{Finalize.everyGC P}` registers a procedure `P` to be invoked eventually after every garbage collection.

In both of these operations, you cannot rely on how soon after the garbage collection the procedure `P` will be invoked. It is in principle possible that the call may only be scheduled several garbage collections late if the system has very many live threads and generates garbage at a high rate.

There is no limitation on what the procedure `P` is allowed to do. This is because `P` is not executed during garbage collection, when the system's internal data structures can be temporarily inconsistent, but is scheduled for execution after garbage collection. `P` can even reference `X` and itself call `Finalize`.

An interesting example is the `everyGC` operation itself, which is defined in terms of `register`:

```
proc {EveryGC P}
   proc {DO _} {P} {Finalize.register DO DO} end
in
   {Finalize.register DO DO}
end
```

This creates a procedure `DO` and registers it using itself as its own handler. When `EveryGC` exits, the reference to `DO` is lost. This means that `DO` will be invoked after the next garbage collection. When invoked, it calls `P` and registers itself again.

Laziness and external resources

To make lazy evaluation practical for external resources like files, we need to use finalization to release the external resources when they are no longer needed. For example, in section 4.5.5 we defined a function `ReadListLazy` that reads a file lazily. This function closes the file after it is completely read. But this is not good enough; even if only part of the file is needed, the file should also be closed. We can implement this with finalization. We extend the definition of `ReadListLazy` to close the file when it becomes inaccessible:

```
fun {ReadListLazy FN}
   {File.readOpen FN}
   fun lazy {ReadNext}
   L T I in
      {File.readBlock I L T}
      if I==0 then T=nil {File.readClose} else T={ReadNext} end
      L
   end
in
   {Finalize.register F proc {$ F} {File.readClose} end}
   {ReadNext}
end
```

This requires just one call to `Finalize`.

6.10 Exercises

1. *The importance of sequences.* Section 6.1 gives a definition of state. For this exercise, compare and contrast this definition with the following definition of comics given by Scott McCloud [138]:

> **com·ics** (kom'iks) **n.** plural in form, used with a singular verb.
> **1.** Juxtaposed pictorial and other images in deliberate sequence, intended to convey information and/or to produce an aesthetic response in the viewer. ...

Hints: Are we interested in the whole sequence or just in the final result? Does the sequence exist in space or time? Is the transition between sequence elements important?

2. *State with cells.* Section 6.1 defines the function `SumList`, which has a state encoded as the successive values of two arguments at recursive calls. For this exercise, rewrite `SumList` so that the state is no longer encoded in arguments, but by cells.

3. *Emulating state with concurrency.* This exercise explores whether concurrency can be used to obtain explicit state.

   (a) First use concurrency to create an updatable container. We create a thread that uses a recursive procedure to read a stream. The stream has two possible commands: `access(X)`, which binds `X` to the container's current content, and `assign(X)`, which assigns `X` as the new content. Here is how it is done:

```
fun {MakeState Init}
   proc {Loop S V}
      case S of access(X)|S2 then
         X=V {Loop S2 V}
      [] assign(X)|S2 then
         {Loop S2 X}
      else skip end
   end S
in
   thread {Loop S Init} end S
end
```

The call `S={MakeState 0}` creates a new container with initial content 0. We use the container by putting commands on the stream. For example, here is a sequence of three commands for the container `S`:

```
declare S1 X Y in
S=access(X)|assign(3)|access(Y)|S1
```

This binds `X` to 0 (the initial content), puts 3 in the container, and then binds `Y` to 3.

(b) Now rewrite `SumList` to use this container to count the number of calls. Can this container be encapsulated, i.e., can it be added without changing the arguments of `SumList`? Why or why not? What happens when we try to add the function `SumCount` as in section 6.1.2?

4. *Implementing ports.* In chapter 5 we introduced the concept of port, which is a simple communication channel. Ports have the operations `{NewPort S P}`, which returns a port `P` with stream `S`, and `{Send P X}`, which sends message `X` on port `P`. From these operations, it is clear that ports are a stateful ADT. For this exercise, implement ports in terms of cells, using the techniques of section 6.4.

5. *Explicit state and security.* Section 6.4 gives four ways to construct secure data abstractions. From these constructions, it seems that the ability to make abstractions secure is a consequence of using one or more of the following three concepts: procedure values (which provide hiding through lexical scoping), name values (which are unforgeable and unguessable), and chunks (which provide selective access). In particular, explicit state seems to have no role with respect to security. For this exercise, think carefully about this assertion. Is it true? Why or why not?

6. *Declarative objects and identity.* Section 6.4.2 shows how to build a declarative object, which combines value and operations in a secure way. However, the implementation given misses one aspect of objects, namely their identity. That is, an object should keep the same identity after state changes. For this exercise, extend the declarative objects of section 6.4.2 to have an identity.

7. *Revocable capabilities.* Section 6.4.5 defines the three-argument procedure `Revocable`, which takes a capability and uses explicit state to create two things: a revocable version of that capability and a revoker. For `Revocable`, the capability is represented as a one-argument procedure and the revoker is a zero-argument procedure. For this exercise, write a version of `Revocable` that is a one-argument procedure and where the revoker is also a one-argument procedure. This allows

Revocable to be used recursively on all capabilities including revokers and itself. For example, the ability to revoke a capability can then be made revocable.

8. *Abstractions and memory management.* Consider the following stateful ADT which allows collecting information together into a list. The ADT has three operations. The call C={NewCollector} creates a new collector C. The call {Collect C X} adds X to C's collection. The call L={EndCollect C} returns the final list containing all collected items in the order they were collected. Here are two ways to implement collectors that we will compare:

- C is a cell that contains a pair H|T, where H is the head of the collected list and T is its unbound tail. Collect is implemented as

```
proc {Collect C X}
H T in
   {Exchange C H|(X|T) H|T}
end
```

  Implement the NewCollector and EndCollect operations with this representation.

- C is a pair H|T, where H is the head of the collected list and T is a cell that contains its unbound tail. Collect is implemented as

```
proc {Collect C X}
T in
   {Exchange C.2 X|T T}
end
```

  Implement the NewCollector and EndCollect operations with this representation.

- We compare the two implementations with respect to memory management. Use the table of section 3.5.2 to calculate how many words of memory are allocated by each version of Collect. How many of these words immediately become inactive in each version? What does this imply for garbage collection? Which version is best?

This example is taken from the Mozart system. Collection in the **for** loop was originally implemented with one version. It was eventually replaced by the other. (Note that both versions work correctly in a concurrent setting, i.e., if Collect is called from multiple threads.)

9. *Call by name.* Section 6.4.4 shows how to code call by name in the stateful computation model. For this exercise, consider the following example, taken from [64]:

```
procedure swap(callbyname x,y:integer);
var t:integer;
begin
   t:=x; x:=y; y:=t
end;
var a:array [1..10] of integer;
var i:integer;
i:=1; a[1]:=2; a[2]=1;
swap(i, a[i]);
writeln(a[1], a[2]);
```

This example shows a curious behavior of call by name. Running the example does not swap `i` and `a[i]`, as one might expect. This shows an undesirable interaction between explicit state and the delayed evaluation of an argument.

- Explain this example by using your understanding of call by name.
- Code the example in the stateful computation model. Use the following encoding of `array[1..10]`:

  ```
  A={MakeTuple array 10}
  for J in 1..10 do A.J={NewCell 0} end
  ```

  That is, code the array as a tuple of cells.
- Explain the behavior again in terms of your coding.

10. *Call by need.* With call by name, the argument is evaluated again each time it is needed. With call by need it is evaluated at most once.

- For this exercise, redo the swap example of the previous exercise with call by need instead of call by name. Does the counterintuitive behavior still occur? If not, can similar problems still occur with call by need by changing the definition of `swap`?
- In the call by need example of section 6.4.4, the body of `Sqr` will always call the function `A`. This is fine for `Sqr`, since we can see by inspection that the result is needed three times. But what if the need cannot be determined by inspection? We do not want to call `A` unnecessarily. One possibility is to use lazy functions. Modify the code of section 6.4.4 so that it uses laziness to call `A` only when needed, even if that need cannot be determined by inspection. `A` should be called at most once.

11. *Evaluating indexed collections.* Section 6.5.1 presents four indexed collection types, namely tuples, records, arrays, and dictionaries, with different performance/expressiveness trade-offs. For this exercise, compare these four types in various usage scenarios. Evaluate their relative performance and usefulness.

12. *Extensible arrays.* The extensible array of section 6.5 only extends the array upward. For this exercise, modify the extensible array so it extends the array in both directions.

13. *Generalized dictionaries.* The built-in dictionary type only works for literal keys, i.e., numbers, atoms, or names. For this exercise, implement a dictionary that

can use any value as a key. One possible solution uses the fact that the `==` operation can compare any values. Using this operation, the dictionary could store entries as an association list, which is a list of pairs `Key#Value`, and do simple linear search.

14. *Loops and invariant assertions.* Use the method of invariant assertions to show that the proof rules for the **`while`** and **`for`** loops given in section 6.6.4 are correct.

15. *The* `break` *statement.* A block is a set of statements with a well-defined entry point and exit point. Many modern imperative programming languages, such as Java and C++, are based on the concept of block. These languages allow defining nested blocks and provide an operation to jump immediately from within a block to the block's exit point. This operation is called `break`. For this exercise, define a block construct with a break operation that can be called as follows:

```
{Block proc {$ Break} ⟨stmt⟩ end}
```

This should have exactly the same behavior as executing ⟨stmt⟩, except that executing `{Break}` inside ⟨stmt⟩ should immediately exit the block. Your solution should work correctly for nested blocks and exceptions raised within blocks. If ⟨stmt⟩ creates threads, then these should not be affected by the break operation. *Hint*: use the exception handling mechanism.

16. *Word frequency application.* Section 6.8.2 gives a version of the word frequency algorithm that uses stateful dictionaries. Rewrite the word frequency application of section 3.9.4 to use this stateful version.

17. *"Small world" simulation.* The word-of-mouth simulation of section 6.8.4 makes some strong simplifying assumptions. For example, the simulation assumes that each user can choose any three users at random to ask them about their performance. This is much too strong an assumption. The problem is that the choice ranges over all users. This gives each user a potentially unbounded amount of knowledge. In actuality, each user has bounded knowledge: a small network of acquaintances that changes but slowly. Each user asks only members of his network of acquaintances. Rewrite the simulation program to take this assumption into account. This can make convergence much slower. With this assumption, the simulation is called a small world simulation [224].

18. *Performance effects in word-of-mouth simulation.* The word-of-mouth simulation of section 6.8.4 assumes that site performance is constant. A better way to take performance into account is to assume that it is constant up to a given number of users, which is fixed for each site. Beyond this threshold, performance goes down in inverse proportion to the number of users. This is based on the premise that for small numbers of users, Internet performance is the bottleneck, and for large numbers of users, site performance is the bottleneck.

19. (advanced exercise) *Test-driven development.* Section 6.7.1 explains why incremental development is a good idea. The section ends with a brief mention of test-driven development, a more radical approach that is also incremental in its own fashion. For this exercise, explore test-driven development and compare it

with incremental development. Develop one or more applications using test-driven development and try to come up with a balanced approach that combines the best of both development techniques.

7 Object-Oriented Programming

The fruit is too well known to need any
description of its external characteristics.
– From the entry "Apple," Encyclopaedia Britannica, 11th edition

Object-oriented programming (OOP) is one of the most successful and pervasive areas in informatics. From its origin in the 1960s it has invaded every area of informatics, both in scientific research and technology development. The first object-oriented language was Simula 67, developed in 1967 as a descendant of Algol 60 [149, 156, 170]. OOP did not become industrially popular, though, until the appearance of C++ in the early 1980s [204]. Another important step was Smalltalk-80, released in 1980 as the result of research done in the 1970s [68]. Both C++ and Smalltalk were directly influenced by Simula [111, 203]. The currently most popular programming languages, Java and C++, are both object-oriented [204, 206]. The most popular "language-independent" design aids, the Unified Modeling Language (UML) and Design Patterns, both implicitly assume that the underlying language is object-oriented [66, 178].

With all this momentum, one might think that OOP is well understood (see the epigraph above). Yet this is far from being the case. The purpose of this chapter is not to cover all of OOP in 100 pages or less. This is impossible. Instead, we give an introduction that emphasizes areas where other presentations are weak: the relationship with other computation models, the precise semantics, and the possibilities of dynamic typing. We also motivate the design choices made by OOP and the trade-offs involved in these choices.

Principles of object-oriented programming

The computation model of OOP is the stateful model of chapter 6. The first principle of OOP is that programs are collections of interacting data abstractions. In section 6.4 we saw a rather bewildering variety of ways to build data abstractions. Object-oriented programming brings order into this variety. It posits two principles for building data abstractions:

1. Data abstractions should be stateful by default. Explicit state is important because of program modularity (see section 6.2). It makes it possible to write programs as independent parts that can be extended without changing their interfaces. The

opposite principle (i.e., declarative by default) is also reasonable, since it makes reasoning simpler (see section 4.8.5) and is more natural for distributed programming (see chapter 11). In our view, both stateful and declarative abstractions should be equally easy to use.

2. The object (PDA) style of data abstraction should be the default. The object style is important because it encourages polymorphism and inheritance. Polymorphism was explained in section 6.4. It allows a program to properly apportion responsibility among its parts. Inheritance is a new concept that we introduce in this chapter. It allows building abstractions incrementally. We add a linguistic abstraction, called class, to support inheritance in the language.

To summarize, we can loosely characterize object-oriented programming as programming with object data abstraction, explicit state, polymorphism, and inheritance.

Structure of the chapter

The chapter consists of the following parts:

- *Inheritance* (section 7.1). We first introduce and motivate the concept of inheritance in a general way and situate it with respect to other program structuring concepts.

- *An object-oriented computation model* (sections 7.2 and 7.3). We define a simple object system that provides single and multiple inheritance with static and dynamic binding. The object system takes advantage of dynamic typing to combine simplicity and flexibility. Messages and attributes are first class, classes are values, and arbitrary scopes can be programmed. This allows us to explore better the limits of OOP and situate existing languages within them. We give the object system syntactic and implementation support to make it easier to use and more efficient.

- *Programming with inheritance* (section 7.4). We explain the basic principles and techniques for using inheritance to construct object-oriented programs. The most important principle is called the substitution property. We illustrate the principles with realistic example programs. We give pointers to the literature on object-oriented design.

- *Relation to other computation models* (section 7.5). From the viewpoint of multiple computation models, we show how and when to use and not use object-oriented programming. We relate it to component-based programming, object-based programming, and higher-order programming. We give additional design techniques that become possible when it is used together with other models. We explain the pros and cons of the often-repeated principle stating that every language entity should be an object. This principle has guided the design of several major object-oriented languages, so it is important to understand what it means.

- *Implementing the object system* (section 7.6). We give a simple and precise semantics of our object system, by implementing it in terms of the stateful computation model. Because the implementation uses a computation model with a precise semantics, we can consider it as a semantic definition.

- *The Java language* (section 7.7). We give an overview of the sequential part of Java, a popular object-oriented programming language. We show how the concepts of Java fit in the object system of the chapter.
- *Active objects* (section 7.8). An active object extends a port object of chapter 5 by using a class to define its behavior. This combines the abilities of object-oriented programming and message-passing concurrency. We show how to program with active objects and we compare them with declarative concurrency.

Object-Oriented Software Construction

For more information on object-oriented programming techniques and principles, we recommend *Object-Oriented Software Construction* by Bertrand Meyer [140]. This book is especially interesting for its detailed discussion of inheritance, including multiple inheritance.

7.1 Inheritance

Inheritance is based on the observation that data abstractions frequently have much in common. Let us take the example of sets. There are many different abstractions that are "set-like," in the sense that they are collections to which we can add and delete elements. Sometimes we want them to behave like stacks, adding and deleting in LIFO (last-in, first-out) order. Sometimes we want them to behave like queues, adding and deleting in FIFO order. Sometimes the order in which elements are added and deleted is unimportant. And so forth, with many other possibilities. All of these abstractions share the basic property of being a collection of elements. Can we implement them without duplicating the common parts? Having duplicate parts does not just make the program longer. It is a nightmare for both programmer and maintainer, since if one copy is changed, then the others must also be changed. What's more, the different copies are usually slightly different, which makes the relationships among all the changes nonobvious.

We introduce the concept of inheritance to reduce the problem of code duplication and to make the relationships between data abstractions clear. A data abstraction can be defined to "inherit" from one or more other data abstractions, i.e., to have substantially the same functionality as the others, with possibly some extensions and modifications. Only the differences between the data abstraction and its ancestors have to be specified. Such an incremental definition of a data abstraction is called a *class*.

A new class is defined by a kind of transformation: one or more existing classes are combined with a description of the extensions and modifications to give the new class. Object-oriented languages support this transformation by adding classes as a linguistic abstraction. The transformation can be seen as a syntactic manipulation, where the syntax of the new class can be derived from the original classes (see section 7.3). In the object system of this chapter, the transformation also makes sense semantically (see section 7.6.4). Since classes are values, the transformation can be seen as a function that takes class values as inputs and returns a new class value as output.

While inheritance has great promise, experience shows that it must be used with great care. First of all, the transformation must be defined with intimate knowledge of the ancestor classes, since they can easily break a class invariant. Another problem is that using inheritance opens an additional interface to a component. That is, the ability to extend a class can be seen as an additional way to interact with that class. This interface has to be maintained throughout the lifetime of the component. For this reason, the default when defining a class should be that it is final, i.e., that it is forbidden for other classes to inherit from it. Making a class (or part of a class) inheritable should require explicit action by the programmer.

Inheritance increases the possibilities of factoring an application, i.e., making sure that common parts exist only once, but this comes at the price of spreading out an abstraction's implementation over large parts of the program. The implementation does not exist in one place; all the abstractions that it inherits from have to be considered together. This makes it harder to understand the abstraction, and paradoxically may make it harder to maintain. Even worse, an abstraction may inherit from a class that exists only as object code, with no access to the source code. The lesson is that inheritance should be used sparingly.

Instead of using inheritance, an alternative is to use component-based programming, i.e., to use components directly and compose them. The idea is to define a component that encapsulates another component and provides a modified functionality. There is a trade-off between inheritance and component composition: inheritance is more flexible but can break a class invariant, whereas component composition is less flexible but cannot break a component invariant. This trade-off should be carefully considered whenever an abstraction must be extended.

Early on, it was believed that inheritance would solve the problem of software reuse. For example, it would make it easier to build libraries that can be distributed to third parties, for use in other applications. This has had some success through software frameworks. A software framework is a software system that has been made generic. Instantiating the framework means giving actual values for the generic parameters. As we will see in this chapter, this can be done with inheritance by using generic classes or abstract classes.

7.2 Classes as complete data abstractions

The heart of the object concept is controlled access to encapsulated data. The behavior of an object is specified by a class. In the most general case, a class is an incremental definition of a data abstraction, that defines the abstraction as a

```
class Counter
   attr val
   meth init(Value)
      val:=Value
   end
   meth browse
      {Browse @val}
   end
   meth inc(Value)
      val:=@val+Value
   end
end
```

Figure 7.1: An example class `Counter` (with **`class`** syntax).

modification of others. There is a rich set of concepts for defining classes. We classify these concepts into two sets, according as they permit the class to define a data abstraction completely or incrementally:

- *Complete data abstraction.* These are all the concepts that permit a class, when taken by itself, to define a data abstraction. There are two sets of concepts:
  - Defining the various elements that make up a class (see sections 7.2.3 and 7.2.4), namely methods, attributes, and properties. Attributes can be initialized in several ways, per object or per class (see section 7.2.5).
  - Taking advantage of dynamic typing. This gives first-class messages (see section 7.2.6) and first-class attributes (see section 7.2.7). This allows powerful forms of polymorphism that are difficult or impossible to do in statically typed languages. This increased freedom comes with an increased responsibility of the programmer to use it correctly.
- *Incremental data abstraction.* These are all the concepts related to inheritance, i.e., they define how a class is related to existing classes. They are given in section 7.3.

To explain what classes are we start by giving an example that shows how to define a class and an object. Section 7.2.1 gives the example using the class syntax and then section 7.2.2 gives its precise semantics by defining it in the stateful model.

7.2.1 An example

To see how classes and objects work in the object system, let us define an example class and use it to create an object. We assume that the language has a new syntactic construct, the **`class`** declaration. We assume that classes are first-class values in the language. This lets us use a **`class`** declaration as either statement or expression, in similar manner to a **`proc`** declaration. Later on we will see how to define classes directly in the stateful model. This means we can consider **`class`** as a linguistic

```
local
   proc {Init M S}
      init(Value)=M in (S.val):=Value
   end
   proc {Browse2 M S}
      {Browse @(S.val)}
   end
   proc {Inc M S}
      inc(Value)=M in (S.val):=@(S.val)+Value
   end
in
   Counter=c(attrs:[val]
             methods:m(init:Init browse:Browse2 inc:Inc))
end
```

Figure 7.2: Defining the `Counter` class (without syntactic support).

abstraction.

Figure 7.1 defines a class referred to by the variable `Counter`. This class has one attribute, `val`, that holds a counter's current value, and three methods, `init`, `browse`, and `inc`, for initializing, displaying, and incrementing the counter. The attribute is assigned with the `:=` operator and accessed with the `@` operator. This seems quite similar to how other languages would do it, modulo a different syntax. But appearances can be deceiving!

The declaration of figure 7.1 is actually executed at run time, i.e., it is a statement that creates a class value and binds it to `Counter`. Replace "`Counter`" by "`$`" and the declaration can be used in an expression. Putting this declaration at the head of a program will declare the class before executing the rest, which is familiar behavior. But this is not the only possibility. The declaration can be put anywhere that a statement can be. For example, putting the declaration inside a procedure will create a new and distinct class each time the procedure is called. Later on we will use this possibility to make parameterized classes.

Let us create an object of class `Counter` and do some operations with it:

```
C={New Counter init(0)}
{C inc(6)} {C inc(6)}
{C browse}
```

This creates the counter object `C` with initial value `0`, increments it twice by `6`, and then displays the counter's value. The statement `{C inc(6)}` is called an object application. The message `inc(6)` is used by the object to invoke the corresponding method. Now try the following:

```
local X in {C inc(X)} X=5 end
{C browse}
```

This displays nothing at all! The reason is that the object application

```
{C inc(X)}
```

```
fun {New Class Init}
   Fs={Map Class.attrs fun {$ X} X#{NewCell _} end}
   S={List.toRecord state Fs}
   proc {Obj M}
      {Class.methods.{Label M} M S}
   end
in
   {Obj Init}
   Obj
end
```

Figure 7.3: Creating a `Counter` object.

blocks inside the method `inc`. Can you see exactly where? Now try the following variation:

```
declare S in
local X in thread {C inc(X)} S=unit end X=5 end
{Wait S} {C browse}
```

Things now work as expected. We see that dataflow execution keeps its familiar behavior when used with objects.

7.2.2 Semantics of the example

Before going on to describe the additional abilities of classes, let us give the semantics of the `Counter` example. It is a straightforward application of higher-order programming with explicit state. The semantics we give here is slightly simplified; it leaves out the abilities of **class** that are not used in the example (such as inheritance and **self**). Section 7.6 gives the full semantics.

Figure 7.2 shows what figure 7.1 does by giving the definition of the class `Counter` in the stateful model without any **class** syntax. We can see that according to this definition, a class is simply a record containing a set of attribute names and a set of methods. An attribute name is a literal. A method is a procedure that has two arguments, the message and the object state. In each method, assigning to an attribute ("`val:=`") is done with a cell assignment and accessing an attribute ("`@val`") is done with a cell access.

Figure 7.3 defines the function `New` which is used to create objects from classes. This function creates the object state, defines a one-argument procedure `Obj` that is the object, and initializes the object before returning it. The object state `S` is a record holding one cell for each attribute. The object state is hidden inside `Obj` by lexical scoping.

```
⟨statement⟩        ::= class ⟨variable⟩ { ⟨classDescriptor⟩ }
                       { meth ⟨methHead⟩ [ ´=´ ⟨variable⟩ ]
                         ( ⟨inExpression⟩ | ⟨inStatement⟩ ) end }
                       end
                     | lock [ ⟨expression⟩ then ] ⟨inStatement⟩ end
                     | ⟨expression⟩ ´:=´ ⟨expression⟩
                     | ⟨expression⟩ ´,´ ⟨expression⟩
                     | ...
⟨expression⟩       ::= class ´$´ { ⟨classDescriptor⟩ }
                       { meth ⟨methHead⟩ [ ´=´ ⟨variable⟩ ]
                         ( ⟨inExpression⟩ | ⟨inStatement⟩ ) end }
                       end
                     | lock [ ⟨expression⟩ then ] ⟨inExpression⟩ end
                     | ⟨expression⟩ ´:=´ ⟨expression⟩
                     | ⟨expression⟩ ´,´ ⟨expression⟩
                     | ´@´ ⟨expression⟩
                     | self
                     | ...
⟨classDescriptor⟩ ::= from { ⟨expression⟩ }+ | prop { ⟨expression⟩ }+
                     | attr { ⟨attrInit⟩ }+
⟨attrInit⟩         ::= ( [ ´!´ ] ⟨variable⟩ | ⟨atom⟩ | unit | true | false )
                       [ ´:´ ⟨expression⟩ ]
⟨methHead⟩         ::= ( [ ´!´ ] ⟨variable⟩ | ⟨atom⟩ | unit | true | false )
                       [ ´(´ { ⟨methArg⟩ } [ ´...´ ] ´)´ ]
                       [ ´=´ ⟨variable⟩ ]
⟨methArg⟩          ::= [ ⟨feature⟩ ´:´ ] ( ⟨variable⟩ | ´_´ | ´$´ ) [ ´<=´ ⟨expression⟩ ]
```

Table 7.1: Class syntax.

7.2.3 Defining classes and objects

A class is a data structure that defines an object's internal state (attributes), its behavior (methods), the classes it inherits from, and several other properties and operations that we will see later on. More generally, a class is a data structure that defines a data abstraction and gives its partial or total implementation. Table 7.1 gives the syntax of classes.

There can be any number of objects of a given class. They are called instances of the class. These objects have different identities and can have different values for their internal state. Otherwise, all objects of a given class behave according to the class definition. An object is created with the operation `New`:

```
MyObj={New MyClass Init}
```

This creates a new object `MyObj` of class `MyClass` and invokes the object with the message `Init`. This message is used to initialize the object. The object `MyObj` is called with the syntax `{MyObj M}`. It behaves like a one-argument procedure, where the argument is the message. The messages `Init` and `M` are represented as records. An object call is similar to a procedure call. It returns when the method has completely executed.

7.2.4 Class members

A class defines the constituent parts that each of its objects will have. In object-oriented terminology, these parts are often called members. There are three kinds of members:

- *Attributes* (declared with the keyword "**attr**"). An attribute is a cell that contains part of the instance's state. In object-oriented terminology, an attribute is often called an instance variable. The attribute can contain any language entity. The attribute is visible only in the class definition and all classes that inherit from it. Every instance has a separate set of attributes. The instance can update an attribute with the following operations:
  - An assignment statement: $\langle\mathsf{expr}\rangle_1$ `:=` $\langle\mathsf{expr}\rangle_2$. This assigns the result of evaluating $\langle\mathsf{expr}\rangle_2$ to the attribute whose name is obtained by evaluating $\langle\mathsf{expr}\rangle_1$.
  - An access operation: `@`$\langle\mathsf{expr}\rangle$. This accesses the attribute whose name is obtained by evaluating $\langle\mathsf{expr}\rangle$. The access operation can be used in any expression that is lexically inside the class definition. In particular, it can be used inside of procedures that are defined inside the class.
  - An exchange operation. If the assignment $\langle\mathsf{expr}\rangle_1$ `:=` $\langle\mathsf{expr}\rangle_2$ is used as an expression, then it has the effect of an exchange. For example, consider the statement $\langle\mathsf{expr}\rangle_3$`=`$\langle\mathsf{expr}\rangle_1$ `:=` $\langle\mathsf{expr}\rangle_2$. This first evaluates the three expressions. Then it it unifies $\langle\mathsf{expr}\rangle_3$ with the content of the attribute $\langle\mathsf{expr}\rangle_1$ and atomically sets the new content to $\langle\mathsf{expr}\rangle_2$.
- *Methods* (declared with the keyword "**meth**"). A method is a kind of procedure that is called in the context of a particular object and that can access the object's attributes. The method consists of a head and body. The head consists of a label, which must be an atom or a name, and a set of arguments. The arguments must be distinct variables, otherwise there is a syntax error. For increased expressiveness, method heads are similar to patterns and messages are similar to records. Section 7.2.6 explains the possibilities.
- *Properties* (declared with the keyword "**prop**"). A property modifies how an object behaves. For example:
  - The property `locking` creates a new lock with each object instance. The lock can be accessed inside the class with the **lock** ... **end** construct. Locking is explained in chapter 8.
  - The property `final` makes the class be a final class, i.e., it cannot be extended

with inheritance. It is good practice to make every class `final` except if it is specifically designed for inheritance.

Attributes and method labels are literals. If they are defined with atom syntax, then they are atoms. If they are defined with identifier syntax (e.g., capitalized), then the system will create new names for them. The scope of these names is the class definition. Using names gives a fine-grained control over object security, as we will see. Section 7.2.5 shows how to initialize attributes.

In addition to these three kinds of members, Section 7.3 shows how a class can inherit members from other classes.

7.2.5 Initializing attributes

Attributes can be initialized in two ways: per instance or per class.

- *Per instance.* An attribute can be given a different initial value per instance. This is done by not initializing it in the class definition. For example:

```
class OneApt
   attr streetName
   meth init(X) @streetName=X end
end
Apt1={New OneApt init(drottninggatan)}
Apt2={New OneApt init(rueNeuve)}
```

Each instance, including `Apt1` and `Apt2`, will initially reference a different unbound variable. Each variable can be bound to a different value.

- *Per class.* An attribute can be given a value that is the same for all instances of a class. This is done by initializing it with "`:`" in the class definition. For example:

```
class YorkApt
   attr
      streetName:york
      streetNumber:100
      wallColor:_
      floorSurface:wood
   meth init skip end
end
Apt3={New YorkApt init}
Apt4={New YorkApt init}
```

All instances, including `Apt3` and `Apt4`, have the same initial values for all four attributes. This includes `wallColor`, even though the initial value is an unbound variable. All instances refer to the same unbound variable. It can be bound by binding it in one of the instances, e.g., `@wallColor=white`. Then all instances will see this value. Be careful not to confuse the two operations `@wallColor=white` and `wallColor:=white`.

- *Per brand.* This is another way to use the per-class initialization. A brand is a set of classes that are related in some way, but not by inheritance. An attribute can be given a value that is the same for all members of a brand by initializing with the same variable for all members. For example[1]:

```
L=linux
class RedHat attr ostype:L end
class SuSE attr ostype:L end
class Debian attr ostype:L end
```

Each instance of each class will be initialized to the same value.

7.2.6 First-class messages

The principle is simple: messages are records and method heads are patterns that match a record. As a consequence, the following possibilities exist for the object call and the method definition. In the object call `{Obj M}`, the following are possible:

1. *Static record as message.* In the simplest case, `M` is a record that is known at compile time, e.g., as in the object call `{Counter inc(X)}`.

2. *Dynamic record as message.* It is possible to call `{Obj M}` where `M` is a variable that references a record that is calculated at run time. Because of dynamic typing, it is possible to create new record types at run time (e.g., with `Adjoin` or `List.toRecord`).

In the method definition, the following are possible:

1. *Fixed argument list.* The method head is a pattern consisting of a label followed by a series of arguments in parentheses. For example:

```
meth foo(a:A b:B c:C)
   % Method body
end
```

The method head `foo(a:A b:B c:C)` is a pattern that must match the message exactly, i.e., the label `foo` and arity `[a b c]` must match. The features (`a`, `b`, and `c`) can be given in any order. A class can only have one method definition with a given label, otherwise there is a syntax error.

2. *Flexible argument list.* The method head is the same as in the fixed argument list except it ends in "`...`". For example:

```
meth foo(a:A b:B c:C ...)
   % Method body
end
```

The "`...`" in the method head means that any message is accepted if it has at least the listed arguments. This means the same as the "`...`" in patterns, e.g., in a **`case`** statement. The given label must match the message label and the given arity must be a subset of the message arity.

3. *Variable reference to method head.* The whole method head is referenced by a variable. This is particularly useful with flexible argument lists, but it can also be

1. With apologies to all omitted Linux distributions.

used with a fixed argument list. For example:

```
meth foo(a:A b:B c:C ...)=M
   % Method body
end
```

The variable M references the full message as a record. The scope of M is the method body.

4. *Optional argument.* A default is given for an argument. The default is used if the argument is not in the message. For example:

```
meth foo(a:A b:B<=V)
   % Method body
end
```

The "<=V" in the method head means that the field b is optional in the object call. That is, the method can be called either with or without the field. With the field, an example call is foo(a:1 b:2), which ignores the expression V. Without the field, an example call is foo(a:1), for which the actual message received is foo(a:1 b:V).

5. *Private method label.* We said that method labels can be names. This is denoted by using a variable identifier:

```
meth A(bar:X)
   % Method body
end
```

The method A is bound to a fresh name when the class is defined. A is initially visible only in the scope of the class definition. If it has to be used elsewhere in the program, it must be passed explicitly.

6. *Dynamic method label.* It is possible to calculate a method label at run time, by using an escaped variable identifier. This is possible because class definitions are executed at run time. The method label has to be known when the class definition is executed. For example:

```
meth !A(bar:X)
   % Method body
end
```

causes the method label to be whatever the variable A was bound to. The variable must be bound to an atom or a name. By using names, this technique can make methods secure (see section 7.3.3).

7. *The* otherwise *method.* The method head with label otherwise is a catchall that accepts any message for which no other method exists. For example:

```
meth otherwise(M)
   % Method body
end
```

A class can only have one method with head otherwise, otherwise there is a syntax error. This method must have just one argument, otherwise a run-time "arity mismatch" error is given. If this method exists, then the object accepts any message. If no other method is defined for the message, then the otherwise(M) method is called with the full message in M as a record. This mechanism allows implementing delegation, an alternative to inheritance explained in section 7.3.4. This mechanism also allows making wrappers around method calls.

All these possibilities are covered by the syntax of table 7.1. In general, for the call {Obj M}, the compiler tries to determine statically what the object Obj and the method M are. If it can, then it compiles a very fast specialized call instruction. If it cannot, then it compiles a general object call instruction. The general instruction uses caching. The first call is slow, because it looks up the method and caches the result. Subsequent calls find the method in the cache and are almost as fast as the specialized call.

7.2.7 First-class attributes

Attribute names can be calculated at run time. For example, it is possible to write methods to access and assign any attributes:

```
class Inspector
   meth get(A ?X)
      X=@A
   end
   meth set(A X)
      A:=X
   end
end
```

The get method can access any attribute and the set method can assign any attribute. Any class that has these methods will open up its attributes for public use. This ability is dangerous for programming but can be very useful for debugging.

7.2.8 Programming techniques

The class concept we have introduced so far gives a convenient syntax for defining data abstractions with encapsulated state and multiple operations. The **class** statement defines a class value, which can be instantiated to give objects. In addition to having a convenient syntax, class values as defined here keep all the advantages of procedure values. All of the programming techniques for procedures also apply to classes. Classes can have external references just like procedure values. Classes are compositional: classes can be nested within classes. They are compatible with procedure values: classes can be nested within procedures and vice versa. Classes are not this flexible in all object-oriented languages; usually some limits are imposed, as explained in section 7.5.

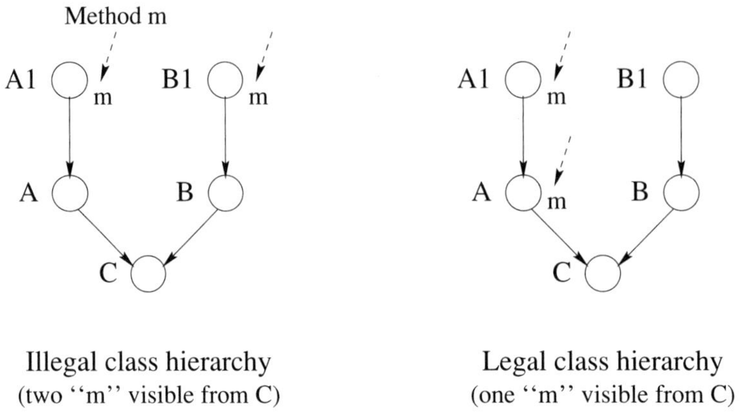

Figure 7.4: Illegal and legal class hierarchies.

7.3 Classes as incremental data abstractions

As explained before, the main addition that OOP adds to component-based programming is inheritance. OOP allows defining a class incrementally, by extending existing classes. Our model includes three sets of concepts for inheritance:

- The first is the inheritance graph (see section 7.3.1), which defines which preexisting classes are extended. Our model allows both single and multiple inheritance.
- The second is method access control (see section 7.3.2), which defines how to access particular methods both in the new class and in the preexisting classes. It is done with static and dynamic binding and the concept of **`self`**.
- The third is encapsulation control (see section 7.3.3), which defines what part of a program can see a classes' attributes and methods. We define the most popular scopes for object members and show how other scopes can be programmed.

We conclude by using the model to express related concepts such as forwarding, delegation, and reflection (see sections 7.3.4 and 7.3.5).

7.3.1 Inheritance graph

Inheritance is a way to construct new classes from existing classes. It defines what attributes and methods are available in the new class. We restrict our discussion of inheritance to methods. The same rules apply to attributes. The methods available in a class `C` are defined through a precedence relation on the methods that appear in the class hierarchy. We call this relation the overriding relation:

- A method in class `C` overrides any method with the same label in all of `C`'s superclasses.

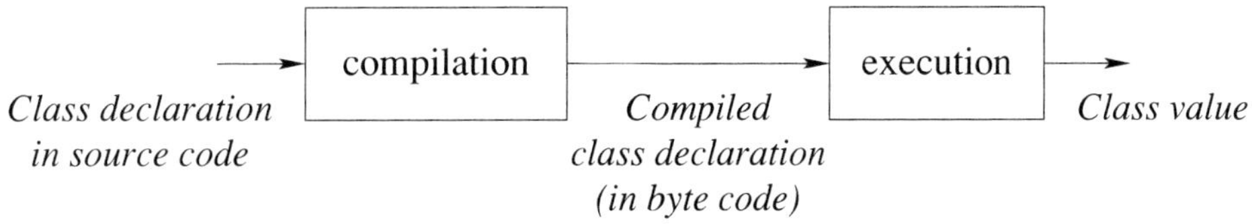

Figure 7.5: A class declaration is an executable statement.

Classes may inherit from one or more classes, which appear after the keyword **from** in the class declaration. A class that inherits from exactly one class is said to use single inheritance (sometimes called simple inheritance). Inheriting from more than one class is called multiple inheritance. A class `B` is a superclass of a class `A` if

- `B` appears in the **from** declaration of `A`, or
- `B` is a superclass of a class appearing in the **from** declaration of `A`.

A class hierarchy with the superclass relation can be seen as a directed graph with the current class being the root. The edges are directed toward the subclasses. There are two requirements for the inheritance to be legal. First, the inheritance relation is directed and acyclic. So the following is not allowed:

```
class A from B ... end
class B from A ... end
```

Second, after striking out all overridden methods, each remaining method should have a unique label and be defined in only one class in the hierarchy. Hence, class `C` in the following example is illegal because the two methods labeled `m` remain:

```
class A1 meth m(...) ... end end
class B1 meth m(...) ... end end
class A from A1 end
class B from B1 end
class C from A B end
```

Figure 7.4 shows this hierarchy and a slightly different one that is legal. The class `C` below is also illegal, since two methods `m` are available in `C`:

```
class A meth m(...) ... end end
class B meth m(...) ... end end
class C from A B end
```

Run time is all there is

If a program containing the declaration of class `C` is compiled in Mozart, then the system will not complain. It is only when the program executes the declaration that the system will raise an exception. If the program does not execute the declaration, then no exception is raised. For example, a program that contains the following source code:

```
fun {StrangeClass}
   class A meth foo(X) X=a end end
   class B meth foo(X) X=b end end
   class C from A B end
in C end
```

can be successfully compiled and executed. Its execution has the effect of defining the function StrangeClass. It is only during the call {StrangeClass} that an exception will be raised. This "late error detection" is not just a property of class declarations. It is a general property of the Mozart system that is a consequence of the dynamic nature of the language. Namely, there is no distinction between compile time and run time. The object system shares this dynamic nature. For example, it is possible to define classes whose method labels are calculated at run time (see section 7.2.6).

The Mozart system blurs the distinction between run time and compile time, to the point where everything is run time. The compiler is part of the run-time system. A class declaration is an executable statement. Compiling and executing it creates a class, which is a value in the language (see figure 7.5). The class value can be passed to New to create an object.

A programming system does not strictly need to distinguish between compile time and run time. The distinction is simply a way to help the compiler perform certain kinds of optimization. Most mainstream languages, including C++ and Java, make this distinction. Typically, a few operations (like declarations) can be executed only at compile time, and all other operations can be executed only at run time. The compiler can then execute all declarations at the same time, without any interference from the program's execution. This allows it to do more powerful optimizations when generating code. But it greatly reduces the flexibility of the language. For example, genericity and instantiation are no longer available to the programmer as general tools.

Because of Mozart's dynamic nature, the role of the compiler is very small. Since the compiler does not actually execute any declarations (it just converts them to executable statements), it needs very little knowledge of the language semantics. The compiler does in fact have some knowledge of language semantics, but this is an optimization that allows earlier detection of some errors and more efficient compiled code. More knowledge could be added to the compiler, e.g., to detect class hierarchy errors when it can deduce what the method labels are.

7.3.2 Method access control (static and dynamic binding)

When executing inside an object, we often want to call another method in the same object, i.e., do a kind of recursive invocation. This seems simple enough, but it becomes slightly more complicated when inheritance is involved. Inheritance is used to define a new class that extends an existing class. Two classes are involved in this definition: the new class and the existing class. Both can have methods with the same name, and the new class might want to call either. This means we need two ways to do a recursive call. They are called static and dynamic binding. We

```
class Account
   attr balance:0
   meth transfer(Amt)
      balance:=@balance+Amt
   end
   meth getBal(Bal)
      Bal=@balance
   end
   meth batchTransfer(AmtList)
      for A in AmtList do {self transfer(A)} end
   end
end
```

Figure 7.6: An example class `Account`.

introduce them by means of an example.

An example

Consider the class `Account` defined in figure 7.6. This class models a simple bank account with a balance. We can transfer money to it with `transfer`, inspect the balance with `getBal`, and do a series of transfers with `batchTransfer`. Note that `batchTransfer` calls `transfer` for each transfer.

Let us extend `Account` to do logging, i.e., to keep a record of all transactions it does. One way is to use inheritance, by overriding the `transfer` method:

```
class LoggedAccount from Account
   meth transfer(Amt)
      {LogObj addentry(transfer(Amt))}
      ...
   end
end
```

where `LogObj` is an object that keeps the log. Let us create a logged account with an initial balance of 100:

```
LogAct={New LoggedAccount transfer(100)}
```

Now the question is, what happens when we call `batchTransfer`? Does it call the old `transfer` in `Account` or the new `transfer` in `LoggedAccount`? We can deduce what the answer must be, if we assume that a class defines a data abstraction in object style. The data abstraction has a set of methods. For `LoggedAccount`, this set consists of the `getBal` and `batchTransfer` methods defined in `Account` as well as the new `transfer` defined in `LoggedAccount` itself. Therefore, the answer is that `batchTransfer` must call the new `transfer` in `LoggedAccount`. This is called dynamic binding. It is written as a call to **self**, i.e., as `{`**self**` transfer(A)}`.

When `Account` was defined, there was no `LoggedAccount` yet. Using dynamic binding keeps open the possibility that `Account` can be extended with inheritance, while ensuring that the new class is a data abstraction that correctly extends the old one. That is, it keeps all the functionality of the old abstraction while adding some new functionality.

However, dynamic binding is usually not enough to implement the extended abstraction. To see why, let us investigate closer how the new `transfer` is defined. Here is the full definition:

```
class LoggedAccount from Account
   meth transfer(Amt)
      {LogObj addentry(transfer(Amt))}
      Account,transfer(Amt)
   end
end
```

Inside the new `transfer`, we have to call the old `transfer`. We cannot use dynamic binding, since this would always call the new `transfer`. Instead, we use another technique, called static binding. In static binding, we call a method by pinpointing the method's class. Here the notation `Account,transfer(Amt)` pinpoints the method `transfer` in the class `Account`.

Discussion

Both static and dynamic binding are needed when using inheritance to override methods. Dynamic binding allows the new class to correctly extend the old class by letting old methods call new methods, even though the new method did not exist when the old method was defined. Static binding allows new methods to call old methods when they have to. We summarize the two techniques:

- *Dynamic binding*. This is written `{self M}`. This chooses the method matching `M` that is visible in the current object. This takes into account the overriding that has been done.
- *Static binding*. This is written `C, M` (with a comma), where `C` is a class that defines a method matching `M`. This chooses the method matching `M` that is visible in the class `C`. This takes overriding into account from the root class up to class `C`, but no further. If the object is of a subclass of `C` that has overridden `M` again, then this is not taken into account.

Dynamic binding is the only possible behavior for attributes. Static binding is not possible for them since the overridden attributes simply do not exist, neither in a logical sense (the only object that exists is the instance of the class that results after all the inheritance is done) nor in a practical sense (the implementation allocates no memory for them).

7.3.3 Encapsulation control

The principle of controlling encapsulation in an object-oriented language is to limit access to class members, namely attributes and methods, according to the

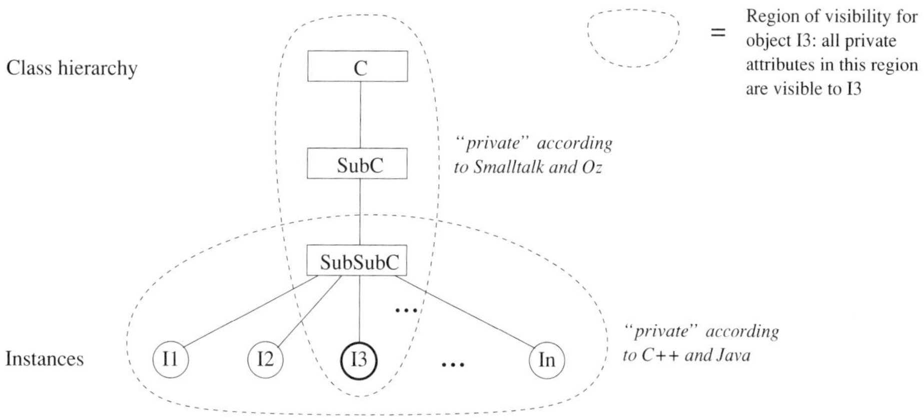

Figure 7.7: The meaning of "private."

requirements of the application architecture. Each member is defined with a scope. The scope is that part of the program text in which the member is visible, i.e., can be accessed by mentioning its name. Usually, the scope is statically defined, by the structure of the program. It can also be dynamically defined, namely during execution, if names are used (see below).

Programming languages usually give a default scope to each member when it is declared. This default can be altered with special keywords. Typical keywords used are `public`, `private`, and `protected`. Unfortunately, different languages use these terms to define slightly different scopes. Visibility in programming languages is a tricky concept. In the spirit of [62], we will try to bring order to this chaos.

Private and public scopes

The two most basic scopes are private and public, with the following meanings:

- A private member is one which is only visible in the object instance. The object instance can see all members defined in its class and its superclasses. Thus private defines a kind of vertical visibility.
- A public member is one which is visible anywhere in the program.

In both Smalltalk and Oz, attributes are private and methods are public according to this definition.

These definitions of private and public are natural if classes are used to construct data abstractions. Let us see why:

- First of all, a class is not the same thing as the data abstraction it defines! The class is an increment; it defines a data abstraction as an incremental modification of its superclasses. The class is only needed during the abstraction's construction.

The data abstraction is not an increment, however; it stands on its own, with all its own attributes and methods. Many of these may come from the superclasses and not from the class.

- Second, attributes are internal to the data abstraction and should be invisible from the outside. This is exactly the definition of private scope.
- Finally, methods make up the external interface of the data abstraction, so they should be visible to all entities that reference the abstraction. This is exactly the definition of public scope.

Constructing other scopes

Techniques for writing programs to control encapsulation are based essentially on two concepts: lexical scoping and name values. The private and public scopes defined above can be implemented with these two concepts. However, many other scopes can also be expressed using name values and lexical scoping. For example, it is possible to express the private and protected scopes of C++ and Java, as well as write programs that have much more elaborate security policies. The basic technique is to let method heads be name values instead of atoms. A name is an unforgeable constant; the only way to know a name is if someone gives you a reference to it (see section 3.7.5 and appendix B.2). In this way, a program can pass the reference in a controlled way, to exactly those areas of the program in which it should be visible.

In the examples of the previous sections, we used atoms as method labels. But atoms are not secure: if a third party finds out the atom's print representation (either by guessing or by some other way), then he or she can call the method too. Names are a simple way to plug this kind of security leak. This is important for a software development project with well-defined interfaces between different components. It is even more important for open distributed programs, where code written at different times by different groups can coexist (see chapter 11).

Private methods (in the C++ and Java sense)

When a method head is a name value, then its scope is limited to all instances of the class, but not to subclasses or their instances. This is exactly private in the sense of C++ and Java. Because of its usefulness, the object system of this chapter gives syntactic support for this technique. There are two ways to write it, depending on whether the name is defined implicitly inside the class or comes from the outside:

- By using a variable identifier as the method head. This implicitly creates a name when the class is defined and binds it to the variable. For example:

```
class C
   meth A(X)
      % Method body
   end
end
```

Method head A is bound to a name. The variable A is only visible inside the class definition. An instance of C can call method A in any other instance of C. Method A is invisible to subclass definitions. This is a kind of horizontal visibility. It corresponds to the concept of private method as it exists in C++ and Java (but not in Smalltalk). As figure 7.7 shows, private in C++ and Java is very different from private in Smalltalk and Oz. In Smalltalk and Oz, private is relative to an object and its classes, e.g., I3 in the figure. In C++ and Java, private is relative to a class and its instances, e.g., SubSubC in the figure.

- By using an escaped variable identifier as the method head. The exclamation point ! indicates that we will declare and bind the variable identifier outside of the class. When the class is defined, then the method head is bound to whatever the variable is bound to. This is a very general mechanism that can be used to protect methods in many ways. It can also be used for other purposes than security (see section 7.2.6). Here is an example that does exactly the same as the previous case:

```
local
   A={NewName}
in
   class C
      meth !A(X)
         % Method body
      end
   end
end
```

This creates a name at class definition time, just as in the previous case, and binds the method head to it. In fact, the previous definition is just shorthand for this example.

Letting the programmer determine the method label allows defining a security policy at a very fine grain. The program can pass the method label to exactly those entities that need to know it.

Protected methods (in the C++ sense)

By default, methods in the object system of this chapter are public. Using names, we can construct the concept of a protected method, including both the C++ version and the Java version. In C++, a method is protected if it is accessible only in the class it is defined or in descendant classes (and all instance objects of these classes). The protected concept is a combination of the Smalltalk notion of private with the C++/Java notion of private: it has both a horizontal and vertical component. Let us show how to express the C++ notion of protected. The Java notion of protected is somewhat different; we leave it to an exercise. In the following class, method A is protected:

```
class C
   attr pa:A
   meth A(X) skip end
   meth foo(...) {self A(5)} end
end
```

It is protected because the attribute pa stores a reference to A. Now create a subclass C1 of C. We can access method A as follows in the subclass:

```
class C1 from C
   meth b(...) A=@pa in {self A(5)} end
end
```

Method b accesses the method with label A through the attribute pa, which exists in the subclass. The method label can be stored in the attribute because it is just a value.

Attribute scopes

Attributes are always private. The only way to make them public is by means of methods. Because of dynamic typing, it is possible to define generic methods that give read and write access to all attributes. The class Inspector in section 7.2.7 shows one way to do this. Any class that inherits from Inspector will have all its attributes potentially be public. Atom attributes are not secure because they can be guessed. Name attributes are secure even when using Inspector, because they cannot be guessed.

Atoms or names as method heads?

When should one use an atom or a name as a method head? By default, atoms are visible throughout the whole program and names are visible only in the lexical scope of their creation. We can give a simple rule when implementing classes: for internal methods use names and for external methods use atoms.

Most popular object-oriented programming languages (e.g., Smalltalk, C++, and Java) support only atoms as method heads, not names. These languages make atoms usable by adding special operations to restrict their visibility (e.g., `private` and `protected` declarations). On the other hand, names are practical too. Their visibility can be extended by passing around references. But the capability-based approach exemplified by names has not yet become popular. Let us look more closely at the trade-offs in using names versus atoms.

Atoms are uniquely identified by their print representations. This means they can be stored in program source files, in emails, on Web pages, etc. In particular, they can be stored in the programmer's head! When writing a large program, a method can be called from anywhere by just giving its print representation. On the other hand, with names this is more awkward: the program itself has somehow to pass the name to the caller. This adds some complexity to the program as well as being a burden for the programmer. So atoms win out both for program simplicity and for the psychological comfort factor during development.

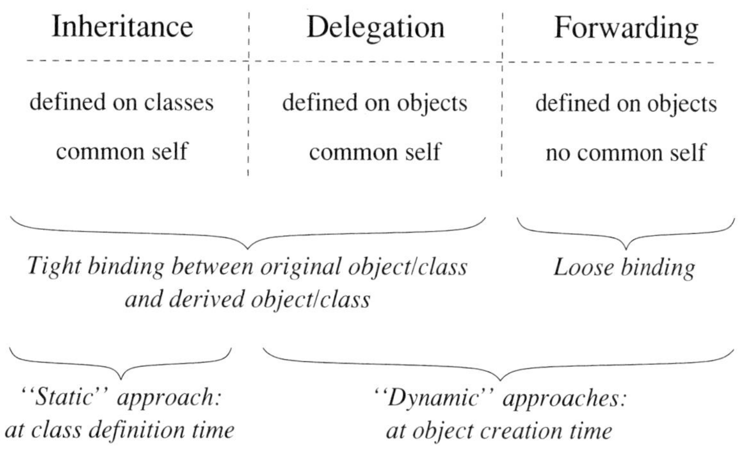

Figure 7.8: Different ways to extend functionality.

Names have other advantages. First, it is impossible to have conflicts with inheritance (either single or multiple). Second, encapsulation can be better managed, since an object reference does not necessarily have the right to call all the object's methods. Therefore, the program as a whole can be made less error-prone and better structured. A final point is that names can be given syntactic support to simplify their use. For example, in the object system of this chapter, it suffices to capitalize the method head.

7.3.4 Forwarding and delegation

Inheritance is one way to reuse already-defined functionality when defining new functionality. Inheritance can be tricky to use well, because it implies a tight binding between the original class and its extension. Sometimes it is better to use looser approaches. Two such approaches are forwarding and delegation. Both are defined at the level of objects: if object `Obj1` does not understand message `M`, then `M` is passed transparently to object `Obj2`. Figure 7.8 compares these approaches with inheritance.

Forwarding and delegation differ in how they treat **`self`**. In forwarding, `Obj1` and `Obj2` keep their separate identities. A self call in `Obj2` will stay in `Obj2`. In delegation, there is just one identity, namely that of `Obj1`. A self call in `Obj2` will call `Obj1`. We say that delegation, like implementation inheritance, implies a common self. Forwarding does not imply a common self.

Let us show how to express forwarding and delegation. We define special object creation functions, `NewF` and `NewD`, for forwarding and delegation. We are helped in this by the flexibility of our object system: we use the `otherwise` method, messages as values, and the dynamic creation of classes. We start with forwarding since it is the simplest.

```
local
   class ForwardMixin
      attr Forward:none
      meth setForward(F) Forward:=F end
      meth otherwise(M)
         if @Forward==none then raise undefinedMethod end
         else {@Forward M} end
      end
   end
in
   fun {NewF Class Init}
      {New class $ from Class ForwardMixin end Init}
   end
end
```

Figure 7.9: Implementing forwarding.

Forwarding

An object can forward to any other object. In the object system of this chapter, this can be implemented with the `otherwise(M)` method (see section 7.2.6). The argument `M` is a first-class message that can be passed to another object. Figure 7.9 gives the implementation of `NewF`, which replaces `New` for creating objects. Objects created with `NewF` have a method `setForward(F)` that lets them set dynamically the object to which they will forward messages they do not understand. Let us create two objects `Obj1` and `Obj2` such that `Obj2` forwards to `Obj1`:

```
class C1
   meth init skip end
   meth cube(A B) B=A*A*A end
end

class C2
   meth init skip end
   meth square(A B) B=A*A end
end

Obj1={NewF C1 init}
Obj2={NewF C2 init}
{Obj2 setForward(Obj1)}
```

Doing `{Obj2 cube(10 X)}` will cause `Obj2` to forward the message to `Obj1`.

Delegation

Delegation is a powerful way to structure a system dynamically [130]. It lets us build a hierarchy among objects instead of among classes. Instead of an object inheriting from a class (at class definition time), we let an object delegate to another object

```
local
   SetSelf={NewName}
   class DelegateMixin
      attr this Delegate:none
      meth !SetSelf(S) this:=S end
      meth set(A X) A:=X end
      meth get(A ?X) X=@A end
      meth setDelegate(D) Delegate:=D end
      meth Del(M S) SS in
         SS=@this this:=S
         try {self M} finally this:=SS end
      end
      meth call(M) SS in
         SS=@this this:=self
         try {self M} finally this:=SS end
      end
      meth otherwise(M)
         if @Delegate==none then
            raise undefinedMethod end
         else
            {@Delegate Del(M @this)}
         end
      end
   end
in
   fun {NewD Class Init}
      Obj={New class $ from Class DelegateMixin end Init}
   in
      {Obj SetSelf(Obj)}
      Obj
   end
end
```

Figure 7.10: Implementing delegation (part 1: creating objects).

(at object creation time). Delegation can achieve the same effects as inheritance, with two main differences: the hierarchy is between objects, not classes, and it can be changed at any time.

Given any two objects `Obj1` and `Obj2`, we suppose there exists a method `setDelegate` such that `{Obj2 setDelegate(Obj1)}` sets `Obj2` to delegate to `Obj1`. In other words, `Obj1` behaves as the "superclass" of `Obj2`. Whenever a method is invoked that is not defined in `Obj2`, the method call will be retried at `Obj1`. The delegation chain can grow to any length. If there is an `Obj3` that delegates to `Obj2`, then calling `Obj3` can climb up the chain all the way to `Obj1`.

An important property of the delegation semantics is that self is always preserved: it is the self of the original object that initiated the delegation chain. It follows that the object state (the attributes) is also the state of the original object. In that sense, the other objects play the role of classes: in a first instance, it is their methods that

Operation	Original syntax	Delegation syntax
Object call	`{`⟨obj⟩` M}`	`{`⟨obj⟩` call(M)}`
Self call	`{`**`self`**` M}`	`{@this M}`
Get attribute	`@`⟨attr⟩	`{@this get(`⟨attr⟩` $)}`
Set attribute	⟨attr⟩`:=X`	`{@this set(`⟨attr⟩` X)}`
Set delegate		`{`⟨obj⟩$_1$` setDelegate(`⟨obj⟩$_2$`)}`

Table 7.2: Implementing delegation (part 2: using objects and attributes).

are important in delegation, not the values of their attributes.

Let us implement delegation using our object system. Figure 7.10 gives the implementation of `NewD`, which replaces `New` for creating objects. We can use delegation with these objects and their attributes if we use them as shown in Table 7.2. The special syntax in this table could be eliminated by an appropriate linguistic abstraction. Now let us give a simple example of how delegation works. We define two objects `Obj1` and `Obj2` and let `Obj2` delegate to `Obj1`. We give each object an attribute `i` and a way to increment it. With inheritance this would look as follows:

```
class C1NonDel
   attr i:0
   meth init skip end
   meth inc(I) i:=@i+I end
   meth browse {self inc(10)} {Browse c1#@i} end
   meth c {self browse} end
end

class C2NonDel from C1NonDel
   attr i:0
   meth init skip end
   meth browse {self inc(100)} {Browse c2#@i} end
end
```

With our delegation implementation we can get the same effect by using the code of figure 7.11. It is more verbose, but that is only because the system has no syntactic support for delegation. It is not due to the concept itself. Note that this just scratches the surface of what we could do with delegation. For example, by calling `setDelegate` again we could change the hierarchy of the program at run time. Let us now call `Obj1` and `Obj2`:

```
{Obj2 call(c)}
{Obj1 call(c)}
```

Doing these calls several times shows that each object keeps its own local state, that `Obj2` "inherits" the `inc` and `c` methods from object `Obj1`, and that `Obj2` "overrides" the `browse` method. Let us make the delegation chain longer:

```
class C1
   attr i:0
   meth init skip end
   meth inc(I)
      {@this set(i {@this get(i $)}+I)}
   end
   meth browse
      {@this inc(10)}
      {Browse c1#{@this get(i $)}}
   end
   meth c {@this browse} end
end
Obj1={NewD C1 init}

class C2
   attr i:0
   meth init skip end
   meth browse
      {@this inc(100)}
      {Browse c2#{@this get(i $)}}
   end
end
Obj2={NewD C2 init}
{Obj2 setDelegate(Obj1)}
```

Figure 7.11: An example of delegation.

```
class C2b
   attr i:0
   meth init skip end
end
ObjX={NewD C2b init}
{ObjX setDelegate(Obj2)}
```

`ObjX` inherits all its behavior from `Obj2`. It is identical to `Obj2` except that it has a different local state. The delegation hierarchy now has three levels: `ObjX`, `Obj2`, and `Obj1`. Let us change the hierarchy by letting `ObjX` delegate to `Obj1`:

```
{ObjX setDelegate(Obj1)}
{ObjX call(c)}
```

In the new hierarchy, `ObjX` inherits its behavior from `Obj1`. It uses the `browse` method of `Obj1`, so it will increment by 10 instead of by 100.

7.3.5 Reflection

A system is reflective if it can inspect part of its execution state while it is running. Reflection can be purely introspective (only reading the internal state, without modifying it) or intrusive (both reading and modifying the internal state). Reflection can be done at a high or low level of abstraction. One example of reflection at a high level would be the ability to see the entries on the semantic stack as closures. It can be explained simply in terms of the abstract machine. On the other hand, the ability to read memory as an array of integers is reflection at a low level. There is no simple way to explain it in the abstract machine.

Meta-object protocols

Object-oriented programming, because of its richness, is a particularly fertile area for reflection. For example, the system could make it possible to examine or even change the inheritance hierarchy while a program is running. This is possible in Smalltalk. The system could make it possible to change how objects execute at a basic level, e.g., how inheritance works (how method lookup is done in the class hierarchy) and how methods are called. The description of how an object system works at a basic level is called a meta-object protocol. The ability to change the meta-object protocol is a powerful way to modify an object system. Meta-object protocols are used for many purposes: debugging, customizing, and separation of concerns (e.g., transparently adding encryption or format changes to method calls). Meta-object protocols were originally invented in the context of the Common Lisp Object System (CLOS) [113, 160]. They are an active area of research in OOP.

Method wrapping

A common use of meta object protocols is to do method wrapping, i.e., to intercept each method call, possibly performing a user-defined operation before and after the call and possibly changing the arguments to the call itself. In our object system, we can implement this in a simple way by taking advantage of the fact that objects are one-argument procedures. For example, let us write a tracer to track the behavior of an object-oriented program. The tracer should display the method label whenever we enter a method and exit a method. Here is a version of `New` that implements this:

```
fun {TraceNew Class Init}
   Obj={New Class Init}
   proc {TracedObj M}
      {Browse entering({Label M})}
      {Obj M}
      {Browse exiting({Label M})}
   end
in TracedObj end
```

An object created with `TraceNew` behaves identically to an object created with `New`, except that method calls (except for calls to **`self`**) are traced. The definition of `TraceNew` uses higher-order programming: the procedure `TracedObj` has the external reference `Obj`. This definition can easily be extended to do more sophisticated wrapping. For example, the message `M` could be transformed in some way before being passed to `Obj`.

A second way to implement `TraceNew` is to do the wrapping with a class instead of a procedure. This gives the following definition:

```
fun {TraceNew2 Class Init}
   Obj={New Class Init}
   TInit={NewName}
   class Tracer
      meth !TInit skip end
      meth otherwise(M)
         {Browse entering({Label M})}
         {Obj M}
         {Browse exiting({Label M})}
      end
   end
in {New Tracer TInit} end
```

This has the same limitation with **`self`** as before. It uses dynamic class creation, the `otherwise` method, and a fresh name `TInit` for the initialization method to avoid conflicts with other method labels. Note that the class `Tracer` has the external reference `Obj`. If your language does not allow this, then you can modify the technique to store `Obj` in an attribute of `Tracer`. Needless to say, the solution with higher-order programming is more concise.

Reflection of object state

Let us show a simple but useful example of reflection in OOP. We would like to be able to read and write the whole state of an object, independent of the object's class. The Mozart object system provides this ability through the class `ObjectSupport.reflect`. Inheriting from this class gives the following three additional methods:

- `clone(X)` creates a clone of **`self`** and binds it to `X`. The clone is a new object with the same class and the same values of attributes.
- `toChunk(X)` binds to `X` a protected value (a "chunk") that contains the current values of the attributes.
- `fromChunk(X)` sets the object state to `X`, where `X` was obtained from a previous call of `toChunk`.

A chunk is like a record but with a restricted set of operations. It is protected in the sense that only authorized programs can look inside it (see appendix B.4). Chunks can be used to build secure data abstractions, as shown in section 3.7.5. Let us extend the `Counter` class we saw before to do state reflection:

```
class Counter from ObjectSupport.reflect
   attr val
   meth init(Value)
      val:=Value
   end
   meth browse
      {Browse @val}
   end
   meth inc(Value)
      val:=@val+Value
   end
end
```

We can define two objects:

```
C1={New Counter init(0)}
C2={New Counter init(0)}
```

and then transfer state from one to the other:

```
{C1 inc(10)}
local X in {C1 toChunk(X)} {C2 fromChunk(X)} end
```

At this point C2 also has the value 10. This is a simplistic example, but state reflection is actually a very powerful tool. It can be used to build generic abstractions on objects, i.e., abstractions that work on objects of any class.

7.4 Programming with inheritance

All the programming techniques of stateful programming and declarative programming are still possible in the object system of this chapter. Particularly useful are techniques that are based on encapsulation and state to make programs modular. See the previous chapter, and especially the discussion of component-based programming, which relies on encapsulation.

This section focuses on the new techniques that are made possible by OOP. All these techniques center around the use of inheritance: first, using it correctly, and then, taking advantage of its power.

7.4.1 The correct use of inheritance

There are two ways to view inheritance:

- *The type view.* In this view, classes are types and subclasses are subtypes. For example, take a `LabeledWindow` class that inherits from a `Window` class. All labeled windows are also windows. The type view is consistent with the principle that classes should model real-world entities or some abstract versions of them. In the type view, classes satisfy the *substitution property*: every operation that works for an object of class `C` also works for objects of a subclass of `C`. Most object-oriented languages, such as Java and Smalltalk, are designed for the type view [68, 71]. Section 7.4.1 explores what happens if we do not respect the type view.

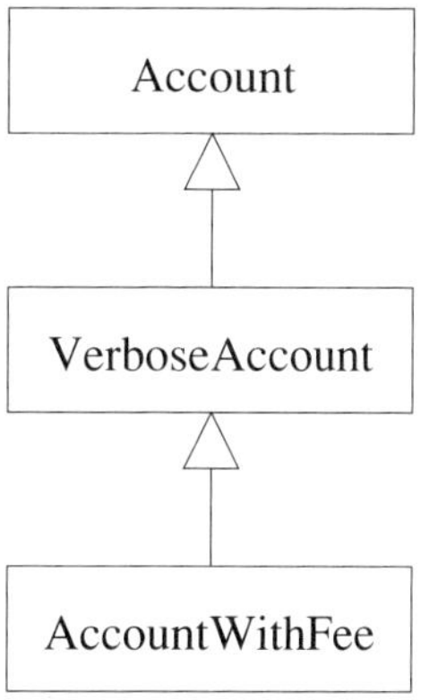

Figure 7.12: A simple hierarchy with three classes.

- *The structure view.* In this view, inheritance is just another programming tool that is used to structure programs. This view is *strongly discouraged* because classes no longer satisfy the substitution property. The structure view is an almost unending source of bugs and bad designs. Major commercial projects, which shall here remain anonymous, have failed for this reason. A few object-oriented languages, notably Eiffel, are designed from the start to allow both the type and structure views [140].

In the type view, each class stands on its own two feet, so to speak, as a bona fide data abstraction. In the structure view, classes are sometimes just scaffolding, which exists only for its role in structuring the program.

An example

In the vast majority of cases, inheritance should respect the type view. Doing otherwise gives subtle and pernicious bugs that can poison a whole system. Let us give an example. We take as base class the `Account` class we saw before, which is defined in figure 7.6. An `Account` object `A` satisfies the following algebraic rule:

$\{$`A getBalance(`b`)`$\}$ $\{$`A transfer(`s`)`$\}$ $\{$`A getBalance(`b'`)`$\}$

with $b + s = b'$. That is, if the initial balance is b and a transfer of s is done, then the final balance is $b + s$. This algebraic rule can be seen as a specification of `Account`, or as we will see later, a contract between `Account` and the program that uses its objects. (In a practical definition of `Account`, there would be other rules as well. We leave them out for the purposes of the example.) According to the type view, subclasses of `Account` should also implement this contract. Let us now extend `Account` in two ways. The first extension is conservative, i.e., it respects the type view:

```
class VerboseAccount from Account
   meth verboseTransfer(Amt)
      {self transfer(Amt)}
      {Browse ´Balance:´#@balance}
   end
end
```

We simply add a new method, `verboseTransfer`. Since the existing methods are not changed, this implies that the contract still holds. A `VerboseAccount` object will work correctly in all cases where an `Account` object works. Let us now do a second, more dangerous extension:

```
class AccountWithFee from VerboseAccount
   attr fee:5
   meth transfer(Amt)
      VerboseAccount,transfer(Amt-@fee)
   end
end
```

Figure 7.12 shows the resulting hierarchy. The open arrowhead in this figure is the usual notation to represent an inheritance link. `AccountWithFee` overrides the method `transfer`. Overriding is not a problem in itself. The problem is that an `AccountWithFee` object does not work correctly when viewed as an `Account` object. Consider the sequence of three calls:

```
{A getBalance(B)} {A transfer(S)} {A getBalance(B2)}
```

If `A` is an `AccountWithFee` object, this implies `B+S-@fee=B2`. If `@fee`$\neq 0$ then the contract no longer holds. This will break any program that relies on the behavior of `Account` objects. Typically, the origin of the break will not be obvious, since it is carefully hidden inside a method somewhere in a large application. It will appear long after the change was made, as a slight imbalance in the books. Debugging such "slight" problems is amazingly difficult and time-consuming.

The rest of section 7.4 primarily considers the type view. Almost all uses of inheritance should respect the type view. However, the structure view is occasionally useful. Its main use is in changing the behavior of the object system itself. For this purpose, it should be used only by expert language implementors who clearly understand the ramifications of what they are doing. A simple example is method wrapping (see section 7.3.5), which requires using the structure view. For more information, we recommend [140] for a deeper discussion of the type view versus the structure view.

Design by contract

The `Account` example is an example of a general technique for designing correct programs and verifying their correctness. We say a program is *correct* if it performs according to its specification. One way to prove the correctness of a program is by reasoning with a formal semantics. For example, with a stateful program we can reason using the axiomatic semantics of section 6.6. We can also reason with algebraic rules, as in the `Account` example. Based on these techniques for formal specification, Bertrand Meyer has developed a method for designing correct programs called *design by contract* and implemented it in the Eiffel language [140].

The principal idea of design by contract is that a data abstraction implies a contract between the abstraction's designer and its users. The users must guarantee that an abstraction is called in the right way, and in return the abstraction behaves in the right way. There is a deliberate analogy with contracts in human society. All parties are expected to follow the contract. The contract can be formulated in terms of algebraic rules, as we did in the `Account` example, or with preconditions and postconditions, as we saw in section 6.6. The user ensures that the preconditions are always true before calling an operation. The data abstraction's implementation then ensures that the postconditions are always true when the operation returns. There is a division of responsibility: the user is responsible for the preconditions and the data abstraction is responsible for the postconditions.

The data abstraction checks whether the user follows the contract. This is especially easy if preconditions and postconditions are used. The preconditions are checked at the boundary between the user and the data abstraction. Once we are inside the data abstraction, we can assume the preconditions are satisfied. No checks are done inside the data abstraction, so its implementation is uncluttered. This is analogous to human society. For example, to enter a country, you are checked at the boundary (e.g., passport control, security checks, and customs). Once you are inside, there are no more checks.

Checking the preconditions can be done either at compile time or at run time. Many industrial systems, e.g., in telecommunications, do checking at run time. They run for long test periods during which all contract violations are logged. Checking at compile time is particularly desirable since contract violations can be determined before running a program. It is an interesting research question to determine just how expressive the preconditions can be and still be checked at compile time.

A cautionary tale

We end the discussion on the correct use of inheritance with a cautionary tale. Some years ago, a well-known company initiated an ambitious project based on OOP. Despite a budget of several billion dollars, the project failed. Among many reasons for the failure was an incorrect use of OOP. in particular concerning inheritance. Two major mistakes were made:

- The substitution property was regularly violated. Routines that worked correctly with objects of a given class did not work with objects of a subclass. This made it much more difficult to use objects: instead of one routine being sufficient for many classes, many routines were needed.
- Classes were subclassed to fix small problems. Instead of fixing the class itself, a subclass was defined to patch the class. This was done so frequently that it gave layers upon layers of patches. Object invocations were slowed down by an

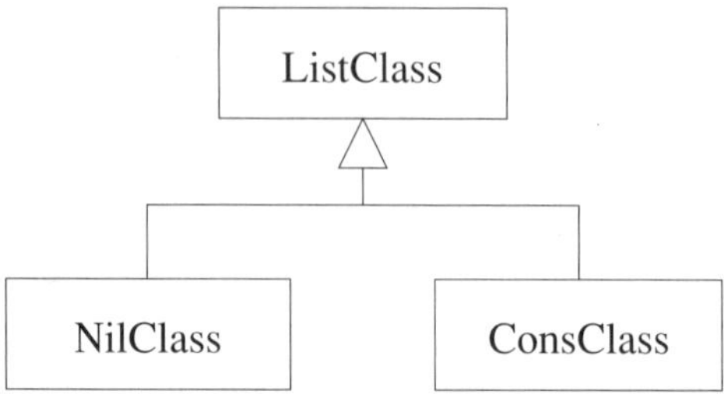

Figure 7.13: Constructing a hierarchy by following the type.

order of magnitude. The class hierarchy became unnecessarily deep, which increased complexity of the system.

The lesson to heed is to be careful to use inheritance in a correct way. Respect the substitution property whenever possible. Use inheritance to add new functionality and not to patch a broken class. Study common design patterns to learn the correct use of inheritance.

Reengineering At this point, we should mention the discipline of reengineering, which can be used to fix architectural problems like these two incorrect uses of inheritance [51, 16]. The general goal of reengineering is to take an existing system and attempt to improve some of its properties by changing the source code. Many properties can be improved in this way: system architecture, modularity, performance, portability, quality of documentation, and use of new technology. However, reengineering cannot resurrect a failed project. It is more like curing a disease. If the designer has a choice, the best approach remains to prevent the disease, i.e., to design a system so that it can be adapted to changing requirements. In section 6.7 and throughout the book, we give design principles that work toward this goal.

7.4.2 Constructing a hierarchy by following the type

When writing programs with recursion, we saw in section 3.4.2 that it is a good idea to define first the type of the data structure, and then to construct the recursive program by following the type. We can use a similar idea to construct inheritance hierarchies. For example, consider the list type ⟨List T⟩, which is defined as

⟨List T⟩ ::= `nil`
          | T ´|´ ⟨List T⟩

This says that a list is either `nil` or a list pair. Let us implement the list abstraction in the class `ListClass`. Following the type definition means that we define two other classes that inherit from `ListClass`, which we can call `NilClass` and `ConsClass`.

```
class ListClass
   meth isNil(_) raise undefinedMethod end end
   meth append(_ _) raise undefinedMethod end end
   meth display raise undefinedMethod end end
end

class NilClass from ListClass
   meth init skip end
   meth isNil(B) B=true end
   meth append(T U) U=T end
   meth display {Browse nil} end
end

class ConsClass from ListClass
   attr head tail
   meth init(H T) head:=H tail:=T end
   meth isNil(B) B=false end
   meth append(T U)
      U2={@tail append(T $)}
   in
      U={New ConsClass init(@head U2)}
   end
   meth display {Browse @head} {@tail display} end
end
```

Figure 7.14: Lists in object-oriented style.

Figure 7.13 shows the hierarchy. This hierarchy is a natural design to respect the substitution property. An instance of `NilClass` is a list, so it is easy to use it wherever a list is required. The same holds for `ConsClass`.

Figure 7.14 defines a list abstraction that follows this hierarchy. In this figure, `ListClass` is an abstract class: a class in which some methods are left undefined. Trying to call the methods `isNil`, `append`, and `display` will raise an exception. Abstract classes are not intended to be instantiated, since they lack some methods. The idea is to define another class that inherits from the abstract class and that adds the missing methods. This gives a concrete class, which can be instantiated since it defines all the methods it calls. `NilClass` and `ConsClass` are concrete classes. They define the methods `isNil`, `append`, and `display`. The call `{L1 append(L2 L3)}` binds `L3` to the concatenation of `L1` and `L2`, without changing `L1` or `L2`. The call `{L display}` displays the list. Let us now do some calculations with lists:

```
L1={New ConsClass
    init(1 {New ConsClass
            init(2 {New NilClass init})})}
L2={New ConsClass init(3 {New NilClass init})}
L3={L1 append(L2 $)}
{L3 display}
```

```
class GenericSort
   meth init skip end
   meth qsort(Xs Ys)
      case Xs
      of nil then Ys = nil
      [] P|Xr then S L in
         {self partition(Xr P S L)}
         {Append {self qsort(S $)}
                 P|{self qsort(L $)} Ys}
      end
   end
   meth partition(Xs P Ss Ls)
      case Xs
      of nil then Ss=nil Ls=nil
      [] X|Xr then Sr Lr in
         if {self less(X P $)} then
            Ss=X|Sr Ls=Lr
         else
            Ss=Sr Ls=X|Lr
         end
         {self partition(Xr P Sr Lr)}
      end
   end
end
```

Figure 7.15: A generic sorting class (with inheritance).

This creates two lists `L1` and `L2` and concatenates them to form `L3`. It then displays the contents of `L3` in the browser, as 1, 2, 3, `nil`.

7.4.3 Generic classes

A generic class is one that only defines part of the functionality of a data abstraction. It has to be completed before it can be used to create objects. Let us look at two ways to define generic classes. The first way, often used in OOP, uses inheritance. The second way uses higher-order programming. We will see that the first way is just a syntactic variation of the second. In other words, inheritance can be seen as a programming style that is based on higher-order programming.

Using inheritance

A common way to make classes more generic in OOP is to use abstract classes. For example, figure 7.15 defines an abstract class `GenericSort` for sorting a list. This class uses the quicksort algorithm, which needs a boolean comparison operation. The boolean operation's definition depends on the type of data that are sorted. Other classes can inherit from `GenericSort` and add definitions of `less`, e.g., for

```
class IntegerSort from GenericSort
   meth less(X Y B)
      B=(X<Y)
   end
end

class RationalSort from GenericSort
   meth less(X Y B)
      '/'(P Q)=X
      '/'(R S)=Y
   in B=(P*S<Q*R) end
end
```

Figure 7.16: Making it concrete (with inheritance).

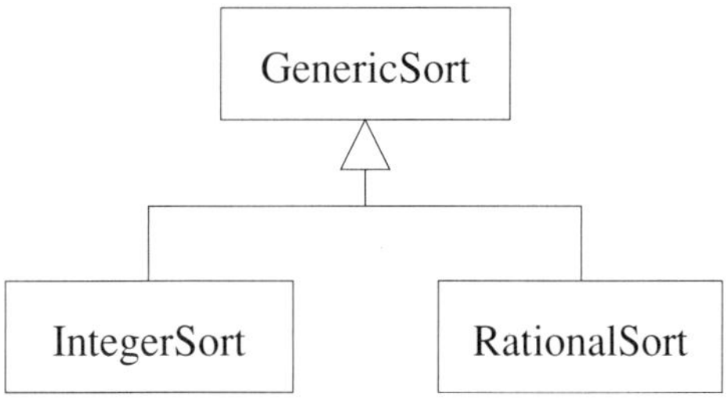

Figure 7.17: A class hierarchy for genericity.

integers, rationals, or strings. In this case, we specialize the abstract class to form a concrete class, i.e., a class in which all methods are defined. Figure 7.16 defines the concrete classes `IntegerSort` and `RationalSort`, which both inherit from `GenericSort`. Figure 7.17 shows the resulting hierarchy.

Using higher-order programming

There is a second natural way to create generic classes, namely by using higher-order programming directly. Since classes are first-class values, we can define a function that takes some arguments and returns a class that is specialized with these arguments. Figure 7.18 defines the function `MakeSort` that takes a boolean comparison as its argument and returns a sorting class specialized with this comparison. Figure 7.19 defines two classes, `IntegerSort` and `RationalSort`, that can sort lists of integers and lists of rational numbers (the latter represented as pairs with label `'/'`). Now we can execute the following statements:

```
fun {MakeSort Less}
   class $
      meth init skip end
      meth qsort(Xs Ys)
         case Xs
         of nil then Ys = nil
         [] P|Xr then S L in
            {self partition(Xr P S L)}
            {Append {self qsort(S $)}
                    P|{self qsort(L $)} Ys}
         end
      end
      meth partition(Xs P Ss Ls)
         case Xs
         of nil then Ss=nil Ls=nil
         [] X|Xr then Sr Lr in
            if {Less X P} then
               Ss=X|Sr Ls=Lr
            else
               Ss=Sr Ls=X|Lr
            end
            {self partition(Xr P Sr Lr)}
         end
      end
   end
end
```

Figure 7.18: A generic sorting class (with higher-order programming).

```
ISort={New IntegerSort init}
RSort={New RationalSort init}

{Browse {ISort qsort([1 2 5 3 4] $)}}
{Browse {RSort qsort(['/'(23 3) '/'(34 11) '/'(47 17)] $)}}
```

Discussion

It is clear that we are using inheritance to "plug in" one operation into another. This is just a form of higher-order programming, where the first operation is passed to the second. What is the difference between the two techniques? In most programming languages, the inheritance hierarchy must be defined at compile time. This gives a static genericity. Because it is static, the compiler may be able to generate better code or do more error checking. Higher-order programming, when it is possible, lets us define new classes at run time. This gives a dynamic genericity, which is more flexible.

```
IntegerSort = {MakeSort fun {$ X Y} X<Y end}

RationalSort = {MakeSort fun {$ X Y}
                            '/'(P Q) = X
                            '/'(R S) = Y
                         in P*S<Q*R end}
```

Figure 7.19: Making it concrete (with higher-order programming).

7.4.4 Multiple inheritance

Multiple inheritance is useful when an object has to be two different things in the same program. For example, consider a graphics package that can show a variety of geometric figures, including circles, lines, and more complex figures. We would like to define a "grouping" operation that can combine any number of figures into a single, composite figure. How can we model this with OOP? We will design a simple, fully working program. We will use multiple inheritance to add the grouping ability to figures. The idea for this design comes from Bertrand Meyer [140]. This simple program can easily be extended to a full-fledged graphics package.

Geometric figures

We first define the class `Figure` to model geometric figures, with methods `init` (initialize the figure), `move(X Y)` (move the figure), and `display` (display the figure):

```
class Figure
   meth otherwise(M)
      raise undefinedMethod end
   end
end
```

This is an abstract class; any attempt to invoke its methods will raise an exception. Actual figures are instances of subclasses of `Figure`. For example, here is a `Line` class:

```
class Line from Figure
   attr canvas x1 y1 x2 y2
   meth init(Can X1 Y1 X2 Y2)
      canvas:=Can
      x1:=X1 y1:=Y1
      x2:=X2 y2:=Y2
   end
   meth move(X Y)
      x1:=@x1+X y1:=@y1+Y
      x2:=@x2+X y2:=@y2+Y
   end
   meth display
      {@canvas create(line @x1 @y1 @x2 @y2)}
   end
end
```

And here is a `Circle` class:

```
class Circle from Figure
   attr canvas x y r
   meth init(Can X Y R)
      canvas:=Can
      x:=X y:=Y r:=R
   end
   meth move(X Y)
      x:=@x+X y:=@y+Y
   end
   meth display
      {@canvas create(oval @x-@r @y-@r @x+@r @y+@r)}
   end
end
```

Figure 7.20 shows how `Line` and `Circle` inherit from `Figure`. This kind of diagram is called a class diagram. It is a part of UML, the Uniform Modeling Language, a widely used set of techniques for modeling object-oriented programs [62]. Class diagrams are a useful way to visualize the class structure of an object-oriented program. Each class is represented by a rectangle with three parts, containing the class name, the attributes it defines, and the methods it defines. These rectangles can be connected with lines representing inheritance links.

Linked lists

We define the class `LinkedList` to group figures together, with methods `init` (initialize the linked list), `add(F)` (add a figure), and `forall(M)` (execute `{F M}` for all figures):

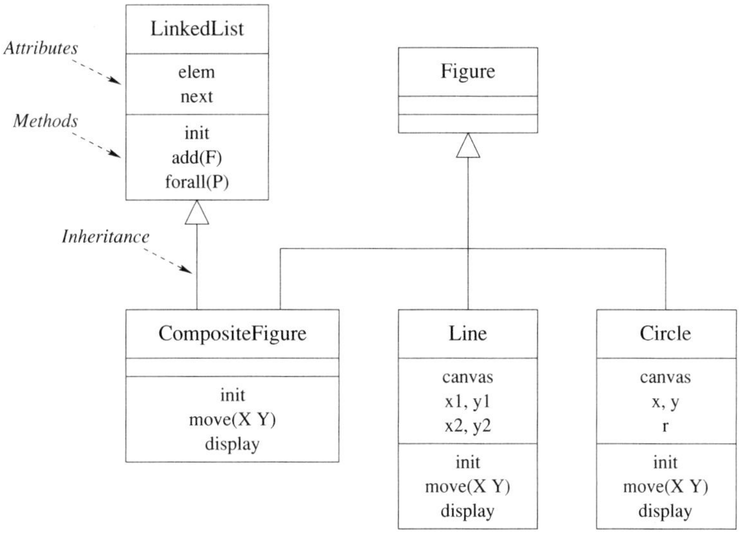

Figure 7.20: Class diagram of the graphics package.

```
class LinkedList
   attr elem next
   meth init(elem:E<=null next:N<=null)
      elem:=E next:=N
   end
   meth add(E)
      next:={New LinkedList init(elem:E next:@next)}
   end
   meth forall(M)
      if @elem\=null then {@elem M} end
      if @next\=null then {@next forall(M)} end
   end
end
```

The `forall(M)` method is especially interesting because it uses first-class messages. A linked list is represented as a sequence of instances of this class. The `next` field of each instance refers to the next one in the list. The last element has the `next` field equal to `null`. There is always at least one element in the list, called the header. The header is not an element that it seen by users of the linked list; it is just needed for the implementation, The header always has the `elem` field equal to `null`. Therefore an empty linked list corresponds to a header node with both `elem` and `next` fields equal to `null`.

Composite figures

What is a composite figure? It is both a figure and a linked list of figures. Therefore we define a class `CompositeFigure` that inherits from both `Figure` and

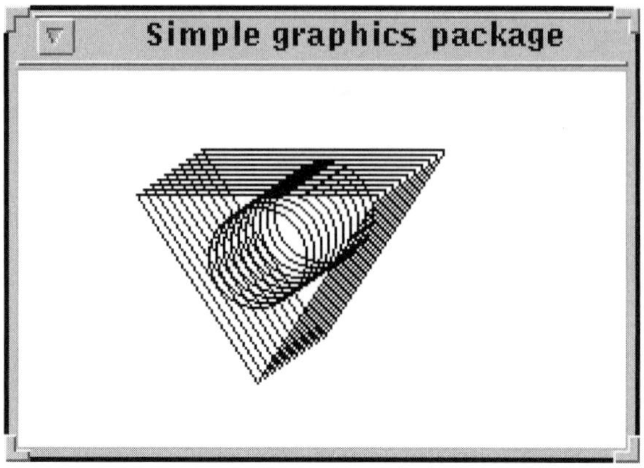

Figure 7.21: Drawing in the simple graphics package.

```
LinkedList:
 class CompositeFigure from Figure LinkedList
    meth init
       LinkedList,init
    end
    meth move(X Y)
       {self forall(move(X Y))}
    end
    meth display
       {self forall(display)}
    end
 end
```

Figure 7.20 shows the multiple inheritance. The multiple inheritance is correct because the two functionalities are completely different and have no undesirable interaction. The `init` method is careful to initialize the linked list. It does not need to initialize the figure. As in all figures, there is a `move` and a `display` method. The `move(X Y)` method moves all figures in the linked list. The `display` method displays all figures in the linked list.

Do you see the beauty of this design? With it, a figure can consist of other figures, some of which consist of other figures, and so forth, to any number of levels. The inheritance structure guarantees that moving and displaying will always work correctly. This is a nice example of polymorphism: the classes `CompositeFigure`, `Line`, and `Circle` all understand the messages `move(X Y)` and `display`.

Example execution

Let us run this example. First, we set up a window with a graphics display field:

```
declare
W=250 H=150 Can
Wind={QTk.build td(title:"Simple graphics package"
                   canvas(width:W height:H bg:white handle:Can))}
{Wind show}
```

This uses the `QTk` graphics tool, which is explained in chapter 10. For now just assume that this sets up a canvas, which is the drawing field for our geometric figures. Next, we define a composite figure `F1` containing a triangle and a circle:

```
declare
F1={New CompositeFigure init}
{F1 add({New Line init(Can 50 50 150 50)})}
{F1 add({New Line init(Can 150 50 100 125)})}
{F1 add({New Line init(Can 100 125 50 50)})}
{F1 add({New Circle init(Can 100 75 20)})}
```

We can display this figure as follows:

```
{F1 display}
```

This displays the figure once. Let us move the figure around and display it each time:

```
for I in 1..10 do {F1 display} {F1 move(3 ~2)} end
```

Figure 7.21 shows the result.

Composite figures with single inheritance

Instead of defining `CompositeFigure` with multiple inheritance, we can define it using single inheritance by putting the list of figures in an attribute. This gives

```
class CompositeFigure from Figure
   attr figlist
   meth init
      figlist:={New LinkedList init}
   end
   meth add(F)
      {@figlist add(F)}
   end
   meth move(X Y)
      {@figlist forall(move(X Y))}
   end
   meth display
      {@figlist forall(display)}
   end
end
```

Figure 7.22 shows the class diagram for this case. The link between `CompositeFigure` and `LinkedList` is called an association. It represents a relationship between the two classes. The numbers attached to the two ends are cardinalities; each number says how many elements there are for a particular instance. The number 1 on the linked list side means that there is exactly one linked list per composite figure, and

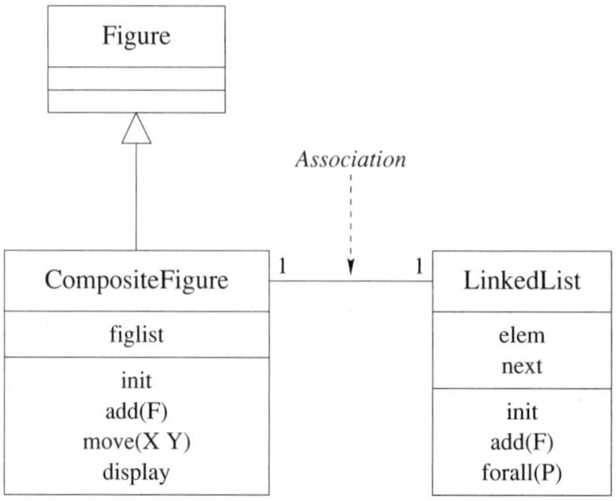

Figure 7.22: Class diagram with an association.

similarly for the other side. The association link is a specification; it does not say how it is implemented. In our case, each composite figure has a `figlist` attribute that references a linked list.

The example execution we gave before will also work in the single inheritance case. What are the trade-offs in using single or multiple inheritance in this example? In both cases, the figures that make up the composite figure are encapsulated. The main difference is that multiple inheritance brings the operations of linked lists up to the same level as figures:

- With multiple inheritance, a composite figure is also a linked list. All the operations of the `LinkedList` class can be used directly on composite figures. This is important if we want to do linked list calculations with composite figures.
- With single inheritance, a composite figure completely hides its structure. This is important if we want to protect the composite figure from any calculations other than those defined in its class.

Scaling it up

It is straightforward to extend this example to be a full-fledged graphics package. Here are some of the changes that should be made:

- Many more figures can be defined to inherit from `Figure`.
- In the current implementation, figures are tied to their canvas. This has the advantage that it allows figures to be spread over multiple canvasses. But usually we will not want this ability. Rather, we would like to be able to draw the same figure on different canvasses. This means that the canvas should not be an attribute of figure objects but be passed as argument to the `display` method.
- A journaling facility can be added. That is, it should be possible to record

sequences of drawing commands, i.e., sequences of calls to figures, and manipulate the recordings as first-class entities. These recordings represent drawings at a high level of abstraction. They can then be manipulated by the application, stored on files, passed to other applications, etc.

- The `display` method should be able to pass arbitrary parameters from the application program, through the graphics package, to the underlying graphics subsystem. In the `Line` and `Circle` classes, we change it as follows:

```
meth display(...)=M
   {@canvas {Adjoin M create(line @x1 @y1 @x2 @y2)}}
end
```

The `Adjoin` operation combines two record arguments, where the second argument overrides the first in the case of conflicts. This allows arbitrary parameters to be passed through `display` to the canvas drawing command. For example, the call `{F display(fill:red width:3)}` draws a red figure of width 3.

7.4.5 Rules of thumb for multiple inheritance

Multiple inheritance is a powerful technique that has to be used with care. We recommend that you use multiple inheritance as follows:

- Multiple inheritance works well when combining two completely independent abstractions. For example, figures and linked lists have nothing in common, so they can be combined fruitfully.

- Multiple inheritance is much harder to use correctly when the abstractions have something in common. For example, creating a `WorkStudy` class from `Student` and `Employee` is dubious, because students and employees are both human beings. They may in fact both inherit from a common `Person` class. Even if they do not have a shared ancestor, there can be problems if they have some concepts in common.

- What happens when sibling superclasses share (directly or indirectly) a common ancestor class that specifies a stateful object (i.e., it has attributes)? This is known as the implementation-sharing problem. This can lead to duplicated operations on the common ancestor. This typically happens when initializing an object. The initialization method usually has to initialize its superclasses, so the common ancestor is initialized twice. The only remedy is to understand carefully the inheritance hierarchy to avoid such duplication. Alternatively, you should only inherit from multiple classes that do not share a stateful common ancestor.

- When name clashes occur, i.e., the same method label is used for adjacent superclasses, then the program must define a local method that overrides the conflict-causing methods. Otherwise the object system gives an error message. A simple way to avoid name clashes is to use name values as method heads. This is a useful technique for classes, such as mixin classes, that are often inherited from by multiple inheritance.

7.4.6 The purpose of class diagrams

Class diagrams are excellent tools for visualizing the class structure of an application. They are at the heart of the UML approach to modeling object-oriented applications, and as such they enjoy widespread use. This popularity has often masked their limitations. They have three clear limitations:

- They do not specify the functionality of a class. For example, if the methods of a class enforce an invariant, then this invariant does not show up in the class diagram.
- They do not model the dynamic behavior of the application, i.e., its evolution over time. Dynamic behavior is both large-scale and small-scale. Applications often go through different phases, for which different class diagrams are valid. Applications are often concurrent, with independent parts that interact in coordinated ways.
- They only model one level in the application's component hierarchy. As section 6.7 explains, well-structured applications have a hierarchical decomposition. Classes and objects are near the base of this hierarchy. A class diagram explains the decomposition at this level.

The UML approach recognizes these limitations and provides tools that partially alleviate them, e.g., the interaction diagram and the package diagram. Interaction diagrams model part of the dynamic behavior. Package diagrams model components at a higher level in the hierarchy than classes.

7.4.7 Design patterns

When designing a software system, it is common to encounter the same problems over and over again. The design pattern approach explicitly recognizes this and proposes solutions to these problems. A design pattern is a technique that solves one of these common problems. This book is full of design patterns in that sense. For example, here are two:

- In declarative programming, Section 3.4.2 introduces the rule of constructing a function by following the structure of a type. A program that uses a complicated recursive data structure can often be written easily by looking at the type of the data structure. The structure of the program mirrors the type definition.
- Section 6.4.2 introduces a series of techniques for making a data abstraction secure by wrapping the functionality in a secure layer. These techniques are independent of what the abstraction does; they work for any abstraction.

Design patterns were first popularized in an influential book by Gamma, Helm, Johnson, and Vlissides [66], which gives a catalog of design patterns in OOP and explains how to use them. The catalog emphasizes patterns based on inheritance, using the type view. Let us look at a typical design pattern of this catalog from the viewpoint of a programmer who thinks in terms of computation models.

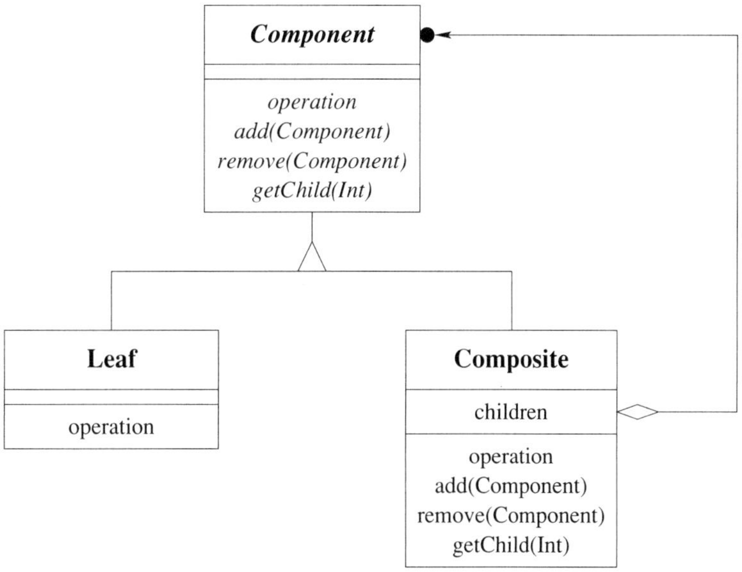

Figure 7.23: The Composite pattern.

The Composite pattern

Composite is a typical example of a design pattern. The purpose of Composite is to build hierarchies of objects. Given a class that defines a leaf, the pattern shows how to use inheritance to define trees. Figure 7.23, taken from Gamma et al, [66] shows the inheritance diagram of the Composite pattern. The usual way to use this pattern is to plug in an initial leaf class, `Leaf`. Then the pattern defines both the `Composite` and `Component` classes. `Component` is an abstract class. The hierarchy is either an instance of `Leaf` or `Composite`.

We can use the Composite pattern to define compound graphic figures. Section 7.4.4 solves the problem by combining a figure and a linked list (either with single or multiple inheritance). The Composite pattern is a more abstract solution, in that it does not assume that the grouping is done by a linked list. The `Composite` class has `add` and `remove` operations but does not say how they are implemented. They could be implemented as a linked list, but they could also be implemented differently, e.g., as a dictionary or as a declarative list.

Given a class that defines a leaf of the tree, the Composite pattern returns a class that defines the tree. When put in this way, this sounds much like higher-order programming: we would like to define a function that accepts a class and returns another class. Most programming languages, such as C++ and Java, do not allow defining this function, however. There are two reasons for this. First, most languages do not consider classes as first-class values. Second, the function defines a new superclass of the input class. Most languages allow defining new subclasses but not new superclasses. Yet despite these limitations we would still like to use the Composite pattern in our programs.

The usual solution to this dilemma is to consider design patterns as primarily a way to organize one's thoughts, without necessarily being supported by the programming language. A pattern might exist only in the mind of the programmer. Design patterns can then be used in languages like C++ or Java, even if they cannot be implemented as abstractions in those languages. This can be made easier by using a source code preprocessor. The programmer can then program directly with design patterns, and the preprocessor generates the source code for the target language.

Supporting the Composite pattern

The object system of this chapter lets us support a grouping pattern very much like Composite from within the computation model. Let us implement a tree structure whose leaves and internal nodes are objects. The leaves are instances of the `Leaf` class, which is provided at run time. The internal nodes forward all method invocations to the leaves in their subtree. The simplest way to implement this is to define a class `Composite` for the internal nodes. This class contains a list of its children, which may be instances of `Composite` or `Leaf`. We assume that all instances have the initialization method `init` and that `Composite` instances have the method `add` for adding a new subtree.

```
class Composite
   attr children
   meth init
      children:=nil
   end
   meth add(E)
      children:=E|@children
   end
   meth otherwise(M)
      for N in @children do {N M} end
   end
end
```

If nodes have many subnodes, then it is inefficient to remove nodes in this implementation. In that situation, using dictionaries instead of lists might be a good choice. Here is an example of how to construct a tree:

```
N0={New Composite init}
L1={New Leaf init} {N0 add(L1)}
L2={New Leaf init} {N0 add(L2)}
N3={New Composite init} {N0 add(N3)}
L4={New Leaf init} {N0 add(L4)}

L5={New Leaf init} {N3 add(L5)}
L6={New Leaf init} {N3 add(L6)}
L7={New Leaf init} {N3 add(L7)}
```

If Leaf is the Figure class of section 7.4.4, then Composite defines composite figures:

Enforcing valid trees This implementation works for any Leaf class because of dynamic typing. The disadvantage of this solution is that the system does not enforce all leaves to be instances of the same class. Let us add such enforcement to Composite:

```
class Composite
   attr children valid
   meth init(Valid)
      children:=nil
      @valid=Valid
   end
   meth add(E)
      if {Not {@valid E}} then raise invalidNode end end
      children:=E|@children
   end
   meth otherwise(M)
      for N in @children do {N M} end
   end
end
```

When an instance of Composite is initialized, it is given a function Valid, which is bound to the stateless attribute valid. The function Valid is used to check the validity of each inserted node.

7.5 Relation to other computation models

The language does not prevent you from deeply nesting classes, but good taste should. ... Nesting more than two levels invites a readability disaster and should probably never be attempted.
– *The Java Programming Language*, 2nd edition,
Ken Arnold and James Gosling (1998)

Object-oriented programming is one way to structure programs, which is most often used together with explicit state. In comparison with other computation models, it is characterized primarily by its use of polymorphism and inheritance. Polymorphism is a general technique that is not limited to OOP, so we will not discuss it further here. Rather, we focus on inheritance and how it relates to other programming concepts. From the viewpoint of multiple computation models, inheritance is not a new concept in the kernel language, but emerges rather from how the **class** linguistic abstraction is defined. This section examines how inheritance relates to other higher-order techniques. This section also examines the commonly stated design goal that "everything should be an object," to find out what it means and to what extent it makes sense.

7.5.1 Object-based and component-based programming

Object-based programming is OOP without inheritance. This is like component-based programming with class syntax. This gives a convenient notation for encapsulating state and defining multiple operations on it. Without inheritance, the object abstraction becomes much simpler. There are no problems of overriding and conflict in multiple inheritance. Static and dynamic binding are identical.

7.5.2 Higher-order programming

Object-oriented programming and higher-order programming are closely related. For example, let us examine the case of a sorting routine that is parameterized by an order function. A new sorting routine can be created by giving a particular order function. In higher-order programming, this can be written as follows:

```
proc {NewSortRoutine Order ?SortRoutine}
   proc {SortRoutine InL OutL}
      % ... {Order X Y} calculates order
   end
end
```

In OOP, this can be written as follows:

```
class SortRoutineClass
   attr ord
   meth init(Order)
      ord:=Order
   end
   meth sort(InL OutL)
      % ... {@ord order(X Y $)} calculates order
   end
end
```

The order relation itself is written as follows:

```
proc {Order X Y ?B}
   B=(X<Y)
end
```

or as follows:

```
class OrderClass
   meth init skip end
   meth order(X Y B)
      B=(X<Y)
   end
end
```

Instantiating the sorting routine is then written as follows:

```
SortRoutine={NewSortRoutine Order}
```

or as follows:

```
SortRoutine={New SortRoutineClass init({New OrderClass init})}
```

Embellishments added by object-oriented programming

It is clear that procedure values and objects are closely related. Let us now compare higher-order and object-oriented programming more carefully. The main difference is that OOP "embellishes" higher-order programming. It is a richer abstraction that provides a collection of additional idioms beyond procedural abstraction:

- Explicit state can be defined and used easily.
- Multiple methods that share the same explicit state can be defined easily. Invoking an object picks one of them.
- Classes are provided, which define a set of methods and can be instantiated. Each instance has a fresh explicit state. If objects are like procedures, then classes are like procedures that return procedures.
- Inheritance is provided, to define new sets of methods from existing sets, by extending, modifying, and combining existing ones. Static and dynamic binding make this ability particularly rich.
- Different degrees of encapsulation can be defined between classes and objects. Attributes and methods can be private, public, protected or have some other, programmer-defined encapsulation.

It is important to note that these mechanisms do not provide any fundamentally new ability. They can be completely defined with higher-order programming, explicit state, and name values. On the other hand, the mechanisms are useful idioms that lead to a programming style that is often convenient.

Object-oriented programming is an abstraction that provides a rich notation to use any or all of these mechanisms together, whenever they are needed. This richness is a double-edged sword. On the one hand, it makes the abstraction particularly useful for many programming tasks. On the other hand, the abstraction has a complex semantics and is hard to reason about. For this reason, we recommend using object orientation only in those cases when it significantly simplifies program structure, e.g., when there is a clear need for inheritance: the program contains a set of closely related data abstractions. In other cases, we recommend using simpler programming techniques.

Common limitations

The object system defined in this chapter is particularly close to higher-order programming. Not all object systems are so close. In particular, the following characteristics are often absent or cumbersome to use:

- Classes as values. They can be created at run time, passed as arguments, and stored in data structures.
- Full lexical scoping. Full lexical scoping means that the language supports procedure values with external references. This allows a class to be defined inside the

scope of a procedure or another class. Both Smalltalk-80 and Java support procedure values (with some restrictions). In Java they are instances of inner classes (i.e., nested classes). They are quite verbose due to the class syntax (see the epigraph at the beginning of this section).

- First-class messages. Usually, the labels of messages and methods both have to be known at compile time. The most general way to remove this restriction is to allow messages to be values in the language, which can be calculated at run time. Both Smalltalk-80 and Java provide this ability, although it is more verbose than the usual (static) method invocations. For example, here is a generic way to add "batching" to a class C:

```
class Batcher
   meth nil skip end
   meth ´|´(M Ms) {self M} {self Ms} end
end
```

Mixing in the class Batcher adds batching ability to any other class:

```
C={New class $ from Counter Batcher end init(0)}
{C [inc(2) browse inc(3) inc(4)]}
```

Section 7.8.5 gives another way to add batching.

Some object-oriented languages, e.g., C++, do not support full higher-order programming because they cannot define procedure values with lexical scoping at run time (as explained in section 3.6.1). In these languages, many of the abilities of higher-order programming can be obtained through encapsulation and inheritance, with a little effort from the programmer:

- A procedure value can be encoded as an object. The object's attributes represent the procedure value's external references and the method arguments are the procedure value's arguments. When the object is created, its attributes are initialized with the external references. The object can be passed around and called just like a procedure value. With a little bit of discipline from the programmer, this allows for programming with procedure values, thus giving true higher-order programming.
- A generic procedure can be encoded as an abstract class. A generic procedure is one that takes procedure arguments and returns a specific procedure. For example a generic sorting routine can take a comparison operation for a given type and return a sorting routine that sorts arrays of that type. An abstract class is a class with undefined methods. The methods are defined in subclasses.

Encoding procedure values as objects

Let us give an example of how to encode a procedure value in a typical object-oriented language. Assume we have any statement ⟨stmt⟩. With procedural abstraction, we can define a procedure with **proc** {P} ⟨stmt⟩ **end** and execute it later as {P}. To encode this in our object system we have to know the external references of ⟨stmt⟩. Assume they are X and Y. We define the following class:

Type definition

⟨T⟩ ::= ⟨T⟩₁ | ⟨T⟩₂ | ⟨T⟩₃

Operations

⟨F⟩₁, ⟨F⟩₂, ..., ⟨F⟩ₙ

Functional decomposition

```
fun {⟨F⟩1 ⟨T⟩ ...}
   case ⟨T⟩
   of ⟨T⟩1 then
      ...
   [] ⟨T⟩2 then
      ...
   [] ⟨T⟩3 then
      ...
   end
end

fun {⟨F⟩2 ⟨T⟩ ...}
   ...
end

 ...

fun {⟨F⟩n ⟨T⟩ ...}
   ...
end
```

Type decomposition

```
class ⟨T⟩ ... end


class ⟨T⟩1 from ⟨T⟩
   ...
   meth ⟨F⟩1(...)
      ...
   end
   meth ⟨F⟩2(...)
      ...
   end
   ...
   meth ⟨F⟩n(...)
      ...
   end
end

class ⟨T⟩2 from ⟨T⟩ ...  end

class ⟨T⟩3 from ⟨T⟩ ...  end
```

Figure 7.24: Functional decomposition versus type decomposition.

```
class Proc
   attr x y
   meth init(X Y) @x=X @y=Y end
   meth apply X=@x Y=@y in ⟨stmt⟩ end
end
```

The external references are represented by the stateless attributes `x` and `y`. We define `P` by doing `P={New Proc init(X Y)}` and call it with `{P apply}`. This encoding can be used in any object-oriented language. With it, we can use almost all the higher-order programming techniques of the book. It has two disadvantages with respect to procedures: it is more cumbersome to write and the external references have to be written explicitly.

7.5.3 Functional decomposition versus type decomposition

How do we organize a data abstraction that is based on a type $\langle\mathsf{T}\rangle$ with subtypes $\langle\mathsf{T}\rangle_1$, $\langle\mathsf{T}\rangle_2$, $\langle\mathsf{T}\rangle_3$ and includes a set of operations $\langle\mathsf{F}\rangle_1, \ldots, \langle\mathsf{F}\rangle_n$? In declarative programming, section 3.4.2 recommends constructing functions by following the type definition. In OOP, section 7.4.2 recommends constructing inheritance hierarchies in similar fashion, also by following the type definition. Both sections give examples based on lists. Figure 7.24 gives a rough schematic overview comparing the two approaches. They result in very different program structures, which we call functional decomposition and type decomposition. These structures correspond to the ADT style and the object style of data abstraction introduced in section 6.4. In functional decomposition, each function definition is a self-contained whole, but the types are spread out over all functions. In type decomposition, each type is a self-contained whole, but the function definitions are spread out over all types. Which approach is better? It turns out that each has its uses:

- In functional decomposition, one can modify a function or add a new function without changing the other function definitions. However, changing or adding a type requires modifying all function definitions.
- In type decomposition, one can modify a type (i.e., a class) or add a new type (including by inheritance) without changing the other type definitions. However, changing or adding a function requires modifying all class definitions.

When designing a program, it is good to ask oneself what kind of modification is most important. If the type is relatively simple and there are a large number of operations, then the functional approach is usually clearer. If the type is complex, with a relatively small number of operations, then the type approach can be clearer. There are techniques that combine some of the advantages of both approaches. See, e.g., [232], which explains some of these techniques and shows how to use them to build extensible compilers.

7.5.4 Should everything be an object?

In discussions about OOP, the principle is often invoked that "everything should be an object." Let us examine this principle to discover what it is really trying to say.

Strong objects

A sensible way to define the principle is as "all language entities should be instances of data abstractions with as many generic properties as possible." In its extreme form, this implies six properties: all language entities should be defined with the object style (see section 6.4), be defined in terms of classes that can be instantiated, be extensible with inheritance, have a unique identity, encapsulate a state, and be accessed with a uniform syntax. The word "object" is sometimes used for entities with all these properties. To avoid confusion, we will call them strong objects. An object-oriented language is called pure if all its entities are strong objects.

The desire for purity can lead to good things. For example, many languages have the concept of "exception" to handle abnormal events during execution. It can be quite convenient for exceptions to be objects within an inheritance hierarchy. This allows classifying them into different categories, catching them only if they are of a given class (or its subclasses), and possibly changing them (adding information) if they are stateful.

Smalltalk-80 is a good example of a language for which purity was an explicit design goal [68, 100]. All data types in Smalltalk, including simple ones like integers, are objects. However, not everything in Smalltalk is an object; the ADT style is used for primitive operations of basic types such as integers and there is a concept called block that is a procedure value used for building control abstractions.

In most languages, not all entities are strong objects. Let us give some examples in Java. An integer in Java is a pure value in the ADT style; it is not defined by a class and does not encapsulate a state. An object in Java can have just `final` attributes, which means that it is stateless. An array in Java cannot be extended with inheritance. Arrays behave as if they were defined in a final class. We summarize this by saying that Java is object-oriented but not pure.

Should a language have only strong objects? It is clear that the answer is no, for many reasons. First, the ADT style is sometimes essential, as we explained in section 6.4.3. Second, stateless entities can play an important role. With them, the powerful reasoning techniques of declarative programming become possible. For this reason, many language designs allow them. We cite Objective Caml [37], which has a functional core, and Java [11], which has immutable objects. In addition, stateless entities are essential for making transparent distributed programming practical (see chapter 11). Third, not all entities need a unique identity. For example, structured entities such as tuples in a database are identified by their contents, not by their names. Fourth, the simplicity of a uniform syntax is illusory, as we explain below.

We seem to be removing each property one by one. We are left with two principles: all language entities should be instances of data abstractions and uniformity among data abstractions should be exploited when it is reasonable. Some data abstractions will have all the properties of strong objects; others will have only some of these properties but also have some other, completely different properties. These principles are consistent with the use of multiple computation models advocated in this book. Building a system consists primarily in designing abstractions and realizing them as data or control abstractions.

Objects and program complexity

Given a particular object, how can one predict its future behavior? It depends on two factors:

1. Its internal state, which potentially depends on all past calls. These calls can be

done from many parts of the program.

2. Its textual definition, which depends on all classes it inherits from. These classes can be defined in many places in the program text.

We see that the semantics of an object is spread out over both time and space. This makes an object harder to understand than a function. The semantics of a function is all concentrated in one place, namely the textual definition of the function. The function does not have a history; it depends only on its definition and its arguments.

We give an example that shows why objects are harder to program with when they have state. Assume that we are doing arithmetic with the IEEE floating point standard and that we have implemented the standard completely. This means, e.g., that we can change the rounding mode of arithmetic operations during execution (round to nearest even, round up, round down, etc.). If we do not use this ability carefully, then whenever we do an addition `X+Y` we have no idea what it will do unless we have followed the whole execution. Any part of the program could have changed the rounding mode. This can wreak havoc on numeric methods, which depend on predictable rounding to get good results.

To avoid this problem as much as possible, the language should not favor explicit state and inheritance. That is, not using them should be easy. For inheritance, this is almost never a problem, since it is always harder to use it than to avoid it. For explicit state, it depends on the language. In the object-oriented model of this chapter, defining (stateless) functions is actually slightly easier than defining (stateful) objects. Objects need to be defined as instances of classes, which themselves are defined with a **class** ... **end** wrapping one or more **meth** ... **end** declarations. Functions just need **fun** ... **end**. In popular object-oriented languages, explicit state is unfortunately almost always the default and functions are usually syntactically cumbersome. For example, in Java there is no syntactic support for functions and object attributes are stateful unless declared to be `final`. In Smalltalk, all attributes are stateful but function values can be defined easily.

Uniform object syntax

A language's syntax should help and not hinder programmers in designing, writing, and reasoning about programs. An important principle in syntax design is form mirrors content. Differences in semantics should be visible as differences in syntax and vice versa. For example, the while loop as used in many languages has a syntax similar to `while` ⟨expr⟩ do ⟨stmt⟩. By writing ⟨expr⟩ before ⟨stmt⟩, the syntax reflects the fact that the condition ⟨expr⟩ is evaluated before executing ⟨stmt⟩. If ⟨expr⟩ is false, then ⟨stmt⟩ is not executed at all. The Cobol language does things differently. It has the perform loop, which can be written `perform` ⟨stmt⟩ `until` ⟨expr⟩. This syntax is misleading since ⟨expr⟩ is tested before ⟨stmt⟩, yet is written after ⟨stmt⟩. The perform loop's semantics are `while not` ⟨expr⟩ do ⟨stmt⟩.

Should all operations on language entities have the same syntax? While this makes program transformation easier (e.g., with macros as done in Lisp [72]), it does not necessarily improve readability. For example, Scheme has a uniform syntax which does not necessarily make it more readable. We find that a uniform syntax just moves the richness of the language away from the syntax and into the names of objects and classes. This adds a second layer of syntax, making the language more verbose. Let us give an example taken from symbolic programming languages. Stateless values can be given a very natural, compact syntax. A list value can be created just by mentioning it, e.g.:

```
LV=[1 2 3]
```

This is approximately the syntax used by languages that support symbolic programming, such as Lisp, Prolog, Haskell, Erlang, and their relatives. This contrasts with the use of a uniform object syntax:

```
ListClass *lv= new ConsClass(1, new ConsClass(2,
               new ConsClass(3, new NilClass())));
```

This is C++ syntax, which is similar to Java syntax. For decomposing a list value, there is another natural notation using pattern matching:

```
case LV of X|LV2 then ... end
```

Pattern matching is commonly used in symbolic languages. This is also cumbersome to do in a uniform object syntax. There is a further increase in verbosity when doing concurrent programming in the object syntax. This is because the uniform syntax requires explicit synchronization. This is not true for the **case** syntax above, which is sufficient for concurrent programming if the computation model does implicit dataflow synchronization.

Another example is the graphical user interface tool `QTk` of chapter 10, which relies heavily on record values and their concise syntax. Inspired by this tool, Christophe Ponsard built a Java prototype of a similar tool. The Java version is more cumbersome to use than the Oz version, primarily because Java has no syntactic support for record values. Unfortunately, this verbosity is an inherent property of Java. There is no simple way around it.

7.6 Implementing the object system

The complete object system can be implemented in a straightforward way from the declarative stateful computation model. In particular, the main characteristics come from the combination of higher-order programming with explicit state. With this construction, you will understand objects and classes completely.

While the construction of this section works well and is reasonably efficient, a real implementation will add optimizations to do even better. For example, a real implementation can make an object invocation be as fast as a procedure call. This section does not give these optimizations.

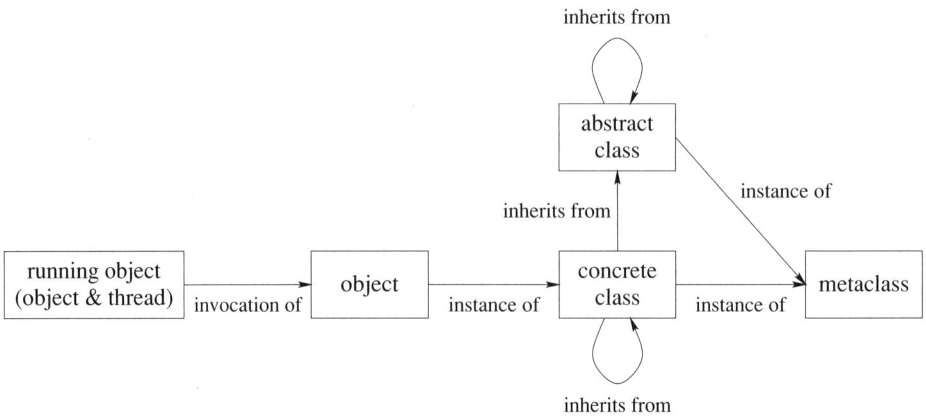

Figure 7.25: Abstractions in object-oriented programming.

7.6.1 Abstraction diagram

The first step in understanding how to build an object system is to understand how the different parts are related. Object-oriented programming defines a hierarchy of abstractions that are related to each other by a kind of "specification-implementation" relationship. There are many variations on this hierarchy. We give a simple one that has most of the main ideas. Here are the abstractions, in order from most concrete to most abstract:

- *Running object.* A running object is an active invocation of an object. It associates a thread to an object. It contains a set of environment frames (the part of the thread's stack that is created while executing the object) as well as an object.
- *Object.* An object is a procedure that encapsulates an explicit state (a cell) and a set of procedures that reference the state.
- *Class.* A class is a wrapped record that encapsulates a set of procedures named by literals and a set of attributes, which are just literals. The procedures are called methods. Methods take a state as argument for each attribute and modify that state. Methods can only call each other indirectly, through the literals that name them. Often the following distinction is useful:
  - *Abstract class.* An abstract class is a class in which some methods are called that have no definition in the class.
  - *Concrete class.* A concrete class is a class in which all methods that are called are also defined.

If first-class messages are supported by the language, then invocations of the form `{Obj M}` are possible where `M` is calculated at run time. If such an invocation exists in the program, then the distinction between abstract and concrete class disappears in the program (although it may still exist conceptually). Executing the invocation

```
class Counter
   attr val
   meth init(Value)
      val:=Value
   end
   meth inc(Value)
      val:=@val+Value
   end
   meth browse
      {Browse @val}
   end
end
```

Figure 7.26: An example class `Counter` (again).

`{Obj M}` raises an exception if `M` does not exist in `Obj`.

- *Metaclass.* A metaclass is a class with a particular set of methods that correspond to the basic operations of a class, e.g.: object creation, inheritance policy (which methods to inherit), method call, method return, choice of method to call, attribute assignment, attribute access, self call. Writing these methods allows customizing the semantics of objects.

Figure 7.25 shows how these concepts are related. There are three relationships, "invocation of," "instance of," and "inherits from." These relationships have the following intuitive meanings:

- A running object is created when a thread invokes an object. The running object exists until the thread's execution leaves it. Multiple invocations of the same object can exist simultaneously.
- An object can be created as an instance of a class. If the object system distinguishes between abstract and concrete classes, then it is usually only possible to create instances of concrete classes. The object exists forever.[2] The object encapsulates a cell that was created especially for it. Multiple instances of the same class can exist simultaneously.
- A class can be created that inherits from a list of other classes. The new class exists forever. Inheritance takes a set of methods and a list of classes and returns a new class with a new set of methods. Multiple classes that inherit from the same class can exist simultaneously. If one class can inherit from several classes, then we have multiple inheritance. Otherwise, if one class can inherit only from one class, we have single inheritance.

2. In practice, until the actively running program loses all references to it. At that point, garbage collection can reclaim its memory and finalization can perform a last action, if necessary.

```
declare Counter
local
   Attrs = [val]
   MethodTable = m(browse:MyBrowse init:Init inc:Inc)
   proc {Init M S Self}
      init(Value)=M
   in
      (S.val):=Value
   end
   proc {Inc M S Self}
      X
      inc(Value)=M
   in
      X=@(S.val) (S.val):=X+Value
   end
   proc {MyBrowse M S Self}
      browse=M
      {Browse @(S.val)}
   end
in
   Counter = {Wrap c(methods:MethodTable attrs:Attrs)}
end
```

Figure 7.27: An example of class construction.

- A class can be created as an instance of a metaclass. The new class exists forever. The basic operations of the class are defined by particular methods of the metaclass. Multiple instances of the same metaclass can exist simultaneously.

7.6.2 Implementing classes

We first explain the class linguistic abstraction. The `Counter` class of figure 7.26 is translated internally into the definition of figure 7.27. This figure shows that a class is simply a value, a record, that is protected from snooping because of the wrapper `Wrap` (see section 3.7.5). (Later, when the class is used to create objects, it will be unwrapped with the corresponding `Unwrap`.) The class record contains:

- A set of methods in a method table. Each method is a three-argument procedure that takes a message `M`, which is always a record, an extra parameter `S` representing the state of the current object, and `Self`, which references the object itself.
- A set of attribute names, giving the attributes that each class instance (object) will possess. Each attribute is a stateful cell that is accessed by the attribute name, which is either an atom or an Oz name.

This example is slightly simplified because it does not show how to support static binding (see Exercises, section 7.9). The `Counter` class has a single attribute accessed by the atom `val`. It has a method table with three methods accessed

```
fun {New WClass InitialMethod}
   State Obj Class={Unwrap WClass}
in
   State={MakeRecord s Class.attrs}
   {Record.forAll State proc {$ A} {NewCell _ A} end}
   proc {Obj M}
      {Class.methods.{Label M} M State Obj}
   end
   {Obj InitialMethod}
   Obj
end
```

Figure 7.28: An example of object construction.

through the features `browse`, `init`, and `inc`. As we can see, the method `init` assigns the value `Value` to the attribute `val`, the method `inc` increments the attribute `val`, and the method `browse` browses the current value of `val`.

7.6.3 Implementing objects

We can use the class `Counter` to create objects. Figure 7.28 shows a generic function `New` that creates an object from any class. It starts by unwrapping the class. It then creates an object state, which is a record, from the attributes of the class. Since the attributes are in general only known at run time, it does dynamic record creation with `MakeRecord`. It initializes each field of this record to a cell (with an unbound initial value). This uses the iterator `Record.forAll` to iterate over all fields of a record.

The object `Obj` returned by `New` is a one-argument procedure. When called as `{Obj M}`, it looks up and calls the procedure corresponding to `M` in the method table. Because of lexical scoping, the object state is visible only within `Obj`. One can say that `Obj` is a procedure that encapsulates the state.

The definition of figure 7.28 works correctly, but it may not be the most efficient way to implement objects. An actual system can use a different, more efficient implementation as long as it behaves in the same way. For example, the Mozart system uses an implementation in which object invocations are almost as efficient as procedure calls [85, 86].

The proof of the pudding is in the eating. Let us verify that the class works as claimed. We now create the `Counter` class and try out `New` as follows:

```
C={New Counter init(0)}
{C inc(6)} {C inc(6)}
{C browse}
```

This behaves in exactly the same way as the example of section 7.2.1.

```
fun {From C1 C2 C3}
   c(methods:M1 attrs:A1)={Unwrap C1}
   c(methods:M2 attrs:A2)={Unwrap C2}
   c(methods:M3 attrs:A3)={Unwrap C3}
   MA1={Arity M1}
   MA2={Arity M2}
   MA3={Arity M3}
   ConfMeth={Minus {Inter MA2 MA3} MA1}
   ConfAttr={Minus {Inter A1 A2} A3}
in
   if ConfMeth\=nil then
      raise illegalInheritance(methConf:ConfMeth) end
   end
   if ConfAttr\=nil then
      raise illegalInheritance(attrConf:ConfAttr) end
   end
   {Wrap c(methods:{Adjoin {Adjoin M2 M3} M1}
           attrs:{Union {Union A2 A3} A1})}
end
```

Figure 7.29: Implementing inheritance.

7.6.4 Implementing inheritance

Inheritance calculates a new class record starting from existing class records, which are combined according to the inheritance rules given in section 7.3.1. Inheritance can be defined by the function `From`, where the call `C={From C1 C2 C3}` returns a new class record whose base definition is `C1` and which inherits from `C2` and `C3`. It corresponds to the following class syntax:

```
class C from C2 C3
   ... % The base class C1
end
```

Figure 7.29 shows the definition of `From`. It uses the set operations in the `Set` module, which can be found on the book's Web site. `From` first checks the method tables and attribute lists for conflicts. If a duplicate method label or attribute is found in `C2` and `C3` that is not overridden by `C1`, then an exception is raised. Then `From` constructs the new method table and attribute lists. Overriding is handled properly by the `Adjoin` function on the method tables (see appendix B.3.2). The definition is slightly simplified because it does not handle static binding and because it assumes that there are exactly two superclasses.

7.7 The Java language (sequential part)

Java is a concurrent object-oriented language with a syntax that resembles C++. This section gives a brief introduction to the sequential part of Java. We explain how to write a simple program, how to define classes, and how to use inheritance. We defer talking about concurrency in Java until chapter 8. We do not talk about the reflection package, which lets one do much of what the object system of this chapter can do (although in a more verbose way).

Java is almost a pure object-oriented language, i.e., almost everything is an object. Only a small set of primitive types, namely integers, floats, booleans, and characters, use the ADT style and so are not objects. Java is a relatively clean language with a relatively simple semantics. Despite their syntactic similarity, there is a major difference in language philosophy between Java and C++ [11, 204]. C++ gives access to the machine representation of data and a direct translation to machine instructions. It also has manual memory management. Because of these properties, C++ is often suitable as a replacement for assembly language. In contrast, Java hides the representation of data and does automatic memory management. It supports distributed computing on multiple platforms. It has a more sophisticated object system. These properties make Java better for general-purpose application development.

7.7.1 Computation model

Java consists of statically typed object-oriented programming with classes, passive objects, and threads. The Java computation model is close to the shared-state concurrent model (which has both threads and cells), minus dataflow variables, triggers, and names. Section 8.6 gives an introduction to the concurrent part of Java. Parameter passing is done by value, both for primitive types and object references. Newly declared variables are given a default initial value that depends on their type. There is support for single assignment: variables and object attributes can be declared as `final`, which means that the variable can be assigned exactly once. Final variables must be assigned before they are used.

Java introduces its own terminology for some concepts. Classes contain fields (attributes, in our terminology), methods, other classes, or interfaces, which are known collectively as class members. Variables are either fields, local variables (declared in code blocks local to methods), or method parameters. Variables are declared by giving their type, identifier, and an optional set of modifiers (e.g., `final`). The **`self`** concept is called `this`.

Interfaces

Java has an elegant solution to the problems of multiple inheritance (see sections 7.4.4 and 7.4.5). Java introduces the concept of interface, which syntactically looks like a class with only method declarations. An interface has no implementation. A class can implement an interface, which simply means that it defines all the methods in the interface. Java supports single inheritance for classes, thus avoiding the problems of multiple inheritance. But to preserve the advantages of multiple inheritance, Java supports multiple inheritance for interfaces.

Java supports higher-order programming in a trivial way by means of the encoding given in section 7.5.2. In addition to this, Java has more direct support for higher-order programming through inner classes. An inner class is a class definition that is nested inside another class or inside a code block (such as a method body). An instance of an inner class can be passed outside of the method body or code block. An inner class can have external references, but there is a restriction if it is nested in a code block: in that case it cannot reference nonfinal variables. We could say that an instance of an inner class is almost a procedure value. The restriction likely exists because the language designers wanted nonfinal variables in code blocks to be implementable on a stack, which would be popped when exiting the method. Without the restriction, this might create dangling references.

7.7.2 Introduction to Java programming

We give a brief introduction to programming in Java. We explain how to write a simple program, how to define classes, and how to use inheritance. This section only scratches the surface of what is possible in Java. For more information, we refer the reader to one of the many good books on Java programming [11].

A simple program

We would like to calculate the factorial function. In Java, functions are defined as methods that return a result:

```
class Factorial {
   public long fact(long n)  {
      long f=1;
      for (int i=1; i<=n; i++) f=f*i;
      return f;
   }
}
```

Statements are terminated with a semicolon ";" unless they are compound statements, which are delimited by braces {...}. Variable identifiers are declared by preceding them with their type, as in `long f`. Assignment is denoted by the equals sign `=`. In the object system of chapter 7 this becomes:

```
class Factorial
   meth fact(N ?X)
   F={NewCell 1} in
      for I in 1..N do F:=@F*I end
      X=@F
   end
end
```

Note that i is an assignable variable (a cell) that is updated on each iteration, whereas I is a value that is declared anew on each iteration. Factorial can also be defined recursively:

```
class Factorial {
    public long fact(long n) {
       if (n==0) return 1;
       else return n*this.fact(n-1);
    }
}
```

In our object system this becomes

```
class Factorial
    meth fact(N ?F)
       if N==0 then F=1
       else F=N*{self fact(N-1 $)} end
    end
end
```

There are a few differences with the object system of chapter 7. The Java keyword `this` is the same as **`self`** in our object system. Java is statically typed. The type of all variables is declared at compile time. Our model is dynamically typed. A variable can be bound to an entity of any type. In Java, the visibility of `fact` is declared to be public. In our model, `fact` is public by default; to get another visibility we would have to declare it as a name.

Input/output

Any realistic Java program has to do input/output (I/O). Java has an elaborate I/O subsystem based on the notion of stream, which is an ordered sequence of data that has a source (for an input stream) or a destination (for an output stream). This should not be confused with the concept of stream as used in the rest of the book: a list with unbound tail. The Java stream concept generalizes the Unix concept of standard I/O, i.e., the standard input (`stdin`) and standard output (`stdout`) files.

Streams can encode many types, including primitive types, objects, and object graphs. (An object graph is an object together with the other objects it references, directly or indirectly.) Streams can be byte streams or character streams. Characters are not the same as bytes since Java supports Unicode. A byte in Java is an 8-bit unsigned integer. A character in Java is a Unicode 2.0 character, which has a 16-bit code. We do not treat I/O further in this section.

Defining classes

The `Factorial` class is rather atypical. It has only one method and no attributes. Let us define a more realistic class. Here is a class to define points in two-dimensional space:

```
class Point {
   public double x, y;
}
```

The attributes `x` and `y` are public, which means they are visible from outside the class. Public attributes are usually not a good idea; it is almost always better to make them private and use accessor methods:

```
class Point {
   double x, y;
   Point(double x1, y1) { x=x1; y=y1; }
   public double getX() { return x; }
   public double getY() { return y; }
}
```

The method `Point` is called a constructor; it is used to initialize new objects created with `new`, as in:

```
Point p=new Point(10.0, 20.0);
```

which creates the new `Point` object `p`. Let us add some methods to calculate with points:

```
class Point {
   double x, y;
   Point(double x1, y1) { x=x1; y=y1; }
   public double getX() { return x; }
   public double getY() { return y; }
   public void origin() { x=0.0; y=0.0; }
   public void add(Point p) { x+=p.getX(); y+=p.getY(); }
   public void scale(double s) { x*=s; y*=s; }
}
```

The `p` argument of `add` is a local variable whose initial value is a reference to the argument. In our object system we can define `Point` as follows:

```
class Point
   attr x y
   meth init(X Y) x:=X y:=Y end
   meth getX(X) X=@x end
   meth getY(Y) Y=@y end
   meth origin x:=0.0 y:=0.0 end
   meth add(P) x:=@x+{P getX($)} y:=@y+{P getY($)} end
   meth scale(S) x:=@x*S y:=@y*S end
end
```

```
class MyInteger {
   public int val;
   MyInteger(int x) { val=x; }
}

class CallExample {
   public static void sqr(MyInteger a) {
      a.val=a.val*a.val;
      a=null;
   }

   public static void main(String[] args) {
      MyInteger c=new MyInteger(25);
      CallExample.sqr(c);
      System.out.println(c.val);
   }
}
```

Figure 7.30: Parameter passing in Java.

This definition is very similar to the Java definition. There are also some minor syntactic differences, such as the operators `+=` and `*=`. Both definitions have private attributes. There is a subtle difference in the visibility of the attributes. In Java, private attributes are visible to all objects of the same class. This means the method `add` could be written differently:

```
public void add(Point p) { x+=p.x; y+=p.y; }
```

This is explained further in section 7.3.3.

Parameter passing and main program

Parameter passing to methods is done with call by value. A copy of the value is passed to the method and can be modified inside the method without changing the original value. For primitive values, such as integers and floats, this is straightforward. Java also passes object references (not the objects themselves) by value. So objects can almost be considered as using call by reference. The difference is that, inside the method, the field can be modified to refer to another object.

Figure 7.30 gives an example. This example is a complete standalone program; it can be compiled and executed as is. Each Java program has one method, `main`, that is called when the program is started The object reference `c` is passed by value to the method `sqr`. Inside `sqr`, the assignment `a=null` has no effect on `c`.

The argument of `main` is an array of strings that contains the command line arguments of the program when called from the operating system, The method call `System.out.println` prints its argument to the standard output.

Inheritance

We can use inheritance to extend the `Point` class. For example, it can be extended to represent a pixel, which is the smallest independently displayable area on a two-dimensional graphics output device such as a computer screen. Pixels have coordinates, just like points, but they also have color.

```
class Pixel extends Point {
   Color color;
   public void origin() {
      super.origin();
      color=null;
   }
   public Color getC() { return color; }
   public void setC(Color c) { color=c; }
}
```

The `extends` keyword is used to denote inheritance; it corresponds to **`from`** in our object system. We assume the class `Color` is defined elsewhere. The class `Pixel` overrides the `origin` method. The new `origin` initializes both the point and the color. It uses `super` to access the overridden method in the immediate ancestor class. With respect to the current class, this class is often called the superclass. In our object system, we can define `Pixel` as follows:

```
class Pixel from Point
   attr color
   meth origin
      Point,origin
      color:=null
   end
   meth getC(C) C=@color end
   meth setC(C) color:=C end
end
```

7.8 Active objects

An active object is a port object whose behavior is defined by a class. It consists of a port, a thread that reads messages from the port's stream, and an object that is a class instance. Each message that is received will cause one of the object's methods to be invoked. Active objects combine the abilities of OOP (including polymorphism and inheritance) and the abilities of message-passing concurrency (including concurrency and object independence). With respect to active objects, the other objects of this chapter are called passive objects, since they have no internal thread.

```
class BallGame
   attr other count:0
   meth init(Other)
      other:=Other
   end
   meth ball
      count:=@count+1
      {@other ball}
   end
   meth get(X)
      X=@count
   end
end

B1={NewActive BallGame init(B2)}
B2={NewActive BallGame init(B1)}
{B1 ball}
```

Figure 7.31: Two active objects playing ball (definition).

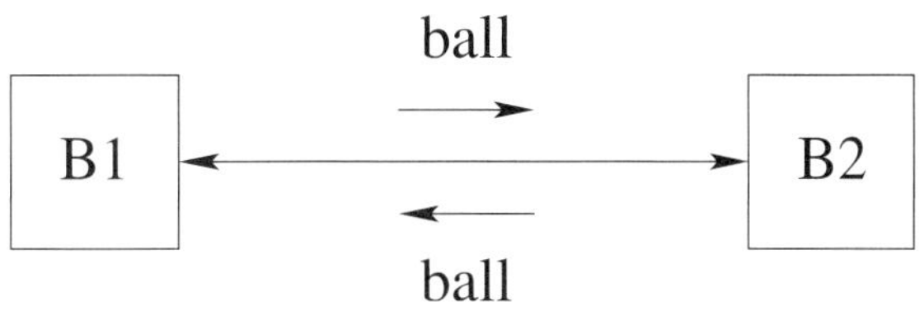

Figure 7.32: Two active objects playing ball (illustration).

7.8.1 An example

Let us start with an example. Consider two active objects, where each object has a reference to the other. When each object receives the message `ball`, it sends the message `ball` to the other. The ball will be passed back and forth indefinitely between the objects. We define the behavior of the active objects by means of a class. Figure 7.31 defines the objects and Figure 7.32 illustrates how the messages pass between them. Each object references the other in the attribute `other`. We also add an attribute `count` to count the number of times the message `ball` is received. The initial call `{B1 ball}` starts the game. With the method `get(X)` we can follow the game's progress:

```
declare X in
{B1 get(X)}
{Browse X}
```

Doing this several times will show a sequence of numbers that increase rapidly.

7.8.2 The `NewActive` abstraction

The behavior of active objects is defined with a class. Each method of the class corresponds to a message that is accepted by the active object. Figure 7.31 gives an example. Sending a message `M` to an active object `A` is written as `{A M}`, with the same syntax as invoking a standard, passive object. In contrast to passive objects, the invocation of an active object is asynchronous: it returns immediately, without waiting until the message has been handled. We can define a function `NewActive` that works exactly like `New` except that it creates an active object:

```
fun {NewActive Class Init}
   Obj={New Class Init}
   P
in
   thread S in
      {NewPort S P}
      for M in S do {Obj M} end
   end
   proc {$ M} {Send P M} end
end
```

This makes defining active objects very intuitive.

7.8.3 The Flavius Josephus problem

Let us now tackle a bigger problem. We introduce it with a well-known historical anecdote. Flavius Josephus was a Roman historian of Jewish origin. During the Jewish-Roman wars of the 1st century A.D., he was in a cave with fellow soldiers, forty men in all, surrounded by enemy Roman troops. They decided to commit suicide by standing in a ring and counting off each third man. Each man so designated was to commit suicide. Figure 7.33 illustrates the problem. Josephus, not wanting to die, managed to place himself in the position of the last survivor.

In the general version of this problem, there are n soldiers numbered from 1 to n and each kth soldier will be eliminated. The count starts from the first soldier. What is the number of the last survivor? Let us model this problem by representing soldiers with active objects. There is a ring of active objects where each object knows its two neighbors. Here is one possible message-passing protocol to solve the problem. A message `kill(X S)` circulates around the ring, where `X` counts live objects traversed and `S` is the total number of live objects remaining. Initially, the message `kill(1 N)` is given to the first object. When object i receives the message `kill(X S)` it does the following:

- If it is alive and $s = 1$, then it is the last survivor. It signals this by binding a global variable. No more messages are forwarded.
- If it is alive and `X` $\bmod k = 0$, then it becomes dead and it sends the message `kill(X+1 S-1)` to the next object in the ring.
- If it is alive and `X` $\bmod k \neq 0$, then it sends the message `kill(X+1 S)` to the

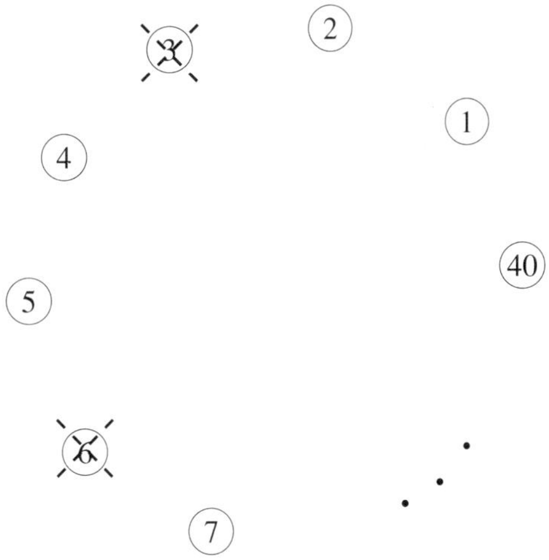

Figure 7.33: The Flavius Josephus problem.

next object in the ring.

- If it is dead, then it forwards the message `kill(X S)` to the next object.[3]

Figure 7.34 gives a program that implements this protocol. The function `Josephus` returns immediately with an unbound variable, which will be bound to the number of the last survivor as soon as it is known.

Short-circuit protocol

The solution of figure 7.34 removes dead objects from the circle with a short-circuit protocol. If this were not done, the traveling message would eventually spend most of its time being forwarded by dead objects. The short-circuit protocol uses the `newsucc` and `newpred` methods. When an object dies, it signals to both its predecessor and its successor that it should be bypassed. The short-circuit protocol is just an optimization to reduce execution time. It can be removed and the program will still run correctly.

Without the short-circuit protocol, the program is actually sequential since there is just a single message circulating. It could have been written as a sequential program. With the short-circuit protocol it is no longer sequential. More than one message can be traveling in the network at any given time.

3. A student made the observation that the dead object is a kind of zombie.

```
class Victim
   attr ident step last succ pred alive:true
   meth init(I K L) ident:=I step:=K last:=L end
   meth setSucc(S) succ:=S end
   meth setPred(P) pred:=P end
   meth kill(X S)
      if @alive then
         if S==1 then @last=@ident
         elseif X mod @step==0 then
            alive:=false
            {@pred newsucc(@succ)}
            {@succ newpred(@pred)}
            {@succ kill(X+1 S-1)}
         else
            {@succ kill(X+1 S)}
         end
      else {@succ kill(X S)} end
   end
   meth newsucc(S)
      if @alive then succ:=S
      else {@pred newsucc(S)} end
   end
   meth newpred(P)
      if @alive then pred:=P
      else {@succ newpred(P)} end
   end
end

fun {Josephus N K}
   A={NewArray 1 N null}
   Last
in
   for I in 1..N do
      A.I:={NewActive Victim init(I K Last)}
   end
   for I in 2..N do {A.I setPred(A.(I-1))} end
   {A.1 setPred(A.N)}
   for I in 1..(N-1) do {A.I setSucc(A.(I+1))} end
   {A.N setSucc(A.1)} {A.1 kill(1 N)}
   Last
end
```

Figure 7.34: The Flavius Josephus problem (active object version).

```
fun {Pipe Xs L H F}
   if L=<H then {Pipe {F Xs L} L+1 H F} else Xs end
end

fun {Josephus2 N K}
   fun {Victim Xs I}
      case Xs of kill(X S)|Xr then
         if S==1 then Last=I nil
         elseif X mod K==0 then
            kill(X+1 S-1)|Xr
         else
            kill(X+1 S)|{Victim Xr I}
         end
      [] nil then nil end
   end
   Last Zs
in
   Zs={Pipe kill(1 N)|Zs 1 N
        fun {$ Is I} thread {Victim Is I} end end}
   Last
end
```

Figure 7.35: The Flavius Josephus problem (data-driven concurrent version).

A declarative solution

As alert programmers, we remark that the solution of figure 7.34 has no observable nondeterminism. We can therefore write it completely in the declarative concurrent model of chapter 4. Let us do this and compare the two programs. Figure 7.35 shows a declarative solution that implements the same protocol as the active object version. Like the active object version, it does short-circuiting and eventually terminates with the identity of the last survivor. It pays to compare the two versions carefully. The declarative version is half the size of the active object version. One reason is that streams are first-class entities. This makes short-circuiting very easy: just return the input stream as output.

The declarative program uses a concurrent abstraction, `Pipe`, that it defines especially for this program. If $l \leq h$, then the function call `{Pipe Xs L H F}` creates a pipeline of $h - l + 1$ stream objects, numbered from l to h inclusive. Each stream object is created by the call `{F Is I}`, which is given an input stream `Is` and an integer `I` and returns the output stream. We create a closed ring by feeding the output stream `Zs` back to the input, with the additional message `kill(1 N)` to start the execution.

7.8.4 Other active object abstractions

Section 5.3 shows some of the useful protocols that we can build on top of message passing. Let us take two of these protocols and make them into abstractions for active objects.

Synchronous active objects

It is easy to extend active objects to give them synchronous behavior, like a standard object or an RMI object. A synchronous invocation {Obj M} does not return until the method corresponding to M is completely executed. Internal to the abstraction, we use a dataflow variable to do the synchronization. Here is the definition of NewSync, which creates a synchronous active object:

```
fun {NewSync Class Init}
P Obj={New Class Init} in
   thread S in
      {NewPort S P}
      for M#X in S do {Obj M} X=unit end
   end
   proc {$ M} X in {Send P M#X} {Wait X} end
end
```

Each message sent to the object contains a synchronization token X, which is bound when the message is completely handled.

Active objects with exception handling

Explicitly doing exception handling for active objects can be cumbersome, since it means adding a **try** in each server method and a **case** after each call. Let us hide these statements inside an abstraction. The abstraction adds an extra argument that can be used to test whether or not an exception occurred. Instead of adding the extra argument in the method, we add it to the object invocation itself. In this way, it automatically works for all methods. The extra argument is bound to normal if the invocation completes normally, and to exception(E) if the object raises the exception E. Here is the definition of NewActiveExc:

```
fun {NewActiveExc Class Init}
P Obj={New Class Init} in
   thread S in
      {NewPort S P}
      for M#X in S do
         try {Obj M} X=normal
         catch E then X=exception(E) end
      end
   end
   proc {$ M X} {Send P M#X} end
end
```

The object Obj is called as {Obj M X}, where X is the extra argument. So the send is still asynchronous and the client can examine at any time whether the call completed successfully or not. For the synchronous case, we can put the **case** statement inside the abstraction:

```
proc {$ M}
X in
   {Send P M#X}
   case X of normal then skip
   [] exception(E) then raise E end end
end
```

This lets us call the object exactly like a passive object.

7.8.5 Event manager with active objects

We can use active objects to implement a simple concurrent event manager. The event manager contains a set of event handlers. Each handler is a triple Id#F#S, where Id uniquely identifies the handler, F defines the state update function, and S is the handler's state. When an event E occurs, each triple Id#F#S is replaced by Id#F#{F E S}. That is, each event handler is a finite state machine, which does a transition from state S to state {F E S} when the event E occurs.

The event manager was originally written in Erlang [7]. The Erlang computation model is based on communicating active objects (see chapter 5). The translation of the original code to the concurrent stateful model was straightforward.

We define the event manager EM as an active object with four methods:

1. {EM init} initializes the event manager.
2. {EM event(E)} posts the event E at the event manager.
3. {EM add(F S Id)} adds a new handler with update function F and initial state S. Returns a unique identifier Id.
4. {EM delete(Id S)} removes the handler with identifier Id, if it exists. Returns the handler's state in S.

Figure 7.36 shows how to define the event manager as a class. We show how to use the event manager to do error logging. First we define a new event manager:

```
EM={NewActive EventManager init}
```

We then install a memory-based handler. It logs every event in an internal list:

```
MemH=fun {$ E Buf} E|Buf end
Id={EM add(MemH nil $)}
```

We can replace the memory-based handler by a disk-based handler during execution, without losing any of the already-logged events. In the following code, we remove the memory-based handler, open a log file, write the already-logged events to the file, and then define and install the disk-based handler:

```
class EventManager
   attr
      handlers
   meth init handlers:=nil end
   meth event(E)
      handlers:=
         {Map @handlers fun {$ Id#F#S} Id#F#{F E S} end}
   end
   meth add(F S ?Id)
      Id={NewName}
      handlers:=Id#F#S|@handlers
   end
   meth delete(DId ?DS)
      handlers:={List.partition
         @handlers fun {$ Id#F#S} DId==Id end [_#_#DS]}
   end
end
```

Figure 7.36: Event manager with active objects.

```
DiskH=fun {$ E F} {F write(vs:E)} F end
File={New Open.file init(name:´event.log´ flags:[write create])}
Buf={EM delete(Id $)}
for E in {Reverse Buf} do {File write(vs:E)} end
Id2={EM add(DiskH File $)}
```

This uses the System module `Open` to write the log. We could use the `File` module, but then the rest of the program could not use it, since it only supports one open file at a time for writing.

Adding functionality with inheritance

The event manager of figure 7.36 has the defect that if events occur during a replacement, i.e., between the delete and add operations, then they will not be logged. How can we remedy this defect? A simple solution is to add a new method, `replace` to `EventManager` that does both the delete and add. Because all methods are executed sequentially in the active object, this ensures no event will occur between the delete and add. We have the choice to add the new method directly, to `EventManager`, or indirectly, to a subclass by inheritance. Which possibility is the right solution depends on several factors. First, whether we have access to the source code of `EventManager`. If we do not, then inheritance is the only possibility. If we do have the source code, inheritance may still be the right answer. It depends on how often we need the replace functionality. If we almost always need it in event managers, then we should modify `EventManager` directly and not create a second class. If we rarely need it, then its definition should not encumber `EventManager`, and we can separate it by using inheritance.

Let us use inheritance for this example. Figure 7.37 defines a new class

```
class ReplaceEventManager from EventManager
   meth replace(NewF NewS OldId NewId
                insert:P<=proc {$ _} skip end)
      Buf=EventManager,delete(OldId $)
   in
      {P Buf}
      NewId=EventManager,add(NewF NewS $)
   end
end
```

Figure 7.37: Adding functionality with inheritance.

`ReplaceEventManager` that inherits from `EventManager` and adds a new method `replace`. Instances of `ReplaceEventManager` have all methods of `EventManager` as well as the method `replace`. The `insert` field is optional; it can be used to insert an operation to be done between the delete and add operations. We define a new event manager:

```
EM={NewActive ReplaceEventManager init}
```

Now we can do the replacement as follows:

```
DiskH=fun {$ E S} {S write(vs:E)} S end
File={New Open.file init(name:´event.log´ flags:[write create])}
Id2
{EM replace(DiskH File Id Id2
            insert:
               proc {$ S}
                  for E in {Reverse S} do
                     {File write(vs:E)} end
               end)}
```

Because `replace` is executed inside the active object, it is serialized with all the other messages to the object. This ensures that no events can arrive between the delete and add methods.

Batching operations using a mixin class

A second way to remedy the defect is to add a new method that does batching, i.e., it does a list of operations. Figure 7.38 defines a new class `Batcher` that has just one method, `batch(L)`. The list `L` can contain messages or zero-argument procedures. When `batch(L)` is called, the messages are passed to **`self`** and the procedures are executed, in the order they occur in `L`. This is an example of using first-class messages. Since messages are also language entities (they are records), they can be put in a list and passed to `Batcher`. We define a new class that inherits from `EventManager` and brings in the functionality of `Batcher`:

```
class BatchingEventManager from EventManager Batcher end
```

```
class Batcher
   meth batch(L)
      for X in L do
         if {IsProcedure X} then {X} else {self X} end
      end
   end
end
```

Figure 7.38: Batching a list of messages and procedures.

We use multiple inheritance because `Batcher` can be useful to any class that needs batching, not just to event managers. Now we can define a new event manager:

```
EM={NewActive BatchingEventManager init}
```

All instances of `BatchingEventManager` have all methods of `EventManager` as well as the method `batch`. The class `Batcher` is an example of a mixin class: it adds functionality to an existing class without needing to know anything about the class. Now we can replace the memory-based handler by a disk-based handler:

```
DiskH=fun {$ E S} {S write(vs:E)} S end
File={New Open.file init(name:´event.log´ flags:[write create])}
Buf Id2
{EM batch([delete(Id Buf)
           proc {$}
              for E in {Reverse Buf} do {File write(vs:E)} end
           end
           add(DiskH File Id2)])}
```

The `batch` method guarantees atomicity in the same way as the `replace` method, i.e., because it executes inside the active object.

What are the differences between the replacement solution and the batching solution? There are two:

- The replacement solution is more efficient because the `replace` method is hard-coded. The `batch` method, on the other hand, adds a layer of interpretation.
- The batching solution is more flexible. Batching can be added to any class using multiple inheritance. No new methods have to be defined. Furthermore, any list of messages and procedures can be batched, even a list that is calculated at run time. However, the batching solution requires that the language support first-class messages.

Combining computation models

The event manager is an interesting combination of the declarative, object-oriented, and stateful concurrent computation models:

- Each event handler is defined declaratively by its state update function. Even stronger, each method of the event manager can be seen as a declarative definition. Each method takes the event manager's internal state from the attribute `handlers`, does a declarative operation on it, and stores the result in `handlers`.

- All methods are executed in sequential fashion, as if they were in a stateful model with no concurrency. All concurrency is managed by the active object abstraction, as implemented by `NewActive`. This abstraction guarantees that all object invocations are serialized. Especially, no locking or other concurrency control is needed.
- New functionality, e.g., replacement or batching, is added by using object-oriented inheritance. Because the new method executes inside the active object, it is guaranteed to be atomic.

The result is that event handlers are defined sequentially and declaratively, and yet can be used in a stateful concurrent environment. This is an example of impedance matching, as defined in section 4.8.7. Impedance matching is a special case of the general principle of separation of concerns. The concerns of state and concurrency are separated from the definition of the event handlers. It is good programming practice to separate concerns as much as possible. Using different computation models together often helps to achieve separation of concerns.

7.9 Exercises

1. *Uninitialized objects.* The function `New` creates a new object when given a class and an initial message. Write another function `New2` that does not require an initial message. That is, the call `Obj={New2 Class}` creates a new object without initializing it. *Hint*: write `New2` in terms of `New`.

2. *Protected methods in the Java sense.* A protected method in Java has two parts: it is accessible throughout the package that defines the class and also by descendants of the class. For this exercise, define a linguistic abstraction that allows annotating a method or attribute as `protected` in the Java sense. Show how to encode this in the model of section 7.3.3 by using name values. Use functors to represent Java packages. For example, one approach might to be to define the name value globally in the functor and also to store it in an attribute called `setOfAllProtectedAttributes`. Since the attribute is inherited, the method name is visible to all subclasses. Work out the details of this approach.

3. *Method wrapping.* Section 7.3.5 shows how to do method wrapping. The definition of `TraceNew2` given there uses a class `Trace` that has an external reference. This is not allowed in some object systems. For this exercise, rewrite `TraceNew2` so that it uses a class with no external references.

4. *Implementing inheritance and static binding.* For this exercise, generalize the implementation of the object system given in section 7.6 to handle static binding and to handle inheritance with any number of superclasses (not just two).

5. *Message protocols with active objects.* For this exercise, redo the message protocols of section 5.3 with active objects instead of port objects.

6. *The Flavius Josephus problem.* Section 7.8.3 solves this problem in two ways, using active objects and using data-driven concurrency. For this exercise, do the following:

(a) Use a third model, the sequential stateful model, to solve the problem. Write two programs: the first without short-circuiting and the second with it. Try to make both as concise and natural as possible in the model. For example, without short-circuiting an array of booleans is a natural data structure to represent the ring. Compare the structure of both programs with the two programs in section 7.8.3.

(b) Compare the execution times of the different versions. There are two orthogonal analyses to be done. First, measure the advantages (if any) of using short-circuiting for various values of n and k. This can be done in each of the three computation models. For each model, divide the (n, k) plane into two regions, depending on whether short-circuiting is faster or not. Are these regions the same for each model? Second, compare the three versions with short-circuiting. Do these versions have the same asymptotic time complexity as a function of n and k?

7. (advanced exercise) *Inheritance without explicit state.* Inheritance does not require explicit state; the two concepts are orthogonal. For this exercise, design and implement an object system with classes and inheritance but without explicit state. One possible starting point is the implementation of declarative objects in section 6.4.2.

8. (research project) *Programming design patterns.* For this exercise, design an object-oriented language that allows "upward" inheritance (defining a new superclass of a given class) as well as higher-order programming. Upward inheritance is usually called generalization. Implement and evaluate the usefulness of your language. Show how to program the design patterns of Gamma et al. [66] as abstractions in your language. Do you need other new operations in addition to generalization?

8 Shared-State Concurrency

Of course, the lock and key is a very small beginning, and language was already highly developed, even perhaps overdeveloped, before this first tiny step on the road to a mechanical equivalent of language was made. It is a long way from the first locks, via looms and mechanical music makers, to the first mechanical computers, and then a long way further to the electronic computer.
– *Invention and Evolution: Design in Nature and Engineering*, Michael French (1994)

The shared-state concurrent model is a simple extension to the declarative concurrent model that adds explicit state in the form of cells, which are a kind of mutable variable. This model is equivalent in expressiveness to the message-passing concurrent model of chapter 5, because cells can be efficiently implemented with ports and vice versa. When we want to cover both models, we speak of the stateful concurrent model. The models are not equivalent in practice because they encourage very different programming styles. The shared-state model encourages programs where threads concurrently access a shared data repository. The message-passing model encourages multi-agent programs. The shared-state model is harder to program than the message-passing model. Let us see what the problem is and how we can solve it.

The inherent difficulty of the model

Let us first see exactly why the shared-state model is difficult. Execution consists of multiple threads, all executing independently and all accessing shared cells. At some level, a thread's execution can be seen as a sequence of atomic instructions. For a cell, these are `@` (access), `:=` (assignment), and `Exchange`. Because of the interleaving semantics, all execution happens as if there was one global order of operations. All operations of all threads are therefore "interleaved" to make this order. There are many possible interleavings; their number is limited only by data dependencies (calculations needing results of others). Any particular execution realizes an interleaving. Because thread scheduling is nondeterministic, there is no way to know which interleaving will be chosen.

But just how many interleavings are possible? Let us consider a simple case: two threads, each doing k cell operations. Thread T_1 does the operations a_1, a_2, ..., a_k and thread T_2 does b_1, b_2, ..., b_k. How many possible executions are there, interleaving all these operations? It is easy to see that the number is $\binom{2k}{k}$. Any interleaved execution consists of $2k$ operations, of which each thread takes k. Consider these operations as integers from 1 to $2k$, put in a set. Then T_1 takes k integers from this set and T_2 gets the others. This number is exponential in k.[1] For three or more threads, the number of interleavings is even bigger (see Exercises, section 8.7).

It is possible to write algorithms in this model and prove their correctness by reasoning on all possible interleavings. For example, if we assume that the only atomic operations on cells are `@` and `:=`, then Dekker's algorithm implements mutual exclusion. Even though Dekker's algorithm is short (e.g., forty-eight lines of code in [50], using a Pascal-like language), the reasoning is already quite difficult. For bigger programs, this technique rapidly becomes impractical. It is unwieldy and interleavings are easy to overlook.

Why not use declarative concurrency?

Given the inherent difficulty of programming in the shared-state concurrent model, an obvious question is why not stick with the declarative concurrent model of chapter 4? It is enormously simpler to program in than the shared-state concurrent model. It is almost as easy to reason in as the declarative model, which is sequential.

Let us briefly examine why the declarative concurrent model is so easy. It is because dataflow variables are monotonic: they can be bound to just one value. Once bound, the value does not change. Threads that share a dataflow variable, e.g., a stream, can therefore calculate with the stream as if it were a simple value. This is in contrast to cells, which are nonmonotonic: they can be assigned any number of times to values that have no relation to each other. Threads that share a cell cannot make any assumptions about its content: at any time, the content can be completely different from any previous content.

The problem with the declarative concurrent model is that threads must communicate in a kind of "lockstep" or "systolic" fashion. Two threads communicating with a third thread cannot execute independently; they must coordinate with each other. This is a consequence of the fact that the model is still declarative, and hence deterministic.

We would like to allow two threads to be completely independent and yet communicate with the same third thread. For example, we would like clients to make independent queries to a common server or to independently increment a shared state. To express this, we have to leave the realm of declarative models. This is because two independent entities communicating with a third introduce an observable nondeterminism. A simple way to solve the problem is to add explicit state to the model. Ports and cells are two important ways to add explicit state. This gets us back to the model with both concurrency and state. But reasoning directly

1. Using Stirling's formula we approximate it as $2^{2k}/\sqrt{\pi k}$.

in this model is impractical. Let us see how we can get around the problem.

Getting around the difficulty

Programming in the stateful concurrent model is largely a matter of managing the interleavings. There are two successful approaches:

- Message passing between port objects. This is the subject of chapter 5. In this approach, programs consist of port objects that send asynchronous messages to each other. Internally, a port object executes in a single thread.
- Atomic actions on shared cells. This is the subject of this chapter. In this approach, programs consist of passive objects that are invoked by threads. Abstractions are used to build large atomic actions (e.g., using locking, monitors, or transactions) so that the number of possible interleavings is small.

Each approach has its advantages and disadvantages. The technique of invariants, as explained in chapter 6, can be used in both approaches to reason about programs. The two approaches are equivalent in a theoretical sense, but not in a practical sense: a program using one approach can be rewritten to use the other approach, but it may not be as easy to understand [125].

Structure of the chapter

The chapter consists of six main sections:

- Section 8.1 defines the shared-state concurrent model.
- Section 8.2 brings together and compares briefly all the different concurrent models that we have introduced in the book. This gives a balanced perspective on how to do practical concurrent programming.
- Section 8.3 introduces the concept of lock, which is the basic concept used to create coarse-grained atomic actions. A lock defines an area of the program inside of which only a single thread can execute at a time.
- Section 8.4 extends the concept of lock to get the concept of monitor, which gives better control on which threads are allowed to enter and exit the lock. Monitors make it possible to program more sophisticated concurrent programs.
- Section 8.5 extends the concept of lock to get the concept of transaction, which allows a lock to be either committed or aborted. In the latter case, it is as if the lock had never executed. Transactions greatly simplify the programming of concurrent programs that can handle rare events and nonlocal exits.
- Section 8.6 summarizes how concurrency is done in Java, a popular concurrent object-oriented language.

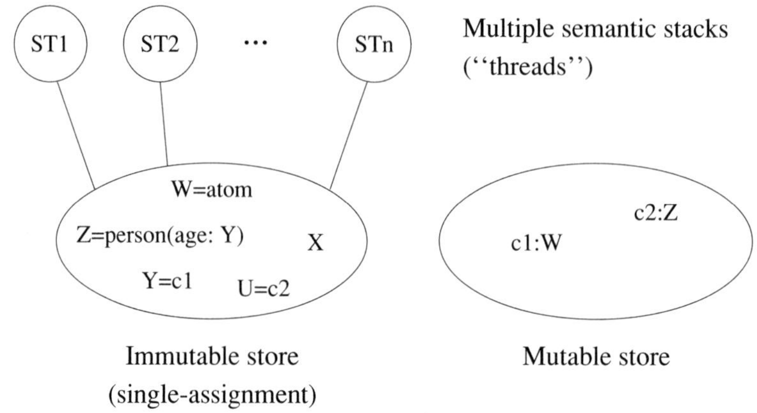

Figure 8.1: The shared-state concurrent model.

⟨s⟩ ::=	
skip	Empty statement
| $\langle s\rangle_1$ $\langle s\rangle_2$	Statement sequence
| **local** ⟨x⟩ **in** ⟨s⟩ **end**	Variable creation
| $\langle x\rangle_1$=$\langle x\rangle_2$	Variable-variable binding
| ⟨x⟩=⟨v⟩	Value creation
| **if** ⟨x⟩ **then** $\langle s\rangle_1$ **else** $\langle s\rangle_2$ **end**	Conditional
| **case** ⟨x⟩ **of** ⟨pattern⟩ **then** $\langle s\rangle_1$ **else** $\langle s\rangle_2$ **end**	Pattern matching
| { ⟨x⟩ $\langle y\rangle_1$ ··· $\langle y\rangle_n$ }	Procedure application
| **thread** ⟨s⟩ **end**	Thread creation
| {NewName ⟨x⟩}	Name creation
| ⟨y⟩=!!⟨x⟩	Read-only view
| **try** $\langle s\rangle_1$ **catch** ⟨x⟩ **then** $\langle s\rangle_2$ **end**	Exception context
| **raise** ⟨x⟩ **end**	Raise exception
| {NewCell ⟨x⟩ ⟨y⟩}	Cell creation
| {Exchange ⟨x⟩ ⟨y⟩ ⟨z⟩}	Cell exchange

Table 8.1: The kernel language with shared-state concurrency.

8.1 The shared-state concurrent model

Chapter 6 adds explicit state to the declarative model. This allows object-oriented programming. Chapter 4 adds concurrency to the declarative model. This allows having multiple active entities that evolve independently. The next step is to add both explicit state and concurrency to the declarative model. One way to do this is given in chapter 5: by adding ports. This chapter gives an alternative way: by adding cells.

The resulting model, called the shared-state concurrent model, is shown in figure 8.1. Its kernel language is defined in table 8.1. If we consider the subset of operations up to `ByNeed` then we have the declarative concurrent model. We add names, read-only variables, exceptions, and explicit state to this model.

8.2 Programming with concurrency

By now, we have seen many different ways to write concurrent programs. Before diving into programming with shared-state concurrency, let us make a slight detour and put all these ways into perspective. We first give a brief overview of the main approaches. We then examine more closely the new approaches that become possible with shared-state concurrency.

8.2.1 Overview of the different approaches

For the programmer, there are four main practical approaches to writing concurrent programs:

- *Sequential programming* (see chapters 3, 6, and 7). This is the baseline approach that has no concurrency. It can be either eager or lazy.
- *Declarative concurrency* (see chapter 4). This is concurrency in the declarative model, which gives the same results as a sequential program but can give them incrementally. This model is usable when there is no observable nondeterminism. It can be either eager (data-driven concurrency) or lazy (demand-driven concurrency).
- *Message-passing concurrency* (see chapter 5 and section 7.8). This is message passing between port objects, which are internally sequential. This limits the number of interleavings. Active objects (see section 7.8) are a variant of port objects where the object's behavior is defined by a class.
- *Shared-state concurrency* (this chapter). This is threads updating shared passive objects using coarse-grained atomic actions. This is another approach to limiting the number of interleavings.

Figure 8.2 gives a complete list of these approaches and some others. Previous chapters have already explained sequential programming and concurrent declarative

Model	Approaches
Sequential (declarative or stateful)	Sequential programming Order–determining concurrency Coroutining Lazy evaluation
Declarative concurrent	Data–driven concurrency Demand–driven concurrency
Stateful concurrent	Use the model directly Message–passing concurrency Shared–state concurrency
Nondeterministic concurrent	Stream objects with merge

Figure 8.2: Different approaches to concurrent programming.

programming. In this chapter we look at the others. We first give an overview of the four main approaches.

Sequential programming

In a sequential model, there is a total order among all operations. This is the strongest order invariant a program can have. We have seen two ways that this order can be relaxed a little, while still keeping a sequential model:

- *"Order-determining" concurrency* (see section 4.4.1). In this model, all operations execute in a total order, as with sequential execution, but the order is unknown to the programmer. Concurrent execution with dataflow finds the order dynamically.
- *Coroutining* (see section 4.4.2). In this model, preemption is explicit, i.e., the program decides when to pass control to another thread. Lazy evaluation, in which laziness is added to a sequential program, does coroutining.

Both of these variant models are still deterministic.

Declarative concurrency

The declarative concurrent models of chapter 4 all add threads to the declarative model. This does not change the result of a calculation, but only changes the order in which the result is obtained. For example, the result might be given incrementally. This allows building a dynamic network of concurrent stream objects connected with streams. Because of concurrency, adding an element to its input stream allows a stream object to produce an output immediately.

These models have nondeterminism in the implementation, since the system chooses how to advance the threads. But to stay declarative, the nondeterminism must not be observable to the program. The declarative concurrent models guarantee this as long as no exceptions are raised (since exceptions are witnesses to an observable nondeterminism). In practice, this means that each stream object must know at all times from which stream its next input will come.

The demand-driven concurrent model, also known as lazy execution (see section 4.5), is a form of declarative concurrency. It does not change the result of a calculation, but only affects how much calculation is done to obtain the result. It can sometimes give results in cases where the data-driven model would go into an infinite loop. This is important for resource management, i.e., controlling how many computational resources are needed. Calculations are initiated only when their results are needed by other calculations. Lazy execution is implemented with by-need triggers.

Message-passing concurrency

Message passing is a basic programming style of the stateful concurrent model. It is explained in chapter 5 and section 7.8. It extends the declarative concurrent model with a simple kind of communication channel, a port. It defines port objects, which extend stream objects to read from ports. A program is then a network of port objects communicating with each other through asynchronous message passing. Each port object decides when to handle each message. The port object processes the messages sequentially. This limits the possible interleavings and allows us to reason using invariants. Sending and receiving messages between port objects introduces a causality between events (send, receive, and internal). Reasoning on such systems requires reasoning on the causality chains.

Shared-state concurrency

Shared state is another basic programming style of the stateful concurrent model. It is explained in this chapter. It consists of a set of threads accessing a set of shared passive objects. The threads coordinate among each other when accessing the shared objects. They do this by means of coarse-grained atomic actions, e.g., locks, monitors, or transactions. Again, this limits the possible interleavings and allows us to reason using invariants.

Relationship between ports and cells

The message-passing and shared-state models are equivalent in expressiveness. This follows because ports can be implemented with cells and vice versa. (It is an amusing exercise to implement the `Send` operation using `Exchange` and vice versa.) It would seem then that we have the choice whether to add ports or cells to the declarative concurrent model. However, in practice this is not so. The two computation models emphasize a quite different programming style that is appropriate for different classes of applications. The message-passing style is of programs as active entities that coordinate with one another. The shared-state style is of programs as passive data repositories that are modified in a coherent way.

Other approaches

In addition to these four approaches, there are two others worth mentioning:

- *Using the stateful concurrent model directly.* This consists in programming directly in the stateful concurrent model, either in message-passing style (using threads, ports, and dataflow variables; see section 5.6), in shared-state style (using threads, cells, and dataflow variables; see section 8.2.2), or in a mixed style (using both cells and ports).
- *Nondeterministic concurrent model* (see section 5.8.1). This model adds a nondeterministic choice operator to the declarative concurrent model. It is a stepping stone to the stateful concurrent model.

They are less common, but can be useful in some circumstances.

Which concurrent model to use?

How do we decide which approach to use when writing a concurrent program? Here are a few rules of thumb:

- Stick with the least concurrent model that suffices for your program. For example, if using concurrency does not simplify the architecture of the program, then stick with a sequential model. If your program does not have any observable nondeterminism, such as independent clients interacting with a server, then stick with the declarative concurrent model.
- If you absolutely need both state and concurrency, then use either the message-passing or the shared-state approach. The message-passing approach is often the best for multi-agent programs, i.e., programs that consist of autonomous entities ("agents") that communicate with each other. The shared-state approach is often the best for data-centered programs, i.e., programs that consist of a large repository of data ("database") that is accessed and updated concurrently. Both approaches can be used together for different parts of the same application.
- Modularize your program and concentrate the concurrency aspects in as few places as possible. Most of the time, large parts of the program can be sequential or use declarative concurrency. One way to implement this is with impedance matching, which is explained in section 4.8.7. For example, active objects can be used as front ends to passive objects. If the passive objects are all called from the same active object then they can use a sequential model.

```
fun {NewStack}
   Stack={NewCell nil}
   proc {Push X}
   S in
      {Exchange Stack S X|S}
   end
   fun {Pop}
   X S in
      {Exchange Stack X|S S}
      X
   end
in
   stack(push:Push pop:Pop)
end
```

Figure 8.3: Concurrent stack.

Too much concurrency is bad

There is a model, the maximally concurrent model, that has even more concurrency than the stateful concurrent model. In the maximally concurrent model, each operation executes in its own thread. Execution order is constrained only by data dependencies. This has the greatest possible concurrency.

The maximally concurrent model model has been used as the basis for experimental parallel programming languages. But it is both hard to program in and hard to implement efficiently (see Exercises, section 8.7). This is because operations tend to be fine-grained compared to the overhead of scheduling and synchronizing. The shared-state concurrent model of this chapter does not have this problem because thread creation is explicit. This allows the programmer to control the granularity. We do not present the maximally concurrent model in more detail in this chapter. A variant of this model is used for constraint programming (see chapter 12).

8.2.2 Using the shared-state model directly

As we saw in the beginning of this chapter, programming directly in the shared-state model can be tough. This is because there are potentially an enormous number of interleavings, and the program has to work correctly for all of them. That is the main reason why more high-level approaches, like active objects and atomic actions, were developed. Yet, it is sometimes useful to use the model directly. Before moving on to using atomic actions, let us see what can be done directly in the shared-state concurrent model. Practically, it boils down to programming with threads, procedures, cells, and dataflow variables. This section gives some examples.

Concurrent stack

A *concurrent data abstraction* is a data abstraction where multiple threads can execute operations simultaneously. The first and simplest concurrent data abstraction we show is a stack in object style. The stack provides nonblocking push and pop operations, i.e., they never wait, but succeed or fail immediately. Using exchange, its implementation is very compact, as figure 8.3 shows. The exchange does two things: it accesses the cell's old content and it assigns a new content. Because exchange is atomic, it can be used in a concurrent setting. Because the push and pop operations each do just one exchange, they can be interleaved in any way and still work correctly. Any number of threads can access the stack concurrently, and it will work correctly. The only restriction is that a pop should not be attempted on an empty stack. An exception can be raised in that case, e.g., as follows:

```
fun {Pop}
X S in
   try {Exchange Stack X|S S}
   catch failure(...) then raise stackEmpty end end
   X
end
```

The concurrent stack is simple because each operation does just a single exchange. Things become much more complex when an operation of the abstraction does more than one cell operation. For the abstraction's operation to be correct in general, the cell operations would have to be done atomically. To guarantee this in a simple way, we recommend using the active object or atomic action approach.

Simulating a slow network

The object invocation {Obj M} calls Obj immediately and returns when the call is finished. We would like to modify this to simulate a slow, asynchronous network, where the object is called asynchronously after a delay that represents the network delay. Here is a simple solution that works for any object:

```
fun {SlowNet1 Obj D}
   proc {$ M}
      thread
         {Delay D} {Obj M}
      end
   end
end
```

The call {SlowNet1 Obj D} returns a "slow" version of Obj. When the slow object is invoked, it waits at least D ms before calling the original object.

Preserving message order with token passing The above solution does not preserve message order. That is, if the slow object is invoked several times from within the same thread, then there is no guarantee that the messages will arrive in the same order they were sent. Moreover, if the object is invoked from several threads, different executions of the object can overlap in time, which could result in an inconsistent object state. Here is a solution that does preserve message order and guarantees that only one thread at a time can execute inside the object:

```
fun {SlowNet2 Obj D}
C={NewCell unit} in
   proc {$ M}
   Old New in
      {Exchange C Old New}
      thread
         {Delay D} {Wait Old} {Obj M} New=unit
      end
   end
end
```

This solution uses a general technique, called token passing, to extract an execution order from one part of a program and impose it on another part. The token passing is implemented by creating a sequence of dataflow variables X_0, X_1, X_2, ..., and passing consecutive pairs (X_0, X_1), (X_1, X_2), ... to the operations that should be done in the same order. An operation that receives the pair (X_i, X_{i+1}) does the following steps in order:

1. Wait until the token arrives, i.e., until X_i is bound ({Wait X_i}).
2. Do the computation.
3. Send the token to the next pair, i.e., bind X_{i+1} (X_{i+1}=**unit**).

In the definition of `SlowNet2`, each time the slow object is called, a pair of variables (`Old`, `New`) is created. This is inserted into the sequence by the call `{Exchange C Old New}`. Because `Exchange` is atomic, this works also in a concurrent setting where many threads call the slow object. Each pair shares one variable with the previous pair (`Old`) and one with the next pair (`New`). This effectively puts the object call in an ordered queue. Each call is done in a new thread. It first waits until the previous call has terminated (`{Wait Old}`), then invokes the object (`{Obj M}`), and finally signals that the next call can continue (`New=`**`unit`**). The `{Delay D}` call must be done before `{Wait Old}`; otherwise each object call would take at least `D` ms, which is incorrect.

8.2.3 Programming with atomic actions

Starting with the next section, we give the programming techniques for shared-state concurrency using atomic actions. We introduce the concepts gradually, starting with locks. We refine locks into monitors and transactions. Figure 8.4 shows the hierarchical relationships between these three concepts.

- Locks allow the grouping of little atomic operations into big atomic operations. With a reentrant lock, the same lock can guard discontiguous parts of the program. A thread that is inside one part can reenter the lock at any part without suspending.
- Monitors refine locks with wait points. A wait point is a pair of an exit and a

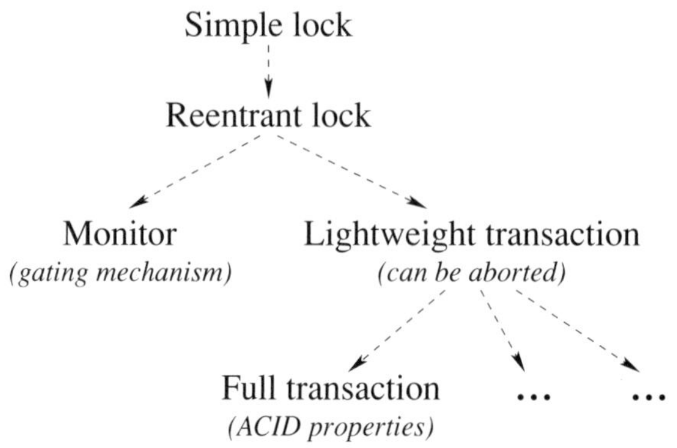

Figure 8.4: The hierarchy of atomic actions.

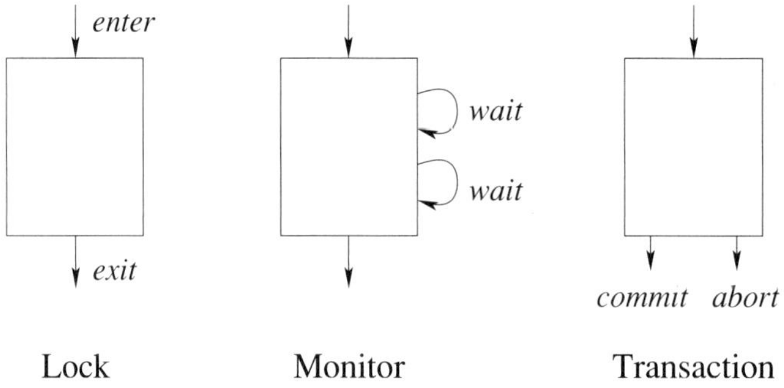

Figure 8.5: Differences between atomic actions.

corresponding entry with no code in between. (Wait points are sometimes called delay points [6].) Threads can park themselves at a wait point, just outside the lock. Exiting threads can wake up parked threads.

- Transactions refine locks to have two possible exits: a normal one (called commit) and an exceptional one (called abort). The exceptional exit can be taken at any time during the transaction. When it is taken, the transaction leaves the execution state unchanged, i.e., as it was upon entry.

Figure 8.5 summarizes the principal differences between the three concepts. There are many variations of these concepts that are designed to solve specific problems. This section only gives a brief introduction to the basic ideas.

Reasoning with atomic actions

Consider a program that uses atomic actions throughout. Proving that the program is correct consists of two parts: proving that each atomic action is correct (when considered by itself) and proving that the program uses them correctly. The first step is to show that each atomic action, e.g., lock, monitor, or transaction, is correct. Each atomic action defines a data abstraction. The data abstraction should have an invariant assertion, i.e., an assertion that is true when there is no thread inside the abstraction. This is similar to reasoning with stateful programs and active objects, except that the data abstraction can be accessed concurrently. Because only one thread can be inside the atomic action at a time, we can still use mathematical induction to show that the assertion is an invariant. We have to prove two things:

- When the data abstraction is first defined, the assertion is satisfied.
- Whenever a thread exits from the data abstraction, the assertion is satisfied.

The existence of the invariant shows that the atomic action is correct. The next step is to show that the program using the atomic actions is correct.

8.2.4 Further reading

There are many good books on concurrent programming. The following four are particularly well-suited as companions to this book. They give more practical techniques and theoretical background for the two concurrent paradigms of message-passing and shared-state concurrency. At the time of writing, we know of no books that deal with the third concurrent paradigm of declarative concurrency.

Concurrent Programming in Java

The first book deals with shared-state concurrency: Concurrent Programming in Java by Doug Lea [127]. This book presents a rich set of practical programming techniques that are particularly well-suited to Java, a popular concurrent object-oriented language (see chapters 7 and 8). However, they can be used in many other languages including the shared-state concurrent model of this book. The book is targeted toward the shared-state approach; message passing is mentioned only in passing.

The major difference between the Java book and this chapter is that the Java book assumes threads are expensive. This is true for current Java implementations. Because of this, the Java book adds a conceptual level between threads and procedures, called tasks, and advises the programmer to schedule multiple tasks on one thread. If threads are lightweight, this conceptual level is not needed. The range of practical programming techniques is broadened and simpler solutions are often possible. For example, having lightweight threads makes it easier to use active objects, which often simplifies program structure.[2]

Concurrent Programming in Erlang

The second book deals with message-passing concurrency: Concurrent Programming in Erlang by Joe Armstrong, Mike Williams, Claes Wikström, and Robert Virding [10]. This book is complementary to the book by Doug Lea. It presents a rich set of practical programming techniques, all based on the Erlang language. The book is entirely based on the message-passing approach.

Concurrent Programming: Principles and Practice

The third book is Concurrent Programming: Principles and Practice by Gregory Andrews [6]. This book is more rigorous than the previous two. It explains both shared state and message passing. It gives a good introduction to formal reasoning with these concepts, using invariant assertions. The formalism is presented at just the right level of detail so that it is both precise and usable by programmers. The book also surveys the historical evolution of these concepts and includes some interesting intermediate steps that are no longer used.

Transaction Processing: Concepts and Techniques

The final book is Transaction Processing: Concepts and Techniques by Jim Gray and Andreas Reuter [73]. This book is a successful blend of theoretical insight and hard-nosed practical information. It gives insight into various kinds of transaction processing, how they are used, and how they are implemented in practice. It gives a modicum of theory, carefully selected to be relevant to the practical information.

8.3 Locks

It often happens that threads wish to access a shared resource, but that the resource can only be used by one thread at a time. To help manage this situation, we introduce a language concept called lock, to help control access to the resource. A lock dynamically controls access to part of the program, called a critical region. The basic operation of the lock is to ensure exclusive access to the critical region, i.e., that only one thread at a time can be executing inside it. If the shared resource is only accessed from within the critical region, then the lock can be used to control access to the resource.

The shared resource can be either inside the program (e.g., an object) or outside it (e.g., an operating system resource). Locks can help in both cases. If the resource is

2. Special cases of active objects are possible if threads are expensive; see e.g., section 5.6.1.

```
fun {NewQueue}
X in
   q(0 X X)
end

fun {Insert q(N S E) X}
E1 in
   E=X|E1 q(N+1 S E1)
end

fun {Delete q(N S E) X}
S1 in
   S=X|S1 q(N-1 S1 E)
end
```

Figure 8.6: Queue (declarative version).

inside the program, then the programmer can guarantee that it cannot be referenced outside the critical region, using lexical scoping. This kind of guarantee can in general not be given for resources outside of the program. For those resources, locks are an aid to the programmer, but he or she must follow the discipline of only referencing the resource inside the critical region.

There are many different kinds of locks that provide different kinds of access control. Most of them can be implemented in Oz using language entities we have already seen (i.e., cells, threads, and dataflow variables). However, a particularly useful kind of lock, the thread-reentrant lock, is directly supported by the language. The following operations are provided:

- `{NewLock L}` returns a new lock.
- `{IsLock X}` returns **`true`** if and only if `X` references a lock.
- **`lock`** `X` **`then`** ⟨stmt⟩ **`end`** guards ⟨stmt⟩ with lock `X`. If no thread is currently executing any statement guarded by lock `X`, then any thread can enter. If a thread is currently executing a guarded statement, then the same thread can enter again, if it encounters the same lock in a nested execution. A thread suspends if it attempts to enter a guarded statement while there is another thread in a statement guarded by the same lock.

Note that **`lock`** `X` **`then`** `...` **`end`** can be called many times with the same lock `X`. That is, the critical section does not have to be contiguous. The lock will ensure that at most one thread is inside any of the parts that it guards.

8.3.1 Building stateful concurrent data abstractions

Now that we have introduced locks, we are ready to program stateful concurrent data abstractions. Let us approach this in steps. We give a systematic way to

```
fun {NewQueue}
   X C={NewCell q(0 X X)}
   proc {Insert X}
   N S E1 in
      q(N S X|E1)=@C
      C:=q(N+1 S E1)
   end
   fun {Delete}
   N S1 E X in
      q(N X|S1 E)=@C
      C:=q(N-1 S1 E)
      X
   end
in
   queue(insert:Insert delete:Delete)
end
```

Figure 8.7: Queue (sequential stateful version).

transform a declarative data abstraction to become a stateful concurrent data abstraction. We also show how to modify a sequential stateful data abstraction to become concurrent.

We illustrate the different techniques by means of a simple example, a queue. This is not a limitation since these techniques work for any data abstraction. We start from a declarative implementation and show how to convert this to a stateful implementation that can be used in a concurrent setting:

- Figure 8.6 is essentially the declarative queue of section 3.4.4. (For brevity we leave out the function `IsEmpty`.) Delete operations never block: if the queue is empty when an element is deleted, then a dataflow variable is returned which will be bound to the next inserted element. The size `N` is positive if there are more inserts than deletes and negative otherwise. All functions have the form `Qout={QueueOp Qin ...}`, taking an input queue `Qin` and returning an output queue `Qout`. This queue will work correctly in a concurrent setting, insofar as it can be used there. The problem is that the order of the queue operations is explicitly determined by the program. Doing these queue operations in different threads will ipso facto cause the threads to synchronize. This is almost surely an undesired behavior.
- Figure 8.7 shows the same queue, but in a stateful version that encapsulates the queue's data. This version cannot be used in a concurrent setting without some changes. The problem is that encapsulating the state requires reading the state (`@`), doing the operation, and then writing the new state (`:=`). If two threads each do an insert, then both reads may be done before both writes, which is incorrect. A correct concurrent version requires the read-operation-write sequence to be atomic.
- Figure 8.8 shows a concurrent version of the stateful queue, using a lock to ensure atomicity of the read-operation-write sequence. Doing queue operations in different

```
fun {NewQueue}
   X C={NewCell q(0 X X)}
   L={NewLock}
   proc {Insert X}
   N S E1 in
      lock L then
         q(N S X|E1)=@C
         C:=q(N+1 S E1)
      end
   end
   fun {Delete}
   N S1 E X in
      lock L then
         q(N X|S1 E)=@C
         C:=q(N-1 S1 E)
      end
      X
   end
in
   queue(insert:Insert delete:Delete)
end
```

Figure 8.8: Queue (concurrent stateful version with lock).

threads will not impose any synchronization between the threads. This property is a consequence of using state.

- Figure 8.9 shows the same version, written with object-oriented syntax. The cell is replaced by the attribute `queue` and the lock is implicitly defined by the `locking` property.

- Figure 8.10 shows another concurrent version, using an exchange to ensure atomicity. Since there is only a single state operation (the exchange), no locks are needed. This version is made possible because of the single-assignment property of dataflow variables. An important detail: the arithmetic operations `N-1` and `N+1` must be done after the exchange. Why?

We discuss the advantages and disadvantages of these solutions:

- The declarative version of figure 8.6 is the simplest, but it cannot be used as a shared resource between independent threads.

- Both concurrent versions of figure 8.8 and 8.10 are reasonable. The use of a lock in figure 8.8 is more general, since a lock can be used to make atomic any set of operations. This version can be written with an object-oriented syntax, as shown in figure 8.9. The version with exchange shown in figure 8.10 is compact but less general; it is only possible for operations that manipulate a single data sequence.

```
class Queue
   attr queue
   prop locking

   meth init
      queue:=q(0 X X)
   end

   meth insert(X)
      lock N S E1 in
         q(N S X|E1)=@queue
         queue:=q(N+1 S E1)
      end
   end

   meth delete(X)
      lock N S1 E in
         q(N X|S1 E)=@queue
         queue:=q(N-1 S1 E)
      end
   end
end
```

Figure 8.9: Queue (concurrent object-oriented version with lock).

8.3.2 Tuple spaces ("Linda")

Tuple spaces are a popular abstraction for concurrent programming. The first tuple space abstraction, called Linda, was introduced by David Gelernter in 1985 [67, 34, 35]. This abstraction plays two very different roles. From a theoretical viewpoint, it is one of the first models of concurrent programming. From a practical viewpoint, it is a useful abstraction for concurrent programs. As such, it can be added to any language, thus giving a concurrent version of that language (e.g., C with Linda is called C-Linda). A tuple space abstraction is sometimes called a coordination model and a programming language that contains a tuple space abstraction is sometimes called a coordination language. In its basic form, the abstraction is simple to define. It consists of a multiset `TS` of tuples with three basic operations:

- `{TS write(T)}` adds the tuple `T` to the tuple space.
- `{TS read(L T)}` waits until the tuple space contains at least one tuple with label `L`. It then removes one such tuple and binds it to `T`.
- `{TS readnonblock(L T B)}` does not wait, but immediately returns. It returns with `B=`**`false`** if the tuple space contains no tuple with label `L`. Otherwise, it returns with `B=`**`true`**, removes one tuple with label `L` and binds it to `T`.

```
fun {NewQueue}
   X C={NewCell q(0 X X)}
   proc {Insert X}
   N S E1 N1 in
      {Exchange C q(N S X|E1) q(N1 S E1)}
      N1=N+1
   end
   fun {Delete}
   N S1 E N1 X in
      {Exchange C q(N X|S1 E) q(N1 S1 E)}
      N1=N-1
      X
   end
in
   queue(insert:Insert delete:Delete)
end
```

Figure 8.10: Queue (concurrent stateful version with exchange).

This slightly simplifies the usual formulation of Linda, in which the read operation can do pattern matching. This abstraction has two important properties. The first property is that it provides a content-addressable memory: tuples are identified only by their labels. The second property is that the readers are decoupled from the writers. The abstraction does no communication between readers and writers other than that defined above.

Example execution

We first create a new tuple space:

```
TS={New TupleSpace init}
```

In `TS` we can read and write any tuples in any order. The final result is always the same: the reads see the writes in the order they are written. Doing `{TS write(foo(1 2 3))}` adds a tuple with label `foo` and three arguments. The following code waits until a tuple with label `foo` exists, and when it does, it removes and displays it:

```
thread {Browse {TS read(foo $)}} end
```

The following code immediately checks if a tuple with label `foo` exists:

```
local T B in {TS readnonblock(foo T B)} {Browse T#B} end
```

This does not block, so it does not need to be put in its own thread.

```
fun {NewQueue}
   X TS={New TupleSpace init}
   proc {Insert X}
   N S E1 in
      {TS read(q q(N S X|E1))}
      {TS write(q(N+1 S E1))}
   end
   fun {Delete}
   N S1 E X in
      {TS read(q q(N X|S1 E))}
      {TS write(q(N-1 S1 E))}
      X
   end
in
   {TS write(q(0 X X))}
   queue(insert:Insert delete:Delete)
end
```

Figure 8.11: Queue (concurrent version with tuple space).

Implementing a concurrent queue

We can show yet another implementation of a concurrent queue, using tuple spaces instead of cells. Figure 8.11 shows how it is done. The tuple space `TS` contains a single tuple `q(N S E)` that represents the state of the queue. The tuple space is initialized with the tuple `q(0 X X)` that represents an empty queue. No locking is needed because the `read` operation atomically removes the tuple from the tuple space. This means that the tuple can be considered as a unique token, which is passed between the tuple space and the queue operations. If there are two concurrent `Insert` operations, only one will get the tuple and the other will wait. This is another example of the token passing technique introduced in section 8.2.2.

Implementing tuple spaces

A tuple space can be implemented with a lock, a dictionary, and a concurrent queue. Figure 8.12 shows a simple implementation in object-oriented style. This implementation is completely dynamic; at any moment it can read and write tuples with any labels. The tuples are stored in a dictionary. The key is the tuple's label and the entry is a queue of tuples with that label. The capitalized methods `EnsurePresent` and `Cleanup` are private to the `TupleSpace` class and invisible to users of tuple space objects (see section 7.3.3). The implementation does correct memory management: a new entry is added upon the first occurrence of a particular label; and when the queue is empty, the entry is removed.

The tuple space implementation uses a concurrent stateful queue which is a slightly extended version of figure 8.8. We add just one operation, a function that

```
class TupleSpace
   prop locking
   attr tupledict

   meth init tupledict:={NewDictionary} end

   meth EnsurePresent(L)
      if {Not {Dictionary.member @tupledict L}}
      then @tupledict.L:={NewQueue} end
   end

   meth Cleanup(L)
      if {@tupledict.L.size}==0
      then {Dictionary.remove @tupledict L} end
   end

   meth write(Tuple)
      lock L={Label Tuple} in
         {self EnsurePresent(L)}
         {@tupledict.L.insert Tuple}
      end
   end

   meth read(L ?Tuple)
      lock
         {self EnsurePresent(L)}
         {@tupledict.L.delete Tuple}
         {self Cleanup(L)}
      end
      {Wait Tuple}
   end

   meth readnonblock(L ?Tuple ?B)
      lock
         {self EnsurePresent(L)}
         if {@tupledict.L.size}>0 then
            {@tupledict.L.delete Tuple} B=true
         else B=false end
         {self Cleanup(L)}
      end
   end
end
```

Figure 8.12: Tuple space (object-oriented version).

```
fun {SimpleLock}
   Token={NewCell unit}
   proc {Lock P}
   Old New in
      {Exchange Token Old New}
      {Wait Old}
      {P}
      New=unit
   end
in
   ´lock´(´lock´:Lock)
end
```

Figure 8.13: Lock (non-reentrant version without exception handling).

```
fun {CorrectSimpleLock}
   Token={NewCell unit}
   proc {Lock P}
   Old New in
      {Exchange Token Old New}
      {Wait Old}
      try {P} finally New=unit end
   end
in
   ´lock´(´lock´:Lock)
end
```

Figure 8.14: Lock (non-reentrant version with exception handling).

returns the size of the queue, i.e., the number of elements it contains. Our queue extends figure 8.8 like this:

```
fun {NewQueue}
   ...
   fun {Size}
      lock L then @C.1 end
   end
in
   queue(insert:Insert delete:Delete size:Size)
end
```

We will extend this queue again for implementing monitors.

8.3.3 Implementing locks

Locks can be defined in the concurrent stateful model by using cells and dataflow variables. We first show the definition of a simple lock, then a simple lock that

```
fun {NewLock}
   Token={NewCell unit}
   CurThr={NewCell unit}
   proc {Lock P}
      if {Thread.this}==@CurThr then
         {P}
      else Old New in
         {Exchange Token Old New}
         {Wait Old}
         CurThr:={Thread.this}
         try {P} finally
            CurThr:=unit
            New=unit
         end
      end
   end
in
   ´lock´(´lock´:Lock)
end
```

Figure 8.15: Lock (reentrant version with exception handling).

handles exceptions correctly, and finally a thread-reentrant lock. The built-in locks provided by the system are thread-reentrant locks with the semantics given here, but they have a more efficient low-level implementation.

A simple lock is a procedure `{L P}` that takes a zero-argument procedure `P` as argument and executes `P` in a critical section. Any thread that attempts to enter the lock while there is still one thread inside will suspend. The lock is called simple because a thread that is inside a critical section cannot enter any other critical section protected by the same lock. It first has to leave the initial critical section. Simple locks can be created by the function `SimpleLock` defined in figure 8.13. If multiple threads attempt to access the lock body, then only one is given access and the others are queued. When a thread leaves the critical section, access is granted to the next thread in the queue. This uses the token passing technique of section 8.2.2.

But what happens if the lock body `{P}` raises an exception? The lock of figure 8.13 does not work since `New` will never be bound. We can fix this problem with a **`try`** statement. Figure 8.14 gives a version of the simple lock that handles exceptions. The **`try`** ⟨stmt⟩$_1$ **`finally`** ⟨stmt⟩$_2$ **`end`** is syntactic sugar that ensures ⟨stmt⟩$_2$ is executed in both the normal and exceptional cases, i.e., an exception will not prevent the lock from being released.

A thread-reentrant lock extends the simple lock to allow the same thread to enter other critical sections protected by the same lock. It is even possible to nest critical sections protected by the same lock. Other threads trying to acquire the lock will queue until `P` is completed. When the lock is released, it is granted to the thread standing first in line. Figure 8.15 shows how to define thread-reentrant locks. This assumes that each thread has a unique identifier `T` that is different from the literal **unit** and that is obtained by calling the procedure `{Thread.this T}`. The assignments to `CurThr` have to be done in exactly the places shown. What can go wrong if `{Wait Old}` and `CurThr:={Thread.this}` are switched or if `CurThr:=unit` and `New=unit` are switched?

8.4 Monitors

Locks are an important tool for building concurrent abstractions in a stateful model, but they are not sufficient. For example, consider the simple case of a bounded buffer. A thread may want to put an element in the buffer. It is not enough to protect the buffer with a lock. What if the buffer is full? The thread enters and can do nothing! What we really want is a way for the thread to wait until the buffer is not full, and then continue. This cannot be done with just locks. It needs a way for threads to coordinate among each other. For example, a thread that puts an element in the buffer can be notified that the buffer is not full by another thread which removes an element from the buffer.

The standard way of coordinating threads in a stateful model is by using monitors. Monitors were introduced by Brinch Hansen [26, 27] and further developed by Hoare [93]. They continue to be widely used; e.g., they are a basic concept in the Java language [127]. A monitor is a lock extended with program control over how waiting threads enter and exit the lock. This control makes it possible to use the monitor as a resource that is shared among concurrent activities. There are several ways to give this control. Typically, a monitor has either one set of waiting threads or several queues of waiting threads. The simplest case is when there is one set; let us consider it first.

The monitor adds a `wait` and a `notify` operation to the lock entry and exit operations. (`notify` is sometimes called `signal`.) The `wait` and `notify` are only possible from inside the monitor. When inside a monitor, a thread can explicitly do a `wait`; thereupon the thread suspends, is entered in the monitor's wait set, and releases the monitor lock. When a thread does a `notify`, it lets one thread in the wait set continue. This thread attempts to get the monitor lock again. If it succeeds, it continues running from where it left off.

We first give an informal definition of monitors. We then program some examples both with monitors and in the declarative concurrent model. This will let us compare both approaches. We conclude the section by giving an implementation of monitors in the shared-state concurrent model.

8.4.1 Definition

There exist several varieties of monitors, with slightly different semantics. We first explain the Java version because it is simple and popular. (Section 8.4.5 gives an alternative version.) The following definition is taken from [126]. In Java, a monitor is always part of an object. It is an object with an internal lock and wait set. Object methods can be protected by the lock by annotating them as `synchronized`. There are three operations to manage the lock: `wait`, `notify`, and `notifyAll`. These operations can only be called by threads that hold the lock. They have the following meaning:

- The `wait` operation does the following:
  - The current thread is suspended.
  - The thread is placed in the object's internal wait set.
  - The lock for the object is released.
- The `notify` operation does the following:
  - If one exists, an arbitrary thread `T` is removed from the object's internal wait set.
  - `T` proceeds to get the lock, just as any other thread. This means that `T` will always suspend for a short time, until the notifying thread releases the lock.
  - `T` resumes execution at the point it was suspended.
- The `notifyAll` operation is similar to `notify` except that it does the above steps for all threads in the internal wait set. The wait set is then emptied.

For the examples that follow, we suppose that a function `NewMonitor` exists with the following specification:

- `M={NewMonitor}` creates a monitor with operations `{M.'lock'}` (monitor lock procedure), `{M.wait}` (wait operation), `{M.notify}` (notify operation), and `{M.notifyAll}` (notifyAll operation).

In the same way as for locks, we assume that the monitor lock is thread-reentrant and handles exceptions correctly. Section 8.4.4 explains how the monitor is implemented.

Monitors were designed for building concurrent data abstractions based on shared state. To make it easier to use monitors, some languages provide them as a linguistic abstraction. This makes it possible for the compiler to guarantee that the wait and notify operations are only executed inside the monitor lock. This can also make it easy for the compiler to ensure safety properties, e.g., that shared variables are only accessed through the monitor [28].

8.4.2 Bounded buffer

In chapter 4, we showed how to implement a bounded buffer declaratively in two ways, with both eager and lazy stream communication. In this section we implement it with a monitor. We then compare this solution with the two declarative implementations. The bounded buffer is an object with three operations:

- `B={New Buffer init(N)}`: create a new bounded buffer `B` of size `N`.

```
class Buffer
   attr
      buf first last n i

   meth init(N)
      buf:={NewArray 0 N-1 null}
      first:=0 last:=0 n:=N i:=0
   end

   meth put(X)
      ... % wait until i<n
      % now add an element:
      @buf.@last:=X
      last:=(@last+1) mod @n
      i:=@i+1
   end

   meth get(X)
      ... % wait until i>0
      % now remove an element:
      X=@buf.@first
      first:=(@first+1) mod @n
      i:=@i-1
   end
end
```

Figure 8.16: Bounded buffer (partial definition of monitor version).

- `{B put(X)}`: put the element `X` in the buffer. If the buffer is full, this will block until the buffer has room for the element.
- `{B get(X)}`: remove the element `X` from the buffer. If the buffer is empty, this will block until there is at least one element.

The idea of the implementation is simple: the put and get operations will each wait until the buffer is not full and not empty, respectively. This gives the partial definition of figure 8.16. The buffer uses an array of n elements, indexed by `first` and `last`. The array wraps around: after element $n-1$ comes element 0. The buffer's maximum size is `n` of which `i` elements are used. Now let's code it with a monitor. The naive solution is the following (where `M` is a monitor record):

```
meth put(X)
   {M.´lock´ proc {$}
      if @i>=@n then {M.wait} end
      @buf.@last:=X
      last:=(@last+1) mod @n
      i:=@i+1
      {M.notifyAll}
   end}
end
```

That is, if the buffer is full, then {M.wait} simply waits until it is no longer full. When get(X) removes an element, it does a {M.notifyAll}, which wakes up the waiting thread. This naive solution is not good enough, since there is no guarantee that the buffer will not fill up just after the wait. When the thread releases the monitor lock with {M.wait}, other threads can slip in to add and remove elements. A correct solution does {M.wait} as often as necessary, checking the comparison @i>=@n each time. This gives the following code:

```
meth put(X)
   {M.´lock´ proc {$}
      if @i>=@n then {M.wait} {self put(X)}
      else
         @buf.@last:=X
         last:=(@last+1) mod @n
         i:=@i+1
         {M.notifyAll}
      end
   end}
end
```

After the wait, this calls the put method again to do the check again. Since the lock is reentrant, it will let the thread enter again. The check is done inside the critical section, which eliminates any interference from other threads. Now we can put the pieces together. Figure 8.17 gives the final solution. The init method creates the monitor and stores the monitor procedures in object attributes. The put and get methods use the technique we gave above of waiting in a loop.

Let us compare this version with the declarative concurrent versions of chapter 4. Figure 4.14 gives the eager version and figure 4.27 gives the lazy version. The lazy version is the simplest. Either of the declarative concurrent versions can be used whenever there is no observable nondeterminism, e.g., in point-to-point connections to connect one writer with one reader. Another case is when there are multiple readers that all read the same items. The monitor version can be used when the number of independent writers is more than one or when the number of independent readers is more than one.

8.4.3 Programming with monitors

The technique we used in the bounded buffer is a general one for programming with monitors. Let us explain it in the general setting. For simplicity, assume that we are defining a concurrent data abstraction completely in a single class. The idea is that each method is a critical section that is guarded, i.e., there is a boolean condition that must be true for a thread to enter the method body. If the condition is false, then the thread waits until it becomes true. A guarded method is also called a conditional critical section.

Guarded methods are implemented using the wait and notifyAll operations. Here is an example in a simple pseudocode:

```
class Buffer
   attr m buf first last n i

   meth init(N)
      m:={NewMonitor}
      buf:={NewArray 0 N-1 null}
      n:=N i:=0 first:=0 last:=0
   end

   meth put(X)
      {@m.´lock´ proc {$}
         if @i>=@n then {@m.wait} {self put(X)}
         else
            @buf.@last:=X
            last:=(@last+1) mod @n
            i:=@i+1
            {@m.notifyAll}
         end
      end}
   end

   meth get(X)
      {@m.´lock´ proc {$}
         if @i==0 then {@m.wait} {self get(X)}
         else
            X=@buf.@first
            first:=(@first+1) mod @n
            i:=@i-1
            {@m.notifyAll}
         end
      end}
   end
end
```

Figure 8.17: Bounded buffer (monitor version).

```
meth methHead
   lock
      while not ⟨expr⟩ do wait;
      ⟨stmt⟩
      notifyAll;
   end
end
```

In this example, ⟨expr⟩ is the guard and ⟨stmt⟩ is the guarded body. When the method is called, the thread enters the lock and waits for the condition in a `while` loop. If the condition is true, then it immediately executes the body. If the condition is false, then it waits. When the wait continues then the loop is repeated, i.e., the condition is checked again. This guarantees that the condition is true when the body is executed. Just before exiting, the method notifies all other waiting threads

```
fun {NewQueue}
   ...
   fun {Size}
      lock L then @C.1 end
   end
   fun {DeleteAll}
      lock L then
      X q(_ S E)=@C in
         C:=q(0 X X)
         E=nil S
      end
   end
   fun {DeleteNonBlock}
      lock L then
         if {Size}>0 then [{Delete}] else nil end
      end
   end
in
   queue(insert:Insert delete:Delete size:Size
         deleteAll:DeleteAll deleteNonBlock:DeleteNonBlock)
end
```

Figure 8.18: Queue (extended concurrent stateful version).

that they might be able to continue. They will all wake up and try to enter the monitor lock to test their condition. The first one that finds a true condition is able to continue. The others will wait again.

8.4.4 Implementing monitors

Let us show how to implement monitors in the shared-state concurrent model. This gives them a precise semantics. Figure 8.20 shows the implementation. It is thread-reentrant and correctly handles exceptions. It implements mutual exclusion using the get-release lock of figure 8.19. It implements the wait set using the extended queue of figure 8.18. Implementing the wait set with a queue avoids starvation because it gives the longest-waiting thread the first chance to enter the monitor.

The implementation only works if `M.wait` is always executed inside an active lock. To be practical, the implementation should be extended to check this at run time. We leave this simple extension up to the reader. Another approach is to embed the implementation inside a linguistic abstraction that statically enforces this.

When writing concurrent programs in the shared-state concurrent model, it is usually simpler to use the dataflow approach rather than monitors. The Mozart implementation therefore does no special optimizations to improve monitor performance. However, the implementation of figure 8.20 can be optimized in many ways, which is important if monitor operations are frequent.

```
fun {NewGRLock}
   Token1={NewCell unit}
   Token2={NewCell unit}
   CurThr={NewCell unit}

   proc {GetLock}
      if {Thread.this}\=@CurThr then Old New in
         {Exchange Token1 Old New}
         {Wait Old}
         Token2:=New
         CurThr:={Thread.this}
      end
   end

   proc {ReleaseLock}
      CurThr:=unit
      unit=@Token2
   end
in
   ´lock´(get:GetLock release:ReleaseLock)
end
```

Figure 8.19: Lock (reentrant get-release version).

Extended concurrent queue

For the monitor implementation, we extend the concurrent queue of figure 8.8 with the three operations: `Size`, `DeleteAll`, and `DeleteNonBlock`. This gives the definition of figure 8.18.

This queue is a good example of why reentrant locking is useful. Just look at the definition of `DeleteNonBlock`: it calls `Size` and `Delete`. This will only work if the lock is reentrant.

Reentrant get-release lock

For the monitor implementation, we extend the reentrant lock of figure 8.15 to a get-release lock. This exports the actions of getting and releasing the lock as separate operations, `Get` and `Release`. This gives the definition of figure 8.19. The operations have to be separate because they are used in both `LockM` and `WaitM`.

8.4.5 Another semantics for monitors

In the monitor concept we introduced above, `notify` has just one effect: it causes one waiting thread to leave the wait set. This thread then tries to obtain the monitor lock. The notifying thread does not immediately release the monitor lock. When it does, the notified thread competes with other threads for the lock. This means that

```
fun {NewMonitor}
   Q={NewQueue}
   L={NewGRLock}

   proc {LockM P}
      {L.get} try {P} finally {L.release} end
   end

   proc {WaitM}
   X in
      {Q.insert X} {L.release} {Wait X} {L.get}
   end

   proc {NotifyM}
   U={Q.deleteNonBlock} in
      case U of [X] then X=unit else skip end
   end

   proc {NotifyAllM}
   L={Q.deleteAll} in
      for X in L do X=unit end
   end
in
   monitor('lock':LockM wait:WaitM notify:NotifyM
           notifyAll:NotifyAllM)
end
```

Figure 8.20: Monitor implementation.

an assertion satisfied at the time of the notify might no longer be satisfied when the notified thread enters the lock. This is why an entering thread has to check the condition again.

There is a variation that is both more efficient and easier to reason about. It is for `notify` to do two operations atomically: it first causes one waiting thread to leave the wait set (as before) and it then immediately passes the monitor lock to that thread. The notifying thread thereby exits from the monitor. This has the advantage that an assertion satisfied at the time of the notify will still be true when the notified thread continues. The `notifyAll` operation no longer makes any sense in this variation, so it is left out.

Languages that implement monitors this way usually allow declaring several wait sets. A wait set is seen by the programmer as an instance of a data abstraction called a condition. The programmer can create new instances of conditions, which are called condition variables. Each condition variable `c` has two operations, `c.wait` and `c.notify`.

We can reimplement the bounded buffer using this variation. The new bounded buffer has two conditions, which we can call nonempty and nonfull. The `put` method waits for a nonfull and then signals a nonempty. The `get` method waits for a nonempty and then signals a nonfull. This is more efficient than the previous implementation because it is more selective. Instead of waking up all the monitor's waiting threads with `notifyAll`, only one thread is woken up, in the right wait set. We leave the actual coding to an exercise.

8.5 Transactions

Transactions were introduced as a basic concept for the management of large shared databases. Ideally, databases must sustain a high rate of concurrent updates while keeping the data coherent and surviving system crashes. This is not an easy problem to solve. To see why, consider a database represented as a large array of cells. Many clients wish to update the database concurrently. A naive implementation is to use a single lock to protect the whole array. This solution is impractical for many reasons. One problem is that a client that takes one minute to perform an operation will prevent any other operation from taking place during that time. This problem can be solved with transactions.

The term "transaction" has acquired a fairly precise meaning: it is any operation that satisfies the four ACID properties [20, 73]. ACID is an acronym:

- A stands for atomic: no intermediate states of a transaction's execution are observable. It is as if the transaction happened instantaneously or did not happen at all. The transaction can complete normally (it commits) or it can be canceled (it aborts).
- C stands for consistent: observable state changes respect the system invariants. Consistency is closely related to atomicity. The difference is that consistency is the responsibility of the programmer, whereas atomicity is the responsibility of the implementation of the transaction system.
- I stands for isolation: several transactions can execute concurrently without interfering with each other. They execute as if they were sequential. This property is also called serializability. It means that the transactions have an interleaving semantics, just like the underlying computation model. We have "lifted" the interleaving semantics up from the model to the level of the transactions.
- D stands for durability: observable state changes survive across system shutdowns. Durability is often called persistence. Implementing durability requires a stable storage (such as a disk) that stores the observable state changes.

This chapter only gives a brief introduction to transaction systems. The classic reference on transactions is Bernstein, Hadzilacos, and Goodman [20]. This book is clear and precise and introduces the theory of transactions with just the right amount of formalism to aid intuition. Unfortunately, the book is out of print. Good libraries will often have a copy. Another good book on transactions is Gray and Reuter [73]. An extensive and mathematically rigorous treatment is given by Weikum and Vossen [225].

Lightweight (ACI) transactions

Outside of database applications, all four ACID properties are not always needed. This section uses the term "transaction" in a narrower sense that is closer to the needs of general-purpose concurrent programming. Whenever there is a risk of confusion, we will call it a lightweight transaction. A lightweight transaction is simply an abortable atomic action. It has all ACID properties except for D (durability). A lightweight transaction can commit or abort. The abort can be due to a cause internal to the program (e.g., because of conflicting access to shared data) or external to the program (e.g., due to failure of part of the system, like a disk or the network).

Motivations

We saw that one motivation for transactions was to increase the throughput of concurrent accesses to a database. Let us look at some other motivations. A second motivation is concurrent programming with exceptions. Most routines have two possible ways to exit: either they exit normally or they raise an exception. Usually the routine behaves atomically when it exits normally, i.e., the caller sees the initial state and the result but nothing in between. When there is an exception this is not the case. The routine might have put part of the system in an inconsistent state. How can we avoid this undesirable situation? There are two solutions:

- The caller can clean up the called routine's mess. This means that the called routine has to be carefully written so that its mess is always limited in extent.
- The routine can be inside a transaction. This solution is harder to implement, but can make the program much simpler. Raising an exception corresponds to aborting the transaction.

A third motivation is fault tolerance. Lightweight transactions are important for writing fault-tolerant applications. With respect to a component, e.g., an application doing a transaction, we define a fault as incorrect behavior in one of its subcomponents. Ideally, the application should continue to behave correctly when there are faults, i.e., it should be fault tolerant. When a fault occurs, a fault-tolerant application has to take three steps: (1) detect the fault, (2) contain the fault in a limited part of the application, and (3) repair any problems caused by the fault. Lightweight transactions are a good mechanism for fault confinement.

A fourth motivation is resource management. Lightweight transactions allow acquisition of multiple resources without causing a concurrent application to stop because of an undesirable situation called deadlock. This situation is explained below.

Kernel language viewpoint Let us make a brief detour and examine transactions from the viewpoint of computation models. The transactional solution satisfies one of our criteria for adding a concept to the computation model, namely that programs in the extended model are simpler. But what exactly is the concept to be added? This is still an open research subject. In our view, it is a very important one. Some day, the solution to this question will be an important part of all general-purpose programming languages. In this section we do not solve this problem. We will implement transactions as an abstraction in the concurrent stateful model without changing the model.

8.5.1 Concurrency control

Consider a large database accessed by many clients at the same time. What does this imply for transactions? It means that they are concurrent yet still satisfy serializability. The implementation should allow concurrent transactions and yet it has to make sure that they are still serializable. There is a strong tension between these two requirements. They are not easy to satisfy simultaneously. The design of transaction systems that satisfy both has led to a rich theory and many clever algorithms [20, 73].

Concurrency control is the set of techniques used to build and program concurrent systems with transactional properties. We introduce these techniques and the concepts they are based on and we show one practical algorithm. Technically speaking, our algorithm does optimistic concurrency control with strict two-phase locking and deadlock avoidance. We explain what all these terms mean and why they are important. Our algorithm is interesting because it is both practical and simple. A complete working implementation takes just two pages of code.

Locks and timestamps

The two most widely used approaches to concurrency control are locks and timestamps:

- Lock-based concurrency control. Each stateful entity has a lock that controls access to the entity. For example, a cell might have a lock that permits only one transaction to use it at a time. In order to use a cell, the transaction must have a lock on it. Locks are important to enforce serializability. This is a safety property, i.e., an assertion that is always true during execution. A safety property is simply a system invariant. In general, locks allow restricting the system's behavior so that it is safe.
- Timestamp-based concurrency control. Each transaction is given a timestamp that gives it a priority. The timestamps are taken from an ordered set, something like the numbered tickets used in shops to ensure that customers are served in order. Timestamps are important to ensure that execution makes progress. For example, that each transaction will eventually commit or abort. This is a liveness property, i.e., an assertion that always eventually becomes true.

Safety and liveness properties describe how a system behaves as a function of time. To reason with these properties, it is important to be careful about the exact meanings of the terms "is always true" and "eventually becomes true." These terms are relative to the current execution step. A property is always true, in the technical sense, if it is true at every execution step starting from the current step. A property eventually becomes true, in the technical sense, if there exists at least one execution step in the future where it is true. We can combine always and eventually to make more complicated properties. For example, a property that always eventually becomes true means that at every step starting from the current step it will eventually become true. The property "an active transaction will eventually abort or commit" is of this type. This style of reasoning can be given a formal syntax and semantics. This gives a variety of logic called temporal logic.

Optimistic and pessimistic scheduling

There are many algorithms for concurrency control, which vary on different axes. One of these axes is the degree of optimism or pessimism of the algorithm. Let us introduce this with two examples taken from real life. Both examples concern traveling, by airplane or by train.

Airlines often overbook flights, i.e., sell more tickets than there is room on the flight. At boarding time, there have usually been enough cancellations that this is not a problem (all passengers have a seat). But occasionally some passengers have no seat, and these have to be accommodated in some way (e.g., by booking them on a later flight and reimbursing them for their discomfort). This is an example of optimistic scheduling: a passenger requesting a ticket is given the ticket right away even if the flight is already completely booked, as long as the overbooking is less than some ratio. Occasional problems are tolerated since overbooking allows increasing the average number of filled seats on a flight and because problems are easily repaired.

Railways are careful to ensure that there are never two trains traveling toward each other on the same track segment. A train is only allowed to enter a track segment if at that moment there is no other train on the same segment. Protocols and signaling mechanisms have been devised to ensure this. This is an example of pessimistic scheduling: a train requesting to enter a segment may have to wait until the segment is known to be clear. Unlike the case of overbookings, accidents are not tolerated because they are extremely costly and usually irreparable in terms of lives lost.

Let us see how these approaches apply to transactions. A transaction requests a lock on a cell. This request is given to a scheduler. The scheduler decides when and if the request should be fulfilled. It has three possible responses: to satisfy the request immediately, to reject the request (causing a transaction abort), or to postpone its decision. An optimistic scheduler tends to give the lock right away, even if this might cause problems later on (deadlocks and livelocks; see below). A pessimistic scheduler tends to delay giving the lock until it is sure that no problems can occur. Depending on how often transactions work on shared data, an optimistic or pessimistic scheduler might be more appropriate. For example, if transactions mostly work on independent data, then an optimistic scheduler may give higher performance. If transactions often work on shared data, then a pessimistic scheduler may give higher performance. The algorithm we give below is an optimistic one; it sometimes has to repair mistakes due to past choices.

Two-phase locking

Two-phase locking is the most popular technique for doing locking. It is used by almost all commercial transaction-processing systems. It can be proved that doing two-phase locking guarantees that transactions are serializable. In two-phase locking a transaction has two phases: a growing phase, in which it acquires locks but does not release them, and a shrinking phase, in which it releases locks but does not acquire them. A transaction is not allowed to release a lock and then acquire another lock afterward. This restriction means that a transaction might hold a lock longer than it needs to. Experience shows that this is not a serious problem.

A popular refinement of two-phase locking used by many systems is called strict two-phase locking. In this refinement, all locks are released simultaneously at the end of the transaction, after it commits or aborts. This avoids a problem called cascading abort. Consider the following scenario. Assume that standard two-phase locking is used with two transactions T1 and T2 that share cell C. First T1 locks C and changes C's content. Then T1 releases the lock in its shrinking phase but continues to be active. Finally T2 locks C, does a calculation with C, and commits. What happens if T1, which is still active, now aborts? If T1 aborts, then T2 has to abort too, since it has read a value of C modified by T1. T2 could be linked in a similar way to another transaction T3, and so forth. If T1 aborts, then all the others have to abort as well, in cascade, even though they already committed. If locks are released only after transactions commit or abort, then this problem does not occur.

8.5.2 A simple transaction manager

Let us design a simple transaction manager. It will do optimistic concurrency control with strict two-phase locking. We first design the algorithm using stepwise refinement. We then show how to implement a transaction manager that is based on this algorithm.

A naive algorithm

We start the design with the following simple idea. Whenever a transaction requests the lock of an unlocked cell, let it acquire the lock immediately without any further conditions. If the cell is already locked, then let the transaction wait until it becomes unlocked. When a transaction commits or aborts, then it releases all its locks. This algorithm is optimistic because it assumes that getting the lock will not give problems later on. If problems arise (see next paragraph!), then the algorithm has to fix them.

Deadlock

Our naive algorithm has a major problem: it suffers from deadlocks. Consider two concurrent transactions T1 and T2 where each one uses cells C1 and C2. Let transaction T1 use C1 and C2, in that order, and transaction T2 use C2 and C1, in the reverse order. Because of concurrency, it can happen that T1 has C1's lock and T2 has C2's lock. When each transaction tries to acquire the other lock it needs, it waits. Both transactions will therefore wait indefinitely. This kind of situation, in which active entities (transactions) wait for resources (cells) in a cycle, such that no entity can continue, is called a deadlock.

How can we ensure that our system never suffers from the consequences of deadlock? As for ailments in general, there are two basic approaches: prevention and cure. The goal of deadlock prevention (also called deadlock avoidance) is to prevent a deadlock from ever happening. A transaction is prevented from locking an object that might lead to a deadlock. The goal of deadlock cure (also called deadlock detection and resolution) is to detect when a deadlock occurs and to take some action to reverse its effects.

Both approaches are based on a concept called the wait-for graph. This is a directed graph that has nodes for active entities (e.g., transactions) and resources (e.g., cells). There is an edge from each active entity to the resource it is waiting for (if any) but does not yet have. There is an edge from each resource to the active entity (if any) that has it. A deadlock corresponds to a cycle in the wait-for graph. Deadlock avoidance forbids adding an edge that would make a cycle. Deadlock detection detects the existence of a cycle and then removes one of its edges. The algorithm we give below does deadlock avoidance. It keeps a transaction from getting a lock that might result in a deadlock.

The correct algorithm

We can avoid deadlocks in the naive algorithm by giving earlier transactions higher priority than later transactions. The basic idea is simple. When a transaction tries to acquire a lock, it compares its priority with the priority of the transaction already holding the lock. If the latter has lower priority, i.e., it is a more recent transaction, then it is restarted and the former gets the lock. Let us define an algorithm based on this idea. We assume that transactions perform operations on cells and that each cell comes with a priority queue of waiting transactions, i.e., the transactions wait in order of their priorities. We use timestamps to implement the priorities. Here is the complete algorithm:

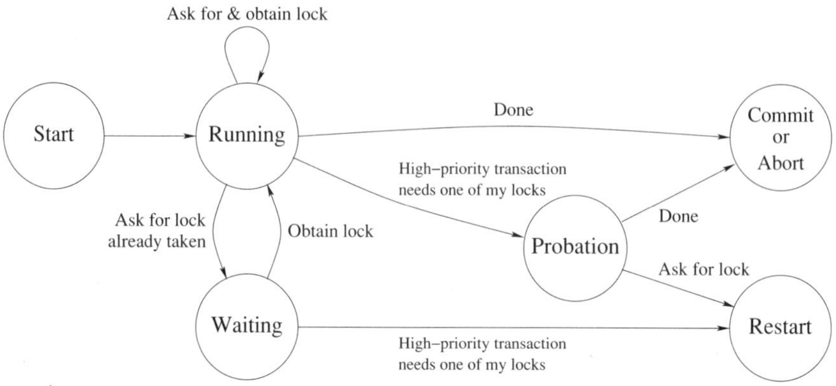

Figure 8.21: State diagram of one incarnation of a transaction.

- A new transaction is given a priority that is lower than all active transactions.
- When a transaction tries to acquire a lock on a cell, then it does one of the following:
    - If the cell is currently unlocked, then the transaction immediately takes the lock and continues.
    - If the cell is already locked by the transaction, then the transaction just continues.
    - If the cell is locked by a transaction with higher priority, then the current transaction waits, i.e., it enqueues itself on the cell's queue.
    - If the cell is locked by a transaction with lower priority, then restart the latter and give the lock to the transaction with higher priority. A restart consists of two actions: first to abort the transaction and second to start it again with the same priority.
- When a transaction commits, then it releases all its locks and dequeues one waiting transaction per released lock (if there is one waiting).
- When a transaction aborts (because it raises an exception or explicitly does an abort operation), then it unlocks all its locked cells, restores their states, and dequeues one waiting transaction per unlocked cell (if there is one waiting).

Restarting at a well-defined point

There is a small problem with the above algorithm. It terminates running transactions at an arbitrary point during their execution. This can give problems. It can lead to inconsistencies in the run-time data structures of the transaction. It can lead to complications in the implementation of the transaction manager itself.

A simple solution to these problems is to terminate the transaction at a well-defined point in its execution. A well-defined point is, e.g., the instant when a transaction asks the transaction manager for a lock. Let us refine the above algorithm to restart only at such points. Again, we start with a simple basic idea: instead of restarting a low-priority transaction, we mark it. Later, when it tries to acquire a lock, the transaction manager notices that it is marked and restarts it. To implement this idea, we extend the algorithm as follows:

- Transactions can be in one of three states (the marks):
  - `running`: this is the unmarked state. The transaction is running freely and is able to acquire locks as before.
  - `probation`: this is the marked state. The transaction still runs freely, but the next time it tries to acquire a lock, it will be restarted. If it asks for no more locks, it will eventually commit.
  - `waiting_on(C)`: this means that the transaction is waiting for the lock on cell `C`. It will obtain the lock when it becomes available. However, if a high-priority transaction wants a lock held by this one while it is waiting, it will be restarted.

Figure 8.21 gives the state diagram of one incarnation of a transaction according to this scheme. By incarnation we mean part of the lifetime of a transaction, from its initial start or a restart until it commits, aborts, or again restarts.

- When a transaction tries to acquire a lock, then it checks its state before attempting to acquire locks. If it is in the state `probation`, then it is restarted immediately. This is fine, since the transaction is at a well-defined point.
- When a transaction tries to acquire a lock and the cell is locked by a transaction with lower priority, then do the following. Enqueue the high-priority transaction and take action depending on the state of the low-priority transaction:
  - `running`: change the state to `probation` and continue.
  - `probation`: do nothing.
  - `waiting_on(C)`: remove the low-priority transaction from the queue it is waiting on and restart it immediately. This is fine, since it is at a well-defined point.
- When a transaction is enqueued on a cell `C`, change its state to `waiting_on(C)`. When a transaction is dequeued, change its state to `running`.

8.5.3 Transactions on cells

Let us define a data abstraction for doing transactions on cells that uses the algorithm of the previous section.[3] We define the abstraction as follows:

---

3. A similar data abstraction can be defined for transactions on objects, but the implementation is a little more complicated since we have to take into account classes and methods. For simplicity we will therefore limit ourselves to cells.

- `{NewTrans ?Trans ?NewCellT}` creates a new transaction context and returns two operations: `Trans` for creating transactions and `NewCellT` for creating new cells.
- A new cell is created by calling `NewCellT` in the same way as with the standard `NewCell`:

```
{NewCellT X C}
```

This creates a new cell in the transaction context and binds it to `C` The cell can only be used inside transactions of this context. The initial value of the cell is `X`.

- A new transaction is created by calling the function `Trans` as follows:

```
{Trans fun {$ T} ⟨expr⟩ end B}
```

The sequential expression ⟨expr⟩ can interact with its environment in only the following ways: it can read values (including procedures and functions) and it can perform operations on cells created with `NewCellT`. The `Trans` call executes ⟨expr⟩ in a transactional manner and completes when ⟨expr⟩ completes. If ⟨expr⟩ raises an exception then the transaction will abort and raise the same exception. If the transaction commits, then it has the same effect as an atomic execution of ⟨expr⟩ and it returns the same result. If the transaction aborts, then it is as if ⟨expr⟩ were not executed at all (all its state changes are undone). `B` is bound to `commit` or `abort`, respectively, depending on whether the transaction commits or aborts.

- There are four operations that can be performed inside ⟨expr⟩:
    - `T.access`, `T.assign`, and `T.exchange` have the same semantics as the standard three cell operations. They must only use cells created by `NewCellT`.
    - `T.abort` is a zero-argument procedure that when called causes the transaction to abort immediately.
- There are only two ways a transaction can abort: either it raises an exception or it calls `T.abort`. In all other cases, the transaction will eventually commit.

An example

Let us first create a new transaction environment:

```
declare Trans NewCellT in
{NewTrans Trans NewCellT}
```

We first define two cells in this environment:

```
C1={NewCellT 0}
C2={NewCellT 0}
```

Now let us increment `C1` and decrement `C2` in the same transaction:

```
{Trans proc {$ T _}
          {T.assign C1 {T.access C1}+1}
          {T.assign C2 {T.access C2}-1}
       end _ _}
```

(We use procedure syntax since we are not interested in the output.) We can repeat this transaction several times in different threads. Because transactions are atomic, we are sure that @C1 + @C2 = 0 will always be true. It is an invariant of our system. This would not be the case if the increment and decrement were executed outside a transaction. To read the contents of C1 and C2, we have to use another transaction:

```
{Browse {Trans fun {$ T} {T.access C1}#{T.access C2} end _}}
```

Another example

The previous example does not show the real advantages of transactions. The same result could have been achieved with locks. Our transaction abstraction has two advantages with respect to locks: aborting causes the original cell states to be restored and the locks can be requested in any order without leading to deadlock. Let us give a more sophisticated example that exploits these two advantages. We create a tuple with 100 cells and do transactional calculations with it. We start by creating and initializing the tuple:

```
D={MakeTuple db 100}
for I in 1..100 do D.I={NewCellT I} end
```

(We use a tuple of cells instead of an array because our transaction abstraction only handles cells.) We now define two transactions, Mix and Sum. Sum calculates the sum of all cell contents. Mix "mixes up" the cell contents in random fashion but keeps the total sum unchanged. Here is the definition of Mix:

```
fun {Rand} {OS.rand} mod 100 + 1 end
proc {Mix} {Trans
   proc {$ T _}
      I={Rand} J={Rand} K={Rand}
      A={T.access D.I} B={T.access D.J} C={T.access D.K}
   in
      {T.assign D.I A+B-C}
      {T.assign D.J A-B+C}
      if I==J orelse I==K orelse J==K then {T.abort} end
      {T.assign D.K ~A+B+C}
   end _ _}
end
```

The random number generator Rand is implemented with the OS module. The mix-up function replaces the contents a, b, c of three randomly picked cells by $a+b-c$, $a-b+c$, and $-a+b+c$. To guarantee that three different cells are picked, Mix aborts if any two are the same. The abort can be done at any point inside the transaction. Here is the definition of Sum:

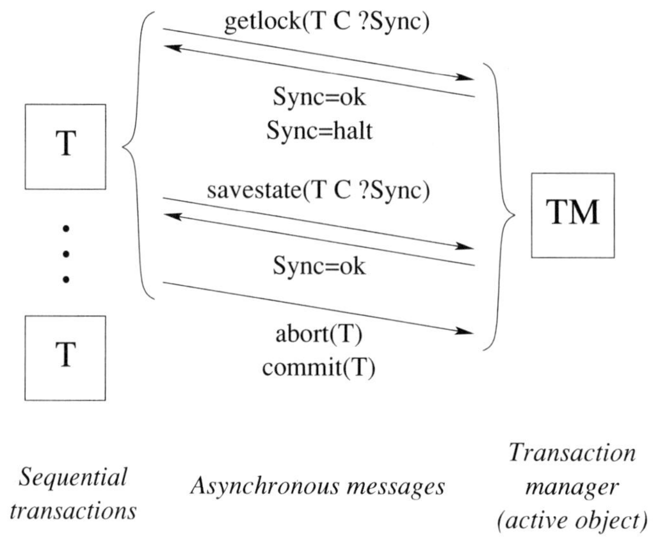

Figure 8.22: Architecture of the transaction system.

```
S={NewCellT 0}
fun {Sum}
   {Trans
    fun {$ T} {T.assign S 0}
       for I in 1..100 do
          {T.assign S {T.access S}+{T.access D.I}} end
       {T.access S}
    end _}
end
```

Sum uses the cell S to hold the sum. Note that Sum is a big transaction since it simultaneously locks all cells in the tuple. Now we can do some calculations:

```
{Browse {Sum}}  % Displays 5050
for I in 1..1000 do thread {Mix} end end
{Browse {Sum}}  % Still displays 5050
```

5050 is the sum of the integers from 1 to 100. You can check that the values of individual cells are well and truly mixed:

```
{Browse {Trans fun {$ T} {T.access D.1}#{T.access D.2} end _}}
```

This initially displays 1#2, but will subsequently display very different values.

8.5.4 Implementing transactions on cells

Let us show how to build a transaction system that implements our optimistic two-phase locking algorithm. The implementation consists of a transaction manager and a set of running transactions. (Transaction managers come in many varieties and are sometimes called transaction processing monitors [73].) The transaction manager and the running transactions each execute in its own thread. This allows terminating a running transaction without affecting the transaction manager. A running thread sends four kinds of messages to the transaction manager: to get a lock (`getlock`), to save a cell's state (`savestate`), to commit (`commit`), and to abort (`abort`). Figure 8.22 shows the architecture.

The transaction manager is always active and accepts commands from the running transactions' threads. When a transaction is restarted, it restarts in a new thread. It keeps the same timestamp, though. We implement the transaction manager as an active object using the `NewActive` function of section 7.8. The active object has two internal methods, `Unlockall` and `Trans`, and five external methods, `newtrans`, `getlock`, `savestate`, `commit`, and `abort`. Figures 8.23 and 8.24 show the implementation of the transaction system. Together with `NewActive` and the priority queue, this is a complete working implementation. Each active transaction is represented by a record with five fields:

- `stamp`: This is the transaction's timestamp, a unique integer that identifies the transaction and its priority. This number is incremented for successive transactions. High priority therefore means a small timestamp.
- `save`: This is a dictionary indexed by cell name (see below) that contains entries of the form `save(cell:C state:S)`, where `C` is a cell record (as represented below) and `S` is the cell's original state.
- `body`: This is the function **`fun`** `{$ T}` ⟨expr⟩ **`end`** that represents the transaction body.
- `state`: This is a cell containing `running`, `probation`, or `waiting_on(C)`. If `probation`, it means that the transaction will be restarted the next time it tries to obtain a lock. If `waiting_on(C)`, it means that the transaction will be restarted immediately if a higher-priority transaction needs `C`.
- `result`: This is a dataflow variable that will be bound to `commit(Res)`, `abort(Exc)`, or `abort` when the transaction completes.

Each cell is represented by a record with four fields:

- `name`: This is a name value that is the cell's unique identifier.
- `owner`: This is either **`unit`**, if no transaction is currently locking the cell, or the transaction record if a transaction is locking the cell.
- `queue`: This is a priority queue containing pairs of the form `Sync#T`, where `T` is a transaction record and `Sync` is the synchronization variable on which the transaction is currently blocked. The priority is the transaction's timestamp. `Sync` will always eventually be bound by the transaction manager to `ok` or `halt`.
- `state`: This is a cell that contains the transactional cell's content.

When a transaction `T` does an exchange operation on cell `C`, it executes the `ExcT` procedure defined in `Trans`. This first sends `getlock(T C Sync1)` to the

```
class TMClass
   attr timestamp tm
   meth init(TM) timestamp:=0 tm:=TM end

   meth Unlockall(T RestoreFlag)
      for save(cell:C state:S) in {Dictionary.items T.save} do
         (C.owner):=unit
         if RestoreFlag then (C.state):=S end
         if {Not {C.queue.isEmpty}} then
         Sync2#T2={C.queue.dequeue} in
            (T2.state):=running
            (C.owner):=T2 Sync2=ok
         end
      end
   end

   meth Trans(P ?R TS) /* See next figure */ end
   meth getlock(T C ?Sync) /* See next figure */ end

   meth newtrans(P ?R)
      timestamp:=@timestamp+1 {self Trans(P R @timestamp)}
   end
   meth savestate(T C ?Sync)
      if {Not {Dictionary.member T.save C.name}} then
         (T.save).(C.name):=save(cell:C state:@(C.state))
      end Sync=ok
   end
   meth commit(T) {self Unlockall(T false)} end
   meth abort(T) {self Unlockall(T true)} end
end

proc {NewTrans ?Trans ?NewCellT}
TM={NewActive TMClass init(TM)} in
   fun {Trans P ?B} R in
      {TM newtrans(P R)}
      case R of abort then B=abort unit
      [] abort(Exc) then B=abort raise Exc end
      [] commit(Res) then B=commit Res end
   end
   fun {NewCellT X}
      cell(name:{NewName} owner:{NewCell unit}
           queue:{NewPrioQueue} state:{NewCell X})
   end
end
```

Figure 8.23: Implementation of the transaction system (part 1).

```
meth Trans(P ?R TS)
   Halt={NewName}
   T=trans(stamp:TS save:{NewDictionary} body:P
           state:{NewCell running} result:R)
   proc {ExcT C X Y} S1 S2 in
      {@tm getlock(T C S1)}
      if S1==halt then raise Halt end end
      {@tm savestate(T C S2)} {Wait S2}
      {Exchange C.state X Y}
   end
   proc {AccT C ?X} {ExcT C X X} end
   proc {AssT C X} {ExcT C _ X} end
   proc {AboT} {@tm abort(T)} R=abort raise Halt end end
in
   thread try Res={T.body t(access:AccT assign:AssT
                            exchange:ExcT abort:AboT)}
          in {@tm commit(T)} R=commit(Res)
          catch E then
             if E\=Halt then {@tm abort(T)} R=abort(E) end
   end end
end

meth getlock(T C ?Sync)
   if @(T.state)==probation then
      {self Unlockall(T true)}
      {self Trans(T.body T.result T.stamp)} Sync=halt
   elseif @(C.owner)==unit then
      (C.owner):=T Sync=ok
   elseif T.stamp==@(C.owner).stamp then
      Sync=ok
   else /* T.stamp\=@(C.owner).stamp */ T2=@(C.owner) in
      {C.queue.enqueue Sync#T T.stamp}
      (T.state):=waiting_on(C)
      if T.stamp<T2.stamp then
         case @(T2.state) of waiting_on(C2) then
         Sync2#_={C2.queue.delete T2.stamp} in
            {self Unlockall(T2 true)}
            {self Trans(T2.body T2.result T2.stamp)}
            Sync2=halt
         [] running then
            (T2.state):=probation
         [] probation then skip end
      end
   end
end
```

Figure 8.24: Implementation of the transaction system (part 2).

```
fun {NewPrioQueue}
   Q={NewCell nil}
   proc {Enqueue X Prio}
      fun {InsertLoop L}
         case L of pair(Y P)|L2 then
            if Prio<P then pair(X Prio)|L
            else pair(Y P)|{InsertLoop L2} end
         [] nil then [pair(X Prio)] end
      end
   in Q:={InsertLoop @Q} end

   fun {Dequeue}
      pair(Y _)|L2=@Q
   in
      Q:=L2 Y
   end

   fun {Delete Prio}
      fun {DeleteLoop L}
         case L of pair(Y P)|L2 then
            if P==Prio then X=Y L2
            else pair(Y P)|{DeleteLoop L2} end
         [] nil then nil end
      end X
   in Q:={DeleteLoop @Q} X end

   fun {IsEmpty} @Q==nil end
in
   queue(enqueue:Enqueue dequeue:Dequeue
         delete:Delete isEmpty:IsEmpty)
end
```

Figure 8.25: Priority queue.

transaction manager to request a lock on the cell. The transaction manager replies with `Sync1=ok` if the transaction successfully gets the lock and `Sync1=halt` if the current thread should be terminated. In the latter case, `getlock` ensures that the transaction is restarted. If the transaction gets the lock, then it calls `savestate(T C Sync2)` to save the original cell state.

Priority queue

The transaction manager uses priority queues to make sure that high-priority transactions get the first chance to lock cells. A priority queue is a queue whose entries are always ordered according to some priority. In our queue, the priorities are integers and the lowest value has the highest priority. We define the priority queue data abstraction as follows:

- `Q={NewPrioQueue}` creates an empty priority queue.
- `{Q.enqueue X P}` inserts `X` with priority `P`, where `P` is an integer.
- `X={Q.dequeue}` returns the entry with the smallest integer value and removes it from the queue.
- `X={Q.delete P}` returns an entry with priority `P` and removes it from the queue.
- `B={Q.isEmpty}` returns true or false depending on whether `Q` is empty or not.

Figure 8.25 shows a simple implementation of the priority queue. The priority queue is represented internally as a cell containing a list of pairs `pair(X P)`, which are ordered according to increasing `P`. The `dequeue` operation executes in $O(1)$ time. The `enqueue` and `delete` operations execute in $O(s)$ time where s is the size of the queue. More sophisticated implementations are possible with better time complexities.

8.5.5 More on transactions

We have just scratched the surface of transaction processing. Let us finish by mentioning some of the most useful extensions [73]:

- Durability. We have not shown how to make a state change persistent. This is done by putting state changes on stable storage, such as a disk. Techniques for doing this are carefully designed to maintain atomicity, no matter at what instant in time a system crash happens.
- Nested transactions. It often happens that we have a long-lived transaction that contains a series of smaller transactions. For example, a complex bank transaction might consist of a large series of updates to many accounts. Each of these updates is a transaction. The series itself should also be a transaction: if something goes wrong in the middle, it is canceled. There is a strong relationship between nested transactions, encapsulation, and modularity.
- Distributed transactions. It often happens that a database is spread over several physical sites, either for performance or organizational reasons. We would still like to perform transactions on the database.

8.6 The Java language (concurrent part)

The introduction in section 7.7 only talked about the sequential part of Java. We now extend this to the concurrent part. Concurrent programming in Java is supported by two concepts: threads and monitors. Java is designed for shared-state concurrency. Threads are too heavyweight to support an active object approach efficiently. Monitors have the semantics of section 8.4. Monitors are lightweight constructs that are associated to individual objects.

Each program starts with one thread, the one that executes `main`. New threads can be created in two ways, by instantiating a subclass of the Thread class or by implementing the Runnable interface. By default, the program terminates when all its threads terminate. Since threads tend to be heavyweight in current Java implementations, the programmer is encouraged not to create many of them. Using the Thread class gives more control, but might be overkill for some applications. Using the Runnable interface is lighter. Both techniques assume that there is a method run

```
public void run();
```

that defines the thread's body. The Runnable interface consists of just this single method.

Threads interact by means of shared objects. To control the interaction, any Java object can be a monitor, as defined in section 8.4. Methods can execute inside the monitor lock with the keyword synchronized. Methods without this keyword are called nonsynchronized. They execute outside the monitor lock but can still see the object attributes. This ability has been strongly criticized because the compiler can no longer guarantee that the object attributes are accessed sequentially [28]. Nonsynchronized methods can be more efficient, but they should be used extremely rarely.

We give two examples. The first example uses synchronized methods just for locking. The second example uses the full monitor operations. For further reading, we recommend [127].

8.6.1 Locks

The simplest way to do concurrent programming in Java is with multiple threads that access shared objects. Let us extend the class Point as an example:

```
class Point {
   double x, y;
   Point(double x1, y1) { x=x1; y=y1; }
   public double getX() { return x; }
   public double getY() { return y; }
   public synchronized void origin() { x=0.0; y=0.0; }
   public synchronized void add(Point p)
      { x+=p.getX(); y+=p.getY(); }
   public synchronized void scale(double s) { x*=s; y*=s; }
   public void draw(Graphics g) {
      double lx, ly;
      synchronized (this) { lx=x; ly=y; }
      g.drawPoint(lx, ly);
   }
}
```

```
class Buffer
   int[] buf;
   int first, last, n, i;

   public void init(int size) {
       buf=new int[size];
       n=size; i=0; first=0; last=0;
   }

   public synchronized void put(int x) {
      while (i<n) wait();
      buf[last]=x;
      last=(last+1)%n;
      i=i+1;
      notifyAll();
   }

   public synchronized int get() {
      int x;
      while (i==0) wait();
      x=buf[first];
      first=(first+1)%n;
      i=i-1;
      notifyAll();
      return x;
   }
}
```

Figure 8.26: Bounded buffer (Java version).

Each instance of `Point` has its own lock. Because of the keyword `synchronized`, the methods `origin`, `add`, and `scale` all execute within the lock. The method `draw` is only partly synchronized. This is because it calls an external method, `g.drawPoint` (not defined in the example). Putting the external method inside the object lock would increase the likelihood of deadlocking the program. Instead, `g` should have its own lock.

8.6.2 Monitors

Monitors are an extension of locks that give more control over how threads enter and exit. Monitors can be used to do more sophisticated kinds of cooperation between threads accessing a shared object. Section 8.4.2 shows how to write a bounded buffer using monitors. The solution given there can easily be translated to Java, giving figure 8.26. This defines a bounded buffer of integers. It uses an array of integers, `buf`, which is allocated when the buffer is initialized. The percent sign `%` denotes the modulo operation, i.e., the remainder after integer division.

8.7 Exercises

1. *Number of interleavings.* Generalize the argument used in the chapter introduction to calculate the number of possible interleavings of n threads, each doing k operations. Using Stirling's formula for the factorial function, $n! \approx \sqrt{2\pi}n^{n+1/2}e^{-n}$, calculate a closed form approximation to this function.

2. *Concurrent counter.* Let us implement a concurrent counter in the simplest possible way. The counter has an increment operation. We would like this operation to be callable from any number of threads. Consider the following possible implementation that uses one cell and an `Exchange`:

```
local X in {Exchange C X X+1} end
```

This attempted solution does not work.

- Explain why the above program does not work and propose a simple fix.
- Would your fix still be possible in a language that did not have dataflow variables? Explain why or why not.
- Give a solution (perhaps the same one as in the previous point) that works in a language without dataflow variables.

3. *Maximal concurrency and efficiency.* In between the shared-state concurrent model and the maximally concurrent model, there is an interesting model called the job-based concurrent model. The job-based model is identical to the shared-state concurrent model, except that whenever an operation would block, a new thread is created with only that operation (this is called a job) and the original thread continues execution.[4] Practically speaking, the job-based model has all the concurrency of the maximally concurrent model, and in addition it can easily be implemented efficiently. For this exercise, investigate the job-based model. Is it a good choice for a concurrent programming language? Why or why not?

4. *Simulating slow networks.* Section 8.2.2 defines a function `SlowNet2` that creates a "slow" version of an object. But this definition imposes a strong order constraint. Each slow object defines a global order of its calls and guarantees that the original objects are called in this order. This constraint is often too strong. A more refined version would only impose order among object calls within the same thread. Between different threads, there is no reason to impose an order. Define a function `SlowNet3` that creates slow objects with this property.

5. *The `MVar` abstraction.* An `MVar` is a box that can be full or empty. It comes with two procedures, `Put` and `Get`. Doing `{Put X}` puts `X` in the box if it is empty, thus making it full. If the box is full, `Put` waits until it is empty. Doing `{Get X}` binds `X` to the box's content and empties the box. If the box is empty, `Get` waits until it is full. For this exercise, implement the `MVar` abstraction. Use whatever concurrency

4. An earlier version of the Oz language used the job-based model [199].

approach is most natural.

6. *Communicating Sequential Processes (CSP).* The CSP language consists of independent threads (called "processes" in CSP terminology) communicating through synchronous channels [94, 184]. The channels have two operations, send and receive, with rendezvous semantics. That is, a send blocks until a receive is present and vice versa. When send and receive are simultaneously present, then they both complete atomically, transferring information from send to receive. The Ada language also uses rendezvous semantics. In addition, there is a nondeterministic receive operation which can listen to several channels simultaneously. As soon as a message is received on one of the channels, then the nondeterministic receive completes. For this exercise, implement these CSP operations as the following control abstraction:

- `C={Channel.new}` creates a new channel `C`.
- `{Channel.send C M}` sends message `M` on channel `C`.
- `{Channel.mreceive [C1#S1 C2#S2 ... Cn#Sn]}` listens nondeterministically on channels `C1`, `C2`, ..., and `Cn`. `Si` is a one-argument procedure **`proc`** `{$ M}` ⟨stmt⟩ **`end`** that is executed when message `M` is received on channel `Ci`.

Now extend the `Channel.mreceive` operation with guards:

- `{Channel.mreceive [C1#B1#S1 C2#B2#S2 ... Cn#Bn#Sn]}`, where `Bi` is a one-argument boolean function **`fun`** `{$ M}` ⟨expr⟩ **`end`** that must return true for a message to be received on channel `Ci`.

7. *Comparing Linda with Erlang.* Linda has a read operation that can selectively retrieve tuples according to a pattern (see section 8.3.2). Erlang has a **`receive`** operation that can selectively receive messages according to a pattern (see section 5.7.3). For this exercise, compare and contrast these two operations and the abstractions that they are part of. What do they have in common and how do they differ? For what kinds of application is each best suited?

8. *Termination detection with monitors.* This exercise is about detecting when a group of threads are all terminated. Section 4.4.3 gives an algorithm that works for a flat thread space, where threads are not allowed to create new threads. Section 5.6.3 gives an algorithm that works for a hierarchical thread space, where threads can create new threads to any nesting level. The second algorithm uses a port to collect the termination information. For this exercise, write an algorithm that works for a hierarchical thread space, like the second algorithm, but that uses a monitor instead of a port.

9. *Monitors and conditions.* Section 8.4.5 gives an alternative semantics for monitors in which there can be several wait sets, which are called conditions. The purpose of this exercise is to study this alternative and compare it with main approach given in the text.

- Reimplement the bounded buffer example of figure 8.17 using monitors with conditions.
- Modify the monitor implementation of figure 8.20 to implement monitors

with conditions. Allow the possibility of creating more than one condition for a monitor.

10. *Breaking up big transactions.* The second example in section 8.5.3 defines the transaction `Sum` that locks all the cells in the tuple while it is calculating their sum. While `Sum` is active, no other transaction can continue. For this exercise, rewrite `Sum` as a series of small transactions. Each small transaction should only lock a few cells. Define a representation for a partial sum, so that a small transaction can see what has already been done and determine how to continue. Verify your work by showing that you can perform transactions while a sum calculation is in progress.

11. *Lock caching.* In the interest of simplicity, the transaction manager of section 8.5.4 has some minor inefficiencies. For example, `getlock` and `savestate` messages are sent on each use of a cell by a transaction. It is clear that they are only really needed the first time. For this exercise, optimize the `getlock` and `savestate` protocols so they use the least possible number of messages.

12. *Read and write locks.* The transaction manager of section 8.5 locks a cell upon its first use. If transactions T1 and T2 both want to read the same cell's content, then they cannot both lock the cell simultaneously. We can relax this behavior by introducing two kinds of locks, read locks and write locks. A transaction that holds a read lock is only allowed to read the cell's content, not change it. A transaction that holds a write lock can do all cell operations. A cell can either be locked with exactly one write lock or with any number of read locks. For this exercise, extend the transaction manager to use read and write locks.

13. *Concurrent transactions.* The transaction manager of section 8.5 correctly handles any number of transactions that execute concurrently, but each individual transaction must be sequential. For this exercise, extend the transaction manager so that the individual transactions can themselves be concurrent. *Hint*: add the termination detection algorithm of section 5.6.3.

14. *Combining monitors and transactions.* Design and implement a concurrency abstraction that combines the abilities of monitors and transactions. That is, it has the ability to wait and notify, and also the ability to abort without changing any state. Is this a useful abstraction?

15. (research project) *Transactional computation model.* Extend the shared-state concurrent model of this chapter to allow transactions, as suggested in section 8.5. Your extension should satisfy the following properties:

- It should have a simple formal semantics.
- It should be efficient, i.e., only cause overhead when transactions are actually used.
- It should preserve good properties of the model, e.g., compositionality.

This will allow programs to use transactions without needing costly and cumbersome encodings. Implement a programming language that uses your extension and evaluate it for realistic concurrent programs.

9 Relational Programming

Toward the end of the thirteenth century, Ramón Llull (Raimundo Lulio or Raymond Lully) invented the thinking machine. ... The circumstances and objectives of this machine no longer interest us, but its guiding principle—the methodical application of chance to the resolution of a problem—still does.
– Ramón Llull's Thinking Machine, Jorge Luis Borges (1899–1986)

In retrospect it can now be said that the *ars magna Lulli* was the first seed of what is now called "symbolic logic," but it took a long time until the seed brought fruit, this particular fruit.
– Postscript to "The Universal Library," Willy Ley (1906–1969)

A procedure in the declarative model uses its input arguments to calculate the values of its output arguments. This is a functional calculation, in the mathematical sense: the outputs are functions of the inputs. For a given set of input argument values, there is only one set of output argument values. We can generalize this to become relational. A relational procedure is more flexible than a functional procedure in two ways. First, there can be any number of results to a call, either zero (no results), one, or more. Second, which arguments are inputs and which are outputs can be different for each call.

This flexibility makes relational programming well-suited for databases and parsers, in particular for difficult cases such as deductive databases and parsing ambiguous grammars. It can also be used to enumerate solutions to complex combinatoric problems. We have used it to automatically generate diagnostics for a RISC microprocessor, the VLSI-BAM [95, 214]. The diagnostics enumerate all possible instruction sequences that use register forwarding. Relational programming has also been used in artificial intelligence applications, such as David Warren's venerable WARPLAN planner [44].

From the programmer's point of view, relational programming extends declarative programming with a new kind of statement called a "choice." Conceptually, the choice statement nondeterministically picks one among a set of alternatives. During execution, the choice is implemented with search, which enumerates the possible answers. We call this "don't know nondeterminism," although the search algorithm is almost always deterministic.

Introducing a choice statement is an old idea. E. W. Elcock [60] used it in 1967 in the Absys language and Floyd [61] used it in the same year. The Prolog language uses a choice operation as the heart of its execution model, which was defined in

1972 [45]. Floyd gives a lucid account of the choice operation. He first extends a simple Algol-like language with a function called *choice(n)*, which returns an integer from 1 to n. He then shows how to implement a depth-first search strategy using flow charts to give the operational semantics of the extended language.

Watch out for efficiency

The flexibility of relational programming has a reverse side. It can easily lead to highly inefficient programs, if not used properly. This cannot be avoided in general since each new choice operation multiplies the size of the search space by the number of alternatives. The search space is the set of candidate solutions to a problem. This means the size is exponential in the number of choice operations. However, relational programming is sometimes practical:

- *When the search space is small.* This is typically the case for database applications. Another example is the above-mentioned VLSI-BAM diagnostics generator, which generated all combinations of instructions for register forwarding, condition bit forwarding, and branches in branch delay slots. This gave a total of about 70,000 lines of VLSI-BAM assembly language code. This was small enough to be used as input to the gate-level simulator.
- *As an exploratory tool.* If used on small examples, relational programming can give results even if it is impractical for bigger examples. The advantage is that the programs can be much shorter and easier to write: no algorithm has to be devised since search is a brute force technique that avoids the need for algorithms. Because of Moore's law this is often practical. It is an example of nonalgorithmic programming. It gives insight into the problem structure that is often sufficient to design an efficient algorithm.

To use search in other cases, more sophisticated techniques are needed, e.g., powerful constraint-solving algorithms, optimizations based on the problem structure, and search heuristics. We leave these until chapter 12. The present chapter studies the use of nondeterministic programming as a tool for the two classes of problems for which it works well. For more information and techniques, we recommend any good book on Prolog, which has good support for nondeterministic programming [44, 201].

Structure of the chapter

The chapter consists of four parts:

- Section 9.1 explains the two basic concepts of the relational computation model, namely choice and encapsulated search. Section 9.2 continues with some more examples to introduce programming in the model.
- Section 9.3 introduces logic and logic programming. It introduces a new kind of semantics for programs, the logical semantics. It then explains how both the

$\langle s \rangle$ ::=	
skip	Empty statement
$\mid \langle s \rangle_1 \ \langle s \rangle_2$	Statement sequence
$\mid$ **local** $\langle x \rangle$ **in** $\langle s \rangle$ **end**	Variable creation
$\mid \langle x \rangle_1 = \langle x \rangle_2$	Variable-variable binding
$\mid \langle x \rangle = \langle v \rangle$	Value creation
$\mid$ **if** $\langle x \rangle$ **then** $\langle s \rangle_1$ **else** $\langle s \rangle_2$ **end**	Conditional
$\mid$ **case** $\langle x \rangle$ **of** $\langle \text{pattern} \rangle$ **then** $\langle s \rangle_1$ **else** $\langle s \rangle_2$ **end**	Pattern matching
$\mid \{ \langle x \rangle \ \langle y \rangle_1 \cdots \langle y \rangle_n \}$	Procedure application
$\mid$ **choice** $\langle s \rangle_1$ [] $\cdots$ [] $\langle s \rangle_n$ **end**	**Choice**
$\mid$ **fail**	**Failure**

Table 9.1: The relational kernel language.

declarative and relational computation models do logic programming.

- Sections 9.4 through 9.6 give large examples in three areas that are particularly well-suited to relational programming, namely natural language parsing, interpreters, and deductive databases.
- Section 9.7 gives an introduction to Prolog, a programming language based on relational programming. Prolog was originally designed for natural language processing, but has become one of the main programming languages in all areas that require symbolic programming.

9.1 The relational computation model

9.1.1 The `choice` and `fail` statements

The relational computation model extends the declarative model with two new statements, **`choice`** and **`fail`**:

- The **`choice`** statement groups together a set of alternative statements. Executing a **`choice`** statement provisionally picks one of these alternatives. If the alternative is found to be wrong later on, then another one is picked. We often say that the **`choice`** statement creates a *choice point*, where a choice point is a part of the abstract machine that encapsulates the information necessary to roll back execution and pick another alternative. This follows the usual implementation strategy in Prolog, a popular language that implements search in this way. However, this is not the only way to implement the **`choice`** statement, as we shall see in chapter 12.
- The **`fail`** statement indicates that the current alternative is wrong. A **`fail`** is executed implicitly when trying to bind two incompatible values, e.g., `3=4`. This

is a modification of the declarative model, which raises an exception in that case. Section 2.8.2 explains the binding algorithm in detail for all partial values.

Table 9.1 shows the relational kernel language.

An example for clothing design

Here is a simple example of a relational program that might interest a clothing designer:

```
fun {Soft} choice beige [] coral end end
fun {Hard} choice mauve [] ochre end end

proc {Contrast C1 C2}
   choice C1={Soft} C2={Hard} [] C1={Hard} C2={Soft} end
end

fun {Suit}
   Shirt Pants Socks
in
   {Contrast Shirt Pants}
   {Contrast Pants Socks}
   if Shirt==Socks then fail end
   suit(Shirt Pants Socks)
end
```

This program is intended to help a clothing designer pick colors for a man's casual suit. `Soft` picks a soft color and `Hard` picks a hard color. `Contrast` picks a pair of contrasting colors (one soft and one hard). `Suit` returns a complete set, including shirt, pants, and socks, such that adjacent garments are in contrasting colors and shirt and socks are of different colors.

9.1.2 Search tree

A relational program is executed sequentially. The **choice** statements are executed in the order that they are encountered during execution. When a **choice** is first executed, its first alternative is picked. When a **fail** is executed, execution "backs up" to the most recent **choice** statement, which picks its next alternative. If there are none, then the next most recent **choice** picks another alternative, and so forth. Each **choice** statement picks alternatives in order from left to right.

This execution strategy can be illustrated with a tree called the search tree. Each node in the search tree corresponds to a **choice** statement and each subtree corresponds to one of the alternatives. Figure 9.1 shows part of the search tree for the clothing design example. Each path in the tree corresponds to one possible execution of the program. The path can lead either to no solution (marked "fail") or to a solution (marked "succeed"). The search tree shows all paths at a glance, including both the failed and successful ones.

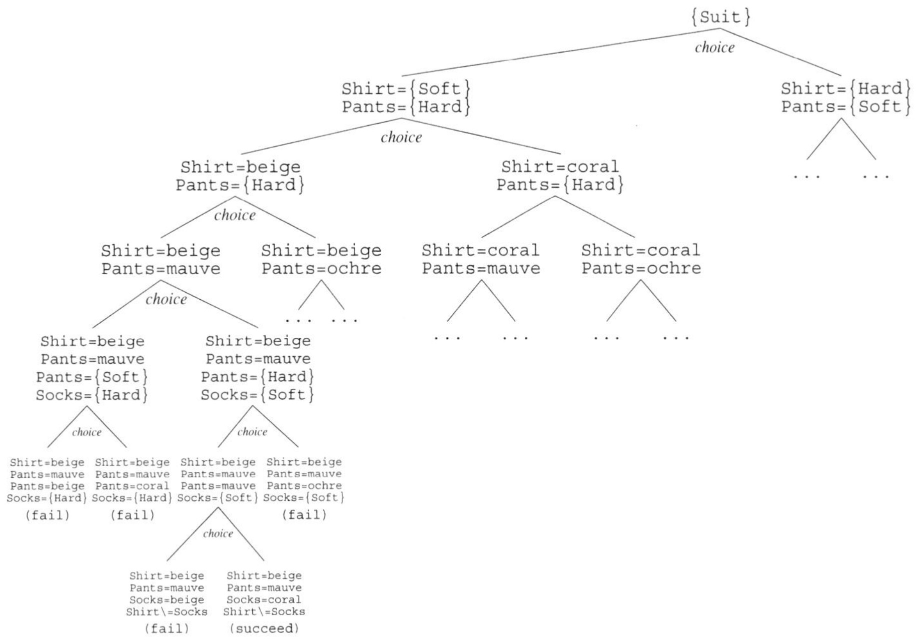

Figure 9.1: Search tree for the clothing design example.

9.1.3 Encapsulated search

A relational program is interesting because it can potentially execute in many different ways, depending on the choices it makes. We would like to control which choices are made and when they are made. For example, we would like to specify the search strategy: depth-first search, breadth-first search, or some other strategy. We would like to specify how many solutions are calculated: just one solution, all solutions right away, or new solutions on demand. Briefly, we would like the same relational program to be executed in many different ways.

One way to exercise this control is to execute the relational program with encapsulated search. Encapsulation means that the relational program runs inside a kind of "environment." The environment controls which choices are made by the relational program and when they are made. The environment also protects the rest of the application from the effects of the choices. This is important because the relational program can do multiple bindings of the same variable when different choices are made. These multiple bindings should not be visible to the rest of the application. Encapsulated search is important also for modularity and compositionality:

- For modularity: with encapsulated search there can be more than one relational program running concurrently. Since each is encapsulated, they do not interfere with each other (except that they can influence each other's performance because they share the same computational resources). They can be used in a program that communicates with the external world, without interfering with that communication.

- For compositionality: an encapsulated search can run inside another encapsulated search. Because of encapsulation, this is perfectly well-defined.

Early logic languages with search such as Prolog have global backtracking, in which multiple bindings are visible everywhere. This is bad for program modularity and compositionality. To be fair to Prolog, it has a limited form of encapsulated search, namely the `bagof/3` and `setof/3` operations. This is explained in section 9.7.

9.1.4 The `Solve` function

We provide encapsulated search by adding one function, `Solve`, to the computation model. The call `{Solve F}` is given a zero-argument function `F` (or equivalently, a one-argument procedure) that returns a solution to a relational program. The call returns a lazy list of all solutions, ordered according to a depth-first search strategy. For example, the call

```
L={Solve fun {$} choice 1 [] 2 [] 3 end end}
```

returns the lazy list `[1 2 3]`. Because `Solve` is lazy, it only calculates the solutions that are needed. `Solve` is compositional, i.e., it can be nested: the function `F` can contain calls to `Solve`. Using `Solve` as a basic operation, we can define both one-solution and all-solutions search. To get one-solution search, we look at just the first element of the list and never look at the rest:

```
fun {SolveOne F}
   L={Solve F}
in
   if L==nil then nil else [L.1] end
end
```

This returns either a list `[X]` containing the first solution `X` or `nil` if there are no solutions. To get all-solutions search, we look at the whole list:

```
fun {SolveAll F}
   L={Solve F}
   proc {TouchAll L}
      if L==nil then skip else {TouchAll L.2} end
   end
in
   {TouchAll L}
   L
end
```

This returns a list of all solutions.

Computation spaces

We have introduced **choice** and **fail** statements and the `Solve` function. These new operations can be programmed by extending the declarative model with just one new concept, the computation space. Computation spaces are part of the constraint-based computation model, which is explained in chapter 12. They were originally designed for constraint programming, a powerful generalization of relational programming. Chapter 12 explains how to implement **choice**, **fail**, and `Solve` in terms of computation spaces. The definition of `Solve` is also given in the supplements file on the book's Web site.

Solving the clothing design example

Let us use `Solve` to find answers to the clothing design example. To find all solutions, we do the following query:

```
{Browse {SolveAll Suit}}
```

This displays a list of the eight solutions:

```
[suit(beige mauve coral) suit(beige ochre coral)
 suit(coral mauve beige) suit(coral ochre beige)
 suit(mauve beige ochre) suit(mauve coral ochre)
 suit(ochre beige mauve) suit(ochre coral mauve)]
```

Figure 9.1 gives enough of the search tree to show how the first solution `suit(beige mauve coral)` is obtained.

9.2 Further examples

We give some simple examples to show how to program in the relational computation model.

9.2.1 Numeric examples

Let us show some simple examples using numbers, to show how to program with the relational computation model. Here is a program that uses **choice** to count from 0 to 9:

```
fun {Digit}
   choice 0 [] 1 [] 2 [] 3 [] 4 [] 5 [] 6 [] 7 [] 8 [] 9 end
end
{Browse {SolveAll Digit}}
```

This displays

```
[0 1 2 3 4 5 6 7 8 9]
```

We can combine calls to `Digit` to count with more than one digit:

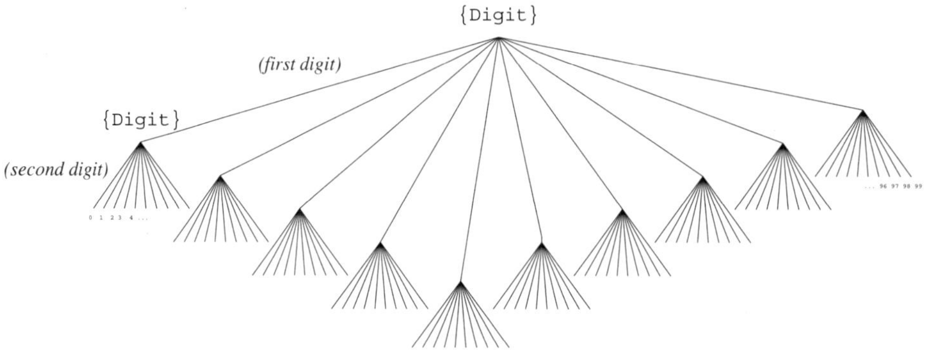

Figure 9.2: Two-digit counting with depth-first search.

```
fun {TwoDigit}
   10*{Digit}+{Digit}
end
{Browse {SolveAll TwoDigit}}
```

This displays

```
[0 1 2 3 4 5 6 7 8 9 10 11 12 13 14 ... 98 99]
```

This shows what it means to do a depth-first search: when two choices are done, the program first makes the first choice and then makes the second. Here the function chooses first the tens digit and then the ones digit. Changing the definition of `TwoDigit` to choose digits in the opposite order will give unusual results:

```
fun {StrangeTwoDigit}
   {Digit}+10*{Digit}
end
{Browse {SolveAll StrangeTwoDigit}}
```

This displays

```
[0 10 20 30 40 50 60 70 80 90 1 11 21 31 41 ... 89 99]
```

In this case, the tens digit is chosen second and therefore changes quicker than the ones digit.

Palindrome product problem

Using `Digit`, we can already solve some interesting puzzles, like the "palindrome product" problem. We would like to find all four-digit palindromes that are products of two-digit numbers. A palindrome is a number that reads the same forward and backward, when written in decimal notation. The following program solves the puzzle:

```
proc {Palindrome ?X}
   X=(10*{Digit}+{Digit})*(10*{Digit}+{Digit})  % Generate
   (X>0)=true                                   % Test 1
   (X>=1000)=true                               % Test 2
   (X div 1000) mod 10 = (X div 1) mod 10       % Test 3
   (X div 100) mod 10 = (X div 10) mod 10       % Test 4
end

{Browse {SolveAll Palindrome}}
```

This displays all 118 palindrome products. Why do we have to write the condition `X>0` as `(X>0)=true`? If the condition returns **`false`**, then the attempted binding **`false`**`=`**`true`** will fail. This ensures the relational program will fail when the condition is false.

Palindrome product is an example of a generate-and-test program: it generates a set of possibilities and then it uses tests to filter out the bad ones. The tests use unification failure to reject bad alternatives. Generate-and-test is a very naive way to explore a search space. It generates all the possibilities first and only filters out the bad ones afterward. In palindrome product, 10000 possibilities are generated.

Chapter 12 introduces a much better way to explore a search space, called propagate-and-search. This approach does the filtering during the generation, so that many fewer possibilities are generated. If we extend palindrome product to six-digit numbers then the naive solution takes 45 seconds.[1] The propagate-and-search solution of chapter 12 takes less than 0.4 second to solve the same problem.

9.2.2 Puzzles and the n-queens problem

The n-queens problem is an example of a combinatoric puzzle. This kind of puzzle can be easily specified with relational programming. The resulting solution is not very efficient; for more efficiency we recommend using constraint programming instead, as explained in chapter 12. Using relational programming is a precursor of constraint programming.

The problem is to place n queens on an $n \times n$ chessboard so that no queen attacks another. There are many ways to solve this problem. The solution given in figure 9.4 is noteworthy because it uses dataflow variables. We can get the first solution of an eight-queens problem as follows:

```
{Browse {SolveOne fun {$} {Queens 8} end}}
```

This uses higher-order programming to define a zero-argument function from the one-argument function `Queens`. The answer displayed is:

```
[[1 7 5 8 2 4 6 3]]
```

This list gives the placement of the queens on the chessboard. It assumes there

1. Using Mozart 1.1.0 on a Pentium III processor at 500 MHz.

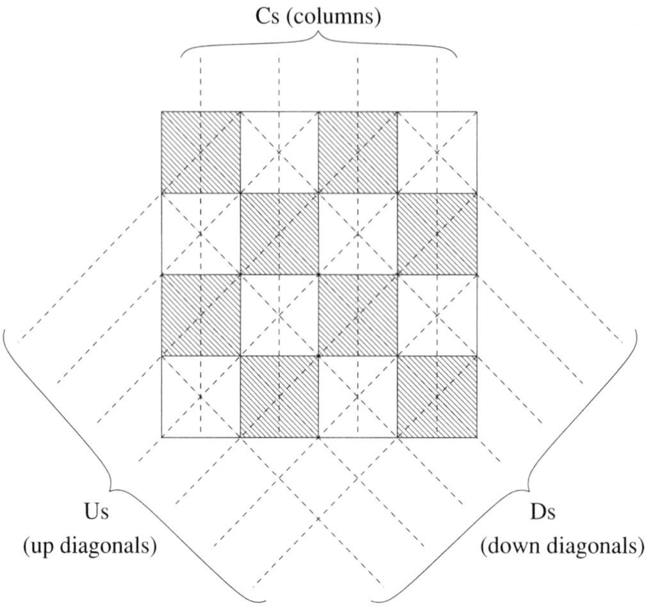

Figure 9.3: The n-queens problem (when n= 4).

is one queen per column. The solution lists the eight columns and gives for each column the queen's position (first square of first column, seventh square of second column, etc.). How many solutions are there to the eight-queens problem (counting reflections and rotations as separate)? This is easy to calculate:

```
{Browse {Length {SolveAll fun {$} {Queens 8} end}}}
```

This displays the number 92, which is the answer. `Queens` is not the best possible program for solving the n-queens problem. It is not practical for large n. Much better programs can be gotten by using constraint programming or by designing specialized algorithms (which amounts almost to the same thing). But this program is simple and elegant.

How does this magical program work? We explain it by means of figure 9.3. Each column, up diagonal, and down diagonal has one dataflow variable. The lists `Cs`, `Us`, and `Ds` contain all the column variables, up variables, and down variables, respectively. Each column variable "guards" a column, and similarly for the variables of the up and down diagonals. Placing a queen on a square binds the three variables to the queen's number. Once the variables are bound, no other queen can bind the variable of the same column, up diagonal, or down diagonal. This is because a dataflow variable can only have one value. Trying to bind to another value gives a unification failure, which causes that alternative to be rejected.

The procedure `PlaceQueens` traverses a column from top to bottom. It keeps the same `Cs`, but "shifts" the `Us` one place to the right and the `Ds` one place to the

```
fun {Queens N}
   fun {MakeList N}
      if N==0 then nil else _|{MakeList N-1} end
   end

   proc {PlaceQueens N ?Cs ?Us ?Ds}
      if N>0 then Ds2
         Us2=_|Us
      in
         Ds=_|Ds2
         {PlaceQueens N-1 Cs Us2 Ds2}
         {PlaceQueen N Cs Us Ds}
      else skip end
   end

   proc {PlaceQueen N ?Cs ?Us ?Ds}
      choice
         Cs=N|_ Us=N|_ Ds=N|_
      [] _|Cs2=Cs _|Us2=Us _|Ds2=Ds in
         {PlaceQueen N Cs2 Us2 Ds2}
      end
   end
   Qs={MakeList N}
in
   {PlaceQueens N Qs _ _}
   Qs
end
```

Figure 9.4: Solving the n-queens problem with relational programming.

left. At each iteration, `PlaceQueens` is at one row. It calls `PlaceQueen`, which tries to place a queen in one of the columns of that row, by binding one entry in `Cs`, `Us`, and `Ds`.

9.3 Relation to logic programming

Both the declarative computation model of chapter 2 and the relational computation model of this chapter are closely related to logic programming. Let us look closer at this relationship. Section 9.3.1 first gives a brief introduction to logic and logic programming. Sections 9.3.2 and 9.3.3 then show how these ideas apply to the declarative and relational computation models. Finally, section 9.3.4 briefly mentions pure Prolog, which is another implementation of logic programming.

The advantage of logic programming is that programs have two semantics, a logical and an operational semantics, which can be studied separately. If the underlying logic is chosen well, then the logical semantics is much simpler than the operational. However, logic programming cannot be used for all computation models. For example, there is no good way to design a logic for the stateful model. For it we can use the axiomatic semantics of section 6.6.

9.3.1 Logic and logic programming

A logic program is a statement of logic that is given an operational semantics, i.e., it can be executed on a computer. If the operational semantics is well designed, then the execution has two properties: it is correct, i.e., it respects the logical semantics (all consequences of the execution are valid logical consequences of the program considered as a set of logical axioms) and it is efficient, i.e., it allows writing programs that execute with the expected time and space complexity. Let us examine more closely the topics of logic and logic programming. Be warned that this section gives only a brief introduction to logic and logic programming. For more information we refer interested readers to other books [132, 201].

Propositional logic

What is an appropriate logic in which to write logic programs? There are many different logics. For example, there is propositional logic. Propositional formulas consist of expressions combining symbols such as p, q, r, and so forth together with the connectors $\wedge$ ("and"), $\vee$ ("or"), $\leftrightarrow$ ("if and only if"), $\rightarrow$ ("implies"), and $\neg$ ("not"). The symbols p, q, r, and so forth are called atoms in logic. An atom in logic is the smallest indivisible part of a logical formula. This should not be confused with an atom in a programming language, which is a constant uniquely determined by its print representation.

Propositional logic allows the expression of many simple laws. The contrapositive law $(p \rightarrow q) \leftrightarrow (\neg q \rightarrow \neg p)$ is a formula of propositional logic, as is De Morgan's law $\neg(p \wedge q) \leftrightarrow (\neg p \vee \neg q)$. To assign a truth-value to a propositional formula, we have to assign a truth-value to each of its atoms. We then evaluate the formula using the usual rules for $\wedge$, $\vee$, $\leftrightarrow$, $\rightarrow$, and $\neg$:

a	b	$a \wedge b$	$a \vee b$	$a \leftrightarrow b$	$a \rightarrow b$	$\neg a$
false	false	false	false	true	true	true
false	true	false	true	false	true	true
true	false	false	true	false	false	false
true	true	true	true	true	true	false

If the formula is true for all possible assignments of its atoms, then it is called a tautology. Both the contrapositive law and De Morgan's law are examples of tautologies. They are true for all four possible truth assignments of p and q.

First-order predicate calculus

Propositional logic is rather weak as a base for logic programming, principally because it does not allow expressing data structures. First-order predicate calculus is much better suited for this. The predicate calculus generalizes propositional logic with variables, terms, and quantifiers A logical formula in the predicate calculus has the following grammar, where $\langle \mathsf{a} \rangle$ is an atom and $\langle \mathsf{f} \rangle$ is a formula:

$$
\begin{array}{lcl}
\langle \mathsf{a} \rangle & ::= & p(\langle \mathsf{x} \rangle_1, \ldots, \langle \mathsf{x} \rangle_n) \\
\langle \mathsf{f} \rangle & ::= & \langle \mathsf{a} \rangle \\
& | & \langle \mathsf{x} \rangle = f(l_1 : \langle \mathsf{x} \rangle_1, \ldots, l_n : \langle \mathsf{x} \rangle_n) \\
& | & \langle \mathsf{x} \rangle_1 = \langle \mathsf{x} \rangle_2 \\
& | & \langle \mathsf{f} \rangle_1 \wedge \langle \mathsf{f} \rangle_2 \mid \langle \mathsf{f} \rangle_1 \vee \langle \mathsf{f} \rangle_2 \mid \langle \mathsf{f} \rangle_1 \leftrightarrow \langle \mathsf{f} \rangle_2 \mid \langle \mathsf{f} \rangle_1 \rightarrow \langle \mathsf{f} \rangle_2 \mid \neg \langle \mathsf{f} \rangle \\
& | & \forall \langle \mathsf{x} \rangle . \langle \mathsf{f} \rangle \mid \exists \langle \mathsf{x} \rangle . \langle \mathsf{f} \rangle
\end{array}
$$

Atoms in predicate calculus are more general than propositional atoms since they can have arguments. Here $\langle \mathsf{x} \rangle$ is a variable symbol, p is a predicate symbol, f is a term label, and the l_i are term features. The symbols $\forall$ ("for all") and $\exists$ ("there exists") are called quantifiers. In like manner as for program statements, we can define the free identifier occurrences of a logical formula. Sometimes these are called free variables, although strictly speaking they are not variables. A logical formula with no free identifier occurrences is called a logical sentence. For example, $p(x, y) \wedge q(y)$ is not a logical sentence because it has two free variables, x and y. We can make it a sentence by using quantifiers, giving, e.g., $\forall x . \exists y . p(x, y) \wedge q(y)$. The free variables x and y are captured by the quantifiers.

Logical semantics of predicate calculus

To assign a truth-value to a sentence of the predicate calculus, we have to do a bit more work than for the propositional calculus. We have to define a model. The word "model" here means a logical model, which is a very different beast than a computation model! A logical model consists of two parts: a domain of discourse (all possible values of the variables) and a set of relations (where a relation is a set of tuples). Each predicate has a relation, which gives the tuples for which the predicate is true. Among all predicates, equality ($=$) is particularly important. The equality relation will almost always be part of the model. The quantifiers $\forall x$ ("for all x") and $\exists x$ ("there exists x") range over the domain of discourse. Usually the logical model is chosen so that a special set of sentences, called the axioms, are all true. Such a model is called a logical semantics of the axioms. There can be many models for which the axioms are true.

Let us see how this works with an example. Consider the following two axioms:

$$
\begin{array}{l}
\forall x, y . \mathrm{grandfather}(x, y) \leftrightarrow \exists z . \mathrm{father}(x, z) \wedge \mathrm{father}(z, y) \\
\forall x, y, z . \mathrm{father}(x, z) \wedge \mathrm{father}(y, z) \rightarrow x = y
\end{array}
$$

There are many possible models of these axioms. Here is one:

Domain of discourse: {george, tom, bill}
Father relation: {father(george, tom), father(tom, bill)}
Grandfather relation: {grandfather(george, bill)}
Equality relation: {george = george, tom = tom, bill = bill}

The relations contain only the true tuples; all other tuples are assumed to be false. With this model, we can give truth-values to sentences of predicate calculus. For example, the sentence $\exists x, y.\text{father}(x, y) \rightarrow \text{father}(y, x)$ can be evaluated as being false. Note that the equality relation is part of this model, even though the axioms might not mention it explicitly.

Logic programming

Now we can state more precisely what a logic program is. For our purposes, a logic program consists of a set of axioms in the first-order predicate calculus, a sentence called the query, and a theorem prover, i.e., a system that can perform deduction using the axioms in an attempt to prove or disprove the query. Performing deductions is called executing the logic program. Can we build a practical programming system based on the idea of executing logic programs? We still need to address three issues:

- Theoretically, a theorem prover is limited in what it can do. It is only guaranteed to find a proof or disproof for queries that are true in all models. This result is known as Gödel's completeness theorem. It was first proved by Kurt Gödel in 1929. Completeness is the ability to find a proof or disproof of any query. In general, completeness depends on the models we are interested in. If we are just interested in some particular models, then there might not exist a proof even though the query is true in those models. For those models, the theorem prover will be incomplete. For example, we might be interested in number theory, so we use the model of integers with integer arithmetic. In that case, Gödel's incompleteness theorem, first proved by Gödel in 1930, states that for any given finite set of consistent axioms in which one can do basic arithmetic (addition and multiplication), there exist true statements about numbers that cannot be proved or disproved with those axioms.
- Even in those cases where the theorem prover could theoretically find a result, it might be too inefficient. The search for a proof might take exponential time. A theorem prover intended for practical programming should have a simple and predictable operational semantics, so that the programmer can define algorithms and reason about their complexity.
- A final point is that the deduction done by the theorem prover should be constructive. That is, if the query states that there exists an x that satisfies some property, then the system should construct a witness to the existence. In other words, it should build a data structure as an output of the logic program.

Two approaches are taken to overcome these problems:

- We place restrictions on the form of the axioms so that an efficient constructive theorem prover is possible. The Prolog language, e.g., is based on Horn clauses, which are axioms of the form

$\forall x_1, \ldots, x_k \,.\, \langle \mathsf{a} \rangle_1 \wedge \cdots \wedge \langle \mathsf{a} \rangle_n \rightarrow \langle \mathsf{a} \rangle$

where $\{x_1, \ldots, x_k\}$ are chosen so that the axiom has no free variables. Horn clauses are interesting because there is an efficient constructive theorem prover for them using an inference rule called resolution [132]. The relational computation model of this chapter also does logic programming, but without using resolution. It uses a different set of axioms and theorem prover, which are discussed in the next section.

- We give the programmer the possibility of helping the theorem prover with operational knowledge. This operational knowledge is essential for writing efficient logic programs. For example, consider a logic program to sort a list of integers. A naive program might consist of axioms defining a permutation of a list and a query that states that there exists a permutation whose elements are in ascending order. Such a program would be short but inefficient. Much more efficient would be to write axioms that express the properties of an efficient sorting algorithm, such as mergesort.

A major achievement of computer science is that practical logic programming systems have been built by combining these two approaches. The first popular language to achieve this goal was Prolog; it was subsequently followed by many other languages. High-performance Prolog implementations are amazingly fast; they can even rival the speed of imperative language implementations [216].

9.3.2 Operational and logical semantics

There are two ways to look at a logic program: the logical view and the operational view. In the logical view, it is simply a statement of logic. In the operational view, it defines an execution on a computer. Before looking at the relational model, let us look first at the declarative model of chapter 2. We will see that programs in the declarative model have a logical semantics as well as an operational semantics. It is straightforward to translate a declarative program into a logical sentence. If the program terminates correctly, i.e., it does not block, go into an infinite loop, or raise an exception, then all the bindings it does are correct deductions from the axioms. That is, the results of all predicates are valid tuples in the predicates' relations. We call this deterministic logic programming.

Table 9.2 defines a translation scheme T which translates any statement $\langle \mathsf{s} \rangle$ in the relational kernel language into a logical formula $T(\langle \mathsf{s} \rangle)$. Procedure definitions are translated into predicate definitions. Note that exceptions are not translated. Raising an exception signals that the normal, logical execution is no longer valid. The logical sentence therefore does not hold in that case. Proving the correctness of

Relational statement	Logical formula
skip	true
fail	false
$\langle s\rangle_1$ $\langle s\rangle_2$	$T(\langle s\rangle_1) \wedge T(\langle s\rangle_2)$
local X **in** $\langle s\rangle$ **end**	$\exists x.T(\langle s\rangle)$
X=Y	$x = y$
X=f(l1:X1 ... ln:Xn)	$x = f(l_1 : x_1, ..., l_n : x_n)$
if X **then** $\langle s\rangle_1$ **else** $\langle s\rangle_2$ **end**	$(x = \text{true} \wedge T(\langle s\rangle_1)) \vee (x = \text{false} \wedge T(\langle s\rangle_2))$
case X	$(\exists x_1, \ldots, x_n.x = f(l_1 : x_1, \ldots, l_n : x_n) \wedge T(\langle s\rangle_1))$
of f(l1:X1 ... ln:Xn)	$\vee((\neg\exists x_1, \ldots, x_n.x = f(l_1 : x_1, \ldots, l_n : x_n)) \wedge T(\langle s\rangle_2))$
then $\langle s\rangle_1$ **else** $\langle s\rangle_2$ **end**	
proc {P X1 ... Xn} $\langle s\rangle$ **end**	$\forall x_1, \ldots, x_n.p(x_1, \ldots, x_n) \leftrightarrow T(\langle s\rangle)$
{P Y1 ... Yn}	$p(y_1, \ldots, y_n)$
choice $\langle s\rangle_1$ [] $\cdots$ [] $\langle s\rangle_n$ **end**	$T(\langle s\rangle_1) \vee \cdots \vee T(\langle s\rangle_n)$

Table 9.2: Translating a relational program to logic.

this table is beyond the scope of this chapter. We leave it as an interesting exercise for mathematically minded readers.

A given logical semantics can correspond to many operational semantics. For example, the following three statements:

X=Y $\langle s\rangle$

$\langle s\rangle$ X=Y

if X==Y **then** $\langle s\rangle$ **else fail end**

all have the exactly same logical semantics, namely:

$x = y \wedge T(\langle s\rangle)$

But their operational semantics are very different! The first statement binds X and Y and then executes $\langle s\rangle$. The second statement executes $\langle s\rangle$ and then binds X and Y. The third statement waits until it can determine whether or not X and Y are equal. It then executes $\langle s\rangle$, if it determines that they are equal.

Writing a logic program consists of two parts: writing the logical semantics and then choosing an operational semantics for it. The art of logic programming consists in balancing two conflicting tensions: the logical semantics should be simple and the operational semantics should be efficient. All the declarative programs of chapters 3 and 4 can be seen in this light. They are all logic programs. In the Prolog language, this has given rise to a beautiful programming style [25, 158, 201].

Deterministic append

Let us write a simple logic program to append two lists. We have already seen the `Append` function:

```
fun {Append A B}
   case A
   of nil then B
   [] X|As then X|{Append As B}
   end
end
```

Let us expand it into a procedure:

```
proc {Append A B ?C}
   case A
   of nil then C=B
   [] X|As then Cs in
      C=X|Cs
      {Append As B Cs}
   end
end
```

According to table 9.2, this procedure has the following logical semantics:

$$\forall a, b, c.append(a, b, c) \leftrightarrow$$
$$(a = \texttt{nil} \wedge c = b) \vee (\exists x, a', c'.a = x \,|\, a' \wedge c = x \,|\, c' \wedge append(a', b, c'))$$

The procedure also has an operational semantics, given by the semantics of the declarative model. The call

```
{Append [1 2 3] [4 5] X}
```

executes successfully and returns `X=[1 2 3 4 5]`. The call's logical meaning is the tuple $append([1, 2, 3], [4, 5], x)$. After the execution, the tuple becomes

$$append([1, 2, 3], [4, 5], [1, 2, 3, 4, 5])$$

This tuple is a member of the *append* relation. We see that `Append` can be seen as a logic program.

Another deterministic append

The above definition of `Append` does not always give a solution. For example, the call `{Append X [3] [1 2 3]}` should return `X=[1 2]`, which is the logically correct solution, but the program cannot give this solution because it assumes `X` is bound to a value on input. The program blocks. This shows that the operational semantics is incomplete. To give a solution, we need to write a version of `Append` with a different operational semantics. To calculate `X` from the last two arguments, we change the definition of `Append` as follows:

```
proc {Append ?A B C}
   if B==C then A=nil
   else
      case C of X|Cs then As in
         A=X|As
         {Append As B Cs}
      end
   end
end
```

This version of Append expects its last two arguments to be inputs and its first argument to be an output. It has a different operational semantics than the previous version, but keeps the same logical semantics. To be precise, its logical semantics according to table 9.2 is

$$\forall a, b, c. append(a, b, c) \leftrightarrow \\ (b = c \wedge a = \texttt{nil}) \vee (\exists x, c', a'. c = x \,|\, c' \wedge a = x \,|\, a' \wedge append(a', b, c'))$$

This sentence is logically equivalent to the previous one.

Nondeterministic append

We have seen two versions of Append, with the same logical semantics but different operational semantics. Both versions return exactly one solution. But what if we want the solutions of {Append X Y [1 2 3]}? There are four different solutions that satisfy the logical semantics. The declarative model is deterministic, so it can only give one solution at most. To give several solutions, we can use the **choice** statement to guess the right information and then continue. This is explained in the next section.

9.3.3 Nondeterministic logic programming

We saw that the Append procedure in the declarative model has a logical semantics but the operational semantics is not able to realize this logical semantics for all patterns of inputs and outputs. In the declarative model, the operational semantics is deterministic (it gives just one solution) and directional (it works for only one pattern of input and output arguments). With relational programming, we can write programs with a more flexible operational semantics, that can give solutions when the declarative program would block. We call this nondeterministic logic programming. To see how it works, let us look again at the logical semantics of append:

$$\forall a, b, c. append(a, b, c) \leftrightarrow \\ (a = \texttt{nil} \wedge c = b) \vee (\exists x, a', c'. a = x \,|\, a' \wedge c = x \,|\, c' \wedge append(a', b, c'))$$

How can we write a program that respects this logical semantics and is able to provide multiple solutions for the call {Append X Y [1 2 3]}? Look closely at the logical semantics. There is a disjunction ($\vee$) with a first alternative ($a = \texttt{nil} \wedge c = b$)

and a second alternative $(\exists x, a', c'.a = x\,|\,a' \wedge c = x\,|\,c' \wedge \mathit{append}(a', b, c'))$. To get multiple solutions, the program should be able to pick both alternatives. We implement this by using the **choice** statement. This gives the following program:

```
proc {Append ?A ?B ?C}
   choice
      A=nil B=C
   [] As Cs X in
      A=X|As C=X|Cs {Append As B Cs}
   end
end
```

We can search for all solutions to the call {Append X Y [1 2 3]}:

```
{Browse {SolveAll
           proc {$ S} X#Y=S in {Append X Y [1 2 3]} end}}
```

To get one output, we pair the solutions X and Y together. This displays all four solutions:

```
[nil#[1 2 3]  [1]#[2 3]  [1 2]#[3]  [1 2 3]#nil]
```

This program can also handle the directional cases. For example,

```
{Browse {SolveAll
           proc {$ X} {Append [1 2] [3 4 5] X} end}}
```

displays [[1 2 3 4 5]] (a list of one solution). The program can even handle cases where no arguments are known at all, e.g., {Append X Y Z}. Since in that case there are an infinity of solutions, we do not call SolveAll, but just Solve:

```
L={Solve proc {$ S} X#Y#Z=S in {Append X Y Z} end}
```

Each solution is a tuple containing all three arguments (X#Y#Z). We can display successive solutions one by one by touching successive elements of L:

```
{Touch 1 L}
{Touch 2 L}
{Touch 3 L}
{Touch 4 L}
...
```

({Touch N L} is defined in section 4.5.6; it simply traverses the first N elements of L.) This displays successive solutions:

```
nil#B#B|
   [X1]#B#(X1|B)|
      [X1 X2]#B#(X1|X2|B)|
         [X1 X2 X3]#B#(X1|X2|X3|B)|_
```

All possible solutions are given in order of increasing length of the first argument. This can seem somewhat miraculous. It certainly seemed so to the first logic programmers, in the late 1960s and early 1970s. Yet it is a simple consequence of the semantics of the **choice** statement, which picks its alternatives in order. Be warned that this style of programming, while it can sometimes perform miracles, is extremely dangerous. It is very easy to get into infinite loops or exponential-time searches, i.e., to generate candidate solutions almost indefinitely without ever finding a good one. We advise you to write deterministic programs whenever possible and to use nondeterminism only in those cases when it is indispensable. Before running the program, verify that the solution you want is one of the enumerated solutions.

9.3.4 Relation to pure Prolog

The relational computation model provides a form of nondeterministic logic programming that is very close to what Prolog provides. To be precise, it is a subset of Prolog called "pure Prolog" [201]. The full Prolog language extends pure Prolog with operations that lack a logical semantics but that are useful for programming a desired operational semantics (see section 9.7, which explains Prolog in more detail). Programs written in either pure Prolog or the relational computation model can be translated in a straightforward way to the other. There are three principal differences between pure Prolog and the relational computation model:

- Prolog uses a Horn clause syntax with an operational semantics based on resolution. The relational computation model uses a functional syntax with an operational semantics tailored to that syntax.
- The relational computation model allows full higher-order programming. This has no counterpart in first-order predicate calculus but is useful for structuring programs. Higher-order programming is not supported at all in pure Prolog and only partially in full Prolog.
- The relational computation model distinguishes between deterministic operations (which do not use `choice`) and nondeterministic operations (which use `choice`). In pure Prolog, both have the same syntax. Deterministic operations efficiently perform functional calculations, i.e., it is known which arguments are the inputs and which are the outputs. Nondeterministic operations perform relational calculations, i.e., it is not known which arguments are inputs and outputs, and indeed the same relation can be used in different ways.

9.3.5 Logic programming in other models

So far we have seen logic programming in the declarative model, possibly extended with a choice operation. What about logic programming in other models? In other words, in how far is it possible to have a logical semantics in other models? To have a logical semantics means that execution corresponds to deduction, i.e., execution can be seen as performing inference and the results of procedure calls give valid tuples in a simple logical model, such as a model of the predicate calculus. The basic principle is to enrich the control: we extend the operational semantics, which allows us to calculate new tuples in the same logical model. Let us examine some other computation models:

- Adding concurrency to the declarative model gives the data-driven and demand-driven concurrent models. These models also do logic programming, since they only change the order in which valid tuples are calculated. They do not change the content of the tuples.

- The nondeterministic concurrent model of section 5.8.1 does logic programming. It adds just one operation, `WaitTwo`, which can be given a logical semantics. Logically, the call `{WaitTwo X Y Z}` is equivalent to $z = 1 \vee z = 2$, since `Z` is bound to 1 or 2. Operationally, `WaitTwo` waits until one of its arguments is determined. `WaitTwo` is used to manage control in a concurrent program, namely to pick an execution path that does not block.
The nondeterministic concurrent model is interesting because it combines two properties. It has a straightforward logical semantics and it is almost as expressive as a stateful model. For example, it allows building a client/server program with two independent clients and one server, which is not possible in a declarative model. This is why the model was chosen as the basis for concurrent logic programming.

- The stateful models are another story. There is no straightforward way to give a logical meaning to a stateful operation. However, stateful models can do logic programming if the state is used in a limited way. For example, it can be encapsulated inside a control abstraction or it can be used as a parameter to part of a program. In the first case we are just enriching the control. In the second case, as long as the state does not change, we can reason as if it were constant.

- The constraint-based computation model of chapter 12 is the most powerful model for doing logic programming that we see in the book. It gives techniques for solving complex combinatoric optimization problems. It is the most powerful model in the sense that it has the most sophisticated mechanisms both for specifying and automatically determining the control flow. From the logic programming viewpoint, it has the strongest deduction abilities.

9.4 Natural language parsing

Section 3.4.8 shows how to do parsing with a difference list. The grammar that it parses is deterministic with a lookahead of one token: it suffices to know the next token to know what grammar rule will apply. This is sometimes a very strong restriction. Some languages need a much larger lookahead to be parsed. This is certainly true for natural languages, but can also be true for programming languages (like PL/I and Fortran, see below).

The one-token lookahead restriction can be removed by using relational programming. Relational programs can be written to parse highly ambiguous grammars. This is one of the most flexible ways to do parsing. It can parse grammars with absolutely no restriction on the form of the grammar. The disadvantage is that if the grammar is highly ambiguous, the parser can be extremely slow. But if the ambiguity is localized to small parts of the input, the efficiency is acceptable.

This section gives a simple example of natural language parsing in the relational style. This style was pioneered by the Prolog language in the early 1970s. It is fair to say that Prolog was originally invented for this purpose [45]. This section only scratches the surface of what can be done in this area with the relational computation model. For further reading, we recommend [56].

Examples in PL/I and Fortran

Using relational programming to parse ambiguous grammars is quite practical. For example, it is being used successfully by Darius Blasband of Phidani Software to build transformation tools for programs written in Fortran and PL/I [23]. These two languages are difficult to parse with more traditional tools such as the Unix lex/yacc family. Let us see what the problems are with these two languages.

The problem with parsing PL/I The following fragment is legal PL/I syntax:

```
IF IF=THEN THEN THEN=ELSE ELSE ELSE=IF
```

This `IF` statement uses variables named `IF`, `THEN`, and `ELSE`. The parser has to decide whether each occurrence of the tokens `IF`, `THEN`, and `ELSE` is a variable identifier or a keyword. The only way to make the distinction is to continue the parse until only one unambiguous interpretation remains. The problem is that PL/I makes no distinction between keywords and variable identifiers.

The problem with parsing Fortran Fortran is even more difficult to parse than PL/I. To see why, consider the following fragment, which is legal Fortran syntax:

```
   DO 10 I = 1,10
   ...
10 CONTINUE
```

This defines a loop that iterates its body 10 times, where I is given consecutive values from 1 to 10. Look what happens when the comma in the `DO` statement is replaced by a period:

```
DO 10 I = 1.10
```

In Fortran, this is legal syntax that has the same meaning as

```
DO10I = 1.10
```

where `DO10I` is a new variable identifier that is assigned the floating point number 1.10. In this case, the loop body is executed exactly once with an undefined (garbage) value stored in I. This is possible because Fortran allows white space within a variable identifier and does not require that variable identifiers be declared in advance. This means that the parser has to look far ahead to decide whether there is one token, `DO10I`, or three, `DO`, `10`, and `I`. The parser cannot parse the `DO` statement unambiguously until the period or comma is encountered.

This is a famous error that was discovered at Nasa during tests with an orbit computation program during the Mercury project in the early 1960s. Other errors just as minor have caused the failure of rocket launches worth tens of millions of dollars, e.g., the Mariner I spacecraft [36]. An important lesson for designing programming languages is that changing the syntax of a legal program slightly should not create another legal program.

9.4.1 A simple grammar

We use the following simple grammar for a subset of English:

⟨Sentence⟩	::=	⟨NounPhrase⟩ ⟨VerbPhrase⟩
⟨NounPhrase⟩	::=	⟨Determiner⟩ ⟨Noun⟩ ⟨RelClause⟩ | ⟨Name⟩
⟨VerbPhrase⟩	::=	⟨TransVerb⟩ ⟨NounPhrase⟩ | ⟨IntransVerb⟩
⟨RelClause⟩	::=	`who` ⟨VerbPhrase⟩ | ε
⟨Determiner⟩	::=	`every` | `a`
⟨Noun⟩	::=	`man` | `woman`
⟨Name⟩	::=	`john` | `mary`
⟨TransVerb⟩	::=	`loves`
⟨IntransVerb⟩	::=	`lives`

Here ε means that the alternative is empty (nothing is chosen). Some examples of sentences in this grammar are:

"john loves mary"
"a man lives"
"every woman who loves john lives"

Let us write a parser that generates an equivalent sentence in the predicate calculus. For example, parsing the sentence "a man lives" will generate the term `exists(X and(man(X) lives(X))` in the syntax of the relational computation model, which represents $\exists x.\text{man}(x) \wedge \text{lives}(x)$. The parse tree is a sentence in predicate calculus that represents the meaning of the natural language sentence.

9.4.2 Parsing with the grammar

The first step is to parse with the grammar, i.e., to accept valid sentences of the grammar. Let us represent the sentence as a list of atoms. For each nonterminal in the grammar, we write a function that takes an input list, parses part of it, and returns the unparsed remainder of the list. For ⟨TransVerb⟩ this gives

```
proc {TransVerb X0 X}
   X0=loves|X
end
```

This can be called as

```
{TransVerb [loves a man] X}
```

which parses "loves" and binds `X` to `[a man]`. If the grammar has a choice, then the procedure uses the **choice** statement to represent this. For ⟨Name⟩ this gives

```
proc {Name X0 X}
   choice X0=john|X [] X0=mary|X end
end
```

This picks one of the two alternatives. If a nonterminal requires another nonterminal, then the latter is called as a procedure. For ⟨VerbPhrase⟩ this gives

```
proc {VerbPhrase X0 X}
   choice X1 in
      {TransVerb X0 X1} {NounPhrase X1 X}
   [] {IntransVerb X0 X}
   end
end
```

Note how `X1` is passed from `TransVerb` to `NounPhrase`. Continuing in this way we can write a procedure for each of the grammar's nonterminal symbols.

To do the parse, we execute the grammar with encapsulated search. We would like the execution to succeed for correct sentences and fail for incorrect sentences. This will not always be the case, depending on how the grammar is defined and which search we do. For example, if the grammar is left-recursive then doing a depth-first search will go into an infinite loop. A left-recursive grammar has at least one rule whose first alternative starts with the nonterminal, like this:

⟨NounPhrase⟩ ::= ⟨NounPhrase⟩ ⟨RelPhrase⟩ | ⟨Noun⟩

In this rule, a ⟨NounPhrase⟩ consists first of a ⟨NounPhrase⟩! This is not necessarily wrong; it just means that we have to be careful how we parse with the grammar. If we do a breadth-first search or an iterative deepening search instead of a depth-first search, then we are guaranteed to find a successful parse, if one exists.

9.4.3 Generating a parse tree

We would like our parser to do more than just succeed or fail. Let us extend it to generate a parse tree. We can do this by making our procedures into functions. For example, let us extend ⟨Name⟩ to output the name it has parsed:

```
fun {Name X0 X}
   choice
      X0=john|X  john
   [] X0=mary|X  mary
   end
end
```

When ⟨Name⟩ parses "john", it outputs the atom `john`. Let us extend ⟨TransVerb⟩ to output the predicate loves(x, y), where x is the subject and y is the object. This gives

```
fun {TransVerb S O X0 X}
   X0=loves|X
   loves(S O)
end
```

Note that ⟨TransVerb⟩ also has two new inputs, `S` and `O`. These inputs will be filled in when it is called.

9.4.4 Generating quantifiers

Let us see one more example, to show how our parser generates the quantifiers "for all" and "there exists." They are generated for determiners:

```
fun {Determiner S P1 P2 X0 X}
   choice
      X0=every|X
      all(S imply(P1 P2))
   [] X0=a|X
      exists(S and(P1 P2))
   end
end
```

The determiner "every" generates a "for all." The sentence "every man loves mary" gives the term `all(X imply(man(X) loves(X mary)))`, which corresponds to $\forall x.\text{man}(x) \rightarrow \text{loves}(x, \text{mary})$. In the call to ⟨Determiner⟩, `P1` will be bound to `man(X)` and `P2` will be bound to `loves(X mary)`. These bindings are done inside ⟨NounPhrase⟩, which finds out what the ⟨Noun⟩ and ⟨RelClause⟩ are, and passes this information to ⟨Determiner⟩:

```
fun {NounPhrase N P1 X0 X}
   choice P P2 P3 X1 X2 in
      P={Determiner N P2 P1 X0 X1}
      P3={Noun N X1 X2}
      P2={RelClause N P3 X2 X}
      P
   [] N={Name X0 X}
      P1
   end
end
```

Since `P1` and `P2` are single-assignment variables, they can be passed to ⟨Determiner⟩ before they are bound. In this way, each nonterminal brings its piece of the puzzle and the whole grammar fits together.

9.4.5 Running the parser

The complete parser is given in figures 9.5 and 9.6. Figure 9.5 shows the simple nonterminals, which enumerate atoms directly. Figure 9.6 shows the compound nonterminals, which call other nonterminals. To run the parser, feed both figures into Mozart. Let us start by parsing some simple sentences. For example:

```
fun {Determiner S P1 P2 X0 X}
   choice
      X0=every|X
      all(S imply(P1 P2))
   [] X0=a|X
      exists(S and(P1 P2))
   end
end

fun {Noun N X0 X}
   choice
      X0=man|X
      man(N)
   [] X0=woman|X
      woman(N)
   end
end

fun {Name X0 X}
   choice
      X0=john|X
      john
   [] X0=mary|X
      mary
   end
end

fun {TransVerb S O X0 X}
   X0=loves|X
   loves(S O)
end

fun {IntransVerb S X0 X}
   X0=lives|X
   lives(S)
end
```

Figure 9.5: Natural language parsing (simple nonterminals).

```
fun {Sentence X0 X}
P P1 N X1 in
   P={NounPhrase N P1 X0 X1}
   P1={VerbPhrase N X1 X}
   P
end

fun {NounPhrase N P1 X0 X}
   choice P P2 P3 X1 X2 in
      P={Determiner N P2 P1 X0 X1}
      P3={Noun N X1 X2}
      P2={RelClause N P3 X2 X}
      P
   [] N={Name X0 X}
      P1
   end
end

fun {VerbPhrase S X0 X}
   choice O P1 X1 in
      P1={TransVerb S O X0 X1}
      {NounPhrase O P1 X1 X}
   [] {IntransVerb S X0 X}
   end
end

fun {RelClause S P1 X0 X}
   choice P2 X1 in
      X0=who|X1
      P2={VerbPhrase S X1 X}
      and(P1 P2)
   [] X0=X
      P1
   end
end
```

Figure 9.6: Natural language parsing (compound nonterminals).

```
fun {Goal}
   {Sentence [mary lives] nil}
end
{Browse {SolveAll Goal}}
```

The `SolveAll` call will calculate all possible parse trees. This displays

```
[lives(mary)]
```

This is a list of one element since there is only a single parse tree. How about the following sentence:

```
fun {Goal}
   {Sentence [every man loves mary] nil}
end
```

Parsing this gives

```
[all(X imply(man(X) loves(X mary)))]
```

To see the unbound variable `X`, choose the **Minimal Graph** representation in the browser. Let us try a more complicated example:

```
fun {Goal}
   {Sentence [every man who lives loves a woman] nil}
end
```

Parsing this gives

```
[all(X
     imply(and(man(X) lives(X))
           exists(Y and(woman(Y) loves(X Y)))))]
```

9.4.6 Running the parser "backward"

So far, we have given sentences and parsed them. This shows only part of what our parser can do. In general, it can take any input to `Sentence` that contains unbound variables and find all the parses that are consistent with that input. This shows the power of the **choice** statement. For example, let us find all sentences of three words:

```
fun {Goal}
   {Sentence [_ _ _] nil}
end
```

Executing this goal gives the following eight parse trees:

```
[all(A imply(man(A) lives(A)))
 all(B imply(woman(B) lives(B)))
 exists(C and(man(C) lives(C)))
 exists(D and(woman(D) lives(D)))
 loves(john john)
 loves(john mary)
 loves(mary john)
 loves(mary mary)]
```

See if you can find out which sentence corresponds to each parse tree. For example, the first tree corresponds to the sentence "every man lives."

The ability to compute with partial information, which is what our parser does, is an important step in the direction of constraint programming. Chapter 12 gives an introduction to constraint programming.

9.4.7 Unification grammars

Our parser does more than just parse; it also generates a parse tree. We did this by extending the code of the parser, "piggybacking" the generation on the actions of the parser. There is another, more concise way to define this: by extending the grammar so that nonterminals have arguments. For example, the nonterminal ⟨Name⟩ becomes ⟨Name⟩(N), which means "the current name is `N`." When ⟨Name⟩ calls its definition, `N` is bound to `john` or `mary`, depending on which rule is chosen. Other nonterminals are handled in the same way. For example, ⟨TransVerb⟩ becomes ⟨TransVerb⟩(S O P), which means "the current verb links subject `S` and object `O` to make the phrase `P`." When ⟨TransVerb⟩ calls its definition, the corresponding arguments are bound together. If `S` and `O` are inputs, ⟨TransVerb⟩ constructs `P`, which has the form `loves(S O)`. After extending the whole grammar in similar fashion (following the parser code), we get the following rules:

⟨Sentence⟩(P)	::=	⟨NounPhrase⟩(N P1 P) ⟨VerbPhrase⟩(N P1)
⟨NounPhrase⟩(N P1 P)	::=	⟨Determiner⟩(N P2 P1 P) ⟨Noun⟩(N P3) ⟨RelClause⟩(N P3 P2)
⟨NounPhrase⟩(N P1 P1)	::=	⟨Name⟩(N)
⟨VerbPhrase⟩(S P)	::=	⟨TransVerb⟩(S O P1) ⟨NounPhrase⟩(O P1 P)
⟨VerbPhrase⟩(S P)	::=	⟨IntransVerb⟩(S P)
⟨RelClause⟩(S P1 and(P1 P2))	::=	`who` ⟨VerbPhrase⟩(S P2)
⟨RelClause⟩(S P1 P1)	::=	ε
⟨Determiner⟩(S P1 P2 all(S imply(P1 P2)))	::=	`every`
⟨Determiner⟩(S P1 P2 exists(S and(P1 P2))	::=	`a`
⟨Noun⟩(N man(N))	::=	`man`
⟨Noun⟩(N woman(N))	::=	`woman`
⟨Name⟩(john)	::=	`john`
⟨Name⟩(mary)	::=	`mary`
⟨TransVerb⟩(S O loves(S O))	::=	`loves`
⟨IntransVerb⟩(S lives(S))	::=	`lives`

These rules correspond exactly to the parser program we have written. You can see the advantage of using the rules: they are more concise and easier to understand than the program. They can be automatically translated into a program. This translation is so useful that the Prolog language has a built-in preprocessor to support it.

This kind of grammar is called a definite clause grammar, or DCG, because each rule corresponds to a kind of Horn clause called a definite clause. Each nonterminal can have arguments. When a nonterminal is matched with a rule, the corresponding arguments are unified together. DCGs are a simple example of a very general kind of grammar called unification grammar. Many different kinds of unification grammar are used in natural language parsing. The practical ones use constraint programming instead of relational programming.

9.5 A grammar interpreter

The previous section shows how to build a simple parser and how to extend it to return a parse tree. For each new grammar we want to parse, we have to build a new parser. The parser is "hardwired": its implementation is based on the grammar it parses. Wouldn't it be nice to have a generic parser that would work for all grammars, simply by passing the grammar definition as an argument? A generic parser is easier to use and more flexible than a hardwired parser. To represent the grammar in a programming language, we encode it as a data structure. Depending on how flexible the language is, the encoding will look almost like the grammar's EBNF definition.

The generic parser is an example of an interpreter. Recall that an interpreter is a program written in language L_1 that accepts programs written in another language L_2 and executes them. For the generic parser, L_1 is the relational computation model and L_2 is a grammar definition.

The generic parser uses the same execution strategy as the hardwired parser. It keeps track of two extra arguments: the token sequence to be parsed and the rest of the sequence. It uses a choice operation to choose a rule for each nonterminal. It is executed with encapsulated search.

9.5.1 A simple grammar

To keep things simple in describing the generic parser, we use a small grammar that defines s-expressions. An s-expression starts with a left parenthesis, followed by a possibly empty sequence of atoms or s-expressions, and ends with a right parenthesis. Two examples are `(a b c)` and `(a (b) () (d (c)))`. S-expressions were originally used in Lisp to represent nested lists. Our grammar will parse s-expressions and build the list that they represent. Here is the grammar's definition:

⟨sexpr⟩(s(As))	::=	'(' ⟨seq⟩(As) ')'
⟨seq⟩(nil)	::=	ε
⟨seq⟩(A|As)	::=	⟨atom⟩(A) ⟨seq⟩(As)
⟨seq⟩(A|As)	::=	⟨sexpr⟩(A) ⟨seq⟩(As)
⟨atom⟩(X)	::=	X & *(X is an atom different from '(' and ')')*

This definition extends the EBNF notation by allowing terminals to be variables and by adding a boolean condition to check whether a rule is valid. These extensions occur in the definition of ⟨atom⟩(X). The argument X represents the actual atom that is parsed. To avoid confusion between an atom and the left or right parenthesis of an s-expression, we check that the atom is not a parenthesis.

9.5.2 Encoding the grammar

Let us encode this grammar as a data structure. We first encode rules. A rule is a tuple with two parts, a head and a body. The body is a list of nonterminals and terminals. For example, the rule defining ⟨sexpr⟩ could be written as

```
local As in
   rule(sexpr(s(As)) ['(' seq(As) ')'])
end
```

The unbound variable `As` will be bound when the rule is used. This representation is not quite right. There should be a fresh variable `As` each time the rule is used. To implement this, we encode the rule as a function:

```
fun {$} As in
   rule(sexpr(s(As)) ['(' seq(As) ')'])
end
```

Each time the function is called, a tuple is returned containing a fresh variable. This is still not completely right, since we cannot distinguish nonterminals without arguments from terminals. To avoid this confusion, we wrap terminals in a tuple with label `t`. (This means that we cannot have a nonterminal with label `t`.) This gives the final, correct representation:

```
fun {$} As in
   rule(sexpr(s(As)) [t('(') seq(As) t(')')])
end
```

Now that we can encode rules, let us encode the complete grammar. We represent the grammar as a record where each nonterminal has one field. This field contains a list of the nonterminal's rules. We have seen that a rule body is a list containing nonterminals and terminals. We add a third kind of entry, a boolean function that has to return **`true`** for the rule to be valid. This corresponds to the condition we used in the definition of ⟨atom⟩(X).

Figure 9.7 gives the complete grammar for s-expressions encoded as a data structure. Note how naturally this encoding uses higher-order programming: rules are functions that themselves may contain boolean functions.

9.5.3 Running the grammar interpreter

Let us define a data abstraction for the grammar interpreter. The function `NewParser` takes a grammar definition and returns a parser:

```
Parse={NewParser Rules}
```

```
r(sexpr:[fun {$} As in
            rule(sexpr(s(As)) [t('(') seq(As) t(')')])
         end]
  seq:  [fun {$}
            rule(seq(nil) nil)
         end
         fun {$} As A in
            rule(seq(A|As) [atom(A) seq(As)])
         end
         fun {$} As A in
            rule(seq(A|As) [sexpr(A) seq(As)])
         end]
  atom: [fun {$} X in
            rule(atom(X)
                 [t(X)
                  fun {$}
                     {IsAtom X} andthen X\='(' andthen X\=')'
                  end])
         end])
```

Figure 9.7: Encoding of a grammar.

`Rules` is a record like the grammar definition in figure 9.7. `Parse` takes as inputs a goal to be parsed, `Goal`, and a list of tokens, `S0`. It does the parse and returns the unparsed remainder of `S0` in `S`:

```
{Parse Goal S0 S}
```

While doing the parse, it can also build a parse tree because it unifies the arguments of the nonterminal with the head of the chosen rule.

The parser is executed with encapsulated search. Here is an example:

```
{Browse {SolveOne
   fun {$} E in
      {Parse sexpr(E)
             ['(' hello '(' this is an sexpr ')' ')'] nil}
      E
   end}}
```

This returns a list containing the first solution:

```
[s([hello s([this is an sexpr])])]
```

9.5.4 Implementing the grammar interpreter

Figure 9.8 gives the definition of the grammar interpreter. `NewParser` creates a parser `Parse` that references the grammar definition in `Rules`. The parser is written as a **case** statement. It accepts four kinds of goals:

- A list of other goals. The parser is called recursively for all goals in the list.

```
fun {NewParser Rules}
   proc {Parse Goal S0 S}
      case Goal
      of nil then S0=S
      [] G|Gs then S1 in
         {Parse G S0 S1}
         {Parse Gs S1 S}
      [] t(X) then S0=X|S
      else if {IsProcedure Goal} then
         {Goal}=true
         S0=S
      else Body Rs in /* Goal is a nonterminal */
         Rs=Rules.{Label Goal}
         {ChooseRule Rs Goal Body}
         {Parse Body S0 S}
      end end
   end
   proc {ChooseRule Rs Goal Body}
      I={Space.choose {Length Rs}}
   in
      rule(Goal Body)={{List.nth Rs I}}
   end
in
   Parse
end
```

Figure 9.8: Implementing the grammar interpreter.

- A procedure, which should be a zero-argument boolean function. The function is called and its result is unified with **true**. If the result is **false**, then the parser fails, which causes another alternative to be chosen.
- A terminal, represented as the tuple `t(X)`. This terminal is unified with the next element in the input list.
- A nonterminal, represented as a record. Its label is used to look up the rule definitions in `Rules`. Then a rule is chosen nondeterministically with `ChooseRule` and `Parse` is called recursively.

This structure is typical of interpreters. They examine the input and decide what to do depending on the input's syntax. They keep track of extra information (here, the arguments `S0` and `S`) to help do the work.

Dynamic choice points

The parser calls `ChooseRule` to choose a rule for a nonterminal. Using the **choice** statement, we could write `ChooseRule` as follows:

```
proc {ChooseRule Rs Goal Body}
   case Rs of nil then fail
   [] R|Rs2 then
      choice
         rule(Goal Body)={R}
      []
         {ChooseRule Rs2 Goal Body}
      end
   end
end
```

This definition creates a series of binary choice points, i.e., choice points with two alternatives. (Note that it calls the rule definition `R` to create a fresh rule instance.) There is another, more flexible and efficient way to write `ChooseRule`. Instead of using the **choice** statement, which implies a statically fixed number of choices, we use another operation, `Space.choose`, which works with any number of choices. `Space.choose` (which is called `Choose` in chapter 12) is part of the `Space` module, which defines operations on computation spaces. The curious reader can skip ahead to chapter 12 to find out more about them. But it is not necessary to understand computation spaces to understand `Space.choose`.

The call `I={Space.choose N}` creates a choice point with `N` alternatives and returns `I`, the alternative that is picked by the search strategy. `I` ranges from 1 to `N`. The number of alternatives can be calculated at run time, whereas in the **choice** statement it is statically known as part of the program's syntax. In fact, the **choice** statement is a linguistic abstraction that is implemented with `Space.choose`. Section 12.5 shows how it is done.

Meta-interpreters

Our interpreter is actually a special kind of interpreter called a meta-interpreter since it uses the relational model's unify operation directly to implement the grammar's unify operation. In general, any interpreter of L_2 that uses operations of L_1 directly to implement the same operations in L_2 is called a meta-interpreter. Writing meta-interpreters is a standard programming technique in languages whose primitive operations are complex. It avoids having to reimplement these operations and it is more efficient. A popular case is Prolog, which has unification and search as primitives. It is easy to explore extensions to Prolog by writing meta-interpreters.

9.6 Databases

A database is a collection of data that has a well-defined structure. Usually, it is assumed that the data are long-lived, in some loose sense, e.g., they survive independently of whether the applications or the computer itself is running. The latter property is often called persistence. In this section we will not be concerned about persistence.

There are many ways to organize the data in a database. One of the most popular ways is to consider the data as a set of relations, where a relation is a set of tuples. A database organized as a set of relations is called a relational database. For example, a graph can be defined by one relation, which is a set of tuples where each tuple represents one edge (see figure 9.9):

```
edge(1 2)   edge(2 1)   edge(2 3)   edge(3 4)
edge(2 5)   edge(5 6)   edge(4 6)   edge(6 7)
edge(6 8)   edge(1 5)   edge(5 1)
```

A relational database explicitly stores these tuples so that we can calculate with them. We can use the relational computation model of this chapter to do these calculations. Typical operations on a relational database are query (reading the data) and update (modifying the data):

- A query is more than just a simple read, but is a logical formula whose basic elements are the relations in the database. It is the role of the DBMS (database management system) to find all tuples that satisfy the formula.
- An update means to add information to the database. This information must be of the right kind and not disturb the organization of the database. The update is usually implemented as a transaction (see section 8.5).

This section touches on just a few parts of the area of databases. For more information, we refer the reader to the comprehensive introduction by Date [49].

Relational programming is well-suited for exploring the concepts of relational databases. There are several reasons for this:

- It places no restrictions on the logical form of the query. Even if the query is highly disjunctive (it has many choices), it will be computed correctly (albeit slowly).
- It allows experimentation with deductive databases. A deductive database is a database whose implementation can deduce additional tuples that are not explicitly stored. Typically, the deductive database allows defining new relations in terms of existing relations. No tuples are stored for these new relations, but they can be used just like any other relation.

The deep reason for these properties is that the relational computation model is a form of logic programming.

9.6.1 Defining a relation

Let us first define an abstraction to calculate with relations. For conciseness, we use object-oriented programming to define the abstraction as a class, `RelationClass`.

- A new relation is an instance of `RelationClass`, e.g., `Rel={New RelationClass init}` creates the initially empty relation `Rel`.
- The following operations are possible:
    - `{Rel assert(T)}` adds the tuple `T` to `Rel`. Assert can only be done outside

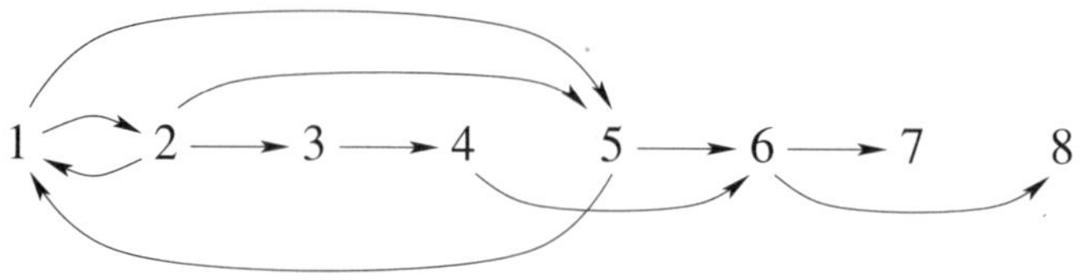

Figure 9.9: A simple graph.

a relational program.

- {Rel assertall(Ts)} adds the list of tuples Ts to Rel. Assertall can only be done outside a relational program.
- {Rel query(X)} binds X to one of the tuples in Rel. X can be any partial value. If more than one tuple is compatible with X, then search can enumerate all of them. Query can only be done inside a relational program.

These operations are similar to what a Prolog system provides. For example, assert is a limited version of Prolog's **assert/1** that can assert facts (i.e., tuples), not complete clauses. (The "/1" suffix means that it has one argument.) For the examples that follow, we assume that Rel has efficiency similar to a good Prolog implementation [101]. That is, the set of tuples is stored in a dictionary that indexes them on their first argument. This makes it possible to write efficient programs. Without this indexing, even simple lookups would need to do linear search. More sophisticated indexing is possible, but in practice first-argument indexing is often sufficient. Section 9.6.3 gives an implementation of RelationClass that does first-argument indexing.

9.6.2 Calculating with relations

An example relation

Let us show an example of this abstraction for doing calculations on graphs. We use the example graph of figure 9.9. We define this graph as two relations: a set of nodes and a set of edges. Here is the set of nodes:

```
NodeRel={New RelationClass init}
{NodeRel
 assertall([node(1) node(2) node(3) node(4)
            node(5) node(6) node(7) node(8)])}
```

The tuple node(1) represents the node 1. Here is the set of edges:

```
EdgeRel={New RelationClass init}
{EdgeRel
 assertall([edge(1 2) edge(2 1) edge(2 3) edge(3 4)
            edge(2 5) edge(5 6) edge(4 6) edge(6 7)
            edge(6 8) edge(1 5) edge(5 1)])}
```

The tuple `edge(1 2)` represents an edge from node 1 to node 2. We can query `NodeRel` or `EdgeRel` with the message `query`. Let us define the procedures `NodeP` and `EdgeP` to make this more concise:

```
proc {NodeP A} {NodeRel query(node(A))} end
proc {EdgeP A B} {EdgeRel query(edge(A B))} end
```

With these definitions of `NodeP` and `EdgeP` we can write relational programs.

Some queries

Let us start with a very simple query: what edges are connected to node 1? We define the query as a one-argument procedure:

```
proc {Q ?X} {EdgeP 1 X} end
```

This calls `EdgeP` with first argument 1. We calculate the results by using `Q` as argument to a search operation:

```
{Browse {SolveAll Q}}
```

This displays

```
[2 5]
```

Here is another query, which defines paths of length three whose nodes are in increasing order:

```
proc {Q2 ?X} A B C D in
   {EdgeP A B} A<B=true
   {EdgeP B C} B<C=true
   {EdgeP C D} C<D=true
   X=path(A B C D)
end
```

We list all paths that satisfy the query:

```
{Browse {SolveAll Q2}}
```

This displays

```
[path(3 4 6 7) path(3 4 6 8) path(2 3 4 6)
 path(2 5 6 7) path(2 5 6 8) path(1 2 3 4)
 path(1 2 5 6) path(1 5 6 7) path(1 5 6 8)]
```

The query `Q2` has two kinds of calls, generators (the calls to `EdgeP`) and testers (the conditions). Generators can return several results. Testers can only fail. For efficiency, it is a good idea to call the testers as early as possible, i.e., as soon as all their arguments are bound. In `Q2`, we put each tester immediately after the generator that binds its arguments.

```
proc {PathP ?A ?B ?Path}
   {NodeP A}
   {Path2P A B [A] Path}
end

proc {Path2P ?A ?B Trace ?Path}
   choice
      A=B
      Path={Reverse Trace}
   [] C in
      {EdgeP A C}
      {Member C Trace}=false
      {Path2P C B C|Trace Path}
   end
end
```

Figure 9.10: Paths in a graph.

Paths in a graph

Let us do a more realistic calculation. We will calculate the paths in our example graph. This is an example of a deductive database calculation, i.e., we will perform logical inferences on the database. We define a path as a sequence of nodes such that there is an edge between each node and its successor and no node occurs more than once. For example, `[1 2 5 6]` is a path in the graph defined by `EdgeP`. We can define path as a derived relation `PathP`, i.e., a new relation defined in terms of `EdgeP`. Figure 9.10 shows the definition.

The relation `{PathP A B Path}` is true if `Path` is a path from `A` to `B`. `PathP` uses an auxiliary definition, `Path2P`, which has the extra argument `Trace`, the list of already-encountered nodes. `Trace` is used to avoid using the same node twice and also to accumulate the path. Let us look more closely at `Path2P`. It has two choices, each of which has a logical reading:

- In the first choice, `A=B`, which means the path is complete. In that case, the path is simply the reverse of `Trace`.
- In the second choice, we extend the path. We add an edge from `A` to another node `C`. The path from `A` to `B` consists of an edge from `A` to `C` and a path from `C` to `B`. We verify that the edge `C` is not in `Trace`.

The definition of `Path2P` is an example of logic programming: the logical definition of `Path2P` is used to perform an algorithmic calculation. Note that the definition of `Path2P` is written completely in the relational computation model. It is an interesting combination of deterministic and nondeterministic calculation: `EdgeP` and `Path2P` are both nondeterministic and the list operations `Reverse` and `Member` are both deterministic.

```
proc {Choose ?X Ys}
   choice   Ys=X|_
   [] Yr in Ys=_|Yr {Choose X Yr} end
end

class RelationClass
   attr d
   meth init
      d:={NewDictionary}
   end
   meth assertall(Is)
      for I in Is do {self assert(I)} end
   end
   meth assert(I)
      if {IsDet I.1} then
         Is={Dictionary.condGet @d I.1 nil} in
         {Dictionary.put @d I.1 {Append Is [I]}}
      else
         raise databaseError(nonground(I)) end
      end
   end
   meth query(I)
      if {IsDet I} andthen {IsDet I.1} then
         {Choose I {Dictionary.condGet @d I.1 nil}}
      else
         {Choose I {Flatten {Dictionary.items @d}}}
      end
   end
end
```

Figure 9.11: Implementing relations (with first-argument indexing).

9.6.3 Implementing relations

Figure 9.11 shows the implementation of `RelationClass`. It is quite simple: it uses a dictionary to store the tuples and the **`choice`** statement to enumerate query results. The choice is done in the procedure `Choose`, which successively chooses all elements of a list. First-argument indexing is a performance optimization. It is implemented by using a new operation, `IsDet`, to check whether the argument is bound or unbound. If the first argument is unbound, then all tuples are possible results. If the first argument is bound, then we can use it as an index into a much smaller set of possible tuples.

⟨s⟩ ::=	
skip	Empty statement
| ⟨s⟩$_1$ ⟨s⟩$_2$	Statement sequence
| **local** ⟨x⟩ **in** ⟨s⟩ **end**	Variable creation
| ⟨x⟩$_1$=⟨x⟩$_2$	Variable-variable binding
| ⟨x⟩=⟨v⟩	Value creation
| **if** ⟨x⟩ **then** ⟨s⟩$_1$ **else** ⟨s⟩$_2$ **end**	Conditional
| **case** ⟨x⟩ **of** ⟨pattern⟩ **then** ⟨s⟩$_1$ **else** ⟨s⟩$_2$ **end**	Pattern matching
| {⟨x⟩ ⟨y⟩$_1$ ⋯ ⟨y⟩$_n$}	Procedure application
| **choice** ⟨s⟩$_1$ [] ⋯ [] ⟨s⟩$_n$ **end**	Choice
| **fail**	Failure
| {NewName ⟨x⟩}	Name creation
| {IsDet ⟨x⟩ ⟨y⟩}	**Boundness test**
| {NewCell ⟨x⟩ ⟨y⟩}	Cell creation
| {Exchange ⟨x⟩ ⟨y⟩ ⟨z⟩}	Cell exchange

Table 9.3: The extended relational kernel language.

Extended relational computation model

The implementation in figure 9.11 extends the relational computation model in two ways: it uses stateful dictionaries (i.e., explicit state) and the operation `IsDet`.[2] This is a general observation: to implement useful relational abstractions, we need state (for modularity) and the ability to detect whether a variable is still unbound or not (for performance optimization). Table 9.3 shows the kernel language of this extended computation model. Because of encapsulated search, a running relational program can only read state, not modify it. The boolean function `{IsDet X}` returns true or false depending on whether `X` is not an unbound variable or is an unbound variable. A variable that is not unbound is called determined. `IsDet` corresponds exactly to the Prolog operation `nonvar(X)`.

9.7 The Prolog language

Despite many extensions and new ideas, Prolog is still the most popular language for practical logic programming [201]. This is partly because Prolog has a quite simple operational model that easily accommodates many extensions and partly because no consensus has yet been reached on a successor. The computation model of the "pure" subset of Prolog, i.e., Prolog minus its extralogical features, is exactly

2. Leaving aside exceptions, since they are only used for detecting erroneous programs.

the relational computation model.

Modern implementations of Prolog are efficient and provide rich functionality for application development (e.g., [101]). It is possible to compile Prolog with similar execution efficiency as C; the Aquarius and Parma systems are constructive proof of this [209, 215]. The successful series of conferences on "Practical Applications of Prolog" is witness to the usefulness of Prolog in industry. For information on the history of Prolog and its implementation technology, see [45, 216].

Prolog is generally used in application areas in which complex symbolic manipulations are needed, such as expert systems, specialized language translators, program generation, data transformation, knowledge processing, deductive databases, and theorem proving. There are two application areas in which Prolog is still predominant over other languages: natural language processing and constraint programming. The latter in particular has matured from being a subfield of logic programming into being a field in its own right, with conferences, practical systems, and industrial applications.

Prolog has many advantages for such applications. The bulk of programming can be done cleanly in its pure declarative subset. Programs are concise due to the expressiveness of unification and the term notation. Memory management is dynamic and implicit. Powerful primitives exist for useful nondeclarative operations. The `call/1` operation provides a form of higher-orderness (first-class procedures, but without lexical scoping). The `setof/3` provides a form of encapsulated search that can be used as a database query language. The arity of a Prolog operation, i.e., its number of arguments, is traditionally given as a suffix of the form `/N` where `N` is a non-negative integer.

The two programming styles

Logic programming languages have traditionally been used in two very different ways:

- For algorithmic problems, i.e., for which efficient algorithms are known. Most applications written in Prolog, including expert systems, are of this kind.
- For search problems, i.e., for which efficient algorithms are not known, but that can be solved with search. For example, combinatoric optimization or theorem proving. Most applications in constraint programming are of this kind.

Prolog was originally designed as a compromise between these two styles. It provides backtracking execution, which is just built-in depth-first search. This compromise is not ideal. For algorithmic problems the search is not necessary. For search problems the search is not good enough. This problem has been recognized to some extent since the original conception of the language in 1972. The first satisfactory solution, encapsulated search, was given by AKL (Andorra Kernel Language) in 1990 [81, 104]. The unified model of the book simplifies and generalizes the AKL solution (see chapter 12).

9.7.1 Computation model

The Prolog computation model has a layered structure with three levels:

1. The first level is a simple theorem prover that uses Horn clauses and that executes with SLDNF resolution [132]. The acronym SLDNF has a long history; it means approximately "selection in linear resolution for definite clauses, augmented by negation as failure." It defines a theorem prover that does backward chaining, i.e., it starts with the query to be proved and works backward one step at a time. With an axiom in the form of a Horn clause

$$\forall x_1, \ldots, x_k \ . \ \langle \mathsf{a} \rangle_1 \wedge \cdots \wedge \langle \mathsf{a} \rangle_n \rightarrow \langle \mathsf{a} \rangle$$

this means that to prove the query $\langle \mathsf{a} \rangle$ we first try to prove $\langle \mathsf{a} \rangle_1$, ..., $\langle \mathsf{a} \rangle_n$. For each $\langle \mathsf{a} \rangle_i$ that is not itself an axiom, we repeat the process. This executes very much like the relational computation model, where proving $\langle \mathsf{a} \rangle$ corresponds to calling the procedure $\langle \mathsf{a} \rangle$ and choosing the right axiom for $\langle \mathsf{a} \rangle$ corresponds to executing a **`choice`** statement. The theorem prover implements negation by using a simple strategy called negation as failure: if trying to prove the atom $\langle \mathsf{a} \rangle$ fails finitely, then deduce $\neg\langle \mathsf{a} \rangle$. Finite failure means that the search tree (defined in section 9.1.2) has only a finite number of leaves (no infinite loops) and all are failed. This can easily be detected in the relational model: it means simply that `Solve` finds no solutions and does not loop. Negation as failure is incomplete: if the theorem prover loops indefinitely or blocks trying to prove $\langle \mathsf{a} \rangle$, then we cannot deduce anything.

2. The second level consists of a series of extralogical features that are used to modify and extend the resolution-based theorem prover. These features consist of the `freeze/2` operation (giving data-driven execution, implemented with coroutining), the `bagof/3` and `setof/3` operations (giving aggregate operations similar to database querying), the `call/1` operation (giving a limited form of higher-order programming), the cut operation "`!`" (used to prune search), and the `var/1` and `nonvar/1` operations (also used to prune search).

3. The third level consists of the `assert/1` and `retract/1` operations, which provide explicit state. This is important for program design and modularity.

The Prolog computation model is the heart of a whole family of extensions. One of the most important extensions is constraint logic programming. It retains the sequential search strategy of Prolog, but extends it with new data structures and constraint-solving algorithms. See chapter 12 for more information.

There is a second family of computation models for logic programming, called concurrent logic programming. These are centered around the nondeterministic concurrent model, which is explained in section 5.8.1. This model allows writing logic programs for long-lived concurrent calculations that interact with each other and with the real world. This makes it possible to write operating systems.

In the late 1980s, the first deep synthesis of these two families was done by Maher and Saraswat, resulting in concurrent constraint programming [135, 182].

This model was first realized practically by Haridi and Janson [81, 104]. The general computation model of the book is a concurrent constraint model. For more information about the history of these ideas, we recommend [217].

Future developments

There are three major directions in the evolution of logic programming languages:

1. *Mercury*. An evolution of Prolog that is completely declarative, statically typed and moded, and higher-order. It focuses on the algorithmic programming style. It keeps the Horn clause syntax and global backtracking.

2. *Oz*. An evolution of Prolog and concurrent logic programming that cleanly separates the algorithmic and search programming styles. It also cleanly integrates logic programming with other computation models. It replaces the Horn clause syntax with a syntax that is closer to functional languages.

3. *Constraint programming*. An evolution of Prolog that consists of a set of constraint algorithms and ways to combine them to solve complex optimization problems. This focuses on the search programming style. Constraint techniques can be presented as libraries (e.g., ILOG Solver is a C++ library) or language extensions (e.g., SICStus Prolog and Oz).

9.7.2 Introduction to Prolog programming

Let us give a brief introduction to programming in Prolog. We start with a simple program and continue with a more typical program. We briefly explain how to write good programs, which have both a logical reading and execute efficiently. We conclude with a bigger program that shows Prolog at its best: constructing a KWIC (keyword in context) index. For more information on Prolog programming, we recommend one of many good textbooks, such as [25, 201].

A simple predicate

Let us once again define the factorial function, this time as a Prolog predicate.

```
factorial(0, 1).
factorial(N, F) :- N>0,
   N1 is N-1, factorial(N1, F1), F is N*F1.
```

A Prolog program consists of a set of predicates, where each predicate consists of a set of clauses. A predicate corresponds roughly to a function or procedure in other languages. Each clause, when considered by itself, should express a property of the predicate. This allows us to do purely logical reasoning about the program. The two clauses of `factorial/2` satisfy this requirement. Note that we identify the predicate by its name and its number of arguments.

A particularity of Prolog is that programs have the same syntax as terms, i.e., tuples in our terminology. This is reminiscent of Lisp and its descendants, which have the same property. The term syntax of Prolog is richer since it allows declaring new syntactic operators at run time.

The term syntax shows up clearly in Prolog's treatment of arithmetic. The second argument `N-1` of the predicate `is/2` is a term. The syntax `N-1` denotes a term with label `'-'` and two arguments `N` and 1. The predicate `is/2` interprets the term and does the subtraction.[3] This is why we have to use the extra variables `N1` and `F1`. Let us call the predicate with `N` bound and `F` unbound:

```
| ?- factorial(10, F).
```

(The notation `| ?-` is part of the Prolog system; it means that we are performing an interactive query.) This returns with `F` bound to 3628800. How is this answer obtained? The Prolog system considers the clauses as precise operational instructions on how to execute. When calling factorial, the system tries each clause in turn. If the clause head unifies with the caller, then the system executes the calls in the clause body from left to right. If the clause head does not unify or a body call fails, then the system backtracks (i.e., undoes all bindings done in the clause) and tries the next clause. If the last clause has been tried, then the whole predicate fails.

Calculating logically with lists

Factorial is a rather atypical Prolog predicate, since it does not use the power of unification or search. Let us define another predicate that is more in the spirit of the language, namely `sublist(L1, L2)`, which is true for lists `L1` and `L2` whenever `L1` occurs as a contiguous part of `L2`:

```
sublist(L1, L2) :- append(V, T, L2), append(H, L1, V).
```

Logically, this says "`L1` is a sublist of `L2` if there exist lists `H` and `T` such that appending together `H`, `L1`, and `T` gives `L2`." These variables do not need an explicit declaration; they are declared implicitly with a scope that covers the whole clause. The order of the `append/3` calls might seem strange, but it does not change the logical meaning. We will see later why this order is important. We define `append/3` as follows:

```
append([], L2, L2).
append([X|M1], L2, [X|M3]) :- append(M1, L2, M3).
```

In Prolog syntax, `[]` denotes the empty list `nil` and `[X|M1]` denotes the list pair `X|M1`. In the relational model of chapter 9, this program can be written as follows:

3. Most Prolog compilers examine the term at compile time and generate a sequence of instructions that does the arithmetic without constructing the term.

```
proc {Sublist L1 L2} H V T in
   {Append V T L2} {Append H L1 V}
end

proc {Append L1 L2 L3}
   choice
      L1=nil  L3=L2
   [] X M1 M3 in
      L1=X|M1 L3=X|M3 {Append M1 L2 M3}
   end
end
```

Each clause is an alternative in a **choice** statement. All the local variables in the clause bodies are declared explicitly.

There are many ways that `sublist/2` can execute, depending on which arguments are instantiated when it is called. Some of these will be efficient; others may go into infinite loops. Let us execute the call:

```
| ?- sublist(L1, [a,b]).
```

Note that list elements are separated by commas in Prolog. We can execute this in the relational model as follows:

```
{Browse {SolveAll proc {$ X} {Sublist X [a b]} end}}
```

This displays a list of six solutions:

```
[nil [a] nil [a b] [b] nil]
```

These are the same solutions in the same order as would be calculated by a Prolog system. Why are the solutions returned in this order? Why is `nil` returned three times? Trace through the execution of the program to find out.

The order of the `append/3` calls in the definition of `sublist/2` might seem strange. The following definition is more intuitive:

```
sublist(L1, L2) :- append(H, L1, V), append(V, T, L2).
```

That is, we first append `H` and `L1` to get `V`, and then we append `V` and `T` to get `L2`. What happens if we execute `sublist(L1, [a,b])` with this definition?

From this example, we can see that programming solely by reasoning about the logic can lead to inefficient programs. To get efficiency, we have to take the execution order into account. The art of programming in Prolog is to write definitions that are both logical and efficient [158, 201]. Let us see how to achieve this.

How to write Prolog programs

One way to write good Prolog programs is to follow these three steps:

1. Write the program as if it were a statement in pure logic. The resulting program is logically correct but it might be inefficient or go into an infinite loop as a result of Prolog's depth-first search strategy.

2. Rewrite (part of) the program for efficiency, taking care not to break the logical semantics. This step introduces algorithmic knowledge into the program's logic. The program remains purely logical, however. In the case of `sublist/2`, changing the order of the `append/3` calls changes efficiency but does not change the logical meaning. The best order is the one in which the `append/3` with fewest solutions comes first.

3. Add extralogical operations where they are needed. These operations are needed for various reasons, such as efficiency, adjusting execution order, modularity, or parameterizing the program. They should be used in a disciplined way, so that the logical view holds as much as possible.

Let us look again at `factorial/2` in the light of this methodology. It needs to be rewritten slightly for efficiency reasons. As it stands, if the first clause is chosen, then the system might still store information allowing backtracking to the second clause.[4] To avoid this inefficiency, we add a pruning operator called "cut" (written as "`!`"). Executing a cut commits to the current clause, by discarding the information needed to backtrack. This gives the following definition:

```
factorial(0, F) :- !, F=1.
factorial(N, F) :- N>0,
   N1 is N-1, factorial(N1, F1), F is N*F1.
```

Note that the cut is placed exactly at the earliest moment that we know the current clause is correct, and any output variables are bound after it. A cut placed in this way does not change the logical semantics; it is called a blue cut (see section 9.7.3 below).

For programs that do complex symbolic manipulations (such as compilers, interpreters, database managers, parsers, and other data processors), this methodology is quite practical. The logical view is usually much easier to understand. Things get complicated only when we try to deduce exactly when the operations are done.

A bigger program

To finish our introduction to Prolog, let us look at a Prolog program that is logical, efficient, and does useful work. The program takes a list of article titles and calculates a KWIC index for them. The program is a modified version of an original from The Art of Prolog [201]. It uses unification, backtracking, and the aggregate operation `setof/3`.

---

4. Whether or not it does so depends on the sophistication of the compiler. Many Prolog compilers index only on the first argument of a predicate and do not look inside clause bodies.

```
kwic(T, K) :-
   setof(Ys, Xs^(member(Xs,T),rotFilter(Xs,Ys)), K).

rotFilter(Xs, Ys) :-
   append(As, [Key|Bs], Xs),
   not insignificant(Key),
   append([Key|Bs], ['.'|As], Ys).

insignificant(a).   insignificant(the).
insignificant(in).  insignificant(of).

member(X, [X|_]).
member(X, [_|L]) :- member(X, L).
```

The predicate `rotFilter(Xs,Ys)` is true if `Ys` is a rotated version of `Xs` whose first element is a reasonable candidate to be a keyword (i.e., it is not insignificant). We translate this program as follows into the relational model:

```
proc {Kwic T K} B in
   {SolveAll
    proc {$ Ys} Xs in {Member Xs T} {RotFilter Xs Ys} end B}
   {Sort B fun {$ X Y} X.1<Y.1 end K}
end

proc {RotFilter Xs Ys}
As Key Bs in
   {Append As Key|Bs Xs}
   {Insignificant Key}=false
   {Append Key|Bs ´.´|As Ys}
end

fun {Insignificant Key}
   Key==a orelse Key==the orelse Key==´in´ orelse Key==´of´
end
```

We translate `setof/3` as an all-solutions search followed by a list sort. This translation is explained in section 9.7.3. We translate `insignificant/1` as a boolean function, which is more efficient than **choice** to express how it is used. We leave the translation of `member/2` up to the reader. Here is an example execution:

```
{Kwic [[the principle ´of´ relativity]
       [the design ´of´ everyday things]] K}
```

Browsing `K` displays

```
[[design ´of´ everyday things ´.´ the]
 [everyday things ´.´ the design ´of´]
 [principle ´of´ relativity ´.´ the]
 [relativity ´.´ the principle ´of´]
 [things ´.´ the design ´of´ everyday]]
```

Given a keyword, scanning this sorted list allows finding the title in which it is used. For more efficiency, we can put the titles in a dictionary indexed by the keywords:

```
D={NewDictionary}
for Key|Ys in K do D.Key:=Key|Ys end
```

If the dictionary is stateful, this lets us access the titles in constant time. If we use a dictionary, we can omit the `Sort` operation without affecting efficiency.

9.7.3 Translating Prolog into a relational program

We show how to translate any pure Prolog program into a relational program with the same logical semantics and operational semantics. The translation is a purely syntactic one. Translating in the opposite direction is not possible because the declarative model is higher-order and compositional, which is not true of pure Prolog. We also show how to translate Prolog programs with cut (if they are properly written) and with `bagof/3` into relational programs. The `Queens` program of section 9.2.2 was originally written in Prolog. We translated it into the relational computation model using the rules of this section.

Translating pure Prolog

To translate a pure Prolog program to a relational program in the declarative model, follow these three rules for each of the program's predicates:

1. Translate deterministic predicates, i.e., those that do not do backtracking, into relational programs using **if** and **case** but not **choice**.

2. Translate nondeterministic predicates, i.e., those that are backtracked into, into procedures with **choice**. Each clause is one alternative of the **choice** statement.

3. If you have doubts whether the predicate is deterministic or nondeterministic, then your Prolog program may have a memory leak. This is because it may be accumulating choice points forever. We strongly suggest that you rewrite the predicate so that it is clearly deterministic or nondeterministic. If you do not or cannot do this, then translate it as if it were nondeterministic. The resulting relational program will have a memory leak if the Prolog program does.

Here are examples of a deterministic and a nondeterministic Prolog predicate, translated according to these rules. Consider the following deterministic Prolog predicate:

```
place_queens(0, _, _, _) :- !.
place_queens(I, Cs, Us, [_|Ds]) :-
   I>0, J is I-1,
   place_queens(J, Cs, [_|Us], Ds),
   place_queen(I, Cs, Us, Ds).
```

This predicate has a blue cut according to O'Keefe [158], i.e., the cut is needed to inform naive implementations that the predicate is deterministic, so they can improve efficiency, but it does not change the program's results. The `factorial/2` predicate of the previous section uses a blue cut. The predicate is translated as

```
proc {PlaceQueens N ?Cs ?Us ?Ds}
   if N==0 then skip
   elseif N>0 then Ds2 Us2=_|Us in
      Ds=_|Ds2
      {PlaceQueens N-1 Cs Us2 Ds2}
      {PlaceQueen N Cs Us Ds}
   else fail end
end
```

The following nondeterministic Prolog predicate:

```
placequeen(N, [N|_],   [N|_],   [N|_]).
placequeen(N, [_|Cs2], [_|Us2], [_|Ds2]) :-
   placequeen(N, Cs2, Us2, Ds2).
```

is translated as

```
proc {PlaceQueen N ?Cs ?Us ?Ds}
   choice N|_   =Cs N|_   =Us N|_   =Ds
   []       _|Cs2=Cs _|Us2=Us _|Ds2=Ds in
      {PlaceQueen N Cs2 Us2 Ds2}
   end
end
```

In both examples, the logical semantics and the operational semantics of the Prolog and relational versions are identical.

The cut operation ("!")

If your Prolog program uses cut "!", then the translation to a relational program is often simple if the cut is a grue cut, i.e., a blue or green cut, as defined by O'Keefe [158]. A green cut removes irrelevant solutions. Grue cuts do not have any effect on logical semantics but they improve the program's efficiency. Let us translate the following predicate:

```
foo(X, Z) :- guard1(X, Y), !, body1(Y, Z).
foo(X, Z) :- guard2(X, Y), !, body2(Y, Z).
```

The guards must not bind any head variables. We say that the guards are quiet. It is good Prolog style to postpone binding head variables until after the cut. The translation has two cases, depending on whether the guards are deterministic or not. If a guard is deterministic (it has no **choice**), then write it as a deterministic boolean function. This gives the following simple translation:

```
proc {Foo X ?Z}
   if      Y in {Guard1 X Y} then {Body1 Y Z}
   elseif Y in {Guard2 X Y} then {Body2 Y Z}
   else fail end
end
```

If a guard is nondeterministic (it uses **choice**), then write it so that it has one input and one output argument, like this: `{Guard1 In Out}`. It should not bind the input argument. This gives the following translation:

```
proc {Foo X ?Z}
   case {SolveOne fun {$} {Guard1 X} end} of [Y] then
      {Body1 Y Z}
   elsecase {SolveOne fun {$} {Guard2 X} end} of [Y] then
      {Body2 Y Z}
   else fail then
end
```

If neither of these two cases apply to your Prolog program, e.g., either your guards bind head variables or you use cuts in other ways (i.e., as red cuts), then it likely does not have a logical semantics. A red cut prunes away logical solutions, i.e., it changes the logical semantics. A program with red cuts is defined only by its operational semantics. When that happens, the translation is not automatic. You will have to understand the program's operational semantics and use this knowledge to translate into an equivalent relational program.

The `bagof/3` *and* `setof/3` *predicates*

Prolog's `bagof/3` predicate corresponds to using `SolveAll` inside a relational program. Its extension `setof/3` sorts the result and removes duplicates. We show how to translate `bagof/3`; for `setof/3` it is straightforward to follow this with the `Sort` operation (see appendix B.5). Consider the following small biblical database (taken from [201]):

```
father(terach,  abraham).
father(terach,  nachor).
father(terach,  haran).
father(abraham, isaac).
father(haran,   lot).
father(haran,   milcah).
father(haran,   yiscah).
```

This can be written as follows as a relational program:

```
proc {Father ?F ?C}
   choice F=terach   C=abraham
   []     F=terach   C=nachor
   []     F=terach   C=haran
   []     F=abraham  C=isaac
   []     F=haran    C=lot
   []     F=haran    C=milcah
   []     F=haran    C=yiscah
   end
end
```

Calling `bagof/3` without existential quantification, e.g.:

```
children1(X, Kids) :- bagof(K, father(X,K), Kids).
```

is defined as follows with `SolveAll`:

```
proc {Children1 X ?Kids}
   {SolveAll proc {$ K} {Father X K} end Kids}
end
```

The `Children1` definition is deterministic; it assumes `X` is known and it returns `Kids`. To search over different values of `X` the following definition should be used instead:

```
proc {Children1 ?X ?Kids}
   {Father X _}
   {SolveAll proc {$ K} {Father X K} end Kids}
end
```

The call `{Father X _}` creates a choice point on `X`. The "_" is syntactic sugar for **local** X **in** X **end**, which is just a new variable with a very small scope.
Calling `bagof/3` with existential quantification, e.g.:

```
children2(Kids) :- bagof(K, X^father(X,K), Kids).
```

is defined as follows with `SolveAll`:

```
proc {Children2 ?Kids}
   {SolveAll proc {$ K} {Father _ K} end Kids}
end
```

The relational solution uses _ to add a new existentially scoped variable. The Prolog solution, on the other hand, introduces a new concept, namely the "existential quantifier" `X^`, which only has meaning in terms of `setof/3` and `bagof/3`. The fact that this notation denotes an existential quantifier is arbitrary. The relational solution introduces no new concepts. It really does existential quantification inside the search query.

In addition to doing all-solutions `bagof/3`, relational programs can do a lazy `bagof/3`, i.e., where each new solution is calculated on demand. Lazy `bagof/3` can be done by `Solve`, which returns a lazy list of solutions.

9.8 Exercises

1. *Natural language parsing and databases.* For this exercise, combine the techniques of sections 9.4 and 9.6 to build a natural language parser with a large vocabulary that can be updated at run time. In other words, write a natural language parser that uses a dynamic database.

2. *Parsing the EBNF syntax.* Section 9.5 shows how to write a generic parser that takes any definite clause grammar and returns a parser for that grammar. Unfortunately, the grammar has to be encoded as a data structure. This makes it harder to read than the usual EBNF (Extended Backus-Naur Form) syntax. For this exercise, write a parser that takes the grammar written in EBNF syntax and returns its encoding. In this way, the grammar input to the generic parser can be written in the usual EBNF syntax instead of encoded. As a first step, give an EBNF definition of the extended EBNF syntax itself.

3. *Flight planning.* This exercise uses the relation class implemented in section 9.6. FlyByNight airlines asks you to write a program that can plan flights for its passengers. We are given a database containing a set of facts of the form

```
data(City1 City2 Distance Connected)
```

The first two arguments represent a pair of cities served by FlyByNight airlines, the third argument is the great circle distance between the two cities, and the fourth argument is a boolean that is true if there is a direct flight between the two cities and false otherwise. For this exercise, do the following:

(a) Write a planner that, given a source city and a destination city, returns a path between the two cities that is noncircular, i.e., no city appears twice in the path. Define the planner as a function {`Plan City1 City2`} that returns a pair `Distance#Path`, where `Distance` is the total distance flown on the path from `City1` to `City2` and `Path` is a list of cities representing the path from `City1` to `City2`. The function should be nondeterministic so that `Solve` can use it to generate different plans.

(b) Use the above planner to compute the shortest path between two cities. Define a function {`BestPlan City1 City2`} that returns the shortest path.

(c) The implementation of `BestPlan` will enumerate all solutions to find the best one. This can be very costly in time. To reduce the time, we can use a heuristic called *best first*. Whenever we need to choose a city, we choose first a connected city that has the shortest direct distance to the destination. Define a function {`GoodPlan City1 City2`} that uses this heuristic.

4. *Scheduling.* This exercise is a problem of resource allocation, allocating workers to different shifts while satisfying a set of requirements. All information about the problem is stored as facts in database relations. We would like to schedule workers for a small departmental library. The library has a morning and an evening shift. For each shift we need two workers to shelve books and one worker to operate the checkout desk. For the morning shift we need a worker to catalog new items. This gives the following relation:

```
slot(WeekDay am cataloger 1)
slot(WeekDay Shift checkoutclerk 1)
slot(WeekDay Shift shelver 2)
```

where `WeekDay` is a member of {`mon`, `tue`, `wed`, `thu`, `fri`} and `Shift` is a member of {`am`, `pm`}. We have also a relation that explains when and how much each person can work, like this:

```
person(alice 6  8 2 [mon tue thu fri])
person(bob   7 10 2 [mon tue wed thu fri])
person(carol 3  5 1 [mon tue wed thu fri])
person(don   6  8 2 [mon tue wed])
person(ellen 0  2 1 [thu fri])
person(fred  7 10 2 [mon tue wed thu fri])
```

The second argument is the minimum number of desired shifts per week, the third argument is the maximum number of shifts, the fourth argument is the number of shifts per day the person can do, and the fifth argument the weekdays the person can work. Finally, we have a relation that gives each person's professional abilities:

```
job(cataloger [fred alice])
job(checkoutclerk [bob carol fred])
job(shelver [bob carol fred don ellen alice])
```

For this exercise, do the following:

(a) Design a program that computes an initial schedule as a set of facts of the form `assignment(WeekDay Shift Job Person)`. The schedule need not satisfy each person's minimum number of shifts per week, nor does it have to assign a job to each person.

(b) Improve the program to satisfy the minimum shift requirement.

(c) Improve the program so that each person has a job.

5. *Dynamic updating of database relations.* Prolog programs often perform non-declarative operations while backtracking, e.g., to print an output or assert a fact in a Prolog database. This allows search branches to learn from previous branches, which is useful in Prolog-style applications. This is not possible in the relational model of this chapter because search is encapsulated and runs in a different thread than the top-level computation. Communication only happens when a solution is found; the solution is added to the list of solutions output by `Solve`. This exercise extends the relational model to get the same effect as Prolog. We will use ports to communicate from inside an encapsulated search to a top-level computation. We add the following operation to a port:

```
{Port.sendRecv P X Y}
```

This adds the pair `X#Y` to `P`'s stream, where `X` is a message that is sent and `Y` is the reply to that message. For this to work from inside an encapsulated search, `X` should be a complete value and `Y` should be unbound. We give an example of how to use `Port.sendRecv` with encapsulated search. Consider first the following program:

```
L={SolveAll fun {$} choice 1 [] 2 [] 3 end end} {Browse L}
```

This displays the list `[1 2 3]`. We extend this program with `Port.sendRecv`:

```
declare S P={NewPort S}
thread for X#Y in S do {Browse p(X)} Y=unit end end
L={SolveAll fun {$}
   choice Y in {Port.sendRecv P 1 Y} {Wait Y} 1
   []     Y in {Port.sendRecv P 2 Y} {Wait Y} 2
   []     Y in {Port.sendRecv P 3 Y} {Wait Y} 3
   end end}
{Browse L}
```

This displays `p(1)`, `p(2)`, and `p(3)` in the browser during the search. For this exercise, use `Port.sendRecv` to extend the relation class of section 9.6 to allow asserting and retracting facts while a search is running. Extend the class by adding a database server and interface procedures that use `Port.sendRecv` to communicate information to the server.

6. *Planning with forward chaining.* For this exercise, we will design a simple block stacking robot that uses a forward chaining production system to plan its actions. A situation in the robot's world is described by a database of facts and goals. The robot reasons by using forward chaining on a set of rules of the form

Condition $\Rightarrow$ Action

The condition is a predicate on the database and the actions add or remove facts and goals from the database. The execution cycle is as follows:

(a) Find the set of rules whose condition is true with respect to the database.

(b) If the set is empty, then exit. Otherwise, select one rule using a conflict resolution strategy.

(c) Execute the action part of the selected rule.

This is called forward chaining since each rule builds on the consequences of previous rules. For this exercise, we will use a combination of the relation class of section 9.6 and a meta-interpreter similar to the one in section 9.5. Each rule is represented as a function that returns a pair of a condition and action. A condition is a sequence of database queries. An action is a sequence of adds and removes. The robot's goal is to stack boxes on top of each other. For example, a possible goal could be `g(stack([a b c d]))` (label `g` means this is a goal), which is a request to make a stack of blocks where `a` is on the floor and `d` is on top. A situation in the robot's world is described by a set of facts of the form `f(support(A B))` (label `f` means this is a fact), which states `B` is on top of `A`. A possible initial situation is

```
f(support(floor a))
f(support(floor b))
f(support(b c))
f(support(c d))
```

with the initial goal we gave before. For this exercise, write a program that tries to satisfy the goal using forward chaining. Use a simple conflict resolution strategy: select the first rule that matches. Figure 9.12 gives one possible rule database for the block stacking robot. Write all necessary code to implement the planner. Complete the rule database (if necessary) by adding rules so that it can solve the problem given above.

As a final point, we explain how negation works in the planner. Negation (`´not´`) is coded with negation as failure. For example,

```
´not´(fun {$} U in f(supports(X U)) end)
```

means $\neg\exists u.\mathtt{supports}(x,u)$. Note that x is free in this logical formula. It will be bound in the part of the condition before the negation. Negation as failure can now be implemented as follows. For each rule, first run `SolveAll` on the part of the condition before the negation, where the negation is `´not´(F)`. This finds a set of solutions, where each solution is simply a set of variable bindings. For each

```
rules(% If the goal is to put Y on X and X supports Y,
      % then remove that goal
      fun {$} X Y Xr in
         [g(stack(X|Y|Xr)) f(supports(X Y))] #
         [remove(g(stack(X|Y|Xr))) add(g(stack(Y|Xr)))]
      end
      % If the goal is to put Y on X and X and Y are free,
      % then put Y on top of X
      fun {$} X Y Z Xr in
         [g(stack(X|Y|Xr))
          ´not´(fun {$} U in f(supports(X U)) end)
          ´not´(fun {$} U in f(supports(Y U)) end)
          f(supports(Z Y))] #
         [remove(f(supports(Z Y))) add(f(supports(X Y)))
          remove(g(stack(X|Y|Xr))) add(g(stack(Y|Xr)))]
      end
      % If the goal is to put Y on X and X supports Z,
      % then create a new goal to move Z to the floor
      fun {$} X Y Xr Z in
         [g(stack(X|Y|Xr)) f(supports(X Z)) notEqual(Y Z)
          ´not´(fun {$} g(move(Z)) end)] #
         [add(g(move(Z)))]
      end
      fun {$} X Y Xr in
         [g(stack(_|X|Xr)) f(supports(X Y))
          ´not´(fun {$} g(move(Y)) end)] #
         [add(g(move(Y)))]
      end
      fun {$} X in
         [g(stack([X])) f(supports(floor X))
          ´not´(fun {$} U in f(supports(X U)) end)] #
         [remove(g(stack([X])))]
      end
      fun {$} X Y in
         [g(move(X)) f(supports(X Y))
          ´not´(fun {$} g(move(Y)) end)] #
         [add(g(move(Y)))]
      end
      fun {$} X Y in
         [g(move(X))
          ´not´(fun {$} U in f(supports(X U)) end)
          f(supports(Y X))] #
         [remove(f(supports(Y X))) add(f(supports(floor X)))
          remove(g(move(X)))]
      end)
```

Figure 9.12: Rule database for a block stacking robot.

solution, run `SolveAll` again for the query `F`. Keep only solutions for which this second `SolveAll` returns `nil`.

7. (advanced exercise) *Meta-interpreters and virtual machines.* Virtual machines achieve efficiency by executing virtual instructions directly on the underlying hardware (see section 2.1.2). Meta-interpreters achieve simplicity by executing interpreted operations directly by the underlying language (see section 9.5.4). For this exercise, compare and contrast these two approaches.

8. (research project) *Relational programming with state.* In the relational computation model of this chapter, explicit state that is created outside of a relational program can only be read, not modified, during the execution of the relational program. This restriction exists because of encapsulated search (see, e.g., [188, 190]). For this exercise, investigate how to remove this restriction while maintaining the desirable properties of the relational computation model, i.e., its simple logical semantics and efficient implementation.

9. (research project) *Relational programming and transactions.* A transaction can do an abort, which cancels the current calculation (see section 8.5). A relational program can do a fail, which says that the current calculation is wrong (see section 9.1). For this exercise, examine the relationship between abort and failure. In what cases can you give a transactional meaning to a relational program or a relational meaning to a transactional program? Can you design a computation model that combines the abilities of the transactional and relational models?

II SPECIALIZED COMPUTATION MODELS

10 Graphical User Interface Programming

Nowadays the growth of a graphic image can be divided into two sharply defined phases. The process begins with the search for a visual form that will interpret as clearly as possible one's train of thought. ... After this, to my great relief, there dawns the second phase, that is the making of the graphic print; for now the spirit can take its rest while the work is taken over by the hands.
– *The Graphic Work of M.C. Escher*, M.C. Escher (1898–1972)

This chapter shows a particularly simple and powerful way to do graphical user interface (GUI) programming. We combine the declarative model together with the shared-state concurrent model in an approach that takes advantage of the good properties of each model. To introduce the approach, let us first summarize the existing approaches:

- *Purely procedural.* The user interface is constructed by a sequence of graphics commands. These commands can be purely imperative, as in `tcl/tk`; object-oriented, as in the Java AWT (Abstract Window Toolkit) package or its extension, the Swing components; or even functional, as in Haskell fudgets. The object-oriented or functional style is preferable to an imperative style because it is easier to structure the graphics commands.
- *Purely declarative.* The user interface is constructed by choosing from a set of predefined possibilities. This is an example of descriptive declarativeness, as explained in section 3.1. A well-known example is HTML, the formatting language used for Web pages.
- *Using an interface builder.* The user interface is constructed manually by the developer, using a direct manipulation interface. A well-known example is Microsoft Visual Studio.

The procedural approach is expressive (anything at all can be done at run time) but is complex to use. The declarative approach is easy to use (a few simple declarations suffice to create an interface) but lacks expressiveness. The interface builder approach is easy to use and gives immediate feedback on the interface, but it lacks expressiveness and the interface is hard to change at run time. None of these approaches is satisfactory. In our view, this is because each is limited to a single computation model.

This chapter gives an approach to building GUIs that combines a declarative base together with a selected set of procedural concepts, including objects and threads. We provide a user interface toolkit that is both expressive and easy to use. In the context of the book, this has two goals:

- To present the ideas underlying a practical tool for GUI design that gives the user a high level of abstraction. It turns out that the combination of declarative and procedural techniques is particularly appropriate for GUI design.
- To give a realistic example that shows the advantages of programming with concepts instead of programming in models. We start from the declarative programming techniques of chapter 3 and add state and concurrency exactly where they are needed. This is a practical example of combining several computation models.

To a first approximation, our user interface specifications are just data structures, which can be calculated at run time. The declarative model makes it easy to calculate with symbolic data structures such as records and lists. This means that we can easily define and manipulate quite sophisticated user interfaces. For example:

- We build a context-sensitive clock widget that changes its shape and presentation depending on an external parameter, which is the window size. Other widgets and external parameters are just as easily programmed.
- We show how to generate user interfaces quickly, starting from program data. It requires just a few simple data structure manipulations.

The ideas in this chapter are embodied in the `QTk` module, which is part of the Mozart system. `QTk` is a full-featured GUI design tool based on the combined declarative/procedural approach [75, 76]. `QTk` ("Quick Tk") is implemented as a front end to the `tcl/tk` graphics package [159]. It has been used to build GUIs for real applications. All the examples we give can be run directly with `QTk`.

This chapter gives most of the key ideas underlying `QTk` but only shows a small fraction of the available widgets. The main idea we do not discuss is the concept of *alias*, which makes it possible to extend `QTk` with new widgets. Aliases are related to macros. For more information we refer the reader to the `QTk` documentation [74].

Structure of the chapter

The chapter consists of five sections:

- Section 10.1 introduces the basic concepts underlying declarative and procedural approaches and how we propose to combine them.
- Section 10.2 gives an introduction to the principles of `QTk` and how to use it to build user interfaces.
- Section 10.3 introduces the Prototyper, an interactive learning tool for `QTk` that is also a good example of a program that uses `QTk`.
- Section 10.4 gives four case studies to progressively illustrate different aspects of the approach: a simple progress monitor, a calendar widget, the automatic

generation of a user interface from a data set, and a context-sensitive clock.

- Section 10.5 says a few words about how QTk is implemented.

10.1 The declarative/procedural approach

What are the relative merits of the declarative and procedural approaches to specifying user interfaces? The trade-off is between expressiveness and manipulability:

- The declarative approach defines a set of possibilities for different attributes. The developer chooses among this set and defines a data structure that describes the interface. A purely declarative approach makes it easy to formally manipulate the user interface definitions, e.g., to translate raw data into a user interface or to change representations. However, the expressiveness is limited because it is only possible to express what the designers initially thought of.
- The procedural approach gives a set of primitive operations and the ability to write programs with them. These programs construct the interface. A purely procedural approach has no limits on expressiveness, since in its general form it defines a full-fledged programming language. However, this makes it harder to do formal manipulations on the user interface definitions, i.e., to calculate the user interface.

This trade-off is not a temporary state of affairs, to be solved by some ingenious new approach. It is a deep property of computation models. As a language becomes more expressive, its programs become less amenable to formal manipulation. This is illustrated by the halting problem.[1]

However, this trade-off is not as bad as it seems at first glance. It is still possible to define a model that is both manipulable and expressive. We can do it by combining the declarative and procedural approaches. We use the declarative approach in those areas where manipulability is important but a limited expressiveness is sufficient. We use the procedural approach for those areas where expressiveness is essential. To be precise, for each window we define four parts declaratively:

1. The static structure of the window as a set of nested widgets, where a widget is a primitive component of a graphical user interface.
2. The widget types.
3. The initial states of the widgets.
4. The resize behavior of the window, i.e., how the widgets change size and relative position when the window size changes.

1. Assume a language as expressive as a Turing machine, i.e., it is based on a general-purpose computer with potentially unbounded memory. Then the halting problem theorem states that it is impossible to write a program that, when given an input program, determines in finite time whether or not the input program will halt.

We define two parts procedurally:

1. Procedures that are executed when external events happen. These procedures are called actions. Events are external activities that are detected by the window.

2. Objects that can be called to change the interface in various ways. These objects are called handlers.

The complete definition of the interface is a nested record value with embedded procedures and objects. Since it is a record, all the declarative parts can be formally manipulated. Since it has procedures and objects, it can do arbitrary computations.

When designing a GUI, we recommend using the declarative approach as the primary approach, and to supplement it with procedural aspects to increase expressiveness exactly where it is needed. There is a standard for Web design, Dynamic HTML, that also makes it possible to combine the declarative and procedural approaches [69]. It uses character strings instead of records for the declarative part. It is not as tightly integrated with a programming language as the approach of this chapter. At the time of writing, the performance of the declarative part was not yet adequate to support the design approach we recommend.

10.2 Using the declarative/procedural approach

As much of the interface as possible is defined declaratively as record values. Records are a good choice for two reasons: they are very general data structures and it is easy to calculate with them. The GUI consists of a set of widgets, where each widget is specified by a record. Specifying a GUI is done not by defining a new language, but by using records in the existing language. Programming a complex GUI then becomes a simple matter of doing calculations with records and lists. Since both are strongly supported by the declarative model, these calculations are easy to specify and efficient.

10.2.1 Basic user interface elements

The GUI model of this chapter has five basic elements:

- *Windows and widgets.* A window is a rectangular area of the screen that contains a set of widgets arranged hierarchically according to a particular layout. A widget is a GUI primitive that is represented visually on the screen and that contains an interaction protocol, which defines its interactions with a human user. A widget is specified by a record, which gives its type, initial state, a reference to its handler, and some of the actions it can invoke (see below). An interaction protocol defines what information is displayed by the widget and what sequences of user commands and widget actions are acceptable.

- *Events and actions.* An event is a well-defined discrete interaction by the external world on the user interface. An event is defined by its type, the time at which it

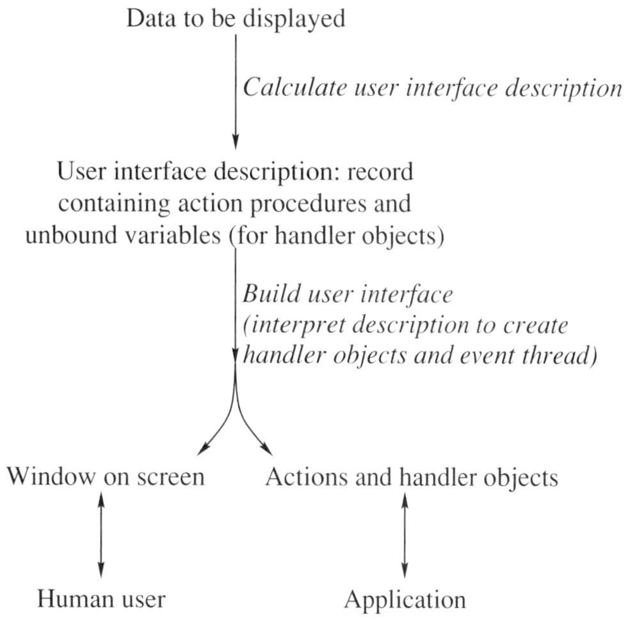

Figure 10.1: Building the GUI.

occurs, and possibly some additional information (such as the mouse coordinates). Events are not seen directly by the program, but only indirectly by means of actions. An event can trigger the invocation of an action. An action is a procedure that is invoked when a particular event occurs.

- *Handlers.* A handler is an object with which the program can control a widget. Each widget can have a corresponding handler.

10.2.2 Building the GUI

Figure 10.1 shows how a GUI is built. It starts with the data to be displayed. These data are manipulated to create a record data structure, the user interface description. This description defines the logical structure of the interface as a nested record. The record contains embedded action procedures and unbound variables which will become references to handler objects. The record is passed to a procedure `QTk.build`, which interprets it and builds the interface. `QTk.build` does two things.

- It builds a window using its underlying graphics package.
- It sets up an internal mechanism so that the application can interact with the window. For this, it creates one handler object per widget and one thread per window. It registers the action procedures with the widgets and the events they are triggered on. The action procedures are executed sequentially in the thread as window events arrive.

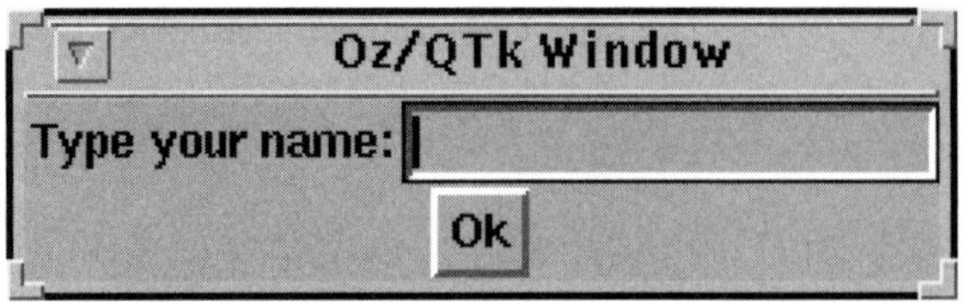

Figure 10.2: Simple text entry window.

```
fun {GetText A}
H T D W in
   D=td(lr(label(text:A) entry(handle:H))
        button(text:"Ok"
               action:proc {$} T={H get($)} {W close} end))
   W={QTk.build D}
   {W show} {W wait}
   T
end
```

Figure 10.3: Implementing the simple text entry window.

An example

The easiest way to see how this works is by means of an example. Here is a simple user interface description defined as a record:

```
D=button(text:"Click this button")
```

The record `D` defines a widget of `button` type and the content of the `text` field gives the initial text in the button. Other widgets follow the same conventions. The record label denotes the widget type, the field names denote widget parameters, and the field contents denote either the parameters' initial values or the procedural parts of the interface (actions or handlers).

Some widgets can contain other widgets. The complete user interface is therefore a nested record that defines all the widgets and their logical organization on the screen. For example, here is a simple interface for doing text entry (see figure 10.2):

```
D=td(lr(label(text:"Type your name:")
        entry(handle:H))
     button(text:"Ok" action:proc {$} {W close} end))
```

The `td` widget organizes its member widgets in top-down fashion. The `lr` widget is similar, but goes from left to right. This example has one action, **proc** `{$} {W close}` **end**, and one handle, `H`, which we explain later. At this point, both `H` and `W` are still unbound variables. We can now create the window by passing `D` to the `QTk.build` procedure. We must first install the `QTk` module:

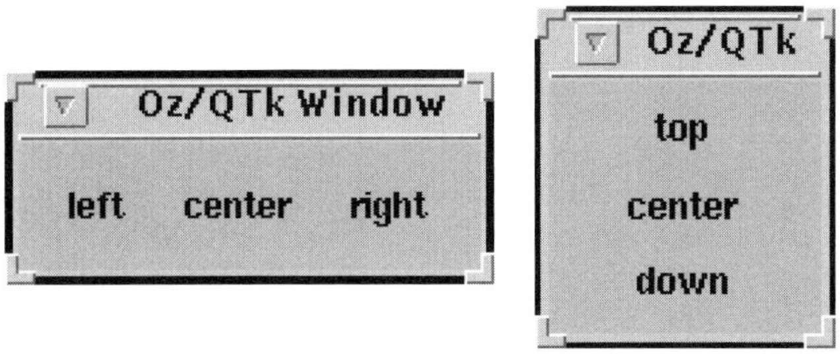

Figure 10.4: Windows generated with the `lr` and `td` widgets.

```
declare [QTk]={Module.link ["x-oz://system/wp/QTk.ozf"]}
```

This command is valid for Mozart 1.3.0; it loads and links `QTk` from the Mozart Standard Library. Now we can call `QTk.build`:

```
W={QTk.build D}
```

This creates a window, a window object `W` that represents it, and a handler object `H`. The top-level widget of `D` has a special status since it is the only widget that is directly in contact with the window itself. `QTk.build` therefore imposes the condition that the top-level widget must be `td` or `lr`. This is not a restriction since any widget can be nested inside `td` or `lr`. The window created by `QTk.build` is initially hidden. We can display it as follows:

```
{W show}
```

The user can type text in this window. At any time, the text in the window can be read by calling the handler `H`:

```
T={H get($)}
```

This is usually done when the window is closed. To make sure it is done when the window is closed, we can put it inside the action procedure.

To complete this example, let us encapsulate the whole user interface in a function called `GetText`. Figure 10.3 shows the resulting code. Calling `GetText` will wait until the user types a line of text and then return the text:

```
{Browse {GetText "Type your name:"}}
```

Note that `GetText` does a `{W wait}` call to wait until the window is closed before returning. Leaving out the wait makes `GetText` asynchronous, i.e., it returns immediately with an unbound variable that is bound later, when the user clicks the button.

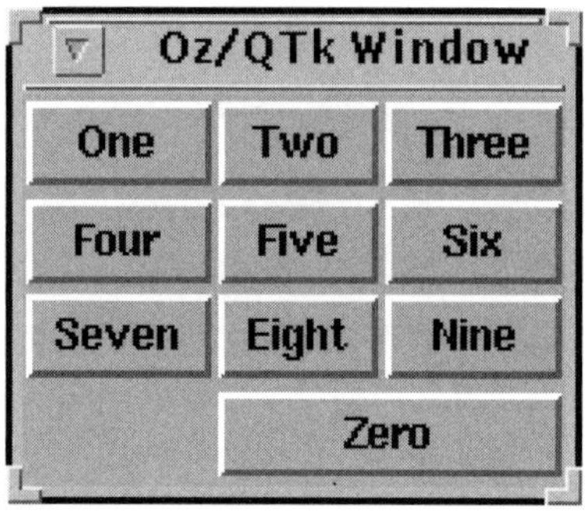

Figure 10.5: Window generated with `newline` and `continue` codes.

10.2.3 Declarative geometry

In addition to the widgets themselves, there are two other aspects of a window that are defined declaratively: the geometric arrangement of its widgets and the behavior of its widgets when the window is resized. We describe each in turn. The geometric arrangement of widgets is defined by means of three special widgets that can contain other widgets:

- The `lr` and `td` widgets arrange their member widgets left-to-right or top-down. Figure 10.4 shows the two windows that are displayed with the following two commands:

```
D=lr(label(text:"left")
     label(text:"center")
     label(text:"right"))
W1={QTk.build D}
{W1 show}
```

```
E=td(label(text:"top")
     label(text:"center")
     label(text:"down"))
W2={QTk.build E}
{W2 show}
```

- The `placeholder` widget defines a rectangular area in the window that can contain any other widget as long as the window exists. The placeholder's content can be changed at any time during execution. A placeholder may be put inside a placeholder, to any level of recursion. In the following example, the window alternatively contains a label and a pushbutton:

```
placeholder(handle:P)
...
{P set(label(text:"Hello"))}
...
{P set(button(text:"World"))}
```

Calling `{P set(D)}` is almost the same as calling `{QTk.build D}`, i.e., it interprets the nested record `D` and creates handler objects, but the visible effect is limited to the rectangular area of the placeholder widget.

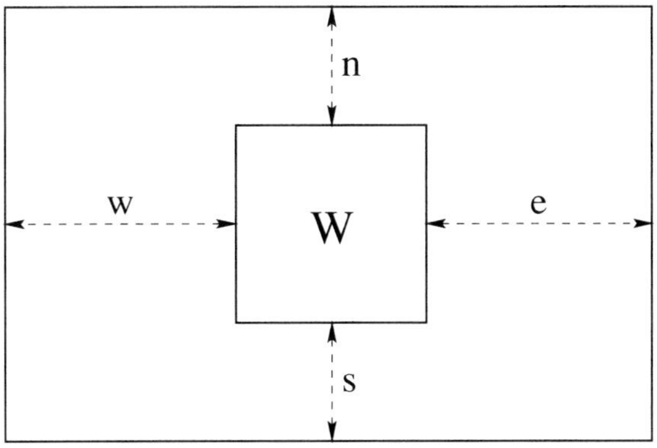

Figure 10.6: Declarative resize behavior.

■ The `lr` and `td` widgets support the special codes `newline`, `empty`, and `continue`, which allows their member widgets to be organized in a grid structure with aligned rows and columns of the same size (see figure 10.5). The code `newline` makes the subsequent contained widgets jump to a new row (for `lr`) or column (for `td`). All the widgets in the new row or column are aligned with the widgets in the previous row or column. The `empty` special code leaves an empty box the size of a widget. The `continue` special code lets the previous widget span over an additional box. The following description:

```
lr(button(text:"One" glue:we)
   button(text:"Two" glue:we)
   button(text:"Three" glue:we) newline
   button(text:"Four" glue:we)
   button(text:"Five" glue:we)
   button(text:"Six" glue:we) newline
   button(text:"Seven" glue:we)
   button(text:"Eight" glue:we)
   button(text:"Nine" glue:we) newline
   empty button(text:"Zero" glue:we) continue)
```

gives the window of figure 10.5.

10.2.4 Declarative resize behavior

When the size of a window is changed, the interface has to define how the internal widgets rearrange themselves. This is called the resize behavior. The resize behavior is dynamic, i.e., it defines a behavior over time. But it is a sufficiently restricted kind of dynamic behavior that we can define it using a descriptive declarative model.

We define the resize behavior of a widget by an optional "glue" parameter, whose value is an atom made up of any combination of the letters `n`, `s`, `w`, and `e`. The glue parameter places constraints on how the widget is placed and how it resizes. As

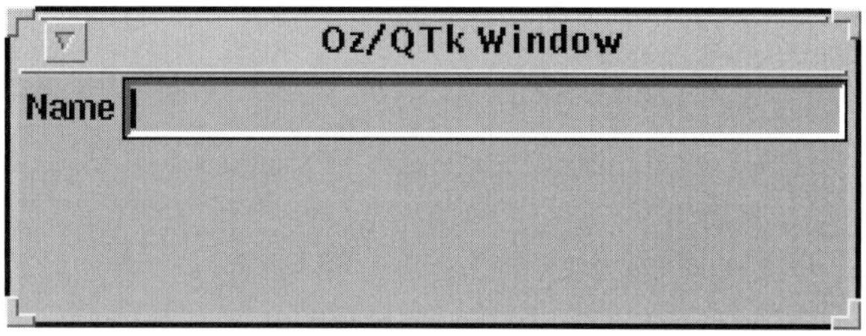

Figure 10.7: Window generated with the `glue` parameter.

figure 10.6 illustrates, a widget W is always placed inside a rectangular area and has a "natural" size defined by its contents. One can choose for the widget to occupy its natural size in either direction (horizontally or vertically) or to be expanded to take as much space as possible in either direction. For the left-to-right direction, the `w` value, when present, will attach the widget to the left side ("west"). The same for the `e` value ("east") and the right side. If `w` and `e` are present simultaneously, then the widget is expanded. Otherwise, it takes up just its natural size. For the top-down direction, the `n` and `s` values play the same roles ("north" and "south"). For example, the description

```
td(lr(label(text:"Name" glue:w) entry(glue:we) glue:nwe))
```

gives the window of figure 10.7. This example nests the `lr` widget inside a `td` widget. This is necessary because the top-level widget of the `QTk.build` description has an implicit glue parameter `nswe`. To use a widget with another glue parameter, such as `nwe` in this example, you have to nest it.

10.2.5 Dynamic behavior of widgets

The dynamic behavior of widgets is defined by means of action procedures and handler objects. Look again at the example of section 10.2.2:

```
declare E D W in
D=td(lr(label(text:"Type your name:")
        entry(handle:E))
     button(text:"Ok" action:toplevel#close))
W={QTk.build D}
{W show}
```

The action `toplevel#close` is part of the button; when the button is clicked, then this causes the window to be closed. Generally, actions are zero-argument procedures, except that shortcuts are given for a few common actions such as closing the window. The handle `E` is an object that allows control of the text entry widget. For example, here's how to set the value of the widget's text entry field:

```
{E set("Type here")}
```

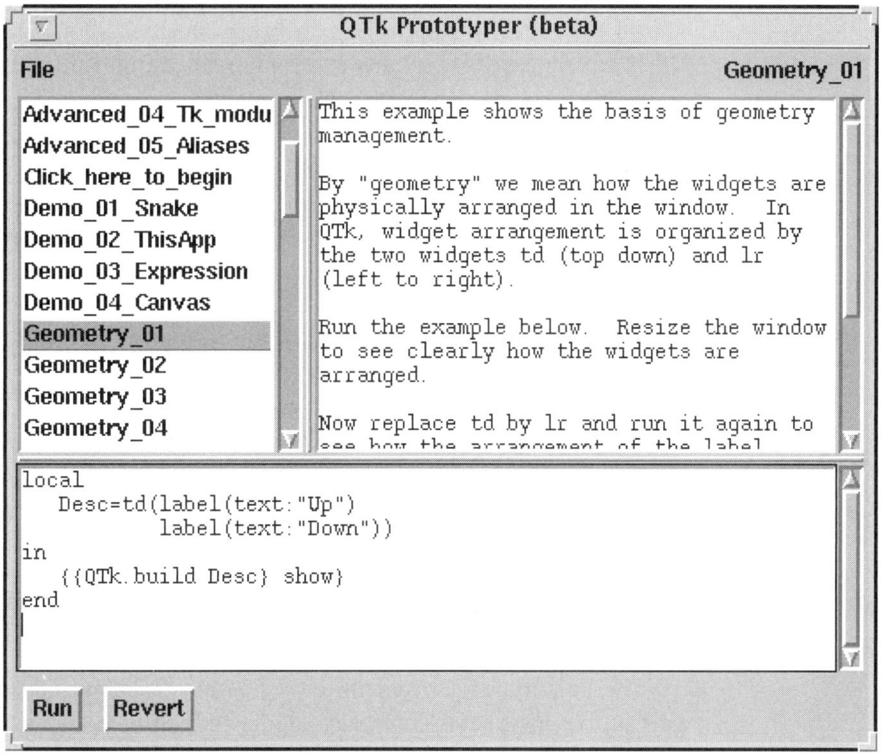

Figure 10.8: The Prototyper interactive learning tool for `QTk`.

Here is how to read and display the value of the field:

```
{Browse {E get($)}}
```

Actions can also be attached to events such as mouse clicks:

```
proc {P} {Browse 'clicked with third mouse button!'} end
{E bind(event:"<3>" action:P)}
```

The event `"<3>"` means a click of the third mouse button. Attaching it to `E` means that the button has to be clicked when the mouse is over `E`'s widget. A complete list of possible events is given in the `QTk` documentation in the Mozart system.

10.3 The Prototyper interactive learning tool

To learn `QTk`, we recommend using the Prototyper, a small but powerful application written by Donatien Grolaux that can be used as an interactive tutorial. Figure 10.8 gives a screenshot. The Prototyper consists of a single window with three panes. The top left pane gives a list of topics on various aspects of `QTk`, including geometry management, interaction, widgets, demos, and advanced topics. Click on a topic (e.g., Geometry_01) and the two other panes display information on the topic. The top right pane explains the topic and the bottom pane gives an editable Oz code fragment that illustrates the topic. Clicking on the `Run` button runs the code. Clicking on the `Revert` button reverts to the original code.

Because the code pane is editable, students can try out ideas and get immediate feedback. This feature is useful for programmers as well, to design user interfaces interactively. By changing the set of topics, the Prototyper could be used for learning other tools, for teaching programming, or even as a simple design tool.

One of the demos is the Prototyper code itself. Pressing `Run` opens a new Prototyper window, identical with the original one, and fully operational. One can recursively open many Prototyper windows by pressing Run in each previous window. An intrepid user could use this to understand the Prototyper's interface and explore any number of variations of the Prototyper itself.

The Prototyper can run user-defined code because it uses Mozart's first-class compiler, which is accessible through the `Compiler` module. Making the compiler accessible to users is a powerful pedagogical technique. Because of this, the Prototyper is more than just a toy that can only execute canned examples. On the contrary, it understands the complete Oz language, including not just `QTk` but everything else as well.

The Prototyper can be run either as a standalone application or started from within the interactive interface. The latter can be done as follows:

```
declare [P]={Module.link ["x-oz://system/wp/Prototyper.ozf"]}
{P.run}
```

Like `QTk` itself, the Prototyper is a compiled functor in the Mozart Standard Library.

10.4 Case studies

We present four case studies that show different techniques of user interface design:

- The first is a simple progress monitor. This example has no special features except to show how simple it is to build a custom display for a particular purpose.
- The second builds a simple calendar widget. It is based on an `lr` widget with gridding ability. It shows the flexibility of the gridding. It also shows how to use a placeholder and how state can be introduced to optimize execution of what is originally a purely declarative calculation.
- The third derives two different GUIs by transforming one data model into two GUI specifications. The user can switch between the two at any time. This shows the advantage of tightly integrating the GUI tool with the language, since different data models can be represented with the same data structures (e.g., records and lists) and transformed with the same operations.
- The fourth defines a clock with an interface that adapts itself according to an

```
fun {NewProgWindow CheckMsg}
   InfoHdl See={NewCell true}
   H D=td(title:"Progress monitor"
          label(text:nil handle:InfoHdl)
          checkbutton(
             text:CheckMsg handle:H init:true
             action:proc {$} See:={H get($)} end))
in
   {{QTk.build D} show}
   proc {$ Msg}
      if @See then {Delay 50} {InfoHdl set(text:Msg)} end
   end
end
```

Figure 10.9: A simple progress monitor.

external condition. The best view of the clock data is chosen dynamically depending on the window size. Because of the mixed declarative/procedural approach, each view can be completely defined in just a few lines of code.

The second through fourth case studies were originally written by Donatien Grolaux.

10.4.1 A simple progress monitor

We start by defining the simple interface that we used in section 5.6.1 to monitor the progress of a message-passing program. The interface has a checkbutton that can be enabled and disabled. Enabling and disabling this button is done concurrently with the monitored program. When enabled, the interface displays a message that can be updated dynamically. The program is slowed down so that each new message appears for at least 50 ms. When disabled, the interface freezes and lets the program run at full speed. This allows the progress of a running program to be monitored without unduly perturbing the program. Figure 10.9 shows the definition. Note that we have set the window title by using the `title` field of the top-level widget.

The Ping-Pong program of section 5.6.1 gives a screenshot of the progress monitor. Calling `InfoMsg={NewProgWindow Msg}` creates a new window with checkbutton message `Msg`. During program execution, `{InfoMsg Msg}` can be called as often as desired to display `Msg` in the window. With the checkbutton, the user can choose to track these calls or to freeze the display.

10.4.2 A simple calendar widget

The grid structure of section 10.2.3 can be used to build widgets with data arranged in rectangular form. We show how by building a simple calendar widget. Figure 10.10 shows what it looks like. We define the procedure `Calendar` that

Figure 10.10: A simple calendar widget.

returns the calendar widget and its display procedure:

```
proc {Calendar ?Cal ?Redraw}
P in
   Cal=placeholder(handle:P)
   proc {Redraw T}
      ...
      {P set(...)}
   end
end
```

The calendar widget is a placeholder that is updated by calling {Redraw T} with a time argument T. The redraw procedure should be called at least once a day to update the calendar. For simplicity, we will redraw the complete calendar each time.

Let us now see what is inside the Redraw procedure. It has a time argument T. Assume that the time has the format of the {OS.localTime} call, which is a record that looks like this:

```
time(hour:11 isDst:0 mDay:12 min:5 mon:11 sec:7
     wDay:2 yDay:346 year:100)
```

For the calendar we need only the fields wDay (weekday, 0 to 6, where 0 is Sunday), mDay (day of month, 1 to 31), mon (month, 0 to 11), and year (years since 1900).

The calendar is a rectangular grid of weekday names and day numbers. Redraw builds this grid by using an lr widget. We first make a list of all the calendar elements and use newline to go to the next line in the calendar. We start by defining the calendar's header:

```
Header=[label newline
        label(text:"Mo") label(text:"Tu") label(text:"We")
        label(text:"Th") label(text:"Fr") label(text:"Sa")
        label(text:"Su") newline
        lrline(glue:we) continue continue continue
        continue continue continue newline]
```

This displays the weekday names and underlines them. We now make a list that contains all calendar numbers. First, we calculate the number of days in the month, taking leap years into account[2]:

```
ML={List.nth [31
      if (T.year div 4)==0 then 29 else 28 end
      31 30 31 30 31 31 30 31 30 31] T.mon+1}
```

Second, we calculate the number of blank spots in the grid before the calendar day with number "1":

```
SD=(((7-(T.mDay mod 7))+T.wDay) mod 7)
```

With these two numbers, we can make a list of calendar days, correctly offset in the month:

```
fun {Loop Skip Col Nu}
   if Nu>ML then nil
   elseif Col==8 then
      newline|{Loop Skip 1 Nu}
   elseif Skip>0 then
      label|{Loop Skip-1 Col+1 Nu}
   elseif Nu==T.mDay then
      label(text:Nu bg:black fg:white)|{Loop 0 Col+1 Nu+1}
   else
      label(text:Nu)|{Loop 0 Col+1 Nu+1}
   end
end
R={Append Header {Loop SD 1 1}}
```

Here, `Col` gives the column (from 1 to 7) and `Nu` is today's day number. Finally, we can update the placeholder:

```
{P set({List.toTuple lr R})}
```

This completes the inside of `Redraw`. Let us now create and display a calendar:

```
declare Cal Redraw W in
{Calendar Cal Redraw}
W={QTk.build td(Cal title:"Calendar")}
{Redraw {OS.localTime}}
{W show}
```

The calendar can be redrawn at any time by calling `Redraw`.

2. This calculation is incomplete. As an exercise, correct the leap year calculation by using the complete rules for the Gregorian calendar: multiples of 4 are leap years; except for multiples of 100, which are not; except for multiples of 400, which are.

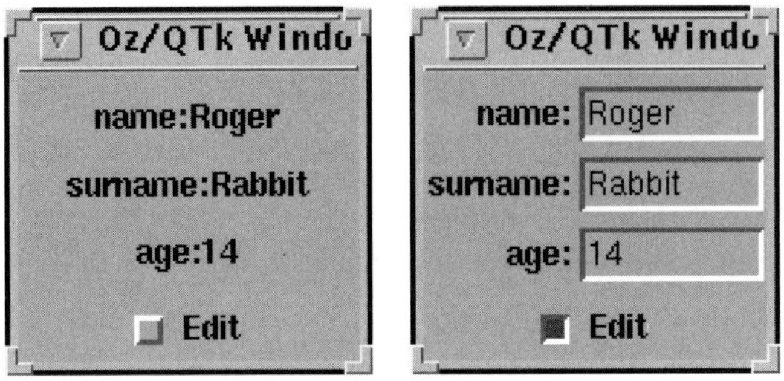

Figure 10.11: Dynamic generation of a user interface.

Memoization: using state to avoid repeating work

This redraw procedure will redraw the whole calendar each time it is called. For many clocks this will be once per second or once per minute. This is very wasteful of computational resources. We can avoid the repetitive redraw by storing the `yDay`, `year`, and `mon` fields together in a cell, and redrawing only if the content changes:

```
proc {Calendar ?Cal ?Redraw}
   P Date={NewCell r(yDay:0 year:0 mon:0)}
in
   Cal=placeholder(handle:P)
   proc {Redraw T}
      TOld=@Date
      TNew=r(yDay:T.yDay year:T.year mon:T.mon)
   in
      if TOld==TNew then skip
      else
         Date:=TNew
         ... % Recalculate and redisplay as before
      end
   end
end
```

If we leave out the final call to `P`, then the original `Redraw` procedure has a declarative implementation and the new `Redraw` procedure has a stateful implementation. Yet, both have identical behavior when viewed from the outside. The state is used just to memorize the previous calendar calculation so that the procedure can avoid doing the same calculation twice. Paraphrasing philosopher George Santayana, we can say this is remembering the past to avoid repeating it. This technique is called memoization. It is a common use of state. It is particularly nice because it is modular: the use of state is hidden inside the procedure (see section 6.7.2).

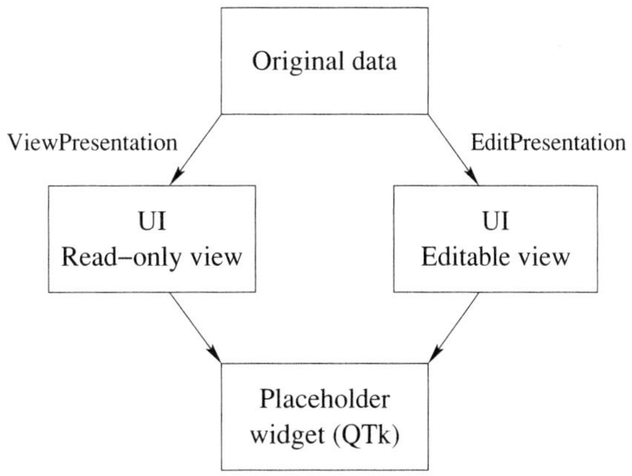

Figure 10.12: From the original data to the user interface.

10.4.3 Dynamic generation of a user interface

Using records to specify the user interface makes it possible to calculate the user interface directly from the data. This is a powerful technique that supports advanced approaches to GUI design. One such approach is model-based design. In this approach, different aspects of a GUI design are specified in separate formalisms called models. A running GUI is then obtained from all the models taken together [163]. Typical models include a domain model, a presentation model, a dialog model, a task model, a user model, a platform model, and a help model. These models can be represented within the language as data structures consisting of nested records and procedure values. From these records, it is possible to calculate `QTk` descriptions. It is particularly easy to translate the domain model into the presentation and dialog models, because the latter are directly supported by `QTk`.

The domain model is very similar to the application's data model. It defines the data entities that the user can manipulate. The presentation model is a representation of the visual, auditive, and other elements that the user interface offers to the users. The dialog model defines how the presentation model interacts with the user. It represents the actions that a user can initiate via the presentation elements and the responses of the application.

We give an example to show how one domain model can be dynamically mapped to two presentation models: a read-only view and an editable view of the data. The user can freely switch between the views by clicking a checkbutton (see figure 10.11). The mapping from the domain model to the presentation models is done in a natural way by means of functions, using declarative programming. There are two functions, `ViewPresentation` and `EditPresentation`, each of which calculates the `QTk` presentation model from the same original data (see figure 10.12). Both functions do dynamic record creation with `MakeRecord` and `Adjoin`. The presentation model is encapsulated in a common interface for the two views. A placeholder is used to

```
fun {ViewPresentation Data}
   Hdl In={NewCell Data}
   HR={MakeRecord hr {Map Data fun {$ D#_} D end}}
in
   r(spec: {Adjoin
            {List.toTuple td
             {Map Data fun {$ D#V}
              label(glue:we handle:HR.D text:D#":"#V) end}}
            td(glue:nswe handle:Hdl)}
     handle: Hdl
     set: proc {$ Ds}
             In:=Ds
             for D#V in Ds do {HR.D set(text:D#":"#V)} end
          end
     get: fun {$} @In end)
end
```

Figure 10.13: Defining the read-only presentation.

dynamically display one of the two views. Because of the common interface, keeping coherence between views is straightforward.

Let us write a simple example program to illustrate these ideas. We use a very simple domain model: a list of pairs of the form `identifier#value`, which represents the known information about some entity. The purpose of the GUI is to display or edit this information. We take the following example information:

```
Data=[name#"Roger"
      surname#"Rabbit"
      age#14]
```

Now let us define the two functions that translate this domain representation into the view information needed by `QTk`. The first function, `ViewPresentation`, builds the read-only view. It builds a representation where each pair `identifier#value` is mapped to a `label` widget whose text is the identifier followed by a colon ":" and the corresponding value. Figure 10.13 gives the source code. The function returns a record with four fields:

- Field `spec`: the interface specification, which describes the widget in `QTk` format.
- Field `handle`: the widget's handle, when the interface is created.
- Field `set`: a one-argument procedure that updates the information displayed by the widget. During execution, this lets us change the data that are displayed.
- Field `get`: a zero-argument function that returns the data that are displayed, in the same format as they were input. Since `ViewPresentation` does not change the data, this simply returns the last information that was set. (In `EditPresentation` it will return the new information that the user has typed.)

The `get` and `set` operations are used to keep coherence of the data when switching

```
fun {EditPresentation Data}
   Hdl Feats={Map Data fun {$ D#_} D end}
   HR={MakeRecord hr Feats}
   fun {Loop Ds}
      case Ds of D#V|Dr then
         label(glue:e text:D#":") |
         entry(handle:HR.D init:V glue:we) |
         newline | {Loop Dr}
      else nil end
   end
in
   r(spec: {Adjoin
            {List.toTuple lr {Loop Data}}
            lr(glue:nswe handle:Hdl)}
     handle: Hdl
     set: proc {$ Ds}
             for D#V in Ds do {HR.D set(V)} end end
     get: fun {$}
             {Map Feats fun {$ D} D#{HR.D get($)} end} end)
end
```

Figure 10.14: Defining the editable presentation.

between the two views. The HR record collects all the data items' handles, for the use of the get and set operations.

The second function, EditPresentation, builds the editable view. It builds a representation where each pair identifier#value is mapped to a label containing the identifier followed by ":" and an entry widget. Figure 10.14 gives the source code. This function also returns a record with four fields, like the ViewPresentation function. This time, the result of the get function is obtained from the widgets themselves.

The main application calls both of these functions on the same data. The main window contains a placeholder widget and a checkbox widget. Once the window is built, the specifications of both views are put in the placeholder widget. Subsequently they can be put back at any time by using just their handles. Checking or unchecking the checkbox switches between the two views. Data integrity between the views is maintained by using their associated set and get operations. Here is the source code:

Figure 10.15: Three views of FlexClock, a context-sensitive clock.

```
P C V1={ViewPresentation Data} V2={EditPresentation Data}
{{QTk.build
   td(placeholder(glue:nswe handle:P)
      checkbutton(text:"Edit" init:false handle:C
         action:
            proc {$}
              Old#New=if {C get($)} then V1#V2 else V2#V1 end
            in {New.set {Old.get}} {P set(New.handle)} end))}
 show}
{P set(V2.spec)} {P set(V1.spec)}
```

This example shows the advantages of tightly integrating an executable model-based GUI with an expressive programming language. The different models can all be expressed as data structures of the language. The mappings between the different models can then be done easily within the language.

10.4.4 A context-sensitive clock

This section defines a simple clock utility, FlexClock, that dynamically displays a different view depending on the size of the window. When the window is resized, the "best" view for the new size is chosen. The application defines six different views and takes about 100 lines of code. It dynamically chooses the best view among the six. The best view is the one that gives the most detailed time information in the available window size. Figure 10.15 shows three of the six views. A more elaborate version with sixteen views, an analog clock widget, and a calendar widget, is available as part of the Mozart demos.

Figure 10.16 shows the architecture of the clock. Each view consists of three parts: a refresh procedure, a widget definition, and a minimum size. A clock calls all the refresh procedures once a second with the current time. A view selector

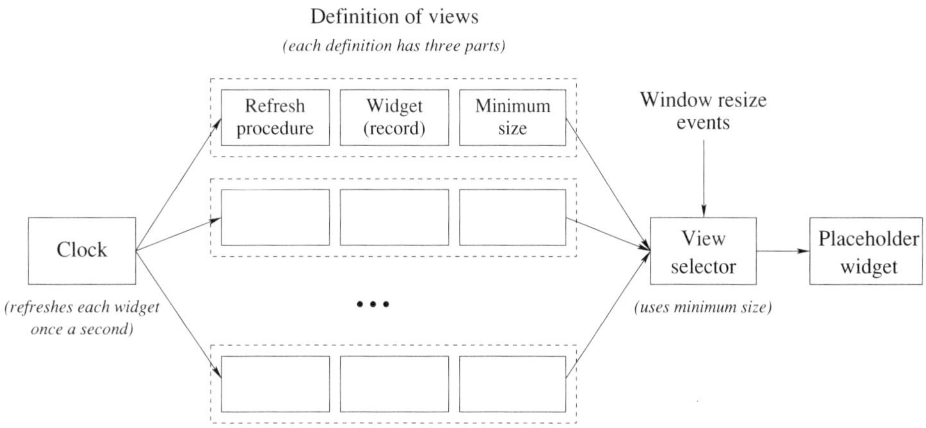

Figure 10.16: Architecture of the context-sensitive clock.

picks one of the views and puts it in a placeholder widget to display it. Each time the window is resized, i.e., whenever a resize event occurs, then the view selector chooses the best view and displays it. The refresh procedures and the view selector run concurrently. This is acceptable because there is no interference between them.

Let us implement the clock according to this architecture. We first set up a small server that periodically calls each procedure in a list of procedures:

```
NotifyClock
local
   Clocks={NewCell nil}
   proc {Loop}
   T={OS.localTime} in
      for I in @Clocks do {I T} end
      {Delay 1000} {Loop}
   end
in
   proc {NotifyClock P} Clocks:=P|@Clocks end
   thread {Loop} end
end
```

The period is almost exactly once per second.[3] Calling `{NotifyClock P}` adds `P` to the list of procedures to be notified. The refresh procedure of each view will be put in this list. The `OS.localTime` call returns a record that contains all the time information. To help in calculating the views, we define some utility functions to format the time information in various ways:

3. Section 4.6.2 explains how to do it exactly once per second.

```
fun {TwoPos I} if I<10 then "0"#I else I end end
fun {FmtTime T} {TwoPos T.hour}#":"#{TwoPos T.min} end
fun {FmtTimeS T} {FmtTime T}#":"#{TwoPos T.sec} end
fun {FmtDate T} {TwoPos T.mDay}#"/"#{TwoPos T.mon+1} end
fun {FmtDateY T} {FmtDate T}#"/"#(1900+T.year) end
fun {FmtDay T}
   {List.nth ["Sunday" "Monday" "Tuesday" "Wednesday"
              "Thursday" "Friday" "Saturday"] T.wDay+1} end
fun {FmtMonth T}
   {List.nth ["January" "February" "March" "April" "May" "June"
              "July" "August" "September" "October" "November"
              "December"] T.mon+1} end
```

Now we define each view as a record with three elements:

- Field `refresh`: a procedure that is called with a time argument to update the view's display.
- Field `spec`: a declarative specification of the widgets constituting the view.
- Field `surface`: the minimal size (horizontally and vertically) that is required to correctly display the view.

Figure 10.17 defines all six views in one list. Alert readers will notice that there is a seventh, empty view that will be displayed in case the window is too small to display a text. The window that displays a view contains just a single placeholder widget. A placeholder, as we saw before, is a container that can contain any widget and that can change the displayed widget at any time as long as the window exists. Here is the window:

```
declare P W in
W={QTk.build
   td(title:"FlexClock demo"
      placeholder(handle:P width:1 height:1 glue:nswe))}
```

To initialize the application, all views are placed once in the placeholder. After this is done, any view can be displayed again in the placeholder by a single command using the view's handle. We also register each refresh procedure with `NotifyClock`. The result is a list, `Views`, that has one triple per view, containing the minimal width, minimal height, and a handle for the view:

```
Views={Map ViewList
       fun {$ R}
          Width#Height=R.surface
       in
          {P set(R.spec)}
          {NotifyClock R.refresh}
          Width#Height#(R.spec).handle
       end}
```

Now we have initialized the placeholder and registered all the refresh procedures. The next step is to set up the mechanism to calculate the best view and display it. We assume the best view is the one that satisfies the following three conditions:

- The window size is big enough to display the view, i.e., window width $\geq$ minimal

```
declare
H0 H1 H2 H3 H4 H5 H6
ViewList=
  [r(refresh:proc {$ T} skip end
     spec:label(handle:H0 glue:nswe bg:white)
     surface:0#0)

   r(refresh:proc {$ T} {H1 set(text:{FmtTime T})} end
     spec:label(handle:H1 glue:nswe bg:white)
     surface:40#10)

   r(refresh:proc {$ T} {H2 set(text:{FmtTimeS T})} end
     spec:label(handle:H2 glue:nswe bg:white)
     surface:80#10)

   r(refresh:
        proc {$ T}
           {H3 set(text:{FmtTime T}#'\n'#{FmtDate T})} end
     spec:label(handle:H3 glue:nswe bg:white)
     surface:40#30)

   r(refresh:
        proc {$ T}
           {H4 set(text:{FmtTimeS T}#'\n'#{FmtDateY T})}
        end
     spec:label(handle:H4 glue:nswe bg:white)
     surface:80#30)

   r(refresh:
        proc {$ T}
           {H5 set(text:{FmtTimeS T}#'\n'#{FmtDay T}#", "#
                         {FmtDateY T})} end
     spec:label(handle:H5 glue:nswe bg:white)
     surface:130#30)

   r(refresh:
        proc {$ T}
           {H6 set(text:{FmtTimeS T}#'\n'#{FmtDay T}#", "#
              T.mDay#" "#{FmtMonth T}#" "#(1900+T.year))}
        end
     spec:label(handle:H6 glue:nswe bg:white)
     surface:180#30)]
```

Figure 10.17: View definitions for the context-sensitive clock.

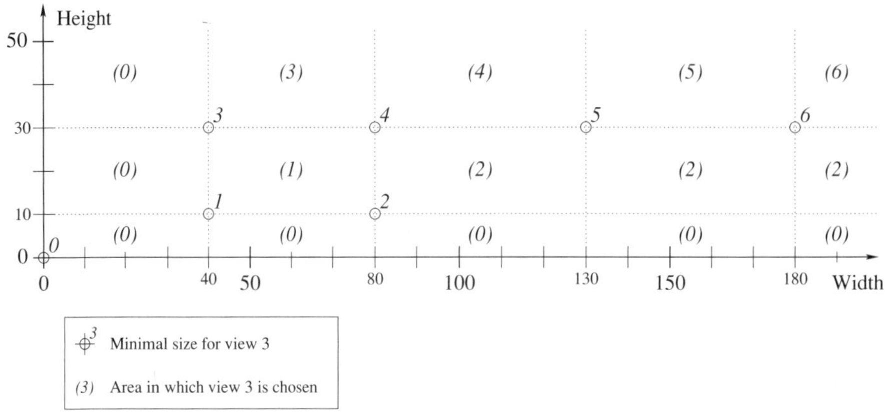

Figure 10.18: The best view for any size clock window.

view width and window height ≥ minimal view height.

- The distance between the bottom right corner of the minimal view and the bottom right corner of the window is minimized. It suffices to minimize the square of this distance.
- If no view satisfies the above two conditions, the smallest view is chosen by default.

Figure 10.18 shows how this divides up the plane among the seven views. The procedure `Place` does the calculation and displays the best view in the placeholder:

```
proc {Place}
   WW={QTk.wInfo width(P)}
   WH={QTk.wInfo height(P)}
   _#Handle={List.foldRInd Views
             fun {$ I W#H#Handle Min#CH}
                This=(W-WW)*(W-WW)+(H-WH)*(H-WH)
             in
                if W<WW andthen H<WH andthen
                   (Min==inf orelse This<Min) then This#Handle
                else Min#CH end
             end
             inf#local (_#_#H)|_=Views in H end}
in
   {P set(Handle)}
end
```

This starts with a minimum of `inf`, representing infinity, and is reduced for each view with a smaller distance. When the window is resized, `Place` has to be called to set the correct view according to the new size of the window. This is done by binding the **`<Configure>`** event of `QTk`:

```
{P bind(event:'<Configure>' action:Place)}
```

The window is now completely set up, but still hidden. We display it by calling `{W show}`.

10.5 Implementing the GUI tool

The GUI tool is implemented as three layers: a front end, a middle layer, and a back end. The front end is the `QTk` module, which is an interpreter for the declarative GUI specifications. The middle layer is the `Tk` module, which offers an object-oriented interface to the underlying graphics package. The front end and middle layer are both implemented in Oz. The back end is the graphics package, which is **tcl/tk** [159]. Mozart and **tcl/tk** run in separate OS processes.

When a specification is given to the interpreter by calling `QTk.build`, the interpreter builds the user interface by giving commands to the graphics package using a model that is almost completely procedural. The interpretation overhead is only paid once. The only overhead in the calls to the handler objects is the run-time type checking of their arguments.

The placeholder widget deserves a mention because a new widget can be put in it at any time during execution. When a widget is first put in, it is like calling `QTk.build`, i.e., there is an interpretation overhead. The placeholder reduces this overhead by caching the interpretation of each widget that is put in. To put a widget in a placeholder again, it suffices to put in the widget's handler. This is enough for the placeholder to identify which widget is meant.

10.6 Exercises

1. *Prototyper tool.* For this exercise, use the Prototyper of section 10.3 to learn `QTk`. Run the examples given and understand their behavior. Edit the examples and run them again to see the effects of your changes.

2. *Geometry management.* Consider the following three windows:

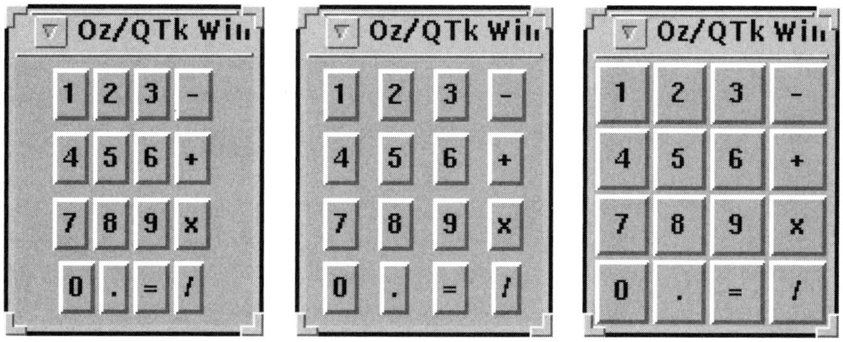

Note the alignment and relative sizes of the buttons in each of these windows, in both the horizontal and vertical directions. Using the `td` and `lr` widgets and the glue parameters, define descriptions to build precisely these windows.

3. *Calculator.* The action parameter of a button can be used to specify a procedure to execute when the user clicks the button.

- Extend one of the declarations above by adding a `label` widget that displays the text of each button when it is clicked.
- When the user clicks on several buttons in sequence, use one or more cells to store the number that this represents.
- Display this number in the `label` widget as it is being entered.
- Extend the program to implement a fully working calculator, i.e., interpret the other buttons (`-`, `+`, `x`, `/`, `.`, `=`) in the proper way.

4. *Events and handles.* Create a window containing a `label` widget and an `entry` widget. When the user inputs something into the `entry`, the `label` should immediately be updated to display the same information. In your solution, use events to trigger an update. To get the text of an `entry`, call the `get` method of its handle. To set the text of a `label`, call the `set` method of its handle.

5. *Dynamic generation of a user interface.* Functional programming is well adapted to transform one data structure into another. Define functions that transform this structured list:

```
[Item1#Value1 Item2#Value2 ... ItemN#ValueN]
```

into a record of the form

```
td(lr(label(text:Item1) entry(text:Value1))
   lr(label(text:Item2) entry(text:Value2))
   ...
   lr(label(text:ItemN) entry(text:ValueN)))
```

Do the same for a record of the form

```
lr(label(text:Item1) entry(init:Value1) newline
   label(text:Item2) entry(init:Value2) newline
   ...
   label(text:ItemN) entry(init:ValueN))
```

Now modify the previous solution so that if `ValueI` is an integer, then the record `numberentry(init:ValueI)` is generated instead of `entry(init:ValueI)`. Add glue parameters to make it look nice to the eye. Finally, add a fresh variable `VI` per entry as the handle parameter, e.g., giving `entry(init:ValueI handle:VI)`. Extend the function to return both the computed record and the list of all the fresh variables, in the same order as the input list. Call this function on the list

```
[name#"Roger" surname#"Rabbit" age#14]
```

The function returns a record `D` and a list of three variables `[V1 V2 V3]`. Build a window by calling `QTk.build`. The list of variables now becomes a list of handles. With these handles we can access any changes the user types in the window.

6. *Calendar widget.* Section 10.4.2 gives a formula for calculating the number of

blank spots in the grid before day 1. Why is this formula correct?

7. *Clock with calendar.* Extend the context-sensitive clock of section 10.4 with a calendar and add views so that the calendar is shown only when the window is big enough. You can use the calendar widget defined in the same section.

8. (research project) *Next-generation interfaces.* Apply the ideas of this chapter to human-computer interfaces in areas such as collaborative virtual environments and ubiquitous computing. Can the ideas be applied to three-dimensional or multimedia interfaces?

11 Distributed Programming

> The distant king of birds, the Simurgh, drops one of his splendid feathers somewhere in the middle of China; on learning of this, the other birds, tired of their present anarchy, decide to seek him. ... Thirty, made pure by their sufferings, reach the great peak of the Simurgh. At last they behold him; they realize that they are the Simurgh, and that the Simurgh is each of them and all of them.
> – *The Book of Imaginary Beings*, Jorge Luis Borges (1899–1986)

A distributed system is a set of computers that are linked together by a network. Distributed systems are ubiquitous in modern society. The canonical example of such a system, the Internet, has been growing exponentially ever since its inception in the late 1970s. The number of host computers that are part of it has been doubling each year since 1980. The question of how to program a distributed system is therefore of major importance.

This chapter shows one approach to programming a distributed system. For the rest of the chapter, we assume that each computer has an operating system that supports the concept of process and provides network communication. Programming a distributed system then means to write a program for each process such that all processes taken together implement the desired application. For the operating system, a process is a unit of concurrency. This means that if we abstract away from the fact that the application is spread over different processes, this is just a case of concurrent programming. Ideally, distributed programming would be just a kind of concurrent programming, and the techniques we have seen earlier in the book would still apply.

Distributed programming is complicated

Unfortunately, things are not so simple. Distributed programming is more complicated than concurrent programming for the following reasons:

- Each process has its own address space. Data cannot be transferred from one process to another without some translation.
- The network has limited performance. Typically, the basic network operations are many orders of magnitude slower than the basic operations inside one process. At the time of writing, network transfer time was measured in milliseconds, whereas

computational operations were done in nanoseconds or less. This enormous disparity is not projected to change in the foreseeable future.

- Some resources are localized. There are many resources that can only be used at one particular computer due to physical constraints. Localized resources are typically peripherals such as input/output (display screen, keyboard/mouse, file system, printer). They can be more subtle, such as a commercial application that can only be run on a particular computer because it is licensed there.
- The distributed system can fail partially. The system consists of many components that are only loosely connected. It might be that part of the network stops working or that some of the computers stop working.
- The distributed system is open. Independent users and computations cohabit the system. They share the system's resources and they may compete or collaborate. This gives rise to problems of security (protection against malicious intent) and naming (finding one another).

How do we manage this complexity? Let us attempt to use the principle of separation of concerns. According to this principle, we can divide the problem into an ideal case and a series of nonideal extensions. We give a solution for the ideal case and we show how to modify the solution to handle the extensions.

The network-transparency approach

In the ideal case, the network is fast, resources can be used everywhere, all computers are up and running, and all users trust one another. In this case there is a solution to the complexity problem: network transparency. That is, we implement the language so that a program will run correctly independently of how it is partitioned across the distributed system. The language has a distributed implementation to guarantee this property. Each language entity is implemented by one or more distribution protocols, which all are carefully designed to respect the language semantics. For example, the language could provide the concept of an object. An object can be implemented as a stationary object, which means that it resides on one process and other processes can invoke it with exactly the same syntax as if it were local. The behavior will be different in the nonlocal case (there will be a round trip of network messages), but this difference is invisible from the programmer's point of view.

Another possible distribution protocol for an object is the cached object. In this protocol, any process invoking the object will first cause the object to become local to it. From then on, all invocations from that process will be local ones (until some other process causes the object to move away). The point is that both stationary and cached objects have exactly the same behavior from the language point of view.

With network transparency, programming a distributed system becomes simple. We can reuse all the techniques of concurrent programming we saw throughout the book. All the complexity is hidden inside the language implementation. It provides all the distribution protocols. It translates data between the address spaces of the processes. Translating to serial form is called marshaling and translating back is called unmarshaling. The term serialization is also used. It does distributed garbage collection, i.e., not reclaiming a local entity if there is still some remote reference.

The idea of making a distributed language operation similar to a local language operation has a long history. The first implementation was the remote procedure call (RPC), done in the early 1980s [22]. A call to a remote procedure behaves in the same way, under ideal conditions, as a local procedure. Recently, the idea has been extended to object-oriented programming by allowing methods to be invoked remotely. This is called remote method invocation (RMI). This technique has been made popular by the Java programming language [206].

Beyond network transparency

Network transparency solves the problem in the ideal case. The next step is to handle the nonideal extensions. Handling all of them at the same time while keeping things simple is a research problem that is still unsolved. In this chapter we only show the tip of the iceberg of how it could be done. We give a practical introduction to each of the following extensions:

- *Network awareness* (i.e., performance). We show how choosing the distribution protocol allows tuning the performance without changing the correctness of the program.
- *Openness.* We show how independent computations can connect together. In this we are aided because Oz is a dynamically typed language: all type information is part of the language entities. This makes connecting independent computations relatively easy.
- *Localized resources.* We show how to package a computation into a component that knows what localized resources it needs. Installing this component in a process should connect it to these resources automatically. We already have a way to express this, using the concept of functor. A functor has an **`import`** declaration that lists what modules it needs. If resources are visible as modules, then we can use functors to solve the problem of linking to localized resources.
- *Failure detection.* We show how to detect partial failure in a way usable to the application program. The program can use this information to do fault confinement and possibly to repair the situation and continue working. While failure detection breaks transparency, doing it in the language allows building abstractions that hide the faults, e.g., using redundancy to implement fault tolerance. These abstractions, if desired, could be used to regain transparency.

This brief introduction leaves out many issues such as security, naming, resource management, and building fault-tolerance abstractions. But it gives a good overview of the general issues in the area of distributed programming.

Structure of the chapter

The chapter consists of the following parts:

- Sections 11.1 and 11.2 set the stage by giving a taxonomy of distributed systems and by explaining our distributed computation model.
- Sections 11.3 through 11.6 show how to program in this distribution model. We first show how to program with declarative data and then with state. We handle state separately because it involves more sophisticated and expensive distribution protocols. We then explain the concept of network awareness, which is important for performance reasons. Finally, we show some common distributed programming patterns.
- Section 11.7 explains the distributed protocols in more detail. It singles out two particularly interesting protocols, the mobile state protocol and the distributed binding protocol.
- Section 11.8 introduces partial failure. It explains and motivates the two failures we detect, permanent process failure and temporary network inactivity. It gives some simple programming techniques, including an abstraction to create resilient server objects.
- Section 11.9 briefly discusses the issue of security and how it affects writing distributed applications.
- Section 11.10 summarizes the chapter by giving a methodology of how to build distributed applications.

11.1 Taxonomy of distributed systems

This chapter is mainly about a quite general kind of distributed system, the open collaborative system. The techniques we give can also be used for other kinds of distributed systems, such as cluster computing. To explain why this is so, we give a taxonomy of distributed systems that situates the different models. Figure 11.1 shows four types of distributed system. For each type, there is a simple diagram to illustrate it. In these diagrams, circles are processors or computers, the rectangle is memory, and connecting lines are communication links (a network). The figure starts with a shared-memory multiprocessor, which is a computer that consists of several processors attached to a memory that is shared between all of them. Communication between processors is extremely fast; it suffices for one processor to write a memory cell and another to read it. Coordinating the processors, so that, e.g., they all agree to do the same operation at the same time, is efficient.

Small shared-memory multiprocessors with one to eight processors are commodity items. Larger scalable shared-memory cache-coherent multiprocessors are also available but are relatively expensive. A more popular solution is to connect a set of independent computers through their input/output (I/O) channels. Another pop-

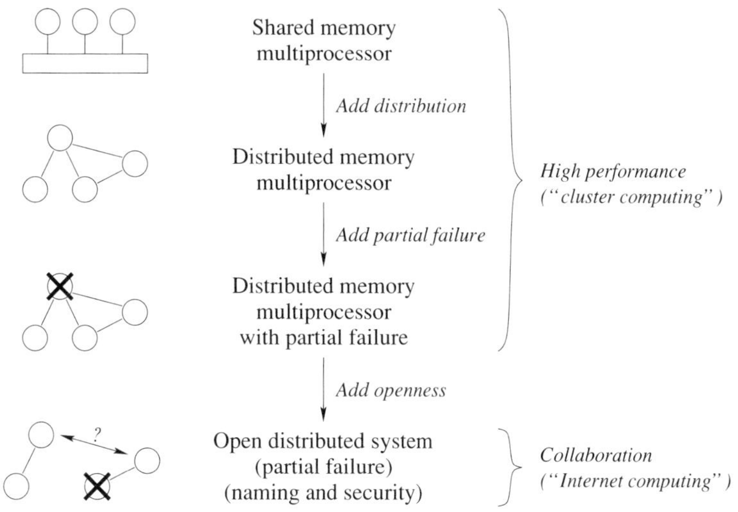

Figure 11.1: A simple taxonomy of distributed systems.

ular solution is to connect off-the-shelf computers with a high-speed network. The network can be implemented as a shared bus (similar to Ethernet) or be point-to-point (separately connecting pairs of processors). It can be custom or use standard LAN (local area network) technology. All such machines are usually called clusters or distributed-memory multiprocessors. They usually can have partial failure, i.e., where one processor fails while the others continue. In the figure, a failed computer is a circle crossed with a large X. With appropriate hardware and software the cluster can keep running, albeit with degraded performance, even if some processors are failed. That is, the probability $A(t)$ that the cluster can provide its service at a given instant of time t, i.e., the availability of the cluster, stays close to 1 even if part of the cluster is failed. This property is called high availability. A cluster with proper hardware and software can combine high performance with high availability. (Availability should not be confused with reliability, which is the probability $R(t)$ that the cluster can provide its service continuously over a time interval of duration t.)

In the last step, the computers are connected through a wide area network (WAN) such as the Internet. This adds openness, in which independent computations or computers can find each other, connect, and collaborate meaningfully. Openness is the crucial difference between the world of high-performance computing and the world of collaborative computing. In addition to partial failure, openness introduces two new issues: naming and security. Naming is how computations or computers find each other. Naming is usually supported by a special part of the system called the name server. Security is how computations or computers protect themselves from each other.

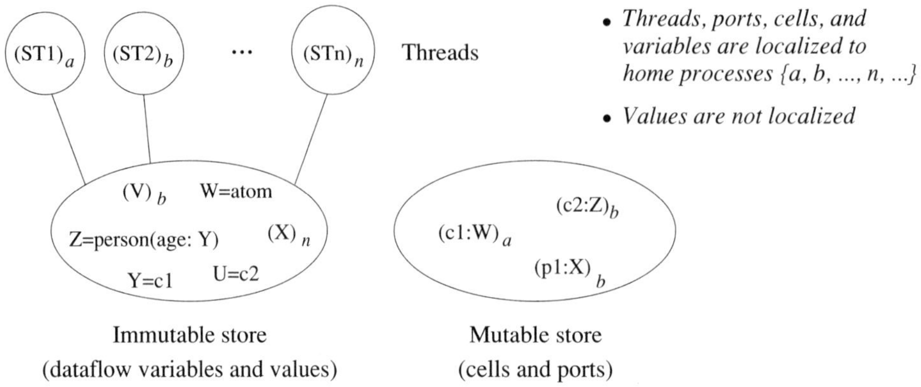

Figure 11.2: The distributed computation model.

11.2 The distribution model

We consider a computation model with both ports and cells, combining the models of chapters 5 and 8. We refine this model to make the distribution model, which defines the network operations done for language entities when they are shared between Oz processes [82, 83, 84, 218, 222]. If distribution is disregarded (i.e., we do not care how the computation is spread over processes) and there are no failures, then the computation model of the language is the same as if it executes in one process.

We assume that any process can hold a reference to a language entity on any other process. Conceptually, there is a single global computation model that encompasses all running Mozart processes and Mozart data worldwide (even those programs that are not connected together!). The global store is the union of all the local stores. In the current implementation, connected Mozart processes primarily use TCP (Transmission Control Protocol) to communicate. To a first approximation, all data and messages sent between processes travel through TCP.

Figure 11.2 shows the computation model. To add distribution to this global view, the idea is that each language entity has a distribution behavior, which defines how distributed references to the entity interact. In the model, we annotate each language entity with a process, which is the "home process" of that entity. It is the process that coordinates the distribution behavior of the entity. Typically, it will be the process at which the entity was first created.[1] We sometimes use the phrase "consistency protocol" to describe the distribution behavior of an entity. The distribution behavior is implemented by exchanging messages between Mozart

1. In Mozart, the coordination of an entity can be explicitly moved from one process to another. This issue will not be discussed in this introductory chapter.

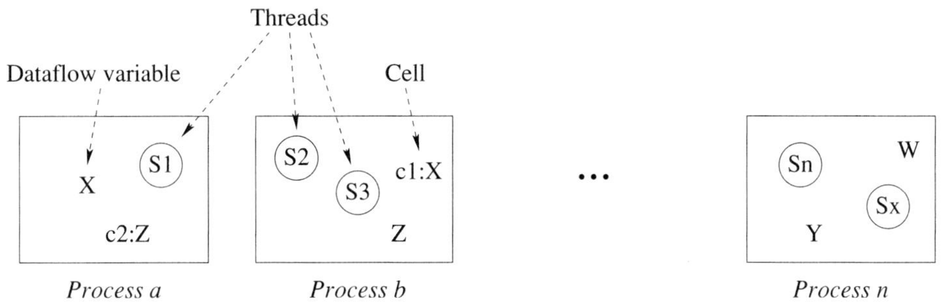

Figure 11.3: Process-oriented view of the distribution model.

processes.

What kinds of distribution behavior are important? To see this, we first distinguish between stateful, stateless, and single-assignment language entities. Each of them has a different distribution behavior:

- Stateful entities (threads, cells, ports, objects) have an internal state. The distribution behavior has to be careful to maintain a globally coherent view of the state. This puts major constraints on the kinds of efficient behavior that are possible. The simplest kind of behavior is to make them stationary. An operation on a stationary entity will traverse the network from the invoking process and be performed on the entity's home process. Other kinds of behavior are possible.
- Single-assignment entities (dataflow variables, streams) have one essential operation, namely binding. Binding a dataflow variable will bind all its distributed references to the same value. This operation is coordinated from the process on which the variable is created.
- Stateless entities, i.e., values (procedures, functions, records, classes, functors) do not need a process annotation because they are constants. They can be copied between processes.

Figure 11.3 shows a set of processes with localized threads, cells, and unbound dataflow variables. In the stateful concurrent model, the other entities can be defined in terms of these and procedure values. These basic entities have a default distributed behavior. But this behavior can be changed without changing the language semantics. For example, a remote operation on a cell could force the cell to migrate to the calling process, and thereafter perform the operation locally.

For all derived entities except for ports, the distributed behaviors of the defined entities can be seen as derived behavior from the distributed behavior of their parts. In this respect ports are different. Their default distributed behavior is asynchronous (see section 5.1). This behavior does not follow from the definition of ports in terms of cells. This means that ports are basic entities in the distribution model, just like cells.

The model of this section is sufficient to express useful distributed programs, but it has one limitation: partial failures are not taken into account. In section 11.8 we extend the basic model to overcome this limitation.

Depending on the application's needs, entities may be given different distributed behaviors. For example, "mobile" objects (also known as "cached" objects) move to the process that is using them. These objects have the same language semantics but a different distributed behavior. This is important for tuning network performance.

11.3 Distribution of declarative data

Let us show how to program with the distribution model. In this section we show how distribution works for the declarative subset of the stateful concurrent model. We start by explaining how to get different processes to talk to each other.

11.3.1 Open distribution and global naming

We say a distributed computation is open if a process can connect independently with other processes running a distributed computation at run time, without necessarily knowing beforehand which process it may connect with nor the type of information it may exchange. A distributed computation is closed if it is arranged so that a single process starts and then spawns other processes on various computers it has access to. We discuss closed distribution later.

An important issue in open distributed computing is naming. How do independent computations avoid confusion when communicating with each other? They do so by using globally unique names for things. For example, instead of using print representations (character strings) to name procedures, ports, or objects, we use globally unique names instead. The uniqueness should be guaranteed by the system. There are many possible ways to name entities:

- *References.* A reference is an unforgeable means to access any language entity. To programs, a reference is transparent, i.e., it is dereferenced when needed to access the entity. References can be local, to an entity on the current process, or remote, to an entity on a remote process. For example, a thread can reference an entity that is localized on another process. The language does not distinguish local from remote references.

- *Names.* A name is an unforgeable constant that is used to implement secure data abstractions. Names can be used for different kinds of identity and authentication abilities (see sections 3.7.5 and 6.4). All language entities with token equality, e.g., objects, classes, procedures, functors, etc., implement their identity by means of a name embedded inside them (see chapter 13).

- *Tickets.* A ticket, in the terminology of this chapter, is a global means to access any language entity. A ticket is similar to a reference, except that it can be used anywhere including outside a Mozart process. It is valid as long as the process containing its reference is running. It is represented by an ASCII (American Standard Code for Information Interchange) string, it is explicitly created and dereferenced, and it is forgeable. A computation can get a reference to an independent computation by getting a ticket from that computation. A common technique is to open socket communication between two processes, just long enough to pass the ticket. However, the ticket can be communicated using any communication protocol between the processes (e.g., TCP, IP [Internet Protocol], SMTP [Simple Mail Transfer Protocol], etc.) or between the users of these processes (e.g., sneakernet, telephone, Post-It notes, etc.) [78, 121]. Usually, these protocols can only pass simple data types, not arbitrary language references. But in almost all cases they support passing information coded in ASCII form. If they do, then they can pass a ticket.

- *URLs (Uniform Resource Locators).* A URL is a global reference to a file. The file must be accessible by a World Wide Web server. A URL encodes the host name of a machine that has a Web server and a file name on that machine. URLs are used to exchange persistent information between processes. A ticket can be stored in a file addressed by URL.

Within a distributed computation, all these four kinds of names can be passed between processes. References and names are pure names, i.e., they do not explicitly encode any information other than being unique. They can be used only inside a distributed computation. Tickets and URLs are impure names since they explicitly encode the information needed to dereference them—they are ASCII strings and can be read as such. Since they are encoded in ASCII, they can be used both inside and outside a distributed computation. We connect different processes together using tickets.

The `Connection` *module*

Tickets are created and used with the `Connection` module. This module has three basic operations:

- `{Connection.offer X ?T}` creates a ticket `T` for any reference `X`. The ticket can be taken just once. Attempting to take a ticket more than once will raise an exception.

- `{Connection.offerUnlimited X ?T}` creates a ticket `T` for any reference `X`. The ticket can be taken any number of times.

- `{Connection.take T ?X}` creates a reference `X` when given a valid ticket in `T`. The `X` refers to exactly the same language entity as the original reference that was offered when the ticket was created. A ticket can be taken at any process. If taken at a different process than where the ticket was offered, then network communication is initiated between the two processes.

With `Connection`, connecting computations in different processes is extremely simple. The system does a great deal of work to give this simple view. It implements the connection protocol, transparent marshaling and unmarshaling, distributed garbage collection, and a carefully designed distribution protocol for each language entity.

11.3.2 Sharing declarative data

Sharing records

We start with a simple example. The first process has a big data structure, a record, that it wants to share. It first creates the ticket[2]:

```
X=the_novel(text:"It was a dark and stormy night. ..."
            author:"E.G.E. Bulwer-Lytton"
            year:1803)
{Browse {Connection.offerUnlimited X}}
```

This example creates the ticket with `Connection.offerUnlimited` and displays it. (To display it as a string, select **Strings** in the **Representation** entry of the browser's **Options** menu and feed the ticket again.) Any other process that wants to get a reference to `X` just has to know the ticket. Here is what the other process does:

```
X2={Connection.take ´...ticket comes here...´}
```

(To make this work, you have to replace the text `´...ticket comes here...´` by what was displayed by the first process.) That's it. The operation `Connection.take` takes the ticket and returns a language reference, which we put in `X2`. Because of network transparency, both `X` and `X2` behave identically.

Sharing functions

This works for other data types as well. Assume the first process has a function instead of a record:

```
fun {MyEncoder X} (X*4449+1234) mod 33667 end
{Browse {Connection.offerUnlimited MyEncoder}}
```

The second process can get the function easily:

```
E2={Connection.take ´...MyEncoders ticket...´}
{Browse {E2 10000}}  % Call the function
```

This executes the function in the second process and displays the result there.

---

2. Here, as in the subsequent examples, we leave out **declare** for brevity, but we keep **declare ... in** for clarity.

Sharing dataflow variables

In addition to records and functions, the ticket can also be used to pass unbound variables. Any operation that needs the value will wait, even across the network. This is how we do distributed synchronization [82]. The first process creates the variable and makes it globally accessible:

```
declare X in
{Browse {Connection.offerUnlimited X}}
```

But the process does not bind the variable yet. Other processes can get a reference to the variable:

```
declare X in
X={Connection.take ´...Xs ticket...´}
{Browse X*X}
```

The multiplication blocks until `X` is bound. Try doing `X=111` in the first process. The binding will become visible on all processes that reference the variable.

11.3.3 Ticket distribution

In the above examples we copied and pasted tickets between windows of the interactive environment. A better way to distribute tickets is to store them in a file. To successfully connect with the ticket, the destination process just has to read the file. This not only makes the distribution easier, it also can distribute over a larger part of the network. There are two basic ways:

- *Local distribution.* This uses the local file system. The destination process has to be connected to the same file system as the source process. This works well on a LAN where all machines have access to the same file system.
- *Global distribution.* This uses the global Web infrastructure. The file can be put in a directory that is published by a Web server, e.g., in a `~/public_html` directory on Unix. The file can then be accessed by URL.

Using a URL to make connections is a general approach that works well for collaborative applications on the Internet. To implement these techniques we need an operation to store and load a ticket from a file or URL. This is already provided by the `Pickle` module as described in chapter 2. Any stateless value can be stored in a file and retrieved by another process that has a read access right to the file.

The `Pickle` module We recall that the `Pickle` module has two operations:

- `{Pickle.save X FN}` saves any value `X` in the file whose name is `FN`.
- `{Pickle.load FNURL ?X}` loads into `X` the value stored in `FNURL`, which can be a file name or a URL.

`Pickle` can store any stateless entity. For example, it can be used to store records, procedures, classes, and even functors, all of which are pure values. An attempt to save stateful data in a pickle will raise an exception. An attempt to save a partial value in a pickle will block until the partial value is complete. The following code:

```
{Pickle.save MyEncoder ´~/public_html/encoder´}
```

saves the function `MyEncoder` in a file. Files in the `~/public_html` directory are often publicly accessible by means of URLs. Anyone who needs the `MyEncoder` function can just load the file by giving the right URL:

```
MyEnc={Pickle.load ´http://www.info.ucl.ac.be/~pvr/encoder´}
```

`MyEncoder` and `MyEnc` are absolutely identical from the program's point of view. There is no way to distinguish them. The ability to store, transfer, and then execute procedure values across a network is the essential property of what nowadays is known as "applets." A value saved in a pickle continues to be valid even if the process that did the save is no longer running. The pickle itself is a file that contains complete information about the value. This file can be copied and transferred at will. It will continue to give the same value when loaded with `Pickle.load`.

The main limitation of pickles is that only values can be saved. One way to get around this is to make a snapshot of stateful information, i.e., make a stateless data structure that contains the instantaneous states of all relevant stateful entities. This is more complex than pickling since the stateful entities must be locked and unlocked, and situations such as deadlock must be avoided.

However, we do not need such a complete solution in this case. There is a simple technique for getting around this limitation that works for any language entity, as long as the process that did the save is still running. The idea is to store a ticket in a pickle. This works since tickets are strings, which are values. This is a useful technique for making any language entity accessible worldwide. The URL is the entry point for the entity addressed by the ticket.

The `Offer` and `Take` operations Using `Pickle` and `Connection`, we define two convenience operations `Offer` and `Take` that implement this technique. These operations are available in the module `Distribution`, which can be found on the book's Web site. The procedure `Offer` makes language entity `X` available through file `FN`:

```
proc {Offer X FN}
   {Pickle.save {Connection.offerUnlimited X} FN}
end
```

The function `Take` gets a reference to the language entity by giving the file `FNURL`:

```
fun {Take FNURL}
   {Connection.take {Pickle.load FNURL}}
end
```

This uses `Pickle.load`, which can load any stateless data from a file. The argument `FNURL` can either be a file name or a URL.

11.3.4 Stream communication

Declarative programming with streams, as in chapter 4, can be made distributed simply by starting the producer and consumer in different processes. They only have to share a reference to the stream.

Eager stream communication

Let us first see how this works with an eager stream. First create the consumer in one process and create a ticket for its stream:

```
declare Xs Sum in
{Offer Xs tickfile}
fun {Sum Xs A}
   case Xs of X|Xr then {Sum Xr A+X} [] nil then A end
end
{Browse {Sum Xs 0}}
```

Then create the producer in another process. It takes the ticket to get a reference to `Xs` and then creates the stream:

```
declare Xs Generate in
Xs={Take tickfile}
fun {Generate N Limit}
   if N<Limit then N|{Generate N+1 Limit} else nil end
end
Xs={Generate 0 150000}
```

This creates the stream `0|1|2|3|...` and binds it to `Xs`. This sends the stream across the network from the producer process to the consumer process. This is efficient since stream elements are sent asynchronously across the network. Because of thread scheduling, the stream is created in "batches" and each batch is sent across the network in one message.

Lazy stream communication

We can run the same example with lazy stream communication. Take the examples with programmed triggers (see section 4.3.3) and implicit triggers (see section 4.5) and run them in different processes, as we showed above with eager streams.

Ports and servers

A port is a basic data type; it is a FIFO channel with an asynchronous send operation. "Asynchronous" means that the send operation completes immediately, without waiting for the network. FIFO means that successive sends in the same thread will appear in the same order in the channel's stream. Ports generalize streams by allowing many-to-one communication. With ports we can build servers. Let us show how by making a simple "Browse server." We create a port, make it globally accessible, and display the stream contents locally:

```
declare S P in
{NewPort S P}
{Offer P tickfile}
for X in S do {Browse X} end
```

The **for** loop causes dataflow synchronization to take place on elements appearing on the stream S. Each time a new element appears, an iteration of the loop is done. Now we can let a second process send to the port:

```
P={Take tickfile}
{Send P hello}
{Send P 'keep in touch'}
```

Since the Send operation is asynchronous, it sends just a single message on the network.

11.4 Distribution of state

Stateful entities are more expensive to distribute than stateless entities in a network-transparent system. It is because changes in state have to be visible to all processes that use the entity.

11.4.1 Simple state sharing

Sharing cells

The simplest way to share state between processes is by sharing a cell. This can be done exactly in the same way as for the other types. Let us create a cell and make it available to other processes:

```
declare
C={NewCell unit}
{Offer C tickfile}
```

Any other process can access C by doing

```
declare
C1={Take tickfile}
```

C and C1 are indistinguishable in the language. Any process that references the cell in this way can do operations on it. The system guarantees that this is globally coherent. That is, if process 1 first puts foo in the cell, and then process 2 does an exchange, then process 2 will see foo. Knowing how the system does this is important for efficiency (e.g., network hops). We will see later how the global coherence is maintained and how the programmer can control what the network operations are.

```
fun {CorrectSimpleLock}
   Token={NewCell unit}
   proc {Lock P}
   Old New in
      {Exchange Token Old New}
      {Wait Old}
      try {P} finally New=unit end
   end
in
   ´lock´(´lock´:Lock)
end
```

Figure 11.4: Distributed locking.

Distributed locking

Now that we know the distributed behavior of cells, let us use it to implement a well-known distributed locking algorithm, also known as distributed mutual exclusion using token passing.[3] When locking a critical section, multiple requests should all correctly block and be queued, independent of whether the threads are on the same process or on another process. We show how to implement this concisely and efficiently in the language. Figure 11.4, taken from section 8.3, shows one way to implement a lock that handles exceptions correctly.[4] If multiple threads attempt to access the lock body, then only one is given access, and the others are queued. The queue is a sequence of dataflow variables. Each thread suspends on one variable in the sequence, and will bind the next variable after it has executed the lock body. Each thread desiring the lock therefore references two variables: one to wait for the lock and one to pass the lock to the next thread. Each variable is referenced by two threads.

When the threads are on different processes, the definition of figure 11.4 implements distributed token passing, a well-known distributed locking algorithm [38]. We explain how it works. When a thread tries to enter the lock body, the `Exchange` gives it access to the previous thread's `New` variable. The previous thread's process is `New`'s owner. When the previous thread binds `New`, the owner sends the binding to the next thread's process. This requires a single message.

Sharing objects and other data types

A more sophisticated way to share state is to share objects. In this way, we encapsulate the shared state and control what the possible operations on it are. Here is an example:

---

3. The built-in locks of Mozart use this algorithm when they are distributed.
4. For simplicity, we leave out reentrancy since it does only local execution.

```
class Coder
   attr seed
   meth init(S) seed:=S end
   meth get(X)
      X=@seed
      seed:=(@seed*1234+4449) mod 33667
   end
end
C={New Coder init(100)}
{Offer C tickfile}
```

This defines the class `Coder` and an object `C`. Any process that takes the object's ticket will reference it. The Mozart system guarantees that the object will behave exactly like a centralized object. For example, if the object raises an exception, then the exception will be raised in the thread calling the object.

11.4.2 Distributed lexical scoping

One of the important properties of network transparency is distributed lexical scoping: a procedure value that references a language entity will continue to reference that entity, independent of where the procedure value is transferred across the network. This causes remote references to be created implicitly, by the simple act of copying the procedure value from one process to another. For example:

```
declare
C={NewCell 0}
fun {Inc X} X+@C end
{Offer C tickfile1}
{Offer Inc tickfile2}
```

`Inc` will always reference `C`, no matter from which process it is called. A third process can take `C`'s ticket and change the content. This will change the behavior of `Inc`. The following scenario can happen: (1) process 1 defines `C` and `Inc`, (2) process 2 gets a reference to `Inc` and calls it, and (3) process 3 gets a reference to `C` and changes its content. When process 2 calls `Inc` again it will use the new content of `C`. Semantically, this behavior is nothing special: it is a consequence of using procedure values with network transparency. But how is it implemented? In particular, what network operations are done to guarantee it? We would like the network behavior to be simple and predictable. Fortunately, we can design the system so that this is indeed the case, as section 11.7 explains.

Distributed lexical scoping, like lexical scoping, is important for reasons of software engineering. Entities that are moved or copied between processes will continue to behave according to their specification, and not inadvertently change because some local entity happens to have the same name as one of their external references. The importance of distributed lexical scoping was first recognized by Luca Cardelli and realized in Obliq, a simple functional language with object-based extensions that was designed for experimenting with network-transparent distribution [32].

11.5 Network awareness

With these examples it should be clear how network transparency works. Before going further, let us give some insight into the distributed behavior of the various language entities. The distributed implementation of Mozart does many different things. It uses a wide variety of distributed algorithms to provide the illusion of network transparency (e.g., see section 11.7). At this point, you may be getting uneasy about all this activity going on behind the scenes. Can it be understood, and controlled if need be, to do exactly what we want it to do? There are in fact two related questions:

- What network operations does the system do to implement transparency?
- Are the network operations simple and predictable, i.e., is it possible to build applications that communicate in predictable ways?

As we will see, the network operations are both few and predictable; in most cases exactly what would be achieved by explicit message passing. This property of the distribution subsystem is called network awareness.

We now give a quick summary of the network operations done by the most-used language entities; later on in section 11.7 we will define the distributed algorithms that implement them in more detail.[5] The basic idea is the following: stateless entities are copied, bindings of dataflow variables are multicast, ports are stationary with FIFO sends, and other stateful entities use a consistency protocol. Here is a more detailed description:

- *Numbers*, *records*, and *literals* are stateless entities with structure equality. That is, separately created copies cannot be distinguished. The values are copied immediately whenever a source process sends a message to a target process. This takes one network hop. Many copies can exist on the target process, one for each message sent by the source process.
- *Procedures*, *functions*, *classes*, and *functors* are stateless entities with token equality. That is, each entity when created comes with a globally unique name. The default protocol needs one message possibly followed by one additional round trip. In the first message, just the name is sent. If this name already exists in the target process, then the value is already present and the protocol is finished. If not, then the value is immediately requested with a round trip. This means that at most one copy of these entities can exist on each process.
- *Dataflow variables.* When binding the variable, one message is sent to the process coordinating the variable protocol. This process then multicasts one message to each process that references the variable. This means that the coordinating process

5. The distribution behavior we give here is the default behavior. It is possible to change this default behavior by explicit commands to the Mozart implementation; we do not address this issue in this chapter.

implicitly knows all processes that reference the variable.

- *Objects*, *cells*, and *locks*. Objects are a particular case of distributed state. There are many ways to implement distributed state in a network-transparent way. This chapter singles out three protocols in particular: mobile cached objects (the default), stationary objects, and asynchronous objects. Each protocol gives good network behavior for a particular pattern of use. The `Coder` example we gave before defines a mobile cached object. A mobile cached object is moved to each process that uses it. This requires a maximum of three messages for each object move. Once the object has moved to a process, no further messages are needed for invocations in that process. Later on, we will redo the `Coder` example with a stationary object (which behaves like a server) and an asynchronous object (which allows message streaming).

- *Streams*. A stream is a list whose tail is an unbound variable. Sending on a stream means to add elements by binding the tail. Receiving means reading the stream's content. Sending on a stream will send stream elements asynchronously from a producer process to a consumer process. Stream elements are batched when possible for best network performance.

- *Ports*. Sending to a port is both asynchronous and FIFO. Each element sent causes one message to be sent to the port's home process. This kind of send is not possible with RMI, but it is important to have; in many cases, one can send things without having to wait for a result.

It is clear that the distributed behavior of these entities is both simple and well-defined. To a first approximation, we recommend that a developer just ignore it and assume that the system is being essentially as efficient as a human programmer doing explicit message passing. There are no hidden inefficiencies.

11.6 Common distributed programming patterns

11.6.1 Stationary and mobile objects

In the `Coder` example given above, the object is mobile (i.e., cached). This gives good performance when the object is shared between processes, e.g., in a collaborative application. The object behaves like a cache. On the other hand, it is often useful to have an object that does not move, i.e., a stationary object. For example, the object might depend on some external resources that are localized to a particular process. Putting the object on that process can give orders of magnitude better performance than putting it elsewhere. A stationary object is a good way to define a server, since servers often use localized resources.

Whether or not an object is mobile or stationary is defined independently of the object's class. It is defined when the object is created. Using `New` creates a mobile cached object and using `NewStat` creates a stationary object. We have already

```
fun {NewStat Class Init}
P Obj={New Class Init} in
   thread S in
      {NewPort S P}
      for M#X in S do
         try {Obj M} X=normal
         catch E then X=exception(E) end
      end
   end
   proc {$ M}
   X in
      {Send P M#X}
      case X of normal then skip
      [] exception(E) then raise E end end
   end
end
```

Figure 11.5: Stationary objects.

defined `NewStat`, in section 7.8 where it is the second version of `NewActiveExc`. Figure 11.5 gives the definition again, because we will use it to understand the distribution behavior. Let us see how the distributed behavior of `NewStat` is derived from the default behavior of its component parts. We define a stationary version of the `Coder` object:

```
C={NewStat Coder init(100)}
{Offer C tickfile}
```

This creates a thread and a port situated on the home process. `C` is a reference to a one-argument procedure. Now assume another process gets a reference to `C`:

```
C2={Take tickfile}
```

This will transfer the procedure to the second process. That is, the second process now has a copy of the procedure `C`, which it references by `C2`. Now let the second process call `C2`:

```
local A in
   {C2 get(A)} {Browse A}
end
```

This creates a dataflow variable `A` and then calls `C2` locally. This does a port send `{Send get(A)#X}`. The references to `A` and `X` are transferred to the first process. At the home process, `{Obj get(A)}` is executed, where `Obj` is the actual `Coder` object. If this execution is successful, then `A` is bound to a result and `X` is bound to `normal`. Both bindings are transferred back to the second process. If the execution would have raised an exception `E`, then it would be transferred back as the tuple `exception(E)`.

What we have described is a general algorithm for remote method invocation of a stationary object. For example, the object on the home process, while serving a request, could call another object at a third process, and so on. Exceptions will be passed correctly.

We can also see that remote calls to stationary objects are more complex than calls to mobile cached objects! Mobile objects are simpler, because once the object arrives at the caller process, the subsequent execution will be local (including any raised exceptions).

How many network hops does it take to call a remote stationary object? Once the caller has a reference to the object, it takes two hops: one to send the tuple `M#X` and one to send the results back. We can see the difference in performance between mobile and stationary objects. Do the following in a second process, preferably on another machine:

```
C2={Take tickfile}
for I in 1..100000 do {C2 get(_)} end
{Browse done}
```

This does 100000 calls to `C2`. Try doing this for both mobile and stationary objects and measure the difference in execution time. How do you explain the difference?

11.6.2 Asynchronous objects and dataflow

We have seen how to share an object among several processes. Because of network transparency, these objects are synchronous. That is, each object call waits until the method completes before continuing. Both mobile and stationary objects are synchronous. Calling a stationary object requires two messages: first from the caller to the object, and then from the object to the caller. If the network is slow, this can take a long time.

One way to get around the network delay is to do an asynchronous object call. First do the send without waiting for the result. Then wait for the result later when it is needed. This technique works very well together with dataflow variables. The result of the send is an unbound variable that is automatically bound as soon as its value is known. Because of dataflow, the variable can be passed around, stored in data structures, used in calculations, etc., even before its value is known. Let us see how this works with the `Coder` object. First, create an asynchronous object:

```
C={NewActive Coder init(100)}
{Offer C tickfile}
```

(We use the definition of `NewActive` given in section 7.8.) This object has exactly the same behavior as a standard object, except that an object call does not wait until the method completes. Assume that the second process needs three random numbers and calls `C` three times:

```
C1={Take tickfile}
X={C1 get($)}
Y={C1 get($)}
Z={C1 get($)}
...
% use X, Y, and Z as usual
```

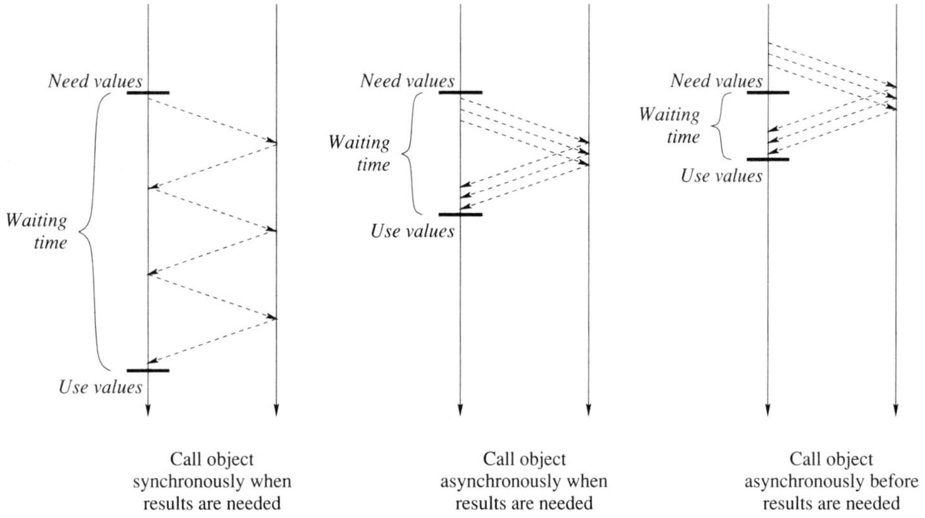

Figure 11.6: The advantages of asynchronous objects with dataflow.

These three calls all return immediately without waiting for the network. The three results, `X`, `Y`, and `Z`, are still unbound variables. They can be used as if they were the results:

```
S=X+Y+Z
{Browse S}
```

Because of dataflow, this addition will automatically block until the three results have arrived. Figure 11.6 shows the three possibilities:

- In the first scenario (using `NewStat`), the program does three synchronous calls at the moment it needs their results. This takes three round-trip message delays before it can calculate with the results.
- The second scenario does better by using asynchronous calls. This takes slightly more than one round-trip message delay before the calculation.
- The third scenario is best of all. Here the asynchronous calls are initiated before we need them. When we need them, their calculation is already in progress. This can take much less than one round-trip message delay.

The first scenario is standard sequential object-oriented programming. Because of dataflow, the second scenario can be done without changing any program code except for using `NewActive` instead of `New` to define the object. Again because of dataflow, the third scenario is possible without changing any program code except for making the calls earlier. For both the second and third scenarios, the dataflow behavior is automatic and can be ignored by the programmer.

Asynchronous objects with exceptions

The asynchronous objects defined above differ in one crucial aspect from standard synchronous objects. They never raise exceptions. We can solve this problem by using `NewActiveExc`, which is also defined in section 7.8. The object call then looks like `{Obj M X}`, where the extra argument `X` is used to inform the caller whether the execution terminated normally or raised an exception. The caller can then catch the exception at a time that is suitable to it.

Separating timing from functionality

Now we have seen most of what the distributed computation model provides for object-oriented programming. Let us summarize the possibilities. We have seen that exactly the same program code can be executed with synchronous objects (either mobile or stationary) or asynchronous objects (either called on need or called early). In other words, the distributed model separates timing issues from programming techniques. This is a remarkable result. It is made possible because of implicit synchronization with dataflow variables.

11.6.3 Servers

A compute server

One of the promises of distributed computing is making computations go faster by exploiting the parallelism inherent in networks of computers. A first step is to create a compute server, which uses its computational resources to do any computation that is given it. Here is one way to create a compute server:

```
class ComputeServer
   meth init skip end
   meth run(P) {P} end
end
C={NewStat ComputeServer init}
```

Assume that a client gets a reference to `C` as shown before. Here is how the client can use the compute server:

```
fun {Fibo N}
   if N<2 then 1 else {Fibo N-1}+{Fibo N-2} end
end
local F in
   {C run(proc {$} F={Fibo 30} end)} {Browse F}
end
local F in
   F={Fibo 30} {Browse F}
end
```

This first does the computation `{Fibo 30}` remotely and then repeats it locally. In the remote case, the variable `F` is shared between the client and server. When the server binds it, its value is immediately sent to the server. This is how the client gets a result from the server.

This compute server can execute almost any statement ⟨stmt⟩ remotely. Just make a zero-argument procedure out of it:

```
P=proc {$} ⟨stmt⟩ end
```

and execute `{C run(P)}`. Because of network transparency, there are few restrictions on ⟨stmt⟩. For example, ⟨stmt⟩ can define new classes that inherit from client classes and ⟨stmt⟩ can have references to variables for passing back results. During the remote execution, these references become distributed.

The only statements that do not work are those that reference entities restricted to one process, e.g., display operations (`Show` and `Browse`), file input/output (`File` module), or OS operations (`OS` module). We will show how to do these in the next section.

Distributed programming with resources

The compute server we defined above does not properly handle entities that are restricted to one process. Let us define a *resource* as a module whose use is restricted to one process. A little thought shows that our compute server has two limitations with respect to resources. First, the statement ⟨stmt⟩, which executes at the server, cannot use client resources (since they are restricted to the client process). Second, the statement ⟨stmt⟩ cannot use server resources either (since ⟨stmt⟩ is created at the client, which cannot specify server resources). In brief, the server cannot use client resources and the client cannot specify server resources to be used.

Some examples of resources in Mozart are the `Open` module (the file system) and the `QTk` module (the graphics display). In Mozart, the rule is that all System modules are resources. On the other hand, Base modules are not resources. Code (procedures, classes, etc.) referencing only Base modules can be passed to any process and it will work correctly. Code referencing a System module will only work on the home process of the System module, unless special care is taken.

Let us remove these two limitations. In the first case, we want the server to use client resources. This can be done with port objects. For example, if we want the server to use the client's browser, then we can pass it a reference to a Browse server. This consists of a port object that browses all messages sent to it:

```
declare S P in
{NewPort S P}
{Offer proc {$ M} {Send P M} end tickfile}
for X in S do {Browse X} end
```

Instead of calling `Browse`, the server calls the Browse server:

```
declare Browse2 in
Browse2={Take tickfile}
{Browse2 message}
```

References to `Browse2` can be passed to any process and they will work correctly.

We can generalize this idea to any resource. The server can access a client resource if the latter is implemented behind a port object, like the Browse server.[6]

The second case is where we want the client to specify server resources, so that ⟨stmt⟩ can execute with them. To be precise, ⟨stmt⟩ has to specify which server resources it needs. This can be done with functors. A functor can be seen as a module specification that defines which resources the module needs. These resources are the modules named in the **import** clause. Since functors are values, the client can define a functor on the fly and pass it to the compute server. For example, the following statement:

```
declare T F in
functor F
   import OS
define
   T={OS.time}
end
```

defines a functor that is referenced by `F`. The functor specifies a module that imports the resource `OS` and binds `T` to the result of calling `OS.time`. The resource `OS` contains basic operating system functionality. The function `OS.time` returns the current time in seconds since January 1, 1970. The purpose of functor `F` is to tell us what time the compute server thinks it is. Note that this functor does not export any references (there is no **export** clause); it returns its result by binding `T`.

To pass this functor to the compute server, we have to modify the server to accept functors instead of procedures. That is, the compute server has to install the functor locally, i.e., create a module that is connected to all the resources mentioned in the **import** clause. As we saw in section 6.7, the System module `Module` is able to do this. The new class `ComputeServer` looks like this:

```
class ComputeServer
   meth init skip end
   meth run(F) {Module.apply [F] _} end
end
```

This compute server is called in exactly the same way as the previous one. `Module.apply` takes a list of functors, installs them in a shared environment, and returns a list of modules. For this application we are not interested in the resulting module, but just in the computation.

This compute server can execute any statement ⟨stmt⟩ remotely. Just make a functor out of it, specifying which resources it needs:

```
F=functor $ import ⟨resourceList⟩ define ⟨stmt⟩ end
```

where ⟨resourceList⟩ is a list of resources. Then execute `{C run(F)}`.

The definition we give here allows the computation to access all the server's resources. This is because it uses the default module manager provided by `Module`. We can use `Module` to create another module manager that allows only restricted

6. In a future Mozart release, the system will do this automatically for all resources.

access to resources. For example, it might allow the computation to do file operations only to a given directory. This can be important for reasons of security.

A dynamically upgradable compute server

Sometimes a server has to be upgraded, e.g., to add extra functionality or to fix a bug. As a final server example, we show how to write a server that can be upgraded without stopping it. The upgrade can even be done interactively. A person sits down at a terminal anywhere in the world, starts up an interactive Mozart session, and upgrades the running server. First define a generic upgradable server:

```
proc {NewUpgradableStat Class Init ?Upg ?Srv}
   Obj={New Class Init}
   C={NewCell Obj}
in
   Srv={MakeStat
        proc {$ M} {@C M} end}
   Upg={MakeStat
        proc {$ Class2#Init2} C:={New Class2 Init2} end}
end
```

(`MakeStat` is defined in the supplements file on the book's Web site.) This definition must be executed on the server process. It returns a server `Srv` and a stationary procedure `Upg` used for upgrading the server. The server is upgradable because it does all object calls indirectly through the cell `C`.

An upgradable compute server is created almost exactly as a fixed compute server, namely by executing the following on the server process:

```
declare Srv Upg in
Srv={NewUpgradableStat ComputeServer init Upg}
```

Now we can upgrade the compute server while it is running. Let us define a new class `CComputeServer`. We upgrade the server with an object of the new class:

```
class CComputeServer from ComputeServer
   meth run(P Prio<=medium)
      thread
         {Thread.setThisPriority Prio}
         ComputeServer,run(P)
      end
   end
end
{Upg CComputeServer#init}
```

That's all there is to it. The upgraded compute server overrides the `run` method with a new method that has a default. The new method supports the original call `run(P)` and adds a new call `run(P Prio)`, where `Prio` sets the priority of the thread doing the computation `P`.

The compute server can be upgraded as many times as desired since garbage collection will remove any unused old compute server code. For example, it would be nice if the client could find out how many active computations there are on the compute server before deciding whether or not to do a computation there. We leave it to the reader to upgrade the server to add a new method that returns the number of active computations at each priority level.

11.6.4 Closed distribution

Closed distribution is when an application completely manages its distribution structure. For example, a server application that runs on a cluster can itself create all the processes that will run on the cluster machines. Just as the `Connection` module provides the basic primitives for open distribution, the `Remote` module provides the basic primitives for closed distribution. `Remote` is an extension of `Module`. It creates a remote process along with the means to install new functors there. Executing

```
R={New Remote.manager init}
```

creates a remote process and a local object `R` which is the remote process's "manager." If no arguments are given, then the remote process is created on the same machine as the caller process. With the right arguments it is possible to create processes on other machines. For example, the call

```
R={New Remote.manager init(host:´norge.info.ucl.ac.be´)}
```

creates a remote process on the host **`norge.info.ucl.ac.be`**. By default, the remote process will be created using **`rsh`** (remote shell). In order for this to work, the host must have been set up properly beforehand. The remote process can also be created with **`ssh`** (secure shell). For information on this and other aspects of `Remote`, please see the Mozart documentation [148].

Once a remote process has been created, it can be controlled through the manager object `R`. This object has an interface that closely resembles that of `Module`, i.e., it controls the instantiation of functors at the remote process. Calling the manager with `{R apply(F X)}` installs functor `F` on the remote process and returns the module in `X`.

There is a kind of "master-slave" relationship between the original process and the new process. The original process can observe the new process's behavior, e.g., to keep track of its resource consumption. The original process can change the new process's process priority, put it to sleep, and even terminate it if necessary. The original process can give the new process limited versions of some critical system modules, so that the new process behaves like a sandbox.

11.7 Distribution protocols

We now briefly summarize the distribution protocols implemented in Mozart. We first give an overview of all the different protocols for the different language entities. We then focus on two particularly interesting protocols: the mobile state protocol (used for cached cells and objects) and the distributed binding protocol (used for dataflow variables). We end with a quick look at the distributed garbage collector.

11.7.1 Language entities

Each language entity is implemented by one or more distributed algorithms. Each algorithm respects the entity's semantics if distribution is disregarded. The language entities have the following protocols:

- Stateful entities are implemented with one of the following three protocols:
  - *Stationary state.* All operations always execute on the process where the state resides, called the target process. Remote invocations send messages to this process. Conceptually, it is as if the invoking thread moves to the target process. When seen in this way, distributed exceptions and reentrant locking work correctly. Operations are synchronous. Asynchronous operations require explicit programming, e.g., by using **thread** ... **end**.
  - *Mobile state.* In this case the invoking thread is stationary. The right to update the state moves from one process to another. We call this right the state pointer or content edge. An exchange operation will first cause the state pointer to move to the executing process, so that the exchange is always local [222, 218]. The mobile state protocol can be seen as implementing a cache, i.e., it is a cache coherence protocol.
  - *Invalidation.* This protocol optimizes the mobile state protocol when reading is much more frequent than updating. A process that wants to read the state sends a message to the target process and gets the state in reply, thus creating a local replica of the state. A process that wants to update the state must first explicitly invalidate all these replicas by sending them an invalidation message. This guarantees that the interleaving semantics of state updates is maintained. The right to update the state still moves from one process to another.
- Single-assignment entities are implemented with a distributed unification algorithm [82]. The key operation of this algorithm is a distributed bind operation, which replaces the variable by whatever it is bound to, on all the processes that know the variable. There are two variants of this algorithm:
  - *Lazy binding* (on demand). The replacement is done on a process only when the process needs the variable. This variant typically reduces the total number of network messages, but increases latency and keeps a dependency on the variable's home process.
  - *Eager binding* (on supply). The replacement is done on a process as soon as the variable is bound, whether or not the process needs the variable.

The Mozart system currently implements just the eager binding algorithm.

- Stateless entities are implemented with one of the following three protocols [3]:
  - *Lazy copying* (on demand). The value is copied to a process only when the

Kind of entity	Algorithm	Entity
Stateless	eager immediate copying	record, integer
	eager copying	procedure, class, functor
	lazy copying	object-record
Single assignment	eager binding	dataflow variable, stream
Stateful	stationary state	port, thread, object-state
	mobile state	cell, object-state

Table 11.1: Distributed algorithms.

process needs it. This reduces the number of network messages, but increases latency and keeps a dependency on the original process.

▫ *Eager copying* (on supply, sent if not present). The value is not sent as part of the message, but if upon reception of the message the value is not present, then an immediate request is made for it. In most cases, this is the optimal protocol, since the value will be present on the receiving process for all except the first message referencing it.

▫ *Eager immediate copying* (on supply, always sent). The value is sent as part of the message. This has minimum latency, but can overload the network since values will be repeatedly sent to processes. It is used to send record structures.

■ In addition to these algorithms, there is a distributed garbage collection algorithm. This algorithm works alongside the local garbage collection. The algorithm does no global operations and is able to remove all garbage except for cross-process cycles between stateful entities. The algorithm consists of two parts, a credit mechanism and a time-lease mechanism. The credit mechanism works well when there are no failures. It is a kind of weighted reference counting [169]. Each language entity with remote references has a supply of "credits." Each remote reference to the entity must have at least one credit. When a local garbage collection reclaims a remote reference, then its credits are sent back. When the entity has no outstanding remote credits and no local references, then it can be reclaimed. In the time-lease mechanism, each distributed entity exists only for a limited time unless it is periodically renewed by a message sent from a remote reference. This handles the case of partial failure.

Table 11.1 shows the algorithms used by the current system for each language entity. In this table, an object consists of two parts, the object-record (which contains the class) and the object-state (the object's internal cell). The invalidation protocol is not implemented in the current system. We conclude that network operations[7] are predictable for all language entities, which gives the programmer the ability to manage network communications.

7. In terms of the number of network hops.

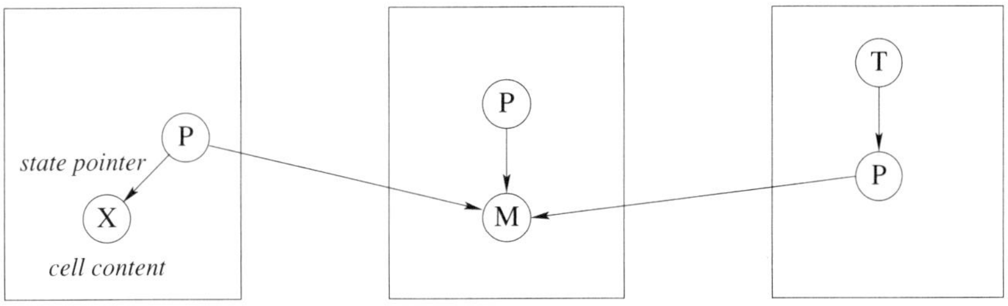

Figure 11.7: Graph notation for a distributed cell.

11.7.2 Mobile state protocol

The mobile state protocol is one of the distributed algorithms used to implement stateful entities. Objects, cells, and locks are implemented with this protocol. This section gives the intuition underlying the protocol and explains the network operations it does. A formal definition of the protocol and a proof that it respects the language semantics are given in [222]. An extension that is well-behaved in case of network and process failure is given together with proof in [24]. The Mozart system implements this extended protocol.

We use a graph notation to describe the protocol. Each (centralized) language entity, i.e., record, procedure value, dataflow variable, thread, and cell, is represented by a node in the graph. To represent a distributed computation, we add two additional nodes, called proxy and manager. Each language entity that has remote references is represented by a starlike structure, with one manager and a set of proxies. The proxy is the local reference of a remote entity. The manager coordinates the protocol that implements the distribution behavior of the entity. The manager is also called the coordinator.

Figure 11.7 shows a cell that has remote references on three processes. The cell consists of three proxies P and one manager M. The cell content X is accessible from the first proxy through the state pointer. A thread T on the third process references the cell, which means that it references the third proxy.

What happens when T does an exchange operation? The state pointer is on a different process from T, so the mobile state protocol is initiated to bring the state pointer to T's process. Once the state pointer is local to T, then the exchange is performed. This implies the remarkable property that all cell operations are always performed locally in the thread that initiates them.

The protocol to move the state pointer consists of three messages: `get`, `put`, and `forward`. Figure 11.8 shows how they are sent. The third proxy initiates the move by sending a `get` request to M. The manager M plays the role of a serializer: all requests pass through it. After receiving the `get`, M sends a `forward` message to the first proxy. When the first proxy receives the `forward`, it sends a `put` to the third proxy. This atomically transfers the state pointer to the third proxy.

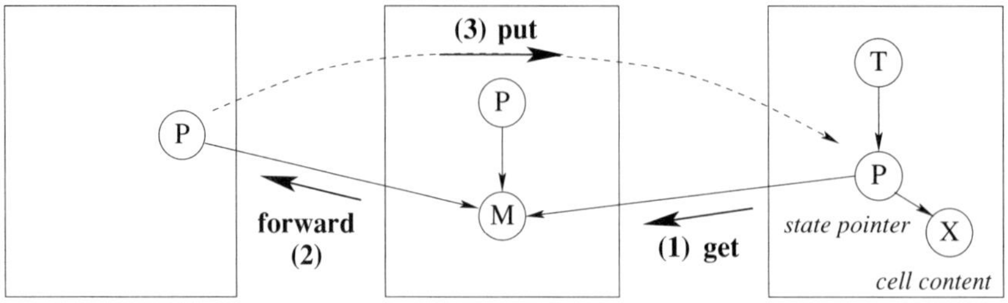

Figure 11.8: Moving the state pointer.

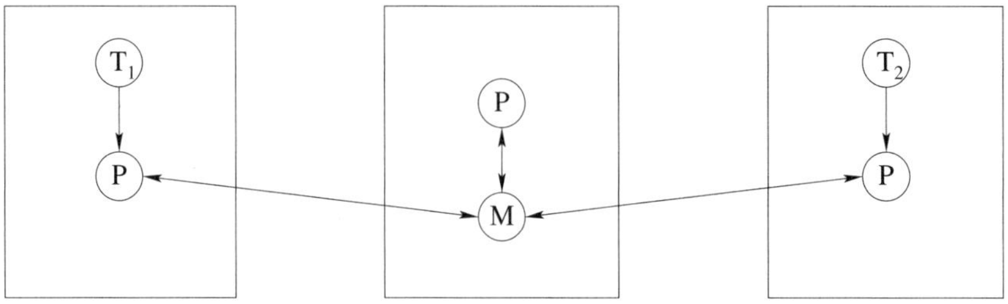

Figure 11.9: Graph notation for a distributed dataflow variable.

11.7.3 Distributed binding protocol

The distributed binding protocol is used to bind dataflow variables that have references on several processes. The general binding algorithm is called unification; the distributed version does distributed unification. A formal definition of the protocol and a proof that it respects the language semantics are given in [82]. The Mozart system implements an extended version of this protocol that is well-behaved in case of network and process failure.

When unification is made distributed it turns out that the whole algorithm remains centralized except for one operation, namely binding a variable. To give the intuition underlying distributed unification it is therefore sufficient to explain distributed binding.

Figure 11.9 shows a dataflow variable V that has remote references on three processes. Like the distributed cell, there are three proxies P and one manager M. The manager has references to all proxies. On the first process, thread T_1 references V and is suspended on the operation `W=V+1`. On the third process, thread T_2 also references V and is about to do the binding `V=10`.

The protocol to bind V consists of two messages: `request`(X) and `binding`(X). Figure 11.10 shows how they are sent. The third proxy initiates the protocol by sending `request`(10) to M. The first such request received by M causes a

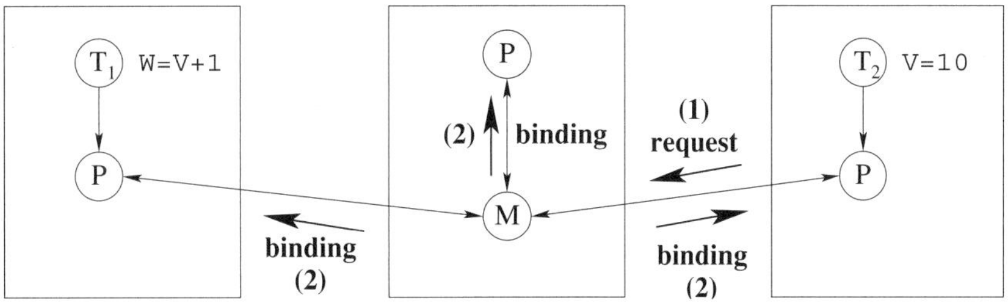

Figure 11.10: Binding a distributed dataflow variable.

`binding`(10) to be sent to all proxies. This action is the heart of the algorithm. The rest is details to make it work in all cases. If M is already bound when it receives the request, then it simply ignores the request. This is correct since the proxy that sent the request will receive a binding in due course. If a new proxy is created on a fourth process, then it must register itself with the manager. There are a few more such cases; they are all explained in [82].

This algorithm has several good properties. In the common case where the variable is on just two processes, e.g., where the binding is used to return the result of a computation, the algorithm's latency is a single round trip. This is the same as explicit message passing. A binding conflict (an attempt to bind the same variable to two incompatible values) will cause an exception to be raised on the process that is responsible for the conflict.

11.7.4 Memory management

When distribution is taken into account, the Mozart system has three levels of garbage collection:

- A local garbage collector per process. This collector coordinates its work with the distributed collectors.
- A distributed garbage collector that uses weighted reference counting.
- A distributed garbage collector based on a time-lease mechanism.

Weighted reference counting The first level of distributed garbage collection uses weighted reference counting [169]. This collector works when there are no failures. It can rapidly remove all distributed garbage except for cross-process cycles between stateful entities on different owner processes. Each remote reference has a nonzero amount of credit as long as it is alive. When the remote reference is reclaimed, the credit is returned to the owner. When the owner sees there is no longer any outstanding credit, then the entity can be reclaimed if there are no more local references.

Weighted reference counting is efficient and scalable. First, creating a new remote reference requires essentially zero network messages in addition to the messages sent by the application. Second, each remote process does not need to know any other process except the owner process. Third, the owner process does not need to know any remote process.

Time-lease mechanism The second level of distributed garbage collection uses a time-lease mechanism. This collector works when there are permanent or long-lived temporary failures. Each remote reference has only a limited lifetime (a "lease on life"), and must periodically send a "lease renewal" message to the owner process. If the owner process does not receive any lease renewal messages after a given (long) time period, then it assumes that the reference may be considered dead.

The time-lease mechanism is complementary to weighted reference counting. The latter reclaims garbage rapidly in the case when there are no failures. The former is much slower, but it is guaranteed in finite time to reclaim all garbage created because of failure. This plugs the memory leaks due to failure.

Programmer responsibility The main problem with distributed garbage collection is to collect cycles of data that exist on several processes and that contain stateful entities. As far as we know, there does not exist an efficient and simple distributed garbage collector that can collect these cycles.

This means that distributed memory management is not completely automatic; the application has to do a little bit of work. For example, consider a client/server application. Each client has a reference to the server. Often, the server has references to the clients. This creates a cycle between each client and the server. If the client and server are on different processes, they cannot be reclaimed. To reclaim a client or a server, it is necessary to break the cycle. This has to be done by the application. There are two ways to do it: either the server has to remove the client reference or the client has to remove the server reference.

Creating a ticket with `{Connection.offerUnlimited X T}` makes `X` a permanent reference. That is, `X` is added to the root set and is never reclaimed. Once-only tickets, i.e., those created with `{Connection.offer X T}`, can only be taken once. As soon as they are taken, `X` is no longer a permanent reference and is potentially reclaimable again.

It is possible to use distribution to reduce the time needed by local garbage collection. With `Remote`, create a small process that runs the time-critical part of the application. Since the process is small, local garbage collection in it will be very fast.

11.8 Partial failure

Let us now extend the distribution model with support for partial failure. We first explain the kinds of failures we detect and how we detect them. Then we show some simple ways to use this detection in applications to handle partial failure.

11.8.1 Fault model

The fault model defines the kinds of distribution faults that can occur in the system and how they are reflected in the language by a failure detection mechanism. We have designed a simple fault model that captures the most common kinds of Internet failures. The Mozart system can detect just two kinds of failures, namely permanent process failure and network inactivity:

- Permanent process failure is commonly known as fail-silent with failure detection. It is indicated by the failure mode `permFail`. That is, a process stops working instantaneously, does not communicate with other processes from that point onward, and the stop can be detected from the outside. Permanent process failure cannot in general be detected on a WAN (e.g., the Internet), but only on a LAN.
- Network inactivity is a kind of temporary failure. It can be either temporary or permanent, but even when it is supposedly permanent, one could imagine the network being repaired. It is different from process failure because the network does not store any state. Network inactivity is indicated by the failure mode `tempFail`. The Mozart system assumes that it is always potentially temporary, i.e., it never times out by default.

These failures are reflected in the language in two ways, either synchronously or asynchronously:

- Synchronous (i.e., lazy) detection is done when attempting to do an operation on a language entity. If the entity is affected by a failure, then the operation is replaced by another, which is predefined by the program. For example, the operation can be replaced by a raised exception.
- Asynchronous (i.e., eager) detection is done independent of any operations. A program first posts a "watcher" on an entity, before any problems occur. Later, if the system detects a problem, then it enables the watcher, which executes a predefined operation in a new thread. Watchers use the well-known heartbeat mechanism for failure detection.

The two failure modes, detected either synchronously or asynchronously, are sufficient for writing fault-tolerant distributed applications. They are provided by Mozart's primitive failure detection module `Fault`.

Network inactivity

The network inactivity failure mode allows the application to react quickly to temporary network problems. It is raised by the system as soon as a network problem is recognized. It is therefore fundamentally different from a time-out. A time-out happens when a part of the system that is waiting for an event abandons the wait. The default behavior of TCP is to give a time-out after some minutes. This duration has been chosen to be very long, approximating infinity from the viewpoint of the network connection. After the time-out, one can be sure that the connection is no longer working.

The purpose of `tempFail` is to inform the application of network problems, not to mark the end of a connection. For example, if an application is connected to a server and if there are problems with the server, then the application would like to be informed quickly so that it can try connecting to another server. A `tempFail` failure mode can therefore be relatively frequent, much more frequent than a time-out. In most cases, a `tempFail` state will eventually go away.

It is possible for a `tempFail` state to last forever. For example, if a user disconnects the network connection of a laptop machine, then only he or she knows whether the problem is permanent. The application cannot in general know this. The decision whether to continue waiting or to stop the wait can cut through all levels of abstraction to appear at the top level (i.e., the user). The application might then pop up a window to ask the user whether to continue waiting or not. The important thing is that the network layer does not make this decision; the application is completely free to decide or to let the user decide.

Where to do time-outs

A surprisingly large number of existing systems (both programming platforms and applications) incorrectly handle prolonged network inactivity. When there is a prolonged network inactivity during an operation, they do a time-out: they abort the waiting operation and invoke an error-handling routine. Often, this abort is irrevocable: it is impossible to continue the operation. Many operating system utilities are of this type, e.g., `ftp` and `ssh`.

The mistake in this approach is that the decision to time-out is made at the wrong level. For example, assume there is a time-out in a lower layer, e.g., the transport layer (TCP) of the network interface. This time-out crosses all abstraction boundaries to appear directly at the top level, i.e., to the user. The user is informed in some way: the application stops, or at best a window is opened asking confirmation to abort the application. The user does not have the possibility to communicate back to the timed-out layer. This limits the flexibility of the system.

The right approach is not to time-out by default but to let the application decide. The application might decide to wait indefinitely (avoiding an abort), to abort immediately without waiting, or to let the user decide what to do. This greatly increases the perceived quality of the system. For example, a hard-mounted resource in the NFS file system offers the first possibility. The Stop button in recent Web browsers offers the third possibility.

11.8.2 Simple cases of failure handling

We show how to handle two cases, namely disconnected operation and failure detection. We show how to use the `Fault` module in either case.

Disconnected operation

Assume that you are running part of an application locally on your machine through a dial-up connection. These connections are not meant to last for very long times; they are made for conversations that usually are short. There are many ways a connection can be broken. For example, you might want to hang up to make an urgent phone call, or you are connected in an airport and your calling card runs out of cash, or the phone company just drops your connection unexpectedly.

You would like your application to be impervious to this kind of fickleness. That is, you would like the application to wait patiently until you reconnect and then continue working as if nothing went wrong. In Mozart, this can be achieved by setting the default failure detection to detect only permanent process failures:

```
% Each process executes this on startup:
{Fault.defaultEnable [permFail] _}
```

This means that operations will only raise exceptions on permanent process failures; on network inactivity they will wait indefinitely until the network problem goes away.

Detecting a problem and taking action

On many computers, booting up is an infuriating experience. How many times have you turned on a laptop, only to wait several minutes because the operating system expects a network connection, and has to time-out before going on? Mozart cannot fix your operating system, but it can make sure that your application will not have the same brainless behavior.

Assume you want to use a remote port. If the remote port has problems (intermittent or no access), then the application should be informed of this fact. This is easy to set up:

```
% Get a reference to the port:
X={Take tickfile}

% Signal as soon as a problem is detected:
{Fault.installWatcher X [tempFail permFail]
   proc {$ _ _}
      {Browse X#' has problems!  Its use is discouraged.'}
   end _}
```

```
fun {NewStat Class Init}
   Obj={New Class Init}
   P
in
   thread S in
      {NewPort S P}
      for M#X in S do
         try {Obj M} X=normal
         catch E then
            try X=exception(E)
            catch system(dp(...) ...) then
                  skip  /* client failure detected */
            end
         end
      end
   end
   proc {$ M}
   X in
      try {Send P M#X} catch system(dp(...) ...) then
         raise serverFailure end
      end
      case X of normal then skip
      [] exception(E) then raise E end end
   end
end
```

Figure 11.11: A resilient server.

The procedure passed to `Fault.installWatcher` is called a watcher; it will be called in its own thread as soon as the system detects a problem. It's up to you to do what's necessary, e.g., set an internal flag to indicate that no communication will be done.

If the problem was `tempFail`, then it is possible that communication with `X` will be restored. If that happens, Mozart allows you to continue using `X` as if nothing wrong had happened.

11.8.3 A resilient server

We saw the `NewStat` operation for creating stationary objects. Let us show how to extend it to be resilient to client failure and at the same time protect the client against server failure. We use the exception-handling mechanism. Attempting to perform an operation on an entity that requires coordination with a remote failed process will raise an exception. We use this behavior to protect both the server and the client from failures. We protect the server by using a **`try`** statement:

```
try {Obj M} X=normal catch ... end
```

This protects the server against a client that shares a variable with the server (in this case `X`). We need a second **try** statement:

```
try X=exception(E) catch _ then skip end
```

since the statement `X=exception(E)` also binds `X`. We protect the client:

```
proc {$ M}
X in
   try {Send P M#X}
   catch _ then raise serverFailure end end
   case X of normal then skip
   [] exception(E) then raise E end end
end
```

The `try {Send P M#X} ... end` signals to the client that the server has failed. In general, any operation on a distributed entity has to be wrapped in a **try**. The complete definition of `NewStat` is given in figure 11.11. Note that distribution faults show up as exceptions of the form `system(dp(...) ...)`.

If `tempFail` detection is enabled, the stationary server defined here will be slowed down if there are communication problems with the client, i.e., it will wait until `tempFail` is raised (e.g., when `try X=exception(E)` is executed). One way around this problem is to provide mutiple server objects to allow serving multiple clients simultaneously.

11.8.4 Active fault tolerance

Applications sometimes need active fault tolerance, i.e., part of the application is replicated on several processes and a replication algorithm is used to keep the parts coherent with each other. Building abstractions to provide this is an active research topic. For example, in Mozart we have built a replicated transactional object store, called GlobalStore [147]. This keeps copies of a set of objects on several processes and gives access to them through a transactional protocol. The copies are kept coherent through the protocol. As long as at least one process is alive, the GlobalStore will survive.

Because of the failure detection provided by the `Fault` module, the Mozart system lets the GlobalStore and other fault-tolerant abstractions be written completely in Oz without recompiling the system. Ongoing research involves building abstractions for active fault tolerance and improved failure detection.

11.9 Security

An application is secure if it can continue to fulfill its specification despite intentional (i.e., malicious) failures of its components. Security is a global problem: a weakness in any part of the system can potentially be exploited. Security is a relative concept: no system is absolutely secure because with sufficient effort it can always be compromised. All we can do is increase the effort required to break the security, until it is not cost-effective for an adversary to attempt it. Security issues appear at each layer of a distributed system. We identify the following layers [83]:

- *Application security.* This is a property of the application program. The application can continue to fulfill its specification despite adversaries whose attacks stay within the permitted operations in the application itself.
- *Language security.* This is a property of the language. In a secure language, applications can continue to fulfill their specifications despite adversaries whose attacks stay within the language. As we explain in section 3.7.7, the kernel languages of the book provide language security because they have a rigorous semantics that permits the construction of secure ADTs.
- *Implementation security.* This is a property of the language implementation in the process. In a secure implementation, applications can continue to fulfill their specifications despite adversaries that attempt to interfere with compiled programs and the language's run-time system. Providing implementation security requires cryptographic techniques that are outside the scope of the book.
- *Operating system security*, *network security*, and *hardware security.* We group these three together, although each of them is a big topic that can be studied separately. The system is secure if applications can continue to fulfill their specifications despite adversaries who attempt to interfere with the operating system, the network, or the hardware. For the operating system and network, we can rely to some degree on off-the-shelf products. Hardware security is another matter entirely. Unless we have a special "hardened" computer, giving physical access to the computer always makes it possible to compromise security.

Each of these layers must be addressed to some degree, or otherwise the application is not secure. To judge how much effort must be put in making each layer secure, a threat model must be set up and a threat analysis done. Then a security policy must be defined, implemented, and verified. These activities are called security engineering. They are beyond the scope of the book. We recommend Anderson's book for an excellent overview [5].

Section 6.4 shows how to build secure data abstractions using language security. These techniques are necessary for building secure applications on the Internet, but they are not sufficient. We also have to address the other layers. For implementation security, we need a secure Mozart implementation. The development of such an implementation is ongoing research. Building implementation-secure systems is a research area with a long tradition. As an entry point in this area, we recommend the work on the E language and its secure implementation [142, 202].

11.10 Building applications

With the examples given in this chapter, you have enough technical knowledge already to build fairly sophisticated distributed applications.

11.10.1 Centralized first, distributed later

Developing an application is done in two phases:

- First, write the application without partitioning the computation between processes. Check the correctness and termination properties of the application on one process. Most of the debugging is done here.
- Second, place the threads on the right processes and give the objects a distributed semantics to satisfy the geographic constraints (placement of resources, dependencies between processes) and the performance constraints (network bandwidth and latency, machine memory and speed).

The large-scale structure of an application consists of a graph of threads and objects. Threads are created on the processes that need them. Objects may be stationary, mobile, or asynchronous. They exchange messages which may refer to objects or other entities. Records and procedures, both stateless entities, are the basic data structures of the application—they are passed automatically between processes when needed. Dataflow variables and locks are used to manage concurrency and dataflow execution.

11.10.2 Handling partial failure

The application must be able to handle partial failure. A good approach is to design for fault confinement. A fault is a failure of part of an application. The application should be designed so that faults can be confined, i.e., their effect will not propagate throughout the whole application but will be limited. Fault confinement has to be part of the initial application design. Otherwise the number of failure modes can be very large, which makes fault confinement infeasible.

There is a trade-off between the communication mode (synchronous or asynchronous) and the fault detection/confinement mechanism. Compared to synchronous communication, asynchronous communication improves performance but makes fault confinement harder. Consider a system with three active objects, T1, T2, and T3. T1 does an asynchronous send to T2 and continues, assuming that T2 is alive. Later, T1 sends a message to T3 under this assumption. But the assumption might have been wrong. T1 might have been executing for a long time under this wrong assumption. With synchronous sends this problem cannot occur. T1 does a synchronous send to T2 and is informed that T2 has a problem before continuing. This confines the fault to an earlier point of the program. The trade-off between early fault detection and asynchronous communication is fundamental, like the choice between optimistic and pessimistic concurrency control. With asynchronous communication, the application must be prepared to correct any false assumptions it makes about the rest of the system working correctly.

There are different ways to realize fault confinement. One way is to build abstractions that do all the fault handling internally. If done well, this can hide completely the complexities of handling faults, at the cost of having to use the particular abstraction. The GlobalStore mentioned before takes this approach. If we cannot hide the faults completely, the next best thing is to have narrow interfaces (say just one port) between processes. A final point is that a message-passing programming style is preferable over a shared-state style. Fault handling of distributed shared state is notoriously difficult.

11.10.3 Distributed components

Functors and resources are the key players in distributed component-based programming. A functor is stateless, so it can be transparently copied anywhere across the net and made persistent by storing a pickle in a file. A functor is linked on a process by evaluating it there with the process resources that it needs ("plugging it in" to the process). The result is a new resource, which can be used as is or linked with more functors. Functors can be used as a core technology driving an open community of developers who contribute to a global pool of useful components.

11.11 Exercises

1. *Implementing network awareness.* Explain exactly what happens in the network (what messages are sent and when) during the execution of the distributed lexical scoping example given in section 11.4. Base your explanation on the distributed algorithms explained in section 11.7.

2. *Distributed lift control system.* Make the lift control system of chapter 5 into a distributed system. Put each component in a separate process. Extend the system to handle partial failure, i.e., when one of the components fails or has communication problems.

3. *A simple chat room.* Use the techniques of this chapter to write a simple server-based chat application. Clients connect to the server, receive all previous messages, and can send new messages. Extend your chat room to handle client failures and server failure. If there is a server failure, the client should detect this and allow the human user to connect to another server.

4. (advanced exercise) *A replicated server.* To make a server resistant to failures, one technique is to replicate it on two processes. Client requests are sent to both replicas, each of which does the computation and returns a result. The client needs only to receive one result. This assumes that the server is deterministic. If one of the replicas fails, the other replica detects this, starts a new second replica using

the `Remote` module, and informs the client. For this exercise, write an abstraction for a replicated server that hides all the fault-handling activities from the clients.

5. (advanced exercise) *Fault tolerance and synchronous communication.* Section 11.10 says that synchronous communication makes fault confinement easier. Section 5.7 says that asynchronous communication helps keep concurrent components independent, which is important when building fault tolerance abstractions. For this exercise, reconcile these two principles by studying the architecture of fault tolerant applications.

12 Constraint Programming

by Peter Van Roy, Raphaël Collet, and Seif Haridi

Plans within plans within plans within plans.
– *Dune*, Frank Herbert (1920–1986)

Constraint programming consists of a set of techniques for solving constraint satisfaction problems. A constraint satisfaction problem, or CSP, consists of a set of constraints on a set of variables. A constraint, in this setting, is simply a logical relation, such as "X is less than Y" or "X is a multiple of 3." The first problem is to find whether there exists a solution, without necessarily constructing it. The second problem is to find one or more solutions.

A CSP can always be solved with brute force search. All possible values of all variables are enumerated and each is checked to see whether it is a solution. Except in very small problems, the number of candidates is usually too large to enumerate them all. Constraint programming has developed "smart" ways to solve CSPs which greatly reduce the amount of search needed. This is sufficient to solve many practical problems. For many problems, though, search cannot be entirely eliminated. Solving CSPs is related to deep questions of intractability. Problems that are known to be intractable will always need some search. The hope of constraint programming is that, for the problems that interest us, the search component can be reduced to an acceptable level.

Constraint programming is qualitatively different from the other programming paradigms that we have seen, such as declarative, object-oriented, and concurrent programming. Compared to these paradigms, constraint programming is much closer to the ideal of declarative programming: to say what we want without saying how to achieve it.

Structure of the chapter

This chapter introduces a quite general approach for tackling CSPs called propagate-and-search or propagate-and-distribute. The chapter is structured as follows:

- Section 12.1 gives the basic ideas of the propagate-and-search approach by means of an example. This introduces the idea of encapsulating constraints inside a kind of container called a computation space.

- Section 12.2 shows how to specify and solve some example constraint problems using propagate-and-search.
- Section 12.3 introduces the constraint-based computation model and its two parts: constraints (including both basic constraints and propagators) and computation spaces.
- Section 12.4 defines computation spaces as an ADT and shows how to program propagate-and-search with them. It introduces the space operations by means of a worked-out example.
- Section 12.5 shows how to implement the **`choice`**, **`fail`**, and `Solve` operations of the relational computation model with computation spaces.

12.1 Propagate-and-search

In this section, we introduce the basic ideas underlying the propagate-and-search approach by means of a simple example. Sections 12.3 and 12.3.2 continue this presentation by showing how the stateful concurrent model is extended to support this approach and how to program with the extended model.

12.1.1 Basic ideas

The propagate-and-search approach is based on three important ideas:

1. Keep partial information. During the calculation, we might have partial information about a solution (such as, "in any solution, X is greater than 100"). We keep as much of this information as possible.
2. Use local deduction. Each of the constraints uses the partial information to deduce more information. For example, combining the constraint "X is less than Y" and the partial information "X is greater than 100," we can deduce that "Y is greater than 101" (assuming Y is an integer).
3. Do controlled search. When no more local deductions can be done, then we have to search. The idea is to search as little as possible. We will do just a small search step and then we will try to do local deduction again. A search step consists in splitting a CSP P into two new problems, $(P \wedge C)$ and $(P \wedge \neg C)$, where C is a new constraint. Since each new problem has an additional constraint, it can do new local deductions. To find the solutions of P, it is enough to take the union of the solutions to the two new problems. The choice of C is extremely important. A well-chosen C will often lead to a solution in just a few search steps.

12.1.2 Calculating with partial information

The first part of constraint programming is calculating with partial information, namely keeping partial information and doing local deduction on it. We give an example to show how this works, using intervals of integers. Assume that x and y measure the sides of a rectangular field of agricultural land in integral meters. We only have approximations to x and y. Assume that $90 \leq x \leq 110$ and $48 \leq y \leq 53$. Now we would like to calculate with this partial information. For example, is the area of the field bigger than 4000 m^2? This is easy to do with constraint programming. We first declare what we know about x and y:

```
declare X Y in
X::90#110
Y::48#53
```

The notation `X::90#110` means $x \in \{90, 91, \ldots, 110\}$. Now let us calculate with this information. With constraint programming, $xy > 4000$ will return with true immediately[1]:

```
declare A in
A::0#10000
A=:X*Y
{Browse A>:4000}   % Displays 1
```

We can also display the area directly:

```
{Browse A}          % Displays A{4320#5830}
```

From this we know the area must be in the range from 4320 to 5830 m^2. The statement `A=:X*Y` is a constraint that multiplies `X` and `Y` and equates the result with `A`. Technically, it is called a propagator: it looks at its arguments a, x, and y, and propagates information between them. In this case, the propagation is simple: the minimal value of a is updated to 90×48 (which is 4320) and the maximal value of a is updated to 110×53 (which is 5830). Note that we have to give the initial information about a, e.g., that it is in the range from 0 to 10000. If we do not give this information, the constraint multiplication `A=:X*Y` will block.

Now let us add some more information about x and y and see what we can deduce from it. Assume we know that the difference $x - 2y$ is exactly 11 m. We know this by fitting a rope to the y side. Passing the rope twice on the x side leaves 11 m. What can we deduce from this fact? Add the constraint:

```
X-2*Y=:11
```

Technically, this new constraint is also a propagator. It does a local deduction with the information we know about x and y. The browser display is automatically updated to `A{5136#5341}`. This considerably increases the accuracy of our mea-

1. The program fragment will display the integer `1`, which means true. The boolean is given as an integer because we often need to do calculations with it.

surement: we know the area must be between 5136 and 5341 m^2 (inclusive). What do we know about x and y? We can display them:

```
{Browse X}
{Browse Y}
```

This displays `X{107#109}` for x and `Y{48#49}` for y. This is a very simple example of calculating with partial information, but it can already be quite useful.

12.1.3 An example

We now look at an example of a complete constraint program, to see how propagate-and-search actually works. Consider the following problem:

> How can I make a rectangle out of 24 unit squares so that the perimeter is exactly 20?

Say that x and y are the lengths of the rectangle's sides. This gives two equations:

$$x \cdot y = 24$$
$$2 \cdot (x + y) = 20$$

The second equation can be simplified to $x + y = 10$. We add a third equation:

$$x \leq y$$

Strictly speaking, the third equation is not necessary, but including it does no harm (since we can always flip a rectangle over) and it will make the problem's solution easier (technically, it reduces the size of the search space). These three equations are constraints. We will implement them as propagators, since we will use them to make local deductions.

To solve the problem, it is useful to start with some information about the variables. We bound the possible values of the variables. This is not absolutely necessary, but it is almost always possible and it often makes solving the problem easier. For our example, assume that X and Y each range from 1 to 9. This is reasonable since they are positive and less than 10. This gives two additional equations:

$$x \in \{1, 2, \ldots, 9\}$$
$$y \in \{1, 2, \ldots, 9\}$$

These equation are also constraints. We will implement them as basic constraints, which can be represented directly in memory. This is possible since they are of the simple form "variable in an explicit set."

The initial problem

Now let us start solving the problem. We have three propagators and two basic constraints. This gives the following situation:

S_1 : `X*Y=:24 X+Y=:10 X=<:Y` || `X::1#9 Y::1#9`

which we will call the computation space S_1. A computation space contains the propagators and the basic constraints on the problem variables. As in the previous example, we use the notation `X::1#9` to mean $x \in \{1, 2, \ldots, 9\}$. We have the three propagators `X*Y=:24`, `X+Y=:10`, and `X=<:Y`. Syntactically, we show that these are propagators by adding the colon `:` to their name.

Local deductions

Each propagator now tries to do local deductions. For example, the propagator `X*Y=:24` notices that since `Y` is at most 9, that `X` cannot be 1 or 2. Therefore `X` is at least 3. It follows that `Y` is at most 8 (since 3*8=24). The same reasoning can be done with `X` and `Y` reversed. The propagator therefore updates the computation space:

S_1 : `X*Y=:24 X+Y=:10 X=<:Y` || `X::3#8 Y::3#8`

Now the propagator `X+Y=:10` enters the picture. It notices that since `Y` cannot be 2, therefore `X` cannot be 8. Similarly, `Y` cannot be 8 either. This gives

S_1 : `X*Y=:24 X+Y=:10 X=<:Y` || `X::3#7 Y::3#7`

With this new information, the propagator `X*Y=:24` can do more deduction. Since `X` is at most 7, therefore `Y` must be at least 4 (because 3*7 is definitely less than 24). If `Y` is at least 4, then `X` must be at most 6. This gives

S_1 : `X*Y=:24 X+Y=:10 X=<:Y` || `X::4#6 Y::4#6`

At this point, none of the propagators sees any opportunities for adding information. We say that the computation space has become stable. Local deduction cannot add any more information.

Using search

How do we continue? We have to make a guess. Let us guess `X=4`. To make sure that we do not lose any solutions, we need two computation spaces: one in which `X=4` and another in which `X`$\neq$`4`. This gives

S_2 : `X*Y=:24 X+Y=:10 X=<:Y` || `X=4 Y::4#6`

S_3 : `X*Y=:24 X+Y=:10 X=<:Y` || `X::5#6 Y::4#6`

Each of these computation spaces now has the opportunity to do local deductions again. For S_2, the local deductions give a value of `Y`:

S_2 : `X*Y=:24 X+Y=:10 X=<:Y` || `X=4 Y=6`

At this point, each of the three propagators notices that it is completely solved (it can never add any more information) and therefore removes itself from the computation space. We say that the propagators are entailed. This gives

S_2 : *(empty)* || `X=4 Y=6`

The result is a solved computation space. It contains the solution `X=4 Y=6`.

Let us see what happens with S_3. Propagator `X*Y=:24` deduces that `X=6 Y=4` is the only possibility consistent with itself (we leave the reasoning to the reader). Then propagator `X=<:Y` sees that there is no possible solution consistent with itself. This causes the space to fail:

S_3 : *(failed)*

A failed space has no solution. We conclude that the only solution is `X=4 Y=6`.

12.1.4 Executing the example

Let us run this example in Mozart. We define the problem by writing a one-argument procedure whose argument is the solution. Running the procedure sets up the basic constraints, the propagators, and selects a distribution strategy. The distribution strategy defines the "guess" that splits the search in two. Here is the procedure definition:

```
proc {Rectangle ?Sol}
   sol(X Y)=Sol
in
   X::1#9    Y::1#9
   X*Y=:24   X+Y=:10   X=<:Y
   {FD.distribute naive Sol}
end
```

The solution is returned as the tuple `Sol`, which contains the two variables `X` and `Y`. Here `X::1#9` and `Y::1#9` are the two basic constraints and `X*Y=:24`, `X+Y=:10`, and `X=<:Y` are the three propagators. The `FD.distribute` call selects the distribution strategy. The chosen strategy (`naive`) selects the first nondetermined variable in `Sol`, and picks the leftmost element in the domain as a guess. To find the solutions, we pass the procedure to a general search engine:

```
{Browse {SolveAll Rectangle}}
```

This displays a list of all solutions, namely `[sol(4 6)]` since there is only one.

All the constraint operations used in this example, namely `::`, `=:`, `=<:`, and `FD.distribute`, are predefined in the Mozart system. The full constraint programming support of Mozart consists of several dozen operations. All of these operations are defined in the constraint-based computation model. This model introduces just two new concepts to the stateful concurrent model: finite domain constraints (basic constraints like `X::1#9`) and computation spaces. All the richness of constraint programming in Mozart is provided by this model.

12.1.5 Summary

The fundamental concept used to implement propagate-and-search is the computation space, which contains propagators and basic constraints. Solving a problem alternates two phases. A space first does local deductions with the propagators. When no more local deductions are possible, i.e., the space is stable, then a search step is done. In this step, two copies of the space are first made. A basic constraint C is then "guessed" according to a heuristic called the distribution strategy. The constraint C is then added to the first copy and $\neg C$ is added to the second copy. We then continue with each copy. The process is continued until all spaces are either solved or failed. This gives us all solutions to the problem.

12.2 Programming techniques

Now that we have seen the basic concepts, let us see how to program with them. A constraint problem is defined by a one-argument procedure. The procedure argument is bound to the solution of the problem. Inside the procedure, next to the usual language operations, two new kinds of operations are possible:

- Posting constraints. These specify the relationships between the different parts of the problem. They can be either basic constraints or propagators.
- Specifying the distribution strategy. This specifies how the search tree is to be formed, i.e., which constraints C and $\neg C$ are chosen at each node when doing a search step.

In contrast to relational programming (see chapter 9), there is no explicit creation of choice points (no **`choice`** statement). This would be too crude a way to search; what actually happens is that choice points are created dynamically in terms of the distribution strategy that is specified.

12.2.1 A cryptarithmetic problem

Now that we have the basic concepts, let us see how we can program with them. As an example we take a well-known combinatoric puzzle, the Send-More-Money problem [193]. The problem is to assign digits to letters such that the following addition makes sense:

```
proc {SendMoreMoney ?Sol}
   S E N D M O R Y
in
   Sol=sol(s:S e:E n:N d:D m:M o:O r:R y:Y)   %1
   Sol:::0#9                                  %2
   {FD.distinct Sol}                          %3
   S\=:0                                      %4
   M\=:0
                1000*S + 100*E + 10*N + D     %5
   +            1000*M + 100*O + 10*R + E
   =: 10000*M + 1000*O + 100*N + 10*E + Y
   {FD.distribute ff Sol}                     %6
end
```

Figure 12.1: Constraint definition of the Send-More-Money problem.

$$\begin{array}{ccccc} & S & E & N & D \\ + & M & O & R & E \\ \hline M & O & N & E & Y \end{array}$$

There are two conditions: each letter is assigned to a different digit and the leading digits of the numbers are different from zero ($S \neq 0$ and $M \neq 0$).

To solve this problem with constraints, the first step is to model the problem, i.e., to set up data structures and constraints that reflect the problem structure. In this problem, it is easy: each digit is a variable and the problem conditions become constraints on the variables. There are eight different letters, and therefore eight variables.

The second step is to define a one-argument procedure that implements this model. Figure 12.1 shows one way to define the procedure. The numbered statements have the following effects:

1. The solution `Sol` is a record with one field for every different letter.
2. The fields of `Sol` are integers in the domain $\{0, \ldots, 9\}$.
3. The fields of `Sol` are pairwise distinct, i.e., no two have the same value. This uses the propagator `FD.distinct`.
4. Since they are leading digits, the values of `S` and `M` are not zero. This uses the inequality constraint `\=:`.
5. All the digits satisfy the equation $SEND + MORE = MONEY$.
6. The distribution strategy tries the letters according to a first-fail strategy (`ff`). This means that the strategy tries first the letter with the least number of possibilities, and with this letter it tries the least value first.

The third step is to solve the problem:

```
{Browse {SolveAll SendMoreMoney}}
```

This computes and displays a list of all solutions. Note that this is done in the same way as search in relational programming (see chapter 9). This displays

```
[sol(d:7 e:5 m:1 n:6 o:0 r:8 s:9 y:2)]
```

In other words, there is just one solution, which is

$$\begin{array}{ccccc} & 9 & 5 & 6 & 7 \\ + & 1 & 0 & 8 & 5 \\ \hline 1 & 0 & 6 & 5 & 2 \end{array}$$

That is all there is to it! In practice, things are a bit more complicated, for the following reasons:

- *Modeling the problem.* Modeling the problem is not always easy. There are often many possible ways to represent the problem with constraints.
- *Making the solution efficient.* The first solution to a realistic problem is usually too inefficient. There are many techniques to improve it. Some possibilities are to take advantage of problem structure, to use redundant constraints, to use different distribution strategies, and to use the Explorer (an interactive graphical search tree exploration tool; see [191]). It is not always obvious which one is best!
- *Understanding the constraints and distribution strategies.* There are many constraints and distribution strategies to choose from. Which ones are best depends strongly on the problem.

12.2.2 Palindrome products revisited

In section 9.2.1, we saw how to find palindrome products with relational programming. The technique used there takes 45 seconds to find all solutions for six-digit palindromes. Here is a smarter solution that takes advantage of constraints and the propagate-and-search approach:

```
proc {Palindrome ?Sol}
   sol(A)=Sol
   B C X Y Z
in
   A::0#999999 B::0#999 C::0#999
   A=:B*C
   X::0#9 Y::0#9 Z::0#9
   A=:X*100000+Y*10000+Z*1000+Z*100+Y*10+X
   {FD.distribute ff [X Y Z]}
end
```

This takes slightly less than two seconds.[2] We can do even better by realizing that a palindrome $XYZZYX$ is always a multiple of 11. That is, $XYZZYX = X \cdot 100001 + Y \cdot 10010 + Z \cdot 1100$, which means $XYZZYX/11 = X \cdot 9091 + Y \cdot 910 + Z \cdot 100$.

2. Using Mozart 1.1.0 on a Pentium III processor at 500 MHz.

Taking advantage of this, we can specify the problem as follows:

```
proc {Palindrome ?Sol}
   sol(A)=Sol
   B C X Y Z
in
   A::0#90909 B::0#90 C::0#999
   A=:B*C
   X::0#9 Y::0#9 Z::0#9
   A=:X*9091+Y*910+Z*100
   {FD.distribute ff [X Y Z]}
end
```

This takes slightly less than 0.4 second to solve the same problem. What can we conclude from this simple example? Many things:

- A constraint-based formulation of a combinatoric problem can be much faster than a a generate-and-test formulation. For palindrome product, the constraint solution is more than 100 times faster than the naive solution.
- To make it fast, you also have to take advantage of the problem structure. A little bit of smarts goes a long way. For palindrome product, taking advantage of the solution being a multiple of 11 makes the program five times faster.
- A fast solution is not necessarily more complicated than a slow solution. Compare the slow and fast solutions to palindrome product: they are about equal in length and ease of understanding.
- Performance can depend strongly on the exact problem formulation. Changing it a little bit can make it much faster or (usually) much slower.
- To write a good specification, you have to understand the operational meaning of the constraints as well as the logical meaning. The latter is enough for showing correctness, but the former is essential to get good performance.

12.3 The constraint-based computation model

In the example of section 12.1.3, we saw that the propagate-and-search approach is supported by three concepts: basic constraints, propagators, and computation spaces. Let us see now what this means in terms of the computation model. Basic constraints and computation spaces are new concepts that are added to the model. Basic constraints are stored in the single-assignment store. Bindings of dataflow variables are one kind of basic constraint; in this chapter we will see other kinds.

Computation spaces are depicted in figure 12.2, which gives an overview of the constraint-based computation model. Each rectangle in this figure represents all the entities in a computation model, like we saw in previous chapters. Each rectangle is called a "computation space." The biggest rectangle contains the entities that can communicate with the outside world. It is called the top-level computation space. The smaller rectangles are created as part of the execution of the constraint

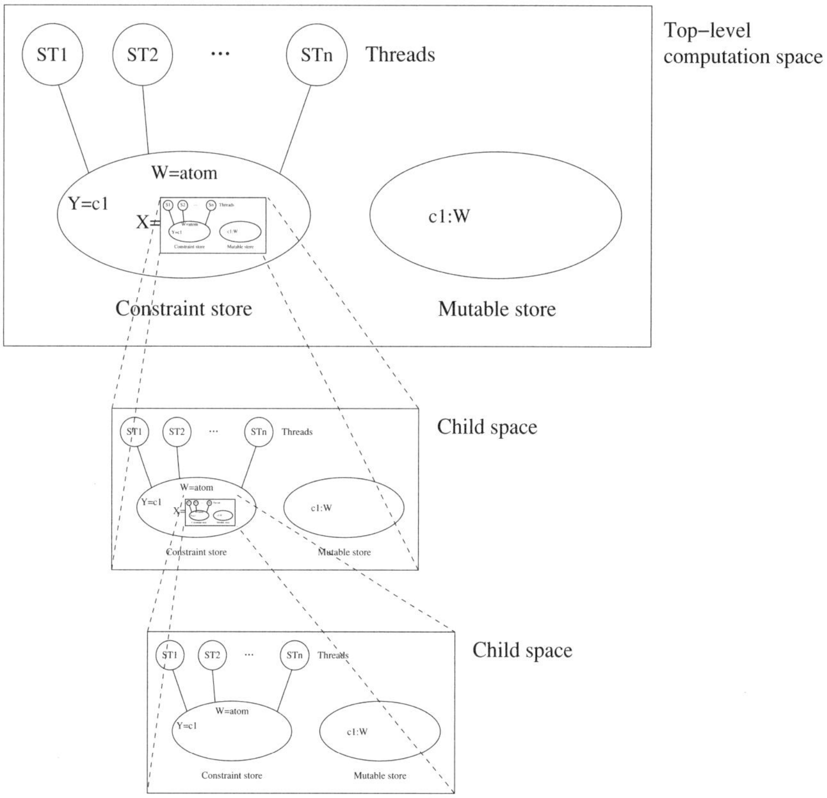

Figure 12.2: Constraint-based computation model.

program. They are called child spaces. They can be nested, i.e., a child space can create further child spaces inside itself.

A computation space collects together basic constraints and propagators, as we saw in the example of section 12.1.3, and puts them inside an encapsulation boundary. A propagator is simply a thread that can add new basic constraints to the store. A computation space is always created inside a parent space; it can see the constraints of its parent. In figure 12.2, X is bound to a computation space that is created inside the top-level space.

12.3.1 Basic constraints and propagators

Basic constraints are constraints that are directly represented in the single-assignment store. An example of a basic constraint is a binding of a dataflow variable, such as x = person(age:y). This gives partial information about x. Chapter 2 shows how these bindings are represented in the store. The binding represents an equality constraint between the dataflow variable and a partial value.

In this chapter, we extend the store with a new kind of basic constraint, namely membership in a finite domain. A finite domain is a finite set of integers. The new basic constraint is an equation of the form $x \in D$, where D is a finite domain. This gives partial information about x: it means that x is an integer in the set D. This basic constraint is added to the store by the statement $x::D$. The domain D is specified with a compact syntax that we showed in the examples of the previous sections. We note that the finite domain constraint $x \in \{n\}$ is equivalent to the binding $x{=}n$.

Adding the constraints $x::D_1$, $x::D_2$, ..., $x::D_n$ restricts the domain of x to $D_1 \cap D_2 \cap \cdots \cap D_n$, provided that the latter is nonempty. Adding a constraint with an empty domain for a variable would result in an inconsistent store (do you see why?), so such an attempt must fail.

The single-assignment store we saw in chapter 2 can be considered as a constraint store. The basic constraints it represents are all of the form $x{=}y$, where x and y are partial values. We call these constraints "bindings," although they can do more than simply bind a variable to a value. The general operation of binding two partial values together is called unification, which is defined in section 2.8.2.

What are all the complete values to which a fresh variable can be bound? This is not an obvious question, since we can add cyclic bindings to the store, e.g., the binding `X=foo(X)`. It turns out that variables can be bound to rational trees. A rational tree generalizes the finite trees of section 3.4.6 to allow certain kinds of infinite trees that can be stored in a finite space. A rational tree can be represented by a rooted directed graph. Unfolding the graph to remove cycles and sharing yields the tree. For example, the graph `X=foo(X)` represents the tree `X=foo(foo(foo(...)))`. This tree is infinite, i.e., it has an infinite number of nodes, but it is stored in a finite space, i.e., as the binding `X=foo(X)`.

When a variable is initially declared, it can potentially be bound to any rational tree. Each basic constraint, i.e., each binding, that we add to the store restricts the set of rational trees to which the variable can be bound. For example, adding the constraint x `=person(age:`y`)` restricts the possible bindings of x, namely to rational trees whose root is a record of label `person` with one field whose feature name is `age`. The single-assignment store therefore implements constraints over rational trees.

The set of complete values to which a variable can be bound is called its domain. This book gives constraints over two domains: rational trees and finite domains. Many other constraint domains are possible, e.g., the Mozart system implements finite sets of integers, fine-grained records, and real intervals.

A propagator is a thread that continually observes the store and occasionally adds new basic constraints to the store. Each time a variable's domain is changed in the store, the propagators that use that variable must be given a chance to execute, so they can propagate new partial information to variables. Waiting for a domain change is a fine-grained variant of waiting for determinacy.

The solution of a constraint problem typically involves many propagators. Since propagators can be identical, this is a multiset. The execution of these propagators must behave in a declarative concurrent fashion, as we defined in section 4.1.4. That is, no matter in what order the propagators execute, the final stores must be logically equivalent. This property is important for defining controlled search with computation spaces.

12.3.2 Programming search with computation spaces

In the previous sections of this chapter we have seen how to do constraint programming with operations that provide search and distribution strategies. In this section and the next we explain how to program these operations with computation spaces. A computation space is a data abstraction that is designed to implement the propagate-and-search technique of section 12.1. All the search abstractions of chapter 9 and this chapter are programmed using spaces.

Computation spaces have the flexibility needed for real-world constraint problems and they can be implemented efficiently: on real-world problems the Mozart implementation using copying and recomputation is competitive in time and memory use with traditional systems using trailing-based backtracking [187]. The computation space abstraction can be made language-independent; [88] describes a C++ implementation of a similar abstraction that provides both trailing and copying.

We outline how computation spaces are used to implement search and distribution strategies. A search strategy defines how the search tree is explored, e.g., depth-first search or breadth-first search. A distribution strategy defines the shape and content of the search tree, i.e., how many alternatives exist at a node and what constraint is added for each alternative. Computation spaces can be used to program search strategies and distribution strategies independent of each other. That is, any search strategy can be used together with any distribution strategy. Here is how it is done:

- Create the space with the correct program inside. This program defines all the variables and constraints in the space.
- Let the program run inside the space. Variables and propagators are created. All propagators execute until no more information can be added to the store in this manner. The space eventually reaches stability.
- During the space's execution, the computation inside the space can decide to create a choice point. The decision of which constraint to add for each alternative defines the distribution strategy. One of the space's threads will suspend when the choice point is created.
- When the space has become stable, execution continues outside the space, to decide what to do next. There are different possibilities depending on whether or not a choice point has been created in the space. If there is none, then execution can stop and return with a solution. If there is one, then the search strategy decides which alternative to choose and commits to that alternative.

The next section defines the operations we need for this approach, by means of a

```
fun {DFE S}
   case {Ask S}
   of failed then nil
   [] succeeded then [S]
   [] alternatives(2) then C={Clone S} in
      {Commit S 1}
      case {DFE S} of nil then {Commit C 2} {DFE C}
      [] [T] then [T]
      end
   end
end

% Given {Script Sol}, returns solution [Sol] or nil:
fun {DFS Script}
   case {DFE {NewSpace Script}} of nil then nil
   [] [S] then [{Merge S}]
   end
end
```

Figure 12.3: Depth-first single-solution search.

concrete example. Section 12.5 gives another example of how to program search with spaces, namely the `Solve` operation of chapter 9. Many other strategies can be programmed than are shown here; for more information see [188, 190].

12.4 Defining and using computation spaces

To explain how computation spaces work, we explain in detail how they are used to implement a search engine on a small problem. We introduce and define the space operations as they are needed (see table 12.1). The discussion in this section follows the model in [188, 190]. This model is implemented in the Mozart system [148] and refines the one presented in the articles [186, 189].

12.4.1 A depth-first search engine

Figure 12.3 shows how to program depth-first single-solution search in the case of binary choice points. This explores the search tree in depth-first manner and returns the first solution it finds. The problem is defined as a one-argument procedure `Script`, whose single argument `Sol` gives a reference to the solution, just like the examples of section 12.2. The solution is returned in a one-element list as `[Sol]`. If there is no solution, then `nil` is returned. In `Script`, choice points are defined with the primitive space operation `Choose`.

The search function uses the primitive space operations `NewSpace`, `Ask`, `Commit`, `Clone`, and `Merge`. Table 12.1 lists the complete set of primitive operations. In

```
⟨statement⟩ ::= {NewSpace ⟨x⟩ ⟨y⟩}
             | {WaitStable}
             | {Choose ⟨x⟩ ⟨y⟩}
             | {Ask ⟨x⟩ ⟨y⟩}
             | {Commit ⟨x⟩ ⟨y⟩}
             | {Clone ⟨x⟩ ⟨y⟩}
             | {Inject ⟨x⟩ ⟨y⟩}
             | {Merge ⟨x⟩ ⟨y⟩}
```

Table 12.1: Primitive operations for computation spaces.

Mozart, these operations are grouped together in the `Space` module. We explain each operation in detail as it appears in the execution.

12.4.2 A script example

Let us run the search engine on the example of section 12.1.3. We specified the problem with a script, which is the procedure `Rectangle`:

```
proc {Rectangle ?Sol}
   sol(X Y)=Sol
in
   X::1#9   Y::1#9
   X*Y=:24  X+Y=:10  X=<:Y
   {FD.distribute naive Sol}
end
```

We start the execution with the statement `Sol={DFS Rectangle}`, where `DFS` and `Rectangle` are defined as above, and `Sol` is a fresh variable. If we expand the body of the function, it should create two variables, say `S` and `L`, leading to a configuration like the following. The box represents the thread that executes the statements, and below it is a representation of the store:

```
S={NewSpace Rectangle}
L={DFE S}
Sol=case L of ... end
```

```
Rectangle=<proc>   Sol   L   S
```

We denote the procedure value by `<proc>` for short.

12.4.3 Space creation

The first primitive space operation we use is `NewSpace`. In our example, it creates a new computation space `S`, with a root variable `Root`, and one thread that executes `{Rectangle Root}`. Both the new thread and the new store are shown inside a box, which delimits the "boundaries" of the space.

```
L={DFE S}
Sol=case L of ... end
```

```
Rectangle=<proc>   Sol   L   S= | {Rectangle Root} |
                                |      Root        |
```

Here is the definition of NewSpace:

- S={NewSpace P}, when given a one-argument procedure P, creates a new computation space and returns a reference to it. In this space, a fresh root variable R and a new thread are created, and {P R} is invoked in the thread.

Recall that a computation space encapsulates a computation. It is thus an instance of the stateful concurrent model, with its three parts: thread store, constraint store, and mutable store. As it can itself nest a computation space, the spaces naturally form a tree structure:

- There is always a top-level computation space where threads may interact with the external world. A thread may create a new computation space. The new space is called a child space. The current space is the child's parent space. At any time, there is a tree of computation spaces in which the top-level space is the root. With respect to a given space, a higher one in the tree (closer to the root) is called an ancestor and a lower one is called a descendant.
- Threads and variables belong to spaces. A thread always belongs to exactly one computation space. A variable always belongs to exactly one computation space.

12.4.4 Space execution

Now let us focus on the space S. The thread inside is runnable, so we will run it. The reduction of the procedure call {Rectangle Root} gives

```
   local sol(X Y)=Root in
      X::1#9   Y::1#9
      X*Y=:24  X+Y=:10  X=<:Y
S=    {FD.distribute naive Root}
   end
                 Root
```

You might have noticed that the variable Rectangle is bound outside the space, which did not prevent the inner thread from reading its value and using it. Computation spaces respect precise visibility rules. Those rules provide a certain degree of isolation from the "external" computation:

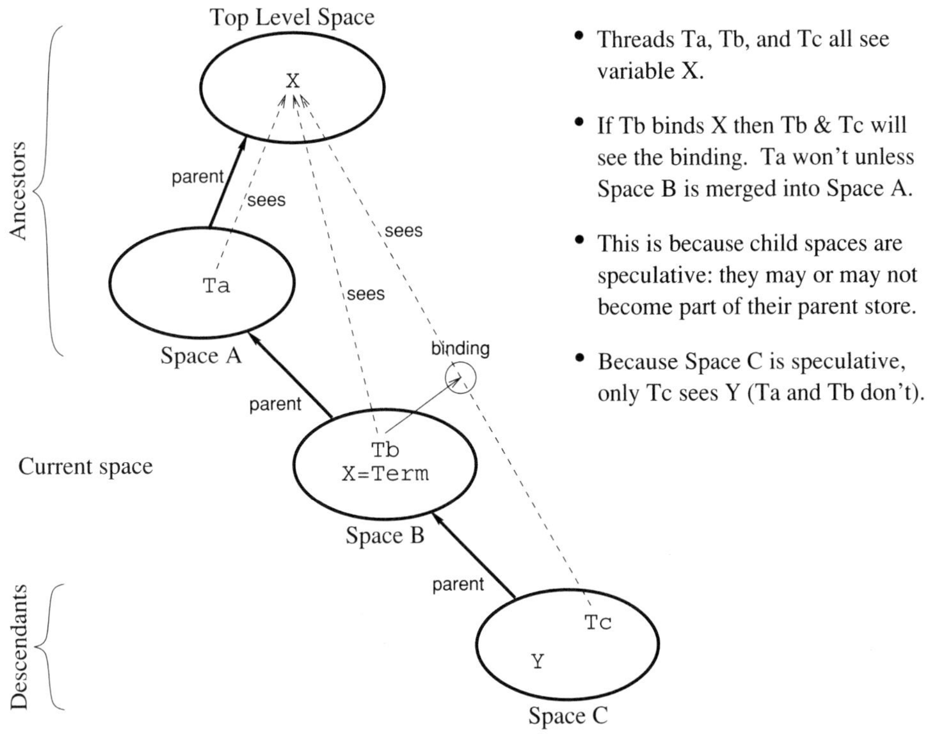
Top Level Space
X
parent
sees
sees
Ta
sees
Space A
binding
parent
Tb
X=Term
Current space
Space B
parent
Tc
Y
Space C
Ancestors
Descendants
• Threads Ta, Tb, and Tc all see variable X.
• If Tb binds X then Tb & Tc will see the binding. Ta won't unless Space B is merged into Space A.
• This is because child spaces are speculative: they may or may not become part of their parent store.
• Because Space C is speculative, only Tc sees Y (Ta and Tb don't).

Figure 12.4: Visibility of variables and bindings in nested spaces.

- Visibility of variables. A thread sees and may access variables belonging to its space as well as to all ancestor spaces. The thread cannot see the variables of descendant spaces. Figure 12.4 gives an example with bindings.
- Visibility of basic constraints. A thread may add basic constraints to variables it sees. This means that it may constrain variables belonging to its space or to its ancestor spaces. The basic constraint will only be visible in the current space and its descendants. That is, the parent space does not see the binding unless the current space is merged with it (see later).

12.4.5 Posting constraints

The thread inside the space continues its execution. It creates two new variables `X` and `Y` inside the space, and binds `Root` to `sol(X Y)`. This gives

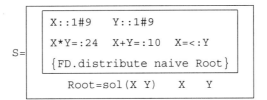

```
S= | X::1#9   Y::1#9
   | X*Y=:24  X+Y=:10  X=<:Y
   | {FD.distribute naive Root}
   |
   |   Root=sol(X Y)   X   Y
```

It then tells the basic constraints `X::1#9` and `Y::1#9` to the constraint store of the space, and creates new propagators, each one in its own thread. We have:

```
     X*Y=:24   X+Y=:10   X=<:Y   {FD.distribute naive Root}
S=
          Root=sol(X Y)    X::1#9    Y::1#9
```

12.4.6 Concurrent propagation

Now propagators enter the scene. As we have seen in section 12.1.3, they propagate concurrently, reducing the domains to `4#6`. The space becomes:

```
     X*Y=:24   X+Y=:10   X=<:Y   {FD.distribute naive Root}
S=
          Root=sol(X Y)    X::4#6    Y::4#6
```

Execution in a computation space is a variant of the maximally concurrent model defined in section 8.2, where each propagator executes in its own thread. It avoids the difficulties usually associated with this model. Let us see why this is possible. Each constraint is implemented as a propagator, i.e., a thread, that executes concurrently with the other propagators. Each propagator adds information to the store until no more information can be added. Constraint programming avoids the difficulties of the maximally concurrent model because propagator execution is monotonic: propagators only add information, they never change or remove information. (This is essentially the same reason why concurrent declarative programming is simpler than concurrent stateful programming.) Furthermore, propagators have a logical semantics. All the information they add is consistent with this semantics. If they are written correctly, then the exact order in which they execute does not matter. When they reach a fixpoint i.e., when no propagator can add any more information, the result is always the same. We say the space is stable.

12.4.7 Distribution (search step)

`FD.distribute` implements the distribution strategy. It first uses `WaitStable` to detect when the space becomes stable. At that point, it picks a variable and a value following a heuristic, in this case `X` and `4`, and proposes a "guess." For this it executes the statement `{Choose 2}`, which creates a choice point with two alternatives, and blocks until a call to `Commit` unblocks it. The interaction between `Choose` and `Commit` is explained in detail later. The whole computation (including the parent space) now looks like

```
L={DFE S}
Sol=case L of ... end

Rectangle=<proc>   Sol   L
```

```
     X*Y=:24     case {Choose 2}
                 of 1 then X=4 {FD.distribute [Y]}
S=   X+Y=:10     [] 2 then X\=:4 {FD.distribute Root}
     X=<:Y       end
          Root=sol(X Y)   X::4#6   Y::4#6
```

`WaitStable` and `Choose` are the only two space operations that are called from inside the space. The remaining operations are all called from outside the space. Here are the definitions of `WaitStable` and `Choose`:

- `{WaitStable}` waits until the current space becomes stable. At that instant, the thread containing `WaitStable` becomes runnable again. This thread should eventually execute a `Choose` operation (see below). Viewed from the outside, the space is not stable until the `Choose` operation is encountered.
- `Y={Choose N}` waits until the current space becomes stable (it should normally already be stable), blocks the current thread, and then creates a choice point with `N` alternatives in the current space. The blocked `Choose` call waits for an alternative to be chosen by a `Commit` operation on the space. The `Choose` call only defines *how many* alternatives there are; it does not specify what to do for any given alternative. Eventually, `Choose` continues its execution and returns with `Y=I` when alternative `I` (with `1≤I≤N`) is chosen. A maximum of one choice point may exist in a space at any time.

12.4.8 State of a space

The space is running concurrently with its parent space. The thread of the search engine, outside the space, now executes the statement `L={DFE S}`, which evaluates `{Ask S}`. This operation asks the space for its status. In this case, it returns `alternatives(2)`, meaning that a choice point with two alternatives has been created inside the space. After reduction of the **case** statement, the whole computation becomes:

```
local C={Clone S} in
   {Commit S 1}
   L=case {DFE S} of ... end
end
Sol=case L of ... end
```

```
Rectangle=<proc>   Sol   L   S=<space>
```

Let us give a precise definition of the various states of a space. A space is runnable if it or a descendant contains a runnable thread, and blocked otherwise. Let us run all threads in the space and its descendants, until the space is blocked. Then the space can be in one of the following further states:

- The space is stable. This means that no matter what additional basic constraints are added in an ancestor, the space will not become runnable. A stable space can be in four further states:
  - The space is succeeded. This means that it contains no choice points. A succeeded space contains a solution to the logic program.
  - The space is distributable. This means that the space has one thread that is suspended on a choice point with two or more alternatives. A space can have at most one choice point; attempting to create another gives an error.
  - The space is failed. This means that the space attempted to tell inconsistent basic constraints, e.g., binding the same variable to two different values. No further execution happens in the space.
  - The space is merged. This means that the space has been discarded and its constraint store has been added to a parent. Any further operation on the space is an error. This state is the end of a space's lifetime.
- The space is suspended. This means that additional basic constraints done in an ancestor can make the space runnable. Being suspended is usually a temporary condition due to concurrency. It means that some ancestor space has not yet transferred all required information to the space. A space that stays not stable indefinitely usually indicates a programmer error.

Here is the definition of `Ask`:

- `A={Ask S}` asks the space `S` for its status. As soon as the space becomes stable, `A` is bound. If `S` is failed, merged, or succeeded, then `Ask` returns `failed`, `merged`, or `succeeded`. If `S` is distributable, then it returns `alternatives(N)`, where `N` is the number of alternatives.

12.4.9 Cloning a space

The next statement of the search engine thread declares a variable `C`, and creates a copy of the space `S`. Note that variables and threads belonging to `S` are copied too, so that both spaces are independent of each other. For the sake of simplicity, we have kept the same identifiers for `S` and `C` in the picture below. But they actually denote different variables in the stores.

```
{Commit S 1}
L=case {DFE S} of ... end
Sol=case L of ... end
```

```
Rectangle=<proc>   Sol   L
```

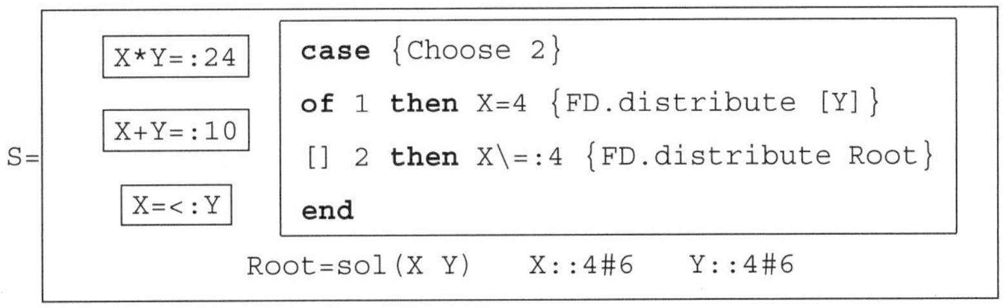

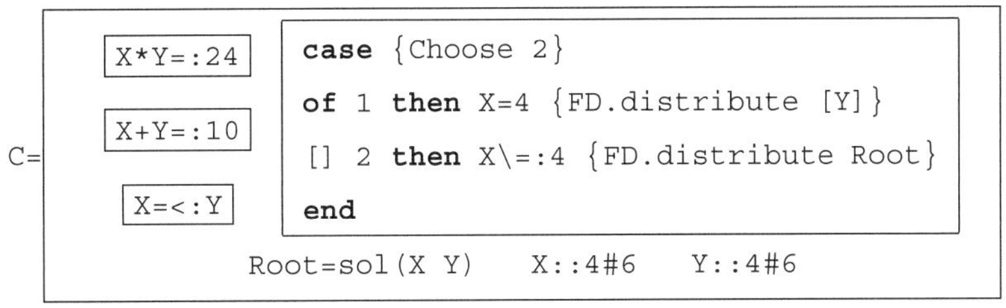

Here is the definition of `Clone`:

- `C={Clone S}` waits until `S` is stable, then creates an identical copy (a clone) of `S` and returns a reference to the clone. This allows both alternatives of a distributable space to be explored.

12.4.10 Committing to an alternative

The search engine then executes `{Commit S 1}`. This indicates to the space `S` to enter the first alternative. So the call to `Choose` inside the space unblocks and returns `1`. The distributor thread then binds `X` to `4`, which leads to the space

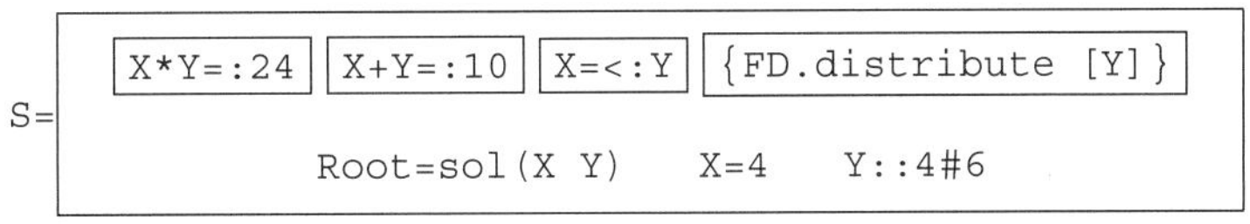

Here is the definition of `Commit`:

- `{Commit S I}`, if `S` is a distributable space, causes the `Choose` call in the space to complete and return `I` as its result. This may cause the space to resume execution. The integer `I` must satisfy `1≤I≤N`, where `N` is the first argument of the `Choose` call.

Now we see precisely how to make the search strategy interact with the distribution strategy. The basic technique is to use `Choose`, `Ask`, and `Commit` to communicate between the inside of a space and the search strategy, which is programmed in the parent space. Figure 12.5 shows how the communication works. Within the space, calling `I={Choose N}` first informs the search strategy of the total number of alternatives (`N`). Then the search strategy picks one (`I`) and informs the space. The synchronization condition between the inside of the space and the search strategy is stability, i.e., that there are no more local deductions possible inside the space.

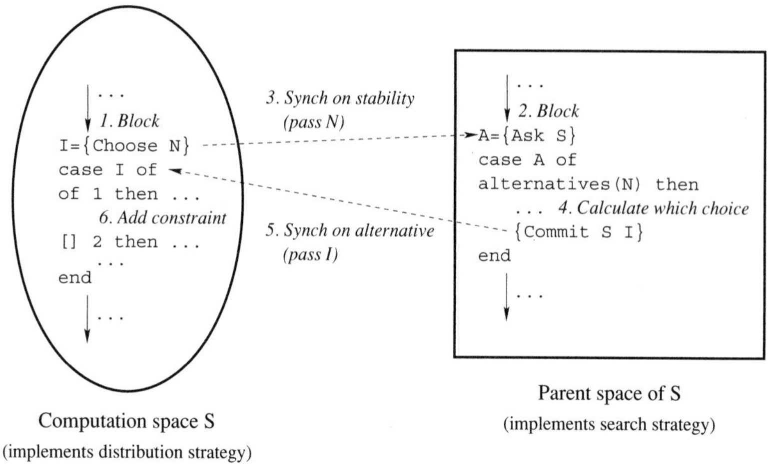

Figure 12.5: Communication between a space and its distribution strategy.

12.4.11 Merging a space

The propagators inside S now run until both variables become determined. Since all the propagators are entailed by the store, they simply disappear from S:

```
S= | {FD.distribute [Y]}
   | Root=sol(X Y)   X=4   Y=6
```

The distributor thread terminates too, because Y is determined, so the whole computation becomes:

```
L=case {DFE S} of ... end
Sol=case L of ... end

Rectangle=<proc>   Sol   L   S= | Root=sol(X Y)   X=4   Y=6 |

C= | X*Y=:24    case {Choose 2}
   | X+Y=:10    of 1 then X=4 {FD.distribute [Y]}
   | X=<:Y      [] 2 then X\=:4 {FD.distribute Root}
   |            end
   | Root=sol(X Y)   X::4#6   Y::4#6
```

The search engine calls again {DFE S}, which performs {Ask S}. The returned value is now succeeded, which means that the computation inside S has terminated with a consistent store. The search engine continues its execution. The call to {DFE S} then returns [S]. The latter matches the second clause in DFS, and the search ends with the statement Sol=[{Merge S}]. The call {Merge S} merges S with the current space, and returns the root variable of S. The computation becomes:

```
Rectangle=<proc>    Sol=Root    L=[S]    S=<merged>
          Root=sol(X Y)    X=4    Y=6
```

```
C=
  X*Y=:24     case {Choose 2}
              of 1 then X=4 {FD.distribute [Y]}
  X+Y=:10     [] 2 then X\=:4 {FD.distribute Root}
              end
  X=<:Y
          Root=sol(X Y)    X::4#6    Y::4#6
```

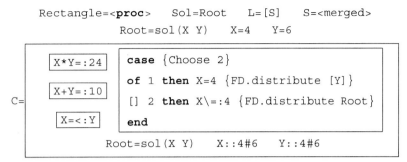

Merging a space is necessary to access the solution. A thread cannot see the variables of a child space unless the child space is merged with its parent. Merging is an explicit program operation. It causes the child space to disappear and all the child's content to be added to the parent space. Here is the definition of Merge:

- {Merge S Y} binds Y to the root variable of space S and discards the space.

12.4.12 Space failure

Suppose now that the search would continue. This would be the case if the first alternative had no solution. The search engine would then execute {Commit C 2} L={DFE C}. The statement {Commit C 2} causes {Choose 2} to return 2, which makes the space C evolve to

```
C=
  X*Y=:24   X+Y=:10   X=<:Y   {FD.distribute Root}

          Root=sol(X Y)    X::5#6    Y::4#6
```

As we have seen, the action of the propagators lead to inconsistencies. For instance, X*Y=:24 propagates the constraints X=6 and Y=4. The propagator X=<:Y cannot be satisfied with those values, which makes the space C fail:

```
C=<failed>
```

In the search engine, the call to {Ask C} would return failed. This means that C contains no solution. The search would then return nil in that case.

Failures, stateful operations, and interaction with the external world are encapsulated in computation spaces in the following way:

- Exceptions and failures. A thread that tries to add an inconsistent basic constraint to its constraint store will raise a failure exception. What happens then in the top-level space is implementation-dependent. If the exception occurs in a child space and is not caught, then the space fails. A failure happening in a propagator immediately results in its space's failure, because propagators are threads by themselves.
- Stateful operations. Operations on stateful entities across spaces are forbidden. For instance, a thread cannot read or change the value of a cell that belongs to its

space's parent. A consequence is that only the top-level space can interact with the external world.

12.4.13 Injecting a computation into a space

There is one primitive operation that we have not used, namely `Inject`. This operation permits adding constraints to an existing space. For instance, you can constrain the solution of a space to be "better" than an already-known solution. The definition of "better" is problem-dependent, of course. Here is the definition of `Inject`:

- `{Inject S P}` is similar to space creation except that it uses an existing space `S`. It creates a new thread in the space and invokes `{P R}` in the thread, where `R` is the space's root variable. This makes a stable space not stable again. Adding constraints to an existing space is necessary for some distribution strategies such as branch-and-bound and saturation [188, 190].

12.5 Implementing the relational computation model

We end this brief introduction to constraint programming by connecting with the relational computation model of chapter 9. The relational model extends the declarative model with **choice** and **fail** statements and with a `Solve` operation to do encapsulated search. We show how to program these operations with computation spaces. We have already shown how to do **fail**; it remains to implement **choice** and `Solve`. Their implementation is independent of the constraint domain. It will work for finite domain constraints. It will also work for the single-assignment store used in the rest of the book, since it is also a constraint system.

12.5.1 The choice statement

We can define the **choice** statement with the `Choose` operation. The following statement:

```
choice ⟨stmt⟩1 [] ⟨stmt⟩2 [] ... [] ⟨stmt⟩n end
```

is a linguistic abstraction that is defined as follows:

```
case {Choose N}
of 1 then ⟨stmt⟩1
[] 2 then ⟨stmt⟩2
...
[] N then ⟨stmt⟩n
end
```

This creates a choice point and then executes the statement corresponding to the choice made by the search engine.

```
% Returns the list of solutions of Script given by a lazy
% depth-first exploration
fun {Solve Script}
   {SolveStep {Space.new Script} nil}
end

% Returns the list of solutions of S appended with SolTail
fun {SolveStep S SolTail}
   case {Space.ask S}
   of failed           then SolTail
   [] succeeded        then {Space.merge S}|SolTail
   [] alternatives(N) then {SolveLoop S 1 N SolTail}
   end
end

% Lazily explores the alternatives I through N of space S,
% and returns the list of solutions found, appended with
% SolTail
fun lazy {SolveLoop S I N SolTail}
   if I>N then
      SolTail
   elseif I==N then
      {Space.commit S I}
      {SolveStep S SolTail}
   else
      C={Space.clone S}
      NewTail={SolveLoop S I+1 N SolTail}
   in
      {Space.commit C I}
      {SolveStep C NewTail}
   end
end
```

Figure 12.6: Lazy all-solution search engine `Solve`.

12.5.2 The `Solve` function

Figure 12.6 shows the implementation of the `Solve` function. It is an all-solution search engine that uses both computation spaces and laziness. The reader should pay attention to where laziness occurs. It is important because of the stateful nature of spaces. For instance, in the **else** clause of `SolveLoop`, a clone of `S` must be created before any attempt to `Commit` on `S`. Because of the lazy nature of `SolveLoop`, we could actually have declared `C` and `NewTail` in reverse order:

```
...
NewTail={SolveLoop S I+1 N SolTail}
C={Space.clone S}
...
```

This works because the value of `NewTail` is not needed before `C` is committed.

12.6 Exercises

1. *Absolute difference triangles.* Write a program to put the integers from 1 to 15 in a triangular table with side 5, such that each entry is the absolute difference between the two neighbors just above it to the left and right. Each integer should appear just once. Your program should find the unique solution (up to mirroring)

```
6   14   15   3   13
  8    1   12   10
     7   11   2
       4    9
          5
```

The following procedures from the `FD` module will be useful:

- `{FD.distinct Xs}` creates a propagator that constrains all the elements of `Xs` to be pairwise distinct. `Xs` is a *vector* of finite domain variables, i.e., either a list or a record of such variables.
- `{FD.distance X Y '=:' Z}` creates a propagator for the distance constraint $|X - Y| = Z$. The third argument defines the arithmetic relation in the constraint (here equality). Other possible values are `'\=:'`, `'<:'`, `'=<:'`, `'>:'` and `'>=:'`.

Generalize your program to triangles of side n. Try it at least for all values of n between 1 and 7.

2. *Grocery puzzle.*[3] A kid goes into a grocery store and buys four items. The cashier charges $7.11, the kid pays and is about to leave when the cashier calls the kid back and says, "Hold on, I multiplied the four items instead of adding them; I'll try again. Hah, when I add them the price still comes to $7.11."

- What were the prices of the four items? Write a program that solves this problem. *Hint*: in your program, assume that the prices are given in cents. This makes the problem expressible with integers only.
- This puzzle has many different solutions since the four prices can be given in any order. We can eliminate this proliferation by imposing an order on the prices, e.g., the prices a, b, c, d should satisfy $a \leq b \leq c \leq d$. With these ordering constraints there is a unique solution. Demonstrate this by adding the order constraints to your program.

---

3. This and the next two exercises are well-known problems that have traditionally been used for teaching Prolog and constraint programming [44, 193]. The versions given here are taken from [193]. Many other problems in a similar style can be found in puzzle books. See, e.g., the classic collections of Sam Loyd, Henry E. Dudeney, and Martin Gardner.

3. *Zebra puzzle.* Five men with different nationalities live in the first five houses of a street. The houses are all on the same side of the street. The men practice distinct professions and each of them has a favorite drink and a favorite animal, all of them different. The five houses are painted with different colors. The following facts are known:

(a) The Englishman lives in a red house.

(b) The Spaniard owns a dog.

(c) The Japanese is a painter.

(d) The Italian drinks tea.

(e) The Norwegian lives in the first house.

(f) The owner of the green house drinks coffee.

(g) The green house comes after the white one.

(h) The sculptor breeds snails.

(i) The diplomat lives in the yellow house.

(j) Milk is drunk in the third house.

(k) The Norwegian's house is next to the blue one.

(l) The violinist drinks juice.

(m) The fox is in the house next to that of the doctor.

(n) The horse is in the house next to that of the diplomat.

(o) The zebra is in the white house.

(p) One of the men drinks water.

Who lives where? *Hint*: you should use a clever problem representation to avoid redundant solutions. We suggest to number the houses from 1 to 5, and to associate a house to each of the 25 properties (e.g., hosting an Englishman, being the green house, hosting a painter, hosting a dog, or hosting someone who drinks juice).

4. *Making change.* Given some bills and coins of different denominations and an amount A, select a minimal number of bills and coins to pay A. For example, assume we want to pay the amount of \$1.42, and that we have 6 one dollar bills (worth 100 cents each), 8 quarters (25 cents each), 10 dimes (10 cents each), 1 nickel (5 cents each), and 5 pennies (1 cent each). The script that solves the problem should be parameterized by the monetary value of each denomination, the number of bills or coins for each denomination, and the amount to pay. Write a function that takes those parameters and returns the corresponding script. *Hint*: to avoid conversions, assume that the amount to pay and all denominations are specified in the same currency unit (e.g., cents). The distribution strategy should give precedence to larger denominations and, within a denomination, to larger numbers of items. The following procedure from the `FD` module will be useful:

- `{FD.sumC Is Xs '=:' Y}` creates a propagator for the scalar product of the vectors `Is` and `Xs`: $\mathtt{I}_1 \cdot \mathtt{X}_1 + \cdots + \mathtt{I}_n \cdot \mathtt{X}_n = \mathtt{Y}$.

Use your program to compare American and European money with respect to making change. American dollars are subdivided into 100, 25, 10, 5, and 1 (as above; there is also a half-dollar worth 50 cents). Euros are subdivided into 100, 50, 20, 10, 5, 2, and 1.

5. *Cryptarithmetic.* Write a program to solve all puzzles of the form "Word1 plus Word2 equals Word3." The words should be input interactively. Use the Send-More-Money program given in section 12.2.1 as a guide. As a refinement, make an interruptible version of the program, which can be stopped at any time if it is taking too long to find a solution. For the interruptible version, use the `Search` module instead of the `Solve` function.

6. (advanced exercise) *Using recomputation to improve* `Solve`. Recomputation is a powerful technique for increasing the performance of abstractions written with computation spaces (see, e.g., [187, 190]). For this exercise, read about recomputation from the above references and then rewrite the `Solve` operation to use recomputation. Compare its performance with the original version.

III SEMANTICS

13 Language Semantics

by Peter Van Roy, Raphaël Collet, and Seif Haridi

This is the secret meaning of the runes; I hid here magic-runes, undisturbed by evil witchcraft. In misery shall he die by means of magic art who destroys this monument.
– Runic inscription, Björketorp Stone

For all the computation models of the previous chapters, we gave a formal semantics as a simple abstract machine. For the declarative model, this abstract machine contains two main parts: a single-assignment store and a semantic stack. For concurrency, we extended the machine to have multiple semantic stacks. For lazy execution we added a trigger store. For explicit state we added a mutable store. For read-only views we added a read-only store.

This chapter brings all these pieces together. It defines an operational semantics for all the computation models of the previous chapters. We use a different formalism than the abstract machine of the previous chapters. The formalism of this chapter is more compact and easier to reason with than the abstract machine definitions. It has four principal changes with respect to the abstract machine that was introduced in chapter 2 and extended in subsequent chapters:

1. It uses a concise notation based on reduction rules. The reduction rules follow the abstract syntax, i.e., there are one or more rules for each syntactic construct. This approach is called structural operational semantics, or SOS for short. It was pioneered by Gordon Plotkin [229].

2. It uses substitutions instead of environments. We saw that statements, in order to be reducible, must define bindings for their free identifiers. In the abstract machine, these bindings are given by the environment in the semantic statement. In this chapter, the free identifiers are directly substituted by references into the store. We have the invariant that in a reducible statement, all free identifiers have been replaced by store references.

3. It represents the single-assignment store as a logical formula. This formula is a conjunction of basic constraints, each of which represents a single variable binding. Activation conditions are replaced by logical conditions such as entailment and disentailment.

4. It replaces the trigger store by a need store. A trigger is a derived concept; the real primitive operation is synchronization on need. A trigger is simply a suspended thread that is waiting on some variable being needed.

Structure of the chapter

The chapter is structured as follows:

- Section 13.1 is the main part. It gives the semantics of the general computation model.
- Section 13.2 gives a formal definition of declarative concurrency, which is an important property of some subsets of the shared-state concurrent model.
- Section 13.3 explains how subsets of this semantics cover the different computation models of the previous chapters.
- Section 13.4 explains how the semantics covers the different programming abstractions and concepts seen in previous chapters.
- Section 13.5 briefly summarizes the historical development of the shared-state concurrent model and its relative, the message-passing concurrent model.

This chapter is intended to be self-contained. It can be understood independently of the previous chapters. However, its mathematical content is much higher than the previous chapters. To aid understanding, we therefore recommend that you connect it with the abstract machine that was defined before.

13.1 The general computation model

This section gives a structural operational semantics for the general computation model, which subsumes all the computation models of the book except for the relational and constraint-based models. It contains all the concepts we saw in the models of previous chapters. The semantics of each earlier model, e.g., the declarative, declarative concurrent, and stateful models, can be obtained by taking just the rules for the language constructs that exist in those models. A configuration in the general computation consists of several tasks connected to a shared store:

$$\begin{array}{ccc} \mathit{task} & \cdots & \mathit{task} \\ \searrow & & \swarrow \\ & \mathit{store} & \end{array}$$

A task, also called thread, is the basic unit of sequential calculation. A computation consists of a sequence of computation steps, each of which transforms a configuration into another configuration. At each step, a task is chosen among all reducible tasks. The task then does a single reduction step. The execution of the different tasks is therefore interleaved. We say that the model has an interleaving semantics.

Concurrency is modeled by reasoning about all possible interleavings.

13.1.1 The store

The store consists of two parts, a single-assignment store and a predicate store:

- The single-assignment store (also called the constraint store) contains variables and their bindings. The constraint store is monotonic: variables and bindings can be added, but never changed or removed.
- The predicate store contains the additional information that is needed for the execution of certain statements. The predicate store consists of the procedure store (containing procedure values), the mutable store (containing cells), the need store (containing need information for by-need synchronization), and the read-only store (containing read-only views). Some of these stores are nonmonotonic. These stores are introduced in step-by-step fashion as we define the reduction rules that need them.

All reduction rules are carefully designed so that task reduction is monotonic: once a task is reducible, then it stays reducible even if information is added to the constraint store or the predicate store is changed.

13.1.2 The single-assignment (constraint) store

The constraint store is a repository of information about the program variables. For instance, the store can contain the information "x is bound to 3 and x is equal to y," which is written $x{=}3 \wedge x{=}y$. Such a set of bindings is called a constraint. It has a logical semantics, which is explained in chapter 9. It gives partial information about the program variables, as explained in section 12.3.1. This is why we also call this store the constraint store. For this chapter we use just a small part of the logical semantics, namely logical conjunction (adding new information to the store, i.e., doing a binding) and entailment (checking whether some information is in the store).

The constraint store entails information. For example, the store $x{=}3 \wedge x{=}y$ entails $y{=}3$, even though that information is not directly present as a binding. We denote the store by σ and we write this as $\sigma \models y{=}3$. More formally, for any constraints σ and β, we say that σ *entails* β if every logical model of σ is also a logical model of β. We also use another relation called disentailment. We say that σ *disentails* β if σ entails the negation of β, i.e., $\sigma \models \neg\beta$. For example, if σ contains $x{=}3$ then it disentails $x{=}4$. We assume that the implementation uses an efficient algorithm for checking both relations. Such an algorithm is given in section 2.8.2.

The constraint store is monotonic, i.e., information can be added but not changed or removed. Consequently, both entailment and disentailment are monotonic too:

when the store entails some information or its negation, this stays true forever.[1] The constraint store provides two primitive operations to the programmer, called tell and ask:

- *Tell.* The tell operation is a mechanism to add information to the store. A task telling the information β to store σ updates the store to $\sigma \wedge \beta$, provided that the new store is consistent. For instance, a task may not tell $y{=}7$ to the store $x{=}3 \wedge x{=}y$. It may however tell $y{=}3$, which is consistent with the store. An inconsistent tell leaves the store unchanged. It is signaled with some mechanism, typically by raising an exception.
- *Ask.* The ask operation is a mechanism to query the store for the presence of some information. A task asking store σ for information β becomes reducible when σ entails either β or its negation $\neg\beta$. For instance, with the store $x{=}3 \wedge x{=}y$, asking for $y{=}3$ will give an affirmative answer (the information is present). Asking for $y{=}4$ will give a negative answer (the information will never be present). An affirmative answer corresponds to an entailment and a negative answer corresponeds to a disentailment. The task will not reduce until either an affirmative or negative answer is possible. Therefore the ask operation is a synchronization mechanism. The task doing the ask is said to synchronize on β, which is called its guard.

Monotonicity of the store implies a strong property: task reduction is monotonic. Assume that a task waits for the store to contain some information, i.e., the task becomes reducible when the store entails some information. Then, once the task is reducible, it stays reducible even if other tasks are reduced before it. This is an excellent basis for dataflow concurrency, where tasks synchronize on the availability of data.

13.1.3 Abstract syntax

Figure 13.1 defines the abstract syntax for the kernel language of the general computation model. Here S denotes a statement, C, P, X, Y denote variable identifiers, k denotes an integer constant, and n is an integer such that $n \geq 0$. In the record $f(l_1{:}X_1 \cdots l_n{:}X_n)$, the label f denotes an atom, and each one of the features l_i denotes an atom or integer constant. We use $\equiv$ to denote equality between semantic objects, to avoid confusion with $=$ in the equality statement.

We assume that in any statement defining a lexical scope for a list of variable identifiers, the identifiers in the list are pairwise distinct. To be precise, in the three

1. Note that "σ disentails β" is not the same as "it is not true that σ entails β." The former is monotonic while the latter is not.

S	::=	**skip**	*empty statement*
	|	S_1 S_2	*sequential composition*
	|	**thread** S **end**	*thread introduction*
	|	**local** $X_1 \cdots X_n$ **in** S **end**	*variable introduction* ($n \geq 1$)
	|	X=Y	*imposing equality (tell)*
	|	X=k	
	|	X=$f(l_1{:}X_1 \cdots l_n{:}X_n)$	
	|	**if** X **then** S_1 **else** S_2 **end**	*conditional statements (ask)*
	|	**case** X **of** $f(l_1{:}X_1 \cdots l_n{:}X_n)$ **then** S_1 **else** S_2 **end**	
	|	{NewName X}	*name introduction*
	|	**proc** {P $X_1 \cdots X_n$} S **end**	*procedural abstraction*
	|	{P $X_1 \cdots X_n$}	
	|	{IsDet X Y}	*explicit state*
	|	{NewCell X C}	
	|	{Exchange C X Y}	
	|	{WaitNeeded X}	*by-need synchronization*
	|	Y=!!X	*read-only variable*
	|	**try** S_1 **catch** X **then** S_2 **end**	*exception handling*
	|	**raise** X **end**	
	|	{FailedValue X Y}	

Figure 13.1: The kernel language of the general computation model.

statements

local $X_1 \cdots X_n$ **in** S **end**

case X **of** $f(l_1{:}X_1 \cdots l_n{:}X_n)$ **then** S_1 **else** S_2 **end**

proc {P $X_1 \cdots X_n$} S **end**

we must have $X_i \not\equiv X_j$ for $i \neq j$. We further assume that all identifiers (including X) are distinct in the record tell X=$f(l_1{:}X_1 \cdots l_n{:}X_n)$. These conditions on pairwise distinctness are important to ensure that statements are truly primitive, i.e., that there are no hidden tells of the form $X = Y$.

13.1.4 Structural rules

The system advances by successive reduction steps. A possible reduction step is defined by a reduction rule of the form

$$\begin{array}{c||c} \mathcal{T} & \mathcal{T}' \\ \hline \sigma & \sigma' \end{array} \quad \text{if } C$$

stating that the computation makes a transition from a multiset of tasks $\mathcal{T}$ connected to a store σ, to a multiset of tasks $\mathcal{T}'$ connected to a store σ'. We call the pair $\mathcal{T}/\sigma$ a configuration. The rule can have an optional boolean condition C, which has to be **`true`** for the rule to reduce. In this notation, we assume that the left-hand side of a rule (the initial configuration $\mathcal{T}/\sigma$) may have patterns and that an empty pattern matches anything. For the rule to reduce, the pattern must be matched in the obvious way.

We use a very light notation for multisets of tasks: the multiset is named by a letter in calligraphic style, disjoint union is denoted by a white space, and singletons are written without curly braces. This allows us to write "$T_1\ \mathcal{T}\ T_2$" for $\{T_1\} \uplus \mathcal{T} \uplus \{T_2\}$. Any confusion with a sequence of statements is avoided because of the thread syntax (see later). We generally write "σ" to denote a store, leaving implicit the set of its variables, say $\mathcal{V}$. If need be, we can make the set explicit by writing the store with $\mathcal{V}$ as a subscript: $\sigma_{\mathcal{V}}$.

We use two equivalent notations to express that a rule has the entailment condition $\sigma \models \beta$. The condition can be written as a pattern on the left-hand side or as an explicit condition:

$$\begin{array}{c||c} \mathcal{T} & \mathcal{T}' \\ \hline \sigma \wedge \beta & \sigma \wedge \beta \end{array} \qquad \text{or} \qquad \begin{array}{c||c} \mathcal{T} & \mathcal{T}' \\ \hline \sigma & \sigma \end{array} \quad \text{if } \sigma \models \beta$$

In the definitions that follow, we use whichever notation is the more convenient.

We assume the semantics has the following two rules, which express model properties that are independent of the kernel language.

$$\begin{array}{c||c} \mathcal{T}\ \mathcal{U} & \mathcal{T}'\ \mathcal{U} \\ \hline \sigma & \sigma' \end{array} \ \text{if}\ \begin{array}{c||c} \mathcal{T} & \mathcal{T}' \\ \hline \sigma & \sigma' \end{array} \qquad\qquad \begin{array}{c||c} \mathcal{T} & \mathcal{T} \\ \hline \sigma & \sigma' \end{array} \quad \text{if } \sigma \text{ and } \sigma' \text{ are equivalent}$$

The first rule expresses concurrency: a subset of the threads can reduce without directly affecting or depending on the others. The second rule states that the store can be replaced by an equivalent one. The second rule can also be written as

$$\begin{array}{c||c} & \\ \hline \sigma & \sigma' \end{array} \quad \text{if } \sigma \text{ and } \sigma' \text{ are equivalent}$$

(using an empty pattern instead of $\mathcal{T}$).

Equivalent stores

A store σ consists of a constraint store σ_c and a predicate store σ_p. We denote this as $\sigma = \sigma_c \wedge \sigma_p$. We say that two stores σ and σ' are equivalent if (1) their constraint stores entail one another, that is, $\sigma_c \models \sigma'_c$ and $\sigma'_c \models \sigma_c$, and (2) their stores entail the other's predicate store, i.e., $\sigma \models \sigma'_p$ and $\sigma' \models \sigma_p$.

We define entailment for the predicate store σ_p as follows. We consider σ_p as a multiset of items called predicates. A predicate can be considered as a tuple of variables, e.g., $\mathit{trig}(x, y)$ is a predicate. We say that $\sigma \models p'_1 \wedge \cdots \wedge p'_n$ if there exists a subset $\{p_1, \ldots, p_n\}$ of σ_p such that for all i, p_i and p'_i have the same labels and number of arguments, and the corresponding arguments of p_i and p'_i are equal in σ_c. For example, if $\sigma \equiv x{=}x' \wedge \mathit{trig}(x, y)$ then $\sigma \models \mathit{trig}(x', y)$.

This definition of equivalence is a form of logical equivalence. It is possible because entailment makes the store independent of its representation: if σ and σ' are equivalent, then $\sigma \models \gamma$ if and only if $\sigma' \models \gamma$.

13.1.5 Sequential and concurrent execution

A thread is a sequence of statements $S_1\ S_2 \cdots S_n$ that we write in a head-tail fashion with angle brackets, i.e., $\langle S_1\ \langle S_2\ \langle \cdots \langle S_n\ \langle\rangle\rangle \cdots \rangle\rangle\rangle$. The abstract syntax of threads is

$$T ::= \langle\rangle \mid \langle S\ T\rangle$$

A terminated thread has the form $\langle\rangle$. Its reduction simply leads to an empty set of threads. A nonterminated thread has the form $\langle S\ T\rangle$. Its reduction replaces its topmost statement S by its reduction S':

$$\frac{\langle\rangle \quad\Big\|\quad }{\sigma \quad\Big\|\quad \sigma} \qquad\qquad \frac{\langle S\ T\rangle \quad\Big\|\quad \langle S'\ T\rangle}{\sigma \quad\Big\|\quad \sigma'} \ \text{if}\ \frac{S \quad\Big\|\quad S'}{\sigma \quad\Big\|\quad \sigma'}$$

(We extend the reduction rule notation to allow statements in addition to multisets of tasks.) The empty statement, sequential composition, and thread introduction are intimately tied to the notion of thread. Their reduction needs a more specific definition than the one given above for S:

$$\frac{\langle \texttt{skip}\ T\rangle \quad\Big\|\quad T}{\sigma \quad\Big\|\quad \sigma} \qquad \frac{\langle (S_1\ S_2)\ T\rangle \quad\Big\|\quad \langle S_1\ \langle S_2\ T\rangle\rangle}{\sigma \quad\Big\|\quad \sigma} \qquad \frac{\langle \texttt{thread}\ S\ \texttt{end}\ T\rangle \quad\Big\|\quad \langle T\rangle\ \langle S\ \langle\rangle\rangle}{\sigma \quad\Big\|\quad \sigma}$$

The empty statement **skip** is removed from the thread's statement sequence. A sequence $S_1\ S_2$ makes S_1 the thread's first statement, while **thread** S **end** creates a new thread with statement S, i.e., $\langle S\ \langle\rangle\rangle$.

13.1.6 Comparison with the abstract machine semantics

Now that we have introduced some reduction rules, let us briefly compare them with the abstract machine. For example, let us consider the semantics of sequential composition. The abstract machine semantics defines sequential composition as follows (taken from section 2.4):

The semantic statement is

$(\langle \mathsf{s} \rangle_1 \ \langle \mathsf{s} \rangle_2, E)$

Execution consists of the following actions:

- Push $(\langle \mathsf{s} \rangle_2, E)$ on the stack.
- Push $(\langle \mathsf{s} \rangle_1, E)$ on the stack.

The reduction rule semantics of this chapter defines sequential composition as follows (taken from the previous section):

$$\frac{\langle (S_1 \ S_2) \ T \rangle}{\sigma} \Bigg\| \frac{\langle S_1 \ \langle S_2 \ T \rangle \rangle}{\sigma}$$

It pays dividends to compare carefully these two definitions. They say exactly the same thing. Do you see why this is? Let us go over it systematically. In the reduction rule semantics, a thread is given as a sequence of statements. This sequence corresponds exactly to the semantic stack of the abstract machine. The rule for sequential composition transforms the list from $\langle (S_1 \ S_2) \ T \rangle$ to $\langle S_1 \ \langle S_2 \ T \rangle \rangle$. This transformation can be read operationally: first pop $(S_1 \ S_2)$ from the list, then push S_2, and finally push S_1.

The reduction rule semantics is nothing other than a precise and compact notation for the English-language definition of the abstract machine with substitutions.

13.1.7 Variable introduction

The **local** statement does variable introduction: it creates new variables in the store and replaces the free identifiers by these variables. We give an example to understand how the **local** statement executes. In the following statement, the identifier `Foo` in S_2 refers to a different variable from the one referred to by `Foo` in S_1 and S_3:

```
local Foo Bar in
   S1                        )
   local Foo in S2 end       }  ≡ S4
   S3                        )
end
```

The outermost **local** replaces the occurrences of `Foo` in S_1 and S_3 but not those in S_2. This gives the following reduction rule:

$$\frac{\texttt{local}\ X_1 \cdots X_n\ \texttt{in}\ S\ \texttt{end} \quad \Big\| \quad S\{X_1 \rightarrow x_1, \ldots, X_n \rightarrow x_n\}}{\sigma_{\mathcal{V}} \quad \Big\| \quad \sigma_{\mathcal{V} \cup \{x_1, \ldots, x_n\}}} \quad \text{if } x_1, \ldots, x_n \text{ fresh variables}$$

In this rule, as in subsequent rules, we use "x" to denote a variable and "X" to denote an identifier. A variable is fresh if it is different from all existing variables in the store. So the condition of the rule states that all the variables x_i are distinct and not in $\mathcal{V}$.

The notation $S\{X_1 \rightarrow x_1, \ldots, X_n \rightarrow x_n\}$ stands for the simultaneous substitution of the free occurrences of X_1 by x_1, X_2 by x_2, ..., X_n by x_n. For instance, the substitution of `Foo` by x and `Bar` by y in the statement S_4 defined above gives

$$\begin{aligned} S_4\{\texttt{Foo} \rightarrow x, \texttt{Bar} \rightarrow y\} \quad \equiv \quad & S_1\{\texttt{Foo} \rightarrow x, \texttt{Bar} \rightarrow y\} \\ & \textbf{local}\ \texttt{Foo}\ \textbf{in}\ S_2\{\texttt{Bar} \rightarrow y\}\ \textbf{end} \\ & S_3\{\texttt{Foo} \rightarrow x, \texttt{Bar} \rightarrow y\} \end{aligned}$$

A substitution is actually an environment that is used as a function. Since variables and identifiers are in disjoint sets, the substitution $S\{X_1 \rightarrow x_1, \ldots, X_n \rightarrow x_n\}$ is equivalent to the composition of single substitutions $S\{X_1 \rightarrow x_1\} \cdots \{X_n \rightarrow x_n\}$. The substitution operation $S\{X \rightarrow x\}$ is defined formally in section 13.1.17.

13.1.8 Imposing equality (tell)

According to section 13.1.7, a variable introduced by **local** has no initial value. The variable exists but the store simply has no information about it. Adding information about the variable is done by the tell operation. Let β denote a statement imposing equality. This statement has three possible forms:

$\beta ::= x{=}y \mid x{=}z \mid x{=}f(l_1{:}x_1 \cdots l_n{:}x_n).$

This states that x is equal to either another variable y, an integer or name z, or a record with label f, features (i.e., field names) l_i, and fields x_i. Doing a tell operation adds the information in β to the store, provided that it does not lead to an inconsistent store. This is also called binding the variable x.

It is possible that the new information in β conflicts with what the store already knows about x. We say that β is inconsistent with σ. This happens whenever $\beta \wedge \sigma \leftrightarrow$ **false**. For example, take $\beta \equiv x{=}10$ and $\sigma \equiv x{=}20$. Instead of adding β to the store, we signal this as an error, e.g., by raising an exception. Therefore the store is always consistent.

In practice, most tell operations are very simple: telling β just binds one variable, x, without binding any others. For example, telling $x{=}23$ where σ has no binding for x. But the tell operation is actually much more general. It can cause many bindings to be done. For example, take $\sigma \equiv x{=}f(x_1\ x_2) \wedge y{=}f(y_1\ y_2)$. Then telling $x = y$ does three bindings: $x{=}y$, $x_1{=}y_1$, and $x_2{=}y_2$.

Naive semantics of tell

The following two rules decide whether to add β to the store.

$$\frac{\beta \;\|\; \texttt{skip}}{\sigma \;\|\; \sigma \wedge \beta} \text{ if } \sigma \wedge \beta \text{ is consistent}$$

$$\frac{\beta \;\|\; \texttt{fail}}{\sigma \;\|\; \sigma} \text{ if } \sigma \wedge \beta \text{ is inconsistent}$$

(Note that β is used to denote both a statement and a constraint.) We could implement tell to follow these rules. However, such an implementation would be complicated and hard to make efficient. The Mozart system uses a slightly more elaborate semantics that can be implemented efficiently. The tell operation is a good example of the trade-off between simple semantics and efficient implementation.

Realistic semantics of tell

We have seen that one tell operation can potentially add many bindings to the store. This generality has an important consequence for inconsistent tells. For example, take $\beta \equiv x{=}y$ and $\sigma \equiv x{=}f(x_1\ x_2) \wedge y{=}f(y_1\ y_2) \wedge x_2{=}\mathtt{a} \wedge y_2{=}\mathtt{b}$. The tell is inconsistent. Does the tell add $x_1{=}y_1$ to the store? It would be nice if the tell did nothing at all, i.e., σ is unchanged afterward. This is the naive semantics. But this is very expensive to implement: it means the tell operation would be a transaction, which is rolled back if an inconsistency is detected. The system would have to do a transaction for each variable binding. It turns out that implementing tell as a transaction is not necessary. If $\beta \wedge \sigma$ is inconsistent, practical experience shows that it is perfectly reasonable that some bindings remain in place after the inconsistency is detected.

For the semantics of a tell operation we therefore need to distinguish a binding that implies no other bindings (which we call a basic binding) and a binding that implies other bindings (which we call a nonbasic binding). In the above example, $x{=}y$ is nonbasic and $x_1{=}y_1$ is basic.

Bindings implied by β

To see whether β is a basic binding, we need to determine the extra bindings that happen as part of a tell operation, i.e., the bindings of variables other than x. For a store σ, we write $\beta \xrightarrow{\sigma} \gamma$ to say that the binding β involves the extra binding γ. The relation $\xrightarrow{\sigma}$ is defined as the least reflexive transitive relation satisfying

$$x{=}f(l_1{:}y_1 \cdots l_n{:}y_n) \xrightarrow{\sigma} x_i{=}y_i \text{ if } \sigma \models x{=}f(l_1{:}x_1 \cdots l_n{:}x_n)$$

$$x{=}y \xrightarrow{\sigma} x_i{=}y_i \text{ if } \sigma \models x{=}f(l_1{:}x_1 \cdots l_n{:}x_n) \wedge y{=}f(l_1{:}y_1 \cdots l_n{:}y_n)$$

We can now define $\mathit{subbindings}_\sigma(\beta)$, the set of bindings strictly involved by β and not yet entailed by σ, as

$$\mathit{subbindings}_\sigma(\beta) = \left\{\gamma \;\middle|\; \beta \xrightarrow{\sigma} \gamma \text{ and } \gamma \not\xrightarrow{\sigma} \beta \text{ and } \sigma \not\models \gamma\right\}.$$

Rules for basic bindings

We refine the naive semantics to allow some nonbasic bindings to remain when the tell is inconsistent. We first give the rules for the basic bindings. They decide whether to add β to the store, in the simple case where β just binds one variable.

$$\begin{array}{c||c} \beta & \texttt{skip} \\ \hline \sigma & \sigma \wedge \beta \end{array} \quad \text{if } \mathit{subbindings}_\sigma(\beta) = \emptyset \text{ and } \sigma \wedge \beta \text{ is consistent}$$

$$\begin{array}{c||c} \beta & \texttt{fail} \\ \hline \sigma & \sigma \end{array} \quad \text{if } \mathit{subbindings}_\sigma(\beta) = \emptyset \text{ and } \sigma \wedge \beta \text{ is inconsistent}$$

If only basic bindings are done, then these rules are sufficient. In that case, the naive semantics and the realistic semantics coincide. On the other hand, if there are nonbasic bindings, we need one more rule, which is explained next.

Rule for nonbasic bindings

The following rule applies when β involves other bindings. It allows β to be decomposed into basic bindings, which can be told first.

$$\begin{array}{c||c} \beta & \gamma\ \beta \\ \hline \sigma & \sigma \end{array} \quad \text{if } \gamma \in \mathit{subbindings}_\sigma(\beta)$$

With the three binding rules, we can now completely explain how a realistic tell operation works. Telling β consists of two parts. If β is basic, then the two basic binding rules explain everything. If β is nonbasic, then the nonbasic binding rule is used to "peel off" basic bindings, until the tell is reduced to basic bindings only. The rule allows basic bindings to be peeled off in any order, so the implementation is free to choose an order that it can handle efficiently.

This rule handles the fact that some bindings may be done even if β is inconsistent with the store. The inconsistency will eventually be noticed by a basic binding, but some previously peeled-off basic bindings may have already been done by then.

13.1.9 Conditional statements (ask)

There is a single conditional statement that does an ask operation, namely the **if** statement. The reduction of an **if** statement depends on its condition variable:

if x **then** S_1 **else** S_2 **end**	S_1
$\sigma \wedge x$=**true**	$\sigma \wedge x$=**true**

if x **then** S_1 **else** S_2 **end**	S_2
$\sigma \wedge x$=**false**	$\sigma \wedge x$=**false**

This statement synchronizes on the value of the variable x. The first rule applies when the store entails x=**true** and the second rule applies when the store entails x=**false**. The value of x can be determined by a boolean function, as in $x=(y<z)$ (see section 13.1.11). What happens if x is different from the atoms **true** and **false** is explained later.

The **if** statement only becomes reducible when the store entails sufficient information to decide whether x is **true** or **false**. If there is not enough information in the store, then neither rule can reduce. The **if** statement is said to do dataflow synchronization. Because store variables are the basis for dataflow execution, they are called dataflow variables.

The case *statement*

The **case** statement is a linguistic abstraction for pattern matching that is built on top of **if**. Its semantics can be derived from the semantics of **if**, **local**, and the record operations `Arity` and `Label`. Because pattern matching is such an interesting concept, though, we prefer to give the semantics of **case** directly as reduction rules:

case x **of** $f(l_1{:}X_1 \cdots l_n{:}X_n)$ **then** S_1 **else** S_2 **end**	$S_1\{X_1 \rightarrow x_1, \ldots, X_n \rightarrow x_n\}$
$\sigma \wedge x=f(l_1{:}x_1 \cdots l_n{:}x_n)$	$\sigma \wedge x=f(l_1{:}x_1 \cdots l_n{:}x_n)$

case x **of** $f(l_1{:}X_1 \cdots l_n{:}X_n)$ **then** S_1 **else** S_2 **end**	S_2	if $\sigma \models x \neq f(l_1{:}x_1 \cdots l_n{:}x_n)$ for any variables $x_1, \ldots, x_n$
σ	σ	

The semantics of pattern matching uses entailment. We say that x matches the pattern $f(l_1{:}X_1 \cdots l_n{:}X_n)$ if there exist x_1, ..., x_n such that the store entails $x=f(l_1{:}x_1 \cdots l_n{:}x_n)$. If the match is successful, then the **case** statement reduces to S_1 where the identifiers X_i are replaced by the corresponding x_i. This implies that the lexical scope of the X_i covers the whole statement S_1. Otherwise, if we can deduce that the match will never succeed, the **case** reduces to S_2. If there is not enough information to decide one way or another, then neither rule can reduce. This is the dataflow behavior of **case**.

Determined variables and the `Wait` *statement*

We say that a variable is determined if it is bound to an integer, a name, or a record. We say an equality determines a variable if it results in the variable becoming determined. We define the predicate $det(x)$ which is entailed by the store when the given variable x is determined.

$$\begin{array}{llll} \sigma \models det(x) & \text{iff} & \sigma \models x{=}z & \text{for some integer or name } z \\ & \text{or} & \sigma \models x{=}f(l_1{:}x_1 \ldots l_n{:}x_n) & \text{for some } f, l_i, x_i \text{ with } n \geq 0 \end{array}$$

It is useful to introduce a statement that blocks until a variable is determined. We call this the `Wait` statement. Its semantics is extremely simple: it reduces to **skip** when its argument is determined.

$$\frac{\{\texttt{Wait}\ x\}}{\sigma} \Bigg\| \frac{\textbf{skip}}{\sigma} \quad \text{if } \sigma \models det(x)$$

`Wait` is a form of ask; like the **case** statement it can be defined with **if**:

```
proc {Wait X}
   if X==unit then skip else skip end
end
```

That is, `{Wait X}` waits until it can be decided whether `X` is the same as or different from **unit**. This reduces when anything definite, no matter what, is known about `X`.

13.1.10 Names

Names are unforgeable constants, similar to atoms but without a print representation. They are used in the semantics to give a unique identity to procedures and cells (see sections 13.1.11 and 13.1.12). But their usefulness goes much beyond this semantic role. They behave as first-class rights, because they do not have a concrete representation and cannot be forged. A thread cannot guess a name value: a thread can know a name only if it references it via one of its variables. We therefore provide names to the programmer as well as use them in the semantics.

There are just two operations on a name: creation and equality test. A name is equal only to itself. New names can be created at will. We use the metavariable ξ to denote a name, and we extend the equality statement for names:

$$\beta ::= \cdots \mid x{=}\xi$$

This statement cannot be typed directly by the programmer, but only created indirectly through the `NewName` operation, which creates a new name:

$$\frac{\{\texttt{NewName}\ x\}}{\sigma} \bigg\| \frac{x{=}\xi}{\sigma} \quad \text{if } \xi \text{ fresh name}$$

The `NewName` operation is not needed for the semantics of procedures and cells.

13.1.11 Procedural abstraction

A procedure is created by the execution of a **proc** statement. This puts a procedure value **proc** $\{\$\ X_1 \cdots X_n\}\ S$ **end** in the procedure store. This value is almost the same as a λ expression in the λ calculus. The difference is a matter of detail: a true λ expression returns a result when applied, whereas a procedure value binds its arguments when applied. This means that a procedure value can return any number of results including none. When the procedure is applied, its procedure value is pushed on the semantic stack and its argument identifiers X_i reference its effective arguments. The procedure value must of course contain no free occurrence of any identifier. This can be proved as a property of the reduction rule semantics.

We associate a procedure to a variable by giving the procedure a name. Names are globally unique constants; they were introduced in the previous section. We pair the name ξ with the procedure value, giving ξ:**proc** $\{\$\ X_1 \cdots X_n\}\ S$ **end**, which is put in the procedure store. The procedure store consists of pairs *name*:*value* which define a mapping from names to procedure values. A variable that refers to the procedure is bound to ξ in the constraint store.

$$\frac{\textbf{proc}\ \{x_p\ X_1 \cdots X_n\}\ S\ \textbf{end}}{\sigma} \bigg\| \frac{x_p{=}\xi}{\sigma \wedge \xi{:}\textbf{proc}\ \{\$\ X_1 \cdots X_n\}\ S\ \textbf{end}} \quad \text{if } \xi \text{ fresh name}$$

$$\frac{\{x_p\ x_1 \cdots x_n\}}{\sigma \wedge x_p{=}\xi \wedge \xi{:}\textbf{proc}\ \{\$\ X_1 \cdots X_n\}\ S\ \textbf{end}} \bigg\| \frac{S\{X_1{\rightarrow}x_1, \ldots, X_n{\rightarrow}x_n\}}{\sigma \wedge x_p{=}\xi \wedge \xi{:}\textbf{proc}\ \{\$\ X_1 \cdots X_n\}\ S\ \textbf{end}}$$

It is interesting to see the dataflow behavior of the procedure call. The invocation statement $\{x_p\ x_1 \cdots x_n\}$ synchronizes on the value of x_p. So the procedure can be created in a concurrent thread, provided that no other thread binds x_p to a value.

Where is the contextual environment?

In the abstract machine, a procedure value consists of two parts: the procedure's source definition and a contextual environment that gives its external references. Where does the contextual environment appear in the procedure value ξ:**proc** $\{\$\ X_1 \cdots X_n\}\ S$ **end**? It is very simple: the contextual environment appears in the procedure body S. When a **local** statement (or another statement that creates variables) executes, it substitutes identifiers by variables in all the statements that it encompasses, including procedure bodies. Take, e.g.:

```
local Add N in
   N=3
   proc {Add A B} B=A+N end
end
```

When the procedure is defined, it creates the value ξ:**proc** {$ A B} B=A+n **end**, where n is the variable that was substituted for N. The contextual environment is $\{n\}$.

Built-in procedures

A practical implementation of the general computation model has to define built-in procedures, such as arithmetic operators, comparisons, etc. For instance, the sum operation can be written as $x{=}x_1 + x_2$, which is actually a shorthand for the procedure call {Add x_1 x_2 x} that is defined by

$$\frac{\{\texttt{Add}\ x_1\ x_2\ x\}}{\sigma \wedge x_1{=}k_1 \wedge x_2{=}k_2} \Bigg\| \frac{x{=}k}{\sigma \wedge x_1{=}k_1 \wedge x_2{=}k_2} \quad \text{if } k = k_1 + k_2$$

Another built-in procedure is the equality test, which is often used in conjunction with an **if** statement. Equality test is the general form of the ask operation defined in section 13.1.2. It is usually written as a boolean function in infix notation, as in $x{=}(x_1{=}{=}x_2)$ which is shorthand for {Equal x_1 x_2 x}.

$$\frac{\{\texttt{Equal}\ x_1\ x_2\ x\}}{\sigma} \Bigg\| \frac{x{=}\textbf{true}}{\sigma} \quad \text{if } \sigma \models x_1{=}x_2$$

$$\frac{\{\texttt{Equal}\ x_1\ x_2\ x\}}{\sigma} \Bigg\| \frac{x{=}\textbf{false}}{\sigma} \quad \text{if } \sigma \models x_1{\neq}x_2$$

An algorithm to implement the Equal operation is given in section 2.8.2.4. Notice that both Add and Equal have dataflow behavior.

13.1.12 Explicit state

There are two forms of explicit state in the model. First, there is the boundness check of dataflow variables, which is a weak form of state. Then there are cells, which is a true explicit state. We explain them in turn. The relationship between the two is explored in an exercise.

Boundness check

The boundness check IsDet lets us examine whether variables are determined or not, without waiting. This lets us examine the instantaneous status of a dataflow variable. It can be defined with the following rules:

$$\frac{\{\texttt{IsDet}\ x\ y\}}{\sigma} \left\| \frac{y\texttt{=}\mathbf{true}}{\sigma} \right. \quad \text{if } \sigma \models det(x)$$

$$\frac{\{\texttt{IsDet}\ x\ y\}}{\sigma} \left\| \frac{y\texttt{=}\mathbf{false}}{\sigma} \right. \quad \text{if } \sigma \models \neg det(x)$$

The first rule, checking whether x is determined, is similar to the rule for `Wait`. It is the second rule that introduces something new: it allows a definite result, y = **false**, for a negative test. This was not possible up to now. This is the first rule in our semantics that has a nonmonotonic condition, i.e., if the rule is reducible, then adding more information to the store can make the rule no longer reducible.

Cells

All the statements introduced up to now define a language that calculates with the constraint store and procedure store, both of which are monotonic. We have now arrived at a point where we need a nonmonotonic store, which we call the mutable store. The mutable store contains entities called cells, which implement explicit state. This is important for reasons of modularity (see section 4.8). It greatly increases the model's expressive power, allowing object-oriented programming, for instance. The reverse side of the coin is that reasoning about programs and testing them become harder.

A cell is named in the same way as a procedure: when the cell is created, a fresh name ξ is associated with it. A pair $\xi{:}x$ is put in the mutable store, where the variable x defines the current value of the cell. One changes a cell's value to y by replacing the pair $\xi{:}y$ in the mutable store by $\xi{:}y$. Cells need two primitive operations only, namely cell creation and exchange:

$$\frac{\{\texttt{NewCell}\ x\ x_c\}}{\sigma} \left\| \frac{x_c\texttt{=}\xi}{\sigma \wedge \xi{:}x} \right. \quad \text{if } \xi \text{ fresh name}$$

$$\frac{\{\texttt{Exchange}\ x_c\ x_{old}\ x_{new}\}}{\sigma \wedge x_c\texttt{=}\xi \wedge \xi{:}x} \left\| \frac{x_{old}\texttt{=}x}{\sigma \wedge x_c\texttt{=}\xi \wedge \xi{:}x_{new}} \right.$$

Having just one operation to use cells, `Exchange`, is rather minimal. It is often convenient to assume that two other operations exist, namely x_c`:=`x (assignment) and x`=@`x_c (access). Since we can define them with `Exchange`, no additional rules are needed for them.

It is interesting to see the dataflow behavior of `Exchange`. It blocks until its first argument references a cell. It never blocks on the second or third arguments. This allows it to manipulate the cell's contents even before they are determined.

Example of a stream

Using cells and dataflow variables together permits some remarkable programming techniques. We give a small example that uses a stream. Assume that the cell `C` contains the tail of a stream. Then the following statement adds the atom `one` to the stream:

```
local X Old New in
   {Exchange C Old New}
   X=one
   Old=X|New
end
```

The three instructions inside this **`local`** statement can be executed in any order and the final result is exactly the same. What's more, several threads can independently add elements to the stream by each executing this **`local`** statement. The order of the elements on the stream is determined by the order in which the `Exchange` statements are executed.

13.1.13 By-need synchronization

Demand-driven execution is defined with one new primitive concept, synchronization on need, which exists as an explicit operation called `WaitNeeded`. Lazy functions and the `ByNeed` operation are defined with `WaitNeeded`. We build the semantics of `WaitNeeded` in three steps:

1. The first step is to define formally the informal notion of "need." We will define "need" in terms of a new relation, $need_\sigma(S, x)$, that is true when statement S needs variable x in the context of store σ.

2. The second step is to introduce one new predicate in the store, called $need(x)$. This predicate is added to the store whenever a statement needs a variable. The predicate is never removed, so that being needed is a monotonic property of a variable. The set of all $need(x)$ predicates is called the need store.

3. The third step is to define {`WaitNeeded` x} so that it waits until $need(x)$ exists in the store.

With `WaitNeeded` we can define the `ByNeed` operation as follows:

```
proc {ByNeed P X}
   thread {WaitNeeded X} {P X} end
end
```

A by-need trigger, as introduced in section 4.5.1, is simply the suspended thread that is created when `ByNeed` is executed. The trigger store is the set of these suspended threads.

The semantics of this section is designed so that the demand-driven concurrent model of chapter 4 is declarative. In particular, we are careful to ensure that the $need(x)$ predicate is monotonic, that the reduction rules introduce no nondeterminism, and that unification never blocks because of by-need execution.

As a final point, we remark that while the semantics of section 4.5.1 is correct according to this section, the semantics of this section is more general (it allows more executions). Section 4.5.1 is more restricted to make it easier to implement.

The $need_\sigma(S, x)$ relation

Intuitively, the relation $need_\sigma(S, x)$ means that reducing S in σ is tied to x becoming determined.[2] Formally, the relation holds between a statement S, a store σ, and a variable x if and only if three conditions hold:

1. No reduction is possible for S with store σ.

2. There exists a constraint c (a set of variable bindings) such that $\sigma \wedge c$ is consistent and a reduction is possible for S with store $\sigma \wedge c$.

3. It is true that $\sigma \models \neg det(x)$ and for all constraints c that satisfy the previous condition, we have $\sigma \wedge c \models det(x)$.

The first condition says that S is suspended. The second condition says that S can be made reducible by adding bindings to the store. The third condition says that these added bindings also make x determined, i.e., making x determined is a necessary condition on the added bindings.

Rules for $need(x)$

We use the $need_\sigma(S, x)$ relation to decide when to add the $need(x)$ predicate to the need store. The first rule implements this idea:

$$\frac{S \;\|\; S}{\sigma \;\|\; \sigma \wedge need(x)} \quad \text{if } need_\sigma(S, x) \text{ and } \sigma \not\models need(x)$$

We need a second rule to ensure that $need(x)$ is monotonic:

$$\frac{\;\|\;}{\sigma \;\|\; \sigma \wedge need(x)} \quad \text{if } \sigma \models det(x) \text{ and } \sigma \not\models need(x)$$

This rules says that even if no statement needs x, the mere fact of x being determined is enough to make it needed. We can use the monotonicity property of the $need(x)$ predicate to show that the demand-driven model is declarative.

---

2. There are other ways to define need, e.g., we could use the more implementation-oriented definition that a variable is needed if there is a suspension on the variable. This can be seen as a conservative extension of the above definition that may result in more variables being needed.

The WaitNeeded *statement*

The following rule defines the operation of the WaitNeeded statement:

$$\frac{\{\texttt{WaitNeeded}\ x\}}{\sigma} \Bigg\| \frac{\texttt{skip}}{\sigma} \quad \text{if } \sigma \models need(x)$$

This is the same as the definition of Wait, except that the condition $det(x)$ is replaced by $need(x)$.

Lazy functions

A lazy function is implemented by attaching a by-need trigger to the variable that will contain the function result. The "lazy" annotation is a syntactic shortcut for this technique. Any lazy function, e.g.,

```
fun lazy {F X1 ... Xn} ⟨expr⟩ end
```

behaves as if it were defined by

```
fun {F X1 ... Xn}
   {ByNeed fun {$} ⟨expr⟩ end}
end
```

When written in full, this becomes

```
proc {F X1 ... Xn X}
   local P in
      proc {P X} X=⟨expr⟩ end
      {ByNeed P X}
   end
end
```

Using WaitNeeded *directly*

It is often more efficient to use WaitNeeded directly rather than using ByNeed. Let us compare the two by showing how to define an infinite list of integers with each of them. With standard lazy functions as defined above, the definition is

```
fun lazy {Ints N}
   N|{Ints N+1}
end
```

When written in full using the definition of ByNeed, this becomes

```
proc {Ints N Xs}
   thread P in
      {WaitNeeded Xs}
      proc {P Xs} Ys in Xs=N|Ys {Ints N+1 Ys} end
      {P Xs}
   end
end
```

We can see that this does too much work: in each iteration it creates a thread, creates a procedure, and applies the procedure.[3] Removing these superfluous operations gives

```
proc {Ints N Xs}
Ys in
   {WaitNeeded Xs}
   Xs=N|Ys
   {Ints N+1 Ys}
end
```

This is faster and generates less garbage. When executed in a producer/consumer configuration, it does coroutining between the producer thread and the consumer thread.

The `WaitQuiet` *statement*

Executing `{Wait X}` causes `X` to be needed, i.e., all by-need triggers will be activated. It is possible to define a variation of `Wait`, called `WaitQuiet`, that has a different behavior:

$$\frac{\texttt{\{WaitQuiet } x\texttt{\}} \;\Big\|\; \textbf{skip}}{\sigma \;\Big\|\; \sigma} \quad \text{if } \sigma \models \mathit{det}(x)$$

This rule is identical with the rule for `Wait`. The difference between the two appears when the variable's value is computed by need. By definition, we stipulate that arguments of `WaitQuiet` are not recognized by the $\mathit{need}_\sigma(S, x)$ relation. This means that while `{Wait X}` causes `X` to be needed, `{WaitQuiet X}` does not. `WaitQuiet` is used in the Mozart system to implement the Browser.

13.1.14 Read-only variables

A read-only variable is a restricted version of a dataflow variable that cannot be made determined by binding it. Any such attempt will block. A read-only variable y is always linked to another variable x that does not have this restriction. When x becomes determined then y is bound to the same partial value. Any blocked bindings of y can then continue.

To define the semantics of read-only variables, we first add the predicate $\mathit{readonly}(x, y)$ to the store. This states that y is a read-only view of x. We can view these predicates as sitting in a new store called the read-only store. Once x is determined, the predicate is removed from the store and replaced by the binding $x{=}y$.

Four rules are needed: one each for the creation and removal of the read-only view, one to block any attempted bindings, and one to handle by-need synchronization.

3. Even if `ByNeed` were implemented as a primitive, this would do too much work.

A read-only view is created by the procedure {`ReadOnly` x x_r}, which binds x_r to a read-only view of x. To be compatible with Mozart syntax, which uses the prefix operator "`!!`", we will always write this procedure as a function call x_r=`!!`x,

$$\begin{array}{c||c} x_r\texttt{=!!}x & x_r{=}y \\ \hline \sigma & \sigma \wedge \mathit{readonly}(x,y) \end{array} \quad \text{if } y \text{ fresh variable}$$

This creates y, a read-only variable for x, and a *readonly* predicate that associates them. The second rule removes the *readonly* predicate when x is determined.

$$\begin{array}{c||c} & \\ \hline \sigma \wedge \mathit{readonly}(x,y) & \sigma \wedge x{=}y \end{array} \quad \text{if } \sigma \models \mathit{det}(x)$$

A third rule is needed to block any attempt to make y determined by binding it. This rule replaces the first basic binding rule given in section 13.1.8. It adds one new condition to the basic binding rule.

$$\begin{array}{c||c} \beta & \textbf{skip} \\ \hline \sigma & \sigma \wedge \beta \end{array} \quad \text{if } \mathit{subbindings}_\sigma(\beta) = \emptyset \text{ and } \sigma \wedge \beta \text{ is consistent and } \neg \mathit{prevent}_\sigma(\beta)$$

Here $\mathit{prevent}_\sigma(\beta)$ prevents a binding in two cases: (1) the variable to be bound is read-only and would be made determined, and (2) two read-only variables would be bound together. We define it as follows:

$$\begin{array}{rcl} \mathit{prevent}_\sigma(\beta) & \equiv & \mathit{pre1}_\sigma(\beta) \vee \mathit{pre2}_\sigma(\beta) \\ \mathit{pre1}_\sigma(\beta) & \equiv & \exists y.\ \sigma \models \mathit{readonly}(\_, y) \text{ and } \sigma \wedge \beta \models \mathit{det}(y) \\ \mathit{pre2}_\sigma(\beta) & \equiv & \exists y, y'.\ \sigma \models \mathit{readonly}(\_, y) \wedge \mathit{readonly}(\_, y') \text{ and } \sigma \wedge \beta \models y{=}y' \end{array}$$

A final rule is needed for by-need synchronization. Read-only views are used to protect dataflow variables used in abstractions, but the dataflow variables should still be effective in lazy calculations. This implies that if y is needed, the need should be propagated to x.

$$\begin{array}{c||c} & \\ \hline \sigma & \sigma \wedge \mathit{need}(x) \end{array} \quad \text{if } \sigma \models \mathit{need}(y) \wedge \mathit{readonly}(x,y) \text{ and } \sigma \not\models \mathit{need}(x)$$

It is possible to add a "quiet" version of the `!!` operation which is opaque to the need condition. The quiet version would not need this final rule.

13.1.15 Exception handling

The exception mechanism is closely bound to sequential composition. Indeed, raising an exception modifies the sequence of statements in the thread where it has been thrown. It skips every statement inside the scope defined by the most enclosing **`try`**/**`catch`** block.

The following rule for the **`try`**/**`catch`** statement is a first attempt toward its semantics:

$$\frac{\texttt{try } S_1 \texttt{ catch } X \texttt{ then } S_2 \texttt{ end} \;\Big\|\; \texttt{try } S_1' \texttt{ catch } X \texttt{ then } S_2 \texttt{ end}}{\sigma \;\Big\|\; \sigma'} \text{ if } \frac{S_1 \;\|\; S_1'}{\sigma \;\|\; \sigma'}$$

It defines the reduction of the nested statement. We then just need to add two rules for the cases where S_1 is **skip** and **raise** x **end**. But this definition is not complete: it does not handle thread creation inside the **try**/**catch** block.

So let us try another approach. We "unfold" the **try**/**catch** statement in order to match the reduction of the nested statement with the usual rules for sequence and thread creation. We say that the statement

$\texttt{try } S_1 \texttt{ catch } X \texttt{ then } S_2 \texttt{ end}$

unfolds to a sequence of two statements, the first one being S_1, and the second one a "**catch**" statement:

$S_1\ (\texttt{catch } X \texttt{ then } S_2 \texttt{ end})$

The new **catch** statement is for semantic use only: it is a marker that stops a **raise** statement exactly at the place it must. The unfolding technique works even when **try**/**catch** blocks are nested. For instance, the statement

$$\begin{array}{l} \texttt{try} \\ \quad \left.\begin{array}{l} \texttt{try } S_1 \\ \texttt{catch } X \texttt{ then } S_2 \texttt{ end} \\ S_3 \end{array}\right\} \equiv \begin{array}{l}\text{scope of outer} \\ \texttt{try/catch}\end{array} \\ \texttt{catch } Y \texttt{ then } S_4 \texttt{ end} \\ S_5 \end{array}$$

when put in a thread unfolds to

$$\overbrace{\langle \underbrace{S_1}_{\substack{\text{scope of nested} \\ \texttt{try/catch}}} \langle \texttt{catch } X \texttt{ then } S_2 \texttt{ end} \langle S_3}^{\substack{\text{scope of outer} \\ \texttt{try/catch}}} \langle \texttt{catch } Y \texttt{ then } S_4 \texttt{ end} \langle S_5 \langle\rangle\rangle\rangle\rangle\rangle\rangle$$

The following two rules define the unfolding of a **try**/**catch** statement and the simplification of a **catch** statement when no exception is raised:

$$\begin{array}{c||c} \texttt{try } S_1 \texttt{ catch } X \texttt{ then } S_2 \texttt{ end} & S_1 \ (\texttt{catch } X \texttt{ then } S_2 \texttt{ end}) \\ \hline \sigma & \sigma \end{array}$$

$$\begin{array}{c||c} \texttt{catch } X \texttt{ then } S_2 \texttt{ end} & \texttt{skip} \\ \hline \sigma & \sigma \end{array}$$

We now define the behavior of a **raise** statement. As we said earlier, it should skip every statement following it, except a **catch** statement. As the following statements reside in the current thread's tail, we must use a "thread-level" reduction:

$$\begin{array}{c||c} \langle \texttt{raise } x \texttt{ end } \langle S \ T \rangle \rangle & \langle \texttt{raise } x \texttt{ end } T \rangle \\ \hline \sigma & \sigma \end{array} \quad \text{if } S \not\equiv \texttt{catch} \ldots \texttt{end}$$

$$\begin{array}{c||c} \langle \texttt{raise } x \texttt{ end } \langle S \ T \rangle \rangle & \langle S_2\{X \rightarrow x\} \ T \rangle \\ \hline \sigma & \sigma \end{array} \quad \text{if } S \equiv \texttt{catch } X \texttt{ then } S_2 \texttt{ end}$$

What happens if the thread's statement sequence is done (i.e., there is only the termination symbol)? The behavior in this case is implementation-dependent. The implementation should have a rule like this one:

$$\begin{array}{c||c} \langle \texttt{raise } x \texttt{ end } \langle\rangle \rangle & \ldots \\ \hline \sigma & \ldots \end{array}$$

The Mozart system has a rule that halts the process with an error message ("`Uncaught exception`").

Sources of exceptions

Exceptions can have three origins: explicitly by executing a **raise**, implicitly through a language operation that is impossible, and implicitly through an event external to the system. This section defines the implicit exceptions that come from language operations. Several statements can raise an exception when their reduction will never be possible. The first case is imposing an equality that would lead to an inconsistent store. This means that **fail** is replaced by **raise** in the second basic binding rule:

$$\begin{array}{c||c} \beta & \texttt{raise failure(...) end} \\ \hline \sigma & \sigma \end{array} \quad \text{if } \mathit{subbindings}_\sigma(\beta) = \emptyset \text{ and } \sigma \wedge \beta \text{ is inconsistent}$$

where the ... stands for some debugging information that is not specified here.[4]

The second case is a type inconsistency. This is defined with the following rules. An exception is raised when the condition variable of an **if** statement is not a boolean:

$$\frac{\textbf{if } x \textbf{ then } S_1 \textbf{ else } S_2 \textbf{ end} \;\Big\|\; \textbf{raise } \texttt{error(...)} \textbf{ end}}{\sigma \;\Big\|\; \sigma} \text{ if } \begin{array}{l} \sigma \models det(x) \wedge \\ x \notin \{\textbf{true}, \textbf{false}\} \end{array}$$

An exception is raised if a procedure application is invoked on something that is not a procedure or is a procedure with a wrong number of arguments:

$$\frac{\{x_p\ x_1 \cdots x_n\} \;\Big\|\; \textbf{raise } \texttt{error(...)} \textbf{ end}}{\sigma \;\Big\|\; \sigma} \text{ if } \sigma \models det(x_p) \wedge (x_p \text{ not a procedure})$$

$$\frac{\{x_p\ x_1 \cdots x_n\} \;\Big\|\; \textbf{raise } \texttt{error(...)} \textbf{ end}}{\sigma \;\Big\|\; \sigma} \text{ if } x_p \text{ is a procedure with arity} \neq n$$

An exception is raised if `Exchange` is executed on something that is not a cell:

$$\frac{\{\texttt{Exchange}\ x_c\ x_{old}\ x_{new}\} \;\Big\|\; \textbf{raise } \texttt{error(...)} \textbf{ end}}{\sigma \;\Big\|\; \sigma} \text{ if } \begin{array}{l} \sigma \models det(x_c) \wedge \\ (x_c \text{ not a cell}) \end{array}$$

We can add analogous rules for the built-in procedures.

13.1.16 Failed values

The semantics of failed values is defined by three rules and some extensions of previous rules. The first rule creates a failed value:

$$\frac{\{\texttt{FailedValue}\ x\ x_f\} \;\Big\|\; x_f{=}y}{\sigma \;\Big\|\; \sigma \wedge y{=}\mathit{failed}(x)} \text{ if } y \text{ fresh variable}$$

The entity $\mathit{failed}(x)$ represents a failed value that encapsulates the variable x. A failed value is not a value, i.e., it is not a member of the set of possible values. It follows that a rule that needs a value to reduce will not reduce with a failed value. However, we do allow a failed value to be bound to an unbound variable. This means it can be passed to and from a procedure and it can be embedded in a data structure. The second rule ensures that needing a failed value raises an exception:

$$\frac{S \;\Big\|\; \textbf{raise } x \textbf{ end}}{\sigma \;\Big\|\; \sigma} \text{ if } need_{\sigma_y}(S, y) \text{ and } \sigma \models y{=}\mathit{failed}(x)$$

4. The **raise** statement in this rule is shorthand for **local** `X` **in** `X=failure(...)` **raise** `X` **end end**.

Here $\sigma_y = \sigma \setminus \{y{=}\mathit{failed}(x)\}$, i.e., y is unbound in σ_y. This allows correct calculation of the need_σ relation. The third rule ensures that attempting to bind a failed value to a nonvariable raises an exception:

$$\frac{\beta \,\|\, \texttt{raise}\ x\ \texttt{end}}{\sigma \,\|\, \sigma} \quad \text{if } \mathit{subbindings}_\sigma(\beta) = \emptyset \text{ and } \mathit{failconflict}_\sigma(\beta, x)$$

This rule is added to the two basic binding rules. We define the condition $\mathit{failconflict}_\sigma(\beta, x)$ to be true in two cases. First, if $\beta \models \mathit{det}(y)$ and $\sigma \models y{=}\mathit{failed}(x)$. Second, if $\beta \equiv y{=}y'$ and at least one of y or y' is bound to a failed value of the form $\mathit{failed}(x)$ and the other is a different failed value or determined.

What's left is to explain what happens when other operations, such as `IsDet`, `WaitQuiet`, and read-only variables, are involved with failed values. Since these operations are used to build specialized control abstractions, we find that a reasonable solution is not to raise an exception for them. We define `IsDet` to return **`false`** for a failed value. We define a new operation `IsFailed` that returns **`true`** for a failed value and **`false`** for all other language entities. We define `WaitQuiet` to succeed for a failed value. For read-only views, failed values behave like normal values.

13.1.17 Variable substitution

This section defines the substitution of identifiers by variables in a statement. The notation $S\theta$, where $\theta = \{X_1{\rightarrow}x_1, \ldots, X_n{\rightarrow}x_n\}$, stands for the substitution of X_1 by x_1, ..., X_n by x_n in the statement S. For convenience, we first define substitutions for variables and identifiers. Let χ denote an identifier or a variable, i.e., $\chi ::= X \mid x$.

$$\chi\theta = \begin{cases} \theta(\chi) & \text{if } \chi \in \mathrm{dom}(\theta) \\ \chi & \text{otherwise} \end{cases}$$

The following substitutions do not involve lexical scoping, so their definition is easy.

$$\begin{aligned}
(\texttt{skip})\theta &\equiv \texttt{skip} \\
(S_1\ S_2)\theta &\equiv S_1\theta\ S_2\theta \\
(\texttt{thread}\ S\ \texttt{end})\theta &\equiv \texttt{thread}\ S\theta\ \texttt{end} \\
(\chi_1{=}\chi_2)\theta &\equiv \chi_1\theta = \chi_2\theta \\
(\chi{=}z)\theta &\equiv \chi\theta = z \\
(\chi{=}f(l_1{:}\chi_1 \cdots l_n{:}\chi_n))\theta &\equiv \chi\theta = f(l_1{:}\chi_1\theta \cdots l_n{:}\chi_n\theta) \\
(\texttt{if}\ \chi\ \texttt{then}\ S_1\ \texttt{else}\ S_2\ \texttt{end})\theta &\equiv \texttt{if}\ \chi\theta\ \texttt{then}\ S_1\theta\ \texttt{else}\ S_2\theta\ \texttt{end} \\
(\{\chi\ \chi_1 \cdots \chi_n\})\theta &\equiv \{\chi\theta\ \chi_1\theta \cdots \chi_n\theta\} \\
(\texttt{raise}\ \chi\ \texttt{end})\theta &\equiv \texttt{raise}\ \chi\theta\ \texttt{end}
\end{aligned}$$

We assume that the primitive operations `Wait`, `NewName`, `IsDet`, `NewCell`, `Exchange`, `WaitNeeded`, `WaitQuiet`, `ReadOnly`, and `FailedValue` are handled by the procedure application case. The remaining substitutions deal with lexical scoping. The notation $\theta_{\{X_1,\ldots,X_n\}}$ stands for the removal of the mappings of $X_1, \ldots, X_n$ from θ, i.e.,

$$\theta_{\{X_1,\ldots,X_n\}} = \left\{X{\rightarrow}x \in \theta \;\middle|\; X \notin \{X_1,\ldots,X_n\}\right\}$$

With this notation, we write:

$$(\texttt{local}\ X_1\cdots X_n\ \texttt{in}\ S\ \texttt{end})\theta \equiv \texttt{local}\ X_1\cdots X_n\ \texttt{in}\ S\theta_{\{X_1,\ldots,X_n\}}\ \texttt{end}$$

$$\begin{pmatrix}\texttt{case}\ \chi\ \texttt{of}\ f(l_1{:}X_1\ldots l_n{:}X_n)\\ \texttt{then}\ S_1\ \texttt{else}\ S_2\ \texttt{end}\end{pmatrix}\theta \equiv \begin{matrix}\texttt{case}\ \chi\theta\ \texttt{of}\ f(l_1{:}X_1\ldots l_n{:}X_n)\\ \texttt{then}\ S_1\theta_{\{X_1,\ldots,X_n\}}\ \texttt{else}\ S_2\theta\ \texttt{end}\end{matrix}$$

$$(\texttt{proc}\ \{\chi\ X_1\cdots X_n\}\ S\ \texttt{end})\theta \equiv \texttt{proc}\ \{\chi\theta\ X_1\cdots X_n\}\ S\theta_{\{X_1,\ldots,X_n\}}\ \texttt{end}$$

$$(\texttt{try}\ S_1\ \texttt{catch}\ X\ \texttt{then}\ S_2\ \texttt{end})\theta \equiv \texttt{try}\ S_1\theta\ \texttt{catch}\ X\ \texttt{then}\ S_2\theta_{\{X\}}\ \texttt{end}$$

13.2 Declarative concurrency

In section 4.1.4 we gave an informal definition of the concept of declarative concurrency. Let us now make this definition formal. Recall how we define a reduction step:

$$\frac{\mathcal{T}}{\sigma} \Bigg\| \frac{\mathcal{T}'}{\sigma'}$$

Here $\mathcal{T}$ is a multiset of threads in execution (i.e., statement sequences) and σ is a set of bindings (a store). Let us assume for this section that σ has no cells. We call $\mathcal{T}$ a program in execution, or program for short, if there is no risk of confusion with the meaning of program as a source text.

13.2.1 Partial and total termination

We say that the configuration $\mathcal{T}/\sigma$ is partially terminated if it cannot be further reduced (no reduction rule applies). The termination is partial since adding bindings to σ might allow some rules to apply and execution to continue. Although it is not needed for defining declarative concurrency, we can also define total termination: no matter what bindings are added to σ, the configuration cannot be reduced further.

We can also consider failed computations as partially terminated if we introduce the following two reduction rules.

$$\frac{\langle \texttt{raise}\ x\ \texttt{end}\ \langle\rangle\rangle}{\sigma} \Bigg\| \frac{}{\texttt{false}} \qquad\qquad \frac{\mathcal{T}}{\texttt{false}} \Bigg\| \frac{}{\texttt{false}}$$

With those rules, any uncaught exception eventually leads to the failure configuration $\emptyset/$**false**.

13.2.2 Logical equivalence

We define logical equivalence between stores as we did in the beginning of the chapter. We extend this to logical equivalence between configurations. Let $\mathcal{V}$ be a set of variables. Two configurations $\mathcal{T}/\sigma$ and $\mathcal{T}'/\sigma'$ are logically equivalent with respect to $\mathcal{V}$ if there exists a bijection r on variables and names such that

- for all x in $\mathcal{V}$, $r(x) = x$,
- $r(\sigma) \equiv \sigma'$ and $\sigma \equiv r^{-1}(\sigma')$,
- $r(\mathcal{T}) = \mathcal{T}'$ and $\mathcal{T} = r^{-1}(\mathcal{T}')$, where r and r^{-1} are used as substitutions.

The mapping r makes the correspondence between variables and names that are not in a common set $\mathcal{V}$.

13.2.3 Formal definition of declarative concurrency

We say that a program $\mathcal{T}$ is declarative concurrent if for all $\sigma_{\mathcal{V}}$,

- $\mathcal{T}/\sigma$ always reduces after a finite number of reduction steps to a partially terminated configuration and all these configurations are logically equivalent with respect to $\mathcal{V}$;
- for every partial termination $\mathcal{T}'/\sigma'$ of $\mathcal{T}/\sigma$, σ' entails σ (monotonicity).

Those two statements also hold for failure configurations. The failed store **`false`** entails all the other stores.

In general, we say that a computation model is declarative concurrent if all its programs are declarative concurrent. Intuitively, we can consider a declarative concurrent program as calculating a partial function $b = f_{\mathcal{T}}(a)$, where $a = \sigma$ and $b = \sigma'$. The function is determined by the program $\mathcal{T}$.

The execution of a declarative concurrent program can always be separated into a sequence of alternating input and output "phases": adding a set of bindings (input phase) and executing until partial termination (output phase).

We can prove that all the declarative concurrent models of chapter 4 are declarative concurrent according to the above definition. In particular, the most general model (which contains both threads and by-need triggers) is declarative concurrent.

From the viewpoint of foundational calculi, this result means that the declarative concurrent model can be seen as an interesting intermediate step between functional calculi such as the λ calculus and process calculi such as the π calculus. The λ calculus is a model of functional programming. This has nice properties such as confluence (see section 4.9.2). The π calculus is a model of concurrent programming: it is not functional but it is able to express many concurrent computations. The declarative concurrent model is both functional and concurrent. It restricts the expressiveness of concurrency compared to the π calculus in such a way that computations become functional again as in the λ calculus.

13.2.4 Confluence property

The above definition of declarative concurrency only considers partial terminations. Nothing is said about infinite executions. Here we propose another way to express declarative concurrency which takes all kinds of computations into account. We use the notation $\mathcal{T}/\sigma \longrightarrow \mathcal{T}'/\sigma'$ to say that there exists a finite execution that begins with configuration $\mathcal{T}/\sigma$ and ends with configuration $\mathcal{T}'/\sigma'$. Partial termination is not required for $\mathcal{T}'/\sigma'$.

A program $\mathcal{T}$ is declarative concurrent if for all $\sigma_{\mathcal{V}}$, and for all executions $\mathcal{T}/\sigma \longrightarrow \mathcal{T}_1/\sigma_1$ and $\mathcal{T}/\sigma \longrightarrow \mathcal{T}_2/\sigma_2$, there exist two further executions $\mathcal{T}_1/\sigma_1 \longrightarrow \mathcal{T}'_1/\sigma'_1$ and $\mathcal{T}_2/\sigma_2 \longrightarrow \mathcal{T}'_2/\sigma'_2$ such that the configurations $\mathcal{T}'_1/\sigma'_1$ and $\mathcal{T}'_2/\sigma'_2$ are equivalent with respect to $\mathcal{V}$.

The property can be depicted by the following diagram, where the configuration $\mathcal{T}'/\sigma'$ is given "up to equivalence with respect to $\mathcal{V}$."

$$\begin{array}{ccc} & \mathcal{T}/\sigma & \\ \swarrow & & \searrow \\ \mathcal{T}_1/\sigma_1 & & \mathcal{T}_2/\sigma_2 \\ \searrow & & \swarrow \\ & \mathcal{T}'/\sigma' & \end{array}$$

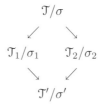

This property is useful for reasoning about infinite executions. It states that all finite executions of a never-ending declarative program must be consistent with each other. For instance, consider a program $\mathcal{T}$ that binds x to an infinite list. If x is bound to `1|2|3|...` during one execution, and to `2|4|6|...` during another execution, then the program is not declarative.

13.3 Eight computation models

The previous section gives the semantics of the general computation model, which is the most expressive general-purpose model of the book. This semantics is factorized so that the semantics of most of the earlier models are subsets of it. To make these subsets easy to understand, we distinguish three properties: concurrency, state, and laziness. Each of these properties is defined by a part of the semantics:

- *Concurrency* is introduced by the **`thread`** statement. Having concurrency implies that there is a multiset of tasks.
- *State* is introduced by the `NewCell` operation and handled by the `Exchange` operation. Having state implies that there is a mutable store. We assume that having *ports* is equivalent to having state.
- *Laziness* is introduced by the `WaitNeeded` operation. Having laziness implies that there is a need store.

C	L	S	Description
			Declarative model (chapters 2 &3, Mercury, Prolog).
		×	Stateful model (chapters 6 & 7, Scheme, Standard ML, Pascal).
	×		Lazy declarative model (Haskell).
	×	×	Lazy stateful model.
×			Eager concurrent model (chapter 4, dataflow).
×		×	Stateful concurrent model (chapters 5 & 8, Erlang, Java, FCP).
×	×		Lazy concurrent model (chapter 4, demand-driven dataflow).
×	×	×	Stateful concurrent model with laziness (Oz).

Table 13.1: Eight computation models.

Each of the three properties can be left out of the model by removing its statements. This gives eight useful models of varying degrees of expressiveness (!). Table 13.1 lists these eight models. All of these models are practical and most have been used in real programming languages. Table 13.1 also situates a number of real languages with respect to the model that in our opinion best fits the intended use of each language. In this table, C means concurrency, L means laziness, and S means state. An × means the property is in the model, a blank means it is not.

In the general computation model, the three properties are all explicit. That is, the programmer controls whether or not they are used by means of explicit commands. This is not true of all the languages mentioned. For example, laziness is implicit in Haskell and concurrency is implicit in FCP (Flat Concurrent Prolog).

Languages can be based on the same computation model and yet "feel" very differently to the programmer:

- Scheme, Standard ML, and Pascal are all based on the stateful model. Pascal is a simple imperative language. Scheme and Standard ML are "mostly functional" languages. By "mostly" we mean that state is intended to be used in a limited way.
- Erlang, Java, and FCP are all based on the stateful concurrent model, either of the shared-state variety or of the message-passing variety. Erlang is based on port objects that are programmed in a functional model and communicate with asynchronous message passing. Java is based on passive objects referenced by threads and that communicate through shared monitors. FCP is based on the process model of logic programming, with predicates in Horn clause syntax that communicate through shared streams.

Whether a language is dynamically or statically typed is independent of its place in the table. Scheme, Prolog, Erlang, FCP, and Oz are dynamically typed. Haskell, Standard ML, Mercury, Java, and Pascal are statically typed.

The table does not give the semantics of the relational computation model of chapter 9 (the declarative model with search). We delay this until we give the semantics of constraint programming in chapter 12. The logical semantics of Prolog and Mercury are closely related to the relational computation model.

13.4 Semantics of common abstractions

We have seen many programming abstractions throughout the book. For example, some of the more general ones are the following:

- Loop abstractions such as the **`for`** loop
- Software components (functors) and their instances (modules)
- Stream objects and declarative concurrency
- Coroutines (non-preemptive threads)
- Lazy functions and list comprehensions
- Secure data abstractions, wrappers, and revocable capabilities
- Incremental definition of data abstractions (classes) and their instances (objects)
- Ports (communication channels) and port objects
- Concurrent components (port objects and their compositions)
- Active objects, both asynchronous and synchronous
- Active objects with mailboxes (as used in Erlang)
- Locks, reentrant locks, monitors, and transactions
- Tuple spaces (similar to the Linda concept)

We showed how to implement these abstractions using the general computation model or a subset of this model. When taken together with this chapter, these implementations can be seen as formal semantic definitions of the abstractions. The choice of which concepts are primitive and which are derived is often a matter of judgment. For example, chapter 5 defines a port as a primitive concept and gives its semantics directly.

For some of the abstractions, we have defined new syntax, thus making them into linguistic abstractions. For the semantics, it is almost irrelevant whether or not an abstraction has syntactic support. We say "almost" because the syntax can guarantee that the abstraction is not used in an incorrect way, which is important when reasoning about programs.

13.5 Historical notes

The computation model of this chapter was developed over many years. We briefly summarize its history. In the late 1980s, a new model of computation known as the concurrent constraint model was developed by Michael Maher and Vijay Saraswat out of concurrent logic programming and constraint logic programming [102, 135,

182]. All computation models of the book are ultimately based on this model.

The concurrent constraint model led to the AKL language [104, 105] and subsequently to Oz 1 [198, 199], a precursor of the Oz language used in the book. AKL adds stateful data (in the form of ports) and encapsulated search to the basic concurrent constraint model. Oz 1 further adds higher-order procedures, a compositional syntax (instead of the Horn clause syntax of AKL), stateful abstractions including an object system, and computation spaces for encapsulated search. Like AKL, Oz 1 has implicit concurrency: when a statement blocks it is put into its own thread that contains only that statement. The direct successor of Oz 1, called Oz 2, replaces implicit concurrency by explicit thread creation, which allows an improved object system and makes it easier to reason about programs.

The kernel languages used in this book are subsets of Oz 3, which this book calls simply *Oz*. Oz 3 extends and simplifies Oz 2 in many ways. It adds by-need execution (an early version is given in [139]), first-class software components called functors [58], and a distributed computation model [83]. It has a simple formal semantics that can be implemented efficiently. The formal semantics of this chapter completes and corrects the semantics given in earlier publications, notably regarding by-need execution and read-only variables.

13.6 Exercises

1. *The* **case** *statement.* Let us investigate the **case** statement, whose semantics is defined in section 13.1.9.

   (a) Show how the semantic rules of **case** can be derived from the rules for **local** and **if**.

   (b) In the first rule for the **case**, we could have explicitly introduced variables for the X_i by

$$\frac{\texttt{case}\ x\ \texttt{of}\ f(l_1{:}X_1 \cdots l_n{:}X_n)\ \texttt{then}\ S_1\ \texttt{else}\ S_2\ \texttt{end}}{\sigma \wedge x{=}f(l_1{:}x_1 \cdots l_n{:}x_n)} \;\Bigg\|\; \frac{\texttt{local}\ X_1 \cdots X_n\ \texttt{in}\ X_1{=}x_1\ \cdots\ X_n{=}x_n\ S_1\ \texttt{end}}{\sigma \wedge x{=}f(l_1{:}x_1 \cdots l_n{:}x_n)}$$

   Do the rules lead to the same possible executions? What are the differences (if any)?

   (c) It is possible to write an **if** statement in terms of a **case** statement. How? This implies that **case** could have been put in the kernel language instead of **if**, and **if** could have been defined as a linguistic abstraction.

2. *Lexically scoped closures.* The rules for procedural abstraction in section 13.1.11 are designed to follow lexical scoping, i.e., procedure introduction creates a lexically scoped closure. Let us look more closely to see how this works:

   (a) Write the consecutive computation steps (rule reductions) for the execution of the `ForAll` and `MakeAdder` definitions in section 13.1.11.

(b) Procedure introduction creates the value **proc** {$ $X_1 \cdots X_n$} S **end** in the store. Explain how the contextual environment is stored in this value.

3. *Implementing cells with* `IsDet`. Section 13.1.12 explains the `IsDet` operation, which can be used to check the status of a dataflow variable. For this exercise, let us examine the expressive power of `IsDet`.

(a) Define the operations `NewCell` and `Exchange` in the declarative model extended with `IsDet`. The semantics of these operations should be identical to their semantics with cells, as given in this chapter. It is straightforward to define a solution, albeit an inefficient one, that works in a sequential model. *Hint*: use the function `LastCons`, defined as

```
fun {LastCons Xs}
   case Xs of X|Xr then
      if {IsDet Xr} then {LastCons Xr} else Xs end
   [] nil then nil end
end
```

Using `LastCons` lets us get around the monotonicity of the store. The idea is to build incrementally a list with unbound tail and use `IsDet` to get its latest known element.

(b) Does the above solution work in a concurrent model, i.e., when exchanges on the same cell are done concurrently? Is such a solution possible? In the light of this result, comment on the relationship between `IsDet` and explicit state.

4. *Reading and writing a cell.* Section 13.1.12 mentions that two more cell operations can be added for programming convenience, namely x_{old}=@x_c to read the content and x_c:=x_{new} to update the content. Define the semantics of these two operations.

5. *Dataflow streams.* Section 13.1.12 gives an example of a **local** statement that adds an element to a stream. Prove that executing two of these statements in different threads always gives exactly the same final result as if they were executed sequentially in the same thread in one order or another.

6. *Stateful streams.* Define a stream data type that does not use dataflow variables. That is, it is a list in which each tail is a cell whose content points to the rest of the list. The last cell contains a marker saying that the stream is not yet complete, e.g., the atom `incomplete`. (This is not the same as the atom `nil` which means that the stream is complete.) There is a global cell `C` whose content is always the last cell in the stream. Write an operation that adds an element to the stream and that works in a concurrent setting. *Hint*: assume that there exists a statement **lock** S **end** such that only one thread at a time can be executing S; all others suspend if needed to make this true. Can you do it without using a **lock** statement? Compare your solution to that of the previous exercise. Which is simpler?

7. *Needing a variable.* Section 13.1.13 gives a definition of what it means to need a variable. Because this need relation is monotonic, we can show that the demand-driven concurrent model is declarative. However, there are other ways to define the need relation that also result in declarative models. For this exercise, try to find at

least one such definition.

8. (advanced exercise) *Lambda calculus*. The book claims that the declarative model and the declarative concurrent model both do functional programming. For this exercise, prove this claim formally. First show that any execution in the declarative model corresponds to an execution in a version of the λ calculus. How do dataflow variables show up? Then show that adding concurrency and laziness do not change this result.

9. (research project) *Trade-offs in language design*. When designing a language, there are often trade-offs between the programmer's mental model, the language semantics, and the implementation. One would like all three to be simple, but that is often impossible. One of the delicate matters is to find the right balance. To make this concrete, let us see how to provide the concept of binding in a dataflow language. Section 13.1.8 defines two semantics for binding, which it calls the naive semantics and the realistic semantics. There is also a third possibility. Let us summarize all three:

- The naive semantics does binding atomically, as a transaction. If adding β would be inconsistent, then the store is unchanged. This gives a simple mental model and a simple semantics, but the implementation is complex. This semantics was much discussed in the context of concurrent logic programming, but was dropped because of problems implementing it efficiently [196, 211].
- The realistic semantics does binding as an incremental tell. That is, if β is inconsistent, then the store might still be changed. This makes the implementation simple, but the semantics somewhat more complex. Experience shows that the mental model is acceptable. This semantics is chosen for the computation models of the book.
- The third semantics is more in line with mainstream programming languages. It jettisons unification in favor of simple bindings only. It allows binding only unbound variables with terms. Variable-variable bindings block and term-term bindings raise an exception. This makes both the implementation and the semantics simple. However, it is less expressive for the programmer. This approach was pioneered, e.g., in dataflow languages with I-structures such as Id and pH [150, 151, 152] and in Multilisp [79] (see section 4.9.4).

For this exercise, reexamine the trade-offs between these three approaches. Which would you recommend?

IV APPENDIXES

A Mozart System Development Environment

Beware the ides of March.
– Soothsayer to Julius Caesar, William Shakespeare (1564–1616)

The Mozart system has a complete IDE (interactive development environment). To get you started, we give a brief overview of this environment here. We refer you to the system documentation for additional information.

A.1 Interactive interface

The Mozart system has an interactive interface that is based on the Emacs text editor. The interfactive interface is sometimes called the OPI, which stands for Oz programming interface. The OPI is split into several buffers: scratch pad, Oz emulator, Oz compiler, and one buffer for each open file. This interface gives access to several tools: incremental compiler (which can compile any legal program fragment), Browser (visualize the single-assignment store), Panel (resource usage), Compiler Panel (compiler settings and environment), Distribution Panel (distribution subsystem including message traffic), and the Explorer (interactive graphical resolution of constraint problems). These tools can also be manipulated from within programs, e.g., the `Compiler` module can compile strings from within programs.

A.1.1 Interface commands

You can access all the important OPI commands through the menus at the top of the window. Most of these commands have keyboard equivalents. The most important commands are listed in table A.1. The notation "`CTRL-x`" means to hold down the Control key and then press the key `x` once. The `CTRL-g` command is especially useful if you get lost. To feed a text means to compile and execute it. A region is a contiguous part of the buffer. It can be selected by dragging over it while holding the first mouse button down. A paragraph is a set of nonempty text lines delimited by empty lines or by the beginning or end of the buffer.

The emulator window gives messages from the emulator. It gives the output of `Show` and run-time error messages, e.g., uncaught exceptions. The compiler window gives messages from the compiler. It says whether fed source code is accepted by

Command	Effect
CTRL-x CTRL-f	Read a file into a new editor buffer
CTRL-x CTRL-s	Save current buffer into its file
CTRL-x i	Insert file into the current buffer
CTRL-. CTRL-l	Feed current line into Mozart
CTRL-. CTRL-r	Feed current selected region into Mozart
CTRL-. CTRL-p	Feed current paragraph into Mozart
CTRL-. CTRL-b	Feed current buffer into Mozart
CTRL-. h	Halt the run-time system (but keep the editor)
CTRL-x CTRL-c	Halt the complete system
CTRL-. e	Toggle the emulator window
CTRL-. c	Toggle the compiler window
CTRL-x 1	Make current buffer fill the whole window
CTRL-g	Cancel current command

Table A.1: Some commands of the Oz programming interface.

the system and gives compile-time error messages otherwise.

A.1.2 Using functors interactively

Functors are software component specifications that aid in building well-structured programs. A functor can be instantiated, which creates a module. A module is a run-time entity that groups together other run-time entities. Modules can contain records, procedures, objects, classes, running threads, and any other entity that exists at run time.

Functors are compilation units, i.e., their source code can be put in a file and compiled as one unit. Functors can also be used in the interactive interface. This follows the Mozart principle that everything can be done interactively.

- A compiled functor can be loaded and linked interactively. For example, assume that the `Set` module, which can be found on the book's Web site, is compiled in the file `Set.ozf`. It will be loaded and linked interactively with the following code:

```
declare
[Set]={Module.link ["Set.ozf"]}
```

This creates and links the module `Set`. The function `Module.link` takes a list of file names or URLs and returns a list of modules.

- A functor is simply a value, like a class. It can be defined interactively with a syntax similar to classes:

```
F=functor $ define skip end
```

This defines a functor and binds `F` to it. We can create a module from `F` as follows:

```
declare
[M]={Module.apply [F]}
```

This creates and links the module `M`. The function `Module.apply` takes a list of functor values and returns a list of modules.

For more functor manipulations, see the documentation of the module `Module`.

A.2 Command line interface

The Mozart system can be used from a command line. Oz source files can be compiled and linked. Source files to compile should contain functors, i.e., start with the keyword **functor**. For example, assume that we have the source file `Set.oz`. We create the compiled functor `Set.ozf` by typing the following command from a command line interface:

```
ozc -c Set.oz
```

We can create a standalone executable `Set` by typing the following:

```
ozc -x Set.oz
```

(In the case of `Set.oz`, the standalone executable does very little: it just defines the set operations.) The Mozart default is to use dynamic linking, i.e., needed modules are loaded and linked at the moment they are needed in an application. This keeps compiled files small. But it is possible to link all imported modules during compilation (static linking) so that no dynamic linking is needed.

B Basic Data Types

Wie het kleine niet eert is het grote niet weert.
He who does not honor small things is not worthy of great things.
– Dutch proverb.

This appendix explains the most common basic data types in Oz together with some common operations. The types explained are numbers (including integers and floating point numbers), characters (which are represented as small integers), literals (constants of two types, either atoms or names), records, tuples, chunks (records with a limited set of operations), lists, strings (which are represented as lists of characters), and virtual strings (strings represented as tuples).

For each data type discussed in this appendix, there is a corresponding Base module in the Mozart system that defines all operations on the data type. This appendix gives some but not all of these operations. See the Mozart system documentation for complete information [57].

B.1 Numbers (integers, floats, and characters)

The following code fragment introduces four variables, `I`, `H`, `F`, and `C`. It binds `I` to an integer, `H` to an integer in hexadecimal notation, `F` to a float, and `C` to the character `t` in this order. It then displays `I`, `H`, `F`, and `C`:

```
declare I H F C in
I = ~5
H = 0xDadBeddedABadBadBabe
F = 5.5
C = &t
{Browse I} {Browse H} {Browse F} {Browse C}
```

Note that ~ (tilde) is the unary minus symbol. This displays the following:

```
~5
1033532870595452951444158
5.5
116
```

Oz supports binary, octal, decimal, and hexadecimal notation for integers, which can have any number of digits. An octal integer starts with a leading `0` (zero), followed by any number of octal digits, i.e., with values from `0` to `7`. A binary

<table>
<tr><td>⟨character⟩</td><td>::=</td><td>(any integer in the range 0 . . . 255)</td></tr>
<tr><td></td><td></td><td>| ´&´ ⟨charChar⟩</td></tr>
<tr><td></td><td></td><td>| ´&´ ⟨pseudoChar⟩</td></tr>
<tr><td>⟨charChar⟩</td><td>::=</td><td>(any inline character except \ and NUL)</td></tr>
<tr><td>⟨pseudoChar⟩</td><td>::=</td><td>(´\´ followed by three octal digits)</td></tr>
<tr><td></td><td></td><td>| (´\x´ or ´\X´ followed by two hexadecimal digits)</td></tr>
<tr><td></td><td></td><td>| ´\a´ | ´\b´ | ´\f´ | ´\n´ | ´\r´ | ´\t´</td></tr>
<tr><td></td><td></td><td>| ´\v´ | ´\\´ | ´\´´ | ´\"´ | ´\`´ | ´\&´</td></tr>
</table>

Table B.1: Character lexical syntax.

integer starts with a leading `0b` or `0B` (zero followed by the letter `b` or `B`), followed by any number of binary digits, i.e., `0` or `1`. A hexadecimal integer starts with a leading `0x` or `0X` (zero followed by the letter `x` or `X`). The hexadecimal digits from 10 to 15 are denoted by the letters `a` through `f` and `A` through `F`.

Floats are different from integers in that they approximate real numbers. Here are some examples of floats:

```
~3.14159265359   3.5E3   ~12.0e~2   163.
```

Note that Mozart uses ~ (tilde) as the unary minus symbol for floats as well as integers. Floats are internally represented in double precision (64 bits) using the IEEE floating point standard. A float must be written with a decimal point and at least one digit before the decimal point. There may be zero or more digits after the decimal point. Floats can be scaled by powers of ten by appending the letter `e` or `E` followed by a decimal integer (which can be negative with a ´~´).

Characters are a subtype of integers that range from `0` to `255`. The standard ISO 8859-1 coding is used. This code extends the ASCII code to include the letters and accented letters of most languages whose alphabets are based on the Roman alphabet. Unicode is a 16-bit code that extends the ASCII code to include the characters and writing specifics (like writing direction) of most of the alphabets used in the world. It is not currently used in Mozart, but may be in the future. There are five ways to write characters:

- A character can be written as an integer in the range `0`, `1`, ..., `255`, in accord with the integer syntax given before.
- A character can be written as an ampersand `&` followed by a specific character representation. There are four such representations:
  - Any inline character except for \ (backslash) and the `NUL` character. Some examples are `&t`, `& ` (note the space), and `&+`. Inline control characters are acceptable.
  - A backslash \ followed by three octal digits, e.g., `&\215` is a character. The

<table>
<tr><td>⟨expression⟩</td><td>::=</td><td>⟨expression⟩ ⟨binaryOp⟩ ⟨expression⟩</td></tr>
<tr><td></td><td>|</td><td>´{´ ⟨expression⟩ { ⟨expression⟩ } ´}´</td></tr>
<tr><td></td><td>|</td><td>...</td></tr>
<tr><td>⟨binaryOp⟩</td><td>::=</td><td>´+´ | ´-´ | ´*´ | ´/´ | div | mod | ...</td></tr>
</table>

Table B.2: Expression syntax (in part).

first digit should not be greater than 3.

▫ A backslash \ followed by the letter `x` or `X`, followed by two hexadecimal digits, e.g., `&\x3f` is a character.

▫ A backslash \ followed by one of the following characters: `a` (= `\007`, bell), `b` (= `\010`, backspace), `f` (= `\014`, formfeed), `n` (= `\012`, newline), `r` (= `\015`, carriage return), `t` (= `\011`, horizontal tab), `v` (= `\013`, vertical tab), \ (= `\134`, backslash), ´ (= `\047`, single quote), " (= `\042`, double quote), ` (= `\140`, backquote), and `&` (= `\046`, ampersand). For example, `&\\` is the backslash character, i.e., the integer 92 (the ASCII code for \) .

Table B.1 summarizes these possibilities.

There is no automatic type conversion in Oz, so `5.0 = 5` will raise an exception. The next section explains the basic operations on numbers, including the primitive procedures for explicit type conversion. The complete set of operations for characters, integers, and floats are given in the Base modules `Char`, `Float`, and `Int`. Additional generic operations on all numbers are given in the Base module `Number`. See the documentation for more information.

B.1.1 Operations on numbers

To express a calculation with numbers, we use two kinds of operations: binary operations, such as addition and subtraction, and function applications, such as type conversions. Table B.2 gives the syntax of these expressions. Table B.3 gives some number operations; more are listed in Table 2.3. All numbers, i.e., both integers and floats, support addition, subtraction, and multiplication:

```
declare I Pi Radius Circumference in
I = 7 * 11 * 13 + 27 * 37
Pi = 3.1415926536
Radius = 10.
Circumference = 2.0 * Pi * Radius
```

The arguments of `+`, `-`, and `*` must both be integers or floats; no implicit type conversion is done. Integer arithmetic is to arbitrary precision. Float arithmetic has a fixed precision. Integers support integer division (**div** symbol) and modulo (**mod** symbol). Floats support floating division (/ symbol). Integer division truncates the fractional part. Integer division and modulo satisfy the following identity:

Operation	Description
`{IsInt I}`	Return boolean saying whether `I` is an integer
`{IsFloat F}`	Return boolean saying whether `F` is a float
`{IntToFloat I}`	Return float closest to integer `I`
`{IntToString I}`	Return string describing integer `I`
`{FloatToInt F}`	Return integer closest to float `F`, to nearest even
`{FloatToString F}`	Return string describing float `F`
`{Round F}`	Return integral float closest to float `F`, to nearest even
`{Floor F}`	Return largest integral float $\leq$ float `F`
`{Ceil F}`	Return smallest integral float $\geq$ float `F`
`{Sin F}`	Return the sine of float `F`
`{Cos F}`	Return the cosine of float `F`
`{Tan F}`	Return the tangent of float `F`
`{Sqrt F}`	Return the square root of float `F`
`{Exp F}`	Return $e^{\mathtt{F}}$ for float `F`
`{Log F}`	Return $\log_e$ `F` for float `F`

Table B.3: Some number operations.

```
A = B * (A div B) + (A mod B)
```

There are several operations to convert between floats and integers.

- There is one operation to convert from an integer to a float, namely `IntToFloat`. This operation finds the best float approximation to a given integer. Because integers are calculated with arbitrary precision, it is possible for an integer to be larger than a representable float. In that case, the float **`inf`** (infinity) is returned.
- There is one operation to convert from a float to an integer, namely `FloatToInt`. This operation follows the default rounding mode of the IEEE floating point standard, i.e., if there are two possibilities, then it picks the even integer. For example, `{FloatToInt 2.5}` and `{FloatToInt 1.5}` both give the integer `2`. This eliminates the bias that would result by always rounding half integers upward.
- There are three operations to convert a float into a float that has zero fractional part: `Floor`, `Ceil` (ceiling), and `Round`.
  - `Floor` rounds toward negative infinity, e.g., `{Floor ~3.5}` gives `~4.0` and `{Floor 4.6}` gives `4.0`.
  - `Ceil` rounds toward positive infinity, e.g., `{Ceil ~3.5}` gives `~3.0` and `{Ceil 4.6}` gives `5.0`.
  - `Round` rounds toward the nearest even, e.g., `{Round 4.5}=4` and `{Round 5.5}=6`. `Round` is identical to `FloatToInt` except that it returns a float, i.e., `{Round X} = {IntToFloat {FloatToInt X}}`.

Operation	Description
`{IsChar C}`	Return boolean saying whether `C` is a character
`{Char.toAtom C}`	Return atom corresponding to `C`
`{Char.toLower C}`	Return lowercase letter corresponding to `C`
`{Char.toUpper C}`	Return uppercase letter corresponding to `C`

Table B.4: Some character operations.

<table><tr><td>⟨expression⟩ ::= unit | true | false | ⟨atom⟩ | ...</td></tr></table>

Table B.5: Literal syntax (in part).

<table>
<tr><td>⟨atom⟩</td><td>::=</td><td>(lowercase char) { (alphanumeric char) } (except no keyword)</td></tr>
<tr><td></td><td></td><td>| ''' { ⟨atomChar⟩ | ⟨pseudoChar⟩ } '''</td></tr>
<tr><td>⟨atomChar⟩</td><td>::=</td><td>(any inline character except ', \, and NUL)</td></tr>
<tr><td>⟨pseudoChar⟩</td><td>::=</td><td>('\' followed by three octal digits)</td></tr>
<tr><td></td><td></td><td>| ('\x' or '\X' followed by two hexadecimal digits)</td></tr>
<tr><td></td><td></td><td>| '\a' | '\b' | '\f' | '\n' | '\r' | '\t'</td></tr>
<tr><td></td><td></td><td>| '\v' | '\\' | '\'' | '\"' | '\`' | '\&'</td></tr>
</table>

Table B.6: Atom lexical syntax.

B.1.2 Operations on characters

All integer operations also work for characters. There are a few additional operations that work only on characters. Table B.4 lists some of them. The Base module `Char` gives them all.

B.2 Literals (atoms and names)

Atomic types are types whose members have no internal structure.[1] The previous section has given one kind of atomic type, namely numbers. In addition to numbers, literals are a second kind of atomic type (see tables B.5 and B.6). Literals can be either atoms or names. An atom is a value whose identity is determined by a sequence of printable characters. An atom can be written in two ways. First, as a sequence of alphanumeric characters starting with a lowercase letter. This sequence may not be a keyword of the language. Second, by arbitrary printable characters enclosed in single quotes. Here are some valid atoms:

```
a foo ´=´ ´:=´ ´Oz 3.0´ ´Hello World´ ´if´ ´\n,\n ´ a_person
```

There is no confusion between the keyword **if** and the atom ´if´ because of the quotes. The atom ´\n,\n ´ consists of four characters. Atoms are ordered lexicographically, based on the underlying ISO 8859-1 encoding for single characters.

Names are a second kind of literal. A name is a unique atomic value that cannot be forged or printed. Unlike numbers or atoms, names are truly atomic, in the original sense of the word: they cannot be decomposed at all. Names have just two operations defined on them: creation and equality comparison. The only way to create a name is by calling the function {NewName}, which returns a new name that is guaranteed to be unique. Note that table B.5 has no representation for names. The only way to reference a name is through a variable that is bound to the name. As section 3.7 explains, names play an important role for secure encapsulation in ADTs.

There are three special names that have keywords reserved to them. The keywords are **unit**, **true**, and **false**. The names **true** and **false** are used to denote boolean true and false values. The name **unit** is often used as a synchronization token in concurrent programs. Here are some examples:

```
local X Y B in
   X = foo
   {NewName Y}
   B = true
   {Browse [X Y B]}
end
```

B.2.1 Operations on atoms

Table B.7 gives the operations in the Base module Atom and some of the operations relating to atoms in the Base module String.

1. But like physical atoms, atomic values can sometimes be decomposed if the right tools are used, e.g., numbers have a binary representation as a sequence of zeros and ones and atoms have a print representation as a sequence of characters.

Operation	Description
`{IsAtom A}`	Return boolean saying whether `A` is an atom
`{AtomToString A}`	Return string corresponding to atom `A`
`{StringToAtom S}`	Return atom corresponding to string `S`

Table B.7: Some atom operations.

⟨expression⟩	::=	⟨label⟩ ´(´ { [⟨feature⟩ ´:´] ⟨expression⟩ } ´)´ | ...
⟨label⟩	::=	**unit** | **true** | **false** | ⟨variable⟩ | ⟨atom⟩
⟨feature⟩	::=	**unit** | **true** | **false** | ⟨variable⟩ | ⟨atom⟩ | ⟨int⟩
⟨binaryOp⟩	::=	´.´ | ⟨consBinOp⟩ | ...
⟨consBinOp⟩	::=	´#´ | ...

Table B.8: Record and tuple syntax (in part).

B.3 Records and tuples

Records are data structures that allow language references to be grouped together. Here is a record that groups four variables:

```
tree(key:I value:Y left:LT right:RT)
```

It has four components and the label `tree`. To avoid ambiguity, there should be no space between the label and the left parenthesis. Each component consists of an identifier, called feature, and a reference into the store. A feature can be either a literal or an integer. Table B.8 gives the syntax of records and tuples. The above record has four features, `key`, `value`, `left`, and `right`, that identify four language references, `I`, `Y`, `LT`, and `RT`.

It is allowed to omit features in the record syntax. In that case, the feature will be an integer starting from `1` for the first such component and incrementing by `1` for each successive component that does not have a feature. For example, the record `tree(key:I value:Y LT RT)` is identical to `tree(key:I value:Y 1:LT 2:RT)`.

The order of labeled components does not matter; it can be changed without changing the record. We say that these components are unordered. The order of unlabeled components does matter; it determines how the features are numbered. It is as if there were two "worlds": the ordered world and the unordered world. They have no effect on each other and can be interleaved in any way. All the following notations denote the same record:

```
tree(key:I value:Y LT RT)      tree(value:Y key:I LT RT)
tree(key:I LT value:Y RT)      tree(value:Y LT key:I RT)
tree(key:I LT RT value:Y)      tree(value:Y LT RT key:I)
tree(LT key:I value:Y RT)      tree(LT value:Y key:I RT)
tree(LT key:I RT value:Y)      tree(LT value:Y RT key:I)
tree(LT RT key:I value:Y)      tree(LT RT value:Y key:I)
```

Two records are the same if the same set of components is present and the ordered components are in the same order.

It is an error if a feature occurs more than once. For example, the notations `tree(key:I key:J)` and `tree(1:I value:Y LT RT)` are both in error. The error is discovered when the record is constructed. This can be either at compile time or at run time. However, both `tree(3:I value:Y LT RT)` and `tree(4:I value:Y LT RT)` are correct since no feature occurs more than once. Integer features do not have to be consecutive.

B.3.1 Tuples

If the record has only consecutive integer features starting from `1`, then we call it a tuple. All these features can be omitted. Consider this tuple:

```
tree(I Y LT RT)
```

It is exactly the same as the following tuple:

```
tree(1:I 2:Y 3:LT 4:RT)
```

Tuples whose label is `´#´` have another notation using the `#` symbol as an "mixfix" operator (see appendix C.4). This means that `a#b#c` is a tuple with three arguments, namely `´#´(a b c)`. Be careful not to confuse it with the pair `a#(b#c)`, whose second argument is itself the pair `b#c`. The mixfix notation can only be used for tuples with at least two arguments. It is used for virtual strings (see section B.7).

B.3.2 Operations on records

Table B.9 gives a few basic record operations. Many more operations exist in the Base module `Record`. This appendix shows only a few, namely those concerning extracting information from records and building new records. To select a field of a record component, we use the infix dot operator, e.g., `tree(key:I value:Y LT RT).value` returns `Y`. To compare two records, we use the equality test operation. Two records are the same if they have the same set of features and the language references for each feature are the same.

The arity of a record is a list of the features of the record sorted lexicographically. The call `{Arity R}` executes as soon as `R` is bound to a record and returns the record arity. This should not be confused with the function `Width`, which returns the number of arguments. Feeding the statement

Operation	Description
R.F	Return field F from R
{HasFeature R F}	Return boolean saying whether feature F is in R
{IsRecord R}	Return boolean saying whether R is of record type
{MakeRecord L Fs}	Return record with label L and features Fs
{Label R}	Return the label of R
{Arity R}	Return the list of features (arity) of R
{Record.toList R}	Return the list of fields of R, in Arity order
{Width R}	Return the number of features (width) of R
{AdjoinAt R F X}	Return R augmented with feature F and value X
{Adjoin R1 R2}	Return R1 augmented with all fields of R2

Table B.9: Some record operations.

```
declare T W L R in
T=tree(key:a left:L right:R value:1)
W=tree(a L R 1)
{Browse {Arity T}}
{Browse {Arity W}}
```

will display

```
[key left right value]
[1 2 3 4]
```

The function {AdjoinAt R1 F X} returns the record resulting from adjoining (i.e., adding) the field X to R1 at feature F. The record R1 is unchanged. If R1 already has the feature F, then the result is identical to R1 except for the field R1.F, whose value becomes X. Otherwise the feature F is added to R1. For example:

```
declare T W L R in
T=tree(key:a left:L right:R value:1)
W=tree(a L R 1)
{Browse {AdjoinAt T 1 b}}
{Browse {AdjoinAt W key b}}
```

will display

```
tree(b key:a left:L right:R value:1)
tree(a L R 1 key:b)
```

The {Adjoin R1 R2} operation gives the same result as if AdjoinAt were called successively, starting with R1 and iterating through all features of R2.

B.3.3 Operations on tuples

All record operations also work for tuples. There are a few additional operations that work only on tuples. Table B.10 lists some of them. The Base module Tuple gives them all.

Operation	Description
`{MakeTuple L N}`	Return tuple with label `L` and features `1`, ..., `N`
`{IsTuple T}`	Return boolean saying whether `T` is of tuple type

Table B.10: Some tuple operations.

⟨expression⟩	::=	´[´ { ⟨expression⟩ }+ ´]´ | ...
⟨consBinOp⟩	::=	´|´ | ...

Table B.11: List syntax (in part).

B.4 Chunks (limited records)

A chunk is Mozart terminology for a record type with a limited set of operations. There are only two basic operations on chunks: create a chunk from a record and extract information with the field selection operator ".":

```
declare
C={Chunk.new anyrecord(a b c)}  % Chunk creation
F=C.2                           % Chunk field selection
```

The `Label` and `Arity` operations are not defined and unification is not possible. Chunks give a way of "wrapping" information so that access to the information is restricted, i.e., only those computations that know the field can access the information. If the field is a name value, then it can only be known by a computation if it is passed explicitly to the computation. It cannot be guessed. This makes chunks and names useful for building secure data abstractions. For example, we use them in section 3.7.5 to define a secure stack ADT. Chunks are used in some library modules to provide secure encapsulation of data, such as in the module `ObjectSupport`.

B.5 Lists

A list is either the atom `nil` representing the empty list or a tuple with infix operator | and two arguments which are respectively the head and the tail of the list. The two arguments have field numbered 1 and 2. The head can be any data type and the tail is a list. We call the tuple a list pair. Often it is called a cons cell because creating one in Lisp is done with an operation called cons. Lisp is the oldest list-processing language and pioneered many list concepts and their terminology. When the second argument is not necessarily a list, then it is often called a dotted pair, because Lisp writes it in infix with a dot operator. In our notation, a list of the letters a, b, and c is written as

```
a|b|c|nil
```

We provide a more concise syntax for complete lists (i.e., when the rightmost argument is nil):

```
[a b c]
```

Table B.11 shows the syntax of these two ways of writing a list. The partial list containing elements a and b and whose tail is the variable X looks like

```
a|b|X
```

One can also use the standard record notation for lists:

```
'|'(a '|'(b X))
```

or even (making the field names explicit):

```
'|'(1:a 2:'|'(1:b 2:X))
```

Circular lists are allowed. For example, the following is legal:

```
declare X in
X=a|b|X
{Browse X}
```

By default, the browser displays the list without taking sharing into account, i.e., without taking into account multiple references to the same part of the list. In the list X, after the first two elements a and b, we find X again. By default, the browser ignores all sharing. It displays X as:

```
a|b|a|b|a|b|a|b|a|b|a|b|a|b|a|b|a|b|a|b|a|b|a|b|
a|b|a|b|a|b|a|b|a|b|a|b|a|b|a|b|a|b|a|b|a|b|,,,
```

To avoid infinite loops, the browser has an adjustable depth limit. The three commas ,,, represent the part of the list that is not displayed. Select Graph in the Representation entry of the browser's Options menu and feed the fragment again. This will display the list as a graph (see figure B.1):

```
C1=a|b|C1
```

The browser introduces the new variable C1 to refer to another part of the list. See the browser manual for more information on what the browser can display.

B.5.1 Operations on lists

Table B.12 gives a few basic list operations. Many more operations exist in the Base module List. Here is a simple symbolic calculation with lists:

```
declare A B in
A=[a b c]
B=[1 2 3 4]
{Browse {Append A B}}
```

Operation	Description
{Append L1 L2}	Return the concatenation of L1 and L2
{Member X L}	Return boolean saying whether X is in L
{Length L}	Return the length of L
{List.drop L N}	Return L minus the first N elements, or nil if it is shorter
{List.last L}	Return the last element of nonempty list L
{Sort L F}	Return L sorted with the boolean comparison function F
{Map L F}	Return the list obtained by applying F to each element of L
{ForAll L P}	Apply the unary procedure P to each element of L
{Filter L F}	Return the list of elements of L for which F gives **true**
{FoldL L F N}	Return the value obtained by inserting F between all elements of L
{Flatten L}	Return the list of all non-list elements of L, at any nesting depth
{List.toTuple A L}	Return tuple with label A and ordered fields from L
{List.toRecord A L}	Return record with label A and features/fields F#X in L

Table B.12: Some list operations.

This displays the list `[a b c 1 2 3 4]`. Like all operations, these all have correct dataflow behavior. For example, `{Length a|b|X}` blocks until `X` is bound. The operations `Sort`, `Map`, `ForAll`, `Filter`, and `FoldL` are examples of higher-order operations, i.e., operations that take functions or procedures as arguments. We talk about higher-order programming in chapter 3. For now, here's an example to give a flavor of what is possible:

```
declare L in
L=[john paul george ringo]
{Browse {Sort L Value.'<'}}
```

sorts `L` according to the comparison function `'<'` and displays the result:

```
[george john paul ringo]
```

As an infix operator, comparison is written as `X<Y`, but the comparison operation itself is in the Base module `Value`. Its full name is `Value.'<'`. Modules are explained in section 3.9.

B.6 Strings

Lists whose elements are character codes are called strings. For example:

```
"Mozart 1.2.3"
```

is the list:

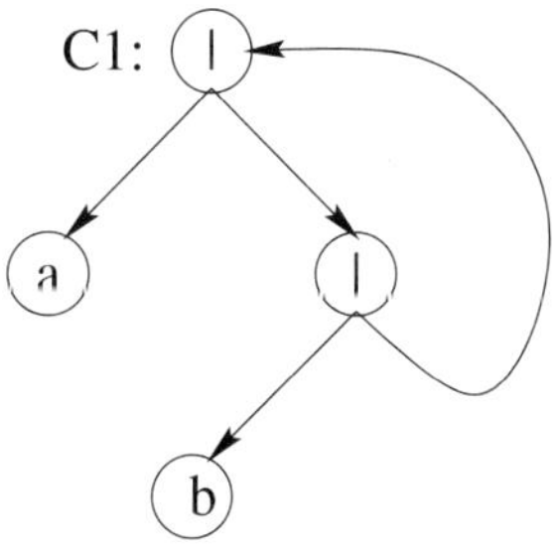

Figure B.1: Graph representation of the infinite list `C1=a|b|C1`.

<table>
<tr><td>⟨expression⟩</td><td>::=</td><td>⟨string⟩ | ...</td></tr>
<tr><td>⟨string⟩</td><td>::=</td><td>'"' { ⟨stringChar⟩ | ⟨pseudoChar⟩ } '"'</td></tr>
<tr><td>⟨stringChar⟩</td><td>::=</td><td>(any inline character except ", \, and NUL)</td></tr>
<tr><td>⟨pseudoChar⟩</td><td>::=</td><td>('\' followed by three octal digits)</td></tr>
<tr><td></td><td></td><td>| ('\x' or '\X' followed by two hexadecimal digits)</td></tr>
<tr><td></td><td></td><td>| '\a' | '\b' | '\f' | '\n' | '\r' | '\t'</td></tr>
<tr><td></td><td></td><td>| '\v' | '\\' | '\'' | '\"' | '\`' | '\&'</td></tr>
</table>

Table B.13: String lexical syntax.

```
[77 111 122 97 114 116 32 49 46 50 46 51]
```

or equivalently:

```
[&M &o &z &a &r &t &  &1 &. &2 &. &3]
```

Using lists to represent strings is convenient because all list operations are available for doing symbolic calculations with strings. Character operations can be used together with list operations to calculate on the internals of strings. String syntax is shown in table B.13. The `NUL` character mentioned in the table has character code 0 (zero). See section B.1 for an explanation of the meaning of `'\a'`, `'\b'`, etc.

There exists another, more memory-efficient representation for character sequences called bytestring. This representation should only be used if memory limitations make it necessary.

B.7 Virtual strings

A virtual string is a tuple with label `'#'` that represents a string. The virtual string brings together different substrings that are concatenated with virtual concatena-

Operation	Description
{VirtualString.toString VS}	Return a string with the same characters as VS
{VirtualString.toAtom VS}	Return an atom with the same characters as VS
{VirtualString.length VS}	Return the number of characters in VS
{Value.toVirtualString X D W}	Return a string representing the partial value X, where records are limited in depth to D and in width to W

Table B.14: Some virtual string operations.

tion. That is, the concatenation is never actually performed, which saves time and memory. For example, the virtual string

```
123#"-"#23#" is "#(123-23)
```

represents the string

```
"123-23 is 100"
```

Except in special cases, a library operation that expects a string can always be given a virtual string instead. For example, virtual strings can be used for all I/O operations. The components of a virtual string can be numbers, strings, virtual strings (i.e., `´#´`-labeled tuples), and all atoms except for `nil` and `´#´`. Table B.14 gives a few virtual string operations.

C Language Syntax

The devil is in the details.
– Traditional proverb.

God is in the details.
– Traditional proverb.

I don't know what is in those details,
but it must be something important!
– Irreverent proverb.

This appendix defines the syntax of the complete language used in the book, including all syntactic conveniences. The language is a subset of the Oz language as implemented by the Mozart system. The appendix is divided into six sections:

- Section C.1 defines the syntax of interactive statements, i.e., statements that can be fed into the interactive interface.
- Section C.2 defines the syntax of statements and expressions.
- Section C.3 defines the syntax of the nonterminals needed to define statements and expressions.
- Section C.4 lists the operators of the language with their precedence and associativity.
- Section C.5 lists the keywords of the language.
- Section C.6 defines the lexical syntax of the language, i.e., how a character sequence is transformed into a sequence of tokens.

To be precise, this appendix defines a context-free syntax for a superset of the language. This keeps the syntax simple and easy to read. The disadvantage of a context-free syntax is that it does not capture all syntactic conditions for legal programs. For example, take the statement **local** X **in** ⟨statement⟩ **end**. The statement that contains this one must declare all the free variable identifiers of ⟨statement⟩, possibly minus X. This is not a context-free condition.

This appendix defines the syntax of a subset of the full Oz language, as defined in [55, 87]. This appendix differs from [87] in several ways: it introduces nestable constructs, nestable declarations, and terms to factor the common parts of statement and expression syntax; it defines interactive statements and **for** loops; it

⟨interStatement⟩	::=	⟨statement⟩
		| **declare** { ⟨declarationPart⟩ }+ [⟨interStatement⟩]
		| **declare** { ⟨declarationPart⟩ }+ **in** ⟨interStatement⟩

Table C.1: Interactive statements.

⟨statement⟩	::=	⟨nestCon(statement)⟩ | ⟨nestDec(⟨variable⟩)⟩
		| **skip** | ⟨statement⟩ ⟨statement⟩
⟨expression⟩	::=	⟨nestCon(expression)⟩ | ⟨nestDec('$')⟩
		| ⟨unaryOp⟩ ⟨expression⟩
		| ⟨expression⟩ ⟨evalBinOp⟩ ⟨expression⟩
		| '$' | ⟨term⟩ | **self**
⟨inStatement⟩	::=	[{ ⟨declarationPart⟩ }+ **in**] ⟨statement⟩
⟨inExpression⟩	::=	[{ ⟨declarationPart⟩ }+ **in**] [⟨statement⟩] ⟨expression⟩
⟨in(statement)⟩	::=	⟨inStatement⟩
⟨in(expression)⟩	::=	⟨inExpression⟩

Table C.2: Statements and expressions.

leaves out the translation to the kernel language (which is given for each linguistic abstraction in the main text of the book); and it makes other small simplifications for clarity (but without sacrificing precision).

C.1 Interactive statements

Table C.1 gives the syntax of interactive statements. An interactive statement is a superset of a statement; in addition to all regular statements, it can contain a **`declare`** statement. The interactive interface must always be fed interactive statements. All free variable identifiers in the interactive statement must exist in the global environment; otherwise the system gives a "variable not introduced" error.

C.2 Statements and expressions

Table C.2 gives the syntax of statements and expressions. Many language constructs can be used in either a statement position or an expression position. We call such constructs nestable. We write the grammar rules to give their syntax just once,

```
⟨nestCon(α)⟩ ::= ⟨expression⟩ ( ´=´ | ´:=´ | ´,´ ) ⟨expression⟩
               | ´{´ ⟨expression⟩ { ⟨expression⟩ } ´}´
               | local { ⟨declarationPart⟩ }+ in [ ⟨statement⟩ ] ⟨α⟩ end
               | ´(´ ⟨in(α)⟩ ´)´
               | if ⟨expression⟩ then ⟨in(α)⟩
                 { elseif ⟨expression⟩ then ⟨in(α)⟩ }
                 [ else ⟨in(α)⟩ ] end
               | case ⟨expression⟩ of ⟨pattern⟩ [ andthen ⟨expression⟩ ] then ⟨in(α)⟩
                 { ´[]´ ⟨pattern⟩ [ andthen ⟨expression⟩ ] then ⟨in(α)⟩ }
                 [ else ⟨in(α)⟩ ] end
               | for { ⟨loopDec⟩ }+ do ⟨in(α)⟩ end
               | try ⟨in(α)⟩
                 [ catch ⟨pattern⟩ then ⟨in(α)⟩
                   { ´[]´ ⟨pattern⟩ then ⟨in(α)⟩ } ]
                 [ finally ⟨in(α)⟩ ] end
               | raise ⟨inExpression⟩ end
               | thread ⟨in(α)⟩ end
               | lock [ ⟨expression⟩ then ] ⟨in(α)⟩ end
```

Table C.3: Nestable constructs (no declarations).

```
⟨nestDec(α)⟩ ::= proc ´{´ α { ⟨pattern⟩ } ´}´ ⟨inStatement⟩ end
               | fun [ lazy ] ´{´ α { ⟨pattern⟩ } ´}´ ⟨inExpression⟩ end
               | functor α
                 [ import { ⟨variable⟩ [ at ⟨atom⟩ ]
                          | ⟨variable⟩ ´(´
                              { (⟨atom⟩ | ⟨int⟩) [ ´:´ ⟨variable⟩ ] }+ ´)´
                          }+ ]
                 [ export { [ (⟨atom⟩ | ⟨int⟩) ´:´ ] ⟨variable⟩ }+ ]
                 define { ⟨declarationPart⟩ }+ [ in ⟨statement⟩ ] end
               | class α { ⟨classDescriptor⟩ }
                 { meth ⟨methHead⟩ [ ´=´ ⟨variable⟩ ]
                   ( ⟨inExpression⟩ | ⟨inStatement⟩ ) end }
                 end
```

Table C.4: Nestable declarations.

⟨term⟩	::=	[´!´] ⟨variable⟩ | ⟨int⟩ | ⟨float⟩ | ⟨character⟩
		| ⟨atom⟩ | ⟨string⟩ | **unit** | **true** | **false**
		| ⟨label⟩ ´(´ { [⟨feature⟩ ´:´] ⟨expression⟩ } ´)´
		| ⟨expression⟩ ⟨consBinOp⟩ ⟨expression⟩
		| ´[´ { ⟨expression⟩ }+ ´]´
⟨pattern⟩	::=	[´!´] ⟨variable⟩ | ⟨int⟩ | ⟨float⟩ | ⟨character⟩
		| ⟨atom⟩ | ⟨string⟩ | **unit** | **true** | **false**
		| ⟨label⟩ ´(´ { [⟨feature⟩ ´:´] ⟨pattern⟩ } [´...´] ´)´
		| ⟨pattern⟩ ⟨consBinOp⟩ ⟨pattern⟩
		| ´[´ { ⟨pattern⟩ }+ ´]´

Table C.5: Terms and patterns.

in a way that works for both statement and expression positions. Table C.3 gives the syntax for nestable constructs, not including declarations. Table C.4 gives the syntax for nestable declarations. The grammar rules for nestable constructs and declarations are templates with one argument. The template is instantiated each time it is used. For example, ⟨nestCon(α)⟩ defines the template for nestable constructs without declarations. This template is used twice, as ⟨nestCon(statement)⟩ and ⟨nestCon(expression)⟩, and each corresponds to one grammar rule.

C.3 Nonterminals for statements and expressions

Tables C.5 and C.6 define the nonterminal symbols needed for the statement and expression syntax of the preceding section. Table C.5 defines the syntax of terms and patterns. Note the close relationship between terms and patterns. Both are used to define partial values. There are just two differences: (1) patterns can contain only variable identifiers, whereas terms can contain expressions, and (2) patterns can be partial (using ´...´), whereas terms cannot.

Table C.6 defines nonterminals for the declaration parts of statements and loops, for unary operators, for binary operators ("constructing" operators ⟨consBinOp⟩ and "evaluating" operators ⟨evalBinOp⟩), for records (labels and features), and for classes (descriptors, attributes, methods, etc.).

C.4 Operators

Table C.7 gives the precedence and associativity of all the operators used in the book. All the operators are binary infix operators, except for three cases. The minus sign ´~´ is a unary prefix operator. The hash symbol ´#´ is an n-ary

```
⟨declarationPart⟩ ::= ⟨variable⟩ | ⟨pattern⟩ ´=´ ⟨expression⟩ | ⟨statement⟩
⟨loopDec⟩         ::= ⟨variable⟩ in ⟨expression⟩ [ ´..´ ⟨expression⟩ ] [ ´;´ ⟨expression⟩ ]
                    | ⟨variable⟩ in ⟨expression⟩ ´;´ ⟨expression⟩ ´;´ ⟨expression⟩
                    | break ´:´ ⟨variable⟩ | continue ´:´ ⟨variable⟩
                    | return ´:´ ⟨variable⟩ | default ´:´ ⟨expression⟩
                    | collect ´:´ ⟨variable⟩
⟨unaryOp⟩         ::= ´~´ | ´@´ | ´!!´
⟨binaryOp⟩        ::= ⟨consBinOp⟩ | ⟨evalBinOp⟩
⟨consBinOp⟩       ::= ´#´ | ´|´
⟨evalBinOp⟩       ::= ´+´ | ´-´ | ´*´ | ´/´ | div | mod | ´.´ | andthen | orelse
                    | ´:=´ | ´,´ | ´=´ | ´==´ | ´\=´ | ´<´ | ´=<´ | ´>´ | ´>=´
                    | ´::´ | ´=:´ | ´\=:´ | ´=<:´
⟨label⟩           ::= unit | true | false | ⟨variable⟩ | ⟨atom⟩
⟨feature⟩         ::= unit | true | false | ⟨variable⟩ | ⟨atom⟩ | ⟨int⟩
⟨classDescriptor⟩ ::= from { ⟨expression⟩ }+ | prop { ⟨expression⟩ }+
                    | attr { ⟨attrInit⟩ }+
⟨attrInit⟩        ::= ( [ ´!´ ] ⟨variable⟩ | ⟨atom⟩ | unit | true | false )
                      [ ´:´ ⟨expression⟩ ]
⟨methHead⟩        ::= ( [ ´!´ ] ⟨variable⟩ | ⟨atom⟩ | unit | true | false )
                      [ ´(´ { ⟨methArg⟩ } [ ´...´ ] ´)´ ]
                      [ ´=´ ⟨variable⟩ ]
⟨methArg⟩         ::= [ ⟨feature⟩ ´:´ ] ( ⟨variable⟩ | ´_´ | ´$´ ) [ ´<=´ ⟨expression⟩ ]
```

Table C.6: Other nonterminals needed for statements and expressions.

mixfix operator. The "`. :=`" is a ternary infix operator that is explained in the next section. There are no postfix operators. The operators are listed in order of increasing precedence, i.e., tightness of binding. The operators lower in the table bind tighter. We define the associativities as follows:

- Left. For binary operators, this means that repeated operators group to the left. For example, `1+2+3` means the same as `((1+2)+3)`.
- Right. For binary operators, this means that repeated operators group to the right. For example, `a|b|X` means the same as `(a|(b|X))`.
- Mixfix. Repeated operators are actually just one operator, with all expressions being arguments of the operator. For example, `a#b#c` means the same as `´#´(a b c)`.
- None. For binary operators, this means that the operator cannot be repeated. For example, `1<2<3` is an error.

Parentheses can be used to override the default precedence.

Operator	Associativity
`=`	right
`:=` "`. :=`"	right
orelse	right
andthen	right
`==` `\=` `<` `=<` `>` `>=` `=:` `\=:` `=<:`	none
`::`	none
`|`	right
`#`	mixfix
`+` `-`	left
`*` `/` **div** **mod**	left
`,`	right
`~`	left
`.`	left
`@` `!!`	left

Table C.7: Operators with their precedence and associativity.

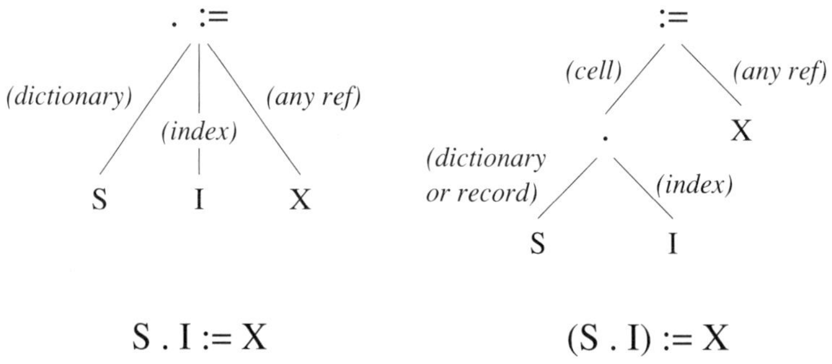

Figure C.1: The ternary operator "`. :=`".

C.4.1 Ternary operator

There is one ternary (three-argument) operator, "`. :=`", which is designed for dictionary and array updates. It has the same precedence and associativity as `:=`. It can be used in an expression position like `:=`, where it has the effect of an exchange. The statement `S.I:=X` consists of a ternary operator with arguments `S`, `I`, and `X`. This statement is used for updating dictionaries and arrays. This should not be confused with `(S.I):=X`, which consists of the two nested binary operators `.` and `:=`. The latter statement is used for updating a cell that is inside a dictionary. The parentheses are highly significant! Figure C.1 shows the difference in abstract

andthen	default	**false**	**lock**	**require** (*)
at	**define**	**feat** (*)	**meth**	return
attr	**dis** (*)	**finally**	**mod**	**self**
break	**div**	**for**	**not** (*)	**skip**
case	**do**	**from**	**of**	**then**
catch	**else**	**fun**	**or** (*)	**thread**
choice	**elsecase** (*)	**functor**	**orelse**	**true**
class	**elseif**	**if**	otherwise	**try**
collect	**elseof** (*)	**import**	**prepare** (*)	**unit**
cond (*)	**end**	**in**	**proc**	
continue	**export**	lazy	**prop**	
declare	**fail**	**local**	**raise**	

Table C.8: Keywords.

syntax between `S.I:=X` and `(S.I):=X`. In the figure, *(cell)* means any cell or object attribute, and *(dictionary)* means any dictionary or array.

The distinction is important because dictionaries can contain cells. To update a dictionary `D`, we write `D.I:=X`. To update a cell in a dictionary containing cells, we write `(D.I):=X`. This has the same effect as **`local`** `C=D.I` **`in`** `C:=X` **`end`** but is more concise. The first argument of the binary operator `:=` must be a cell or an object attribute.

C.5 Keywords

Table C.8 lists the keywords of the language in alphabetic order. Keywords marked with (*) exist in Oz but are not used in the book. Keywords in boldface can be used as atoms by enclosing them in quotes. For example, `'then'` is an atom, whereas **`then`** is a keyword. Keywords not in boldface can be used as atoms directly, without quotes.

C.6 Lexical syntax

This section defines the lexical syntax of Oz, i.e., how a character sequence is transformed into a sequence of tokens.

<table>
<tr><td>⟨variable⟩</td><td>::=</td><td>(uppercase char) { (alphanumeric char) }</td></tr>
<tr><td></td><td></td><td>| ´`´ { ⟨variableChar⟩ | ⟨pseudoChar⟩ } ´`´</td></tr>
<tr><td>⟨atom⟩</td><td>::=</td><td>(lowercase char) { (alphanumeric char) } (except no keyword)</td></tr>
<tr><td></td><td></td><td>| ´'´ { ⟨atomChar⟩ | ⟨pseudoChar⟩ } ´'´</td></tr>
<tr><td>⟨string⟩</td><td>::=</td><td>´"´ { ⟨stringChar⟩ | ⟨pseudoChar⟩ } ´"´</td></tr>
<tr><td>⟨character⟩</td><td>::=</td><td>(any integer in the range 0...255)</td></tr>
<tr><td></td><td></td><td>| ´&´ ⟨charChar⟩ | ´&´ ⟨pseudoChar⟩</td></tr>
</table>

Table C.9: Lexical syntax of variables, atoms, strings, and characters.

<table>
<tr><td>⟨variableChar⟩</td><td>::=</td><td>(any inline character except `, \, and NUL)</td></tr>
<tr><td>⟨atomChar⟩</td><td>::=</td><td>(any inline character except ', \, and NUL)</td></tr>
<tr><td>⟨stringChar⟩</td><td>::=</td><td>(any inline character except ", \, and NUL)</td></tr>
<tr><td>⟨charChar⟩</td><td>::=</td><td>(any inline character except \ and NUL)</td></tr>
<tr><td>⟨pseudoChar⟩</td><td>::=</td><td>´\´ ⟨octdigit⟩ ⟨octdigit⟩ ⟨octdigit⟩</td></tr>
<tr><td></td><td></td><td>| (´\x´ | ´\X´) ⟨hexdigit⟩ ⟨hexdigit⟩</td></tr>
<tr><td></td><td></td><td>| ´\a´ | ´\b´ | ´\f´ | ´\n´ | ´\r´ | ´\t´</td></tr>
<tr><td></td><td></td><td>| ´\v´ | ´\\´ | ´\'´ | ´\"´ | ´\`´ | ´\&´</td></tr>
</table>

Table C.10: Nonterminals needed for lexical syntax.

<table>
<tr><td>⟨int⟩</td><td>::=</td><td>[´~´] ⟨nzdigit⟩ { ⟨digit⟩ }</td></tr>
<tr><td></td><td></td><td>| [´~´] 0 { ⟨octdigit⟩ }+</td></tr>
<tr><td></td><td></td><td>| [´~´] (´0x´ | ´0X´) { ⟨hexdigit⟩ }+</td></tr>
<tr><td></td><td></td><td>| [´~´] (´0b´ | ´0B´) { ⟨bindigit⟩ }+</td></tr>
<tr><td>⟨float⟩</td><td>::=</td><td>[´~´] { ⟨digit⟩ }+ ´.´ { ⟨digit⟩ } [(´e´ | ´E´) [´~´] { ⟨digit⟩ }+]</td></tr>
<tr><td>⟨digit⟩</td><td>::=</td><td>0 | 1 | 2 | 3 | 4 | 5 | 6 | 7 | 8 | 9</td></tr>
<tr><td>⟨nzdigit⟩</td><td>::=</td><td>1 | 2 | 3 | 4 | 5 | 6 | 7 | 8 | 9</td></tr>
<tr><td>⟨octdigit⟩</td><td>::=</td><td>0 | 1 | 2 | 3 | 4 | 5 | 6 | 7</td></tr>
<tr><td>⟨hexdigit⟩</td><td>::=</td><td>⟨digit⟩ | ´a´ | ´b´ | ´c´ | ´d´ | ´e´ | ´f´</td></tr>
<tr><td></td><td></td><td>| ´A´ | ´B´ | ´C´ | ´D´ | ´E´ | ´F´</td></tr>
<tr><td>⟨bindigit⟩</td><td>::=</td><td>0 | 1</td></tr>
</table>

Table C.11: Lexical syntax of integers and floating point numbers.

C.6.1 Tokens

Variables, atoms, strings, and characters

Table C.9 defines the lexical syntax for variable identifiers, atoms, strings, and characters in strings. Unlike the previous sections which define token sequences, this section defines character sequences. An alphanumeric character is a letter (uppercase or lowercase), a digit, or an underscore character. Single quotes are used to delimit atom representations that may contain nonalphanumeric characters and backquotes are used in the same way for variable identifiers. Note that an atom cannot have the same character sequence as a keyword unless the atom is quoted. Table C.10 defines the nonterminals needed for table C.9. "Any inline character" includes control characters and accented characters. The `NUL` character has character code 0 (zero).

Integers and floating point numbers

Table C.11 defines the lexical syntax of integers and floating point numbers. Note the use of the `'~'` (tilde) for the unary minus symbol.

C.6.2 Blank space and comments

Tokens may be separated by any amount of blank space and comments. Blank space is one of the characters tab (character code 9), newline (code 10), vertical tab (code 11), form feed (code 12), carriage return (code 13), and space (code 32). A comment is one of three possibilities:

- A sequence of characters starting from the character `%` (percent) until the end of the line or the end of the file (whichever comes first).
- A sequence of characters starting from `/*` and ending with `*/`, inclusive. This kind of comment may be nested.
- The single character `?` (question mark). This is intended to mark the output arguments of procedures, as in

```
proc {Max A B ?C} ... end
```

where `C` is an output. An output argument is an argument that gets bound inside the procedure.

D General Computation Model

The removal of much of the accidental complexity of programming means that the intrinsic complexity of the application is what's left.
– *Security Engineering*, Ross J. Anderson (2001)

If you want people to do something the right way, you must make the right way the easy way.
– Traditional saying.

This appendix brings together all the general concepts introduced in the book.[1] We call the resulting computation model the general computation model. Its semantics are given in chapter 13. While this model is quite general, it is certainly not the final word in computation models. It is just a snapshot that captures our current understanding of programming. Future research will certainly change or extend it. The book mentions dynamic scoping and transaction support as two areas which require more support from the model.

The general computation model was designed in a layered fashion, by starting from a simple base model and successively adding new concepts. Each time we noted a limitation in the expressiveness of a computation model, we had the opportunity to add a new concept. There was always a choice: either to keep the model as is and make programs more complicated, or to add a concept and keep programs simple. The decision to add the concept or not was based on our judgment of how complicated the model and its programs would be, when considered together. "Complexity" in this sense covers both the expressiveness and ease of reasoning of the combination.

There is a strong element of creativity in this approach. Each concept brings something novel that was not there before. We therefore call it the creative extension principle. Not all useful concepts end up in the general model. Some concepts were added only to be superseded by later concepts. For example, this is the case for nondeterministic choice (see section 5.8.1), which is superseded by explicit state. The general model is just one among many possible models of similar expressiveness. Your judgment in this process may be different from ours. We would be interested

1. Except for computation spaces, which underlie the relational computation model and the constraint-based computation model.

to hear from any reader who has reached significantly different conclusions.

Because earlier computation models are subsets of later ones, the later ones can be considered as frameworks inside of which many computation models can coexist. In this sense, the general computation model is the most complete framework of the book.

D.1 Creative extension principle

We give an example to explain and motivate the creative extension principle. Let us start with the simple declarative language of chapter 2. In that chapter, we added two concepts to the declarative language: functions and exceptions. But there was something fundamentally different in how we added each concept. Functions were added as a linguistic abstraction by defining a new syntax and showing how to translate it into the kernel language (see section 2.6.2). Exceptions were added to the kernel language itself by adding new primitive operations and defining their semantics (see section 2.7). Why did we choose to do it this way? We could have added functions to the kernel language and defined exceptions by translation, but we did not. There is a simple but profound reason for this: functions can be defined by a local translation but exceptions cannot. A translation of a concept is local if it requires changes only to the parts of the program that use the concept.

Starting with the declarative kernel language of chapter 2, the book added concepts one by one. For each concept we had to decide whether to add it as a linguistic abstraction (without changing the kernel language) or to add it to the kernel language. A linguistic abstraction is a good idea if the translation is local. Extending the kernel language is a good idea if there is no local translation.

This choice is always a trade-off. One criterion is that the overall scheme, including both the kernel language and the translation scheme into the kernel language, should be as simple as possible. This is what we call the creative extension principle. To some degree, simplicity is a subjective judgment. This book makes one particular choice of what should be in the kernel languages and what should be outside. Other reasonable choices are certainly possible.

An additional constraint on the kernel languages of the book is that they are all carefully chosen to be subsets of the full Oz language. This means that they are all implemented by the Mozart system. Users can verify that the kernel language translation of a program behaves in exactly the same way as the program. The only difference between the two is efficiency. This is useful both for learning the kernel languages and for debugging programs. The Mozart system implements certain constructs more efficiently than their representation in the kernel language. For example, classes and objects in Oz are implemented more efficiently than their kernel definitions.

<table>
<tr><td>⟨s⟩ ::=</td><td></td></tr>
<tr><td>skip</td><td>Empty statement</td></tr>
<tr><td>| ⟨s⟩$_1$ ⟨s⟩$_2$</td><td>Statement sequence</td></tr>
<tr><td>| local ⟨x⟩ in ⟨s⟩ end</td><td>Variable creation</td></tr>
<tr><td>| ⟨x⟩$_1$=⟨x⟩$_2$</td><td>Variable-variable binding</td></tr>
<tr><td>| ⟨x⟩=⟨v⟩</td><td>Value creation</td></tr>
<tr><td>| {⟨x⟩ ⟨y⟩$_1$ ··· ⟨y⟩$_n$}</td><td>Procedure application</td></tr>
<tr><td>| if ⟨x⟩ then ⟨s⟩$_1$ else ⟨s⟩$_2$ end</td><td>Conditional</td></tr>
<tr><td>| case ⟨x⟩ of ⟨pattern⟩ then ⟨s⟩$_1$ else ⟨s⟩$_2$ end</td><td>Pattern matching</td></tr>
<tr><td>| thread ⟨s⟩ end</td><td>Thread creation</td></tr>
<tr><td>| {WaitNeeded ⟨x⟩}</td><td>By-need synchronization</td></tr>
<tr><td>| {NewName ⟨x⟩}</td><td>Name creation</td></tr>
<tr><td>| ⟨y⟩=!!⟨x⟩</td><td>Read-only view</td></tr>
<tr><td>| try ⟨s⟩$_1$ catch ⟨x⟩ then ⟨s⟩$_2$ end</td><td>Exception context</td></tr>
<tr><td>| raise ⟨x⟩ end</td><td>Raise exception</td></tr>
<tr><td>| {FailedValue ⟨x⟩ ⟨y⟩}</td><td>Failed value</td></tr>
<tr><td>| {NewCell ⟨x⟩ ⟨y⟩}</td><td>Cell creation</td></tr>
<tr><td>| {Exchange ⟨x⟩ ⟨y⟩ ⟨z⟩}</td><td>Cell exchange</td></tr>
<tr><td>| {IsDet ⟨x⟩ ⟨y⟩}</td><td>Boundness test</td></tr>
</table>

Table D.1: The general kernel language.

D.2 Kernel language

Table D.1 gives the kernel language of the general computation model. For clarity, we divide the table into five parts:

- The first part is the descriptive declarative model. This model allows the building of complex data structures (rooted graphs whose nodes are records and procedure values) but does not allow calculating with them.
- The first and second parts taken together form the declarative concurrent model. This is the most general purely declarative model of the book. All programs written in this model are declarative.
- The third part adds security: the ability to build secure data abstractions and program with capabilities.
- The fourth part adds exceptions: the ability to handle exceptional situations by doing nonlocal exits.
- The fifth part adds explicit state, which is important for building modular programs and programs that can change over time.

Taking all parts gives the general computation model. This is the most general model of the book. Chapter 13 gives the semantics of this model and all its subsets.

D.3 Concepts

Let us now recapitulate the design methodology of the general model by starting with a simple base model and briefly explaining what new expressiveness each concept brings. All models are Turing complete, i.e., they are equivalent in computing power to a Turing machine. However, Turing completeness is only a small part of the story. The ease with which programs can be written or reasoned about differs greatly in these models. Increased expressiveness typically goes hand in hand with increased difficulty to reason about programs.

D.3.1 Declarative models

Strict functional model

The simplest practical model is strict functional programming with values. This model is defined in section 2.8.1. In this model there are no unbound variables; each new variable is immediately bound to a value. This model is close to the λ calculus, which contains just procedure definition and application and leaves out the conditional and pattern matching. The λ calculus is Turing complete but is much too cumbersome for practical programming.

Sequential declarative model

The sequential declarative model is defined in chapter 2. It contains all concepts in table D.1 up to and including procedure application, conditionals, and pattern matching. It extends the strict functional model by introducing dataflow variables. Doing this is a critical step because it prepares the way for declarative concurrency. For binding dataflow variables, we use a general operation called unification. This means that the sequential declarative model does both deterministic logic programming and functional programming.

Threads

The thread concept is defined in section 4.1. Adding threads allows the model to express activities that execute independently. This model is still declarative since the result of a calculation is unchanged. Only the order in which the calculations are done is more flexible. Programs become more incremental: incrementally building an input results in an incrementally built output. This is the first form of declarative concurrency.

By-need synchronization

The concept of by-need synchronization (the `WaitNeeded` operation) is defined in section 13.1.13. Adding it allows the model to express demand-driven execution. Lazy functions and `ByNeed` are defined in terms of `WaitNeeded`. A trigger, as defined in section 4.5.1, is simply the suspended thread created by executing `ByNeed`. This model is still declarative since the result of a calculation is unchanged. Only the amount of calculation done to achieve the result changes (it can become smaller). Sometimes the demand-driven model can give results in cases where the data-driven model would go into an infinite loop. This is a second form of declarative concurrency.

D.3.2 Security

Names

The name concept is defined in section 3.7.5. A name is an unforgeable constant that does not exist outside of a program. A name has no data or operations attached to it; it is a first-class "key" or "right." Names are the basis of programming techniques such as unbundled data abstraction (see section 6.4) and encapsulation control (see section 7.3.3).

In the declarative model, secure data abstractions can be built without names by using procedure values to hide values. The hidden value is an external reference of the procedure. But names add a crucial additional expressiveness. They make it possible to program with rights, e.g., separating data from operations in a secure data abstraction or passing keys to programs to enable secure operations.

Strictly speaking, names are not declarative since successive calls to `NewName` give different results. That is, the same program can return two different results if names are used to identify the result uniquely. But if names are used only to enforce security properties, then the model is still declarative.

Read-only views

The read-only view concept is defined in section 3.7.5. A read-only view is a dataflow variable that can be read but not bound. It is always paired with another dataflow variable that is equal to it but that can be bound. Read-only views are needed to construct secure data abstractions that export unbound variables. The abstraction exports the read-only view. Since it cannot be bound outside the abstraction, this allows the abstraction to maintain its invariant property.

D.3.3 Exceptions

Exception handling

The exception concept is defined in section 2.7.2. Adding exceptions allows exiting in one step from an arbitrarily large number of nested procedure calls. This allows programs to be written that treat rare cases correctly, without complicating the program in the common case.

Failed values

The failed value concept is defined in section 4.9.1. A failed value is a special kind of value that encapsulates an exception. Any attempt to use the value or to bind it to a determined value will raise the exception. While exception handling happens within a single thread, failed values allow exceptions from the thread that detected the problem to be passed to other threads.

Failed values are useful in models that have both exceptions and by-need computation. Assume that a program does a by-need computation to calculate a value, but the computation raises an exception instead. What should the value be? It can be a failed value. This will cause any thread that needs the value to raise an exception.

D.3.4 Explicit state

Cells (explicit state)

Explicit state is defined in section 6.3. Adding state gives a program a memory: a procedure can change its behavior over successive calls. In the declarative model this is not possible since all knowledge is in the procedure's arguments.

The stateful model greatly improves program modularity when compared to models without state. It increases the possibilities for changing a module's implementation without changing its interface (see section 4.8).

Ports (explicit state)

Another way to add explicit state is by means of ports, which are a kind of asynchronous communication channel. As explained in section 7.8, ports and cells are equivalent: each can implement the other in a simple way. Ports are useful for programming message passing with active objects. Cells are useful for programming atomic actions with shared state.

Boundness test (weak state)

The boundness test `IsDet` lets us use dataflow variables as a weak form of explicit state. The test checks whether a variable is bound or still unbound, without waiting when the variable is unbound. For many programming techniques, knowing the binding status of a dataflow variable is unimportant. However, it can be important when programming a time-dependent execution, i.e., to know what the instantaneous state is of an execution (see section 4.8.3).

Object-oriented programming

Object-oriented programming is introduced in chapter 7. It has the same kernel language as the stateful models. It is based on three principles: programs are collections of interacting data abstractions, the data abstractions should be stateful by default (which is good for modularity), and the data abstractions should use the object (PDA) style by default (which encourages polymorphism and inheritance).

D.4 Different forms of state

Adding explicit state is such a strong change to the model that it is important to have weaker forms of state. In the above models we have introduced four forms of state. Let us summarize these forms in terms of how many times we can assign a variable, i.e., change its state. In order of increasing strength, they are:

- No assignment, i.e., programming with values only (monotonic execution). This is functional programming as it is usually understood. Programs are completely deterministic, i.e., the same program always gives the same result.
- Single assignment, i.e., programming with dataflow variables (monotonic execution). This is also functional programming, but is more flexible since it allows declarative concurrency (with both lazy and eager execution). Programs are completely deterministic, but the result can be given incrementally.
- Single assignment with boundness test, i.e., programming with dataflow variables and `IsDet` (nonmonotonic execution). Programs are no longer deterministic.
- Multiple assignment, i.e., programming with cells or ports (nonmonotonic execution). Programs are no longer deterministic. This is the most expressive model.

We can understand these different forms of state in terms of an important property called monotonicity. At any time, a variable can be assigned to an element of some set S of values. Assignment is monotonic if as execution progresses, values can be removed from S but not added. For example, binding a dataflow variable `X` to a value reduces S from all possible values to just one value. A function f is monotonic if $S_1 \subset S_2 \implies f(S_1) \subset f(S_2)$. For example, `IsDet` is nonmonotonic since `{IsDet X}` returns **`true`** when `X` is bound and **`false`** when `X` is unbound, and `{`**`true`**`}` is not a subset of {**false**}. A program's execution is monotonic if all its operations are monotonic. Monotonicity is what makes declarative concurrency possible.

D.5 Other concepts

D.5.1 What's next?

The general computation model of the book is just a snapshot of an ongoing process. New concepts will continue to be discovered in the future using the creative extension principle. What will these new concepts be? We cannot tell for sure, since anticipating a discovery is tantamount to making that discovery! But there are hints about a few of the concepts. Three concepts that we are fairly sure about, even though we do not know their final form, are dynamic scoping, membranes, and transaction support. With dynamic scoping the behavior of a component depends on its context. With membranes an enclosure can be defined around part of a program, such that "something happens" when any reference crosses it. This is true even for references hidden inside a data structure or procedure value. With transaction support the execution of a component can be canceled if it cannot complete successfully. According to the creative extension principle, all these concepts should be added to the computation model.

D.5.2 Domain-specific concepts

This book gives many general concepts that are useful for all kinds of programs. In addition to this, each application domain has its own set of concepts that are useful only in that domain. These extra concepts complement the general concepts. For example, we can cite artificial intelligence [155, 179], algorithm design [47], object-oriented design patterns [66], multi-agent programming [226], databases [49], and numerical analysis [171].

D.6 Layered language design

The general computation model has a layered design. Each layer offers its own special trade-off of expressiveness and ease of reasoning. The programmer can choose the layer that is best adapted to each part of the program. From the evidence presented in the book, it is clear that this layered structure is beneficial for a general-purpose programming language. It makes it easier for the programmer to say directly what he or she wants to say, without cumbersome encodings.

The layered design of the general computation model can be found to some degree in many languages. Object-oriented languages such as Smalltalk, Eiffel, and Java have two layers: an object-oriented core and a second layer providing shared-state concurrency [68, 140, 11]. The functional language Erlang has two layers: an eager functional core and a second layer providing message-passing concurrency between active objects [10] (see also section 5.7). Active objects are defined within the functional core. The logic language Prolog has three layers: a logical core that is a simple theorem prover, a second layer modifying the theorem prover's operation, and a third layer providing explicit state [201] (see also section 9.7). The functional language Concurrent ML has three layers: an eager functional core, a second layer providing explicit state, and a third layer providing concurrency [176]. The multiparadigm language Oz has many layers, which is why it was used as the basis for the book [199].

References

[1] Harold Abelson, Gerald Jay Sussman, and Julie Sussman. *Structure and Interpretation of Computer Programs.* MIT Press, Cambridge, MA, 1985.

[2] Harold Abelson, Gerald Jay Sussman, and Julie Sussman. *Structure and Interpretation of Computer Programs,* 2nd edition. MIT Press, Cambridge, MA, 1996.

[3] Iliès Alouini and Peter Van Roy. Le protocole réparti du langage Distributed Oz (The distributed protocol of the Distributed Oz language). In *Colloque Francophone d'Ingénierie de Protocoles (CFIP 99)*, pages 283–298, Nancy, France, April 1999.

[4] Edward G. Amoroso. *Fundamentals of Computer Security Technology.* Prentice Hall, Englewood Cliffs, NJ, 1994.

[5] Ross J. Anderson. *Security Engineering: A Guide to Building Dependable Distributed Systems.* John Wiley & Sons, 2001.

[6] Gregory R. Andrews. *Concurrent Programming: Principles and Practice.* Addison-Wesley, Menlo Park, CA, 1991.

[7] Joe Armstrong. Higher-order processes in Erlang, January 1997. Unpublished talk.

[8] Joe Armstrong. Concurrency oriented programming in Erlang, November 2002. Invited talk, Lightweight Languages Workshop 2002.

[9] Joe Armstrong. *Making reliable distributed systems in the presence of software errors.* PhD thesis, Royal Institute of Technology (KTH), Kista, Sweden, November 2003.

[10] Joe Armstrong, Mike Williams, Claes Wikström, and Robert Virding. *Concurrent Programming in Erlang.* Prentice-Hall, Englewood Cliffs, NJ, 1996.

[11] Ken Arnold and James Gosling. *The Java Programming Language,* 2nd edition. Addison-Wesley, 1998.

[12] Arvind and R. E. Thomas. I-Structures: An efficient data type for functional languages. Technical Report 210, MIT, Laboratory for Computer Science, Cambridge, MA, 1980.

[13] John Backus. Can programming be liberated from the von Neumann style? A functional style and its algebra of programs. *Communications of the ACM*, 21(8):613–641, August 1978.

[14] John Backus. The history of FORTRAN I, II, and III. *ACM SIGPLAN Notices*, 13(8):165–180, August 1978.

[15] Henri E. Bal, Jennifer G. Steiner, and Andrew S. Tanenbaum. Programming languages for distributed computing systems. *ACM Computing Surveys*, 21(3):261–322, September 1989.

[16] Holger Bär, Markus Bauer, Oliver Ciupke, Serge Demeyer, Stéphane Ducasse, Michele Lanza, Radu Marinescu, Robb Nebbe, Oscar Nierstrasz, Michael Przybilski, Tamar Richner, Matthias Rieger, Claudio Riva, Anne-Marie Sassen, Benedikt Schulz, Patrick Steyaert, Sander Tichelaar, and Joachim Weisbrod. *The FAMOOS Object-Oriented Reengineering Handbook.* October 1999. Deliverable, ESPRIT project FAMOOS.

[17] Victor R. Basili and Albert J. Turner. Iterative enhancement: A practical technique for software development. *IEEE Transactions on Software Engineering*, 1(4):390–396, December 1975.

[18] Kent Beck. *Test-driven development: by example.* Addison-Wesley, 2003.

[19] Joseph Bergin and Russel Winder. Understanding object-oriented programming, 2000. Available at `http://csis.pace.edu/~bergin/`.

[20] Philip A. Bernstein, Vassos Hadzilacos, and Nathan Goodman. *Concurrency Control and*

Recovery in Database Systems. Addison-Wesley, Reading, MA, 1987.

[21] Richard Bird. *Introduction to Functional Programming using Haskell,* 2nd edition. Prentice Hall, Englewood Cliffs, NJ, 1998.

[22] Andrew D. Birrell and Bruce Jay Nelson. Implementing remote procedure calls. *ACM Transactions on Computer Systems*, 2(1):39–59, February 1984.

[23] Darius Blasband. Language engineering: From a hobby, to a research activity, to a trade, March 2002. Unpublished talk.

[24] Per Brand, Peter Van Roy, Raphaël Collet, and Erik Klintskog. Path redundancy in a mobile-state protocol as a primitive for language-based fault tolerance. Technical Report RR2000-01, Département d'Ingénierie Informatique, Université catholique de Louvain, Belgium, 2000. Available at `http://www.info.ucl.ac.be`.

[25] Ivan Bratko. *Prolog Programming for Artificial Intelligence,* 3rd edition. Addison-Wesley, 2000.

[26] Per Brinch Hansen. Structured multiprogramming. *Communications of the ACM*, 15(7):574–578, July 1972.

[27] Per Brinch Hansen. *Operating System Principles.* Prentice Hall, Englewood Cliffs, NJ, 1973.

[28] Per Brinch Hansen. Java's insecure parallelism. *ACM SIGPLAN Notices*, 34(4):38–45, April 1999.

[29] Frederick P. Brooks, Jr. *The Mythical Man-Month: Essays on Software Engineering.* Addison-Wesley, 1975.

[30] Frederick P. Brooks, Jr. *The Mythical Man-Month: Essays on Software Engineering, Anniversary Edition.* Addison-Wesley, 1995.

[31] Timothy A. Budd. *Multiparadigm Programming in Leda.* Addison-Wesley, 1995.

[32] Luca Cardelli. A language with distributed scope. In *Principles of Programming Languages (POPL)*, pages 286–297, San Francisco, CA, January 1995. ACM Press.

[33] Luca Cardelli and Peter Wegner. On understanding types, data abstraction, and polymorphism. *Computing Surveys*, 17(4):471–522, December 1985.

[34] Nicholas Carriero and David Gelernter. Linda in context. *Communications of the ACM*, 32(4):444–458, 1989.

[35] Nicholas Carriero and David Gelernter. Coordination languages and their significance. *Communications of the ACM*, 35(2):96–107, February 1992.

[36] Paul E. Ceruzzi. *Beyond the Limits: Flight Enters the Computer Age.* MIT Press, Cambridge, MA, 1989.

[37] Emmanuel Chailloux, Pascal Manoury, and Bruno Pagano. *Développement d'applications avec Objective Caml.* O'Reilly & Associates, Paris, 2000.

[38] Randy Chow and Theodore Johnson. *Distributed Operating Systems and Algorithms.* Addison-Wesley, San Francisco, CA, 1997.

[39] Keith L. Clark. PARLOG: The language and its applications. In A. J. Nijman, J. W. de Bakker, and P. C. Treleaven, editors, *Proceedings of the Conference on Parallel Architectures and Languages Europe (PARLE), volume 2: Parallel Languages*, volume 259 of *Lecture Notes in Computer Science*, pages 30–53, Eindhoven, the Netherlands, June 1987. Springer-Verlag.

[40] Keith L. Clark and Frank McCabe. The control facilities of IC-Prolog. In D. Michie, editor, *Expert Systems in the Micro-Electronic Age*, pages 122–149. Edinburgh University Press, Edinburgh, 1979.

[41] Keith L. Clark, Frank G. McCabe, and Steve Gregory. IC-PROLOG — language features. In Keith L. Clark and Sten-Åke Tärnlund, editors, *Logic Programming*, pages 253–266. Academic Press, London, 1982.

[42] Arthur C. Clarke. *Profiles of the Future,* revised edition. Pan Books, 1973.

[43] William Clinger and Jonathan Rees. The revised^4 report on the algorithmic language Scheme. *LISP Pointers*, 4(3):1–55, July-September 1991.

[44] Helder Coelho and José C. Cotta. *Prolog by Example: How to Learn, Teach, and Use It.* Springer-Verlag, Berlin, 1988.

[45] Alain Colmerauer. The birth of Prolog. *ACM SIGPLAN Notices*, 28(3):37–52, March 1993.

Originally appeared in History of Programming Languages Conference (HOPL-II), 1993.

[46] William R. Cook. Object-oriented programming versus abstract data types. In *REX Workshop/School on the Foundations of Object-Oriented Languages*, volume 173 of *Lecture Notes in Computer Science*, pages 151–178. Springer-Verlag, 1990.

[47] Thomas H. Cormen, Charles E. Leiserson, and Ronald L. Rivest. *Introduction to Algorithms*. MIT Press, McGraw-Hill, Cambridge, MA, 1990.

[48] Charles Darwin. *On the Origin of Species by means of Natural Selection, or the Preservation of Favoured Races in the Struggle for Life.* Harvard University Press (originally John Murray, London, 1859).

[49] C. J. Date. *An Introduction to Database Systems.* Addison-Wesley, 1994.

[50] Harvey M. Deitel. *An Introduction to Operating Systems.* Addison-Wesley, 1984.

[51] Serge Demeyer, Stéphane Ducasse, Oscar Nierstrasz, and Ralph E. Johnson. *Object Oriented Reengineering Patterns.* Morgan Kaufmann, 2002.

[52] J. B. Dennis and E. C. Van Horn. Programming semantics for multiprogrammed computations. *Communications of the ACM*, 9(3), March 1966.

[53] Edsger W. Dijkstra. *A Primer of Algol 60 Programming.* Academic Press, 1962.

[54] Edsger W. Dijkstra. Go To statement considered harmful. *Communications of the ACM*, 11(3):147–148, March 1968.

[55] Denys Duchier. Loop support. Technical report, Mozart Consortium, 2003. Available at `http://www.mozart-oz.org/`.

[56] Denys Duchier, Claire Gardent, and Joachim Niehren. Concurrent constraint programming in Oz for natural language processing. Technical report, Saarland University, Saarbrücken, Germany, 1999. Available at `http://www.ps.uni-sb.de/Papers/abstracts/oznlp.html`.

[57] Denys Duchier, Leif Kornstaedt, and Christian Schulte. The Oz base environment. Technical report, Mozart Consortium, 2003. Available at `http://www.mozart-oz.org/`.

[58] Denys Duchier, Leif Kornstaedt, Christian Schulte, and Gert Smolka. A higher-order module discipline with separate compilation, dynamic linking, and pickling. Technical report, Programming Systems Lab, DFKI and Saarland University, Saarbrücken, Germany, 1998. Available at `http://www.mozart-oz.org/papers/`.

[59] R. Kent Dybvig, Carl Bruggeman, and David Eby. Guardians in a generation-based garbage collector. In *SIGPLAN Conference on Programming Language Design and Implementation (PLDI)*, pages 207–216, Albuquerque, NM, June 1993.

[60] E. W. Elcock. Absys: The first logic programming language—a retrospective and a commentary. *Journal of Logic Programming*, 9(1):1–17, 1990.

[61] Robert W. Floyd. Nondeterministic algorithms. *Journal of the ACM*, 14(4):636–644, October 1967.

[62] Martin Fowler and Kendall Scott. *UML Distilled: A Brief Guide to the Standard Object Modeling Language.* Addison-Wesley Longman, 2000.

[63] Michael J. French. *Invention and Evolution: Design in Nature and Engineering.* Cambridge University Press, Cambridge, UK, 1988.

[64] Daniel P. Friedman, Mitchell Wand, and Christopher T. Haynes. *Essentials of Programming Languages.* MIT Press, Cambridge, MA, 1992.

[65] Tetsuro Fujise, Takashi Chikayama, Kazuaki Rokusawa, and Akihiko Nakase. KLIC: A portable implementation of KL1. In *Fifth Generation Computing Systems (FGCS '94)*, pages 66–79, Tokyo, December 1994. Institute for New Generation Computer Technology (ICOT).

[66] Erich Gamma, Richard Helm, Ralph Johnson, and John Vlissides. *Design Patterns: Elements of Reusable Object-Oriented Software.* Addison-Wesley, 1994.

[67] David Gelernter. Generative communication in Linda. *ACM Transactions on Programming Languages and Systems*, 7(1):80–112, January 1985.

[68] Adele Goldberg and David Robson. *Smalltalk-80: The language and its implementation.* Addison-Wesley, 1983.

[69] Danny Goodman. *Dynamic HTML: The Definitive Reference,* 2nd edition. O'Reilly & Associates, Sebastopol, CA, 2002.

[70] James Edward Gordon. *The Science of Structures and Materials.* Scientific American

Library, 1988.

[71] James Gosling, Bill Joy, and Guy Steele. *The Java Language Specification*. Addison-Wesley, 1996. Available at `http://www.javasoft.com`.

[72] Paul Graham. *On Lisp*. Prentice Hall, Englewood Cliffs, NJ, 1993. Available for download from the author.

[73] Jim Gray and Andreas Reuter. *Transaction Processing: Concepts and Techniques*. Morgan Kaufmann, San Mateo, CA, 1993.

[74] Donatien Grolaux. QTk: Graphical user interface design for Oz, 2003. Available at `http://www.mozart-oz.org/mozart-stdlib/index.html`.

[75] Donatien Grolaux, Peter Van Roy, and Jean Vanderdonckt. `QTk`—a mixed declarative/procedural approach for designing executable user interfaces. In *8th IFIP Working Conference on Engineering for Human-Computer Interaction (EHCI'01)*, volume 2254 of *Lecture Notes in Computer Science*, pages 109–110, Toronto, Canada, May 2001. Springer-Verlag.

[76] Donatien Grolaux, Peter Van Roy, and Jean Vanderdonckt. `QTk`—an integrated model-based approach to designing executable user interfaces. In *8th Workshop on Design, Specification, and Verification of Interactive Systems (DSV-IS 2001)*, pages 77–91, Glasgow, Scotland, June 2001. GIST Technical Report G-2001-1.

[77] Carl A. Gunter and John C. Mitchell, editors. *Theoretical Aspects of Object-Oriented Programming*. MIT Press, Cambridge, MA, 1994.

[78] Fred Halsall. *Data Communications, Computer Networks, and Open Systems*, 4th edition. Addison-Wesley, 1996.

[79] Robert H. Halstead, Jr. MultiLisp: A language for concurrent symbolic computation. *ACM Transactions on Programming Languages and Systems*, 7(4):501–538, October 1985.

[80] Richard Hamming. *The Art of Doing SCIENCE and Engineering: Learning to Learn*. Gordon and Breach Science Publishers, Amsterdam, the Netherlands, 1997.

[81] Seif Haridi and Sverker Janson. Kernel Andorra Prolog and its computation model. In *7th International Conference on Logic Programming*, pages 31–48. MIT Press, June 1990.

[82] Seif Haridi, Peter Van Roy, Per Brand, Michael Mehl, Ralf Scheidhauer, and Gert Smolka. Efficient logic variables for distributed computing. *ACM Transactions on Programming Languages and Systems*, 21(3):569–626, May 1999.

[83] Seif Haridi, Peter Van Roy, Per Brand, and Christian Schulte. Programming languages for distributed applications. *New Generation Computing*, 16(3):223–261, May 1998.

[84] Seif Haridi, Peter Van Roy, and Gert Smolka. An overview of the design of Distributed Oz. In the *2nd International Symposium on Parallel Symbolic Computation (PASCO 97)*. ACM, July 1997.

[85] Martin Henz. *Objects for Concurrent Constraint Programming*, volume 426 of *International Series in Engineering and Computer Science*. Kluwer Academic Publishers, Boston, November 1997.

[86] Martin Henz. Objects in Oz. Doctoral dissertation, Saarland University, Saarbrücken, Germany, May 1997.

[87] Martin Henz and Leif Kornstaedt. The Oz notation. Technical report, Mozart Consortium, 2003. Available at `http://www.mozart-oz.org/`.

[88] Martin Henz, Tobias Müller, and Ka Boon Ng. Figaro: Yet another constraint programming library. In *Workshop on Parallelism and Implementation Technology for Constraint Logic Programming, International Conference on Logic Programming (ICLP 99)*, Las Cruces, NM, November 1999.

[89] Martin Henz, Gert Smolka, and Jörg Würtz. Oz—a programming language for multi-agent systems. In Ruzena Bajcsy, editor, *13th International Joint Conference on Artificial Intelligence*, pages 404–409, Chambéry, France, August 1993. Morgan Kaufmann.

[90] Martin Henz, Gert Smolka, and Jörg Würtz. Object-oriented concurrent constraint programming in Oz. In Pascal Van Hentenryck and Vijay Saraswat, editors, *Principles and Practice of Constraint Programming*, pages 29–48, Cambridge, MA, 1995. MIT Press.

[91] Carl Hewitt. Viewing control structures as patterns of passing messages. *Journal of Artificial Intelligence*, 8(3):323–364, June 1977.

[92] Carl Hewitt, Peter Bishop, and Richard Steiger. A universal modular ACTOR formalism

for artificial intelligence. In *3rd International Joint Conference on Artificial Intelligence (IJCAI)*, pages 235–245, August 1973.

[93] Charles Antony Richard Hoare. Monitors: An operating system structuring concept. *Communications of the ACM*, 17(10):549–557, October 1974.

[94] Charles Antony Richard Hoare. Communicating sequential processes. *Communications of the ACM*, 21(8):666–677, August 1978.

[95] Bruce K. Holmer, Barton Sano, Michael Carlton, Peter Van Roy, and Alvin M. Despain. Design and analysis of hardware for high performance Prolog. *Journal of Logic Programming*, 29:107–139, November 1996.

[96] Paul Hudak. Conception, evolution, and application of functional programming languages. *Computing Surveys*, 21(3):359–411, September 1989.

[97] Paul Hudak, John Peterson, and Joseph Fasel. A gentle introduction to Haskell, version 98, June 2000. Available at `http://www.haskell.org/tutorial/`.

[98] John Hughes. Why functional programming matters. *Computer Journal*, 32(2):98–107, 1989.

[99] Robert A. Iannucci. *Parallel Machines: Parallel Machine Languages. The Emergence of Hybrid Dataflow Computer Architectures.* Kluwer, Dordrecht, the Netherlands, 1990.

[100] Daniel H. H. Ingalls. Design principles behind Smalltalk. *Byte*, 6(8):286–298, 1981.

[101] Intelligent Systems Laboratory, Swedish Institute of Computer Science. SICStus Prolog user's manual, April 2003. Available at `http://www.sics.se/sicstus/`.

[102] Joxan Jaffar and Michael Maher. Constraint logic programming: A survey. *Journal of Logic Programming*, 19/20:503–581, May/July 1994.

[103] Raj Jain. *The Art of Computer Systems Performance Analysis: Techniques for Experimental Design, Measurement, Simulation, and Modeling.* John Wiley & Sons, New York, 1991.

[104] Sverker Janson. *AKL—A Multiparadigm Programming Language.* PhD thesis, Uppsala University and SICS, 1994.

[105] Sverker Janson and Seif Haridi. Programming paradigms of the Andorra Kernel Language. In *International Symposium on Logic Programming*, pages 167–183, October 1991.

[106] K. Jensen and N. Wirth. *Pascal: User Manual and Report,* 2nd edition. Springer-Verlag, 1978.

[107] Richard Jones and Rafael Lins. *Garbage Collection: Algorithms for Automatic Dynamic Memory Management.* John Wiley & Sons, New York, 1996.

[108] Andreas Kågedal, Peter Van Roy, and Bruno Dumant. Logical State Threads 0.1, January 1997. Available at `http://www.info.ucl.ac.be/people/PVR/implementation.html`.

[109] Gilles Kahn. The semantics of a simple language for parallel programming. In *IFIP Congress*, pages 471–475, 1974.

[110] Gilles Kahn and David B. MacQueen. Coroutines and networks of parallel processes. In *IFIP Congress*, pages 993–998, 1977.

[111] Alan C. Kay. The early history of Smalltalk. *ACM SIGPLAN Notices*, 28(3):69–95, March 1993. Originally appeared in History of Programming Languages Conference (HOPL-II), 1993.

[112] B. W. Kernighan and D. M. Ritchie. *The C Programming Language (ANSI C),* 2nd edition. Prentice Hall, Englewood Cliffs, NJ, 1988.

[113] Gregor Kiczales, Jim des Rivières, and Daniel G. Bobrow. *The Art of the Metaobject Protocol.* MIT Press, Cambridge, MA, 1991.

[114] Donald E. Knuth. *The Art of Computer Programming: Seminumerical Algorithms*, volume 2. Addison-Wesley, Reading, MA.

[115] Donald E. Knuth. *The Art of Computer Programming: Fundamental Algorithms*, volume 1. Addison-Wesley, Reading, MA, 1973.

[116] Donald E. Knuth. Structured programming with **go to** statements. *Computing Surveys*, 6(4):261–301, December 1974.

[117] Leif Kornstaedt. Gump–a front-end generator for Oz. Technical report, Mozart Consortium, 2003. Available at `http://www.mozart-oz.org/`.

[118] S. Rao Kosaraju. Analysis of structured programs. *Journal of Computer and System Sciences*, 9(3):232–255, December 1974.

[119] Robert A. Kowalski. Algorithm = logic + control. *Communications of the ACM*, 22(7):424–436, July 1979.

[120] Robert A. Kowalski. *Logic for Problem Solving.* North-Holland, 1979.

[121] James F. Kurose and Keith W. Ross. *Computer Networking: a Top-down Approach Featuring the Internet.* Addison-Wesley, 2001.

[122] Raymond Kurzweil. *The Singularity is Near.* Viking/Penguin Books, 2003. Expected publication date.

[123] Leslie Lamport. *LaTeX: A Document Preparation System,* 2nd edition. Addison-Wesley, 1994.

[124] Craig Larman and Victor R. Basili. Iterative and incremental development: A brief history. *IEEE Computer*, 36(6):47–56, June 2003.

[125] Hugh C. Lauer and Roger M. Needham. On the duality of operating system structures. In *Second International Symposium on Operating Systems, IRIA*, October 1978. Reprinted in *Operating Systems Review*, 13(2), April 1979, pp. 3–19.

[126] Doug Lea. *Concurrent Programming in Java.* Addison-Wesley, 1997.

[127] Doug Lea. *Concurrent Programming in Java,* 2nd edition. Addison-Wesley, 2000.

[128] Nancy Leveson and Clark S. Turner. An investigation of the Therac-25 accidents. *IEEE Computer*, 26(7):18–41, July 1993.

[129] Henry M. Levy. *Capability-Based Computer Systems.* Digital Press, Bedford, MA, 1984. Available for download from the author.

[130] Henry Lieberman. Using prototypical objects to implement shared behavior in object-oriented systems. In *1st Conference on Object-Oriented Programming Languages, Systems, and Applications (OOPSLA 86)*, pages 214–223, September 1986. Also in Object-Oriented Computing, Gerald Peterson, editor, IEEE Computer Society Press, 1987.

[131] Barbara Liskov. A history of CLU, April 1992. Technical Report, Laboratory for Computer Science, MIT.

[132] John Lloyd. *Foundations of Logic Programming,* 2nd, extended edition. Springer-Verlag, New York, 1987.

[133] Nancy Lynch. *Distributed Algorithms.* Morgan Kaufmann, San Francisco, CA, 1996.

[134] Bruce J. MacLennan. *Principles of Programming Languages,* 2nd edition. WB Saunders, Philadelphia, 1987.

[135] Michael Maher. Logic semantics for a class of committed-choice programs. In *International Conference on Logic Programming (ICLP 87)*, pages 858–876, Melbourne, Australia, May 1987. MIT Press.

[136] Zohar Manna. *The Mathematical Theory of Computation.* McGraw-Hill, New York, 1974.

[137] John McCarthy. *LISP 1.5 Programmer's Manual.* MIT Press, Cambridge, MA, 1962.

[138] Scott McCloud. *Understanding Comics: The Invisible Art.* Kitchen Sink Press, 1993.

[139] Michael Mehl, Christian Schulte, and Gert Smolka. Futures and by-need synchronization for Oz. Technical report, DFKI and Saarland University, Saarbrücken, Germany, May 1998. Available at `http://www.mozart-oz.org/papers/`.

[140] Bertrand Meyer. *Object-Oriented Software Construction,* 2nd edition. Prentice Hall, Englewood Cliffs, NJ, 2000.

[141] George A. Miller. The magical number seven, plus or minus two: Some limits on our capacity for processing information. *The Psychological Review*, 63:81–97, 1956.

[142] Mark Miller, Marc Stiegler, Tyler Close, Bill Frantz, Ka-Ping Yee, Chip Morningstar, Jonathan Shapiro, and Norm Hardy. E: Open source distributed capabilities, 2001. Available at `http://www.erights.org`.

[143] Mark Miller, Ka-Ping Yee, and Jonathan Shapiro. Capability myths demolished. Draft available at `http://zesty.ca/capmyths`, 2003.

[144] Mark S. Miller, Chip Morningstar, and Bill Frantz. Capability-based financial instruments. In *Financial Cryptography 2000*, Anguilla, British West Indies, February 2000.

[145] Robin Milner, Mads Tofte, and Robert Harper. *Definition of Standard ML.* MIT Press,

Cambridge, MA, 1990.

[146] J. Paul Morrison. *Flow-Based Programming: A New Approach to Application Development.* Van Nostrand Reinhold, New York, 1994.

[147] Al-Metwally Mostafa, Iliès Alouini, and Peter Van Roy. Fault tolerant global store module, 2001. Available at `http://www.mozart-oz.org/mogul/info/mostafa/globalstore.html`.

[148] Mozart Consortium. The Mozart Programming System, version 1.3.0, 2003. Available at `http://www.mozart-oz.org/`.

[149] Peter Naur, John W. Backus, Friedrich L. Bauer, Julien Green, C. Katz, John L. McCarthy, Alan J. Perlis, Heinz Rutishauser, Klaus Samelson, Bernard Vauquois, Joseph Henry Wegstein, Adriaan van Wijngaarden, and Michael Woodger. Revised report on the algorithmic language ALGOL 60. *Communications of the ACM*, 6(1):1–17, 1963.

[150] Rishiyur S. Nikhil. ID language reference manual version 90.1. Technical Report Memo 284-2, MIT, Computation Structures Group, Cambridge, MA, July 1994.

[151] Rishiyur S. Nikhil. An overview of the parallel language Id–a foundation for pH, a parallel dialect of Haskell. Technical report, Digital Equipment Corporation, Cambridge Research Laboratory, 1994.

[152] Rishiyur S. Nikhil and Arvind. *Implicit Parallel Programming in pH.* Morgan Kaufmann, 2001.

[153] Donald A. Norman. *The Design of Everyday Things.* Basic Books, New York, 1988.

[154] Theodore Norvell. Monads for the working Haskell programmer—a short tutorial. Available at `http://www.haskell.org/`.

[155] Peter Norvig. *Paradigms of Artificial Intelligence Programming: Case Studies in Common Lisp.* Morgan Kaufmann, 1992.

[156] K. Nygaard and O. J. Dahl. *The Development of the SIMULA Languages*, pages 439–493. Academic Press, 1981.

[157] Chris Okasaki. *Purely Functional Data Structures.* Cambridge University Press, Cambridge, UK, 1998.

[158] Richard A. O'Keefe. *The Craft of Prolog.* MIT Press, 1990.

[159] John K. Ousterhout. *Tcl and the Tk Toolkit.* Professional Computing Series. Addison-Wesley, Reading, MA, 1994.

[160] Andreas Paepcke, editor. *Object-Oriented Programming: The CLOS Perspective.* MIT Press, Cambridge, MA, 1993.

[161] David Lorge Parnas. Teaching programming as engineering. In *9th International Conference of Z Users*, volume 967 of *Lecture Notes in Computer Science.* Springer-Verlag, 1995. Reprinted in *Software Fundamentals*, Addison-Wesley, 2001.

[162] David Lorge Parnas. *Software Fundamentals.* Addison-Wesley, 2001.

[163] F. Paternò. *Model-based Design and Evaluation of Interactive Applications.* Springer-Verlag, Berlin, 1999.

[164] David A. Patterson and John L. Hennessy. *Computer Architecture: A Quantitative Approach,* 2nd edition. Morgan Kaufmann, 1996.

[165] Simon L. Peyton Jones. Tackling the awkward squad: Monadic input/output, concurrency, exceptions, and foreign-language calls in Haskell. In Tony Hoare, Manfred Broy, and Ralf Steinbruggen, editors, *Engineering theories of software construction*, pages 47–96. IOS Press, 2001. Presented at the 2000 Marktoberdorf Summer School, Marktoberdorf, Germany.

[166] Simon L. Peyton Jones, editor. *Haskell 98 Language and Libraries: The Revised Report.* Cambridge University Press, Cambridge, UK, 2003. Also published as the January 2003 special issue of Journal of Functional Programming.

[167] Simon L. Peyton Jones, Andrew Gordon, and Sigbjorn Finne. Concurrent Haskell. In *Principles of Programming Languages (POPL)*, pages 295–308, St. Petersburg Beach, FL, January 1996. ACM Press.

[168] Shari Lawrence Pfleeger. *Software Engineering: The Production of Quality Software,* 2nd edition. Macmillan, 1991.

[169] David Plainfossé and Marc Shapiro. A survey of distributed garbage collection techniques. In *International Workshop on Memory Management*, volume 986 of *Lecture Notes in*

Computer Science, pages 211–249, Berlin, September 1995. Springer-Verlag.

[170] R. J. Pooley. *An Introduction to Programming in SIMULA*. Blackwell Scientific Publishers, 1987.

[171] William H. Press, Brian P. Flannery, Saul A. Teukolsky, and William T. Vetterling. *Numerical Recipes: The Art of Scientific Computing*. Cambridge University Press, Cambridge, UK, 1986.

[172] Roger S. Pressman. *Software Engineering*, 6th edition. Addison-Wesley, 2000.

[173] Mahmoud Rafea, Fredrik Holmgren, Konstantin Popov, Seif Haridi, Stelios Lelis, Petros Kavassalis, and Jakka Sairamesh. Application architecture of the Internet simulation model: Web Word of Mouth (WoM). In *IASTED International Conference on Modelling and Simulation MS2002*, May 2002.

[174] Eric Raymond. *The Cathedral and the Bazaar: Musings on Linux and Open Source by an Accidental Revolutionary*. O'Reilly & Associates, January 2001.

[175] Juris Reinfelds. Teaching of programming with a programmer's theory of programming. In *Informatics Curricula, Teaching Methods, and Best Practice (ICTEM 2002, IFIP Working Group 3.2 Working Conference)*, Boston, 2002. Kluwer Academic Publishers.

[176] John H. Reppy. *Concurrent Programming in ML*. Cambridge University Press, Cambridge, UK, 1999.

[177] John C. Reynolds. User-defined types and procedural data structures as complementary approaches to data abstraction. In David Gries, editor, *Programming Methodology, A Collection of Papers by Members of IFIP WG 2.3*, pages 309–317. Springer-Verlag, 1978. Originally published in New Directions in Algorithmic Languages, INRIA Rocquencourt, 1975.

[178] James Rumbaugh, Ivar Jacobson, and Grady Booch. *The Unified Modeling Language Reference Manual*. Addison-Wesley, 1999.

[179] Stuart Russell and Peter Norvig. *Artificial Intelligence: A modern approach*. Prentice Hall, Englewood Cliffs, NJ, 1995.

[180] Oliver Sacks. *The Man Who Mistook His Wife for a Hat And Other Clinical Tales*. Harper & Row, Publishers, 1987.

[181] Jakka Sairamesh, Petros Kavassalis, Manolis Marazakis, Christos Nikolaos, and Seif Haridi. Information cities over the Internet: Taxonomy, principles and architecture. In *Digital Communities 2002*, November 2001.

[182] Vijay A. Saraswat. *Concurrent Constraint Programming*. MIT Press, Cambridge, MA, 1993.

[183] Vijay A. Saraswat, Martin C. Rinard, and Prakash Panangaden. Semantic foundations of concurrent constraint programming. In *Principles of Programming Languages (POPL)*, pages 333–352, Orlando, FL, January 1991.

[184] Steve Schneider. *Concurrent and Real-time Systems: The CSP Approach*. John Wiley & Sons, New York, 2000.

[185] Bruce Schneier. *Applied Cryptography*. John Wiley & Sons, New York, 1996.

[186] Christian Schulte. Programming constraint inference engines. In Gert Smolka, editor, *Proceedings of the Third International Conference on Principles and Practice of Constraint Programming*, volume 1330 of *Lecture Notes in Computer Science*, pages 519–533, Schloss Hagenberg, Austria, October 1997. Springer-Verlag.

[187] Christian Schulte. Comparing trailing and copying for constraint programming. In *International Conference on Logic Programming (ICLP 99)*, pages 275–289. MIT Press, November 1999.

[188] Christian Schulte. *Programming Constraint Inference Services*. PhD thesis, Saarland University, Fachbereich Informatik, Saarbrücken, Germany, 2000.

[189] Christian Schulte. Programming deep concurrent constraint combinators. In Enrico Pontelli and Vítor Santos Costa, editors, *Practical Aspects of Declarative Languages, Second International Workshop, PADL 2000*, volume 1753 of *Lecture Notes in Computer Science*, pages 215–229, Boston, January 2000. Springer-Verlag.

[190] Christian Schulte. *Programming Constraint Services: High-Level Programming of Standard and New Constraint Services*, volume 2302 of *Lecture Notes in Computer Science*. Springer-Verlag, 2002.

[191] Christian Schulte. Oz Explorer—visual constraint programming support. Technical report, Mozart Consortium, 2003. Available at `http://www.mozart-oz.org/`.

[192] Christian Schulte and Gert Smolka. Encapsulated search for higher-order concurrent constraint programming. In *1994 International Symposium on Logic Programming*, pages 505–520. MIT Press, November 1994.

[193] Christian Schulte and Gert Smolka. Finite domain constraint programming in Oz. A tutorial. Technical report, Mozart Consortium, 2003. Available at `http://www.mozart-oz.org/`.

[194] Ehud Shapiro. A subset of Concurrent Prolog and its interpreter. Technical Report TR-003, Institute for New Generation Computer Technology (ICOT), Cambridge, MA, January 1983.

[195] Ehud Shapiro, editor. *Concurrent Prolog: Collected Papers*, volume 1-2. MIT Press, Cambridge, MA, 1987.

[196] Ehud Shapiro. The family of concurrent logic programming languages. *ACM Computing Surveys*, 21(3):413–510, September 1989.

[197] Daniel P. Siewiorek, C. Gordon Bell, and Allen Newell. *Computer Structures: Principles and Examples*. McGraw-Hill, New York, 1982.

[198] Gert Smolka. The definition of Kernel Oz. In Andreas Podelski, editor, *Constraints: Basics and Trends*, volume 910 of *Lecture Notes in Computer Science*, pages 251–292. Springer-Verlag, Berlin, 1995.

[199] Gert Smolka. The Oz programming model. In *Computer Science Today*, volume 1000 of *Lecture Notes in Computer Science*, pages 324–343. Springer-Verlag, Berlin, 1995.

[200] Guy L. Steele, Jr. *Common Lisp: The Language*, 2nd edition. Digital Press, Bedford, MA, 1990.

[201] Leon Sterling and Ehud Shapiro. *The Art of Prolog: Advanced Programming Techniques*. Series in Logic Programming. MIT Press, Cambridge, MA, 1986.

[202] Marc Stiegler. *The E Language in a Walnut*. 2000. Draft available at `http://www.erights.org`.

[203] Bjarne Stroustrup. A history of C++. *ACM SIGPLAN Notices*, 28(3):271–297, March 1993. Originally appeared in History of Programming Languages Conference (HOPL-II), 1993.

[204] Bjarne Stroustrup. *The C++ Programming Language*, 3rd edition. Addison-Wesley, 1997.

[205] Giancarlo Succi and Michele Marchesi. *Extreme Programming Examined*. Addison-Wesley, 2001.

[206] Sun Microsystems. *The Java Series*. Sun Microsystems, Mountain View, CA, 1996. Available at `http://www.javasoft.com`.

[207] Sun Microsystems. *The Remote Method Invocation Specification*, 1997. Available at `http://www.javasoft.com`.

[208] Clemens Szyperski. *Component Software: Beyond Object-Oriented Programming*. Addison-Wesley and ACM Press, 1999.

[209] Andrew Taylor. *High-Performance Prolog Implementation*. PhD thesis, Basser Department of Computer Science, University of Sydney, Australia, June 1991.

[210] Gerard Tel. *An Introduction to Distributed Algorithms*. Cambridge University Press, Cambridge, UK, 1994.

[211] Evan Tick. The deevolution of concurrent logic programming. *Journal of Logic Programming*, 23(2):89–123, May 1995.

[212] Kasunori Ueda. Guarded Horn Clauses. In Eiti Wada, editor, *Proceedings of the 4th Conference on Logic Programming*, volume 221 of *Lecture Notes in Computer Science*, pages 168–179, Tokyo, July 1985. Springer-Verlag.

[213] Jeffrey D. Ullman. *Elements of ML Programming*. Prentice Hall, Englewood Cliffs, NJ, 1998.

[214] Peter Van Roy. VLSI-BAM Diagnostic Generator, 1989. Prolog program to generate assembly language diagnostics. Aquarius Project, University of California at Berkeley.

[215] Peter Van Roy. *Can Logic Programming Execute as Fast as Imperative Programming?* PhD thesis, Computer Science Division, University of California at Berkeley, December 1990. Technical Report UCB/CSD 90/600.

[216] Peter Van Roy. 1983–1993: The wonder years of sequential Prolog implementation. *Journal of Logic Programming*, 19/20:385–441, May/July 1994.

[217] Peter Van Roy, Per Brand, Denys Duchier, Seif Haridi, Martin Henz, and Christian Schulte. Logic programming in the context of multiparadigm programming: The Oz experience. *Theory and Practice of Logic Programming*, 3(6):715–763, November 2003.

[218] Peter Van Roy, Per Brand, Seif Haridi, and Raphaël Collet. A lightweight reliable object migration protocol. In Henri E. Bal, Boumediene Belkhouche, and Luca Cardelli, editors, *Internet Programming Languages*, volume 1686 of *Lecture Notes in Computer Science*. Springer Verlag, October 1999.

[219] Peter Van Roy and Alvin Despain. High-performance logic programming with the Aquarius Prolog compiler. *IEEE Computer*, pages 54–68, January 1992.

[220] Peter Van Roy and Seif Haridi. Teaching programming broadly and deeply: The kernel language approach. In *Informatics Curricula, Teaching Methods, and Best Practice (ICTEM 2002, IFIP Working Group 3.2 Working Conference)*, Boston, 2002. Kluwer Academic Publishers.

[221] Peter Van Roy and Seif Haridi. Teaching programming with the kernel language approach. In *Workshop on Functional and Declarative Programming in Education (FDPE02), at Principles, Logics, and Implementations of High-Level Programming Languages (PLI2002)*. University of Kiel, Germany, October 2002.

[222] Peter Van Roy, Seif Haridi, Per Brand, Gert Smolka, Michael Mehl, and Ralf Scheidhauer. Mobile objects in Distributed Oz. *ACM Transactions on Programming Languages and Systems*, 19(5):804–851, September 1997.

[223] Arthur H. Veen. Dataflow machine architecture. *ACM Computing Surveys*, 18(4):365–396, December 1986.

[224] Duncan J. Watts. *Small Worlds: The Dynamics of Networks between Order and Randomness*. Princeton University Press, Princeton, NJ, 1999.

[225] Gerhard Weikum and Gottfried Vossen. *Transactional Information Systems: Theory, Algorithms, and the Practice of Concurrency Control and Recovery*. Morgan Kaufmann, 2002.

[226] Gerhard Weiss, editor. *Multiagent Systems: A Modern Approach to Distributed Artificial Intelligence*. MIT Press, Cambridge, MA, 1999.

[227] Claes Wikström. Distributed programming in Erlang. In the *1st International Symposium on Parallel Symbolic Computation (PASCO 94)*, pages 412–421, Singapore, September 1994. World Scientific.

[228] Herbert S. Wilf. *generatingfunctionology*. Academic Press, 1994.

[229] Glynn Winskel. *The Formal Semantics of Programming Languages*. Foundations of Computing Series. MIT Press, Cambridge, MA, 1993.

[230] Noel Winstanley. What the hell are Monads?, 1999. Available at `http://www.haskell.org`.

[231] David Wood. Use of objects and agents at Symbian, September 2000. Talk given at the Newcastle Seminar on the Teaching of Computing Science, Newcastle, UK.

[232] Matthias Zenger and Martin Odersky. Implementing extensible compilers. In *1st International Workshop on Multiparadigm Programming with Object-Oriented Languages*, pages 61–80, Budapest, Hungary, June 2001. John von Neumann Institute for Computing (NIC). Workshop held as part of ECOOP 2001.

Index